lonely planet

Australia

Josh West, Brett Atkinson, Andrew Bain, Kat Barber, Natasha Bazika, Rosamund Brennan, Ivy Carruth, Peter Dragicevich, Emmylou Dzubiel, Anthony Ham, Paul Harding, Jessica Korteman, Ashlyn Oswalt, Charles Rawlings-Way, Chantae Reden, Rachel Tolosa Paz, Tiare Tuuhia, Steve Waters

CONTENTS

Plan Your Trip

The Guide

Toolkit

Storybook

Acknowledgement of Country

Lonely Planet would like to acknowledge all First Nations people throughout this country, who have nurtured and maintained the land since time immemorial. This guide was written on, and is written about, the lands of many diverse nations. We recognise the unique and ongoing connection that First Nations peoples have to land and waters and thank them for their efforts to preserve them. We pay our respects to Elders past and present and extend this respect to any Aboriginal or Torres Strait Islander people who may be reading this guide. We also recognise the ongoing efforts of Aboriginal and Torres Strait Islander peoples for reconciliation, justice, and social, cultural and economic self-determination. Sovereignty was never ceded. Australia always was, and always will be, Aboriginal land.

Cultural Sensitivity Warning

Aboriginal and Torres Strait Islander readers are advised that this guide may contain names and images of people who have since passed away.

ADAM GORMLEY/SHUTTERSTOCK

Flinders Ranges (p786)

AUSTRALIA

THE JOURNEY BEGINS HERE

I still remember my first flight over Australia. I was eight, leaving Adelaide to visit the Sydney cousins. Nose to the window, I watched the Murray River's green-brown waters coil through the Mallee plains, then the hazy blue peaks of the Great Dividing Range lift towards the East Coast. More recently, on a Brisbane–Alice Springs hop, the view felt like another country entirely: north Queensland's floodwaters spread in silvery sheets across sunburnt soils, inching thousands of kilometres to the continent's lowest point, Kati Thanda-Lake Eyre in South Australia. Australia is a vast, shape-shifting place: rainforest spilling to reefs, alpine highlands that ice over each winter, the vineyard-draped south and desert sands that spool on forever. Threading these contrasts is an enduring First Nations custodianship, a quiet through-line across a land that's nearly impossible to grasp – and that's half the magic. This place is always larger, stranger and more wonderful than you expect.

Josh West

@trekkingwest

Josh is an Australian-based writer, photographer and habitual wanderer of the world's wild edges. He wrote the Adelaide & South Australia chapter.

My favourite experience is waking to the **Flinders Ranges'** (p786) ancient ironstone walls glowing red at first light.

WHO GOES WHERE

Our writers and experts choose the places that, for them, define Australia.

WEBPD/SHUTTERSTOCK

Despite plenty of recent visits to other parts of Australia from New Zealand, Queensland was actually off my radar for too long. My highlight of getting back to the Sunshine State was visiting **Minjerribah** (North Stradbroke Island; p300). The North Gorge Walk is supremely scenic and it was a privilege to learn about the island's Indigenous heritage and culture. Next time, I won't wait so long for a return visit.

Brett Atkinson

@travelwriternz

Brett Atkinson is an Auckland-based travel, beer and food writer who's always eager to cross the Tasman and explore Australia. He co-wrote the Brisbane & South Queensland chapter.

ANDREW BAIN/ALAMY

There's something almost ethereal about **Takayna / Tarkine** (p687). As you kayak down the Pieman River at dawn, the reflections of the largest temperate rainforest in Australia are so perfect as to be disorientating, yet one of the wildest stretches of coastline in the country is just a band of trees away. It speaks volumes about the yin and yang of Tasmania – so classically beautiful on the one hand and so wildly wondrous on the other.

Andrew Bain

@bainonbike

Andrew is a travel writer who was drawn to Tasmania almost 20 years ago by the presence of so many outdoor opportunities. He co-wrote the Tasmania chapter.

RAGIL HTP/SHUTTERSTOCK

Ever since my first visit for a school excursion in grade seven, I've felt an air of reverence in Canberra. Whether it's the rush of power during Question Time in **Parliament House** (p232) or watching the touching Last Post Ceremony at the War Memorial, these feelings stay with you.

Kat Barber

katbarberwriter.wordpress.com

Kat is a writer from Geelong who grew up in Wagga Wagga and loves finding the best coffee, views and swimming spots wherever she goes. She wrote the Canberra & Country New South Wales chapter.

FROM LEFT: ELECTRA/SHUTTERSTOCK, STEPHEN DOREY/ALAMY

I grew up road-tripping the Central and South Coast on family summer holidays, so this region is personal for me. But on this research trip, Batemans Bay surprised me most, thanks to the new 15km **Munjip Trail Hike** (p206), with headland lookouts, shady bush sections and beaches where I didn't see another person. The murals and carved message poles created by the Walbunja people added a layer of culture and connection to Country.

Natasha Bazika

@natashagracebazika

Natasha is a Sydney-based writer who loves a road trip, especially one fuelled by regional bakery stops and adventure. She wrote the Coastal New South Wales chapter.

In summer, Fremantle's **South Beach** (p905) becomes a kind of floating commons. The pontoon bobs offshore, drawing kids, teenagers and the perpetually young out into the water, while south of the groyne dogs flail joyfully through the shallows. Back on land, everyone picnics on the grass. There's an easy-going community feel to it: smiley people lingering well past sunset, fish and chips in hand, as the giant orange orb melts into the Indian Ocean.

Rosamund Brennan

@rosamundbrennan

Based in Fremantle, Rosamund is a freelance journalist focusing on travel, culture and society. She finds the stories buried in the bush, hidden in the archives or carved into ancient rock faces. She co-wrote the Perth & Western Australia chapter.

FROM LEFT: ALAN BENGE/SHUTTERSTOCK, JAMES WK/SHUTTERSTOCK

I love the long, quiet journeys in the Northern Territory because they make you earn the awe. Hours unspool under a wide and indifferent sky and somewhere between leaving Alice Springs and approaching Yulara, seeing roadhouses and red horizons, you realise you've settled into a rhythm. The places are the reward: **Ormiston Gorge** (p867), Ellery Creek, Standley Chasm – all unspoiled and still as wild as the country that surrounds them. Nowhere else feels the same.

Ivy Carruth

@ivy_carruth

Ivy is a US-Australia dual citizen and Sydney-based writer fluent in the wonder of wandering and catching details. She wrote the Uluṟu & the Red Centre chapter.

Melbourne's (p468) historic core blends the corporate with the cool more successfully than any other urban centre in Australia. Grand old buildings are connected by lanes covered in colourful streetart, charge-account restaurants compete with Chinatown noodle shops and pricey cocktail bars rub shoulders with grungy rock venues. This dense grid of streets and laneways remains the most thrilling part of the city.

Peter Dragicevich

@peterdragnz

Peter is a travel writer whose work has appeared in major newspapers, magazines and dozens of Lonely Planet guidebooks. He wrote the Melbourne & Surrounds chapter.

FROM LEFT: LEANNE IRVIN/SHUTTERSTOCK, GENEVIEVE VALLEE/ALAMY

The Margaret River region is a wine- and food-lover's paradise, but it's the coastal wonders that keep me coming back. Walking sections of the **Cape to Cape** (p927), fishing off the shores of Meelup Beach and watching whales peep up for a hello amongst the waves really grounds you in the present. It was taking my first surf lesson here that solidified the magic of this place as an outdoor wonderland.

Emmylou Dzubiel

@emmylou.marie

Emmylou writes about food and culture, covering Australia, Japan and the Philippines. She co-wrote the Perth & Western Australia chapter.

Kakadu and Garig Gunak Barlu National Park are among my favourite places on the planet for their mix of soulful landscapes and Indigenous presence. But I love the sense of discovery that comes when I travel in the Top End. On my most recent trip, my detour to Jasper Gorge down the Buchanan Hwy in **Judbarra / Gregory National Park** (p838) was like stumbling into paradise – the lush landscapes, dramatic escarpments and ancient stories left me spellbound.

Anthony Ham

anthonyham.com

Anthony has been travelling the Top End and deep into the outback for more than two decades – his book The Last Desert Woman *takes readers into Warlpiri Country in the Tanami and Great Sandy Deserts. He wrote the Darwin & the Top End chapter.*

FROM LEFT: NICOLE PATIENCE/SHUTTERSTOCK, DZUNG VU/SHUTTERSTOCK

You don't need to ski to enjoy Victoria's Alps. I love the summer drive from **Bright to the Gippsland coast** (p592) – on a clear day the views from Mt Hotham to Mt Feathertop and across the Alps is special and the Razorback-Feathertop trail snaking off into the distance is magnetic. It's surreal to head down the other side and be sitting on Gippsland's 90-mile beach in less than two hours!

Paul Harding

@paulhtravel

Paul is a Melbourne-based travel writer and photographer specialising in Australia, Southeast Asia and India. He co-wrote the Greater Victoria chapter.

That breathtaking moment you emerge onto an open escarpment in the **Grampians** (p583) is what hiking in this part of the world is all about for me. With sheer slopes of sandstone, rocky outcrops and panoramic views, you can chase the thrill of grand reveals for weeks here without encountering the same trail twice. It's no wonder there's no official tally on the number of hikes in the park – 'a lot' seems about right!

Jessica Korteman

@jessicakorteman

Jessica is an Australian travel writer based in Melbourne, passionate about raising the profile of women in the travel industry. She co-wrote the Greater Victoria chapter.

Magnetic Island (p438) was a pleasant surprise. Just a half-hour ferry ride from Townsville, north Queensland's largest city, the island provided the perfect rugged retreat. With plenty of hikes to fill my days and great restaurants with ocean views, it was the kind of place where you could quickly feel like a local. Not to mention, seeing koalas in the wild on the Forts Walk was a real highlight.

Ashlyn Oswalt

@ashlynoswalt

Curious about food, travel and the outdoors, Ashlyn is an American writer based in New Zealand. She co-wrote the Cairns & North Queensland chapter.

FROM LEFT: FRANK FICHTMUELLER/SHUTTERSTOCK, MICK2770/SHUTTERSTOCK

The ancient Celts talked about 'thin places' – special locations where the divide between their everyday lives and the 'other' world of spirits and dreams seemed to narrow. **South Street** (p649) in Hobart's Battery Point is my 'thin place'. I can't explain it, but every time I walk down here, I'm awash with maritime vibes and memories that are my own, but feel much older. South St has got soul. If I could only afford to buy a house here...

Charles Rawlings-Way

@crawlingsway

Based in Hobart, Charles writes about travel, cricket, food, education and music – inspired and haunted by Tasmania's history, landscapes and maritime soul. He co-wrote the Tasmania chapter.

The coolest cosmopolitan coastal walk in Sydney is the stretch between **Bondi and Coogee** (p116). I struggle to estimate how long it takes. I'm always stopping to watch the surfers or diving in for 'just a quick' dip. Coffee at Bronte Beach, a cold drink at Clovelly Bowling Club and a lazy brunch at Coogee are all mandatory in my eyes. Yes, there are lesser-known walks, but this one is quintessentially Sydney.

Chantae Reden

@TheSaltSirens

Chantae is a surfer, scuba diver and freediver whose hair is permanently salt-soaked and tangled from time in the water. She wrote the Sydney & Surrounds chapter.

FROM LEFT: GENUS PHOTOG/SHUTTERSTOCK AUSTRALIANCAMERA/SHUTTERSTOCK

Chillagoe (p397) is a speck on the north Queensland map, but what a heart this dusty desert town has. It's an otherworldly landscape – limestone rocks jut out where you least expect them and underground adventures reveal sparkling stalactites and stalagmites! There are huge cubes of marble by the roadside (remnants of the marble industry), freshwater swimming spots and an observatory to gaze up at that awe-inspiring sky.

Rachel Tolosa Paz

@racheltolosapaz

Rachel Tolosa Paz is a writer and photographer, the author of The Food of Argentina *and contributor to Lonely Planet titles on Argentina and Buenos Aires. She co-wrote the Cairns & North Queensland chapter.*

FROM LEFT: BEN JEAYES/SHUTTERSTOCK, BTP AUS/SHUTTERSTOCK

I love **Great Keppel Island** (p365), off the coast of Yeppoon in Queensland. It's one of the Southern Great Barrier Reef islands that's still a little under the radar, but has absolutely everything you want in an island getaway. Long stretches of white-sand beaches without the crowds, pristine snorkelling and diving spots, and great bush walking tracks too. Plus it's only a 30-minute ferry ride away from the mainland.

Tiare Tuuhia

authory.com/tiaretuuhia

Tiare is a freelance journalist and travel writer who grew up on the beautiful Sunshine Coast in Queensland. She co-wrote the Brisbane & South Queensland chapter.

I just love the rawness of the **Kimberley** (p994), the bright primary colours of blue sky, red earth, yellow ochre. I love the vast savannah plains and hidden gorges, Livistona palms, secret swimming holes, rock art and Indigenous culture. And boabs, they are the funkiest tree ever! I love sleeping on warm rocks under the Milky Way. And the wet season! Man, if you thought sunsets were good from Cable Beach, try watching an electrical storm.

Steve Waters

Steve has been travelling through, volunteering in and writing about northern Western Australia for over 15 years. He co-wrote the Cairns & North Queensland and Perth & Western Australia chapters.

CONTRIBUTING WRITERS

Sudeshna Ghosh

@travelnow_world

Sudeshna is a Sydney-based editor and writer.

Briar Jensen

@briarstravelbeat

An award-winning travel journalist based in Sydney.

Lisa Martin

@lmarti_journo

Originally from Australia, Lisa is a freelance journalist and writer based in Copenhagen, Denmark.

Olivia Pozzan

@theruggedbikini

A veterinarian on Queenland's Sunshine Coast, Olivia has contributed to more than 25 Lonely Planet titles.

Jo Stewart

@jostewartwriter

Jo covers pop culture, food, travel and community from her home base in Victoria.

Max Veenhuyzen

@maxveenhuyzen

Culinary and travel journalist lives lives on Whadjuk Nyoongar Country in Perth.

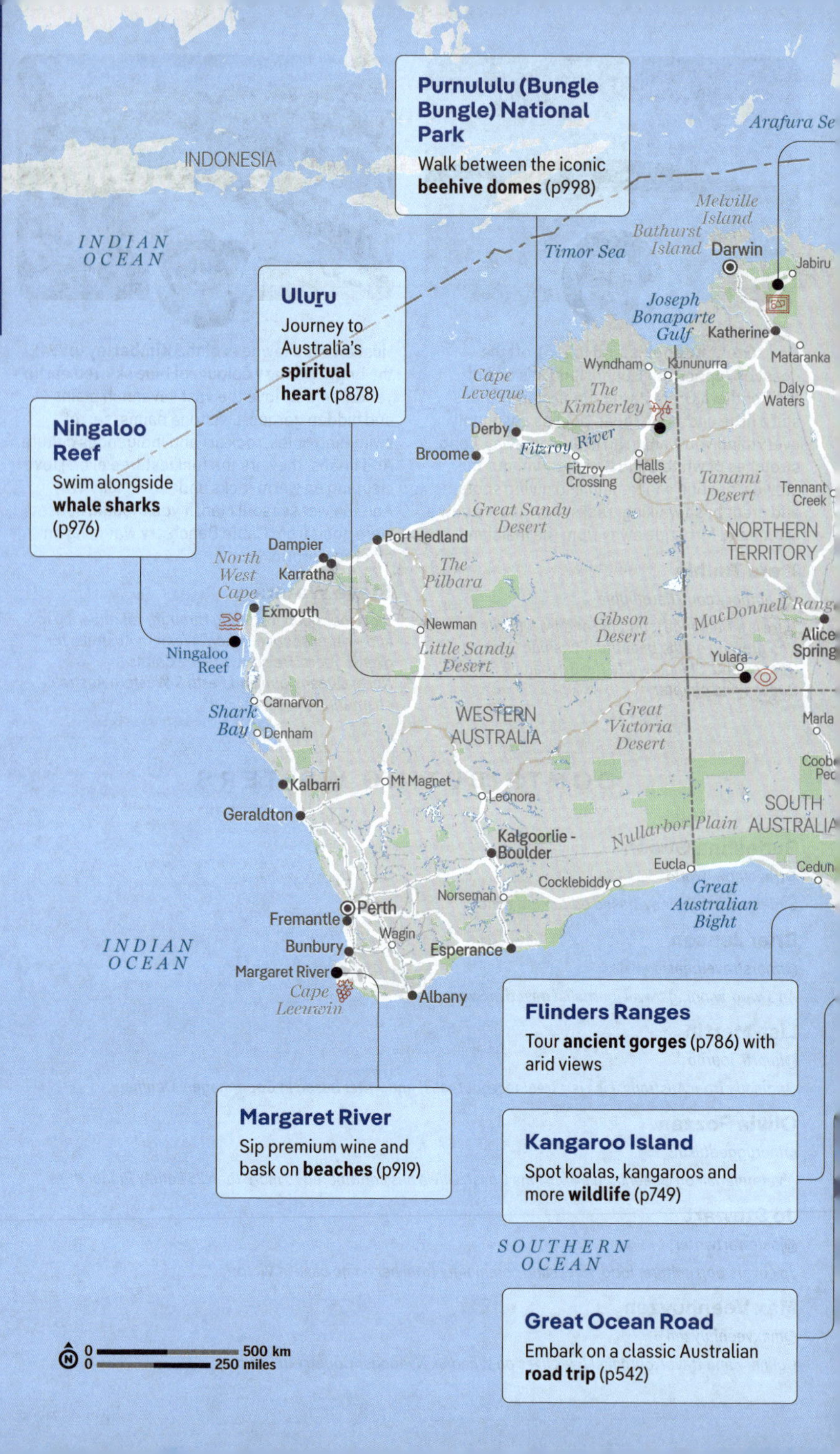
Purnululu (Bungle Bungle) National Park
Walk between the iconic beehive domes (p998)
Uluṟu
Journey to Australia's spiritual heart (p878)
Ningaloo Reef
Swim alongside whale sharks (p976)
Margaret River
Sip premium wine and bask on beaches (p919)
Flinders Ranges
Tour ancient gorges (p786) with arid views
Kangaroo Island
Spot koalas, kangaroos and more wildlife (p749)
Great Ocean Road
Embark on a classic Australian road trip (p542)
INDONESIA
INDIAN OCEAN
Arafura Se
Timor Sea
Melville Island
Bathurst Island
Darwin
Jabiru
Joseph Bonaparte Gulf
Katherine
Mataranka
Wyndham
Kununurra
Cape Leveque
The Kimberley
Daly Waters
Derby
Broome
Fitzroy River
Fitzroy Crossing
Halls Creek
Tanami Desert
Tennant Creek
Great Sandy Desert
NORTHERN TERRITORY
Port Hedland
Dampier
Karratha
The Pilbara
North West Cape
Exmouth
Newman
Gibson Desert
MacDonnell Rang
Alice Spring
Ningaloo Reef
Little Sandy Desert
Yulara
Carnarvon
Shark Bay
Denham
WESTERN AUSTRALIA
Great Victoria Desert
Marla
Coob Ped
Kalbarri
Mt Magnet
Leonora
Geraldton
SOUTH AUSTRALIA
Kalgoorlie - Boulder
Nullarbor Plain
Eucla
Cedun
Cocklebiddy
Norseman
Perth
Great Australian Bight
Fremantle
Wagin
Bunbury
Esperance
INDIAN OCEAN
Margaret River
Cape Leeuwin
Albany
SOUTHERN OCEAN
0 500 km
0 250 miles

Kakadu National Park
Go bush for mesmerising **rock art** (p814)
Great Barrier Reef
Immerse in the world's largest **coral reef** (p382)
K'gari
Explore the world's largest sand **island** (p344)
Byron Bay
Bliss out in an iconic **surf town** (p177)
Lord Howe Island
Laze by a turquoise **lagoon** (p216)
Sydney
Scale the **Sydney Harbour Bridge** (p78)
Melbourne
Rock out at **live-music venues** (p463)
Cradle Mountain-Lake St Clair National Park
Hike into Tasmania's **alpine splendour** (p691)
Port Moresby
PAPUA NEW GUINEA
SOLOMON ISLANDS
Thursday Island
Torres Strait
Cape York
Nhulunbuy
Weipa
Coral Sea
Groote Eylandt
Cape York Peninsula
Cape Melville
Gulf of Carpentaria
Great Barrier Reef
Cooktown
Port Douglas
Cairns
Innisfail
Normanton
Ingham
Townsville
Camooweal
Charters Towers
Bowen
Airlie Beach
Whitsunday Islands
Cloncurry
Mt Isa
Flinders River
Mackay
Winton
Longreach
Barcaldine
Great Dividing Range
Rockhampton
Gladstone
Simpson Desert
Birdsville
QUEENSLAND
Bundaberg
Hervey Bay
K'gari
Charleville
Innamincka
Maroochydore
Lake Eyre
St George
Toowoomba
Brisbane
Surfers Paradise
Barwon River
Byron Bay
Bourke
Armidale
Broken Hill
Darling River
Coffs Harbour
Port Augusta
Flinders Ranges
NEW SOUTH WALES
Nyngan
Tamworth
Port Macquarie
Lord Howe Island (NSW)
SOUTH PACIFIC OCEAN
Whyalla
Dubbo
Mildura
Bathurst
Newcastle
Adelaide
Murray Bridge
Griffith
Hay
Sydney
Tasman Sea
Swan Hill
Wagga Wagga
Wollongong
Murray River
CANBERRA
Kangaroo Island
Horsham
VICTORIA
Albury
Batemans Bay
Mt Gambier
Ballarat
Melbourne
Warrnambool
Geelong
Wilsons Promontory
King Island
Bass Strait
Flinders Island
Devonport
Launceston
TASMANIA
Hobart
NEW ZEALAND
Queenstown

UNDERWATER MAGIC

Australia's reefs are among the most extraordinary ecosystems on Earth, from the coast-hugging sea gardens of Western Australia to the tropical expanse of Queensland's Great Barrier Reef. Together they form vibrant worlds of colour, movement and marine life. Swim among coral wonderlands, drift on a glass-bottom boat or take in the patterns from the air. These fragile yet resilient reef systems are an unforgettable world waiting to be discovered. Go on, dive in.

FROM LEFT: PHMARCOSBORSATTO/SHUTTERSTOCK, JANA JONES/SHUTTERSTOCK, EMILY HAMLEY/SHUTTERSTOCK

Australia's Coral Contribution

Australia's reef network represents roughly 16% to 20% of all coral reefs on Earth – close to one-fifth of the planet's total, underscoring its global importance.

Cultural Connections

The Great Barrier Reef forms part of the Sea Country of over 70 Aboriginal and Torres Strait Islander groups who maintain deep cultural connections to the reef.

Regions to Explore

Cairns is the main gateway to the Great Barrier Reef, but more than a dozen other access points offer a rich range of experiences.

Ningaloo Reef (p976)

BEST REEF EXPERIENCES

Admire the majestic manta rays that glide around family-friendly ❶ **Lady Elliot Island Eco Resort** (p357) at the Great Barrier Reef's southern tip.

Camp on Lady Musgrave Island on the Southern Great Barrier Reef following a day trip from Bundaberg with ❷ **Lady Musgrave Experience** (p358).

Snorkel or dive the Coral Greenhouse, part of the ❸ **Museum of Underwater Art** (p432), then explore the surrounding John Brewer Reef, off Townsville.

Give back to the reef on a citizen-science experience such as the Marine Conservation Program at ❹ **Fitzroy Island** (p384), just off Cairns.

Dive into the world's largest coast-fringing coral at ❺ **Ningaloo Reef** (p976) in WA, and meet the resident whale sharks from March to August.

RAISE A GLASS

Big reds, zesty whites, fancy fizz: Australia's wine industry has grown to become a global behemoth and touring the country's many wine regions is an indulgent experience. Adventurous foodie culture and high-end accommodation go hand-in-hand (wine-in-glass?) with the viticulture. Recruit a designated driver (or book a tour) and swing by some winery cellar doors – even balmy Queensland has some.

FROM LEFT: BENNY MARTY/SHUTTERSTOCK, VINCENT_NGUYEN/SHUTTERSTOCK, ANNA SOELBERG/SHUTTERSTOCK

Au Naturel

Popularity of minimal-intervention organic and biodynamic wine is growing across the country – get a taste anywhere from Tasmania (pictured) to the Adelaide Hills.

Wine & Dine

Some of Australia's best restaurants are located in wineries, particularly in McLaren Vale (South Australia; pictured), Margaret River (WA) and the Hunter Valley (New South Wales).

That's the Spirit

Not big on wine? Australia is also home to booming craft beer and distilling scenes, with Australian botanical gin among the top drops.

Hunter Valley (p170)

BEST WINE EXPERIENCES

Begin an SA wine adventure at the towering ❶ **d'Arenberg Cube** (p743), a McLaren Vale landmark with a penthouse tasting room.

Raise a glass of cool-climate pinot noir or chardonnay in Victoria's ❷ **Yarra Valley** (p528).

Sip superb semillon in the ❸ **Hunter Valley** (p170), Australia's oldest wine region.

Cellar-door-hop to your heart's content around ❹ **Margaret River** (p922), which produces 25% of Australia's premium wine.

Uncover an unexpected wine region in Queensland's high-altitude ❺ **Granite Belt** (p305), known for its rare Strange Bird wines.

WIDE OPEN ROAD

There's a heckuva lot of empty tarmac across this wide brown land. From Fremantle to Cooktown, Jabiru to Dover, the best way to experience Australia is to hit the open road. Car hire is affordable, road conditions are good and beyond the big cities the traffic fades away. Pick up a campervan and explore the national parks, or hire a 4WD and stir up some outback dust.

Bakery Stop

Among the highlights of an Aussie road trip is visiting the bakeries en route – every town has one, with time-honoured treats including the classic meat pie.

Hop on a Tour

If you're travelling solo or nervous about driving, consider a tour. Operators in Cairns and Cooktown make the classic trip to the Tip (of Cape York Peninsula).

Safety First

The Australian landscape is beautiful yet unforgiving. If you're headed down remote roads or 4WD tracks, inform someone and ensure you're prepared for emergencies.

FROM LEFT: ALIZADA STUDIOS/SHUTTERSTOCK, CHAMELEONSEYE/SHUTTERSTOCK, SUMMER360/SHUTTERSTOCK

Great Ocean Road (p554)

BEST ROAD-TRIP EXPERIENCES

Take the 2700km trip from Perth to Adelaide, via ❶ **Kalgoorlie-Boulder** (p953), across the epic emptiness of the Nullarbor Plain.

Enjoy an easy yet spectacular drive along Victoria's dramatic ❷ **Great Ocean Road** (p554).

Embark on the 4WD-only ❸ **Oodnadatta Track** (p796), a former rail route in the arid SA outback featuring 615km of red dust and dry lakes.

Cruise the Pacific Hwy between Sydney and Brisbane, stitching together surf towns, hinterland detours and the ❹ **Mid North Coast** (p172).

Set off from Broome or Kununurra for an epic drive through the Kimberley via the 4WD-only ❺ **Gibb River Road** (p1003) in WA.

ANCIENT, LIVING CULTURES

There are some fine ways to experience 65,000 years of Aboriginal and Torres Strait Islander cultures. Peel back the big-city layers on a Traditional Custodian-guided tour of spiritually rich urban sites, watch an Indigenous dance troupe, hike to rock art and hit the art galleries where a new generation of First Nations artists are making their mark.

BEST INDIGENOUS EXPERIENCES

Marvel at the world's oldest freshwater aquaculture systems at coastal Victoria's UNESCO-listed ❶ **Budj Bim Cultural Landscape** (p560).

Tour the famous rock-art sites and wildlife-rich waterways of the Northern Territory's ❷ **Kakadu National Park** (p814) with an Aboriginal guide.

Explore the rich Aboriginal arts scene in the desert city of ❸ **Alice Springs** (p850).

Trace 50,000 years of history at ❹ **Murujuga National Park** (p979) in Western Australia, home to the world's largest collection of petroglyphs.

Walk in the footsteps of Tasmania's Palawa people on the immersive multiday ❺ **Wukalina Walk** (p677).

FROM LEFT: JAMES DAVIS PHOTOGRAPHY/SHUTTERSTOCK, TOTAJLA/SHUTTERSTOCK

Many Tongues

At the time of colonisation there were thought to be around 300 Indigenous languages spoken across Australia. Approximately half are still spoken to some extent.

Land of Plenty

Remnants of great feasts enjoyed by the First Nations people of Australia's coastlines and waterways are still visible in the form of middens, piles of calcified shells and bones.

Indigenous Population

The latest census figures show that 3.8% of the population, or approximately one million Australians, identify as Aboriginal or Torres Strait Islander.

650S SHOP/SHUTTERSTOCK

Quokka and its joey, Rottnest Island (p907)

BEST ISLAND EXPERIENCES

Ferry between ❶ **Torres Strait Islands** (p420), experiencing their vibrant, sea-rooted Indigenous cultures.

Hangout with adorable quokkas and laze on the azure beaches of WA's ❷ **Rottnest Island** (p907).

Venture to NSW's ❸ **Lord Howe Island** (p216) to hike, swim, snorkel and paddle in a natural paradise.

Escape to Queensland's epic sand islands: **K'gari** (p344), **North Stradbroke** (p300) or ❹ **Moreton** (p299).

Find koalas, sea lions, wombats, echidnas and goannas on SA's wildlife-rich ❺ **Kangaroo Island** (p749).

ISLAND LIFE

Australia's territory encompasses more than 8200 islands, each with their own draws. Magical bushwalks, rampant wildlife, cinematic reefs, luxe resorts, convict history and footprint-free beaches are just a few of the lures. And of course, mainland Australia is an island, too: think of your time here as one big atoll adventure.

Wildlife Havens

Many Australian islands help to safeguard threatened species. Koalas thrive on Magnetic Island and wildlife abounds on rat-free Maria and Lord Howe Islands.

Culture Isles

A popular day trip from Darwin, the Tiwi Islands are home to the Tiwi people, a distinct First Nations group renowned for its vibrant printed textiles.

URBAN BUZZ

Sydney is home to the blockbuster sights – the Sydney Harbour Bridge and the Sydney Opera House top most people's lists – but its fellow state and territory capitals have plenty of unique selling points. Darwin is Australia's only tropical capital, Perth moves to its own beat (and time zone) and Melbourne's unpredictable weather has birthed cosy cafe and live-music scenes. Regional cities, too, are packed with history, foodie finds and opportunities to meet the locals.

Fabulous Festivals

From Sydney's world-renowned Mardi Gras (pictured) to music festivals hosted across the country, there's always something to celebrate in Australia's cities.

Game On

From the AFL Grand Final in Melbourne to the State of Origin rugby league series between NSW and Queensland, Australia's top sporting events play out on the East Coast.

On Song

Known for its diverse range of independent musicians and a plethora of live-music venues, Adelaide is Australia's only UNESCO City of Music.

FROM LEFT: FIMINA ANNA/SHUTTERSTOCK, NEALE COUSLAND/SHUTTERSTOCK, DANIELBBOZEK/SHUTTERSTOCK

Sydney Harbour Bridge (p78)

BEST BIG-CITY EXPERIENCES

Choose from seven different ways to climb the ❶ **Sydney Harbour Bridge** (p78), including an Indigenous-guided climb.

Visit showpiece art galleries and museums including the engaging ❷ **WA Museum Boola Bardip** (p897) in Perth.

Throw yourself into the rich array of festivals hosted by the likes of Adelaide, home of the huge ❸ **Adelaide Fringe** (p728).

Watch footy or cricket in any city during the season, or sweat it out courtside at the Australian Open in ❹ **Melbourne Park** (p496) in January.

Dive into the rich and diverse food scenes of Australia's capitals – small-but-mighty ❺ **Hobart** (p638) is a food city to watch.

OUTBACK WONDERS

There's big. And then there's Australia's outback. Covering more than 70% of the continent, the outback spans 10 deserts, swathes of subtropical savannah and the largest temperate woodland on Earth – WA's Great Western Woodlands. Dotted with dramatic dunes, geological oddities, Aboriginal art centres and quirky outback pubs, roamed by hardy wildlife and laced with Dreaming tracks and epic 4WD trails, its savage beauty is spellbinding.

FROM LEFT: EDWARD HAYLAN/SHUTTERSTOCK, CHAMELEONSEYE/SHUTTERSTOCK, NICK FOX/SHUTTERSTOCK

Outback Roadhouses

A huge part of the charm of Australia's outback is its collection of rustic pubs and the colourful characters you'll find in them.

Follow the Dots

Dot painting on canvas emerged in central Australia in the 1970s as a result of Aboriginal people working together with non-Indigenous schoolteacher Geoffrey Bardon.

Gone Feral

Considered an invasive species, over one million camels (first introduced in the 1840s) currently roam central Australia.

Mungo National Park (p628)

BEST OUTBACK EXPERIENCES

Marvel at the incredible changing colours of ❶ **Uluṟu** (p878) at sunset.

Uncover fossils that mark the very beginning of Earth's complex life at ❷ **Nilpena Ediacara National Park** (p789) in SA's Flinders Ranges.

Feel like you're walking on the moon in the surreal landscape of active archaeological site ❸ **Mungo National Park** (p628) in outback NSW.

Clamber through the sandstone gorges of WA's ❹ **Karijini National Park** (p983) to discover hidden plunge pools and waterfalls beneath the Pilbara's peaks.

Visit the site of the world's only known ❺ **fossilised dinosaur stampede** (p456) near Winton in outback Queensland.

ANNALUCIA/SHUTTERSTOCK

Port Arthur Historic Site (p662), Tasmania

SETTLER STORIES

The relatively recent colonisation of Australia means that many of its early-19th-century buildings still stand today alongside relics from gold rushes, abandoned settlements and the nation's seafaring heritage. A cornucopia of sites around the country offer an evocative taste of colonial-era life – for both settlers and First Nations peoples.

It Takes a Village

Some of Australia's best-preserved historic buildings are found in country towns such as Berrima in NSW, Australia's oldest Georgian village.

First European Settlers

The *Batavia* shipwreck sparked mutiny and massacre off WA's coast in 1629, leaving two teen castaways to live out their days with Indigenous locals.

BEST HISTORY EXPERIENCES

Join the ❶ **Kurrah Mia** (p941) walking tour in Albany to learn how colonisation has reshaped Noongar Country (WA).

Learn how the Eureka Stockade influenced Australian politics at the ❷ **Eureka Centre** (p575) in Victoria's goldfields.

Uncover the harrowing convict stories connected to Tasmania's ❸ **Port Arthur Historic Site** (p662).

Spend a creepy night at ❹ **Fremantle Prison** (p904), Australia's best-preserved convict-built jail.

Soak up the history of modern Australia's first neighbourhood in ❺ **the Rocks** (p78), Sydney.

AUSTRALIA FROM ABOVE

Climb, float or fly – Australia's enormous scale only reveals itself from above. It might be a scenic flight skimming across outback plains, a hot-air balloon drifting over vineyard valleys or a summit lookout opening onto ancient horizons. However you rise, expect the landscape to take on an entirely new shape from the top.

Sunrise over the Vines

Australia's wine regions are prime ballooning territory – drift over the Yarra (pictured) or Barossa Valleys at dawn for misty vineyard views.

Australia's Icons

The country's biggest drawcards shine from above, including flights over the Twelve Apostles (pictured) and Uluṟu, and climbing the Sydney Harbour Bridge.

Hangar History

Aviation museums are well covered nationwide, from Port Adelaide's South Australian Aviation Museum to the Qantas Founders Museum in outback Queensland.

BEST ELEVATED EXPERIENCES

Catch a scenic flight over the vast salt pans of SA's ❶ **Kati Thanda-Lake Eyre** (p792) and the marbled folds of Anna Creek Painted Hills.

Drive to the summit of ❷ **Kunanyi / Mt Wellington** (p651), rising 1271m above Hobart's harbour.

Ride a hot-air balloon over ❸ **Canberra** (p228) to see the nation's parliamentary skyline at its most photogenic.

Hop a chopper above ❹ **Kings Canyon** (p871) and watch its sandstone walls carve a spectacular cleft through the outback.

Climb WA's ❺ **Bluff Knoll** (p946) for a ridge-stacked panorama atop the Stirling Range's tallest mountain (1095m).

FROM LEFT: ALONA_HRINCHENKO/SHUTTERSTOCK,

TAKE A DIP

There are thought to be more than 10,000 beaches fringing Australia's vast coastline and they're all for public use. From cute coves to seemingly endless stretches of sand, the diversity of options is astounding. Find an empty beach for refreshing solitude, or spend a day on some urban sand where locals mix up their morning surf with macchiatos and people-watching. Stay safe and swim at patrolled beaches wherever possible.

FROM LEFT: 365 FOCUS PHOTOGRAPHY/SHUTTERSTOCK, OZBEACHES/SHUTTERSTOCK, JAM TRAVELS/SHUTTERSTOCK

Reality Star

Following the daily routines of Bondi Beach's (pictured) professional lifeguards, *Bondi Rescue* is one of Australia's longest-running reality TV shows, with over 200 episodes filmed since 2006.

Swimwear Options

Topless sunbathing is widely accepted across Australia, but nude bathing is restricted to certain beaches. Queensland is the only state without a dedicated nude beach.

First Surfer

Hawaiian Duke Kahanamoku is thought to have introduced surfing to Sydney in 1915, but photos prove a merchant seafarer was surfing in Manly at least six summers earlier.

Whitehaven Beach (p444), Whitsunday Island

BEST BEACH EXPERIENCES

See and be seen on Sydney's famous ❶ **Bondi Beach** (p118), linked to Coogee Beach by a scenic clifftop walk.

Sail for the swirls of turquoise water and silica sand framing ❷ **Whitehaven Beach** (p444), the jewel of the Whitsundays.

Hike to a lookout point and perhaps even take a heart-starting dip at Tasmania's most beautiful beach, ❸ **Wineglass Bay** (p672).

Learn to surf the waves rolling into the iconic beaches of NSW's ❹ **Byron Bay** (p177), perhaps alongside a local dolphin or two.

Take in a mesmerising Top End sunset as camels carry tourists along the sands of ❺ **Cable Beach** (p986) in Broome.

INTO THE WILD

There's nowhere like Australia to bask in Mother Nature's creation. This massive, sparsely populated country plays host to some astonishing national parks, wild places and remote frontiers, where solitude is the daily experience. Rediscover your natural state with brilliant bushwalks, from arid outback ranges to craggy Tasmanian clifftops and wild WA coastlines.

Indigenous Stewardship

Australia's wild places are not just ecologically significant, they are also living cultural landscapes carefully managed by Traditional Custodians for millennia.

Blockbuster Rainforests

The Gondwana Rainforests (pictured) contain the world's largest remaining stands of subtropical rainforest and Antarctic beech cool temperate rainforests.

UNESCO Pride

Australia is home to 16 World Heritage Sites listed for their natural heritage, including another five sites recognised solely for their cultural value.

FROM LEFT: STEVE WATERS/LONELY PLANET, JAKUB MACULEWICZ/SHUTTERSTOCK, LEAH-ANNE THOMPSON/SHUTTERSTOCK

Blue Mountains (p138)

BEST WILDERNESS EXPERIENCES

Chase waterfalls, cassowaries and sweaty adventures in the Wet Tropics of Queensland, home to the ❶ **Daintree Rainforest** (p404).

Hike into the Tasmanian Wilderness on the famous ❷ **Overland Track** (p692) beginning in Cradle Mountain-Lake St Clair National Park.

Walk among the surreal rock formations of ❸ **Purnululu National Park** (p998), deep in WA's Kimberley region.

Explore ❹ **Wilsons Promontory Marine National Park** (p594) for white beaches and roaming wildlife at the southern tip of mainland Australia.

Traverse the network of trails in the cool, eucalypt-scented air of NSW's ❺ **Blue Mountains** (p140).

CREATURES GREAT & SMALL

Australia's wilderness is animated by a cohort of native animals found nowhere else on Earth. Between the sea lions cavorting on Kangaroo Island and the otherworldly critters of the Daintree Rainforest is a panoply of weird and wonderful species from koalas to kangaroos, wombats to platypuses. There's great whale watching along the East, West and South Coasts, plus the omnipresent cackle of kookaburras, to say nothing of the marine life of the Great Barrier Reef.

Koala Country

Native to eastern states, koalas are officially listed as endangered, but there are plenty of places to spot them in the wild. Try Magnetic Island and Kangaroo Island.

Kangaroo Etymology

Among the first Aboriginal words collected by the First Fleet from the Guugu Yimithirr of present-day Cooktown was *ganguru*, recorded as 'kangaroo'.

When the Lights Go Out

Most of Australia's native wildlife is nocturnal, making camping in national parks a great way to see it. BYO red-light torch!

FROM LEFT: SEBW/SHUTTERSTOCK, DAVID HAVEL/SHUTTERSTOCK, FERRY FERDINANDUS/SHUTTERSTOCK

Penguin Parade (p590), Phillip Island

BEST WILDLIFE EXPERIENCES

Observe nesting turtles along Exmouth's beaches on a summer tour with the ❶ **Jurabi Turtle Centre** (p978) in WA.

Walk among wombats and Tasmanian devils in ❷ **Maria Island National Park** (p668), dubbed 'Australia's Noah's Ark'.

Hop aboard a wintertime whale-watching boat trip in ❸ **Hervey Bay** (p339) in Queensland.

Witness giant cuttlefish turn the quiet waters of SA's ❹ **Eyre Peninsula** (p780) into a psychedelic love-in each winter.

Watch little penguins waddle ashore at the famous ❺ **Penguin Parade** (p590) on Phillip Island, just offshore from Melbourne.

REGIONS & CITIES

Find the places that tick all your boxes.

Canberra & Country New South Wales

CAPITAL CHARM, WINES AND COLOURFUL COUNTRYSIDE

Alpine walks, wonderful wineries, historic towns and glorious country drives lure travellers beyond the bright lights of the nation's sophisticated capital.

Greater Victoria

COAST, MOUNTAINS AND COUNTRY ESCAPES

Drive the Great Ocean Road, camp out in the Grampians, step back into Victoria's gold rush and cycle across Gippsland – or simply relax with a glass of Yarra Valley pinot noir.

Melbourne & Surrounds

AUSTRALIA'S CAPITAL OF COOL

Consistently ranked among the world's most liveable cities, Melbourne (Narrm) has it all – its thriving arts, music, dining and sporting scenes make Victoria's capital endlessly exciting.

Canberra & Country NSW p222
Greater Victoria p536
Melbourne Surround p463

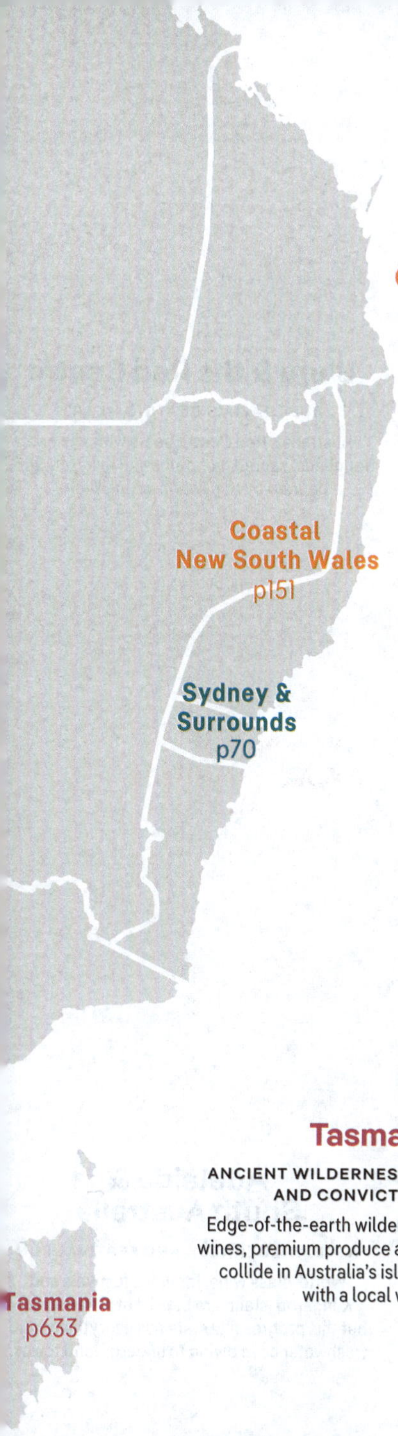

Coastal New South Wales

COASTLINE, CULTURE AND ADVENTURE

From rolling southern shores to the subtropical north, this dreamy strip passes surf towns and hinterland hideaways along a ribbon of beach and bush.

Sydney & Surrounds

OZ'S GLEAMING EMERALD CITY

Sydney (Warrane) loves to show off its sparkling harbour, golden beaches and buffed bodies, but that's just the entrée.

Tasmania

ANCIENT WILDERNESS, GASTRONOMY AND CONVICT HISTORY

Edge-of-the-earth wilderness, cool-climate wines, premium produce and wacky museums collide in Australia's island state. Ease in with a local whisky.

Uluṟu & the Red Centre

AUSTRALIA'S BEATING HEART

Australia's Red Centre beats with ancient Songlines, sacred monoliths and living culture, defined by the awe-inspiring Uluṟu.

Perth & Western Australia

ETERNAL LANDSCAPES, ENDLESS COASTLINE AND RAW BEAUTY

Australia's most remote capital moves to its own beat, with Rottnest Island on its doorstep and pristine reefs and vast outback gorges beyond.

Adelaide & South Australia

WINE, WILDERNESS AND FESTIVAL FUN

World-class wine, fabulous festivals and Kangaroo Island are big-ticket attractions, but this progressive state has everything from freshwater cave diving to underground towns.

Darwin & the Top End

OUTBACK WONDERS AND WILD ADVENTURES

Big in scale and rich in story, the Top End spans Darwin's streetart energy, Kakadu's red-rock landscapes and the Tiwi Islands' deep culture.

Cairns & North Queensland

CORAL REEFS, RAINFOREST AND THE OUTBACK

Stretching from Yeppoon north to the Torres Strait Islands and encompassing the bulk of the mesmerising Great Barrier Reef, this wild and sultry region reels you right in.

Brisbane & South Queensland

URBAN THRILLS AND FUN IN THE SUN

Welcome to the holiday capital of Australia, where lush rainforest, buzzing cities and epic sand islands stretch along a sparkling coast tracking north to the Tropic of Capricorn.

WIRESTOCK CREATORS/SHUTTERSTOCK

Daintree Fan Palm Farm (p413)

ITINERARIES

Best of Australia

Allow: 8 days **Distance:** 5000km

When you want a taste of the big hitters but time is tight, get (jet) set for an action-packed itinerary that takes you from East Coast Australia's blockbuster harbour city to Queensland's main Great Barrier Reef gateway, then out to Uluru, the beating heart of the Australian outback.

1

SYDNEY ⏱ 2 DAYS

Kick-start your tour in the New South Wales **capital** (p70), checking out the big-ticket sights, seeing and being seen on Bondi Beach, bar-hopping and shopping. Don't miss the Bondi to Coogee coastal walk (pictured) and lap up Sydney's fabulous restaurants. Thirsty? Take a day trip to the Hunter Valley wine region, but you might want an extra day if the pours are generous.

2

BLUE MOUNTAINS ⏱ 1 DAY

Dart inland to explore the **Blue Mountains** (p138), beginning with misty Katoomba's cache of Art Deco architecture and the amazing Three Sisters lookout. Choose from dozens of walking trails (pictured) lacing the bush landscape, take a ride on the hair-raising Scenic Railway down to Dinosaur Valley, or put your feet up and enjoy a gourmet mountain meal.

FROM LEFT: JAMES_DAVIES/SHUTTERSTOCK, ALEXANDRE.ROSA/SHUTTERSTOCK

3

CAIRNS ⏱ 3 DAYS

Get a taste of Queensland and Australia's tropical north in the vibrant coastal hub of **Cairns** (p378). A three-hour flight from Sydney, it's the perfect base to explore the Great Barrier Reef and the Daintree Rainforest, learn about First Nations culture and eyeball a saltwater crocodile in its natural habitat. If you're visiting between Friday and Sunday, swing by Rusty's Markets for a street-food feast.

4

ULUṞU ⏱ 2 DAYS

Another three-hour flight lands you in the heart of Australia's Red Centre. Take your pick from the myriad ways to experience **Uluṟu-Kata Tjuṯa National Park** (p876; pictured), from sunrise- and sunset-viewing tours to the Wintjiri Wiṟu Aboriginal drone show and British artist Bruce Munro's mesmerising Field of Light. The tiny Uluṟu service town of Yulara is home to the airport and a handful of accommodation options.

OZITRAVELER/SHUTTERSTOCK, MICHAEL LINGBERG/SHUTTERSTOCK

ITINERARIES

Central Australia

Allow: 2 weeks
Distance: 3000km

This classic 3000km dash up the Stuart Hwy takes you from coast to coast and right into Australia's desert heart. Have a ball getting to know two of Australia's most underrated capitals at either end and lean into the wild and quirky attractions along the way.

Coober Pedy (p793)

1

ADELAIDE ⏱ 4 DAYS

Spend a day or two enjoying the eat streets and old stone pubs of South Australia's **capital** (p716). Then venture out to explore local wine regions, with the Adelaide Hills (known for its chardonnay and pinot noir) as well as the Barossa Valley (world renowned for its reds) both within easy reach. Or even take a trip to wildlife-rich Kangaroo Island.

2

FLINDERS RANGES ⏱ 1 DAY

Consider a stop in the Clare Valley (the home of Australian riesling) en route to the rust-coloured **Ikara-Flinders Ranges National Park** (p790). Here Ikara (Wilpena Pound) jags up from the semidesert and two dozen hiking trails take you deep into this storied landscape. Camp or stay at the resort inside the park or bed down nearby to watch the ranges glowing red at sunrise.

3

COOBER PEDY ⏱ 1 DAY

It's a full day's drive across the red sands and salt flats of SA's outback to the iconic opal-mining town of **Coober Pedy** (p793), aka Australia's underground city. Spend a day fossicking and museum-hopping, then settle into a subterranean hotel. Travelling by 4WD? You can shave 100km by rerouting along the legendary Oodnadatta Track past Kati Thanda-Lake Eyre.

FROM LEFT: MYPHOTOBANK.COM.AU/SHUTTERSTOCK, ALEXANDRE.ROSA/SHUTTERSTOCK, KWEST/SHUTTERSTOCK, SKYMEDIA AUSTRALIA/SHUTTERSTOCK

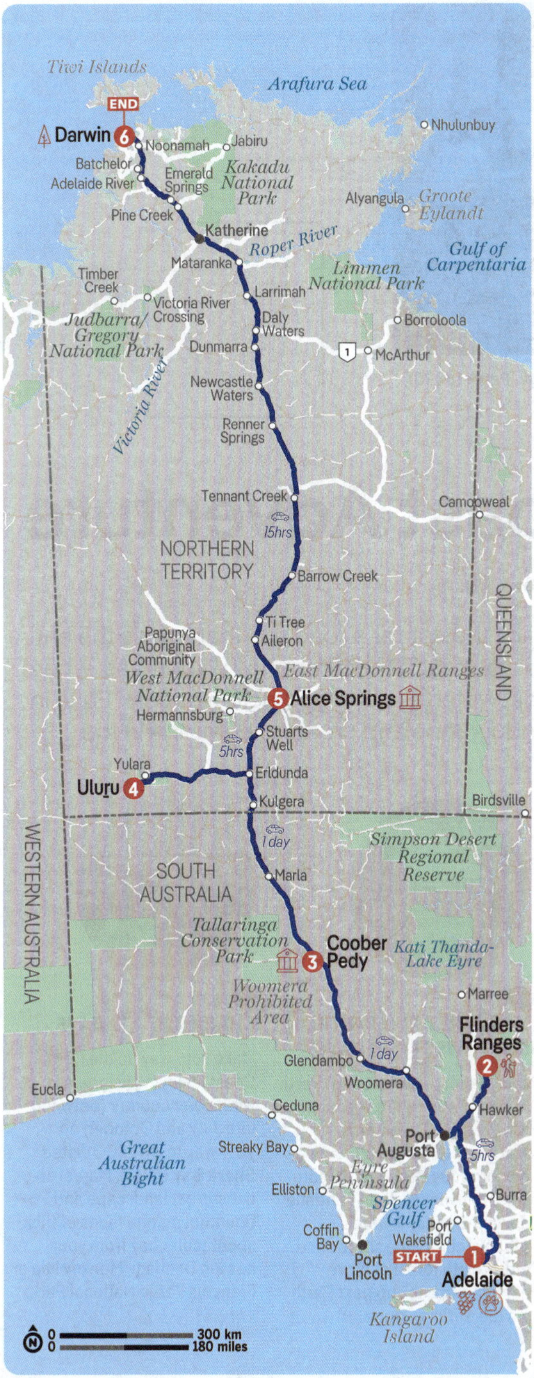

4 ULURU 2 DAYS

Gain a new appreciation for the wide open road as you travel roughly the same distance north again to Uluru. With a huge variety of ways to explore **Uluru-Kata Tjuta National Park** (p876), you'll need at least two days to sample a few from your base in the tiny Uluru service town of Yulara.

5 ALICE SPRINGS 2 DAYS

It's 470km or a five-hour drive to **Alice Springs** (p850), but if you have extra time up your sleeve, it's worth taking the long way past Watarrka National Park and its famed Kings Canyon. In Alice there's a wonderful cultural precinct and a collection of museums to explore along with the nearby West MacDonnell Ranges.

6 DARWIN 4 DAYS

With 1500km to cover to **Darwin** (p804), you'll want to break up the trip; don't miss the thermal pools of Elsey National Park, nor Katherine's magnificent Nitmiluk Gorge. It's easy to day-trip to Litchfield National Park from the sultry capital of Darwin, but you'll want at least two days to visit Kakadu National Park.

Elizabeth Bridge, Perth (p890)

ITINERARIES

West Coast Adventure

Allow: 3–4 weeks **Distance:** 3200km

Feeling adventurous? Pack the car for a road trip that traces the entire West Coast, at least until you reach the Kimberley wilderness, where side roads lead to magical waterfalls and geologic wonders. Ease in with a slice of gourmet indulgence and creature comforts in the Perth area.

1

PERTH 2 DAYS

Fly into Western Australia's **capital** (p890) and see the sights: stroll Elizabeth Quay, visit the museums at the Perth Cultural Centre, spend a spooky night at Fremantle Prison (pictured) and ride the ferry to Rottnest Island to meet the famous quokkas. Then hire a car and hit the road.

2

MARGARET RIVER & THE SOUTHWEST 4 DAYS

Take a short drive south of Perth to one of Australia's premium wine regions (pictured), **Margaret River** (p919). Laze on gorgeous beaches, explore limestone caves, then continue down the coast towards Albany for pristine shores and old-growth forests before hammering back up past Perth via the Stirling Range.

3

SHARK BAY 2 DAYS

Make your way up the Coral Coast, enjoying wanders in wildflower country (between late July and October) on your way to UNESCO-listed **Shark Bay** (p967). Marvel at the surreal landscape and bountiful marine fauna of this spectacular bay from your base in Denham, Monkey Mia or Francois Peron National Park.

BENNY MARTY/SHUTTERSTOCK, GAGLIARDIPHOTOGRAPHY/SHUTTERSTOCK, JAKUB MACULEWICZ/SHUTTERSTOCK

4

EXMOUTH & NINGALOO REEF ⏱ 3 DAYS

The Coral Coast reaches its climax at **Ningaloo Reef** (p976), just steps from the desert landscape of Cape Range National Park (pictured) near Exmouth. Spend your days exploring the park and snorkelling on the reef, perhaps in the company of whale sharks between March and August. And look out for emus on the road.

5

KARIJINI NATIONAL PARK ⏱ 1 DAY

Turn inland and let the Pilbara take over – red earth, spinifex plains and long, heat-hazed miles. After a day's drive, **Karijini** (p983) emerges between the folds of Hamersley Range, its chiselled gorges and shaded plunge pools a sharp break from the furnace outside. Dry off, dust off and roll north back to the coast, through Port Hedland and on to Broome.

6

BROOME & THE KIMBERLEY ⏱ 1–2 WEEKS

Now the real adventure begins! Soak up the frontier vibe and dazzling sunsets of **Broome** (p986) before heading into the heart of the Kimberley (dry season only). You'll need a 4WD to tackle the famous Gibb River Road, but the Great Northern Hwy to Kununurra is sealed (pictured). No sense turning back now, so push on to Darwin – arrange one way car hire in advance.

DARKYDOORS/SHUTTERSTOCK, ADELINE HELG/SHUTTERSTOCK, PHILIP SCHUBERT/SHUTTERSTOCK

ITINERARIES

Best of the East Coast

Allow: 10 days

Distance: 3600km

It's more carbon-friendly to drive this classic East Coast Australian van-life route in four to six weeks, but the trip can also be undertaken in less than two weeks by plane, with airports in every hub. Travel through a staggering array of landscapes from moody Melbourne to the tropical north.

Art Gallery of NSW (p90), Sydney

1

MELBOURNE ⏱ 2 DAYS

Melbourne (p463) can keep visitors engaged for months with its bars, live music, shopping, AFL football and other delights. Fuel up with a coffee in the city's famous laneways and get stuck into the highlights, from wandering the National Gallery of Victoria to tucking into some of Australia's top restaurants.

2

SYDNEY ⏱ 2 DAYS

If you've visited the NSW **capital** (p70) before, check out newer attractions including the revamped Art Gallery of NSW and the proliferation of new restaurants and bars that have transformed the city centre. Or pop inland and stretch your legs in the glorious Blue Mountains (pictured); it's just two hours on the train from the city to Katoomba.

CLOCKWISE FROM TOP LEFT: JANE RIX/SHUTTERSTOCK, AUTUMN STARRA/SHUTTERSTOCK, THERESA J GRAHAM/SHUTTERSTOCK, ROBERT HARDING VIDEO/SHUTTERSTOCK, SABELLA PURWOKO/SHUTTERSTOCK

3

HUNTER VALLEY 1 DAY

Book a day trip or make your own way two hours northwest of Sydney to the vineyards of the **Hunter Valley** (p170) for tastings and other gourmet pleasures. Treat yourself to a sumptuous winery lunch or dinner and sleep off the indulgence at a boutique hotel.

4

BYRON BAY 2 DAYS

Road trippers will love the journey north to **Byron Bay** (p177), with its many tempting coastal and hinterland diversions. When you arrive, there are iconic surf beaches, an epic headland walk, good diving and an enticing array of restaurants to try. Explore another side of Byron on an Aboriginal tour.

5

CAIRNS 3 DAYS

You can fly direct from the Gold Coast, a 45-minute drive north of Byron, to Australia's reef-diving **capital** (p378) and gateway to the Wet Tropics World Heritage Area. Spend a day on the outer Great Barrier Reef (pictured), explore the rainforest on an Indigenous-guided tour, then dive into the tropical city's vibrant food scene.

OLGA KASHUBIN/SHUTTERSTOCK

Cradle Mountain-Lake St Clair National Park (p691)

ITINERARIES

Southern Splendour

Allow: 12 days **Distance:** 1600km

Seen Sydney before? Not big on tropical heat? This itinerary takes you from Melbourne along the most scenic section of Victoria's coast, before dropping into Tasmania for wine, wildlife and the most spectacular edge-of-the-world landscapes you could dream of.

1 MELBOURNE ⏱ 2 DAYS

Drink in the cosmopolitan Victorian **capital's** (p463) acclaimed bars, restaurants, museums, music and sports events to your heart's content. Enjoy the simple pleasure of getting lost in the city centre's winding alleys, or venture out to the Yarra Valley for a day of wine tasting before retiring in a hip hotel.

2 GREAT OCEAN ROAD ⏱ 3 DAYS

Tick off one of Australia's most iconic **road trips** (p542; pictured). Tracing a spectacular section of Victoria's coastline, the 680km round trip from Melbourne is manageable in three days, but allow four or five to enjoy more walks, waterfalls, surf and geological marvels along the way.

3 LAUNCESTON & CRADLE MOUNTAIN ⏱ 2 DAYS

Take an overnight ferry from Geelong to Devonport and make the hour's drive to **Launceston** (p679), or fly from Melbourne. Admire the city's historic buildings (pictured) and get a taste for Tasmanian sparkling wine before heading to the state's blockbuster national park for a gorgeous day hike and maybe an encounter with Tasmanian devils.

FROM LEFT: PRIYANTO MISPAN/SHUTTERSTOCK, JANE RIX/SHUTTERSTOCK, TRABANTOS/SHUTTERSTOCK

4

FREYCINET PENINSULA ⏱2 DAYS

It's a scenic two-hour drive from Launceston to **Freycinet National Park** (p672), home of the stunning Wineglass Bay (pictured). Take a hike to a lookout (or down to its powder-white sands), kayak along the glorious coastline, or simply sit back and slurp fresh oysters from local farms. The little fishing town of Bicheno waits nearby for further refreshments.

5

HOBART & SURROUNDS ⏱3 DAYS

It takes less than three hours to drive directly to **Hobart** (p638), but you should definitely detour to Port Arthur Historic Site (pictured) and nearby Tasman National Park. The emerging culinary capital of Hobart wows with its cosy restaurants and epic art museum. But there's more to explore nearby, from Bruny Island to Mt Field National Park.

WHEN TO GO

It's always a good time to be somewhere in Australia. As a general rule, go north in winter, south in summer, and east and west anytime.

Summer is synonymous with beach weather, but it's not always the case in Australia. In the southern states, summer is short and sweet, with January and February bringing the most comfortable conditions for a dip. Snow falls in the alpine regions of New South Wales, Victoria and Tasmania from May to September, while winter temperatures grow milder (and summers hotter) the further north you travel. In Tropical North Queensland, Darwin and the Kimberley, winter is the most comfortable time to visit – during the southern summer, these northern regions are deep in their wet (and low) season (November to April).

The winter months also have their benefits (beyond skiing) in the lower mainland states, with superb whale watching along East and West Coasts (roughly between May and November) and cooler, less humid weather ideal for coastal bushwalking. Autumn foliage is best experienced anywhere south of Sydney, especially in Tasmania, while spring wildflowers light up the desert fringe.

Forum Theatre (p475), Melbourne

I LIVE HERE

GIG-READY MELBOURNE

Ryan Egan is a Melbourne-based music nerd, broadcaster, radio manager and musician.

Melbourne's chilly winters are often cited as a reason for its strong live-music scene. I'll warm up at a sweaty punk show at the Tote in Collingwood or see an international act heat up the Corner Hotel or the **Forum Theatre**. Winter festivals like Rising draw eclectic lineups, while smaller venues and bars nurture not just the next hot act or DJ but an active community of music lovers.

CYCLONE SEASON

Australia's tropical cyclone season is typically November to April, although cyclones can form outside these bounds. On average, the nation experiences 11 cyclones a year, although typically only four to five reach land, including one or two Category 5 (most severe) cyclones. Heed official warnings and advice.

Weather Through the Year (Sydney)

JANUARY	FEBRUARY	MARCH	APRIL	MAY	JUNE
Ave. daytime max: **26°C**	Ave. daytime max: **25.8°C**	Ave. daytime max: **24.8°C**	Ave. daytime max: **22.5°C**	Ave. daytime max: **19.5°C**	Ave. daytime max: **17.0°C**
Days of rainfall: **8.6**	Days of rainfall: **9.0**	Days of rainfall: **9.9**	Days of rainfall: **8.9**	Days of rainfall: **8.6**	Days of rainfall: **8.8**

BEATING THE HEAT

If you prefer your summer days on the mild side, Tasmania is your spot. From December to February, average highs sit around 20°C, perfect for long rambles and lazy picnics. Even on hot days, keep a jumper handy.

Big-Ticket Festivals

Sydney Gay & Lesbian Mardi Gras Parade (p110) Australia's biggest and most iconic Pride festival paints a rainbow across Sydney, culminating in a joyous parade along Oxford St.
February–March

Adelaide Fringe (p728) The world's second-largest fringe festival is an absolute hoot, with hundreds of shows over an entertaining month.
February–March

Melbourne International Comedy Festival (p480) Laugh until your sides hurt at Australia's largest comedy festival, with more than 500 shows to choose from.
March–April

Rising (p480) Victoria's flagship festival of music, food, art and culture spills into the streets of Melbourne over 16 wonderful days at the beginning of winter. **June**

Dark Mofo (p647) Hobart's midwinter festival paints the town red with boundary-pushing art, up-late performances and fiery rituals.
June

Offbeat Events

Adelaide Cabaret Festival (p729) A three-week burst of sass and satire, from international burlesque stars to up-and-coming circus acts.
June

Mary Poppins Festival (p352) Maryborough in Queensland hosts a free, joy-filled day of nanny races, chimney-sweeping and pavement art.
June/July

Beer Can Regatta (p808) Cheer on homemade-boat captains at this family-friendly one-day festival in Darwin.
June/July

Jumpers & Jazz in July (p306) Queensland's quirkiest festival sees 'Yarntopians' decorate the communities of the Southern Downs. **July**

Shinju Matsuri Festival of the Pearl (p988) Broome pays homage to its pearling heritage with dragon-boat races, fireworks and more.
August–September

I LIVE HERE

BAROSSA VALLEY'S VINES

Joseph Evans is the winemaker and viticulturist at Ballycroft Vineyard and Cellars. *@ballycroft*

For a winemaker, summertime is about watching the grapes change colour in the vineyard while pruning rows in the sun. It's a time of collective anticipation in the valley. Preparation for vintage has begun and soon we'll be bringing in the harvest. At the end of a long, hot day, nothing beats a slightly chilled bottle of Montepulciano shared with family and friends.

Adelaide Fringe (p728)

SUNSHINE STATE

Queensland's tagline is particularly accurate on the Gold Coast in the state's subtropical southeast, which receives around 300 days of sunshine annually. The city receives most of its rain during summer, which is still a lovely time to visit.

JULY	AUGUST	SEPTEMBER	OCTOBER	NOVEMBER	DECEMBER
Ave. daytime max: **16.4°C**	Ave. daytime max: **17.9°C**	Ave. daytime max: **20.1°C**	Ave. daytime max: **22.2°C**	Ave. daytime max: **23.7°C**	Ave. daytime max: **25.3°C**
Days of rainfall: **7.4**	Days of rainfall: **7.1**	Days of rainfall: **7.1**	Days of rainfall: **7.9**	Days of rainfall: **8.3**	Days of rainfall: **7.9**

FROM LEFT: ENEEMS/SHUTTERSTOCK, ZAK KACZMAREK/GETTY IMAGES

GET PREPARED FOR AUSTRALIA

Useful things to load in your bag, your ears and your brain.

Clothes

Light waterproof jacket It can, and does, rain anytime in most coastal regions. And even summer evenings can be chilly, especially in the southern states.

Walking shoes Bring a pair with enough support for pounding city pavements. For more serious bushwalking, breathable walking shoes or boots with ankle coverage are best.

Casual and smart casual clothes Nicer restaurants and bars command a dress code. Shorts and smart sandals are fine, but thongs/flip-flops are not – south of the Tropic of Capricorn, at least.

Swimwear Have you even been to Australia if you didn't take a dip in the sea?

Layers Handy if you're visiting cooler zones or multiple regions.

Manners

Civilities Australians might be relaxed, but manners remain important. Use 'please', 'thank you' and 'excuse me'.

Queues Like the British, Australians are sticklers for queuing, but less reserved about telling off queue-jumpers.

Ordering It's polite to say hello to service staff or even ask how their day is going before placing an order.

Headphones Respecting people's personal space includes wearing headphones.

Sunscreen Slip, slop and slap SPF30 or above before you head out during the day (even when it's overcast).

READ

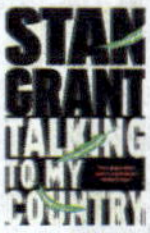

Talking to My Country (Stan Grant; 2016) Powerful meditation on race, culture and national identity by a Wiradjuri media identity.

Carpentaria (Alexis Wright; 2006) First Nations fiction, blending humour, politics and magical realism with Queensland's Gulf Country.

Where Song Began (Tim Low; 2014) Insightful study of Australia's unique birdlife and its role in reshaping global evolutionary history.

Tracks (Robyn Davidson; 1980) The author's epic 2700km journey across the Australian outback makes for an inspiring holiday read.

Words

Arvo Afternoon
Bail Leave ('I'm gonna bail.')
Bludger Someone who is lazy ('Bob's a bludger.')
Bonza Great
Booze bus Random breath-testing police unit
Bottle-o Liquor store
Brekkie Breakfast
Buckley's No chance
Cactus Dead or broken
CBD Central Business District
Cellar door Tasting room
Coldie/stubby Cold beer
Devo Devastated ('I'm devo I have to work tomorrow.')
Galah Person who doesn't know what they're doing
How ya goin'? How are you? (equivalent to 'How you doin'?' in the US)
Old mate A bloke (man) whose name you don't know ('old mate over there')
Pineapple and lobster Australian $50 note and $20 note
Sanga Sandwich
Servo Petrol station
Shout Round of drinks ('It's your shout, mate.')
Snag Sausage
Stuffed Full of food or tired (or both)
Tinny Can of beer or a small boat ('Let's crack a tinny in the tinny.')
Too easy/no worries/no wuckas/no dramas No problem
Tucker/grub Any type of food
Woop woop Middle of nowhere ('Pam lives out in woop woop.')
Yarn A conversation ('having a yarn')
Yeah, nah No
You little ripper That's excellent
You right? Are you OK? (enquiring about a person's welfare, or calling out bad manners)

WATCH

The Dressmaker (Jocelyn Moorhouse; 2015; pictured) Wickedly funny revenge drama set in dust-bowl Australia.

The Adventures of Priscilla, Queen of the Desert (Stephan Elliot; 1994) Powerful presentation of positive LGBTIQ+ themes.

The Castle (Rob Sitch; 1997) Aussie comedy about family, home and fighting city hall – deadpan and endlessly quotable.

Rabbit-Proof Fence (Phillip Noyce; 2002) Drama based on a true story confronts Australia's devastating Stolen Generations policy.

The Dry (Robert Connolly; 2020) Taut cop-returns-home mystery-thriller set in drought-stricken Victoria.

LISTEN

Back in Black (AC/DC; 1980) A thunderous hard-rock icon and one of the world's best-selling albums, packed with recognisable riffs.

Better in Blak (Thelma Plum; 2019) A catchy debut album mixing polished folk-pop with identity, heartbreak and Gamilaraay womanhood.

Conversations (ABC) A long-running radio-segment-come-podcast uncovering the stories behind everyday Aussies.

Full Story (Guardian Australia) Guardian journalists go behind the headlines every weekday on the podcast.

ROSE MARINELLI/SHUTTERSTOCK

A schooey and a parmy

HOW TO... Speak Strayan

Wanna go t' the local for a few schooies and a parmy? Aussies understand this phrase as an invitation to go to the pub for a few beers and a chicken parmigiana (a popular pub meal). But it's likely to leave visitors scratching their heads. Welcome to the mysterious world of Australian slang, where no word in the English language is safe from being butchered and one of the most offensive swear words in the dictionary is commonly used to refer to a friend.

Get Shorty

A nationwide love of shortening words sits at the heart of Aussie slang; the most common endings are *-ie/-y* and *-o*. The earliest examples date to the 19th century and referred to a person's trade – for example, 'milko' (milkman) or 'bottle-o' (bottle collector). Over time, these terms have taken on new meaning: today, a 'bottle-o' is a bottle shop (liquor store) and a 'milko' is most commonly associated with a vanilla-flavoured lolly (candy).

When it comes to names, a shortening often doubles as affection: 'Robert' might become 'Robbie' or 'Robbo'. But not all slang is friendly – there's nothing warm about calling someone a 'sicko' (sadistic person). And while there's no strict rule about which ending a word receives, some shortenings are non-negotiable. Australians always fill the car at a 'servo' (service station) and breakfast is 'brekkie/brekky' – never 'brekko'.

Modern slang has sprouted, too, including 'iso' (isolation) and the now-global 'selfie'. But watch for traps – 'avo' means avocado, not afternoon (that's 'arvo') and a 'smoko' is a work break, not a cigarette endorsement.

Regional quirks add another layer. Order a 285mL beer in New South Wales and you'll get a 'middy'; in South Australia, a 'schooner' (schooey). Accents shift as you travel, too: Adelaide's rounded lilt, Queensland's longer drawl, Melbourne's subtle merging of vowels. Listen closely and you'll also hear the retroflex curls of Indigenous languages in names like Uluṟu.

So how do you learn Australian? With many slang words now universally understood – from 'mozzie' to 'greenie' – it's certainly getting easier. Like with any language, though, immersion is the key. So whaddya waitin' for? Head to the local, order a schooey and a parmy and get amongst it.

AUSSIE ENGLISH

When English washed up on these shores barely two centuries ago, it didn't stay pristine for long. Dozens of regional dialects were crammed into convict camps and rural outposts – speakers simply sanded off the edges so they could understand one another. By the 1880s, a burst of elocution fever tried steering everyone towards polished southern English, but the bush had other ideas. Slang, convict lingo, Indigenous words and a storehouse of rural expressions all seeped in, giving the Australian accent its unmistakable twang. Australian English wasn't taught so much as weathered, scuffed and made entirely its own.

MARTIN MECNAROWSKI/SHUTTERSTOCK

Tasmanian devil

HOW TO... Spot Native Wildlife

You won't need to travel far to see a kangaroo or a kookaburra, but tracking down other iconic species can be a bit of a treasure hunt. Start at the national parks.

In the Rainforest

Dinosaur-like cassowaries are regularly seen in **Cape Tribulation** (p408) and the **Cassowary Coast** (p426) of Tropical North Queensland. For a chance to see tree kangaroos and platypuses, head to the **Atherton Tablelands** (p391). In the **Gondwana Rainforests** (p186) of southeast Queensland and North Coast New South Wales, look out (and listen) for lyrebirds with their extravagant tail feathers and mimicking cry.

In the Ocean

Southern right and humpback whales migrate along the East and West Coasts, trading Antarctic cold for Australia's warmer waters, roughly between May and November. Southern right whales also gather in the **Great Australian Bight** (p785) in spring, while orca tours (p948) run in southwest Western Australia from January to April. Whale sharks cruise WA's **Ningaloo Reef** (p976) from March to August; sea lions and fur seals frequent southern coastlines.

In the Desert

If you're visiting in a drought year, you might not see much more than the odd mob of kangaroos and emus, and maybe a few feral camels. Return after big rains, however, and you'll encounter vast salt lakes filled with millions of waterbirds. Keep an eye out for **desert lizards** (p854) including the thorny devil and perentie (Australia's largest monitor lizard). Head further north for frill-necked lizards.

On the Coast

One of the trickiest native critters to spot is the koala. Listed as endangered (in Queensland, New South Wales and the Australian Capital Territory) in 2022, they live in eucalypt forests along the East Coast and also inland. For near-guaranteed sightings in the wild, head to **Kangaroo Island** (p749) or **Magnetic Island** (p438). Tasmania is jam-packed with wallabies, wombats, possums and the endangered Tasmanian devil. Fox-free landscapes and conservation programs, like in **Maria Island National Park** (p668), offer hope for the devil.

TWILIGHT ENCOUNTERS

Australia's wildlife is easiest to see when you match the habitat to the hour. At dusk and dawn, watch for kangaroos and wallabies grazing on golf courses or open grassy verges. This is also an excellent time to spot koalas; scan the ground for fresh green scat. Just after dark, seek out possums, gliders and bandicoots in parks and bushland. Use a red-light torch to stay unobtrusive – bright white beams and camera flashes can confuse and disturb nocturnal creatures, especially little penguins searching for their rocky burrows. Above all, move slowly, stay quiet and give every animal plenty of space.

CHAMELEONSEYE/SHUTTERSTOCK

Laura Quinkan Dance Festival (p417)

TRIP PLANNER

INDIGENOUS AUSTRALIA

Aboriginal and Torres Strait Islander cultures have evolved over 65,000 years, kept alive from one generation to the next through storytelling, song, art, dance and other cultural traditions. Right across Australia, there are opportunities to learn from ways of life still practised by the world's oldest living cultures.

LAND OF MANY NATIONS

The Aboriginal peoples of mainland Australia and Torres Strait Islander peoples hailing from the eponymous Queensland archipelago are two ethnically and culturally distinct Indigenous cultures. Within them are many subgroups with their own languages, traditions and customs. Language groups are commonly described as 'Nations' and groups within Nations as 'clans' or 'mobs'. While terminology preferences differ between individuals (when in doubt, ask), 'Aboriginal' is typically used to refer to Aboriginal peoples, while 'Indigenous' or 'First Nations' is used for Indigenous Australians or groups/individuals who may have mixed Aboriginal and Torres Strait Islander heritage. Many First Nations peoples include their Nation and/or clan name as a prefix to their given name and may use the term Blackfella/Blackfulla to describe themselves. The term 'Aborigine' is now widely considered to be derogatory and should be avoided.

WHOSE COUNTRY?

Every part of Australia (except for a few remote islands) lies on the traditional land and sea territory of at least one First Nations group. The Traditional Custodians (or Owners) of these landscapes, also known as 'Country', have a cultural obligation to safeguard them.

Understanding whose Country you're on as you explore Australia forms the basis of respect for its Traditional Custodians.

HANDY RESOURCES

Welcome to Country *(welcometocountry.com)* Browse and book First Nations experiences across the country via this not-for-profit marketplace.

Discover Aboriginal Experiences *(discoveraboriginalexperiences.com)* Tourism Australia's premium range of First Nations experiences; click through to book direct.

Indigenous Art Code *(indigenousartcode.org)* Members listed on the website commit to ensuring the artwork they purchase comes from ethical sources and that artists are paid and treated fairly.

Creative Spirits *(creativespirits.info)* Articles and resources covering everything from the Stolen Generations to Indigenous languages.

Blak Out *(abc.net.au/triplej/programs/blak-out)* Tune into Triple J radio every Sunday from 5pm to 6pm to listen to Indigenous artists. You can also listen online.

This information is typically found on the local government website (the shire or municipal council) in the form of an acknowledgement. Another helpful resource is the Australian Institute of Aboriginal and Torres Strait Islander Studies' (AIATSIS) map of Indigenous Australia *(aiatsis.gov.au/explore/map-indigenous-australia),* which attempts to represent the language and social groups of Australia's First Nations.

CHOOSING AN INDIGENOUS EXPERIENCE

Australia now offers an incredible array of Indigenous-guided tourism experiences. And the unique ancestral traditions of each Indigenous group – and families within them – mean that no two experiences are ever the same. Many tours are geared towards families, with storytelling and opportunities to sample bush tucker always a hit with kids big and small. Booking Indigenous-owned and operated experiences means your tourism dollars directly support Indigenous communities.

Smoking ceremony, Gadigal Country (p1027)

David Unaipon on the $50 note

THE IMPORTANCE OF STORYTELLING

Indigenous Australians historically had an oral culture, so storytelling was an important way to learn. Stories gave meaning to life and were used to teach the messages of the spirit ancestors. Although beliefs and cultural practices vary according to region and language groups, there's a common worldview that these ancestors created the land, the sea and all living things. This is often referred to as the Dreaming. Through stories, knowledge and beliefs are passed on from one generation to another, setting out the community's social mores and recording events from the past.

Today, artists have continued this tradition with new media such as film and literature. The first published Indigenous Australian was David Unaipon (1872–1967), a Ngarrindjeri man from South Australia who was a writer, a scientist and an advocate for his people and the author of *Aboriginal Legends* (1927) and *Native Legends* (1929). You can see Unaipon's portrait on the $50 note.

WELCOME 101

You may be welcomed to the traditional lands of Indigenous Australians with a Welcome to Country – a typically brief but always moving ceremony performed by a Traditional Custodian of the place you are visiting. It is also common for Australian festivals and events to be opened with an Acknowledgement of Country – this is delivered by a non-Traditional Custodian as a gesture of respect to the Traditional Custodians of the land.

VISITING INDIGENOUS COMMUNITIES

Many remote Indigenous communities are 'closed', which means the general public can't visit without permission – always check before you go. You may also need a permit to enter national parks on Aboriginal lands, which are typically acquired through the local Indigenous land council. If you have the privilege of visiting any type of Indigenous community, it's polite to avoid wearing revealing clothing and always ask before taking photos of people or sacred places (including rock art) as it may not be allowed, or welcomed. Most First Nations guides are happy to answer any questions about Indigenous culture and history, so don't be shy. But be mindful that English may be your host's second, third or even fourth language and don't be deterred by avoidance of eye contact – this is customarily a gesture of respect in Aboriginal and Torres Strait Islander cultures.

INDIGENOUS ART & CULTURAL CENTRES

Big-city museums such as the Australian Museum (p107) in Sydney, the South Australian Museum (p725) in Adelaide and the Bunjilaka Aboriginal Culture Centre within the Melbourne Museum (p505) have excellent displays on Australia's Indigenous cultures. Major art events like Adelaide's

BEATA URMOS/SHUTTERSTOCK

Worimi Conservation Lands (p169)

Best Rock Art

KAKADU NATIONAL PARK
Two of Australia's best and most accessible rock-art galleries are found at **Ubirr** (p814) and **Nourlangie** (p816) in the Northern Territory.

MURUJUGA NATIONAL PARK
The rocky landscape of Western Australia's Burrup Peninsula contains more than a million **petroglyphs** (p979).

QUINKAN COUNTRY
Paintings of spirit figures are found on many of the **sandstone escarpments** (p417) surrounding the small Queensland town of Laura.

Tarnanthi *(agsa.sa.gov.au)* reveal the depth and diversity of contemporary First Nations works, but stepping inside a community-run art or cultural centre is another experience entirely. These centres are among the best places to buy work ethically and many offer the opportunity to meet or watch artists at work, from the Kimberley art co-ops (p996) spread across northern WA to hands-on workshops at Maruku Arts (p877) in Uluru. Cultural centres, which typically also have art and other Indigenous-made products for sale, offer hyperlocal insights into Indigenous history and culture, making them a great first stop before exploring the region you're visiting. Indigenous art and cultural centres aren't only found in the outback, but also in coastal and urban areas – such as the Minjungbal Aboriginal Cultural Centre (p189) in Tweed Heads (New South Wales), Perridak Arts (p575) in Ballarat (Victoria) and Jellurgal Aboriginal Cultural Centre (p314) on the Gold Coast (Queensland).

INDIGENOUS FESTIVALS

There's nothing like attending an Indigenous festival on Country to connect with First Nations cultures. Typically held in remote destinations, these events generally require a high degree of preparation. The big ones include the Garma Festival (p830), Barunga Festival (p841) and Parrtjima (p875) in the NT; and the Laura Quinkan Dance Festival (p417) and Thursday Island's Winds of Zenadth Cultural Festival (p422), both in Queensland. There's always Indigenous art for sale at festivals, with some of the best opportunities to purchase art including the Cairns Indigenous Art Fair (p379), the Darwin Aboriginal Art Fair (p808), the Tiwi AFL Grand Final and Art Sale (p813) on the Tiwi Islands and **Desert Mob** *(desertmob.com)* in Alice Springs.

INDIGENOUS TOURISM OPTIONS

Walking Tours
Accessible for families and very ecofriendly, walking tours typically include storytelling, bush-tucker tasting, visiting sacred sites and opportunities to get hands-on with traditional tools, instruments or weapons.

Rock art Tours
Rock art isn't only found in the outback, with carvings, paintings and other works to be uncovered along the coast and surrounds. Some tours are conducted on foot, others by car.

Cultural Cruises
See the Great Barrier Reef through Indigenous eyes, pair bush-tucker insights with Ngarrindjeri culture in SA's **Coorong National Park** (p748) and more.

Cultural/Art Centres
Great places to learn about the local mob and shop for Indigenous-made products; most regional centres have one. Some art centres also offer art classes.

Indigenous Dining
Get a taste of Indigenous Australia at slick urban restaurants helmed by Indigenous chefs, at cultural-centre cafes, or at traditional campfire cook-ups included on tours.

Adventure & Adrenaline
Tear around the sand dunes of the **Worimi Conservation Lands** (p168) near Newcastle on an Aboriginal-guided quad-bike ride, or hike deep into the Tasmanian bush on the **Wukalina Walk** (p677).

INJALAK HILL
Guided tours take visitors to an incredible **collection of rock shelters** (p829) in West Arnhem Land, slathered in layers of ancient X-ray art.

SYDNEY
Aboriginal rock carvings can be found in the likes of **Ku-ring-gai Chase National Park** (p137) and **Royal National Park** (p144).

FLINDERS RANGES
See ancient **Adnyamathanha art** (p791) tucked into caves and overhangs, revealing outback SA's prehistoric creatures.

KIMBERLEY
The **Mitchell Plateau** (p1004) is home to examples of both the Gwion Gwion and Wandjina art traditions.

CHAMELEONSEYE/SHUTTERSTOCK

Great Barrier Reef (p382)

TRIP PLANNER

VISITING THE GREAT BARRIER REEF

There are numerous ways to experience the magnificent spectacle of the Great Barrier Reef, stretching over 2300km from just below the Tropic of Capricorn (near Bundaberg) to just south of Papua New Guinea. Diving and snorkelling are the best ways, but you can also enjoy the reef without getting wet.

PICKING YOUR SPOT

There are multiple gateways to the reef, all offering different experiences. It's generally more affordable to base yourself at a mainland gateway and travel out to the reef for a day or longer (with an average journey time to the outer reef of 90 minutes), but there are also dozens of islands you can stay on, with camping costing as little as $7.25 per person per night in national parks, though the cost of transfers can add to that significantly. Islands with resorts include Lady Elliot Island, Heron Island, Wilson Island and Great Keppel Island (Southern Great Barrier Reef); Hamilton Island, Daydream Island, Hayman Island and Long Island (Whitsundays/Central Great Barrier Reef); and Orpheus Island, Green Island, Fitzroy Island and Lizard Island (Northern Great Barrier Reef). Of these, Lady Elliot, Heron and Lizard Islands have the best snorkelling straight off the beach.

SAFEGUARDING THE REEF

It's no secret that the reef faces unprecedented challenges in the face of the climate crisis; in 2025 it endured its sixth mass bleaching in a decade. But you only need to don a snorkel to discover that it's far from 'dead'. The outer reef tends to have the best snorkelling and diving. Operators generally visit healthier sections where bleaching

WHEN TO GO

High Season
High season on the reef is from June to November, which coincides with the best underwater visibility.

Wet Season
From December to March, northern Queensland (north of Townsville) has its wet season, bringing oppressive heat and abundant rainfall (it's cooler from July to September).

Stinger Season
Stinger (jellyfish) season is between November and May; most reef operators offer Lycra stinger suits to snorkellers and divers, or bring your own.

Other Times
Winter (June to August) can be pleasantly warm, but you'll occasionally need a jumper (sweater). Anytime is generally good to visit the Whitsundays and the Southern Great Barrier Reef (between Yeppoon and Lady Elliot Island).

and other damage (for example, from cyclones) is minimal to unnoticeable. Healthy coral can come in shades of olive, green, brown, tan and pale yellow – check with the onboard marine biologist (all good operators have one) before jumping to conclusions.

Every visitor to the reef can play a role in its protection by uploading images and observations (such as the location of invasive crown-of-thorns starfish) via the Eye on the Reef app, which is monitored by scientists. A growing number of operators offer their own citizen-science projects, such as Fitzroy Island's full-day Marine Conservation Program and the marine-biologist-for-a-day program offered by Passions of Paradise, which also operates from Cairns (Gimuy). Read up on responsible reef tourism at *www2.gbrmpa.gov.au/access/responsible-reef-practices*.

TANYA PUNTTI/SHUTTERSTOCK

Airlie Beach (p440)

MAINLAND GATEWAYS

Here's a brief overview of the gateways and the reef experiences they offer, from south to north.

Bundaberg
Excellent day and overnight tours to Lady Musgrave Island's coral lagoon (diving available), plus flights to Lady Elliot Island.

Agnes Water & Town of 1770
Snorkelling tours to Lady Musgrave Island and diving in the Capricorn Bunker area.

Gladstone
Boat and heli transfers to Heron Island resort and Wilson Island glamping.

Yeppoon
Snorkelling day tours to Keppel Bay Islands National Park.

Mackay
Snorkelling tours to local islands including Brampton and Keswick; outer reef diving available by private charter.

Airlie Beach
The big attraction is spending several days aboard a boat and seeing some of the Whitsundays' fringing coral reefs. Outer reef trips on big boats also available.

Townsville
Diving the wreck of the SS *Yongala* and snorkelling or diving the Museum of Underwater Art (particularly the outer-reef Coral Greenhouse) are highlights. Boats tend to be smaller (read: bumpier).

Mission Beach
This small, relaxed town offers a few snorkelling and diving tours to the outer reef.

Cairns
The main launching pad for reef tours, with myriad operators offering everything from affordable day trips on large boats to intimate multiday luxury charters. Lizard Island is reached by small plane from Cairns.

Port Douglas
Higher-end gateway to the Low Isles and Agincourt Reef, one of the nicer sections of the outer reef. Plenty of activities and operators to choose from.

BOAT EXCURSIONS

Unless you're staying on a coral-fringed island, you'll need to join a boat excursion to experience the reef's real beauty. Day trips leave from many places along the coast, as well as from island resorts, and typically include the use of snorkelling gear, snacks and a buffet lunch, with scuba diving an optional extra. On some boats, naturalists or marine biologists present talks on the reef's ecology.

Boat trips vary dramatically in passenger numbers, type of vessel and quality – which is reflected in the price – so get all the details before committing. When selecting a tour, consider the vessel (motorised catamaran or sailing ship), the number of passengers (from six to 400), what extras are offered and the destination. The outer reefs are usually more vibrant. Inner reefs often show signs of damage from humans and coral-eating crown-of-thorns starfish. Coral bleaching is a major issue in the far northern sections of the reef. Some operators offer the option of a trip in a glass-bottom boat or semisubmersible.

Many boats have underwater cameras for hire, although you'll save money by hiring these on land (or using your own). Some boats also have professional photographers on board who will dive and take high-quality shots of you in action.

LIVEABOARDS

If you're eager to do as much diving as possible, a liveaboard is an excellent option as you'll do three dives per day, plus some night dives, all in more remote parts of the Great Barrier Reef. Trip lengths vary from one to 12 nights. The three-day/three-night

RABAN/SHUTTERSTOCK

Fitzroy Island (p384)

Best Great Barrier Reef Island Camping

WHITSUNDAY ISLANDS
Nearly a dozen beautifully sited camping areas, scattered on Hook, Whitsunday, South Molle and Lindeman Islands.

CAPRICORNIA CAYS
Camping available on three separate coral cays – Masthead Island, North West Island and Lady Musgrave Island.

DUNK ISLAND
On the Cassowary Coast, it's easy to get to, with good swimming, kayaking and hiking.

voyages, which allow up to 11 dives (nine day and two night dives), are among the most common.

Some boats offer specialist itineraries, following marine life and events such as minke whales or coral spawning, or offer trips to less-visited spots like the far northern reefs, Pompey Complex, Coral Sea Reefs or Swain Reefs. Go with operators who are **Dive Queensland** *(dive-queensland.com.au)* members – this ensures they follow a minimum set of guidelines. Ideally, they'll also be accredited by **Ecotourism Australia** *(ecotourism.org.au)*.

Popular departure points for liveaboard dive vessels, along with the main locales they visit, are: **Bundaberg** (p354; the Bunker Island group, including Lady Musgrave Island and Lady Elliot Island, possibly Fitzroy Reef, Llewellyn Reef and the rarely visited Boult Reef, or Hoskyn Islands and Fairfax Islands); **Airlie Beach** (p440; the Whitsundays, Knuckle Reef and Hardy Reef); **Townsville** (p430; SS *Yongala* wreck, plus canyons of Wheeler Reef and Keeper Reef); **Cairns** (p378; Cod Hole, Ribbon Reefs, the Coral Sea and possibly far northern reefs); and **Port Douglas** (p403; Osprey Reef, Cod Hole, Ribbon Reefs, Coral Sea and possibly the far northern reefs).

EQROY/SHUTTERSTOCK

Scuba diving, Port Douglas (p403)

LEAVE ONLY BUBBLES

The Great Barrier Reef may be big, but it's incredibly fragile. Follow these easy steps to minimise your impact.

- It is an offence to damage or remove coral in the marine park.
- If you touch or walk on coral, you'll damage it (and probably get some nasty cuts).
- Don't touch or harass marine animals and don't enter the water near a dugong.
- If you have a boat, be aware of the rules in relation to anchoring around the reef.
- If you're diving, check that you're weighted correctly before entering the water, maintain good buoyancy control and ensure that equipment such as secondary regulators aren't dragging over the reef.
- Wear reef-safe sunscreen, or hire a wetsuit or a 'rashie'.
- Watch where your fins are – try not to stir up sediment or disturb coral.
- Take all litter away with you – even biodegradable materials like apple cores – and dispose of it back on the mainland.

SAFE DIVING

Your last dive should be completed 24 hours before flying – even in a balloon or for a parachute jump – to minimise the risk of residual nitrogen in the blood that can cause decompression injury. It's fine to dive soon after arriving by air.

Find out whether your insurance policy classifies diving as a dangerous-sport exclusion. For a nominal annual fee, the **Divers Alert Network** *(diversalertnetwork.org)* provides insurance for medical or evacuation services required in the event of a diving accident.

FITZROY ISLAND
Resort and national-park camping with short walking trails through bush and coral just off the beaches.

FRANKLAND ISLANDS
Coral-fringed national park with white-sand beaches awaits just south of Cairns.

LIZARD ISLAND
Eye-popping beaches, magnificent coral and abundant wildlife; visitors mostly arrive by plane.

ORPHEUS ISLAND
Secluded island (accessible by air) with pretty tropical forest and superb fringing reef.

Fish and chips

THE FOOD SCENE

Food critics claim there has never been a better time to eat out in Australia. Dig in and you'll soon find out why.

We hope you've packed your appetite, because you're going to want to take a seriously big bite out of Australia. With 87% of the population living by the coast, relaxed coastal dining reigns supreme, but this can mean anything from fish and chips on the beach to a multicourse extravaganza served in a fancy restaurant overlooking the sea. Local seafood is ever-present on menus, from barramundi in northern Australia to fresh oysters plucked from South Coast New South Wales, also known as Australia's Oyster Coast. And there's no shortage of land-based proteins either, including opportunities to sample kangaroo, wallaby, crocodile and even emu, paired with farm-fresh local produce.

Chefs across the region are increasingly looking to their local backyards to highlight hyperlocal produce, including punchy native ingredients harvested by First Nations peoples for millennia. Fermenting and pickling has also taken off across the country, adding another element of zing to menus flavoured by the four corners of the planet.

An Evolving Cuisine

Australians have been borrowing bits from other cuisines since well before the British arrived (with Makassan traders thought to have introduced *blachan*, the spicy fermented shrimp paste that remains a staple in Darwin kitchens), creating a food culture that can't really be pinned down

Best Australian Dishes

SMASHED AVO
Avocado on sourdough. The king of Aussie brunch dishes, best paired with poached eggs.

FISH AND CHIPS
Battered or grilled, with chips (fries), salad, tartare sauce and lemon.

MEAT PIE
Bakery staple with choices spanning plain beef to Thai chicken curry.

SAUSAGE SANGA
Barbecued beef sausage in bread, topped with onions and tomato sauce (ketchup).

because it's always changing and evolving.

Australia's food scene reads like a world map, nowhere more so than in Melbourne where Chinatown, Little Italy, Little Saigon and strong Jewish, Greek and Indian communities shape what ends up on the plate. Chinese migrants played a defining role early on – a third of chefs in the 1890s were Chinese, paving the way for sweet-and-savoury favourites now served right across the country. Even so, meat-and-three-veg largely ruled dinner tables until the 1940s. The mass arrival of emigrants from postwar Europe, Southeast Asia and beyond sparked an era of culinary experimentation that never ended. Sit down at any contemporary fine-dining restaurant and the menu will invariably feature cooking techniques or entire dishes borrowed from a dozen different nations – with a subtle Australian twist.

Vegetarians, Vegans & Food Intolerances

There has never been a better time to be a plant-based traveller in Australia, where many restaurants have introduced entire degustation menus catering to vegetarians and vegans. Even the classic meat-and-wheat pub scene now typically includes a few options for different dietary needs. Farmers markets are ubiquitous and great places to pick up fresh produce. Australia's love of dairy products can make eating out as a vegan slightly more challenging at times, but most restaurants can cater to your needs, especially in urban centres. Food intolerances from gluten to nuts are increasingly well managed.

JACKSON STOCK PHOTOGRAPHY/SHUTTERSTOCK

Smashed avo

MINIMINAMUM/SHUTTERSTOCK

Narooma Oyster Festival (p209)

FOOD & DRINK FESTIVALS

Taste of Summer (p636) Coinciding with the Sydney to Hobart yacht race in December/January, this celebration of Tassie food, drink and music sees waterfront streets blocked off for foodie festivities.

Melbourne Food & Wine Festival (p480) Take your pick from over 300 foodie events hosted across the city over 10 days in March.

Tasting Australia (p728) The country's longest-running food festival takes over Adelaide's Victoria Sq for 10 mouth-watering days in May.

Narooma Oyster Festival (p209) A NSW South Coast favourite shelling out chef demos, shucking classes and live music across a May long weekend.

Truffle Kerfuffle (p938) The 'black gold' of Manjimup in Western Australia is celebrated over an aromatic weekend in June.

CHICKEN PARMIGIANA
Pub classic: breaded chicken topped with tomato pasta sauce and cheese.

PAVLOVA
Meringue dessert topped with tropical fruit, synonymous with summer celebrations.

SALT 'N PEPPER SQUID
Crunchy, lightly deep-fried calamari, served with lemon and aioli.

LOT BURGER
Beef patty, bacon, cheese, lettuce, tomato, beetroot, egg and grilled pineapple.

KANGAROO
Lean, gamey meat, usually served medium-rare – grilled, seared or as a steak.

Specialities

Dare to Try

Witchetty grubs These protein-rich outback grubs taste like eggs when cooked. Can also be eaten raw.
Crocodile Tastes a bit like chicken crossed with swordfish.
Green ants Bite off the abdomen for a citrus burst, or steep ants in boiling water to make a lemony tea.
Vegemite Spread lightly: the strong umami flavour of this popular breakfast spread can take some getting used to.
Dawgood dog This nostalgic festival staple is a hot dog on a stick, dipped in batter, then deep-fried in hot oil.
Curried scallop pie Tassie scallops swimming in creamy curry under a flaky lid. Hangover cure in pastry form.
Dim sim The thicker-skinned cousin of the dim sum dumpling is Melbourne's gift to snack culture.
Pie floater Meat pie plonked upside-down in pea soup. Adelaide's late-night icon.

Sweet Treats

Lamington Square of sponge cake coated in chocolate sauce and rolled in coconut.

Vanilla slice

Vanilla slice Aka the 'snot block' – a bakery staple made with vanilla custard and puff pastry.
Anzac biscuits Sweet biscuits originally sent to soldiers abroad because the ingredients, including rolled oats and maple syrup, kept well.
Cherry Ripe Cadbury chocolate bar made with cherries and coconut covered in dark chocolate.
Tim Tams Milk-chocolate-covered biscuits made for hot-drink dunking.
Fairy bread Kids' party-food dish consisting of white bread with margarine and rainbow sprinkles called 'hundreds and thousands'.

MEALS OF A LIFETIME

Fig Tree (p756) Mediterranean menu meets arboreal architecture inside a 120-year-old fig tree on remote Kangaroo Island, off South Australia's coast.

Tali Wiru (p881) Combined with a didgeridoo performance and Aboriginal storytelling, this alfresco dune-top dining experience is a wonderful way to experience Uluṟu.

Bennelong (p84) Enjoy the best of contemporary Australian flavours at the Sydney Opera House, where fresh heirloom produce takes center stage.

Wildflower (p894) The creation of every dish at this Perth degustation restaurant honours the six seasons of the Noongar calendar. The two-course lunch offers a more affordable taste.

THE YEAR IN FOOD

SPRING

Asparagus is cheap and ricotta-stuffed zucchini flowers are a seasonal starter highlight. It's also a top time to try wild-caught barramundi, mud crab, king prawns and Moreton Bay bug (slipper lobster; pictured).

SUMMER

Stone fruits including mangoes (pictured), nectarines and cherries hit market shelves in the lead-up to Christmas. Sydney rock oysters are at their peak and if you're lucky, you might get to sample bunya nuts.

AUTUMN

Strawberries are switched for Hass avocados (the most popular variety; pictured) and an abundance of mushrooms, pumpkins, beans and herbs inspire warming dishes.

WINTER

Hearty winter menus showcase freshly harvested truffles, rhubarb (pictured), spinach, broccoli, cauliflower and oranges alongside heavier proteins like beef, duck and lamb.

TOP: PHOTOGRAPHY BY ROB D/SHUTTERSTOCK; FROM LEFT: THP CREATIVE/SHUTTERSTOCK, AVPHOTOSALES/SHUTTERSTOCK, ERMAN GUNES/SHUTTERSTOCK, DAMIAN HERDE/SHUTTERSTOCK

JOMPHOL/SHUTTERSTOCK

Finger limes

HOW TO... Embrace Bush Tucker

There are more than 5000 edible plant species in Australia, known as bush tucker or bush foods. Australia's First Nations people have been dining out on the landscape for millennia, guided by the seasons and 65,000 years of ancestral knowledge. These native ingredients are now increasingly turning up on restaurant menus in innovative ways as chefs around the country seek to elevate their dishes with the punchy, distinctive flavours of the Aussie bush.

Seasonal Bounty

Indigenous groups living in different environments and climatic zones across the country observe unique seasonal calendars, all of which have associated plant and animal seasonal markers. The Noongar people in Western Australia's southwest observe six seasons, for example, while the Kuku Yalanji people of Queensland's Daintree region recognise five main seasons. Thought to be the world's first bakers, Australia's First Nations people have developed complex systems for harvesting and preparing native foods that are otherwise unpalatable or even poisonous. It's for this reason that foraging without an expert guide in Australia is not recommended. Indigenous-guided bush-tucker tours – such as Dale Tilbrook's **Bush Tucker Talks & Tastings** (p911) in WA – are among the most memorable (and safe) ways to sample Australia's native bounty.

Native Protein

Bush tucker also encompasses a variety of seafood and native game meat. Wild kangaroo and farmed crocodile are the most widely available meats and both can be delicious when cooked correctly, which can take a little practice. Like many native meats, kangaroo is so lean that all it needs is a light searing. Boutique farms in some states also produce emu meat (which tastes more like beef than poultry), while Tasmania is the only state where it is legal to harvest wallaby. Some Indigenous groups are exempt from laws prohibiting the harvest of protected species for cultural reasons; you won't see these on restaurant menus.

BUSH TUCKER DECODER

Lemon myrtle: The herbaceous, lemony leaves can be used to flavour everything from cakes to tea.

Davidson plum: Intensely tart fruit perfect for relishes, jams, yoghurts and ice creams.

Pepperberry: Punchy native peppercorn that becomes sweeter and less spicy when cooked for longer.

Finger lime: The fruit's 'pearls' pop in the mouth with a burst of sweet-tart flavours.

Quandong: Drought-tolerant desert fruit prized for its peach-like tang.

Saltbush: The salty, herbaceous leaves add depth of flavour to fish, meat and vegetable dishes.

Wattleseed: Used like poppyseeds, these ubiquitous seeds have a rich, nutty flavour.

FROM LEFT: IAN CROCKER/SHUTTERSTOCK, EMMA JONES/SHUTTERSTOCK

Florence Falls (p822), Litchfield National Park

THE OUTDOORS

Australian culture is geared around the great outdoors, offering some of the world's most memorable opportunities to step outside.

Blessed with a warm and sunny climate, thousands of beaches and hundreds of national parks, as well as a vast outback to explore, Australia is practically designed for life outside. There are hidden beaches to uncover, tropical reefs to snorkel and dive, and even snowcapped mountains to ski and snowboard. Coastal national parks teeming with wildlife are laced with bushwalking and biking trails, Indigenous tourism experiences from the outback to the coast invite travellers to get hands-on and more adventurous travellers can sign up for an array of thrills and spills.

The Life Aquatic

Australia was made for days on the beach. But you don't even need to get sandy to enjoy the spectacular coastal landscape. Sailing tours in the calm waters of Sydney and the Whitsundays are a great way to soak up the sunshine and coastal views; flightseeing and glass-bottom boat tours offer a glimpse of the Great Barrier Reef; and whale-watching tours on the East and West Coasts get you up close to the gentle giants of the sea. Opportunities for kayaking in rivers and the sea also abound. Most travellers will agree that diving right in is the best way to experience Australia's aquatic

More Outdoor Thrills

CROC CRUISES
Eyeball an apex predator on a croc-spotting cruise in **Kakadu** (p814) or the **Daintree region** (p408).

SHARK DIVING
Swim among docile grey nurse sharks in **South West Rocks** (p175), or in a cage alongside great whites in the **Neptune Islands** (p781).

SEAL SNORKELLING
Swim among the playful fur seals of **Barunguba Montague Island** (p209) or the sea lions that cavort off **Port Lincoln** (p780).

FAMILY ADVENTURES

Climb aboard a wintertime whale-watching boat trip at dozens of locations along the East and West Coasts, including **Dunsborough** (p928).

Learn about Indigenous connections to coastal Country as a family on a **Kuku Yalanji–guided fishing tour** (p406) near Port Douglas.

Coo over little penguins, koalas, kangaroos and other wildlife at **Phillip Island Nature Parks** (p587).

Seek out waterfalls and waterholes in **Litchfield National Park** (p821) for a thrilling day out from Darwin with older kids.

Go wild-koala-spotting in **Lismore** (p186) and **Port Stephens** (p168) or get a close-up at koala sanctuaries in these North Coast NSW destinations.

playground, with the best surfing beaches found in southeast Queensland, New South Wales, southern Western Australia and Victoria's Surf Coast. While beach swimming is off-limits outside designated croc-free areas of northern Australia, the Great Barrier Reef can be visited year-round and there are some seriously idyllic freshwater waterholes hidden across outback regions.

Walking & Hiking

Australia is a hiker's utopia, with thousands of trails crisscrossing its rich collection of well-maintained and highly protected national parks. A growing network of urban coastal trails also offer an accessible breath of fresh air, many of them suitable for wheelchairs and prams.

If you're self-driving, you'll need a parks pass to pull up in national parks in some states and territories – check official websites before you go. Camping fees also apply in most parks, with an online reservation typically required (expect basic facilities). Serious hikers can choose from a diverse range of multiday epics, including Australia's longest-marked walking track, the Heysen Trail (p734) in South Australia. Familiarise yourself with bushwalking safety before you set off along any trail (p1015).

Saltwater crocodile

Cycling & Mountain Biking

Australia's relatively flat coastline and picturesque countryside lend beautifully to cycling. While urban cycleways are still a work in progress, particularly in big cities, recent years have seen considerable investment in making Australia more cycling-friendly. Bike-sharing schemes are available in capital cities as well as some regional centres, e-bike tours proliferate and disused rail trails across the country have been transformed into trails for cyclists and walkers. And while Tasmania may be the home of mountain biking, the mainland states also have a rich collection of mountain biking parks and trails. Bicycle helmets are a legal requirement nationwide.

KITESURFING
WA's breezy coast offers prime kitesurfing conditions, with **Rockingham** (p914) and **Lancelin** (p960) among the best spots.

RAFTING
Embark on a multiday rafting expedition on the **Franklin River** (p706), deep in the Tasmanian Wilderness.

STAND-UP PADDLEBOARDING
Skim Shoal Bay's seagrass shallows on a SUP rental or guided excursion with **Port Stephens Paddlesports** (p169).

DOWNHILL SKIING
Carve fresh tracks at ski resorts in the **Snowy Mountains** (p246) and Victoria's **High Country** (p606).

ACTION AREAS

Where to find Australia's best outdoor activities.

Snorkelling/Diving

1. Great Barrier Reef (p382)
2. Ningaloo Reef (p976)
3. Byron Bay (p177)
4. South West Rocks (p175)
5. Limestone Coast (p757)
6. Lord Howe Island (p216)

Walking/Hiking

1. Overland Track (p692)
2. Blue Mountains (p140)
3. Jatbula Trail (p835)
4. Larapinta Trail (p865)
5. Cape to Cape Track (p927)
6. The Grampians (p583)
7. Gondwana Rainforests World Heritage Area (p186)

Cycling

1. Blue Derby Trail Network (p677)
2. Murray to Mountains Rail Trail (p612)
3. Mt Remarkable National Park (p774)
4. Central Coast (p156)
5. Northern Rivers Rail Trail (p189)
6. Falls Creek (p608)
7. Pemberton Mountain Bike Park (p939)

Surfing
1 Sydney (p70)
2 Byron Bay (p180)
3 Margaret River (p924)
4 Gold Coast (p315)
5 Newcastle (p166)
6 Surf Coast (p547)
Kayaking/Canoeing
1 Murray River National Park (p767)
2 Glenelg River (p562)
3 Sydney Harbour (p89)
4 Shark Bay (p967)
5 Ord River (p1002)
6 Eurimbula National Park (p360)
7 Freycinet National Park (p672)
PAPUA NEW GUINEA
Port Moresby
Torres Strait
Thursday Island
Cape York
Coral Sea
Nhulunbuy
Weipa
Groote Eylandt
Cape York Peninsula
Cape Melville
Gulf of Carpentaria
Great Barrier Reef
Cooktown
Port Douglas
Cairns
Normanton
Innisfail
Ingham
Great Barrier Reef Marine Park
Camooweal
Charters Towers
Townsville
Cloncurry
Bowen
Mt Isa
Flinders River
Airlie Beach
Whitsunday Islands
Mackay
Winton
Longreach
Barcaldine
Great Dividing Range
Rockhampton
Gladstone
Birdsville
QUEENSLAND
Bundaberg
Hervey Bay
K'gari
Charleville
Innamincka
Maroochydore
Lake Eyre
St George
Toowoomba
Brisbane
Surfers Paradise
Barwon River
Byron Bay
Flinders Ranges
Bourke
Armidale
Broken Hill
Darling River
Coffs Harbour
Port Augusta
NEW SOUTH WALES
Nyngan
Tamworth
Lord Howe Island (NSW)
Dubbo
Port Macquarie
SOUTH PACIFIC OCEAN
Mildura
Newcastle
Adelaide
Hay
Griffith
Wagga Wagga
Sydney
Tasman Sea
Murray Bridge
Swan Hill
Albury
CANBERRA
VICTORIA
Horsham
Batemans Bay
Mt Gambier
Geelong
Melbourne
Warrnambool
Wilsons Promontory
King Island
Bass Strait
Flinders Island
Devonport
Launceston
TASMANIA
Hobart
NEW ZEALAND
Queenstown

AUSTRALIA

THE GUIDE

Chapters in this section are organised by hubs and their surrounding areas. We see the hub as your base in the destination, where you'll find unique experiences, local insights, insider tips and expert recommendations. It's also your gateway to the surrounding area, where you'll see what and how much you can do from there.

Whitehaven Beach (p444), Whitsunday Island

JAKUB MACULEWICZ/SHUTTERSTOCK

Researched by
Chantae Reden

Sydney & Surrounds

OZ'S GLEAMING EMERALD CITY

Not the shy and retiring type, Sydney is more than happy to show off, bedazzling visitors with its glistening harbour, golden beaches and gregarious attitude.

THE MAIN AREAS

Compared with the rest of Australia, Sydney (Warrane) thrives on spectacle. Bodies are more buffed here, heels are higher, contact sports more brutal, starlets shinier and drag queens out-glitter them all. Visitors find it an easy place to love, its sunny attitude infectious.

For a city of 5.5 million people and a state capital to boot, it's surprisingly wild. National parks line its edges and penetrate right into its core. Great swathes of the harbour are still fringed with bush and native critters turn up when you least expect them. Oversized spiders scuttle over car dashboards, possums rattle over suburban roofs, water dragons rustle through parks, cockatoos bleat from railings and great clouds of flying foxes glide by at twilight.

Yet make no mistake, Sydney is no slouch on the urban front either. A lively bar scene encompasses everything from 19th-century pubs to tucked-away speakeasies and from swanky rooftop cocktail bars to beachfront beer gardens. Sydney's large migrant communities (40% of residents were born overseas) have spiced up the dining scene, creating a vast variety of cuisines and inspiring international flavours paired with indigenous ingredients in the city's most fashionable restaurants.

While highbrow arts may not be the first thing that springs to mind when you think of Australia, it's not a complete accident that the most recognisable symbol of Sydney is an opera house. World-class theatre, music and dance are performed here nightly and the city has many notable art galleries, large and small.

Aboriginal culture is gradually taking a more prominent place in Sydney's public institutions and, increasingly, in everyday life. Warrane (the original name for Sydney Cove, now used broadly for the entire city) was the site of the First Fleet's landing in 1788, which marked the beginning of British colonisation. This event brought profound and lasting devastation to the local Indigenous communities, a legacy that is now widely acknowledged. Learning about their stories – along with those of the unfortunate convicts who were unceremoniously brought to their land – helps to fill in the picture of what makes this flashy, sometimes frivolous, always fabulous city unique.

For places to stay in Sydney & Surrounds, see p148

ELIAS BITAR/SHUTTERSTOCK

Sydney Opera House (p82)

Find Your Way

Sydney's suburbs sprawl all the way to the national parks that enclose it, but most places of interest cluster along the coastline and the fringes of the city centre. Central Sydney can easily be explored on foot, with excellent public transport connections getting you anywhere else you'd like to go.

FROM THE AIRPORT

Taxis to the city are capped at $60, rideshares cost around $45. Trains depart from beneath the terminal but charge an $18 fee on top of the normal train fare; they take around 15 minutes to get from the airport to the city centre.

CAR, TAXI & RIDESHARE

Parking and traffic headaches make private cars a liability in central Sydney, but they're useful for getting to the beaches, mountains and Royal National Park. Taxis and rideshares (Uber and DiDi) are easy to arrange and particularly handy for late-night journeys.

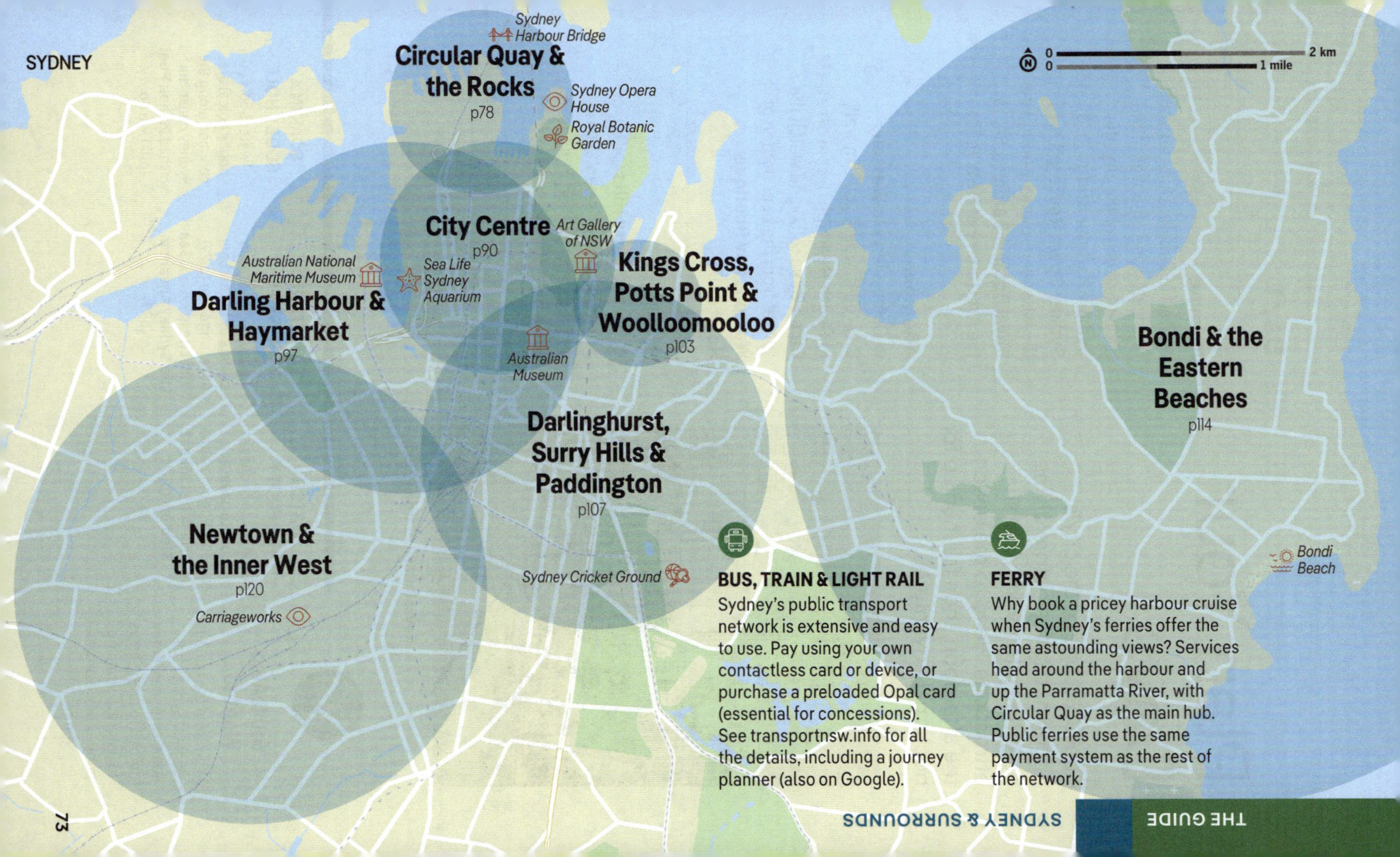

BUS, TRAIN & LIGHT RAIL
Sydney's public transport network is extensive and easy to use. Pay using your own contactless card or device, or purchase a preloaded Opal card (essential for concessions). See transportnsw.info for all the details, including a journey planner (also on Google).

FERRY
Why book a pricey harbour cruise when Sydney's ferries offer the same astounding views? Services head around the harbour and up the Parramatta River, with Circular Quay as the main hub. Public ferries use the same payment system as the rest of the network.

Plan Your Days

Fuel up at one of the city's acclaimed cafes before diving headfirst into Sydney's star attractions. Head to the beach in the afternoon, then freshen up for nocturnal adventures.

MAJONIT/SHUTTERSTOCK

Royal Botanic Garden (p84)

Day 1

Morning

- Start in Circular Quay for your first wide-eyed glimpses of the absolute icons of the city: the **Sydney Harbour Bridge** (p78) and **Sydney Opera House** (p82). Circle the latter and wander through the **Royal Botanic Garden** (p84) to the **Art Gallery of NSW** (p90).

Afternoon

- Catch a ferry to **Watsons Bay** (p114), where you can walk to **South Head** (p117), cool off at **Camp Cove** (p117) and watch the sunset from the beer garden of **Watsons Bay Boutique Hotel** (p117).

Evening

- Head to **Surry Hills** (p107) for a taste of Sydney's best dining neighbourhood, then indulge in some bar hopping.

You'll Also Want to...

Away from the famous sights, Sydney has some surprises. From football to drag shows to natural swimming pools, buckle up and jump on in.

WATCH THE FOOTY

Experience Sydney's favourite game at a National Rugby League (NRL) match at **Allianz Stadium** (p112).

MEET WILD AUSSIES

Encounter Australian critters by the harbour at **Taronga Zoo** (p129), **Wild Life** (p99) and **Sea Life Sydney Aquarium** (p99).

SOAK IN A BOGEY HOLE

Saltwater pools (aka bogey holes) are common along the Sydney coast; surf-washed **Mahon Pool** (p117) is a doozy.

Day 2

Morning

- Kick off in the City Centre with our walking tour of Victorian **George St** (p94). Continue up Martin Place to **Macquarie St** (p93) and pause to visit **Hyde Park Barracks** (p93), **St James' Church** (p95) and **St Mary's Cathedral** (p95). Take a stroll through **Hyde Park** (p95) to the **ANZAC Memorial** (p95).

Afternoon

- Take the bus along Oxford St to **Bondi Beach** (p118) for an afternoon alternating between sand, surf and sustenance at nearby cafes and bars. If you've still got energy, tackle the **Bondi to Coogee Coastal Walk** (p116).

Evening

- Wind up by wining and dining in **Newtown** (p120).

Day 3

Morning

- Take a look around **Chinatown** (p102) before continuing down past the **Chinese Garden of Friendship** (p102) to **Darling Harbour** (p97). Trace the waterline to **Barangaroo** (p99) and on to **Walsh Bay** and **The Rocks** (p78). Learn more about the area's history (pre- and postcolonial) at the **Rocks Discovery Museum** (p85).

Afternoon

- Catch the ferry to **Manly** (p131) for an afternoon spent pretty much like yesterday's in Bondi. Swap beaches if you get restless.

Evening

- Finish up in **Kings Cross** (p103), Sydney's semi-rambunctious nightlife precinct. There's excellent dining to be found around neighbouring **Potts Point** (p103).

PUSH YOUR ARTISTIC BOUNDARIES

Galleries such as **White Rabbit** (p124) and **Artspace** (p106) nibble at the edges of contemporary art.

EXPLORE SYDNEY'S MUSIC SCENE

See what's on at **Oxford Art Factory** (p111), **Enmore Theatre** (p123) and dozens of other venues.

SEE SOME DRAG SHOWS

The classic movie *The Adventures of Priscilla, Queen of the Desert* kicked off at the **Imperial Erskineville** (p120), where drag shows are still a staple.

HEAD TO THE MOUNTAINS

A favourite escape for locals, the **Blue Mountains** (p138) offers cooler temperatures and extravagant scenery.

Sydney Harbour

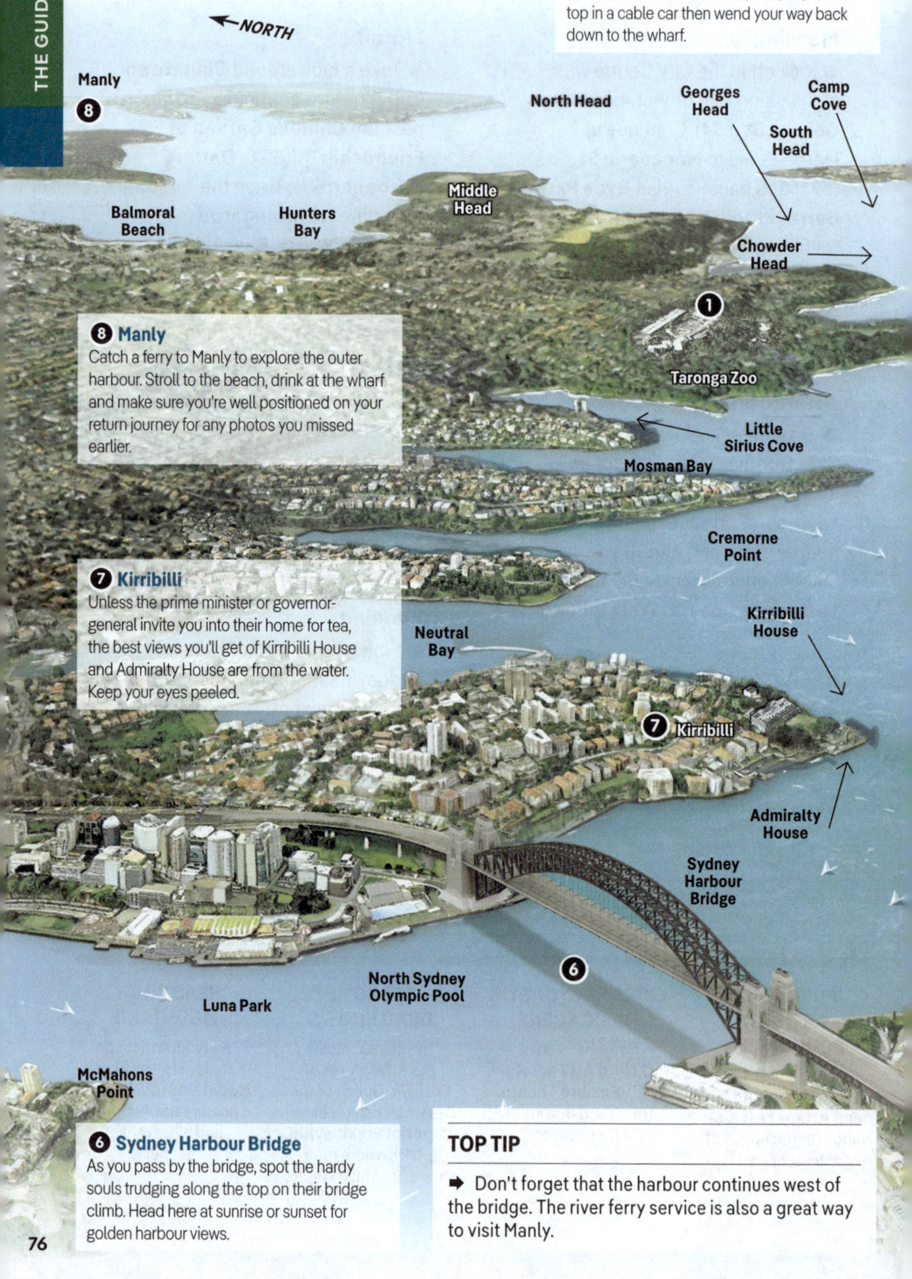

1 Taronga Zoo

Even if you've hired a car, the best way to reach this excellent zoo is by ferry. Zip to the top in a cable car then wend your way back down to the wharf.

8 Manly

Catch a ferry to Manly to explore the outer harbour. Stroll to the beach, drink at the wharf and make sure you're well positioned on your return journey for any photos you missed earlier.

7 Kirribilli

Unless the prime minister or governor-general invite you into their home for tea, the best views you'll get of Kirribilli House and Admiralty House are from the water. Keep your eyes peeled.

6 Sydney Harbour Bridge

As you pass by the bridge, spot the hardy souls trudging along the top on their bridge climb. Head here at sunrise or sunset for golden harbour views.

TOP TIP

➡ Don't forget that the harbour continues west of the bridge. The river ferry service is also a great way to visit Manly.

ILLUSTRATION BY JAVIER ZARRACINA

❷ Watsons Bay

As you pull into its sheltered wharf, imagine Watsons Bay as the isolated fishing village it once was. Stroll around South Head for views up the harbour and over ocean-battered cliffs.

❸ Fort Denison

Known as Pinchgut, this fortified speck was once a place of fearsome punishment. The bodies of executed convicts were left to hang here as a grisly warning to all; the local Aboriginal people were horrified.

DINOZZAVER/SHUTTERSTOCK

Ferries

Circular Quay is the hub for state-run Sydney Ferries; 10 separate routes leave from here, journeying to 36 different wharves.

❺ Sydney Opera House

You can wander inside it and walk around it, but nothing beats the perspective you get as your ferry glides past the Opera House's dazzling sails. Have your camera at the ready.

❹ Circular Quay

Circular Quay has been at the centre of Sydney life since the First Fleet dropped anchor here in 1788. Book your ferry ticket, check the indicator boards for the correct pier and get on board.

Circular Quay & the Rocks

HISTORIC-LADEN HARBOURSIDE SHOWPIECE

GETTING AROUND

A car is a burden in these parts, as traffic crawls and parking is expensive. The best way to explore this compact area is on foot, though you'll contend with stairs and hills around The Rocks. The only train station is at Circular Quay; several bus routes and the light rail terminate here.

TOP TIP

The City of Sydney operates a tourist information desk in the old **Customs House**, which is well stocked with maps and brochures, including self-guided walking tours. It's worth calling in just to check out the building (completed in 1885) and the fascinating 1:500 model of the city centre under the glass floor.

Bookended by the two architectural icons of the city – the Opera House and the Harbour Bridge – Circular Quay is a logical starting point for Sydney explorations. Distinctive yellow and green ferries shuttle constantly from its five wharves, making it the gateway to Sydney Harbour.

Known to the Gadigal people as Warrane, it was here, in 1788, that the ragtag First Fleet unloaded its cargo of convicts, renaming it Sydney Cove in the process. The rugged headland called Tallawoladah to the west eventually grew into the gritty harbourside neighbourhood known as The Rocks. Once an unsanitary slum, it's now one of the city's premier tourist areas. On weekends, The Rocks Markets fill the bottom end of George St, with stallholders selling handicrafts and street-food.

The heritage precinct extends west to Dawes Point and Millers Point, incorporating a performing arts enclave centred on the revitalised Edwardian wharves of Walsh Bay.

Hangout on 'The Coathanger'

Traverse Sydney Harbour Bridge

Before the Opera House was built, the **Sydney Harbour Bridge** was the defining emblem of the city. Stretching for 1149m, it connects Dawes Point on the city side to Milsons Point on the North Shore via a footpath on its eastern side, a bike path on the west, and a roadway and train tracks along the centre. **Bonza Bike Tours** *(bonzabiketours.com)* hires bikes for $20 per hour at the bridge. Walk north to south to see Sydney's icons come into view. It's one of the tallest steel arch bridges in the world and weighs 52,800 tonnes.

To learn more about its construction and to enjoy the views from the top, climb to the **Pylon Lookout & Museum** *(pylonlookout.com.au)* housed in the southeastern pylon and accessed from the bridge's footpath. The panorama of the skyline more than justifies the 200-plus steps to the top.

STEPHEN D. GARD/SHUTTERSTOCK

Sydney Harbour Bridge

However, the very best views are saved for those with a penchant for heights on the **BridgeClimb** *(bridgeclimb.com)*. Several climb options are on offer, catering to a different level of thrill and lasting between 2½ and 3½ hours. All of them head to the apex of the arch, 134m above Sydney Harbour. An interesting option is the Burrawa Aboriginal Climb Experience, led by an Indigenous storyteller. For those prone to vertigo, the scariest part is crossing the mesh catwalk underneath the bridge; once you get onto the actual arch the track is wide enough that you don't see straight down. The other scary part is the price, climbing from $335 for an adult, with premium prices at dawn and twilight.

History amid the Greenery

Explore the Royal Botanic Garden

Mere metres away from the high-rise heart of Sydney, this large expanse of lawns, tree-shaded lanes and formal botanical collections provides a welcome break from the big-city buzz. On weekday lunch breaks, office workers can be spotted jogging the paths or just escaping their coworkers in quiet corners. On weekends, groups of friends congregate for picnics, parents let their toddlers off the leash and young lovers canoodle in shady nooks.

Continued on p84

BUILDING THE BRIDGE

Construction started on Sydney Harbour Bridge in 1923, overseen by chief engineer John Job Crew Bradfield (his actual given name, as unlikely as that seems). When the Great Depression kicked in six years later, the project was a major source of employment, with 1400 workers involved in its construction.

The mighty arches were built outwards from both sides simultaneously. The two sides were finally bolted together in 1930, but not before 100km/h winds sent them swaying when they were only centimetres apart. Work then commenced on the granite-faced pylons; although they look like they're shouldering most of the weight, they're largely decorative.

Two years later, on 19 March 1932, the bridge was officially opened.

EATING IN CIRCULAR QUAY & THE ROCKS: BUDGET BITES

Dutch Smuggler: Delicious Indonesian-inspired sandwiches and excellent coffee, served between skyscrapers. *6am-4pm Mon-Fri, 8am-3pm Sat & Sun* $

El Camino Cantina: Tacos and margarita specials every Tuesday, with decently priced Tex-Mex food the rest of the week. *noon-10pm Sun-Thurs, to midnight Fri & Sat* $

Fine Food Store: Contemporary cafe in The Rocks with great coffee, brunch classics, sandwiches and salads. *7am-3pm Mon-Fri, 7.30am-3pm Sat & Sun* $

Malay-Chinese: Serving up laksa, fried noodles, Hainanese chicken rice and spicy curries to hungry office workers and travellers in the know. *11am-4.30pm Mon-Fri* $

CIRCULAR QUAY & THE ROCKS

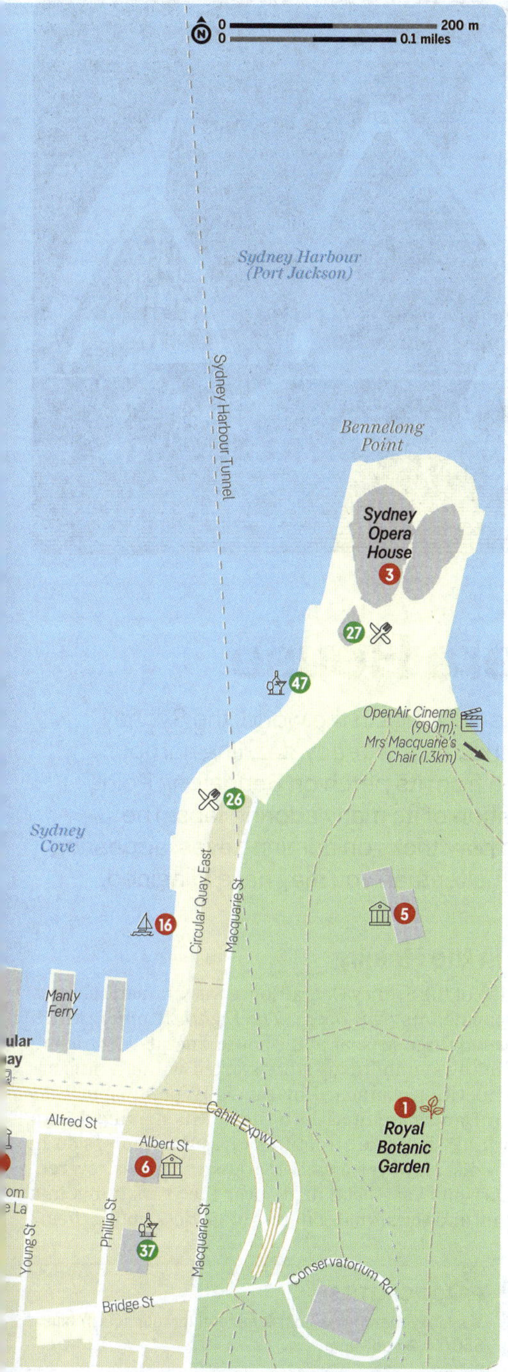

HIGHLIGHTS
1 Royal Botanic Garden
2 Sydney Harbour Bridge
3 Sydney Opera House

SIGHTS
4 Customs House
5 Government House
6 Justice & Police Museum
7 Museum of Contemporary Art
8 Observatory Hill
9 Pylon Lookout & Museum
10 Rocks Discovery Museum
11 SH Ervin Gallery
12 Susannah Place

ACTIVITIES
13 Bonza Bike Tours
14 BridgeClimb
15 Captain Cook Cruises
16 Mari Nawi
17 Sydney Harbour Tall Ships
18 Sydney Observatory

SLEEPING
19 Four Seasons Hotel
20 Lord Nelson Brewery Hotel
21 Park Hyatt
22 Pier One
23 Russell Boutique Hotel
24 Sydney Harbour YHA

EATING
25 6Head
26 Aria
27 Brew Cafe
28 Canvas
29 Dutch Smuggler
30 El Camino Cantina
31 Fine Food Store
32 La Renaissance Patisserie
33 Malay-Chinese
34 Pancakes on the Rocks
35 Quay
36 The Garden

DRINKING & NIGHTLIFE
37 Aster
38 Australian Heritage Hotel
39 Doss House
40 Fortune of War
41 Frank Mac's
42 Glenmore Hotel
43 Henry Deane
44 Hero of Waterloo
45 Le Foote
see 20 Lord Nelson Brewery Hotel
46 Maybe Sammy
47 Opera Bar

ENTERTAINMENT
48 Australian Theatre for Young People
49 Bangarra Dance Theatre
50 Roslyn Packer Theatre
51 Sydney Dance Company
52 Sydney Theatre Company

JAMES WK/SHUTTERSTOCK

TOP EXPERIENCE

Sydney Opera House

One of the most recognisable buildings in the world, the Sydney Opera House adds extra sparkle to an already dazzling harbour. It gazes confidently out to sea from its perch on Bennelong Point, brazenly accepting the adulation of its many adoring fans. The captivating curves of its sails play tricks on admiring eyes, appearing simultaneously bigger and smaller than you may have imagined.

DON'T MISS

- The Forecourt
- Concert Hall
- Joan Sutherland Theatre
- Utzon Room
- Opera Bar
- Seagull Patrol
- Guided tours

Drama in the Making

The creation of the Sydney Opera House was dramatic enough to have spawned its own opera, *The Eighth Wonder,* which has completed three seasons at the house since its 1995 debut.

The building's tumultuous story started with an international competition, launched by the NSW premier in 1955 and won by Danish architect Jørn Utzon. His striking design of interlocking shell-like structures gives the impression of billowing sails. However, this being Australia, less reverential comparisons have been made over the years (nuns in a rugby scrum and the sexual congress of turtles, among them).

PRACTICALITIES

● *sydneyoperahouse.com* ● general 1hr tour adult/child $50/30 ● 9am-11pm

At first sight, under the summer sun, the sails appear as a dazzling expanse of solid white. But come closer and you'll see that they're actually clad with alternating matte-cream and glossy-white tiles, arranged in chevron patterns – nearly a million of them in total.

Construction started in 1959 and was expected to last four years, but after cost blowouts and much politicking, Utzon quit in 1966. The building was eventually opened in 1973 by a windblown Queen Elizabeth II, without any of Utzon's original interior designs.

Utzon famously never saw the finished building. In 2004, he and his son Jan were commissioned to work on renovations to the interior, but he never made it back to Sydney and died in Denmark in 2008.

Beneath the Sails

Of the various performance spaces within the Opera House, the largest and grandest is the **Concert Hall**, with seating for 2679 people. Home to the Sydney Symphony Orchestra, it was thoroughly renovated in 2022 in preparation for the building's 50th birthday and its angular golden-hued interior is now looking and sounding better than ever. Its 10,000-pipe tracker-action organ is the largest of its kind in the world.

Next up, size-wise, is the 1507-seat **Joan Sutherland Theatre**, named after Sydney's greatest-ever opera singer. Both Opera Australia and the Australian Ballet make themselves at home here. Three smaller theatres are tucked away downstairs: the **Studio**, **Playhouse** and **Drama Theatre**. Smaller ensembles also perform in the intimate **Utzon Room**, an open space with views over the harbour and a colourful tapestry designed by the great man himself.

Forecourt & Broadwalks

Utzon credited Mayan and Aztec temples with his inspiration for the **Monumental Steps** leading up to the Opera House from the **Forecourt**. This large open space has played host to royalty, pop stars and a pope. Up to 6000 people can be accommodated here for ticketed events, although a charity gig by Crowded House in 1996 was said to have drawn a crowd of around 150,000.

Events are also held on the **Northern** and **Western Broadwalks**, which wrap around the house and offer remarkable city and harbour views.

Tours

A range of guided tours of the building is offered, the most popular being the daily, hour-long **Sydney Opera House Tour** *(multiple languages; adult/child $50/30)*. The most comprehensive is the two-hour **Backstage Tour** *(English only; $199)*, run daily at 7am; bookings essential. There's also an hour-long **Architectural Tour** *(adult/child $60/33)*, which kicks off at 8.15am and 10am on Saturday mornings.

SEAGULL PATROL

The Lower Concourse on the Circular Quay side is home to the memorable **Opera Bar**, a large, partly open-air establishment serving refreshments to buzzing tourists and locals alike. A novel solution to the problem of pesky seagulls is provided by the Opera House's happiest workers, the border collies and kelpies of the **Seagull Patrol**, employed to chase the birds away.

TOP TIPS

- Check the website for the screening times of *Badu Gili*, a regularly changing First Nations video-art installation projected onto the sails multiple times most evenings.
- Look out for Benny the fur seal (named after Bennelong Point), who regularly hangs out on the VIP steps leading from the water to the Northern Broadwalk.
- The Opera House is committed to accessibility and a schedule of Access Events is offered, including audio-described, sign-language-interpreted and captioned performances.
- An hour-long **Mobility Tour** *(adult/child $50/30)* is offered at 11.30am and 2.45pm daily.
- French, German, Spanish, Japanese, Korean and Mandarin tours can be arranged.

WALSH BAY ARTS PRECINCT

Before the arrival of container shipping saw the working harbour move to Botany Bay, the wharves of Walsh Bay were Sydney's busiest. The elegant Federation-era piers have since become a staging ground for some of the city's most acclaimed arts organisations.

Chief among them is the prestigious **Sydney Theatre Company**, which has complemented its two Wharf Theatres with the custom-built **Roslyn Packer Theatre** across the road. **Sydney Dance Company**, Australia's top contemporary ensemble, has its own Wharf Studios but also uses the Roslyn Packer Theatre for performances. Lauded as the nation's leading Indigenous arts company, **Bangarra Dance Theatre** is based at the wharf and performs all over the country. The **Australian Theatre for Young People** also has a home here.

ARLIFTATOZ2205/SHUTTERSTOCK

Rocks Discovery Museum

Continued from p79

The **Royal Botanic Garden** sprawls along Farm Cove, the next bay over from the Opera House. It was here, in 1788, that the earliest colonists attempted to plant Australia's first European-style vegetable patch; it was a dismal failure. Now those First Farm beds are complemented by the neighbouring 'Cadi Jam Ora: First Encounters' display, featuring native plants and boards telling the story of the local Gadigal people. There are also fascinating hour-long **Aboriginal Harbour Heritage Tours** and **Aboriginal Bush Tucker Tours** *(botanicgardens.org.au; adult/child $32/21. Book ahead).*

Other garden highlights include the wildflower meadow, succulent garden, rose garden, herb garden, Oriental garden, palm grove, fernery, Australian native rockery and the Calyx, a curving glasshouse with a living wall devoted to temporary botanical displays.

After exploring the garden, continue wandering along the harbour to the tip of the neighbouring headland. Originally known as Yurong, this was an important initiation site for Gadigal men. The lawn on the city side is now the picturesque setting for **OpenAir Cinema** *(westpacopenair.com.au),* which screens movies here in January and February. Just around the point is **Mrs Macquarie's Chair**, a seat carved out of the sandstone in 1810 by convicts so that Governor Macquarie's wife, Elizabeth, could sit back and admire the views.

Iconically Australian cuisine on the bow of the Sydney Opera House

EATING IN CIRCULAR QUAY & THE ROCKS: FINE DINING

Aria: Refined restaurant with stylish decor, faultless service and windows framing the Opera House. Reservations recommended. *hours vary* $$$

6Head: Top-notch steakhouse in one of the Campbell's Stores buildings in The Rocks, with views to the Opera House. *5-9.30pm Mon, noon-10pm Tue-Sun* $$$

Canvas: In the Museum of Contemporary Art, diners enjoy harbour views paired with innovative fine dining from seasonal chefs in residence. *11am-4.30pm Wed-Sun* $$$

Bennelong: Contemporary Australian dining inside the Sydney Opera House, with seasonal and heirloom produce at the centre of the menu. *hours vary* $$$

Enter Sydney's Colonial Past

Bijou museums exploring local life

Sydney's story is fascinating and multilayered, and a set of free museums does an excellent job of unpeeling the onion. Hidden along a back lane, the **Rocks Discovery Museum** *(rocksdiscoverymuseum.com; free)* partly occupies a stone cottage built in 1844. Displays cover the history of the immediate area, starting with its original inhabitants, the Gadigal people, and continuing through the arrival of convicts, the establishment of the port and the battle to preserve The Rocks' unique heritage.

While the Discovery Museum brings life to the stories of local identities, **Susannah Pl** *(mhnsw.au; 1hr tour adult/child $20/10)* offers an immersive take on working-class existence in The Rocks. Also dating from 1844, this block of four terrace houses and a corner store and can be visited on hour-long guided tours. Each of the houses has been decorated to reflect a different era, with the guides sharing the stories of the real people who once lived here. Extensive conservation works completed in late 2025 led to the creation of new tours, making the experience even more intriguing.

For a darker side of Sydney life, visit the **Justice & Police Museum** *(mhnsw.au; free)*, housed in the old Water Police headquarters near Circular Quay. Gangs, bandits, murderers and notorious underworld figures all feature, along with a section devoted to the police themselves – with a frank overview of the force's interactions with Indigenous Australians over the years. It's open daily in January but only on weekends in other months.

Spectacularly Illuminated Landmarks

Colourful wonders of Vivid Sydney

For 23 nights from mid-May, inner Sydney is transformed with large-scale illuminations projected onto structures, skyscrapers, the Sydney Harbour Bridge (p78) and the Opera House (p82). **Vivid Sydney** *(vividsydney.com)* is an incredible spectacle and one that draws large crowds to the waterfront. While the light shows and many interactive art installations are free, it's backed up with ticketed events, showcasing the work of innovative thinkers, artists, musicians and chefs.

THE ROCKS' BEST WALKING & CYCLING TOURS

Sydney Architecture Walks: Themed small-group architecture walks with options including 'Utzon and the Sydney Opera House' and 'Harbourings' (Circular Quay to Walsh Bay).

Bonza Bike Tours: Cruises over the Harbour Bridge and visits the main sights, ending with a cold beer at an old pub.

Dave's Tours: Various brewery, winery, distillery and bar tours are on offer, including 'The Rocks Pub Tour'.

I'm Free: Young guides run these tours for tips, with a 90-minute stroll around The Rocks kicking off at 6pm daily.

The Rocks Walking Tours: Two daily 90-minute tours through The Rocks, replete with interesting tales.

EATING IN THE ROCKS: BEST BREAKFASTS

Pancakes on the Rocks: Hearty breakfasts and triple pancake stacks, plus pizzas and grilled meats later on. *7.30am-midnight Sun-Thu, 7.30am-2am Fri & Sat* $

La Renaissance Patisserie: Decadent fruit tarts, croissants and pastries both savoury and sweet are found at this cute cafe with a courtyard. *7am-6pm* $

The Garden: Set inside the courtyard of a heritage building, thoughtfully plated breakfasts are made with fresh, seasonal ingredients. *7am-10pm* $$

Brew Cafe: Despite its industrial decor, this cafe serves up comforting fare, with a varied and satisfying breakfast menu. *7am-4pm Mon-Fri, 7am-1pm Sat* $$

ROAMING AROUND THE ROCKS

Wander through Sydney's edgy 19th-century past on this self-guided walk through The Rocks' historic lanes and landmarks.

START	END	LENGTH
First Fleet Park	Sydney Observatory	1.5km; 1hr

Start at 1 **First Fleet Park** and walk past the striking 2 **Museum of Contemporary Art** building to 3 **Cadmans Cottage**, inner Sydney's oldest surviving house (built in 1816).

Take Argyle St to 4 **George St** and turn left to admire its old shops and pubs. The 5 **Suez Canal**, on the right, is a name play on 'sewers' and a reference to its narrow size, tapering to 1m at the George St end. It was once a hangout for the notorious Victorian-era gang The Rocks Push.

Follow the lane to Harrington St and turn right to Argyle St. Continue to the 6 **Argyle Cut**, a canyon-like road carved through sandstone by convicts between 1843 and 1867, first with hand tools, later with dynamite. The Cut exits near the 7 **Garrison Church** (1843). Pop in to admire the hushed interior and collection of regimental flags. In front of it is 8 **Argyle Pl**, where you'll find Georgian terraced houses.

Take the steps up 9 **Observatory Hill** for expansive views over the harbour. The colony's first windmill was built here in 1796, operating until its sails were stolen and it fell into decay. The centrepiece of the hilltop park is the copper-domed, Italianate 10 **Sydney Observatory**. The rooftop time ball once dropped daily at 1pm to signal the correct time to ships in the harbour.

The Eclectic Edges of Australian Art

MCA and SH Ervin Gallery

Looking like it has been beamed in from Batman's Gotham City, the **Museum of Contemporary Art** *(MCA; mca.com.au; adult/child $35/free)* occupies a prime slice of Circular Quay waterfront. Combined with the Opera House, just across the water, it provides a sophisticated riposte to *Crocodile Dundee* clichés of Australian life.

The gallery of over 4700 items features Aboriginal and Torres Strait Islander works prominently, both in the permanent and temporary exhibitions. Once you've browsed, head to the rooftop cafe for Opera House views.

For a broader slice of Australian art, visit the National Trust's **SH Ervin Gallery** *(shervingallery.com.au; $15)* inside the old Fort St School on **Observatory Hill**. The building dates from 1856 and it houses a collection of Australian art through the ages. It also plays host to three annual art competitions, including the always entertaining Salon des Refusés (showcasing portraits rejected by the Archibald Prize). It's closed on Mondays.

Visit the Governor's Gaff

Tour Government House's stately rooms

Built between 1837 and 1841, the grand Gothic pile that serves as the official residence of the Governor of NSW sits within park-like grounds adjacent to the Royal Botanic Garden. Free guided tours of **Government House** head through the public sections of the palace, including the dining room, drawing room and ballroom, all of which are hung with grandiose royal and viceregal portraits. Tours leave on the half-hour from 10.30am to 3pm on Fridays, Saturdays and Sundays; bring ID and register at the gatehouse.

Starry-Eyed in the City

Peer through telescopes at the Sydney Observatory

It was built on the highest point in Sydney in 1858, so it'll come as no surprise that one of the best places to admire the skyline and the cosmos above is from the **Sydney Observatory** *(powerhouse.com.au; free)*. Home to Australia's oldest working telescope, the observatory also highlights the deep connections between astronomy and Indigenous traditions through its thoughtful exhibits. Entry to the museum is free and guided night tours run Wednesday to Saturday (adult/child $36/24),

A ROCKY ROAD TO PRESERVATION

In the early 19th century, whalers and sailors rubbed shoulders with ex-convicts in The Rocks – and inns and brothels sprang up to entertain them. With the settlement filthy and overcrowded, wealthier people started building houses on the upper slopes, their sewage flowing to the slums below. The lower lanes festered with disease and drunken lawlessness.

Bubonic plague broke out in 1900, killing 103 people and leading to the razing of entire streets. The construction of the Harbour Bridge in the 1920s wiped out even more streets. It wasn't until the 1970s that the area's historical significance was finally recognised.

Many of the remaining heritage buildings survived by being converted into tourist-focused businesses.

DRINKING IN CIRCULAR QUAY & THE ROCKS: TOP VIEWS

Glenmore Hotel: Downstairs it's a predictably nice 1920s pub, but head to the rooftop and the harbour views are beyond fabulous. *11am-midnight*

Henry Deane: Enjoy bridge views from this cocktail bar on the top two levels of the historic Hotel Palisade. *4-10pm Tue & Wed, noon-11pm Thu-Sun*

Opera Bar: Right on Circular Quay, with the Opera House on one side and the Harbour Bridge on the other. *11am-11pm*

Aster: Sip cocktails and admire panoramic views of the harbour from the 32nd storey of the InterContinental Sydney; reservations recommended. *4-10pm Tue-Sun*

THE FIRST FLEET

The 11 ships of the First Fleet arrived at Botany Bay in January 1788, but the site was quickly dismissed as inappropriate due to a lack of fresh water. Instead they continued north to a harbour that James Cook had named Port Jackson but never explored. They eventually dropped anchor in a horseshoe bay with a freshwater stream running into it. Governor Phillip renamed it Sydney Cove, after the British Home Secretary. It was here that the motley crew of convicts, sailors, marines and officials disembarked; 1373 people in total. The convicts were allocated the rocky land to the west of the stream, while the governor and other officials pitched tents to the east.

JHVEPHOTO/SHUTTERSTOCK

with special sessions for families with children over six. Be aware it's a long and steep stair climb to the dome, but the ground-floor exhibits and surrounding gardens are accessible to everyone.

See Sydney by Sea

Venture out on the harbour

Circular Quay is the launch point for many of Sydney's best harbour cruises, offering a new perspective of the Harbour Bridge and Opera House. **Sydney Harbour Tall Ships** *(sydneytallships.com.au; adult/child $119/55)* has three impressive sailboats departing throughout the day, where you'll sail around with champagne and sea shanties. Those with a penchant for heights can request to climb up into the crow's nest.

Whales cruise through the Sydney Harbour from late May to November, following the East Australian Current. If you visit during this time, go whale watching with **Captain Cook Cruises** *(captaincook.com.au; adult/child $95/65)*, which runs a 2½-hour cruise twice daily and often has a cetacean expert on board providing commentary.

DRINKING IN THE ROCKS: BEST OLD PUBS

Fortune of War: Operating since 1828 (rebuilt since), this bar hosts live music from Wednesday to Saturday nights and on weekend afternoons. *9am-late*

Lord Nelson Brewery Hotel: Continuously licensed since 1841, the Lord Nelson produces a range of natural ales in its microbrewery. *11am-11pm Mon-Sat, noon-10pm Sun*

Hero of Waterloo: Enter this rough-hewn 1843 sandstone pub to meet some locals and listen to folk and jazz bands (Friday to Sunday). *noon-11pm Tue-Sun*

Australian Heritage Hotel: This heritage pub serves over 130 Australian craft beers and does a nice line of kangaroo, emu and crocodile pizzas. *11am-midnight*

Circular Quay

Onboard the **Mari Nawi** *('Big Canoe'; tribalwarrior.org; adult/child $83/55),* Aboriginal guides tell stories of the Eora Nation, which Sydney Harbour is a part of, from the lens of history that spans back long before the first Europeans dropped anchor. On the two-hour cruise, listen to songs, and learn traditional fishing and food-gathering methods, and about plant-based medicines.

If you prefer to see Sydney Harbour under your own steam, hop in a kayak and paddle your way around. Tours led by Sophie from **Ozpaddle Sydney** *(ozpaddle.com.au; 2½hr tours $250)* come with paddling lessons and get nice and close to the Opera House. Tours are weather dependent; all experience levels are welcome. **Sydney Kayak Experience** *(sydneykayakexperience.com.au; 2hr tours from $150)* runs sunrise, morning, sunset and special-occasion nighttime tours.

For a budget-friendly alternative, hop aboard the **Manly Ferry** – it glides past all the icons, including Kirribilli House, the Prime Minister's residence, for the cost of a public transport ticket (BYO snacks).

PUBLIC TRANSPORT

Transport NSW *(transportnsw.info)* operates Sydney's train, light-rail, bus and ferry network. Purchase tickets by tapping the readers with your contactless credit card, debit card or mobile device. If you're eligible for a concession or you'd prefer to avoid international transaction fees, purchase an Opal smart card (available at the airport and many newsagencies and convenience stores) that comes preloaded with credit. You can then top up your balance at the machines at the stations.

Whether you're using your personal card or Opal, fares cap out at $19.30 per day (Monday to Thursday, falling to $9.65 from Friday to Sunday) or $50 per week. The cap doesn't include the Sydney Airport station access fee ($18).

DRINKING IN THE ROCKS: SPECIALITY BARS

Doss House: There's a serious whisky menu at this little gem in an atmospheric basement in The Rocks. *5pm-1am Tue-Thu, 3pm-2am Fri & Sat, 3pm-midnight Sun*

Frank Mac's: Try the gin flights for a guided tasting experience at a bar that evokes an old-timey Irish pub. *5pm-1am Tue-Thu, 4pm-2am Fri & Sat, 3pm-midnight Sun*

Maybe Sammy: A cocktail bar merging mixology with bold aesthetics, where cocktails come with over-the-top theatrical flair. *4.30pm-1am Wed-Sun*

Le Foote: Browse through the extensive wine list at this Parisian-inspired wine bar, where the open-air courtyard adds an element of romance. *noon-midnight Wed-Sun*

City Centre

SYDNEY'S HIGH-RISE HEART

TOP TIP

The city centre's best restaurants are pricey establishments catering to the expense-account crowd. Some offer set 'express lunch' or 'pretheatre' menus, which can be a cheaper way to experience the top places. If you're seeking a quick, inexpensive feed, head to the food courts within the shopping centres and malls.

The cavernous streets of Sydney's Central Business District (CBD) aren't just the preserve of besuited office workers. Even with stiff competition from suburban malls, the city centre remains Sydney's premier retail hub and there are plenty of excellent restaurants and bars tucked among the skyscrapers.

The main artery is George St, which ditched cars in favour of light rail in 2019. Impressive buildings, new and old, are strung along its entire length. Running parallel to it, Pitt St is a prime shopping strip, especially along the pedestrianised section known as Pitt St Mall. Further east again is Macquarie St, where a row of gracious sandstone buildings harkens back to the early days of the colony. Beyond here, a green corridor formed by Hyde Park, the Domain and the Royal Botanic Garden creates breathing space between the CBD and the first of the Eastern Suburbs.

One of Australia's Great Galleries

Supersized Art Gallery of NSW

The **Art Gallery of NSW** *(artgallery.nsw.gov.au; free)* is an impressive home to one of Australia's largest collections of art. The setting is lovely, tucked away on the edge of the grassy expanse of **The Domain**, overlooking Woolloomooloo Finger Wharf. Allow half a day to do it justice, although art aficionados could easily spend longer.

The revered Naala Nura building has a Neoclassical frontage and a modern rear end. In the Grand Courts on the ground

GETTING AROUND

The city centre is flat and easily explored on foot. Public transport is excellent and a much better option than driving. City Circle trains loop in both directions through Central, Town Hall, Wynyard, Circular Quay, St James and Museum stations, while Eastern Suburbs trains stop at Martin Place. Light rail runs along George St and bus routes pass through as well. You could stroll to all major landmarks within the CBD in around three hours.

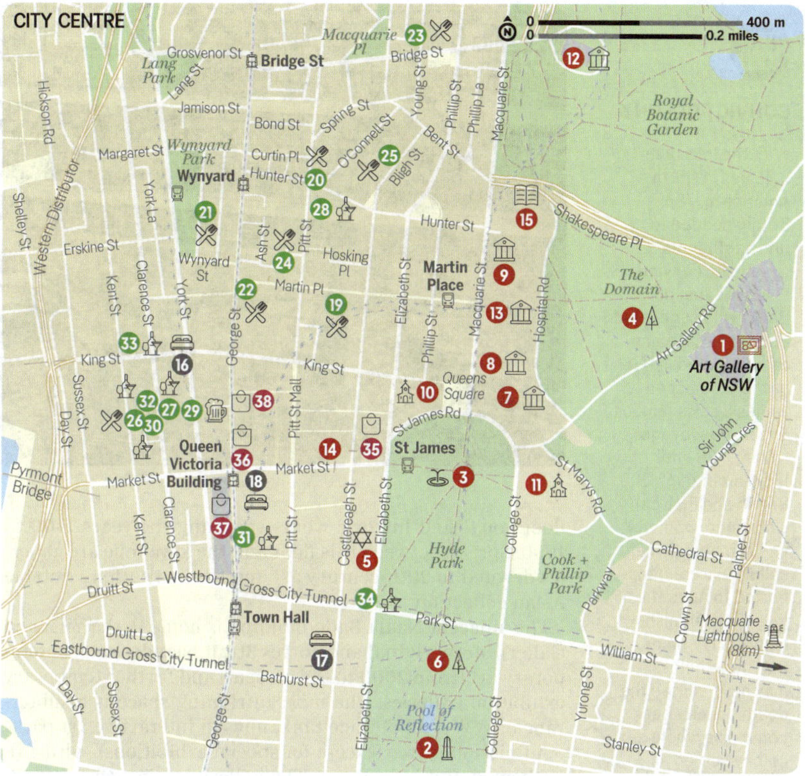

★ **HIGHLIGHTS**
1 Art Gallery of NSW

SIGHTS
2 Anzac Memorial
3 Archibald Memorial Fountain
4 Domain
5 Great Synagogue
6 Hyde Park
7 Hyde Park Barracks
8 Mint
9 Parliament House
10 St James' Church
11 St Mary's Cathedral
12 Sydney Conservatorium of Music
13 Sydney Hospital
14 Sydney Tower

ACTIVITIES
15 State Library of NSW

SLEEPING
16 Grace Hotel
17 Porter House Hotel
18 QT Sydney

EATING
19 Aalia
20 Bentley
21 Maydanoz
22 Morena
23 Neptune's Grotto
24 Ragazzi
25 Restaurant Hubert
26 Towzen

DRINKING & NIGHTLIFE
27 Barber
28 Door Knock
29 Duke of Clarence
30 Lobo
31 Marble Bar
32 Old Love's
33 PS40
34 Ramblin' Rascal

SHOPPING
35 David Jones
36 Myer
37 Queen Victoria Building
38 Strand Arcade
see 14 Westfield Sydney

EATING IN THE CITY CENTRE: MOST INVENTIVE RESTAURANTS

Maydanoz: This contemporary spin on Turkish cuisine serves lavish meze in an intimate setting, showcasing inventive dishes. *noon-3pm & 5.30-10pm* **$$$**

Aalia: Interesting twists on Middle Eastern and North African dishes. Cheaper express-lunch and pretheatre menus are offered. *noon-3pm & 5.30-11pm Mon-Sat* **$$$**

Bentley: Modern Australian cuisine in chic surrounds, with native fruits and seeds lending their unique flavours. *6-11pm Tue-Sat, plus noon-3pm Thu & Fri* **$$$**

Neptune's Grotto: An underground restaurant offering spins on traditional Italian. *noon-11pm Sun-Thu, noon-midnight Fri & Sat* **$$$**

CONVICT COLONY

With the loss of its colonies in North America in 1783, Britain needed to find another place to send its convicts. It was Sir Joseph Banks who suggested Botany Bay, a place he had visited in 1770 as the botanist on James Cook's famous *Endeavour* voyage.

From 1788 until 1868, around 162,000 British and Irish convicts (men, women and sometimes their children) were transported to Australia, many for astonishingly petty crimes that nonetheless may have carried the death penalty back home. The whole colony served as an open-air gaol, with convicts put to work clearing land, constructing roads and raising buildings. When their term ended, most then stayed on in Australia as free settlers.

SOFTVISUAL/SHUTTERSTOCK

floor you'll find historic works spanning the years 1400 to 1900. Spread between this floor and the lower one are galleries devoted to 20th-century art and the institution's notable Asian collection.

The adjacent Naala Badu building is home to the Yiribana Gallery of Aboriginal and Torres Strait Islander art, contemporary art (from 2000 to the present) and further temporary exhibition galleries. The most intriguing space is a subterranean WWII oil-storage tank, now an interactive art park.

Admission is free (except for special exhibitions), with daily themed and kids' tours. The gallery is wheelchair accessible and offers aids for visitors with low or colour-vision impairment.

Elegant Edwardian Temple to Knowledge

Delve into the State Library

Even if you're not particularly scholarly, the **State Library of NSW** *(sl.nsw.gov.au)* is worth a look for the decor of the Neoclassical Mitchell Wing (1910) and for its free galleries. Among the six million tomes housed here are journals and logs by the likes of James Cook and Joseph Banks. Reflecting that era of exploration, the decor features bronze relief doors

Try the truffle ramen with walnut-milk broth

EATING IN THE CITY CENTRE: OUR PICKS

Ragazzi: This tiny trattoria serves delicious handmade pasta dishes alongside an extensive Italian-leaning wine list. *11.30am-midnight Mon-Sat, to 10pm Sun* **$$**

Morena: Peruvian chef Alejandro Saravia brings dishes from Latin America to Sydney in this effortlessly elegant restaurant. *7am-9pm Mon-Fri, 5.30-9.30pm Sun* **$$$**

Restaurant Hubert: French fare comes in old-fashioned portions and with an old-time ambience in this candlelit subterranean restaurant. *noon-3pm & 5pm-1am* **$$$**

Towzen: A beloved Kyoto eatery, serves generous bowls of ramen loaded with vegetables. *5-9pm Wed-Sun, plus 11.30am-2.30pm Thu-Sun* **$$**

State Library of NSW

illustrating famous European voyages and period portrayals of Aboriginal Australian life. There's also an intricate mosaic in the atrium depicting Abel Tasman's travels. A design highlight is the light-filled reading room, clad in milky marble.

Sydney's Most Evocative Convict Site

History-filled Hyde Park Barracks

Between 1819 and 1848, around 50,000 convicts passed through **Hyde Park Barracks** *(mhnsw.au; free),* which despite its refined appearance was then a miserable, overcrowded and rat-infested place. A visit to this UNESCO World Heritage Site, designed by convict architect Francis Greenway, provides a poignant insight into life in the penal colony.

Visitors can request a free audio-guide, which provides essential background information as you take the self-directed tour. Each floor has a theme: 'Control' on the 2nd, 'Fear' on the 1st and 'Hope' on the ground level. Along the way, intricate dioramas tell the story of expanding colonial settlement and its devastating effect on the lives of Indigenous Australians. Artefacts also illustrate the building's subsequent use as a women's immigration depot and asylum. The tour ends with inspiring video testimonies from Indigenous Elders and the descendants of those who passed through these doors.

MACQUARIE ST

Locally, this street is synonymous with political machinations, with one of its grand sandstone buildings home to the NSW Parliament. At the Hyde Park end, large statues of Queen Victoria and her consort, Prince Albert, are perched on opposite corners. On Albert's side are Hyde Park Barracks, **The Mint, Sydney Hospital, Parliament House** and the State Library of NSW, while Victoria has St James' Church (p95).

Parliament House and The Mint were once part of the infamous Rum Hospital, built in 1816 by two merchants in return for a monopoly on rum (then Sydney's currency). Hardly a shock, the liquor barons' build quality left something to be desired. The politicians shifted here in 1829, making it Australia's oldest continually operating parliament building.

DRINKING IN THE CITY CENTRE: BEST SUBTERRANEAN BARS

Ramblin' Rascal: Head downstairs to this darkened den where indie musicians perform from Wednesday to Saturday. *5pm-2am Mon-Thu, noon-2am Fri, 4pm-2am Sat*

Lobo: Step down into a sumptuous prerevolution Cuban fantasy in this louche cocktail bar, with tropical wallpaper and club-style seating. *5pm-2am*

Door Knock: Beneath the chaos of the city lies a serene, Parisian-style speakeasy serving inventive cocktails and small plates. *4pm-1am Mon-Sat, plus noon-3pm Thu & Fri*

Marble Bar: This ornate underground bar, built in 1893, is a hidden jewel box, with live music every night. *4pm-midnight Mon-Sat, 4-10pm Sun*

STROLLING THROUGH THE PAST ON GEORGE ST

Wander past the city centre's most fascinating landmarks, from rowdy convict-era relics to striking examples of Art Deco design.

START	END	LENGTH
St Andrew's Cathedral	Archibald Memorial Fountain	1.5km; 1½hr

Start at 1 **St Andrew's Cathedral** (built in 1868), a salubrious sandstone building with twin spires inspired by England's York Minster. Its exuberant neighbour, 2 **Sydney Town Hall**, was completed the following year.

Behind an imperious statue of its namesake (transported here from Dublin in 1987), the 3 **Queen Victoria Building** (p96) takes up an entire city block. It opened in 1898 and remains the city's swankiest shopping centre, with Romanesque arches and Byzantine domes. Cut through to admire its tiled floors, multiple mezzanines, stained-glass dome and two kitsch animated clocks.

Turn right onto Market St to the ostentatiously ornate 4 **State Theatre**. Built in 1929 as a movie palace, it's an exceptional setting for concerts, musicals and comedy shows, with faux-medieval decor in the foyer.

Turn left onto 5 **Pitt St Mall**, lined with shopping centres, then walk through the gorgeous 6 **Strand Arcade** (p96; built in 1891), to return to George St. Continue to Martin Place, a promenade lined with imposing bank and insurance buildings.

At its bottom end is the 7 **Cenotaph**, commemorating Australia's war dead. The colonnaded building beside it is the former 8 **General Post Office**, built in 1874 in a style inspired by Italian Renaissance palaces, with Queen Victoria gazing over the thoroughfare. Continue along Martin Place and turn right to reach Hyde Park's 9 **Archibald Memorial Fountain**.

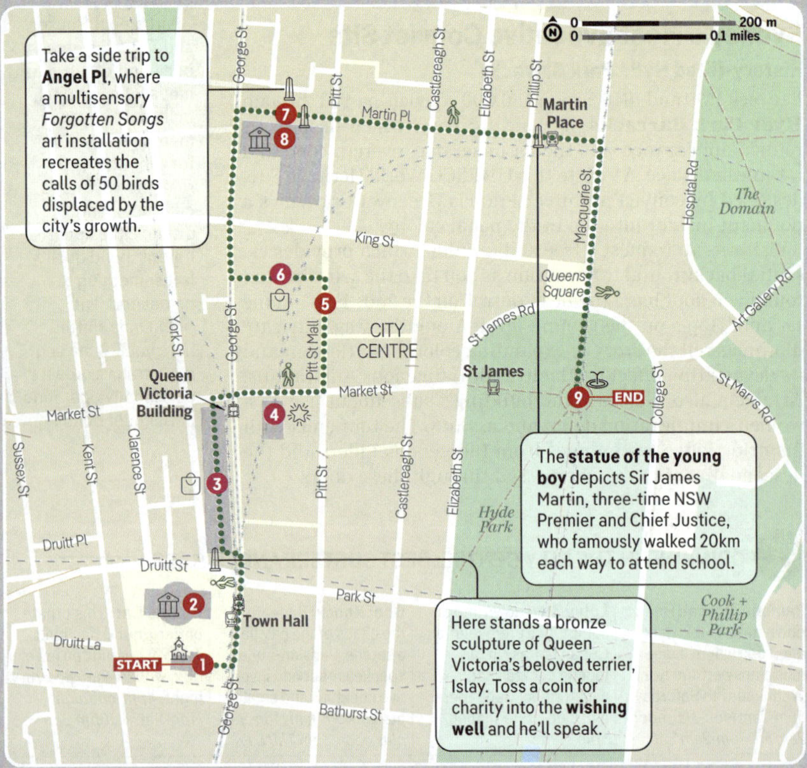

Leafy Corridor Linking Art Deco Memorials

Stroll through Hyde Park

With a broad tree-formed path running along its centre, **Hyde Park** provides a dramatic approach to the city, made magical at night with twinkling fairy lights. On the northern end is the over-the-top **Archibald Memorial Fountain**, liberally adorned with naked Greek deities and water-spouting turtles.

At the southern end, behind a shallow Pool of Reflection, is the exquisite Art Deco **ANZAC Memorial** *(anzacmemorial.nsw.gov.au; free)*. It opened in 1934 to commemorate the troops of the Australia and New Zealand Army Corps (ANZACs) who fought in WWI, but has been expanded to include those who served in subsequent conflicts.

In the central hall, a bronze statue of a naked fallen soldier lies under a canopy of 120,000 stars set into the domed ceiling, one for every NSW soldier who served. Downstairs there's a military-themed museum, which includes a section on the construction and symbolism of the memorial. There's also an exhibition of soil samples from all the NSW places of origin of WWI soldiers. One-hour **guided tours** *(booking fee per person $2)* of the memorial reveal its history.

Hyde Park's Houses of the Holy

Sydney's most beautiful religious buildings

Facing off across the northern end of Hyde Park are a trio of exquisite places of worship dating from the first century of the colony. Between them they capture a sense of the diverse peoples who came to call Australia home.

The oldest is **St James' Church**, designed by architect Francis Greenway and built by his fellow convicts between 1820 and 1824, making it Sydney's oldest surviving church. It was originally intended as a courthouse, which explains its somewhat austere exterior. Along the way the brief changed: a steeple sprouted, the cells became a crypt and an Anglican church appeared in its place. The interior is a simple rectangle offset with Romanesque arches and a dark-wood choir loft, and enlivened by a gilded mosaic above the altar and vivid stained-glass windows.

The most spectacular of the three structures is **St Mary's Cathedral**, on the eastern edge of the park. Catholics arrived in Australia with the First Fleet, most of them convicts and many of them Irish, and their numbers were to swell with subsequent transportations following various Irish rebellions.

THE CONVICT ARCHITECT

Francis Greenway was a notable architect working in Bath and Bristol before being sentenced to death in 1812 for forging financial documents.

The sentence was commuted to transportation and in 1814 he found himself in Australia serving a 14-year sentence. He received his first Australian commission while still on the boat. Upon arrival, he swiftly formed a close working relationship with ambitious Governor Lachlan Macquarie.

Many of the elegant Georgian buildings Greenway designed are still beloved in Sydney today, such as the **Macquarie Lighthouse** in Vaucluse, Hyde Park Barracks (p93), the extravagant Government House stables block (now the **Sydney Conservatorium of Music**) and, especially, St James' Church, which is widely regarded as his masterpiece.

DRINKING IN THE CITY CENTRE: SPECIALITY BARS

Duke of Clarence: An 18th-century English pub, complete with overstuffed armchairs, a roaring fireplace and portraits of nobles. *noon-1am Mon-Sat, to 11pm Sun*

The Barber Shop: A moody speakeasy hidden in a courtyard, serving gin flights, with gin cocktails as the star sip. *4pm-midnight Mon-Thu, 4pm-2am Fri & Sat*

Old Love's: A fun and funky vintage tiki bar with flamboyant rum cocktails (you can then hop upstairs to brother bar Old Mate's for rooftop drinks). *5pm-2am Tue-Sun*

PS40: Adventurous drinkers will feel right at home in this innovative cocktail bar where trusting the process pays off. *5pm-midnight Tue-Sat*

BEST SHOPPING CENTRES & DEPARTMENT STORES

Queen Victoria Building: The QVB features nearly 200 shops on five levels, including high-end boutiques and speciality stores; it's worth visiting for the Art Deco architecture alone.

Strand Arcade: Australian designers have boutiques on the upper level, while downstairs you can pick up an Aussie classic at Strand Hatters.

Westfield Sydney: This massive maze of a complex has gobbled up Sydney Tower and hosts a fair number of pop-up shops.

David Jones: DJs is Sydney's premier department store, with high-quality clothing, a highbrow food court and a whole kids' floor.

Myer: With seven storeys, Myer is one of Sydney's largest department stores, selling fashion, beauty products, homewares and much more.

MAURIZIO DE MATTEI/SHUTTERSTOCK

St Mary's Cathedral (p95)

Catholics gained freedom to worship in 1820, with the first St Mary's founded soon after. The current 106m-long sandstone Gothic Revival cathedral was begun in 1868, consecrated in 1905, completed in 1928 and crowned with its 75m-high spires in 2000. Unusually aligned north–south rather than facing the rising sun, the building glows with golden light emanating through its stained-glass windows each morning and afternoon. Free guided tours take place Sundays at 2pm.

The First Fleet also carried with it a small number of Jews, mostly from London's working-class East End. The **Great Synagogue** on the western edge of Hyde Park was completed in 1878. The building combines Romanesque, Gothic, Moorish and Byzantine elements and the interiors are magnificent, with golden stars set onto a deep-blue ceiling. Sadly, it can only be visited as part of a pricey guided tour ($350 for up to 35 people), which must be arranged a week in advance.

Head to the Heights

Shoot up Sydney Tower

Despite the proliferation of skyscrapers, the 309m-tall **Sydney Tower** (completed in 1981) is still Sydney's highest structure.

Naturally, the main drawcard is the 360-degree vista from the 250m-high observation level branded as **Sydney Tower Eye** *(sydneytowereye.com.au; adult/child $29/21)*. Adrenaline chasers can opt to tackle the **Skywalk** *(from $95)*, a guided walk along a ledge circumnavigating the roof. Sydney Tower Eye is run by the same company as Sea Life, Wild Life and Madame Tussauds, with a baffling number of combo ticket options available. It stays open for the sunset views in the evening.

The tower features two revolving restaurants (a mediocre buffet and fine dining option) and **Bar 83**, where the $30-per-person minimum rivals the Sydney Tower Eye fee but includes food and drinks.

Darling Harbour & Haymarket

WATERFRONT ATTRACTIONS AND CHINATOWN

The historic docklands to the west of the city centre have been completely transformed into a dedicated entertainment precinct, with big-name tourist attractions, flashy hotels and two gargantuan casino complexes. It all kicked off with the redevelopment of Darling Harbour, timed around the bicentenary in 1988. Since then, the gentrification has spread along the waterfront in both directions, culminating in the just-out-of-its-wrapper Barangaroo enclave.

Step back from the water and things are less glitzy in the city-fringe neighbourhoods of Pyrmont, Ultimo and Haymarket. Ultimo is dominated by the University of Technology Sydney (UTS), with a profusion of statement buildings ranging in style from brutalist to the crumpled magnificence of Frank Gehry's 'brown paper bag' building.

Office blocks give way to high-rise apartment blocks in Haymarket, at the southern end of the city centre. Here you'll find Central Station, Sydney's lively Chinatown and the curated chaos of Paddy's Markets.

TOP TIP

Darling Harbour and Haymarket are livelier than many other parts of the city after dark. In Darling Harbour, a free fireworks show takes place most Saturday nights and dancers practise their performances nightly in Dancers' Alley (Moriarty Walk). Chinatown also illuminates after dark, with night markets every Friday.

Wildlife by the Water

Sharks, koalas and wax figurines

You can tick a whole swag of Aussie critters off your list in Darling Harbour at the trio of attractions at the city end of Pyrmont Bridge.

GETTING AROUND

Central Station is the hub of Sydney's public transport system, making this one of the best-connected areas in the city. The light rail heads up George St and loops around Pyrmont. Adding to the mix are buses and ferries. Some of the Darling Harbour attractions offer discounted parking at the large car parks near the Convention Centre (check when you're booking your tickets online). Alternatively, you can walk from Central to Barangaroo in 30 minutes or from Wynyard Station to Barangaroo in five minutes.

HIGHLIGHTS
1 Australian National Maritime Museum
2 Sea Life Sydney Aquarium

SIGHTS
3 Chinatown
4 Chinese Garden of Friendship
5 Crown Sydney
6 Golden Water Mouth
7 Madame Tussauds
8 Wild Life

ACTIVITIES
9 Sydney Harbour Kayaks

SLEEPING
10 Darling, The
11 Hotel Woolstore 1888
12 Pod Sydney
13 Sydney Central YHA
14 Wake Up! Sydney

EATING
15 Boon Cafe
16 City Oltra
17 Gumshara
18 Ho Jiak Haymarket
19 Kowloon
20 LuMi
21 Mamak
22 Meat & Wine Co
see 17 Nanjing Dumpling
23 Royal Palace
24 Social Brew
25 Sokyo

DRINKING & NIGHTLIFE
see 5 Cirq
26 Home
27 Smoke
28 Untied

ENTERTAINMENT
29 ARA Darling Quarter Theatre
30 Capitol Theatre
31 ICC Sydney
32 IMAX Sydney
33 Sydney Lyric Theatre

SHOPPING
34 Paddy's Markets

Walk through perspex tunnels under the capacious tanks at **Sea Life Sydney Aquarium** *(visitsealife.com; online tickets from $39)* while immense rays and sharks glide overhead. If you'd like to make their acquaintance, cage-less shark dives are on offer (from $349). Corals and disco-lit jellyfish add Day-Glo colour and kids love the short boat ride through the gentoo and king penguin enclosure. The star attraction, a dugong named Pig, was rescued after washing up as a youngster on a Queensland beach. Attempts to return him to the wild failed, so he found a home at Sea Life.

Head next door to meet the stars of Australian fauna that prefer dry land. **Wild Life** *(wildlifesydney.com.au; online tickets from $39)* has all the famous Aussie critters - from wallabies to wombats, kangaroos to koalas, platypuses to possums - and plenty of other mammals, birds, reptiles and insects that you may not have heard of. Walk-through aviaries and enclosures allow you to get close to the animals that are less likely to kill you.

The third place showcases a different kind of beast altogether. This branch of London's famous **Madame Tussauds** *(madametussauds.com; online tickets from $39)* is heavy on the Aussie quotient, featuring the likes of Kylie Minogue, Heath Ledger, Steve Irwin and the Hemsworths in hyper realistic waxwork form.

The same company that runs these attractions also runs Sydney Tower Eye and combo tickets are available in various permutations.

Sea, Surf & Submarines

Breeze through the 'Mu-sea-um'

Housed in a curvy building reminiscent of a scaled-down Opera House, the **Australian National Maritime Museum** *(sea.museum)* - ANMM or Mu-sea-um for short - isn't constrained by what's beneath its sail-like roofline. Many of the displays are docked outside in the form of tall ships, three naval vessels and other classic craft. The 'See It All Ticket' (adult/child $35/25) allows access to all galleries and the bigger vessels, including the replica of James Cook's HMB *Endeavour*, the naval destroyer HMAS *Vampire* and the submarine HMAS *Onslow*.

Exhibitions range from Indigenous seafaring to surf culture and from immigration to ocean science. There's plenty to fill half a day here, or you can bump it out further by booking a

BENNELONG & BARANGAROO

Early Sydney's most well-known Indigenous couple - Bennelong and Barangaroo - first met in 1790 in Banarung (Rose Bay). Bennelong had been kidnapped the previous year by Governor Phillip, who hoped to learn from him the local people's language and customs. Bennelong was a Wangal man, from the Inner West, while Barangaroo was Cammeraygal, from the lower North Shore - both Darug clans.

While Bennelong continued a close association with the settlers after he escaped, even travelling to London with Phillip in 1792, Barangaroo preferred to live with her own people. Phillip built a hut for Bennelong at what became Bennelong Point (where the Sydney Opera House stands), while a new waterfront development has been named after Barangaroo.

EATING IN DARLING HARBOUR: OUR PICKS

Social Brew: Small cafe serving big flavours with top-tier coffee and hearty breakfasts and doling out decadent lunchtime salads and burgers. *7am-3.30pm* $

Sokyo: Bringing Toyko glam to the Star, Sokyo serves well-crafted Japanese fare, including delicious eight-dish *orizume* lunches. *5-10pm daily, plus noon-3pm Fri-Sun* $$$

LuMi: Offering innovative degustation menus of Japanese-influenced Italian cuisine at Pyrmont Bay pier. *5.30-8.30pm Thu-Sun, plus noon-2.30pm Sat & Sun* $$$

Meat & Wine Co: Quality Aussie steaks and impeccably paired wines served in a moody venue with harbour views. *noon-10pm* $$$

Try the coffee-marinated kangaroo skewers

HAYMARKET'S FOODIE HIT LIST

Justin Steele, local guide and owner of Local Sauce Tours. *@localsaucetours*

Chinatown isn't just for Chinese food anymore; you'll always find something a little different here. Start your day with *fan tuan,* a sticky rice roll filled with egg, pork floss, pickled vegetables and crunchy bread. Family-run Mother Chu's has been perfecting it for over 30 years. You also can't go wrong with a banh mi from Marrickville Pork Roll, a crisp baguette stuffed with herbs, vegetables and roast pork. Cool off with a Purple Rice Yoghurt from Milkflower, an icy drink of yoghurt and black rice sipped through a thick straw. For something sweet, try the hot, freshly made custard puffs at Emperor's Garden Bakery.

DHW688/SHUTTERSTOCK

Crown Sydney tower (left)

cruise on one of the Sydney Heritage Fleet. The most romantic craft is the *James Craig,* a three-masted iron barque built in England in 1874, which heads out past the Heads a couple of times a month (from $180; minimum age 12).

Sea-kayaking tours with **Sydney Harbour Kayaks** *(sydney harbourkayaks.com.au; adult/child $89/69)* depart out front.

Sydney's Shiny New Precinct

Dock yourself at Barangaroo

Barangaroo divides opinion among Sydneysiders, its skyline dominated by the glitzy **Crown Sydney tower**. Critics argue the waterfront precinct favours developers over the public, but it's best to visit and decide for yourself. The southern end brims with upscale bars, shops and restaurants around the Three International Towers, while the centre remains under construction. At the northern tip, Barangaroo Reserve offers native gardens and harbour views, plus Marrinawi Cove, refreshed in 2025 with swim steps and outdoor showers.

DRINKING IN DARLING HARBOUR: BEST CLUBS & BARS

Smoke: On the 2nd-floor rooftop of Barangaroo House, Smoke delivers views and seasonal cocktails. *3-10pm Tue, 3pm-midnight Wed-Sat, 2-10pm Sun*

Cirq: Hit this pricey bar on the 26th floor of Crown Sydney for happy-hour cocktails and dizzying sunset views. *4pm-midnight Wed-Fri, noon-1am Sat, noon-10pm Sun*

Untied: A whimsical rooftop bar with brunches, creative cocktails and seasonal pop-up events and drinks. *noon-10pm Mon-Thu, noon-midnight Fri & Sat, noon-9pm Sun*

Home: This multilevel Cockle Bay Wharf nightclub has plenty of space to party, with dance floors, chill spots and a reputation for top-notch house music. *hours vary*

WANDER ALONG THE WATERFRONT

Stroll the flat waterfront promenade and take in the sights, or step inside the attractions to fill a full day.

START	END	LENGTH
The Star light-rail stop	Marrinawi Cove	3.7km; 2hr

Catch the light rail to ❶ **The Star** stop and stroll through ❷ **Pyrmont Bay Park**. As you enter Darling Harbour you'll pass the ❸ **Welcome Wall** migration monument, followed by the moored vessels that form part of the ❹ **Australian National Maritime Museum** (p99).

Cross under ❺ **Pyrmont Bridge**, the world's first electric swing bridge (1902) and trace the waterline past the ❻ **International Convention Centre** (ICC Sydney; p102) and the ❼ **Ribbon**, a lopsided curve containing IMAX Sydney and the W Sydney hotel. As you pass the restaurants and bars of ❽ **Cockle Bay Wharf**, note the brolga cranes perpetually dancing in their fountain.

After scooting under Pyrmont Bridge again you'll pass ❾ **Sea Life** (p99), ❿ **Madame Tussauds** (p99) and ⓫ **Wild Life** (p99). Next up, ⓬ **King Street Wharf** is lined with restaurants and bars. It morphs into the still-being-developed Barangaroo complex, dominated by Sydney's tallest skyscraper, 271m-high ⓭ **Crown Sydney**. Locals cheekily call it 'Packer's Pecker', after billionaire James Packer's casino company that built it. As part of the deal, the developers restored the pre-1836 shoreline using large sandstone blocks.

Walk through the ⓮ **Barangaroo Reserve** on one of its upper walkways; it's a welcome retreat into nature with over 75,000 native trees and plants along its paths. Beneath it, ⓯ **Marrinawi Cove** has a shark-netted swimming area, should you fancy a dip.

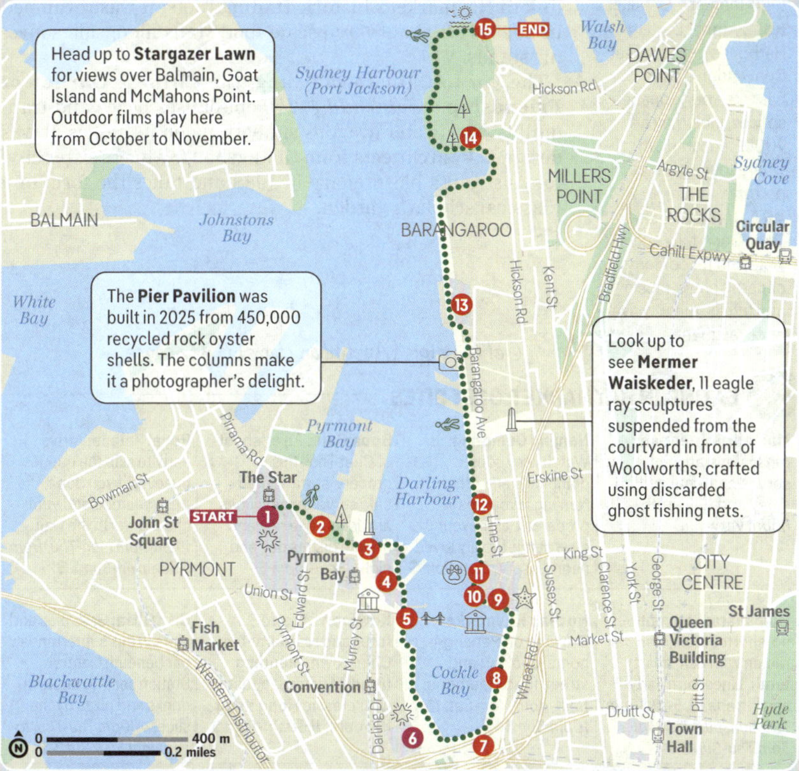

DARLING HARBOUR & HAYMARKET ENTERTAINMENT VENUES

Capitol Theatre: This large, lavishly restored Haymarket theatre is home to big-budget musicals and the occasional ballet or concert.

Sydney Lyric Theatre: The high-quality 2000-seat theatre within the Star casino also stages high-profile musicals and sporadic concerts.

IMAX Sydney: It's pricey ($40 for a standard adult ticket) but IMAX's vast 692-sq-metre movie screen is the third-largest ever built.

ICC Sydney: Darling Harbour's International Convention Centre has three performance spaces, including a 9000-seat stadium where touring bands perform.

ARA Darling Quarter Theatre: A fully accessible hub for comedy, cabaret, plays, music and family-friendly live entertainment.

Chaos & Serenity in Chinatown

The heart of Chinese Sydney

Ornate *paifang,* ornamental archways decorated with fake bamboo tiles and guardian lions, mark each end of the car-free section of Dixon St, standing as the heart of **Chinatown**. However, the whole of Haymarket is now a Pan-Asian dining destination, with Chinatown morphing into a tiny Koreatown (around Goulburn and George Sts) and larger Thaitown (Pitt and Campbell Sts).

Dixon St is Sydney's third Chinatown, following earlier enclaves in The Rocks and Market St. Chinese migration began in 1818 and grew in the 1840s with labourers and gold-miners, who faced discrimination under racist laws formalised in 1901 with the White Australia policy. By the 20th century, Chinese cooks made up around a third of the culinary work-force, heavily influencing Australia's cuisine. **Local Sauce Tours** *(localsaucetours.com.au; $75)* offers walking food tours through Haymarket, blending delicious tastings with fascinating local history.

On Hay St, the **Golden Water Mouth** sculpture provides a visual reminder of the early Chinese gold-miners. Nearby **Paddy's Markets** *(closed Mondays and Tuesdays)* is the last link to Haymarket's historic trading roots; it was revamped in 2025 with about 50 upscale food stalls alongside souvenir stands.

The yin to Chinatown's yang, the **Chinese Garden of Friendship** *(adult/child $12/8)* epitomises peace and tranquillity with water dragons sunbathing on its stones. It was designed by architects from Guangzhou (Sydney's sister city) for Australia's bicentenary in 1988 and takes the form of a Classical scholar's garden.

EATING IN HAYMARKET: BEST BITES

Get the pipis (Australian clams) in XO sauce (Royal Palace)

Mamak: This eat-and-run Malaysian joint serves charcoal-grilled satay and flaky roti. *hours vary*

Nanjing Dumpling: Watch juicy soup dumplings and other Nanjing favourites prepared before your eyes at this locally loved neon-lit spot. *8am-9pm* $

Boon Cafe: An offshoot of Chat Thai, this grocery-store-turned-cafe serves sandwiches and Isan-style rice and noodle dishes day and night. *8am-10pm* $

Royal Palace: Arrive early to skip the queues – but even if you don't, the fresh seafood and yum cha are worth the wait. *10am-11pm Mon-Thu, from 9.30am Fri-Sun* $$

Gumshara: Scrumptious, no-shortcut tonkotsu ramen with rich, hearty broth. Lines form early, so plan ahead. *5-10.30pm Tue-Sun, plus 11.30am-3pm Thu-Sun* $$

Ho Jiak Haymarket: Drawing on Penang home-cooking and street-food traditions. *11am-11pm Mon-Sat, to 10pm Sun* $$

Kowloon: A retro-futuristic restaurant in Chinatown, blending trendy Australian tastes with classic Hong Kong flavours. *11.30am-9pm* $

City Oltra: Grab pies and pints in this subterranean bar beneath Central Station serving endless drinks and pizza by the slice. *4-10pm Tue-Thu, to midnight Fri & Sat* $$

Kings Cross, Potts Point & Woolloomooloo

CITY-FRINGE NEIGHBOURHOODS WITH EDGE

Once notorious for its strip clubs, easy-to-access narcotics and well-heeled gangsters, Kings Cross has shed much of its seedy character over the past decade. It still has one of the city's liveliest bar scenes, but trendy cafes, chic restaurants and upmarket homeware stores are also in the mix. Truth be told, the Cross's unsavoury side often overshadowed its role as one of Sydney's earliest and most inclusive neighbourhoods, while the densely packed suburbs of Potts Points and Elizabeth Bay that surround it have always had more than their fair share of multimillion-dollar sea-view homes.

Nestled in the bay separating Potts Point from the city centre is the historic working-class suburb of Woolloomooloo. Its back streets have retained their social housing and the navy still has a presence here, but the heritage-listed wharf at the heart of the bay has long since been converted into a luxury hotel, restaurants and apartments.

TOP TIP

Much of what most people call Kings Cross falls within the suburb of Potts Point. Businesses tend to use a Potts Point address if they want to sound classy and Kings Cross if they want to emphasise their party cred. Either way, you'll know Kings Cross when you see it.

GETTING AROUND

Potts Point occupies a ridge that slopes steeply down to Woolloomooloo, Elizabeth Bay and Rushcutters Bay. The most atmospheric route to Woolloomooloo is the 113-step McElhone Stairs, built in 1870 and popular with masochistic joggers. Kings Cross Station is at the centre of the strip, with regular trains to the city centre and Bondi Junction. The 311 bus from the city loops through Woolloomooloo, up through Potts Point to Elizabeth Bay and back through the heart of the Cross. William St is also a busy bus route. Parking is difficult, so avoid bringing a car.

THE FIRST MARDI GRAS

Sydney had seen gay rights protests before, with activists arrested in Martin Place in 1973, but the 24 June 1978 parade was different. Timed around the ninth anniversary of New York's Stonewall Riots, this march had a carnival-like spirit. On that Saturday night, around 2000 revellers on Oxford St heeded the call to 'get out of the bars and into the streets'.

After being harassed by the police for much of the route, the remaining marchers were corralled in Kings Cross, where some were beaten and 53 arrested. Their names were published in the *Sydney Morning Herald* newspaper and many lost their jobs.

In 2018, four decades later, the NSW Police Commissioner issued a formal apology for the abuse during the 1978 Mardi Gras.

SIGHTS
1 Artspace
2 Coca-Cola Sign
3 Elizabeth Bay House
4 Fitzroy Gardens
5 Woolloomooloo Finger Wharf

SLEEPING
6 Hotel 59
7 Pacific House Hostel
8 Regents Court
9 Spicers Potts Point

EATING
10 Cho Cho San
11 Fratelli Paradiso
12 Harry's Cafe de Wheels
13 PIÑA
14 Yellow

DRINKING & NIGHTLIFE
15 Bar Lucia
16 Dulcie's
17 Holey Moley
18 Kings Cross Hotel
19 Kit & Kaboodle
20 Old Fitzroy Hotel
21 Piccolo Bar
22 Tilbury

Bright Lights & Boozy Bars

Wander the Darlinghurst Rd strip

Technically Kings Cross is just the intersection of William and Victoria Sts, where the thoroughfares named after two 'kings' cross (it was known as Queen's Cross during Victoria's reign). However, the area popularly known as Kings Cross today is centred on the busy 350m-long strip of businesses on Darlinghurst Rd that starts here.

Go for the sourdough pancakes

EATING IN POTTS POINT: OUR PICKS

Yellow: This sunflower-coloured former artists' residence is Sydney's most ambitious vegan restaurant, serving only multicourse degustation menus. *hours vary* $$$

Cho Cho San: The food is just as artful as the chic surrounds at this chic *izakaya*-style Japanese restaurant. *5.30pm-midnight Mon-Thu, from noon Fri-Sun* $$

Fratelli Paradiso: A balance between cosy trattoria and upmarket restaurant, with a short menu and street-side tables. *noon-11pm Mon-Sat, noon-10pm Sun* $$$

PIÑA: All-day breakfasts, plus burgers and salads served in a relaxed laneway; the chefs don't skimp on the good stuff. *7am-3pm* $

A giant **Coca-Cola sign** has been flashing over the 'Top of the Cross' since 1974 and has become synonymous with the neighbourhood. This is actually the 2016 model; when the previous incarnation was replaced, it was auctioned off letter by letter for fundraising for the Wayside Chapel, a local charity for people experiencing homelessness.

As you wander past the bars, fast-food joints, porn shops, clothing boutiques and strip bars, keep an eye out for the inscriptions in the footpath offering snatches of local history. Darlinghurst Rd terminates at **Fitzroy Gardens**, a once-dodgy park that now hosts genteel markets on the weekends. Here you'll find sulphur-crested cockatoos and the dandelion-esque El Alamein Fountain (1961), the Cross' other much-loved emblem.

Relic of a Salubrious Past

Step into Elizabeth Bay House

Now ringed by multistorey apartments, elegant **Elizabeth Bay House** *(mhnsw.au; free)* gives a window into a time when the colonial well-to-do were beginning to shift out of the central city, seeking a peaceful escape from the convicts and open sewers of Sydney Cove. It's open from 10am to 4pm Sundays and Mondays.

Built for Colonial Secretary Alexander Macleay, this gracious Greek Revival mansion was considered the finest house in the colony when it was completed in 1839. The architectural highlight is the curved, cantilevered staircase in the domed oval saloon at the centre of the house. An interesting video in one of the upstairs bedrooms tells the tragic story of how Macleay, after falling into debt, was turfed out of the house by his own ruthless son.

A stroll through nearby Rushcutters Bay winds past elegant yachts and manicured lawns where locals escape the city's concrete edges for fresh air and harbour views.

THE END OF SIN SYDNEY

Kings Cross reigned as Sydney's capital of vice for a century, ruled by underworld figures like Abe Saffron, who vied to be 'Boss of the Cross' with an empire of bars, hotels and strip clubs. During WWII it became the go-to playground for off-duty soldiers. By the 2000s, Kings Cross was a place where anyone could party beneath the glow of the Coca-Cola sign, though a darker undercurrent ran beneath the fun. After several alcohol-fuelled deaths, the city rolled out lockout laws in 2014, banning bar entry after 1.30am, shuttering hundreds of venues and dimming the city's nightlife. The laws were lifted in 2021, with Kings Cross the last to be freed. Today it's a tamer version of what it once was.

DRINKING IN KINGS CROSS & WOOLLOOMOOLOO: BEST BARS

Piccolo Bar: Piccolo has transitioned from old-Cross cafe to hip aperitivo bar, but otherwise it looks much as it did in 1952. *4pm-midnight Mon-Sat, to 10pm Sun*

Kings Cross Hotel: This grand old brick pub has a 1st-floor balcony bar, a 3rd-floor club (Friday and Saturday only) and a 5th-floor rooftop. *10am-3.30am*

Old Fitzroy Hotel: This unpretentious theatre pub is a good old-fashioned boozer, with a great variety of natural wines and beers. *noon-midnight*

Tilbury: This old Woolloomooloo pub now sparkles with bright interiors, street-side tables and a garden bar. *11am-midnight Wed-Sat, 11am-10pm Sun-Tue*

Holey Moley: No one will judge you if your swing is askew at this boozy 18-hole mini-golf course. *5-11pm Mon-Wed, 2-11pm Thu-Sun*

Bar Lucia: A low-lit Spanish tavern that serves tapas, sangria, fine wines and crisp cocktails. *5-11pm Wed-Fri, noon-midnight Sat, noon-10pm Sun*

Kit & Kaboodle: A nightclub paying homage to the neighbourhood's wild past, with a relaxed rooftop bar to recharge before the next banger. *9.30pm-4am Thu-Sat*

Dulcie's: This subterranean bar, pours icy cocktails and hosts intimate cabaret and burlesque performances. *5pm-midnight Sun-Thu, to 2am Fri & Sat*

Woolloomooloo Finger Wharf

Pier, Pie Cart & Pubs

Explore Old Woolloomooloo

One of the few old port suburbs to retain some of its working-class population, Woolloomooloo is an intriguing place to explore. Beautiful **Woolloomooloo Finger Wharf** is the obvious starting point. Built between 1910 and 1915, it served as a wool and cargo dock before the advent of shipping containers saw it fall into disuse. It was only saved from demolition by a 2½-year demolition workers' union ban. Despite the luxury apartments now here, large parts of the structure are still a public space, so feel free to wander around.

Another survivor is **Harry's Cafe de Wheels** *(harryscafedewheels.com.au)*, a legendary meat-pie cart that first opened for business in 1938. In its time it has served the likes of Frank Sinatra and Colonel Sanders.

Across the road, an old brick warehouse now houses **Artspace** *(artspace.org,au; free)*, one of the city's boldest galleries. Once home to the *Sydney Morning Herald*'s distribution hub, then a naval gunnery and later an artists' squat, the building was formally transformed into Artspace in 1983, with a full restoration in 2023.

THE MACLEAY COLLECTION

Alexander Macleay was an enthusiastic amateur entomologist who amassed a large zoological collection, both from his own endeavours and through acquisitions. This now forms the basis of the natural history section of Sydney University's **Chau Chak Wing Museum** (p123).

Darlinghurst, Surry Hills & Paddington

LGBTIQ+ BARS AND GREAT RESTAURANTS

Row upon row of Victorian terrace houses fill the streets of these city-fringe suburbs that were once notorious slums but are now hugely sought-after neighbourhoods. Darlinghurst ('Darlo' for short) is closely associated with Sydney's LGBTIQ+ communities and has the city's largest concentration of gay bars. While Oxford St, its main thoroughfare, is more shabby than chic, it swirls with sequins and feathers in early March when tens of thousands descend to watch the Sydney Gay & Lesbian Mardi Gras parade.

To the south, Surry Hills is an undulating suburb of terrace houses and old warehouses. Historically it was home to the newspaper publishing and rag trade, but in recent decades it has become one of the city's premier dining districts, with exciting new places opening all the time.

Head east and you'll hit Paddington ('Paddo' to many), a more upmarket neighbourhood with grander terrace houses, swankier stores and fancier pubs.

GETTING AROUND

Here you can get anywhere you need to go by public transport or on foot. Museum and Kings Cross are the closest train stations to Darlinghurst, while Central Station sits at the base of Surry Hills. Light rail runs from Central through Surry Hills and into Moore Park and all three suburbs are well connected by bus. Street parking is possible with patience, but it's usually metered and limited in duration.

Treasures of Australia & the Pacific

The Australian Museum's eclectic collections

Established in 1827, the venerable **Australian Museum** *(australian.museum; 10am-5pm daily; free)*, is a key contender for any Sydney itinerary. A wonderfully diverse array of objects is displayed in the 200 Treasures exhibition, ranging

DRINKING IN DARLINGHURST: BEST BARS

Love, Tilly Devine: Named after a 1930s madam and crime boss, this dark, good-looking, split-level wine bar lurks down a back alley. *5pm-midnight Mon-Sat*

Riley Hotel: This cosy corner pub (established in 1860) offers a quieter option on the Oxford St strip. *8am-2am*

Darlo Bar: Something of a locals' lounge room, this triangular pub has a retro vibe and a rooftop bar. *noon-midnight*

Bitter Phew: A down-to-earth bar showcasing a constantly evolving lineup of craft beers and boutique wines. *3pm-midnight Tue-Thu, 2pm-2am Fri & Sat, 2-10pm Sun*

DARLINGHURST, SURRY HILLS & PADDINGTON

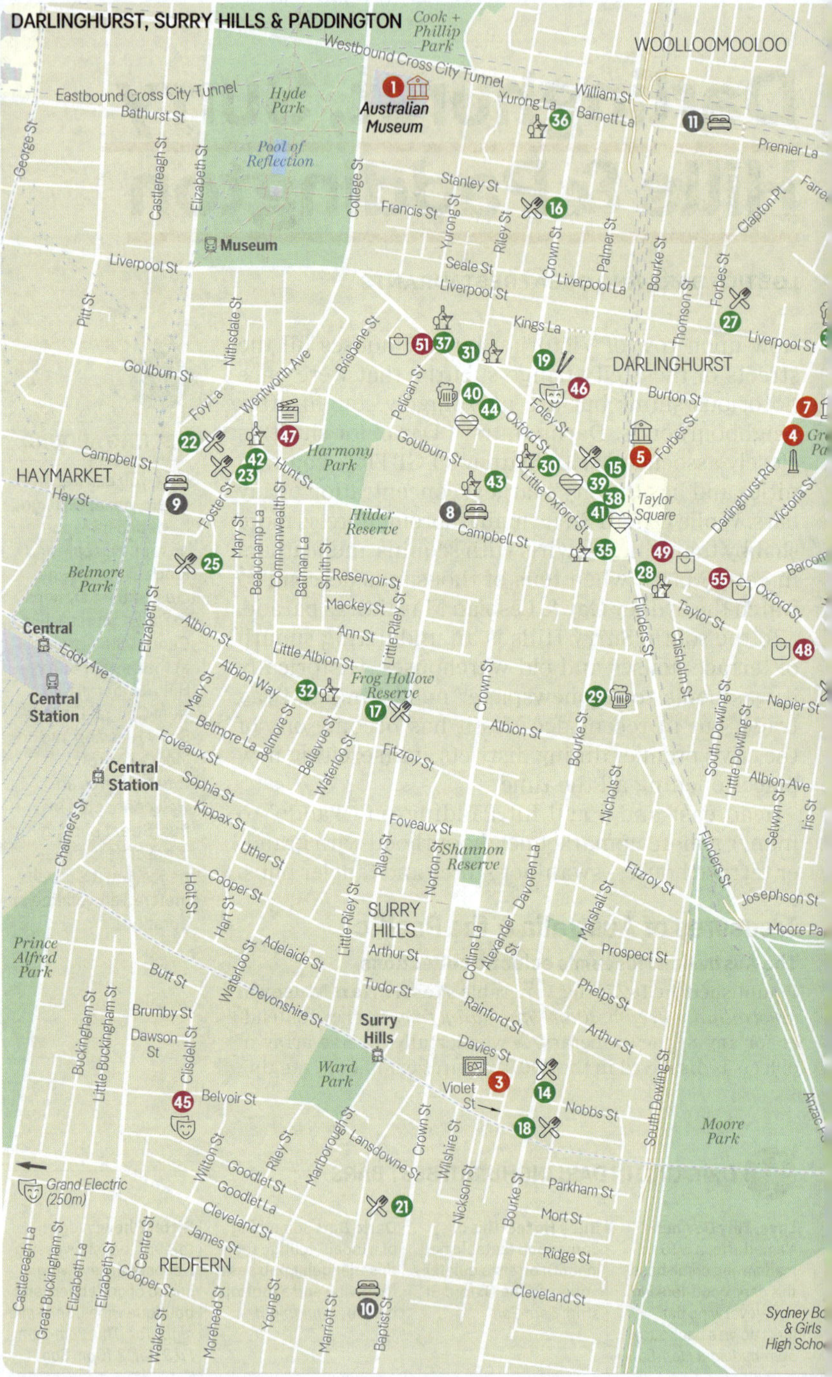

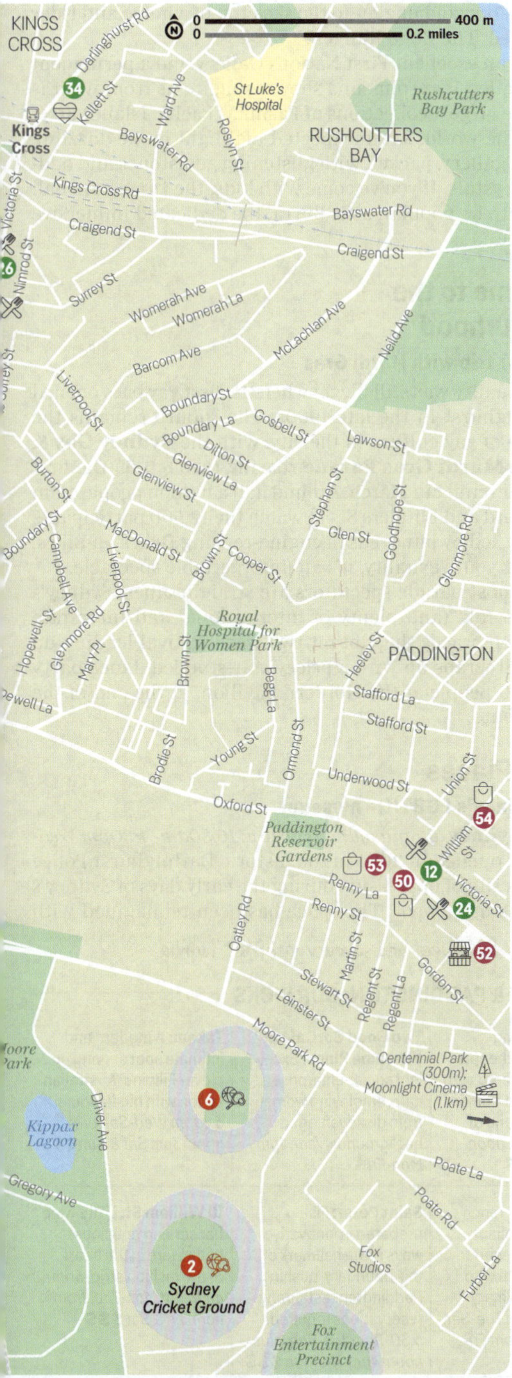

HIGHLIGHTS
1 Australian Museum
2 Sydney Cricket Ground

SIGHTS
3 Brett Whiteley Studio
4 Gay & Lesbian Holocaust Memorial
5 Qtopia Sydney
6 Sydney Football Stadium
7 Sydney Jewish Museum

SLEEPING
8 ADGE Hotel + Residences
9 Big Hostel
10 Eve Hotel
11 Nate's Place

EATING
12 10 William Street
13 Ampersand Cafe & Bookstore
14 Arthur
15 Avia
16 Bar Reggio
17 Bessie's
18 Bourke Street Bakery
19 Chaco Ramen
20 GAZI
21 Kurumba
22 NEL Restaurant
23 Nomad
see 47 Paramount Coffee Project
24 Saint Peter
25 Single O
26 Takam
27 Two Good Co. Cafe at Yirranma Place

DRINKING & NIGHTLIFE
28 Aura
29 Beresford Hotel
30 Bitter Phew
31 Cliff Dive
32 Copains
33 Darlo Bar
34 Grove Bar
35 Kinselas
36 Love, Tilly Devine
37 Oxford Art Factory
38 Oxford Hotel
39 Palms on Oxford
40 Riley Hotel
41 Stonewall
42 Tio's
43 Tucano's
44 Universal

ENTERTAINMENT
45 Belvoir St Theatre
46 Eternity Playhouse
47 Golden Age Cinema & Bar

SHOPPING
48 Berkelouw Books
49 Bookshop Darlinghurst
50 Dinosaur Designs
51 House of Priscilla
52 Paddington Markets
53 Parlour X
54 Poepke
55 Sax Fetish
see 49 Tattoora

from a 10.7kg gold nugget to the skeleton of a horse and rider nicknamed 'The Bone Ranger'.

There's an excellent First Nations Gallery and a permanent gallery called Wansolmoana showcasing items from what is one of the largest collections of Pasifika (Pacific Island) artefacts in the world. An unexpected highlight is the dazzling Minerals gallery, packed with glistening gemstones and odd-shaped crystals. If you've come with kids, the Dinosaurs hall is bound to be popular, as is Burra, the dedicated immersive play space.

Welcome to the Gaybourhood

Time your trip with Mardi Gras

Homosexuality was still illegal when the first gay bars opened in Darlinghurst in the late 1960s. The suburb remains the epicentre of gay culture in the city, with the **Sydney Gay & Lesbian Mardi Gras Parade** roaring through on the first Saturday evening in March. Around half a million people cram onto Oxford and Flinders Sts to watch the 12,500 participants sashay by, led by hundreds of engine-revving Dykes on Bikes. Whatever your sexuality, it's an unforgettable spectacle.

While most parade spectators are straight allies, Sydney's LGBTIQ+ folk (and plenty of international and interstate visitors) embraces the vibrant two-week festival leading up to it. It all wraps up with a pricey star-studded dance party for 10,000 people at the Hordern Pavilion, at the end of the parade route.

Proud Places

Visit Sydney's LGBTIQ+ museum

Qtopia Sydney *(qtopiasydney.com.au; 10.30am-4.30pm Wed-Sun; $15)* opened in 2024 in the historic Darlinghurst Police Station, a site of oppression during the early days of Sydney's gay rights movement. The space has been reimagined with

BEST THEATRES & CINEMAS IN DARLINGHURST & SURRY HILLS

Belvoir St Theatre: This intimate venue with two small stages is the home of an often-experimental and consistently excellent theatre company.

Grand Electric: From cabaret to comedy to circus performances and more, there's a show for everyone in this retro parlour theatre.

Eternity Playhouse: Based in a beautifully restored 1887 Baptist tabernacle, this 200-seat theatre brings intelligent Australian scripts to the stage.

Golden Age Cinema & Bar: A heartwarming small cinema in what was the Sydney HQ of Paramount Pictures. The bar hosts free gigs on weekends.

Moonlight Cinema: Take a picnic and join the bats for movies under the stars during summertime in magnificent Centennial Park.

EATING IN DARLINGHURST & PADDINGTON: OUR PICKS

Try the sweet and savoury jackfruit 'humba'

Chaco Ramen: This simple but chic little place specialises in ramen, serving some seriously good broth. *11.30am-2.30pm & 5.30-8.30pm* $

Bar Reggio: Long-running Italian cheapie with walls plastered with Ferrari flags and Roman murals and a menu of simple classics. *noon-10pm Mon-Sat* $

Two Good Co. Cafe at Yirranma Place: Excellent social-enterprise cafe, employing women from disadvantaged backgrounds. *7am-4pm Mon-Fri* $

Takam: A modern and intimate spot serving up clever Filipino-Australian fusion with big flavours. *6-10pm Wed-Sat, plus noon-3pm Sat & Sun* $$

GAZI: Swap the stuffy fine-dining scene for a more social vibe with Mediterranean meals at this moody supper club with regular entertainment. *6pm-midnight Tue-Sat* $$

Avia: Elevated French-, Spanish- and Italian-inspired cuisine with chefs at the helm who have serious culinary cred. *5-10.30pm Tue-Sat, plus noon-3.30pm Fri-Sun* $$

Saint Peter: Fish prepared in innovative ways is the hallmark of this boundary-pushing Paddington restaurant; reservations required. *5.30-11pm Tue-Sun, plus noon-4pm Thu-Sun* $$$

10 William St: Little wine bar serving delicious Italian fare in the heart of the fashion strip. *5pm-midnight Mon-Thu, from noon Fri & Sat* $$$

Sydney Cricket Ground

powerful exhibitions on queer art, modern day activism and a sombre reflection on the AIDS crisis in Sydney.

In nearby Green Park, near the Jewish Museum, the **Gay & Lesbian Holocaust Memorial** takes the form of a stylised pink triangle backed by black pillars. It was founded by the late Dr Kitty Fischer, who was kept alive as a young Jewish girl in Auschwitz by food smuggled to her by a gay inmate.

Catch a Match in Moore Park

See the SCG in action

Sydneysiders, like most Australians, go nuts for their sports teams. If you want to witness all of the power and the passion unleashed, Moore Park's two large stadiums are convenient places to do it.

The legendary **Sydney Cricket Ground** *(SCG; sydneycricketground.com.au; 1hr tour adult/child $30/20)* can hold 48,000 for the oval-pitch games: cricket and Australian Football League (AFL, aka Aussie Rules) matches. It's the home of the Sydney Swans (AFL), NSW (state cricket) and the Sydney Sixers (T20 cricket) and international cricket test matches regularly take place here. Cricket obsessives should consider a tour, which includes the dressing rooms, heritage-listed pavilions, the SCG Museum and various exhibition spaces.

BEST CLUBS IN DARLINGHURST

Oxford Art Factory: Indie kids watch bands and party against an arty backdrop at this two-room multipurpose venue modelled on Andy Warhol's Factory.

Cliff Dive: Head downstairs to a dance club with rough-hewn stone walls, tropical-fish lanterns, Polynesian knick-knacks and tiki cocktails.

Palms on Oxford: Good silly fun; the 1980s never ended in this basement gay club, where Kylie Minogue rules supreme.

Aura: Kitted out with an epic sound and light system for a multisensory music experience the A-list clubbers come out for.

Universal: There's drag every night at this longstanding gay venue, either downstairs in the bar, upstairs in the club or at both.

DRINKING IN THE EASTERN SUBURBS: BEST LGBTIQ+ BARS

Kinselas: This colourful converted funeral parlour incorporates an Art Deco chapel and has the best balcony for posing and people-watching. *9am-6am*

Stonewall: A stalwart of the Oxford St strip, Stonewall has three levels of bars and dance floors. *4pm-2am Sun, Wed & Thu, to 4.30am Fri & Sat*

Oxford Hotel: A Sydney gay institution (up for heritage listing at the time of writing), it spans four levels plus a terrace. *10am-4am Sun-Thu, to 6am Fri & Sat*

Grove Bar: A laid-back Kings Cross gay bar with sultry lounge vibes and a soundtrack soft enough for conversation. *6pm-2am Wed-Sat*

SHOPPING IN PADDINGTON

Paddington Markets: Originating in the 1970s, these popular Saturday markets are worth exploring for their new and vintage clothing, crafts and jewellery.

Dinosaur Designs: Locally made, richly coloured, translucent, resin jewellery sits among technicoloured vases and bowls, along with chunky sterling-silver rings and necklaces.

Poepke: On the William St fashion strip, this is one of Paddington's more interesting women's boutiques, stocking Australian and global designers.

Parlour X: Paddington is full of designer boutiques, but this sandstone church shines with a curated mix of Australian and international labels.

Berkelouw Books: Browse through three floors of preloved tomes, new releases, antique maps and Australia's largest collection of rare books.

SEBASTIAN REATEGUI/SHUTTERSTOCK

Centennial Park

The **Sydney Football Stadium** *(Allianz Stadium; allianz stadium.com.au)* can accommodate upwards of 42,000 devotees and is the home ground for the Sydney Roosters rugby league (NRL) team, the NSW Waratahs (Super Rugby) team and the Sydney FC (A-League) soccer team. In this rugby-league-mad town, you can't beat a Roosters game for atmosphere.

Ramble Through Sydney's Biggest Park

Stretch out in Centennial Park

Big enough to accommodate dog walkers, joggers, cyclists, horse riders, ball kickers and many picnickers, 189-hectare **Centennial Park** includes ponds, playgrounds and the domed Federation Pavilion, marking the spot where, on 1 January 1901, Australia was officially proclaimed a nation.

Visit the Home of an Iconic Aussie Artist

Stop in at the Brett Whiteley Studio

Brett Whiteley (1939–1992) spent his life travelling, but his last home was a spacious studio in Surry Hills. His paintings, sculptures, sketches and personal memorabilia will be on display at the **Brett Whiteley Studio** *(artgallery.nsw.gov.au),*

DRINKING IN SURRY HILLS: BEST BARS

Get here early to secure a table

Beresford Hotel: Art Deco pub with a handsome front bar, a club upstairs and a terrific beer garden. Gay-centred on Sunday afternoons. *noon-midnight Tue-Sun*

Tio's: An atmospheric margarita bar, attracting a young free-popcorn-munching crowd. *5pm-midnight Tue-Thu, from 4pm Fri & Sat*

Tucano's: Killer cocktails keep the energy high at this tropical bar spinning everything from house to '70s disco. *5pm-midnight Thu, to 2am Fri & Sat*

Copains: Appealing little wine bar with tables spilling out onto the street and spot-on staff recommendations. *4pm-midnight Mon-Thu, from noon Fri & Sat, 1-10pm Sun* due to reopen to visitors in 2026 to offer an intimate look at his creative process and artistic legacy. The studio has regularly hosted drawing workshops for all experience levels.

Telling the Australian Jewish Story

Thought-provoking museum displays

Striking a balance between sobering and celebratory, the community-run **Sydney Jewish Museum** *(sydneyjewish museum.com.au)* explores Jewish history, culture and traditions through a local lens. Jews arrived with the First Fleet but their numbers expanded greatly in the aftermath of WWII, when Australia became home to the greatest number of Holocaust survivors per capita after Israel. The museum is currently being redeveloped and will reopen in early 2027 with a new cultural centre alongside its legacy Holocaust exhibits, which feature personal testimonies and artefacts. The expanded space will also explore contemporary human-rights issues, including those affecting Indigenous peoples, refugees, asylum seekers, people with disabilities and LGBTIQ+ communities.

NEVER FORGET

Honour the six million lives lost in the Holocaust through powerful survivor testimonies, evocative artefacts, and award-winning architecture at the **Melbourne Holocaust Museum** (p493). From the harrowing 'Everybody Had a Name' exhibition to the inspiring 'Hidden' for children, experience a deeply sobering journey.

SHOPPING AROUND DARLINGHURST

Ampersand Cafe & Bookstore: A multilevel bookshop brimming with tales for every taste, with a cafe and outdoor tables perfect for perusing your new find.

Bookshop Darlinghurst: This outstanding bookshop specialises in gay and lesbian books, with everything from queer crime to glossy pictorials.

House of Priscilla: Run by some of the city's leading drag artistes, Priscilla is the place for sequinned frocks to fit even the burliest queens.

Sax Fetish: Exceptionally helpful staff to assist with finding you quality leather and rubber adult gear, much of it Aussie made.

Tattoora: Come home with a tattoo or piercing from one of the talented, caring artists at this modern new tattoo parlour.

Regulars love the Moreton Bay bug sandwich

EATING IN SURRY HILLS: BEST RESTAURANTS

Bourke Street Bakery: There are branches across Sydney, but this original bakery remains a must-visit Surry Hills staple. *7am-6pm Mon-Fri, to 5pm Sat & Sun* $

Paramount Coffee Project: Rotating coffees and adventurous dishes in the former headquarters of the Paramount film company are an excellent choice. *7am-4pm* $

Bessie's: A smoky kiss from the woodfire defines the meat and seafood at this easy-going restaurant. *5-10pm Mon-Wed, noon-10pm Thu-Sun* $$$

Single O: Sitting on the corner of a graffitied lane, this roastery cafe serves coffee 'flights' and hefty brunches. *7am-3pm Mon-Fri, from 8am Sat & Sun* $$

Arthur: Creative plates with solely Australian ingredients and produce, paired with exclusively Aussie wines. *6-11pm Wed-Sun, plus 12.30-3pm Sat & Sun* $$$

Nomad: Full of bold Mediterranean flavours, it specialises in share plates cooked using fire and smoke. *5.30-9.30pm daily, plus noon-2.30pm Wed-Sun* $$$

Kurumba: Tuck into Sri Lankan street-food at this family-run spot spread over two terraces on Crown St. *5.30-10pm Tue-Thu, to 11pm Fri & Sat* $$

NEL Restaurant: Arrive open-minded and linger over 12 inventive courses from an ever-changing degustation in this sleek underground spot. *5-10pm Tue-Sat* $$$

Bondi & the Eastern Beaches

FAMOUS BEACHES AND DRAMATIC CLIFFS

TOP TIP

These are dangerous beaches, prone to rips, holes and large surf. Always swim between the red-and-yellow flags, as these are the areas patrolled by surf life-savers. Long-running reality TV show *Bondi Rescue* amply illustrates the fate of those who fail to head the safety warnings; try not to star in it.

Bondi doesn't let its status as one of the most famous beaches in the world go to its head. It's a laid-back, egalitarian kind of place where everyone is welcome, from the buffed bodies stretched out in their barely-there swimwear on North Bondi to the Hassidic Jewish community that has made its home in the back streets. Backpackers pour out of the hostels onto the sands, rubbing shoulders with old-timers who have been surfing here for decades.

In any case, Bondi is just one of many outrageously beautiful beaches on this coastline. Heading south you'll hit Tamarama, Bronte, Clovelly, Coogee, Maroubra and Malabar, each of which has its own unique appeal. In the opposite direction, surf-battered sandstone cliffs stretch all the way to the South Head of Sydney Harbour. Tucked just inside the harbour is pretty Watsons Bay, with its sheltered beaches and memorable views back over the city skyline.

Beaches, Cliffs & Sunset Views

A half-day in Watsons Bay

As an excursion from central Sydney, a trip to **Watsons Bay** on a sunny afternoon is hard to top. It's reachable by bus, but the ferry ride from Circular Quay offers unforgettable views of all of Sydney Harbour's most famous sights for a fraction of the cost of a cruise.

GETTING AROUND

Trains only make it as far as Bondi Junction, 2.5km from Bondi Beach. Buses will get you everywhere else. Bondi Junction is a major hub, with the bus station sitting directly above the train station. This part of Sydney is very hilly; you'll likely work up a sweat hiking or cycling around. Parking is a challenge on weekends but somewhat less so midweek. Ferries provide a highly scenic means of travelling from Circular Quay to Watsons Bay. The bus also provides a direct connection from Circular Quay to the sands of Bondi Beach.

HIGHLIGHTS
1 Bondi Beach
2 Watsons Bay

SIGHTS
3 Bondi Pavilion
4 Bronte Beach
5 Camp Cove
6 Clovelly Beach
7 Coogee Beach
8 Gap Lookout
9 Hornby Lighthouse
10 Lady Bay
see 5 South Head Heritage Trail
11 Tamarama Beach

ACTIVITIES
12 Bondi Beach Public School
13 Bondi Icebergs
14 Giles Baths
15 Let's Go Surfing
16 McIver's Ladies Baths
17 Wylie's Baths

SLEEPING
18 Bondi 38
19 Bondi Beach House
20 Wake Up! Bondi Beach
see 2 Watsons Bay Boutique Hotel

EATING
21 Bondi Trattoria
22 Gertrude & Alice
23 Little Jack Horner
24 Louie
25 Lox Stock & Barrel
26 Mimi's
27 Solar Cafe
28 Speedos Cafe

DRINKING & NIGHTLIFE
29 Beach Road Hotel
30 Hotel Ravesis
31 Rocker
32 Shop & Wine Bar

SHOPPING
33 Budgy Smuggler
34 Wayside Chapel Op Shop

STROLL & SWIM ON THE BONDI TO COOGEE COASTAL WALK

This coastal walk connects two lively beaches with coves, swim spots and stunning sights in between.

START	END	LENGTH
Bondi Beach	Coogee Beach	6km; 2hr (one way)

Starting at 1 **Bondi Beach** (p118), take the stairs up the south end, passing above 2 **Bondi Icebergs** (p118), Sydney's iconic saltwater pools. Step onto the clifftop trail at the end of Notts Ave, with the wild Tasman Sea raging against the rocks below.

Next up is narrow 3 **Tamarama Beach**, nicknamed 'Glamarama' for its long-held reputation as a haven for beautiful beachgoers.

Then it's back up the cliffs before descending onto larger 4 **Bronte Beach**. This is a perfect midway stop to take a dip in the bogey hole or ocean pool, picnic under the Norfolk Island pines, or relax with a coffee at a nearby cafe. The path then skirts the astonishing cliff-edge 5 **Waverley Cemetery**, its white tombstones dazzling in the summer sun. Pass the locals enjoying a beer after lawn bowls at 6 **Clovelly Bowling Club**, then breeze past the cockatoos and canoodling lovers in 7 **Burrows Park** to the narrow channel of 8 **Clovelly Beach**.

Follow the footpath around the car park then down the steps to the upturned dinghies lining 9 **Gordons Bay**, one of Sydney's best shore-dive spots.

The trail continues past 10 **Dolphins Point**, where you can watch the waves crash while swimming in tranquil Giles Bath below, before ending on glorious 11 **Coogee Beach**. Prefer not to backtrack? Hop on the bus linking Coogee and Bondi.

MADISON_IMAGES/SHUTTERSTOCK

Maroubra Beach (p119)

Watsons Bay was once an isolated fishing village and it retains vestiges of those times in the boats pulled up on the beach and in the back streets peppered with Victorian cottages. Once you arrive, cut across to the **Gap Lookout** on the ocean side for awe-inspiring views from some of Sydney's most precipitous sea cliffs. You might spot whales cruising by from May to November.

The best swimming beach is pretty **Camp Cove**. It was here that the First Fleet first dropped anchor when they reached Sydney Harbour. At the northern end of the beach, the **South Head Heritage Trail** kicks off, leading into a section of Sydney Harbour National Park distinguished by harbour views and crashing surf. The trail skirts a naval base, passing old fortifications en route to the candy-striped **Hornby Lighthouse** and the sandstone Lightkeepers' Cottages (1858). Along the way a path leads down to tiny **Lady Bay**, one of the city's most popular gay and nudist beaches.

Finish off in the beer garden of the **Watsons Bay Boutique Hotel**, watching the sun set over the distant city skyline.

BEST SALTWATER POOLS

Bondi Icebergs: There are terrific views over Bondi Beach from this attractive pair of saltwater swimming pools.

Giles Baths: At Coogee Beach's northern end, Giles Baths is a 'bogey hole' – a semiformal rock pool open to the surging surf.

McIver's Ladies Baths: Perched against the cliffs south of Coogee Beach, this sea pool has been designated for women's bathing since the 1870s.

Wylie's Baths: On the rocky coast south of Coogee Beach, this superb seawater pool (dating from 1907) is suited to swimming laps.

Mahon Pool: Surf crashes over the edges of this idyllic bogey hole 500m north of Maroubra Beach.

DRINKING IN BONDI: BEST BARS

Shop & Wine Bar: This diminutive space morphs from daytime cafe into a food-focused wine bar. *6am-3pm Mon, 6am-10pm Tue-Sat, 7am-8pm Sun*

Rocker: Bondi's best bottomless brunch and their drink list features standout cocktails and a solid range of craft beers. *11.30am-midnight Thu-Sun, from 5pm Wed*

Beach Road Hotel: Weekends at this big boxy pub are a boisterous multilevel 'alcoholiday', with live bands and DJs. *11am-late Mon-Sat, 10am-10pm Sun*

Hotel Ravesis: Big corner pub with views over the beach from the upstairs balcony and DJs or bands most nights. *noon-midnight*

Go early for a spot on the balcony

TOP EXPERIENCE

Bondi Beach

Bondi Beach is a beauty to behold year-round. On a glorious summer's day, join the bronzed throngs on the sands and in the surf. On a blustery winter's day, wrap up and witness the Tasman Sea crashing against the shore. Standing as a testimony to nature's power, a 235-tonne boulder near Ben Buckler Point was hurled ashore by a 1912 storm.

SASANAN TRAKANSUEBKUL/SHUTTERSTOCK

Bondi Icebergs

Take a Dip

Rotate between sand and sea and cool off in the waters of Bondi Beach. Surf clubs patrol the beach between red-and-yellow flags, positioned to avoid the worst rips. For gentler dips, try the free ocean bath at the northern end, ideal for families and beachgoers with limited mobility, or head south to the famous pools of **Bondi Icebergs** *(icebergs.com.au; adult/child $10/7)* for a few laps and a post-swim drink.

Catch a Wave

The northern end and smaller summer swells are ideal for beginners, while the southern sandbank draws larger waves to thrill experienced surfers. Open to most swells yet sheltered from strong winds, Bondi is one of the most consistent surf spots in the city. If you're keen to give it a go, **Let's Go Surfing** *(letsgosurfing.com.au; adult/child $140/59)* offers two-hour small-group beginner lessons.

Picnics & People-Watching

At the centre of the beach stands the attractive **Bondi Pavilion**, built in 1929. Here you'll find cafes, an art gallery, a theatre, beachwear stores and changing rooms with showers and lockers. Nearby, there's an outdoor gym, shaded playground and skatepark. Sunset Cinema screens films in November and December.

TOP TIPS

- The council offers free beach wheelchairs that can be booked via *waverley.nsw.gov.au* or by calling 9083 8400.
- Bondi gets busy: arrive before 9am for tranquillity.
- Apply sun protection, even when it's overcast.

Practicalities

- free
- metered parking $11.60 per hour
- average summertime water temperature 23°C

Local Labels & Stylish Souvenirs

Shop for souvenirs in Bondi

Go beyond the cute koala stuffies and felt hats you'll never actually wear and shop for seriously cool souvenirs in Bondi. Weekends are when the markets are on at **Bondi Beach Public School**, with a farmers market doling out produce, baked goods, marmalades, seasonings and snacks on Saturdays from 9am to 1pm. On Sundays from 10am to 4pm regional designers sell their clothing, jewellery and home goods – some of the east coast's biggest labels got their start here.

Along the main drag, you'll find a handful of surf and clothing shops. Buy skimpy swimwear that's Aussie made at **Budgy Smuggler** or score a breezy beach outfit at the **Wayside Chapel Op Shop**, a thrifter favourite known for its budget-friendly designer finds.

Cool Coastal Neighbourhood

Relax at Coogee Beach

Coogee embodies the relaxed spirit of Sydney's Eastern Suburbs, where life moves at an easy pace and cafe owners often pull up a chair for a chat. A rainbow walkway marks the entrance to its spacious beachfront, where the water is generally calm. Pools on both ends of the beach offer a safe place to swim year-round.

A Coastal Walk Without the Crowds

Wander around Maroubra

The kilometre-long stretch of **Maroubra Beach** might have a scruffy rep from the Bra Boys (there was even a documentary about the '90s surf gang) but it's actually a peaceful place to swim and sunbathe. Due south, the beach leads into Malabar Headland National Park, where scenic coastal trails trace sandstone cliffs and often see less foot traffic than the walks further north. Some sections close during ANZAC Rifle Range operations; check *nationalparks.nsw.gov.au* for updates before visiting.

WHY I LOVE BONDI

Chantae Reden, Lonely Planet writer

When I show videos and tell stories about Bondi Beach to my mother-in-law, she says it's just the same as when she visited as a German backpacker in the 1980s. The mornings still start quietly, with surfers catching the first light's waves and joggers tracing the coastal path, before the sun draws an international crowd to sprawl along the sand. The nights still hum with parties, friendships form in hostel rooms and beach barbecues remain the best way to eat on a budget. Sure, the apartments are flashier, the cocktails more intricate and parking's now a nightmare, but the experience you're bound to have as a traveller here is iconically Australian.

EATING IN COOGEE BEACH: OUR PICKS

Pair their pão de queijo with a pistachio latte

Mimi's: This white-linen restaurant serves seasonal fare and fresh seafood with ocean views. *noon-10pm Wed, Thu & Sun, to midnight Fri & Sat* **$$$**

Little Jack Horner: This breezy restaurant with beach views keeps up the holiday vibes with live music and Aussie bites. *5.15am-3pm Mon & Tue, to 11pm Wed-Sun* **$$**

Louie: Just off Coogee Beach, this cosy spot serves Italian and seafood dishes in a charming setting. *5-9.30pm Tue-Fri, noon-2.30pm & 5-9.30pm Sat & Sun* **$$**

Solar Cafe: A local favourite with a chatty duo doling out delicious coffee, sandwiches and baked goods. *6.30am-3pm Mon-Fri, from 7am Sat & Sun* **$**

Newtown & the Inner West

GLOBETROTTERS' FOOD HEAVEN AND BOHEMIAN NIGHTLIFE

GETTING AROUND

Various train lines head through the Inner West, with useful stops at Newtown, Erskineville, St Peters and Marrickville. Light rail circles through Glebe, while buses fill in the rest of the gaps. Street parking is possible, although many of the back streets are narrow. Pedestrians will find it reasonably flat, but this is a large, spread-out area. It takes around 50 minutes to walk from the start of King St to St Peters Station.

With a reputation as one of the most progressive parts of Sydney, the city fringe of the Inner West is one of its most idiosyncratic and interesting areas. The sleeve-tattoo, Day-Glo hair and beard quotient is high here, particularly along King St, Newtown's busy main thoroughfare. King St is a reliable bet for buzz most nights of the week, with the energy extending along Enmore Rd.

On the other side of Sydney Uni, Glebe's leafy streets are lined with Victorian terraces, where a significant Indigenous community rubs shoulders with students, alternative lifestylers and city workers. Neighbouring Chippendale has transformed beyond belief in recent years, with a major urban-renewal project adding starchitect sparkle to a formerly forsaken nook.

To the west, the sprawling suburb Marrickville was once known mainly for its Greek and Vietnamese restaurants, but nowadays it's one of Sydney's hippest neighbourhoods, with thriving cafe, craft-beer and bar scenes.

Storybook Structures

Treasures of Sydney Uni

The campus of the **University of Sydney** *(sydney.edu.au)* takes up a big chunk of Camperdown and Darlington, but its effect is felt more broadly in terms of the large student

DRINKING IN THE INNER WEST: BEST LGBTIQ-FRIENDLY BARS

Imperial Erskineville: The 'Home of Priscilla' still offers drag and regular trivia nights. *4-10pm Mon & Tue, to midnight Wed-Fri, noon-3am Sat, noon-midnight Sun*

Miss Wolf: Don't be fooled by its size – this glittery cocktail lounge always delivers a good time. *4.30-10pm Mon-Thu, to midnight Fri & Sat, 5-9pm Sun*

Newtown Hotel: The crowd skews young and straight, but there's drag from Wednesday to Sunday. *11.30am-midnight Sun-Wed, to 1am Thu-Sat*

Bank Hotel: Multilevel pub attracting a mixed crowd, with 'les and queer' Wednesdays and bears on Thursdays. 10am-2am Mon & Tue, to 4am Wed-Sat, noon-midnight Sun

NEWTOWN & THE INNER WEST

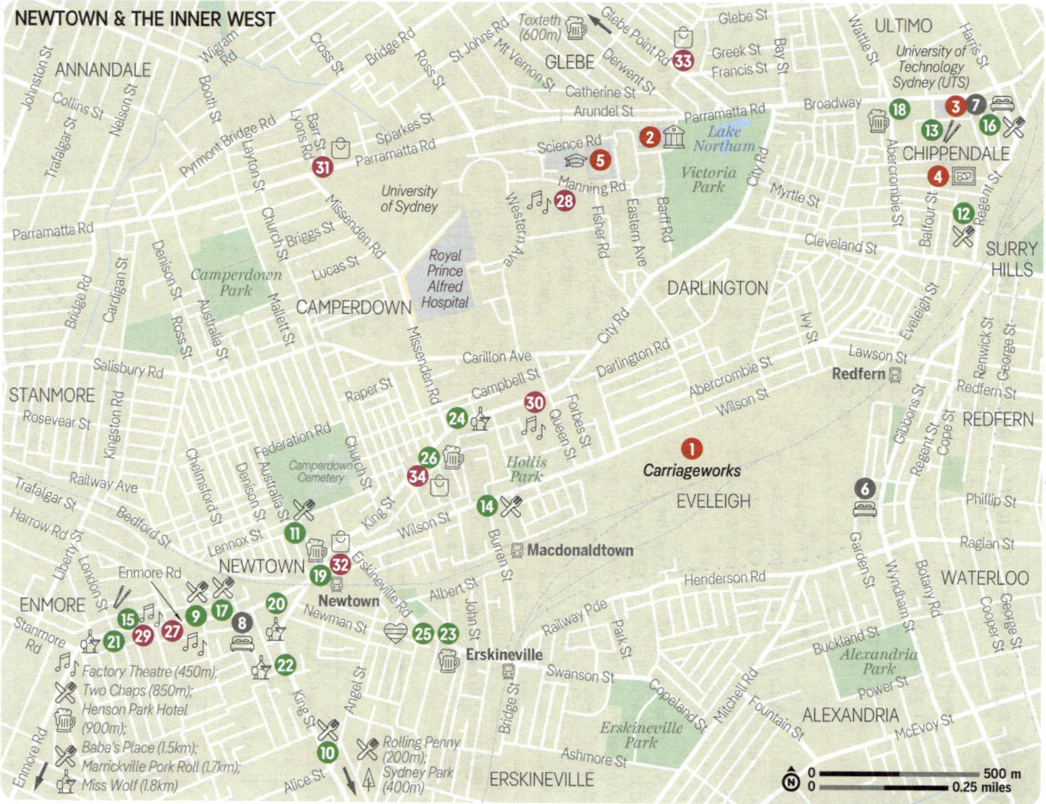

HIGHLIGHTS
1 Carriageworks

SIGHTS
2 Chau Chak Wing Museum
3 One Central Park
4 White Rabbit

ACTIVITIES
5 University of Sydney

SLEEPING
6 Hoteloco
7 Old Clare Hotel
8 Urban Newtown

EATING
9 Cairo Takeaway
10 Comeco
11 Continental Delicatessen
12 Ester
13 Hongdae Pocha
14 One Another
15 Queen Chow
16 Spice Alley
17 Vandal Taqueria

DRINKING & NIGHTLIFE
18 Abercrombie
19 Bank Hotel
20 Bar Planet
21 Deadwax
22 Earl's Juke Joint
23 Erskineville Hotel
24 Huelo
25 Imperial Erskineville
26 Newtown Hotel

ENTERTAINMENT
27 Enmore Theatre
28 Manning Bar
29 Trocadero Room
30 Vanguard

SHOPPING
see 19 Affends
31 Deus Ex Machina
32 Egg Records
33 Sappho Books, Cafe & Bar
34 Social Outfit

ALES & ARTWORK: MARRICKVILLE ON FOOT

In Marrickville, creativity flows as freely as the beer, so pause for a schooner between murals on this colourful crawl.

START	END	LENGTH
Bracket Brewing	Post Café	2.6km; 2hr

Start your stroll at 1 **Bracket Brewing** off Addison Rd, a nanobrewery led by a science-minded squad. Then head to 2 **Village**, the joint taproom of Wildflower and Mountain Culture Beer Co – there's a brew for every palate.

Wander along Victoria Rd, past the groovy blue-hued animal mural, to 3 **Mixtape Brewing** microbrewery. They've got an epic wine list if you're keen to switch things up. Loop through 4 **Faversham La**, one of the best laneways for streetart in town and a canvas for resident artist Stuart Sale. Cross under the shady trees of Wicks Park.

5 **Philter Brewing** offers guided 30-minute tours if you'd like to add in a further stop. Otherwise, continue to the 6 **Bob Hawke Beer & Leisure Centre** for a peek at 1980s Australia and a semi-shrine dedicated to former prime minister Bob Hawke, who's somewhat of a national folk hero. A portion of each pour goes to charity.

Turn onto 7 **Marrickville Rd**, or 'Little Greece', where you'll find Hellenic restaurants, boutiques and secondhand shops. Pass the 8 **Marrickville Hotel**, an emblem of the classic Aussie pub experience.

Further on, there's a hidden mural behind the 9 **Post Café**; find it on the intersection of Silver La and Marrickville La. The giant portrait of a woman is a nod to the neighbourhood's Greek heritage and influence.

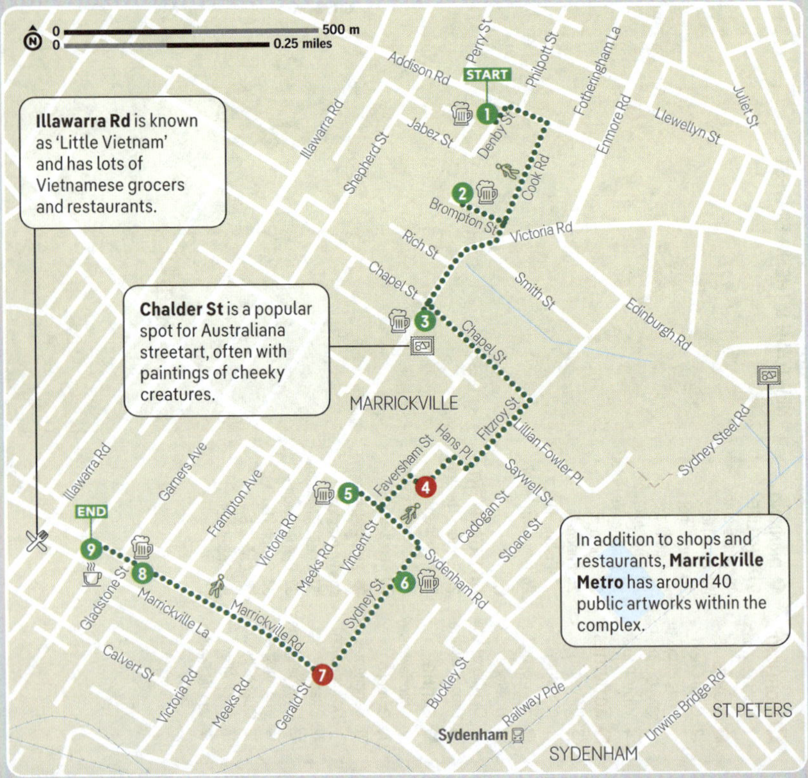

population that adds both a boozy and a bookish bent to the surrounding suburbs. Completed in 1859, the main building has more than a touch of a fairy-tale feeling about it. Feel free to wander through the central quadrangle, but to access either of the grand halls you'll need to take a campus tour ($20; bookings required).

The main reason to visit is one of Sydney's best but least-heralded museums, the free **Chau Chak Wing Museum** *(sydney.edu.au/museum; 10am-5pm Mon-Fri, noon-4pm Sat & Sun)*. This striking building opened in 2020 as a new home to the university's collections of art, antiquities, Indigenous and Pasifika artefacts and natural history. The ancient-history displays are particularly good, showcasing an astonishing volume of Egyptian, Etruscan, Greek and Roman relics, ranging from beautifully painted sarcophagi to penis-shaped votive offerings.

Food for the Belly & Soul

Get carried away in Carriageworks

There are varied reasons to visit the vast Victorian brick warehouses comprising the former Eveleigh Railyards. The tastiest is the Saturday morning Farmers Market, where stallholders sell all manner of fruits, vegetables, meats, artisan products, baked goods and cooked meals. There's often a pop-up themed market held simultaneously in a neighbouring hall, selling anything from pottery to paintings.

Carriageworks *(carriageworks.com.au)* is also home to various theatre and dance companies, staging an impressive program of inventive performances and visual art installations, often on a monumental scale.

BEST MUSIC VENUES IN THE INNER WEST

Enmore Theatre: Originally a vaudeville playhouse, the Art Deco Enmore is an atmospheric showcase for midsized gigs.

Factory Theatre: Good sightlines characterise this purpose-built Marrickville venue that hosts medium-sized touring bands and more intimate cabaret and comedy gigs.

Trocadero Room: Boogie under the glow of the disco balls to live music, or take a seat for the regular comedy shows.

Vanguard: This moody Newtown venue operates as a 'stage for hire' for intimate gigs and hosts a regular burlesque review.

Manning Bar: Within the grounds of Sydney Uni, this former women's college is now a 950-capacity venue with multiple levels and spaces.

EATING IN NEWTOWN & CHIPPENDALE: OUR PICKS

You can't beat the set menu

Cairo Takeaway: You may need to queue at this favourite, but the charcoal chicken is worth the wait. *noon-10pm Mon-Fri, 11am-10pm Sat & Sun* $

Comeco: Meals sell out quickly at this Japanese restaurant serving vegan sushi, curry, ramen and sweets. *11.30am-3pm Tue-Sun, plus 6-9pm Thu-Sat* $

One Another: Off the main strip on a sunny corner, this Newtown cafe serves a modern menu full of interesting twists. *7am-3pm Mon-Fri, from 8am Sat & Sun* $

Vandal Taqueria: Colourful murals capture attention, but it's the plant-based LA-Mex fare that truly makes this spot shine. *5-10pm Tue-Fri, from noon Sat & Sun* $$

Rolling Penny: Everything's made from scratch at this artfully dishevelled little cafe down the St Peters end of King St. *7.30am-2pm* $

Hongdae Pocha: Seoul street-food and BBQ served in a former brewery, where sharing plates is recommended. *5-10pm daily, plus noon-3pm Sat & Sun* $$

Continental Delicatessen: Attractive deli-style bistro on a Newtown side street that makes its own sausages and cans everything from fish parfait to cocktails. *noon-11pm* $$

Ester: Exemplifies Sydney's contemporary dining scene: informal but professional; innovative without being gimmicky. *6-11pm Mon-Fri, noon-11pm Sat, noon-4pm Sun* $$$

BEST INNER WEST SHOPPING

Sappho Books, Cafe & Bar: Lose track of time in this cosy secondhand bookstore with a courtyard cafe and bar.

Deus Ex Machina: A hybrid motorcycle workshop, cafe and offbeat boutique, this kooky Camperdown warehouse stocks Deus-branded men's and women's clothing.

Social Outfit: A sustainable Sydney label creating well-made pieces locally, with proceeds supporting training and employment for refugee communities.

Egg Records: Just off King St, this long-running music store sells new and secondhand albums, band T-shirts and music-related gifts.

Affends: Effortlessly cool clothing brand from NSW with lots of staple clothing pieces made from hemp and sustainable materials.

Green-Fingered Architecture

Sky-high Central Park

To get an idea of a potential Sydney of the future, head to the Chippendale end of Broadway, where an old brewery site has been transformed by leading architects into a shopping and residential development. It's a stark contrast to the bleak streetscape immortalised in David Bowie's 1983 *Let's Dance* music video, which powerfully depicted racism in Australia at the time.

The most striking structure here is Jean Nouvel's award-winning 177m-tall garden-draped skyscraper, **One Central Park**. The unusual cantilevered platform is angled to bounce light to the lower levels of the building.

Shift your gaze from the skies and you'll find a shopping centre, a treelined park, a supermarket, cinemas and restaurants (don't miss **Spice Alley**, a Singapore-style hawker lane dishing up all manner of tasty treats).

Go down an Artistic Rabbit Hole

Chase the White Rabbit

If you're not familiar with China's contemporary art scene, be prepared to be surprised, challenged, amused and delighted by Chippendale's extraordinary **White Rabbit** *(whiterabbitcollection.org; 10am-5pm Wed-Sun; free)*. Despite the gallery being spread over four floors, it can house only a fraction of the collection of billionaire philanthropist Judith Neilson at any one time. Since 2000 she has been purchasing new work by cutting-edge Chinese artists, amassing one of the world's largest and most significant collections of its kind.

Music request nights on Tuesdays and Thursdays

DRINKING IN THE INNER WEST: BEST BARS

Toxteth: Head to the rooftop of this old Glebe corner pub for spectacular views of the city skyline. *noon-midnight Mon-Sat, to 10pm Sun*

Abercrombie: Art Deco Chippendale pub/club zhooshed with pops of neon and a rooftop cocktail bar. *4pm-midnight Tue & Wed, noon-2am Thu, to 5am Fri & Sat*

Earl's Juke Joint: Swinging Earl's serves craft beers and killer cocktails to the cool set in a former butcher's shop. *6pm-midnight Tue-Sun*

Deadwax: A trippy and intimate bar for music heads who'll appreciate vinyl records and incredible cocktails. *4pm-midnight Tue-Thu & Sun, to 2am Fri & Sat*

Henson Park Hotel: This excellent Marrickville pub sums up the modern Inner West vibe; craft ale, a beer garden and a children's play area. *11.30am-11pm*

Erskineville Hotel: One of the area's best pubs. The Erko's Art Deco glory is something to behold and the food is excellent. *10am-midnight Mon-Sat, to 10pm Sun*

Huelo: Part corner store, part speakeasy, part pub – this watering hole has a vibe for everyone. *5pm-midnight Wed & Thu, 4pm-1am Fri & Sat, 4-10pm Sun*

Bar Planet: Head to this galactic cocktail bar where martinis are the standout sip. *5pm-midnight Mon-Thu, to 2am Fri, 3pm-3am Sat, 3pm-midnight Sun*

One Central Park

Playgrounds for All

Take a break in Sydney Park

Spanning 40 hectares, urban **Sydney Park** is a green escape packed with family fun. Kids can hop across nature-inspired stepping stones over the wetlands, ride the bike track or test the skatepark. Shaded playgrounds, barbecues and picnic lawns invite lazy afternoons. A small kiosk serves coffee, juice and sandwiches.

MORE ASIAN ART

White Rabbit isn't Sydney's only significant collection of Asian art. The **Art Gallery of NSW** (p90) has over 4400 items in its Asian collection and can display around 250 at a time in its two Asian Lantern galleries in the South Building.

STREETART IN THE INNER WEST

King St, Newtown: Slow your stroll along King St's mural-lined lanes, where the iconic 'I Have a Dream' MLK Jr mural reimagines comments on a colonial past.

Wilson St, Darlington: A mural by Fintan Magee shows blurred portraits of Patyegarang and William Dawes, forgotten figures who first documented the Gadigal language.

May La, St Peters: For half a century, this paint-splashed laneway has served as a creative canvas for artists with sharp social commentary.

Marrickville Rd, Marrickville: Marrickville's main road is lined with bold murals, while its laneways hide creative hubs and smaller streetart gems.

Holt St, Newtown: Spot the fiery mural commenting on climate change, then follow the road for Marrickville's beloved cats and colourful laneway artworks.

EATING IN ENMORE & MARRICKVILLE: OUR PICKS

Marrickville Pork Roll: A little hole in the wall serving only banh mi with various fillings. The crispy bread rolls are baked on-site. *6.30am-5.30pm* $

Two Chaps: Tasty sandwiches, baked goods and coffee for brunch, with weekend pasta nights and it's all made from scratch. *7am-2pm daily, plus 7-9pm Fri & Sat* $$

Baba's Place: This quirky warehouse eatery serves Mediterranean comfort food. *5.45-11.30pm Thu-Sat, 5.15-10pm Sun, plus noon-4pm Sat & Sun* $$

Queen Chow: Fizzing with moody elegance, this trendy restaurant serves Cantonese share plates. *5-10pm Tue-Thu, noon-11pm Fri & Sat, noon-9pm Sun* $$$

North Shore

BEACHES, CREATURES AND HARBOUR VIEWS

TOP TIP
Time your trip to the North Shore with the Kirribilli Markets (the first and second Sundays and the fourth Saturday of each month, open 8.30am to 3pm). Located beside the Harbour Bridge, there's exotic food, market stalls and a lively harbourside hubbub. There tend to be more art stalls at the Sunday markets.

The chunk of Sydney traditionally known as the North Shore (as distinct from the Northern Beaches) stretches along the harbour from Greenwich to The Spit and extends to the city's northern limits. For visitors, it's the bit around the harbour that's the most interesting, containing scenic walks, some cosmopolitan beaches and a couple of famous sights.

Milsons Point, at the northern end of Sydney Harbour Bridge, has a duo of Art Deco delights in the form of Luna Park and North Sydney Olympic Pool. North of here is the suburb officially known as North Sydney, a second high-rise business district. To the east are a series of salubrious harbourside suburbs containing some of Sydney's most expensive real estate. The first of them, Kirribilli, is home to the official Sydney residences of Australia's Governor General (Admiralty House, built in 1846) and Prime Minister (Kirribilli House, dating to 1854); both are best seen from the water.

Old-Time Amusements

Lunacy at Luna Park

A leering clown face provides a strangely sinister welcome to 1930s **Luna Park** *(lunaparksydney.com; day pass adult/child $44/34)*, located just below the Harbour Bridge in Milsons Point. Other old-fashioned treats include a carousel, a swing ride, the Coney Island funhouse and traditional sideshow stalls.

GETTING AROUND

North Sydney is a large area, so getting around solely on foot isn't practical. Thankfully, it's well connected by public transport, particularly by bus. Ferries from Circular Quay stop at Greenwich Point, McMahons Point, Milsons Point, Kirribilli, North Sydney, Neutral Bay, Kurraba Point, Cremorne Point, Old Cremorne, Mosman Bay, South Mosman and Taronga Zoo. Two train lines head from the city to Milsons Point, North Sydney and points north.

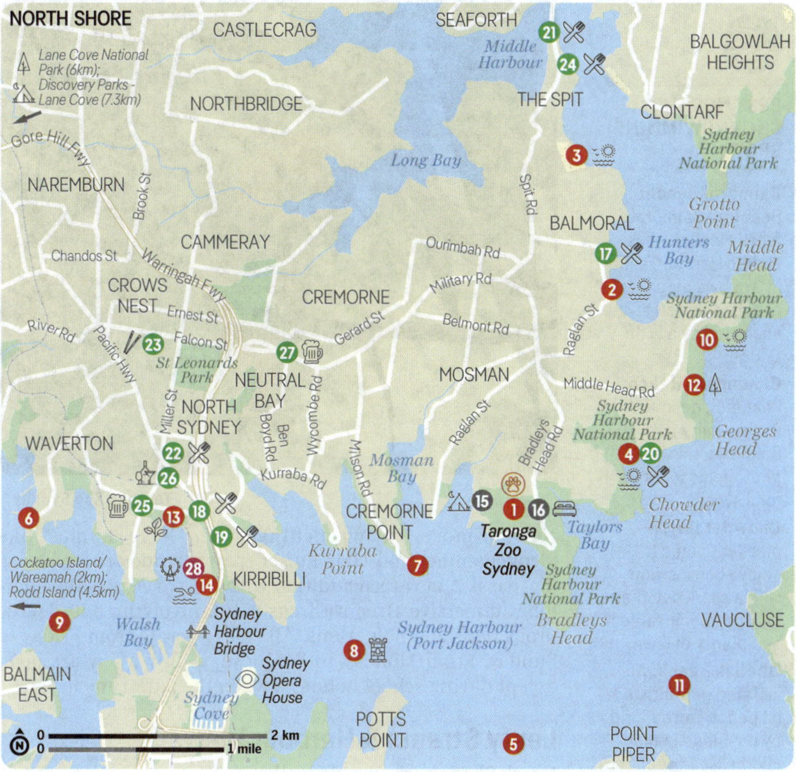

HIGHLIGHTS
1 Taronga Zoo Sydney

SIGHTS
2 Balmoral Beach
3 Chinamans Beach
4 Chowder Bay
5 Clark Island
6 Coal Loader Wharf
7 Cremorne Point
8 Fort Denison
9 Goat Island
10 Obelisk Beach
11 Shark Island
12 Sydney Harbour National Park
13 Wendy Whiteley's Secret Garden

ACTIVITIES
14 North Sydney Olympic Pool

SLEEPING
15 Roar & Snore
16 Wildlife Retreat at Taronga

EATING
17 Bathers' Pavilion
18 Bay Ten Espresso
19 Botanist
20 L'Héritage
21 Ormeggio at The Spit
22 Poetica Bar & Grill
23 Ryo's Noodles
24 St Siandra

DRINKING & NIGHTLIFE
25 Commodore Hotel
26 Greenwood Hotel
see 19 Kirribilli Hotel
27 Oaks Hotel

ENTERTAINMENT
28 Luna Park

DRINKING ON THE NORTH SHORE: BEST PUBS

Oaks Hotel: Locals love this Neutral Bay pub for its craft beer, food and spacious terrace cocktail bar. *10am-1.30am Mon-Sat, to 11.30pm Sun*

Commodore Hotel: On a leafy corner near North Sydney Station, this large pub has a substantial and attractive beer garden. *10am-midnight Mon-Sat, to 10pm Sun*

Kirribilli Hotel: Near the Harbour Bridge, this curvaceous Art Deco pub offers an excellent craft-beer selection. *10am-midnight Mon-Sat, to 10pm Sun*

Greenwood Hotel: A slate-roofed sandstone schoolhouse (1878) transformed into an atmospheric bar in workaday North Sydney. *noon-10pm Mon-Sat*

BEST NORTH SHORE SWIMMING SPOTS

Balmoral Beach: Beautiful Balmoral faces Manly across Middle Harbour, split in two by a picturesque rocky islet accessed by a little bridge.

Chinamans Beach: Peaceful, despite its proximity to busy Balmoral, this is a photogenic location for a swim.

Chowder Bay: A pleasant place to enjoy scenic swims, with a shark net, playground, picnic tables and plenty of lawn.

Obelisk Beach: An isolated gay and nudist beach surrounded by bushland in the Middle Head section of Sydney Harbour National Park.

North Sydney Olympic Pool: Renovated in 2025, this Art Deco complex next to Luna Park has an Olympic-sized outdoor pool, a 25m indoor pool, a kids pool and splash-pad, plus unbelievable harbour views.

Taronga Zoo Sydney

Newer, more gut-wrenching rides have names like Sledgehammer and Hair Raiser (pay per ride or purchase a day pass). A new-tech addition with a retro edge is the hour-long immersive Dream Circus ($19), involving 360-degree projections and holograms. All rides operate from Friday to Sunday. From Monday to Wednesday, only a few are open except during school holidays, when the park runs in full.

Leafy Streets & Harbour Views

North Shore harbourside walks

Memorable walks abound on the North Shore, especially those suburbs hugging the Sydney Harbour shoreline. Many pop in and out of pockets of Sydney Harbour National Park, a non-contiguous reserve covering nearly 400 hectares of coast and scrubby headlands.

One great half-day option is to catch a ferry to **Cremorne Point** and take a four-hour walk to **Balmoral Beach** via Mosman Bay, Little Sirius Cove, Whiting Beach, Bradleys Head, Taylors Bay and **Chowder Bay**.

If you've got the time, the four-day Sydney Harbour Circle Walk is a fantastic way to explore the inner harbour, following the northern shoreline from the Sydney Harbour Bridge

EATING ON THE NORTH SHORE: OUR PICKS

Bay Ten Espresso: Excellent cafe in a warehouse tucked under the approach to the Harbour Bridge with a co-working space attached. *7am-3pm Mon-Fri* $

Ryo's Noodles: People seek out this humble bright-orange place in Crows Nest for what is reputedly Sydney's best ramen. *11.30am-2pm & 5-8.30pm Thu-Tue* $

Poetica Bar & Grill: Famed for their Australian steaks, this modern restaurant also impresses with its seafood dishes. *noon-10pm Mon-Sat* $$

Botanist: The menu skews towards seasonal Australian ingredients at this moody Kirribilli restaurant with killer cocktails. *hours vary* $$

to the Gladesville Bridge and then returning via Drummoyne and Balmain.

The five-hour first leg to Greenwich Wharf makes a superb day walk, tracing the lower North Shore's deep bays and the little headlands that separate them. Take in the view from the heritage-listed **Coal Loader Wharf**, a favourite spot for sunset picnics with sweeping harbour views. The historic MV *Cape Don* is docked here; it once worked to service lighthouses and now is part of the salt-misted scenery.

The Zoo with the View

Harbourside Taronga Zoo

A visit to **Taronga Zoo Sydney** *(taronga.com.au; adult/child $50/30, cheaper online)* is about more than just the animal enclosures, although they're up there with the best in the world. First, there's the opportunity to arrive by ferry from Circular Quay, a fantastic experience. Then there are the million-dollar views, gazing straight back over the harbour towards the Opera House and city skyline.

As for the animals, the zoo is not-for-profit and Australian natives are showcased in the immersive Nura Diya Australia section. Here you can walk through aviaries filled with chattering parrots and enclosures where emus strut about officiously while wallabies laze in the sun.

Elsewhere, the chimpanzees, gorillas, elephants and lions are habitual show stealers. Other highlights include the aquatic enclosures where you can watch seals and penguins from below the waterline. Put aside at least three hours to get around everything.

Zookeeper talks and presentations are held throughout the day, with the free-flight bird show a must-see. These are included in the ticket price, but there is also a range of add-ons available, including animal encounters, a high-ropes course and options to stay overnight (in the swanky Wildlife Lodge or the Roar and Snore glamping tents).

The City's Semi-Secluded Sanctuary

Wander through Wendy Whiteley's Secret Garden

Wendy Whiteley's Secret Garden *(wendyssecretgarden.org.au)* is a fairy-tale garden that was once described largely as a wasteland until Wendy lovingly tended to it after the passing of her husband, Australian artist Brett Whiteley. Free to

NORTHSIDE NATIONAL PARKS

North Sydney is home to two national parks and parts of a third, Sydney Harbour National Park. Surrounded by suburbia, **Lane Cove National Park** is a wild pocket of bushland flanking the Lane Cove River, 10km northwest of the Harbour Bridge. It's a good place for bushwalking and kayaking from the boat shed. Exponentially bigger, Ku-ring-gai Chase National Park (p137) protects nearly 150 sq km on Sydney's northern boundary. Remnants of precolonial Aboriginal life are visible today, thanks to the preservation of more than 800 sites, including rock engravings and cave art. The **Sydney Harbour National Park** encompasses a large amount of the harbour foreshore and its islands with no shortage of picnic, swimming and camping spots, along with scenic coastal walks.

EATING ON THE NORTH SHORE: OUR PICKS

Book a table by the water

Ormeggio at The Spit: Acclaimed Italian seafood restaurant overlooking the marina at the end of The Spit. *11.30am-3pm & 5.30-10pm Wed-Sun* **$$$**

Bathers' Pavilion: Spanish Mission architecture, harbour views and outstanding food coalesce with a cafe and bistro under the same roof. *8am-10pm* **$$$**

L'Héritage: Quaint and elegant, this Chowder Bay bistro delights with traditional French food and ocean views. *11am-3.30pm & 5.30-10pm Wed-Sun* **$$$**

St Siandra: With fresh seafood and crisp spritzers, it feels like you're living the luxe life. *11.30am-5pm Wed & Sun, 11.30am-10pm Thu-Sat* **$$$**

THE OTHER HARBOUR ISLANDS

Sydney Harbour's islands shaped the city's story, serving as penal sites, shipyards and quarantine stations. **Rodd Island**, which once had a team led by French microbiologist Louis Pasteur running rabbit-control experiments, is now a favourite picnic spot. **Shark Island** (Boowambillee), a former quarantine site, draws kayakers seeking a peaceful retreat, while neighbouring **Clark Island** (Billong-olola) grew vegetables for the First Fleet – its isolation keeping thieves at bay. **Fort Denison**, built in 1840 as a British-style fort, juts from the harbour like an artificial blemish and occasionally hosts private events. **Goat Island** (Me-Mel), rich in Aboriginal heritage and later used as a penal colony and naval depot, is in the process of being returned to Aboriginal ownership.

visit, the garden occasionally hosts complimentary drawing classes beneath its leafy fig trees. Trails throughout the garden are generally uneven and steep. Signage is limited, but several entrances exist and are easy to find along Lavender St.

An Island of Ships & Convicts

Visit or camp at Cockatoo Island

Just a short ferry ride from the city, **Cockatoo Island** (Wareamah) is layered with history. Long before European colonisation, it was a gathering place for the Wareamah people. From 1839 to 1869, it became a convict prison where inmates endured harsh conditions of scorching summers and frigid winters and their guards hardly fared better. From 1857 to 1992, the island was one of Australia's key shipyards – its workers' perilous contributions largely overlooked in the nation's maritime history.

Discover Cockatoo Island through a guided or self-guided audio tour that brings each era to life. Choose from themes covering the convict years, shipbuilding heritage or an all-in-one highlights route. The convict tour suits families with older kids, while the shipyard tour is wheelchair accessible. Tech-minded visitors can interact with digital characters scattered around the island, each revealing stories from Wareamah's past.

Allow half a day to explore and enjoy lunch at one of the island's two restaurants. To dive deeper and tick each tour off your list, stay overnight and camp on the northern foreshore. While you can BYO tent, the ones provided have decently comfortable cots. It's one of Sydney's most unique and affordable waterfront stays. If you prefer to sleep with a roof overhead, book into one of the heritage houses or apartments, some with Harbour Bridge views.

INDIGENOUS NORTH SHORE

Darug Country meets Kuringgai Country on the North Shore, with the latter traditionally occupying the area from Broken Bay north to the NSW Central Coast. Ku-ring-gai Chase National Park takes its name from them. For more on Sydney's **First Nations**, see p139.

Manly & the Northern Beaches

WORLD-FAMOUS URBAN SURF BREAKS

An outstanding day-trip destination or a superb base if you plan to spend a lot of time on the beach, Manly deserves to make its way onto most Sydney itineraries. Regular ferry services mean that you can easily flit backwards and forwards to the city from here and what a memorable voyage it is.

Manly has a scrappy charm all its own, not as flashy as its Eastern Suburbs counterparts or as stuffy as its monied neighbours on the lower North Shore. The vibe is relaxed, unpretentious and outdoorsy.

It's also the gateway to the Northern Beaches region, which takes up a big chunk of northeast Sydney, stretching 35km from the North Head of Sydney Harbour to the narrow peninsula where Pittwater joins Broken Bay at the mouth of the Hawkesbury River. It's an area defined by a succession of spectacular beaches, each with its own surf-gazing suburb.

Manly Beach (p134)

PIC MEDIA AUS/SHUTTERSTOCK

GETTING AROUND

The highly scenic ferry trip to Manly is well worth taking. Regular Sydney Ferries takes 30 minutes for the journey, while privately run fast ferries take just 18 minutes. Once you arrive, it's easy to walk to cafes, bars and beaches. As for the rest of the Northern Beaches, this is a part of Sydney where having a car is an asset. There are buses to all the beach suburbs but it's far easier to hop between them with your own vehicle. Parking is metered and can be expensive.

TOP TIP

Just outside the ferry terminal, the Manly Visitor Information Centre is your go-to for maps, brochures, local tips and current happy hour or dining specials. At the beaches be sure to swim between the flags. These patrolled zones ensure a safe and enjoyable dip.

HIGHLIGHTS
1 Manly Beach

SIGHTS
2 Avalon
3 Barrenjoey Lighthouse
4 Basin, The
5 Bilgola
6 Bungan Beach
7 Corso
8 Curl Curl
9 Dee Why
10 Fairy Bower Beach
11 Freshwater Beach
12 Ku-ring-gai Chase National Park
13 Manly Cove
14 Manly Dam
15 Mona Vale Beach
16 Narrabeen
17 Newport Beach
18 North Head Sanctuary
19 Palm Beach
20 Shelly Beach
21 Store Beach
22 Turimetta Beach
23 Warriewood Beach
24 Whale Beach
25 Winnererremy Bay

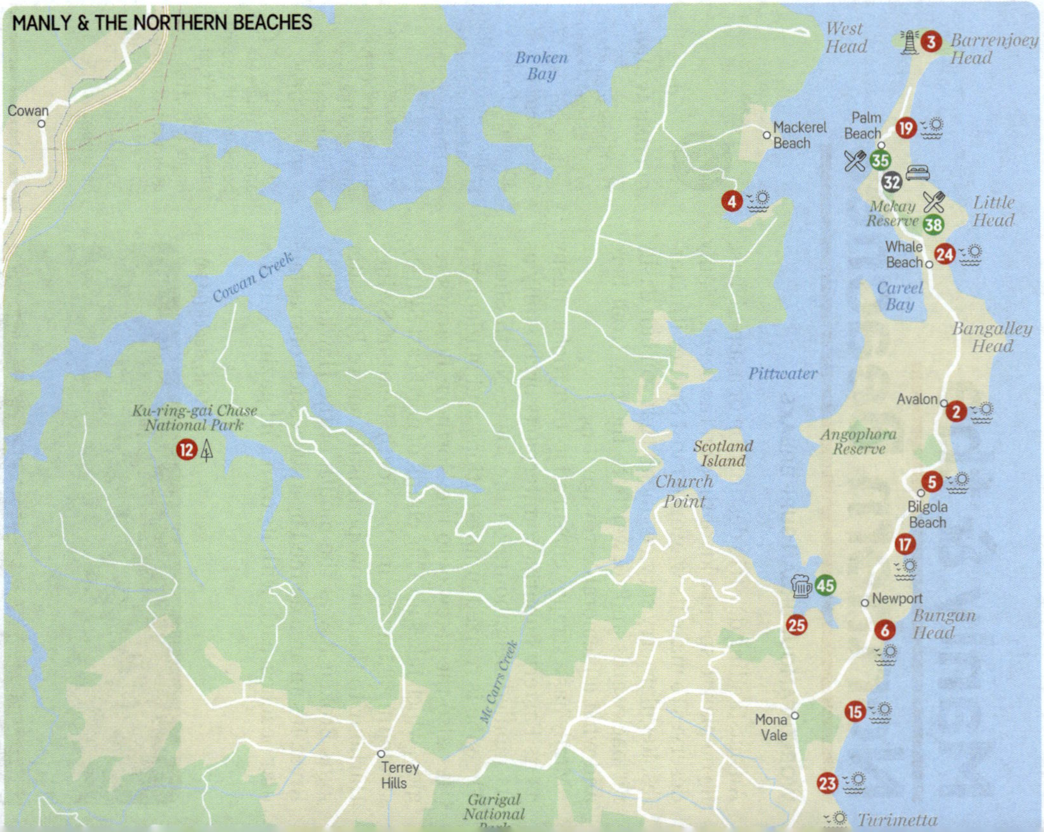

ACTIVITIES
26 Dive Centre Manly
27 Manly Kayak Centre
28 Manly Ocean Adventures
29 Manly Surf School
30 Manly Surfboards
31 Pro Dive

SLEEPING
32 Palm Beach B&B
33 Q Station
34 Stoke Beach House

EATING
35 Barrenjoey House
see 15 Basin Dining Room
36 Belgrave Cartel
37 Fika the Cafe
38 Jonah's
39 Norma's Deli
40 Pantry, The
41 Pilu at Freshwater

DRINKING & NIGHTLIFE
42 4 Pines Brewpub
43 Donny's Bar
44 New Brighton Hotel
45 Newport

INFORMATION
46 Manly Visitor Information Centre

TRANSPORT
47 Manly Bikes

Sydney's Other Famous Beach Suburb

Dive headfirst into Manly

Bondi may be more famous but **Manly** isn't relying on just one (admittedly amazing) surf beach for its appeal. Straddling a narrow isthmus, it offers the choice of gentle harbour dips or rough-and-tumble ocean swims.

As soon as you step off the ferry at **Manly Cove**, you're greeted with a calm swimming beach to your left and a calm place to kayak to your right. Alternatively, go straight ahead past the tourist office and follow the **Corso**, Manly's part-pedestrianised shopping strip, to Manly Beach. Stretching for two golden kilometres and lined with Norfolk Island pines, Manly's surf beach is a stirring sight. Three separate surf life-saving clubs (South Steyne, North Steyne and Queenscliff) set out their flags in front of their clubrooms and patrol the waves between them. Manly Beach also has a beach wheelchair available at South Steyne Lifesaving Station and the North Steyne playground has a wheelchair swing.

Continue along the promenade at the southern end of Manly Beach and you'll first reach **Fairy Bower Beach**, where there's a pretty, triangular ocean pool set into the rocky shoreline. The life-size sea nymphs of Helen Leete's bronze sculpture *Oceanides* (1997) stand on the edge, washed by the surf. Continue on and you'll come to little **Shelly Beach**, a more sheltered scoop of sand gazing back at Manly Beach that's a great spot for snorkelling.

If those aren't enough options, hire a kayak from Manly Wharf and paddle to **Store Beach**, only accessible from the water. It's a breeding ground for Australian little penguins, so access is prohibited from dusk when the birds waddle in to settle down for the night.

At the City's Edge

Walks and whale watching around North Head

North Head, a bush-covered peninsula laced with 10km of walking trails, marks the entrance to Sydney Harbour. Follow the flat, paved 1km Fairfax Walk to its two lookout points, a top spot for whale watching between May and November. For a stroll into history, walk or take the bus to North Head Quarantine Station, which was used to attempt to quell disease outbreaks in the 1830s. Now, there's a hotel, a cafe and a

OTHER MANLY ACTIVITIES

Manly Kayak Centre: Hires kayaks, paddleboards and small boats for trips to otherwise inaccessible beaches around North Head. Guided kayaking tours, too.

Dive Centre Manly: Offers snorkel safaris, two-day PADI courses and guided shore dives and boat dives (including night dives).

Pro Dive: Based in nearby Brookvale and offering boat and shore dives, along with three-day open-water courses.

Manly Bikes: Hires out a wide selection of bikes (including e-bikes) and provides maps and suggested routes for self-guided tours.

Manly Ocean Adventures: Blast out to sea in a speedboat; whale watching is on offer from mid-May to November.

EATING IN MANLY: OUR PICKS

Norma's Deli: This Manly bakery/cafe/deli has quite possibly the most tempting array of counter food in Sydney; from cakes to rotisserie chickens. *8am-5pm* $

Belgrave Cartel: This place peddles cafe fare by day and Italian food and cocktails at night. *6.30am-1pm Mon, 6.30am-1pm & 3-10pm Tue-Thu, 6.30am-10pm Fri-Sun* $

Fika the Café: Stop in for Swedish pastries and strong coffee, or stay for a Skagen Toast with creamy prawn mix heaped onto sourdough. *7am-2pm* $$

The Pantry: Watch the waves roll in from this beachside restaurant serving modern Aussie meals. *8am-9pm* $$$

STROLLING THE SHORELINE FROM MANLY TO SPIT

This spectacular coastal walk runs from Manly past extravagant waterfront homes and through a rugged section of national park.

START	END	LENGTH
Manly Visitor Information Centre	Spit Bridge	10km; 4hr

Before setting off, pack water and wear sunscreen, a hat and sturdy shoes. Start at the ❶ **Manly Visitor Information Centre** to pick up a map. Head along ❷ **Manly Cove** to the path at the end of the beach. After 700m you'll reach ❸ **Fairlight Beach** and enjoy the view straight through the Heads. After 2km you'll come to ❹ **Forty Baskets Beach**. At high tide, cross the bridge or go for a paddle. Kookaburras cackle as you enter the Sydney Harbour National Park and head towards ❺ **Reef Beach**.

The trail grows steeper and rougher deeper into the park – slow down and spot the wildflowers, spiders nestled in bottlebrush trees and fat goannas sunning themselves. The view from ❻ **Dobroyd Head** reveals incredible blues. Look for the deserted 1930s shacks at the base of the cliff at ❼ **Crater Cove**. Further along, examine the ❽ **Aboriginal rock engravings** on a ledge to the left of the track before the turn off to the ❾ **Grotto Point Lighthouse**.

Calm ❿ **Castle Rock Beach** marks the western end of the national park. From here the path winds around the rear of houses to broad and sandy ⓫ **Clontarf Beach**. Next up is ⓬ **Sandy Bay**, ⓭ **Fisher Bay** and then the ⓮ **Spit Bridge**. Return to Manly by bus or Uber.

FAMILY-FRIENDLY FUN IN THE NORTHERN BEACHES

Winnererremy Bay: A spacious grassy area, calm waters, a fenced playground, barbecues and plenty of shade make this a top spot for kids of all ages.

The Basin: Take a day trip or camp to visit the resident wallabies at this sheltered beach area, the only campground in Ku-ring-gai Chase National Park.

Manly Dam: Swim and paddle in freshwater at this protected area surrounded by calm beaches and easy bushwalks.

Curl Curl Rock Pool: A stair-free rock pool perfect for toddlers to paddle in the shallows while parents take turns clocking 50m laps.

Mona Vale Rock Pool: This striking rock pool pairs a shallow section for kids with a deeper one for adults, all bordered by the drama of crashing waves.

JAMES WK/SHUTTERSTOCK

Manly Beach

museum hosting guided tours, including an after-dark experience. After you've seen it all, head down to Quarantine Beach.

Take a Surfin' Safari

Explore the Northern Beaches

When the Beach Boys chose to namecheck 'Australia's Narrabeen' among a list of surfing spots rattled off in their 1963 hit 'Surfin' USA' they were just confirming what serious surfers already knew: that the breaks along Sydney's Northern Beaches are some of the best. Some are even declared National Surfing Reserves.

Manly Surfboards *(manlysurfhire.com.au)* has a range of beginner and performance surfboards for hire, plus lockers, near the waterfront. **Manly Surf School** *(manlysurfschool.com; lessons adult/child $85/75)* runs daily 1½-hour lessons and coaching sessions in front of the North Steyne Lifesaving Club for those who want to give it a go.

After Manly, beach after glorious golden-sand beach lines up all along this coast. Many have saltwater ocean pools and

EATING IN THE NORTHERN BEACHES: OUR PICKS

Barrenjoey House: A breezy spot with Pittwater views serving fresh seafood, pizza and steak. *11.30am-9pm Sun-Fri, to 10.30pm Sat* $$

Basin Dining Room: Inside Mona Vale Surf Club; come for a glass of wine and fresh pasta and seafood. *noon-3pm & 5-10pm* $$

Pilu at Freshwater: Housed within a heritage-listed house overlooking the ocean, this restaurant serves Sardinian specialities. *noon-10pm Wed-Sat, to 9pm Sun* $$$

Jonah's: Perched above Whale Beach, luxurious Jonah's pairs modern Australian seafood dishes with ocean views. *noon-3pm & 6.30-10.30pm Thu-Sun* $$$

a surf-life-saving service, making them just as appealing for swimming as surfing.

Starting from Manly and heading north, you'll hit **Freshwater Beach** followed by **Curl Curl**, **Dee Why**, **Narrabeen**, **Turimetta**, **Warriewood**, **Mona Vale**, **Bungan**, **Newport**, **Bilgola**, **Avalon** and **Whale Beach**. Take your pick; they're all appealing in their own way.

Last but definitely not least is **Palm Beach**, famous as the setting for long-running TV soap *Home and Away*. It's located on the narrow spit of land that divides the Pittwater inlet from the ocean. The headland terminates at the 1881 **Barrenjoey Lighthouse**, which forms part of Ku-ring-gai Chase National Park, although the main part of the park is just across Pittwater, accessible by ferries operated by **Fantasea Cruising** *(fantasea.com.au; one way adult/child $10/5)*. A steep 2km loop leads from Palm Beach to the top of Barrenjoey Lighthouse.

Rock Art & Big Views

Trek through Ku-ring-gai Chase National Park

Australia's second-oldest **national park** spans around 150 sq km of quietly underrated bushland just north of Sydney. Trails here are rarely crowded, winding through bushland to hidden bays and beaches you can only reach on foot. If you've time for just one walk, make it the Aboriginal Heritage Walk (4.5km loop, about three hours). Within the first 10 minutes you'll reach Red Hands Cave, where ochre handprints mark the sandstone, a link to the area's long human history – though it's unknown how old the prints are. The path continues past rock engravings and cave shelters, with opportunities to take a short and steep side trip to Resolute and West Head Beach.

One of the easiest parts of the park to reach without a car is Ku-ring-gai's 14km stretch of the Great North Walk, a 260km trail linking Sydney to Newcastle. Starting at Cowan Station, the trail winds past creeks and along gentle ridgelines before finishing at Hawksbury River Station in Brooklyn, where your reward is a cold drink by the water. Along the way, side trails lead to secluded bays and sweeping lookouts. Come springtime, the area is blanketed with wildflowers.

ABORIGINAL ROCK ENGRAVINGS

While colonisation erased many of the artistic and cultural expressions of the Indigenous peoples who lived in and around what is now Sydney, one aspect survived by being literally written into the city's bedrock. All over Sydney there are places where the outlines of animals, marine life and humanoid forms have been carved onto prominent shelves of rock.

Although many have been lost, built over or forgotten, several prominent sites remain and are accessible. These include an extensive set of carvings on a patch of rock within the **Bondi Golf & Diggers Club**, north of Bondi Beach and others at **Jibbon Head** (near Bundeena in Royal National Park) and near **Grotto Point** on the Manly Scenic Walkway.

DRINKING IN MANLY & THE NORTHERN BEACHES: OUR PICKS

4 Pines Brewpub: Near the ferry in Manly, this remodelled pub attached to a local microbrewery is a perfect spot for sunny afternoon beers. *11am-11pm*

Donny's Bar: This two-level loft-style Manly bar with a low-lit speakeasy vibe is an atmospheric spot for a cocktail. *4pm-2am Mon-Sat, 3pm-midnight Sun*

New Brighton Hotel: This refurbished 1929 Manly boozer has bars on four levels, with a wraparound balcony and rooftop. *10am-3am Mon-Sat, 9am-midnight Sun*

Newport: An enormous complex overlooking the bobbing boats of Pittwater, with acres of appealing outdoor seating, several bars and good food. *noon-midnight*

Blue Mountains

EUCALYPT-FOREST HIKES | BIRD WATCHING | COSY NIGHTS

Places

TOP TIP

The fastest route from Sydney to the Blue Mountains is the M4 Motorway, but there is an alternative route that can turn the journey into a scenic loop. Bells Line of Road connects North Richmond with Lithgow and passes through Mt Tomah, home to the Blue Mountains Botanic Garden.

On the edge of Western Sydney, the Blue Mountains are Sydney's favourite cool-climate escape, popular for weekenders and midwinter Christmas escapes (with a chance of snow in July and August).

The foothills start 65km inland from the city centre and rise to a 1100m-high sandstone plateau slashed by broad valleys cut through the stone. Within their depths are dense eucalyptus forests that release a fine mist of oil, resulting in the bluish haze that gives the mountains their name. The views over the valleys from the edge of the escarpments are unforgettable – the type of landscape you'll only find in Australia.

A series of small towns, some little more than villages, are spread out along the main highways. Leura is the prettiest, it's genteel streets lined with trees, cottages and well-tended gardens. Katoomba is the main hub, with the most dining, drinking and shopping options. Other appealing contenders include Wentworth Falls, Blackheath and Mt Victoria.

Katoomba

TIME FROM SYDNEY: 1½HR

Katoomba makes an ideal base for exploring the Blue Mountains, offering small-town charm that feels worlds away from Sydney's city centre. Its mural-lined main street brims with cosy cafes, pocket gardens and vintage shops that have resisted the plague of fast fashion.

Hazy blue-tinged views

The essential Blue Mountains experience is standing at a clifftop lookout, taking in eucalyptus-scented valleys and sculpted horizons. One of the most memorable places for doing

GETTING AROUND

It's possible to travel between the main towns such as Leura, Katoomba and Blackheath by public bus or train, the latter of which run from Central Station hourly. Another option is the Blue Mountains Explorer Bus, which offers a pricey hop-on, hop-off service on a Katoomba–Leura loop ($55 per day). A car is the best option for getting to remote trailheads and viewpoints.

MAJONIT/SHUTTERSTOCK

View of the Three Sisters

this is **Echo Point** in Katoomba, which offers the added thrill of views over the magical trio known as the **Three Sisters**, an enigmatic rock formation sacred to the local Gundungurra people. Echo Point's attractiveness comes at a price and that's the great gaggles of fellow travellers regularly disgorged here by idling tour buses; arrive early or late if you'd prefer serenity. It's fully wheelchair accessible.

Scenic World's dizzying rides

While the best things in the Blue Mountains are free, **Scenic World** *(scenicworld.com.au; adult/child from $69/41)* offers extra frisson if the views alone aren't cutting it for you. Two of its attractions are billed as the steepest of their kind in the world, which helps justify the correspondingly steep prices.

The **Scenic Railway** descends on a hair-raising 52-degree gradient to the Jamison Valley floor (aka Dinosaur Valley), where a herd of lifelike animatronic dinosaurs has been let loose in the ancient rainforest. There are over 25 species for junior rangers to spot among the trees. After completing a circuit of the forest boardwalks, catch the 510m **Scenic Cableway** back to the top.

Continued on p143

SYDNEY'S ABORIGINAL NATIONS

The Indigenous peoples on whose country Sydney was built were by no means a homogenous group. In fact, the land was divided up between several Aboriginal nations, each speaking a different language. Hence, the Dharawal people James Cook encountered in Botany Bay were entirely different from the Darug people that Governor Phillip met in Sydney Harbour.

The Darug were further split into clans such as the Gadigal, Wangal and Cammeraygal. They were bordered by the Kuringgai and Darkinjung people to the north, the Wiradjuri and Gundungurra to the west and the Dharawal to the south. Six different nations have territory in the vast Greater Blue Mountains World Heritage Area. Learn more at the fascinating **Blue Mountains Cultural Centre** *(bluemountainscultural centre.com.au)* in Katoomba.

Save room for the zucchini flowers

EATING IN THE BLUE MOUNTAINS: OUR PICKS

Basil Nut: Hidden down a shopping arcade, this unassuming place serves modern Southeast Asian and fusion fare. *noon-3pm & 5-8pm Wed-Mon* **$$**

Ateş: A delectable modern Mediterranean sharing menu makes this Blackheath restaurant the best in the Blue Mountains. *5.30-10pm Wed-Sun, plus noon-2.30pm Sat* **$$$**

Rustico: Cheesy woodfired pizzas and delicious eggplant parmigiana are favourites at this Italian restaurant in Katoomba. *5-9pm daily, plus 11.30am-2.30pm Sat & Sun* **$$**

Blaq: There's a cool 1970s vibe going on in this Blackheath spot serving meals made with local produce on the terrace. *5-9pm daily, plus noon-3pm Sat & Sun* **$$$**

HELP ME PICK:

Blue Mountains Hikes

The crisp scent of eucalyptus always seems to spark a burst of energy the moment you step onto the trail. Here, colours defy expectation. From afar, the forest appears a hazy blue, yet up close there's fiery red waratah blooms, bottlebrush trees and flashes of crimson rosellas in the canopy. With over 140km of trails winding through the Blue Mountains National Park, here's how to choose the right hike for you.

Where to Hike if You Love...

Long Journeys

Grand Cliff Top Walk The relatively flat 19km walk traces the dramatic rim of the Blue Mountains, offering panoramic views the entire way. With convenient access points to Wentworth Falls, Leura and Katoomba, it's easy to tackle the route in sections or enjoy a multiday trek without lugging a heavy pack.

Mount Solitary loop Experienced hikers with their own gear can take on the 33km loop from Katoomba. The route is steep and exposed, but the sweeping views make up for the challenge.

OLGA KASHUBIN/SHUTTERSTOCK

Wentworth Falls (p143)

Fairy-Tale Forests

Grand Canyon Track Get ready for stairs (lots of them) that plunge you deep into a misty, fern-filled canyon with trickling waterfalls, grottoes and caves on the 6km Grand Canyon Track loop from Blackheath. While steep, this trek isn't technically challenging and has one of the few canyons you can explore without fiddling with ropes and a harness.

Interesting Geography

Wentworth Falls (p143) Start at the falls for the 3.5km Overcliff-Undercliff Track that loops beneath sandstone overhangs – offering welcome shade on sunny days – and opens to views of Wentworth Falls and the Valley of the Waters. Though there are a few stairs, this is one of the flatter, easier hikes in the area.

Wandering Among Waterfalls

Katoomba Falls An easy 1.5km loop from Katoomba leads to clifftop views of the dramatic falls and close-up views of Katoomba Cascades. After dark, the path is illuminated until 11pm, revealing the trail in a whole new light. The section from Katoomba Falls Park to Cliff View Lookout is also wheelchair accessible.

The 3km Horseshoe Falls Track in Hazelbrook loops past seven waterfalls along the creek, with Horseshoe Falls as the highlight. The trail can get muddy and slippery, so wear sturdy shoes. After dark, thousands of glowworms light up the walls behind Horseshoe and Glow Worm Nook Falls; use a red torch and keep the beam low to protect them.

High-Adrenaline Adventure

High and Wild *(highandwild.com.au)* For an extra hit of adrenaline, opt for abseiling, canyoning or rock climbing. The company also runs bush-survival courses to sharpen your outdoor skills, with adventures tailored to your fitness level and experience – including beginner-friendly options.

BRUCE GRAHAM/SHUTTERSTOCK

Terrace Falls, Blue Mountains National Park

HOW TO

When to go Spring (September–November) brings mild weather and wildflowers. Autumn (March–May) is also pleasant. Crowds surge and the sun scorches in summer (December–February). Winter (June–August) occasionally sees snow.

Entry Free at most trailheads, though an $8 park entry fee applies to vehicles in the Glenbrook area.

Alerts Trail closures are common throughout the year. Check for relevant updates with National Parks *(nationalparks.nsw.gov.au)* before you hike.

Visitor Centre Found at Govetts Leap and Echo Point, the Visitor Centre is a worthwhile stop for personalised trail recommendations and answering any questions about plant and animal life.

Guided Tour vs On Your Own

A range of tour companies offer day trips to the Blue Mountains, from 12-person group outings to large bus tours. Accounting for the drive from Sydney, expect a fast-paced hop-on, hop-off experience covering highlights like Katoomba Cascades, Echo Point, the Three Sisters and Scenic World. Some itineraries include a stop at a wildlife park. It's a good choice if you're short on time and want transport handled for you. Those on a budget or who crave independence can catch an early train from Sydney and complete this itinerary using the public bus, returning late afternoon.

Those who are already in the region should consider a National Parks ranger-led **guided tour** *(around adult/child $55/25)*, which is much more informative than going at it alone. One of the most popular is the three-hour Grand Cliff Top Walk tour at Wentworth Falls, which runs every other Saturday. Large groups can also request park-hosted Aboriginal culture and art workshops, arranged in advance.

Trails are graded by difficulty on the National Parks website: grade 1 tracks are short and wheelchair accessible, grades 2 and 3 suit most walkers, grade 4 routes are steeper and less maintained and grade 5 trails are reserved for experienced bushwalkers who have a high level of fitness and navigation skills. When in doubt, choose the lower-graded treks if going without a guide.

JUSTIN MCKINNEY/SHUTTERSTOCK

Evans Lookout

Continued from p139

The top station is also the starting point for the **Scenic Skyway**, a glass-floored gondola strung across the valley for 384m, with the forest 270m below. If that's not enough of a thrill, you can clamber onto the roof of the gondola at sunset for the open-air **Beyond Skyway** *($369)* experience.

For a complete change of pace, book the 90-minute **Buunyal Tour** *(incl rides adult/child from $82/50)*, where local Gundungurra guides introduce their culture and Country.

Blackheath

TIME FROM SYDNEY: **1HR 40MIN**

Grose Valley lookouts

There are several spots in Blackheath providing majestic views over the Grose Valley, notably **Evans Lookout** and **Govetts Leap Lookout**. Govetts Leap can be reached via one of the national park's best wheelchair-accessible tracks, the Fairfax Heritage Walking Track, running for 2km from the **Blue Mountains Heritage Centre** via regenerating native bush.

Leura

TIME FROM SYDNEY: **1HR 20MIN**

Sublime views

The sharp, triangular outcrop at **Sublime Point** narrows to a dramatic lookout with sheer cliffs on each side. You can still spot the Three Sisters from here, although they're far away. Nearby Elysian Rock Lookout also offers deep valley views.

Wentworth Falls

TIME FROM SYDNEY: **1HR 20MIN**

Wander among waterfalls

There's something very *Lost World* looking and sounding about the Valley of the Waters, an idyllic expanse of rainforest replete with creeks, waterfalls and cascades near the town of Wentworth Falls. At the namesake falls, Jamison Creek plummets 297m from an escarpment in two separate drops. It's most easily viewed (from a distance) from the Princes Rock Lookout, reached by a 20-minute walk. Other options include a two-hour loop on the Overcliff-Undercliff Track.

BEST GARDENS & HISTORIC HOUSES

Norman Lindsay Gallery: The Faulconbridge home and garden of Norman Lindsay is now a gallery devoted to his life and saucy artworks.

Everglades: A Leura property with fabulous 1930s interiors and a magnificent 5-hectare garden laid out by Danish landscape designer Paul Sorensen.

Campbell Rhododendron Garden: A pretty 18-hectare garden in Blackheath maintained by the local rhododendron society, lovingly planted with rhododendrons and azaleas.

Blue Mountains Botanic Garden Mt Tomah: This 252-hectare botanic garden between Bilpin and Bell is the cool-climate sibling of Sydney's Royal Botanic Garden.

Mayfield Garden: Australia's largest privately owned cool-climate garden; near Oberon, to the west of the mountains.

DRINKING IN THE BLUE MOUNTAINS: BEST BARS

Station Bar: Upbeat Katoomba spot combining three things: craft beer, wood-fired pizza and live music (on weekends). *noon-10pm Sun-Thu, to midnight Fri & Sat*

Aunty Ed's: Descend the stairs to travel in time, with craft beer, cocktails and artfully retro food in Katoomba. *noon-9pm Sun-Thu, to 11pm Fri & Sat*

Bootlegger Bar: Under a vaulted ceiling, this cellar-like Katoomba bar hosts everything from Irish sessions to drag bingo. *noon-midnight Wed-Sat, to 10pm Sun*

Mountain Culture Brewery: Raise a glass on the terrace of this heritage-listed Katoomba brewpub. *4-9pm Mon-Wed, 11am-9pm Thu-Sun*

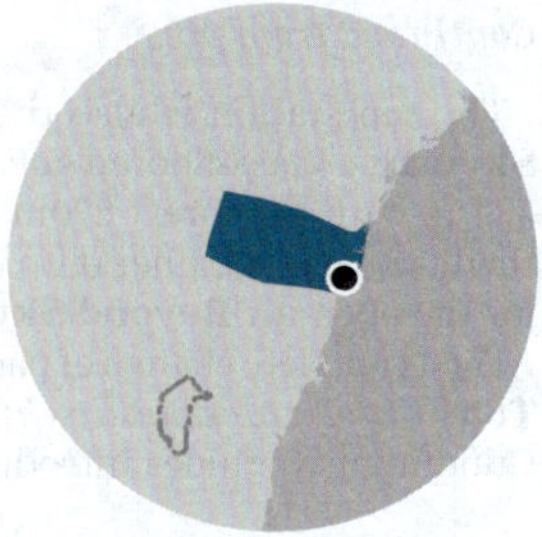

Royal National Park

WILDERNESS AND RUGGED BEACHES

TOP TIP
Check *nationalparks.nsw.gov.au* for information about track and campground closures. Rockfalls, erosion, maintenance and pest-control programs make closures within the park frequent. Most beaches are unpatrolled and can be treacherous. Phone service is spotty; download maps ahead of time. There's free wi-fi at the visitor centre.

The second-oldest national park in the world (established in 1879), 151-sq-km Royal National Park adds a wild edge to Sydney's southern border.

Precipitous cliffs broken up by secluded beaches stretch for 32km along its wave-pummelled coastline. Inland from here is a prime expanse of wilderness with pockets of subtropical rainforest, sandstone gullies filled with gum trees, scrubby heathland and wetlands fed by rivers and creeks. This is part of the traditional lands of the Dharawal people and their legacy can be felt strongly at places like Jibbon Head (near Bundeena), where their ancestors carved images of turtles, rays, whales and kangaroos into the stone.

The main visitor centre is at Audley on the Hacking River, right where it connects with Kangaroo Creek. Call in to pick up maps and get track advice. Rowboats, canoes and kayaks can be hired from the nearby Audley Boatshed for paddles along the two waterways.

Cool Coastal Hikes

Spot sights along the Coast Track

On this spectacular 26km trail tracing the coastline of **Royal National Park** *(nationalparks.nsw.gov.au)*, you'll quickly forget that there's a major metropolis nearby. It's bookended by Bundeena and Otford, with few facilities in between.

GETTING AROUND

There's a $12-per-vehicle daily fee to enter Royal National Park and having a car is by far the easiest way to get around. Vehicles have three main entry points: Farnell Ave in Loftus, Lady Wakehurst Dr in Otford and McKell Ave in Waterfall. Mountain biking is also an option; take your bike on a train (for free) to Loftus, Engadine, Heathcote or Waterfall. Alternatively, take the train to Cronulla and then catch the ferry across Port Hacking to Bundeena, the main village on the park's northern coast, which is the start of the Coast Track.

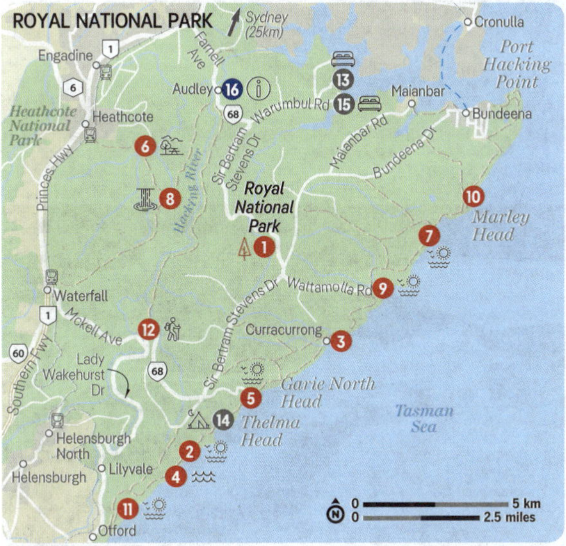

HIGHLIGHTS
1 Royal National Park

SIGHTS
2 Burning Palms Beach
3 Eagle Rock
4 Figure Eight Pools
5 Garie Beach
6 Karloo Pool
7 Little Marley Beach
8 Uloola Falls
9 Wattamolla Beach
10 Wedding Cake Rock
11 Werrong Beach

ACTIVITIES
12 Forest Path

SLEEPING
13 Hilltop Cottage
14 North Era Campground
15 Weemalah Cottage

INFORMATION
16 Royal National Park Visitor Centre

From May to November, whales are often spotted from the cliffside trails, while summer brings the chance to cool off at the many beaches along the way. Most beaches and swimming sites are unpatrolled; consider the swell and tides when venturing onto them.

Those who want to cover it in its entirety usually tackle it in two days, with an overnight stay at the basic **North Era Campground**. Though most of it is along a raised platform, there are steep, technical sections, best for experienced hikers. Water availability is limited, so you'll need to carry plenty and pack a filter or purification tablets. Both ends are accessible by public transport; hiking north to south will keep the sun out of your eyes. Closures are common along the trail, including the North Era Campground, so check ahead on the National Parks website, which is also where you'll book your stay. Though the trail is easy to follow, it's wise to download the NPWS app, which has offline map guidance.

BEST BEACHES IN ROYAL NATIONAL PARK

Little Marley Beach: The only way to get to this secluded little beach is to walk; you may have it all to yourself.

Wattamolla Beach: Accessible by car, Wattamolla has the great advantage of having both a surf beach and a lagoon.

Garie Beach: This picturesque surf beach, accessible by road, has life-saving patrols on summer weekends and throughout January.

Burning Palms Beach: Idyllic golden-sand beach reached by a steep 2km walk. At low tide you can walk to Figure Eight Pools.

Werrong Beach: A tucked-away peaceful nudist beach reached by a very steep 2km walk.

KEN GRIFFITHS/SHUTTERSTOCK

Wedding Cake Rock

Sandstone Suspended Above the Sea

Half-day hike to Eagle Rock

Eagle Rock earned its name from a sandstone overhang that juts out like a giant beak above the cliffs near where Curracurrong Falls flows into the ocean. On blustery days, the water is blown towards the sky, defying gravity. There are three trails leading to Eagle Rock (Wattamolla, Curra Moors and Garie Beach), though the best step-to-view ratio is via Wattamolla along the Coast Track. The 9km out-and-back trail starts in Wattamolla Beach car park and takes about 3½ hours to complete. The cool pools next to Eagle Rock are a tranquil place to picnic.

A Slice of Sydney's Geology

Sea stack views at Wedding Cake Rock

If you just want to get a taste of the Coast Track, a one-hour, 2.8km walk from Bundeena will bring you to **Wedding Cake Rock**, a large fenced-off slab of gleaming white sandstone, only just clinging on the cliff edge. This out-and-back walk spans 5.6km and includes a few steep sections. Crowds are heaviest around noon; early trekkers will enjoy a quieter trail. Continue another 1.5km to reach the golden sands of Marley Beach, then return to Bundeena either back along the Coast Track or inland along the Big Marley Fire Trail, which can be muddy, for a 7.7km loop.

Seaside Pools

Soak in Figure Eight Pools

Many Instagrammers make a beeline for the **Figure Eight Pools**, a striking natural rock pool on a shelf near **Burning Palms Beach**. The most famous pool is the namesake figure eight shape, though there are a handful of other pools around the area. Long queues form at the figure eight, but you'll find spots to yourself at sunrise or during the winter months. The trailhead begins at the Garrawarra Farm car park and winds 6km out and back along the coastline; allow two hours each way. It can be dangerous here: you should only visit (with caution) at low tide. Prepare for slippery scramble sections and leave before the tide returns. The National Parks website *(nationalparks.nsw.gov.au)* has a risk forecast factoring the tide and swell, giving a green light on when to go. Check it the day of your visit.

From Rocks to Rainforest

Family-friendly hiking on the Forest Path

The **Forest Path** is an easy, 4km loop following the Hacking River and Bola Creek through a forest of eucalyptus and turpentine trees, where cabbage palm trees and Gymea lilies, endemic only in the Sydney region, line the trail. In spring, their crimson flowers add a vibrant contrast to all the greenery. Those keen to trek on can add another 4km along Lady Carrington Drive, a popular route for mountain bikers, to Palona Cave, which has a neighbouring waterfall after heavy rains. The region is notorious for leaches, so be sure to cover up. The Forest Path Loop plus Palona Cave covers 8km, taking most people around 2½ hours.

Heathland Hike & Freshwater Swimming

Scenic bushwalk to wild swimming holes and waterfalls

Only half an hour's walk via the Karloo walking track from Heathcote Station, **Karloo Pool** is a pretty spot for a picnic and refreshing swim. This natural swimming hole sits on a bend of Kangaroo Creek, surrounded by stone platforms where you can stretch out and dry off. The track then continues to **Uloola Falls**, where there's a rudimentary campground near a picturesque set of cascades. It's a 10km return track; allow around three hours. Alternatively, you can turn right at the falls and continue on the Uloola walking track to Waterfall Station, which takes around 90 minutes.

This area of the park is particularly lovely in springtime when the wildflowers are in bloom.

FEATHERED FRIENDS OF THE PARK

Azure kingfisher: Spot this bright blue and yellow feathered kingfisher near waterways and listen for its 'seeep' call.

Royal spoonbill: A white bird with long legs and a black spoon-shaped bill; usually found in wetland shallows searching for fish and crustaceans.

Crimson rosella: Easy to spot with their red and blue feathers, these cheeky parrots are often heard making a ruckus in the treetops.

Superb lyrebird: The males of this long-tailed songbird woo with complex calls, even imitating a kookaburra's laugh.

Yellow-tailed black cockatoo: A large parrot with charcoal plumage and yellow cheeks, its call sounds like a creaky door hinge.

Places We Love to Stay

$ Budget $$ Midrange $$$ Top End

Circular Quay & the Rocks

MAP p80

Sydney Harbour YHA $ Any qualms about the un-hostel-like prices will be shelved the moment you check out the rooftop of this sprawling, modern hostel.

Lord Nelson Brewery Hotel $$ Built in 1836, this atmospheric pub has a tidy set of upstairs rooms, with exposed stone walls and dormer windows.

Russell Boutique Hotel $$ A cosy boutique hotel in the heart of The Rocks that feels like staying with a long-lost relative.

Park Hyatt $$$ A luxurious Sydney experience in an unbeatable location. From the rooftop pool, the Harbour Bridge seems almost close enough to touch.

Pier One $$$ Harbourside but away from the Circular Quay crowds in one of the Walsh Bay piers. The decor has a light maritime theme.

Four Seasons Hotel $$$ Five-star luxury in a tower block at the heart of things, with harbour views, comfortable rooms, first-class amenities and attentive staff.

City Centre

MAP p91

Grace Hotel $$ The sumptuous skyscraper-Gothic exterior and Art Deco features makes this 1920s building a Sydney landmark. By contrast, the commodious rooms are generically modern.

Porter House Hotel $$$ A heritage building hosting modern rooms and moody lounge rooms steps from Hyde Park.

QT Sydney $$$ Fun, sexy and relaxed, this theatrical, effortlessly cool hotel is located in the State Theatre complex. Rooms are decorated with flair.

Darling Harbour & Haymarket

MAP p98

Wake Up! Sydney $ Flashpackers sleep soundly in this converted 1900 department store on top of Sydney's busiest intersection, now a convivial, colourful 520-bed hostel.

Sydney Central YHA $ By Central Station, this 565-bed mega-hostel has brilliant facilities, including workspaces for digital nomads and a rooftop pool.

Pod Sydney $ Offers a mix of comfy dorm beds (individual lights and privacy curtains) and private doubles. Facilities are shared, including a small kitchen.

Hotel Woolstore 1888 $$ Once a 19th-century wool store, now an industrial-chic boutique hotel in Pyrmont.

The Darling $$$ Above the bling of the Star casino, the elegant Darling offers fancy sheets, floor-to-ceiling windows and remote-control operation of basically everything.

Kings Cross, Potts Point & Woolloomooloo

MAP p104

Pacific House Hostel $$ A beautifully renovated 1892 building converted into an atmospheric and very clean hostel with all the facilities you could wish for.

Hotel 59 $$ With just nine simple, spotless, comfortable rooms, the family-run Hotel 59 offers great bang for your buck.

Regents Court $$$ Great for longer stays, these Art Deco–inspired studio apartments come with access to a rooftop lounge.

Spicers Potts Point $$$ This expert conversion of three Victorian-era terraces into a hotel is a classy choice on leafy Victoria St.

Darlinghurst, Surry Hills & Paddington

MAP p108

Big Hostel $ A bright and breezy, no-frills Surry Hills hostel with lockers, a rooftop terrace, a decent communal area and a 24-hour kitchen.

Nate's Place $ This refreshingly clean hostel has a rooftop lounge and is well connected to the rest of the city.

ADGE Hotel + Residences $$ Modern and bold, ADGE puts an upbeat twist on the ubiquitous serviced-apartment experience, with quality kitchens and appealing balconies.

Eve Hotel $$$ A sophisticated stay with mid-century flair, where guests are drawn to the loungers by the rooftop pool.

Bondi & the Eastern Beaches

MAP p115

Wake Up! Bondi Beach $ Wake up to views of crashing waves at this clean hostel on the main strip. Large rooftop terrace, too.

Bondi Beach House $$ In a tranquil pocket behind Campbell Pde, this charming guesthouse offers a home-like atmosphere, decorated in botanical style with rustic-chic furnishings.

Bondi 38 **$$$** Check the surf from the window of a serviced apartment overlooking the shores of Bondi.

Newtown & the Inner West

MAP p121

Hoteloco **$$** This cool boutique hotel has spacious, modern rooms and fun train-themed decor.

Urban Newtown **$$** A couple of minutes' walk from Newtown Station, this casual hotel in a former RSL club offers industrial-styled studio accommodation.

Old Clare Hotel **$$$** A sensitive brewery conversion is now a 69-room hotel in a prime Chippendale location. Rooms are attractive, with high ceilings.

North Shore

MAP p127

Discovery Parks – Lane Cove **$** Have a back-to-nature experience in the heart of suburbia in this Lane Cove National Park campground.

Wildlife Retreat at Taronga **$$$** Gaze out your window at koalas and wallabies in this memorable luxury lodge within Taronga Zoo.

Roar & Snore **$$$** Luxury harbourside glamping within earshot of the lions and tigers at Taronga Zoo. Prices include dinner, breakfast and up-close animal encounters.

Manly & the Northern Beaches

MAP p132

Stoke Beach House **$** An attractive hostel close to Manly Beach, with comfy rooms, a well-equipped kitchen, soap dispensers in the showers and great staff.

Q Station **$$** Formerly a quarantine station, now a four-star stay with breezy views of Store Beach.

Palm Beach B&B **$$$** A family-run B&B hosting dreamy beach stays where all rooms have sea views.

Blue Mountains

No. 14 Lovel St **$** This hostel in a 1913 Katoomba cottage has a friendly vibe, colourful interiors, polished floorboards and helpful managers.

La Maison Boutique Hotel **$$** A short walk from Echo Point, this stay has spacious, cosy rooms and plenty of lounge spaces.

Carrington Hotel **$$** Like stepping into a game of Cluedo, this 1883 gem has a billiard room, ballroom, wood-panelled library and a dome-roofed bar.

Royal National Park

MAP p145

Hilltop Cottage **$$$** A wildlife-lover's retreat, this three-bedroom Royal National Park cottage overlooks peaceful Port Hacking.

Weemalah Cottage **$$$** Rented out by the national park, this self-contained timber house sits by the river at Warumbul.

SOFTVISUAL/SHUTTERSTOCK

Park Hyatt, The Rocks

For places to stay in Coastal New South Wales, see p220

DANIELA CONSTANTINESCU/SHUTTERSTOCK

Above: Fitzroy Falls (p194), Kangaroo Valley; Right: Cape Byron Lighthouse (p179), Byron Bay

THE MAIN AREAS

CENTRAL COAST
Coastal national parks.
p156

NEWCASTLE
History, food and surf beaches.
p163

COFFS HARBOUR & THE MID NORTH COAST
Coastal nature galore.
p172

BYRON BAY
Lush hinterland and buzzy beach towns.
p177

THE TWEED
Subtropical surf town with creative edge.
p187

Researched by
Natasha Bazika

Coastal New South Wales

COASTLINE, CULTURE AND ADVENTURE

Set out on a spectacular coastal journey, where rivers meet the sea, forests hug the shore and adventure is never far away.

Welcome to the coast of New South Wales, a stretch running from the quieter beaches of the far South Coast on the Victorian border to the subtropical shores bordering Queensland. This coastline has always drawn people to the water. For millennia, Aboriginal communities lived along beaches and estuaries, moving with seasonal food sources. Traces of this deep history remain in cultural sites and place names. European settlement later followed the shoreline, with ports, whaling stations and lighthouses shaping many of the coastal towns you'll visit today.

GARY YIM/SHUTTERSTOCK

The South Coast is defined by rolling hills, seaside villages and thriving oyster farms. The Mid North Coast brings forested hinterlands, sleepy fishing towns and sunlit estuaries. Further north, beaches stretch longer and waves grow bigger, with places like Coffs Harbour and Byron Bay known for surf breaks, coastal walks and an evolving local food scene.

The hinterlands hold national parks, rainforests and farmland producing cheeses, wines and fresh produce you can taste straight from the source. Wildlife is never far away, with dolphins playing in bays, kangaroos wandering near beaches and birds filling the skies.

From surf towns to hinterland villages, the NSW coast presents a landscape that moves at its own pace. Walk the beaches, paddle an estuary or simply watch the tide roll in. Everywhere you go, you'll feel the rhythm of the land, the sea and the stories they hold.

Find Your Way

The NSW coastline runs the length of the state, from Tweed Heads to Eden, over 1000km of beaches and bushland that can easily be explored in shorter, scenic drives.

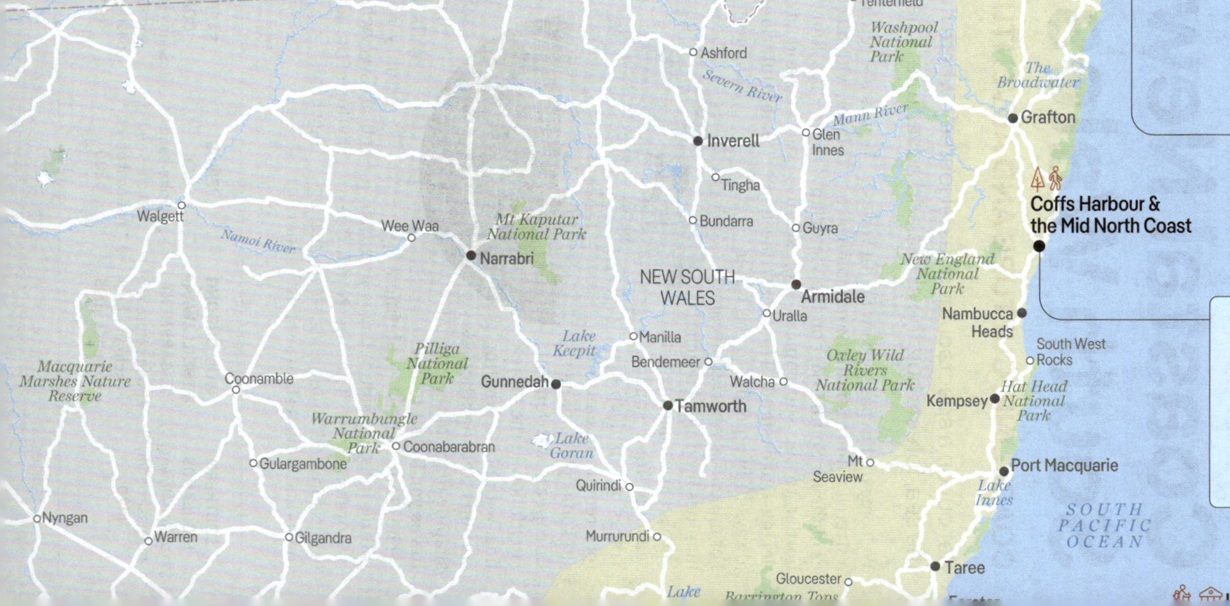

The Tweed, p187

A chill border town where surf beaches, subtropical rivers and creative communities drift between NSW and Queensland.

Byron Bay, p177

Beautiful beaches at NSW's northeastern tip; hinterland towns also lure foodies, writers, cyclists, hikers and hippies-at-heart.

Coffs Harbour & the Mid North Coast, p172

Tiny surf towns, deserted beaches and hinterlands dominated by coastal national parks.

CAR

The best way to explore the coast is by car. The Pacific Hwy and Princes Hwy make it easy to cruise between beaches, towns and national parks.

BUS

Long-distance buses including **Premier** *(premierms.com.au)* and **Greyhound Australia** *(greyhound.com.au)* run between Sydney and Byron Bay, though services are more limited along the South Coast.

TRAIN

NSW TrainLink *(nswtrainlink.info)* trains head north to Tweed Heads and south to Bomaderry, with connecting buses linking smaller coastal towns all the way to Eden.

Newcastle, p163
Australia's second-oldest city feels renewed, with beaches, great food and the Hunter Valley nearby.

Central Coast, p156
A classic summer escape for Sydney families, mixing beaches, national parks and lively towns.

Southern Highlands, p190
A favourite weekend escape for destination dining, wine tasting and heritage villages.

Wollongong & the Illawara Escarpment, p195
A rejuvenated city, where mountains meet the sea and a waterpark is a family road-trip highlight.

Jervis Bay, p200
Cross the border for white-sand beaches, blue waters and camping adventures.

Batemans Bay & Eurobodalla, p204
Waterways, cycle paths and scenic drives lead to national parks, estuaries and beaches.

Sapphire Coast, p210
Twin towns Merimbula and Pambula shine on the Sapphire Coast, with beaches and lakes to explore.

Plan Your Time

Make a plan, but be prepared to change it. Sometimes it's best to see where the wind takes you and this is one of those places.

CONSTANTIN STANCIU/SHUTTERSTOCK

Cave Beach (p202), Jervis Bay

If You Only Visit One Place

- No doubt **Byron Bay** (p177), the legendary Far North Coast beach town, is high on your list, with its world-class surf beaches, vibrant cafes and wellness offerings. From here, it's easy to hire a car and explore the lush hinterland and **Tweed** (p187) region, full of rainforest walks, waterfalls and charming towns. Non stop daily flights from Sydney to Ballina make getting there quick and easy.

- Alternatively, on the South Coast, **Jervis Bay** (p200) is unmissable. Its soft white sands and clear waters are unlike anywhere else along this coastline. Compact enough to explore by bike or car, the area has scenic walks, quiet beaches and camp sites within the national park for easy access to its natural wonders.

Seasonal Highlights

North Coast offers winter bargains and summer surf, Central Coast is busy in summer, while the South Coast stays quiet, sunny in summer, cooler and wet in winter.

JANUARY

Summer brings long, hot days and buzzing **beaches** along the NSW coast. Expect busy highways, booked-out resorts and packed motels, especially during school holidays. Plan ahead, book early and allow extra travel time.

MARCH

As summer heat eases in March, days become milder and more comfortable. Southern coastal air feels crisp, **walking tracks** reopen and hinterlands enter **fruit-picking season**, making it a great time to explore beyond the beach.

APRIL

April delivers autumn warmth, quieter beaches and a slower pace. **Whale sightings** begin, festivals like **Byron Bay Bluesfest** (p179) return and **coastal walks** shine. Further south, cooler winds appear, so layered clothing is useful.

A Week up Your Sleeve

- A week lets you explore stretches of the coast, an easy drive from Sydney. Head south along the Grand Pacific Drive, following it all the way down to **Merimbula** (p221) to slurp fresh oysters and enjoy a laid-back beach holiday. Slowly drive back to Sydney, stopping at **Batemans Bay** (p204) or **Mollymook** (p221) for a night or two for more seafood, walks and swims.

- Alternatively, a road trip along the **Central Coast** (p156) is perfect for families, with a few days hopping between **The Entrance** (p158), **Terrigal** (p159) and other seaside towns.

- Extend your trip up to **Port Stephens** (p168) for kayaking, dolphin spotting and bushwalks. A week gives you time to get a feel for each destination. Travel off-peak for flexibility and easier last-minute bookings.

Longer to Travel Around

- Pack the car or campervan and hit the open road for the ultimate North Coast adventure, with plenty of detours to keep things interesting. Stop in the **Hunter Valley** (p170) to taste wines, wander through tiny **Central Coast** (p156) beach towns and don't forget a photo at the **Big Banana** (p173), an iconic halfway point.

- On the Far North Coast, explore the hinterlands around **Byron Bay** (p177) and **Tweed Heads** (p189), with lush rainforests, quiet beaches and small towns along the way. Spend your days swimming, hiking, spotting wildlife and diving into local history and Aboriginal culture. Treat yourself to fresh regional produce and relaxed coastal dining.

- You can keep heading into Queensland or turn back to discover different towns. There's no way to see everything, but there's no harm in trying.

JUNE

Winter varies along the NSW coast, with sunny, mild conditions in the north and cooler, wetter weather in the south. **Whales** migrate close to shore, crowds thin out and towns feel empty without fully closing.

JULY

Winter swells arrive in Byron Bay. Beach towns quieten, accommodation deals improve and clear days create ideal conditions for peaceful **coastal walks and hikes**.

SEPTEMBER

Spring is ideal for exploring **coastal tracks**, with wildflowers in bloom and wildlife more active. Regional towns host **food and wine festivals**, waterfalls run well after spring rains and days feel fresh without peak-season crowds.

NOVEMBER

Enjoy prime **beach weather** before holiday crowds return. Expect long, warm days, clearer roads and waterfalls still flowing after spring rain, making it one of the most balanced times to visit.

Central Coast

BEACHES | NATIONAL PARKS | MOUNTAIN BIKING

Places

TOP TIP

The Central Coast is home to some of Australia's most accessible beaches, with beach wheelchairs available for free hire at a dozen locations; arrange at individual **Surf Life Saving Clubs** *(sls.com.au)*. Beach matting is installed at four beaches, including Terrigal, during the patrol season (September to April).

The Central Coast runs between Sydney and Newcastle and includes some gorgeous beaches, sizeable swaths of national park, and inlets and saltwater lagoons that make the geography here fascinating. There's demographic diversity, too, with working-class coastal communities combined with weekending Sydney socialites and a solid corpus of lifestyle retirees and property-price refugee commuters. The area's largest town is the transport and services hub of Gosford, but visitors tend to flock to the coastal holiday towns of Avoca and Terrigal, while Ettalong has some of the region's best dining options. Further south, towards the mouth of the Hawkesbury River, are picturesque national park enclaves including Patonga, Pearl Beach and Killcare. To the north, salt 'lakes' like Tuggerah and Lake Macquarie are popular for paddleboarding.

Ettalong

TIME FROM SYDNEY: **1HR 20MIN**

Two big national parks

The Central Coast has several national parks and conservation areas, but two are especially easy to reach from the seaside town of Ettalong. Cradling the region's southeastern tip, **Bouddi National Park** *(nationalparks.nsw.gov.au)* has a collection of walking trails leading to isolated beaches and dramatic lookouts, with views towards Barrenjoey Head at Sydney's northern end. There are NSW National Parks & Wildlife Service (NSW NPWS) camping grounds at **Little Beach**, **Putty Beach** and **Tallow Beach**. From Putty Beach, the easy **Bouddi Coastal Walk** runs 8km to **Macmasters Beach**.

GETTING AROUND

The southernmost points of the Central Coast can be accessed by ferry from Sydney's Palm Beach, while **NSW TrainLink** *(nswtrainlink.info)* trains from Sydney to Newcastle stop in Woy Woy and Gosford. A network of buses connects the Central Coast with interchange hubs at Gosford, Wyong, Tuggerah and Woy Woy railway stations. See **Busways** *(busways.com.au)* for timetables and maps; pay with an Opal card or a credit or debit card. **Central Coast Ferries** *(centralcoastferries.com.au)* operates a local ferry service between Woy Woy and Empire Bay, via Saratoga and Davistown. Self-service **Boomerang Bikes** *(boomerangbikes.com.au)* kiosks are found in Umina, Ettalong and The Entrance.

MERRILLIE REDDEN/SHUTTERSTOCK

Ettalong

Brisbane Water National Park *(nationalparks.nsw.gov.au)* is known for its spring wildflowers and Aboriginal rock engravings. The most impressive gallery is the **Bulgandry Art Site Aboriginal Place**, 3km south of the Pacific Hwy on Woy Woy Rd. The 2km **Girrakool loop track** also has an Aboriginal engraving site. Remember not to walk on or touch the art, for its preservation.

On your bike

Hire a bike from **Ride Ettalong** *(rideettalong.com.au; per 2-4hr adult/child $35/25)* on Ocean View Rd and cruise along the 7km shared coastal pathway, the **Esplanade**. This flat route takes you to neighbouring Umina, the Peninsula Recreation Precinct and back, hugging the beaches for a 1½-hour round trip.

Brisbane Water National Park has three scenic mountain biking trails, while the 10km **Bouddi Ridge Explorer MTB trail** in Bouddi National Park offers great variety and scenery.

ITALIAN CINEMA

Ettalong's laid-back, sun-soaked charm owes a lot to its postwar immigrants. In the 1950s and '60s, Italian and Greek families moved to the Central Coast, drawn by fishing, farming and the promise of coastal life. They brought their food, architecture and love of community, shaping Ettalong into a place that feels like a little slice of the Med. You'll notice it in the cafes serving espresso and gelato, the tiled roofs and colourful facades, and the weekend markets filled with handmade goods and fresh produce. Locals still celebrate traditions from the old countries, including oyster festivals and a weekend dedicated to the local Italian community, giving Ettalong a uniquely Aussie-Mediterranean vibe, blending heritage architecture with a modern, relaxed coastal town.

The cinnamon rolls are heavenly!

EATING & DRINKING ON THE CENTRAL COAST: OUR PICKS

Bay Road Brewing: Microbrewery in Gosford with beer garden, craft beer on tap and lobster rolls. *noon-10pm Thu-Sat, noon-7pm Sun, from 4pm Tue* $$

Burnt Honey: BYO cup to this eco-conscious bakery near Copacabana Beach; the coffee is as good as the pastries. *7am-2pm Tue-Sat, to 12.30pm Sun* $

Woy Woy Fishermen's Wharf: Get the best fish and chips from the kiosk (from 11am) or grab a table overlooking Empire Bay. *noon-3pm Sun-Thu, to 8pm Fri & Sat* $

Chillis Cottage: All-purpose cafe in Ettalong with jetty views and house-baked sourdough. Lunch based on local seafood and produce. *8am-4pm Wed-Sun* $$

PELICAN TIME

The Entrance wouldn't be the same without its pelicans. Originally drawn by fish scraps from a local fish and chip shop, they became so popular that in 1990 a dedicated platform (called Pelican Plaza) was built so people could gather to watch these huge birds in action.

Australian pelicans are the country's largest flying birds, with wingspans up to 2.5m and expandable pouches that hold over 1L of water or fish. Mostly white with black-tipped wings, they are very different from North American brown pelicans, like Nigel in *Finding Nemo*.

Visit **Memorial Park** for **Pelican Time**, a free 3.30pm talk on weekends and during school holidays run by Marine Wildlife Rescue volunteers, who share stories about feeding, behaviour and the pelicans' longstanding connection to the foreshore.

RUSSELL MORRIS/SHUTTERSTOCK

Toowoon Bay

Local art and treasures

Ettalong is a small town with big ideas for sustainable shopping. Start at **Bay Gallery** *(artstudioscooperative.org)*, opposite **Mantra Ettalong Beach**, for rotating local art; it's open Friday to Sunday. Each weekend, the **Galleria** mall hosts the **Ettalong Beach Markets** with handmade fashion and homewares. While you're there, check out **Cinema Paradiso** *(cinemaparadiso.com.au)*, a six-screen cinema with Art Deco design and Italian Renaissance murals, showing new releases and classics for a relaxed family-friendly afternoon.

The Entrance

TIME FROM SYDNEY: 1½HR

Stroll scenic loops connecting beaches and lakes

The Coast to Lake Walk is a scenic 7.6km loop around The Entrance, linking lakes, beaches, parks and ocean baths. It's split into four sections; most are accessible for wheelchairs, prams, scooters and bikes, with toilets, picnic spots and water stations along the way. Begin at the Ocean Baths, Memorial Park or Waterfront Playground, cross the Entrance Channel bridge to Picnic Point and continue south to Long Jetty or **Toowoon Bay**. Beach wheelchairs and matting are available seasonally and dogs on leads are welcome on all but section two.

EATING IN THE ENTRANCE: CUTE COFFEE SPOTS

Arcady: Great community vibe and even better coffee. Grab a toastie or pastry to go. *6am-1pm Wed-Thu, to 2pm Fri-Sun* $

Albie's Coffee Bar: Go for a cup of Veneziano coffee and fresh pastries. Limited seating options. *6am-noon* $

Flour & Co: Beach cafe with good coffee and menus written on butcher's paper. The pies are a classic. *6am-3pm Mon-Sat, from 6.30am Sun* $$

Cafe 2261: A local favourite; friendly service and great coffee near Long Jetty. *4am-1pm Mon-Fri, 4.30am-2pm Sat & Sun* $

Dive into historic baths and pristine beaches

Cool off at the historic **Grant McBride Ocean Baths**, beside The Entrance's heritage-listed Surf Life Saving Club. The baths have shallow, child-friendly sections and longer laps for more serious swimmers. Nearby, **Roberts Beach** is a quieter spot to paddle, sunbathe or take in the views. Around the corner, curved **Little Bay** is calm, with small waves; further south, **Toowoon Bay Beach** is a spacious, open stretch popular with surfers and fishers. **North Entrance Beach** is one of the area's most popular beaches, with powerful surf and lifeguards on duty Monday to Friday.

Pier views and boutique shopping

No trip to The Entrance is complete without a walk along **Long Jetty**, the pier stretching into Tuggerah Lake. It's perfect for spotting wetland birds or enjoying a Central Coast sunset. The nearby foreshore has wide concrete paths for wheelchairs and prams, with barbecues and picnic tables dotted around. After the walk, explore the township's boutiques and antique stores. Pop into **Sadie Lou** *(sadielou.com.au)* for coastal-inspired daywear, or browse **Plain Janes** *(plainjanesstore.com.au)* for ceramics, homewares and fashion finds.

Terrigal

TIME FROM SYDNEY: **1HR 25MIN**

Surround yourself with golden sands and headland views

Terrigal has long been the Central Coast's golden child. **Terrigal Beach** stretches just 700m of the 2.8km sand linking to Wamberal and is patrolled from September to April. Surf schools like **Central Coast Surf Academy** *(centralcoastsurfacademy.com; adult beginners & kids $50)*, founded by former World Tour surfer Amee Donohoe, run beginner-friendly lessons on the beach.

A rock pool hugs the southern end, while **Terrigal Lagoon** to the north lets you paddle at a leisurely pace. Behind the sand, the Esplanade is lined with cafes and shops. Make the short, steep climb up the **Skillion** for views of the headlands and ocean.

Explore underwater wrecks and vibrant marine life

Just off the coast lies the former HMAS *Adelaide*, a retired naval ship that was deliberately sunk in 2011 to create an artificial reef. Now it's home to rays, octopuses and countless

Continued on p162

WHY I LOVE THE CENTRAL COAST

Natasha Bazika, Lonely Planet writer

For Sydney families, the Central Coast has always been a bit of a rite of passage and my family was no exception. I can still picture piling into the car, the back seat stacked with bags and an Esky full of drinks and snacks.

Back then, it was all about the simple joys: swimming, paddleboarding, chasing pelicans and bumping into school friends.These days, the Coast still draws families every school holiday, though it's grown up a bit, with trendier restaurants and stylish new stays replacing some of the old motels. But there's still something for every budget, from holiday homes to resorts. I love that it's still where Sydney families unwind, laugh and make memories, just like we did back then.

EATING & DRINKING IN TERRIGAL: OUR PICKS

Swells: Come for the seafood, stay for the view. Great wine list. *noon-9pm Wed, Thu & Sun, to 11.30pm Sat & Fri* **$$**

Void Bar: Dark bar with delicious cocktails and live music on weekends. Ask for anything with mezcal. *5pm-midnight Wed-Sat, to 10pm Sun* **$**

Meribella: Glamorous place to celebrate good food and good company. Located inside a hotel. *12.30-3.30pm & 5-10.30pm Wed-Sat, 1-3.30pm Sun* **$$$**

Pocket Bar: Local favourite for casual drinks and bar food like tacos and burgers. Great atmosphere. *4pm-midnight Mon-Thu, hours vary Fri-Sun* **$**

ROAD TRIP

Tourist Drive 33

Despite the name, Tourist Drive 33 isn't exactly packed with tourists. This scenic, lesser-known route follows parts of the old convict-built Great North Road, linking Sydney to the Hunter Valley through rolling farmland, forest and quiet country towns. Take your time, stop for fresh local produce, stretch your legs on a waterfall walk and turn it into a full day or even an overnight adventure in the Central Coast hinterland.

1 Mt White

Wedged between national parks, Mt White is the most scenic part of this road trip. Meet rescued wildlife at **Walkabout Wildlife Sanctuary**, then explore the **Mt Penang Gardens & Sculpture Trail** with themed sections like Misty Mountains and Bottle Trees. The **Wondabyne Stone Sculptures** is a trail of sandstone works by artists from around the world. Walk paths are wide and smooth, featuring a 35m cantilevered steel footbridge and off-path routes. Stop at **Saddles Mount White** restaurant to fuel up with a hearty breakfast or grab a pie for the road.

The Drive: A 15-minute drive north brings you to Somersby, a popular wedding destination with beautiful venues and rainforest walking trails.

2 Somersby

Turn off the main road to Somersby, where you'll spot Australian Reptile Park's bright-yellow dinosaur Ploddy (p162) from the highway. Take the 30-minute walk from

WORLDSWILDLIFEWONDERS/SHUTTERSTOCK

Somersby Falls

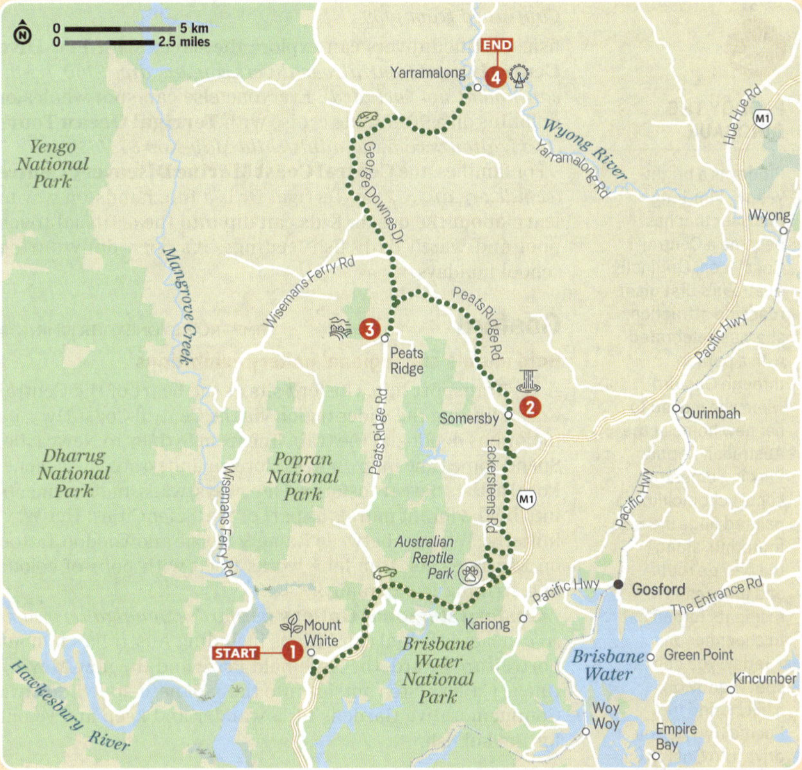

the picnic area to **Somersby Falls**, an 800m return track with some steep, slippery sections to a tiered waterfall. Along the way, listen for kookaburras and keep you r eyes peeled for water dragons. In summer, it's common to see people splashing in the shallows. After the walk, relax at the accessible picnic area in a rainforest setting with plenty of shade and public BBQs.

The Drive: Take the easy 15-minute drive to the small hinterland town of Peats Ridge to pick fresh produce and flowers.

3 Peats Ridge

Welcome to the Central Coast's fruit bowl. Start at **Meliora Farm**, where you can pick juicy oranges or avocados from August to December and bring a picnic to have among the trees. Entry is free. A three-minute drive down the road, you can pick seasonal sunflowers at the **Bloom Barn**. Tickets are $2, with every dollar donated to Coast Shelter. To meet the locals, visit **Mangrove Mountain Market** on the first Sunday of the month – a great spot to pick up local honey, condiments and handmade knick-knacks.

The Drive: The 18-minute drive to Yarramalong winds past orchards and small farms, with the traffic and the noise starting to fade.

4 Yarramalong

This peaceful hinterland spot has some of the Central Coast's oldest European settlements. Driving along Yarramalong Rd, you'll pass turf huts serving coffee and bacon rolls, fruit barns and alpacas grazing by the roadside. At **Amazement Farm & Fun Park** kids can get lost in mazes, enjoy rides, watch wildlife and reptile shows, and meet monkeys and meerkats at the adjoining **Central Coast Zoo**. For bigger thrills, **Treetops Adventure** is just down the road, with rope courses, a 500m zip-coaster, and trampolines and ball pits for younger kids.

PLODDY THE DINOSAUR

Ploddy is a bright-yellow, 14m-long dinosaur that has become a Central Coast icon. Originally Australia's first giant roadside attraction, she was celebrated with a parade through Gosford when she moved to her new home at the Australian Reptile Park in Somersby. Local schoolchildren painted huge life-size footprints along the parade route and thousands of residents turned out to cheer her on.

Today, you can spot Ploddy on a hill beside the Pacific Hwy as you drive into Gosford, visible to millions of passing vehicles each year. The nearby **Australian Reptile Park** *(reptilepark.com.au)* is a fun, family-friendly day out with activities for all ages. Don't forget to wave to Ploddy on the drive in.

Continued from p159

fish. Certified divers can explore the wreck with **Pro-Dive Central Coast** *(centralcoastdivers.com.au; dive $160, rental equipment not included)*. Everyone else can spot whales or dolphins on a 90-minute cruise with **Terrigal Ocean Tours** *(terrigaltours.com.au; adult/child May-Nov $75/65)*.

For families, the **Central Coast Marine Discovery Centre** *(ccmdc.org.au; $12)* on Terrigal Dr is a fun, hands-on way to learn about the ocean. Kids can dip into the artificial touch pool and watch daily fish feedings. It's open daily during school holidays.

Gosford

TIME FROM SYDNEY: **1HR 10MIN**

Bold murals and regional gallery exhibitions

A key transport hub, Gosford sits at the heart of the Central Coast, linking the wider region via the Central Coast Hwy, its major bus depot and the train line from Sydney to Newcastle. Spend some time in town to explore an underrated arts scene. Local artists have transformed laneways, walls and pavements into bold, vibrant murals as part of the 'Safer Cities: Her Way' initiative. Wander between Raine & Horne and Voodoo Tattoo on **Mann St** for 40m-long works filled with pops of colour and striking iconography.

Gosford Regional Gallery *(gosfordregionalgallery.com; free)* hosts seasonal exhibitions including Australia's famous portraiture award, the Archibald Prize and the new Moving Image Gallery. Step outside into the Japanese-style Edogawa Commemorative Gardens for a wander and keep an eye out for the koi fish.

Hike scenic estuaries and lush rainforest trails

A short 1½-hour return hike to **Yaruga Picnic Area** takes you to the best vantage point of Brisbane Water, one of the most scenic estuaries in the state. The reserve also connects to the 11km **Railway to Rainforest Walk** towards Holgate. Begin at the **Rumbalara Environmental Education Centre** *(rumbalara-e.schools.nsw.gov.au)* to learn about local flora and fauna before hitting the trails.

For something flatter, the 8.2km **Gosford Foreshore** walk runs through two parks. Start at **Gosford Sailing Club**, where there's parking and a playground.

EATING IN GOSFORD: BEST CAFES

South End Social: Coffee lab by day, wine bar in the afternoon; breakfast is served until 11.30am. *6am-3pm Mon-Fri, from 8am Sat & Sun* **$$**

Good Bits Co: Grab coffee and a freshly baked pastry; for something substantial, the loaded toasties are a hit. *6am-3pm Mon-Fri, 7am-1pm Sat* **$**

Have It Franks Way: Your one-stop shop for coffee, loaded croissants, fresh flowers and locally made gifts. *7am-2pm Mon-Fri* **$**

Legend Coffee & Culture: Try global blends at this industrial roastery. Arguably the Central Coast's best coffee. *6.30am-2pm Mon-Fri, 7am-noon Sat & Sun* **$$**

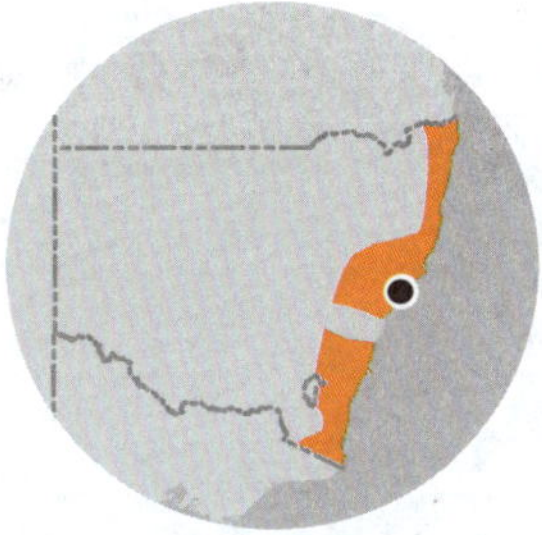

Newcastle

BEACHES & SURFING | HISTORY | FOOD & DRINK

The salt-licked port city of Newcastle may be a fraction of Sydney's size, but Australia's second-oldest city – on the traditional lands of the Awabakal and Worimi peoples – punches well above its weight. Superb surf beaches, historical architecture and a sun-drenched climate are only part of its appeal. A flourishing dining scene now plays a starring role in the city's revival, with entire food streets, buzzing bars, cool cafes and hatted restaurants adding serious foodie appeal.

But Newcastle's appeal goes beyond food. Creative energy pulses through its streets, from streetart and galleries to boutique shops and design-focused projects. The 2023 revitalisation of the historical ocean baths has further cemented its status as a vibrant coastal hub, while music, festivals and local markets reveal a community proud of its heritage yet unafraid to reinvent itself.

With endless ways to explore both surf and city, Newcastle is constantly in motion, making every visit feel unexpectedly inspiring.

TOP TIP

Some of the best things to do in Newcastle won't cost you a cent, from bouncing between the city's beaches to admiring the Newy's diversity of architectural styles, from Gothic Revival to Art Deco, on a self-guided walking tour of the city; download the map from *visitnewcastle.com.au*.

Pack Your Swimwear

Newcastle's blissful beaches and pools

At the eastern end of town is lovely **Newcastle Beach**. Reopened in 2023 after a major renovation, the Art Deco ocean baths at the northern end are a mellow alternative,

GETTING AROUND

Sydney Trains *(transportnsw.info)* runs regular services to Newcastle Interchange (Station St, Wickham; three hours). From here, the Newcastle Light Rail covers the 2.7km to Newcastle Beach. There's an extensive network of local buses and a ferry operates between Queens Wharf and Stockton. Use an Opal card or pay-and-go credit or debit card on local services. The EasyPark app allows you to pay for parking remotely and gives you 15 minutes free in 1P and 2P parking areas (all parking meters accept cards; some take coins). Newcastle's airport in Williamtown services a handful of eastern Australian destinations, including Lord Howe Island.

HIGHLIGHTS
1 Bathers Way
2 Newcastle Beach
3 Newcastle Museum

SIGHTS
4 Bogey Hole
5 Christ Church Cathedral
6 Fort Scratchley
7 Newcastle Art Gallery
8 Nobby's Beach

ACTIVITIES
9 Newcastle Surf School

SLEEPING
10 Lucky Hotel
11 Newcastle Beach YHA
12 QT Newcastle

EATING
13 Antojitos
14 Arno Deli
15 Bistro Penny
16 Humbug
17 Lock's Paddock
18 Newy Burger Co
19 Papa's Bagels

DRINKING & NIGHTLIFE
20 Coal & Cedar
21 Falcon
22 King Street
23 Koutetsu

SHOPPING
24 Abicus
25 Olive Tree Market
26 Palinopsia

INFORMATION
27 Newcastle Visitor Information Centre

with a shallow pool for toddlers and a backdrop of heaving ocean and chugging cargo ships. Around the headland to the north is **Nobby's Beach**, a popular beginner surf spot with small swells.

South of Newcastle Beach, below King Edward Park, is Australia's oldest ocean bath – the convict-carved **Bogey Hole**, an atmospheric place to splash about when the surf's crashing over its edge. The most popular surf breaks are at **Bar Beach** and **Merewether Beach**, two ends of the same beach further south. Merewether has huge ocean baths (Australia's largest) of its own. Opposite the popular **Merewether Surfhouse** *(surfhouse.com.au)*, don't miss the **Merewether Aquarium**, an underpass transformed into a pop-art underwater world by local artist Trevor Dickinson, complete with quirky details including the artist as a diver and an autographed painting of legendary local surfer Mark Richards.

The city's famous annual surfing festival, **Surfest** *(surfest.com)*, takes place in Merewether in February.

Trace the Coast

Traverse clifftop boardwalks and historic coastal paths

Breathe in the ocean on the scenic **Bathers Way** *(visitnewcastle.com.au)* coastal path from Nobby's Beach to Merewether Beach, which winds along spectacular cliff-scapes and the city's finest stretches of sand. Interpretative signs describing Aboriginal, convict and natural history dot the 6km trail. The most spectacular section is the stretch of boardwalk known as Memorial Walk between Bar Beach and Strzelecki Lookout; it offers magical sea views. A refreshed section south of Newcastle Beach weaves past a new skate park that opened in 2024.

From Coal to Cannons

Discover historic museums and legendary military forts

Housed in the restored Honeysuckle rail workshops in the city centre, the **Newcastle Museum** *(newcastlemuseum.com.au; free; closed Mon)* tells the city's tale from its first Awabakal residents to its rough-and-tumble social history, shaped by a cast of convicts, coal miners and steelworkers. Exhibitions are interactive and engaging, ranging from geology to local legends like the band Silverchair (fans will love the neon sign near the bathrooms) and the Newcastle Knights rugby league club. If you're travelling with kids, check out hands-on science centre Supernova and the hourly sound-and-light Fire

NEWCASTLE'S BEST SHOPPING

Abicus: Fashion and footwear, books and vinyl in Darby St, just south of Newcastle Art Gallery.

Newcastle City Farmers Market: Stock up on everything from fresh oysters to Hunter Valley wines at the Newcastle Showground on most Sunday mornings.

Olive Tree Market: With a focus on art and design, Newcastle's most stylish market is held in Civic Park on the first Saturday of each month.

Palinopsia: Homemade ceramics and homewares products, from Japanese-style ceramics to organic tea towels. Located in Darby St.

Retro Wardrobe: Browse colour-popping vintage fashions and homewares in Hamilton.

EATING IN NEWCASTLE: OUR PICKS

Bistro Penny: Perfect for a date night, this French bistro is the hottest table in town, centred around wood-fired cooking. *5pm-late Mon-Sat* $$

Humbug: Buzzy neighbourhood Italian with a standout wine list and knowledgeable staff. *5.30-9pm Wed & Thu, noon-2.30pm & 5-9.30pm Fri & Sat* $$

Flotilla: Artistic small plates pair with a global wine list in a fine-dining setting that never feels pretentious. *5.30-11pm Thu-Sat, noon-2pm Fri-Sun* $$$

Lock's Paddock: Europe meets Australia in this restaurant filled with locals. Order bits and bobs to share. *5-10pm Tue-Thu, noon-10pm Fri & Sat* $$

SURFING NEWCASTLE

Dan Frodsham, owner of **Newcastle Surf School** *(newcastlesurfschool.com.au)*, recommends some of the area's surf spots.

Blacksmiths Beach: Just south of Newcastle, this is hands-down the best spot for beginners. It's a safe, easy wave, with a breakwall that protects it from southerly swells.

Bar Beach and Merewether Beach: There are so many breaks along this 1.3km stretch that you can almost always find a wave to yourself. The right-hander that peels along the rocky reef off Merewether is best suited to intermediate to expert riders.

Caves Beach: I grew up surfing here, south of Blacksmiths Beach, where you'll find a huge range of beach breaks suitable for all levels.

PASKARAN.T/SHUTTERSTOCK

and Earth show about the steelmaking process. A few blocks away on Lamman St, the expansion of the **Newcastle Art Gallery** *(newcastleartgallery.nsw.gov.au; free)* – featuring a 7000-strong collection of works by luminaries ranging from Margaret Preston to Brett Whiteley to Newcastle-born John Olsen – reopened in early 2026.

Perched above Newcastle Harbour on Nobbys Rd, **Fort Scratchley** *(newcastle.nsw.gov.au; free; closed Tue)* was constructed during the Crimean War to protect the city against a feared Russian invasion. During WWII, this intriguing military site returned fire on a Japanese submarine, making it the only Australian fort to have engaged in a maritime attack. Daily 90-minute guided **tours** *(adult/child $15.80/9)*, led by passionate volunteers from the Fort Scratchley Historical Society, add valuable context as you explore the fort's underground tunnels; book online.

If You Only See One Church

Historic cathedrals and golden wartime treasures

Newcastle's huge Anglican **Christ Church Cathedral** *(newcastlecathedral.org.au)* is filled with treasures, including 11 gold artworks made from jewellery donated by locals who lost loved ones in WWI. The self-guided tour offers an insight into special features, such as the fine Pre-Raphaelite stained-glass

The focaccia is baked fresh daily

EATING IN NEWCASTLE: BEST CHEAP EATS

Newy Burger Co: Local favourite for a stacked burger (gluten-free available). Get $1 wings on Wednesdays. *11am-8pm Wed & Thu, hours vary Fri-Sun* $

Antojitos: Fun Mexican taqueria with a California twist and big portions. Spot the combi van. *11am-9pm Mon-Sat* $

Papa's Bagels: Fresh-baked New York-style bagels with all the toppings; plenty of seating inside and out. *7am-3pm Mon-Fri, 6.30am-4pm Sat & Sun* $

Arno Deli: Focaccia paninis filled with meat, cheese and veggies (No5 is a classic). Prepare to wait in line. *8am-2.30pm Mon-Fri, 8.30am-3pm Sat & Sun* $

Fort Scratchley

window by Edward Burne-Jones and William Morris. Climb the claustrophobic spiral stairs to the **tower** *(by appointment, tel 02-4929 2052; donation $10)* for views across the mouth of the Hunter River and the long dunes beyond. It's on Church St, uphill from Queens Wharf.

Art in Alleys

Wander vibrant laneways and large-scale city murals

Newcastle's streetart is interesting not just for its scale or colour, but for how closely it reflects the city itself. Murals appear on warehouses, skate parks and laneways, telling stories of place, renewal and community. The best way to see it is on foot, particularly around the city centre, Civic Theatre, Wickham and Newcastle South Skate Park, where large-scale murals are clustered.

Start in Civic La and the Evolve Housing Corridor behind the **Visitor Information Centre** for colourful murals, illegal streetart, stickers and paste-ups. Walk towards Newcastle Museum to strike a pose in front of artist Trevor Dickinson's famously fun interactive murals. Other highlights include Aboriginal artworks such as Adnate's mural in Wickham, which reimagines a First Nations boy and Nobby's Head landscape in pre-colonial times. For navigating it all, **Pin the City's Art** *(newcastle.mysocialpinpoint.com/art-mapping)* maps murals across town, with the help of public spottings.

BLACKROCK

Silverchair may be Newcastle's most famous cultural export, but one of Australia's most culturally significant films also came out of Newy. Adapted from a play by Nick Enright that was inspired by the brutal 1989 murder of Newcastle schoolgirl Leigh Leigh, *Blackrock* hit screens in 1995. Holding an uncomfortable mirror to the dark side of Australian youth culture, set against the backdrop of a working-class beachside suburb, the gritty drama was like a *Puberty Blues* (Australian coming-of-age 1979 novel) for the 1990s. Premiering at the Sundance Film Festival, *Blackrock* marked the late Heath Ledger's first feature-film credit.

DRINKING IN NEWCASTLE: BEST BARS

Coal & Cedar: Text the number posted at the Hunter St entrance to this Prohibition-style bar serving Newcastle's best cocktails. *5pm-2am Mon-Sat*

Koutetsu: The quirky vibe of this West End bar hints at its former life as a pawn shop. Pair cracking cocktails with gyoza. *6pm-2am Wed-Sat*

Falcon: Too nice to be called a dive bar; North American-style food keeps it real. *5pm-late Wed-Sat*

King Street: This tri-level live music venue with several bars was enlarged and renovated in 2023. *8pm-3.30am Fri & Sat, to midnight Sun*

Beyond Newcastle

The coastal idyll of Port Stephens and one of Australia's most famous wine regions both lie within an hour's drive of Newcastle.

Places

GETTING AROUND

Hunter Line *(transportnsw.info)* train services run between Newcastle and the Hunter Valley fringe towns of Maitland and Singleton. Enlisting a designated driver or booking a tour is the best way to get around the region if you're here for the wine. **Port Stephens Coaches** *(pscoaches.com.au)* zips around Port Stephens' townships, heading to Newcastle and Newcastle Airport. Cycling is a great way to experience the area, with a self-serve **Boomerang Bikes** *(boomerangbikes.com.au)* kiosk in Nelson Bay among local rental options.

North of Newcastle, the Hunter Valley spreads across rolling hills dotted with vineyards, cellar doors and farm-to-table restaurants, ideal for leisurely lunches and wine tastings. Families can entertain children at a wildlife park or race go-karts around an outdoor track.

Heading east, the coastal road leads to Port Stephens, a broad natural harbour framed by sandy beaches and Worimi Conservation Lands, the southern hemisphere's largest moving dunes. Hop on a quad bike to learn about Indigenous history and cultural sites.

Nelson Bay is the main base, with a marina, seafood eateries, dolphin cruises and ferry access to a nearby island inhabited by penguins and muttonbirds, with holiday towns including Shoal Bay, Fingal Bay and Anna Bay nearby.

Port Stephens

TIME FROM NEWCASTLE: **35MIN**

Koala sightings and glamping to support wildlife rescue

Port Stephens sits in an important koala corridor and while spotting them in the wild is tricky, the **Port Stephens Koala Sanctuary** *(portstephenskoalasanctuary.com.au; adult/child $28/15)* near **One Mile Beach** guarantees sightings. Its wheelchair-accessible Skywalk provides close-up views of sick and injured koalas. Visitors can peer through the hospital window or stay overnight in a glamping tent, suite or studio with early Skywalk access. All visits help fund the sanctuary's vital work.

Walk and swim in Tomaree National Park

Tomaree National Park *(nationalparks.nsw.gov.au)*, a 20-minute drive from the township of Nelson Bay, inside the Port Stephens region, offers beautiful hiking in an area that feels more remote than it is. The park harbours angophora forests, threatened species including koalas and outcrops of rare volcanic rhyodacite. Its beaches and trails are superb. Watching sunrise from **Tomaree Head** (161m) is the reward for doing the summit walk (2.2km return), while **Zenith Beach** is great for a post-hike dip.

Island escape with pristine diving, wildlife and camping

Remote **Broughton Island**, 14km off Port Stephens, forms part of Myall Lakes National Park and is uninhabited except for muttonbirds and little penguins, with surrounding waters harbouring diverse fish. The diving is excellent and the beaches are secluded. If you don't have a boat, **Moonshadow-TQC Cruises** *(moonshadow-tqc.com.au; adult/child $129/69)* runs day trips from Nelson Bay. As with all NSW NPWS sites, the five island camp sites must be reserved online in advance.

Vast moving dunes with cultural tours and 4WD trails

The blinding white dunes of the **Stockton Bight** at the southern end of Port Stephens are the longest moving sand dunes in the southern hemisphere, stretching more than 35km to Newcastle. The dunes form part of the **Worimi Conservation Lands** *(worimiconservationlands.com)*, cared for by the Worimi people, the Traditional Custodians of the land. Visitors can explore certain areas on foot, drive along the beach (4WD only; three-day permit $33), or stay overnight at **Ganyamalbaa Campground**. Before you set off, check the latest conditions online; the sand can change quickly with wind and tide.

For those without a 4WD, safari-style tours depart from Birubi Beach at **Anna Bay**. The most memorable is with Worimi-owned **Sand Dune Adventures** *(sanddune adventures.com.au; adult/adult & child $119/180)*, a one-hour experience combining quad biking with stories of the land's deep cultural significance. Pay close attention to the shell middens around, which date back tens of thousands of years. At the far western end of the beach, the rusting MV *Sygna* shipwreck marks where sea and sand meet in constant motion, a fitting symbol for a place always on the move.

BEST AQUATIC ACTIVITIES IN NELSON BAY

Dolphin Swim Australia: Operates the only tour of its kind in NSW – it sees you harnessed to a catamaran as dolphins play around you.

Original Tea Gardens Ferry: Historical ferry ride, with a daily return service between Nelson Bay and Tea Gardens, across the bay.

Let's Go Adventures: Runs regular diving trips around Broughton Island.

Port Stephens Surf School: Offers surfing lessons for adults and kids at Fingal Bay and One Mile Beach. Board hire is also available.

Port Stephens Paddlesports: In Shoal Bay, with a range of kayaks and stand-up paddleboards for hire, plus excursions.

EATING & DRINKING IN PORT STEPHENS: OUR PICKS

Little Nel: Try the local Medowie mushrooms at this popular, sun-drenched Nelson Bay cafe. *6.30am-2.30pm Tue-Fri, from 7am Sat & Sun* **$$**

Cheeky Dog: Mediterranean bistro and bar at Bannisters hotel in Soldiers Point. *noon-10pm Sun-Thu, to 11pm Fri & Sat* **$$**

Shoal Bay Country Club: Cafe, Greek restaurant, bistro and bar in one. Pumps on weekends. *6.30am-2am Mon-Sat, to midnight Sun* **$$**

Little Beach Boathouse: Generous plates of local seafood served Nelson Bay side. *5-8.45pm Tue-Sat, noon-2pm Sat & Sun* **$$**

BEN GI51/SHUTTERSTOCK

TOP EXPERIENCE

Hunter Valley

Just west of Newcastle, the Hunter Valley is Australia's oldest wine region, its rolling hills lined with vineyards producing some of the country's best drops. Beyond wine tastings, you can float over the valley in a hot-air balloon, go horse riding or catch an open-air concert. No surprise it's one of Sydney's favourite weekend escapes, with plenty to sip, see and slow down for.

DON'T MISS

- Hunter Valley Gardens
- Hunter Valley Wildlife Park
- Balloon Aloft
- Comyns & Co

Hop-on, Hop-off Wine Tasting

With 150-plus wineries, the Hunter Valley is best explored at your own pace and **iHop** *(ihophuntervalley.com.au; adult/child full-day pass $79/40, half-day pass $59/29)* hop-on, hop-off bus makes it easy. Running hourly from Wednesday to Monday, it stops at popular wineries and gourmet shops like **Leogate Estate** *(leogate.com.au)*, **Ben Ean** *(benean.com.au)* and **Fat Cow Hunter Valley**. At Pokolbin village, meet the next-generation winemakers at **Comyns & Co** *(comynsandco.com.au)*. There's onboard storage and cooler boxes for your purchases. Book online before 6pm for the next day.

PRACTICALITIES

- *winecountry.com.au*
- 2hr drive from Sydney, 50min drive from Newcastle

Float Above the Valley

One of the best ways to see the valley is from above. **Balloon Aloft** *(balloonaloft.com; from $310)* flights lift off as the first light spills over vineyards, farmland and misty ridgelines. From the basket, you might spot kangaroos hopping through the vines while the valley slowly comes to life. Once you touch down, there's a sparkling-wine breakfast waiting. Flights with access for wheelchairs are available. Flights run year-round, weather permitting; bookings essential.

Wander the Gardens

At **Hunter Valley Gardens** *(huntervalleygardens.com.au; adult/child $39/31)*, a 14-hectare horticultural playground in Pokolbin, themed sections range from Japanese and rose gardens to storybook landscapes for kids. Wander winding paths, cross archways of seasonal blooms and pull up a bench at water features, fountains or the quiet seating areas. Christmas lights, autumn displays and seasonal festivals keep the gardens lively all year.

Taste the Region

While the valley is famous for gourmet restaurants like **Muse** *(musedining.com.au)* and **Margan** *(margan.com.au)*, there's a budget-friendly alternative – foraging for your own ingredients. At **Binnorie Dairy** *(binnorie.com.au)*, a small family-run producer, get a free cheese tasting and stock up on award-winning brie and labna plus cured meats and crackers. Stop at Pokolbin Village Shops to browse local food products, including olive oils and vinegars from **Pukara Estate** *(pukaraestate.com.au)*. For dessert, **Cocoa Nib** *(cocoanib.com.au)*, near Keith Tulloch Wines, has colourful bonbons.

Meet the Wildlife

Hunter Valley Wildlife Park *(huntervalleywildlifepark.com.au; adult/child $49/29)* is a must for families. Start near the entrance to see kangaroos, emus and other Australian animals, then wander further to see meerkats, lions and other exotic species. Daily keeper talks are a hit, offering insights into koala sleeping habits, conservation challenges and fun facts about the animals. There are plenty of spots to take photos and keep the kids entertained.

Zoom Along a Race Track

For something different, **Go Karts Go Hunter Valley** *(gokartsgo.com.au; 1/2 sessions $37.50/65)* has an 850m long track, with a mix of fast straights and bendy corners, where you can race in four-stroke go-karts. There are specially designed junior go-karts and twin-seaters for the younger kids; for the older children, the go-karts reach top speeds of 70km/h. Bookings are required.

WINE HOUSE

The Hunter Valley's **Wine House** *(winehousehuntervalley.com.au)* streamlines the wine experience, bringing the region's standout labels and new releases under one roof. From shiraz and semillon to boutique varietals, it's an easy way to explore the region's diversity without hopping between cellar doors. Knowledgeable staff guide tastings like Hunter Unearthed or the Icon Wine Journey, with optional tasting plates for nibbles alongside your wine.

TOP TIPS

- In spring, see the gardens in bloom and catch a concert, including **A Day on the Green** *(adayonthegreen.com.au)* at Bimbadgen Estate. The **Lovedale Long Lunch** *(lovedalelonglunch.com.au)* in May is a foodie highlight.
- Avoid driving at dawn or dusk when kangaroos and other animals are most active.
- Cycle Palmers Lane picking up a rental bike from the **Grapemobile** *(grapemobile.com.au; per day $65)* bike shed and visit six family-run wineries including Moorebank.
- An all-inclusive full-day wine tour with **Boutique Tours Australia** *(boutiquetoursaustralia.com.au)* or **Autopia Tours** *(autopiatours.com.au)* includes tastings, lunch and transport to/from Sydney.

Coffs Harbour & the Mid North Coast

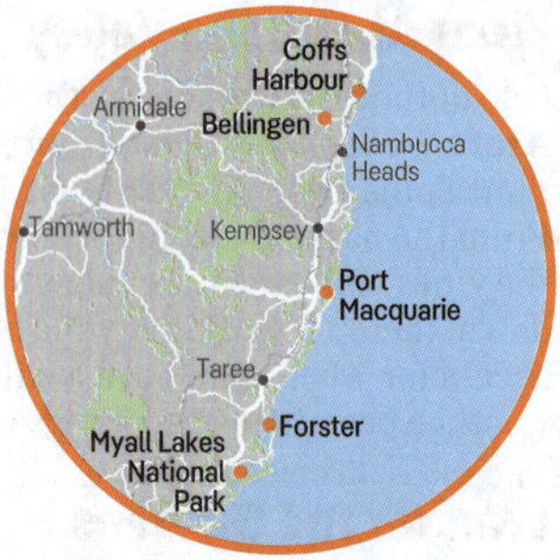

BEACHES & SURFING | COASTAL NATURE | FAMILY FUN

Places

☑ TOP TIP

The Mid North Coast heaves during school holidays, particularly over summer and Easter, which can leave accommodation in short supply. With dozens of excellent camping grounds on this stretch of coast, pitching a tent is a great budget alternative. Book national-park sites online in advance.

The New South Wales' Mid North Coast stretches roughly 400km from Myall Lakes National Park north of Port Stephens to Woolgoolga, just beyond Coffs Harbour. The landscape is textured by sclerophyll forests, subtropical rainforest and sparkling lakes and estuaries, which glisten under an annually high concentration of sunny days.

The Pacific Hwy runs inland from the coast, with winding byways branching off through bushland and farmland to sleepy seaside hamlets where surfing and fishing are central to life.

Coffs Harbour, the largest northern city, is intersected by a busy highway, contrasting with the quiet stretches beyond. Port Macquarie, the second-largest city, is often seen as a retirement hub but this historic place offers plenty to explore.

Coffs Harbour

TIME FROM SYDNEY: **5HR 40MIN**

Island walk with migratory whales and muttonbirds

Joined to Coffs Harbour by the northern breakwall in 1935, **Muttonbird Island** *(nationalparks.nsw.gov.au)* – known as Giidany Miirlarl (Place of the Moon) to the Gumbaynggirr people – has a steep 1km walk (around an hour return) to the viewpoint overlooking the Solitary Islands. From late August to early April, thousands of wedge-tailed shearwaters (muttonbirds) nest here. Take a self-guided audio tour with Elder Uncle Mark Flanders (download the Muttonbird Island Nature Reserve app on App Store and Google Play) to learn the Aboriginal significance of this seabird rookery. The

GETTING AROUND

The main airports are in Port Macquarie (serving Sydney, Lord Howe Island, Brisbane and Melbourne) and Coffs Harbour (serving Sydney and Brisbane). **Greyhound** *(greyhound.com.au)* operates long-distance routes, with other buses connecting major towns along the Pacific Hwy, but a car is needed to reach smaller villages and national parks. Road trippers can enjoy the scenic Old Pacific Hwy and coastal drives such as Lakes Way via Forster-Tuncurry. Larger towns also provide local buses, taxis and rideshare options.

ROBERT HARDING VIDEO/SHUTTERSTOCK

Muttonbird Island

island is also an excellent vantage point for whale migration from May to November.

Marine-life encounters

On weekends, the small **Solitary Islands Aquarium** *(solitary islandsaquarium.com; adult/child $18/12)* in Charlesworth Bay – belonging to Southern Cross University's Marine Science Centre – is open to the public. The touch-tanks and enthusiastic, well-qualified guides provide close encounters with an octopus and the fish and coral that inhabit the waters of the Solitary Islands Marine Park just off the coast, where the warm waters of the East Australian Current meet cooler waters from the south, bringing together a cornucopia of marine life. Visits are offered in 90-minute slots; book in advance.

Bellingen

TIME FROM COFFS HARBOUR: **30MIN**

Explore historic towns and riverside wildlife

In the heart of Bellinger Valley, Bellingen charms with riverside views, organic markets and a creative community hosting events like the **Bellingen Readers & Writers Festival** *(bell ingenwritersfestival.com.au)* in June. Its historical buildings reflect its logging past, showcased at the **Bellingen Museum** *(bellingenmuseum.org.au; adult/child $5/free)* on Hyde St. At

BIG BANANA

The **Big Banana** *(big banana.com)* didn't start out as a national icon. It was born as a clever idea by banana grower John Landi in 1964 to draw visitors to his roadside fruit stand. Builder Alan Harvey completed the 13m-long, 5m-high, 2.4m-wide timber-framed, ferroconcrete banana in just three months.

Over the decades, it became arguably Australia's most famous 'Big Thing'; it was even voted the world's most bizarre tourist attraction in 1995, beating the Big Pineapple and Amsterdam's Giant Penis seat. Contrary to rumours, it hasn't shrunk; visitors have just grown. Today, the Big Banana anchors a full-fledged fun park, visited by over a million people a year, with attractions like a huge indoor slide, mini golf, a toboggan ride – as well as treats like chocolate-coated frozen bananas.

EATING & DRINKING ON THE COFFS COAST: OUR PICKS

Aanuka Beach House: Delicious wood-fired pizzas served beneath palm trees, steps from the beach. Go for weekend bottomless brunch. *7am-late* $$

Hilltop Store: Great coffee and refined cafe fare served in a lovely former general store in Sawtell. *6am-2pm Mon-Fri, 7am-2.30pm Sat & Sun* $$

Treeo: Beneath one of the giant fig trees on Sawtell's main drag, this popular cafe turns out great coffee, homemade cakes and cafe fare. *6am-5pm* $$

Latitude 30: Sumptuous seafood platters and steaks by the water in Coffs Harbour, with indoor and outdoor seating. *11am-10pm* $$$

BELLINGEN'S BEST SHOPPING

A Chair in There: Tiny vintage shop with upcycled furniture and random knick-knacks such as candelabras and baskets.

Handmade Tania Angeli: Locally designed women's clothing crafted from natural fabrics and plant-based dyes.

Habitat Indoor Nursery: This former petrol station turned nursery sells plants, pots, crystals, gifts, plus very good coffee.

Potters Collective: Local ceramicists sell their pieces in this design store, which occasionally offers two-hour workshops.

Silver Mill: One-of-a-kind silver and gold jewellery pieces, handmade on-site. Some have gems and stones inlaid.

Retro Bello: Large collection of secondhand clothing and homewares in a bright shopfront. Everything is neat and categorised.

CHAMELEONSEYE/SHUTTERSTOCK

Port Macquarie Coastal Walk

dusk, **Lavenders Bridge** provides a spectacular view of thousands of fruit bats emerging from Bellingen Island on the river.

Drive through rainforests and past spectacular waterfalls

Considered NSW's most scenic drive, the 200km **Waterfall Way** *(nationalparks.nsw.gov.au)* links national parks between Bellingen and Armidale, winding through subtropical rainforest and lush valleys and past spectacular waterfalls. You can drive from Coffs Harbour to Armidale in just over two hours. If you're short on time, the highlight is the 115km stretch from Bellingen to the Wollomombi Falls Picnic Area. From Bellingen, the road winds through rainforest to Dorrigo National Park, where you can swim in the deep (but cold) pool at **Dangar Falls**. From there, it's a 40-minute drive to **Ebor Falls** with gorge-edge platforms and a further 30 minutes to **Wollomombi Falls**, the tallest along the route, viewed from a platform.

Port Macquarie

TIME FROM BELLINGEN: 1½HR

Lighthouse walk with eight beaches and whale watching

The wonderful **Port Macquarie Coastal Walk** *(nationalparks.nsw.gov.au)* begins at Westport Park near the Town Green foreshore and winds for about 9km along the coast to **Tacking Point Lighthouse** on the southern fringe of Sea Acres National Park. There are plenty of opportunities for

EATING & DRINKING IN BELLINGEN: OUR PICKS

Bellingen Gelato Bar: Made from scratch with local ingredients, gelato flavours span passionfruit sorbet to Persian *bastani. 11am-5pm* **$**

Bruno's: Serving modern-Mediterranean plates like Dorrigo beef carpaccio are best shared – you'll want to try them all. *5-8.30pm Wed & Thu, from 4pm Fri & Sat* **$$**

Charlie's at Church: Rustic, handmade Italian pastas, sourdough pizzas and a wicked tiramisu. *Bellissimo. 5-8pm Wed-Sat* **$$**

Bellingen Brewery & Co: Pair artisan brews with wood-fired pizzas in this cosy back-lane brewery. *5-10pm Mon-Thu, 4-11pm Fri, from noon Sun* **$$**

swimming (it takes in eight beaches) and between May and November, you can view the whale migration. The walk can be divided into shorter 2km to 3km sections, with buses 323, 155, 325 and 340 stopping at key points to return to town or your starting point.

See the sharks of Fish Rock Cave

A 25-minute drive north of Hat Head, the larger yet relaxed coastal town of **South West Rocks** is the launch point for one of Australia's best scuba dives. Running 125m through Fish Rock, a rocky outcrop 2km southeast of Smoky Cape, Fish Rock Cave is one of the only places in the world where critically endangered grey nurse sharks can be seen year-round, with large numbers known to congregate around the cave entrance in the summer months. You'll need to be Advanced Open Water (AOW) certified to dive the deep end of the cave. **South West Rocks Dive Centre** *(swrdive.com.au; per day $260)* can take you there.

Historic gaol with coastal walks and wildlife sightings

Trial Bay, named after the 1816 shipwreck of the *Trial*, stretches east from the township. Its eastern half is protected by Arakoon National Park, popular with kangaroos, kookaburras and campers. On the headland sits the sandstone **Trial Bay Gaol** *(nationalparks.nsw.gov.au; adult/child $11/8)*, built betweem 1877 and 1886 for convicts constructing a breakwall that was later washed away. Used briefly in WWI to intern German and Austrian men, it now operates as a museum offering insight into colonial prison life. Even without going inside, the 4km beach walk from town has sweeping coastal views and regular kangaroo sightings.

Forster

TIME FROM SYDNEY: **3½HR**

Cruise golden sands and endless coastal towns

Forster is a classic Aussie beach town, attracting retirees and young families with its easy pace and endless coastline. With beaches in every direction, you'll find one for every mood. **Forster Beach** is popular for swimming and surf lessons, while **One Mile Beach**, a few minutes away, is where locals walk dogs and kids race the giant 1.6km sand dune. Cross the bridge to Tuncurry for quieter sands and calm water. Walk the **Forster Breakwater** to spot dolphins.

BEST MID-NORTH COASTAL WALKS

Yuraygir Coastal Walk, Yuraygir National Park: This 65km epic walk (four days; moderate) follows a waymarked trail from Angourie to Red Rock.

Look at Me Now Headland Walk, Moonee Beach Nature Reserve: Watch whales in winter and kangaroos year-round; 1.6km (30 minutes; easy) loop, north of Coffs Harbour.

Port Macquarie Coastal Walk, Sea Acres National Park: The ultimate 9km (three hours; moderate) workout.

Diamond Head Loop Walk, Crowdy Bay National Park: Expect coastal views aplenty on this 4.3km (1½ hours; moderate) loop.

Booti Walking Track, Booti Booti National Park: An 8km loop (two to three hours; moderate) from the sea to Wallis Lake, north of Seal Rocks.

EATING & DRINKING IN PORT MACQUARIE: OUR PICKS

Little Shack: Coffee, cocktails and casual dining by the river. *6.30am-9pm Tue-Sun, to 2.30pm Mon* $

Stick Bar: A cute cocktail and yakitori bar in an alley beside Bill's Fishhouse. *5-10pm Tue-Thu, 4-11pm Fri & Sat* $

Stunned Mullet: Opposite Town Beach, Port Macquarie's top restaurant serves the region in its seasonal degustation menu. *noon-2.30pm & 5.30-9pm Tue-Sat* $$$

Zebu Bar & Grill: For a perfect summer day, sip cocktails and eat Italian. Live music on Fridays and Saturdays. *7am-9pm Sun-Thu, to 1pm Fri & Sat* $

BRIDGING TWO TOWNS

Before the Forster–Tuncurry bridge opened in 1959, crossing Wallis Lake required patience and timing. Cars queued for a vehicular punt, passengers paid to ride the *Alma G II* and a launch towed ferries across sandbars that shifted daily. Surfers arrived in station wagons, slept in cars or on the beach and filled the picture theatre at night.

When the bridge opened, it changed how people arrived and how locals lived. Work, school, shopping and surfing no longer depended on tides or timetables. Tourism scaled up, the towns knitted together and habits slowly changed. Today, the low concrete bridge looks unremarkable, but its impact was lasting. Walk across at sunset and you'll see fisherfolk casting lines, pelicans cruising below and traffic whizzing overhead.

Explore coastal lakes and ancient indigenous sites

Less than an hour inland from Forster, **Myall Lakes National Park** *(nationalparks.nsw.gov.au)* is a 400-sq-km haven of lakes, islands, rainforest and beaches. It's great for bird watching or exploring coastal trails around Mungo Brush for wildflowers or dingoes. Over 20 car-accessible camping grounds dot the park; check the **Bombah Ferry** *(nationalparks.nsw.gov.au; per car/pedestrian $6.50/2.50)* if you're travelling between Bombah Point and Mungo Brush. At the southern end, **Dark Point Aboriginal Place** near Hawks Nest has a short walk across dunes to sacred Worimi artefacts and middens dating back 4000 years.

Uncrowded beaches and historic lighthouse views

One of the prettiest spots on this coast, Seal Rocks is a small village surrounded by Myall Lakes National Park, which protects it from development. Hugging Sugarloaf Bay, it has three beautiful, uncrowded beaches. A steep 660m walk to the **Sugarloaf Point Lighthouse** provides epic views, with a path to **Lighthouse Beach** for surfing. **Number One Beach** has rock pools, gentle surf and white sand. Nearby Seal Rocks islets once hosted fur seals. Accommodation is limited to cabins, camping grounds and lighthouse cottages, so booking ahead is advised.

Traverse rugged cliffs and scenic mountain lookouts

Known for its rock formations and rugged cliffs, **Crowdy Bay National Park** *(nationalparks.nsw.gov.au)*, north of Forster, backs onto a long beach, with seven walking tracks including a serene 4.3km (1½ hours) track looping Diamond Head. The roads running through the park are unsealed and can be bumpy, but the dappled light through the gum trees makes it a lovely drive. Camping is available at a few spots, including the popular Diamond Head, Indian Head and Kylie's Beach.

Immediately north of Crowdy Bay, **Dooragan National Park** *(nationalparks.nsw.gov.au)* on the shores of Watson Taylors Lake is dominated by North Brother Mountain. A sealed road leads to the lookout at the top, which has incredible views of the coast, or you can try the challenging 3km **Laurieton Track** (1½ hours one way) through blackbutt and eucalypt forest to the summit.

EATING IN FORSTER: BEST CAFES

Beach Bums: A no-frills local favourite for a takeaway coffee for morning walks. Try the bacon and egg roll. *5.45am-2pm* **$**

Tarrt: Small cafe roasting its own coffee blend and serving generous breakfast dishes. *7am-3pm Mon-Sat, to 2.30pm Sun* **$**

Nineteen 59: Great spot for a caffeine fix and delicious breakfast favourites. Grab takeaway and enjoy it by the waterfront. *6.30am-2pm* **$**

Cafe Toscano: More greenhouse than cafe, with a lovely atmosphere for a long brunch. *8am-8.30pm* **$$**

Byron Bay

BEACHES & NATURE | WELLNESS | BRUNCH

At the point where the Northern Rivers meet the Pacific, Byron Bay is a sun-soaked town famous for surf, sand, a bohemian vibe – and yes, a few celebrity homes too. In summer, the beaches fill with surfers, paddleboarders and families; year-round, cafes, galleries and boutique shops keep the town buzzing. The hinterland climbs into rolling hills, rainforest and historic villages including Bangalow and Mullumbimby, linked by winding roads and scenic trails. The entire region (also known as the Northern Rivers) is situated on Bundjalung Country, which stretches from Grafton up into southeast Queensland and west towards the Great Dividing Range.

Today, life revolves around both coast and hinterland: summer waves, winter whale migrations, farmers markets, artisanal cafes and farm-to-table dining. If you're after a quieter pace, nearby Brunswick Heads and Lennox Head deliver calm beaches and fashion-forward shops. Still, Byron Bay remains the Northern Rivers' crown jewel – a mix of natural beauty, creative energy and laid-back coastal charm that keeps visitors coming back.

TOP TIP

Byron Bay recently became Australia's first destination to ban surfing without a leg rope. You can also help to keep others and yourself safe in the surf by following the key rules of the surfer's code: give right of way, don't drop in and don't let go of your board.

GETTING AROUND

The region's main domestic airport is in Ballina, 740km north of Sydney, but Gold Coast International Airport, just across the border from Tweed Heads in Coolangatta, offers more flight options. Shuttle buses run from both airports to Byron, but services are limited – early or late flights typically require a taxi or private transfer. Local rideshare services are also limited. Cycling is popular along the coast and on the new **Northern Rivers Rail Trail** *(northernriversrailtrail.com.au)*, with bike hire available in most towns. Byron can get choked with traffic during school holidays, making central accommodation a worthwhile splurge.

HIGHLIGHTS
1 Cape Byron Walking Track
2 Tallow Beach
3 Three Blue Ducks

SIGHTS
see 3 Balloon Aloft
4 Belongil Beach
5 Cape Byron Distillery
6 Cape Byron Lighthouse
7 Clarkes Beach
8 Cozy Corner
9 Little Wategos Beach
10 Main Beach
11 Wategos Beach

ACTIVITIES
12 Bende Byron Bay
13 Black Dog Surf School
14 Byron Bay Ballooning
15 Byron Yoga Centre
see 17 Cape Byron Kayaks
16 Comma
17 Go Sea Kayaks
18 Nimbus & Co
19 Skydive Byron Bay
20 Soma
21 Soul Surf School
22 Sundive
23 Whale Watching Byron Bay

SLEEPING
24 Byron Bay YHA
25 Sunseeker

EATING
26 Bang Bang
27 Bayleaf
28 Folk
29 Frankies Gelato
30 Il Buco
31 Japonaise Kitchen
32 No Bones
33 Pixie Food & Wine
34 Raes Dining Room
35 Vagabond
36 Yulli's

DRINKING & NIGHTLIFE
37 Bar Heather
38 Beach Hotel
39 Casa Luna
40 Railway Friendly Bar

ENTERTAINMENT
41 Byron Bay Bluesfest

SHOPPING
42 Byron Beachside Market
43 Byron Farmers Market
44 Byron Twilight Market

EATING IN BYRON BAY: BEST VEGAN & VEGETARIAN EATS

No Bones: A talked-about vegan restaurant even carnivores will love. Dishes are tapas-style and best shared around the table. *5-9pm Sun-Thu, to 10pm Fri & Sat* **$$**

Yulli's: Vegan Asian dishes with a Mediterranean twist and lots of flavour. *noon-10pm Tue-Sun* **$$**

Vagabond: Pick from colourful, nutritious smoothie bowls to mushrooms on toast with vegan feta. *6.30am-3pm Mon-Sat, 7am-2pm Sun* **$**

Folk: Has a great selection of vegan and vegetarian breakfast dishes in a rustic setting. Expect dogs and owners. *7.30am-2.30pm* **$$**

Channel Your Inner Yogi

Dip into Byron's wellness scene

You could spend a lifetime sampling every offering in this well-established wellness hub. Choose from yoga, Pilates (mat and Reformer) and *barre* at **Bende Byron Bay** *(bende.com.au; mat/Reformer $30/40)*, while course-based **Byron Yoga Centre** *(byronyoga.com)* offers free classes hosted by trainees. Top off an infrared sauna session with an ice bath at **Nimbus & Co** *(nimbusco.com.au; hot-cold/standard sauna session $45/35)*, or wind down with a nourishing massage at **Comma** *(commaspaces.com; bath house $80, massages from $160)*. Escape to a hinterland retreat, such as **Gaia Retreat & Spa** *(gaiaretreat.com.au)* or **Soma** *(somabyron.com.au)*, the retreat featured in the US TV drama series *Nine Perfect Strangers*.

A Scenic Caper

Stand on mainland Australia's most easterly point

Spectacular views reward those who climb up to Cape Byron (Walgun) from the Captain Cook Lookout on the **Cape Byron Walking Track** *(nationalparks.nsw.gov.au)*. Ribboning around the headland and through rainforest, the track dips and (mostly) soars its way to the 1901 **lighthouse** perched atop the Cape. Look out for dolphins (year-round) and migrating whales (June to October). Koalas are also occasionally spotted along the trail. Allow about two hours for the entire 3.7km loop.

Rural Foodie Fun

Spend a day at the Farm

This photogenic, 32-hectare farm near the Pacific Hwy turn off to Byron Bay is shared by the **Three Blue Ducks** *(thefarm.com.au/threeblueducks)* all-day restaurant, a produce store, the Bread Social bakery, the Baylato gelato bar, a florist and a nursery. With loads of space for kids to run wild and easy parking, it's particularly popular with families. Download a map from the Farm's website and roam the veggie plots and cattle-and-pig-dotted fields; kids love joining farmers to feed the animals at 10.30am. Book in advance for guided tours and workshops for adults and kids.

BYRON'S BEST FESTIVALS

Byron Bay Bluesfest: Held over the Easter long weekend, attracting huge international acts and local heavyweights.

Mullum Roots Festival: A multi-venue festival with ARIA winners and local talent performing in Mullumbimby.

Byron Bay Writers' Festival: Gathers together big-name, predominantly Australian writers in Bangalow in August.

Byron Bay International Film Festival: Showcases independent films from Australia and abroad at cinemas across the Northern Rivers region.

Byron Music Festival: Celebrating Northern Rivers artists, this event takes over Byron's Dening Park for a day in June.

Caper Byron Bay: Food and culture fest hosted at multiple local venues in May.

DRINKING IN BYRON BAY: OUR PICKS

Railway Friendly Bar: Head to 'the Rails' from 4pm on Friday for happy hour with local Byron Bay characters. *10am-midnight*

Cape Byron Distillery: Swing by for a Brookie's Gin cocktail or take a rainforest gin-tasting tour. Just out of town. *10.45am-6pm Thu-Sun*

Beach Hotel: Byron's sprawling 'Top Pub' is touristy, but has sea views and daily live music. *11am-10pm Sun-Thu, to 12.45am Fri & Sat*

Casa Luna: There's a Mediterranean-inspired menu, but it's more about the drinks and DJs at this late-night spot. *5.30pm-late Wed-Mon*

CONNECT WITH CULTURE

Delta Kay, Arakwal Bundjalung guide with **Explore Byron Bay** *(explorebyronbay.com)*, names the top places to experience local Aboriginal culture in Byron.

Join Delta on Country: Gain a deeper knowledge of this place on a walking tour. Learn the stories of the Arakwal Bundjalung people, visit sacred sites and taste bush tucker.

Discover Native Plants: After sampling raw bush tucker, learn about the medicinal uses of local plants and how they were used to make jewellery, tools and weapons.

Admire Bundjalung art: Beautiful outdoor artworks by local Arakwal artists Nickolla Clark and Kaitlyn Clark in Byron's new Jarjumirr Park showcase the cultural significance of this land.

AURELIEN DUCOS/SHUTTERSTOCK

Soak up the Splendour

Byron's beautiful beaches

One of the toughest choices in Byron Bay is deciding which beach to visit. Northwest of the town centre, **Belongil Beach** is popular with dog owners and local surfers, offering sweeping views towards Cape Byron (Walgun). At its eastern end lies **the Wreck**, a powerful right-hand surf break.

Immediately in front of town, **Main Beach** is the busiest, with lifesaver patrols and a park sloping down to the sand that often hosts buskers. The beach stretches east into **Clarkes Beach** before becoming **the Pass** at the eastern headland, home to one of the world's longest right-hand breaks.

Around the rocks, linked by the Cape Byron Walking Track, is **Wategos Beach**, a crescent of white sand fringed by rainforest and Byron's most affluent enclave. It also has a great point break. A further 400m walk leads to **Little Wategos**, a secluded beach beneath rocky Cape Byron, inaccessible by car – perfect for sunset and moonrise.

Tucked under the south side of the Cape (entry via Tallow Beach Rd) is **Cosy Corner**, a popular surf spot with a sheltered beach to escape northerly winds. This forms part of **Tallow Beach**, a 7km-long stretch of wild sand extending south from the Cape. The northern end is backed by Arakwal

EATING IN BYRON BAY: OUR PICKS

Frankies Gelato: Upping Byron's gelato game with flavours like sticky chai, or blood orange and basil sorbet, with lots of vegan options. *10.30am-late* $

Il Buco: An Italian pizza chef does his homeland proud at this casual laneway pizzeria. BYO booze. *5.30pm-late Wed-Mon* $$

Bayleaf: Byron's original brunch spot remains as popular as ever, with a takeaway counter if you can't wait for a table. *7am-1pm* $$

Japonaise Kitchen: Generous portions of great-value Japanese comfort food (choices range from sushi to *kaa rage*), served lightning-fast. *11am-8pm* $$

Main Beach

National Park, while the south reaches the suburb of Suffolk Park and scenic **Broken Head Beach**. Just south of here, **Kings Beach** is a popular nude beach.

A New Way to See Wildlife

Take a night-vision walk

One of Australia's most innovative wildlife tours sees you don night-vision goggles to view nocturnal critters in a local reserve, from pademelons to microbats. Advance Ecotourism–certified **Vision Walks** *(visionwalks.com.au; adult/child $189/160)* also offers a range of daytime tours, from platypus-spotting excursions to waterfall adventure tours.

Rainforest Trails & Glamping

Trek ancient rainforests and lush coastal headlands

Venture into the wild on the **Gidjuum Gulganyi Walk**, a four-day, 48km trek through lush headlands and ancient Gondwana rainforest. The second day is the toughest: 18.4km with 1035m of ascent. Stop along the way for a detour to **Unicorn Falls** (3km return), a hidden cascade spilling into a turquoise pool. Rain brings leeches, so spray boots, socks and pants with DEET, wear gloves and keep a saltshaker handy for easy removal.

BYRON'S BEST OUTDOOR THRILLS

Diving and snorkelling: Explore marine life of the Julian Rocks Nguthungulli Nature Reserve, 2.5km offshore, on a dive/snorkel with Sundive.

Kayaking with dolphins: Cape Byron Kayaks and Go Sea Kayaks offer paddling tours off Clarkes Beach to spot turtles and dolphins.

Surfing lessons: Learn how to ride waves with Black Dog Surf School or Soul Surf School.

Whale watching: Boat tours of the annual whale migration with Whale Watching Byron Bay (June to October).

Skydiving: Clock Byron from 15,000ft with Skydive Byron Bay.

Hot-air ballooning: Float above Byron with Balloon Aloft or Byron Bay Ballooning.

EATING IN BYRON BAY: OUR PICKS

Bang Bang: Pan-Asian crowd-pleasers, moody lighting and a fun vibe make this a popular spot for celebrations. *5-11pm Mon-Sat, to 10pm Sun* $$

Pixie Food & Wine: When only a classic homemade pasta will do, this nostalgic Jonson La Italian delivers. *5-11pm Mon-Thu, from noon Fri-Sun* $$

Bar Heather: You'll find Byron's best, natural-focused wine list and an ever-changing menu of elegant contemporary dishes. *5pm-midnight Tue-Sat* $$$

Raes Dining Room: Special occasions call for a Mediterranean-inspired affair, with Wategos Beach views. *noon-2.15pm & 6-8.15pm Mon-Sat, noon-4pm Sun* $$$

ANCIENT SUSTAINABLE DINING

Middens (piles of shells and bones left by Aboriginal people) found along the North Coast show the deep connection between local Aboriginal groups and this abundant landscape. They're an ancient form of sustainable dining, revealing how people used the land and even traded with other groups.

About 30 minutes' drive north of Coffs Harbour, Arrawarra Headland has an Aboriginal fish trap, a low-impact hunting technique, visible at low tide. Many middens contain burials, making them culturally significant, but they're fragile and threatened by erosion, off-road vehicles and unregulated tracks.

The **Yarrawarra Aboriginal Cultural Centre** *(yarrawarra.com.au)* at Corindi Beach and Minjungbal Aboriginal Cultural Centre (p189) in Tweed Heads, along with Aboriginal-guided tours, provide a richer understanding of these historic sites.

GLEN BERLIN/SHUTTERSTOCK

Byron Farmers Market

Self-guided hikers pay around $173 for three nights, while guided glamping tours with **Connect Adventures** *(connectadventures.com.au; $1800)* include meals, tents and hot showers.

The Market Beat

The flavours, crafts and community of Byron Bay

Visiting Byron Bay's markets is a great way to get a feel for the town and its local producers, makers and creatives. On the first Sunday of each month, the **Byron Bay Community Market** takes over the Main Beach (p180) foreshore. With around 300 stalls, you'll find everything from handmade crafts to global foods, plus busking and face-painting for the kids.

If you're after something smaller and arts-focused, check out the **Byron Twilight Market** at Railway Park. Running at 4pm every Saturday from October to May, it's a relaxed spot to browse jewellery, leather goods, clothing and accessories while listening to live local music.

For fresh produce, the **Byron Farmers Market** on Thursday mornings is the place to go. Started in 2002 by local farmers, it's where you can grab oysters, cheese, bread, honey and seasonal fruit and vegetables.

The **Byron Beachside Market**, held east of the surf club during school holidays, showcases local makers with ceramics, textiles, fashion and art. There's live music and wellness practitioners, making it easy to spend a couple of hours exploring, tasting and chatting with the people behind the stalls.

Beyond Byron Bay

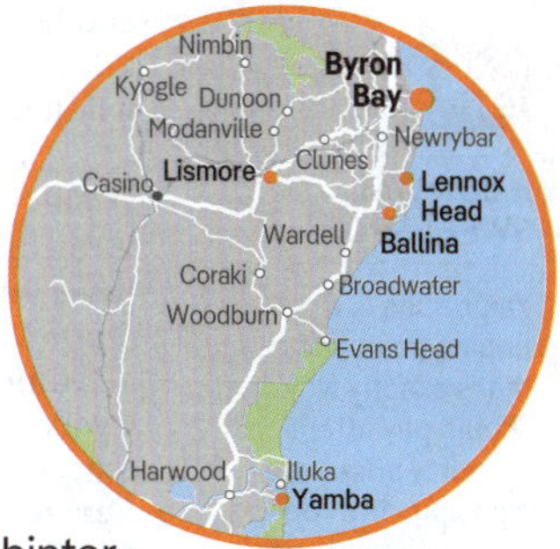

You'll find surf breaks, quiet beaches, lush hinterland, historic villages and farm-fresh cafes across the Northern Rivers.

Beyond Byron Bay, the Northern Rivers reveal a quieter, low-key side of the coast. Yamba, often called the 'new Byron Bay', sits at the mouth of the Clarence River and remains refreshingly low-rise, with a string of beaches, surf breaks, headlands and pools, plus fresh-off-the-trawler seafood. Ballina and Lennox Head have a relaxed coastal lifestyle, fishing spots and surf-friendly beaches, while inland, Lismore and the hinterland rise into rolling hills, rainforest and villages like Bangalow and Mullumbimby, complete with markets, walking trails and farm-to-table cafes. From coast to hinterland, the region delivers a slower-paced, authentic Northern Rivers experience, one to enjoy before gentrification reshapes the landscape.

Places

GETTING AROUND

Getting around towns near Byron Bay, like Yamba, Lismore and Ballina, is easiest by car, giving you freedom to explore the beaches and hinterland at your own pace. **NSW TrainLink** *(transportnsw.info)* coach services connect Byron Bay to surrounding towns, but services can be infrequent, especially in early mornings or evenings. Plan ahead if taking public transport. Walking and cycling are ideal within town centres, with bike hire widely available.

Yamba

TIME FROM BYRON BAY: **1HR 25MIN**

A surfer's paradise

There are waves for every kind of surfer along Yamba's coastline. **Pippi Beach** and ., near the breakwall, pick up a north wind well, while a southerly favours **Angourie Point**, Turners or Main Beach. Most beaches work when the wind is from the west. For calmer waters or safe paddling for kids, **Whiting Beach** is a 10-minute walk from town and is also popular with kayakers and stand-up paddleboarders.

A 10-minute drive north brings you to Angourie, home to one of the world's top point breaks – not for beginners. Nearby **Blue & Green Pools** offer stunning freshwater swimming, but reaching them requires scrambling down a rocky, unmarked cliff, so it's best to wait for a local to guide the way.

Ancient emu trails and ochre cliffs

The 65km **Yuraygir Coastal Walk** *(nationalparks.nsw.gov.au)* stretches from Angourie to Red Rock along ancient emu trails. Tackle the full multiday trek with camping or choose sections via seven car-accessible beachside camping grounds. Discover sea caves, rock pools, hidden beaches and ochre-cliff views. The track crosses beaches, trails, rocky platforms

A COASTAL SWEET SPOT

Yamba sits at a tipping point and that's exactly why you should pay attention. Property prices are climbing, developers are circling and comparisons to Byron Bay are starting to surface, but for now, this fishing town at the mouth of the Clarence River still feels refreshingly low-key. Just 15km east of the Pacific Hwy,

Yamba delivers the kind of classic coastal escape that's getting harder to find. Founded in 1908, its Surf Life Saving Club is one of Australia's oldest and the coastline is stitched together with surf breaks, ocean pools and headlands. Fresh-off-the-trawler seafood remains part of daily life rather than a menu buzzword. With gentrification creeping in but not yet taking hold, visit now, while this beach town still feels like itself.

and headlands, marked by the coastal emu footprint. Watch tides, pack extra food if seas are rough and enjoy the wildlife, wildflowers and scenery of Gumbaynggirr and Yaegl Country.

Wander coastal rainforests and UNESCO-listed trails

Stretching for 25km along the coast north of the Clarence River to South Evans Head, **Bundjalung National Park** *(nationalparks.nsw.gov.au)* is a wonderfully wild slice of coastal rainforest, with some great walks, paddling routes (BYO kayak) and camping grounds. The southern parts can be easily reached from Yamba via the passenger-only **Clarence River Ferries** *(clarenceriverferries.com; adult/child $11.60/5.80)* to Iluka (at least four daily). This section of the park includes Iluka Nature Reserve, where the **Iluka Rainforest Walking Track** (5.2km return, two hours, hard) takes you through UNESCO-listed Gondwana rainforest to Iluka Bluff for superb views and the option for a swim at **Ten Mile Beach**, which unfurls on the other side of the bluff.

Ballina

TIME FROM BYRON BAY: **30MIN**

Enjoy Northern Rivers art

The excellent regional **Northern Rivers Community Gallery** *(nrcgballina.com.au; free)* in Ballina represents the area's strong creative community. Housed in the former Ballina Municipal Council Chambers, built in 1927, it hosts a roster of exhibitions that showcase local artists and craftspeople and has a great cafe. The adjacent Ignite Studios offers daylong beginners' **workshops** *(from $150)* in ceramics, weaving and painting with local artists.

Walk from Ballina to Lennox Head

The **Ballina Shire Coastal Path** links beaches and headlands for 8km between East Ballina's North Wall and Lennox Head's **Pat Morton Lookout**. Views are especially stunning from June to October when migrating whales can be spotted. The 6km **Aboriginal Cultural Ways** section, from Angels Beach to Pat Morton, features 22 panels with Bundjalung stories and artwork. Scan QR codes for audio stories, or join a guided cultural experience with Ngangbul Bundjalung woman Lois Cook, whose great-grandfather survived the East Ballina massacre.

EATING & DRINKING IN YAMBA & ANGOURIE: OUR PICKS

Bay St Local: Cute local corner cafe slinging coffees and tasty burgers for lunch. *7am-2pm* **$$**

Beachwood Cafe: Cookbook author Sevtap Yüce delivers her bold Turkish flavours to the plate at this wonderful little cafe. *7am-2pm Tue-Sat* **$$**

Paradiso: Wash down the likes of dumplings, bao and pan-Asian share plates with cool cocktails. *5-11pm Wed, to 11.30pm Thu-Sat* **$$**

Kiosk: Sip coffee with the best view in town from this tiny kiosk with outdoor seating and umbrellas. *6.30am-noon Mon & Fri, to 1pm Sat & Sun* **$**

CHRIS HAMLIN/SHUTTERSTOCK

Seven Mile Beach and Lake Ainsworth

Lennox Head

TIME FROM BYRON BAY: **20MIN**

Swim in tea-tree-stained waters and healing lakes

At the northern end of the tiny beach town of Lennox Head, just behind **Seven Mile Beach**, large **Lake Ainsworth** is a popular picnic spot, protected somewhat from the northeasterly winds that can batter the beach. Stained dark brown by tannins from the melaleuca trees surrounding the freshwater lake, its waters are said to have healing properties. Signage is erected when occasional blue-green algae blooms make swimming a bad idea.

Browse historic boutiques and farm-gate stalls

Swing off the highway and into Newrybar, a historic one-street village. Grab a coffee and a pastry at the **Little General**, then browse the **Flower House** *(ourlittleflowerfarm.com)* for fragrant bouquets or bespoke arrangements. Step into **Newrybar Merchants** to find some local homewares in a beautifully restored 1890s homestead. Take a short drive through the surrounding countryside to peek into coffee and macadamia plantations, or stop at farm-gate stalls along Broken Head, Brooklet and Piccadilly Hill roads.

SAVING THE BIG PRAWN

Constructed in 1989 to honour the local prawning industry, Ballina's **Big Prawn** was nearly thrown on the BBQ in 2009, but no one had the stomach to dispatch it. After a $400,000 restoration in 2013 by hardware giant Bunnings to add a much-needed tail, the 9m, 35-tonne crustacean rising from the edge of the Bunnings car park on River St is looking good enough to eat following a fresh paint job in 2023.

Ballina is well known for its sweet and juicy prawns, which you can purchase fresh or cooked from the **Fishermen's Co-op** *(ballinafishermenscoop.com.au)*, a short hop along River St. In East Ballina, **Richmond Oysters** *(richmondoystersballina.com.au)* specialises in fresh prawns and oysters (Pacific and Sydney rock varieties).

EATING & DRINKING IN BALLINA & LENNOX HEAD: OUR PICKS

Belle General: Bliss out over wholesome bowls and free-range egg-and-bacon rolls at this destination cafe opposite Shelly Beach in East Ballina. *8am-2pm* $

Shelter: Tasty offerings, with a superb scallop dish on high rotation. Opposite the beach in Lennox. *7am-2pm Mon-Wed, to 9pm Thu-Sat, to 3pm Sun* $$

Hey Lady Bar & Diner: Japanese-inspired diner fare paired with refreshing cocktails. *8am-9pm Wed & Thu, to 10pm Fri & Sat, to 2pm Sun* $$

Seven Mile Brewing: Next to Ballina's airport, this family-run warehouse brewery has a cracking signature ale, the Cali Cream. *noon-6pm Fri-Sun*

EL PACO 33/SHUTTERSTOCK

Koala

BEST SURF SPOTS BEYOND BYRON BAY

Lennox Point: Famous right-hand point with serious power, delivering long, heavy waves; best for advanced surfers confident in strong swell.

Lennox Reef: A quieter alternative to Lennox Point, it offers hollow rights and fun lefts over a rock shelf, needing full tide.

Skennars Beach: A short drive from Ballina's airport, it dishes out exposed, punchy A-frames; a lively beach break for confident intermediates.

Boulder Beach: Steep, hollow waves with lots of rock underfoot; a challenging spot suited to advanced surfers, south of Skennars Beach.

Flat Rock: Calm, steady waves softened by a rocky outcrop; an easy, confidence-building spot for beginners, just north of East Ballina.

Lismore

TIME FROM BYRON BAY: **45MIN**

Go koala spotting

Lismore has a high concentration of koalas living in the region, making sightings in and around town surprisingly common. **Robinson's Lookout** is a popular picnic area where koalas can be seen dozing in treetops. For a more reliable encounter, **Vision Walk** *(visionwalks.com.au; adult/child $130/100)* runs a 3½-hour koala-spotting tour, taking you into their natural habitat to view them from a safe distance, learn of their behaviour from expert guides and enjoy morning tea. Each booking supports a local koala organisation.

Volcanic cliffs and World Heritage rainforests

The spectacular waterfalls, sheer volcanic cliffs and dense rainforest of 80-sq-km **Nightcap National Park** *(nationalparks.nsw.gov.au)* are expected in NSW's wettest area. About 45 minutes from Byron Bay or Lismore, it's part of the World Heritage–listed Gondwana Rainforests and home to many protected creatures.

The **Historic Nightcap Track** (18km, one day), originally carved by postal workers, runs from Mt Nardi to Rummery Park. The **Minyon Loop** (7.5km, 4½ hours) circles **Minyon Falls**, with a wheelchair-accessible lookout just 50m from the car park. A scenic unsealed road leads to Terania Creek Picnic Area and the 1.4km **Protesters Falls Track**; swimming is not permitted.

EATING & DRINKING IN LENNOX HEAD: OUR PICKS

Baraka: Award-winning hot spot for modern Middle Eastern cuisine (like spanner-crab sambousik and falafel). *5-8.30pm Thu & Fri, from noon Sat & Sun* $$$

Williams St: Neighbourhood hangout with live music, healthy bowls and fish tacos, for a relaxed weekend vibe. *6.30am-2.30pm daily, plus 3.30-10pm Fri & Sat* $$

Kopi: Follow the brunch crowd to the blue-and-white striped awning and order the jaffles (toasted sandwiches) and a coffee. *6.30am-2pm* $

Shelter: Beachfront dining with locally sourced food, casual breakfast and lunch. Sundowners (Thursday) are a vibe. *7am-9pm Thu-Sat, to 2pm Mon-Wed* $$

The Tweed

ART & CULTURE | ADVENTURE | GASTRONOMY

Tweed Heads sits right on the border of New South Wales and Queensland, where the Tweed River meets the ocean. It's a laid-back town with a surprisingly lively edge, blending surf culture with a growing food, cafe and craft beer scene. The riverfront is perfect for a stroll, paddleboarding or spotting dolphins, while nearby beaches cater to families and boarders alike. A short drive along the coast leads to Cabarita Beach, known for day spas and cocktail bars, and Fingal Head, where a rocky outcrop mirrors Ireland's famous Giant's Causeway.

Head inland from Tweed Heads and you'll find rolling hills, waterfalls and small towns like Murwillumbah. Spend a day walking the streets, checking out the Art Deco architecture, browsing shops and the art gallery. You'll leave knowing a little more about the people and creativity that the Tweed region is known for.

Get a Culture Hit

Arts hub with studios, galleries and Art Deco legacy

A 30-minute drive from Tweed Heads, Murwillumbah is the creative heart of the Tweed. On the riverbanks, the **M-Arts Precinct** *(m-arts.com.au)* has transformed an old industrial warehouse into a buzzing arts hub where local makers, jewellers and emerging artists showcase their talents. Grab a coffee or a bite while wandering studio pop-ups in colourful shipping containers, or head upstairs to Gallery DownTown, part of the Tweed Regional Gallery. Pick up a brochure for a self-guided walk past Art Deco shopfronts and historical buildings. Above the valley, the **Tweed Regional Gallery** *(gallery.tweed.nsw.gov.au; free; Wed - Sun)* has seven exhibition spaces and the Margaret Olley Art Centre – it's dedicated to Australia's celebrated painter known for her richly coloured still lifes and interiors and lasting influence on modern Australian art.

GETTING AROUND

Public transport in Tweed Heads is reliable, with buses covering most local routes. Walking and cycling are the best ways to explore; coastal paths provide an easy route between beaches and scenic spots. Rideshares are limited, making taxis useful for late nights or short hops. To venture beyond town and explore the wider region, hiring a car is best.

TOP TIP

From October to April, NSW is on Daylight Saving Time, but Queensland is not. If you cross the border into Coolangatta, you'll jump back an hour. Double-check your dinner reservations or flight times at Gold Coast Airport, as your phone might flip-flop between time zones.

HIGHLIGHTS
1 M-Arts Precinct
2 Northern Rivers Rail Trail

SIGHTS
3 Burringbar Range Tunnel
4 Fingal Head
5 Minjungbal Aboriginal Cultural Centre
6 Tweed Regional Gallery
7 Wollumbin National Park

ACTIVITIES
see 7 Lyrebird Track
8 Northern Rivers Bike Hire

SLEEPING
9 Blue Water Motel
10 Halcyon House

EATING
see 10 Paper Daisy
11 Pipit
12 Potager
13 Tweed River House

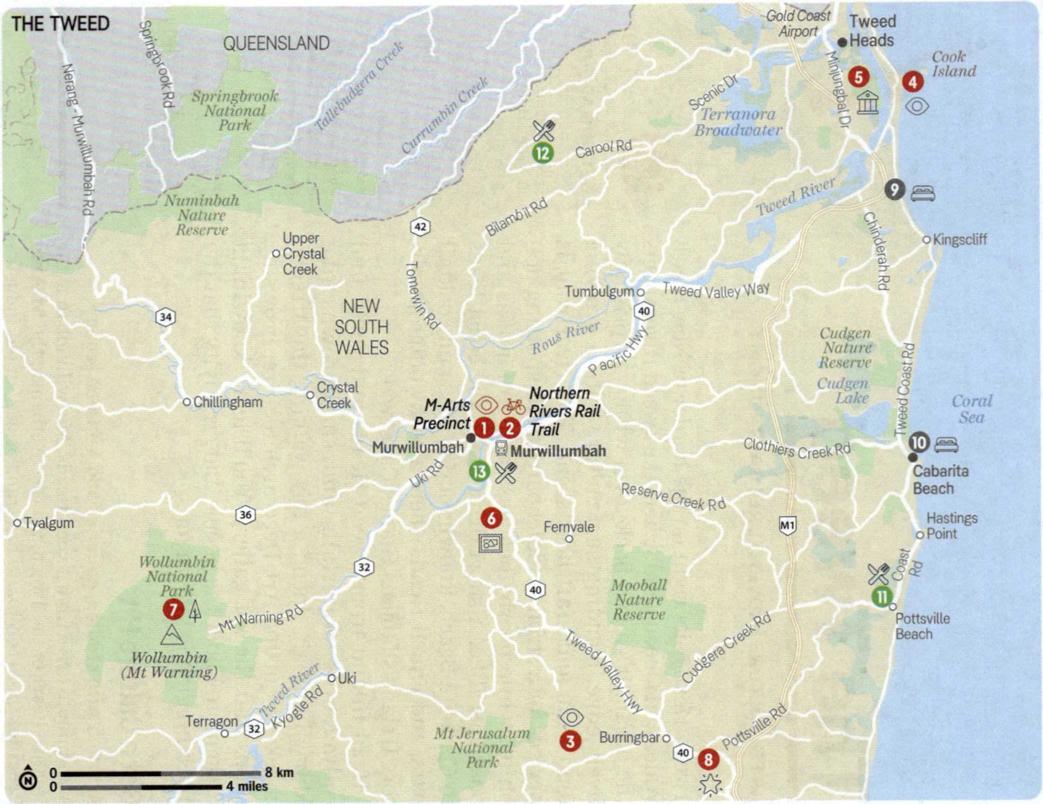

Hidden Highlight of Tweed Heads

Visit a sacred Aboriginal site

Most road trippers blaze through **Tweed Heads**, but the **Minjungbal Aboriginal Cultural Centre** *(minjungbal museum.com.au; trail free, museum adult/child $10/5)*, set in bushland in Tweed Heads South, is a great cultural stop. Browse museum panels and artefacts before strolling the 1km wheelchair-accessible nature trail with interpretative signage. Along the way, pass a bora ring, a sacred site traditionally used for men's initiation ceremonies and an important ancestral link for Minjungbal Bundjalung people.

Ride the Rails

Cycle historic railways through a glowworm-filled tunnel

Two decades after the last train, the Murwillumbah–Crabbes Creek railway corridor has been transformed into a 24km cycling trail. The **Northern Rivers Rail Trail** *(northern riversrailtrail.com.au)* follows the gentle gradients of the former train line, making an e-bike the smart choice for covering more ground. It winds through sugarcane fields and pockets of subtropical rainforest, crossing 18 bridges and tunnels including the 524m **Burringbar Range Tunnel**, home to glowworms. Bike hire and shuttle services are available through **Northern Rivers Bike Hire** *(northernriversbikehire.au; per 4hr e-bike/premium cruiser $89/49)*.

Another Giant's Causeway

Explore basalt columns and striking volcanic coastlines

Fingal Head, the Tweed's answer to Ireland's Giant's Causeway, earned its name from early explorers for its resemblance to the Northern Irish formation. The basalt columns formed when hot lava met the cool sea, creating a striking coastline that's great for wandering and taking in the views. Surf breaks and fishing spots appeal to water lovers and there are cafes and beachside stays.

WOLLUMBIN'S ENDURING SPIRIT

Rising 1157m from the lush hills of the Tweed Range, the distinctive hooked peak of **Wollumbin (Mt Warning)** can be seen from just about everywhere in this coastal region. Forming the central remnant (plug) of the ancient Tweed Volcano, it's a deeply spiritual place for its Bundjalung Traditional Custodians of the land and it's for this reason, combined with safety concerns, that the once-popular hiking route to the summit was quietly and permanently closed by NSW NPWS in 2020. Leading from Mt Warning Rd to a rainforest lookout near the base of Wollumbin, the easy 300m-return **Lyrebird Track** through **Wollumbin National Park** *(nationalparks.nsw.gov.au)* provides a taste of the ecological and cultural significance of this rainforest landscape.

EATING IN THE TWEED: BEST DESTINATION RESTAURANTS

Pipit: Chef Ben Devlin's creative uses of local produce shine at this Pottsville fine diner. *noon-3pm Fri-Sun, 6-10pm Mon & Thu* $$$

Potager: Feel like you're dining at a friend's home at this highly awarded paddock-to-plate restaurant in Carool. *noon-10.30pm Fri & Sat, to 6pm Sun* $$$

Paper Daisy: Feast on fine contemporary fare steps from Cabarita Beach in one of the Tweed's best-decorated dining rooms. *noon-10.30pm* $$$

Tweed River House: Nouvelle French dining in a restored riverside Queenslander-style house in Murwillumbah. *noon-5pm Thu & Sun, to 10pm Fri & Sat* $$$

Southern Highlands

WINE | ANTIQUE SHOPPING | WATERFALLS

Places

TOP TIP

The humble pie becomes the main attraction during Pie Time, a celebration of the meat-filled pastry in June as part of the **Winter's Wonderful** festivities. Alternatively, eat your way along 30 of the best spots on the **Pie Trail** *(visitsouthernhighlands.com.au/trip-ideas/pie-trail)*.

This small region, with Bowral sitting pretty at its centre, is a magnet for well-heeled day-trippers, lifestyle migrants and remote workers. It's just 90 minutes' drive from Sydney but feels like a world away. There's no hustle here and the only bustle you'll see is on a wedding dress at one of the many wedding venues dotted around the countryside.

Bowral's antique shops, cafes and boutiques invite you to nosy around, but there's more than just the good life. Down the road, Mittagong is like a younger sibling sitting in its shadow. Berrima has charm, Moss Vale has the amenities and saleyards, and the towering Fitzroy Falls in the divine Kangaroo Valley is perfect for wanderers.

While it's tempting to stick to the coast, if you can tear yourself away from those views, you'll find peace in this idyllic rural corner.

Bowral

TIME FROM SYDNEY: **1HR 20MIN**

Where shopping meets sports

A draw for antique shoppers and sports fans alike, charming Bowral is a thriving hub for vintage stores, antiques, homeware boutiques and galleries lining Bong Bong St. On the other end of the spectrum is the International Cricket Hall of Fame, incorporating the **Bradman Museum** *(bradman.com.au; adult/child $30/16.50)* that honours the boy from Bowral. Cricket, the interactive displays and memorabilia (including Bradman's Baggy Green hat) will keep anyone engaged for at least an hour. Walk by Donald Bradman's childhood home around the corner at 52 Shepherd St to see where he honed his batting skills by hitting a ball at a water tank for hours on end.

GETTING AROUND

This is a great destination for a car-free escape. The train from Sydney takes about 2½ hours, stopping at Bowral, Mittagong and Moss Vale, all within easy walking distance of main streets. A number of tour companies offer wine tours from Sydney. If you want to get to some smaller towns or Kangaroo Valley, you'll need a car. The roads are generally well maintained but windy.

MARTHA ALMEYDA/SHUTTERSTOCK

Bradman Museum

Farmer for a day

Step onto a true working farm in the Southern Highlands at **Mussett Holdings** *(mussettholdings.com.au; admission/semi-private tour $25/120)*; it's open on Saturdays. Guided by passionate owners Will and Connie, you'll get hands-on with the land and its produce. Walk through a vegetable garden, picking and tasting fresh crops straight from the soil, and see how mushrooms grow in carefully tended beds. Sample raw honey collected on the property and meet the resident farm animals, including pasture-raised chickens, cows, goats, sheep and Maremma dogs keeping watch. Learn about off-grid living, sustainable practices and the philosophy behind regenerative farming.

Sip cool-climate wines at elegant cellar doors

The Southern Highlands' wine scene is a mix of history, cool-climate vintages and relaxed cellar-door culture. Early attempts at winemaking in the 1800s struggled against harsh winters and frosts, despite a long, mild growing season, but by the 1980s expertise and enthusiasm revived the region. Today, Bowral's **Centennial Vineyards** *(centennial.net.au)*, first planted in 1996, stands out with its Tuscany-inspired cellar door and a portfolio of around 40 wines, including dry sparkling, Grüner Veltliner and Traminer; it also hosts festivals and concerts.

BOWRAL, BRADMAN & CRICKET

Sir Donald Bradman, widely regarded as the greatest batsman in cricket history, spent his childhood in Bowral. Dominating the sport in the 1930s and '40s, he achieved a Test batting average of 99.94. Bradman's exceptional skills and humility made him an icon and after retirement he continued to help develop the game. He was recognised with a knighthood in 1949 for his services to the game. Today, cricket is one of the most popular sports in Australia, with Test matches (lasting five days), one-day matches and short T20 (20 overs) games played year-round. The Ashes, a biennial Test match between Australia and England, is the highlight of the cricket calendar evoking intense competition and national pride.

EATING & DRINKING IN THE SOUTHERN HIGHLANDS: OUR PICKS

Press Shop: Brunch destination in Bowral with Parisian vibes, in a heritage building attached to a letterpress studio. *6am-4pm Mon-Sat, from 7am Sun* $$

Paste: Sydneysiders drive to Mittagong just for a dinner at this award-winning Thai restaurant. *noon-2.30pm & 5.30-10pm Mon & Thu-Sat, to 8pm Sun* $$$

Bendooley Estate: Dine among books at the Berkelouw Book Barn on the estate winery. The menu is sophisticated and fresh. *hours vary* $$

Eschalot: Elegant dining in a historic stone cottage in Berrima; the ingredients are sourced from its kitchen garden. *noon-11pm Fri-Sun, from 6pm Thu* $$$

BEST VINTAGE SHOPPING

Dirty Jane's, Bowral: Curated antiques, fancy homewares, handmade crafts and some tat in a lofty industrial warehouse.

Sticky Beaks Vintage Emporium, Berrima: Kitsch decor, china sets and retro furniture fill this marketplace where 15 different sellers set up booths.

Bendooley Estate, Berrima: Fifth-generation book dealers, the Berkelouw Book Barn has thousands of new, secondhand and rare books.

Grandpa's Shed, Fitzroy Falls: Like rummaging through your grandparents' shed – this place is filled with fun collectibles and retro gems.

Reviva Centre, Moss Vale: This social enterprise works with the council to help turn other people's trash into your next treasure.

WILLOWTREEHOUSE/SHUTTERSTOCK

Berrima Courthouse

Mittagong's **Artemis Wines** *(artemiswines.com.au)*, one of the first local cellar doors, is known for its pinot noir and weekend wood-fired pizzas, while **Sondara Estate** *(sondara.com.au)* in Woodlands produces elegant pinot, sauvignon blanc and rosé amid 100 acres of vineyard and art.

In Berrima, **Bendooley Estate** *(bendooleyestate.com.au)* pairs wine with fine dining, and **PepperGreen Estate** *(peppergreenestate.com.au)* offers pinot noir, riesling and its own award-winning olive oil alongside a contemporary French restaurant. Nearby villages host small-batch wineries like **Cherry Tree Hill** *(cherrytreehill.com.au)* in Sutton Forest.

Berrima

TIME FROM BOWRAL: **10MIN**

Explore sandstone cottages and historic convict cells

Berrima's picture-postcard streets lined with sandstone cottages from the 1830s now house homeware, pottery and lolly shops. While it's tempting to just wander aimlessly, check out the prison cells and impressive sound-and-light show inside **Berrima Courthouse** *(berrimacourthouse.org.au; free)* to get

EATING IN SOUTHERN HIGHLANDS: BEST CAFES

Flour Bar: Go for croissants and coffee in the morning, shared plates for lunch and pizza for dinner. In Moss Vale. *7am-3pm daily, plus 9pm Fri & Sat* $$

What If Society: Moss Vale's cosy cafe with a 'blind menu' dependent on the available produce of the day. *6am-3pm Tue & Wed, to 9pm Thu-Sat, to 5pm Sun* $

Plantation Cafe: Light, plant-filled venue next to an antique shop in Bowral, popular for breakfast. Expect a line on weekends. *8am-4.30pm* $$

Harrys on Green Lane: Enjoy a long lunch in this whimsical Bowral cafe; the menu leans on the season. *noon-4.30pm Sun-Thu, to 10pm Fri & Sat* $$

an insight into the region's convict heritage. You can also get lost in the hedge maze at the Georgian **Harper's Mansion** *(nationaltrust.org.au; adult/child $15/12)* on Saturdays and Sundays, or follow the gentle 1.8km **Berrima River trail** with signage detailing how WWI internees stationed here survived in the harsh conditions.

Mittagong

TIME FROM BOWRAL: **10MIN**

Discover mountain reserves and hidden swimming holes

A short drive from Bowral, Mittagong is sandwiched between vineyards and mountain reserves. In addition to slightly cheaper accommodation options, it has plenty to see. Pop into the **Southern Highlands Visitor Information Centre** *(visitsouthernhighlands.com.au)*, which has maps and a great selection of local wine and produce. One of the best walks in the region starts in Mittagong – it's unmarked, so follow the wide, gentle fire trail from the corner of Leopold and Beatrice Sts to the river bed. Follow the river for another 2km to **Sixty Foot Falls**, a sweet waterfall with a refreshing swimming hole at the bottom.

Scale a volcanic summit for panoramic highland views

At 863m, **Mt Gibraltar** is the highest point between the Illawarra Coast and the Great Dividing Range. This 150-million-year-old volcanic core features rugged trachyte summits shaped by wind and erosion. Short loops from 10 to 45 minutes take you past lookouts offering panoramic views of the Southern Highlands. Maps and trail information are available from the visitor information centre in Mittagong.

Joadja

TIME FROM BOWRAL: **25MIN**

Ghost town and distillery tour

Joadja was once the site of a major kerosene mining operation that saw more than 1000 Scottish immigrants move here. But today, it's a ghost town. Fascinating guided 100-minute **tours** *(joadjatown.com.au; adult/child $39/19)* of the ruined buildings are offered on select weekends and include a whisky tasting at **Joadja Distillery** *(joadjadistillery.com.au)*. The Scottish heritage in the valley inspired the Jimenez family to establish the single-malt distillery in 2014. It's open Thursday to Monday, offering free distillery tours and tastings upon arrival (no booking required).

SOUTHERN HIGHLANDS' BEST GARDENS

Corbett Gardens: Open year-round, this garden in the centre of Bowral is a pretty place to sit and people-watch, especially during the Tulip Time festival in September.

Leighton Gardens: A small, old-cottage-style garden opposite Moss Vale's main shopping strip is beloved for its tulips, which bloom from September to October.

Red Cow Farm Garden: Stroll through 20 garden rooms across this 2.5-hectare Sutton Forest property, taking in English-style gardens, rose beds, woodlands and herb gardens.

Retford Park: In Bowral, admire the pink mansion before walking through a manicured garden with sculptures and seasonal florals. Buy tickets online before visiting.

DRINKING IN SOUTHERN HIGHLANDS: BEST DISTILLERIES

Millsheds Distillery: Crafting vodka and gin, with tastings and a 'make your own gin' masterclass; in Bowral. *11am-5pm Wed & Thu, to 7pm Fri, to 8pm Sat*

Renegade Spirits: Taste and shop its range, from banana pudding moonshine to Australian plum gin; at Eden Brewery. *noon-8pm Wed, Thu, Sat & Sun, to 1pm Fri*

Artemis Wines: A Highlands favourite for wine and craft gin, based in Mittagong. Book wine and spirits tastings for the full experience. *11am-4pm*

SoHi Spirits: Book a private tasting at this bottleshop in Bowral, featuring a negroni fountain and ready-to-go martinis. *11am-5pm Thu-Sat, to 3pm Sun*

A WEE TASTE OF SCOTLAND

With the Southern Highlands' fine country manors sporting names like Balmoral and Braemar, rolling hills cloaked with morning mists and the mature European trees painted with the changing seasons, you'd be forgiven for thinking you're in the Scottish Highlands. And it's not purely a coincidence. Many of the early pioneer settlers here were from Scotland, brought to this remote British colony as convicts, miners or migrants in search of greener pastures. In honour of this history, **Bundanoon** turns into the fictional Scottish town of Brigadoon one day in April, swathing the town in tartan. Accompanying the Highlands games, parades, haggis and whisky is the ever-present skirl of the bagpipes.

ROGER NICHOL/SHUTTERSTOCK

Kangaroo Valley

Kangaroo Valley

TIME FROM BOWRAL: **35MIN**

Paddle pristine waterways and spot elusive platypuses

You haven't really seen Kangaroo Valley until you've seen it from the water. **Kangaroo Valley Outdoors** *(valleyoutdoors.com.au; min 4 people $195)* offers several canoe tours, but the half-day 'Time in Nature by Canoe' tour is a great option for families with young kids. The guided paddle takes you through some of the most scenic stillwater in Australia; no experience is needed, just a sense of curiosity. You'll learn the basics, drift through pristine waterways, stop for morning tea, maybe take a dip and even spot a platypus if you're lucky.

A towering waterfall

If you only visit one waterfall in the region, make it **Fitzroy Falls**. It's a simple five-minute stroll from the visitor centre to the main lookout, where water plunges 80m into a deep, forested gorge. The paths are well marked and accessible for most ages, making it great for families or anyone needing to stretch their legs. If you have more time, continue along the **West Rim Track**, a 3.5km walk through eucalypt forest with several lookouts. Expect some stairs and uneven ground.

EATING & DRINKING IN KANGAROO VALLEY: OUR PICKS

Friendly Inn: True to its name, this heritage pub is where locals tuck into chicken schnitzels and pints in the dog-friendly beer garden. *11am-10pm* $$

General: Grab a seat on the verandah and order a breakfast dish. The Korean-style wok-fried eggs are great. *8am-12.30pm Mon, to 1.30pm Fri-Sun* $

Maddison's in the Valley: There's only one thing you need to order, the chicken schnitzel. Daily specials on the chalkboard. *6.30am-3pm Mon-Thu, to 4pm Fri-Sun* $

Lookout Cambewarra: Has the best view in town, overlooking the Shoalhaven region. Go for the scones and waffles. *10am-3pm Mon-Fri, from 9am Sat & Sun* $$

Wollongong & the Illawara Escarpment

BEACH | RAINFOREST | OCEAN ROCK POOLS

Kicking off this South Coast sojourn is Wollongong. Home to the Wodi Wodi people for 40,000 years, 'the Gong' evolved from a 19th-century coal hub into a steel-city powerhouse, imbuing it with a distinct industrial edginess. Today, it's about as laid-back as you can get without falling over, with 17 beautiful beaches and a serious brunch culture.

Pushing south, the landscape shifts from industrial to the Shoalhaven Coast's highlights reel. Here, Norfolk Island pines line a route towards basalt blowholes, hidden waterfalls and sand so rich in quartz it twinkles against turquoise waters. Whether you're skydiving over the escarpment or whale watching in winter, the collision of bush and sea is a powerful draw in this region. It even inspired DH Lawrence to pen his novel *Kangaroo* here in 1922. With 50 villages and countless beaches to explore, roll the windows down and discover why locals never want to leave.

Places

TOP TIP

The Gong has a lively music scene that has produced some great Aussie bands. Check out the homegrown talent at **Hotel Illawarra**, downstairs at **La La La's** or **Music Lounge** on weekends, or at **Seeker Brewing** on Sundays.

Wollongong

TIME FROM SYDNEY: **1HR 20MIN**

Cruise iconic coastal bridges and scenic harbor lookouts

One of Australia's most scenic drives, the **Grand Pacific Drive** stretches 140km from Sydney's Royal National Park down to Nowra, passing Wollongong on the way. About 20km north of town, the road wraps itself along the 665m-long **Sea Cliff Bridge**, perched over the ocean.

Watch for road signs to **Sublime Point Lookout**, before arriving in Wollongong. The observation deck offers stunning views of the Illawarra Escarpment and coastline. Picnic shelters and public toilets are available on-site. The lookout marks the

GETTING AROUND

The free Gong Shuttle Bus loops around the city every 10 to 20 minutes. If you're driving, parking is free on Sundays; you can also walk this hilly city, ride the bike trails or rent an e-scooter.

The **South Coast Line** *(transportnsw.info)* trains and **Premier Motor Service** *(premierms.com.au)* bus services from Sydney connect to many of the coastal towns in the region. If you're driving, the main roads are smooth and wide, but some of the roads to more secluded beaches are dirt tracks with limited parking. With no public transport, most towns are suited for walking.

WOLLONGONG TO SEVEN MILE BEACH

Take a scenic drive around Wollongong's must-see spots.

START	END	LENGTH
Wollongong	Seven Mile Beach	56km; 1hr

Start your South Coast drive in ❶ **Wollongong** and follow the Princes Hwy south to ❷ **Minnamurra Point**, around 20 minutes away. Follow the short boardwalk to the headland, where you'll get ocean views and a good chance of spotting seabirds. In winter, the ❸ **Minnamurra whale-watching platform** is a reliable spot for seeing humpbacks on their migration.

Continue 10 minutes south to the ❹ **Kiama Blowhole** (p198), where waves surge through a basalt tunnel and erupt with spectacular force. Its spray can reach more than 30m high when conditions are right. Viewing platforms circle the site, with the eastern outlook offering the best perspective. The boardwalk is accessible and you'll find toilets, barbecues and parking nearby.

The ❺ **Kiama Lighthouse**, built in 1887, stands just above the blowhole. While you can't go inside, it's 36m above sea level and offers memorable views of the town and ocean. Grab coffee or lunch at ❻ **Diggies** (p198) or pick up tips at the visitor centre.

Finish with a 20-minute drive to ❼ **Seven Mile Beach**, a long sandy stretch ideal for swimming, surfing or a relaxed stroll. Along the way, keep an eye out for lookouts and photo stops; this short drive has some of the most stunning coastal scenery in Illawarra.

start of the **Sublime Point track**, a challenging forest walk with steep climbs, regarded as one of the region's top hikes.

In Wollongong, explore the calm harbour around **Flagstaff Hill** and its **lighthouse**, once a thriving cargo port in the 1800s. Strolling the **Blue Mile** waterfront promenade, you will be lured in for a dip by the turquoise sea. Keep an eye out for skydivers, hang-gliders and paragliders drifting through the sky.

Enjoy rustic ocean pools and golden surf beaches

In a city with 17 beaches, you don't have to go far to find a good one. Closest to the centre is **City Beach** with soft wide sand and surfable waves. At the northern end, behind the lighthouse is a rustic ocean pool. Further north towards the coastal villages, **Thirroul Beach** is a favourite with surfers, while **Austinmer Beach** has twin rock pools where locals swim laps and kids splash about. Families will feel at home at **Coledale Beach**, which sits beside a popular camp site. Keep your eyes on the water: dolphins often play in the waves and the coastline glows with golden light at sunrise or sunset.

Peaceful temple and traditional pagoda calligraphy

The **Nan Tien Temple** *(nantien.org.au; free; closed Mon)* is one of the largest Buddhist temples in the southern hemisphere and its peaceful surrounds. Try calligraphy in the pagoda for a donation, or ring the gratitude bell atop the hill. Modest dress code dictates no leggings, shorts, singlets or thongs (flip-flops).

Stroll botanical trails and lush plant collections

Wollongong Botanic Garden *(wollongongbotanicgarden.com.au; free)* spans a variety of plant collections, from roses and succulents to rainforest species. Trails link picnic areas, a cafe and outdoor libraries, making it easy to explore at your own pace.

Illawarra Escarpment

TIME FROM WOLLONGONG: **45MIN**

Zip through treetops and ancient rainforest canopies

Minnamurra Rainforest Centre *(nationalparks.nsw.gov.au; per vehicle $12)* is a remnant of the ancient growth that once covered the East Coast prior to European colonisation.

WOLLONGONG'S BEST VIEWPOINTS

Mt Keira Lookout: Soak up the mesmerising vista, then take a 15-minute loop walk for more panoramic views in every direction.

Port Kembla Lookout: Best place to watch paragliders launch, check out the steelworks or enjoy the sunset.

Stanwell Tops Lookout: The ocean, beach, mountains and nature stretch out in front of you from this incredible high lookout.

Sea Cliff Bridge: Park at the southern end of the bridge and take a walk to get a closer look at this engineering marvel.

Wollongong Visitor Info Centre: Step outside for sweeping coastal views and learn about the traditional places of the Dharawal people.

EATING & DRINKING IN WOLLONGONG: OUR PICKS

Lee & Me: A funky brick-walled cafe with a brunch menu that goes beyond your standard smashed avo. *7am-2pm Mon-Fri, from 8am Sat & Sun* $

Bulli Beach Cafe: Perched on the headland, a great place to enjoy a casual lunch and watch swimmers paddling in the rock pool. *7am-4pm* $$

Scarborough Hotel: Pull up a pew on the expansive terrace overlooking the sea and enjoy classic pub food. *11am-4pm Thu-Mon* $$

Kinn Thai: A casual Thai eatery in the city centre with delicious soft-shell crab and massaman curry. *11.30am-3pm & 5-9pm* $$

SWIMMING AROUND ILLAWARRA

Rachel Tolosa Paz, Lonely Planet writer, has been living on the NSW South Coast for eight years but spending summer holidays here for a lifetime. Here are her top three spots to take a dip.

Boneyard, Kiama Downs: Park at the end of Cliff Dr and follow the short trail through the trees to find the Boneyard, a pebbly beach surrounded by lush lawns. Pack the snorkel – and your shoes – for a heavenly swim in the bay.

Minnamurra River Mouth, Minnamurra: This headland is a top spot for whale watching. Swim at the river mouth during low tide but take care with the currents.

Kiama Rock Pool: My favourite rock pool; you'll often see seals frolicking in the waves just offshore.

The 1.6km **Loop Walk** takes you across suspension bridges and along wide boardwalks as you relax to the meditative birdsong and flowing water.

Further up the escarpment, **Illawarra Fly Treetop Walk** *(illawarrafly.com.au; adult/child $30/20, zipline & walk $110)* is a family-friendly series of treetop boardwalks through the canopy of tall eucalypts and rainforest. Look out for the tree hollows that are home to marsupials such as ringtail possums and sugar gliders. The pinnacle is **Knights Tower**, where 106 steps lead to views of the coast, Lake Illawarra, Wollongong and Shellharbour. Kids four years and older can try the zipline, suspended 35m above the forest floor.

Berry

TIME FROM WOLLONGONG: **50MIN**

A historic village with boutique shopping

It's worth taking a detour inland to Berry, a historic village with a stylish, relaxed vibe. In 2024, it won gold in the NSW Top Tourism Awards (Small Town category). Spend a few hours exploring the main street, which is full of boutique clothing and homeware stores, cafes and restaurants. **Bliss & Co** *(blissandcoberry.com.au)* stocks local designers across women and baby fashion, plus homewares and gifts. Pop into the **Berry Tea Shop** *(theberryteashop.com.au)* for handmade teas and try one of the daily cake specials. Nearby, grab breakfast or coffee at the **Berry General Store** *(theberrygeneralstore.au)*, or browse local condiments and ceramics. Don't miss the **Berry Donut Van** on Queen St, serving cinnamon doughnuts to locals and travellers for over 50 years.

Kiama

TIME FROM WOLLONGONG: **30MIN**

Marvel at dramatic blowholes and basalt columns

Two vastly different natural sights sit at each end of Kiama's bay, 40km south of Wollongong. In the north, the landscapes of **Bombo Headland** feel otherworldly. The towering basalt columns at **Cathedral Rocks** are as photogenic as any grand European church. The rocks are part of the Kiama Coast Walk, but for a shorter route, park on North Kiama Dr and start at the southern end of Jones Beach. Follow the path to the headland, where the rocks rise dramatically from the ocean. Climb around to find different vantage points.

At the other end, the **Kiama Blowhole** roars and whispers as the waves crash through it all day long. An easy 4km walk

EATING BEYOND WOLLONGONG: OUR PICKS

Diggies: Breezy cafe perfectly positioned next to the Kiama Blowhole. Great for brunch through to afternoon ice cream. *7am-3pm Sun-Fri, to 5pm Sat* $

Penny Whistlers: All-day dining in Kiama: coffee and brunch, fresh lunches and seafood or steaks for dinner. *7am-3pm Sun-Wed, to 10am Thu-Sat* $$

Blue Swimmer: Unassuming cottage on the river in Gerroa, known for seafood and healthy brunches. *7.30am-2.30pm Wed, Thu & Sun, 5-8.30pm Fri & Sat* $$

Hill Bar & Kitchen: Gerringong seafood restaurant/bar open for lunch and dinner, with views of Werri Beach and rolling farmlands. *noon-11pm* $$

BG2023/SHUTTERSTOCK

Kiama Blowhole and lighthouse (p196)

joins the two capes through Kiama's bustling main street, or you can drive and park at each end. This walk is part of the longer **Kiama Coastal Walk**, which stretches for 20km from Minnamurra River all the way to Gerringong. From Kiama, continue past a series of scenic bays. The final section has a steep, rough track as you descend to **Werri Beach**; it's best to call ahead *(1300 654 262)* to check if the tidal lagoon is safe to cross. Add a few extra kilometres to Gerringong Station, then catch the train back.

High-octane slides and water adventures

Cool off at the **Jamberoo Action Park** *(jamberoo.net; adult/child $74/64; open Sep - Apr)*, a high-octane water park for adventure lovers of all ages, only 10 minutes from Kiama. With dozens of waterslides, a wave pool, a chairlift, mini golf and bobsleds, plus a kids' area, you can easily spend a whole day here. Many areas are wheelchair-accessible, though there are some steep hills. A water wheelchair is available for hire, but must be booked in advance.

OCEAN ROCK POOLS AROUND WOLLONGONG

Austinmer Ocean Pool: Twin pools at the south end of the beach, with the shallower of the two perfect for little ones.

Bulli Rock Pool: A 50m rock pool on the headland, with white sand stretching out from either side.

Wollongong Head Lighthouse Rock Pools: Take the rough stone steps behind the lighthouse to this small, pristine natural rock pool.

Kiama Rock Pool: Built in the 1880s near the famous blowhole, its irregular shape only adds to its charm.

Ourie Ocean Pool, Gerringong: This rectangular pool is nestled in the middle of a flat rock bed at Werri Beach.

DRINKING ON THE SOUTH COAST: OUR PICKS

Reub Goldberg Brewing Machine: In Tarrawanna, self-confessed beer nerds tinker away with the brewing process to create magic. *hours vary Wed-Sun*

Seeker Brewing: Great beer and wood-fired pizza under one big industrial roof in Unanderra. *3-9pm Thu, noon-10pm Fri & Sat, to 8pm Sun*

Stoic Brewing: Father-and-son team from Gerringong founded this brewery in 2018 with a focus on high-quality ingredients. *hours vary*

South Yeast Brewing: Grab a tasting paddle and enjoy Nowra's rotating food trucks and live music on weekends. *2-7pm Thu & Sun, noon-9pm Fri & Sat*

Jervis Bay

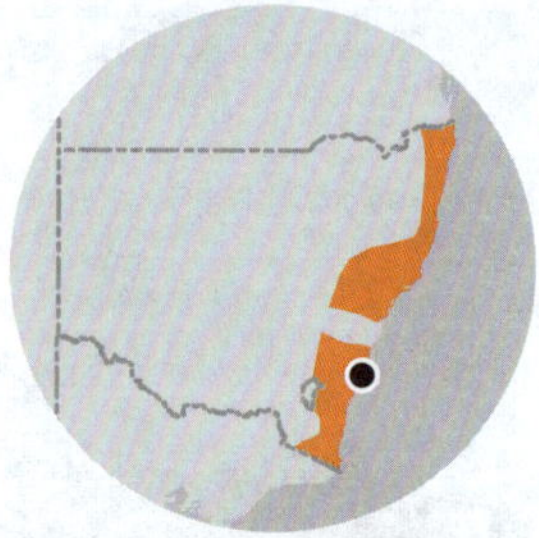

MARINE LIFE | CAMPING | BEACH

GETTING AROUND

Public transport in Jervis Bay is limited, with buses operating routes between residential areas and main towns, but journeys can be long and require multiple changes. A car is the easiest way to explore the national park, especially for reaching remote beaches and hiking trails.

Straddling the Shoalhaven and Eurobodalla regions on the NSW South Coast, Jervis Bay was once worked by whalers and timber cutters and is best known for its white sand and clear, sheltered waters. Wrapped around a wide natural bay, the area takes in the easy-going towns of Huskisson and Vincentia, the much-photographed Hyams Beach and the wild, protected landscapes of Booderee National Park.

Life here still revolves around the water. Swim in sheltered coves, snorkel along rocky headlands or paddle across the bay, where dolphins are such regulars they barely draw attention. In the cooler months, migrating whales cruise past the coastline.

Jervis Bay doesn't have a single town centre or a flashy resort strip and that's part of the appeal. Cafes, casual eateries, holiday parks and beach houses are scattered along the shoreline. Coastal roads and walking tracks link beaches, bushland and lookout points.

TOP TIP

Before setting off on any hike, check the national park's alerts for closed tracks and roads; tell someone where you're going if hiking solo. Watch for snakes and never approach them. The bay's waters are unpatrolled, so stay within your comfort depth and avoid swimming at dawn or dusk when sharks are more active.

A Marine Playground

Dive, snorkel and spot wildlife

This massive natural harbour, called Jervis Bay Marine Park, 100km south of Wollongong, is a protected marine park. It's home to a pod of around 60 bottlenose dolphins, fur seals, little penguins, weedy sea dragons and over 220 fish species. It's no surprise the Traditional Custodians of the land named this place Booderee, meaning 'bay of plenty'. You can snorkel, scuba dive, swim and surf, but there are areas where fishing is prohibited.

Dolphin Watch Cruises *(dolphinwatch.com.au; adult/child $60/41)* takes you straight into Jervis Bay's marine playground. You can spot pods of dolphins and from May to November the bay is frequented by a super pod of whales. Cruises run twice daily (10am and 1pm).

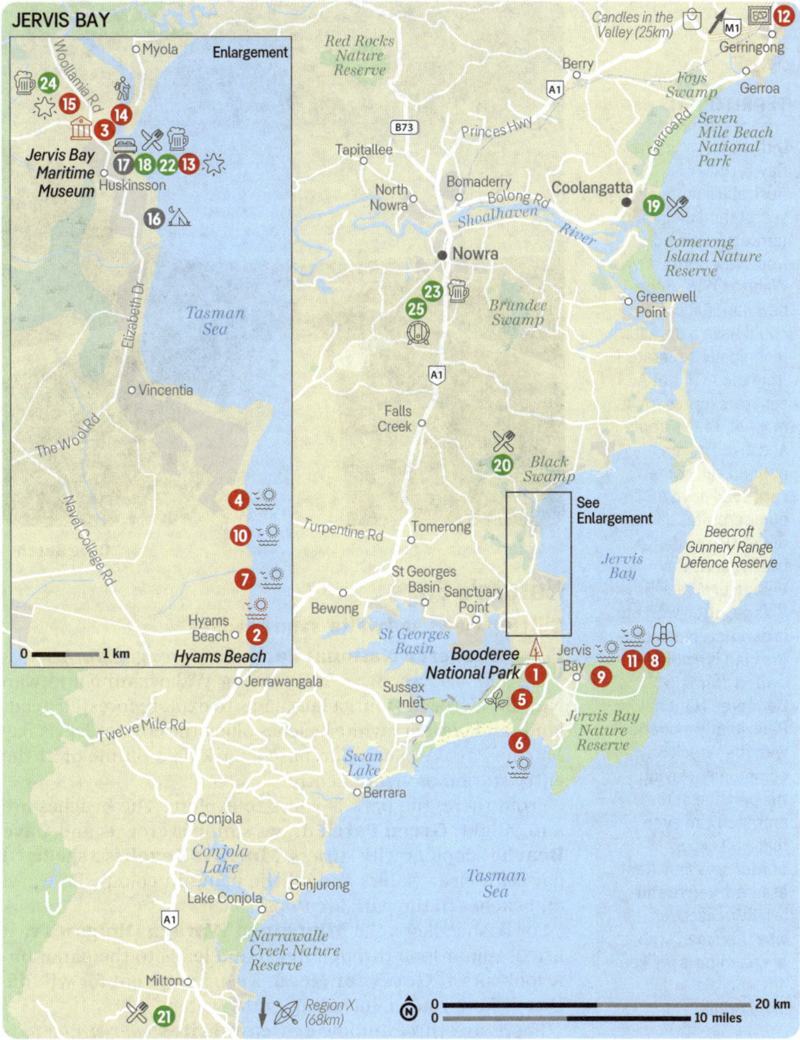

HIGHLIGHTS
1 Booderee National Park
2 Hyams Beach
3 Jervis Bay Maritime Museum

SIGHTS
4 Blenheim Beach
5 Booderee Botanic Gardens
6 Cave Beach
7 Chinamans Beach
8 Governor Head
9 Green Patch
10 Greenfield Beach
11 Murrays Beach
12 Soul Clay Studios

ACTIVITIES
13 Dolphin Watch Cruises
14 Jervis Bay Mangrove Boardwalk
see 9 Munyunga Waraga Dhugan Trail
see 4 White Sands Walk
15 Woebegone Freedive

SLEEPING
16 Holiday Haven Huskisson Beach
17 Jervis Bay Motel

EATING
18 5 Little Pigs
19 Bangalay Dining
20 Gunyah at Paperbark Camp
21 Milkhaus

DRINKING & NIGHTLIFE
22 Huskisson Hotel
23 Husky Brewing
24 Jervis Bay Brewing Co
25 Old Salt

TERRITORIAL

Did you know Jervis Bay Territory is Australia's tiny, secret third mainland territory? Carved from New South Wales in 1915 so the new national capital could have a port, it's technically separate from the ACT, but ACT senators represent it, most ACT laws apply and if you haven't noticed yet, some cars even have ACT numberplates. Most of the 391 residents live in Jervis Bay Village or Wreck Bay Village, often working in defence. Much of the land is Aboriginal-owned, forming Booderee National Park, jointly managed with the Wreck Bay community. Paying the park fee at the entrance can even feel a bit like a border crossing. Rest assured, you're still in NSW. Discover why this small strip of coastline is unlike anywhere else in Australia.

SCENERY AND SUBURBIA/SHUTTERSTOCK

Cave Beach

Nature's Edge

Clifftop views and white-sand beaches

Enter **Booderee National Park** *(booderee.gov.au; per vehicle $20, walkers & cyclists free)*, or Walawaani Njindiwan Njin Booderee in Dhurga language, to explore forested headlands and powdery white beaches along the edge of Jervis Bay Marine Park. You can purchase a park pass online or at the entry station or visitor centre.

From there, the park is yours to explore. The beaches are a highlight. **Green Patch** draws summer crowds and **Cave Beach** is popular with surfers. **Murrays Beach** is a sheltered bay with clear waters and a little penguin colony. Be wary: all beaches in the park are unpatrolled.

For bushwalkers, the **Munyunga Waraga Dhugan Trail** is a 2½-hour loop through forest and leads to the panoramic lookouts at **Governor Head**. Keep an eye out for wildlife everywhere you go, including in the waters.

There are three unpowered **camp sites** *(per night $55-180)* for overnight stays. Clear signage makes it easy to explore beaches and walking tracks. Don't miss the **Booderee Botanic Gardens** *(free)*, Australia's only Aboriginal-owned

EATING & DRINKING IN JERVIS BAY: OUR PICKS

Huskisson Hotel: The revamped 'Husky Pub' is the go-to place in the area for a cold drink in a chilled atmosphere. *11am-10pm Sun-Thu, to late Fri & Sat*

Jervis Bay Brewing Co: Sustainable brewery tucked away in the industrial estate with a kids' playground, food truck and tasting paddles. *noon-9pm Wed-Sun*

5 Little Pigs: This busy little cafe in Huskisson is renowned for its delicious brunches (try the hash browns) and decent coffee. *7am-4pm* **$$**

Gunyah at Paperbark Camp: A three-course bush dining experience under candlelight on the verandah. Bookings essential. *5.30-8.30pm Sep-May* **$$**

and managed botanic gardens. Walk the paths, photograph the colourful wildflowers and read the signposts to learn about local bush tucker (edible plants).

Footprints in the Sand

Walking the white beaches

Many people think **Hyams Beach** is the only white-sand beach in Jervis Bay, but in fact, most beaches in Booderee National Park have powdery white sand that squeaks underfoot. The **White Sands Walk** is the easiest way to experience several in a single outing. This 2.5km loop (about one hour) can start at Nelsons Beach in Vincentia, where bright-orange rock formations create striking contrast against the soft sand, or at **Greenfield Beach** for a slightly shorter hiking experience. Take time to admire the orange rocks. The main trail continues along the headland, passing **Chinamans Beach** and **Blenheim Beach** before finishing at Hyams Beach, which has a playground, picnic facilities and public toilets. For those wanting to venture further into the bush, the optional **Scribbly Gum Track** branches off, featuring steeper sections and more secluded forest scenery. All tracks are clearly marked.

Mangrove Meander

Explore a lush mangrove forest

The **Jervis Bay Mangrove Boardwalk** is an elevated boardwalk managed by the Jervis Bay Maritime Museum. The trail winds through the mangroves and mudflats of Currambene Creek, providing a close-up look at this delicate ecosystem. Start at Dent St or Woollamia Rd and follow the wide, accessible path through grey and river mangroves. Stop at interpretive panels to learn about local birds, ecology and Aboriginal culture while enjoying views of Huskisson, Callala Beach and passing boats. Keep your eyes peeled for stingrays and crabs below.

Nearby, check out the **Jervis Bay Maritime Museum** *(jervisbaymaritimemuseum.asn.au; adult/child $14/free)* to learn about the region's seafaring past and Aboriginal history. Take your time wandering the expansive grounds, which include a native garden and be sure to climb the lighthouse's winding staircase. Its lantern gallery, dating from the mid-1800s, is one of only four surviving examples in Australia.

SOUTH COAST ADVENTURES

Kate from South Coast Experiences *(@southcoastexperiences)* shares off-the-beaten-track things to do led by locals.

Soul Clay Studios: Get your hands dirty and play with clay at a pottery class in Gerringong.

Candles in the Valley: Candle-making classes in a garden studio, a 20-minute drive from Shellharbour. By appointment only.

Region X: Bespoke ecofriendly adventures like oyster shucking and glass-bottom kayak tours.

Fishing with a Local: Catch a fish from the sand in Shoalhaven with local fisherman George. *(fishingwithalocal.com)*

Jervis Bay Stargazing: An astrophysicist takes you stargazing on the beach. *(jervisbaystargazing.com.au)*

Woebegone Freedive: Freediving courses, snorkelling tours, and dolphin, seal and whale swims in Jervis Bay.

EATING & DRINKING IN SHOALHAVEN: OUR PICKS

Bangalay Dining: A must-visit in Ulladulla for native ingredients, with a five-course degustation. *5-8pm Mon, Tue & Thu-Sat, 7.30am-noon Sun* $$$

Milkhaus: In Milton, this former cheese factory serves creative garden-grown breakfasts and lunches in a bright space. *8.30am-2.30pm Thu-Mon* $$

Husky Brewing: South Nowra microbrewery with food trucks serving wood-fired pizzas. Try the blood orange and apple cider. *noon-8pm Thu-Sat*

Old Salt: A distillery in Nowra's industrial estate run by two former fine-dining chefs crafting great spirits and snacks. *hours vary*

Batemans Bay & Eurobodalla

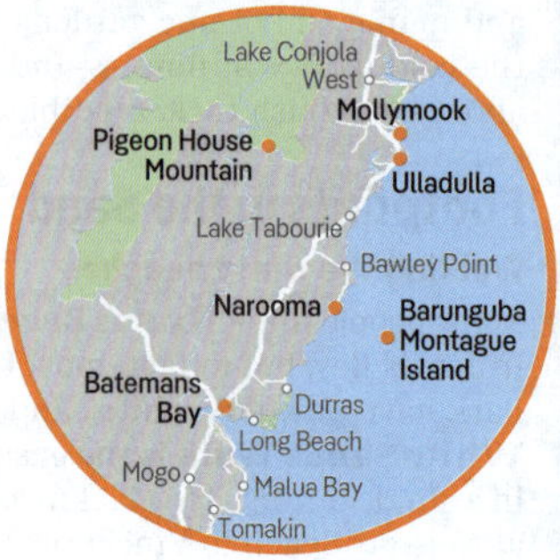

OYSTERS | WATER SPORTS | WILDLIFE

TOP TIP

The town and roads heave during school holidays as landlocked Canberrans escape to the South Coast beaches, with Batemans Bay acting as the main thoroughfare. If you can, visit outside the main holidays to explore and drive in peace.

The journey into Eurobodalla – a Yuin name meaning 'land between waters' – begins where the Clyde River spills into the sea at Batemans Bay. This former gold-rush port has traded steamships for oyster farms, serving as a practical, salt-of-the-earth base camp with seafood restaurants, supply shops and renovated motels. Its estuaries are one of the most popular places to go kayaking, preferably while tasting oysters.

Beyond the bay, the coastline gets wilder and hinterland villages show off their gold-rush heritage. Cycling trails, scenic drives and river paths lead to secluded beaches and national parks. Summer bushfires are common in this area, which you can see from the blackened bark of gum trees, but life bounces back quickly.

Keep your eyes open for kangaroos hopping along the sand, seals in the surf and whales drifting past the cliffs, and set out to explore this corner of the South Coast for yourself.

Batemans Bay

TIME FROM SYDNEY: **3HR 40MIN**

Feast along the Oyster Coast

Batemans Bay's clear fresh water supports a world-class oyster industry, with Sydney rock oysters, Pacific oysters and the rare Angasi flat oysters all grown here. For a food crawl around the bay, start with freshly shucked oysters at the rustic **Oyster Shed** *(oystershed.com.au)* on the banks of the Clyde River. Then cross the new bridge for the **Pearly Oyster Bar** to try its farm-fresh oysters, before ending at the **Innes' Boatshed** *(innesboatshed.com.au)*. This casual family-run

GETTING AROUND

A four-hour drive south of Sydney, Batemans Bay is easiest reached by car. The closest airport is the small regional **Moruya Airport**, 25km south. The town is highly walkable and bike-friendly, with a dedicated cycleway hugging the bay. Local buses and taxis are available, but rideshares are fairly limited.

You'll need a car to explore these parts, as there's limited public transport. Drive carefully along winding national park roads at dawn and dusk – the best chance of spotting wildlife. Boat tours must be booked to visit Barunguba Montague Island.

SASANAN TRAKANSUEBKUL/SHUTTERSTOCK

Oyster Shed

eatery in the heart of town has been serving fresh seafood for three generations.

Region X (*regionx.com.au; adult/child $139/119*) runs daily two-hour oyster-tasting tours by kayak along the Clyde River. Paddle gently between oyster farms, chat with fourth-generation oyster farmers and learn the best shucking technique. For a more 'out-of-the-box' experience, book the **Sunset Pizza Paddle** *($129)*, where hot pizza is delivered straight to your kayak as you watch the sunset. It's a unique date night.

Snorkel rocky reefs and cycle scenic coastal pathways

The **Batemans Bay Snorkelling Trail** takes in three fantastic spots at Maloneys Beach, Sunshine Cove and Guerilla Bay, where you can spot schools of fish, lobsters and abalone on the rocky reefs. Bring your own gear or stop by the **Mossy Point Boat Shed** *(theboatshedmossypoint.com.au; snorkel $15)*, near Guerilla Bay, to pick up snorkelling gear, dry bags, and kayaks and to book guided tours. The sheltered estuary on the Tomaga River makes for a scenic, gentle paddle.

Grab your bike and hit the **Batemans Bay Cycleway**, a flat, family-friendly 9km path that hugs the coast from Batehaven to the wetlands. Hire a bike from **Batemans Bay Cycles** *(batemansbaycycles.com.au; town bike per 3hr $40)*.

Continued on p208

VIEWPOINTS NEAR BATEMANS BAY

Observation Point, Batehaven: The paths between the three lookouts have 180-degree views stretching out to Snapper Island.

Melville Point, Tomakin: Long sandy beaches, inlets and tiny islands create a magical vista; good for whale watching.

Guerrilla Bay Lookout: Check out the coastline and see the family of seals frolicking in the water below.

Mossy Point, Broulee: At the bend of the Tomaga River, this calm area is also a great place to kayak.

Toragy Point, Moruya Heads: On a still day, a great spot for a BBQ or a picnic. Also a good place to spot migrating whales.

EATING IN BATEMANS BAY: OUR PICKS

Innes' Boatshed: Beloved local fish and chip shop, with fresh oysters and seafood. Grab takeaway and watch for stingrays and pelicans. *9am-7.30pm* $$

JJ's at The Marina: Follow the sculpture walk from town to this spacious seafood restaurant with floor-to-ceiling windows. *hours vary Tue-Sun* $$

Catalina Club: Enjoy a seafood platter or wood-fired pizza and watch the kangaroos hop across the golf course. *11.30am-2.30pm & 5-8.15pm Mon-Sun* $$

Crumb Cafe: Open early for breakfast through to lunch. Try its huge bacon and egg rolls and good coffee. *5am-2pm Fri-Wed* $

HIKE

Munjip Trail Hike

A 15km coastal walk from Batehaven to McKenzies Beach near Batemans Bay, the Munjip Trail passes beaches, headlands, bushland and rocky platforms, with interpretive signage, murals and audio posts sharing the culture, stories and history of the Walbunja people. The full trail can be completed in half a day, but taking your time allows for stops to swim and explore.

1 Observation Point

Park at **Observation Point** in Batehaven and admire views of the Great Dividing Range, the Clyde River, Batemans Bay, the Tollgate Islands and the coastline stretching south. At the trailhead, murals like *Two Sea Eagles* by Leanne Brook and timber message poles featuring artwork from local students, Elders and community groups introduce the Walbunja people's culture.

The Hike: Enjoy views of Caseys Beach, then spot the mural on the amenities block by Bronwen Smith and Gavin Chatfield before continuing around the headland.

2 Denhams Beach & Surf Beach

The first beaches come into view, starting with **Sunshine Bay**, a popular spot for snorkelling. The headland lookout has views reaching all the way to Snapper Island. Keep walking around the headland and you'll hit **Denhams Beach**, a scenic stretch of sand for a quick swim. From there, the trail dips back into suburbia at

HIBIKT/SHUTTERSTOCK

Observation Point

Surf Beach. Stop at its cafe for a coffee and a snack.

The Hike: Expect the trail to feel most remote here, with steep, loose terrain and lookouts from every high point.

❸ Lilli Pilli Beach

Around 1km in from Surf Beach, you'll come across **Bulday Gagurr (Grandfather's Gully Beach)**, surrounded by pink spotted gums and home to a freshwater creek. Pay attention to the layered rock walls revealing millions of years of geological activity. Continue around to **Lilli Pilli**, a horseshoe bay with soft sand and gentle waves.

The Hike: Climb back up the headland for another stretch of bushwalking and beach hopping.

❹ Malua Bay

Malua Bay is where the trail shifts from bush to beach. After rounding **Garden Bay** and following the message poles to a headland lookout, you get a wide-angle view south across Malua's long sweep of sand and out to Pretty Point. The southern headland lookout has excellent interpretive signs explaining the Walbunja people's long relationship with the ocean.

The Hike: The final stretch delivers coastal views, with waves smashing on rocks and bays curving quietly below.

❺ McKenzies Beach

Before rounding out the Munjip Trail, detour to **Pretty Point**. The 1.4km return walk peels off the main route to an opening, with clear views north to Durras Mountain and out to the Tollgate Islands. Return to the main trail and follow it to **McKenzies Beach**, a quiet cove marked by a whale's tail sculpture by local artist Daryl Harbrow. It's a satisfying way to wrap up the walk.

BEST PLACES TO SPOT WILDLIFE

Murramarang National Park: This national park is full of kangaroos. Spot them on Merry Beach, Pebbly Beach and Pretty Beach.

Boat Harbour Beach, Bendalong: A small beach full of friendly stingrays who glide around the shallow bay at the southern side.

Seal Rocks, Narooma: A colony of playful fur seals has taken up residence on the rocks of this sea wall.

Batemans Bay: During the day, you'll see pelicans perched on top of pylons along the river's edge.

Bendeela Recreation Area, Kangaroo Valley: Plenty of wombats wander around this camping ground at dusk.

BRAYDEN STANFORD PHOTO/SHUTTERSTOCK

Ulladulla

Continued from p205

In Batehaven, **Corrigans Beach Reserve** has a wheelchair-friendly boardwalk to the shore. The fenced playground is accessible, with a liberty swing.

Mollymook & Ulladulla

TIME FROM BATEMANS BAY: **50MIN**

Stroll around the bay

North of Batemans Bay lie the twin towns of Ulladulla and Mollymook. A highlight is the 4km coastal walk around **Mollymook Beach** and the sparkling bay, a mostly flat loop that starts and ends at the Mollymook Surf Life Saving Club. Walk at a relaxed pace, watch for dolphins cruising just offshore and time your visit for low tide, when conditions are best underfoot and along the shoreline.

Visit Ulladulla's harbour

Ulladulla, meaning 'safe harbour' in the local Yuin language, does in fact have a tiny harbour at its centre. Grab the pie of the day at **Hayden's Pies** *(haydenspies.com.au)*, a road-trip classic, or eat fish and chips from the popular **Fishermans Co-Op** on the wharf, swim laps in the sea pool or hunt for the fossils in the rocks on the easy 500m **Gondwana Coast Fossil Walk**. Head to the **Shoalhaven Visitor Centre** *(shoalhaven.com)* to book an interactive volunteer-led tour; times vary.

EATING & DRINKING IN ULLADULLA & MOLLYMOOK: OUR PICKS

Ruse: Brunch by day, cocktails and Mexican fare by night, views over the Ulladulla harbour all day long. *7am-2pm & 5-10pm Fri & Sat* **$$**

Pilgrims Cafe: Vegetarian restaurant in Milton serving delicious, wholesome meals since the 1980s. *9am-5pm Mon-Fri, from 8am Sat & Sun* **$$**

Cupitt's Estate: This award-winning Ulladulla winery has all bases covered: fromagerie, restaurant, brewery and cellar door. *hours vary* **$$$**

Rick Stein at Bannisters: Celebrity chef's gourmet seafood restaurant in Mollymook with coastal views. *6-9.30pm daily, plus 12.30-4pm Sat & Sun* **$$$**

Summit hike in Morton National Park

Summit **Pigeon House Mountain (Didthul)**, the most striking feature in Morton National Park, on a steep walk (5km return) through forest and spectacular sandstone boulders and cliffs. There's a series of ladders to climb on the way to the peak (720m), but the views from the top stretch right to the horizon, with valleys and escarpments carved into the earth. There's parking and toilets at the trailhead on Yadboro Rd. Allow three to four hours in total, including a decent break at the top to take it all in. Didthul is 33km west of Ulladulla by road.

Narooma

TIME FROM BATEMANS BAY: 1HR

Savour fresh oysters and explore geological formations

A series of sweeping bends wrap Narooma in a sea of clear blue water. It really comes alive in May for the **Narooma Oyster Festival** *(naroomaoysterfestival.com)*, a long weekend of oyster tastings, cooking demonstrations and live music; book tickets in advance.

Narooma is also home to a range of ancient geological sights, around 440 to 510 million years old. **Glasshouse Rocks** at the southern end of Narooma Beach is a photographer's dream thanks to the unique chevron-patterned rocks and pillow lava dotting the beach. Best time to visit is at low tide when the path around the headland is accessible. The walk isn't signposted, so set off from the surf beach car park along the dirt track around the headland.

Island wildlife encounters

The small **Barunguba Montague Island** *(nationalparks.nsw.gov.au)*, 9km offshore from Narooma, was a significant ceremonial and gathering site for the Yuin people for thousands of years. Seals, little penguins and hundreds of birds inhabit the island and visits are only possible on a guided tour. Plenty of operators from Narooma run morning or afternoon tours (weather permitting) that include a visit to the island's lighthouse, a walk around its perimeter, optional swimming with seals in summer and whale watching in season (May to early November). **Narooma Charters** *(naroomacharters.com.au; adult/child $150/130)* runs several Montague Island tours including a sunset and penguin tour, whales and seals, and a lighthouse tour.

BEST PLACES TO LEARN TO SURF

North Broulee Beach: The best place to learn to surf on the East Coast; book a lesson with Broulee Surf School.

Tomakin Beach: A soft, sandy bottom in a sheltered location, just up the road from North Broulee.

Shelly Beach, Moruya Heads: If everywhere else is too big, you can catch a small wave here.

Bar Beach North, Narooma: This stretch of sand is exposed, but when the waves are small it's great for learners.

Cookies Beach, Durras: This sheltered beach is protected from big swells and has minimal rips.

EATING IN EUROBODALLA: OUR PICKS

Tuross Boatshed & Cafe: Watch the fishers at Tuross Lake while enjoying fresh seafood, or coffee and breakfast rolls. *8am-4pm Sun-Thu, to 7pm Fri & Sat* $

Oyster Farmer's Daughter: An oyster-farmer's daughter has set up a seafood cafe on the Wagonga inlet selling Dad's oysters. *11.30am-4pm Fri-Tue* $

Quarterdeck: After a tiki-style revamp, this Narooma fave is back. Fresh seafood plus killer cocktails on the over-water deck. *hours vary Wed-Sun* $$

River: Award-winning Moruya restaurant celebrating local produce and matched wines; five-course tasting menu. *noon-1.30pm Wed-Sun, plus 6-8pm Thu-Sat* $$$

Sapphire Coast

BEACHES | WHALES | OYSTERS

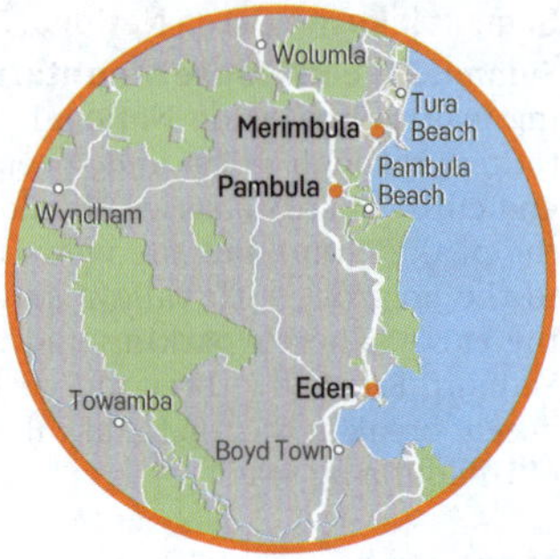

Places

TOP TIP

Visit between September and November for peak whale-watching season. Book outdoor activities like kayaking early and pack layers – the Sapphire Coast can swing from cool mornings to warm afternoons.

Welcome to the Sapphire Coast, where New South Wales meets the Victorian border and the pace of life slows to match the tide. Here forests roll down to the sea, lakes glimmer under big skies and beaches stretch for kilometres, mostly uncrowded. The region's showpiece is Merimbula, a laid-back seaside town with countless beaches and a longstanding oyster-industry heritage. Just down the road, set in the Pambula River valley, Pambula is known for small galleries, good food and creative energy. The two are linked by one long, white shoreline and an easy-going attitude. For the Yuin people, this coast has always been a gathering place, rich in food and meaning. Later came whalers, gold miners and farmers, each shaping the region in different ways. These days, life still centres around the water. Summer brings paddleboards and surfboards, while winter sees humpback whales passing close to shore.

Merimbula

TIME FROM SYDNEY: **5¾HR**

Oyster trail

Merimbula's lakes and estuaries have sustained its famous oyster industry for generations. For the ultimate oyster experience, head to the **Oyster Barn** on Merimbula Lake, run by second-generation farmers Pip and Dom Boyton. They're among the few in Australia cultivating the rare native Angasi oyster, available from May to September. Learn how Sydney rock and Angasi oysters are farmed, then grab an outdoor table overlooking the lake to taste them fresh from the lease, natural or with seasonal toppings. You can BYO bubbly to pair with the seasonal seafood menu.

GETTING AROUND

The Sapphire Coast is best explored by car, with coastal drives along the Princes Hwy, the Sapphire Coast Dr and the Tathra-Bermagui Rd linking beaches, towns and hinterland. **Sapphire Coast Buslines** *(scbuslines.com.au)* and **Bega Valley Coaches** *(begavalleycoaches.com.au)* run buses between towns but services are limited, so driving remains the most flexible way to get around.

Flights with **Regional Express** *(rex.com.au)* and **QantasLink** *(qantas.com)* operate from Sydney and Melbourne to **Merimbula Airport**, where you'll find car hire, taxis and a cafe.

CHARLESTONDAVID/SHUTTERSTOCK

Merimbula Boardwalk

Navigate Expeditions *(navigateexpeditions.com; adult/child $200/160)* runs a 'Kayak and Shuck' tour on Pambula Lake. Paddle past mangroves and oyster leases, stop for a swim and morning tea with local treats, then finish at **Broadwater Oysters** *(broadwateroysters.com.au)* to shuck and taste oysters fresh from the water. The four-hour tour requires moderate fitness and good balance. Booking in advance is recommended.

Stroll the lake's edge

The **Merimbula Boardwalk** is an easy trail (3.4km return) that follows the lake's edge from Market Street Bridge. The wooden path, suitable for prams and wheelchairs, winds past mangroves, oyster leases and bird-filled shallows, with benches and viewing platforms along the way. Go early or late in the day for the best light and keep an eye out for farmers tending their oyster beds.

Find your perfect stretch of sand

Merimbula's **Main Beach** stretches for 5km of sparkling blue ocean. Patrolled in summer, it's family-friendly, has an off-leash area for dogs and is backed by a bush reserve of heathland and forest. Dolphins and seals are regular visitors, with humpback whales passing through in spring.

At the northern end, Main Beach meets Merimbula Lake, with sandy inlets like Bar Beach and Spencer Park. Rent a kayak or SUP from **Mitchies Jetty** *(mitchiesjetty.com; per*

Continued on p214

THE LOCAL MUSIC SCENE

Many of Australia's most popular musicians hail from NSW, from rockers AC/DC to children's entertainers The Wiggles. The live music scene is alive and kicking, with many pubs all along the coast hosting gigs on weekends. It's a great way to check out some up-and-coming local artists. While you're on the road, hit play on some of these formidable Aussie artists who all hail from the NSW South Coast: The Rubens and Tyne-James Organ play catchy soulful rock tunes that you'll want to turn up; Hockey Dad and The Terrys pump out Aussie surf rock tunes; while Satin Cali and The Vanns are popular names in indie rock.

EATING & DRINKING IN MERIMBULA: OUR PICKS

Fishpen Takeaway: In the middle of the Fishpen Peninsula, this popular takeaway joint has delicious fish and chips and big burgers. *11am-7.30pm* **$**

Merimbula Wharf: Dine on the deck, then visit the aquarium featuring Port Jackson sharks, rays, starfish and seahorses. *hours vary Wed-Sun* **$$**

Wheelers: Seafood lovers will love the enormous platter on offer here; it's between Merimbula and Pambula. *noon-2pm & 5.45-8pm Wed-Mon* **$$**

Bar Superette: Cosy wine bar, restaurant and bottle shop with impressive share plates. Swordfish skewers are a must. *noon-9pm* **$$$**

ROAD TRIP

Central Tilba to Tathra

The road trip from Sydney to Merimbula doubles as a slow introduction to the South Coast's rural side. You'll pass dairy country and pockets of coastal forest, with historic villages breaking up the drive. Pull over for local cheese or a cafe stop, then wander Central Tilba's preserved streets or the working wharf at Tathra to see how farming, fishing and small-town life still shape this stretch of coast.

1 Central Tilba

Start your journey in one of the South Coast's most intact heritage towns, with a main street lined by 19th-century weatherboard shops. Local galleries, craft stores, antiques and gourmet producers fill the strip. The **Dromedary Hotel** has been pouring beers here for more than 120 years and families love the old-school lolly shop. At the bottom of the main street, **Tilba Dairy** serves award-winning cheeses made from local Jersey cows.

An optional four-minute drive north, **Tilba Valley Winery & Ale House** is open daily except Mondays for lunch and tastings of local wines and ciders.

The Drive: A 20-minute drive south along the coast will take you to the Bermagui Blue Pool.

2 Bermagui Blue Pool

Bermagui Blue Pool is one of the prettiest rock pools on the NSW coast. Stretching 50m across a rocky ledge, it's accessed via 75 steep steps from the car park. Families

BRAYDEN STANFORD PHOTO/SHUTTERSTOCK

Bermagui Blue Pool

with young children can enjoy the adjacent wading pool, while adults will find the deeper blue pool ideal for laps. The clifftop footpath and nearby grassy picnic area have the best views of the pool and coastline. At low tide, it's possible to walk around the pool's perimeter, but beware that the rocks are slippery and rogue waves can form at any time.

The Drive: Turn the wheel inland for a 50-minute scenic drive through the countryside.

3 Bega

Dotted with small farming communities, the route opens up upon reaching the Bega Valley and the country town of Bega. Stop at the **Bega Cheese Heritage Centre**, the factory that put the region in every Australian fridge. Upstairs, a small free museum showcases vintage cheesemaking equipment, while downstairs, the cafe serves the famous cheddar. Pick up blocks, spreads or local dairy treats and drive to the **Bega Valley Lookout** for a picnic. There's a shaded picnic table at the top, with great views.

The Drive: Emerge from the valley and head back to the coast to reach Tathra Wharf in 20 minutes.

4 Tathra Wharf

The final stop is **Tathra Wharf**, one of the last remaining deep-sea timber wharves in NSW. Built in the 1860s, the heritage-listed structure remains a working pier, popular with fishers and walkers alike. Between August and November, humpback and southern right whales pass through the calm bay. Have lunch or grab a coffee to go at the **Wharf Local**. You can browse a small gallery or step into the **Tathra Wharf Museum** to learn about the region's maritime history.

EDEN & THE WHALES

Whale oil was once a valuable commodity, but the discovery of substitutes such as kerosene and vegetable oil saw an end to whaling in Australia. The last whale was taken in Twofold Bay in 1926. After that, fishing – notably a tuna cannery – took over in Eden. At the height of the industry, 40 boats were fishing in the rich waters off the coast, but overseas competition forced the cannery to close its doors in 1999. Today, the town's incredibly deep natural harbour makes it a popular destination for large cruise ships, and whales still play a central role in Eden, with a number of whale-watching operators departing from the wharf in Snug Cove.

Continued from p211

1hr SUP & kayak $30, double kayak $50, kids kayak $20) and paddle around the calm lake. **Fishpen Charters** *(fishpencharters.com; adult/child $100/75)* runs three- or four-hour family fishing trips (maximum eight to 10 people per boat), with gear and bait supplied. Nearby, Ford Park has a playground, picnic facilities and a seaside market held every third Sunday of the month.

Pambula

TIME FROM MERIMBULA: **10MIN**

Explore Panboola wetlands

This 82-hectare **wetland** *(panboola.com)* is a special example of community-led conservation. A group of passionate volunteers rehabilitated the old racetrack area as a wetland for birds and indigenous flora and fauna. A series of walking and cycling trails guides you through the billabongs, salt marsh and mangroves, past picnic tables and lookouts. The 3.4km loop is best for native bird watching.

Meet furry friends at Potoroo Palace

The **Potoroo Palace** *(potoroopalace.com; adult/child/under 3yr $27/18/5, train ride $5)* is a not-for-profit animal sanctuary that rehabilitates native animals – emus, koalas, kangaroos, potoroos, dingoes and wombats. Keeper talks are at 11am and 2pm daily and you can hand-feed the roos. Pat the farm animals at **Oaklands Barn** *(oaklandsbarn.com)* in the south of Pambula, which is also home to a fantastic craft brewery, **Longstocking Brewery** *(longstocking.com.au)*, small local artists' gallery and a garden centre.

Eden

TIME FROM PAMBULA: **20MIN**

Tour the Killer Whale Trail

This self-drive day tour links five key sites from Eden's whaling history. Start at the **Killer Whale Museum** *(killerwhalemuseum.com.au; adult/child/under 5yr $15/5/free)* before heading to **Rotary Park**, one of the region's top whale-watching lookouts. Continue south to Boydtown and the historic **Seahorse Inn** *(seahorseinnhotel.com.au)* built by entrepreneur Benjamin Boyd in the 1840s, a scenic stop for lunch overlooking the bay. From there, it's a 25-minute drive to **Davidson Whaling Station**, the preserved homestead where

EATING BEYOND MERIMBULA: OUR PICKS

Honorbread: Artisan bakery in Bermagui with delicious croissants, cinnamon buns, sourdough bread and great coffee. *7am-5pm Mon-Sat* **$**

Wild Orchid Cafe: Chill on the bean bags and enjoy a coffee or a healthy brunch at this friendly cafe opposite the beach in Tathra. *7am-3pm* **$$**

Tathra Hotel: Perched on the headland, this bright pub has a lunch/dinner menu that caters for gluten-free, vegetarians and kids. *7am-8pm* **$$**

Mimosa Wines: Try the three-course lunch or six-course dinner menu; spectacular setting in Bermagui. *noon-2.30pm Thu-Sun, plus 6-10pm Fri & Sat* **$$$**

whale carcasses were once hauled ashore and processed. The final stop is **Boyd's Tower**, perched above the coastline, where whalers once kept watch for the telltale 'rusho' of spouting whales. It's an easy walk to the tower and lookout from the car park ($8 per day) via a 350m wheelchair-accessible bitumen track and boardwalk.

Gravity biking

A five-minute drive from Eden, **Gravity Eden** *(gravityeden.com.au; free)* in Nullica State Forest has 58km of machine-built mountain-bike trails with 300m of elevation. The gravity-fed park is divided into beginner, intermediate and advanced zones. Bring your own bike or hire one from **Bike Station Eden** *(0409 307 639; e-bike per day $175)* located inside Supply Central, a pet store in town. Trails can be accessed via the main trailhead off Storey Ave, the midpoint on Nethercote Rd, or the 4WD-only Bimmil Fire Trail (avoid in wet weather). **Eden Shuttles** *(edenshuttles.com.au)* operates from 9am to 3.45pm, with free town pickup available for the first morning run. After that, shuttle passes can be purchased from $15 for additional rides throughout the day.

Walk the Story Trail

Follow the ancient steps of the **Bundian Way** *(bundianway.com.au)* on the easy 1.8km Story Trail south of Eden. This relaxed coastal walk traces a small section of a 365km pathway Yuin-Monaro peoples have travelled for thousands of years, linking Twofold Bay with the high country around Mt Kosciuszko.

Eight interpretive signs explain how the route once connected spring whale ceremonies on the coast with summer gatherings in the mountains for the Bogong moth season. Starting at **Cocora Beach**, the trail passes through native bushland to a ceremonial Bunang Ring, climbs gently to Budginbro Lookout, then continues past Sealers Lookout, along Bungo Beach and finishes at **Quarantine Bay**.

It's an easy outing to plan, with free parking, toilets and a playground. For deeper insight, a three-hour **guided experience** *(adult/child $145/95)* with a local Aboriginal guide includes a smoking ceremony, storytelling, transport and park fees; book on the website.

SAPPHIRE COAST'S BEST SWIMMING SPOTS

Aslings Beach Rock Pool, Eden: Stunning rock pool built into the pink-hued cliff at the southern end of Aslings Beach, a short walk across the sand.

Nullica River: Head to the mouth of the Nullica River at low tide to watch swarms of soldier scabs scuttle across the sand.

Cocora Beach: This calm, family-friendly beach in the bay, south of Eden, has a playground, BBQs and toilets.

Severs Beach: Find this hidden gem on the stunning Pambula River after a 10-minute walk from the car park.

Bittangabee Bay: Cove in Beowa National Park with turquoise waters that's great for kayaking and paddleboarding.

EATING IN EDEN: OUR PICKS

Toast Cafe: Get a quick gourmet toastie, including a mushroom truffle, or if you have time, try the Mexican street salad. *8am-2.30pm* $$

Fig Cafe & Bar: Friendly local service, with an extensive menu of cafe classics. *6am-3pm Mon-Fri, from 8am Sat & Sun* $

Rusty Plough: Roadside cafe serving huge portions of fish and chips and burgers. Grab a milkshake to go. *4am-6.30pm Mon-Sat, to 6pm Sun* $

Great Southern Inn: Eden's go-to pub meal in a sports-bar atmosphere with TV screens and punting (betting) facilities. *10am-midnight* $$

Lord Howe & Norfolk Islands

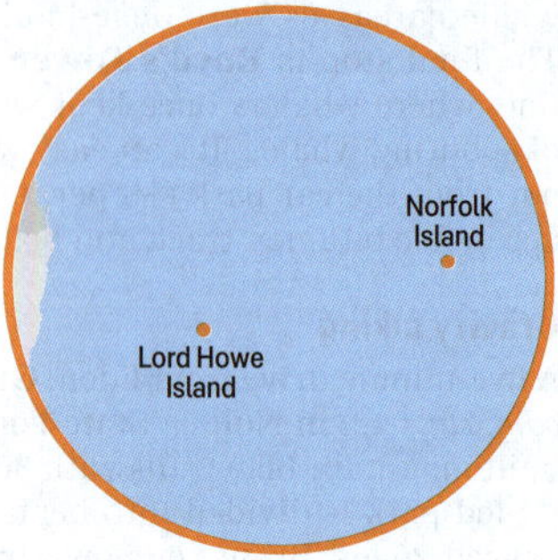

NATURE | COLONIAL HISTORY | HIKING

Places

Lord Howe Island p216
Norfolk Island p218

TOP TIP

With limited wi-fi and no mobile-phone signal on Lord Howe, it's a great opportunity to switch off. Norfolk Island isn't on the Australian mobile network, but global roaming might be available to you, or purchase a local SIM. Most Norfolk Island accommodation providers offer serviceable wi-fi and there are several hot spots in town.

Hundreds of kilometres off the coast of NSW lie two utterly fascinating – if very different – islands, ideal for a splurge-y side trip.

Dramatically rising from the Pacific, 780km northeast from Sydney, little Lord Howe's tropical, World Heritage–listed beauty and its forward-thinking approach to sustainable tourism (only 400 visitors are allowed on the 14.55-sq-km island at any one time) have thrust this isle into the international spotlight. From above, it could be mistaken for a Bond villain's lair, with two lofty mountains overlooking an idyllic lagoon, gorgeous white-sand beaches and a lush subtropical jungle interior crisscrossed with walking trails.

Some 900km northeast of Lord Howe, Norfolk Island has a rugged natural beauty of its own. But it's the island's colonial relics and storied history that draw most visitors to this remote outpost. Unlike Lord Howe, which is part of NSW, 34.6-sq-km Norfolk is an external (Commonwealth-run) Australian territory.

Lord Howe Island

TIME FROM SYDNEY: **2HR**

Hiker's heaven

Lord Howe's volcanic birth around seven million years ago gives it a unique ecosystem, with about half its plants and animals found nowhere else on Earth. Bird watchers should keep an eye out for nesting terns and an ear out for the eerie calls of mutton birds at night.

GETTING AROUND

Qantas *(qantas.com)* flies to Lord Howe from Sydney and Brisbane and **Eastern Air Services** *(easternairservices.com.au)* flies from Newcastle and Port Macquarie, with a flight time of around two hours. Flights are expensive, typically costing over $1000 return. Bicycles are the main form of local transport, with bike rental available from your accommodation or **Wilson's Hire Service** on Lagoon Rd.

Qantas flies to Norfolk Island from Sydney (2½ hours) and Brisbane (2¼ hours). Most visitors to this larger island hire a car to explore; the main town of Burnt Pine sits at the island's centre.

Walking is the island's top land activity, with **Mt Gower** the standout. The challenging 14km (eight hour) hike to the summit isn't for the faint-hearted: you'll edge cliff faces and use ropes to heave yourself up. But the view from the summit makes every effort worth it. Jack Shick of **Sea to Summit Expeditions** *(lordhoweislandtours.net; $170)* has done over 2000 climbs, following in his father's and grandfather's footsteps.

Shorter walks, like **Malabar Hill** (1.5km one way) or the coastal tracks, have viewpoints and hidden beaches. Download the Walking Track Map from *lordhoweisland.info* and choose your pace.

Underwater wonderland

Lord Howe sits where five ocean currents meet, creating a marine hot spot with 447 fish species, of which 10% are found only here, including the blue doubleheader wrasse. The island has plenty of beaches and snorkelling spots to explore.

The easiest and most family-friendly option is **Ned's Beach**, where schools of fish swim just metres from the shore. Grab fish food from the small shed on the beach, operating on an honesty box ($1 per serving). **Lagoon Beach** is another favourite, with colourful corals and reef fish just a short swim from shore. The calm, clear waters make it perfect for snorkelling on your own.

For guided tours, **Islander Cruises** *(islandercruises.com.au; adult/child $90/45)* runs reef and glass-bottom trips, while **ReefN Beyond** *(visitlordhowe.com.au; from $240)* heads further out into the deep blue to the towering **Ball's Pyramid**. Serious divers can join guided dives with **Dive Lord Howe** *(divelordhowe.com; from $260)*, which runs weekly trips to experience the surrounding underwater world.

Discover island heritage

The **Lord Howe Island Museum** *(lhimuseum.com; free)* is a small but captivating treasure at the heart of the island's community. Run by the Lord Howe Island Historical Society, it preserves the stories, objects and traditions that make this World Heritage–listed island unique.

The museum began in 1951 as the RSL Hall, a gathering place for locals. By 1978, it had been transformed into a museum to house artefacts collected by the island's first curator, Jim Dorman. Over the years, Dorman built an impressive collection of photographs, tools and objects that reveal daily life

WAR ON RATS

Once infested by more than 360,000 rodents thought to have hitchhiked to the island on ships, Lord Howe launched a world-first, island-wide rodent eradication program in 2019. The project was a success, with no live rodents detected on island in the two years prior to July 2023. More than 30 threatened plant and wildlife species, including the ground-dwelling Lord Howe Island woodhen, whose numbers had dwindled to around 200 individuals before the project, are now recovering, with more than 1100 woodhens recorded on the island in early 2023. Learn more about Lord Howe's unique ecology at the **Lord Howe Island Museum**, a great place to begin your exploration.

EATING & DRINKING ON LORD HOWE ISLAND: OUR PICKS

Coral Cafe: Casual terrace cafe and restaurant adjacent to the Lord Howe Island Museum. *9am-2.30pm & 6-8pm Mon, Wed & Thu* **$$**

Driftwood: Try Asian-fusion favourites, from beef brisket bao to hibachi-grilled king prawns. *4-10pm Wed-Sat, from 1pm Sun* **$$$**

Crooked Post: Small bar, great cocktails. Pick up daily breakfast or lunch/dinner BBQ packs for the beach. *hours vary* **$$**

Lord Howe Island Brewery: Enjoy a lager or pale ale in the beer garden, surrounded by glasshouses of veggies. *4-9pm Thu-Sat*

PALM LEGACY

Lord Howe Island is home to over 240 native plants and nearly half are found nowhere else in the world, as are most of its birds and insects. But in the plant category, the Kentia palm is the most famous. Originally noticed during the whaling era in the 1800s, it soon caught the world's attention. By the early 20th century, it had become one of the island's most important exports, prized for its ability to thrive indoors, which is why you'll find them in hotels around the world. Keep an eye out for Kentias growing along walking tracks and all around the island. They're impossible to miss.

CHRIS ANDREWS FERN BAY/SHUTTERSTOCK

Kingston

on the island – from early colonists to modern times. By the mid-1980s, the growing collection needed a purpose-built space, which opened in 2001 and remains the museum you can visit today.

Inside, you'll find engaging displays on local history, culture and natural heritage, including rare plants, animals and marine life. Artefacts and photographs bring the past to life, while knowledgeable staff are on hand to answer questions. Open daily, the museum is easy to explore without a guide and most areas allow photography.

Norfolk Island

TIME FROM SYDNEY: **2½HR**

Colonial relics

Established in 1825, Norfolk Island's second convict settlement earned a grim reputation for its harsh conditions. Prisoners built the Georgian buildings of **Kingston**, now the island's main heritage site. **Baunti Tours** *(bauntitours.com; $60)* runs convict tours twice weekly.

Visit Kingston mid-morning to watch fisherfolk cleaning their catch on the pier as reef sharks circle below, emerging for the scraps. Nearby, Emily Bay's clear, sheltered waters and floating raft are perfect for a swim or snorkel. There's no need to worry about sharks here.

Pop into the **Bounty Museum** *(bountymuseum.com; $15)*, an independent museum tracing the island's story from the mutiny on the *Bounty* to today.

Immersive circular painting of *Bounty* mutiny history

Step inside **Fletcher's Mutiny Cyclorama** *(norfolkcyclorama.com; adult/child $17/5)*, a giant circular painting that brings the story of the HMS *Bounty* mutineers to life, from their voyage to Tahiti to the mutiny and their settlement on Norfolk Island. The painting was created by four local artists, all of whom either live on the island or have spent time working here.

There's a flat accessible boardwalk around the painting, making it easy to read the storyboard panels explaining each historical scene. Music, sound effects and perspective tricks add to the atmosphere. Most visitors spend about 30 minutes here, but you can take as long as you like. Photography isn't allowed. Opening hours change throughout the year, so it's best to check ahead. Tickets can be purchased at the entrance, which also houses the **Gallery Guava**. After descending into the basement to the Cyclorama, browse the shelves of the gallery for paintings, ceramics, recycled driftwood artworks and smaller souvenir gifts like postcards.

Scenic forest walks and island views

Over 9km of walking tracks weave through towering Norfolk pines, giant tree ferns and other endemic plants. The **Mt Bates Summit Walk** *(norfolkislandnationalpark.gov.au)* along the ridge between Mt Pitt and Mt Bates is a popular 1.3km walk (around 30 minutes return); it's relatively flat.

The **Mt Pitt Lookout** is the best viewpoint on Norfolk Island, with 360-degree views across the island, Kingston and even nearby islets on a clear day. The best part is that you can drive up to it, or take the short walk nearby. Keep your ears open for the island's wildlife too, including the green parrot and the morepork owl, which call the forest home. Listen for the morepork's distinctive 'ke ke ke' at dawn or dusk.

The Norfolk Island's **Botanic Garden** *(norfolkisland nationalpark.gov.au; free)* on Mission Rd provides a gentler walk with sealed paths, informative signage and a **Discovery Centre** *(open 24/7)* with information about the park's plants, animals and conservation efforts.

NORFOLK ISLAND'S PAGE-TURNING HISTORY

Norfolk Island's original Polynesian seafaring inhabitants had vanished more than a century before the isle was colonised by the British in March 1788, just five weeks after the First Fleet arrived in Sydney. Despite its early success as an agricultural centre, this colony wasn't to last, abandoned in 1814 largely due to the island's isolation. Norfolk's second, notorious penal settlement lasted 30 years until 1855. In 1856 the island was handed over to Pitcairn Islanders – descendants of the infamous HMS *Bounty* mutineers and their Tahitian wives. English is the island's main language, but you can expect to hear some of its 2188 residents speaking Norf'k laengwij, a mix of Tahitian and 19-century English inherited from their mutineering ancestors.

EATING ON NORFOLK ISLAND: OUR PICKS

Olive Cafe: Breakfast and light lunches, from Mediterranean toasties to chicken satay salad. *6.30am-2pm Mon, Tue & Thu-Sat, 7am-1.30pm Sun* $

Hilli Restaurant: Come for morning tea and scones, or for lunch/dinner of local fish, meat and veggies. *10-11.45am, noon-2pm & 6-8pm Fri-Tue* $$$

Homestead: Contemporary dishes cooked on a custom-made Argentinian grill, accompanied by wood-fired sourdough. *6-8pm Thu-Sat* $$$

Baunti Tours: The Fish Fry, set up on a cliff, is a must. Tuck into fried local trumpeter and Fijian sides. BYO wine or buy there. *5-7pm Thu & Sat* $$$

Places We Love to Stay

$ Budget $$ Midrange $$$ Top End

Central Coast

Tiarri on Terrigal $$ Modern eight-room apartment-hotel in a leafy gully just above Terrigal; four rooms have cooking facilities.

Kims Beachside Retreat $$$ Boardwalks through lush palms connect the 36 bungalows at this longstanding retreat on Toowoon Bay's main beach.

Newcastle p164

Newcastle Beach YHA $ Sprawling, heritage-listed building with comfortable dorms, a huge common area and complimentary surfboards and bikes.

Lucky Hotel $$ A slick revamp of this 1880s grand dame means it's an upbeat place to stay above a great pub, with 28 rooms.

QT Newcastle $$$ The playful brand has nailed Newcastle cool with its transformation of the former David Jones building into a 104-room hotel.

Port Stephens

Melaleuca Surfside Backpackers $ Pitch your tent among bushland, nab a dorm bed or kick back in cosy cabins set amid peaceful scrub behind One Mile Beach.

Anchorage $$$ Marina-fronted resort and Port Stephens' most stylish place to stay. Rooms with crisp, coastal charm, all with either a balcony or a terrace.

Hunter Valley

Vine Valley Inn $ Charmingly eclectic budget hotel in Cessnock with a bit of a hostel vibe. Rates include a help-your-self breakfast in the shared kitchen.

Hermitage Lodge $$ Great value for its central Pokolbin location, this freshly renovated lodge with on-site Italian restaurant offers a huge choice of rooms.

Longhouse $$$ Architecture students designed this chic woolshed-inspired Pokolbin pad. Three huge two-room units overlook chardonnay vines.

Coffs Harbour

Woopi Backpackers $ In Woolgoolga, a 25-minute drive north of Coffs Harbour, this modern hostel is the region's best, with pod-like dorms and private twins.

BIG4 Sawtell Beach Holiday Park $$ Backing onto Sawtell's Bonville Creek, this holiday park with cabins and leafy sites is an easy stroll from town.

Bellingen

Lodge Bellingen $$ Just north of town, this 30-room, understated country-chic boutique hotel also has a Three Blue Ducks restaurant.

Promised Land Retreat $$$ A 10-minute drive from town, three stylish chalets have spa baths and superb views. Complimentary mountain bikes.

Port Macquarie

Port Macquarie Backpackers $ This heritage-listed house has dorms and private rooms and a leafy backyard with a small pool. Free bodyboard hire.

Mid Pacific $$ Free bike hire, hot tubs and a saltwater pool are welcome bonuses at this central and pleasant 38-room waterfront motel.

Byron Bay p178

Byron Bay YHA $ With dorms and private rooms wrapping around a tropical pool, this hostel is the pick of central Byron's budget sleeps.

Bangalow Guesthouse $$ Stately timber villa housing four guest rooms, all with en-suites, on the river's edge in Bangalow, 14km from Byron.

Sunseeker $$$ An '80s brick hotel on Bangalow Rd has been reimagined into a '70s-inspired palm-fringed oasis for the modern traveller.

Yamba

Pacific Hotel $$ Stylishly renovated queen rooms (shared bathrooms) at this old pub are a bargain. Also kings/queens with en-suites.

Surf $$$ Perched above Main Beach, this boutique hotel blends modern design with nostalgia in its 12 rooms and rooftop pool deck.

Ballina & Lennox Head

Cubana $$ A playful '60s-style makeover of this Ballina motor inn comes complete with a vintage caravan pool bar.

Reflections Holiday Park Lennox Head $$ By Lake Ainsworth and Seven Mile Beach, with a range of units, spacious sites and good amenities.

The Tweed p188

Blue Water Motel $$ Soothing retro-blue tones set up a nostalgic seaside escape at this stylish hotel in Kingscliff, just south of Tweed Heads.

Halcyon House $$$ The transformation of this original Cabarita Beach hotel into a whimsical-chic boutique stay kicked off an East Coast trend.

Southern Highlands

Motel Melrose $ These simple rooms in a cosy retro motel are walking distance to everything Mittagong has to offer.

Mittagong Hotel $$ Beautifully presented, sleek rooms make for a comfortable stay above the pub on Mittagong's main drag.

Berida Hotel $$$ Recently restored, elegant 1920s boutique hotel in Bowral with a restaurant, gin bar and day spa on-site.

Wollongong & the Illawara Escarpment

Hotel Totto $$ Right in the town centre, with casual-cool minimalist rooms, comfy beds, parking and a Mediterranean bar and restaurant.

SAGE Hotel Wollongong $$ Centrally located rooms with beach views, balconies, an activities room for kids, Friday night movies and a pool bar.

Berry View Hotel $$ Renovated drive-in motel in Berry with a mid-century look and an infinity pool worthy of a magazine cover.

Lodge Jamberoo $$$ Just outside Kiama, this rainforest hideaway is perfect for families. Pool, playground, spa, gym, tennis court, even a chapel!

Jervis Bay p201

Holiday Haven Huskisson Beach $$ Camping ground by the beach, with a safe bike path to town and well-maintained cabins and shady sites.

Jervis Bay Motel $$ Stunning location in Huskisson with beach views from the balcony. Spacious, clean, modern rooms with kitchenettes are great value.

Batemans Bay

Bay Breeze $$ With a chic nautical design and all the amenities, this is a lovely boutique motel within walking distance to town.

Isla $$ This cleverly renovated retro roadside motel stands out for its trendy decor, fun vending machines and a poolside clubhouse.

Mollymook

Mollymook Motel $$ Renovated retro motel at the top of the hill, with on-site parking; the rooms have kitchen facilities and a private balcony.

Bannisters by the Sea $$$ Enjoy coastal luxury with panoramic views from the infinity pool, dine at Rick Stein's or unwind in a private spa.

Merimbula

NRMA Merimbula Beach Holiday Resort $ Caravan park with camp sites, cabins and spa villas, a huge pool, playground, kids' club and e-bike rental.

Hillcrest Merimbula $$ Retro '70s decor and great private-balcony views, plus a pool, tennis court and heavenly body products.

Eden

Coast Motel Eden $$ Fresh, colourful rooms in central Eden; this is a great-value option.

Hotel Australasia $$ Eden's grand dame renovated in 2022 and its eight rooms exude charm and history.

Lord Howe & Norfolk Islands

Paradise Hotel & Resort $$ On Norfolk Island and walking distance to town, with a pool and large, basic rooms. Great on-site restaurant.

Pinetrees Lodge $$$ Just steps from the lagoon on Lord Howe, this elegant long-standing family-run resort is Australia's first carbon-neutral hotel.

Beachcomber Lodge $$$ Handsome, family-run centenarian bungalow on the hill above Lord Howe's 'downtown', with great-value self-catering apartments.

Researched by
Kat Barber

Canberra & Country New South Wales

CAPITAL CHARM, WINES & COLOURFUL COUNTRYSIDE

Canberra's bold museums meet country NSW's big open skies, heritage towns and cool-climate vineyards. It's a mix of culture, countryside and classic Australian road-tripping.

While almost 90% of Australians live within 50km of the coastline, its inland regions tell a different story. With endless space, out here, necessity is the mother of invention: from the Snowy Hydro Scheme that redirected melting snow to drought-plagued farms in the 1940s to Rev. John Flynn's pioneering Royal Flying Doctor Service, which connects rural communities to urgent medical care. More recently, the Silo Art Trails have injected much-needed colour and connection into outback towns that were once on the brink of decline.

MERRILLIE REDDEN/SHUTTERSTOCK

In the capital of Canberra, national galleries, monuments and museums chart Australia's remarkable evolution, alongside trendy restaurants, breweries and cool-climate wineries. Cruise through country NSW, encompassing Australia's highest peak, its flattest plains and the underground tunnels of the colourful mining towns Lightning Ridge and Broken Hill. The region's fertile agricultural fields and farms produce the majority of Australia's citrus, rice and poultry and the endless rows of vines ensure you're never far from a good drop.

Country folk know how to party and you can join them at festivals such as Deniliquin's Ute Muster in October, the Tamworth Country Music Festival in January and the Balloon Spectacular in Canberra in March.

For thousands of years before European arrival, these lands were home to First Nations peoples, whose stories live on in place names, cultural sites and vibrant art trails.

THE MAIN AREAS

CANBERRA
Politics, Australian history and trendy dining.
p228

SNOWY MOUNTAINS
Winter playground with summertime hiking and biking.
p246

WAGGA WAGGA
The heart of NSW's agricultural region.
p250

For places to stay in Canberra & Country New South Wales, see p273

Left: Lake Burley Griffin (p238), Above: Namadgi National Park (p245)

ORANGE
Colourful regional town and historic villages.
p256

NEW ENGLAND
Leafy countryside and country-music capital.
p263

BROKEN HILL & SILVERTON
Quirky mining towns in the remote outback.
p267

Find Your Way

NSW is bigger than it looks. It takes 10 hours to drive from the southern border to the north. Outside of Canberra, the region consists of small country towns and long stretches of highway in between.

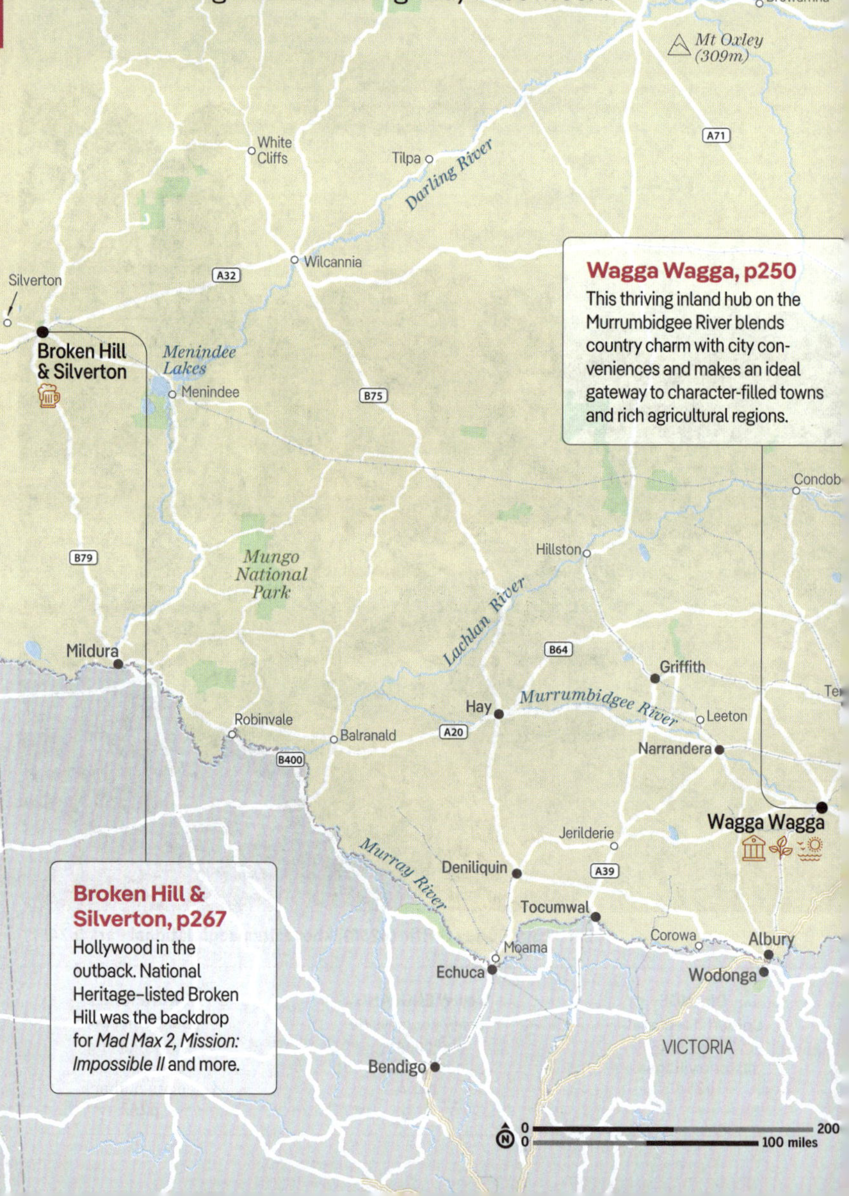

Wagga Wagga, p250

This thriving inland hub on the Murrumbidgee River blends country charm with city conveniences and makes an ideal gateway to character-filled towns and rich agricultural regions.

Broken Hill & Silverton, p267

Hollywood in the outback. National Heritage–listed Broken Hill was the backdrop for *Mad Max 2*, *Mission: Impossible II* and more.

New England, p263

Narrow roads wind through lush green countryside dotted with historic buildings and little churches, with a country-music soundtrack playing on repeat.

Orange, p256

Pretty as a picture, Orange is a hub for shopping, the arts, restaurants and wineries, and it's surrounded by quaint historic villages.

Canberra, p228

Australia's purpose-built capital is home to museums, iconic landmarks like Parliament House and the Australian War Memorial, and cool-climate wineries.

Snowy Mountains, p246

Home to Australia's highest peak, Mt Kosciuszko, this range attracts skiers and boarders in winter and hikers and mountain-bikers in summer.

CAR

Having your own wheels gives you the freedom to get off the highway and into the heart of country NSW. If you're towing a caravan or driving a campervan, you'll find plenty of camping grounds and free camp sites throughout the state.

BUS

Bus routes stretch across the state, from Broken Hill to Tenterfield. Greyhound, Murrays and FlixBus are generally comfortable and the vehicles have toilets on board. In small towns, local buses are usually the only public-transport option.

TRAIN

Plenty of trains depart from Sydney, but they're not much quicker than driving. The XPT runs from Sydney to Melbourne via Albury, Wagga Wagga, Yass and Goulburn; the Southern NSW line goes from Sydney to Canberra. The North Western line runs to Tamworth and Armidale.

Plan Your Time

Plan your stops to ensure you don't spend too long behind the wheel. Highway driving is smooth and fast, but don't rush – this region has so much to see.

PAPAWADEE VARUNPAIJIT/SHUTTERSTOCK

National Gallery of Australia (p228)

If You Only Do One Thing

- Forget what you've heard about **Canberra** (p228); it is not boring and it would be remiss to skip the nation's capital. Get a dose of art and culture at one of the many free national museums, such as the **National Gallery of Australia** (p228) or the **National Capital Exhibition** (p237), before wandering through the halls of **Parliament House** (p232). Observe the moving Last Post Ceremony at the **Australian War Memorial** (p234) and walk or cycle along the shores of **Lake Burley Griffin** (p238).

- When your stomach starts to rumble, head to popular restaurants and pubs, such as **BentSpoke Brewing Co** (p239) or **Lazy Su** (p237) in Braddon.

- If you have an extra day, explore the wineries in **Murrumbateman** (p241) and sip some cool-climate wines while soaking up the region's rolling, bush-fringed landscape.

Seasonal Highlights

This region has distinct seasons. Snow falls in the Snowy Mountains from June to September, which is also the best time to head for the outback. Visit Canberra in spring or autumn.

JANUARY

Toe-tapping Tamworth comes alive over 10 rollicking days at the **Tamworth Country Music Festival** (p264), as Australia's home of country music fills up with live tunes, street performances and music lovers from all over.

MARCH

The **Canberra Balloon Spectacular** (p238) is a sight to behold, as over 50 hot-air balloons brighten up the city over nine days. Book early to get a seat in a basket.

APRIL

The treelined streets in Orange and its surrounds are a picturesque kaleidoscope of autumn colours, making it the perfect time to sip your way through the region's wineries and explore historic villages.

Long Weekend

- Smell the fresh country air with a long weekend in trendy **Orange** (p256), a 3½-hour drive from Canberra. Arrive on a Friday and head straight to boutique hotel **Oriana** (p273) to get your mind into holiday mode. Check out trendy stores such as **Jumbled** (p258) and **Dirty Jane's** (p258) on a wander through town.

- The next day, enjoy a wine tasting at cellar doors **Philip Shaw Wines** (p257) or **Colmar Estate** (p257) then take in the views atop **Mt Canobolas** (p257). Continue exploring the quaint neighbouring villages, such as **Carcoar** (p258) and **Millthorpe** (p258). When the sun goes down, enjoy a memorable dinner under twinkling lights at **Union Bank** (p257).

- A lazy Sunday involves coffee and brunch at **Byng Street Local Store** (p257) or a stroll along the shores of Lake Canobolas.

Weeklong Road Trip

- A week gives you time to see a bit of everything. Explore the Riverina hubs of **Albury** (p253) and **Wagga Wagga** (p250) before heading to the nation's capital **Canberra** (p228).

- Once you've had your fill of great food, wine, art and culture, head north, stopping to enjoy wineries in **Orange** (p256) and the open-range zoo in **Dubbo** (p259).

- It's just a hop, skip and boot-scoot to **Tamworth** (p264), the home of country music, or tackle the long drive north to the opal mines in quirky **Lightning Ridge** (p260) via **Coonabarabran** (p262) for a night of stargazing.

- Follow the **Silo Art Trail** (p261) to get off the highway and see towering artworks that are injecting colour into tiny outback towns.

JULY

Hit the slopes, as the best snow is usually found in July and August at **Thredbo** (p248) and **Perisher** (p248) ski resorts in the Snowy Mountains. Check the local school holiday dates to avoid the crowds.

AUGUST

Much of the region becomes a golden heartland, as **canola fields** around Wagga Wagga and Junee burst into vivid yellow between August and September, creating a breathtaking countryside drive and superb photo opportunities.

SEPTEMBER

The tulips are in full bloom for the country's biggest spring festival, **Floriade** (p239) in Canberra, while the colourful **Broken Heel festival** (p267), inspired by *Priscilla Queen of the Desert* takes over Broken Hill.

OCTOBER

Car lovers converge on Bathurst each October for the epic **Bathurst 1000** (p259) supercar race at Mt Panorama, while citrus lovers head to Griffith in spring to celebrate a fruitful harvest at the Spring Fest.

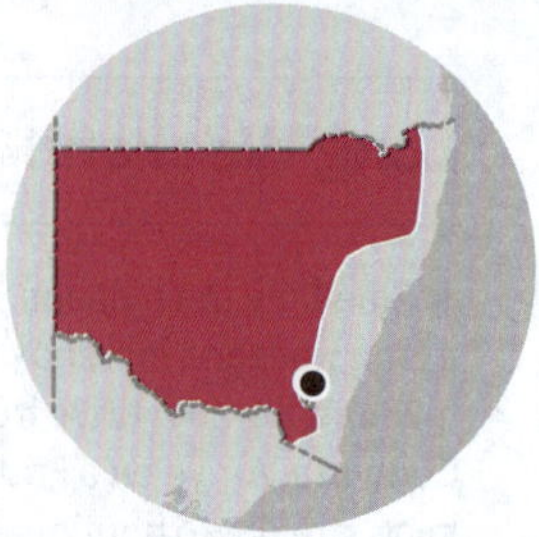

Canberra

MODERN HISTORY | ART | POLITICS

TOP TIP
Most of the national museums and attractions offer free tours daily. These tours give great insights into the history and stories that you might otherwise miss, so it's worth planning your day around them.

Canberra is a smart, bold capital that has come a long way since city folk dismissed it as little more than a sheep paddock when it was chosen as the nation's seat of power. Locals happily lean into the joke, even selling 'Canberra thinks you're boring too' mugs around town.

This purposefully designed and ever-evolving city in the Australian Capital Territory (ACT) continues to raise the bar in food, culture, accessibility and inclusivity. It's the heart of Australian democracy, so you might brush past suited-and-booted politicians on your morning coffee run, then watch them in action later at Parliament House.

With an impressive collection of world-class museums and galleries, Canberra isn't a place to rush. Plan to spend a few days soaking up its history, culture and cuisine. And if you stay longer, you may even get used to its 800-plus roundabouts.

Cultural Icons

Explore national galleries

Perched on the edge of Lake Burley Griffin, the **National Gallery of Australia** *(nga.gov.au; free)* is spread over two

GETTING AROUND

Canberra is an easy drive along the Hume Hwy from Sydney or Melbourne. **Canberra Airport** connects to major cities in Australia. Trains and Greyhound and Murray buses connect Canberra to Sydney and the South Coast.

In the city, buses are your best transport option and a light rail runs along Northbourne Ave (with major extension work underway since 2024, scheduled for completion in 2028). Parking is expensive in the centre of town and at galleries, but many car parks offer free parking on weekends. Canberra is a bike-friendly city, with plenty of bike trails, and the city centre is walkable, although distances are further than they might appear on a map.

GREG BRAVE/SHUTTERSTOCK

National Portrait Gallery

floors of light-filled galleries with soaring ceilings. Its collection includes sculptures, installations, paintings and photography by Australian and international artists, including Francis Bacon, Pablo Picasso, Mark Rothko, Sidney Nolan (famed for his series on infamous bushranger/outlaw Ned Kelly) and Jackson Pollock – whose piece *Blue Poles* was a source of public derision when acquired in 1973. Free, volunteer-led one-hour guided tours at 10.30am and 1pm are recommended. Allow a couple of hours to explore inside before wandering through the sculpture garden filled with monolithic abstract and realist pieces.

Continue your art journey next door at the **National Portrait Gallery** *(portrait.gov.au; free)*, where a rotating display of striking portraits celebrates famous Australians and international icons. From wax cameos of Indigenous Australians to early career photographs of AC/DC's Bon Scott and Angus Young, to the Tasmania-born Princess Mary of Denmark, the many faces that have shaped the nation are easily worth an hour or two's viewing.

DRINKING IN CANBERRA: CUTE COFFEE SPOTS

Cupping Room: Offering a variety of roasts, this is a coffee-lover's paradise, with a decent breakfast menu. *7am-2.30pm Mon-Fri, from 8am Sat & Sun* $

Močan & Green Grout: Tucked away in a corner of New Acton, it has cheap eats, cosy industrial interiors and great coffee. *7am-2pm* $

Walter Cafe: Next door to the Canberra and Region Visitors Centre, Walter is the perfect spot to plan your itinerary with views over the lake. *8am-4pm* $$

Bookplate: This charming cafe inside the National Library serves great coffee with lake views. *8.30am-4pm Mon-Fri, 9am-4.30pm Sat & Sun* $

CANBERRA
Alivio Tourist Park (1km); GIO Stadium (2.5km)
Tilley's Devine Cafe Gallery (2.5km)
Canberra Distillery (8km); Hartley Hall Markets (15km)
Masson St
Haig Park
BRADDO
Elouera Street
Mort St
Torrens St
Donaldson S
Barry Dr
Clunies Ross St
Northbourne Ave
Alinga Street
Cooyong St
Ainslie
Bunda St
Childers St
Marcus Clarke St
CIVIC
City Hill
London Cct
Allara St
Amaro
Constitution Ave
Australian National Botanic Gardens
Black Mountain Dr
Black Mountain Nature Reserve
National Arboretum (2.5km)
Parkes Way
Sullivans Creek
ACTON
Australian National University
Liversidge St
Pier
Commonwealth Park
West Basin
Springbank Island
Acton Peninsula
Lennox Crossing
Lake Burley Griffin
Commonwealth Ave
Regatta Point
Central Basin
National Gallery o Australia
PARKES
Stirling Park
Alexandrina Dr
King Edward Tce
King George Tce
Kings Ave
Forster Cres
Schlich St
Perth Ave
Arkana St
State Cir
Parliament Dr
Parliament House
Hopetoun Cct
Empire Cct
YARRALUMLA
BARTON
National Cct
Brisbane Ave
Tidbinbilla Nature Reserve (40km)
Adelaide Ave
Grey St
Somers Cres
Hobart Ave
National Cct
Dominion Cct
Empire Cct
Melbourne Ave
FORREST
Franklin St
Canberra Ave
Fitzroy St
Telopea Park West
Telopea Park East
Manuka Oval
La Trobe Park
Collins Park
MANUKA
0 1 km
0 0.5 miles
1 2 3 4 5 7 8 9 10 11 13 14 16 17 18 19 21 22 24 25 26 28 29 30 31 32 33 34 35 36 38 39 40 41 42 43 44 45 46 47

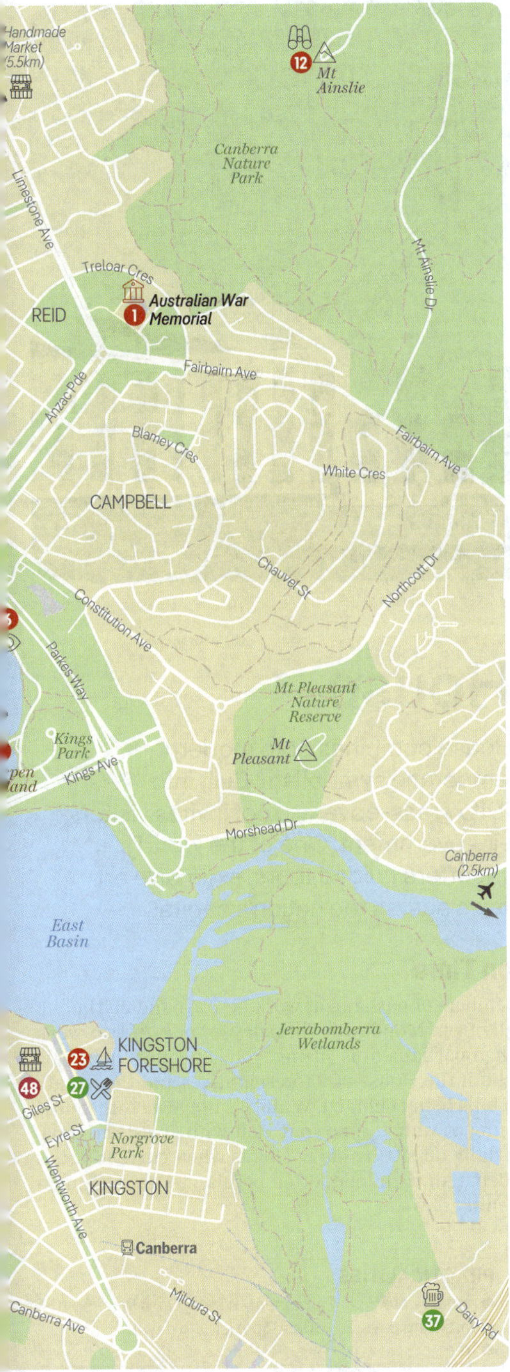

HIGHLIGHTS
1 Australian War Memorial
2 National Gallery of Australia
3 Parliament House

SIGHTS
4 Australian of the Year Walk
see 37 Big River Distilling Co
5 Black Mountain
6 Blundell's Cottage
7 Captain Cook Memorial Water Jet
8 Commonwealth Park
9 International Flag Display
10 Lake Burley Griffin
11 Manuka Oval
12 Mt Ainslie
13 Museum of Australian Democracy
14 National Capital Exhibition
15 National Carillon
16 National Museum of Australia
17 National Portrait Gallery
18 Questacon
19 RG Menzies Walk
20 Rond Terrace

ACTIVITIES
21 Balloon Aloft
22 Canberra Yacht Club
23 GoBoat

SLEEPING
24 East Hotel
25 Little Drifter
26 Little National Hotel

EATING
see 37 Brodburger
27 Dock
28 Eightysix
29 Lazy Su
30 Queen's Terrace Cafe
31 Raku
32 Tiger Lane
33 Verity Lane Market

DRINKING & NIGHTLIFE
34 BentSpoke Brewing Co
35 Blackbird
36 Bookplate
37 Capital Brewing Co
38 Cupping Room
39 Eighty/Twenty Food
40 Močan & Green Grout
41 Molly
42 Smith's Alternative
see 14 Walter Cafe

ENTERTAINMENT
43 Canberra Balloon Spectacular
44 Dissent Cafe & Bar
45 Floriade

SHOPPING
46 Haig Park Market
47 Little Burley Market
48 Old Bus Depot Markets

INFORMATION
see 14 Canberra & Region Visitors Centre

MAX BLAIN/SHUTTERSTOCK

TOP EXPERIENCE

Parliament House

Opened in 1988, Parliament House combines bold modern architecture with powerful democratic symbolism. Built into Capital Hill rather than atop it, its grass-covered roof invites visitors to quite literally walk over their government. One of the world's most accessible parliaments, it offers guided tours, extensive art collections and panoramic views across the nation's capital.

DON'T MISS

- Question Time
- The Rooftop
- The Clocks
- The Lego House
- Iconic Portraits
- The Forecourt

Question Time

Elected members of parliament work here around 20 times a year, usually from Monday to Thursday for one- or two-week blocks. When parliament is sitting, you can enter the public gallery in both the House of Representatives and the Senate and watch bills being debated. While it's not always the most riveting thing to watch, time your visit with Question Time, from 2pm daily on sitting days. This is when current issues are hotly debated, with loud, often petulant outbursts making the evening news.

PRACTICALITIES

● *aph.gov.au/Visit_Parliament/Whats_On* ● 9am–5pm (non-sitting days) & 8.30am–6pm (sitting days) ● free

The Rooftop

Take the lift up to the rooftop to get a closer look at the gigantic Australian flag, one of the building's most identifiable symbols. At 12.8m wide, it's larger than the side of a double-decker bus. The flag mast stand 81m high and it takes three people to raise and lower the flag when it's changed every four to six weeks. From the rooftop, sweeping views extend across the lake to the Australian War Memorial.

The Clocks

Notice the clocks? The building has more than 2700 of them lining every corridor. When a green or red light flashes on the clock face and the bell sounds, all members must race into the chambers within four minutes to cast their vote on an important topic. If they don't make it, they're locked out.

The Lego House

Don't miss checking out the incredible scale-model Lego recreation; made of over 158,000 bricks by renowned Lego artist -6Ryan 'Brickman' McNaught, it took over 740 hours to complete. You can find it in the Queen's Terrace Gallery, on level 1. Can you spot Batman and Yoda hiding among the hundreds of figures?

Iconic Portraits

An impressive art collection lines the walls throughout the building. Don't miss Tom Roberts' *Big Picture*, one of the most famous paintings on display in the Main Committee Room Foyer. It depicts the first-ever sitting of the Australian parliament, held not in Canberra but at the Royal Exhibition Building in Melbourne in 1901. It includes 269 portraits of the people who attended the historic occasion, including Australia's first prime minister, Edmund Barton. Just next door is the gallery of parliamentary 'firsts', where important portraits of the first women and the first Indigenous Australian elected to the federal parliament hang.

The prime ministers' portraits lining the Members' Hall are also worth a look. All are painted at the end of each prime minister's term in office in their chosen style.

The Forecourt

Outside on the forecourt is the stunning mosaic pavement designed by Warlpiri artist Michael Nelson Jagamara AM. It is a significant symbolic reminder of the 65,000 years of Aboriginal and Torres Strait Islander peoples' presence in this country. The sprawling artwork measures 196 sq metres and is surrounded by a ceremonial pool of water, referencing Australia's position surrounded by the sea.

OLD PARLIAMENT HOUSE

A five-minute walk down the hill, **Old Parliament House** was the official parliamentary building from 1927 to 1988 and is now home to the Museum of Australian Democracy (p237). It's free and well worth a visit to learn more about Australian politics over the past century, the role of the media and the public service, and to get a whiff of history in the charmingly vintage offices and musty corridors.

TOP TIPS

- Free 30-minute 'House of the Heart' guided tours are offered six times a day and give a great introduction to Australian parliament. Book online in advance to avoid missing out. Or you can join one of the more in-depth art, architecture or history tours for a fee.
- **Queen's Terrace Cafe** on level 1 has decent food and coffee at surprisingly reasonable prices and a large sunny terrace to take in the view. There's even an indulgent high tea on Fridays, Saturdays and Sundays at 11am.

HOW CANBERRA CAME TO BE

Australia achieved federation on 1 January 1901, but the question of the location of the new capital almost thwarted efforts to create the new nation.

The rivalry between Sydney and Melbourne was fierce, and New South Wales demanded the capital be within its borders, while Victoria stipulated it had to be at least 100 miles (161km) from Sydney. The search began and townships throughout NSW submitted proposals highlighting their landscapes and resources.

After a seven-year search, the site we know as Canberra was chosen. Its abundant water supply, natural beauty, fertile soil and bracing climate were the main reasons why the judges thought it was the perfect spot for the new capital.

ALEX CIMBAL/SHUTTERSTOCK

The Science of Play

Hands-on fun for curious minds

Questacon *(questacon.edu.au; adult/child from $23/17.50)*, is a spiralling science centre that will keep kids of all ages entertained for hours with hands-on exhibits, science experiments, a toddler play area and sideshow games. Don't miss the two-storey free-fall drop in the popular Excite@Q zone and the earthquake simulator. Witty and wacky 30-minute live-science shows (included in your entry) are held daily in the theatre; check times upon arrival.

Honouring the Past

Stories of sacrifice from the battlefield

Learn stories of service, sacrifice and courage at the **Australian War Memorial** *(awm.gov.au; free)*. The wheelchair-accessible site houses a huge collection of war memorabilia from WWI and WWII through to recent conflicts in Afghanistan and Iraq. Immersive 4D dioramas bring battlefields to life with realistic soundscapes and evocative scents.

Pick up a poppy at the entrance for $1 and add it to the Roll of Honour wall, a record of members of the Australian armed forces who lost their lives in war.

If you visit in the afternoon, don't miss the moving Last Post Ceremony at 4.30pm daily, when the life of one veteran is honoured and a bugle plays the haunting 'Last Post'. The site is being extensively expanded, with two new wings expected to be finished by 2028.

National Museum of Australia

After exploring the memorial, stroll along Anzac Pde, a 2.5km boulevard leading down to Lake Burley Griffin. Stroll one side and return along the other to see all 13 memorials dedicated to special forces, peacekeeping missions and key battles in Australia's military history.

Walk Through Australian History

The people and events that shaped a nation

The **National Museum of Australia** *(nma.gov.au; free)* occupies a prime position on a promontory on the lake's northwestern edge and traces defining moments in Australian history through engaging exhibits. Start in the immersive Great Southern Land gallery, where you can wander through a Queensland rainforest and see a steel electricity pole, bent and twisted by winds of Cyclone Tracy in Darwin in 1974. Learn more about Australia's Indigenous history in the First Australians gallery and check out the PS *Enterprise*, one of

BEST CANBERRA VIEWPOINTS

National Arboretum: Rolling hills and landscaped terraces make for stunning views. Head up early to see kangaroos and hot-air balloons.

Mt Ainslie: The viewpoint at Mt Ainslie is the best place to watch the sunset and appreciate the city's symmetrical design.

Parliament House Rooftop: Don't miss the views from the grassy rooftop of Parliament House and marvel at the 12m-wide flag flying above.

Black Mountain: Home to Telstra Tower (closed for renovations until late 2027), but you can still get great views from Black Mountain lookout.

Hot-air Balloon: Canberra is among the rare cities where you can drift in a hot-air balloon over its centre, offering a view few capitals can match.

You can also get 100% vegan and gluten-free burgers

EATING IN CANBERRA: CHEAP EATS

Eighty/Twenty Food: A casual cafe with great coffee and an extensive all-day menu, with sandwich and coffee deals on weekdays. *6am-3pm* $

Verity Lane Market: This casual food hall has Indonesian, Japanese, pizza and fried chicken at reasonable prices. *noon-2pm & 5-9pm Mon-Sat* $

Tiger Lane: Ignite your senses at this vibrant Pan-Asian dining precinct, featuring 10 stalls inspired by Asia's hawker centres. *hours vary daily* $

Brodburger: Started as a lakeside food truck, this burger joint now has three permanent sites, including one next door to Capital Brewery. *11.30am-8pm or later* $

WALKING LAKE BURLEY GRIFFIN

The Bridge to Bridge walk is a popular, flat loop that follows Lake Burley Griffin's shoreline.

START	END	LENGTH
National Capital Exhibition	National Capital Exhibition	5km; 1½–2hr

Park at the Canberra and Region Visitors Centre and start at the 1 **National Capital Exhibition**, a free museum detailing how this location was picked as the nation's capital more than 100 years ago. You can also hire bikes here.

Head towards the lake where you'll see the 2 **Captain Cook Memorial Water Jet** spouting water 150m into the air between 11am and 2pm. Walk clockwise. On your left is 3 **Commonwealth Park** (p239), home to spring festival Floriade. This section of the lake is known as 4 **RG Menzies Walk**, honouring former prime minister Robert Menzies, who was instrumental in Canberra's growth in the 1950s.

Cross the red gravel of 5 **Rond Terrace**, originally designed as military parade grounds at the end of Anzac Pde. 6 **Blundell's Cottage** is on the left, an original 1860 workers' cottage. Nip over to Queen Elizabeth II Island, which houses the 7 **National Carillon**, a towering musical bell tower gifted by the British Empire.

Cross Kings Ave Bridge and continue along the lake. Soon, you'll see the 8 **National Gallery of Australia** (p228) and its peaceful outdoor sculpture garden. The 9 **National Portrait Gallery** (p229) is next door. The national science centre, 10 **Questacon** (p234) is also in this block.

Wander between the fluttering 11 **International Flag Display**. Continue past the 12 **Australians of the Year Walk**. Walk across the Commonwealth Ave Bridge to complete the loop.

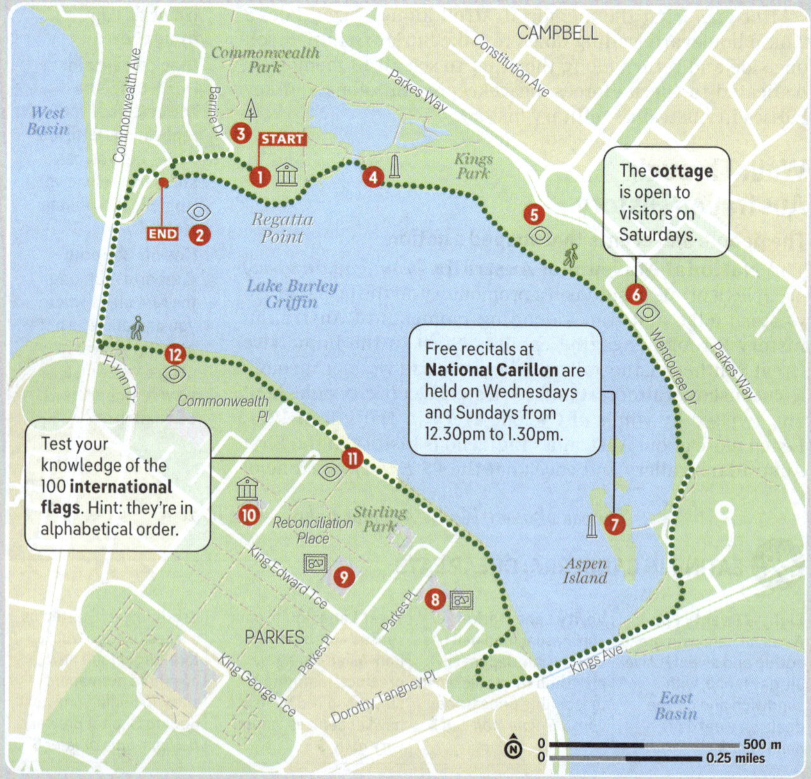

the oldest working paddle steamers in the world. To get the most out of your visit, join a daily **tour** *(adult/child $20/10)*: the Museum Highlights tour at 1pm or the First Australians tour at 3pm. The Tim and Gina Fairfax Discovery Centre is a dedicated kids' soft-play and art space for families (book tickets in 75-minute time slots online). End your visit with a wander through the Garden of Australian Dreams, full of symbols of Australian suburban life like the local invention, the Hills Hoist clothesline.

Canberra's Story

Learn about the making of a city

Get a grasp on local history at the **National Capital Exhibition** *(nca.gov.au/attractions/national-capital-exhibition; free)* inside the **Canberra and Region Visitors Centre**. This interactive space tells the story of how and why a sheep paddock was turned into the nation's capital. It also covers how American architects Walter Burley Griffin and Marion Mahony Griffin came up with the distinctive axis design for the city without ever having visited the site.

Australia's Old White House

Inside a well-preserved political past

Before parliament moved into its swish building in 1988, this old white building just a couple of hundred metres down the hill was the seat of the nation for 61 years. Old Parliament House is now the **Museum of Australian Democracy** *(moadoph.gov.au; free)*.

Where Parliament House has style, this place has the atmosphere. The old chambers have been turned into interactive exhibits about media, democracy, referendums and changemakers. Roam through the prime minister's suite and see the worn-out leather chairs in the decision-making war room of the Cabinet. The free 45-minute guided tour (four times daily) explores the building's highlights while revealing fascinating stories of its occupants.

Kids can play in the dress-up lounge and the make-your-own magazine space, as well as join in free craft sessions (10.30am daily).

CANBERRA'S BEST MARKETS

Haig Park Market: Craft markets take place on Sundays from 8am to 2pm, with live music and kids' activities.

Old Bus Depot Markets: Spend a lazy Sunday hunting for bargains in this old transport depot in Kingston. Open from 9.30am to 2.30pm.

Little Burley Market: This small Saturday-morning lakeside market has food stalls and local crafts, and attracts walkers and their pooches.

Hartley Hall Markets: On the first Sunday of the month from 10am to 3pm, the Hall Showgrounds hosts a large market of homemade wares.

Handmade Market: Held quarterly at Exhibition Park, the Handmade Market supports over 260 small businesses selling homewares, fashion, artworks and gourmet food.

EATING & DRINKING IN CANBERRA: OUR PICKS

Lazy Su: Come for the nori tacos, stay for the relaxed vibes at this trendy Asian-fusion venue in Braddon. *5-10pm Tue-Sun, plus noon-3pm Thu-Sun* **$$**

Eightysix: A dark, moody fit-out with an eclectic menu scribbled on the chalkboard wall. Give the caramel popcorn sundae a go. *6-9pm Mon-Thu, to 11pm Fri & Sat* **$$**

Raku: A Canberra icon, Raku's modern fine-dining sushi bar serves up fresh Japanese dishes using local ingredients. *11.30am-2.30pm & 5.30-9.30pm* **$$$**

Dock: Overlooking the Kingston waterfront, this friendly sports pub serves up large meals. *hours vary, closed Mon*

CANBERRA'S QUIRKY ICONS

As you drive through Canberra's suburbs (most named after former prime ministers), you might notice some peculiarities. First, the orange-and-cream-coloured bus shelters; they were designed by Canberra architect Clem Cummings in 1974 and are equal parts ugly, Brutalist, iconic and practical. Close to 500 are still standing 50 years later and have become a symbol of the city. Secondly, there are no billboards lining the roads. Billboards are banned; they go against Canberra's intentional urban planning and detract from the bush views. And thirdly, are you dizzy yet? Canberra has more roundabouts (over 800) per capita than anywhere else in Australia, earning it the name 'the Roundabout Capital'.

SASANAN TRAKANSUEBKUL/SHUTTERSTOCK

Canberra Balloon Spectacular

Smooth Sailing on the Lake

Cruising Lake Burley Griffin

Lake Burley Griffin is Canberra's glistening centrepiece, covering 664 hectares with 40km of curvaceous shoreline and a towering 114m waterjet in its centre (operating 11am to 2pm). You can walk or cycle its entire shoreline, or cruise across its still waters in an electric **GoBoat** *(goboat.com.au/location/canberra; from $139)* from Kingston Foreshore. Pack a picnic and set off with the freedom to choose your destination. You don't need a licence, but bookings are required.

For a more active experience, rent a SUP or small sailboat from the **Canberra Yacht Club** *(canberrayc.com; per hr from $60; 11am-4pm Tue-Sun Oct-Apr)*.

Catch a Match

Cheer on the local team

Canberra is a sports-mad city. The ACT Brumbies play in the national rugby union competition and the Canberra Raiders compete in rugby league, with both teams playing matches at **GIO Stadium Canberra** *(giostadiumcanberra.com.au)*. Australian Football League (AFL) club GWS Giants often plays home matches at **Manuka Oval** *(manukaoval.com.au)*. All codes play in winter (April to September) and break over summer, so make sure you rug up. Grab tickets online for all matches at *premier.ticketek.com.au* or at the gate.

A FOOTY-MAD NATION

Learn more about Australia's obsession with the odd-shaped ball on p1038. Rugby union and rugby league are popular sports here, but it's the game of Aussie Rules that has truly captured the nation.

Up, up & Away

Hot-air balloon flights over Canberra

Each March, the nine-day **Canberra Balloon Spectacular** *(canberraballoonspectacular.com)* fills the dawn sky with colourful characters and patterns, as up to 50 hot-air balloons rise from the lawns near the National Library. Book early to get a spot in a basket at **Balloon Aloft** *(balloonaloftcanberra.com.au; adult/child from $453/326)*, or head to the National Arboretum (p235) for the best views.

Outside the festival, Balloon Aloft has year-round sunrise flights (weather permitting), giving a bird's-eye view of Canberra's architecture as they glide gently above treetops and lakes, ending with a champagne toast and optional buffet breakfast.

Spring Has Sprung

Floriade blooms to life

Floriade *(floriadeaustralia.com; free)* draws crowds of garden lovers to its annual festival in **Commonwealth Park** from mid-September to mid-October. Tiptoe through intricate tulip displays, shop at market stalls and take part in craft and garden workshops. The ticketed illuminated after-dark sessions run over four nights, and live music and performances in the Spiegeltent create a party atmosphere.

Wildlife & Wilderness at Tidbinbilla

Nature on Canberra's doorstep

If you've got wheels, take the 40-minute drive to **Tidbinbilla Nature Reserve** *(tidbinbilla.act.gov.au; per car from $15)*. Strap on your boots and explore its two most popular trails: the Sanctuary Loop and the Eucalypt Forest.

The 2km Sanctuary Loop follows flat paths and boardwalks that wind around tranquil lakes, where you might spot turtles, black swans and even a shy platypus. Keep an eye out for bandicoots, kangaroos and colourful birdlife, including laughing kookaburras and screeching cockatoos.

Next, wander the 700m Koala Path through the Eucalypt Forest. You're guaranteed to see koalas here – four resident 'Conservation Ambassadors' live in the enclosed area at the entrance. Look up as you stroll, you might spot a few more koalas snoozing high in the trees.

Both trails are flat, wide and accessible for prams and wheelchairs, with toilets located along the paths.

LIVE MUSIC IN CANBERRA

Ryan Vernon, local musician with *@flowermarketband*, shares his favourite live-music spots.

Dissent Cafe & Bar@: Open all week, with either live music, drag shows, stand-up or open-mic nights.

Molly: This speakeasy jazz bar is popular, thanks to its live jazz Tuesday to Saturday and killer cocktails.

Blackbird: This basement bar has live music, karaoke, retro tunes, board-game nights, and great drinks and pizzas.

Smith's Alternative: A bookshop by day and live-music venue by night – with a bunch of pianos out the front that invite anyone to have a tinker.

Tilley's Devine Cafe Gallery: This LGBTIQ-friendly spot in Lyneham features Canberra's best jazz musicians on Saturdays from 6pm.

Try the popular, award-winning Crankshaft IPA

DRINKING IN CANBERRA: LOCAL BREWS

Canberra Distillery: Visit this cellar door in Mitchell to sample flavoursome gin, rum, schnapps and vodka. *10am-4pm Mon-Sat*

Capital Brewing Co: Beloved local brewery pouring 'good-natured' pints from its carbon-neutral brewpub in Fyshwick. *11.30am-9pm or later*

Big River Distilling Co: Pop in at the weekend to sample gin and spirits or join a guided tour; next to Capital Brewing. *hours vary Wed-Sun*

BentSpoke Brewing Co: This microbrewery in Braddon has been brewing since 2014, offering a rotating selection of 18 beers and ciders. *11am-11pm*

Beyond Canberra

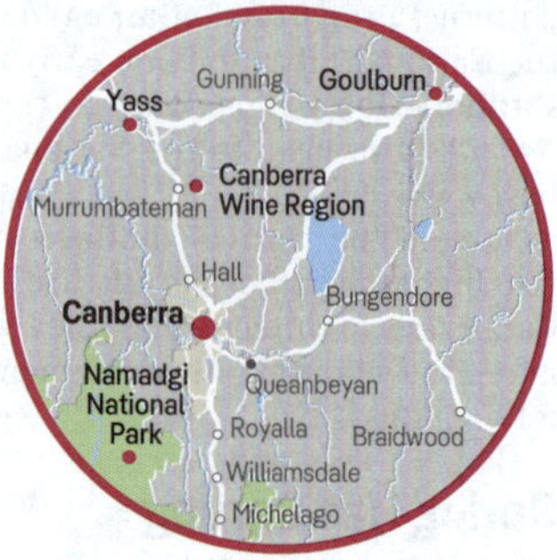

Places

GETTING AROUND

There's limited public transport, so you'll need a car to get around the region surrounding the 'Bush Capital'. The historic towns and wineries are often connected to the main highway by smaller country lanes, so take it slowly and watch out for kangaroos at dawn and dusk. If you plan on visiting Canberra's wineries, designate a driver or jump on board one of the many wine tours leaving from the city.

Drive through bushy surrounds, fertile regions producing elegant cool-climate wines and quaint villages with a country atmosphere.

Throughout the ACT and crossing into NSW, the seasons are as distinct as they are beautiful. Falling leaves turn the roads into a kaleidoscope of colours in autumn, and winter brings snow-dusted mountains. In summer, the lakes and the Molonglo River offer welcome relief, and spring's mild weather makes everything bloom and heralds the arrival of playful lambs and calves.

Among the sheep and cattle farms, many of the hills surrounding Canberra are adorned with meticulously aligned rows of grapevines and this cool-climate region is best known for its riesling and shiraz varieties.

Within an hour's drive from Canberra, you can explore the large town of Goulburn or tiny historic villages on a scenic country drive.

Canberra Wine Region

TIME FROM CANBERRA: **40MIN**

With 40 wineries scattered throughout the region, Canberra is becoming a major player in Australia's wine scene. The first grapes were planted in 1971 by Commonwealth Scientific and Industrial Research Organisation (CSIRO) scientists, yet this young industry is already producing incredible wine. A unique climate with cool evenings and hot, dry days means flavours have longer to develop. Local vintners produce riesling, chardonnay, shiraz, cabernet sauvignon and pinot noirs that are full of personality.

DRINKING IN CANBERRA WINE REGION: BEST CELLAR DOORS

Clonakilla Wines: One of Oz's best wineries: family business in Murrumbateman was one of the region's first. *11am-4pm Mon-Fri, 10am-5pm Sat & Sun*

Helm Wines: Leading regional winemaker (five-star rating by James Halliday). Renowned for riesling and cabernet sauvignon. *10am-4pm Sat-Mon*

Four Winds Vineyard: Sit back and enjoy a tasting paddle and a wood-fired pizza on the large outdoor patio. *11am-4pm or later*

Shaw Estate: Sprawling estate with cellar door overlooking vines and Mediterranean-inspired restaurant. *11am-9pm Wed-Sat, to 5pm Sun*

CHRIS HOWEY/SHUTTERSTOCK

Canberra Wine Region

Cellar-door hopping

Cellar doors cluster in three main hubs, so it's best to pick one region and spend the day exploring. Most of the wineries are boutique, family-run operations, where you're likely to meet the owners pouring wines.

Murrumbateman is north of Canberra. This former gold-mining town has a lovely rural backdrop and several gourmet producers, a chocolate shop, cafes and 15 wineries. An undulating 14km wine trail loops past the wineries and **Canberra Wine Region E-Bike Tours** *(winerides.com.au; from $75)* allow you to enjoy the ride without breaking a sweat.

The second main winegrowing region is to the north of Canberra, set among the rolling landscapes surrounding the towns of **Bungendore** and **Lake George**, as well as the historic towns of **Gundaroo** and **Collector**. The cool-climate vineyards specialise in elegant riesling, pinot noir and shiraz.

The third wine region is set within the bounds of the ACT, around Hall. This peaceful area surrounded by bushland is the closest to Canberra, so it's the best option if you're short on time.

Lake George Winery: Family-owned and operated winery on the beautiful lake shores for over 40 years. *10am-5pm Wed-Sun*

Mount Majura: Only 15 minutes from Canberra, Mount Majura is a leading Australian producer of the Spanish variety tempranillo. *10am-5pm*

Nick O'Leary: Views over Brindabella Ranges, paddock-to-plate menu, complimentary wine tastings: must-do for riesling fans. *11am-5pm Thu-Sun*

Eden Road Wines: Boutique winery producing award-winning shiraz since 2006. Cheese platters and tastings. *10am-4.30pm Thu-Sun*

DRIVING TOUR

Driving Canberra's Countryside

Setting off from Canberra, enjoy this half-day country drive through historic gold-rush towns. Start in Queanbeyan, with its colonial streets and Mt Jerrabomberra views. Continue onto Bungendore for antique shops and historic Lake George Hotel. Tiny Gundaroo tempts with its 19th-century inn, while Braidwood delights with heritage architecture and galleries. Look for grazing kangaroos along the way.

1 Queanbeyan

Queanbeyan has been home to the Ngunnawal people for thousands of years before the first Europeans arrived. A freed convict named Timothy Beard settled in the area in 1828 naming it 'Quinbean', an Aboriginal word meaning 'clear water'. The satellite town is an easy 20 minutes from Canberra's city centre.

Stroll along the historic Monaro St, grab a coffee at **thirty4** and check out the immersive artworks at No Name Lane (off Monaro St). Before you leave town, head up to **Mt Jerrabomberra lookout** for some sweet views.

The Drive: Head 20 minutes north of Queanbeyan through lush green paddocks along single-lane country roads for plenty of free parking in Bungendore.

2 Bungendore

Bungendore's charming walkable main streets, Gibraltar and Molonglo, are lined with eclectic gift shops and antique stores, such as The Malbon, tucked between cosy

CHRIS ANDREWS FERN BAY/SHUTTERSTOCK

Bungendore

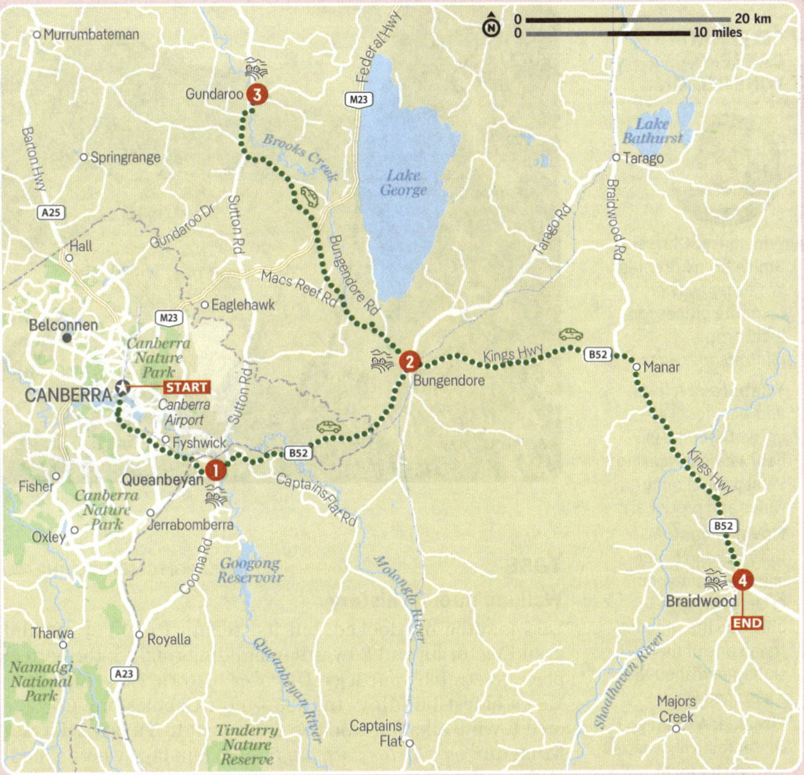

cafes like The Gathering, which delights with a whimsical rear garden. Among the historic shopfronts is the **Lake George Hotel**, one of Australia's oldest continuously licensed pubs (est. 1838), featuring a roaring fireplace for winter and a family-friendly beer garden to enjoy summer days.

The Drive: Continue for 30 minutes along country roads, past grazing sheep and colourful letterbox-lined lanes.

3 Gundaroo

An optional detour, **Gundaroo** is a blink of a town that flourished during the gold-rush era. The Gundaroo Inn, established in 1872, sits proudly on the main street, with old wooden tables lining the verandah. Don't miss the chance to drop into **Lark Hill Winery** for a tasting if you're passing on Friday, Saturday or Sunday.

The Drive: The next stop is only 30 minutes from Bungendore (or an hour from Gundaroo, if you take the detour) along gumtree-lined, single-lane roads. Watch out for kangaroos and wombats.

4 Braidwood

Braidwood is renowned for its picturesque wrought-iron colonial buildings lining Wallace St. The little gold-rush town is a popular pit stop between Canberra and the South Coast. It was the first town in NSW to be added to the State Heritage register and its rustic beauty has turned it into a popular escape for creatives. It has even been immortalised in film; Mick Jagger starred in *Ned Kelly*, shot here in the 1970s.

Take a walk down the main street to check out the art galleries and vintage shops and pop into **Dojo Bread** for delicious sourdough bread or **Smokey Horse** for Nepali cuisine and local craft beers.

CELEBRATING CANBERRA'S WINE REGION

Winemaker **Chrissie Smith** from Intrepidus Wines names her favourite places for local drops. *@intrepidus.wines*

Tumbafest: A food and wine festival in Tumbarumba in February showcasing local cool-climate wines and produce.

Moving Feast: A fun weekend event in Murrumbateman in October: rove between the wineries trying one of their signature dishes with a matched wine.

Fireside: A great winter festival, where you can try local wines suited for the cooler months (such as the region's beloved shiraz), while warming up by a roaring fire.

Canberra Wine & Spirit Merchants: Free wine tastings on Thursday nights.

Thyme to Taste: A great little wineshop in Murrumbateman.

RYANRYN VAGABOND/SHUTTERSTOCK

Yass

TIME FROM CANBERRA: **1HR**

Walking through history

Yass is often overlooked, but its treelined main street and grand Victorian and Edwardian buildings make it the perfect place to stretch your legs. Discover historic sites, including Yass's oldest building, the 1836-built Cobblestone Cottage on a town walk. You can also pay a visit to **Yass & District Museum** *(yasshistory.org.au; free)* on Sundays, where a model recreation of the main street illustrates the changes in the streetscape over the preceding century.

A pioneer's cottage

Cooma Cottage *(nationaltrust.org.au/places/cooma-cottage; adult/child $12/10)* was the grand home of famed Australian explorer Hamilton Hume. You can explore Hume's original house, stables and gardens while learning about pioneering life in the 19th century. Open Sundays, the cottage has picnic spots with sweeping valley views and is just five minutes from Yass town centre. It also serves as the starting point of the 440km Hume and Hovell Walking Track, retracing the route Hume and William Hovell took in 1824.

EATING IN GOULBURN: OUR PICKS

Paragon Cafe: Classic Greek-inspired cafe with hearty breakfasts, mains and delicious baklava. *9am-8.30pm Wed-Sat, 8am-3pm Sun* $$

Hibernation Hotel: This pub has cheap meal deals, live music on weekends and happy hour (4pm-6pm) daily. *10am-1am Mon-Sat, to 10pm Sun* $$

Maltings Bar: Located in the restored malt house of the Goulburn Brewery, this cosy bar features craft-beer tastings and pub meals. *noon-8.30pm Wed-Sat* $

Trappers Bakery: The award-winning bakery next to the Big Merino serves delicious pies, sweet pastries and excellent coffee. *5.30am-6pm* $

Kangaroos, Namadgi National Park

Goulburn

TIME FROM CANBERRA: **1HR**

Exploring Australia's first inland city

As a traditional meeting place for First Nations groups and Australia's first inland city to be settled, Goulburn has a deep history. Wander the 2.5km Heritage Tour to get a glimpse into the town's historic sites and impressive architecture, with maps available at the Tourist Information Centre. Take a peek at the **Goulburn Rail Heritage Centre** *(roundhouse.org.au; adult/child $15/5),* where you can learn how the rail system helped the city grow and see the biggest operating rail turntable in NSW.

The mighty merino of Goulburn

If you're on the hunt for Australia's big things, Goulburn's **Big Merino** is a towering 15m-high sheep statue on the main drag into town. Surrounded by service stations and fast-food outlets, it's not a place you want to linger too long, but worth snapping a quick photo.

Namadgi National Park

TIME FROM CANBERRA: **40MIN**

Hiking rugged landscapes with ancient rock art

Namadgi National Park *(parks.act.gov.au; free)* covers almost half of the Australian Capital Territory total land area, with over 100,000 hectares of rugged landscapes. It's extremely popular with hikers and favoured walks include the Yankee Hat Rock Art Walk, an easy 2km return trail that reveals ancient Aboriginal rock art; and the Mt Tennent Summit Trail, a challenging 11km hike with panoramic views of the Brindabella Ranges. Pack lunch and enjoy a picnic in the bushy surrounds.

BEST REGIONAL TOURS

Tim the Yowie Man: Join one of 10 after-dark tours around Canberra led by crypto-naturalist Tim. *(yowieman.com.au)*

Merry Heart CBR: Take a winery (or brewery and distillery) tour around Canberra's wine region. *(merryheartcbr.com.au)*

Canberra Tracks: Eight self-drive tour routes lead to many of Canberra's important Indigenous sites. *(canberratracks.act.gov.au)*

Canberra Wine Region E-Bike Tours: Take a self-guided e-bike tour through Murrumbateman and choose from six cellar doors to visit. *(winerides.com.au)*

She Shapes History: Learn about the badass women who have been written out of the history books on a two-hour walking tour. *(sheshapeshistory.com.au)*

Snowy Mountains

SNOW SPORTS | MOUNTAIN BIKING | HIKING

Places

TOP TIP

In winter, snow chains for tyres are mandatory on some alpine roads and you can rent them from petrol stations throughout the area. Check local alerts and conditions on *nationalparks.nsw.gov.au/visit-a-park/parks/kosciuszko-national-park* before setting out, as roads can be closed due to snow and ice.

Australia's major alpine region, the Snowy Mountains is a breathtaking expanse of natural beauty and outdoor adventure. With the country's highest point, Mt Kosciuszko, at its centre, 'the Snowies' are dusted in white in winter. While it's no match for major European ski fields, June to October offers decent skiing and boarding.

Historic Cooma and laid-back Jindabyne have all the amenities and act as handy launchpads to the mountains. You can easily occupy yourself for a few days here in all seasons.

As the snow retreats – lending its power to the Snowy Mountains Scheme, a hydroelectric engineering marvel – wildflowers bloom and the mountains reveal their greenery. Hiking and mountain biking are the main drawcards in the warmer months, as well as water sports, fishing and boating on the crystal-clear lakes.

For thousands of years, Aboriginal people, largely the Ngarigo, lived and gathered on these mountains and were largely displaced when Europeans arrived.

Cooma

TIME FROM CANBERRA: **90MIN**

Snow much to see

Cooma is a surprising gem of a town at the base of the Snowy Mountains. Along Sharp St, the town's main drag, you'll find cafes, snow-sports shops and parklands, as well as the **Charles Davis Gallery** *(charlesdavisphotography.com; free)*. Housed in an old Methodist church, the gallery showcases the work of acclaimed local wildlife-photographer Charles Davis, who specialises in capturing extreme closeups of cute Australian wildlife in the snow.

GETTING AROUND

Although you can fly to **Snowy Mountains Airport**, 17km from Cooma, it's best to drive so that you can enjoy the scenery, especially along the Snowy Mountains Hwy.

Parking is free once you've paid for a National Park pass inside the resorts, and the towns have ample parking. Some snow shuttle buses from Jindabyne operate during ski season. If you're driving from Jindabyne, leave early to avoid traffic, especially on weekends.

Tour a unique museum charting prison history

On the grounds of Cooma Correctional Centre, the **NSW State Correctional Museum** *(correctiveservices.dcj.nsw.gov.au/about-us/museums-and-galleries.html; $2)* is a one-of-a-kind museum that charts the history of NSW jails, from the arrival of Europeans on the First Fleet through to modern times, and tours are offered throughout the day. There's the opportunity for interaction, such as pulling the lever on a real hangman's noose, used to end the lives of 34 prisoners at Bathurst.

Offenders serving time at the minimum-security jail work at the museum, leading tours and making products for the gift shop.

Jindabyne

TIME FROM COOMA: **30MIN**

Water sports on the lake

Glistening Lake Jindabyne, a byproduct of the Snowy Mountains Scheme, dominates the laid-back mountain town of the same name. You can walk or cycle its foreshore, or swim, water-ski or boat on its crystal-blue waters in summer. Hire canoes, kayaks, SUPs, water-bikes and bikes from **Sacred Ride** *(sacredride.com.au; per hr from $20)* at the main boat ramp.

Jindabyne is a 30-minute drive from the snowfields and has plenty of hotels, bars and restaurants, making it a more affordable option than staying on the mountain.

Saddle up

Perhaps due to the deep impression that Banjo Paterson's 'Man From Snowy River' has left on the Australian psyche, horse riding is a popular pursuit in these parts. You can channel your inner jackaroo/jillaroo on a multiday back-country trek with **Snowy Wilderness** *(snowywilderness.com.au; 2hr ride from $210)*, a sprawling sanctuary for brumbies south of Jindabyne. Snowy Wilderness offer short two-hour rides for beginners, as well as multiday treks including meals, camping accommodation and joyful evenings by the campfire. Rides set out from the family-run ranch at Ingebyra, 27km from Jindabyne.

LET IT SNOW

Australia's other major ski fields are in Victoria. You can hit the slopes at **Falls Creek** (p606) or take to the steeper runs of **Mt Hotham** (p606); both are around 4½hrs from Melbourne.

SNOWY MOUNTAINS HYDRO SCHEME

The Snowy Mountains Hydro Scheme is a civil engineering wonder of the modern world, conceived as a way to deliver melted snow inland to combat drought. It's also a major energy producer, powering more than one million customers with 16 dams, nine power stations and 145km of underground tunnels.

The scheme welcomed workers from more than 30 countries and construction took 25 years. Small towns for workers popped up along the mountains and only three remain today: Khancoban, Talbingo and Cabramurra. Learn about how the ambitious plan came to life at the free exhibition at the **Snowy Hydro Discovery Centre** *(snowyhydro.com.au/visit)* in Cooma. The 10-minute video explains it best.

EATING AROUND THE SNOWY MOUNTAINS: OUR PICKS

Miss Heidi's Tea House: This Austrian log cabin near Mt Gladstone Lookout is the place to go for warm apple strudel and goulash. *10am-4pm* **$**

Alpine Hotel: The fireplace at this Cooma pub will keep you warm. Enjoy a glass of local red and a hearty steak. *noon-2pm & 6-9pm* **$$**

Bacco: Fuel up on pizza and pasta after a day on the slopes at this longstanding Jindabyne Italian joint. *noon-2pm & 5-9pm Tue-Sun* **$$**

Wildbrumby Distillery: Hearty food on the road to Kosciuszko, plus award-winning gin, vodka and schnapps. *10am-5pm* **$$**

SHU BA/SHUTTERSTOCK

TOP EXPERIENCE

Kosciuszko National Park

Kosciuszko National Park is the largest park in NSW, stretching 150km in length and covering 690,000 hectares. It is home to Mt Kosciuszko, the country's tallest point, and incredible mountain landscapes. The park shifts seasonally from snow-covered ski slopes in winter to wildflower-filled trails in summer, giving you the chance to ski, board, hike, cycle, drive or gallop through the rugged terrain.

DON'T MISS

- Hitting the Slopes
- Hiking Australia's Highest Peak
- Mountain Biking
- Caves and Thermal Waters

Hit the Slopes

Mt Kosciuszko ('Kozzie' to locals) has two major ski resorts: **Thredbo** on the southern slopes and **Perisher** on the eastern side (and tiny **Charlotte Pass** higher up on this side). Ski lifts normally run June to October, with most snowfall in July and August and snow machines pumping out extra cover throughout.

Thredbo has over 50 ski runs, including the longest – Supertrail – at 3.7km, suitable for beginners to advanced skiers and boarders. Costs are high compared to Europe and the US;

PRACTICALITIES
● *nationalparks.nsw.gov.au/visit-a-park/parks/kosciuszko-national-park* ● per vehicle Jun-Oct/rest of year $29/17 ● 7am-7pm

adult lift passes start from $203 per day. Book online seven days in advance to save up to 30%. Perisher sits higher, so gets more reliable snow and has a family-friendly toboggan run, but it's usually more crowded and its town is mainly lodges, so expect less apres-ski nightlife.

Hike Australia's Highest Peak

The Mt Kosciuszko Summit Walk is one of Australia's most accessible high-country hikes. The hike is open year-round, however the snow-covered trail can only be tackled on cross-country skis or snowshoes from June to October. At 2228m, Mt Kosciuszko is no Everest, but sweeping Snowy Mountains views, alpine wildflowers and glacial lakes impress, nonetheless.

There are two ways to the top. The easiest is via Thredbo Alpine Village: ride the 15-minute **Kosciuszko Express Chairlift** *(thredbo.com.au; adult/child from $48/14)*, then follow a sturdy boardwalk on a 13km return walk with a gentle 300m elevation gain.

If you're on a budget, start from Charlotte Pass, hiking 18.6km return along a gravel trail past the Snowy River, with double the elevation gain.

Mountain Biking

Even if the resort seems busy with hikers, they're wildly outnumbered by mountain bikers, who flock to **Thredbo Mountain Bike Park**'s gravity trails in summer.

Four chairlifts whisk bikers to the trailheads looping across the mountain. Trails are available for all levels, including first-timers, with Paparazzi being the most popular. A couple of tracks sit at valley level for those who don't want to fork out for a lift pass.

Riders can also play at the skills park and there is a jump zone, a pump track and lessons for future daredevils. Hire bikes and gear from Thredbo MTB Rental from $189 per day, while lift passes will set you back $125 per day. Book online seven days in advance *(thredbo.com.au/passes-rentals)* to save.

Caves & Thermal Waters

A scenic two-hour drive north of Thredbo, passing the remains of ghost town Kiandra and scores of wild brumbies, leads to the limestone heart of Kosciuszko's northern reaches. A winding 5km road drops to **Yarrangobilly Caves Visitor Centre** *(nationalparks.nsw.gov.au; per car $4)*, where you can grab maps and day passes or book guided tours (from $22 per adult) of six impressive caves.

South Glory Cave can be explored independently before 4pm. Afterwards, stretch your legs on the easy 1.5km River Walk and soak in the natural spring-fed thermal pool, built by prisoners in 1969. The turquoise water stays a blissful 27°C year-round. Entry is free and open 24/7, with basic bathroom facilities for changing. Just save some energy for the brutally steep climb back to the car park.

WHERE TO EAT

Brunelli's Cafe Warm up with its rich coffee blends, selection of hot chocolates or tasty treats. *7am-5pm Jul-Sep* $

Guthega Inn Ski in for lunch on Perisher and try the giant wiener schnitzel, Belgian beers and sausages. *10.30am-10pm Jul-Sep* $$

Eagles Nest Enjoy Italian classics with a view at Australia's highest restaurant at the top of the Kosciuszko chairlift. *hours vary* $$

TOP TIPS

- If you plan to visit several national parks in NSW, an annual vehicle pass is your best option. It's valid for 12 months from the date of purchase. The All Parks Pass includes entry to all parks and costs $190. The Multi Parks Pass is valid for all parks except Kosciuszko and costs $65. Purchase online at *pass.nationalparks.nsw.gov.au*.
- Bikes and pedestrians enter national parks for free.
- Save money by renting gear off-mountain in Cooma, buying lift tickets online in advance and visiting midweek. Check out Thredbo's season pass *(thredbo.com.au/passes-rentals)* or Perisher's Epic Australia Pass *(epicaustraliapass.com.au)* if you plan on hitting the slopes regularly.

Wagga Wagga

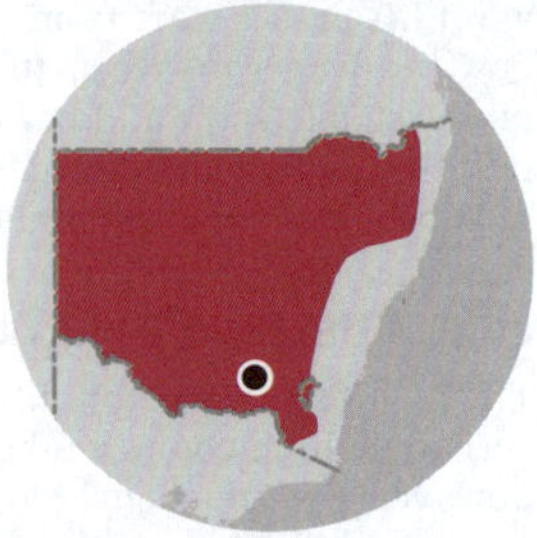

RIVERSIDE WALKS | GLASS GALLERY | BOTANIC GARDENS

GETTING AROUND

Wagga has a small airport with connections to cities around Australia on Rex and Qantaslink. It is also a stop on the NSW TrainLink XPT train service from Sydney to Melbourne, which runs twice daily.

With almost no public transport in town, you need a car, although the downtown area is walkable or suitable for riding a bike. Parking is never a problem.

TOP TIP

Pick up a floatable device from Kmart and join the locals on a river float in summer. Walk upstream on the Murrumbidgee riverside trail 600m from the beach and then jump in from the rocks. Be warned: the current is surprisingly strong.

In the heart of the Riverina region, Wagga Wagga is a thriving country town. Halfway between Sydney and Melbourne, but still a good five-hour drive from both, it's a proud farming district with big-city amenities.

In spring, fields of canola bloom a brilliant yellow across the region and lambs bounce around paddocks. You're spoiled with great cafes, bars and pubs; a thriving culture and arts scene; and relaxing walking tracks by the water. With excellent playgrounds, a free zoo and miniature railway, and a huge indoor pool, this place has plenty to keep the kids busy.

Most of the action is centred on the lengthy main street. The top end of Baylis St starts at the train station and has chain stores, supermarkets and some small malls. Cross the river and it becomes Fitzmaurice St, home to trendy cafes, bars, boutique clothing and homeware stores and plenty of pubs.

Nature Trails

Waterside walks by the river and lake

Even though it's 400km from the coast, Wagga has a **beach**. Set on the banks of the Murrumbidgee River, it's a pleasant spot to swim, picnic, walk or let kids play on the towering playground. You can also take a stroll or cycle a section of the 42km Wiradjuri Trail, which follows the river under shady red gums and loops around Wagga.

On the opposite end of town is **Lake Albert**, a popular spot for water-skiing and barbecues. The 5km loop is a favourite walk among locals and their pooches.

Family Fun at the Gardens

Miniature trains and free zoo

Visit the **Wagga Wagga Botanic Gardens** *(wagga.nsw.gov.au/parks-and-recreation; free)* to say hi to kangaroos, wallabies, emus, dingoes and camels at the large free zoo and aviary, open Thursday to Monday. Kids will love the two large

HIGHLIGHTS
1 Wagga Beach

SIGHTS
2 Wagga Wagga Art Gallery

ACTIVITIES
3 Oasis Aquatic Centre

SLEEPING
4 Mantra Pavilion Hotel
5 Townhouse Hotel

EATING
6 Mr Lawrence
see 5 Oakroom Kitchen & Bar
7 Trail Street Coffee Shop

DRINKING & NIGHTLIFE
8 Bar Olivette
9 Thirsty Crow Brewing Co
10 Tilly's

EATING & DRINKING IN WAGGA WAGGA: OUR PICKS

Mr Lawrence: At the beach end of the main drag, this popular brunch spot has great coffee and chic decor. *6.30am-2pm* $$

Trail Street Coffee Shop: Arguably Wagga's best coffee. Popular brunch menu. *6.30am-3pm Mon-Fri, 7.30am-1pm Sat, 8am-1pm Sun* $$

Magpies Nest: Enjoy views and modern Australian set menus celebrating local produce. Ten minutes out of town. *5.30-11pm Tue-Sat* $$$

Oakroom Kitchen & Bar: Choose between small plates to share or mouth-watering mains. Superb wine list. *hours vary Tue-Sun* $$$

Bar Olivette: Speakeasy-style spot. Incredible cocktails and light meals in a moody basement bar. *4-10pm Wed & Thu, 3pm-2am Fri & Sat*

Thirsty Crow Brewing Co: Independent brewery with gourmet pizzas and Thursday night trivia. Tours/tastings 2pm weekends. *hours vary, Wed-Sun* $$

Palm & Pawn: Pub in North Wagga with great meals, huge beer garden and undercover kids' playground. *11.30am-late* $

Tilly's: Amazing cocktails, great music, a nightclub and a sprawling terrace make this a winning night out. *hours vary Wed-Sat* $$

SO GOOD THEY NAMED IT TWICE

Wagga Wagga (*wo*-ga *wo*-ga) is certainly one of the more unique names in Australia. 'Wagga' means crow in the local Wiradjuri language and it's said twice to indicate plural, so the name means 'place of many crows'. Locals affectionately shorten it to 'Wagga', despite Ted Egan's playful song 'Don't Call Wagga Wagga Wagga'. The song celebrates the region's unique naming traditions and offers a lyrical way to learn about the colourful, tongue-twisting heritage of Australia's rural towns.

Australia has 250 other double-barrelled place names, including nearby Walla Walla, Grong Grong and Gumly Gumly.

DOUBLELEE/SHUTTERSTOCK

Wagga Wagga Botanic Gardens (p250)

playgrounds and the miniature train that runs on the first and third Sunday of the month.

Afterwards, cool off in the indoor and outdoor pools at the **Oasis Aquatic Centre** *(waggaleisure.com.au; adult/child $7.50/5)*, one of the best in the state.

The Cultural Precinct

Browse glass art and sporting legends

Art lovers should check out the 200-plus glass artworks on display at the National Art Glass Gallery, set within the **Wagga Wagga Art Gallery** *(waggaartgallery.com.au; free; closed Mon)* The building is inspired by a large glass shard, welcoming in natural light.

Wagga has a proud history as the home of many Aussie sporting legends and they're honoured at the Sporting Hall of Fame at the **Museum of the Riverina** *(museumriverina.com.au; free, closed Mon)* The museum has uniforms, equipment and storyboards from leading local athletes including AFL player Paul Kelly and former Australian cricket captain Mark Taylor.

Beyond Wagga Wagga

Strap on your boots and venture into the quintessential Aussie countryside, where the skies are big and the fields are fertile.

Places

Agriculture has long been a way of life out here, from the Wiradjuri people who used the Lachlan, Murrumbidgee and Macquarie rivers as abundant sources of food to the drovers who once plodded along the ancient Cobb Hwy and the Italian immigrants who introduced Australia to viticulture.

Wagga Wagga sits at the heart of the Riverina, an extremely productive region, thanks to an ample water supply and warm climate. It's a central jumping-off point for exploring regional towns showcasing contemporary country life and strong community spirit. Farming is no longer the only industry and with an abundance of fresh produce, the region is brimming with cafes, restaurants, providores and wineries.

GETTING AROUND

You need a car to get around this region. Most of the roads are well-maintained bitumen highways and day trips can mean an hour or two of driving each way. Towns have ample free parking. Pay attention to 'cattle ahead' road signs, as drovers may be moving cattle along the highways and they have right of way.

Junee

TIME FROM WAGGA WAGGA: **30MIN**

Licorice and chocolate wonderland

Travellers with a sweet tooth should pay a visit to the **Junee Licorice & Chocolate Factory** *(juneelicoriceandchocolate.com)* in the small town of Junee. Set in an old flour mill that was famously leased for just $1, this family-run business produces delicious organic treats.

Make your own giant chocolate freckle (a chocolate disc covered in sprinkles) for $6 or grab lunch in the cafe and explore the beautifully restored building.

Albury

TIME FROM WAGGA WAGGA: **1HR**

Walk or paddle along the Murray River

The border town of Albury straddles the Murray River on the NSW side. Little ones will love the natural space at **Oddies Creek Park**, or you can grab a canoe from **Murray River Canoe Hire** *(murrayrivercanoehire.com.au, per 1½hr from $35)* situated at Noreuil Park and paddle along the river.

Stretch your legs along the Wagirra Trail, an 8km path that includes the **Yindyamarra Sculpture Walk**, where 12 sculptures tell First Nations stories through contemporary art.

THE DOG ON THE TUCKERBOX

On a plain stretch of the Hume Hwy just outside Gundagai, a little dog sits on a tuckerbox (an old metal lunchbox). Since 1932, the dog has been a pit stop for travellers on the way through, collecting donations for the Gundagai Hospital.

But who is he? Legend has it that a man named Bill was leading his wagon and bulls across the nearby creek in the 1850s when he got stuck in the mud. After unsuccessfully trying to free his wagon and then losing a yoke, he gave up in frustration and went to have lunch, only to discover his dog sitting on top of his tuckerbox doing his business. The story of Bill's ruined lunch spread far and wide.

Just south of town, detour to **Huon Hill** for stunning views of the landscape.

Get artsy

The **MAMA** (Murray Art Museum Albury) is a superb regional gallery that has earned a reputation for innovative, original exhibitions and it also puts on art classes and fascinating live events. Regular special exhibitions present an array of surprising and often challenging art, and the adjacent Canvas Eatery has a very relaxed ambience. Local schools sometimes showcase art competitions at MAMA.

Griffith

TIME FROM WAGGA WAGGA: **2HR**

A taste of Italy

The Murrumbidgee River meanders through the flat landscapes of this lush agricultural region, known for its sweet navel oranges and wine. The region has 66 grape varieties, a legacy largely shaped by a surge of Italian immigrants after WWII.

Taste this history at the cellar doors of **De Bortoli** *(debortoli.com.au)*, home of the renowned Noble One dessert wine; and **Calabria Family Wines** *(calabriawines.com.au)*, best known for its highly awarded robust Durif red wine.

In August, the **Taste of Italy** *(atasteofitalygriffith.com.au)* festival celebrates Italian culture through cooking demonstrations, music and wine.

Meet the animals at Altina Wildlife Park

Spot white lions, rhinos, giraffes, deer, buffalo and more on a guided tour of **Altina Wildlife Park** *(altinawildlife.com; adult/child from $40/20)*. Set on 207 hectares of bushland, the park can be explored by safari vehicle daily (9am and 11am, plus 1pm on weekends) or by horse-drawn cart on weekends. Knowledgeable keepers share fascinating animal facts and breeding success stories as you journey through this open-range sanctuary.

Hay

TIME FROM WAGGA WAGGA: **2HR**

Hear the click of the shears

The outback town of Hay was once a major stop on the Cobb Hwy drovers' trail. Today, the **Shear Outback** *(shearoutback.com.au; adult/child $20/10)* interactive museum celebrates the shearers who helped build the nation's wool industry. Explore

EATING IN ALBURY: OUR PICKS

Bended Elbow: Large menu with decent $22 lunch specials. Take a seat in the bistro, courtyard or rooftop bar. *11am-11pm Sun-Thu, to 1am Fri & Sat* $

Nannina's: A cosy spot for great coffee, brunch or a simple lunch. *7am-3pm Tue-Fri, 8am-2pm Sat* $

River Deck: This sleek venue uses local ingredients and has a large dog-friendly outdoor terrace to soak up the river breeze. *9am-3pm* $$

Yardbird: This Mediterranean-inspired restaurant in the centre of town dishes up flavoursome meals cooked over an open fire. *hours vary Tue-Sat* $$

MAMA (Murray Art Museum Albury)

interactive exhibits and films revealing the tough realities of life on the shearing circuit, then step into the historic shed to watch live-shearing demonstrations at 10.30am and 1pm daily and meet the shearers' trusty working dogs.

Pedal power

Pick up a free bike at the **Hay Visitor Information Centre** and set off to explore Hay on two wheels. The flat landscape and small town lends itself to a relaxing ride. Explore the Bidgee Riverside Trail, right along the edge of the Murrumbidgee and check out the stunning water-tower art on Pine St, commemorating the people of Hay's service during the world wars. If you've worked up a sweat, just down the road, the **John Houston Memorial Pool** is free for everyone.

Endless sunset vistas

Before sundown, head 16km out of town on the Cobb Hwy to the **Hay Plains Sunset Viewing Area** to see an epic sunset in the flattest place in Australia. Pack a picnic to enjoy the 360-degree view as the sky comes alive with orange and pink hues.

WHAT IS THE DENI UTE MUSTER?

Deniliquin, or Deni, is the self-proclaimed 'ute capital of the world'. This classic Australian vehicle, with a chassis up front and a handy tray out the back, is celebrated yearly at the **Deni Ute Muster** *(deniutemuster.com.au)*. The country festival was established in 1999 with a vision to put Deniliquin on the map. Held over one wild weekend in October, the festival now attracts up to 20,000 people. It celebrates all things outback: music, whip-cracking, bull rides, bogan bingo and ute races.

In town, the *Ute on a Pole* sculpture commemorates Deniliquin's *Guinness Book of Records* entry for hosting the largest parade of utes ever recorded, with 2839 vehicles.

EATING & DRINKING IN GRIFFITH: OUR PICKS

La Scala: Since 1977, La Scala has been offering authentic Italian dining, house-made pasta, wood-fired pizza and delicious gelato. *6-9pm Tue-Sat* $$

Limone: Farm-to-fork dining using local, seasonal ingredients served in a stunning rustic interior. *7am-2pm Mon-Sat* $$

De Bortoli: Stop at this third-generation winery for a tasting and cheese platter. Don't miss its signature drop, Noble One. *9am-5pm Mon-Sat* $

Calabria Family Wines: Book for a tasting flight of eight wines with small platter in the Tuscan-style cellar door. *9am-4pm Mon-Fri, from 10am Sat & Sun* $$

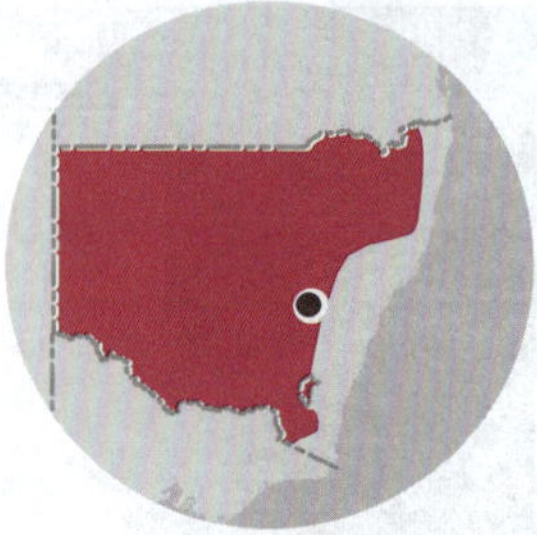

Orange

WINE | SHOPPING | QUAINT VILLAGES

GETTING AROUND

The regional airport has flights to Melbourne, Sydney and Brisbane most days. You can also get to Orange on the XPT train or Australia Wide Coaches bus service.

Orange is a 3½-hour drive from Sydney. The town is walkable and parking is plentiful but often limited to two hours.

TOP TIP

The Orange Wine Festival in spring and the FOOD festival in autumn are the best times to see the town come alive to celebrate the local culinary scene. Plus the autumn landscape of red, gold and orange hues makes it a picturesque time to visit the local wineries.

Known as the town of colours, Orange has long punched above its weight, but in recent years it's become a favourite escape for Sydneysiders seeking fresh country air, either just for a weekend or for good. Driving in beneath treelined streets and twinkling fairy lights feels a little magical. Though its name might suggest otherwise, Orange wasn't inspired by the coloured autumn leaves, but likely chosen by Major Thomas Mitchell in honour of Prince William of Orange.

In spring, the region bursts into green and gold, with canola fields and blooming gardens blanketing the landscape. Fertile farmland fuels a thriving food and wine scene that will be sure to delight visiting gourmets. Beautiful homewares stores and boutique shops, both in town and nearby villages, may tempt you into indulgent spending.

Mt Canobolas

ALF MANCIAGLI/SHUTTERSTOCK

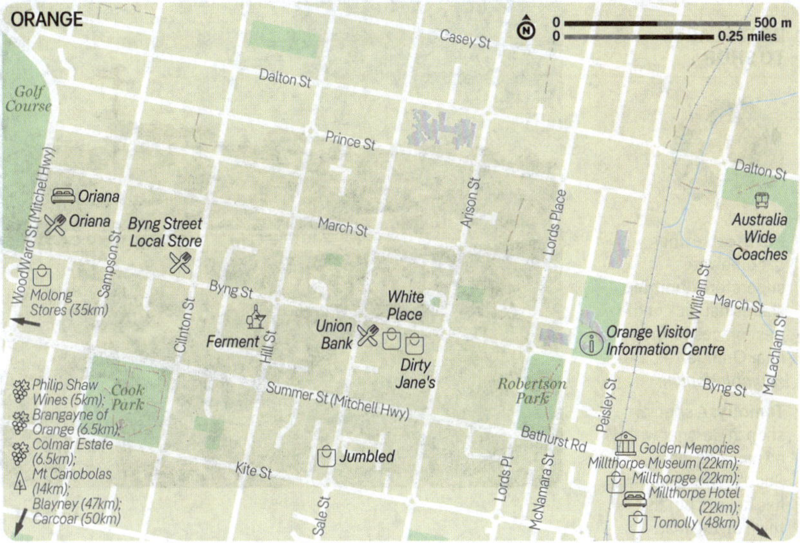

Orange in a Bottle

High-altitude wines with attitude

More than 40 cellar doors are tucked off winding country lanes and rolling hills, with a few breweries and cider houses thrown in for good measure. The cellar doors of **Philip Shaw Wines** *(philipshaw.com.au)*, **Colmar Estate** *(colmarestate.com.au)* and **Brangayne of Orange** *(brangayne.com)* can be easily visited on a self-guided drive along Pinnacle Rd or on a tour with **Orange Wine Tours** *(orangewinetours.com.au; $215)*. If you don't have time to visit them all, pop into **Ferment** *(orangewinecentre.com.au)*, a wine bar that features a huge selection of wines from 19 local wineries.

Views from Above

An ancient volcano lookout

Take in the scenic views atop **Mt Canobolas/Gaanha bula lookout**, an ancient volcano 1395m above sea level. The volcanic soil helps support the incredible wines produced on its slopes. At ground level, walk the 2.5km track around the **Lake**

EATING & DRINKING IN ORANGE: OUR PICKS

Byng Street Local Store: Behind a large red door, this local fave serves up excellent coffee and delicious food on a big corner block. *7am-3pm* $

Oriana: Relaxed vibes on the sprawling lawns; enjoy tapas, wood-fired pizzas and oyster nights at this retro hotel. *hours vary* $$

Union Bank: Great food, drinks and friendly service in the twinkling leafy courtyard or under the high ceilings of this former bank. *noon-11pm* $$

Ferment: Sample a huge selection of local wines during the daily guided wine tastings or from the fancy wine vending machine. *noon-9pm Mon-Sat* $

BEST PLACES TO SHOP

Pip Brett, owner of homewares superstore **Jumbled**, shares her pick of the best places to shop near Orange. *@jumbledonline*

Tomolly: A special shop in Carcoar with an amazing vibe. Shopkeeper Belinda has helped put the town on the map.

Molong Stores: Town larrikin Rob fits amazing hats from his shop in an 1876 Federation building in the tiny town of Molong.

Dirty Jane's: A really cool vintage store with retro collectibles, books, records, toys, jewellery and clothes and a delicious on-site cafe.

White Place: An entire home filled with stylish furniture and fashion with a predominantly white hue in Orange.

CHRIS ANDREWS FERN BAY/SHUTTERSTOCK

Carcoar

Canobolas reservoir or take a dip to cool off. With plenty of picnic areas and a playground, it's a great spot for kids – the turn off to the lake is on the extension of Coronation Rd, 8km west of town.

A Country Drive

Historic villages and charming gold-rush towns

While Orange has modern amenities, its endearing neighbouring villages have a more historic bent. Just a 20-minute drive away is heritage-listed **Millthorpe**, a charming town with art galleries, boutiques and fine dining alongside cosy providores. Walk the cobbled streets and pop into the **Golden Memories Millthorpe Museum** *(millthorpemuseum.com; adult/child $10/5)* to see colonial artefacts and historic items.

Continue along country roads to **Blayney**. The town's rich farming history meant its railway was once a busy station for passengers and goods. Pick up a Blayney Heritage Walk guide from the **Orange Visitor Information Centre** and wander the historic streets.

Time stands still in **Carcoar**, listed by the National Trust for its beautifully preserved 19th-century buildings from the town's gold-rush era. A 40-minute drive from Orange, this picture-perfect town is a breath of fresh country air and charm. The best views of the rolling countryside are from the train station.

Beyond Orange

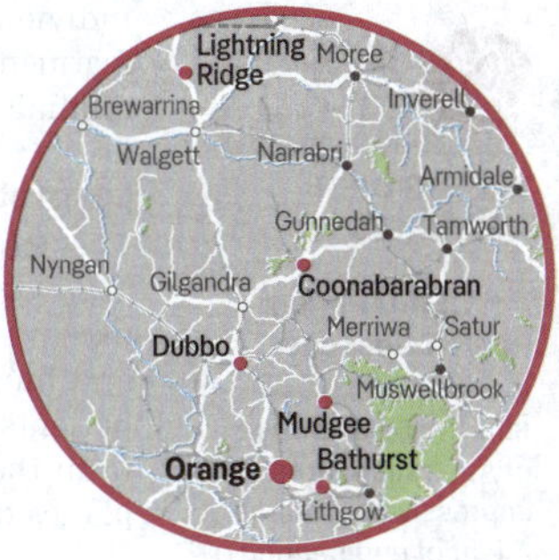

Orange is a great hub for exploring quaint villages – look further afield to discover fascinating towns in every direction.

This northern section of NSW is as varied as it is vast. East of Orange, Bathurst is synonymous with car racing for most Australians. To the south, canola fields stretch out towards Cowra and the cherry-picking capital of Young. To the west, Parkes' big dish is an engineering marvel; while in the north, you'll find Dubbo's plains and Mudgee's refined wineries. Push further north into outback Australia, where the quirky mining town of Lightning Ridge will have you looking down; and the stargazing capital of Australia in Coonabarabran will turn your gaze skywards.

To get off the beaten track, explore the Silo Art Trail and the tiny towns with towering art projects putting them on the map.

Places

Bathurst

TIME FROM ORANGE: **50MIN**

A hot lap of the track

Cruise the circuit at **Mt Panorama**, a public road that hosts major car races in Bathurst. The most famous is the **Bathurst 1000** in October.

Download the Bathurst 'Step Beyond' app and listen to the audio-guide from racecar driver Craig Lowndes as you circle the track. Afterwards, visit the **National Motor Racing Museum** *(museumsbathurst.com.au/nmrm; adult/child $15/7.50)* next to the track and learn more about the history of racing.

Dubbo

TIME FROM ORANGE: **2HR**

Animal spotting on a 'zoo-fari'

Dubbo's must-see attraction is the sprawling **Taronga Western Plains Zoo** *(taronga.org.au; adult/child $49.50/29.70)*, home to more than 350 species, including lion cubs and rhino calves.

Drive your own car, walk or ride bikes (hire available) around the 6km circuit or upgrade to a 'safari vehicle'. The variety of transport options available makes the zoo accessible for

GETTING AROUND

The only way to get around this region is with your own car. The roads are in good condition, but watch out for kangaroos around dawn and dusk. Distances are further than they appear, so plan for regular stops.

Mt Panorama in Bathurst is a public road with a 60km/h speed limit outside of race days.

THE BIG DISH AT PARKES

The **CSIRO Parkes Radio Telescope**, the star of the 2000 film *The Dish*, is one of Australia's more impressive big things. A feat of engineering, it allows astronomers to explore the universe in greater detail. The telescope was famously used to receive live TV images of the *Apollo 11* moon landing, even withstanding 100km/h gusts during the 2½-hour broadcast.

Spanning 64m in diameter and balanced atop a three-storey concrete tower in the middle of a paddock, it's a sight to behold. In its shadow, the Visitor Discovery Centre explains the telescope's importance through hands-on displays and an immersive 3D theatre show. It's free to visit.

individuals with mobility challenges. The open-range design, featuring concealed moats instead of fences, makes spotting animals easy for everyone.

Learn about Australia's Flying Doctors

The **Royal Flying Doctor Service Visitor Experience** *(dubbo.experience.flyingdoctor.org.au; adult/child $25/15)* uses ultramodern interactive exhibits, a giant movie screen and immersive spaces to tell the stories of the doctors and patients who rely on the roving medical service. Get a photo in the pilot's seat or head up to the sky lounge to watch planes take off and land.

Mudgee

TIME FROM ORANGE: **2HR**

A taste of wine country

Mudgee is a refined country town that attracts well-heeled weekenders and former Sydney folk. Despite a population of more than 25,000, the town still has no traffic lights, adding to its relaxed, small-town charm.

The **Mudgee Visitor Information Centre** provides winery maps showcasing the region's 35-plus family-owned wineries, along with three breweries and the Baker Williams distillery. Don't miss **Logan Wines** *(loganwines.com.au)* for the views and **De Beaurepaire** *(debeaurepairewines.com)* for its French flair. Many wineries close on Mondays and Tuesdays and weekends can be busy, so check listings at *mudgeewine.com.au* and book tastings in advance.

For a full day of guided wine tasting across five wineries, join a **Mudgee Wine Explorer Tour** *(mudgeeexplorertours.com.au; from $152)*.

Lightning Ridge

TIME FROM ORANGE: **5HR**

Discover rare black opals in unusual mine tunnels

Lightning Ridge is a quirky outback opal-mining town less than an hour's drive from the Queensland border. It's one of the few places in the world where 'black opals' can be found. Learn more at the town's opal shops or the **Australian Opal Centre** *(australianopalcentre.com; free)*, in the final stages of completing a huge new facility at the time of writing. Go underground in the former mine tunnels at **Opal Mine Adventure** *(opalmineadventure.com.au; adult/child $20/8)* and then try your luck searching for opals at the fossicking heap.

EATING BEYOND ORANGE: OUR PICKS

Ling Ling Thai: In the Orana Hotel in Dubbo, this casual venue serves delicious, authentic Thai meals in generous portions. *5-9.30pm* $$

Press: You can't go wrong at leafy cafe Press, a local favourite in Dubbo with great coffee, big serves and vegan options. *7am-2.30pm Mon-Sat, 8am-2pm Sun* $$

Norma Joan: A bar-restaurant featuring local ingredients and wines tucked away in a festooned courtyard in Bathurst. *hours vary Thu-Mon* $$

Lightning Ridge Bowling Club: Everything under one roof: Asian meals, pizza, pub classics, a bar, cafe, bingo, raffles and a bottle shop. *10am-10pm* $$

DRIVING THE SILO ART TRAIL

This tour takes you past some of the most impressive grain silos and water tanks adorned with oversize artworks across NSW. See more at *australiansiloarttrail.com*.

START	END	LENGTH
Harden	Lightning Ridge	825km; 10+hr

Starting in 1 **Harden**, the Murrumburrah Silo Art by Heesco depicts rural Australia on the eastern side, while the western side reflects the gold-rush period. From here, continue 130km northwest to another Heesco artwork – the 2 **Grenfell** Silos, adorned with sheep, cattle and native birds representing the shire's farming industry.

Continue 180km northeast to 3 **Portland** Old Cement Works. Known as *The Foundations*, these incredibly detailed portraits depict five former workers of the town's cement plant.

Another 230km north is the 4 **Dunedoo** Silo Art, depicting champion racehorse Winx, her trainer and her rider, Hugh Bowman, who was born in Dunedoo. Travel another 160km north to tiny 5 **Gulargambone**, where you'll find colourful water towers adorned with kingfishers, murals and an impressive wire bullock sculpture. A straight 50km stretch takes you past the 25m 6 **Coonamble** Water Tower, painted with pink galahs against a starry sky.

From Coonamble, drive 120km to 7 **Walgett**, where the colourful water tower is a tribute to one of Australia's most cherished Aboriginal musicians, Jimmy Little.

The final straight leg leads to quirky 8 **Lightning Ridge**, with legendary local artist John Murray's street murals.

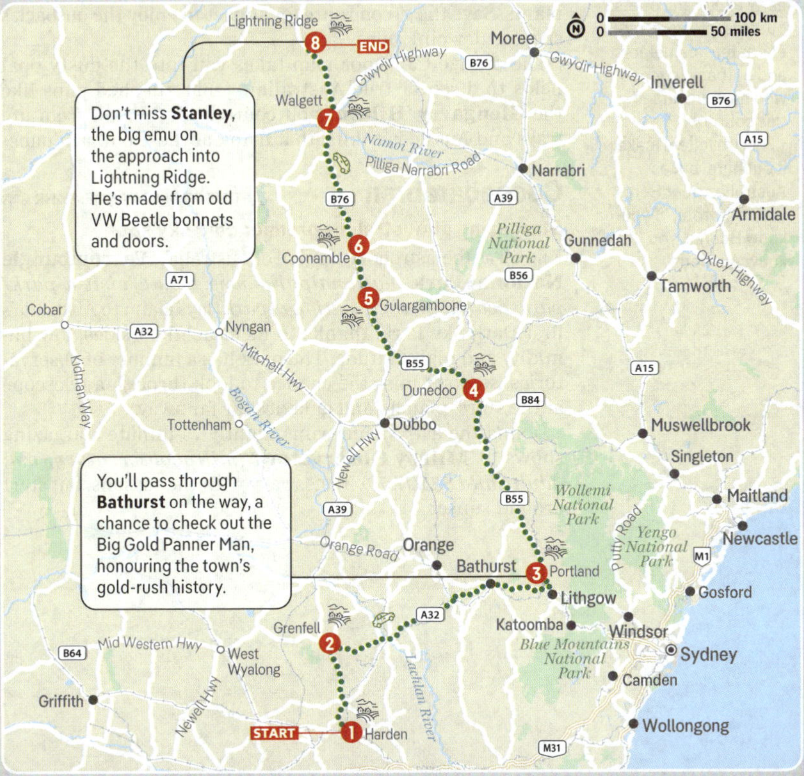

BACK O' BOURKE

When you picture the dusty Australian outback, far from any major city, that's pretty much 'back o' Bourke'. As the last outback hub before the bush stretches out endlessly into the vast interior, Bourke has become part of Australian vernacular.

Back o' Bourke refers to not one place, but a collective 'out there'. The **Back O' Bourke Exhibition Centre** tells engaging stories of the First Nations peoples, early explorers, poets, outlaws, graziers, river boaters, cameleers and outback legends who have traversed this country.

Few travellers make it out here, but as Australian poet Henry Lawson wrote, 'If you know Bourke, you know Australia'.

Vibrant outback art and local murals

Local artist John Murray has painted murals on every street and his vibrant **John Murray Art Gallery** *(johnmurrayart.com.au; free)* is worth a visit. Murray's vibrant, humorous paintings capture the spirit of the Australian outback: emus in utes, dusty roads and surreal desert scenes layered with Aussie wit.

Soothing artesian baths beneath a starry sky

Relax in a natural artesian **bore bath**, where the mineral-rich water is drawn from the Great Artesian Basin, 1200m below ground. Maintaining 40–50°C water temperature, this free community bath is open year-round and is especially magical under a starry night sky.

Self-drive tours through quirky outback opal fields

Visit the **Lightning Ridge Visitor Information Centre** and pick up a Car Door Tour self-drive map. Four short routes are marked out with painted car doors, leading you to the colourful highlights of 'the Ridge', such as the **Chambers of the Black Hand** *(chambersoftheblackhand.com.au; adult/child $48/16)*, an incredible underground sculpture museum (online bookings essential), and **Bevan's Cactus Nursery** *(bevanscactus.com; $10)*, home to more than 2500 prickly plants. Save the green route for sunset to enjoy the outback's spectacular pink hues.

The orange Car Door map takes you into the dusty opal fields to discover true Australian gems: tin-shed pubs like the **Glengarry 'Hilton'**, golf courses that tee off from ute trays and Aussie larrikins that drink at these outback pubs.

Coonabarabran

TIME FROM ORANGE: **3½HR**

Stargazing at Australia's premier dark sky spot

Known as the 'astronomy capital of Australia', **Warrumbungle National Park** *(nationalparks.nsw.gov.au/visit-a-park/parks/warrumbungle-national-park)* lays claim to Australia's first Dark Sky Park, thanks to its clear night skies, low humidity and high altitude. The park has a number of observatories, so don't miss the chance to look through a telescope at the stars, planets and galaxies far far away.

Donna the astronomer runs nightly 75-minute stargazing shows at **Milroy Observatory** *(milroyobservatory.com; adult/child $35/17.50)*. Times vary with the seasons, but start around sunset.

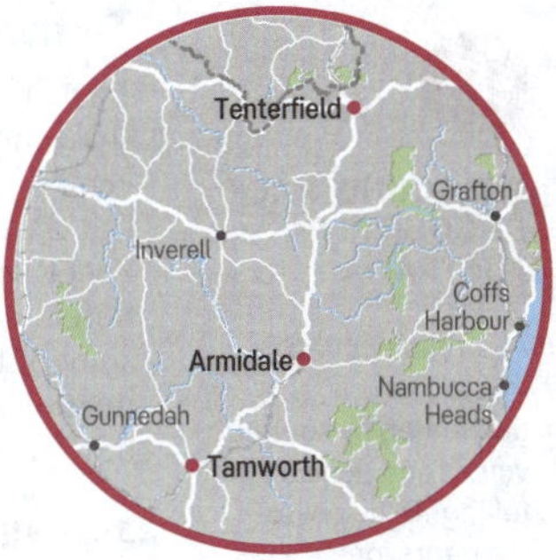

New England

HISTORIC TOWNS | COUNTRY LIFE | NATIONAL PARKS

Despite its unfamiliarity, the verdant scenery of this highland region prompted its first British occupiers to name it 'New England'. While visitors may squint hard to see the likeness, the forested uplands of the Northern Tablelands reminded the homesick colonisers of Scotland and Wales, and the landscape bears 'Celtic' names and the label of 'Celtic country' to this day. It's a stretch, but there's no denying its rustic beauty when mist settles in the hilltops and fertile valleys, little churches are glimpsed in oak-studded paddocks and narrow roads wind through cool green landscapes. Dotted with historic buildings, regional centres including Tamworth, Armidale and Tenterfield have plenty to offer those seeking culture, food and comfort.

The region straddles the traditional lands of several Aboriginal groups, including the Gamilaroi around Tamworth, the Anaiwan around Armidale and the Bundjalung around Tenterfield, among others. Venture beyond the towns to discover a rich collection of national parks and cool-climate wineries.

Tenterfield School of Arts (p266)

ROBERT WALLACE/WALLACE MEDIA NETWORK/ALAMY

Places

GETTING AROUND

The New England region stretches from Tamworth (400km northwest of Sydney) to Tenterfield (700km northwest of Sydney), with the main towns located on the scenic New England Hwy.

NSW TrainLink runs a daily service from Sydney Central to Armidale (eight hours) via Tamworth (six hours), with coach connections to Glen Innes and Tenterfield. With limited public transport beyond these main hubs, most travellers visit on a New England Hwy road trip.

Tamworth and Armidale have tourism information centres – the Big Golden Guitar marks the entrance to the Tamworth branch.

THE SOUNDTRACK OF COUNTRY AUSTRALIA

Australia's country-music scene is dominated by soulful voices and rich storytelling. To discover the genre, press play on Australian legend Slim Dusty, whose classics like 'A Pub with No Beer' you'll hear playing in country pubs. Or tune into popular artists Troy Cassar-Daley, John Williamson, Lee Kernaghan and Kasey Chambers – the backbone of the Australian country music scene for decades – while The Wolfe Brothers add a fresh, rock-infused energy and The McClymonts offer a lighter sound.

The Tamworth Country Music Festival was the launching platform of Aussie superstar Keith Urban, while Peter Allen's famous song 'Tenterfield Saddler' was inspired by his grandfather's saddlery shop in Tenterfield.

Tamworth

TIME FROM ORANGE: **4HR 40MIN**

Australia's country-music capital has a good deal more to it than the annual festival and a reverence for Slim Dusty. The centre of a bounteous farming district traditionally owned by the Gamilaroi people, its broad streets range back from the Peel River, laid out in a grid studded with museums, Art Deco hotels, cafes and restaurants. Tamworth's infatuation with the song of the cowboy is evident throughout town, while to the northeast sit modest uplands offering comprehensive views of rich farmland spreading out in all directions.

Australia's country-music capital

Held over 10 rollicking days from mid-January, the **Tamworth Country Music Festival** *(tcmf.com.au)* is the undisputed king of Australian country music events. It features hundreds of performers across dozens of venues, with around 1000 single events entertaining tens of thousands of visitors.

Outside the festival period, you can follow the town's **Country Music Trail** *(destinationtamworth.com.au/country-music-trail)*. The main stop is the **Country Music Hall of Fame** *(countrymusichalloffame.com.au; adult/child $10/7)* at the southern end of Peel St, housing a trove of artefacts and dioramas exploring Australia's rich country-music story. Two principal exhibitions – the memorabilia-filled Walk a Country Mile and the Country Music Hall of Fame – are housed inside the giant guitar-shaped building.

The Big Golden Guitar

Arguably Tamworth's most photographed sight, this iconic 12m-high golden guitar glitters proudly out front of the Tamworth Visitor Information Centre. The **Big Golden Guitar** is a replica of the famous Golden Guitar Award handed out to the year's best country music artist at the Tamworth Country Music Festival. It's on the southern stretch of the highway leading into town, about 5km from the city centre, with ample parking. The complex is also home to a souvenir shop and cafe, but you can happily skip the underwhelming Country Music Wax Museum.

Tour the Powerstation Museum

Run by infectiously passionate volunteers, this wonderful **Powerstation Museum** *(tamworthpowerstationmuseum.com.au; adult/child $5/3; Wed-Sat)* on Peel St

Try the tasting menu to sample all the most popular dishes

EATING IN TAMWORTH: OUR PICKS

Hopscotch: With fantastic coffee and extensive menu, this prime location right next to a playground makes it a favourite for families. *7am-3pm* **$$**

Le Pruneau: This cottage-style cafe in West Tamworth does spot-on French country cooking, coffee and baked goods. *6.30am-4pm Tue-Fri, 7am-2pm Sat* **$$**

Dragon Palace: Fans of country-town Chinese restaurants will find all the classics here in Tamworth. *noon-2pm & 5-9pm* **$$**

Glasshouse at Goonoo Goonoo: A historic sheep station outside Tamworth is the region's home of fine dining. *hours vary* **$$$**

Big Golden Guitar

commemorates Tamworth's status as the 'City of Light' – the first town in Australia to get electric light (16 years before Sydney!).

Housed in a 1907 power station packed to the rafters with electrotherapy machines, early communications devices and other fascinating electricity-powered artefacts, the museum also has two working steam dynamos, one identical to that used to first deliver power to the town in 1888.

Armidale

TIME FROM TAMWORTH: **90MIN**

Sitting high on New South Wales' Northern Tablelands, surrounded by prime grazing country traditionally owned by the Anaiwan people, Armidale – with its broad streets, lattice-wrapped pubs and distinctive blue-brick buildings – is the de-facto capital of this region. Its physical charms are augmented by four distinct seasons and the proximity of ravishingly beautiful forests and highlands. Home to some of Australia's best boarding schools and the University of New England, Armidale is accustomed to welcoming visitors and gaining admirers, year-round.

RE-EMERGING WINE REGION

New England has a history of viticulture dating back to its first European colony. The *Sunday Mail* described Inverell, 124km northwest of Armidale, as home to 'one of the foremost wine-producing neighbourhoods in the colony' in 1882. But it wasn't to last and the region's last winery reportedly closed during WWII.

Yet the local industry is slowly re-emerging and cool-climate estates are dotting the region. **Topper's Mountain Wines** in Tingha, between Armidale and Inverell, has bagged many awards for its German-style gewurztraminer; **Petersons Guesthouse & Winery** in Armidale is the place to go to sample a range of local wines, housed in the former stables of a historic homestead.

The weekday $20 lunch specials are a steal

EATING & DRINKING IN ARMIDALE: OUR PICKS

Goldfish Bowl: Follow the aroma of fresh coffee to this Armidale cafe or come for Friday wood-fired pizzas. *hours vary* **$$**

Welder's Dog: Build your own grazing platter to enjoy with a craft brew at this Armidale brew bar. *2pm-midnight Tue-Sat, to 10pm Sun & Mon*

Great Hops Brewery: Join the revelry at this huge, eclectic Armidale brewery, with great burgers to mop up the suds. *4-11pm Fri, 12.30-11pm Sat, 12.30-4pm Sun*

Whitebull Hotel: A country pub with an above-average menu and emphasis on local produce. *10am-midnight Mon-Sat, 11am-10pm Sun*

NEW ENGLAND'S BEST NATIONAL PARKS

Bald Rock National Park: The eponymous feature of this park northeast of Tenterfield is Australia's largest granite monolith.

New England National Park: Lichen-draped wilderness area, east of Armidale, spills over the edge of dramatic escarpment.

Oxley Wild Rivers National Park: The park's showpiece, Dangar Falls, is a 25-minute drive south of Armidale. Take a gorge tour with Fleet Helicopters.

Washpool National Park: Rainforest-fringed swimming holes tempt the hour-long detour northeast of Glen Innes.

Boonoo Boonoo National Park: Poet Banjo Paterson famously proposed to his sweetheart, Alice Walker, at the waterfall lookout in this park northeast of Tenterfield.

Queen of the arts

If Tamworth is the king of country music, Armidale is the queen of the arts. The **New England Regional Art Museum** *(neram.com.au; free)* is the home of the Howard Hinton Collection, a veritable thesaurus of Australian art from the 1880s to the 1940s, including works by Arthur Streeton, Margaret Preston and Norman Lindsay. It's closed Mondays. The **Museum of Printing** next door opens on Tuesday and Sunday and traces the history of printing in Australia.

Next door again is the not-for-profit **Aboriginal Cultural Centre & Keeping Place** *(acckp.com.au; free)*, which displays a growing permanent collection, of art and Aboriginal crafts, alongside regularly changing exhibitions of works for sale.

Inside Armidale's Edwardian gem

A masterpiece of Edwardian architecture 9km west of Armidale, **Saumarez Homestead** *(nationaltrust.org.au/places/saumarez-homestead; adult/child $15/12)* was built between 1888 and 1906 on one of the first sheep stations in the area. Be guided through the 30-room time capsule of family life on Wednesdays, Fridays and Sundays. Or you can wander the gardens and peek through the windows for a reduced fee.

Tenterfield

TIME FROM ARMIDALE: **2HR**

Home to a clutch of charming heritage buildings, peaceful Tenterfield serves as the regional hub for a smattering of villages surrounded by picturesque national parks. High altitude means cooler climes in summer and occasional ground-snow accumulations in winter. The Bundjalung are the traditional owners of this land.

Birth of a nation

The leafy highland town of Tenterfield is often hailed as the birthplace of the Australian nation. It was here, in the Banquet Hall at the Tenterfield **School of Arts** in 1889, that Sir Henry Parkes delivered his famous Tenterfield Oration, the speech that ignited the movement leading to the Federation of Australia in 1901. You can step inside the building and explore memorabilia from Parkes' personal life, including a compelling portrait by Julian Ashton, ivory carvings and journals.

Hear the sound of Tenterfield

The free **Tenterfield Soundtrail** *(soundtrails.com.au/tenterfield)* guides you through the heart of town, on a 2.5km audio tour blending history with local storytelling. Hear tales of jailhouse ghosts, brass bands, talking cats and hometown hero Peter Allen's 'manna from heaven'. You'll pass the workshop immortalised in his popular 'Tenterfield Saddler' song, now a living museum full of leather goods and historical tools, as well as the **Centenary Cottage Museum** *(centenarycottagemuseum.com.au)* on Logan St (generally Saturday to Monday). It offers an evocative taste of the town's pioneer days, especially when the volunteer staff wind up the gramophone in the sitting room.

Broken Hill & Silverton

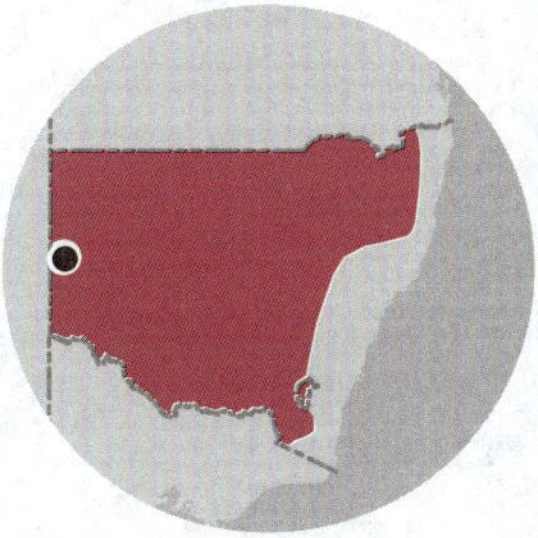

MINING HISTORY | ART SCENE | OUTBACK LANDSCAPES

The discovery of silver ore in this remote corner of outback NSW in the 1880s brought about the establishment of two of Australia's most influential mining towns. Broken Hill stands today as one of Australia's longest continually mined cities and the first city to be included in its entirety on the National Heritage List. Together with Silverton, 25km west, the region is known for its strong history in trade unionism and where significant improvements to miners' rights were fought and won.

Nowadays, it's the flourishing artistic scene that's making headlines, with sweeping outback landscapes inspiring many of the works in the 30-plus art galleries and a growing list of film accolades that includes *Mission: Impossible 2*, *Mad Max 2* and Australian classic *The Adventures of Priscilla, Queen of the Desert*, all filmed on location here. Out of *Priscilla* grew a thriving drag culture; celebrated at the Palace Hotel and the fabulous Broken Heel Festival.

TOP TIP

From around mid-November to mid-March, many outdoor tour operators suspend operations because of the heat – temperatures are routinely above 35°C. If you're planning to travel during this time, do your research and contact businesses directly to check what's running.

Flying for Your Life

Tour an outback institution

The **Royal Flying Doctor Outback Heritage Experience** *(brokenhill.experience.flyingdoctor.org.au; adult/child $25/15)* in Broken Hill is the only working RFDS base in the country

GETTING AROUND

While Broken Hill's downtown area is walkable, explorations beyond are far easier with your own vehicle. Broken Hill's wide streets, many named after minerals, are a dream to drive. Check parking options for hotels along Argent St; a two-hour daytime limit typically applies.

Pay special attention to the road between Silverton and Broken Hill at night. It's sealed, but an 11km section is unfenced grazing land. Depending on your itinerary, expect to travel along unsealed roads at some point. Those without their own wheels can join a tour or use the CDC public bus service.

HIGHLIGHTS
1 Broken Hill City Art Gallery

SIGHTS
2 Absalom's Gallery
3 Big Bench
4 Day Dream Mine
5 John Dynon Gallery
6 Line of Lode Miners Memorial
7 Living Desert State Park
8 Mad Max 2 Museum
9 Pro Hart Gallery
10 Royal Flying Doctor Outback Heritage Experience
11 Silver City Mint & Art Centre
12 Willy Nilly Art

ACTIVITIES
13 Broken Hill City Sights Tours
14 Outback Astronomy
15 Silverton Outback Camels

SLEEPING
16 Imperial Fine Accommodation
17 Red Earth Motel

EATING
18 Astra
19 Bell's Milk Bar
20 Old Salt Bush
21 Silly Goat
22 Silverton Bakery

DRINKING & NIGHTLIFE
23 Broken Hill Pub
24 Palace Hotel
25 Silverton Hotel

INFORMATION
26 Broken Hill Visitor Information Centre

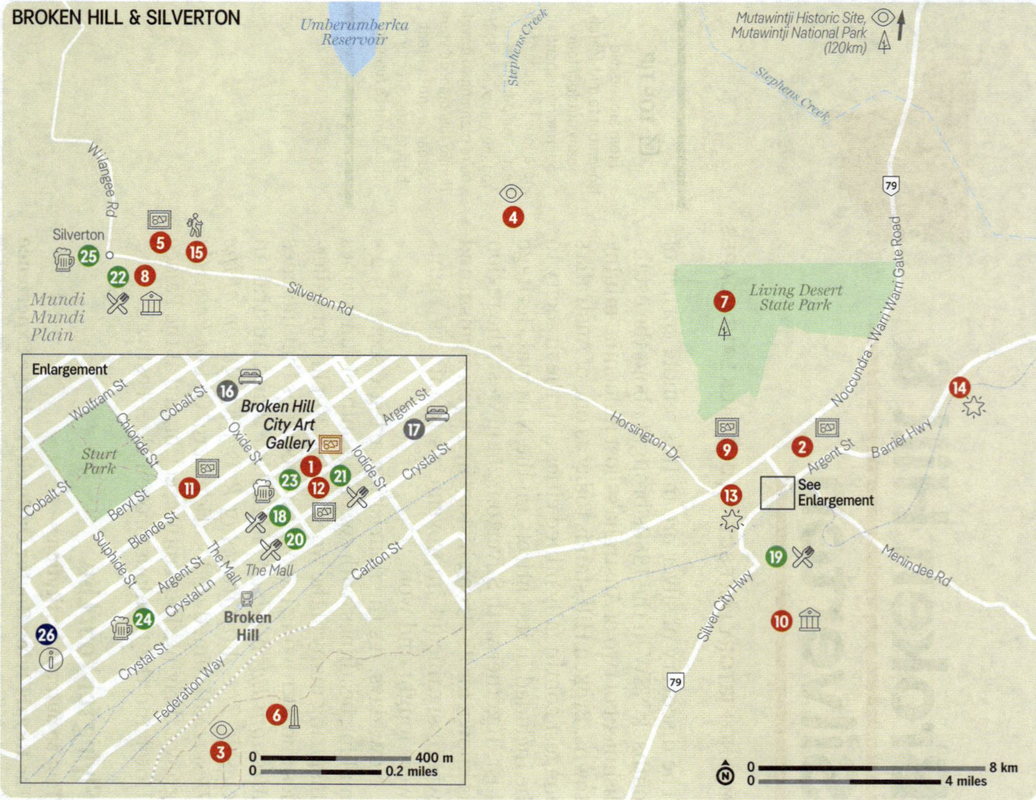

that visitors can tour. Every year, the RFDS travels the equivalent of 35 round-trips to the moon, delivering emergency extraction and primary care services to remote outback communities. Inside the interactive museum, you can see what's happening in real-time in the working control room, explore the aeromedical aircraft in the hangar, tune into real-life medical help calls from remote stations to the Broken Hill base and learn more about the everyday heroes who work for the RFDS. Guided volunteer-led tours operate on a rolling basis throughout the day.

Broken Hill's Reason for Existence

Atop the city's 'mineralogical rainforest'

An imposing backdrop to Broken Hill's Argent St is a huge pile of mounded earth above the Line of Lode: it's locally called the 'slagheap' (meaning the leftover material from the mining process). The Line of Lode is where a rich silver-lead-zinc ore body, one of the world's largest, was first mined in 1885, prompting the founding of Broken Hill. Nearly a century and a half later, this 7.5km-long, 1.6km-deep underground network remains one of Australia's longest continually operated mines and, thanks to the area's diversity of about 300 mineral species, is considered one of the world's great mineral 'rainforests'.

Take the road to the top for views over the entire city and the novelty-sized **Big Bench**. The **Line of Lode Miners Memorial** pays tribute to the more than 800 lives lost in the mine since its inception.

Sunset Sculptures

Towering desert artworks

One of the most memorable Broken Hill experiences is viewing the sunset from the **Living Desert State Park Sculpture Symposium** *(visitbrokenhill.com; adult/child $10/7)*, on the highest hilltop 12km from town. The sculptures are the work of 12 international artists who carved the huge sandstone blocks on-site in 1993. The 24-sq-km park is also home to a flora-and-fauna sanctuary, featuring a 2.2km Cultural Walk Trail and a 1km Flora Trail. Drive up to the sculpture summit or walk up from the sanctuary (around 20 minutes). Pay your entry at the gate and beware park gates close about 30 minutes after sunset.

From Silver to the Silver Screen

The village that keeps innovating

The tiny town of Silverton, just 20 minutes from Broken Hill, once set the stage for the region's mining prowess. The discovery of silver and lead in 1883 saw Silverton's quick establishment and by 1885, it supported a busy community of 3000 miners. However, the discovery of Broken Hill's Line of Lode led to a mass exodus shortly after.

WHY THE TIME DIFFERENCE?

While geographically located in NSW, Broken Hill and Silverton are actually on South Australian time, half an hour behind the rest of the state. It may seem an oddity, but in a city that's never been afraid of standing tall in its differences, it's a quirk that seems rather befitting.

The actual reason is not so unconventional: Adelaide is Broken Hill's nearest capital and SA's Port Pirie has historically been the city's rail link for transporting ore. Born out of practicality, it simply made sense for origin and destination points to be operating in the same time zone. The slightly more exciting local tale is that it's to keep visitors on their toes.

THE REGION'S BEST TOURS

Silverton Outback Camels: Sightsee from the back of a camel with Petah Devine.

Outback Astronomy: Have an expert interpret the spectacular desert night sky while enjoying a cheeseboard and glass of bubbly.

Heritage Walk Tours: Dive into Broken Hill's history with an informative volunteer-led walking tour. Book at the Visitor Information Centre.

Heroes, Larrikins & Visionaries Tour: The 2.5km walking trail introduces you to stories of people who shaped Broken Hill. Pick up a map at the Visitor Information Centre.

Broken Hill City Sights Tours: Tours through Broken Hill, Silverton, Menindee Lakes and White Cliffs, and Day Dream Mine.

SUE MARTIN/SHUTTERSTOCK

But there was no moving the **Silverton Hotel**, now one of Australia's most renowned outback pubs and where mining giant BHP was formed. Say hi to the town's four freely roaming resident donkeys making a scene for carrots at the pub's entrance.

As the set of the 1971 thriller *Wake in Fright*, the hotel kick-started the region's foray into cinema, cemented a decade later with *Mad Max 2* filmed on the nearby Mundi Mundi Plains. Film buff Adrian Bennett is behind the hugely popular **Mad Max 2 Museum** *(silverton.org.au/mad-max-museum; adult/child $10/7.5)*, filled with authentic and replica items from the postapocalyptic set.

The Big Picture

A stunning outback panorama

Silver City Mint & Art Centre *(08 8088 6166; adult/child $8.50/free)* is home to locally made gourmet chocolate, as well as unique silver jewellery and opals, but the real reason to pay the entry fee is to see *The Big Picture*, one of the world's largest canvas paintings. Local artist Peter Anderson used

Say hi to the four friendly donkeys who laze on the pub's verandah most days

EATING & DRINKING IN BROKEN HILL & SILVERTON: OUR PICKS

Silverton Bakery: Delicious selection of in-house baked goods. Try the pies, sourdough or slices. *8.30am-2pm Wed-Sun* $

Old Salt Bush: Upscale restaurant with a menu of regionally sourced produce, infused with rich flavours of native bush foods. *6.30-8.30pm Fri & Sat* $$$

Broken Hill Pub: A classic outback watering hole occupying a main street corner; expect friendly locals and cold beer. *11am-10pm Sun-Thu, to midnight Fri & Sat*

Silverton Hotel: Enjoy pub classics for breakfast, lunch and dinner in this iconic pub in the heart of town. *8am-9pm*

Silverton Hotel

9 tonnes of paint on this 100m-long, 12m-high U-shaped outback panorama. Grab a coupon from the Tourist Info Centre to save money.

Go Underground

Inside a historic mine

Experience what life was like for the early outback miner at the **Day Dream Mine** *(0427 885 682: daydreammine.com.au; adult/child from $33/13)* from the 1880s. Back then, miners worked 12-hour days, six days a week, by candlelight. Electric lights and head torches will guide your way today and rather than staying underground all day, tours last about 90 minutes. Guides give plenty of fascinating details about life in the mines and the harsh conditions miners endured. The tunnels are quite squeezy – not recommended for anyone who suffers from claustrophobia. The above-ground tour through a replica miners' hut is another option. Sturdy footwear is essential.

Afterwards, tuck into the famous fresh scones at the on-site tearoom. It's a scenic 13km dirt drive off the Silverton road; follow the signs. Bookings are essential.

EXPLORE BROKEN HILL'S ART SCENE

Kathy Graham, manager at **Broken Hill City Art Gallery**, shares her favourite arty spots.

Pro Hart Gallery: It doesn't get any more Broken Hill than legendary former-miner-turned-artist Pro Hart.

Absalom's Gallery: Another Broken Hill icon, outback survivalist Jack Absalom was one of the 'Brushmen of the Bush', a collective of local artists in the '70s.

John Dynon Gallery: Out in Silverton, expect brightness, colour and whimsy from this contemporary painter, along with an emu or two.

Willy Nilly Art: Stop into the studio of Broken Hill local Amanda Johnson, whose love of her hometown informs much of her work.

EATING & DRINKING IN BROKEN HILL: OUR PICKS

Silly Goat: A standout, this edgy, modern cafe is *the* place for coffee and brunch in Broken Hill. *6am-2pm Tue-Fri, 7am-1.30pm Sat* $$

Astra: Serving classic pub fare in the Trinders bistro and cocktails in the wine bar on Broken Hill's main street. *5.30-8.30pm* $$

Bell's Milk Bar: A buzzing 1950s retro-style milk bar. Try the signature green lime spider (ice cream float). *10am-5pm Tue-Sun* $

Palace Hotel: Of *Priscilla* film fame; snap photos of the iconic lobby by donation. Regular karaoke, two-up and drag bingo nights. *hours vary*

JASON_L/SHUTTERSTOCK

Mutawintji National Park

A Sacred Journey in Mutawintji

Indigenous rock art sanctuary with cultural tours

A 1½-hour drive northeast of Broken Hill, **Mutawintji National Park** was the first national park in NSW to be handed back to its Traditional Custodians (the Malyangapa and Pantjikali clans of the Barkandji nation) through state legislation. Largely regarded as the most significant Aboriginal ceremony and law business place in western NSW, Mutawintji features 300 recorded art sites with 5000 Panaramitee engravings, a petroglyph style of rock etching that acts as an intergenerational Indigenous cultural library.

In contrast to the open outback terrain of Broken Hill, cleared of vegetation to sustain the mining industry, here you stand among giant leopardwood, beefwood, mulga, cypress pines and river red gumtrees. The park has numerous walking tracks, from Grade 2 to 5, but access to the **Mutawintji Historic Site** in Nootumbulla Gorge, which contains the Main Engraving Site and the innermost ceremonial sanctum, is with an authorised Aboriginal guide only.

Places We Love to Stay

$ Budget $$ Midrange $$$ Top End

Canberra

MAP p230

Little Drifter $ Upmarket hostel with beautifully designed privates and dorms, a rooftop terrace, communal kitchen, games room; in central location.

Alivio Tourist Park $ A budget option with apartments, cabins, caravan sites, playgrounds and a pool; 4km from the city centre.

Little National Hotel $$ With a 24-hour spa and gym, bikes and a library space perfect for remote working, this hotel offers luxury on a budget.

East Hotel $$$ These family-friendly apartments are comfortable and stylish, with extras like free to Manuka Pool, laundry, kitchenettes and three on-site restaurants.

Snowy Mountains

Kookaburra Lodge $$ One of the cheapest options in Jindabyne with no minimum stay. Free hot breakfast and a large cosy lounge with a fireplace.

Thredbo Alpine Hotel $$$ If you want to stay on the mountain, this is the best spot in Thredbo. Big breakfast, parking, sauna, bike and ski storage included.

Wagga Wagga

MAP p251

Townhouse Hotel $$ Good-value rooms in the centre of town with free to the Oasis pool and gym. The on-site restaurant, Oakroom, is impressive.

Mantra Pavilion Hotel $$ Stylish hotel with some pet-friendly rooms; it's close to dining options at the bottom end of town.

Albury

Astor $$ This revamped retro hotel exudes a fun Palm Springs vibe. It has 40 rooms and a great pub menu.

Atura Albury $$ An art-inspired design hotel in central Albury without the high price tag. Generous breakfast, free parking and a pool.

Griffith

Gem Hotel $$ Super stylish suites and rooms, secure parking and great meals in the Bull & Bell Steakhouse.

Coro Club $$ Simple, budget-friendly, spacious rooms with plenty of parking; adjacent to a club with great-value meals and specials.

Orange

MAP p257

Millthorpe Motel $$ Enjoy a relaxing stay in a beautiful boutique property with kitchenettes in the heart of historic Millthorpe.

Oriana $$$ This revamped drive-up motel is the epitome of retro cool. Huge beer garden, pool bar and upmarket restaurant inside.

Dubbo

NRMA Dubbo Holiday Park $ If you're travelling with kids or a van, this dog-friendly park offers clean cabins, units, glamping tents and van sites, plus a playground and pool.

Lightning Ridge

Carinya Station $ Spend a night under the stars in the glamping tents or your own van or tent on this family farm 10 minutes out of the Ridge.

BIG4 Opal Holiday Park $ A well-maintained park with a range of cabins and sites, also with a pool; just a short drive to town.

Tamworth

CH Boutique Hotel $$ Tamworth's swankiest hotel, with 33 rooms in a modern annex and 29 rooms in the original building, decorated in sleek monochrome.

Tenterfield

Tenterfield Lodge & Caravan Park $ This pleasant, pet-friendly place has camp sites and cabins, a camp kitchen, laundry, book exchange and even a self-serve dog wash.

Commercial Boutique Hotel $$ Handsome Art Deco pub reinvented as a glamorous boutique hotel, with eight stylish en-suite rooms. Good gastropub fare served downstairs.

Broken Hill

MAP p268

Imperial Fine Accommodation $$ A short walk from Argent St, this elegant, heritage building with a pool is a respite after a day's sightseeing.

Red Earth Motel $$ Immaculate apartment-style rooms at the end of Argent St; easy walk to cafes and downtown attractions.

For places to stay in Brisbane & South Queensland, see p370

Above: View from South Bank (p289), Brisbane; Right: Dingo, K'gari (p344)

THE MAIN AREAS

Researched by
Brett Atkinson
and Tiare Tuuhia

Brisbane & South Queensland

URBAN THRILLS AND FUN IN THE SUN

Discover city culture, iconic beaches, vast sand islands and rugged hinterlands on a journey from Brisbane to the tropics.

Anchoring this vast region stretching from the New South Wales (NSW)–Queensland border to the Tropic of Capricorn is Brisbane (Meanjin). The capital of Queensland is infused with dynamism as the city prepares to host the Summer Olympics in 2032. After Melbourne (1956) and Sydney (2000), it's just the third opportunity for this sports-obsessed country to host the biggest game in town. The leviathan Queen's Wharf riverside development is more proof of Brisbane's global ambition and there's corresponding aspiration to the south on the Gold Coast, traditionally known for beaches and family-friendly theme parks, but now also enlivened with excellent cafes and restaurants. To the west is a slice of rugged countryside so picturesque it's called the Scenic Rim, while east and north of Brisbane lie the world's three biggest sand islands; rugged Moreton (Mulgumpin), relaxed North Stradbroke (Minjerribah) and surprising K'gari (formerly Fraser Island). Stretching from Brisbane north to the quintessential Australian beach town of Noosa is the Sunshine Coast, one of the fastest-growing regions of Australia and also packed with surf-lined beaches and family attractions. Noosa's own scenic hinterland includes quiet towns with markets, breweries and distilleries, while there's also outdoor adventures nearby on Lake Cootharaba. From Noosa, the Fraser Coast takes over, a natural playground known for whale watching and 4WD adventures on K'gari. Keep heading north and Rockhampton's riverside location flags Queensland's transition to the tropics.

CYNTHIA A JACKSON/SHUTTERSTOCK

SUNSHINE COAST
The name says it all.
p328

HERVEY BAY
4WD island adventures.
p339

BUNDABERG
Legendary rum and ginger beer.
p354

ROCKHAMPTON & YEPPOON
Historic river city and easy-going beach town.
p362

Find Your Way

Southern and central Queensland occupy a vast area, with each regional hub offering a different menu of experiences. Using the highlights of each area, plan and embark on your own personal itinerary.

Rockhampton & Yeppoon, p362
Relaxed, historic river city and charming coastal town with easy access to nearby Southern Great Barrier Reef islands.

Bundaberg, p354
The largest centre north of the Fraser Coast is known for its sugar-cane fields, rum and ginger beer.

Hervey Bay, p339
Watch whales breach on a boat tour from Hervey Bay and take your 4WD (or join a tour) on the ultimate island adventure on K'gari.

Noosa, p321
Ease into a coastal vibe, kayak a labyrinthine river system and enjoy Queensland's best market.

CAR

Hitting the road is the best way to experience the region beyond Brisbane, especially Toowoomba, the Scenic Rim, Granite Belt, the Gold Coast Hinterland, the Sunshine Coast and Rockhampton. A 4WD is essential for K'gari.

TRAIN

This is the easiest way to get around urban Brisbane and down to the Gold Coast to link up with the G:link light rail service. Heading north, Queensland Rail's Tilt Train links Brisbane to Rockhampton.

BUS

Translink buses operate in urban Brisbane. Greyhound buses run between the Gold Coast and Brisbane, west to Toowoomba and to the north linking Brisbane to the Sunshine Coast, Noosa and Rockhampton.

Sunshine Coast, p328

Hit the beach, detour to cafes and craft breweries and be immersed in lush rainforest.

Brisbane, p280

Queensland's capital city brims with the state's best museums, galleries, bars, restaurants and shopping. There's also plenty of riverside fun.

Gold Coast Hinterland, p316

Feel renewed after waterfall hikes and lap up gourmet treats and temptations in this mountainous, rainforest-clad region.

Surfers Paradise & the Gold Coast, p307

Hit the surf (or the theme parks), relax in cafes or bounce between bars. Options abound in this coastal playground.

Plan Your Time

For beaches, head to the Gold Coast, Noosa and the Sunshine Coast. Brisbane provides urban energy, while hinterland scenery and adventures await inland. K'gari is an essential destination further north.

PABOUV/SHUTTERSTOCK

Noosa National Park (p323)

Pressed for Time

- Choose between the bounty of history, arts and opportunities for gastronomic indulgence in **Brisbane** (p280) or hit the glittering beaches, easy-going cafes and nightlife of the **Gold Coast** (p307). While these twin cities are only an hour apart by car, it's easier to stick with one spot if you only have two or three days to spare, as there's plenty to keep you busy in both.

- If the weather isn't ideal, Brisbane offers a wider range of indoor attractions within a more compact area. Down on the Gold Coast, relaxed **Burleigh Heads** (p311) is a good base, easily reached on the G:link light rail extension and home to some of the GC's best cafes, restaurants and craft breweries.

Seasonal Highlights

Temperatures (in and out of the water) are comfortably warm year-round along the coast, but the heat and humidity of the summer months can be a bit overwhelming for some visitors.

APRIL

Watch the world's top surfers shred Snapper Rocks at the **Gold Coast Pro** (p315). After a good laugh? The **Brisbane Comedy Festival** (p287) usually kicks off later in the month and runs into May.

JUNE

Travelling foodies and wine and craft-beer fans enjoy the local provenance at the **Noosa Food & Wine Festival** (p322). May to June is the best time to see manta rays, especially on Lady Elliot Island.

JULY

Winters are wonderfully mild on the Sunshine Coast, which hosts its signature food festival, **The Curated Plate**, over 10 days in July/August. Humpback whales are beginning to reach Hervey Bay.

Five Days to Work With

- Spend a couple of days getting to know **Brisbane** (p280) or the **Gold Coast** (p307), depending which city you arrive in, then switch. You could alternatively base yourself in Brisbane and take day trips to the Gold Coast, **Moreton Island** (p299) and **North Stradbroke Island** (p300).

- Alternatively, use the Gold Coast as a base to explore the walking trails and waterfalls of **Tamborine Mountain** (p316) and the **Gold Coast Hinterland** (p316).

- It's then back to Brisbane and a detour north to **Noosa** (p321) for a couple of nights, taking in the highlights of the **Sunshine Coast** (p328) en route and then enjoying markets and distilleries in **Eumundi** (p324) and **Pomona** (p325). A kayaking or cruising experience on **Lake Cootharaba** (p326) is always a good idea.

Longer to Travel Around

- After **Brisbane** (p280) and the **Gold Coast** (p307), head inland to the rolling hills of the **Scenic Rim** (p303) and the **Granite Belt** (p305). Wine buffs will find plenty of interest around **Tamborine Mountain** (p316) and the rural town of **Stanthorpe** (p305).

- Then head north to **Noosa** (p321) via the **Sunshine Coast** (p328). For travelling families, there's plenty to see and do here. Then cast away to **K'gari** (p344) for 4WD adventures and floating in crystalline lakes. There's also whale watching around **Hervey Bay** (p339) and in humid climes near the Tropic of Capricorn, there's world-famous-in-Australia rum and ginger beer in **Bundaberg** (p352).

- Three hours north, is the relaxed and historic river city of **Rockhampton** (p362), while **Yeppoon** (p362) is an easy-going base for visiting **Great Keppel Island** (p365).

AUGUST

In Brisbane, townies meet their country cousins at **Ekka** (p287), the Royal Queensland Show and it's time for country, blues and folk at the **Gympie Music Muster** (p352). Peak season for Hervey Bay whale watching.

SEPTEMBER

The **Brisbane Festival** (p287) runs for three weeks, entertaining the city's culture vultures at events held at venues around the city. The whole shebang kicks off with the spectacular Riverfire fireworks display.

OCTOBER

Brisbane's jacaranda trees burst into bloom, bathing the city in a dreamy purple haze. It's festival time at the city's Powerhouse with the **Brisbane Writers Festival** (p287)l and then the **Melt** (p287) LGBTIQ+ celebration beginning later in the month.

NOVEMBER

Starting in November, it's loggerhead-turtle nesting season at **Mon Repos Beach** (p356), northeast of Bundaberg. Rooftop bars and pools in Brisbane and the Gold Coast come into their own as the mercury inevitably rises.

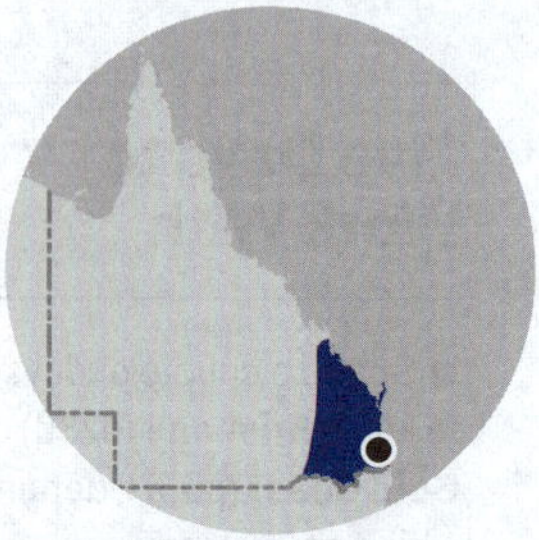

Brisbane

RIVER VISTAS | ARTS | RESTAURANTS

TOP TIP

Located in central Brisbane's heritage-listed former Regent Theatre, the **Brisbane Visitor Information & Booking Centre** has a wealth of information and advice. The building's actually worth a visit just to see its opulent interior. Online, see *visit.brisbane.qld.au* and *@visitbrisbane* on Instagram.

In Brisbane (Meanjin), the charms of Queensland's capital include sunny weather, cool cafes and restaurants, and thriving sports, arts and cultural scenes imbued with the relaxed vibe of a big country town. Through it all flows the river that gives the city its name, a serpentine channel coursing through the traditional lands of the Jagera and Turrbal peoples. Known to locals as the 'Brown Snake', it carves the city into a patchwork of urban villages, each with their own distinct style, including bohemian West End, raffish Fortitude Valley and arts-forward South Bank.

Welcome to a subtropical capital of diversity, sophistication and charm, all refreshed with an expectant energy as the city prepares to host the 2032 Summer Olympics. The spectacular Queen's Wharf precinct may be getting all the coverage, but there's also innovation and dynamism infusing new restaurants and craft breweries in up-and-coming Newstead and Teneriffe. A golden-hued global stage awaits.

Hallowed Hall

MAP P282

Grand heritage, iconic towers and local history

Fronted by sequoia-sized Corinthian columns, Australia's largest **city hall** was built between 1920 and 1930 – the second-largest construction project of its time after the Sydney

GETTING AROUND

Roma St Station is the hub of Brisbane's transport network. All city train lines (including the Gold Coast and the airport line) travel through here and long-distance trains also leave from here. The Brisbane Coach Terminal is located adjacent to the station. Fares on southeast Queensland's integrated Translink *(translink.com.au)* system – excluding the Airtrain from the airport – are standardised at 50c and include buses, trains and CityCat ferries. All forms of contactless payment are accepted. Bikes and e-scooters can be taken on trains and ferries. Rideshare services include Uber and DiDi. Unlock e-scooters and e-bikes through the Lime app.

ARDANME/SHUTTERSTOCK

Brisbane City Hall

Harbour Bridge. Book in advance for free 45-minute heritage tours. Also book online for free 15-minute tours of the 85m-high clock tower. Check out the grand foyer with mosaic tiles and marble staircases and take in 1st-floor views of the ostentatious auditorium.

Clock-tower tours begin at the **Museum of Brisbane** *(museumofbrisbane.com.au)* on the 3rd floor, which explores historic and modern aspects of Brisbane through changing exhibitions. The city's Indigenous and colonial histories are covered in the museum's introductory galleries and the gift shop features art and design by makers around the state.

Birth of a Capital

MAP P282

History, art and architecture around Gardens Point

Near today's central city, Gardens Point is the birthplace of modern Brisbane. At its centre stands **Old Government House** *(ogh.qut.edu.au; free)*. Queensland's most important heritage building (1862) was designed as a private residence for Sir George Bowen, Queensland's first governor. The sparsely furnished interior is open to the public from Tuesday to Friday and on Sundays. Book ahead online for one-hour guided tours at 10.30am on Tuesday, Thursday and Friday. The 1st floor

Continued on p285

BRISBANE'S KEY RETAIL PRECINCTS

Queen St Mall: Brisbane's original and most central shopping strip features big-name brands and high-street favourites.

Brisbane Arcade: Just off Queen St Mall, this historic arcade brims with timeless elegance and boutique and luxury goods.

James St, Fortitude Valley: The tree-lined charm of Brisbane's boutique shopping HQ has a way of loosening the purse strings.

Latrobe Tce, Paddington: Fuel up at a cafe before browsing the fashion boutiques and vintage stores on this strip northwest of Suncorp Stadium.

Oxford St, Bulimba: Catch the CityCat to this East Brisbane homewares hub. There's also an emerging dining scene.

EATING IN THE CITY CENTRE: BAKING & MEZE

MAP P282

Cinnamon and orange zest morning buns are equally addictive

Golden Avenue: Opened in 2025 and enlivening Edward St as a stylish showcase of Middle Eastern cuisine. Lots of vegetarian options. *11.30am-10pm* $$$

Exhibition: Special occasion? Be wowed by peak-season produce reimagined in six-course degustation experiences. *5.30-11pm Tue-Sat* $$$

Opa Bar & Mezze: Greek flavours including meze and a seafood bar combine at a riverside location with Story Bridge views. *11am-10pm* $$$

Lune: Yes, it's worth forking out at least $7 for a speciality croissant. *7.30am-3pm Mon-Fri, from 8am Sat & Sun* $

CENTRAL BRISBANE
Latrobe Tce (450m);
Naim (1.4km);
D'Aguilar National Park (10km)
PETRIE TERRACE
Spring Hill Baths (200m)
Cricket St
Caxton St
Roma Street Parkland
Wickham Tce
Castlemaine St
Hale St
Petrie Tce
Countess St
Roma Street
Albert St
Heussler Tce
Brisbane Botanic Gardens Mt Coot-tha (3.5km);
Sir Thomas Brisbane Planetarium (3.5km);
Mt Coot-tha Forest (4km);
Summit Cafe (6km);
Summit Restaurant & Bar (6km)
Upper Roma St
Roma St
Makerston St
Quay St
Quay St
Milton Rd
Pacific Mwy
Herschel St
Tank St
William Jolly Bridge
Milton
MILTON
Kurilpa Bridge
M3
North Quay
Go Between Bridge
Gallery of Modern Art
Coronation Dr
Montague Rd
Stanley Pl
Bouquet St
Park Rd
Queensland Art Gallery
Victoria Bridge
Peel St
Riverside Dr
Montague Rd
Cordelia St
Merivale St
Melbourne St
Peel St
Norfolk Rd
Boundary St
South Brisbane
Donkin St
Buchanan St
Anthony St
Musgrave St
Melbourne St
Manning St
SOUTH BRISBANE
South Bank Parklands
Mollison St
Bank St
Edmondstone St
Davies Park
Jane St
Boundary St
Russell St
Musgrave Park
Glenelg St
Scott St
Browning St
Ernest St
WEST END
Besant St
Vulture St
SOUTH BRISBANE
Skinner St
Turin St
Exeter St
Cambridge St
Princhester St
Thomas St
Sussex St
Franklin St
Vulture St
Corbett St
Victoria St
Hardgrave Rd
Granville St
Boundary St
Brighton Rd
Hampstead Rd
Gladstone Rd
Spring St
Whynot St
Baynes St
HIGHGATE HILL
0 500 m
0 0.25 miles
University of Queensland Art Museum (3km)

HIGHLIGHTS
1 Gallery of Modern Art
2 Museum of Brisbane
3 Queensland Art Gallery

SIGHTS
4 Birrunga Gallery
5 City Botanic Gardens
6 City Hall
7 Commissariat Store Museum
8 Fish Lane
9 MacArthur Museum Brisbane
10 Mangrove Walkway
11 Memorial Galleries
12 Neville Bonner Bridge
13 Old Government House
14 Old Windmill
15 Parliament House
16 Pillars Project
17 Queen's Wharf Brisbane
18 Queensland Museum Kurilpa
19 QUT Art Museum
20 Raphael, the Traveller
21 Roma Street Parkland
22 Stanley St Plaza
23 Suncorp Stadium
24 What Becomes of the Clouds
25 Wheel of Brisbane
26 Woolloongabba Art Gallery

ACTIVITIES
27 Brisbane Greeters
28 Jet Ski Brisbane
29 Streets Beach

SLEEPING
30 Hotel Indigo
31 Inchcolm by Ovolo
32 Westin Brisbane

EATING
33 Bar Francine
34 Bar Rosa Vini & Piatti
35 Clarence
36 Exhibition
37 Golden Avenue
38 Kafenio
39 Lune
40 Marlowe
41 Morning After
42 Opa Bar & Mezze
43 Yamas Greek + Drink

DRINKING & NIGHTLIFE
44 Antico
45 Come to Daddy
46 Dr Gimlette
47 Gresham Bar
48 Lina Rooftop
49 Little Miss Sunshine Bistro Brewery
50 Maker
51 Next Episode
52 Saccharomyces Beer Cafe
53 Ship Inn
54 Sportsman Hotel

ENTERTAINMENT
55 Moonlight Cinema
56 Queensland Performing Arts Centre
57 Riverstage
58 South Bank Piazza

SHOPPING
59 Brisbane Arcade
60 Brisbane Riverside Markets
61 Collective Markets South Bank
62 Delvene Cockatoo-Collins Art
63 Queen St Mall

INFORMATION
64 Brisbane Visitor Information & Booking Centre

TRANSPORT
65 North Quay
66 South Bank Terminal 3

BRISBANE BY FERRY

Board the popular and frequent F1 CityCat service on this self-guided journey ferry-hopping along the Brisbane River.

START	END	LENGTH
North Quay	Northshore Hamilton	12km; 4hr

Begin at the ❶ **North Quay** ferry terminal on the edge of the central city, conveniently close to Brisbane's new Queen's Wharf precinct.

After a quick hop across the river to ❷ **South Bank**, get a culture hit at the Queensland Cultural Centre or enjoy a dip at Streets Beach. It's also a short walk to the streetart of Fish La.

Continue from South Bank to ❸ **Howard Smith Wharves** (p293). This route passes under the Story Bridge and is especially spectacular at dusk when the central city lights up against a tangerine sky. After braving a bridge climb experience, enjoy bridge views from Felons Brewing Co before boarding another CityCat ferry to ❹ **New Farm Park** (p293), home of the Brisbane Powerhouse.From here it's a short hop two stops to ❺ **Teneriffe** for excellent craft breweries and restaurants. Green Beacon Brewing Co, Working Title Brew Co and Zero Fox can all be reached within a 400m stroll.

Back on board continue past waterfront mansions to ❻ **Northshore Hamilton**, marking the northeastern (upstream) end of Brisbane's CityCat service. From 4pm to 9pm on Friday, Saturday and Sunday afternoons, Eat Street Northshore's street-food market offers global flavours aplenty and regular live music. Hop back to the central city by ferry or catch bus 300 nearby at Macarthur Ave, which will get you there faster.

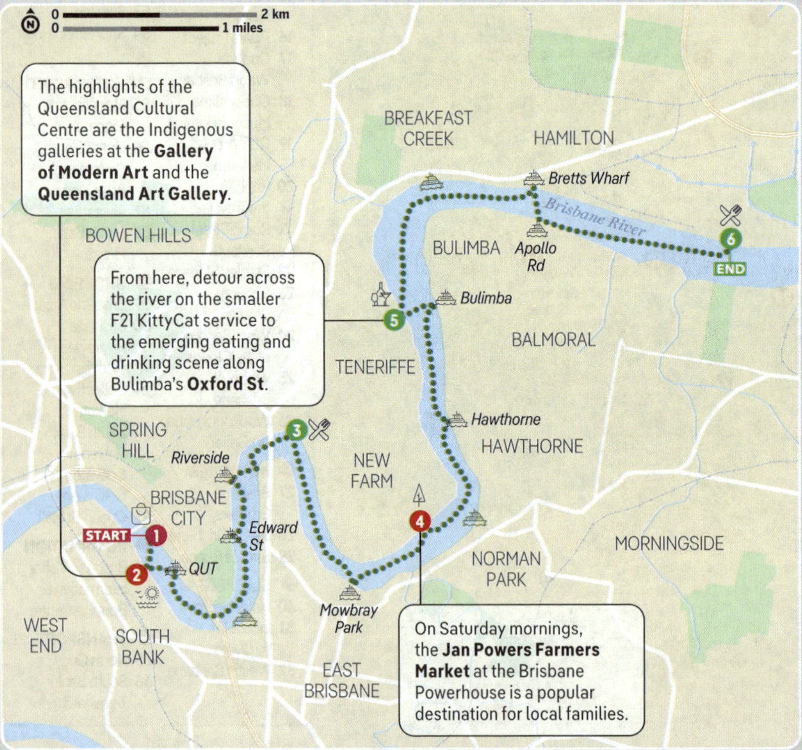

Continued from p281
houses the **William Robinson Gallery** *(wrgallery.qut.edu.au; free)*, dedicated to the Australian artist and displaying his paintings, prints, drawings, sculpture and ceramics. It's open from Tuesday to Friday and on Sundays.

Nearby is **Parliament House** *(parliament.qld.gov.au)*. With a roof clad in Mt Isa copper, this French Renaissance–style building was completed in 1867. Free 30-minute tours leave on the hour from 1pm to 3pm, Monday to Friday. Bring photo ID. Tours depart from the Parliamentary Annexe on Alice St. When parliament is sitting, tours are usually suspended, but visitors can view proceedings from the Parliamentary Gallery.

Brilliant Botanic Gardens

MAP P282

An urban escape, weekend markets and big concerts

Both Old Government House and Parliament House overlook the **City Botanic Gardens**. Originally a collection of food crops planted by convicts in 1825, it's now Brisbane's favourite green space and manicured lawns, tangled Moreton Bay figs, bunya pines, rainforest and mangroves are a soothing elixir for urbanites. Free one-hour guided tours leave from the information kiosk at 11am and 1pm Monday to Saturday. From 8am to 3pm on Sundays, the gardens host the **Brisbane Riverside Markets** *(queenslandmarkets.com.au)*, while the **Riverstage** hosts large-scale concerts and community events. Past performers include Australian music legend Paul Kelly and New Zealand's Lorde. In preparation for the 2032 Olympics, significant expansion of the Riverstage precinct is planned across upcoming years.

Memories of Convict Beginnings

MAP P282

Explore Brisbane's earliest convict-built stone landmarks

Brisbane was established as the Moreton Bay convict settlement in 1824, but only two convict-built structures remain in today's modern city. Built in 1829 as a storehouse, the **Commissariat Store Museum** *(commissariatstore.org.au; adult/child $10/5)* is the city's oldest occupied building. Open from Tuesday to Friday, the museum has a focus on convict and colonial history.

One challenging task delegated to convicts was walking on a treadmill for up to 14 hours a day to grind corn and wheat. The treadmill was installed at the base of the **Old Windmill**

A BRIEF BACKSTORY OF BRISBANE

Grassy forests once stretched across the plains of the Brisbane region, offering an ideal hunting ground for game including kangaroo, wallaby and possum that sustained the Aboriginal groups of the area for around 22,000 years. The Jagera and Turrbal peoples both claim the site of modern-day Brisbane as their traditional homelands, known as Meeanjin in the Yuggera language. To the Turrbal people, it means 'place of the blue water lilies' – once a common sight on the Brisbane River. The British colonisation of Brisbane as a penal colony in 1825 led to interracial tensions that left few First Nations survivors, particularly among the Turrbal group, which counts fewer than 50 members today.

DRINKING IN THE CITY CENTRE: COCKTAILS & CRAFT BEER

MAP P282

Antico: This split-level spot proves there can never be too many old-world cocktail bars in Burnett La. *4pm-1am Sun-Thu, to 2am Fri & Sat*

Dr Gimlette: Named for the surgeon who inspired the famed gin elixir, this vintage-style bar takes cocktails very seriously. *3pm-1am*

Gresham Bar: When you just want a casual drink with a bit of atmosphere, this bar in an 1885 former bank hits the spot. *11am-2am Mon-Fri, from 3pm Sat*

Little Miss Sunshine Bistro Brewery: Quaffable beers brewed on-site and good-value bar food served in a breezy and leafy pavilion. *10am-9pm Mon-Fri*

BRISBANE FUN FOR KIDS

Queensland Museum & Sciencentre: The SparkLab has 40 interactive exhibits designed for kids aged six to 13.

Lone Pine Koala Sanctuary: After the daytime crowds have departed, experience Australia's native nocturnal wildlife on a Twilight or Night Tour.

Story Bridge: Kids aged six and up can get a kick climbing this iconic Brisbane landmark.

New Farm Park: Kids love getting active in New Farm's treehouse-themed playground.

Children's Art Centre (QAGOMA): Queensland Art Gallery's (p288) kid-friendly space has exhibitions and activities created in collaboration with artists, and programs for children under six.

Sir Thomas Brisbane Planetarium: Travel through the galaxy without leaving Mt Coot-tha.

RIBEIROANTONIO/SHUTTERSTOCK

Neville Bonner Bridge

on Wickham Tce. Built by convicts in 1828, the sandstone windmill was positioned poorly to catch the breeze, making its primary function redundant. The building was later used as a signal tower and was the first home of the Queensland Museum. The interior isn't open to the public, but you can walk around the base.

Dominating the River

MAP P282

Views and good eating at Queen's Wharf

On the riverside edge of the the central city, it's impossible to miss Brisbane's newest urban development. Opened in 2025, the multibillion-dollar lifestyle and entertainment precinct known as **Queen's Wharf Brisbane** *(queenswharfbrisbane.com.au)* includes The Star Hotel and a casino complex. It's massive – *almost* too big in the context of its riverside surroundings – but thankfully, adjacent heritage-listed buildings dating from the city's convict and colonial beginnings have been integrated thoughtfully.

For visitors to contemporary Brisbane, Queen's Wharf's essential highlights include the new **Neville Bonner Bridge**, named after the first Aboriginal person to become an Australian Member of Parliament and offering convenient pedestrian-only access across the river to South Bank. There's also the **Sky Deck**, a 100m-high, 250m-long walkway offering brilliant views along the river. Best of all, it's free to access and both the Sky Deck and level 4, where the Neville Bonner Bridge links to, include diverse cafes, bars and restaurants.

On a more human level, Queen's Wharf also features riverside bikeways, parks and playgrounds, and the 450m-long **Mangrove Walkway** is enlivened with art and interpretive signage about the river from an Indigenous perspective.

Tap into Local Intel

MAP P282

Meet the Brisbane Greeters

The team from **Brisbane Greeters** *(brisbane.qld.gov.au; free)* are an authoritative collective of volunteer local guides sharing Brisbane's stories on free walking tours. Bookable until 4pm the day before, the daily 10am **Greeter's Choice** *(2-3hr)* visits under-the-radar central city highlights.

Usually beginning at Brisbane City Hall, other tours focus on 21st-century Brisbane, or explore the city's colonial and convict history. There's also a Greeters Choice dementia-friendly option, shorter, more relaxed and open to all participants. A recent addition is the RiverCity Vistas tour, getting high above the city on Queen's Wharf's spectacular Sky Deck. Neighbourhood tours explore Fortitude Valley, West End, Kangaroo Point and Bulimba.

While free, all tours must be booked online. There is no requirement or expectation to tip.

Exploring Queensland History & Culture

MAP P282

Significant state treasures at Queensland Museum Kurilpa

Queensland Museum Kurilpa *(museum.qld.gov.au/kurilpa; free, open daily)* provides an engaging journey through the state's history. The institution's collection includes a skeleton of the state's own dinosaur, Muttaburrasaurus and the *Avian Cirrus,* the tiny plane in which Queensland's Bert Hinkler made the first England-to-Australia solo flight, in 1928. The fascinating natural history galleries include many taxidermied examples of only-in-Australia wildlife species.

A surprising highlight of the museum's **Anzac Legacy** military gallery is *Mephisto,* a German tank, captured by Aussie diggers (soldiers) on the Western Front in France in 1918 and brought back to Australia following the end of WWI. The iron behemoth is the only surviving example of a Sturmpanzerwagen A7V and is regarded as the world's rarest tank.

One-off exhibitions at the museum could include everything from the cultural impact of migrants from Papua New Guinea in Queensland to the intersection of fashion, club culture and the LGBTIQ+ scene in 1990s Brisbane. Check online to see what's currently scheduled.

Free one-hour guided tours (weekdays from 11am and weekends from 3pm) provide an overview of the museum's collections. Tours depart from the museum's cavernous Whale Mall underneath three extremely lifelike fibreglass whales. It's a good idea to register online before joining a tour. Look for the signage with a handy QR code.

For younger visitors, the museum's **SparkLab** features interactive exhibits delving into STEM (science, technology, engineering and mathematics) disciplines. Expect queues of aspiring scientists and engineers during school holidays.

BIG-TICKET FESTIVALS

Ekka: Country and city coexist at the Royal Queensland Show, the state's largest annual event (and including a public holiday) in August.

Brisbane Festival: Showcasing arts events aplenty, Queensland's premier arts festival runs for three weeks in September.

Brisbane Comedy Festival: Laugh until you cry at more than 100 events hosted across four venues over a month across April and May.

Melt: Two weeks of LGBTIQ+ art, music, dance and cabaret held from late October to early November at New Farm's Powerhouse.

Brisbane Writers Festival: Big-name authors (local literary hero Trent Dalton was a 2025 guest) interact with readers for four days in October. Also held at the Powerhouse.

Indigenous & International Art

MAP P282

Celebrating Australian and global masters at QAG

Like Queensland Museum Kurilpa, the adjacent **Queensland Art Gallery** *(QAG; qagoma.qld.gov.au; free)* is also part of South Bank's Queensland Cultural Centre.

Opened in 1982 as the first major structure of the newly established cultural precinct – the museum's Brutalist building followed a few years later in 1986 – QAG features a fine permanent collection, mostly of domestic artists. This includes works by Australian heavyweights like Sir Sidney Nolan, Russell Drysdale, Arthur Boyd, Charles Blackman, William Dobell, Margaret Olley and Howard Arkley. The gallery also has works by international artists including Picasso, Degas and van Dyck.

A diverse collection of Indigenous Australian works features paintings and pottery by artists from the Hermannsburg School art movement. Highlights include vivid and vibrant landscapes by the great Albert Namatjira, the first Indigenous person to be granted conditional Australian citizenship, in 1957.

WHERE TO ADMIRE SPRINGTIME JACARANDAS

City Botanic Gardens: The first jacaranda grown in Australia was planted here in 1864. They're at their blooming best from mid-October to mid-November.

New Farm Park: Roll out a picnic rug and feast below the lavender blooms in this pleasant park.

Roma Street Parkland: After stumbling across a white jacaranda in a suburban street, former parkland curator Robert Dobbs installed a path of these pale blooms.

Kangaroo Point: Jacarandas have been tastefully planted in many suburbs, including along the riverside at Kangaroo Point.

Brisbane Botanic Gardens Mt Coot-tha: Like its inner-city counterpart, these lofty gardens have an array of jacarandas just waiting to be photographed.

Contemporary Art at GOMA

MAP P282

Culture amid the calm at the Gallery of Modern Art

Adjacent to the Queensland Art Gallery is the conjoined **Gallery of Modern Art** *(GOMA; qagoma.qld.gov.au; free)*. Opened in 2006 and constructed in glass and black metal, it's a striking architectural counterpoint to QAG's hulking amalgam of concrete and cement. Inside the gallery, relaxing pools create a calm and Zen-influenced vibe.

One of Brisbane's must-see cultural institutions celebrates modern and contemporary art, with a particular emphasis on Australian, Asian and Pacific artists. Regularly changing exhibitions spotlight everything from painting, sculpture and photography to video and installation art, while GOMA's Australian Cinémathèque screens unique, often rare films and video several times weekly. The gallery also includes a Children's Art Centre, a well-stocked book-and-design shop and both a casual cafe and a smarter bistro with river views.

Guided experiences ($95 per person) incorporating QAG, GOMA and lunch at GOMA Bistro can be booked online for specific Tuesdays and Fridays. Confirming seven days prior is essential.

Riverside Music, Opera, Ballet & More

MAP P282

World-class performances and vibrant nightlife at QPAC

Also part of South Bank's cultural precinct, the **Queensland Performing Arts Centre** *(QPAC; qpac.com.au)* hosts the Queensland Ballet, the Queensland Symphony Orchestra and Opera Queensland. Its 2000-seat Lyric Theatre hosts Broadway musicals and internationally renowned performers. Check online for upcoming events and for bookings, and make a night of it with dinner and drinks at nearby Fish La before or after the show.

RICHIE CHAN/SHUTTERSTOCK

Streets Beach

Day at the Urban Beach

MAP P282

Dive into South Bank Parklands

Star attractions amid South Bank Parkland's 17 hectares include a Nepalese peace pagoda; **Streets Beach**, an artificial, lagoon-style swimming beach that's packed on weekends; and the 60m-high **Wheel of Brisbane** *(thewheelofbrisbane.com.au; adult/child $22/18)*, delivering 360-degree views of the city.

Nearby is **Stanley St Plaza** with restaurants, shops and the historic pub (1865) **Ship Inn** *(theshipinn.com.au)*. On Friday night, Saturday and Sunday, the plaza hosts the tourist-heavy **Collective Markets South Bank** *(collectivemarkets.com.au)*. Close by, **South Bank Piazza** is an outdoor performance space with regular events.

To reach the parklands catch a CityCat ferry to South Bank, or walk across the pedestrian Neville Bonner Bridge from Queen's Wharf.

Seek out Fish Lane

MAP P282

A laneway revived

Connecting South Bank to raffish West End is **Fish Lane** *(explorefishlane.com.au)*. Just 200m northwest of South Brisbane train station, a formerly disused laneway once known

Continued on p292

MORE MEMORABLE BRISBANE GALLERIES

University of Queensland Art Museum: This university gallery in St Lucia has one of Queensland's most important collections, including a collection of self-portraits.

Institute of Modern Art: An excellent noncommercial gallery in Fortitude Valley with regular showings by local and international names from the art world.

Pillars Project: Admire the vibrant collection of murals on the Merivale Bridge linking South Brisbane to Milton.

QUT Art Museum: The star of this contemporary university gallery is the William Robinson collection, also showcased in the adjacent Old Government House.

Woolloongabba Art Gallery: Top spot to purchase, or just admire, contemporary Australasian art.

DRINKING ON FISH LANE: OUR PICKS

MAP P282

Belgian-style bar food is also available

Bar Rosa Vini & Piatti: Unfussy and contemporary Italian bar/restaurant with a great wine list. *5-9.30pm Tue-Thu, to 10.30pm Fri, noon-10.30pm Sat*

Maker: The type of cocktail bar where bartenders go to drink. It's intimate with no signage, so look for the black bar stools outside. *4pm-midnight Tue-Sun*

Next Episode: Check the bar's socials for the code to enter this fun hip-hop-inspired bar hidden behind a barber shop. *5pm-midnight Wed-Sun*

Saccharomyces Beer Cafe: Serving the best of independent Aussie craft brewers and from further afield. *3-10pm Mon-Thu, noon-midnight Fri & Sat, noon-8pm Sun*

SIGHTS
1 Brisbane Powerhouse
2 Gabba
3 Institute of Modern Art
4 Kangaroo Point
5 New Farm Park
6 Newstead Air Raid Shelter
7 Story Bridge

ACTIVITIES
8 Riverlife Adventure Centre
9 Story Bridge Adventure Climb

SLEEPING
10 Constance
11 Miss Midgely's

EATING
12 Agnes
13 Bar Alto
14 Biànca
15 GRECA
16 Himalayan Cafe
17 Hôntô
18 Joey's
19 Melrose Restaurant & Rooftop Bar
20 Pawpaw
21 Short Grain
22 Stanley
23 Vertigo
24 Yoko
25 Zero Fox

DRINKING & NIGHTLIFE
26 Alfred St Bar & Bottlo
27 Balfour Kitchen & Bar
28 Beat MegaClub
29 Black Bear Lodge
30 Cielo Rooftop

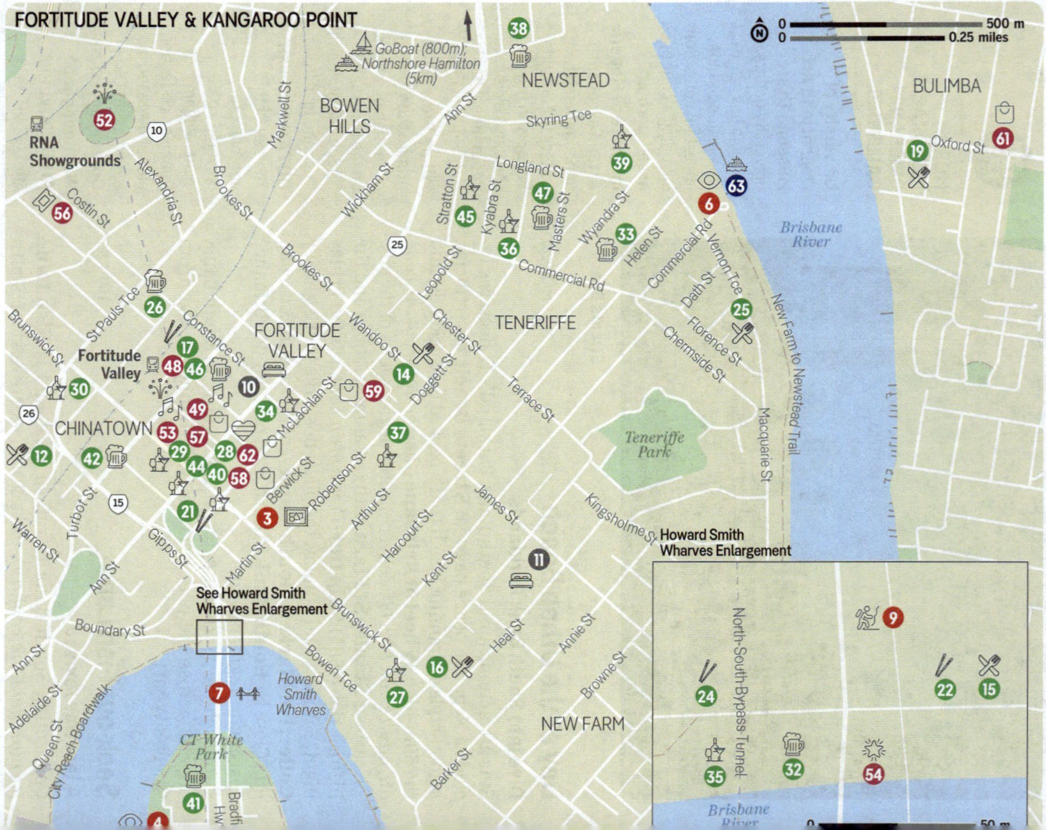

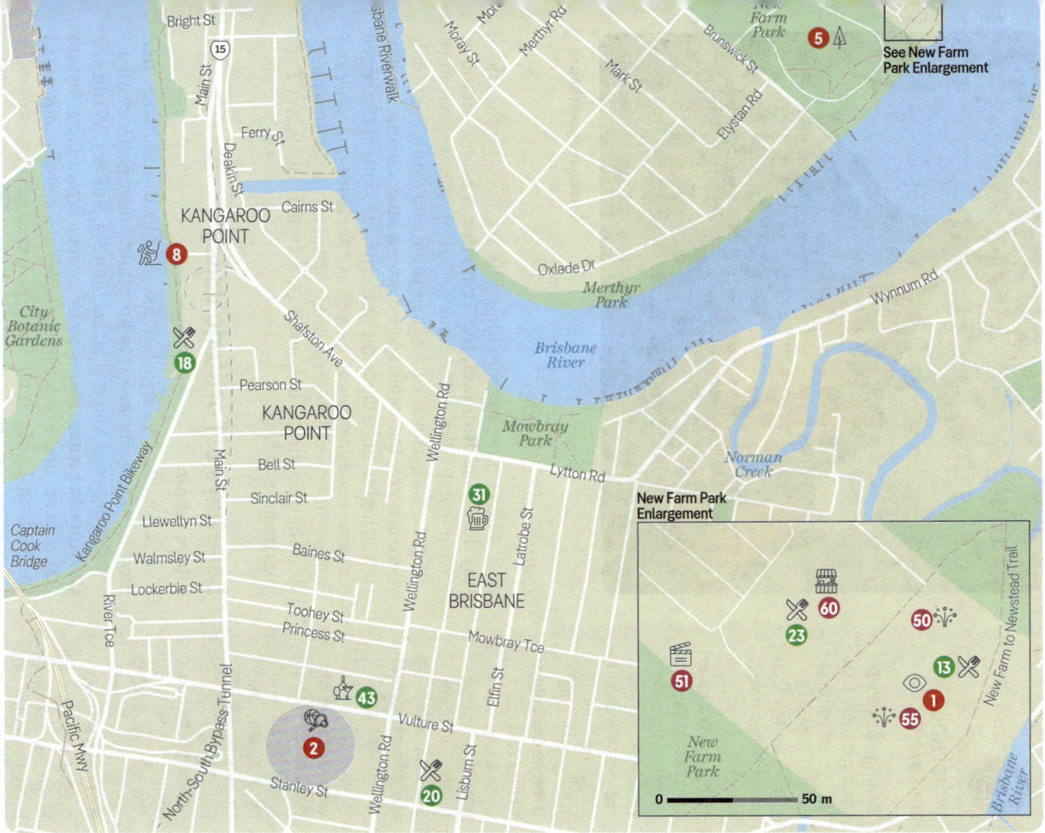

31 E.B. by Hiker Brewing
32 Felons Brewing Co
33 Green Beacon Brewing Co
34 Maya
35 Mr Percival's
36 Niky Wine Bar
37 Nixon Room
38 Range Brewing
39 Ruby, My Dear
40 Savile Row
41 Sea Legs Brewing Co
42 Soapbox Beer
43 Sunsets
44 Suzie Wongs Good Time Bar
45 Triffid
46 Wickham Hotel
47 Working Title Brew Co

ENTERTAINMENT

48 Big Gay Day
49 Brightside
50 Brisbane Comedy Festival
51 Dendy Powerhouse
52 'Ekka' Royal Queensland Show
53 Fortitude Music Hall
54 Howard Smith Wharves
55 Melt
56 Tivoli

SHOPPING

57 Bakery Lane
58 California Lane
59 James St
60 Jan Powers Farmers Market
61 Oxford St
62 Winn Lane

TRANSPORT

63 Teneriffe

INDIGENOUS BRISBANE

Birrunga Gallery & Dining: Browse First Nations art and enjoy a coffee at this welcoming spot relocated to near Milton train station.

Mangrove Walkway: Showcasing Indigenous stories and wildlife, this 450m river pathway is part of the new Queen's Wharf development.

Delvene Cockatoo-Collins Art: Central Brisbane retail outlet for the North Stradbroke Quandamooka artist. Homewares, apparel, accessories and design.

What Becomes of the Clouds: Thought-provoking public art by world-renowned Quandamooka artist Megan Cope. On the ground floor of Heritage Lanes at 80 Ann St. Only viewable during office hours.

Gallery of Modern Art: Admire an incredible showcase of works by leading Indigenous Australian artists.

ALEX CIMBAL/SHUTTERSTOCK

Brisbane Powerhouse

Continued from p289

as Soda La is now awash with public art. Look for the trio of tiny doors and **Raphael, the Traveller**, a bronze statue by French sculptor Bruno Catalano. Colourful murals also feature.

Fish La is also lined with places to eat and drink. Some only open at night, but cafes keep the area busy during the day. Dining highlights include the modern bistro vibe of **Clarence** *(clarencerestaurant.com)* as well as **Marlowe** *(marlowebne.com.au)*, for savvy interpretations of Australian culinary classics; the restaurant is housed in a stylish 1930s Art Deco apartment building.

Laneways of Fortitude Valley

MAP P290

Alleys reborn

One of Fortitude Valley's best assets is its disused lanes that have been transformed into hospitality destinations. All accessible between Ann and McLachlan Sts, **Bakery**, **Winn** and **California Lanes** *(thelanesfortitudevalley.com.au)* feature places to eat and drink. On the laneways' website, download the Hidden Lanes Small Bar Trail map and go exploring. Accessible from nearby Warner St, grungy Warner La features more late-night destinations and a wall mural of proto-punk rocker Iggy Pop.

Charcoal-grilled meat and seafood are highlights

EATING IN WEST END: GREEK FLAVOURS & MORE

MAP P282

Yamas Greek + Drink: Even the small *souvla* could feed a king at this chic Greek restaurant in West Village. *11am-10pm* $$

Morning After: The all-day brunch menu is more creative than most, with more dishes available from 11am. Try the Polish potato pancakes. *7am-3pm* $

Bar Francine: The evolving daily menu means there's always something new to love about this charming Euro bistro. *5.30-10pm Wed & Thu, from 5pm Fri & Sat* $$

Kafenio: Authentic Greek cuisine is dished up at the unpretentious HQ of the Cypriot Community Association of Queensland. *11am-8pm Tue-Sun, to 2pm Mon* $$

Power to the Park

MAP P290

Highlights of New Farm

East of Fortitude Valley, leafy and upscale New Farm features the **Brisbane Powerhouse** *(brisbanepowerhouse.org)*, formerly a 1920s power station but now hosting theatre, music, comedy, dance and more. Festivals, events and exhibitions are also scheduled.

Year-round there's outdoor cinema at **Dendy Powerhouse** (p294), while the **Jan Powers Farmers Market** *(janpowersfarmersmarkets.com.au)* features food trucks on Saturdays from 6am to noon. Dine 17m above the ground at **Vertigo** *(vertigobrisbane.com.au)*, dubbed Australia's first vertical restaurant and offering a similar menu to the Powerhouse's Italian restaurant **Bar Alto** *(baralto.com.au)*. Diners at Vertigo are secured by safety harnesses and after a three-course meal, there's the option of making a controlled jump off the Powerhouse's heritage facade.

Surrounding the Powerhouse is the vast **New Farm Park**, one of Brisbane's best spots for a picnic and easily reached by the CityCat.

Hangout at Howard Smith Wharves

MAP P290

Riverside views, food and fun

Under the northern pylons of the Story Bridge, the precinct **Howard Smith Wharves** *(howardsmithwharves.com)* is Brisbane's shining star of urban regeneration. The heritage-listed wharves on prime riverside real estate were abandoned in the 1960s after the port moved downstream, but after careful restoration, opened in 2018 as a stunning dining and entertainment destination. Reached by cliffside elevators, Howard Smith Wharves are a short walk from Fortitude Valley and also have their own CityCat ferry landing.

Anchored by **Felons Brewing Co** *(felonsbrewingco.com.au)*, the precinct encompasses a dozen drinking and dining options. Standouts include **GRECA** *(greca.com.au)* for contemporary Greek fare, **Stanley** *(stanleyrestaurant.com.au)* for refined Cantonese and **Yoko** *(yokodining.com.au)* for fun Japanese dining. Try **Mr Percival's** for a sexy sundown cocktail and check out Felons' Barrel Hall for weekend DJs and live gigs.

Friday and Saturday nights can be uncomfortably busy at Howard Smith Wharves. A weeknight visit will give you a much better chance of securing an alfresco beanbag for

GLITZ TO GRUNGE & BACK AGAIN

The decommissioning of Brisbane's tram network in 1969 was the death knell for Fortitude Valley, which by the 1980s had declined from a thriving high-end shopping precinct into a derelict state.

By the end of that decade it was already re-emerging as Brisbane's premier late-night entertainment district. And while the early days were decidedly seedy, they paved the way for the Valley to become a hub of creativity and counterculture, as well as a safe place for the LGBTIQ+ community. In 2010, a group of property stakeholders joined forces to transform the industrial area of James St into a lifestyle precinct to rival the Valley's glory days. The rest is history.

EATING IN FORTITUDE VALLEY: OUR PICKS

MAP P290

Try the eggplant polpette (meatballs)

Short Grain: Chef Martin Boetz (of Longrain, Sydney, fame) delivers punchy Thai flavours in his hometown. *5-9pm Wed-Sat & noon-3pm Fri-Sun* $$$

Hôntô: Brisbane's best contemporary Japanese? Judge for yourself in this ultra-moody space in a nondescript laneway. *5.30pm-late Mon-Thu, from 5pm Fri-Sun* $$$

Agnes: The city's temple to wood-fired cookng. Wood-roasted Murray River cod is a menu standout. *5.15-10pm daily, plus 11.30am-3pm Fri-Sun* $$$

Biànca: Dusty pink furniture and terracotta tiles set a stylish scene for on-point Italian. Zingy spritzes and a great wine list, too. *5-10pm Mon-Thu, 11.30am-11pm Fri-Sun* $$

HAPPENING 'HOODS

Karen Inglis, Director of Brisbane Food & Wine Tours, shares some local insight. *@brisbanefoodandwinetours*

Just beyond Fortitude Valley, the Brisbane suburbs of Teneriffe and Newstead are really happening for eating and drinking. New cafes and restaurants are popping up, along with neighbourhood wine bars serving Australian wines. Brisbane Food & Wine Tours runs a progressive long-lunch tour in this area where you are spoiled for options. It's then an easy stroll to James St for great shopping and more restaurants and bars, or a walk along the river to New Farm where the Brisbane Riverwalk connects to the central city. Its newest walking tour explores central city restaurants and bars before crossing to the exciting Fish La precinct in South Bank.

spectacular bridge views at Felons. A wood-fired pizza and their crushable Galaxy Haze pale ale is a recommended after-dark combo.

Brisbane's Own Bridge Climb

MAP P290

Scale the Story Bridge

It's not as iconic as the Sydney Harbour Bridge, but Brisbane's showpiece **Story Bridge**, linking the central city to Kangaroo Point, also offers a thrilling adventure. **Story Bridge Adventure Climb** *(storybridgeadventureclimb.com.au; from $160)* offers a variety of climbing options. Definitely book ahead for the popular twilight tour, to make your way to a summit platform for superb views of the twinkling city.

Also available are dawn and night climbs and the experience is open to children from ages six to 16 if they're accompanied by an adult. Story Bridge's **Accessible Climb** option uses a specially-designed motorised wheelchair to make the experience available to wheelchair users.

Movies by Moonlight

MAPS P282 & P290

Movie magic under the stars at Brisbane's parks

Over summer, **Moonlight Cinema** *(moonlight.com.au)* takes over Roma Street Parkland on the edge of the central city from late November to the end of March. Films including mainstream releases and the odd cult classic usually screen from Tuesday to Sunday, flickering to life at around 7.15pm. Food and drinks are available for purchase. Booking tickets online is recommended as popular films sell out.

Open year-round is the alfresco **Dendy Powerhouse** *(powerhouse.dendy.com.au)*, screening an eclectic program from Thursday to Sunday. Look forward to comfy armchairs, wireless headphones and hand-scooped choc-top ice-creams. Even getting here is fun, arriving on a CityCat ferry at the New Farm Park jetty.

Game On

MAP P290

Experience Brisbane's championship-winning sports

During 2032, the world will be focused on Brisbane, but in the lead-up to the Olympics, the city offers other ways to experience the sporting passion of locals.

Known as the **Gabba** *(thegabba.com.au)*, the Brisbane Cricket Ground in East Brisbane is a good place to catch a

Small plates include French, Italian and Vietnamese flavours

EATING & DRINKING IN NEWSTEAD & TENERIFFE: OUR PICKS

MAP P290

Himalayan Cafe: This prayer-flag-draped Nepali stalwart was born to cure *momo* (dumpling) cravings. Also serves a great goat curry. *5.30-10pm Tue-Sun* $

Ruby, My Dear: Inspired by Japan's jazz *kissaten* (bars), this neighbourhood bar also has a seriously satisfying menu. *5-9pm Wed & Thu, noon-11pm Fri & Sat, noon-8pm Sun* $$

Zero Fox: Korean- and Japanese-inspired small plates and bowls partner with a great Aussie-centric wine, gin and craft-beer selection. *noon-10pm* $$

Niky Wine Bar: A no-reservations policy makes it worth a shot trying to snag a table at this pastel-pink wine cave. *3-10pm Wed-Sat, 2-8pm Sun*

game of cricket. If you're new to the sport, take in an explosive and entertaining Twenty20 (T20) match. The season runs from late September to March.

The Gabba also hosts Australian Rules (AFL) football matches from late March to September. In 2024 and 2025, the **Brisbane Lions** *(lions.com.au)* were crowned AFL Premiers – quite an achievement in a sporting code traditionally dominated by teams from Victoria.

Despite the Lions' achievements, Queensland's most popular football code is still rugby league. Matches are hosted at **Suncorp Stadium** *(suncorpstadium.com.au)*, west of the central city, from March to October. Playing in the NRL (National Rugby League), both the men's and women's teams of the **Brisbane Broncos** *(broncos.com.au)* won NRL premierships in 2025.

The annual three-game State of Origin rugby league series between Queensland (the Maroons) and NSW (the Blues) is one of Australia's most popular sporting contests. Usually held between May and July, the Queensland home game is best experienced at Suncorp Stadium, but watching a game at a local pub is also highly recommended. Just remember to barrack (cheer) for Queensland.

Booming Brews

MAP P290

Toast Newstead's brewing scene

Once the domain of Castlemaine XXXX, a local icon established in 1924, Brisbane now features many craft breweries. Brews tend to have a lower ABV (alcohol by volume) and are relatively unchallenging – a good fit with Brisbane's warmer weather – but two Newstead breweries offer a wider range of beer styles.

Head along to **Range Brewing** *(rangebrewing.com)* for hop-forward and hazy IPAs, while the remit of **Working Title Brew Co** *(workingtitlebrew.co)* often includes stouts, sour beers and farmhouse ales. With Asian-inspired skewers and bowls, Working Title's food menu also stands out. Range Brewing is closed on Mondays while Working Title takes a break on Monday and Tuesday.

For a fun time experiencing Brisbane's brewing scene, join a tour with **Hop On Brewery Tours** *(hoponbrewerytours.com.au)*. Tours focused on the city's northern, southern and eastern suburbs visit breweries further away from the central city. They can also arrange Brisbane distillery visits or a hop-fuelled beer adventure to the Gold Coast.

WHERE TO CATCH A GIG

Fortitude Music Hall: Recent gigs at this 3000-seat venue include Crowded House and the Pixies. Also hosts major Australian touring acts.

Triffid: This former WWII aircraft hangar in Newstead hosts a gig nearly every night. Sunday afternoon events are in the adjacent beer garden.

Black Bear Lodge: This cosy Fortitude Valley space features everything from intimate touring gigs to queer dance parties.

Brightside: In Fortitude Valley, with everything from New Zealand heavy metal to Australian outback country. Opening a larger laneway space in 2026.

Tivoli: First opened in 1989, this Art Deco auditorium in Fortitude Valley has hosted everyone from Nick Cave to Bob Dylan.

DRINKING IN FORTITUDE VALLEY: OUR PICKS

MAP P290

Alfred St Bar & Bottlo: Full of local and global craft beers and four curated taps combine with Asian-inspired bar snacks. *10am-10pm Tue-Fri, 11am-11pm Sat*

Savile Row: A giant chandelier dangles over this classy, old-world bar known for its cocktails and whisky list. *6pm-2am Sun-Thu, to 3am Fri & Sat*

Suzie Wongs Good Time Bar: Hawaiian-surf-shack-inspired dive bar with live music every night. *8pm-1am Wed & Thu, 6pm-3am Fri & Sat*

Nixon Room: Hidden behind a bronze door in a leafy alley, this bar is pure escapism. Don't miss the stellar martini menu. *4pm-midnight Wed-Fri, 3pm-midnight Sat*

Next door, check out their sibling restaurant, essa

BRISBANE'S LGBTIQ+ SCENE

Beat MegaClub: Six dance floors and drag performers every night (Wednesday to Sunday) guarantee a good time at this Fortitude Valley icon.

Wickham Hotel: This historic Fortitude Valley pub hosts events from Friday to Sunday (balls-out bingo, anyone?). It's more low-key and relaxed from Monday to Thursday.

Big Gay Day: Alden St is energised by this fabulous one-day festival held on the first Sunday in May. Based nearby at the Wickham.

Sportsman Hotel: Gay-owned pub in Spring Hill with fun events including drag nights and riotous karaoke sessions. Open from Tuesday to Sunday.

Come to Daddy: Inclusive West End bistro/wine bar with a focus on artisanal Australian producers. Check online for events including karaoke, trivia nights and drag shows. Open Wednesday to Sunday.

KNYCX JOURNEYING/SHUTTERSTOCK

Brisbane Botanic Gardens Mt Coot-tha

Head up Mt Coot-tha

MAP P282

Survey the city from high

A 15-minute drive west of the central city, the huge eucalypt **Mt Coot-tha Forest** is topped by 287m Mt Coot-tha, Brisbane's highest point. There's a good road right to the summit car park, but if you're keen to explore on two legs, park the car further down at the JC Slaughter Falls Picnic Area and tackle the 1.9km (30 minutes) Mt Coot-tha Summit Lookout trail. Look forward to plenty of steps. Download the Mt Coot-tha Forest Track Map on *brisbane.qld.gov.au* for details of other trails.

At the top are the relaxed **Summit Cafe** *(summitbrisbane.com.au)*, open from 6am, and the recently renovated **Summit Restaurant & Bar**. A contemporary bistro menu features local produce and ingredients. Open for lunch and dinner.

Along the road to the summit, attractions include the gentle walking trails of the **Brisbane Botanic Gardens Mt Coot-tha** and the family-friendly celestial learning opportunities of the **Sir Thomas Brisbane Planetarium**. Both are open daily with free admission.

Quiz nights on the second and fourth Sundays of the month

DRINKING IN BRISBANE: CRAFT BEER

MAP P290

E.B. by Hiker Brewing: East Brisbane taproom of popular Salisbury craft brewery. Latin American street-food; conveniently near the Mowbray Park ferry terminal. *hours vary*

Sea Legs Brewing Co: Welcoming warehouse space on Kangaroo Point serving seasonal specials. Close to Holman St ferry terminal. *noon-9pm Sun-Thu, to 11pm Fri & Sat*

Soapbox Beer: The weekday lunch menu makes a good case for starting your night early. Good satay and *momos* (Nepalese dumplings). *noon-late Wed-Sat*

Green Beacon Brewing Co: In Teneriffe, this 2013 craft pioneer still brews some of Brisbane's best beer and serves banging burgers. *2-9pm Mon-Thu, from noon Fri-Sun*

Scope out Streetart

Discover vibrant streetart and local urban culture

Brisbane has a vibrant streetart scene, with council-led initiatives including **Artforce Brisbane** *(artforcebrisbane.com.au)*, which enables local artists to adorn traffic signal boxes. Running for a week in May, the annual **Brisbane Street Art Festival** *(bsafest.com.au)* features workshops at Maritime Green's Superordinary multi-arts space. Local and international artists transform surfaces across the city. See the website for a map of works completed to date.

Fortitude Valley has an ever-evolving gallery of public art in its laneways and other hot spots include Fish La near South Bank and Burnett La in the central city.

Local Sauce Tours *(localsaucetours.com.au; from $60)* offers guided walking tours exploring both streetart and small bars in areas including Fish La, West End and the central city.

Lest We Forget

MAPS P282 & P290

Hidden WWII history and wartime relics

Brisbane played an important role in WWII, when 80,000 Allied soldiers – mainly from the United States – were stationed in the city. Stories of secret bunkers and tunnels created during this era are local folklore, but keen-eyed travellers may also notice wartime relics hidden in plain sight. Near the Teneriffe ferry terminal, a former **air-raid shelter** is now a Newstead bus stop. Also easily missed are the free-to-visit **Memorial Galleries** *(anzacsquare.qld.gov.au)* accessed via the pedestrian tunnel linking Anzac Sq to Central Station. Located underneath the square's Shrine of Remembrance, the gallery (closed Saturdays) features touch-screen displays showcasing the war stories of Brisbane.

Also visit the **MacArthur Museum Brisbane** *(mmb.org.au; adult/child $10/5)*, 400m away on Edward St. Directing Allied efforts in the southwest Pacific, US General Douglas MacArthur was based in Brisbane from July 1942 to October 1944. Open on Tuesday, Thursday and Sunday, his restored 8th-floor office showcases the legacy of the Coastwatchers – Indigenous Pacific Islanders recruited to support Allied intelligence efforts – and the often harrowing stories of Australian prisoners of war throughout the conflict.

For exhibits remembering Australia's WWI history, visit the Anzac Memories galley at Queensland Museum Kurilpa (p287).

OUTDOOR ADVENTURES AROUND BRISBANE

Riverlife Adventure Centre: Kayaking adventures along the 'Brown Snake' and abseiling and rock climbing on the Kangaroo Point cliffs. Also bike rental for Brissie's brilliant bikeways.

GoBoat: Hire a drive-yourself electric boat and embark on an on-the-water picnic. Boats launch from Newstead and an Esky is provided to keep drinks cold.

Jet Ski Brisbane: Guided Jet Ski experiences on the Brisbane River and out into Moreton Bay. Late-afternoon sunset tours are especially scenic. Trips depart from near the Botanic Gardens.

Brisbane Whale Watching: Departing from Redcliffe northeast of Brisbane and offering viewing of humpbacks in the sheltered waters of Moreton Bay from June to October. Pickups available from central Brisbane.

EATING IN BRISBANE: BEST OF THE REST

MAP P290

Pawpaw: Breakfast and lunch are available all day at this oasis of pan-Asian goodness near the Gabba. *7am-3pm daily, plus 5-9pm Wed-Sat* $

Naïm: This popular Middle Eastern restaurant in Paddington includes a neighbouring wine bar dubbed the Hamsa Room. *8am-2pm Tue-Sun, plus 5-10pm Tue-Sat* $$

Joey's: The Brisbane River shimmies beneath this summery bistro perched on the Kangaroo Point cliffs. *6-11am daily, noon-9pm Mon-Fri, to 10pm Sat & Sun* $$

Melrose Restaurant & Rooftop Bar: Cambodian- and Thai-influenced fusion flavours. *5-9pm Tue, noon-3pm & 5-9pm Wed & Thu, noon-10pm Fri & Sat, noon-5pm Sun* $$

TOP SPOTS TO COOL OFF

Streets Beach: Feel the sand between your toes without leaving the city centre at South Bank's urban beach.

Nautilus Pool & Bar: Brisbane's only swim-up pool bar, in the Westin Brisbane, opens to the public on weekends.

Spring Hill Baths: Dive into Brisbane's history as you swim laps at this heritage-listed 23m indoor heated pool, built in 1886.

Suttons Beach: Laze in the artificial Settlement Cove Lagoon or paddle in the sheltered waters of Redcliffe, a 40-minute drive from central Brisbane.

Lina Rooftop: Sip cocktails between refreshing dips at this Mediterranean-styled rooftop pool bar in South Bank.

JAKUB MACULEWICZ/SHUTTERSTOCK

D'Aguilar National Park

Walks & Wombats

MAP P282

Go wild at D'Aguilar National Park

Slake any wilderness cravings at 400-sq-km **D'Aguilar National Park** *(parks.qld.gov.au/parks/daguilar)* 12km northwest of central Brisbane. Pronounced 'dee-ag-lar', its mix of open eucalypt woodlands, scribbly gum forests and subtropical rainforests claim over 800 plant species. Maps are available at the **Walkabout Creek Discovery Centre** at the park's entrance on Mt Nebo Rd, on the shores of the Enoggera Reservoir. Also here is the **Wildlife Centre** *(adult/child $8.90/4.25),* with reptiles and nocturnal marsupials and mammals including a wombat and a rare Lumholtz's tree kangaroo. During school holidays, ranger-led experiences are fun and educational.

Beginning just downhill from the Discovery Centre, the **Araucaria Track** (5km, two hours) traces a path around the forested banks of the Enoggera Reservoir. Look out for Pacific kingfishers amid the eucalypt forest. Other walking trails range from a few hundred metres to a 25km loop shared with mountain bikers. Among them is the 6km-return **Morelia Track** at the Manorina day-use area and the 4.3km-return **Greenes Falls Track** at Mt Glorious. Horse riding is also an option, along with remote, walk-in bush camp sites.

To get here, catch bus 385 from Brisbane's King George Sq to The Gap Park 'n' Ride, then walk 650m up the road. Bring your swimming costume for a swim in the reservoir, or hire a kayak or paddleboard from **Walkabout Creek Adventures** *(walkaboutcreekadventures.com.au; per hr $35).*

DRINKING IN BRISBANE: ROOFTOP BARS

MAP P290

Cielo Rooftop: Potted olive trees and a dedicated spritz list give this Fortitude Valley bar a Mediterranean vibe. *4-10pm Thu & Fri, from noon Sat & Sun*

Sunsets: Pair cool cocktails with Mediterranean plates in a desert oasis above Kangaroo Point. *noon-10pm Thu-Sun*

Maya: Sip margaritas above Fortitude Valley at this Mexican-inspired spot. *noon-11pm Wed & Thu, until late Fri-Sun*

Balfour Kitchen & Bar: Watch the Story Bridge light up from this lovely little bar atop a New Farm boutique hotel. *5-9pm*

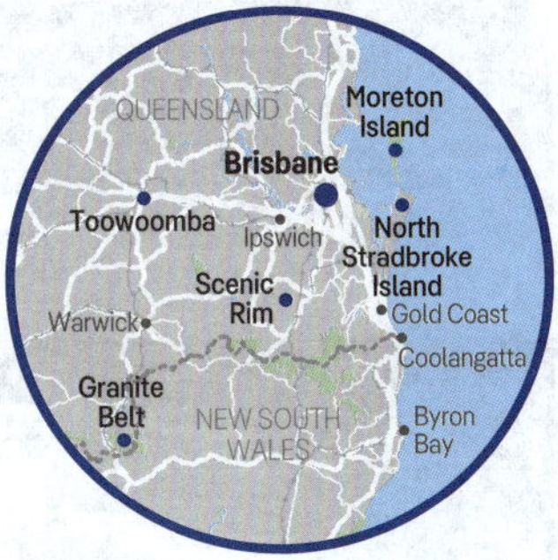

Beyond Brisbane

Head east for spectacular sand islands, or west for charming country towns, rural life, wine and nature.

One of the best things about Brisbane is the diversity of easily accessible adventures on the city's doorstep. North Stradbroke Island (Minjerribah) serves up glorious powdery white beaches, freshwater lakes, Indigenous culture and whale watching, while the wild beauty of Moreton Island (Mulgumpin) is protected by Moreton Island National Park and Recreation Area. Steer a kayak along its protected shores or go snorkelling at the Tangalooma Wrecks.

To the west, Toowoomba is a cool country town (in every sense), while to the southwest, rainforest-clad mountains cradle the agricultural heartland of the Scenic Rim. Head further southwest for a taste of Australia's most northerly – and arguably most relaxed – wine region, in the Granite Belt.

Places

Moreton Island

TIME FROM BRISBANE: **75MIN**

Parks and recreation

The world's third-largest sand island after K'gari and North Stradbroke Island, Moreton Island (Mulgumpin) is popular with fishing fans and 4WD folk. For others, options include catching the Tangalooma Ferry to **Tangalooma Island Resort** *(tangalooma.com)*, either as a day trip for kayaking, quad-bike adventures and fishing *(tangatours.com)*, or to stay overnight. From Tangalooma, it's 1km along the beach for kayaking or snorkelling above the 15 sunken ships of the **Tangalooma Wrecks**. You can also visit the wrecks on day trips from Brisbane or the Gold Coast with **Australian Sunset Safaris** *(sunsetsafaris.com.au; from $259)*.

Leaving from the Port of Brisbane, the **Micat Ferry** from **Moreton Island Adventures** *(moretonislandadventures.com.au)* is a combined passenger and vehicle ferry (4WD only). Check online for day tours to the Tangalooma Wrecks, for sandboarding on giant dunes and for accommodation, including self-contained holiday homes. In the tiny settlement of Bulwer, a 20-minute 4WD journey from the Micat Ferry,

Continued on p302

GETTING AROUND

Vehicle and passenger ferries connect Brisbane with North Stradbroke Island (25 to 45 minutes) from the suburb of Cleveland, while the Tangalooma passenger ferry (75 minutes) to Moreton Island leaves from Pinkenba east of the city. Moreton Island's Micat vehicular ferry (90 minutes; 4WD vehicles only) departs from the Port of Brisbane. Toowoomba is easily accessible by Greyhound bus, but it's handy to have a car. Your own vehicle is essential for exploring the Scenic Rim and Granite Belt independently.

ZSTOCK/SHUTTERSTOCK

Main Beach

TOP EXPERIENCE

North Stradbroke Island

Known to the Quandamooka people as Minjerribah, North Stradbroke Island – aka 'Straddie' – is the world's second-largest sand island after K'gari. Fisherfolk and 4WD enthusiasts flock to its beaches and sandy tracks, but Straddie's combination of clifftop walks, Indigenous culture and spectacular beaches is also easily accessed by other visitors. All this a short ferry ride from Brisbane.

DON'T MISS

- North Gorge Walk
- Cylinder Beach swimming
- Learning about Indigenous history and culture
- Straddie Brewing Co craft beers
- Famous Minjerribah prawn roll
- North Stradbroke's excellent museum

An Astonishing Coastal Walk

At Point Lookout, the spectacular 1.2km **North Gorge Walk** is an essential Minjerribah experience. It's an easy 20-minute loop around the headland, offering incredible views of roiling surf crashing up into the rocky and slender gorge. Views of Main Beach are equally epic and lookouts along the boardwalk are the best vantage points to see migrating humpback whales from June to October. At around 30m high, the gorge's lookouts are regarded as Australia's best place to see humpbacks

PRACTICALITIES

● *stradbrokeisland.com* ● return ferry adult/child/car $17/12.50/$158 ● whale-watching season Jun-Oct from the land. Year-round you might also see dolphins, sea turtles and manta rays in the waters below. Eastern grey kangaroos graze on the side of the trail; their numbers are greatest around dawn and dusk.

A First Nations Perspective

North Gorge Walk is visited with Quandamooka woman Elisha Kissick from **Yura Tours** *(yuratours.com.au; adult/child $150/130)*. Guided experiences explore the history, culture, flora and fauna of the island from an Indigenous perspective. Also visited is **Brown Lake** (Lake Bummiera), its waters rich in soothing tannins from surrounding forests of paperbark eucalypts and, in Indigenous stories, home to the spirit of a giant snake. Elisha's guiding and storytelling are rich in local knowledge and she has a consistent hit rate in seeking out the island's koalas.

North Stradbroke Island Historical Museum

Once the 'Dunwich Benevolent Asylum' – a home for the destitute – this engaging **museum** *(stradbrokemuseum.com.au; adult/child $8/5)* describes shipwrecks and harrowing voyages. Island artefacts include the impressive shell of a green turtle and there's also an interesting video on the history of Amity Point, including the story of Straddie tourism pioneers. Minjerribah's Indigenous heritage is explored in the 'Ngali Dullan – We Remain' exhibition (open Wednesday to Sunday), curated by world-renowned Quandamooka visual artist Megan Cope.

Island Beaches

Fringing Straddie's northern coast are beaches where you'll often have the sea and sand all to yourself. **Main Beach** attracts experienced surfers. Only swim here if it is being patrolled. Near the North Gorge Walk, new boardwalks and steps provide improved access to **Frenchman's Beach**, a good picnic spot. Bordered by Cylinder and Home Beach headlands, family-friendly **Cylinder Beach** generally has smaller waves than nearby bays. It is patrolled, so always swim between the flags.

Welcome to Quandamooka Country

The waters and lands of Moreton Bay lie on the traditional territory of the Quandamooka peoples, including the Ngugi of Mulgumpin (Moreton Island) and the Gorenpul and Nunukal of Minjerribah (North Stradbroke Island). Visit the **Salt Water Murris Quandamooka Aboriginal Art Gallery** *(facebook.com/SWMQuandamooka)* in Dunwich for contemporary art and design. Opened in late 2025, **QUAMPI** (Quandamooka Arts & Culture Centre) showcases Indigenous heritage, culture and art. The centre also hosts September's annual **Quandamooka Festival** *(quandamookafestival.net.au)*.

EATING WELL

Enjoy craft beers and fish tacos at **Straddie Brewing Co** *(straddiebrewing.com.au)* in Dunwich. After the North Gorge Walk, buy an ice cream from **Whale Tail Gelati & Coffee Bar** *(whaletailgelati.com)* or a prawn roll from the **Prawn Shack** *(theprawnshack.com.au)*. Also at Point Lookout, **Six Beaches Fish Grill & Bar** *(sixbeaches.com.au)* is recommended for lunch and dinner, while Amity Point's **Bo Beans Coffee** *(bobeanscoffee.com.au)* serves coffee and breakfast toasties.

TOP TIPS

- Weekends and public holidays are busy; try to visit on a weekday.
- Busy day trips are possible but staying at least a night is recommended.
- Ferries leave from Cleveland, southeast of Brisbane.
- **Sealink** *(sealink.com.au)* takes vehicles and passengers (45 minutes). Book for vehicles well in advance. **Stradbroke Flyer** *(flyer.com.au)* is for passengers only (25 minutes).
- Buses link Dunwich, Amity Point and Point Lookout.
- To explore further, arrive by car or rent a scooter *(scootersonstraddie.com.au)*.
- To explore off sealed roads and on beaches, rent a 4WD vehicle from **Straddie 4WD Hire** *(straddie4wdhire.com)*.

AFTER-DINNER ENTERTAINMENT IN TOOWOOMBA

Empire Theatre: This magnificent Art Deco theatre precinct hosts a variety of performances, from touring musical acts to plays, comedy, circus and more.

Toowoomba Repertory Theatre: The Toowoomba Repertory Theatre Society presents four major productions here per year.

Volcanic Brewing: Toowoomba's best craft beer and occasional live gigs. Check Facebook for what's on.

Fitzy's: Enjoy live music and DJ sets from Thursday through Sunday at this popular main-street pub.

Strand Theatre: This lovely old Art Deco theatre now forms part of a Birch Carroll & Coyle cinema complex.

RIBEIROANTONIO/SHUTTERSTOCK

Ju Raku En Japanese Garden

Continued from p299

Castaways *(castawaysmoretonisland.com.au)* offers glamping and holiday houses. There's a cafe, bottle shop and small grocery store on-site, and 4WD tours – including to **Cape Moreton Lighthouse** – can be arranged.

Toowoomba

TIME FROM BRISBANE: 2HR

A surprising transport museum

Founded in 1848 on the traditional lands of the Jagera, Giabal and Jarowair peoples, Toowoomba is one of Australia's oldest inland cities. Historical insights feature at the **Queensland Museum Cobb+Co** *(museum.qld.gov.au/cobb-and-co; adult/child $12.50/6.50)*, showcasing the transport company that connected Australia's bush settlements from the 1850s to the 1920s. Highlights of Australia's finest collection of horse-drawn vehicles include a 19th-century Cobb & Co Royal Mail coach and a war wagon used on the Western Front in WWI. Excerpts from poems by Australian bush poet Henry Lawson add context and colour to the collection. The broader museum complex includes a First Nations section featuring stories, artefacts and artwork from the region's Indigenous peoples.

Fixed-price Wednesday and Thursday Supper Club specials are good value

EATING & DRINKING IN TOOWOOMBA: OUR PICKS

Bakers Duck: Famed for its sourdough bread and pastries including superb cinnamon morning buns. Good coffee, too. *7am-4pm* $

Loulaki: Modern Greek flavours served in a high-ceilinged and airy ambience. Try the slow-cooked lamb shoulder. *noon-9pm Tue-Sat* $$

Uva Wine Bar: Select from more than 20 wines by the glass at this cute wine bar. *4-10pm Wed & Thu, to 11.45pm Fri & Sat, 5-9pm Tue*

Host: Come for fine wine and elevated snacks or add a hibachi-grilled main at this smart urban bistro. *4-9pm Thu-Sat* $$

Historic masterpieces and vibrant streetart

Also offering historical glimpses into life in the Australian countryside is the **Toowoomba Regional Art Gallery** *(tr.qld.gov.au, Wed-Sun)*, particularly its Lionel Lindsay Gallery, featuring works by significant 19th-century Australian painters including Rupert Bunny, Frederick McCubbin, Tom Roberts and Arthur Streeton. Call ahead to view the gallery's notable library, a treat of rare books, maps and travel journals, including letters written by early European explorers to Australia.

As Queensland's biggest inland city – population 185,000 – Toowoomba's more modern arts vision is expressed by a vibrant collection of streetart. Check out the alleys and laneways along Ruthven and Duggan Sts.

Admire cooler climate gardens

Adorned with green spaces and located 700m above sea level, Toowoomba is known as the Garden City. Wander in the serene **Ju Raku En Japanese Garden** *(unisq.edu.au)*, located in the University of Southern Queensland's sprawling campus. Vermillion-hued bridges and lakeside pavilions are highlights of Australia's largest traditional Japanese gardens (open from 6am to dusk).

Enjoy a picnic in **Queens Park & Botanic Gardens** or be immersed in the scented garden at **Laurel Bank Park**. The collection of fragrant blooms, herbs and shrubs is a sensory feast.

To enjoy Toowoomba's gardens at their peak, visit for the **Toowoomba Carnival of Flowers** *(tcof.com.au)*. Four consecutive weekends of events kick off in mid-September.

Scenic Rim

TIME FROM BRISBANE: **3HR**

Hike on the edge

Hugging the peaks of the Great Diving Range, which cradles the western fringe of the Scenic Rim, **Main Range National Park** is the northernmost park in the UNESCO-listed Gondwana Rainforests of Australia. While some areas of the park affected by the 2019–20 bushfires continue to recover slowly, there are some spectacular day walks to be bagged in all four sections of the mountainous park, including Cunninghams Gap, Spicers Gap, Queen Mary Falls and Goomburra. Top day walks include the **Cascades Circuit** (Goomburra, 6.5km, three hours), **Queen Mary Falls Circuit** (2km return, 40 minutes) and the 12.4km-return slog up the **Bare Rock Track** and **Morgans Walk** (4½ hours) for awe-inspiring panoramas in all directions. But the park's top trek is the **Scenic Rim Trail**, which traces the ridgeline from north to south for 47km. There are three basic walkers' camps en route (book ahead) or you can upgrade to private lodge accommodation on the luxury guided **Spicers Scenic Rim Trail** *(scenicrimtrail.com)*. With nearly 30 camp sites in the national park, overnight adventures beckon.

SCENIC RIM MARKETS & FESTIVALS

Towri Sheep Cheeses Growers Market: A dairy farm hosts a market on the first Saturday of the month; family-friendly fun.

Winter Harvest Festival: The Eat Local Month in June culminates in this one-day market at the Aratula Community Sports Complex.

Kalbar Sunflower Festival: Snap sunflower selfies and enjoy fine food, live music and more at this three-day fest in early May.

Boonah Country Markets: Shop the pop-up stalls in Springleigh Park on the second and fourth Saturdays of each month.

Beaudesert Markets: Find a bargain at this classic country market held on the first Saturday of each month.

SCENIC RIM ROAD TRIP

Start your engine for a leisurely two-day drive around this picturesque rural region southwest of Brisbane.

START	END	LENGTH
Summer Land Camels	O'Reilly's Canungra Valley Vineyards	220km; 2 days

Drive through rural paddocks on the one-hour drive from Brisbane to 1 **Summer Land Camels**. Meet the camels, sample camel cheese and purchase camel-milk skincare products at the homestead's farm store. It's then just 15 minutes to the 2 **Scenic Rim Farm Shop** for elderflower cordial and a lovely garden cafe shaded by a towering jacaranda tree. Continue 30 minutes south to Mt Alford's 3 **Kooroomba Vineyards & Lavender Farm**, for wine tasting, lavender selfies and perhaps lunch with stellar views at the vineyard's restaurant. For a more casual lunch, it's 15 minutes northeast to 4 **Boonah Brewing Co** at Boonah's Commercial Hotel. Continue south for 45 minutes to overnight at 5 **Mt Barney Lodge**. Accommodation options include camping, cabins and a historic Queenslander homestead.

Enjoy a morning ramble in Mt Barney National Park before driving one hour north to the 6 **Overflow Estate 1895**, a historic grazing property turned lakeside winery. There's a French-British-inspired restaurant and Italian wine varietals including vermentino and fiano. Double back through Beaudesert (15 minutes), where the 7 **Beaudesert Historical Museum** showcases the region's pioneer days. Returning leisurely to Brisbane, take the scenic route via Canungra and Tamborine Mountain, making a short detour to 8 **O'Reilly's Canungra Valley Vineyards** to enjoy a picnic basket under the estate's oak trees. Adjacent is the Mountainview Alpaca Farm.

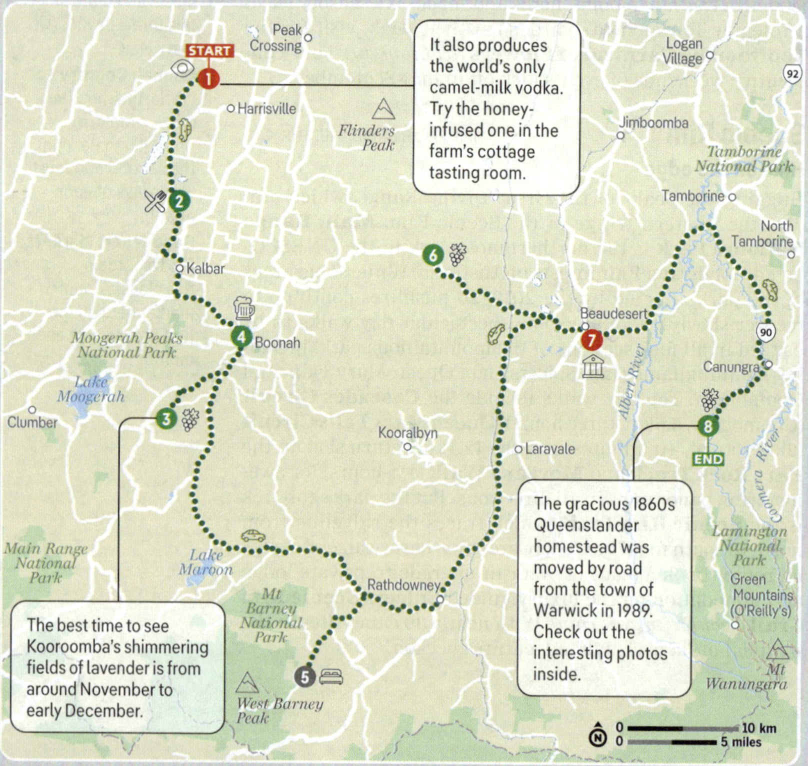

Granite Belt

TIME FROM BRISBANE: **3HR**

Savour Strange Bird wines and cellar-door charm

You could easily spend a week touring the 50-odd wineries of this cool-climate region known for its Strange Bird wines, harnessing lesser-known varieties including fiano and malvasia (white) and durif and sagrantino (red).

Most Granite Belt wineries have cellar doors, but it's usually best to call smaller cellar doors and check they're open. Following are a few of our favourites. See *granitebeltwinecountry.com.au* for touring information, including for restaurants and accommodation, and drop into the friendly **Stanthorpe Visitor Information Centre** for more authoritative guidance. They usually have copies of the Granite Belt Wine Country's *Little Black Book* available, the definitive guide to the region.

For a guided experience visiting a diverse range of wineries and cellar doors, contact **Filippos Wine Tours** *(stanthorpetours.com.au)*.

The Granite Belt's most esteemed and established vineyards include those we've described here.

With the region's highest-elevation vines, **Symphony Hill Wines** *(symphonyhill.com.au)* is a family-owned estate near Ballandean. Their wines have been served on Qantas business-class flights and signature drops include shiraz, nero d'Avola and gewürztraminer. Symphony Hill's recent focus is their Amphora range, fermented in Tuscan terracotta.

Quality eclipses quantity at **Tobin Wines** *(tobinwines.com)*, the top-rated single-vineyard Ballandean winery and a focused operation only producing up to 160 cases of each wine annually. Hosted at a long bench atop a row of barrels, the tasting experience is both informative and intimate. Booking ahead is required.

Winemaker Peter McGlashan at **Ridgemill Estate** *(ridgemillestate.com)*, in Severnlea, co-established the region's Strange Bird Wine Trail, and Georgian Saperavi and Italian nebbiolo are among the vineyard's stars. Stay in their boutique cabin accommodation, enjoy cellar-door experiences including wine and cheese pairings, and don't forget to say 'Hi' to Ridgemill's friendly goats.

Get festive in the Granite Belt

The Southern Downs region celebrates a handful of weird and wonderful festivals worth planning a visit around. Among the

RANGER OF THE NORTH

Australia's longest-roaming bushranger (outlaw) once hid out in the Granite Belt. After escaping from Sydney's Cockatoo Island Prison in 1863, convicted horse thief Frederick Wordsworth Ward (1835–70) embarked on a robbing spree as he headed north, earning himself the nickname Captain Thunderbolt. A 20-minute drive northwest of Stanthorpe, a granite outcrop known as **Donnellys Castle** was one of his hideouts. It's easy to imagine a bushranger taking refuge here as you wander between the lichen-encrusted granite boulders in this public reserve and climb up to a lookout over the rural landscape. After Captain Thunderbolt was finally shot and killed by police near Uralla in 1870, hundreds flocked to see his bullet-ridden body.

EATING IN THE GRANITE BELT: OUR PICKS

Sutton's Juice Factory: Wash down a slice of its famous apple pie with a homemade apple juice. North of Stanthorpe. *9.30am-4.30pm* $

Jamworks of Glen Aplin: Come for produce-driven cafe fare or to stock up on delicious preserves. Between Stanthorpe and Ballandean. *9am-4pm Wed-Sun* $$

Varias: Relaxed dining bistro and served by the savvy student team at Stanthorpe's Queensland College of Wine Tourism. *11am-2pm Tue-Sat, plus 5.30-9pm Fri & Sat* $$

Essen: An innovative kitchen in Stanthorpe serves sumptuous set menus highlighting Granite Belt produce. BYO beer and wine. *6-9pm Thu-Sat* $$$

best is the biennial **Stanthorpe Apple & Grape Harvest Festival** *(appleandgrape.org)*, which celebrates the harvest of Granite Belt region produce with 10 days of foodie festivities held across February and March on even-numbered years.

A 45-minute drive north of Stanthorpe, Warwick and surrounding communities are yarn-bombed (decorated with crocheted or knitted material) in midwinter by a passionate group of local 'Yarntopians' as part of the 10-day **Jumpers & Jazz in July** *(jumpersandjazz.com.au)*, which features more than 100 cultural and community events.

Wildflowers, balancing boulders and ancient forest trails

Girraween is an Aboriginal word meaning 'place of flowers' and if you visit its namesake **national park** *(parks.qld.gov.au/parks/girraween)*, east of Ballandean on the Queensland–NSW border between late winter and summer, you'll be rewarded with bursts of wildflowers. Year-round, other highlights of this eucalypt-forest-dominated park include giant boulders balancing precariously on rocky outcrops and cool streams gushing into rock pools. Look forward to a bush soundtrack provided by more than 170 bird species.

There are three main entrances to the park, with the best of 12 walking trails and the most accessible of 16 camping areas all found in the northern section accessed by the sealed Pyramids Rd. Opened in 2022, the modern **visitor information centre** here has displays on natural history and the cultural history of the park's Traditional Custodians, the Kambuwal people. New interpretative panels near trailheads also enhance the park's enjoyment.

The park's high elevation (approximately 1000m above sea level) means it can get pretty nippy, especially if you're camping.

TOP TRAILS TO TACKLE IN GIRRAWEEN NATIONAL PARK

The Pyramid: Make the 3.6km-return slog up this granite hill for sublime views across the bush landscape.

Bald Rock Creek Circuit: This 2.2km creek-side circuit is a great meander to stretch the legs, with native flowers framing rock pools.

Granite Arch: Marvel at a natural stone archway created by massive balancing boulders on this easy 1.6km circuit suitable for the whole family.

The Junction: The spring wildflower displays and the birdlife they attract are highlights of this easy 5.2km-return ramble.

Castle Rock: Allow around two hours to complete this 5.2km scramble for more great views.

DRINKING AT OTHER GRANITE BELT WINERIES: OUR PICKS

Twisted Gum Wines: Near Ballendean, with a commitment to minimal irrigation and using no chemical insecticides. Try the pink moscato. *10am-4pm Sat & Sun*

Golden Grove Estate: Family-run Golden Grove craft award-winning vermentino and barbera, both lesser-known Italian wine varietals. *10am-4pm Thu-Tue*

Dear Vincent: Modern and unpretentious, with skin-contact pinot gris, and zesty and sparkling pét-nat wines. Often features an on-site food truck. *11am-4pm Fri-Sun*

New Tricks: Family-owned cellar door, with good pinot noir, Mediterranean-inspired lunches, and gin and vodka from their Brisbane distillery. *11am-5pm Sat & Sun*

Surfers Paradise & the Gold Coast

BEACHES | BRONZED BODIES | RESTAURANTS

Built for pleasure and a place dedicated to sun, surf and the body beautiful, this sublime strip of coastline is the Australia that visitors from cooler climes often fantasise about. Affectionately known as the 'Goldie', the coast has shimmering high-rises that often seem incongruous against the beach, but with 300 sunny days a year and countless surf breaks along 52km of sand, it's still very easy to admire. There's a reputation for tackiness that's occasionally deserved, but this is counter-balanced by a youthful spirit and startling coastal beauty. Surfers Paradise's bars and nightclubs might entertain the party kids, but to the south along the Gold Coast Hwy, highlights include Burleigh's booming culinary scene and the more relaxed beach-holiday vibe of Currumbin, Kirra and Coolangatta. The Goldie lies on the traditional lands of the Yugambeh people, whose rich legacy you can connect with at an excellent cultural centre in Burleigh Heads.

TOP TIP

Held over 11 days in October, the Gold Coast's essential festival is **Bleach**. This contemporary arts festival hosts a range of edgy, free and ticketed arts events (from live music to performance art) at a handful of festival hubs across the city. See *hota.com.au* for all the goss.

GETTING AROUND

Gold Coast Airport is 21km south of Surfers Paradise, near Coolangatta. Brisbane Airport is 84km northwest of Surfers Paradise and accessible by train (the final stop is Varsity Lakes). Con-X-ion Airport Transfers runs shuttle services to/from both airports. Since 2026 the G:link light rail has run from Helensvale train station along the Gold Coast Hwy all the way south to Burleigh Heads. Frequent Translink buses are another option on this route. Buses and G:link both cost 50c. All forms of contactless payment are accepted. Neon-green Lime e-bikes are another handy way to get around, especially along quieter roads near the beach.

HIGHLIGHTS
1 Burleigh Beach

SIGHTS
2 Burleigh Head National Park
3 Cavill Mall
4 Currumbin Alley
5 Currumbin Creek
6 Currumbin Wildlife Sanctuary
7 Duranbah Beach
8 Evandale Lake
9 Jellurgal Aboriginal Cultural Centre
10 Main Beach Pavilion
11 Mariner's Cove
12 SkyPoint

ACTIVITIES
see 6 Astra Lumina
13 Bathhouse at Ground
14 Cheyne Horan School of Surf
see 4 Currumbin Alley Surf School
15 Federation Walk
16 Greenhouse the Bathhouse
17 Greenmount Point
18 Kirra Point
see 11 Kokomo Cruises
19 Native State Bathhouse & Studio Gym
see 6 Outback Springs
20 Snapper Rocks
21 Soak Bathhouse
22 Tallebudgera Creek
23 Vikasati

SLEEPING
24 Cheshire Cat
25 QT

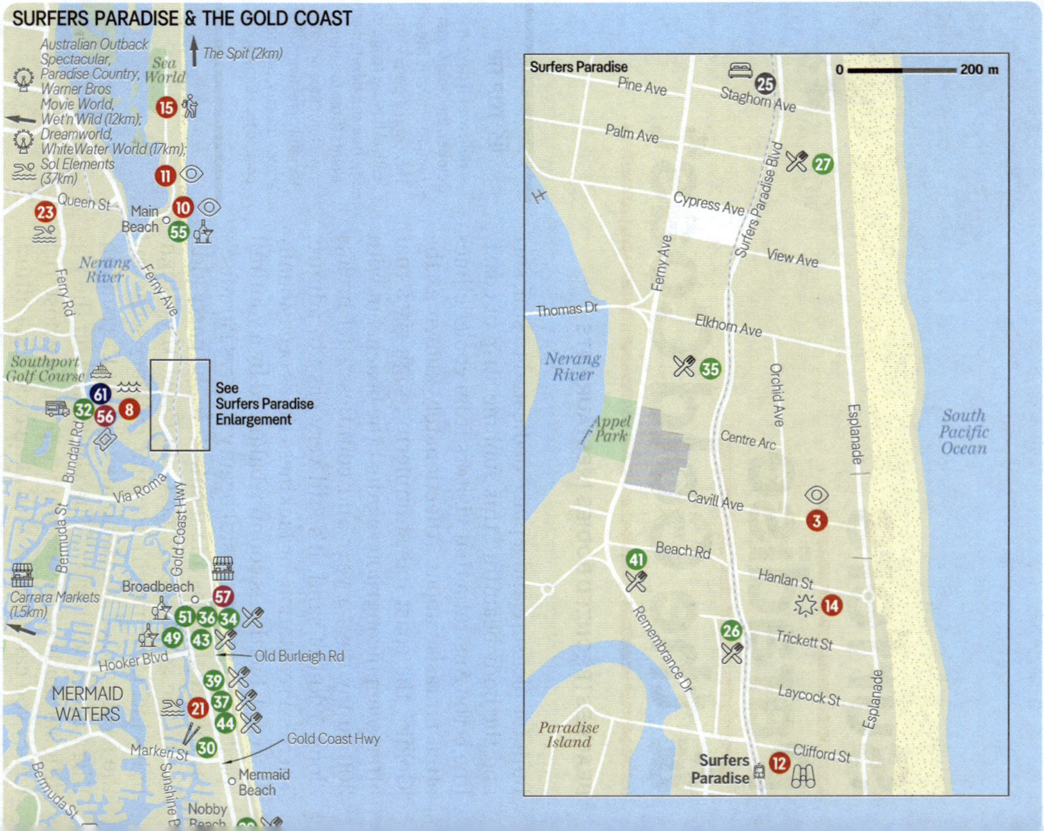

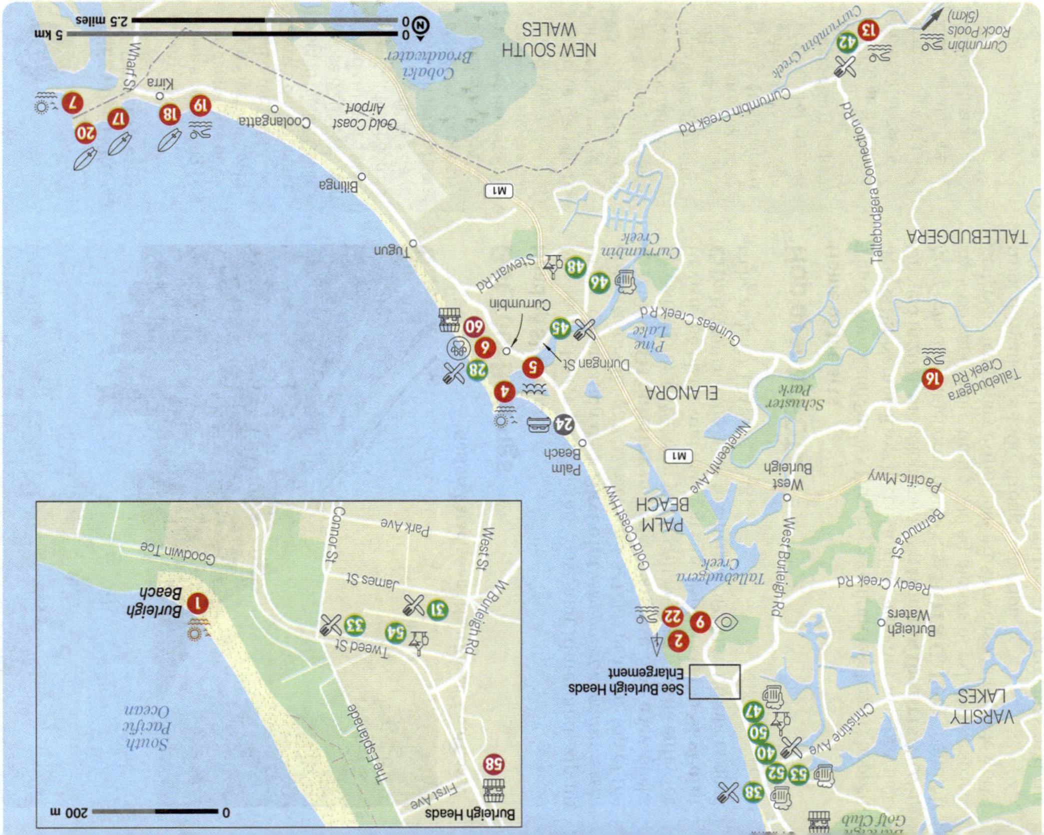

● **EATING**
- **26** Baba Joon Persian Grill
- **27** Coast
- **28** Currumbin Beach Vikings SLSC
- **29** Eska
- **30** Etsu Izakaya
- **31** Golosi Food Emporium
- **32** HOTA Farmers & Artisan Markets
- **33** Justin Lane
- **34** Kurrawa Surf Club
- **35** Little Bali
- **36** Luna's
- **37** Mermaid Beach SLSC
- **38** North Burleigh SLSC
- **39** North Room
- **40** Paddock Bakery
- **41** Paradox Coffee Roasters
- **42** Pasture & Co
- **43** Social Eating House & Bar
- **44** Sunnyboy Espresso
- **45** Tarte Beach House

● **DRINKING & NIGHTLIFE**
- **46** Balter
- **47** Black Hops Brewing
- **48** Burly Gin
- **49** Garden Kitchen & Bar
- **50** Hard Fizz
- **51** Loose Moose
- **52** Precinct Brewing
- **53** Roji Cat Beer Bar
- **54** Rosella's
- **55** Southport Surf Lifesaving Club

● **ENTERTAINMENT**
- **56** HOTA

● **SHOPPING**
- **57** Broadbeach Sunday Market
- **58** Burleigh Farmers Market
- **59** Miami Marketta
- **60** Sanctuary Markets

● **TRANSPORT**
- **61** hopo HOTA jetty

THE EVOLUTION OF CAVILL AVE

Love it or hate it, there's no denying the central role of the pedestrian **Cavill Mall** in the Gold Coast's development. Named for Jim Cavill, whose 1920s Surfers Paradise Hotel gave the neighbourhood its name, Cavill Ave developed into the heart of the city's economy. By the end of 1990s, however, Surfers Paradise – and its famous promenade – was in decline. Despite attempts to revive it, Cavill Mall still retains a tackiness with chain fast-food outlets, nightclubs and carnival rides.

Visit on a day trip to check out the famous Surfers Paradise sign at the end of the mall, but do also recognise that from mid-afternoon, shadows from Surfers' skyscrapers are usually blocking sunshine from the beach.

VISUAL COLLECTIVE/SHUTTERSTOCK

Surfers Paradise and Main Beach, Gold Coast

Get Your Bearings

Head up SkyPoint

For an eagle-eye view of the coast and hinterland, zip up to the observation deck **SkyPoint** *(skypoint.com.au; weekday adult/child $33/25, weekend $41/33)* near the top of the 322m-high **Q1 building** in Surfers Paradise. Save a few bucks by visiting on a weekday; you'll still need to pay the entry fee to visit the bistro and bar. You can also tackle the **SkyPoint Climb** *($99)* up the spire to a height of 270m. Climbers need to be at least 12 years of age.

Hop over to HOTA

Home of the arts

Those who brand Surfers Paradise as cultureless haven't hopped across the Nerang River to the Goldie's signature arts precinct. Opened in 2021, the colour-popping **Home of the Arts** *(HOTA; hota.com.au)* is anchored by the vast **HOTA Gallery** spanning six levels and more than 2000 sq metres of exhibition space. Zeitgeisty temporary exhibitions are showcased alongside works from the gallery's 4500-strong collection.

The complex also has two theatres, two cinemas and the **Palette** fine-dining restaurant. **The Exhibitionist** is a rooftop bar with cracking views. Saturday night's **Comedy**

Thursday to Sunday three-course lunch specials are good value

EATING IN SURFERS PARADISE: OUR PICKS

Paradox Coffee Roasters: Excellent coffee and all-day brunch. The chilli scrambled eggs are a great way to start the day. *7am-2pm* $

Little Bali: Skip Cavill Mall's fast-food chains for a taste of Kuta in the Chevron Renaissance shopping centre. *11.30am-8.30pm* $$

Baba Joon Persian Grill: A haven of authenticity and well-priced meals. Excellent dips and meze and plate-covering lamb and chicken skewers. *11.30am-9pm* $$

Coast: Bringing sophistication to Surfers, this oceanside fine diner specialises in seafood and charcoal-broiled steaks. *noon-10pm Thu-Sun, 3-10pm Tue & Wed* $$$

Underground Saturday Showcase is always popular and there's an outdoor stage with seats and lawn space for 5000 people.

HOTA also hosts a Sunday morning **farmers market** with food stalls and food trucks. Near the market is **Evandale Lake**, a sheltered spot ideal for a picnic or a swim. Nearby, the sky-blue Chevron Island pedestrian bridge links to walking access to Surfers Paradise (1.5km). Another option to reach HOTA is on the **hopo ferry** *(hopo.com.au; $5)*, a hop-on, hop-off service linking to Surfers Paradise on Sunday mornings from 7am to 10am. Beyond the HOTA Sunday service, the hopo ferries' daily schedule includes Southport's Broadwater Parklands and Sea World (fares adult/child from $10/6).

Glimpse of Gold Coast Past

Relaxed coastal charm and scenic nature walks

North of Surfers Paradise, the pace eases up but the apartment towers are only slightly less lofty. **Main Beach** is a relaxing base for views, beach time and taking it easy. Next to the **Southport Surf Lifesaving Club** *(sslsc.com.au)*, the Spanish Mission–style **Main Beach Pavilion** (1934) offers a glimpse of the Goldie's pre-boom days. Inside the pavilion's cafe are B&W photos of the coast before the skyscrapers. For better beach views with your coffee, head next door to the surf club bistro.

Further north, **The Spit** separates the Southport Broadwater from the Pacific Ocean, stretching for 5km to almost meet South Stradbroke Island. Its southern end is home to **Mariner's Cove**, a base for aquatic activities. Backed with dunes and a serene coastal reserve, the 3.7km **Federation Walk** *(federationwalk.org)* takes you through it. Promoted as the 'green beside the gold' the walk is a lovely natural haven very close to the high-rise energy of Surfers Paradise.

Hit the Beach

Enjoy your own patch of sand

There is little separating the Goldie's beaches – literally, with the longest section stretching for some 17km from **The Spit** to **Burleigh Heads**. Forming a small cove, **Burleigh Beach** is arguably the most scenic, with great views of the Surfers Paradise skyline. It's now easily reached on the recent extension of G:link, the Gold Coast's light rail network and just a short walk from good restaurants and cafes.

RISE & SHINE!

Launched in mid-2025, the region's current marketing slogan, 'Get up and Gold Coast' reflects the inclination of more than a few locals to rise at dawn and go for a walk, bike ride or swim.

Cafes often open at 5.30am for the first coffee of the day and because Queensland doesn't adopt daylight saving – unlike NSW just to the south – it starts to get dark around 6.30pm, even in summer. Restaurants open at around 5pm for dinner, and cocktail bars and pubs are usually more crowded earlier in the evening.

Night owls might want to head down to Sydney or Melbourne, but on both the Gold Coast and the Sunshine Coast, early birds should feel right at home.

A well-curated wine and craft beer selection

EATING & DRINKING IN BROADBEACH: OUR PICKS

Luna's: Wood-fired pizzas, decadent pastas and mini meals for kids hungry after theme-park adventures. *5-9pm Wed-Sun, plus noon-3pm Fri-Sun* **$$**

Garden Kitchen & Bar: At The Star hotel complex and channelling a relaxed and beachy vibe. Good for bar snacks and cocktails. *5-9pm daily, plus noon-3pm Sat & Sun*

Loose Moose: Laid-back Americana-themed bar with wings, tacos and a dizzying range of whisky and craft beer. *noon-late Mon-Fri, from 11am Sat & Sun*

Social Eating House & Bar: Pricey but beautifully executed modern Australian dining. Bring friends to share the slow-cooked lamb shoulder. *noon-9pm* **$$$**

To the south, the azure **Tallebudgera Creek** meets the sea on the southern side of Burleigh Hill. Protected from the surf, it's popular with families and surf-shy beachgoers. The surf beach from Tallebudgera to Coolangatta at the Gold Coast's southern tip is broken only by **Currumbin Creek**, which also has swimming areas sheltered from the waves.

Thrills & Spills

High-octane thrills and family fun at theme parks

Centred in Coomera, a 30-minute drive northwest from Surfers Paradise, the Gold Coast's theme parks offer seriously dizzying action. Multiday passes grant unlimited entry to the four theme parks by **Village Roadshow** *(themeparks.com.au)*. Note: Lonely Planet chooses not to publicise parks that keep captive cetaceans, such as performing dolphins.

Venture to the outback at **Australian Outback Spectacular** *(outbackspectacular.com.au; adult/child $119/89)*, a high-tech evening show (with real cattle mustering) including a three-course dinner.

Australia's biggest theme park, **Dreamworld** *(dreamworld.com.au; from adult/child $124/114)* has stomach-churning thrill rides, whiz-bang multisensory rides and entertainment aplenty for smaller kids. Animal rights groups continue to urge Dreamworld to shut down its Tiger Island experiences.

Younger kids love **Paradise Country** *(paradisecountry.com.au; adult/child $69/59)*, the 'Aussie Farm Experience', featuring native animals alongside farm animals and foreign species.

Warner Bros Movie World *(movieworld.com.au; adult/child $109/99)* has movie-themed shows, rides and attractions, while actors dressed as Wonder Woman, Batman and Bugs Bunny roam through the crowds.

At **Wet'n'Wild** *(wetnwild.com.au; adult/child $119/119)* the ultimate water slide is the Kamikaze and this sprawling water park also has white-water rapids and wave pools.

Next door to Dreamworld, **WhiteWater World** *(adult/child $89/69)* features the Cave of Waves, Pipeline Plunge and numerous other water activities and slides. Some tickets grant entry to both Dreamworld and WhiteWater World.

THEME PARK TIPS

Arrive early: The parks can get very crowded, so arrive early or face a long walk from the far side of the car park.

Take public transport: The Surfside Buslines TX7 bus (from Coomera Station) stops at the main theme parks, as does Con-X-ion Airport Transfers.

Book online: This will usually save you from $10 to $15 per person.

Prepare to fork out for food: The parks don't generally let you bring in your own food or drinks.

Water park seasonal hours: Note that Wet'n'Wild is open year-round, but WhiteWater World is only open from September to April.

Check what's on: Some parks also host seasonal events, including Dreamworld's Happy Halloween 'spook-tacular'.

Street-Food Feast

Street-food, live music and coastal vibes

The vibe becomes more relaxed as you head from Surfers Paradise south to Broadbeach and through Mermaid Beach,

EATING FROM MERMAID BEACH TO NOBBY BEACH: OUR PICKS

Look for the white barn doors and the single red lantern

Sunnyboy Espresso: Underneath an apartment building near the Mermaid Beach sands is this locals' favourite. Try the avocado and asparagus toast. *7am-2pm* $

Eska: Seafood specialists with a Japanese accent. One of the recent eating options opening around Nobby Beach's Lavarack Rd. *11.30am-9.30pm Thu-Sat, to 8pm Wed & Sun* $$

North Room: Innovative menus for lunch and dinner. Queensland produce and seafood. Bookings essential. *5-9pm Thu, 12.30-2.30pm & 5-9pm Fri & Sat* $$$

Etsu Izakaya: Shared plates spanning sashimi to yakitori skewers are served under a striking curved feature wall in Mermaid Beach. *5pm-midnight* $$

CHAMELEONSEYE/SHUTTERSTOCK

WhiteWater World

Miami and Nobby Beach (Nobbys). The entire strip features places to eat and drink, but for the ultimate taste of the Gold Coast, head to **Miami Marketta** *(miamimarketta.com)*, a hawker-style street market (from 5pm Wednesday to Saturday) in a huge warehouse.

On offer is everything from Turkish *gözleme* (stuffed turnover) to Japanese *okonomiyaki* (savoury pancakes). Grab a drink at the cocktail bar and browse the cool gift shop. There are hip souvenirs and designs on offer and the market's own craft gin is also available.

You can look forward to buskers and live music most nights, but Australian touring bands and the occasional international act also play Miami Marketta's bigger concert space. Check online for listings. Friday and Saturday nights offer the widest selection of food and the market is a just a five-minute walk from the new Miami North G:link light rail station.

Sacred Hill

Indigenous culture and coastal beauty at Burleigh Head

The 27-hectare **Burleigh Head National Park** is known to the local Kombumerri group of the Yugambeh people as Jellurgal; they trace its formation to a creation spirit called Jabreen. As you walk the 1.2km (one way) **Oceanview Track** that edges the reserve, look out for the six-sided basalt columns Jabreen is said to have left in his wake. Sidetracks lead to lookouts.

TOP GOLD COAST MARKETS

Gold Coast Art & Craft Sunday Markets: Held on alternate Sundays in Broadbeach, Coolangatta and Burleigh Heads. See *artandcraft.com.au* for weekly locations.

HOTA Farmers & Artisan Markets: Essential Sunday morning destination for food-truck treats enjoyed beside Evandale Lake.

Carrara Markets: The coast's biggest market is more like a country fair, complete with farm animals and over 300 stalls (held Saturdays and Sundays).

Burleigh Farmers Market: Prep the ultimate picnic at this popular Saturday market.

Sanctuary Markets: Food trucks aplenty for a Friday night feast (from 4pm to 9pm) at the Currumbin Wildlife Sanctuary.

From Hard Fizz, it's just a 250m walk to the three other bars

DRINKING IN BURLEIGH'S TAPROOM PRECINCT: OUR PICKS

Roji Cat Beer Bar: Tokyo-style laneway bar with beers brewed on-site. Excellent sashimi, ceviche and gyoza (dumplings). *4-10pm Thu & Fri, from noon Sat & Sun*

Precinct Brewing: Warehouse-style taproom with diverse brews crafted locally. Wood-fired pizza and gigs and events most nights. *4-10pm Mon-Thu, from noon Fri-Sun*

Black Hops Brewing: At this hyper-local taproom with a streetart vibe, its 16 taps often feature seasonal specials. *noon-7pm Sun-Thu, to 9pm Fri & Sat*

Hard Fizz: Pastel-hued and playful taproom pouring fruit-based hard seltzers and guest beers from local breweries. *2-7pm Thu, noon-9pm Fri & Sat, 1-5pm Sun*

SURF-LIFE-SAVING CLUBS

Right throughout coastal Queensland, surf-life-saving clubs (SLSCs) are at the heart of their local communities. Kids can join as 'nippers' from as young as five, learning skills that will eventually see them patrolling flagged safe-swimming areas on beaches. Surf-life-saving clubs often enjoy the best of coastal real estate – especially along the Gold Coast – making their good-value bistros a great place for lunch or dinner. Non-members are welcome and they're a good place to meet the locals. Recommended clubs on the Gold Coast include **Kurrawa Surf Club** *(kurrawasurf.com.au)* at Broadbeach, **Mermaid Beach SLSC** *(mermaidslsc.org.au)* and **North Burleigh SLSC** *(surfclubaustralia.com)*. Further south, the **Currumbin Beach Vikings SLSC** *(currumbinslsc.com.au)* has absolute billion-dollar beach views.

ALEX CIMBAL/SHUTTERSTOCK

Currumbin Rock Pools

At the headland's base, **Jellurgal** *(jellurgal.com.au)* is the Goldie's only Aboriginal cultural centre. Their **Jellurgal Walkabout Tour** *(adult/child $59/29)* takes guests on a fascinating walk around the 'Dreaming Mountain'. It's a gentle two-hour stroll imbued with Indigenous culture, history and storytelling. Look forward to brilliant views across Tallebudgera Creek and north to Surfers Paradise.

Also available are **Jellurgal Journey Tours** *(adult/child $149/139)*, run on Wednesdays and including boomerang making and an interactive art class. Outside of the humpback whale season, check online for details of when Jellurgal's **Cruise with Culture** *(adult/child $69/59)* experience is offered in conjunction with **Kokomo Cruises** *(kokomocruises.com.au)*.

Wild Swims & Wildlife

Riverside rock pools and iconic animal encounters

Burleigh merges into Palm Beach before becoming Currumbin. From its lovely beach, take the serpentine road inland along Currumbin Creek to the natural **Currumbin Rock Pools**. They're a shaded place to cool off or have a picnic.

Just south of Currumbin Creek, the **Currumbin Wildlife Sanctuary** *(currumbinsanctuary.com.au; adult/child $70/50)*

Has Blinky Bill cocktails with eucalyptus vodka and quandong (native peach)

EATING & DRINKING IN BURLEIGH: OUR PICKS

Golosi Food Emporium: Deli serving toasted sandwiches and fresh bread and picnic fixings for a feast by the surf. *8am-6pm Mon-Sat, to 4pm Sun* $

Justin Lane: Sourdough pizza and handmade pasta downstairs, cocktails upstairs and a party vibe throughout. *5pm-late Mon-Thu, from noon Fri-Sun* $$

Paddock Bakery: It's hard to beat the garden setting and baked goods at Burleigh's OG brunch spot. *6am-3pm* $$

Rosella's: It's not easy to nail Australiana without being naff, but this Burleigh bar succeeds. *4pm-midnight Mon-Fri, from 2pm Sat & Sun* includes Australia's biggest rainforest aviary. Hand-feed a technicolour blur of rainbow lorikeets. Australian animals include bilbies, koalas and Tasmanian devils. Recent additions to Currumbin include **Outback Springs**, a family-friendly experience including a bush-tucker garden and gemstone panning and **Astra Lumina**, a sound, light and laser walking experience through Currumbin's native bushland.

Surf's Up

Learning to surf and the Goldie's best breaks

The Gold Coast has some of the world's best waves and in 2015 the 16km stretch of beaches from Burleigh Point to Snapper Rocks on the Queensland–NSW border was declared a **World Surfing Reserve**.

Beyond world-class waves attracting gun riders, gentle waves for a body bash or whitewash for learning the ropes are also easy to find. Contact **Cheyne Horan School of Surf** *(cheynehoran.com.au; from $55)* for beginners' lessons at Surfers Paradise or Burleigh.

The following are the region's legendary surf breaks. If you're experienced enough to be on the best waves, you won't be alone out the back. Local surfers have a reputation for being territorial and once you've seen the drop-ins, you'll understand why. Be respectful. Even if you're not a surfer, it's worthwhile getting along to these spots and watching all the action.

An advanced point break at the southern end of Coolangatta, **Snapper Rocks** is home to the **Gold Coast Pro**, the first stop on the World Surf League's Challenger Series, held in April or May. Key to Snapper's iconic break status is the Superbank, a sand bar stretching for 2km from the Queensland–NSW border and encompassing the similarly iconic breaks of **Greenmount Point** and **Kirra Point**.

Universally known as D-bah (and, officially, just over the Queensland–NSW border), Duranbah point and the peaky beach break are good for those who like their waves technical and punchy. **Currumbin Alley**, a point break at the mouth of Currumbin Creek, creates a walling wave that's popular with longboarders. There's a surf school here too, with **Currumbin Alley Surf School** *(currumbinalleysurfschool.com.au; from $55)* running beginners' lessons on more forgiving smaller waves.

BRILLIANT BATHHOUSES

Soak Bathhouse: In Mermaid Beach, hop between hot tubs, mineral baths, plunge pools, steam room and sauna, or unwind with a signature spa treatment.

Greenhouse the Bathhouse: The Goldie's original bathhouse celebrates a relaxed location in Tallebudgera Valley. There's also a good cafe (open Wednesday to Sunday).

Bathhouse at Ground: Unwind in the traditional cedar hot tub at this bathhouse set in a Currumbin Valley eco-village.

Native State Bathhouse & Studio Gym: Wind down after a workout at this intimate, European-inspired sanctuary in Coolangatta.

Vikasati: Head north to Southport for Vikasati's relaxing combo of ice baths, cold and hot magnesium plunger pools, and a Finnish rock sauna.

EATING & DRINKING IN CURRUMBIN: OUR PICKS

Ask about seasonal and one-off brews

Pasture & Co: Flavour-packed brunch dishes served in a serene, sustainability-focused Currumbin Valley venue. Packed on weekends. *7am-3pm* $$

Tarte Beach House: Choose between the ground-floor cafe and upstairs restaurant, both with Currumbin Creek views. *6.30am-3pm Mon-Fri, to 4pm Sat & Sun* $$

Burly Gin: Superior bar snacks and shared plates team with cocktails at this chic Currumbin bar. Try a tasting flight of different gins. *4pm-late Tue-Sat*

Balter: Sample one of Australia's favourite craft beers (Balter XPA), launched by pro surfers, at this Currumbin brewery and taproom. *3-8pm Wed-Fri, from noon Sat & Sun*

Gold Coast Hinterland

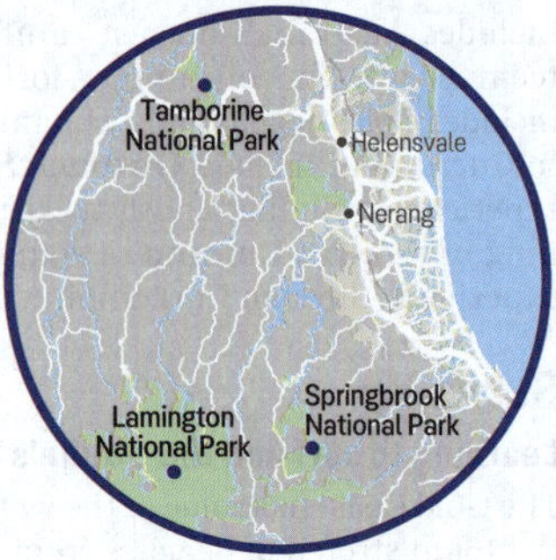

RAINFOREST | WALKS | CRAFT DRINKS

Places

TOP TIP
Hinterland national park trails, picnic areas and sometimes also roads can close at short notice for maintenance, making it a good idea to check park websites for the latest closures – as well as the weather forecast – before you head up here. Camp sites should be booked online, in advance.

Rising up beyond the Goldie's glittering beaches is a forested and blissfully cool hinterland region that feels a million miles away from the energy of the coast.

Misty Tamborine Mountain sits 550m above the Pacific on the northern fringe of this region broadly known as the Gold Coast Hinterland. Forested settlements and an emerging craft-brewing and distilling scene are tucked between lush swathes of Tamborine National Park, known for its waterfall walks.

Clinging to the McPherson Range – a spur of the Great Dividing Range – to the south lie Springbrook and Lamington National Parks. Stretching to the Queensland–NSW border, these mountainous subtropical rainforest havens are packed with waterfalls, walking trails, lookouts and native wildlife, and home to two of Australia's oldest and most iconic rainforest lodges. There's also camping, glamping and endless opportunities for escapism. Pack a picnic, lace your boots and venture in.

Tamborine National Park

TIME FROM SURFERS PARADISE: **45MIN**

Refresh in the rainforest

Just 35km inland from Surfers Paradise, the rainforest community of **Tamborine Mountain** is reached via a serpentine, narrow road that eventually fulfils the promise of cooler weather than the coast's. With this more forgiving microclimate – especially during spring and summer – forest walking is an attraction for many visitors.

GETTING AROUND

With no regular scheduled transport from the Gold Coast (or Brisbane) to Tamborine Mountain or the region's national parks, you'll need your own car. Fuel up before you leave the coast, as the hinterland's only petrol station is a 24hr BP between the Binna Burra and Green Mountains sections of Lamington National Park. **Binna Burra Lodge** (p320) and **O'Reilly's Rainforest Retreat** (p320) both offer one way Border Track transfers; book ahead. For pre-booked shuttle transport from the Gold Coast or Brisbane to Tamborine Mountain, contact **Pineapple Tours** *(pineappletours.com.au)*. They also offer hop-on, hop-off services taking in the town's wineries, breweries and distilleries.

ZSTOCK/SHUTTERSTOCK

Tamborine National Park

Tamborine National Park *(parks.qld.gov.au/parks/tamborine)* comprises 14 sections stretching across the 8km plateau, offering waterfalls and superb Gold Coast views. Six sections offer 11 walking trails between them. While some trails have steep sections, they're all quite short. Download a walking-tracks map from the website, or drop into the excellent **Tamborine Mountain Visitor Information Centre** *(visittamborinemountain.com.au)* for maps and tips.

Soothing experiences at SOL Elements

After hitting the trails, ease into Zen-infused relaxation at **SOL Elements** *(solelements.com.au; communal/private sessions from $80/190)*. Inspired by Japanese *onsen* (bathing) culture, this stylish bathhouse complex opened in 2025 to add an enhanced level of sophistication to Tamborine Mountain. Relax in communal facilities including mineral-rich thermal pools, saunas and plunge pools, or enjoy a private experience in a Secluded Suite. Flotation therapy and spa and massage treatments are equally blissful.

Getting crafty

Tamborine Mountain is an emerging hub for brewing and distilling. Combine a visit to **Witches Falls Winery**

FAMILY-FRIENDLY THUNDERBIRD PARK

Canyon Flyer: Australia's longest zip-line experience, with eight sections spanning 1.4km. Children must weigh at least 40kg.

Digi IT: Kids (and adults) get the chance to operate a mini-excavator. Pint-sized hi-vis vests provided for maximum authenticity.

Treetop Challenge Adventure Park: There's 140 challenges across various courses and four levels. There's also a junior ropes course for kids aged four to seven.

Bird Feeding: A colourful kaleidoscope of vibrant rainbow lorikeets and other native birds fly in to enjoy an avian forest buffet.

Geological fun and entertainment: Fossick for 200-million-year-old 'thundereggs' and learn about panning for crystals and gems.

Adjacent eating options make this Tamborine Mountain's good-dining hub

EATING AT TAMBORINE MOUNTAIN: OUR PICKS

Franquette: Gorgeous pastries, loaded baguettes and gourmet toasties. Good coffee and sunny outdoor seating, too. *7am-2pm Thu-Mon* $

Picnic Real Food Bar: Wholefood brunch dishes and takeaway options in the sustainability-focused North Stores complex. *8am-3pm Wed-Sun* $

Mason Winery Restaurant: Great spot for a long lunch, paired with estate wines. Verdelho, merlot, sauvignon blanc and chardonnay grapes feature. *10am-4pm Wed-Sun* $$$

MANA: Huge souvlakis and other Greek treats feature at this family-owned favourite. Very popular, so book for dinner. *5-9pm Tue-Sat, plus noon-2.30pm Fri & Sat* $$

TOP TAMBORINE MOUNTAIN TRAILS

Curtis Falls Track, Tamborine National Park: Enchanting 1.1km-return trail to a gorgeous waterfall. For a longer walk, branch off onto the Lower Creek Circuit (2.5km return).

Cedar Creek Falls Track, Tamborine National Park: Enjoy a dip in the rock pools on this popular 1.1km-return rainforest ramble.

Glow Worm Caves: Take a guided tour through a purpose-built glowworm cave at Cedar Creek Estate.

Tamborine Rainforest Skywalk: Get eye level with the canopy on this 1.5km trail through a privately owned patch of rainforest.

Witches Falls Circuit, Tamborine National Park: This 3.6km walk offers great views of Witches Falls, which flow after recent rain.

JAKUB MACULEWICZ/SHUTTERSTOCK

Lamington National Park

(witchesfalls.com.au) with wood-fired pizza and craft beers at the adjacent **Boxer Brewing Co** *(boxerbrewing.com.au)*. At the other end of town, stylish tasting room **Loborn** *(loborn.com)* showcases its own distilled spirits, including gin and Italian-style *amaro,* harnessing native botanicals. It's open Friday to Sunday. South of town, **Cauldron Distillery** *(cauldrondistillery.com.au)* crafts its own gin, whisky, vermouth and Mexican-style agave. Wood-fired pizza, food trucks and live music on Saturday and Sunday afternoons combine with vineyard views (closed Mondays).

Embark on a two-wheeled DIY adventure

Hire an e-bike from **Peddly Picnics** *(peddlypicnics.com.au; half-/full day $70/110)* to explore around Tamborine Mountain. Bubbly co-owner Jools and her friendly dogs are full of ideas about where to go. With Peddly Picnics' handy map. set out on well-maintained, top-of-the-line e-bikes to destinations including wineries, distilleries and Tamborine Mountain's famous hang-glider lookout. Riding is a mix of roads and shared pedestrian/bike paths. Picnic hampers can also be arranged.

Springbrook National Park

TIME FROM SURFERS PARADISE : **40MIN**

Spring into nature

Like neighbouring Lamington National Park, **Springbrook National Park** is a remnant of the huge Tweed Shield volcano that centred on nearby Wollumbin (Mt Warning) in NSW. Forming part of the Gondwana Rainforests of Australia World Heritage Area, it's a wonderland for hikers, with excellent trails through cool-temperate, subtropical and eucalypt forests, offering a mosaic of gorges, cliffs and waterfalls.

The park is divided into four sections. The 900m-high Springbrook Plateau is home to the tiny township of

Springbrook *(parks.qld.gov.au/parks/springbrook)*. Laced with waterfalls, trails and eye-catching lookouts, this section receives the most visitors. **Mt Cougal**, accessed via Currumbin Creek Rd, has several waterfalls and swimming holes (watch for submerged logs and slippery rocks). The **Natural Bridge** section has a 1km walking circuit leading to a scenic waterfall-cave formation, while **Numinbah Valley** to the north is the park's most heavily forested section.

Excellent viewpoints in the park include the appropriately named **Best of All Lookout** (Repeater Station Rd); **Canyon Lookout** (Canyon Pde), which is also the start of the 4km Twin Falls Circuit; and the superb lookout beside the 60m-high **Goomoolahra Falls** (Springbrook Rd). There are toilets and gas BBQs at **Settlement Campground**, but no showers.

The ultimate rainforest ramble

Linking Springbrook and Lamington National Parks is the 54km (three-day) **Gold Coast Hinterland Great Walk**. It is recommended that you walk west to east, commencing the walk from O'Reilly's in Lamington National Park and ending at Settlement Campground in Springbrook National Park. Most walkers spend their first night on the trail at Binna Burra Lodge (p320) and the second night at the basic **Woonoongoora Walkers' Camp**, which has no drinking water. Visit the website of the **Queensland National Parks & Wildlife Service** *(parks.qld.gov.au)* for more information and safety advice.

Lamington National Park

TIME FROM SURFERS PARADISE: **1HR**

Step into Gondwana

Dense rainforest cloaks the deep valleys and steep cliffs of the McPherson Range, reaching elevations of 1100m on the Lamington Plateau. Like Springbrook National Park, the 206-sq-km **Lamington National Park** is part of the vast Gondwana Rainforests of Australia World Heritage Area (GWHA). The park's forests were severely damaged by Australia's devastating 2019–20 bushfires – approximately 34% of the GWHA was impacted – but ongoing regrowth and the return of teeming wildlife is restoring the region's natural grandeur. The area is known as Woonoongoora to the local Yugambeh people, meaning 'quiet and timeless' and

TOP DAY WALKS IN LAMINGTON & SPRINGBROOK NATIONAL PARKS

Border Track: Trace the rim of an ancient volcano linking Binna Burra to O'Reilly's on this 21.4km (one way) epic.

Coomera Circuit: This 17.4km loop is the best trail for waterfalls in the Binna Burra section.

Warrie Falls Circuit: Gurgling creeks and gushing waterfalls are constant companions on this 14km loop on the Springbrook Plateau.

Purling Brook Falls Circuit: Expect lots of steps on this 4km-return trail to a superb waterfall viewpoint. It can be extended with the 2km Warringa Pool Track.

Toloona Creek Circuit: Chase great views and misty waterfalls on this 17.4km circuit in Green Mountains.

There's also luxury cottage accommodation available

EATING & DRINKING AT LAMINGTON NATIONAL PARK: OUR PICKS

Flying Bean Cafe: Coffee, snacks, burgers and breakfasts served in Beechmont's former headmaster's house. *6.30am-2pm Thu-Sun* $

Binna Burra Tea House: Crowd-pleasing breakfast and lunch options steps from the Binna Burra trailhead. Local wine, craft beer and excellent views. *8am-3pm* $$

O'Reilly's Canungra Valley Vineyards: Stop in for a tasting or a pre-booked picnic, with just maybe Queensland's biggest jacaranda tree. *10am-4pm*

Paddock Restaurant: Top off a hike with a fancy paddock-to-plate meal at Beechmont Estate on Binna Burra Rd. *noon-3.30pm & 5.30pm-late Wed-Sun* $$$

VIRGINIJA MEILUNE/SHUTTERSTOCK

Binna Burra Lodge

you could spend days exploring this impressive part of the hinterland on its 160km of walking trails. But it offers plenty of short walks, waterfalls, bird watching and picnic areas for day-trippers, too.

The two most accessible sections of the park are Binna Burra on the eastern side and Green Mountains (O'Reilly's) on the western side. **O'Reilly's Campground** (formerly Green Mountains Campground) is adjacent to the day-use visitor car park; book through **O'Reilly's Rainforest Retreat** *(oreillys.com.au),* where diverse attractions also open to day visitors include guided e-bike tours, a tree-top walk – the world's first when launched more than 30 years ago – and a highly regarded spa.

There's also camping and accommodation at **Binna Burra Lodge** *(binnaburralodge.com.au)* next to the Binna Burra section's main trailhead. At Binna Burra, an impressive new lodge opened in 2026, replacing the heritage lodge lost to fire in 2019, and a new visitor centre also acts as reception for diverse accommodation options including Sky Lodge apartments and cosy Tiny Wild Houses bunk rooms. Binna Burra's safari tents were damaged by Cyclone Alfred in March 2025, but are also scheduled to reopen. Check online for the latest.

As well as Binna Burra"s celebrated short walks and day walks – options for most visitors include the Rainforest Circuit (1.2km) and the Tullawallal Circuit (5km) through Antarctic beech forest – an outdoor adventure park opened in early 2026. Experiences at **Happitat** *(happitat.com.au)* incorporate spectacular zip lines and a *via ferrata* cliff-face adventure.

MORE RAINFOREST HIKING

Keen hikers can find another excellent collection of rainforest trails in **Main Range National Park** (p303) on the western fringe of the Scenic Rim region, a two-hour (170km) drive west of the Gold Coast.

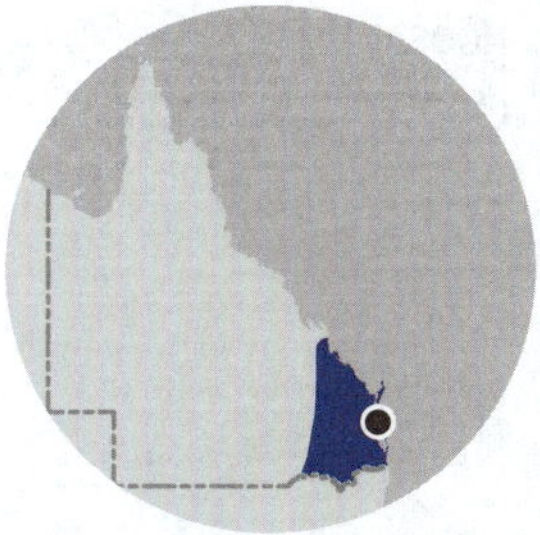

Noosa

BEACHES | CRAFT BEER | FAMILY-FRIENDLY FUN

Enjoying perennial inclusion on annual lists of 'Australia's Best Towns', Noosa crowns the northern end of the Sunshine Coast. Unlike Mooloolaba to the south – or, heaven forbid, the Gold Coast – there are no high-rise buildings. Instead, Noosa's lush, low-rise centre backs onto pristine subtropical rainforest and crystalline waters. Designer boutiques and destination restaurants may line Noosa Heads' Hastings St, but even from there it's just a short drive to the compact coastal wilderness that is Noosa National Park. Continue up the Noosa River and relaxed Noosaville is more unpretentious, making it the ideal base for day trips north to Lake Cootharaba, south to Sunshine Beach and Peregian, or into the Noosa Hinterland for the Eumundi Markets. Noosa is on the traditional lands of the Kabi Kabi (or Gubbi Gubbi) people, whose Country stretches from K'gari south to the Pumicestone Passage and west towards the Conondale and Blackall Ranges.

Noosaville (p322)

EGROY/SHUTTERSTOCK

GETTING AROUND

Both Noosa Heads and Noosaville are very walkable and around sunrise you'll see many locals enjoying a dawn-breaker walk or jog. Regular Translink buses (just 50c) link Noosa Heads to Noosaville and with parking at a premium around Main Beach and Hastings St, it's worth catching public transport if you're headed that way. E-bikes and mountain bikes are also popular to get around on and can be rented from Bike On (p323). The **Noosa Ferry & Cruise Co** *(noosaferry.com; adult/child from $9/4.50)* runs a hop-on, hop-off service linking Hastings St to Tewatin via Noosaville.

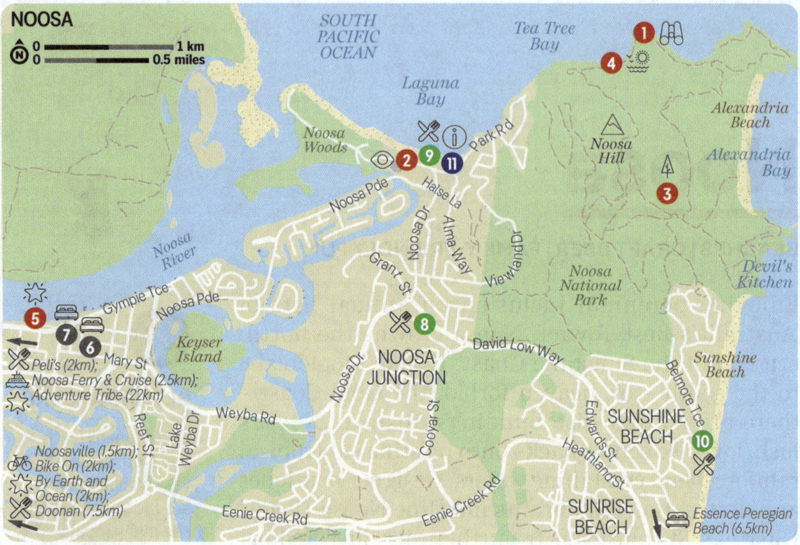

SIGHTS
1 Dolphin Point
2 Noosa Heads
3 Noosa National Park
4 Tea Tree Bay

ACTIVITIES
5 Flite School Noosa

SLEEPING
6 Bounce Noosa
7 Twin Quays

EATING
8 Coya
9 Noosa Heads SLSC
10 Sunshine Beach Surf Club

INFORMATION
11 Noosa Visitor Information Centre

Noosa Heads vs Noosaville

Very different vibes just 5km apart

Hastings St, the main drag of **Noosa Heads**, is a glam cavalcade of cafes and fashion boutiques, and the adjacent stretch of sand known as Main Beach is very popular. At the beach's eastern end, the **Noosa Heads SLSC** has stellar views from its upstairs bar and bistro – open to visitors – and downstairs are showers and changing rooms for freshening up after time on the beach. Noosa's helpful **visitor information centre** *(visitnoosa.com.au)* is also adjacent. For travellers with restricted mobility, the centre hires beach wheelchairs and other facilities include beach matting and accessible bathrooms.

Upstream along the Noosa River, **Noosaville** is a more relaxed and inclusive alternative to Hastings St's mini-Melbourne vibe. Accommodation is better value and there's a diverse strip of more affordable cafes and restaurants one block back from the river. Join the locals around 6am for riverside walks and the first coffee of the day, or ease into twilight when shimmering sunsets are often lighting up the river horizon to the west.

TOP TIP

Noosa is one of Australia's most popular festival destinations. Visit for June's **Noosa Food & Wine Festival** or for the Noosa Jazz Festival in late August/ early September. Some of the world's best surfers arrive to ride local breaks at the Noosa Festival of Surfing in March.

PABOUV/SHUTTERSTOCK

Noosa National Park

Hidden Coves & Fairy Pools

Lush trails, hidden pools and panoramic headlands

This protected headland of **Noosa National Park** is small enough to fully explore in a morning, but despite its diminutive size, its biodiversity includes eucalypt forest, colourful wallum heathland, rainforest and incredible ocean views. The entire 10.8km (one way) walk around its edges is worthwhile, but the best section is from the park's entrance to Hell's Gate (4.2km one way).

Bring your bathing suit for the first stop, **Tea Tree Bay**. Fringed with pandanus palms, this unpatrolled surf beach contrasts sharply with Noosa Heads' busy Main Beach. Once the spot to see koalas, they're now rarely sighted, but other wildlife often includes dolphins and whales. **Dolphin Point** offers the best coastal lookout. Travellers with limited mobility may want to turn around here as the track beyond includes steps and steep sections. Beyond Dolphin Point, there's another opportunity to cool down at the headland just beyond **Picnic Cove**. Below the park bench as the track turns right are 'fairy pools': you'll need to scramble down rocks to enjoy these natural swimming pools.

Reach the park by walking around 1km from town along the boardwalk running alongside Park Rd, or park directly at its entrance, where you'll find an info centre. Arrive early (around 6.30am) to secure a car park.

GETTING ACTIVE AROUND NOOSA

Epic Ocean Adventures: Kayak or paddleboard through mangroves and estuaries surprisingly close to Noosa Heads. There are also 4WD and dolphin kayak experiences.

Flite School Noosa: Tuition in riding a Fliteboard (a motorised foiling surfboard) or an easier-to-master Flitescooter.

Bike On: Mountain bike and e-bike hire to explore more than 100km of bike trails around Noosa.

By Earth and Ocean: Guided e-bike and mountain biking tours and stingray kayak experiences around Lake Weyba. Same location as Bike On.

Adventure Tribe: Based at Boreen Point, with abseiling and rock climbing, plus kayak tours (as Kanu Kayaks) in the Lake Cootharaba everglades.

EATING IN NOOSA: SUNSETS & SEAFOOD

Sunshine Beach Surf Club: The food is pretty standard surf-club fare; instead, head here for sundowners and epic ocean views. *11.30am-8pm* $$

Coya: Blending Japanese and Peruvian flavours, the highlights of Coya's Nikkei menu include kingfish ceviche and lobster tacos. *noon-2pm & 5-9pm* $$$

Peli's: Mediterranean cuisine served at Noosa marina. Italian, Greek and Balkan flavours all enhance and elevate local seafood. *noon-2.30pm & 5-8.45pm Thu-Mon* $$$

Relaxed location a 15-minute drive southwest of Noosa

Doonan: Wood-fired pizzas and fresh seafood in a sprawling indoor-outdoor venue; there's also an ice creamery and kids' playground. *11am-late* $$

Beyond Noosa

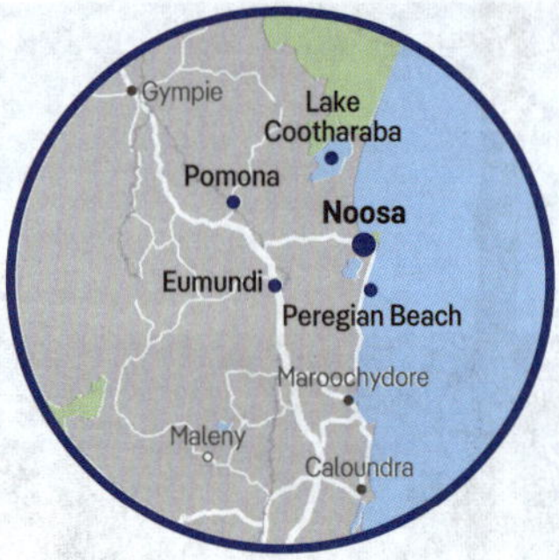

Beyond Noosa's low-key glamour, outdoor adventures await at Lake Cootharaba and there's good eating in the market town of Eumundi.

Places

GETTING AROUND

You can catch Translink bus services from Noosa to Eumundi and Peregian, but having your own vehicle is essential for exploring more remote areas of the Noosa Hinterland. You'll definitely need a car to attend a Sunday afternoon live music session at the Apollonian Hotel in Boreen Point. If you're joining an experience on Lake Cootharaba with Everglades Ecosafaris, the company offers free shuttle transfers from pickup points in Noosa Heads, Noosaville and Sunshine Beach.

The beaches around Noosa are rightly lauded, but sometimes it makes more sense to leave them behind and head off into the Noosa Hinterland. Craft beer and artisan gin are highlights in the hinterland hamlets of Cooran and Pomona respectively and Eumundi is worth a visit any day of the week, not just for the town's popular markets on Wednesday and Saturday. If your active routine while in Noosa is joining lululemon- and Under Armour-clad locals on a coastal walk in Noosa National Park, shake things up with an everglades kayaking adventure on Lake Cootharaba. Rock climbing and abseiling are also on offer and on Sundays there's live music nearby at Boreen Point.

Eumundi

TIME FROM NOOSA: **20MIN**

Meet the makers

With good cafes and restaurants, a great pub and an equally fine bookstore, Eumundi is charming any day of the week, but it really comes alive on Saturday and Wednesday mornings when hundreds throng to the hinterland town for the **Original Eumundi Markets** *(eumundimarkets.com.au)*.

Operating since 1979, the market features around 600 vendors selling artisanal crafts, artwork and jewellery under the shade of fig trees. Of course, reiki aficionados and the occasional Native American dreamcatcher do feature, but there's also fashion and homewares from emerging Sunshine Coast designers. The plentiful food stalls dish up everything from Argentinean empanadas to Vietnamese banh mi and Mexican birria tacos.

Of the two market days, Wednesday is slightly quieter, but still be prepared for crowds, with the markets (deservedly) attracting over a million visitors each year. On non-market days, visit the **Eumundi Brewery** *(eumundibrewery.com.au)* at the Imperial Hotel and browse the storied shelves of **Berkelouw Books** *(berkelouw.com.au)*.

From Noosa to Eumundi takes around 45 minutes by bus on Translink's 631 service.

HYSERB/SHUTTERSTOCK

Original Eumundi Markets

Peregian Beach

TIME FROM NOOSA: **15MIN**

Is this the new Noosa?

Of course, Noosa's own tourism star is in no danger of fading, but a short drive south on a coast-fringed road, **Peregian Beach** is being seen by some as the heir apparent to its more famous neighbour to the north. With barbecues, sheltered picnic areas and an undeniably gorgeous beach, it's very family-friendly, but there's also a very grown-up eating and drinking scene emerging. Visit for the **Peregian Beach Markets** on the first and third Sundays of the month, or jump on Translink bus service 620 from Noosa to see what all the fuss is about.

Pomona

TIME FROM NOOSA: **35MIN**

Gin and a famous footrace

Due west of the hype of Hastings St, the Noosa Hinterland is an elevated region of relaxed rural hamlets. Make a trip to Pomona and the **Pomona Distilling Co** *(pomonadistilling.com.au)*, open Wednesday to Sunday. Its gin harnesses native botanicals foraged from the distillery's own farm, while vodka

The prawn sando with Marie Rose sauce: a Sunshine Coast classic

EATING & DRINKING IN EUMUNDI & PEREGIAN BEACH: OUR PICKS

Outer Square: Beloved by Peregian locals with just maybe the Sunshine Coast's best all-day brunch menu. Mimosa cocktails, too. *5.30am-3pm* **$$**

Matso's Sunshine Coast Brewery: Based in Broome, but now also serving their zesty mango beer in Eumundi. Good burgers and pizza, too. *10am-late*

Popina: Paddock-to-plate culinary excellence with an Italian accent. Savour a curated wine list. Bookings recommended. *5.30-9pm Wed-Sat, noon-3pm Sun* **$$$**

Bask: Fine dining with intensely seasonal modern Australian menus served in an elegant dining room. *noon-3.30pm & 5-9pm Wed-Sat, noon-3.30pm Sun* **$$$**

WHY I LOVE EUMUNDI

Brett Atkinson, Lonely Planet writer

Sure it gets busy on Wednesdays and Saturdays, but the temporary arrival of market-goers to the Eumundi Markets would be a small price to pay for living in my favourite Noosa Hinterland town. With good cafes and restaurants, one of Australia's best bookshops and a choice of two craft breweries, it certainly ticks all my boxes. That's probably why I couldn't resist having a peek at real estate prices when I was last there. The bright(ish) lights of Noosa are a short drive away, while there's outdoor adventures aplenty, with kayaking on Lake Cootharaba and walking on forested hinterland trails. And when I need a day at the beach, it's almost an unbroken line of sand and surf highlights from Noosa south to Coolum.

RN STUDIO/ALAMY

and liqueurs are also produced. Housed in Pomona's original early-20th-century bakery, the distillery's Smokehouse restaurant turns out American-style barbecue. Gin-tasting paddles are also available.

Looming west of town is **Mt Cooroora**, a 439m-high volcanic plug that was traditionally the location of a famous running race. The event was cancelled in 2025, but lives on as the subject of 'King of the Mountain', a song by Aussie rockers Midnight Oil.

Lake Cootharaba

TIME FROM NOOSA: **35MIN**

Paddle into the wild

In 2022, the Sunshine Coast was awarded UNESCO Biosphere status, in no small part thanks to the unique network of waterways and wetlands found within its reaches. No place perhaps illustrates this better than **Lake Cootharaba**. Formed by the tidal Noosa River, it's Queensland's biggest natural saltwater lake.

The lake's shallow tannin-stained waters are favoured by paddlers, primarily because it's also the access point for the **Noosa Everglades**. Unlike its similarly named American cousin, there are no alligators or even crocodiles here, but if you're lucky, you may spot a koala. Instead, the serene river mirrors its surroundings perfectly, including lush forests of cabbage palms on its shores.

It's possible to canoe nearly the entire 60km length of the Everglades, with basic camp sites situated along the way.

Noosa Everglades

Contact **Kanu Kapers** *(kanukapersaustralia.com)* for guided and self-guided one-day and multiday kayaking experiences. Camping gear is also available for hire. Most popular is a 5km section from Fig Tree Point to Harry's Hut, a historic logging camp.

Feel the serenity

Based at **Habitat Noosa**, a fully accessible glamping village on the shores of Lake Cootharaba, **Everglades Ecosafaris** *(evergladesecosafaris.com.au)* runs two boat cruises on the lake. Morning **Explorer cruises** *(adult/child $165/119)* include an optional 5km canoe paddle, while afternoon **Serenity cruises** *(adult/child $94/79)* focus only on the cruise. Both are very relaxing options. Swimming in the river is encouraged at the end of the Explorer canoeing section, and experiences end at Habitat's **CootharaBAR**, a relaxed spot serving its own craft beer. Return shuttle transport from Noosa is available.

Boreen Point's perfect pub

Another spot for a cold beer is Boreen Point's **Apollonian Hotel** (*apollonianhotel.com.au*). Framed by palms, jacarandas and quandong trees, this atmospheric pub – complete with shady verandahs and a beautifully preserved interior – dates back to the late 19th century. Moved here from its original Gympie location in 1985, the Apollonian is famous for its Sunday smokehouse lunch accompanied by live blues and country music.

BANANA BENDERS

Driving north to Noosa along the Bruce Hwy, it's impossible to miss the garish glow of the **Banana Bender Pub** *(thebananabender pub.com)*. Its name isn't just a play on words – it's also a nod to the nickname for Queenslanders. According to the Australian National University's *Australian National Dictionary*, 'the term derives from the joking notion (as perceived from the southern states of Australia) that Queenslanders spend their time putting bends into bananas'. It's thought the phrase dates back to the 1937 royal visit to Australia. Asked his occupation by the queen, one man responded that bananas grew straight on trees and that he was responsible for adding their characteristic curve.

Sunshine Coast

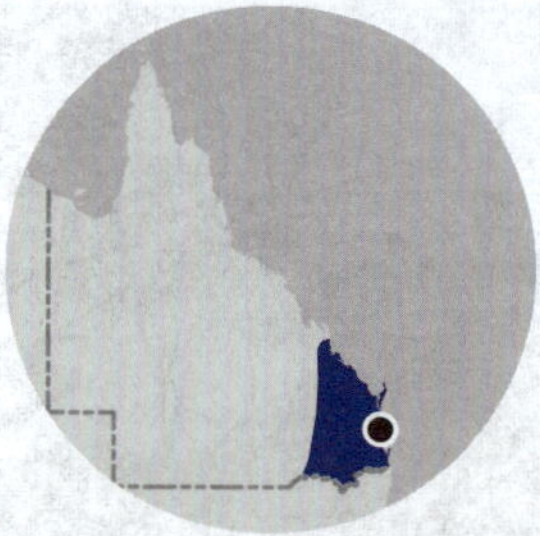

BEACHES | WATERFALLS | CRAFT BEER

Places

Bathed in sunshine 300 days of the year, the Sunshine Coast lives up to its name. With sandy beaches backed by lush hinterland and family-friendly attractions, it's easy to draw comparisons to the Gold Coast. However, unlike Surfers Paradise and the Goldie, the Sunny Coast has nary a nightclub to be found and a legitimate life goal for many is to spend the morning swimming, biking or surfing and then having a casual beer with your mates in the arvo (afternoon).

When you're tired of saltwater sticking to your skin, take a plunge in one of the Sunshine Coast Hinterland's many waterfalls. You'll find them high in the Blackall Range, a cool and lush area thick with rainforest that's long been a haven for artisans, alternative types and elusive platypuses. Mix and match a hinterland sojourn with time in Maleny, Montville or Mapleton – in close proximity, but all very different.

Caloundra

TIME FROM NOOSA: **1HR**

Rainy-day diversions

Renowned for its year-round sunshine, the Sunshine Coast is an outdoor lover's paradise. But when it rains – typically between November and February – it pours.

When the weather cries foul, head to the volunteer-run **Queensland Air Museum** *(qldair.museum; adult/child $25/12.50)* just outside Caloundra. Aviation enthusiasts will appreciate over 80 lovingly restored historic aircraft on display, making this one of Australia's largest and most diverse collections.

GETTING AROUND

Getting along the coast from Mooloolaba and Maroochydore up to Noosa is relatively easy on public transport, with Translink's 622 service also taking in Sunshine Coast International Airport. From Brisbane to the Sunshine Coast, Translink trains run to Nambour, from where bus services extend to other coastal and inland destinations. To explore further afield and especially to take in the Sunshine Coast Hinterland towns of Maleny, Montville and Mapleton, you'll definitely need your own set of wheels.

THE SUNSHINE COAST'S BEST MARKETS

Yandina Country Markets: Huge Saturday markets selling plants and antiques, with food trucks rounding out the scene.

Peregian Beach Markets: The bougiest of markets; everything from clothing to jewellery comes in a shade of sand. First and third Sundays of the month.

Witta Markets: Locals love this market, held every third Saturday of the month, for its fresh bread and produce.

Mooloolaba Sunset Markets: Every Thursday evening food hawkers take over the Esplanade, making for a cheap night out.

GATHAA First Nations Markets: Have a yarn with Indigenous makers at different Sunshine Coast locations each month. Check details on Facebook.

Afterwards, pop into the small but well-curated **Caloundra Regional Gallery** *(gallery.sunshinecoast.qld.gov.au)*. Open Tuesday to Sunday, it features regularly rotating exhibits and a shop selling goods by renowned local artists, including Kabi Kabi (Gubbi Gubbi) man Lyndon Davis.

For more local artwork, there's the **Butter Factory Arts Centre** *(cooroybutterfactory.com.au)*, open Tuesday to Sunday in Cooroy, 30 minutes west of Noosa. Check online if any pottery workshops are scheduled, typically held on weekends.

Big selection of craft beers from 10 Toes Brewing

EATING NEAR THE COAST: PIZZA & SEAFOOD

Goodslice: Down a quiet alley in Maroochydore, this pizzeria serves exemplary Neapolitan-style slices. *4-8.30pm Wed & Thu, noon-8.30pm Fri & Sat, 3-8pm Sun* **$$**

Psari Seafood Bar & Grill: Famous local prawns and other briny-fresh treats in Mooloolaba. Lots of Greek touches, too. *10.30am-10pm Tue-Sat* **$$$**

Riceboi: A Sunshine Coast institution, this hip restaurant specialises in Asian street-food including dumplings, baos and curries. *11.30am-9pm* **$$**

Local Flow Eatery: Mediterranean-inspired and flavour-packed shared plates and pizzas in Maroochydore. *11.30am-2pm & 5.30-8pm Tue-Sat* **$$**

MARTIN VALIGURSKY/SHUTTERSTOCK

Mt Ngungun

Glass House Mountains

TIME FROM NOOSA: **1HR**

Sunrise summits

There's no better place to watch sunrise than from atop one of the Sunshine Coast's iconic Glass House Mountains, like 278m **Mt Beerburrum** (3.5km return; 230m elevation gain). The last 750m of the track are paved, but make no mistake – with an exceptionally steep gradient, the only thing that makes this a walk in the park is that it's literally in a national park. Adventurous families may prefer 253m **Mt Ngungun** (2.8km return; 170m elevation gain), outside the Glass House Mountains township along Fullertons Rd.

Closer to Noosa is 208m **Mt Coolum** (1.6km return; 176m elevation gain). While not technically part of the Glass House Mountains, it's arguably the region's most popular hike, with 360-degree views at its summit. The blood-pumping climb may challenge your fear of heights, but it's safe for beginners. Food trucks at the trailhead (near the intersection of Tanah St and Jarnahill Dr) sell smoothies to those who have smashed out their rise-and-grind.

The wave-shaped 305m **Mt Ninderry** (2.8km return; 185m elevation gain) is largely a local's track – but one you don't want to miss. More sheltered with less exposed edges, it offers similar sweeping summit views. Arrive in the morning and you'll see kangaroos bouncing along the road to its car park, found at the end of Ninderry Rd outside Yandina.

All four hikes will take between 45 minutes and two hours to complete. For an accessible option, try the **Glass House Mountains Lookout**, 10 minutes outside the town of the same name. Information about ascending the natural features is available at the award-winning **Glass House Mountains Visitor & Interpretive Centre**.

TOP TIP

Many holidaymakers base themselves in holiday apartment rentals near the Sunshine Coast's beaches and then take day trips to destinations and attractions further inland. Look towards the elevated hinterland, however, and more interesting accommodation options include cottages, glamping and eco-resorts.

Mooloolaba

TIME FROM NOOSA: **45MIN**

Cruise the canals

With its recently redeveloped oceanfront esplanade and Gold Coast–lite phalanx of apartment buildings, Mooloolaba is the most developed section of the Sunshine Coast. Good accommodation and restaurants make it a convenient family base for day trips.

To see the multimillion-dollar homes lining the canal systems of the Mooloolah River, join a cruise with **Saltwater Eco Tours** *(saltwaterecotours.com.au)*. On board a century-old Huon pine ketch, guests enjoy bush-tucker canapes and lemon-myrtle cocktails while learning about the Kabi Kabi (Gubbi Gubbi) Indigenous heritage of the region.

The **Bushtucker Cruise** *($99)* departs at 11.30am from Tuesday to Sunday. Other Saltwater Eco options include two-hour **sunset cruises** *($85)* with live music and **guided canoe tours** *($120)* on Thursday and Sunday mornings. Jetty infrastructure and adapted canoes make the experience accessible for wheelchair users.

Currimundi Lake

TIME FROM NOOSA: **1HR**

Kayak and SUP on sheltered waters

Actually, 'lake' is a misnomer, as Currimundi is a sheltered and sandy-bottomed coastal lagoon with bathtub-warm waters year-round. This makes it an ideal spot for little ones to play and splash. With the lake's gentle tidal flow, older kids and adults may prefer exploring its beginner-friendly tributaries on a stand-up paddleboard (SUP) or kayak. Equipment can be rented from **KiteThrills** *(kitethrills.com)*. No pre-booking is necessary. The nearby surf beach is popular for kitesurfing and hydrofoiling. Contact KiteThrills for lessons (from $180).

Coolum

TIME FROM NOOSA: **30MIN**

Beach walks and laid-back Coolum

Heading north from Mooloolaba and neighbouring Maroochydore, the beaches at **Marcoola** and **Mudjimba** are both more exposed stretches of sand better suited to stronger swimmers. Both are great for a walk along the beach, however. Further north, **Coolum** stretches inland in suburban fashion, but its arcing **surf beach** is undeniably spectacular, and there's good accommodation and eating and drinking. It's also a more local and low-key scene compared to Noosa.

From the rocky outcrop at Coolum's northern end, the coastline is an unbroken 15km stretch of beaches via **Sunshine Beach** and **Peregian** all the way to Noosa National Park. From June to October, keep an eye out for humpback whales migrating to and from their traditional nurseries around Hervey Bay.

HISTORY OF THE GLASS HOUSE MOUNTAINS

The distinctive craggy peaks of the Glass House Mountains signal your arrival at the Sunshine Coast. Named by Lieutenant (later Captain) James Cook in 1770 because of their resemblance to glass kilns, they're not technically mountains but rather remnants of volcanic activity from 25 million years ago. It's up for debate which mountains belong to the group, but there are at least a dozen peaks scattered across the landscape – many of which you can summit. Two to avoid, however, are **Mt Beerwah** and **Mt Tibrogargan**: both are considered sites of spiritual significance to the Jinibara and Kabi Kabi (Gubbi Gubbi) peoples, who request that visitors don't climb them out of respect.

HELP ME PICK:

Craft Beer on the Sunshine Coast

With more than 20 breweries, craft beer is a big deal on the Sunshine Coast, but don't expect strong or assertively hopped beers. Queenslanders' focus on early rising and fitness on the beach means the emphasis is more on lower ABV, sessionable beers, ideal for enjoying in warmer weather and in taprooms with a strong community focus. From wood-fired pizza and shared plates or visiting food trucks, there's usually food available and weekends often showcase live music.

Where to Drink if You Like...

Well-Crafted Lagers & Saisons

Heads of Noosa Standout beers at their industrial-style taproom in Noosa include a lean and precise Japanese rice lager. The refreshing brew is also on tap at many Noosa restaurants.

Noosa Hinterland Brewing Co Equally refreshing is the summer-friendly kaffir lime saison at this heritage former joinery workshop in Cooran. Look forward to also enjoying regular guest beers from other Queensland breweries.

Hoppy IPAs (India Pale Ales)

Moffat Beach Brewing Company Packed with citrusy and piney American hops, Moffat Beach's Trilogy West Coast IPA is a good choice for travelling hopheads. It's just a short walk downhill to Moffat Beach's arcing cove.

Boiling Pot Brewing Co Boiling Pot's 22 Patels IPA was named after a Yorkshire cricket match where every player from both teams was named 'Patel' (yes, really) – its hop-forward flavours are best enjoyed on the brewery's shaded garden terrace.

Food-Truck Flavours

10 Toes Brewery Just north of Mooloolaba at Alexandra Headland, 10 Toes hosts local food trucks from Friday to Sunday, and live music starts at 3pm most Sunday afternoons. Ask for 10 Toes' refreshingly sour Culture Kick blueberry beer.

Terella Brewing Live music, food trucks and a family-friendly petting zoo all feature at this rural spot southwest of Noosa. With 14 different beers on tap, Terella is a great option for a tasting flight. Definitely include the Mango XPA (Extra Pale Ale) in the mix.

Good Eating

Brouhaha Brewery The region's best brewery food is served at Brouhaha's Maleny taproom. Team the prawn ceviche with the Hinterland pale ale.

Sunshine Brewery Near Maroochydore, the Sunshine Brewery serves great wood-fired pizza and often uses grassy New Zealand hops in their excellent beer. Co-owner Daryle Cook is a proud Kiwi.

Cool Merch

Land & Sea Brewery T-shirts, hoodies and caps all feature at Noosa's first craft brewery. Definitely linger in their cavernous taproom for a lush and creamy Juicebox IPA. Book online for brewery tours ($129) from Thursday to Saturday. Tours include lunch and generous tastings.

Your Mates Brewing The easy-drinking Larry pale ale is the Sunshine Coast in a schooner and equally laid-back is Your Mates' array of Oz-style merch including beanies, surf hats and stubby holders.

HOW TO

When to go Weekends offer the widest range of opening hours and on-site food options. Check breweries' socials for specific opening hours, special events and tap takeovers

Tours Contact **Sunshine Coast Craft Beer Tours** *(sunshinecoastcraftbeertours.com.au)* to visit the best of the region's breweries and taprooms. Tours focus on either the Sunshine Coast or around Noosa.

Map Download a detailed map of Sunshine Coast breweries, taprooms and distilleries from *visitsunshinecoast.com/craftbeercapital.* The map is often also available at local visitor information centres.

Sampling Try a variety of beers with a tasting flight of smaller glasses, a great way to learn about beer styles and different hop flavours.

DRINKING & NIGHTLIFE

1 10 Toes Brewery
2 Beachtree Distilling Co
3 Boiling Pot Brewing Co
4 Brouhaha Brewery
5 Buchi Fermentary
6 Heads of Noosa
7 Land & Sea Brewery
8 Moffat Beach Brewing Company
9 Noosa Heads Distillery
10 Noosa Hinterland Brewing Co
11 Sunshine Brewery
12 Sunshine Coast Cidery's Cider Hub
13 Terella Brewing
14 Your Mates Brewing

More than Beer

The Sunshine Coast's focus on fermentation extends well beyond beer. In cafes, wholefood shops and specialist grocery stores around the region, look for locally brewed (non-alcoholic) kombucha from **Ok Boocha** *(okboocha.com.au)* and Buchi. Buchi also offers a handy fill-your-own station at their **Buchi Fermentary** *(buchi.com.au)* in Eumundi. Stop in when visiting the Eumundi Markets on a Wednesday or Saturday morning.

Based in Kunda Park west of Mooloolaba, **Sunshine Coast Cidery's Cider Hub** cellar door is open for tours and guided tastings from 10am to 4pm on Fridays and Saturdays. Their Méthode Traditionnelle (champagne-style) cider won a Gold Medal and Best in Class at the 2024 Australian Cider Awards.

To discover the Sunshine Coast's growing focus on craft-distilled spirits, see the map at *visitsunshinecoast.com/craftbeercapital*. Based at Land & Sea Brewery, **Noosa Heads Distillery** crafts artisan gin, vodka and whisky, while the First Nations–owned **Beachtree Distilling Co** near Caloundra harnesses native botanicals for gin, whisky, vodka and liqueurs. In the relaxed Noosa Hinterland town of Pomona, forest botanicals also feature in the gin at the Pomona Distilling Co (p325). Pineapple gin is the fresh and fruity star at Sunshine & Sons (p334) near the Big Pineapple in Woombye. Plan your own spirited itinerary around the region or join a Noosa Hinterland Drinks Tour with Sunshine Coast Craft Beer Tours to also incorporate distillery and winery visits.

THE SUNSHINE COAST FOR KIDS

QCamel Dairy: Learn how camels are milked, before heading into the pasture for camel cuddles.

Aussie World: This amusement park is pint-sized, which means you won't have to worry about anyone getting lost.

Ginger Factory: Best for toddlers; the main drawcard is the short train ride around the Yandina factory's lush gardens.

Amaze World: A massive hedge maze, mini golf and more make for a solid half-day of play.

Cooroy Hinterland Adventure Playground: This accessible nature-based park features a splash area, sensory tunnels and swings for children with limited mobility.

Woombye

TIME FROM NOOSA: **45MIN**

An Aussie icon reinvented

First opened in 1971, Woombye's 16m-high **Big Pineapple** *(bigpineapple.com.au)* has been given a makeover to emerge shiny and new. Ascend to the top ($12) and view the interior's nostalgic **museum**, ride the train through the plantation ($12), or say 'G'day' to the native menagerie at the **zoo** *(whqzoo.com; adult/child $49/35)*, including Tasmanian devils, dingoes and koalas. Other nearby attractions include high-ropes courses and zip lines at **Treetop Challenge** *(treetopchallenge.com.au; adult/child $70/60)* and pineapple gin at the distillery of **Sunshine & Sons** *(sunshineandsons.com.au)*.

If you're visiting the Sunshine Coast from November to February, pineapples are plentiful and great value. Look out for roadside stalls.

Maleny

TIME FROM NOOSA: **1¼HR**

Gourmet grazing

High in the hinterland and surrounded by dairy pastures, Maleny is now a popular wedding destination, but was once a haven for hippies and counter-culture types. Today's population is more diverse, but evidence of its alternative edge lingers in its main-street collection of art galleries and op shops (thrift stores). The town has the hinterland's best collection of cafes and restaurants, with the **Maleny Food Co** *(malenyfoodco.com)* a great spot to pick up picnic supplies, local cheeses and award-winning gelato. Formerly a plant nursery, the narrow main-street alley of **Maleny La** *(facebook.com/MalenyLane)* has food stalls offering Thai, Korean, Brazilian and Greek cuisine. Hours vary, but most places open for brunch and lunch from Thursday to Monday.

Platypus encounters

With a **viewing platform** on Maleny's **Obi Obi Creek**, the hinterland's waterways are good places to see the elusive platypus. Follow the easy and accessible 1km path starting from the roundabout at Bunya and Coral Sts, or park at the Maleny District Sport and Recreation Club, just 100m from the platform.

Platypuses can be seen at any time of the day, but dawn and dusk is when they're most active. Stay very quiet and look for low and slow ripples across the water's surface. Local Neil

EATING BETWEEN BEERWAH & PALMWOODS: OUR PICKS

Just five minutes' drive from Australia Zoo

Eudlo General Store: This cute cafe in Eudlo has incredible pies and pastries. There are also pre-made meals and picnic fixings for on-the-road treats. *7am-4pm* $

Rick's Garage: Americana vibes at this sprawling Palmwoods family restaurant; expect diner favourites like burgers and shakes. *11am-9pm* $$

Warrior Restaurant & Bar: This restaurant in Crocodile Hunter Lodge, near Australia Zoo, has views of an enclosure with emus, koalas and kangaroos. *7am-9pm* $$$

Landsborough Pub: Plate-covering steaks and parmas with frosty beers at this locals' favourite. Established in 1888 and still going strong. *11.30am-2.30pm & 5.30-8pm* $$

TOP EXPERIENCE

Australia Zoo

Look for the huge billboard of Steve Irwin, continue along Steve Irwin Way in Beerwah and you'll reach Australia Zoo, the hugely popular legacy of the late conservationist/TV entertainer/zookeeper. Arrayed across 300 rather idyllic hectares of grasslands and small lakes, the Sunshine Coast's top attraction includes both exotic species – Sumatran tigers and giraffes – and Aussie-as critters like dingoes, quokkas, cassowaries and kangaroos.

Kangaroo, Australia Zoo

Make the Most of Your Day

Plan your day by checking out the website's schedule of conservation shows. To (hopefully) get a seat for the very popular Tigers LIVE! experience, arrive at Tiger Temple 30 minutes before it starts. Other popular shows include Elephants LIVE! and Koalas LIVE! Book ahead for behind-the-scenes encounters with diverse species including quokkas, wombats, Komodo dragons and lemurs. Additional costs apply.

It's Definitely a Family Business

He died in 2006, but through photos, signage and video, the legacy of Steve 'the Crocodile Hunter' Irwin is very evident as you explore the zoo. Wildlife photography by his son, Robert Irwin, is sold in the gift shop and there are interesting museum galleries displaying how Steve and his wife, Terri, expanded Australia Zoo and established the Crocodile Hunter brand globally.

CJUR/SHUTTERSTOCK

Kick Back at the Crocoseum

Held daily at 1.15pm in the Crocoseum, a 5000-seat outdoor auditorium, the Wildlife Warriors Show is the day's focus for many visitors. Highlights include raptors swooping across the auditorium, colourful parrots and macaws, and the climax of a massive crocodile entering the arena along a narrow canal and then rising up for a late lunch of raw meat.

TOP TIPS

- The zoo's grounds are surprisingly large. Be prepared for a good walk, or catch the zoo's shuttles.
- Visit on a weekday and get here before the zoo opens at 9am.
- After exiting, don't miss visiting the Australia Zoo Wildlife Hospital near the external car park.

Practicalities

- *australiazoo.com.au*
- adult/child $75/50, family from $225
- 9am-5pm

THE SUNSHINE COAST'S BEST FESTIVALS

Rangebow Festival: The Sunshine Coast Hinterland's very own Pride Festival, complete with drag and cabaret shows, in October.

The Curated Plate: The Sunshine Coast's official food festival is held over 10 days in July/August, with tastings, workshops and long table lunches.

Maleny Music Festival: Held over three days in November and celebrating Maleny's bohemian heritage with a diverse musical lineup. Also has market stalls and food trucks.

Woodford Folk Festival: Hippies and city dwellers alike flock to Woodford over the New Year's period for this multi-day music festival.

Big Pineapple Festival: In early November, Australia's biggest acts take to the stage in the shadow of Woombye's fruity icon.

ALEX CIMBAL/SHUTTERSTOCK

Maleny Botanic Gardens & Bird World

Andison, owner of **Platypus Whispers** *(platypuswhispers.com.au; adult/child $75/free)*, offers educational walking tours with commentary on their behaviour and ecology.

Birds of feather

Yellow-tailed black cockatoos often soar above the Blackall Range. To learn about these and other native birds, head to **Maleny Botanic Gardens & Bird World** *(malenybotanicgardens.com.au; adult/child $47/32)*. The centre's four walk-through aviaries provide respite for rescue birds, with frequent 50-minute guided tours offering visitors close encounters with both native species and exotic birds, including South American macaws. Allow around two hours to also wander through the adjacent botanic gardens. The immaculately-groomed 9 hectares are fully accessible on purpose-designed golf carts and, with a rose garden, waterfall and Glass House Mountains views, are a popular backdrop for wedding photos.

Montville

TIME FROM NOOSA: **50MIN**

With its fudge stores, crystal and candle shops, clockmakers and chocolatiers, the pretty mountain village of Montville is probably the Sunshine Coast's most touristy place. It's still a very pleasant place to while away an afternoon, so treat

Order the Not Your Average Parmy with buttermilk fried chicken

EATING & DRINKING IN MAPLETON, MONTVILLE & MALENY: OUR PICKS

Maleny Hotel: Established in 1908 with over a century of bistro meals and frosty brews. In summer, enjoy the spacious beer garden. *11.30am-midnight* $$

Fiorio & Co: Serving comforting French bistro classics, it's easy to overlook this popular Montville restaurant. *hours vary* $$

Long Apron: French-inspired restaurant at the Spicers Clovelly Estate. Live music on some Sundays. *7.30-9.30am & 5.30-8.30m daily & noon-2pm Fri-Sun* $$$

Mapleton Public House: Paddock-to-plate dining at this country pub; tied to a nearby organic farm. *11am-7pm Sun-Tue, to 8.30pm Wed & Thu, to 10pm Fri & Sat* $$

BLACKALL RANGE TOURIST DRIVE

Explore the highlights of the Sunshine Coast Hinterland on this driving adventure along the supremely scenic Blackall Range Tourist Drive.

START	END	LENGTH
Kenilworth	Mapleton Public House	80km; 6hr

Begin in the country town of ❶ **Kenilworth**, stocking up on doughnuts at the Kenilworth Bakery, or sampling cheese at Kenilworth Dairies. Drive south for 6km, and from the riverside car park at Mary River walk across the bridge to admire towering fig trees along the gentle 15-minute loop trail of the ❷ **Fig Tree Walk**.

Passing through the rural hamlet of Conondale, continue southeast for 35km for a coffee stop in ❸ **Maleny**. From Maleny, drive south along Mountain View Rd for exceptional views and photos of the Glass House Mountains at ❹ **McCarthy's Lookout**. Drive for another 9km to reach ❺ **Gardners Falls** (at the end of Obi La Sth), a fine place for a picnic and a swim. From Gardners Falls, drive back to the Maleny–Montville Rd and continue north for elevated and impressive views of Mt Coolum and the coastline beyond. Pretty ❻ **Montville** is a worth a quick stop for its cafes and gift shops before you continue to ❼ **Mapleton Falls National Park**. From the car park it's a short 50m return walk to the park's 120m-high waterfall.

Make the 4km drive back to Mapleton for a late lunch or dinner at ❽ **Mapleton Public House**, a historic pub serving paddock-to-plate food. Heading back to the coast, it's then around 40km via Nambour and Yandina to Coolum.

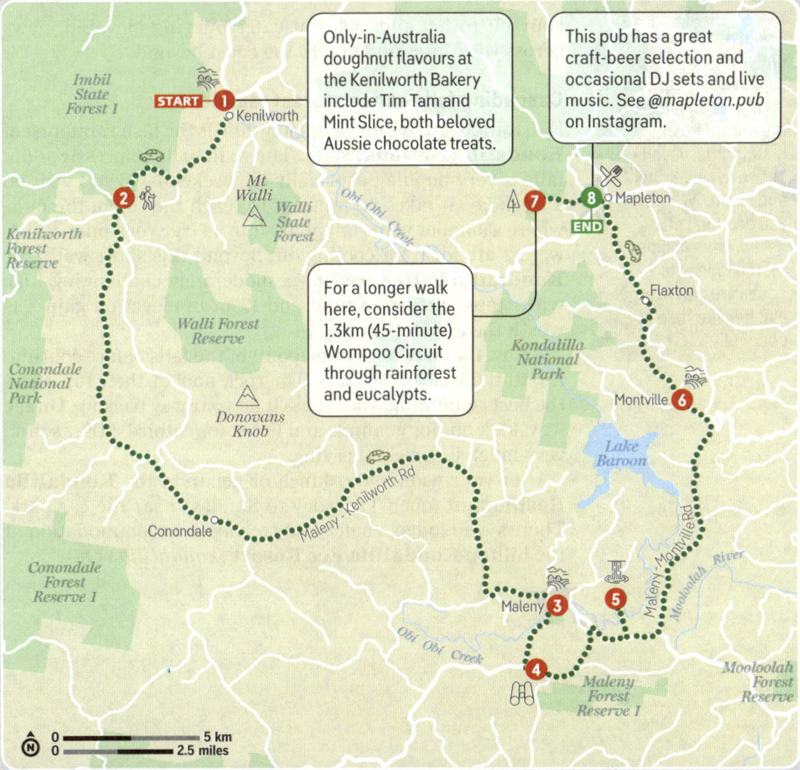

BUNYA PINES

The Blackall Range was a site of spiritual significance for Aboriginal peoples throughout southeast Queensland, as well as an important source of food, thanks to the abundance of bunya pines. With tall spiky canopies, they're one of the most distinctive features of the region.

To protect the food source, it was illegal to settle or clear land where bunya pines grew from 1842 to 1860, and every three years – when crops would peak – large gatherings would be held at **Lake Baroon**. Today you can taste the nuts at local restaurants, usually between December and March. Whatever you do, don't stand below a bunya pine for too long – its cones are much larger and heavier than a coconut.

FILEDIMAGE/SHUTTERSTOCK

Kondalilla Falls Circuit

yourself to tea and cakes at cafes offering elevated views across the hinterland and to the coast beyond.

Cascading falls and rainforest rambles

Five minutes' drive north of Montville is the lush rainforest of **Kondalilla National Park**. The walk to its impressive 90m falls is very popular, especially on weekends. Try to visit on a weekday. It takes 20 minutes to reach the top of the falls, where a smaller waterfall pours into a large rock pool. Chilly waters are ideal for cooling off. Beyond this short walk, the **Kondalilla Falls Circuit** – a moderately challenging hike with steps, uneven ground and 175m in elevation gain – is worth the extra effort.

Follow the circuit to a viewpoint of the falls before continuing to the base of the falls. The rock pool at their top offers the best swimming; you'll pass it on your way back up. On the way, look out for goannas and listen for catbirds: they sound very much like a child crying.

After your walk, enjoy lunch or gelato at the **Kondalilla Restaurant** (open Thursday to Sunday) near the car park. There's also lodge, chalet and treehouse accommodation at the hilltop **Kondalilla Eco Resort** *(kondalilla.com)*.

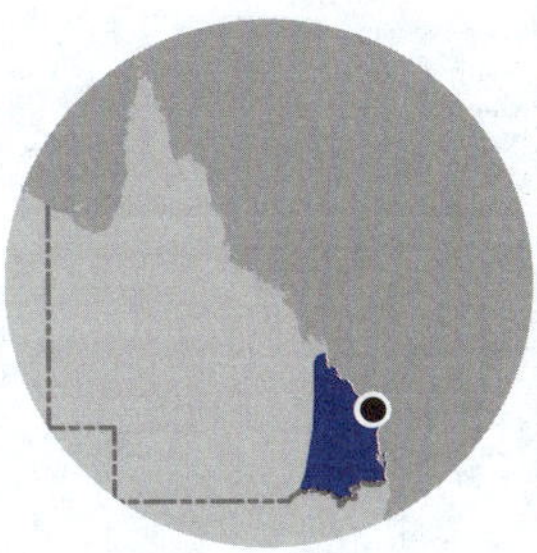

Hervey Bay

ISLAND EXPLORATION | WHALE WATCHING | 4WD ADVENTURE

Hervey Bay, located just under 300km north of Brisbane, is a laid-back coastal town with an alluring stretch of seaside suburbs – Pialba, Torquay, Scarness and Urangan – linked by the Esplanade along a calm waterfront. A great home base for some of Queensland's best nature-based experiences, it's renowned for whale-watching trips from July to October, when migrating humpback whales pass close by. This is also the main jumping-off point for K'gari, where backpackers with 4WD dreams rub shoulders with grey nomads crowding seafront camping grounds. Other activities range from fishing charters to sunset cruises and hiking.

K'gari shelters Hervey Bay from the ocean surf and the sea here is shallow and usually calm. A series of small piers are popular for fishing, but the big one is Urangan Pier – at almost 1km, it's one of the longest in Australia. The Butchulla people are the Traditional Custodians here.

Whale Watching & Cruises

Marine nature tours in season

Whale-watching tours operate out of Hervey Bay every day (weather permitting) during the annual migrations between late July and late October. Thousands of humpback whales pass through here each year, allowing operators to 'guarantee' sightings from August to mid-October (a subsequent trip is free if the whales don't show).

Boats cruise from **Whale Bay Marina** or the adjacent **Great Sandy Straits Marina** in Urangan out to Platypus Bay, then zip around from pod to pod to find the most active whales. Half-day tours are the most popular option, departing at 8am or 1pm and usually including refreshments. Tours start at around $160/70 per adult/child.

'Swimming with whales' experiences are also on offer. Operators adhere to strict whale welfare regulations, but conservationists say the activity may affect the whales' natural

GETTING AROUND

Qantas and Jetstar fly in to **Hervey Bay Airport**. Greyhound and Premier Motor Service operate regular bus services connecting Hervey Bay to east-coast towns. The most useful **Wide Bay Transit** local buses run along the Esplanade between Pialba and Urangan and out to Maryborough. Hervey Bay is fun to explore by bike, e-bike or motor scooter. Purple electric scooters (via the Beam app) can be found on the streets: they're useful for cruising the Esplanade. **Sealink** ferries to K'gari leave from River Heads; whale-watching and tour boats leave from Whale Bay Marina and Great Sandy Straits Marina in Urangan. The main 4WD-hire companies are near the airport.

SIGHTS
1 Dayman Park
2 Hervey Bay Botanic Gardens
3 Hervey Bay Historical Village & Museum
4 Hervey Bay Regional Art Gallery
5 Nala
6 Scarness Beach
7 Tooan Tooan Creek
8 Torquay Beach
9 Urangan Pier

ACTIVITIES
see 11 Blue Dolphin Marine Tours
10 Hervey Bay Dive Centre
see 11 Pacific Whale Foundation
see 11 Salty Safaris
see 13 Spirit of Hervey Bay
11 Tasman Venture
12 Torquay Reef
13 Whalesong Cruises

SLEEPING
14 Beachfront Tourist Park
15 Kondari Hotel
16 Pier One

EATING
17 Boat Harbour Fisheries
18 Hungry Pelican Cafe
19 Migaloo's Seafood Market
20 Odyssey
21 Urangan Fisheries

DRINKING & NIGHTLIFE
22 Aquavue

ENTERTAINMENT
23 Wetside Water Park

SHOPPING
24 Eastons' Anglers Den
25 Markets at the Pier

TRANSPORT
26 Great Sandy Straits Marina
27 Whale Bay Marina

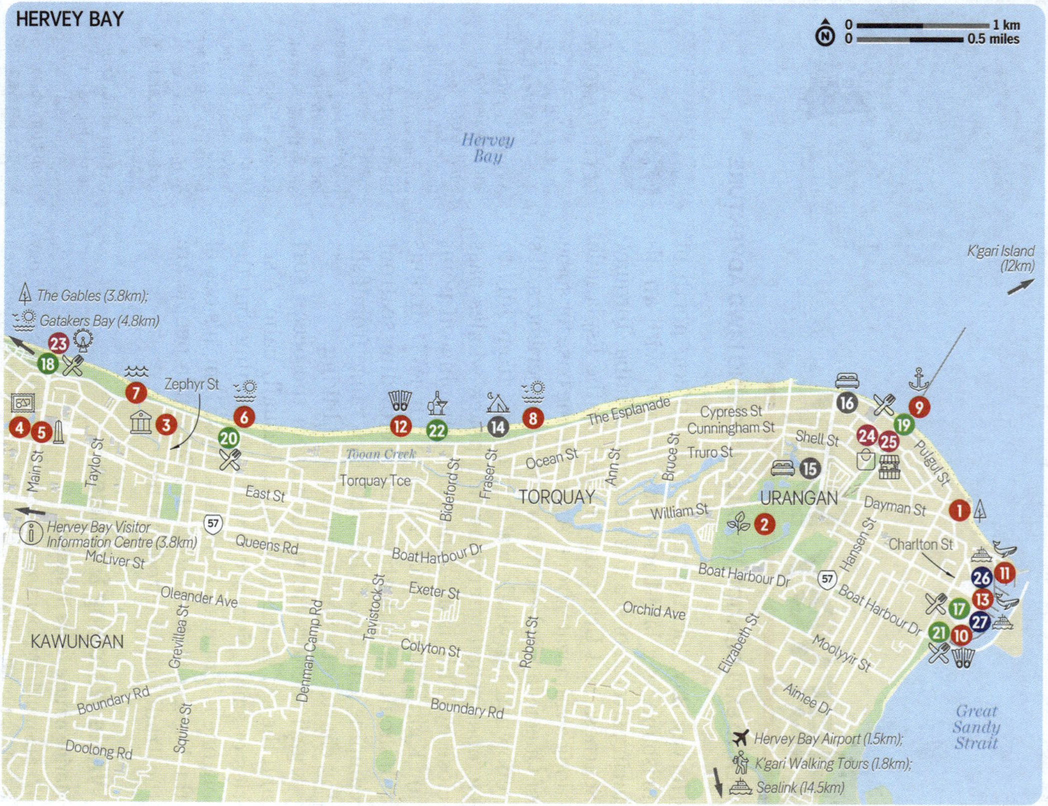

behaviours. If you're intent on getting in the water, book between July and early September – after this period, calf sightings are more common and it's prohibited to swim with calves in Queensland.

Outside the whale season, dolphin-spotting tours and sunset cruises are popular. Book tours online, at the marina or through your accommodation.

Take in Some Art & Culture

Hervey Bay's gallery and museum

The **Hervey Bay Regional Art Gallery** *(hrbg.com.au; free)* is the city's cultural flagship, with three refurbished galleries hosting changing exhibitions that feature local and visiting artists, in addition to a collection of contemporary Australian art. Open from 10am to 4pm Tuesday to Friday, to 2pm Saturday and Sunday.

The **Hervey Bay Historical Village & Museum** *(herveybaymuseum.com.au; adult/child $15/5),* open Friday to Sunday and on school holidays, comprises 21 heritage buildings and exhibits that tell the story of the early days of local settlement. There's a church, school, railway station and a blacksmith.

In Search of Seafood

Fresh from the boat

Hervey Bay is renowned for its fresh-from-the-boat seafood and fishing charters. Locals regularly fish from the numerous piers along the waterfront, particularly Urangan Pier. Fishing enthusiasts can rent gear from **Eastons' Anglers Den** *(eastonsanglersden.com.au),* 500m from the pier.

Fishing charters offer half- or full-day trips, departing from the Great Sandy Straits Marina (p339). **Hot Reels Pro Fish Charters** *(fishingcharterherveybay.com.au)* and **Hervey Bay Fly & Sportfishing** *(herveybaysportfishing.com.au)* are reputable local operators. Expect to pay around $500 per person for a full day trip; book in advance.

For fresh seafood, head to the Fisherman's Wharf area of Urangan, where you'll find wholesalers **Urangan Fisheries** *(uranganfisheries.com.au)* and **Boat Harbour Fisheries** selling direct from their retail shops.

TOP WHALE-WATCHING TOURS

Blue Dolphin Marine Tours: Small groups aboard an 11.6m sailing catamaran. Dolphin tours are offered outside the whale season.

Spirit of Hervey Bay: The four-level *Spirit* is Hervey's largest whale-watching vessel.

Tasman Venture: Three-level catamaran; also offers K'gari day trips to the remote west coast combined with whale-swimming experiences.

Pacific Whale Foundation: Three-hour small group tours aboard a research vessel, run by a conservation NGO. The most affordable option.

Whalesong Cruises: Midsize boat with wheelchair ramps and accessible toilets; also offers sunset cruises and K'gari BBQ tours.

Salty Safaris: Small group adventure tours combining whale watching, swimming and K'gari west coast beaches.

Hervey Bay Dive Centre: Dedicated tours for swimming with whales.

Get takeaway and eat it by the beach

EATING & DRINKING IN HERVEY BAY: OUR PICKS

Odyssey: Elegant bistro and bar serving modern Australian food with a focus on local, seasonal produce. *5pm-late Wed & Thu, noon-late Fri & Sat* $$$

Aquavue: Kick back with a beer and an ocean view. Live music on Sunday afternoons. *6am-3pm Mon-Thu, to 7pm Fri & Sat, to 6pm Sun* $$

Hungry Pelican Cafe: Lovely beachside cafe next to Westside water park in Pialba. Great coffee and even better food. *7am-1.30pm* $$

Migaloo's Seafood Market: Popular fish and chippery facing Urangan Pier, offering dine-in and takeaway. Good-value seafood packs. *11am-7.50pm Wed-Sun* $

KATE JANE/SHUTTERSTOCK

Urangan Pier

EXPLORE HERVEY BAY'S ESPLANADE & BEACHSIDE SUBURBS

Cruise along Hervey Bay's Esplanade and discover the region's sheltered coastline and beachside suburbs on this cycling tour.

START	END	LENGTH
Gatakers Bay	Dayman Park	17km; 3hr

Start at ❶ **Gatakers Bay** and follow the esplanade path around Point Vernon. On the way check out ❷ **The Gables**, a small park with beach access, and explore the rock pools at low tide or spot the resident ospreys.

Continue south to Pialba's ❸ **Wetside Water Park**, a free water playground for all ages. Take a quick detour down Main St to visit ❹ **Nala**, the life-size statue of a humpback whale breaching out of the ground, located in front of the Hervey Bay Regional Art Gallery.

Back on the esplanade head to ❺ **Scarness Beach** for a stroll on the short jetty. Continue to ❻ **Torquay Beach**, home to the surf-life-saving club, and go for a swim or wander around the shops and cafes.

Keep going along the waterfront until you see the sea wall, then turn down Elizabeth St for the ❼ **Hervey Bay Botanic Gardens**; it's worth a visit for the Orchid House.

Once again back on the esplanade, continue to the unmissable ❽ **Urangan Pier**, stretching almost 1km into the bay. The original pier, built in the early 1900s, was a base for exporting sugar, timber and coal abroad.

Finish the ride by taking in the views of K'gari and the Great Sandy Strait from ❾ **Dayman Park**.

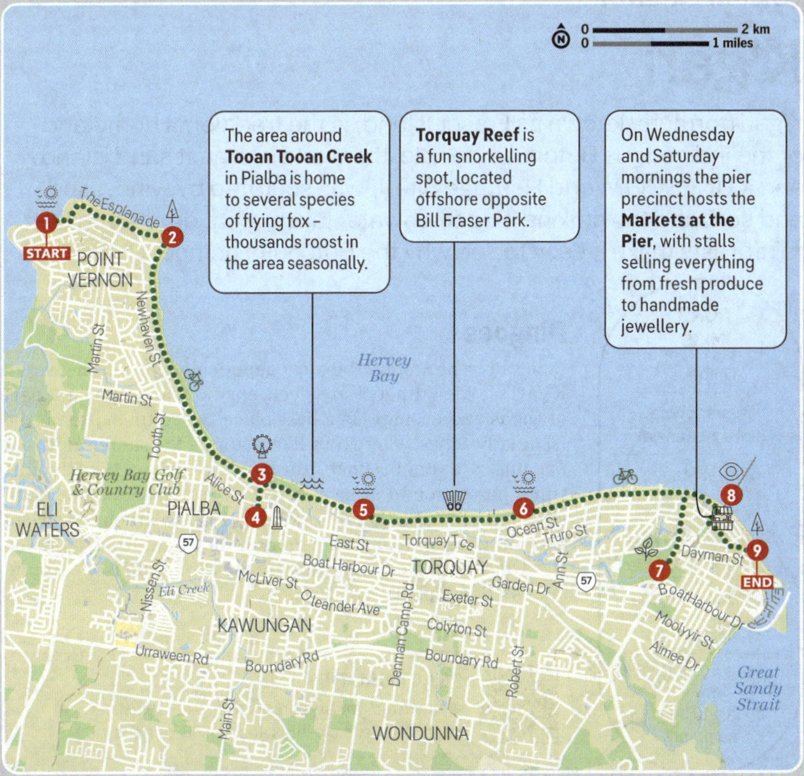

FOGAAS/SHUTTERSTOCK

Maheno wreck (p347)

TOP EXPERIENCE

K'gari

K'gari (formerly known as Fraser Island) is the traditional homeland of the Indigenous Butchulla people, the world's largest sand island and a UNESCO World Heritage Site. It was sculpted by wind, sand and surf, and the striking blue freshwater lakes, giant dunes and lush rainforests make it easy to see why the Butchulla named it 'paradise'.

DON'T MISS

- Dingoes
- Boorangoora (Lake McKenzie)
- Central Station walks
- Kingfisher Bay and Eurong
- Eli Creek
- *Maheno* wreck
- Lake Wabby
- Bush and beach camping

Dingoes

Believed to be among the most genetically pure in the world, K'gari's golden dingoes are sleek, spry and an important part of the island ecology. The best place to see them are on the islands' beaches, where they like roaming the shoreline; dawn and dusk are your best bets. Dingoes are curious; they'll sometimes hang around areas where there's a lot of people gathered and/or where there's the smell of food. Although you can spot dingoes on K'gari year-round, they tend to be more active when its cooler; sightings are very common from around June to September.

PRACTICALITIES

- *parks.qld.gov.au/parks/kgari-fraser* for island conditions, site closures and vehicle permits

K'GARI

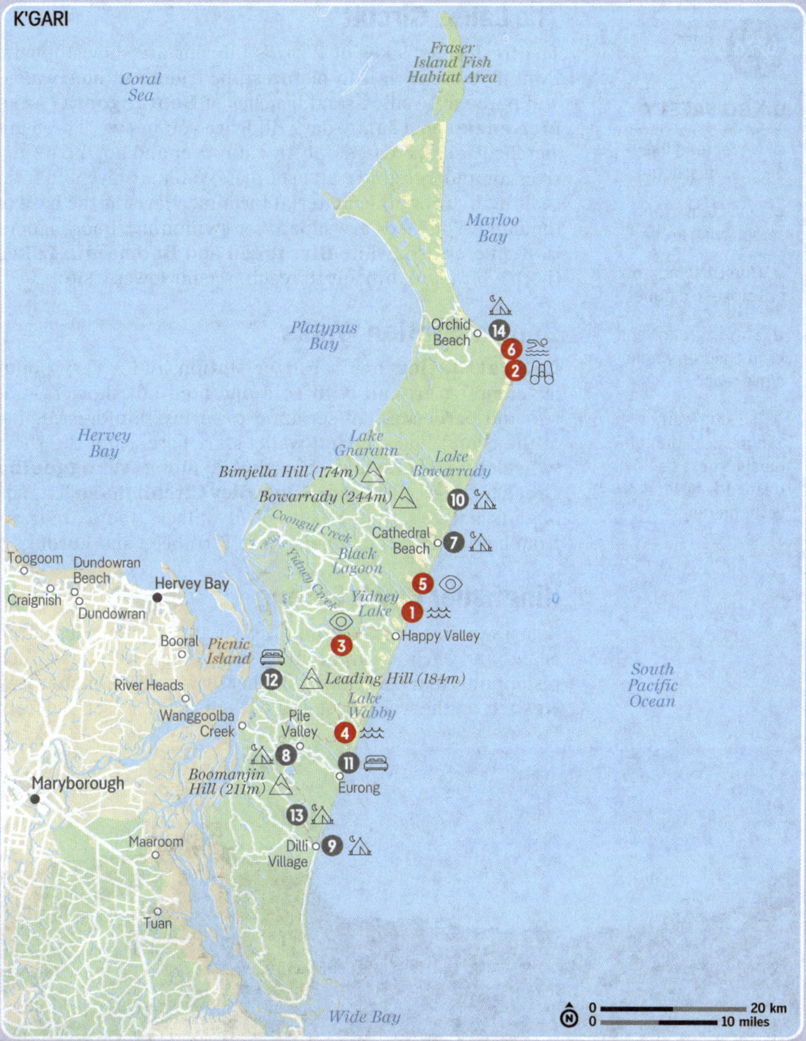

SIGHTS
1 Eli Creek
2 Indian Head
3 K'gari
4 Lake Wabby
5 Maheno Wreck

ACTIVITIES
6 Champagne Pools

SLEEPING
7 Cathedrals on Fraser
8 Central Station Camp Site
9 Dilli Village
10 Dundubara Camping Ground
11 K'gari Beach Resort
12 Kingfisher Bay Resort
13 Lake Boomanjin Camping Area
14 Waddy Point Camping Ground

DINGO SAFETY

- Never feed the dingoes; it's illegal.
- Don't leave food scraps lying around.
- Don't attempt to get close to dingoes.
- Stay in groups and keep children within arm's reach.
- If hiking, carry a 'dingo stick' (orange plastic sticks can be found at island settlements).

The Lakes Circuit

The freshwater lakes of K'gari's interior are showstoppers. Even if you've seen it in pictures, the iridescent blue waters and pure-white silica-sand beaches of **Boorangoora (Lake McKenzie)** on a sunny day will leave you in awe. These are 'perched' lakes, created only by rainwater and not fed by any rivers or underground water sources. Water is prevented from soaking in by organic material forming a layer at the base of the dune. The lakes are superb for swimming: Boorangoora is often crowded, while **Birrabeen** and **Boomanjin Lakes** (both a bit more difficult to reach) see far fewer visitors.

Central Station Walks

Central Station has a ranger station and a very popular camping ground with coin-operated hot showers, toilets and barbecues, all set amid towering rainforest. Some of the island's best inland walks start here, from the short (wheelchair-accessible) boardwalk along **Wanggoolba Creek** to the excellent 4km **Pile Valley Circuit** through stands of giant native satinay trees. For fit walkers, there are trails from here to Lake McKenzie, Lake Birrabeen and Eurong.

Kingfisher Bay & Eurong

K'gari's main resort communities sit at opposite sides of the island and each are mini villages with general stores, fuel, restaurants, tour operators and other services. **Kingfisher Bay Resort**, on the west coast and with direct ferry service from

PAULINE MONGARNY/SHUTTERSTOCK

The Pinnacles

River Heads, is a spectacular rainforest resort with a soaring main building housing several restaurants and bars, a store, fine-art gallery, 4WD hire, and comfortable rooms and villas in native gardens. Island tours leave from here. On the east coast, Eurong has the ageing but comfortable **K'Gari Beach Resort**, with the advantage of easy access to 75 Mile Beach. About 20km north of Eurong, **Happy Valley** is another small community with accommodation, a restaurant and store.

Lake Wabby

About 4km north of Eurong, a signposted walking trail off the beach (4.8km return) leads across sand blows to the beautiful **Lake Wabby**, the most accessible of K'gari's lakes from the beach. An easier route is driving to the **Lake Wabby Lookout** from the inland side off Cornwell's Break Rd. Lake Wabby is surrounded on three sides by eucalyptus forest, while the fourth side is a massive sand blow.

Maheno Wreck

The rusty hulk of the **Maheno wreck** is a fascinating sight, with its photogenic, oxidised ribs wedged firmly in the sand for almost a century. It was a decommissioned passenger liner that was blown ashore by a cyclone in 1935 while being towed to a Japanese scrap yard. A signboard tells the story. The 9km stretch of Maheno Beach runs from the Pinnacles to Eli Creek.

Eli Creek

Eli Creek is a popular stop for families and picnickers along 75 Mile Beach thanks to the crystal-clear stream that flows down from the interior and carves a path to the ocean (take care crossing the waterway by car). Walk the boardwalk upstream and swim or float back to the beach with the current.

The Pinnacles & Red Canyon

The Pinnacles and **Red Canyon**, both on the east coast of the island, are richly coloured sand dunes formed over thousands of years. Over time, weather and erosion have formed these dunes into interesting sculptures and shapes, hence the name 'pinnacles'. To find these geological formations, head along 75 Mile Beach north of Eli Creek and keep an eye out; they're easy to spot from the beach and are signposted.

K'GARI FERRIES

Two main vehicle ferry services operate daily to K'gari from River Heads, 10km south of Hervey Bay and from Inskip Point near Rainbow Beach. From River Heads, Sealink sails regularly to Wanggoolba Creek (30 minutes) and Kingfisher Bay (45 minutes). One way fares are $45/30 per adult/child and $123 for a 4WD vehicle. Check schedules and book ahead online. From Inskip Point, Mantaray barges operate daily (from 6am to 5pm) on demand to Hook Point (10 minutes); payment is per vehicle not per passenger. One way for a 4WD is $105 and walk-ins are welcome. Bring cash.

TOP TIPS

- Book ferry trips and camping permits online in advance (4WD-hire companies can do this for you).
- Be aware of tide times and plan to be off the beach well before high tide.
- Plan where you're going to camp and allow plenty of time to get there (don't drive at night).
- If camping, stock up on food and drinks to avoid higher island prices.
- Don't attempt to swim in the ocean; currents are deadly and the waters are inhabited by sharks and stingers.
- Mobile-phone coverage is poor on K'gari, except in townships such as Eurong and Kingfisher Bay.

Indian Head & Champagne Pools

At the far northern end of the eastern beach, **Indian Head** offers good sea views and occasional whale sightings, accessible via a short walking track. Between here and Waddy Point the trail branches inland to **Champagne Pools**, foaming rock pools that are the only spot on the island for safe saltwater swimming. This is as far as 4WD-hire companies and most tour operators will allow you to go and many tracks from here are closed for environmental protection.

Sand Driving

The majority of visitors to K'gari come with their own 4WD vehicle as much for the adventure of beach driving as for the island's natural attractions. If you don't have one, you can still join the fun by hiring a 4WD in Hervey Bay or Rainbow Beach (or on the island at Kingfisher Bay). It's not cheap, but with a group it can be affordable – count on $200 to $400 per day plus the barge fee – and the hire companies will give you a briefing, tide times, a map of where *not* to go and an introduction to handling the 4WD vehicle. Most companies also offer camping kits for an extra fee. You don't need to be experienced in 4WD or sand driving but people get bogged every year and it can be costly and time-consuming to be rescued, or (worse) there's the risk of being swamped by the tide. Accidents also occur on tight inland bends and single-lane tracks, usually due to excessive speed.

Stressbusting Tours

If you don't want the stress of driving on sand or you're short on time, a tour is the best way to see K'gari. There are essentially two types of tours.

The tag-along tours are where you get to share the driving with other participants on a guided convoy drive of the island, usually over two or three days with camping. These are popular with backpackers as they're affordable, usually all-inclusive, social, safe and good fun. Operators depart from Rainbow Beach and Hervey Bay.

Organised bus tours range from day tours, packing the island's hot spots into a single day, to multiday tours with overnight stops at island resorts, with Kingfisher Bay Resort (p346) being home to a visitor centre and the main departure point for many day-trip buses. Tours also depart from Hervey Bay or Rainbow Beach and include the ferry crossing.

No 4WD? No Problem

If you have no 4WD and you'd like to plan your own trip to K'gari without doing a multiday tour, it's possible. Take the Sealink passenger ferry from Hervey Bay to Kingfisher Bay Resort (p346). The easiest option from here is to purchase a **'day away' package** *(adult/child $99/69)*, which includes lunch and activities such as swimming, or stay a night or two and choose from the wide range of tours and activities the

K'GARI LOCAL KNOWLEDGE

Peter Meyer, a 30-year resident of K'gari, tour guide and fine-art photographer, shares tips on visiting the sand island. *petermeyerphotography.com*

Don't miss: Lake McKenzie and the Southern Lakes Circuit; Pile Valley Circuit Walk at Central Station; Lake Wabby – walk down from the lookout; and Kirrar Sandblow walk.

Best time to visit: April–May and October–November are ideal for the climate, with fewer visitors. Avoid Christmas, New Year's and Easter – it's too crowded! February is the worst for March flies.

Photography: The best light is just after sunrise and just before sunset. Camp as close as possible to your subject (such as the *Maheno* wreck) so you don't need to drive in the dark. It's OK to photograph dingoes from a distance; use a zoom lens.

ALEXANDRE.ROSA/SHUTTERSTOCK

Indian Head

resort offers, including island tours, guided walks and even whale-watching tours (in season).

Another option is to choose alternative accommodation. It's best to book any tours and activities in advance; pickups and drop-offs can be arranged through **Fraser Island Taxi Service** *(+61 429 379 188)*. Be aware that it will be difficult to get around the island from any accommodation without a tour or 4WD. The exception is if you're on K'gari to hike; there are a few day-hike options from Kingfisher Bay Resort, including the 8km return Beerillbee trail leading to impressive views of the Great Sandy Strait. Multiday hikes such as the K'gari Great Walk usually start at either Dilli Village or Happy Valley on the eastern side of the island. Be prepared – never hike alone and book camp sites in advance.

Island Camping

Camping is the best way to soak up the true essence of K'gari. You can camp above the high-tide mark in designated zones along the eastern beach except near freshwater sources (such as Eli Creek) and where signs prohibit it, but there are no facilities, so you must be self-sufficient. You need a camping permit to stay at any of the 45 National Parks camp sites. The most developed sites, with coin-operated hot showers, toilets and BBQs, are at **Waddy Point**, **Dundubara** and **Central Station**. Campers with vehicles can also use the smaller camping grounds with fewer facilities at **Lake Boomanjin**. There are private, dingo-fenced camping grounds at **Cathedrals on Fraser** and **Dilli Village**.

BEST K'GARI TOURS

K'gari Explorer Tours: Well-established 4WD bus tours for all group sizes and ages. Offers both one-day and multiday all-inclusive tours to all the main sights.

Pippies and **Dropbear Adventures:** Fun three-day, two-night tag-along and camping tours geared towards the backpacker set. Departing from Rainbow Beach.

K'gari Walking Tours: Fully supported pack-free, adventure and luxury hiking tours. Everything from short two-day hikes to the seven-day K'gari Great Walk, a 90km hike around the island.

Tasman Venture: Adventure tours by catamaran to K'gari's less-visited west coast. Includes activities such as kayaking, swimming and snorkelling, and whale watching in season.

Air Fraser Island: See incredible K'gari from above with a scenic flight and feel the thrill of landing on the beach. Leaves from Hervey Bay and K'gari; choose between 15-, 30- and 60-minute flights.

Beyond Hervey Bay

Places

While K'gari rightfully commands the majority of traveller interest in this region, there's plenty to entice visitors to linger on the mainland.

The Fraser Coast region is worth lingering in for its coastal beauty, beachfront national parks, seaside villages and sugar-cane fields surrounding old-fashioned country towns. Between Hervey Bay and the Sunshine Coast, the Cooloola Coast is a dramatic stretch of 4WD-able beach, national parks and remote camping, culminating in the backpacker-friendly surf enclave of Rainbow Beach. A little further lies the small coastal town of Tin Can Bay, a great wildlife and boating destination. Inland along the old Bruce Hwy, historic Gympie and Maryborough are well worth a stop for their heritage buildings, museums and Australian country charm. This is the traditional lands of the Butchulla, Kabi Kabi (Gubbi Gubbi) and Gureng Gureng peoples.

GETTING AROUND

Greyhound and Premier Motor Service both have regular coach services along the Bruce Hwy (A1), with stops at all the major towns including Gympie and Maryborough, and diversions to Rainbow Beach and Hervey Bay. The Cooloola Coast is best explored with your own vehicle, on foot or on a tour. Wide Bay Transit runs hourly buses between Hervey Bay and Maryborough. Both the *Spirit of Queensland* and Tilt Train stop at Gympie and Maryborough.

Tin Can Bay

TIME FROM HERVEY BAY: 1½HR

Dolphins of Tin Can Bay

Tin Can Bay is a sleepy fishing town and close-knit community where a pod of Australian humpback dolphins have been showing up outside **Barnacles Cafe** *(barnaclesdolphins.com.au)* at the **Norman Point Marina** most mornings for more than 50 years. From around 8am you can watch the wild dolphins over breakfast at the cafe; entry is $10 for viewing and $15 if you want to hand-feed the dolphins. Arrive early if you'd like to feed them; the cafe opens at 7am.

Feeding wild animals, including dolphins, is a controversial subject and is illegal in Australia. It can interfere with the dolphins' regular hunting habits and affect their health if the feed is not part of their regular diet. The feedings at Barnacles are regulated and overseen by Queensland's Department of Environment (and thus exempt). For more information on the impact of feeding dolphins, check out **Action for Dolphins** *(afd.org.au)*, an Australian marine conservation organisation.

JOHN O'FLAHERTY/SHUTTERSTOCK

Carlo Sand Blow

Rainbow Beach

TIME FROM HERVEY BAY: 1½HR

Coloured cliffs and sand dunes

Named for cliffs of colourful, mineral-rich sand, Rainbow Beach is an idyllic end-of-the-road town on Butchulla land at the base of the Inskip Peninsula. A dramatic beach-driving approach from the south is possible only by 4WD; it's more conventionally accessed by sealed roads from Gympie, 73km southwest. Rainbow is a great place to try your hand at various outdoor activities, from surfing and diving to paragliding and hiking.

A 600m track through forest at the southern end of Cooloola Dr leads to the **Carlo Sand Blow**, a spectacular 120m-tall dune with views across the scope of Wide Bay. You can walk out onto the dune for amazing views over the cliffs, beaches, ocean and islands; heed warning signs for the sake of your own safety and for the preservation of the dune. The Blow is at its most magical at sunset and sunrise.

EATING IN RAINBOW BEACH: OUR PICKS

Little Parliament: This main-street cafe is the place for coffee and a light breakfast or lunch. *6am-3pm* $

Rainbow Beach Hotel: The local pub serves reliable steaks and seafood, with good street views from the upstairs balcony. *10am-late* $$

Deck at Sea Salt: Prime location, a breezy deck and consistently good food; takeaway fish and chips, tapas and more. *7.30am-7.30pm Wed-Sun, to 3pm Mon & Tue* $$

Rainbow Beach Surf Lifesaving Club: The location of this unpretentious bar and bistro, overlooking the beach, can't be beaten. *10am-9pm* $$

MARY POPPINS

Maryborough is the birthplace of Pamela Lyndon (PL) Travers, creator of the umbrella-wielding Mary Poppins character, and though she only spent the first three years of her life here, the town understandably dines out on the connection – even the pedestrian traffic lights on the main street depict Mary: red has an umbrella folded, green is umbrella up!

The former bank building where Travers was born as Helen Lyndon Goff in 1899, on the corner of Kent and Richmond Sts, is now the **Story Bank** *(ourfrasercoast.com.au/The-Story-Bank; adult/child $15/5)*, an interactive museum dedicated to all things Mary Poppins (open 9.30am to 3.30pm Tuesday to Friday and until 2pm on weekends). The **Mary Poppins Festival** enlivens Maryborough in June/July, with storytelling, music and pop-up events around town.

WILLIAM IBBOTT/SHUTTERSTOCK

Great Sandy National Park

TIME FROM HERVEY BAY: **3HR**

Remote beach driving

Extending from Lake Cootharaba north to Rainbow Beach, the Great Sandy National Park section of the Cooloola Coast offers wide ocean beaches, soaring cliffs of richly coloured sands and one of Australia's most exhilarating beach drives – from Noosa North Shore to Double Island Point, around 50km to the north, then on to Rainbow Beach.

The route is only accessible to 4WDs with a vehicle permit (available from *parks.des.qld.gov.au*) and forms part of the **Great Beach Drive**, a coastal touring route linking Noosa and Hervey Bay via K'gari. **Great Beach Drive 4WD Tours** *(greatbeachdrive4wdtours.com; adult/child from $215/140)* offers day trips between Noosa and Rainbow Beach as well as private charters.

Gympie

TIME FROM HERVEY BAY: **1½HR**

Music Muster and museums

Gympie is best known for its annual country music festival, the **Gympie Music Muster** *(muster.com.au; tickets adult/child from $400/free)*, held in August. The ticket prices include the four-day festival and camping. For the rest of the year, the former gold-rush town, largely bypassed by the Bruce Hwy, has some fine heritage architecture, lush parkland and interesting historical sights. Spread over 15 historical buildings, the **Gympie Gold Mining & Historical Museum** *(gympiegoldmuseum.com.au; adult/child $15/10)* displays a diverse collection of mining equipment and steam engines,

Rainbow Beach (p351)

and activities such as gold panning. On the highway north of town, the **Woodworks Museum** *(woodworksmuseum.com.au; $10)* has memorabilia and equipment from the region's old logging days, including an impressive steam-driven sawmill. Train buffs will love the **Mary Valley Rattler** *(maryvalleyrattler.com.au; from $69)*, a three-hour historic rail journey aboard century-old steam trains.

Maryborough

TIME FROM HERVEY BAY: **30MIN**

Heritage celebrated

Founded in 1847 to take advantage of the broad Mary River, Maryborough is one of Queensland's oldest towns. Its role as a major 19th-century river port is visible in its heritage-listed buildings, Victorian parks and handsome Queenslander dwellings lining the streets. History is celebrated in a clutch of intriguing and photogenic local museums and sites in the **Portside Heritage Precinct** around Wharf St, located by the river. Don't miss a visit to the **Cistern Chapel**, working public toilets at the side of the town hall that have been painted inside with lively murals – volunteers known as 'flusher ushers' ensure the loos can be both admired and utilised.

RAINBOW BEACH ADVENTURES

Surf & Sand Safaris: Half-day 4WD tours along the beach to the coloured sands and lighthouse at Double Island Point.

Wolf Rock Dive Centre: Trips to Wolf Rock pinnacles off Double Island Point, to dive with grey nurse sharks and rays.

North Side Paragliding: Rainbow Beach is renowned for paragliding. This Noosa outfit offers tandem flights in a range of locations, including Rainbow Beach.

Epic Ocean Adventures: Surf lessons and tours to Double Island Point and dolphin-spotting kayak tours, departing from Noosa and Rainbow Beach.

Hiking: Rainbow's two best day hikes depart from the Carlo Sand Blow (p351). Trek to Double Island Point for stunning clifftop views (30km return) or head inland for a dip in the tea-coloured waters of Lake Poona (20km return).

EATING IN MARYBOROUGH: OUR PICKS

Tinana Hot Bread Shop: Country-style pies, sandwiches, sausages rolls, cakes and more. *5.30am-5pm Mon-Fri, 6am-2pm Sat* $

Alowishus Delicious: This cafe serves up classics like eggs Benedict and fish and chips in central Maryborough. *7am-4.30pm Mon-Fri, 8am-4pm Sat & Sun* $

Old Sydney Hotel: Classic Queensland pub with hearty meals and beers on tap. *11.30am-2pm & 5.30-9pm* $$

Portside Cafe: Sit outside for views of the Mary River or inside the historic building; for everything from Devonshire tea to lunches. *7.30am-9pm Wed-Sat, 7am-noon Sun* $$

Bundaberg

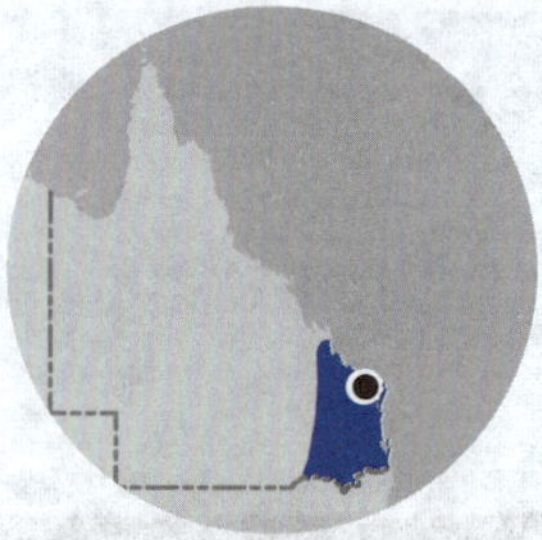

TURTLES | RUM | BEACH COMMUNITIES

TOP TIP

Book online well in advance for the nightly Turtle Encounters (November to March), especially during holiday periods. Bookings can made online at *parks.qld.gov.au/parks/mon-repos* and can also be made through the **Bundaberg Visitor Information Centre**, located next to the Botanic Gardens.

Bundaberg is a vibrant regional centre in the heart of rich agricultural and sugar-cane farmland, fed by the broad Burnett River and its tributaries. The region has an array of attractions – led by its iconic rum distillery and nesting turtles at Mon Repos – and an easy-going ambience with parks, gardens and a decent regional art gallery. Backpackers are drawn here in search of farmwork, so there's a good network of 'working' backpacker hostels in town. Although 'Bundy', as it's known for short, is not on the coast, the beach hamlets of Bargara, Burnett Heads and Elliot Heads are less than half an hour away by car, with their own accommodation and dining options. Boat tours to Lady Musgrave Island depart daily from the marina at Burnett Heads and flights to Lady Elliot leave from Bundaberg's airport. The Traditional Custodians are the Taribelang people; the name comes from Bunda (a kinship group) while 'berg' means 'town'.

The Bundaberg Bowl

Agriculture, farms and food

The Bundaberg region is one of Queensland's richest food bowls – its iconic 'red dirt' (rich volcanic soil) provides the perfect conditions for growing all kinds of fresh fruit and

GETTING AROUND

Greyhound and Premier Motor Service have regular bus services connecting Bundaberg with Brisbane (eight to nine hours), Hervey Bay (2½ hours) and Rockhampton (3½ to five hours). Translink has regular weekday bus services to Bargara (20 minutes) and other beach communities, leaving from Woongarra St. The Queensland Rail Tilt Train runs from Brisbane to Bundaberg (4½ hours). The *Spirit of Queensland* (5½ hours) also stops here between Brisbane and Cairns. Bundaberg's small airport has daily flights to/from Brisbane.

HIGHLIGHTS
1 Mon Repos Turtle Centre

SIGHTS
2 Bundaberg Botanic Gardens
3 Bundaberg Rum Distillery
4 Burnett Heads Lighthouse
5 Elliot Heads Main Beach
6 Kalki Moon
7 Kellys Beach
8 Macadamias Australia

ACTIVITIES
9 Barolin Rocks
see 18 Bundy Belle River Cruise
10 Lady Musgrave Experience
11 Monsoon Aquatics
12 Taribelang Bunda Cultural Tours

SLEEPING
13 AAOK Riverdale Caravan Park
14 Bundaberg Spanish Motor Inn
15 Turtle Sands

EATING
16 Alowishus Delicious
17 At James's Place
18 Grunskes by the River
19 Moon Japanese
20 Red Chilli Thai
21 Rick's at Bargara
22 Tinaberries
23 Water Street Kitchen

DRINKING & NIGHTLIFE
24 Ballistic Bargara
25 Bundaberg Barrel

INFORMATION
see 3 Bundaberg Visitor Information Centre

EATING IN BUNDABERG: OUR PICKS

Grunskes by the River: Grunkes is a fresh seafood market and restaurant that has become a local institution. *10am-3pm Wed-Sun, plus 5-8pm Fri & Sat* $$

Alowishus Delicious: This upbeat cafe in an arcade off Bourbong St is the place for coffee, with good breakfasts and lunches, too. *7am-4pm Mon-Fri, 8am-1pm Sat* $

At James's Place: Can't decide between a burger or bibimbap? This place does both well. *8.30am-1.30pm daily, plus 4.30-8.30pm Mon-Sat* $

Water Street Kitchen: Sophisticated dining that highlights regional produce. *11am-3pm & 5.30-9pm Wed & Thu, 9am-3pm & 5.30-10pm Fri & Sat* $$$

THE RUM STORY

Bundaberg's rum distillery was established in 1888 on the back of the sugar-cane industry. Molasses, the sweet, sticky by-product of sugar refining, is used in many foods, flavourings and even industry, but so much was produced that most of it was going to waste until a forward-thinking group of local citizens hit on the idea of distilling it to make rum. The distillery was built right next to the sugar mill (still in operation – the molasses is pumped directly from the factory to the distillery) and Bundaberg rum was born, using the local molasses, yeast and Bundaberg town water. It's this combination that goes into Bundaberg Original Rum, though today there are many variations.

vegetables as well as meat and dairy production. Stop at one of the many roadside stalls in and around Bundaberg for the best fresh produce.

Macadamias Australia *(macadamiasaustralia.com; tours from $45)* is a working macadamia farm south of Bundaberg open to tourists. It's free to walk around the main building and learn about macadamia farming; on guided tours you can walk through the orchards and have a go cracking your own nuts.

Pick your own strawberries at **Tinaberries** *(tinaberries.com.au)* from the end of August until October or go anytime for a taste of their mouth-watering fresh fruit ice cream. Open daily from 10am to 5pm.

Bundy Brews

Rum, gin and ginger beer

It's not the only brew in town, but Bundaberg is nationally famous for its rum. You can't miss the unmistakable polar bear mascot on billboards and at pubs, while the giant rum bottle stands proudly outside the **Bundaberg Rum Distillery** *(bundabergrum.com.au; guided tours adult/child $30/15)*. Do the self-guided tour through the museum and theatre or join an entertaining hour-long guided distillery tour.

Kalki Moon *(kalkimoon.com)*, open from 10am daily, is a boutique distillery producing gin, vodka, rum and liqueurs. Complimentary tours are held at noon daily, or you can call in for tastings.

For non-alcoholic drinks, **Bundaberg Barrel** *(bundabergbarrel.com; adult/child $20/7)* is the home of Bundy's famous ginger beer, which comes in a surprising range of other flavours. Take a self-guided tour of the small museum, taste the 14 varieties and take a six-pack home.

Loggerheads on the Beach

See the turtles of Mon Repos

The largest population of marine turtles, mostly loggerheads, on Australia's east coast arrives on **Mon Repos Beach** to lay eggs every summer, roughly between mid-October and January. All being well, the hatchlings struggle out of the sand and towards the sea eight weeks later (between January and March). The arriving turtles and nests are carefully monitored by rangers and an impressive ecotourism project has been established at the state-of-the-art **Mon Repos Turtle Centre** *(parks.qld.gov.au/parks/mon-repos/attractions/mon-repos-turtle-centre; free)*. Every evening from around 6.30pm in season, informative guided **Turtle Encounters** *($30)* take visitors to unobtrusively view turtles laying eggs or to watch hatchlings emerge and scurry down the beach. Book ahead online as numbers are limited. Sightings are highly likely but there's no schedule and you may have a long wait before being called out to the beach (turtles can only be observed once they've dug their nest and begun laying). The beach is closed from 6pm to 6am in turtle season, except for those on a tour.

PAUL HARDING 00/SHUTTERSTOCK

Bundaberg Rum Distillery

Coastal Bundaberg

Village by the sea

There are a number of enchanting beach communities east of Bundaberg, including Elliot Heads, Mon Repos and Burnett Heads (port for trips to Lady Musgrave), but the best known is Bargara, popular for its surf beach, cruisy esplanade and low-key atmosphere. Traditional home of the Taribelang people, Bargara was settled by South Pacific Islanders brought in to work on the canefields in the late 19th century. Today it's populated by retirees, long-time locals and holidaymakers.

The best way to orient yourself is by strolling or riding along the 12km paved walking track connecting most of the communities: it starts at the **Burnett Heads Lighthouse** in the north, passes through Mon Repos and Bargara, and then down to **Kellys Beach**, taking in stunning views over tropical beaches and shoreline coral reefs. Past Kellys Beach there's good diving and snorkelling at **Barolin Rocks**. Further down, **Elliot Heads Main Beach** is a windsurfing hot spot.

Coral Farming

Coral reef education

Monsoon Aquatics *(monsoonaquatics.com.au; per person around $30),* located in Burnett Heads, owns Australia's largest coral farm. It's worth booking (in advance) one of their one-hour educational tours to learn more about the reef and coral propagation. It's a great tour for the whole family.

Coral Cay Escape

Tiny island paradise

The Great Barrier Reef's southernmost coral cay, **Lady Elliot**, is renowned for its fringing coral reef, visiting manta rays and some of the southern reef's best snorkelling. Migrating whales can also be seen between June to October. Lady Elliot is too

BEST BUNDY TOURS & WALKS

Taribelang Bunda Cultural Tours: Half-day small group tours of Bundaberg and surrounds with a family-owned business. Learn from the land's Traditional Custodians and be immersed in the region's Indigenous culture and history.

Bundy Belle River Cruise: Hop aboard Bundaberg's repurposed historic river ferries for a sunset or lunch cruise along the Burnett River.

Bundaberg Story Walks: Self-guided walks in North Bundaberg and the city centre. Maps are available from the visitor centre or on the Bundaberg Council website *(bundaberg.qld.gov.au).*

Bundaberg Botanic Gardens: Stroll around the 27-hectare Botanic Gardens, which includes several beautiful lakes, Australian rainforest, a Japanese garden and much more. The gardens are also home to ticketed attractions including the Hinkler Hall of Aviation and Fairymead House.

WHAT IS A CORAL CAY?

Some of the Great Barrier Reef's most breathtaking islands are coral cays; tiny sand islands formed over time as coral and debris collect on top of the reef. Heron Island is a well-known cay that is estimated to be around 6000 years old. Cays are very low elevation islands, usually only a few metres above the high tide mark and can be fragile when subjected to weather extremes and changing ocean currents. They are important ecosystems; coral cays provide homes for nesting turtles and seabirds and are often surrounded by lagoons that support a huge variety of marine life. There are around 300 coral cays in the Great Barrier Reef.

RUGLIG/SHUTTERSTOCK

Green sea turtle, Lady Elliot Island (p357)

remote for regular boat visits, so day-trippers and guests of the **Lady Elliot Island Eco Resort** *(ladyelliot.com.au)* are flown in by light aircraft. Day trips can be booked through the resort; book in advance if you're travelling during school-holiday periods. The tours include a glass-bottom boat and snorkelling tour, snorkelling gear and wetsuit, buffet lunch and optional education tours. Prices start at $545/399 per adult/child. There's also a PADI dive shop on the island offering dive courses.

Boat Tour on the Reef

Snorkelling and marine life

Part of the Capricornia Cays National Park, this tiny cay sits on the western rim of a stunning, turquoise-blue reef lagoon known for its safe swimming, snorkelling and diving. A white-sand beach fringes a dense canopy of pisonia forest brimming with birdlife. Birds nest from October to April, while green turtles nest from November to February. Most people get here via a day trip on the **Lady Musgrave Experience** *(ladymusgraveexperience.com.au; adult/child $300/210)* from Bundaberg (taking two hours) or with **1770 Reef** *(1770reef.com.au; adult/child $280/195)* from the Town of 1770 (90 minutes). Lady Musgrave Experience also offers overnight stays aboard the *Lady Musgrave HQ*, a floating pontoon with above- and below-water accommodation.

EATING IN BARGARA: OUR PICKS

Rick's at Bargara: This beachside cafe and restaurant is popular with locals; live music Friday and Saturday nights. *6.30am-3pm Sun-Thu, 6.30am-10pm Fri & Sat* $$

Moon Japanese: Great sushi and mains at the main shopping centre in Bargara. *8.30am-8pm* $

Red Chilli Thai: All the Thai favourites including pad thai, red curry and *larb gai*. Choose your spiciness level. *5-8pm Thu-Sat* $$

Ballistic Bargara: A craft brewery and taproom with pizzas, sliders and other pub grub, plus a variety of brews. *11.30am-9pm Wed & Thu, 11.30am-10pm Fri & Sat* $$

Beyond Bundaberg

The Wide Bay region extends north and south of Bundaberg, encompassing small coastal communities and inland agricultural towns.

The low-key region around Bundaberg is an area that most travellers whiz through, but which deserves a longer look. The standout attraction on the coast is Agnes Water and the tiny historic Town of 1770. Backpackers gather here to try their hand at surfing or to take the day trip out to Lady Musgrave Island, while campers take advantage of the seafront caravan parks and camping areas, in addition to local national park hiking. Nearby are two remote national parks (Eurimbula and Deepwater), popular with 4WD off-road adventurers. Inland, Childers is a charming little town on the Bruce Hwy surrounded by farmland and a popular stop on the drive north from Brisbane.

Places

GETTING AROUND

The Bruce Hwy runs inland between Maryborough and Rockhampton. Greyhound buses operate daily and stop in Childers and also detour to Bundaberg and Agnes Water. The closest train station to Agnes Water is Miriam Vale on the Bruce Hwy, about 55km southwest. The Miriam Vale Train Station shuttle travels from Miriam Vale to Agnes Water. With your own vehicle, take Rosedale Rd north of Bundaberg for the backroad shortcut to Agnes Water.

Childers

TIME FROM BUNDABERG: **45MIN**

Heritage charm, poignant history and seasonal farm work

Surrounded by lush green fields and the rich red soil of an area traditionally owned by the Dunaburra of the Kabi Kabi (Gubbi Gubbi) people, Childers is a charming little community with grand old pubs and heritage buildings that line the Bruce Hwy through town. The most notable buildings include the early-20th-century Federal Hotel (p360) and the rebuilt Palace Hotel, which an arsonist burnt down in 2000. It's now home to a poignant memorial to the 15 backpackers who tragically perished in the blaze; look for it above the **visitor centre**.

Backpackers still flock to Childers for fruit-picking and farm work. Macadamia nuts, mangoes, lychees, strawberries, tomatoes and avocados are some of the produce planted, harvested and packaged in the area. The best way to get started in farm work and arrange accommodation is to contact one of the local backpacker hostels; try the **Childers Eco Lodge** or **Farmgate Backpackers**.

Agnes Water & the Town of 1770

TIME FROM BUNDABERG: 1½HR

Surf's up

Tucked away on gorgeous coastal lands owned traditionally by the Gureng Gureng people, Agnes Water is a former milling town turned holiday and surfing destination. Bordered by the Eurimbula and Deepwater National Parks, red-rock coves, paperbark wetlands and the rolling Pacific, Agnes Water has a sleepy commercial centre and some excellent backpacker hostels and camping grounds, as well as the east coast's most northerly surf beach.

Gnarly Tours Surf School *(gnarlysurftours.com.au)* and **Stylz Surf School** *(stylezsurfschool.com.au)* run surf lessons for all ages and abilities at Agnes Main Beach. Expect to pay around $30 for an hour or up to $80 for a half-day lesson. Beautiful Agnes Main Beach is also popular for swimmers and sunbathers, with a patrolled swimming area. Wake up early and head here for the best sunrise spot in town.

Just 8km up the road, at the end of a narrow promontory, the tiny Town of 1770 is the site of Cook's first landing in Queensland. The town is little more than a marina, a lovely pub and seafront camping, but it's also a launching point for kayaking, paddleboarding and fishing excursions around the inlets of the 'Discovery Coast' and the departure point for boat trips to the Great Barrier Reef, Lady Musgrave Island and **Eurimbula National Park**.

The calm water around 1770 lends itself to stand-up paddleboarding and it's a fun way to spend a morning or afternoon. **1770 SUP** *(1770sup.com.au; 1hr board hire $25, lessons per person from $35)* rents paddleboards and offers lessons; it's located right on the beach.

Walking trails and bush tucker

Discover great views and native bushland on one of the many walking trails around Agnes and 1770. For ocean views, the Bustard Bay Lookout is a great short walk from the car park at the tip of the peninsula and you can also hike along the beach between the two settlements. The 2.5km **Red Rock Walking Trail** starts near Springs Beach, traversing picturesque beaches and headlands along the way. Finally, about 3km south of Agnes Water, the 400m **Paperbark Forest Boardwalk** meanders through the coastal floodplain and native forest.

COOK'S LANDING

The Town of 1770's unusual name comes from its association with Lieutenant (later Captain) James Cook, who came ashore here in May 1770 during his exploration of Australia's east coast. It was only his second landing, after Botany Bay. His party named nearby Bustard Bay after they shot and ate a large bird here. From 1802 the area was known as Round Hill, but the name was officially changed to 'Seventeen Seventy' by the state government in 1936, though locals prefer the Town of 1770 or simply 1770. If you follow Captain Cook Dr up to Bustard Bay Lookout, you'll pass the Captain Cook Memorial, a stone cairn commemorating the landing site.

EATING IN CHILDERS: OUR PICKS

Paragon Theatre Espresso Bar: A charming cafe in the Paragon Theatre (c 1927), serving toasties, muffins and espresso. *7.30am-12.30pm* $

Insane Caffeine: This cosy, well-decorated cafe has a nice outside garden area, plus good coffee and breakfast items. *7am-3pm* $

Federal Hotel: Classic two-storey Federation-era hotel, the Feddy is a quintessential Australian pub with ice-cold draught beer and pub favourites. *10am-midnight* $$

Mollydookers Cafe: About 5km west of Childers in Apple Tree Creek, Mollydookers is a Canadian-themed cafe and bar. *11.30am-7pm Wed-Sat, 9am-1pm Sun* $$

JAKUB MACULEWICZ/SHUTTERSTOCK

Deepwater National Parks

Learn more about native flora and fauna and bush tucker on a Bushtracks walking tour with **Traveller's Rest 1770** *(travellersrest1770.com.au; tour adult/child $72/36)*, a camping ground located just outside Agnes Water and 1770. These two-hour tours include tastings and run from April to October.

National park adventures

Eurimbula and **Deepwater National Parks** are located north and south of Agnes Water respectively. They're a nature-lovers, wonderland and a haven for boating, fishing, camping and wildlife, with long pristine beaches, rock pools, mangrove estuaries and woodlands. You'll need a 4WD to access these national parks, though canoeing or kayaking is a great way to explore Eurimbula. From 1770 it's a 5km paddle to the beachside **Eurimbula Creek Campground** *(parks.qld.gov.au)*: make sure you book camping in advance on the website. **Moondoggie Beach & Bush Tours** *(moondoggietours.wordpress.com; tours from $165)* offers adventure 4WD tours of the parks; half- and full-day options are available.

MORE AGNES TOURS

Agnes and the Town of 1770 are both great places to join a tour, either on the water or land.

1770 Liquid Adventures: Guided kayak tours around Eurimbula National Park as well as kayak hire.

1770 LARC Tours: Explore Bustard Bay and Eurimbula National Park in a pink amphibious vehicle.

Agnes Water Air Services: Take a flying lesson over beautiful Agnes Water and 1770; no experience required.

1770 Sunset Cruises: End the day by cruising in a pontoon boat and watching the sunset with a drink in hand.

Salty Life Luxury Boat Hire: Hire your own luxury houseboat or fishing boat and tour the 1770 Inlet for a fun day on the water.

EATING IN AGNES WATER & THE TOWN OF 1770: OUR PICKS

Agnes Water Tavern: Aussie pub fare is served at this hilltop local, with live music on weekends. *10.30am-2pm & 5.30-8pm* $$

Round Hill Road Pizza: In Agnes Water, pizza is all they do and they do it well. Fresh ingredients and simple combinations. *4-8.30pm Tue-Sun* $$

1770 Rusty Pelican: Delicious fish and chips right next to the 1770 camping ground by the beach. *7am-3pm Sun-Tue, to 8pm Wed-Sat* $$

Barraca by the Sea: Mediterranean dishes in a lovely spot at the 1770 marina. *noon-2pm & 4-7pm Wed-Sun* $$

Rockhampton & Yeppoon

HISTORIC BUILDINGS | CULTURE | ISLAND GATEWAYS

TOP TIP

Drop into the **Explore Rockhampton Visitor Centre** at the town's southern entrance to pick up local information and see the Tropic of Capricorn spire.

Rockhampton ('Rocky' to locals) was a gold-rush town founded in 1858 along the broad Fitzroy River on land traditionally owned by the Darumbal people. Today it's the administrative and commercial hub of central Queensland, with many fine Victorian buildings and pubs reflecting the region's 19th-century mining and beef-rearing heyday. Although 40km inland from the coast, Rocky has an interesting array of museums, cultural centres and gardens in town, and natural features such as Mt Archer and the Capricorn Caves on the outskirts, as well as good dining and transport connections. For many, though, it's a stopover on the way to Yeppoon, a breezy coastal town 45km northeast of Rocky and gateway to the Keppel Islands. About 100km southeast of Rockhampton, the major port town of Gladstone is an industrial powerhouse with easy access to Curtis and Heron Islands on the Southern Great Barrier Reef.

Gardens & Lookouts

Botanic Gardens and mountain viewpoints

Rockhampton's heritage-listed **Botanic Gardens** offers an escape from the city heat, with shady tropical and subtropical rainforest, landscaped gardens and a small (free) zoo. **Kershaw Gardens** is another excellent park showcasing Australian native plants and an adventure playground. If you

GETTING AROUND

Virgin and Qantas fly from Rockhampton to Brisbane, Cairns, Townsville and Mackay. Rockhampton's airport is about 4km west of the town centre. Greyhound and Premier Motor Service have regular bus services through Rockhampton, connecting to Brisbane and Cairns. Queensland Rail trains between Brisbane and Cairns also stop here. Translink (Kinetic) runs a reasonably comprehensive city bus network from Monday to Saturday; these buses also run out to Yeppoon, Rosslyn Bay and Emu Park. Taxis are available from **Rocky Cabs** *(13 10 08)*.

HIGHLIGHTS
1 Great Keppel Island

SIGHTS
2 Botanic Gardens
3 Bulletin Building
4 Customs House
5 Dreamtime Cultural Centre
6 Emu Park Main Beach
7 Kemp Beach
8 Kershaw Gardens
9 Kinka Beach
10 Koorana Crocodile Farm
11 Lammermoor Beach
12 Mt Archer
13 Rockhampton Museum of Art
see 14 Yeppoon Lagoon
14 Yeppoon Main Beach

ACTIVITIES
15 Capricorn Caves

SLEEPING
16 Criterion Hotel-Motel
17 Denison Boutique Hotel
18 Heritage Hotel
19 Yeppoon Beach House

EATING
20 Beaches Restaurant
see 16 Criterion Hotel-Motel
21 Drapes Deli
22 Headrick's Lane
23 Riverston Tea Rooms

DRINKING & NIGHTLIFE
24 Big Rock Brewing
25 Great Western Hotel
26 The Alley

ENTERTAINMENT
27 Footlights Theatre Restaurant

INFORMATION
28 Capricorn Coast Visitor Information Centre
29 Explore Rockhampton Visitor Centre

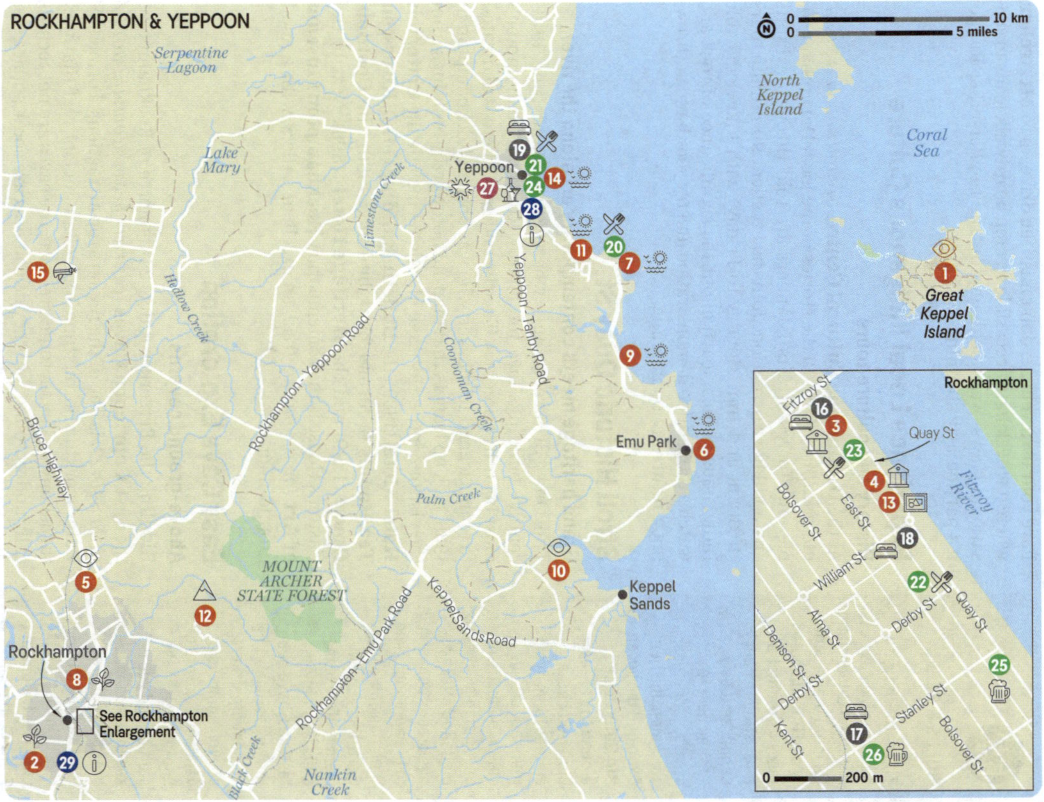

BULLS & BEEF

The cattle industry has been big business in central Queensland for more than a century and Rockhampton takes its reputation as Australia's beef capital seriously.

Come here for steaks, saddleries, stockmen, the Beef Expo and the seven **Big Bulls** dotted around town. The life-sized cattle statues loom over roundabouts and startle pedestrians on footpaths – they're modelled after various breeds common to the area, including Brahman and Santa Gertrudis. A prominent feature of the bulls' anatomy, the testicles, have been the target of theft by student pranksters, souvenir hunters and vandals in the past. Look closely at the statues and you'll see that the testicles are now anchored to the ground with steel rods! The best bull for photos is the one at Frank Forde Park.

have your own vehicle, don't miss the drive up to **Mt Archer**, where a wheelchair-accessible treetop boardwalk leads to sensational views over Rockhampton and the Berserker Range; it's particularly stunning at sunset.

Experience Local Indigenous Culture

History and culture tours

At the **Dreamtime Cultural Centre** *(dreamtimecentre.com.au; adult/child $16/8)* the stories of the local Darumbal people and Torres Straits Islanders are told through exhibits and a village re-creation. Join the excellent 90-minute tours (10.30am and 1pm Monday to Friday) with knowledgeable Indigenous guides: learn about the significance of rock art, watch a didgeridoo demonstration and try your hand at throwing a returning boomerang.

Stroll Historic Quay St

Grand heritage meets contemporary art along the river

The Quay St streetscape, where grand sandstone 19th-century buildings face the Fitzroy River, is Rockhampton's most beautiful precinct. The riverside park here is dedicated to tennis legend Rod Laver, who was born in Rockhampton in 1938. Pick up leaflets that map out noteworthy buildings from the visitor centre. Heritage highlights include the **Criterion Hotel-Motel** (1889), the **Bulletin Building** (1926), **Riverston Tea Rooms** (a former bank building; 1880), the **Customs House** (1899) and the **Heritage Hotel** (1898). Next to the Customs House is the contemporary **Rockhampton Museum of Art** *(moa.com.au; free)*, an excellent gallery with a good ground-floor cafe.

Easy Cave Exploration

Above-ground caverns

Riddling the Berserker Range 24km north of Rockhampton, the vast **Capricorn Caves** *(capricorncaves.com.au; adult/child $40/22)* is one of the region's top attractions. Formed by water working on the limestone of an ancient reef that was thrust upward by tectonic pressure, the caves are not technically underground, but they do contain cave coral, stalactites, dangling fig-tree roots and insectivorous bats. One-hour tours showcase their remarkable acoustics with a classical-music recording in Cathedral Cave.

EATING & DRINKING IN ROCKHAMPTON: OUR PUB PICKS

Great Western Hotel: This iconic heritage pub hosts events such as concerts, rodeos and line dancing; Thursday nights are all-you-can-eat. *11am-late Wed-Sun* $$

Criterion Hotel-Motel: Homestyle pub grub in a lovely 19th-century building by the Fitzroy River. *11am-9pm daily, plus 7-10am Tue-Sun* $$

Big Rock Brewing: A new family-owned brewery in a beautiful industrial heritage building, serving great craft beers. *4-9pm Wed, noon-10pm Thu-Sat, noon-8pm Sun* $$

Headrick's Lane: All industrial decor, this high-ceilinged restaurant and microbrewery is the most urbane place to eat in town. Dress sharp. *5pm-late Tue-Sun* $$$

TOP EXPERIENCE

Great Keppel Island

Known as Wop-pa to its Woppaburra Traditional Custodians, Great Keppel Island is the largest of the group of 18 islands that bears its name and the easiest to reach. Small enough to explore on foot, big enough that you can easily find a secluded bit of beach and beautiful enough that you might never want to leave, Great Keppel makes a perfect day trip.

TOP TIPS

- Book ferries and activities in advance if you're travelling during Queensland school holidays.
- The best time to visit is from July to September.
- Mt Wyndham and the Lighthouse have the best views (accessible on foot).

Picture-Perfect Beaches

Great Keppel is home to 17 white sand beaches. The most easily accessible and popular are Fisherman's Beach, where the ferries disembark, and Putney Beach – a 10-minute walk from Fisherman's. Both have calm swimming areas and access to amenities. Butterfish Bay, Shelving Beach and Monkey Beach offer great snorkelling. Head to Second Beach or Wreck Beach for a secluded patch of paradise. Taxi boats offer one way or return beach drop-offs (around $100 return).

Get on the Water

One of the best ways to experience Great Keppel is on the water. Hire a kayak or paddleboard at one of the water sports huts at Fisherman's Beach and explore the bays (around $25 for one hour). Day tours (from $180) are another fun way to explore the island and usually include activities like snorkelling and swimming plus lunch.

Hiking

Pick up a hiking map from Capricorn Coast Visitor Information Centre (p366) in Yeppoon or Great Keppel Island Hideaway (p371) and spend a day discovering the island on foot. The two-hour-return trail to Long Beach via Monkey Beach is spectacular; pack a picnic and snorkelling gear. Avid hikers will love the strenuous full-day walk to remote Wreck Beach.

Practicalities

- return ferry transfers Rosslyn Bay–Great Keppel
- *freedomfastcats.com* adult/child $60/38
- *greatkeppelisland hideaway.com.au* adult/child $55/30

BEST BEACHES AROUND YEPPOON

Yeppoon Main Beach: Families will love this stretch of beach with a wonderful water playground (The Keppel Kraken), BBQs, sheltered areas and everyone's favourite – the Yeppoon Lagoon.

Emu Park Main Beach: Check out the quirky streetart on the toilet block by the surf life-saving club, go for a swim and check out the famous singing ship nearby.

Lammermoor Beach: Take in sweeping views of Lammermoor Beach from the Wreck Lookout on Matthew Flinders Dr.

Kinka Beach: Keppel Island views and calm waters – kayak from here to Causeway Lake for a bit of fun on the water.

Kemp Beach: A nice beach and a good place to relax after hiking up to Bluff Point.

Swim & Shop in Yeppoon

Beach base and island gateway

Yeppoon is a breezy, laid-back town with good sleeping, dining and shopping options and a long, beautiful beach. On the first Sunday of the month stop by the **Figtree Creek Markets**, a craft-and-produce bazaar held in the grounds outside the **Capricorn Coast Visitor Information Centre**.

The focus of Yeppoon's foreshore, **Yeppoon Lagoon** is a free 'resort-style' swimming lagoon with vistas of the ocean and Keppel Bay Islands, life-savers, BBQs, a cafe and shady lawns.

Bluff Point, 20 minutes' drive south of Yeppoon, is home to a pleasant 2.3km circuit walk around the headland with remarkable views over the coast and islands. Do the circuit before or after a day trip to Great Keppel Island; it's close to the marina.

Meet the Local Crocs

Modern-day dinosaurs

Koorana Crocodile Farm *(koorana.com.au; tours adult/child from $42/22)* is a commercially operated farm 25 minutes' drive south of Yeppoon. It's home to some 3000 saltwater and freshwater crocodiles, the region's apex predators. Excellent educational tours run at 10.30am and 1pm daily – book in advance, especially during school holidays; see crocodile hatching from around March to May. Before or after your tour, you can also try crocodile-meat dishes such as steak and kebabs at their on-site restaurant.

Crocodile farming is a controversial practice; Koorana is an approved farm under the Australian government's strategic conservation program. For more information on crocodile farming and conservation, search for 'crocodile farming' on the Queensland government website *(qld.gov.au)*.

The focaccia here is baked fresh daily

EATING IN YEPPOON: OUR PICKS

Beaches Restaurant: Locally sourced farm-to-table dining in Rosslyn Bay. *7am-late* **$$$**

The Alley: Cafe, restaurant and bar with great coffee and modern Australian food. *6.30am-10.30pm Fri & Sat, to 8pm Sun, to 2pm Mon-Thu, plus 5-8pm Wed & Thu* **$$**

Footlights Theatre Restaurant: A show-stopping three-course meal and two-hour comedy-variety show; book ahead. *hours vary* **$$$**

Drapes Deli: Delightful cafe in downtown Yeppoon. Don't miss the delicious range of focaccia sandwiches. *6.30am-2pm Wed-Sun* **$**

Beyond Rockhampton & Yeppoon

Dreamy coral atolls, extraordinary marine life without the crowds and authentic regional communities.

Places

Gladstone p367
Southern Great Barrier Reef p368

The islands are the main attraction, but Gladstone's quiet seaside communities and natural environment are well worth a look too. Located 100km south of Rockhampton and known as the 'engine room' of Queensland, Gladstone is an industrial centre boasting Australia's finest alumina refineries, cement manufacturers and a huge multicommodity port. But don't let that put you off; it's also a great stepping stone for exploring Southern Great Barrier Reef islands such as Heron, Wilson and North West. The southern section of the reef begins in Bundaberg and stretches all the way up past Yeppoon; an area remarkable for its abundance of marine life, alluring coral cays and off-the-beaten-track adventures.

Gladstone

TIME FROM ROCKHAMPTON: 1½HR

Catch the markets, marinas and barramundi

Gladstone, nicknamed 'Gladdy' or 'Happy Rock' by locals, is more than just an industrial town; spend a day here and you'll be surprised by the wealth of things to see and do. **East Shores**, located close to the marina, is a well-maintained public park with a water playground, sports facilities, a waterfront boardwalk and a fine lookout; the steep walk up to the **Auckland Point Lookout** is worth it for sweeping views over Gladstone Harbour and its offshore islands. On the outskirts of town, the **Tondoon Botanic Gardens** are spread out over 83 hectares with a magnificent array of native and regional plants.

Located 25km south of Gladstone are the twin coastal communities of Boyne Island and Tannum Sands, with a few lovely beaches and parks; the first Saturday of every month (from 2pm to 7pm) sees the Tannum Sands main beach area come alive during the BAM (Beach, Arts, Music) Markets, featuring the best in local food, handicrafts and live music.

GETTING AROUND

Gladstone Airport has flights from Brisbane. Queensland Rail trains and Greyhound buses stop at Gladstone. It's easiest to get around with your own vehicle; the airport has car rental. Ferries leave from Gladstone Marina to Southern Great Barrier Reef Islands. Resort guests can reach Heron Island by ferry or helicopter. Freedom Fast Cats and Keppel Konnections run ferries from Rosslyn Bay to Great Keppel Island. The other Keppel Islands are more difficult to access; there are boat charters and helicopter transfers to some.

GLADSTONE FISHING CULTURE

In Gladstone, fishing is akin to religion and with its freshwater dams, rivers and the Pacific Ocean on its doorstep, it's not hard to see why. Line fishing is most common, though spear fishing and crabbing are popular too. Coveted local species found in the area include trevally, barramundi and black kingfish as well as mud crabs and prawns. Throughout the year the region hosts fishing competitions, including Australia's biggest family fishing competition, the Boyne Tannum HookUp. Held in May, the three-day event attracts competitors from around the country and includes senior, junior and family categories. Other events include the Awoonga Barra Nationals in April, the Baffle Creek Family Fishing Festival in September and the Tannum Crab Classic held in May.

The impressive Awoonga Dam at **Lake Awoonga**, just 20 minutes inland from Tannum Sands, is a renowned freshwater barramundi fishing spot; it's easy to spend a few hours here swimming, having a BBQ or wandering around the dam bird spotting.

Silo art trail

Around a decade ago the first silo was painted in a small country town in Western Australia, a project led by a non-profit with the goal of bringing art to rural communities. Since then, the movement has expanded across the country, revitalising regional and outback Australia and creating a country-wide open-air art gallery. Today they're a tourist attraction and popular with road trippers, some of whom travel just to see these massive murals. For something different, take a trip west of Gladstone and discover regional Australia. Head first to Biloela (1½ hours) to see the **Spirit of the Land mural**, depicting native animals, then continue west to Moura (50 minutes) for the captivating **pink galah mural**. Finish further south in Monto (two hours) and check out the legendary **3 Moon silo art**: the work by Australian artists Zookeeper and Drapl depicts a Gooreng Gooreng Elder telling the story of three moons to his granddaughter.

Southern Great Barrier Reef

TIME FROM ROCKHAMPTON: 1½HR + 2½HR

Marine wonderland at Heron Island

Heron Island may be small but it is an absolute gem. The coral cay is consistently ranked among the world's finest scuba-diving regions, with a majority of the Great Barrier Reef's fish and coral species found here, as well as turtles, sharks, rays and more. There's excellent snorkelling straight off the beach and numerous dive sites that are accessible by boat; the 'Heron Bommie' is one of the best. You need to be a guest of **Heron Island Resort** *(heronisland.com)* to visit the island. While it's a somewhat exclusive experience, deals are sometimes available online; you'll often get a good discount on longer stays. Transfers by ferry or air from Gladstone cost extra. From October to May, Heron Island is a nesting and hatching site for green and loggerhead turtles; seeing the mothers and their hatchlings is a once-in-a-lifetime experience.

Try the Gladstone-brewed craft beers

EATING IN GLADSTONE: OUR PICKS

Junction Cafe: Charming cafe in the Tondoon Botanic Gardens. Come for brunch or coffee alfresco. *7am-4pm Mon-Fri, 6am-2pm Sat & Sun* $

Swains Fish & Chips: This unassuming South Gladstone place has the best fish and chips in town – it's a local favourite. *11am-2pm & 4-6.45pm Tue-Fri* $

MJ's on Boyne: Neighbourhood corner shop serving classic Aussie hot snacks, fish and chips, burgers and more. *5-9pm Tue, 10am-9pm Wed-Fri, 9am-9pm Sat & Sun* $

Auckland House: A restaurant and brewery in a lovely spot overlooking Gladstone Harbour. *7am-11pm* $$

RUGLIG/SHUTTERSTOCK

Heron Island

More reef adventures

Islands like Heron and Lady Elliot may be the jewels in the crown of the Southern Great Barrier Reef but there are plenty of lesser-known islands that still offer incredible natural experiences. Wild camping on these remote islands is a bucket-list-worthy adventure that's still fairly off the radar, though it's not for the faint-hearted. Campers must be self-sufficient and bring all their supplies with them. It's possible to go camping on **North West**, **Mast Head** and Lady Musgrave Island – camping permits must be purchased in advance from the National Parks website *(parks.qld.gov.au)*. Transfers from Gladstone to all three islands are available through **Curtis Ferry Services** *(curtisferryservices.com.au)*. The **Lady Musgrave Experience vessel** also offers camping transfers from Bundaberg to Lady Musgrave Island. Expect to pay $500 or more for a return trip, depending on your group size, gear and destination.

For a remote island getaway with a bit more luxury head to either **Pumpkin Island** in the Keppels or **Wilson Island** off the Gladstone coast; to visit you'll need to book in at the island eco-resorts. Pumpkin is cheaper, more low-key and great for families and groups looking for an off-the-beaten-track island not far off the coast. Wilson is an adults-only off-grid paradise and known for its bounty of marine creatures and birdlife. Transfers are organised by the resorts.

ISLAND CAMPING TIPS

Damon Shearer, Senior Ranger, Capricorn Coast Management Unit.

Be prepared Bring everything you'll need, including fresh water, food, reef booties, first aid, a marine radio or satellite phone, sun cream, earplugs (birds can be noisy during summer months) and a camera – you'll see some amazing stuff and you'll want to capture those memories.

Best time to go January is the best time to see laying and hatching turtles, and seabirds like black noddies and nesting shearwaters. Winter is great for whale watching and manta rays.

Environmental tip Don't bring anything that might impact the environment and the wildlife on the islands. Take care to bring clean gear and double-check that you're not bringing any insects or pests with you.

Places We Love to Stay

$** Budget **$$** Midrange **$$$ Top End

Brisbane MAPS p282 & p290

Constance $$ Fans of streetart will appreciate this 65-room Fortitude Valley hotel, complete with a rooftop cafe and glass-panelled lift.

Miss Midgely's $$$ Luxury guesthouse in a historic 19th-century residence in leafy New Farm. A strong commitment to sustainability and a short walk to James St restaurants.

Hotel Indigo $$$ Awash with murals and quirky art pieces, the Brisbane Indigo offers a boutique experience in a central city location.

Inchcolm by Ovolo $$$ With luxe, vintage-style furnishings, its 50 suites pay homage to the heritage-listed Wickham Terrace building the hotel is named for.

North Stradbroke Island

Manta Lodge $ One of the only Straddie properties taking one-night bookings. No-frills dorms and private rooms. Attached to a dive centre.

Sea Shanties $$ This waterfront oasis at Straddie's Amity Point offers seven, lovely, self-contained cabins. Koalas linger in nearby trees and dolphins swing by at dusk.

Scenic Rim

Country Mile Escape $$ Wake up to wallabies grazing at this 28-hectare farm outside Canungra. Two private cottages: The Shay sleeps two and The Aerial sleeps up to four.

Nightfall $$$ Four luxe glamping tents on the southwestern fringe of Lamington National Park. Glorious nature immersion and organic meals are included.

Granite Belt

Ridgemill Estate $$ Cosy up with a complimentary bottle of estate wine at these 12 contemporary, self-contained cabins overlooking the vines. Friendly goats, too.

Girraween Environmental Lodge $$$ Switch off (there's no wi-fi) at these ecofriendly, self-catering bush chalets just outside the Girraween National Park.

Surfers Paradise & the Gold Coast MAP p308

Cheshire Cat $$$ Retro style abounds at this renovated 1960s Palm Beach property with six individually styled queen rooms and a two-bedroom apartment.

QT $$$ In Surfers Paradise, the Goldie's original retro-chic boutique hotel is still one of the region's hippest places to stay. Cosy cabins offer relaxed Zen luxury.

Gold Coast Hinterland

Binna Burra Lodge $$ Choose between tiny house cabin rooms and 'sky lodge' apartments at this historic Lamington National Park property. Its resurrected lodge (after bushfires) reopened in 2026.

O'Reilly's Rainforest Retreat $$ BYO bedding for the safari tents or upgrade to a studio or villa. O'Reilly's recently opened Pat's Farm features six luxury self-contained chalets.

Tamborine $$$ A 1970s motel has been reinvented as a chic place to stay. There's a lovely pool area, a commitment to local Tamborine Mountain producers and stellar views.

Noosa & Peregian Beach MAP p322

Bounce Noosa $ A flashpackers with shared dorms, private rooms and a pool, 3km from the beach.

Twin Quays $$ Spotless self-contained apartments offering great value just a short walk from the river in Noosaville.

Essence Peregian Beach $$$ Across the street from the ocean, this luxurious retreat offers studios and apartments.

Eumundi

Imperial Hotel $$ An art-forward boutique hotel on Eumundi's main street, highlighting the work of renowned local painters, ceramicists and sculptors.

Lake Cootharaba

Habitat Noosa $ Camp sites, glamping tents and accessible cabins set on the shores of Lake Cootharaba.

Caloundra & Around

Motel Caloundra $$ A classic motel that's been reimagined as the Sunshine Coast's first net-zero-energy hotel, a short walk from the beach in Caloundra.

LOEA $$ With just 10 rooms decorated in coastal shades, this new hotel features free bike hire and a magnesium pool opposite the Maroochy River.

Montville & Around

Secrets on the Lake $$$ Handcrafted in wood and nestled in the rainforest, these treehouses overlook Lake Baroon, with easy access to hiking trails.

Spicers Clovelly $$$ An intimate luxury escape high in the hinterland, with an award-winning on-site restaurant.

Mapleton Springs $$$ The three self-contained villas and infinity pool are lovely. But it's the native rescue animals – including koalas and wallabies – that you'll remember most.

Hervey Bay

MAP p340

Beachfront Tourist Park $ A series of excellent council-run shorefront caravan and camp sites along the Esplanade here at Torquay as well as Pialba and Scarness.

Kondari Hotel $$ Part budget motel, part resort, with a pool, restaurant, bar, bottle shop and easy access to the marinas and airport.

Pier One $$$ Swish apartments with sea views at the cool end of town on the Esplanade near Urangan Pier.

Rainbow Beach

Pippies Beach House $ It's all about the backpackers here, with pool and group activities including tag-along K'gari tours.

Debbie's Place $$ Meticulously kept Queenslander and Rainbow Beach's finest accommodation, with motel- and apartment-style rooms. Debbie is a mine of information.

Bundaberg

MAP p355

AAOK Riverdale Caravan Park $ Comfortable mobile homes and rooms with shared kitchen, BBQ and picnic areas.

Bundaberg Spanish Motor Inn $$ Hacienda-style motel in a quiet but central location.

Turtle Sands $$ Beachside villas, camp sites and glamping tents next to the Mon Repos Turtle Centre.

Agnes Water & the Town of 1770

1770 Caravan Park & Campgrounds $ A well-maintained beachfront camping ground with camp and van sites.

Agnes Water Beach Club $$ Spacious rooms and apartments ideally located within walking distance of the main beach, shops and cafes.

Rockhampton & Yeppoon

MAP p363

Criterion Hotel-Motel $ Stay the night in one of Rockhampton's grand heritage pubs (1889); clean rooms with shared bathrooms.

Yeppoon Beach House $ Budget accommodation across the road from the beach, with clean dorms and private rooms.

Denison Boutique Hotel $$ A handsome two-storey Victorian heritage-listed building (dating to 1886) in Rockhampton, with four-poster beds and spa baths.

Great Keppel Island

Great Keppel Island Holiday Village $ Beachfront budget accommodation in all styles, from camping to safari tents.

Great Keppel Island Hideaway $$ A variety of well-spaced rooms and cabins, plus the island's main restaurant-bar.

ALEXANDER JUNG/SHUTTERSTOCK

Binna Burra Lodge, Gold Coast Hinterland

Researched by Ashlyn Oswalt, Rachel Tolosa Paz, and Steve Waters

Cairns & North Queensland

CORAL REEFS, RAINFOREST AND THE OUTBACK

THE MAIN AREAS

Incredibly diverse, north Queensland stretches from Mackay north to the Torres Strait Islands and from the peerless Great Barrier Reef to the outback.

Get ready for adventure. This vast arena of natural wonders holds many of Australia's greatest drawcards – the 2300km-long submarine kingdom of the Great Barrier Reef, the teal waters and white-sand beaches of the Whitsunday Islands, tropical rainforests like the Daintree that really do come down to meet the sea, plus First Nations civilisations that have existed unbroken for over 50,000 years. Throw in intriguing wildlife, such as tree kangaroos and cassowaries and this place really is an attention-grabber.

It is well and truly the tropics. The city of Mackay is just north of the Tropic of Capricorn, while Thursday Island in the Torres Strait is only 10° south of the equator. Occasional tropical cyclones barrel into the coast from the Coral Sea in summer; the best season for visitors is 'the Dry', from April to October. Temperatures, humidity and plenty of rain can make things a tad uncomfortable during 'the Wet', which turns trickling streams into raging rivers.

With the Great Barrier Reef tantalisingly close, Cairns is a major traveller base and an obligatory stop on any east-coast itinerary. Divers and snorkellers swarm here and to upmarket Port Douglas for easy access to the reef. The cooler Atherton Tablelands, with volcanic craters, waterfalls and gourmet food producers, is a short drive inland, while real adventurers will enjoy delving into the outback.

For places to stay in Cairns & North Queensland, see p460

TRACEY JONES PHOTOGRAPHY/SHUTTERSTOCK

Oak Beach, Port Douglas (p403)

Find Your Way

North Queensland is huge. The main cities, all on or within shouting distance of the coast, are, from south to north, Mackay, Townsville and Cairns. By road, it's 733km from Mackay to Cairns.

Crocodiles can inhabit all waterways in tropical areas. Swimming is not recommended.

Torres Strait Islands, p420

The 274 islands scattered across dazzling blue water make up Australia's most northern frontier, nestled between the Tip and Papua New Guinea.

Cooktown & Cape York, p414

Cooktown is a small place with a big history, while driving to the Tip of Cape York is a 4WD adventurer's dream.

The Daintree & Cape Tribulation, p408

The oldest rainforest on the planet; explore where it meets the sea in this ancient and vital ecosystem.

Port Douglas, p403

The north's most glamorous resort town; great shopping, eating, pristine Four Mile Beach and intimate access to some of the Reef's most beautiful spots.

Cairns, p378

Easy access to the Great Barrier Reef and an unmissable stop on any east-coast travel itinerary.

Mission Beach, p426

Pristine, palm-fringed beaches and cassowary spotting.

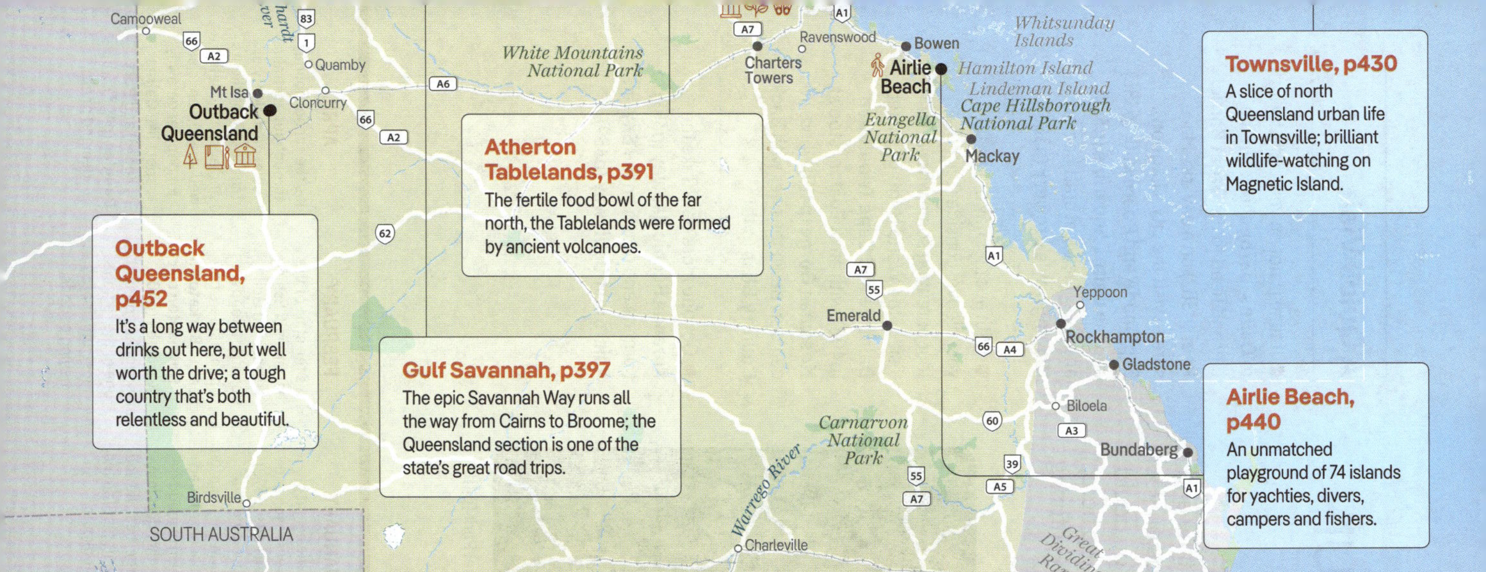

CAR

Having your own wheels is the best way to get around and explore. Get a 4WD if you're planning to go off sealed roads and check with the rental company about which destinations you can travel to.

AIRPLANE

There are some big distances to cover up here. If it's about the destination rather than the journey, consider flying from Cairns or Townsville to remote spots like Cooktown, Cape York, the Torres Strait Islands, Normanton or Mt Isa.

TRAIN

Queensland Rail has a good network, linking Cairns with Brisbane and many towns in between. Separate regional lines head west to Mt Isa. The *Savannahlander* scenic train operates from Cairns and the *Gulflander* runs between Normanton and Croydon.

Plan Your Time

Where you go, at what time and for how long all depends on your interests and budget. You could while away a lot of time up here, especially if you like adventuring, walking and wildlife.

EL PACO 33/SHUTTERSTOCK

Daintree National Park (p410)

A Quick Visit

- If time is not on your side, fly in to **Cairns** (p378), check out the city and head to the **Great Barrier Reef** (p382) on a day trip. Make sure to visit the city's **Lagoon, Esplanade and Boardwalk** (p385) and the **Cairns Aquarium** (p384) and try some local craft beer at **Hemingway's Brewery** (p385).

- With another day or two up your sleeve, consider taking a tour or renting some wheels for a visit to the World Heritage–listed **Daintree and Cape Tribulation** (p408), with an obligatory stop at **Mossman Gorge** (p410) where you can drift down the river with **Back Country Bliss** (p411).

- Got one more day? Take the **Kuranda Scenic Railway** (p389) to Kuranda and return on the **Skyrail Rainforest Cableway** (p389).

Seasonal Highlights

North Queensland is best visited during the dry season (April to October). November to March is hotter, wetter and also cyclone and stinger season.

JANUARY

It's the height of the wet season and **Barron Falls** (p390) are pumping near Kuranda in the Atherton Tablelands; a broad curtain of muddy water thunders into the gorge, best viewed from rainforest-fringed lookouts.

FEBRUARY

It's the start of the barramundi fishing season in Gulf Country. If roads are open, anglers can head to **Burketown**, **Normanton** or **Karumba** (p401), marking the opening of one of the region's most anticipated fishing periods.

APRIL

It's the school holidays throughout Australia, so expect plenty of families. Book flights and accommodation well ahead, especially for popular getaway spots like **Cairns** (p378) and **Port Douglas** (p403), where demand peaks.

Road Trip!

- If you've got wheels and time to explore, it's around 1700km by road from Brisbane to Cairns, or 20 hours of driving up the coast. There's plenty to see and explore along the way. Stop in **Mackay** (p449), then take a few days to play in the **Whitsunday Islands** (p444).

- Continuing north, stop off in Townsville to visit **Magnetic Island** (p438), then drop into **Mission Beach** (p426) to look for a cassowary before reaching **Cairns** (p378). Take the inland road north to visit the Quinkan rock-art sites at **Laura** (p417).

- If you've got a 4WD, tackle the **Bloomfield Track** (p413) and keep heading north until you get to the **Tip of Cape York** (p418), one of Australia's great rough-and-ready driving adventures.

Going the Whole Hog

- If time isn't an issue, consider a round trip of north Queensland from Brisbane with some rental wheels. Drive up the coast to Cairns as per the previous itinerary, then carry on north to **Port Douglas** (p403). Check out the **Daintree Rainforest** (p408), before continuing north to historic **Cooktown** (p414).

- Head back south and inland to check out the waterfalls and crater lakes of the **Atherton Tablelands** (p391) before driving west on the Savannah Way (check your rental-car terms and conditions before driving this epic route).

- Get up close with some lava tubes before reaching **Karumba Point** (p401) on the Gulf of Carpentaria. It's time to turn south again, stopping at **Mt Isa** (p453) then returning to Brisbane via **Outback Queensland** (p452).

JUNE

Book well ahead as the Australian winter school holidays run from late June to mid-July. With dry days, mild temperatures and low humidity, this is one of the most popular times to visit.

JULY

There's plenty happening in Cairns during the three-day **Cairns Show** (p379), a celebration of the region's agriculture, with woodchopping, and fruit-and-vegetable and livestock displays. The final day is a citywide public holiday.

AUGUST

Prime time for a 4WD adventure to the tip of **Cape York** (p418). With dry-season conditions, firm tracks and comfortable temperatures, it's the safest and most enjoyable time to explore this remote region.

NOVEMBER

The outer Great Barrier Reef hosts its annual (but unpredictable) **mass coral spawning event** (p386), usually between November and December's full moons. Plan a dive to witness the reef's extraordinary underwater snowstorm.

Cairns

GREAT BARRIER REEF | FUN ACTIVITIES | RESTAURANTS & BARS

TOP TIP
Time your visit. Head to Cairns from April to October, when the weather is lovely (though you'll want to book well ahead during school holiday periods). November to March brings rain, high humidity, the occasional hurricane, plus box and irukandji jellyfish (known locally as stingers).

Since its humble beginnings as a boggy swamp and rollicking goldfields port, touristy Cairns (Gimuy; population 170,000) has come a long way. As the number-one base for Tropical North Queensland and the Great Barrier Reef, Cairns heaves under the weight of an ever-growing number of resorts, tour agencies, souvenir shops, backpacker bars and clubs, reef boats and visiting cruise ships. This is a tourist town and unashamedly so.

The city centre is more boardshorts than briefcases. You'll find yourself throwing away all notions of speed here, thanks to heady humidity and a hearty hospitality. There's no beach in town, but spend time at the enticing Esplanade Lagoon or the Pier and you'll understand why many travellers fall for Cairns. The city has plenty of attractions in addition to the reef and outdoor adventures, including a thriving arts and cultural scene, plus gorgeous botanical gardens.

Experience a Living Wonder

Visit the Great Barrier Reef

Cairns is one of Australia's most accessible gateways to the Great Barrier Reef – and for many, the main reason to visit. Just offshore lies the world's largest living structure, stretching 2300km and home to over 9000 species of marine life. From affordable day trips on spacious catamarans to intimate

GETTING AROUND

Central Cairns is easy enough to get around on foot. From Cairns Central Shopping Plaza and Cairns Railway Station, it's a five-block walk (10 to 15 minutes) along Shields St to the Lagoon and the waterfront. Taxis and rideshare operators can take you further afield. Cairns has an efficient and comprehensive city-bus system run by Translink. The airport is about 6km north of central Cairns ($25 to $30 in a taxi or $25 per person for the shuttle bus). Cairns Airport sees arrivals from major Australian and international cities and has departures to centres across Tropical North Queensland.

multiday charters, there's a reef experience for every traveller. Snorkel among rainbow fish, dive with rays and reef sharks, cruise in a glass-bottom boat, delve into citizen science or relax on a pontoon. Most tours depart in the morning from **Reef Fleet Terminal**. You can check in with operators' tours desks at the marina for pricing and availability, but it's best to book in advance. For help narrowing the options, see p382.

Under the Water

Get scuba certified

Cairns is world-renowned for scuba diving and one of the few places where you can earn a PADI open-water certification on a World Heritage reef. **Pro Dive Cairns Dive Centre** *(prodivecairns.com; from $995)* and **Divers Den** *(diversden.com.au; from $945)* are respected schools offering beginner, advanced and professional courses, including liveaboard options. A dive medical certificate is required, which operators can help arrange.

Certified divers are spoiled for choice: night dives, the spectacular annual coral spawning, Cod Hole and Ribbon Reefs trips, or swimming with dwarf minke whales. Multiday liveaboards offer maximum immersion, with **Mike Ball Dive Expeditions** *(mikeball.com; from $2500)* leading adventurous Coral Sea trips and expeditions (book well ahead) to the far northern reefs bordering Papua New Guinea.

Island Adventures

Cairns' most accessible reef trips

Just 45 minutes from Cairns, Green and Fitzroy Islands are the reef's most accessible escapes. Although they are technically part of the Great Barrier Reef Marine Park, you won't see the variety of fish seen on the outer reef, but these islands are still home to green turtles, giant clams and some tropical fish species. Green is gentle and family-friendly, while Fitzroy is wilder and more adventurous.

Compact **Green Island** caters to all ages. Calm, shallow water is perfect for young children and snorkelling is beginner-friendly from the beach or jetty. Circuit the island in under an hour, or go on a glass-bottom boat trip, helmet dive, or heli flight. Day visitors can also use the resort pool. Ferries run regularly: **Great Adventures** *(greatadventures.com.au;*

Continued on p384

CAIRNS' BEST FESTIVALS

Cairns Festival: Held annually in late August and early September, this festival takes over the city with a packed arts, comedy and music program.

Cairns Indigenous Art Fair: Curators and collectors descend on Cairns each July for this world-class showcase of First Nations art and culture.

Shine On Gimuy Festival: Each October, the city celebrates local Aboriginal and Torres Strait Islander stories with a 10-day program of music, art, light installations and talks.

Cairns Ecofiesta: Held in the lovely Munro Martin Parklands in June each year, this long-running sustainability festival has workshops, music and markets.

Cairns Show: Celebrate agriculture at this three-day extravaganza held annually at the Cairns Showgrounds in mid-July; the last day is a public holiday in Cairns.

EATING IN CAIRNS: OUR PICKS

Perrotta's at the Gallery: Tuck into top Italian on the deck beside the Cairns Art Gallery; don't miss the Matteo pizza. *6.30am-10pm* **$$**

Guerilla: Edge Hill favourite serving Mexican with plenty of veg and vegan options; corn ribs are a taste sensation. *3-9pm Wed-Fri, from noon Sat & Sun* **$$**

Floriana: Mediterranean meets tropical at the Floriana boutique Art Deco hotel. *6.30am-2.30pm Sun & Mon, to 8pm Tue & Wed, to 9pm Thu-Sat* **$$$**

Ochre: Cairns classic with views over Trinity Inlet; modern Australian with Indigenous-inspired dishes, croc and kangaroo. *11.30am-9.30pm Mon-Sat* **$$$**

CAIRNS
Centenary Parklands Nature Play (1km);
Tanks Markets (1.5km);
Tanks Arts Centre (1.5km);
Mt Whitfield Track (1.5km);
Aussie Macro Photos (1.7km);
Cairns Botanic Gardens (1.7km);
Guerilla (2km);
Goomboora Park (6.5km);
Crystal Cascades (17km)
31
12
4
Esplanade
McKenzie St
James St
Thomas St
Digger St
25
Trinity Bay
Lake St
9
Cairns Foreshore Promenade
Charles St
Sheridan St
21
42
23
18
22
Grafton St
Grove St
Martyn St
Upward St
1
Munro Martin Park
47
Minnie St
Florence St
Severin St
Water St
McLeod St
Grafton
Aplin St
Upward St
Draper St
Bruce Hwy
13
27
Martyn St
Mulgrave Rd
Parramatta Park
Shields
A1
Terminus St
Cairns Central
Loeven St
Bruce Hwy
48
Scott St
Buchan St
Cairns Showgrounds
20
Bunda St

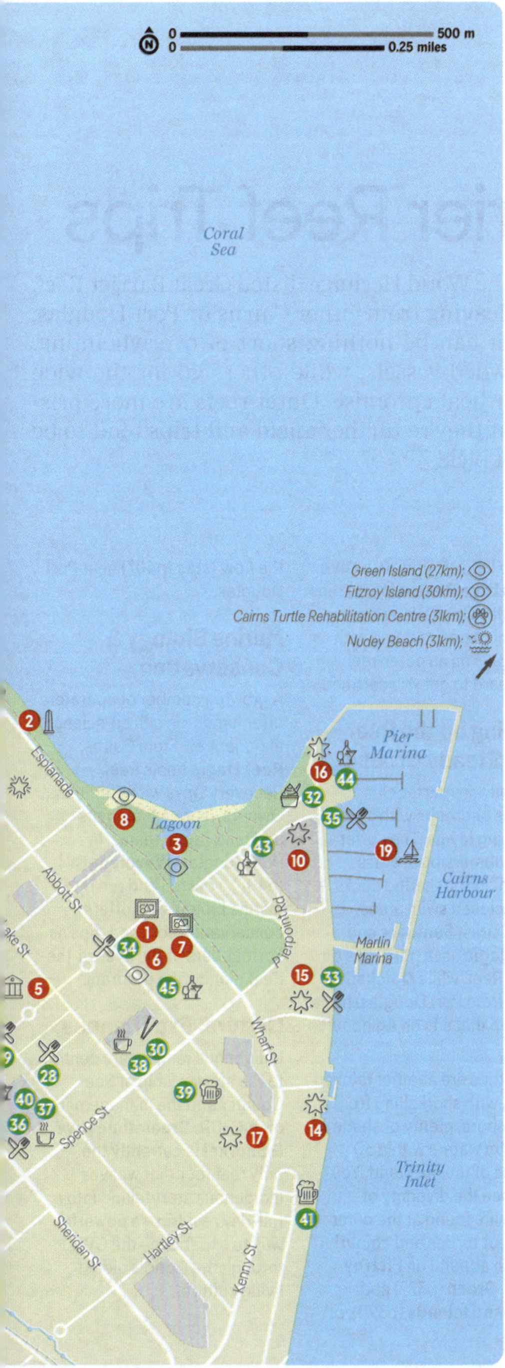

SIGHTS

1 Cairns Art Gallery
2 Cairns Cenotaph
3 Cairns Esplanade, Boardwalk & Lagoon
4 Cairns Foreshore Mudflats
5 Cairns Museum
6 Court House Gallery
7 Mulgrave Gallery
8 Reef Eye

ACTIVITIES

9 Boulder Park
10 Bricks in the Breeze
11 Cairns Aquarium
12 Cairns Esplanade Fun Ship Playground
13 Divers Den
see 15 Dreamtime Dive & Snorkel
14 Fig Tree Playground
15 Great Adventures
16 Mandingalbay Authentic Indigenous Tours
17 Mike Ball Dive Expeditions
18 Muddy's Playground
19 Ocean Free
20 Pro Dive Cairns Dive Centre
see 15 Reef Magic
see 15 Sunlover

SLEEPING

21 Bay Village Tropical Retreat
22 Cairns Plaza Hotel
23 Caravella Backpackers
24 Doubletree by Hilton
25 Floriana Boutique Hotel
26 Mad Monkey Jungle
27 Southern Cross Atrium Apartments

EATING

28 Caffiend
29 Fetta's Greek Taverna
see 25 Floriana
30 Ganbaranba
31 Guyala Cafe
32 Mooz Gelato & Juice Bar
33 Ochre
34 Perrotta's at the Gallery
35 Prawn Star
36 Rusty's Markets

DRINKING & NIGHTLIFE

37 ANNEES
38 Bang & Grind
39 Coral Sea Brewing Company
40 Gilligan's
41 Hemingway's Brewery
42 Muddy's Cafe
43 Pier Bar
44 Salt House
45 Three Wolves

ENTERTAINMENT

46 Bulmba-ja Arts Centre
47 Cairns Ecofiesta
48 Cairns Show

TRANSPORT

see 15 Reef Fleet Terminal

HELP ME PICK:

Great Barrier Reef Trips

Everyone wants to experience the World Heritage–listed Great Barrier Reef, but with a multitude of tours leaving from either Cairns or Port Douglas, choosing how to experience it can be nothing short of overwhelming. Some prefer smaller, less-crowded vessels, while others go for the wide range of inclusions that bigger boats promise. Outer reefs are more pristine, with greater diversity, but they're further afield and trips tend to be more expensive. Let's help you pick.

Where to Go If You Love...

Snorkelling

With 90% of reef life in the top few metres, snorkelling is one of the best ways to experience the GBR. Snorkel-only trips – **Pure Snorkelling** (Cairns) and **ABC Reef Safaris** (p406) and **Wavelength** (p406; Port Douglas) – maximise time in the water and visit reefs chosen specifically for snorkellers. Open-water snorkelling requires confidence in currents; for a gentler option, pontoon trips offer enclosed swimming areas ideal for beginners and kids.

Diving

For experienced divers, a liveaboard delivers the most immersive reef experience. **Spirit of Freedom** and **Mike Ball Dive Expeditions** (p379) offer three- to seven-night itineraries to world-class sites such as Cod Hole, the Ribbon Reefs and Osprey, with multiple daily dives and night diving. Mike Ball also heads to the Torres Strait, including dives on the RMS *Quetta*. If you're keen to learn, Cairns' **Pro Dive Cairns Dive Centre** (p379) runs a five-day Open Water course combining pool training with three days on an outer-reef liveaboard to get you certified.

Soaking up the Reef from Steady Ground

Pontoons are perfect for families or groups with mixed swimming levels. They offer semi-submersibles, glass-bottom boats, shaded decks and enclosed swim areas. From Cairns, **Sunlover** and **Reef Magic** have pontoons on Moore Reef, while **Quicksilver** (p407; from Port Douglas) has a pontoon that sits on Agincourt Reef.

Island trips are another relaxed option, with snorkelling from a sandy shore, plenty of shade and calm waters within 30 minutes of the mainland. You won't see the diversity of marine life found at the outer reefs, but turtles and colourful reef fish abound on **Fitzroy** (p384), **Green** (p379) and **Frankland Islands** (p390), or the **Low Isles** (p407) near Port Douglas.

Marine Biology & Conservation

A growing number of operators offer hands-on citizen-science experiences. From Cairns, **Reef Magic** hosts Reef Recovery Days with Traditional Owners, marine biologists and restoration teams. In Port Douglas, **Wavelength** (p406) – owned and run by marine biologists – offers conservation-focused trips as co-founders of the Eye-on-the-Reef monitoring program.

Cultural Experiences

Indigenous rangers are central to the stewardship of Sea Country and the management of the GBR. **Dreamtime Dive & Snorkel** is currently the only reef tour that weaves Indigenous storytelling into a full-day reef trip – a powerful way to experience the GBR through the world's oldest living culture.

IMAGINE EARTH PHOTOGRAPHY/SHUTTERSTOCK

Potato Cod, Great Barrier Reef

HOW TO

When to go The Dry (May–October here) is peak season, with great visibility. The Wet (November–April) offers fewer crowds, warmer water and changeable weather; stinger suits required.

Budget Pontoon trips: from $295 per person, with smaller boats with more personalised attention costing from $500 per person. Liveaboard experiences: from $800 per person (one night), increasing to over $2200 for premium, multiday adventures.

Motion sickness If this is an issue, opt for tours with shorter travel times or larger boats for greater stability. Pack medication if you're prone to seasickness.

Checking in Most boats depart from Cairns' Reef Fleet Terminal at around 8am; allow plenty of time for check-in.

Top Tips

With preparation, you'll make the most of your time on the reef. If your priority is colourful coral and abundant sealife, head to the outer reef. Out in the open ocean, swells and currents can be challenging, so choose tours that match your ability – guided snorkelling safaris often require you to swim unassisted in open water for up to an hour.

For first-timers, a pontoon tour is a comfortable choice. Large vessels make the journey smoother and once on the reef there are activities for everyone.

If you know *how* you want to experience the reef, consider a tour that specialises in that activity (such as snorkel-only) for the best value.

Cairns offers the widest range of operators, making it busier and generally more budget friendly. Port Douglas provides more intimate experiences and faster access to Agincourt Ribbon Reef, considered one of the GBR's most photogenic day-trip locations. If you're keen to learn to dive, Cairns is better.

Weather can differ from shore to reef; cloudy days reduce visibility, while land-based rain may not affect conditions offshore.

Your visit helps – the Environmental Management Charge included in your ticket supports reef protection. Wear reef-safe sunscreen, take all rubbish with you and treat this remarkable ecosystem with respect so it remains a vibrant biodiverse environment for all.

OFF-THE-BEATEN-TRACK, FAMILY-FRIENDLY ACTIVITIES

Goomboora Park: An obstacle playground with a crystal-clear creek swimming hole perfect for the whole family; 10 minutes' drive from Cairns' city centre.

Aussie Macro Photos: Personalised small group day or night walks to photograph weird and wonderful insects; cameras available to hire.

Crystal Cascades: Swim in the cool waters of this local's favourite. Best for young ones willing to walk a little and confident in the water; 25 minutes' drive from Cairns' city centre.

Bricks in the Breeze: Located in the Pier shopping complex, this community hub offers Lego building and 'art of kite flying' workshops.

Centenary Parklands Nature Play: Part of the Botanic Gardens, this excellent nature-play playground has plenty on offer for kids to get dirty in the city.

Continued from p379

adult/child return $107/54) offers flexibility with multiple departures, while **Ocean Free** *(oceanfree.com.au; adult/child $279/220)* combines sailing and Pinnacle Reef snorkelling.

Fitzroy Island rewards adventurers. Hike to **Nudey Beach** (45 minutes return; shoes essential) or tackle the steep 4km Lighthouse and Summit Walk for Coral Sea views. Learn about reef life at the **Cairns Turtle Rehabilitation Centre** *(fitzroyisland.com/tours-day-trips/turtle-rehabilitation-tours; adult/child $20/12),* at 2.15pm and 2.45pm Tuesday to Sunday, or help gather citizen-science data in the full-day **Marine Conservation Program** *(fitzroyisland.com/marine-conservation-program; adult $199)* – Mondays only. On Saturdays, kids can join the **Junior Marine Biologist program** *(fitzroyisland.com/junior-marine-biologist; from $65);* bookings essential. Hire snorkel gear or stay overnight in the resort (camping available) – once the last ferry leaves, the island is blissfully quiet.

Life Beneath the Sea

North Queensland's ecosystems at Cairns Aquarium

Even if you're heading offshore, spending a couple of hours at the impressive **Cairns Aquarium** *(cairnsaquarium.com.au; adult/child $58/33)* deepens your understanding of the reef and its challenges. Its vast tanks and immersive displays trace north Queensland's ecosystems. Highlights include the giant ocean tank, shark tunnel and reptiles – big and small! Free talks are held throughout the day and guided twilight and after-dark visits *(adult/child $85/49)* shine a different light.

Wander Art Galleries & Museums

Art, culture and history in the tropics

With its strong focus on Aboriginal and Torres Strait Islander art, Cairns' vibrant gallery scene is a great chance to see the work of some of Australia's most celebrated artists.

Cairns Art Gallery *(cairnsartgallery.com.au; free)* highlights First Nations and local artists, including works by Mirdidingkingathi Juwarnda Sally Gabori, alongside national touring shows. The gallery shop is a must-visit for unique local souvenirs like prints, textiles and First Nations pieces.

EATING IN CAIRNS: OUR PICKS

Rusty's Markets: Indoor food and produce market with endless international eats; including excellent Lao, Thai and Vietnamese. *5am-6pm Fri & Sat, to 3pm Sun* $

Ganbaranba: Cairns' best Japanese joint has been serving soothing ramen for around a decade; be prepared to line up. *11am-2pm & 5-8pm Thu-Tue* $

Prawn Star: Jump aboard one of three atmospheric trawlers moored at the marina to dine on fresh prawns and oysters. *11am-9pm* $

Fetta's Greek Taverna: Straight out of Greece with delicious home-style cooking; best on a Friday or Saturday night. *11.30am-2.30pm & 5-9pm Mon-Sat* $$

EXPLORE CAIRNS' ESPLANADE & FORESHORE

Get your bearings and walk the waterfront; cool off in the purpose-built lagoon and let the kids play.

START	END	LENGTH
Guyala Cafe	Hemingway's Brewery	3.5km; 2-3hr

Start at the quieter northern end of the Esplanade with a coffee in hand from 1 **Guyala Cafe** (p387). Head towards the mudflats; just keep clear of the shore – it's home to abundant birdlife and saltwater crocs!

Kids will love the 2 **Cairns Esplanade Fun Ship Playground** and further along, rock climbing at the 3 **Boulder Park** beside the impressive skatepark. Make sure they save some energy for 4 **Muddy's Playground** (water play from 9am daily), a sprawling, shady spot that hugs either side of the ever-busy 5 **Muddy's Cafe**.

Follow the boardwalk, get a bird's-eye view at the top of the 6 **Reef Eye** Ferris wheel, then plunge into the sandy-edged 7 **Lagoon**, effectively a mammoth saltwater pool. The perfect swim spot (it's free and open from 6am to 9pm), here visitors can cool off without worrying about stingers, crocodiles or sharks. There are lifeguards, water fountains and plenty of grass to chill out on.

Follow the boardwalk east from the lagoon and you'll soon reach Cairns Yacht Club. Grab an ice cream at 8 **Mooz Gelato & Juice Bar** or relax in the beer garden at 9 **Salt House**, then follow the boardwalk south up the river for a different view. The area is home to the marina, Reef Fleet Terminal and dining hot spots with options like 10 **Ochre** (p379). Or finish your saunter with a local brew and burger at 11 **Hemingway's Brewery** (p407).

SEX ON THE REEF

Keen divers and romantics at heart can try to time their visit with the annual coral spawning, an all-in orgy in which reef corals simultaneously release millions of eggs and sperm into the water. The ejaculatory event, which some describe as a psychedelic snowstorm, leaves trails of reproductive matter streaking the sea in rainbow colours visible from kilometres away.

The spawning occurs in November or December; the exact date depends on water temperature (it must be 26°C or above), the date of the full moon, the stillness of the water, and the perfect balance between light and darkness. Most diving outfits offer special spawning night dives for those looking to get in on the action.

MARTIN VALIGURSKY/SHUTTERSTOCK

Nudey Beach (p384)

It also manages the nearby **Court House** and **Mulgrave Galleries** (both closed Sundays).

At the **Bulmba-ja Arts Centre** *(arts.qld.gov.au/bulmba-ja)*, multiple galleries sit under one roof, including NorthSite, north Queensland's leading contemporary art space. Deeply committed to Indigenous voices, it's a great choice for purchasing local works. Closed on Sundays.

For a deeper understanding of Cairns and the tropical north, the **Cairns Museum** *(cairnsmuseum.org.au; $15)* is a must-visit. Spread across four galleries, diverse personal stories and collections bring the region's history to life. Children will enjoy the scavenger hunt and Super Sleuth Challenge. Closed Sundays.

Alongside the Cairns Botanic Gardens, the **Tanks Arts Centre** *(tanksartscentre.com; free)* hosts concerts and exhibitions, framed by lush rainforest. There are also historic tours at 10am on Thursdays. Each July, it hosts the exceptional Cairns Indigenous Art Fair (p379). On the last Sunday of the

DRINKING IN CAIRNS: OUR PICKS

Coral Sea Brewing Company: Character-filled hole-in-the-wall hidden away in a laneway; a local brewery with tropical influences. *noon-midnight*

Three Wolves: Superb cocktails, decor and atmosphere at this boutique bar just off Shields St; just open the door. *4pm-midnight*

Pier Bar: Good old-fashioned fun awaits at this Cairns institution; with DJs and live music on the weekends the dance floor gets packed. *11am-3am*

Gilligan's: Chock-full of backpackers, Gilligan's parties hard seven days a week; don't miss the pool-side Sunday sessions and weekend night club, Attic. *11am-3am*

month (April to November), the **Tanks Markets** are held on the leafy promenade.

Stroll Around the Botanical Gardens

Wander the wetlands and winding rainforest boardwalks

A 10-minute drive from the city centre, the **Cairns Botanic Gardens** *(botanicgardens.cairns.qld.gov.au; free)* showcases one of Australia's finest collections of tropical plants. It's easy to spend a couple of hours wandering shady trails filled with giant palms, orchids and gingers. Tag along on free guided walks (10am Monday to Friday) and bird watching tours (7.30am Tuesday).

Across Collins Ave, the Rainforest Boardwalk meanders to Saltwater Creek and Centenary Lakes, a haven for birdlife. Most areas are wheelchair accessible, except for some parts of Flecker Gardens. For expansive views over the airport and out to sea, head behind the visitor centre to climb the Red Arrow **Mt Whitfield Track** (one hour return).

Connect with Country

Ancient culture and smoking ceremonies on Mandingalbay

Just south of Cairns lies the Country of the Mandingalbay Yidinji people, whose stories, knowledge and traditions are deeply rooted in the land and sea. Indigenous-owned and operated, the small-group Hands on Country Eco Tour with **Mandingalbay Authentic Indigenous Tours** *(mandingalbay.com.au; $149)* offers a rare chance to connect with this ancient culture.

A 15-minute cruise through mangroves leads to traditional lands, where visitors are welcomed with a smoking ceremony before joining a guided rainforest walk exploring bush foods, medicines and tools. Stories of Country bring the experience to life, ending with a morning tea of coconut damper, tropical fruit and bush tea. The tours run on Mondays, Wednesdays and Fridays. For another perspective, their **Deadly After Dark Sunset Cruise** *($99; Fri only)*, pairs cultural storytelling with a sunset Trinity Inlet journey, complete with delicious locally sourced canapés and mocktails.

THE TASTE OF MULTICULTURAL CAIRNS

Originally home to the Gimuy-Walubarra Yidi people, Cairns (Gimuy) saw successive waves of immigration after British colonisation in 1876. Lured by backbreaking but lucrative work on the goldfields, in timber and sugar-cane industries and on the wharves, these migrants helped shape the city's multicultural character.

Today, Cairns is a vibrant, diverse city and one of the best ways to experience this mix of cultures is to eat up! Head to Rusty's Markets (p384) for a sensory feast – operating since the mid-1970s, it features over 180 stalls overflowing with exotic fruit, vegetables, flowers and international eats. Arrive early to sample the freshest produce or grab a bargain towards closing time on Sundays.

EATING & DRINKING IN CAIRNS: OUR PICKS

Guyala Cafe: Head north on the Esplanade for lip-smacking local ingredients and locally roasted coffee. *7am-2.30pm Mon-Sat, from 8am Sun* $$

Bang & Grind: Serving great coffee for over 10 years, this cafe has a top-notch brekkie too. *6.30am-2pm Mon-Fri, to noon Sat & Sun*

ANNEES: Delicious traditional Vietnamese iced coffee combined with condensed milk at Rusty's Grafton St entrance. *6.30am-3pm Mon-Fri, from 7am Sat & Sun*

Caffiend: This charming spot has passionate baristas; don't miss the Davidson Plum eggs Benedict. *6.30am-4pm Mon-Fri, from 7am Sat & Sun* $$

Beyond Cairns

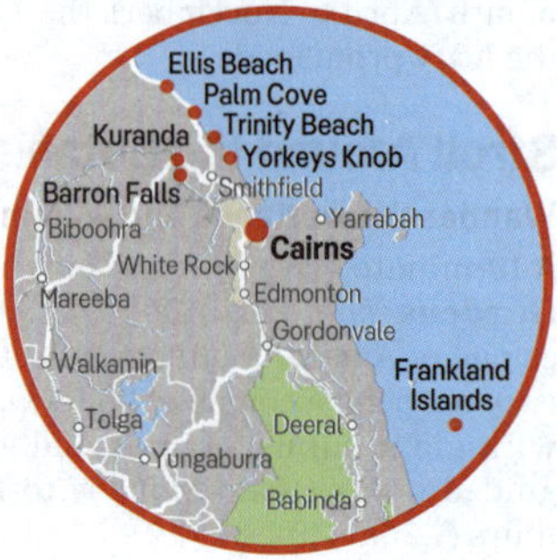

There's plenty to do outside of Cairns – take the train to Kuranda, see thundering Barron Falls or snorkel the southern islands.

Places

GETTING AROUND

For Kuranda, options abound – take the scenic train, Skyrail or bus. Trans North's Cairns–Cooktown (Coastal) route stops in at the Northern Beaches. Having your own wheels offers more flexibility; most rental companies are based near Cairns Airport, 6km north of the city.

Take a day trip up to the village in the rainforest to wander the markets and gawk at the sheer amount of water gushing over the gorge at Barron Falls. Or stay at sea level, beach-hopping north along the Captain Cook Hwy. If you're travelling with small children or just prefer a trip to the reef without the crowds, head south to the Frankland Islands. With the shortest open-water crossing (just 15 minutes from the river mouth to the island), snorkelling with turtles and friendly clownfish, and a river cruise to spot crocs in the mangroves, this ticks a lot of Tropical North Queensland bucket-list boxes.

Northern Beaches

TIME FROM CAIRNS: **15-30MIN**

A string of tropical escapes

If you're craving sand after Cairns' mudflats, head north to the string of beaches between the city and Ellis Beach. Stinger nets are in place from November to March, though you're still swimming at your own risk.

On Yirrganydji Country, **Yorkeys Knob** is a laid-back community just 15 minutes from central Cairns, known for its marina, golf course and occasional croc sightings. There's a long white-sand beach: swim at the northern end of Sims Esplanade.

Framed by headlands, **Trinity Beach** is a favourite for locals, with a pretty palm-dotted esplanade, reasonable cafes and a relaxed holiday vibe that's never too touristy.

The most polished of the lot, **Palm Cove** pairs barefoot luxury with a tropical-village feel. Its melaleuca-lined promenade and white-sand beach front chic resorts and fine-dining spots. Beach strolls, long lunches and general lazing are the main pursuits, but you can hire kayaks or stand-up paddleboards (SUPs).

Last stop is **Ellis Beach**, a sheltered palm-fringed bay right beside the Captain Cook Hwy. It can be packed out with beachfront camping, but locals love to swim in this protected spot. Volunteer lifeguards patrol the beach on weekends from April to November.

TOP EXPERIENCE

Kuranda

Kuranda is a very popular Cairns day trip, not least because half the fun is getting here. Choose between the 19th-century scenic railway (with 55 bridges, 15 hand-carved tunnels and a jaw-dropping view of Barron Falls) or soaring above the rainforest on one of the world's longest gondola cableways. Combine the two or drive the winding curves to the village in the rainforest.

Skyrail Rainforest Cableway

Soar over the Rainforest

Glide silently above a sea of green on the 7.5km **Skyrail Rainforest Cableway** linking Cairns and Kuranda. Allow around 90 minutes one way from Smithfield Terminal (15 minutes' drive from Cairns). The six-seat gondola rises to Red Peak (545m), where a short boardwalk and ranger talks reveal the forest's ancient heart. From here, it sweeps to Barron Falls Station (340m) and the Edge Lookout – a glass-floored perch above the roaring falls – before descending to Kuranda.

Take the Historic Train

Opened in 1891 after four tough years of construction, the **Kuranda Scenic Railway** is now one of Queensland's great day trips. The heritage train climbs slowly from Cairns through tunnels and across bridges, with dizzying glimpses of Barron Gorge below. Depart Cairns Central at 8.30am or 9.30am, returning from Kuranda at 2pm or 3.30pm. Combine the train and Skyrail for the full loop.

Wander the Town & Markets

Kuranda's rainforest village hums with cafes, galleries and wildlife attractions like **Birdworld**, **Australian Butterfly Sanctuary** and **Kuranda Koala Gardens**. The **Kuranda Original Rainforest Markets** *(10am-3pm Wed-Sun)* remain its bohemian heart, alive with local artists, buskers and handmade treasures.

TOP TIPS

- Purchase the **Kuranda Wildlife Experience** *(adult/child $202/110)* for all-in-one fun; it includes the train, Skyrail and entry to Kuranda's wildlife attractions.
- Train and Skyrail bookings are essential; it isn't possible to just turn up.
- If you're intent on seeing butterflies, pick a sunny, cloudless day.

Practicalities

- *ksr.com.au*
- *skyrail.com.au*
- 8.30am-3.15pm

STAYING SAFE IN CROC COUNTRY

Tropical North Queensland is crocodile country, so it's important to be 'croc-wise' when travelling anywhere in the region. There are two types: saltwater (or estuarine) crocodiles, known as 'salties' and freshwater crocodiles, known as 'freshies'.

Freshies aren't as big, have a longer, narrower snout and are deemed relatively harmless; they will only bite if provoked. Salties are much larger (up to 6m in length!) and are aggressive, with jagged, uneven teeth. They are quick to ambush unsuspecting prey. While they prefer saltwater, they can also live in freshwater. Obey all crocodile warning signs, stay vigilant and never swim where crocodiles may be present, even if there are no signs – crocs can't read!

Tip: QWildlife is a great app for tips and recent sightings.

Frankland Islands

TIME FROM CAIRNS: **40MIN** + **30MIN**

Secluded snorkelling and glass-bottom wonders

The Frankland Islands are national-park protected and with exclusive access with **Frankland Islands Reef Cruises** *(franklandislands.com.au; adult/child/family $250/125/625)*, you'll be the only ones here. Full-day trips include a river cruise, lunch, snorkel safari and a glass-bottom-boat cruise. It makes a great trip for smaller children – there are kayaks and SUPs, plenty of shade, a treasure hunt around the rock pools, a sandy beach for swimming and a short open-water crossing of only 15 minutes. Cairns transfers are available (or you can self-drive to Deeral), complete with a magnificent view of the iconic Walsh's Pyramid – known for its near-perfect triangular profile that looks more architectural than natural.

Barron Falls

TIME FROM CAIRNS: **40MIN**

Ancient rainforest canopy and the roar of the falls

A torrent in the wet season and a trickle in the dry, **Barron Falls** is a must-visit at any time of the year – its sheer scale must be seen to be believed. Both the scenic railway and Skyrail offer incredible views (from either side of the gorge), but to soak it up on your own time walk the 600m elevated Budaadji Canopy Walk (3.5km from Kuranda along Barron Falls Rd; follow signs to the car park). The canopy walk takes 15 to 20 minutes one way. You'll hear the falls booming as you wind your way through the rainforest and pop out at the Barron Falls station platform.

EATING BEYOND CAIRNS: OUR PICKS

Hayabusa of Kuranda: Japanese lunch, sushi and sweets are served at this tiny, authentic spot in the Kuranda Original Rainforest Markets. *10am-2.30pm Wed-Sun* $

Trinity Beach Tavern: Overlooking the beach, this popular pub keeps everyone happy with decent pub meals and drinks. *10am-1.30am* $$

Yorkeys Knob Boating Club: Top views from the deck, plus excellent food and drinks, live music and a friendly atmosphere. *10am-10pm Mon-Sat, from 8am Sun* $$

Miguel's: There's top-notch Spanish tapas at this lively Palm Cove beachfront spot; book ahead and bring your friends. *5-9.30pm Mon-Fri, from noon Sat & Sun* $$$

Atherton Tablelands

INTRIGUING WILDLIFE | COOLER TEMPERATURES | LOCAL PRODUCE

Inland from Cairns and the coastal plain is the fertile upland food bowl of the far north, the Atherton Tablelands. Here you'll find quaint country towns, eco-wilderness lodges and luxurious B&Bs dotting greener-than-green hills between patchwork fields, pockets of rainforest, spectacular lakes, waterfalls and Queensland's highest mountains. Formed by ancient volcanic action, this region makes for a great getaway from the swelter of the coast: it's almost always a few degrees cooler than Cairns and on winter nights things can get downright chilly. Twitchers flock for the significant birdlife, and wildlife abounds – it's the only place to spot a Lumholtz's tree kangaroo (yes, a kangaroo that climbs trees!) and there are very real chances to see platypuses in the wild. The Tablelands is the traditional home of several different Indigenous groups.

Places

TOP TIP

For first-timers who want to get the most out of their trip, stay in either Yungaburra or Malanda. Both are within 20 minutes of almost all of the must-visit spots.

Mareeba

TIME FROM CAIRNS: **1HR**

Gateway to Cape York to the north and Chillagoe to the west – this irrigated, prime growing region has a multicultural population, the rollicking **Mareeba Rodeo** *(mareebarodeo.com.au)* each July, the long-running **Mareeba Drive-In** *(mareebadrivein.com.au)* and the four-day music festival **Savannah in the Round** *(savannahintheround.com.au)* each October.

Soar over Mareeba

Mareeba has the most stable air conditions in the country, making it a top spot for hot-air ballooning. **Hot Air** *(hotair.com.au; from $450)* offers 30-minute early-morning flights with the obligatory glass of bubbles. Enquire about transfers from Cairns.

GETTING AROUND

The Tablelands cover a large area but the distance between sites is relatively small. **Trans North** *(transnorthbus.com.au)* operates buses between Cairns and Atherton, via Kuranda and Mareeba, but to make the most of the region, a rental vehicle from Cairns is your best option. Roads in the Tablelands are generally sealed and in good condition, though you'll want to watch out for wildlife. If you suffer from motion sickness, avoid Australia's curviest road, the Gillies Range Rd, with 263 corners! Some of the bigger Tableland towns have taxis and rideshare operators.

WHAT'S GROWN IN THE TABLELANDS?

With its rich, fertile soils and steady, irrigated water supply, the Atherton Tablelands is an important food bowl, but what can you find here?

Bananas: Australians are crazy about bananas – as a nation they eat five million a day! Here they're grown around Mareeba and Lake Tinaroo.

Blueberries and strawberries: Berries can be harvested here during the winter to ensure year-round supply. Find them in Tolga, Yungaburra and Herberton.

Avocados: The Tablelands is Australia's largest avocado-growing region. Mareeba, Ravenshoe and Lake Tinaroo all grow avos.

Mangoes: Half of Queensland's crop of mangoes comes from Mareeba each year.

Coffee: Mareeba is home to Australia's oldest coffee plantation and today 70% of the national crop comes from here.

Brews, bubbles and boutique local produce

An estimated 70% of Australia's coffee crop is grown here. Learn all about it over a cup at **Coffee Works** *(coffeeworks.com.au)* in town, or visit either **Jaques Coffee Plantation** *(jaquescoffee.com.au)* or Australia's oldest commercial coffee grower, **Skybury** *(skybury.com.au)*, outside of Mareeba.

For a taste of the region, shop at **Tablelands to Tabletop** *(tablelandstotabletop.com.au)*, an innovative local produce store. To sip a local mango bubbly, visit the cellar door of the **Golden Drop Winery** *(goldendrop.com.au)*, one of Australia's largest mango plantations.

EATING & DRINKING IN THE ATHERTON TABLELANDS: OUR PICKS

Mt Uncle Distillery: Award-winning gins, rums and whiskys; its Palladium has been voted one of the world's best. A 15-minute drive south of Mareeba. *10am-6pm*

Eventide Hills Distillery: Scenic views and a great range of in-house crafted spirits, two minutes' drive north of Tolga. *11am-5pm Wed & Thu, to 9pm Fri & Sat, to 6pm Sun*

Mungalli Creek Dairy Cafe: Visit this Millaa Millaa farmhouse cafe with delicious produce; try the ploughman's platter and a milkshake. *10am-4pm* $

Gallo Dairyland: Serving their in-house ice-cream, chocolate and cheese on the road between Atherton and Malanda. *10am-4pm Wed-Sun* $

Atherton & Tolga

TIME FROM CAIRNS: **1HR 20MIN**

A spirited country town and the largest Tablelands settlement, Atherton lies 5km south of the charming tiny village of Tolga.

Up close with flying foxes and winged wonders

Atherton is a rewarding stop for wildlife lovers. At the **Tolga Bat Hospital** *(tolgabathospital.org; adult/child $25/15)*, 6km south of Tolga visitors, can meet the region's remarkable flying foxes and minuscule microbats up close. One-hour guided tours share the stories of injured and orphaned bats cared for here and the important role these animals play in pollinating the rainforest. Open 3pm to 6pm; book online.

On the way back to Atherton stop by **Hastie's Swamp National Park** (it's best in the early mornings or late afternoons). The two-storey hide overlooks a seasonal wetland that attracts hundreds of species of birds, from magpie geese and spoonbills to jacanas that skip across the lily pads.

Tracing the region's recent history

During WWII, the Australian Army headquarters was moved from Townsville to Atherton and Tolga. The Tablelands' population boomed with an additional 100,000 troops, and nearby Rocky Creek was the largest field hospital in the southern hemisphere. Trace that story at the **Tolga Museum** *(tolgamuseum.com.au; donation)*, which has a fascinating collection of military artefacts, including a section on women during the war.

Built in 1903, the beautifully restored timber **Hou Wang Miau Temple & Museum** *(nationaltrustqld.com.au/visitor-sites/Hou-Wang-Chinese-Temple-and-Museum; adult/child $10/5)* is the only one of its kind left in Australia. The museum celebrates the Chinese community's vital contribution to pioneering life on the Tablelands. Pay an extra $5 for the guided tour.

Yungaburra & the Crater Lakes

TIME FROM CAIRNS: **1HR 10MIN**

A very quaint village with historic buildings, Yungaburra can be sleepy during the week. Market weekend (on the fourth Saturday of the month) sees it in full force.

IRRIGATION IN THE TABLELANDS

Irrigation has transformed Mareeba's dry savannah into a patchwork of green. Originally built to support the region's once-thriving tobacco industry, the network of channels and dams draws water from the Barron River, fed by Lake Tinaroo, to sustain crops like citrus, mangoes, avocados and coffee through long, hot seasons.

Channels, storage ponds and tailwater discharge from the Mareeba-Dimbulah Irrigation Area feed an array of artificial wetland lagoons in the Mareeba Wetlands, which have come to support a rich array of birdlife – over 300 species of birds have been recorded in a 15km radius. Once open to the public, these wetlands are now only accessible via overnight stays at Wild Nature Lodge.

For bird watching in town, Bicentennial Lakes is a popular spot.

EATING IN MAREEBA & ATHERTON: OUR PICKS

Savannah Cafe: Mareeba Heritage Centre cafe with great coffee and relaxed vibes; profits go towards museum exhibits. *9am-4pm Mon-Fri, 8am-3pm Sat & Sun* $

Emerald Creek Ice Creamery: Stop in on the road back to Kuranda for delicious ice creams made on farm; Davidson plum, lilly pilly and gluten-free cones. *10am-4.30pm* $

Northern Star Thai Restaurant: Authentic Thai cuisine in Atherton with vegetarian options and fresh local ingredients. *11am-2pm & 5-8pm Mon-Fri, 5-8pm Sat* $

Dolce Vita Tablelands: Modern Australian-Italian dining in Atherton; try the Tablelands eye fillet. *8am-8.30pm Tue-Sat* $$$

TABLELAND MARKETS

The scattered small towns of the Tablelands host an assortment of monthly markets.

Atherton Markets: Lion's Club market with food, produce, books and bric-a-brac. Held on the second Sunday of the month at the Atherton Showgrounds.

Herberton Market: Fruit and veg, cakes, jams, leatherwork and plants. At the Wondecla Sports Ground on the third Sunday of the month.

Malanda Markets: Community market with an easy-going vibe; third Saturday of the month at the Malanda Showgrounds.

Mareeba Markets: Buy seasonal fruit and veg direct from local growers, plus hand-crafted objects. At Centenary Park Mareeba; second and fifth Saturdays of the month.

Yungaburra Markets: The region's largest market with 250+ stalls; fourth Saturday of the month, Bruce Jones Park.

Spot a platypus

Volunteer locals have worked hard to regenerate the land beside Peterson Creek, resulting in improved water quality and plenty of biodiversity. Walk to the end of Penda St to start the **Peterson Creek Wildlife & Botanical Walking Track**. Kids will love it, as you are almost guaranteed to see platypuses, water dragons, birds, flying foxes and butterflies. For a longer trail, walk the loop to the Old Yungaburra Railway Bridge and back to town. Tip: late afternoon is a good time for platypus spotting.

Swim in a volcano crater

Crater Lakes National Park protects two volcanic lakes – Barrine and Eacham – both are small and surrounded by rainforest. There is no private boating at either lake.

A 12-minute drive north of Yungaburra, **Lake Barrine** is a tranquil spot. Tackle the 5km rainforest trail that circles the crater, leaving from and returning to the Lake Barrine Teahouse. Cool off with a dip near the jetty.

Around 10 minutes east of Yungaburra, park at the day-use area and dive into the luminous waters of **Lake Eacham**. Although it keeps its distance, beware of the resident freshwater crocodile. Past the jetty, look for turtles gliding near the edge. The 3km track around the lake is shaded and wheelchair accessible.

Malanda & Millaa Millaa

TIME FROM CAIRNS: **1HR 20MIN**

Malanda is home to a Bega dairy factory and Nerada Tea, but what's of real interest to visitors is the opportunity to spot tree kangaroos in the wild. There are also some picturesque heritage buildings like the charming (and operational!) cinema, the **Majestic Theatre** and the century-old **Malanda Hotel** (p396).

Spot a tree kangaroo and have a swim

Remarkable tree kangaroos are only found in the tropical forests of New Guinea and in the Wet Tropics of northern Queensland. The Wet Tropics is home to two species: Lumholtz's tree kangaroo, known as mupee by the local Ngadjon people around Malanda, can be seen around the central Atherton Tablelands, while the rare Bennett's tree kangaroo is found north of the Daintree River.

EATING IN YUNGABURRA & CRATER LAKES: OUR PICKS

Lake Barrine Teahouse: A serene and scenic spot; sit on the deep deck overlooking the crater lake and eat the treats. *9am-3pm* **$**

Mr Belson: Locally owned farm-to-plate cafe with a cosy vibe and the best coffee in Yungaburra. *6am-3pm Sat-Thu, to 8pm Fri* **$**

Our Place: Intimate Yungaburra restaurant with a creative menu and top service; try the focaccia. *5.30-8.30pm Thu-Mon, plus noon-1.45pm Fri-Sun* **$$$**

Little Eden: A fine-dining dinner spot with a lovely atmosphere on Yungaburra's main street; the slow-cooked Tablelands ribs are a must. *5.30-9pm Wed-Sat* **$$$**

A TASTE OF THE CENTRAL TABLELANDS

A flavours-first Tablelands loop serving strawberries, cheese, chocolate and craft beer, with crater-lake swims and wildlife stops in between.

START	END	LENGTH
Atherton	Billycart Brewing	56km; half-day

Kick off the day in 1 **Atherton**, the largest settlement and unofficial capital of the Tablelands, and head east towards 2 **Shaylee Strawberries**, a good spot for an early sorbet should you need one. Around 6km further, follow signage to 3 **Curtain Fig**. There's a boardwalk here to an amazing fig tree; its extensive aerial roots drop 15m to the forest floor. Back on the main road, stop at the 4 **Platypus Viewing Platform** over Peterson Creek. Wee 5 **Yungaburra** ticks every box on the country-cute checklist: within one lap of its tree-lined streets, you'll find 19 heritage-listed sites, including a welcoming 1910 corner pub.

Drive east of town to Crater Lakes National Park, taking the road up to 6 **Lake Eacham**, where you can take a dip in the fresh waters of the crater. Follow the road south to 7 **Malanda** and take a coffee break at Moni's Botanical Cafe. West of town, 8 **Malanda Falls** (p396) has an accommodating visitor centre, your best chance to see a tree kangaroo, beautiful cascades, plus the 'pool' for swimming. Return towards Atherton, stopping at 9 **Gallo Dairyland** (p392) to try cheese, chocolate or ice cream, or drive a bit further north to 10 **Billycart Brewing**, a craft brewery with refreshing tasting paddles, to round off your day.

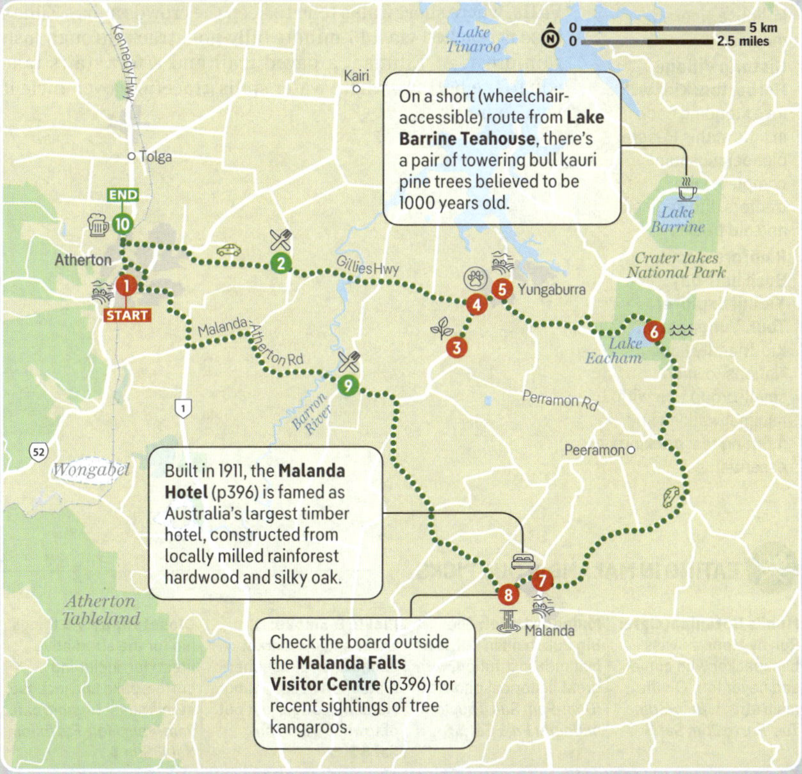

BEST FAMILY-FRIENDLY ACTIVITIES IN THE TABLELANDS

Granite Gorge Nature Park, Mareeba: Private camping ground with day admission. Giant boulders, swimming and friendly Mareeba rock wallabies.

Crystal Caves, Atherton: Crack a geode at this incredible collection of crystals housed in a labyrinth.

Australian Platypus Park at Tarzali Lakes, Minbun: Guaranteed platypus spotting with a delicious lunch of in-house smoked meats.

Historic Village Herberton: Kids will love stepping back in time at this 16-acre pioneer museum complete with tractors, fire engines and old trucks.

Rainforest to Bush half-day Yidinji Explorer Tour, Yungaburra: Kid-friendly First Nations-owned small-group tour with minimal walking and morning tea; bookings essential.

A five-minute drive from Malanda, the excellent **Malanda Falls Visitor Centre** has informative displays plus up-to-date info on the local tree-kangaroo population. There are short 1.2km loop trails through the rainforest on both sides of the road, offering excellent opportunities to spot these elusive creatures, even in the middle of the day. Watching a tree kangaroo, with its thick long tail, hop vertically up a skinny tree and into the tops is an enthralling experience.

Afterwards take the stairs by the car park to swim in the stunning **Malanda Falls**. Built over a century ago, the pool here is concrete-sided with good access for smaller children. Bring a towel.

Chasing waterfalls

A 20-minute drive south of Malanda, pass through the tiny township of Millaa Millaa and turn left at Theresa Creek Rd for the 15km Waterfalls Circuit. The drive through rolling hills and dairy farmland is utterly quaint and the three waterfalls themselves are the icing on the cake. First stop is the easy-access **Millaa Millaa Falls**, where you can park right in front of the cascade. Steps lead down to the pool if you're tempted to swim beneath the curtain of water – but for good reason, it's often busy.

For a quieter experience, head to **Zillie Falls** and **Ellinjaa Falls**, where short walks tend to keep the crowds at bay. Zillie's base is reached via a 15-minute billy-goat track through lush rainforest. At Ellinjaa, a paved trail and a few stairs take you to the bottom, where water spills gracefully over ancient lava columns.

EATING IN MALANDA: OUR PICKS

Moni's Botanical Cafe: Run by Moni, a Swiss backpacker who came and never left. On the main street. *8am-3pm Tue-Fri, to 2pm Sat* $

Malanda Hotel: The Big Pub, built in 1911, is a Malanda institution, with great historical photos. *10am-9pm Sun-Thu, to midnight Fri & Sat* $$

Pickle & Smoke: Excellent, up-market dining in an atmospheric restaurant at sprawling Malanda Lodge, just out of town. *5-9pm Thu-Sat* $$

Closet Hippy: All things hip for the alternative lifestyler, including coffee, cake and incense, at this small organic cafe. *9am-4pm Mon-Fri, to 1pm Sat & Sun* $

Gulf Savannah

OUTBACK ADVENTURE | GEOLOGICAL WONDERS | HISTORIC TOWNS

The epic 3500km Savannah Way runs all the way from Cairns to Broome in Western Australia, skirting the top of the country. The Queensland section, linking Cairns with the Gulf of Carpentaria, is one of the state's great road trips. These days, it's a fully sealed road from Cairns to Normanton and Karumba, achievable in a 2WD, but west of there, you're onto dirt roads or taking the long way around. The world has a different tint out here: the east coast's green, cloud-tipped mountains and sugar-cane fields give way to a flat, red-dust-coated landscape of sweeping grass plains, termite mounds, scrubby forest and mangroves engraved by an intricate network of seasonal rivers and croc-filled tidal creeks that drain into the Gulf of Carpentaria. The fishing here is legendary, particularly for barramundi ('barra' season is February to September). The Savannah Gulf is a real outback adventure.

Places

Chillagoe

TIME FROM CAIRNS: **2HR 40MIN**

The tiny desert town of Chillagoe packs a punch, with stunning underground caves, rock art, stargazing and local hospitality.

Caves and rock formations

Excellent ranger-led guided tours run daily into the spectacular **Royal Arch** (kids will love the thrilling drop down the

GETTING AROUND

The Gulf Savannah is a place to have your own wheels, preferably 4WD but 2WD is sufficient during the Dry. If renting a car, note that only Europcar and Avis currently allow their cars to drive the Savannah Way. **Trans North** *(transnorthbus.com.au)* runs buses three times a week both ways between Cairns and Karumba.

The *Savannahlander* and *Gulflander* scenic-train services run weekly trips during the Dry. Rex Airlines flies between Cairns and Normanton. The **Savannahlander** *(savannahlander.com.au; 4-day trip from $2000)* is one of Australia's great rail journeys. Departing Cairns weekly from April to October, this classic 1960s 'silver-bullet' train winds through the Kuranda range and into the outback. A six-day combo tour with the **Gulflander** *(gulflander.com.au; from $2300)*, known as the train 'from nowhere to nowhere' (Normanton to Croydon), takes you all the way to the Gulf. Both trains offer short day trips. Note: the Cairns–Mareeba and Einasleigh–Forsayth sections are temporarily replaced by buses due to track repairs.

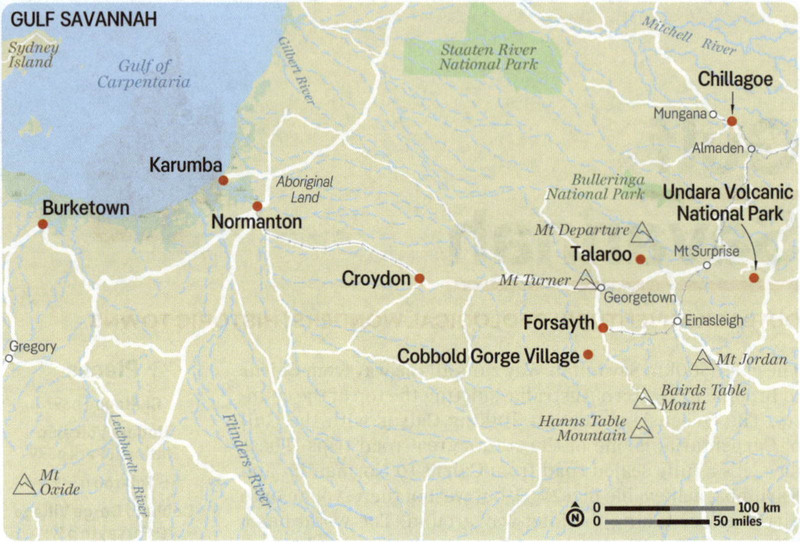

laundry shute!), **Donna** and **Trezkinn Caves**. Book ahead as **tours** *(parks.qld.gov.au/parks/chillagoe-caves/journeys/cave-tours; per cave from $32.50)* fill fast. Call **Chillagoe Hub** *(07-4094 7111)* to book. Royal Arch suits small children or less mobile visitors; Donna and Trezkinn have very steep steps. Archways, Pompeii and Bauhinia Caves can be entered without guides. Archways is a semi-open cave system (and there's Indigenous rock art on the gravel road before the car park), the other two are more challenging.

Don't miss spectacular **Balancing Rock**, a 20-minute loop walk from the car park (1.8km from Chillagoe) and the **Ramparts** (the turn off is 5km south on Burke Developmental Rd), a 200m rock scramble to an incredible viewing point.

TOP TIP

Bring a SIM card from Telstra as it is the only provider with (limited) reception out this way: it's mostly only available in towns. Plan ahead; know where you will refuel and always carry water, physical maps and supplies.

Stargazing

With its expansive desert skies, Chillagoe is the perfect spot to look up at the Milky Way. **Chillagoe Observatory** *(coel.com.au/chillagoe-observatory; $40)* runs nightly, weather-dependent sessions. Bookings essential.

EATING & DRINKING ON THE SAVANNAH WAY: OUR PICKS

Post Office Hotel: Chillagoe's lovely old outback hotel, with a piano and classic pub fare. *11.30am-9pm, kitchen hours vary* $

Chillagoe Gallery 29: Chillagoe's laundromat, gallery space and coffee joint. Service with a smile and superb custard tarts! *8.30am-12.30pm* $

Gulf Country Coffee: Vintage coffee van based in Georgetown beside Venies Fruit & Vegies; epic Tattooed Sailor coffee. *8.30am-1.30pm Mon-Thu* $

Fettler's Iron Pot Bistro: Railway-car dining at Discovery Parks Undara, with bush breakfasts (complete with billy tea) and top-notch barramundi. *7-8am, noon-1.30pm & 6-8pm* $$

Undara Volcanic National Park

TIME FROM CAIRNS: 3½HR

Clamber into ancient lava tubes

One of inland Queensland's most dramatic natural features, the Undara shield volcano erupted about 190,000 years ago, sending molten lava coursing through the surrounding landscape and leaving the world's oldest lava tube system. Entry is by pre-booked, guided tour only – either with **Discovery Parks Undara** *(Apr-Oct)* or **Cobbold Gorge Tours** *(May-Oct)*. The two-hour **Archway Explorer Tour** *(discoveryholidayparks.com.au/resorts/undara; adult/child $71/46)* is a great intro tour while the **Wind Tunnel Explorer** *(adult/child $73/48)* is for more spirited explorers. The three-hour **Cobbold Gorge tour** *(undaralavatubetours.com.au; adult/child $120/60)* explores three tunnels. The **Savannah Way Adventure Pass** *(adult/child $238/119)* covers both Cobbold Gorge and the Lava Tubes.

Talaroo

TIME FROM CAIRNS: 4½HR

Healing hot springs

Owned and operated by the Ewamian people, **Talaroo Hot Springs** *(talaroo.com.au)* are culturally significant, 65-million-year-old hot springs that are also home to aquatic life found nowhere else on earth. Entry (from April to September) is by guided tour only – choose from the 90-minute Discovery Tour ($40, including communal pool) or a 40-minute private soaking session ($50). Other highlights include the 7km mountain bike trail through Ewamian Country and swimming in the Einasleigh River. Two-person glamping tents are also available. Take water and food as supplies are limited. Note: no mobile-phone reception.

Cobbold Gorge Village & Forsayth

TIME FROM CAIRNS: 6HR

Cobbold Gorge oasis

Cobbold Gorge *(cobboldgorge.com.au)*, accessible from April to October, is one of those unexpectedly beautiful outback finds. Follow the 45km good, unsealed road from Forsayth to Cobbold Gorge Village. Lined by 30m sandstone cliffs and narrowing to just 2m wide in places, the gorge is a breathtaking natural wonder. Access is by **guided tour** only and includes

CHILLAGOE'S COPPER & MARBLE

Chillagoe's rich copper outcrops established the town in the late 1800s and the distinctive Chillagoe Smelter chimneys still stand as a reminder of the large-scale industry that existed here until 1943. Visit the viewing area at sunset for a glowing red scene, perfect for photos.

The town was also once home to a bustling marble industry, with over 70 marble quarries. You'll spot some blocks on the drive into town from Mareeba and holding up the bar at the Post Office Hotel. Chillagoe marble was used in the building of Parliament House (although it was first shipped to Italy and then resupplied as Italian marble) and it adorns the floor of the impressive Cairns Art Gallery and the walls of Cairns Airport.

EATING ON THE SAVANNAH WAY: OUR PICKS

MacDonalds Deck: The impressive bar and bistro at Cobbold Gorge Village is open for breakfast, lunch and dinner. *7-8.30am, noon-2pm & 5.30-7.30pm* **$$**

Albion Hotel: The Albion has both pub meals and its Green Room Cafe in Normanton. Also serves coffee, juice and beer. *11am-10pm* **$$**

Sunset Tavern: Savour the sunset with a cold beer and local seafood at Karumba Point. *noon-8pm Mon-Thu, 11am-8pm Fri-Sun* **$$**

Club Hotel: Decent pub meals with a daily special in Croydon; top atmosphere in the 'gutter bar'. *noon-2pm & 5.30-8pm* **$$**

EWAMIAN PRIDE ON DISPLAY

Sharon Prior, General Manager of Ewamian Ltd, an organisation dedicated to preserving and practising Ewamian culture. *ewamian.com.au*

Our native-title rights over Country were recognised by the Federal Court in 2013. That's over 26,000 sq km of land around the Georgetown area. We wanted to do something with the land to provide employment, training and opportunities for our people, so after a lot of hard work, we opened the Talaroo Hot Springs complex in 2021. This was our first venture into tourism. We're all learning what works and have lots of ideas for expansion. We've added a 7km bike trail and a walking trail to the Einasleigh River to attract more guests. We feel proud of our accomplishments and have positive aspirations for the whole of Country.

AUSTRALIANCAMERA/SHUTTERSTOCK

a cruise, guided walk and glass-bridge crossing (adult/child $144/72; discounts for overnight guests; bookings essential). Explore the escarpment further and fossick for agates on a full-day tour (from $220). Optional extras: helicopter flights (from $410 per person) and SUPing (adult/child $68/34).

Ghost stories in Forsayth

Mystery and intrigue abound in the **Forsayth by Night Lantern Tour** *(undaralavatubetours.com.au; adult/child $79/39)*, held on Wednesdays and Thursday and combining dinner, ghost stories and gold-rush history. By day, Charlestown Dam (4.5 km from town) is a must for swimming and fishing.

Croydon

TIME FROM CAIRNS: **6HR 20MIN**

Gold-rush history

Once the beating heart of the Gulf during the 1880s gold rush, Croydon is packed with history and a good place to pause on the way to Karumba. A stroll along Samwell and Brown Sts takes in the **True Blue Visitor Centre & Museum**, the **Club Hotel** (p399) and the heritage precinct. **Diehm's Lookout** offers sweeping sunset views. Check out the **Chinese Temple Archaeological Site** on the way out of town or hop aboard the **Gulflander** (p397) for the 1½-hour **Croydon Golden Sunset Tour** *(gulflander.com.au; adult/child $58.50/30.50)*.

EATING & DRINKING ON THE SAVANNAH WAY: OUR PICKS

Brick Oven at Pinnarendi Station: Wood-fired pizzas and meals served at this working cattle station. Bookings essential. *dinner Mon, Wed, Thu & Sat Apr-Oct* $

Goldfields Hotel: Tiny Forysath's all-in-one venue, with fuel, store supplies, a bar, decent pub food and a world-class agate display. *10am-10pm* $$

Einasleigh Hotel: As far as classics go, this one is a must; over a century old and still serving cold ones. *hours vary* $$

Burketown Pub: Fresh grilled barra and superb steaks at one of Australia's most remote pubs. *10am-10pm Tue-Thu, to midnight Fri & Sat, noon-6pm Sun & Mon* $$

Cobbold Gorge (p399)

Normanton & Karumba

TIME FROM CAIRNS: **8HR**

Wander the port

This delightful, outback town started life as a port for the Gulf's cattle industry and grew with the discovery of gold at Croydon in 1885. Wander the Normanton Town Walk to marvel at its 19th-century buildings, go fishing on the Norman River and gasp at **Krys**, the big croc statue. **Burke & Wills' last camp (119)** is 36km southwest on the road to Burketown.

Karumba sunsets

A further 70km along is Karumba, the only town accessible by sealed road on the entire Gulf coast. Stay at **Karumba Point** to watch the sun set into the Gulf. Hop aboard a sunset cruise with **Karumba Cruises** *(karumbacruises.com.au; from $90)*. Fishing enthusiasts shouldn't miss the **Les Wilson Barramundi Discovery Centre** *(barracentre.com.au; free, tours & feeding $35)*.

Burketown & Beyond

TIME FROM CAIRNS: **11HR**

Burketown and beyond is best reached by 4WD. Check conditions, as the route is often impassable in the Wet.

The back of Burketown

Burketown can feel like the end of the Earth but the barra fishing is legendary – either on the Albert River or 30km north at the Gulf (the season is from February to September). There are plenty of other reasons to visit; between September and November adventurous cloud-spotters stop by, hoping to catch a glimpse of the extraordinary 'morning glory' clouds. First

KRYS THE CROC

There's not much to excite visitors in dusty Normanton, apart from **Krys the Crocodile**. This life-size statue commemorates the 8.63m 'saltie' shot by crocodile hunter Krystina Pawlowski on the Norman River downstream in 1957.

The single shot made Krystina a worldwide celebrity and earned her the nickname 'One Shot'. Her husband, Ron, took photos of the original Krys so comparisons of size could be made but they were unfortunately lost in the floods of 1974. Despite present-day lack of evidence, Krys is recognised in the Guinness World Records as the world's largest-ever recorded croc. Positively enormous; a photo of it is practically obligatory. You'll find the statue right on Landsborough St, the town's main drag.

MORNING GLORY CLOUDS

Roughly between September and October (some sightings are possible in November), when 'morning glory' clouds occasionally (but unpredictably) roll in, Burketown, and to a lesser extent Karumba, becomes the home of intrepid cloud-spotters.

A rare meteorological phenomenon, these tubular clouds typically form in the early morning and come in wavelike sets of up to eight. Each can be up to 1000km long and 2km wide and they travel at speeds of up to 60km/h. Burketown has become a highlight for those wishing to surf the ultimate atmospheric wave. As the sun rises, gliders head up from Burketown Aerodrome, hoping to catch one. For the best morning glory predictions and a close-up look at the clouds aboard a light plane, contact **Savannah Aviation**.

TYRRANNOID/SHUTTERSTOCK

Boodjamulla National Park

Nations-owned **Yagurli Tours** *(yagurlitours.com.au)* offers unique tours, such as soaring over Australia's largest salt flats in a hot-air balloon ($299; July to August) or stargazing with Indigenous storytelling ($150, from May to August). Yagurli can also arrange fishing and self-drive guided 4WD tours.

Gorges and fossils

An alternate Savannah Way route heads south from Burketown to **Boodjamulla National Park** *(boodjamullanationalpark.com.au)*, an outback oasis and home to a sacred, flame-red sandstone gorge and the luminous green, spring-fed Lawn Hill Creek. Following 2023 flood damage, parts of the park are now reopening. Highlights include Indarri Falls and heading south, the **Riversleigh World Heritage Site**, Australia's richest fossil mammal site and the only section of the World Heritage Site open to the public. Travel lightly through Country and do not enter areas of spiritual and sacred significance to the Waanyi people.

Port Douglas

LUXURY STAYS | REEF SAILING | TOP SHOPPING

Port Douglas (Port or PD) is Tropical North Queensland's most glamorous resort town and a fabulous gateway to the Great Barrier Reef – the outer reef is just an hour offshore. Apart from the multimillion-dollar marina, dreamy Four Mile Beach and five-star resorts big enough to warrant their own postcode, the town itself is lovely. The main drag is Macrossan St, filled with excellent restaurants, stylish boutiques and earthy pubs. It's flash, fun and a fine place for discovering all that's good about the north, plus it's also an excellent base for visiting the Daintree and Cape Tribulation. The peninsula that Port Douglas occupies is the traditional home of the Yirrganydji people.

TOP TIP

Plan your stay around the weekly Sunday morning arts and crafts markets on the waterfront. The vibe and products are second-to-none; it's the most buzzing market in the far north.

Port Douglas Sunday Markets

Arts and crafts on the waterfront

Plan your trip around the excellent **Port Douglas Markets**, held on Sundays from 8.30am to 1.30pm at Anzac Park. It's arguably the most atmospheric market on this stretch of coast and you'll find plenty of quality goods, like unique local and Indigenous arts and crafts, jewellery and produce. Stalls spill out beneath shady palms, tunes drift through the breeze and with the Coral Sea glittering just beyond, there's nothing quite like it around here.

GETTING AROUND

The closest airport is Cairns. **SR Coaches** *(srcoaches.com.au; one way from $58)* offers transfers from the airport to Port Douglas (one hour; bookings essential). Alternatively, hire a car at the airport and drive the scenic 68km yourself. Trans North buses stop at Port Douglas on the coastal Cairns–Cooktown route three times a week.

Port Douglas' city centre is compact and easy to walk but some resorts are further from town. SR Coaches runs a minibus shuttle (unlimited day pass $26) from 6am to midnight. Otherwise, hire bikes (including kids bikes), e-bikes and e-scooters from **Bike Shop & Hire** *(bikeshopandhire.com; from $32)*.

SIGHTS
1 Flagstaff Hill
2 Four Mile Beach
3 Lady Douglas
4 Port Douglas Markets
5 Trinity Bay Lookout

ACTIVITIES
6 Bike Shop & Hire
7 Calypso
8 Crystalbrook Marina
see 7 Quicksilver
see 8 Sailaway
see 8 Wavelength

SLEEPING
9 Port Douglas Motel

EATING
10 Iron Bar
see 6 Jungle Fowl
11 Pasta e Vino
12 Salsa Bar & Grill
13 Zinc

DRINKING & NIGHTLIFE
14 Court House Hotel
see 7 Hemingway's Brewery
15 Tin Shed

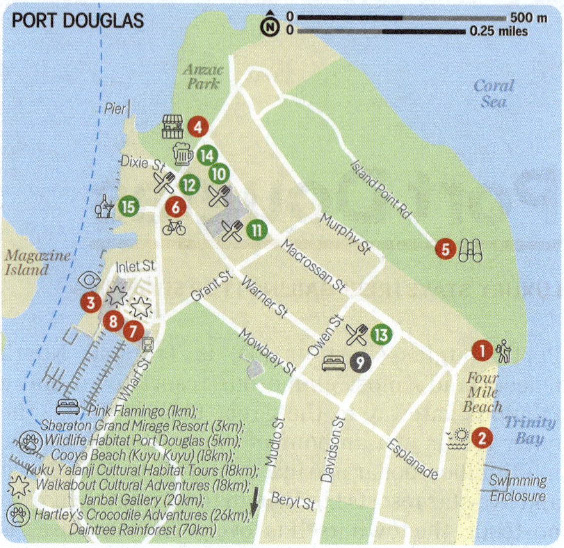

Carnivale on the Coast

Festival and foodie fun

If you're planning a trip around local events, time your visit for the three-day **Port Douglas Carnivale** *(carnivale.com.au)* in late May. The festival fills the town with live music, a colourful street parade and lashings of good food and wine. For foodies, **Taste Port Douglas** *(tasteportdouglas.com.au)* is a four-day feast held every August.

Spectacular Views & Swimming

Stunning Four Mile Beach

The beauty of Port Douglas is the stretch of **Four Mile Beach** where you can swim between the flags or simply laze the day away on deckchairs. Stinger nets are set on the beach from early November to late May but you should wear a stinger suit during this time. Make sure to visit **Trinity Bay Lookout** for sensational views down the length of Four Mile Beach and out over the Coral Sea. Drive or walk up Flagstaff Hill from Macrossan St via Wharf St, or take the path leading up from the north end of Four Mile Beach.

Go Crabbing with the Professionals

Indigenous tours of the coast and rainforest

Highly reputable **Walkabout Cultural Adventures** *(walkaboutadventures.com.au/ngana-julaymba-dungay; half-/full-day tours $190/245)* runs guided tours of the **Daintree Rainforest**'s southern section along the Mossman

DRIVE THE COAST FROM CAIRNS TO PORT DOUGLAS

A spectacular coastal drive skirting rainforest-clad mountains, picture-postcard-perfect beaches and the Coral Sea's shifting blues.

START	END	LENGTH
Cairns	Surfy	68km; half-day

Starting in ❶ **Cairns**, head north on the Captain Cook Hwy, one of Australia's great coast roads. Just 15 minutes away, stop at ❷ **Cattana Wetlands** to wander the peaceful, flat (wheelchair-accessible) paths around the lakes and bird watch from the hides.

Back on the road, be sure to stop at one of Cairns' Northern Beaches – our pick is idyllic ❸ **Trinity Beach** (p388), where palm trees dot the grassy esplanade beside the sand. Or for more action, try ❹ **Palm Cove** (p388) for plenty of cafes, and hire a kayak and tackle the trip to Double Island.

From here, the road hugs the shore – you'll be hard-pressed to find a more picturesque stretch. Stop at ❺ **Ellis Beach** (p388) – weekends are busy but it's worth a pause to stroll on the sand, take a dip or refuel at beachfront Ellis Beach Bar 'n Grill.

The road then starts to wind up towards ❻ **Rex Lookout**, a sensational spot with Coral Sea views. If you're looking to spot a lurking croc, stop by the public viewing platform at ❼ **Mowbray River Foot Bridge**. Time it for low tide if you can; you might just see some salties sunning themselves on the mudflats. Driving in to Port Douglas, head to the beach and treat yourself to the quintessential fish and chips on the deck at ❽ **Surfy**.

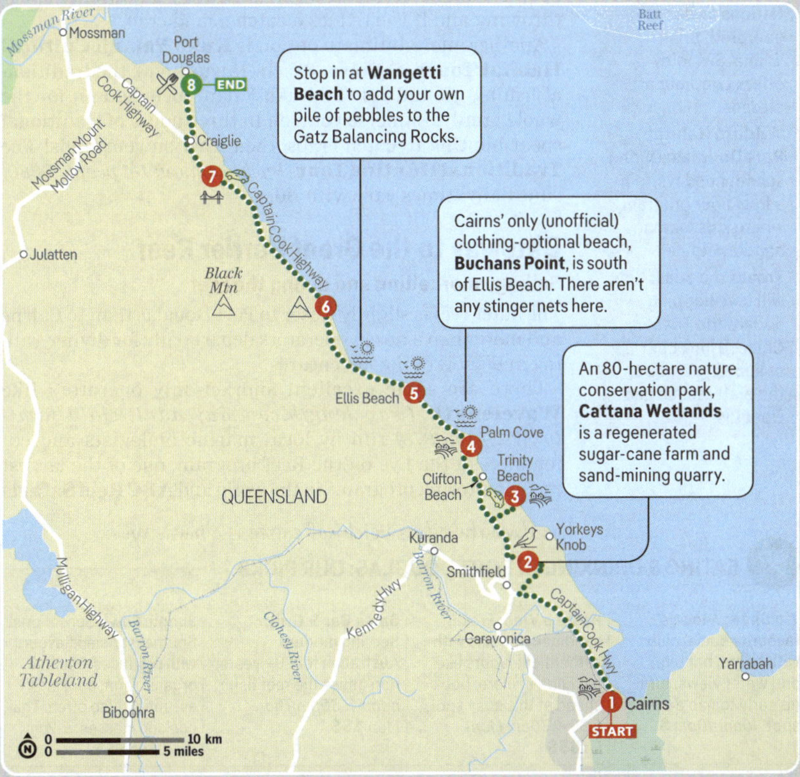

BEST FAMILY-FRIENDLY ACTIVITIES IN PORT DOUGLAS

Hartley's Crocodile Adventures: Marvel at the crocs, snakes and cassowaries; additional wildlife encounters require pre-booking.

Bike Shop & Hire's Treasure Hunt: Maps are available from the Warner St shop; this 13km loop with a stretch on the beach will keep kids busy for hours.

Janbal Gallery, Mossman: First Nations owned and operated; Brian 'Binna' Swindley offers two-hour art classes.

Wildlife Habitat Port Douglas: During school holidays, join a four-hour program where kids learn to handle wildlife.

Travel the seas: Kids will love hopping aboard the Shaolin Chinese junk boat or spotting crocs on the picturesque Lady Douglas.

EQROY/SHUTTERSTOCK

Gorge and coastal habitats. Gain insights into the Kuku Yalanji people, sample seasonal bush tucker, try traditional spear throwing and if you're lucky, catch a mud crab.

Another, more intimate option is **Kuku Yalanji Cultural Habitat Tours**, at Cooya Beach (Kuyu Kuyu), the traditional fishing grounds of the Kuku Yalanji people. Fun for the whole family; immerse yourself in three hours of traditional spear hunting to catch crabs, then feast on your finds! The **Traditional Hunting Tour** *(kycht.com.au; 1-4 people $880)* runs daily; times vary with tides.

Gateway to the Great Barrier Reef

Sailing, snorkelling and diving the reef

The outer reef is slightly closer to Port Douglas than to Cairns and more than a dozen operators depart daily for diving, sailing and snorkelling adventures.

There are some excellent snorkel-only operators like **Wavelength** *(wavelength.com.au; adult/child/family $298/208/878)* run by local marine biologists and co-founders of the Eye on the Reef program, one of the largest reef-monitoring programs in the world and **ABC Reef Safaris**

EATING & DRINKING IN PORT DOUGLAS: OUR PICKS

Tin Shed: A locals' favourite social club with beers, bar bites and water views; turn up early to nab a sunset spot. *10am-10pm* $

Pasta e Vino: Fresh, handmade pastas with authentic flavours like *paccheri di mare;* book ahead at this cosy spot. *5.30-9.30pm Mon-Fri* $$$

Salsa Bar & Grill: Serving modern Australian for 20+ years; don't miss the reef fish. *noon-11.30pm Thu-Mon* $$$

Jungle Fowl: Sensational Southeast Asian flavours, with produce from their organic farm; bookings essential. Also offers Thai cooking classes. *5-9pm Wed-Sun* $$$

The flavourful citrus betel-leaf entrée is a must-try!

Snorkelling off Port Douglas

(abcreefsafaris.com.au; $547), which offers intimate tours with just 12 guests.

If a big boat and a pontoon is more your thing, **Quicksilver** *(quicksilver-cruises.com; adult/child/family $325/172/830)* spends the day at its Agincourt pontoon. If you're more confident in the water, their **Silversonic boat** *(silverseries.com.au/silversonic; adult/child $315/228, diving extra)* takes a smaller group and visits three Agincourt sites.

A great option for kids or for those short on time, the **Low Isles** – a postcard-perfect coral cay complete with lighthouse and sandy beach – are just 30 minutes northeast of PD by boat. **Calypso** *(calypsoreefcruises.com; adult/child $259/205)* offers a half-day snorkelling adventure, while **Sailaway** *(sailawayportdouglas.com; adult/child/family $340/238/1040)* runs full-day small-group sail and snorkel tours, plus an adults-only sunset sail and snorkel ($340). Expect to float over corals spotting plenty of turtles and reef fish.

Most tours depart from Crystalbrook Marina and include transfers, snorkelling gear, lunch and refreshments. For more detailed info to help you pick, see p382. For a quintessential Port Douglas moment, don't miss the **Sailaway Sunset Sail** *($94, 90 minutes)* on the Coral Sea.

STINGERS

If you're in Tropical North Queensland between October and June, you'll want to take precautions when swimming at beaches. The biggest worries are box jellyfish and irukandji. Box jellyfish can be large, with tentacles stretching up to 3m behind them; irukandji, the smallest of the box jellyfish family, may only be the size of your thumbnail, but the tentacles can be 1m in length and its venom is incredibly strong.

Beach towns set up stinger nets to keep them out, though to stay safe swimmers are advised to wear stinger suits: irukandji can be small enough to pass through the mesh of stinger nets. Follow all signage and advice from lifeguards.

EATING & DRINKING IN PORT DOUGLAS: OUR PICKS

Court House Hotel: A popular and lively pub at the northern end of Macrossan St perfectly located to catch the breeze. *10am-midnight* **$$**

Iron Bar: A steakhouse offering grilled and smoked meats, oysters and cocktails; it's hard to walk past this one on Macrossan St. *noon-midnight* **$$**

Hemingway's Brewery: Top spot for beers on the marina; head upstairs for more sophisticated bar, Sails Port Douglas by Hemingway's. *noon-9pm*

Zinc: Modern Australian dining in a vibrant, atmospheric setting with great service; at the southern end of Macrossan St. *2-11pm* **$$$**

The Daintree & Cape Tribulation

ANCIENT RAINFOREST | OUTDOOR ADVENTURE | WILDLIFE SPOTTING

GETTING AROUND

There are plenty of packaged trips to the Daintree and Cape Trib from both Cairns and Port Douglas daily. For some freedom, get rental wheels and explore along the way. Drive slowly to avoid wildlife and slippery conditions. The road is sealed to Cape Tribulation but after that it's 4WD-only on the Bloomfield Track north. There may be some delays during peak periods crossing the Daintree River on the car ferry. Tune in to 87.6FM Daintree Radio for up-to-date info. Fill up with petrol before you leave and carry supplies; there are limited facilities in the park.

TOP TIP

Stock up on supplies at the Woolworths in Mossman; it's the last one before Weipa (nine hours' drive away)!

The oldest rainforest on the planet, the UNESCO World Heritage–listed Daintree Rainforest is one of Australia's most beautiful corners. Sheltered within this vast and extraordinary forest is all manner of wildlife – especially along the Daintree River – from cassowaries to tree kangaroos. Here, the rainforest tumbles right down to the coast, where remote and deserted beaches seem to go on forever, while offshore lies the peerless Great Barrier Reef, another World Heritage site. Combine all of this and we challenge you to find another place where so many world-class natural attractions come together.

The secret, however, is well and truly out. Avoid busloads of day-trippers by visiting under your own steam and spending a few days here. Off-grid Cape Tribulation is the most popular place to stay, with the vibe ranging from luxury to backpacker.

Detour to Daintree Village

Croc spotting on the Daintree River

Before crossing the Daintree River on the ferry, explorers and wildlife lovers will enjoy the short detour from the ferry turn off on the Mossman–Daintree Rd to tiny Daintree Village. Set on a plateau of farmland on the southern side of the Upper Daintree River, this cute township has little more than a village hotel and general store, but successful croc spotting cruises on the river are the main event. Long-running **Crocodile Express** *(crocodileexpress.com; adult/child/family $38/19/88)* has a top reputation for its one-hour boat trips, enjoyed by both bird watchers and croc spotters. You'll see a diverse range of birdlife, including wading birds fossicking on exposed mudflats, and get up close and personal with some big saltwater crocs! Further east on the river towards the car ferry, **Bruce Belcher's Daintree River Cruises** *(daintreerivercruises.com.au; adult/child/family $35/16/89)* is another excellent option.

THE DAINTREE & CAPE TRIBULATION

HIGHLIGHTS
1 Daintree National Park

SIGHTS
2 Bloomfield Track
3 Buchanan Creek Rd
4 Daintree Discovery Centre
5 Daintree Tea Company
6 Mossman Gorge
7 Mt Alexandra Lookout

ACTIVITIES
8 Bruce Belcher's Daintree River Cruises
9 Cape Trib Farm
10 Cape Trib Horse Rides
11 Cooper Creek
12 Crocodile Express
13 Jindalba Boardwalk
14 Madja Boardwalk
see 23 Ngadiku Dreamtime Walk
15 Ocean Safari

SLEEPING
16 Cape Trib Beach House
17 Daintree Beach Resort
18 Rainforest Hideaway

EATING
19 Cassowary Bar & Restaurant
20 Daintree Fan Palm Farm
21 Daintree Ice Cream Company
22 Mason's Cafe
see 16 Tides Bar & Restaurant

INFORMATION
23 Mossman Gorge Culture Centre

TRANSPORT
24 Daintree River Ferry

SKYBOUNDTJ/SHUTTERSTOCK

TOP EXPERIENCE

Daintree National Park

Older than the Amazon, the Daintree is a living link to Earth's deep past – a refuge for some of the planet's earliest flowering plants. Logging and development threats in the 1970s and '80s sparked fierce protests, leading to its inclusion in the Wet Tropics World Heritage Area in 1988. Today, joint management with Eastern Kuku Yalanji Traditional Owners helps safeguard its future.

DON'T MISS

- Mossman Gorge
- Ngadiku Dreamtime Walk
- Backcountry Bliss' River Drift Experience
- Daintree Discovery Centre
- Madja Boardwalk
- Cape Trib Farm's Fruit Tasting Tours
- Daintree Ice Cream Company
- Kulki Lookout

Accessibility

Located between 80km and 150km north of Cairns, Daintree National Park has two main visitor gateways: Mossman Gorge and Cape Tribulation. Each offers a very different rainforest experience.

Mossman Gorge

Just 20 minutes north of Port Douglas, **Mossman Gorge** is a boulder-strewn valley with clear, ice-cold swimming pools and walking trails through dense rainforest. Entry is via the Kuku Yalanji-managed **Mossman Gorge Cultural Centre**

PRACTICALITIES

● *parks.qld.gov.au/parks/daintree* ● Mossman Gorge shuttle bus adult/child $15/7.50 (8am-4.30pm) ● Daintree River Ferry return $51 (5am-midnight) *(mossmangorge.com.au)*, with buses running every 15 minutes from 8am to 4.30pm and from where you can park and catch the 10-minute shuttle to the gorge (no walk-in access; adult/child $15/7.50). Wander the 2.4km rainforest circuit or simply relax and swim in the river. Note: Mossman River conditions can change quickly, especially during the Wet.

To deepen your experience, the 1½-hour **Ngadiku Dreamtime Walk** *(mossmangorge.com.au/things-to-do/dreamtime-walks; adult/child $100/50)* is highly recommended. Local Indigenous guides prepare a smoking ceremony, tea and damper, and accompany you through the rainforest. There are four tours daily; book ahead.

For a splash of adventure, **Back Country Bliss** *(backcountry bliss.com.au)* offers a two-hour **River Drift Experience** *(adult/child $145/110)* where you float down the river, snorkelling with turtles, water dragons and platypuses. Children aged four and up can join when river levels are low; during the Wet, the tour suits fit swimmers aged 14 and older. Bookings essential. The **Mossman Gorge Adventure Day** *(adult/child $270/225)* combines river drift, walks, lunch and a smoking ceremony in one day.

Cape Tribulation

North of the Daintree River (and Mossman Gorge) the rainforest becomes more remote. The only way to access the Cape Tribulation section of the Daintree National Park from the south is to cross the river via the **Daintree River Ferry**. Here, rainforest-clad mountains meet long sandy beaches, and although the winding 38km road from the ferry crossing to Cape Tribulation can be driven in under an hour, you'll find that you will want to stop often. Do allow time for the **Daintree Discovery Centre** and then there are plenty of boardwalks to wander along and tropical treats to eat. Allow at least half a day (or better still, a full day or overnight) to enjoy this part of the park.

Cape Trib is the area to stay in if you're looking to get away from it all, with options ranging from luxury retreats to simple camping grounds. One thing they all have in common is the fact that there is no mains-grid electricity supply north of the Daintree River. Everyone relies on generators or solar power.

Wildlife Spotting

The Daintree is a critical stronghold for the endangered southern cassowary, with one of the largest remaining populations in Australia. While sightings are never guaranteed, patient visitors have a genuine chance, particularly in the early morning or late afternoon. Try the **Jindalba Boardwalk** or **Buchanan Creek Rd** at Cow Bay.

Other commonly seen wildlife include Boyd's forest dragon, often seen clinging motionless to tree trunks, and the brilliant blue Ulysses butterfly, on sunny mornings. The birdlife is prolific, while tree kangaroos are particularly hard to spot. A guided night walk is highly recommended – you'll be amazed at the abundant nocturnal life in this ancient rainforest.

SLOW DOWN

The Daintree rewards patience. Don't race from lookout to lookout – linger at the **Madja Boardwalk** or at the canopy at the Daintree Discovery Centre. The key is to listen first: to the soft slap of fruit falling or the sudden rustle that might be a tiny frog. The Daintree isn't a sight to see but a state to slip into – slow, sensory and alive.

TOP TIPS

- Visit early or late in the day for cooler temperatures and fewer tour buses.
- To miss peak hours at the Daintree River Ferry, make the crossing before 10am or after 5pm.
- Stick to boardwalks and marked tracks to protect fragile rainforest and to avoid snakes.
- The highly elusive Bennett's tree kangaroo is found in the north of the Daintree, while the smaller Lumholtz's tree kangaroo dwells in the south.
- Swimming is possible at Mossman Gorge and near Mason's Cafe at Cape Tribulation; otherwise heed crocodile warnings.
- Mobile-phone reception is limited once you cross over the Daintree River and head north to Cape Tribulation.

MOSSMAN TO CAPE TRIBULATION

The drive from Mossman to Cape Trib is deceptively short; you'll want to stop everywhere along the way.

START	END	LENGTH
Mossman	Cape Trib Beach House	64km; 1 day

Starting out in the sugar-cane town of ❶ **Mossman**, stock up on supplies – the Woolworths here is the last supermarket you'll see. A 25-minute drive alongside the ocean and through plantations brings you to the ❷ **Daintree River Ferry** (p411), the only way to enter the rainforest from the south.

Wind through tropical rainforest to the ❸ **Mt Alexandra Lookout** for sweeping coastal views, then make a longer stop at the ❹ **Daintree Discovery Centre** (p411). Its 23m canopy tower, aerial walkway and jungle bug room make it a hit with kids and it is packed with vital info on the park's biodiversity and conservation.

Just 5km down the road, settle into the lush surrounds at the ❺ **Daintree Ice Cream Company** (with flavours like wattle seed to enjoy). Slow down near ❻ **Cooper Creek** – you might spot a cassowary.

Then stretch your legs at the ❼ **Madja Boardwalk** (p411), an excellent 1.2km wheelchair-accessible loop through rainforest and moody mangroves. Next up, 10 minutes further on, ❽ **Mason's Cafe** croc burgers and jackfruit smoothies. For more tropical flavours, sample exotic fruit at ❾ **Cape Trib Farm**.

Finish where the rainforest meets the sea at ❿ **Cape Trib Beach House** (p460), the end of the sealed road, with dining and direct beach access.

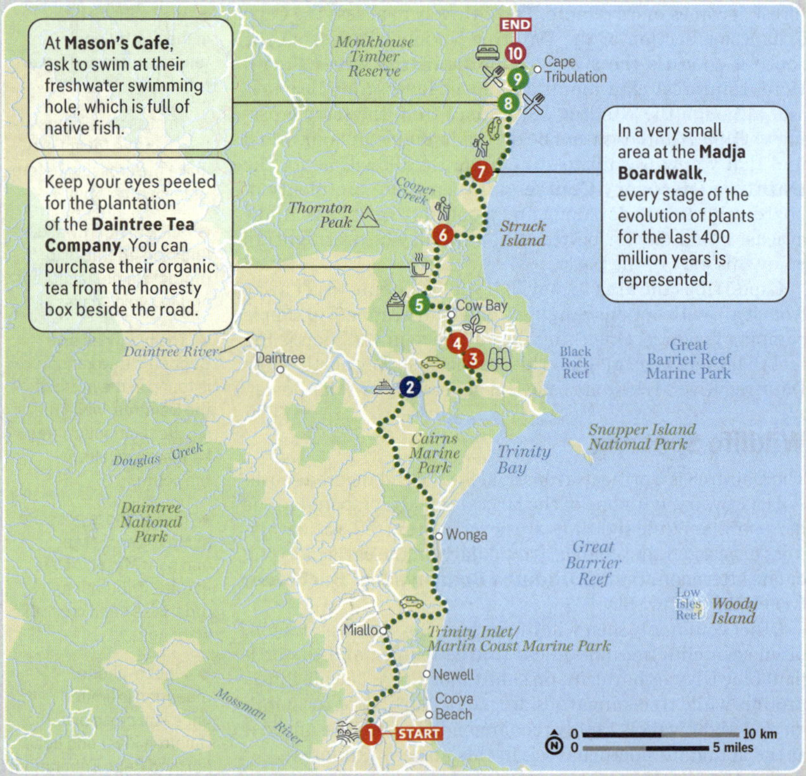

Off-Grid Adventure

Escape to Cape Trib

At the end of the winding sealed road from the Daintree River and, with its two magnificent beaches, laid-back vibe and rainforest walks, Cape Trib is a little slice of tropical paradise. 'Discovered' by backpackers in the early 1980s, it became a part of the India–Goa–Bali trail and continues to lure east-coast travellers. There are a few more up-market offerings these days but there's still plenty of off-grid adventure to be had. The Great Barrier Reef is just 30 minutes offshore (by thrilling inflatable) from Cape Trib, making half-day snorkel tours with **Ocean Safari** *(oceansafari.com.au; adult/child $207/141)* an alluring option (7.30am and 11.30am daily; bookings essential). Or for a slower pace, **Cape Trib Horse Rides** *(capetribhorserides.com.au; adult/child aged 10+ $184/138)* offers ride horses along the pristine beach (11am and 2.30pm daily; bookings essential). Or simply set the alarm for sunrise. If there's a place to take in the beauty of the beach at first light, it's here.

4WD Fun in the Rainforest

Tackle the Bloomfield Track

If you plan to head north to Cooktown, consider your choices. If you're in a 2WD, turn around at Cape Trib, head back to Mossman and head west to the sealed Mulligan Hwy. If you're experienced, well prepared and up for 4WD excitement, consider the legendary **Bloomfield Track**, originally planned as a coastal road to Cooktown. The 32km unsealed road is packed with steep terrain and a couple of hairy creek crossings and is a must-do for adventurous 4WDers. Check conditions before you go at *cook.qld.gov.au/services/roads/road-conditions-closures*.

BIRD WATCHING IN THE DAINTREE

The Daintree hosts over 430 bird species, making it a hot spot for spectacular sightings. Birds tend to vary depending on the season. Winter is a great time to spot a Wompoo fruit dove, a marvellously multicoloured pigeon. In November, you might catch the striking buff-breasted paradise kingfisher when it migrates to the rainforest from New Guinea. It's bright blue and yellow plumage is a sight to behold.

The southern cassowary, a towering, flightless ancient bird, can appear along creeks year-round and is vital for seed dispersal. The shy mangrove robin can often be seen among the roots of tidal flats. Lots of birds depart for warmer climates in the dry season, but dollarbirds and rainbow bee-eaters arrive to show off their colours.

EATING NORTH OF THE DAINTREE RIVER: OUR PICKS

Daintree Fan Palm Farm: Organic coffee, cakes, pies, whole foods and ready-made meals are offered at this idyllic Diwan farm. *hours vary* $

Mason's Cafe: A Cape Trib institution, Mason's has been serving up rustic, no-frills (croc and emu) burgers for years. *11am-3pm* $

Tides Bar & Restaurant: This Cape Trib Beach House open-air restaurant with beach access offers all-day dining and kids meals. *8am-10pm* $$

Cassowary Bar & Restaurant: Modern Australian at the Ferntree Rainforest Lodge. *bar 4pm-late, restaurant 5-8pm* $$

Cooktown & Cape York

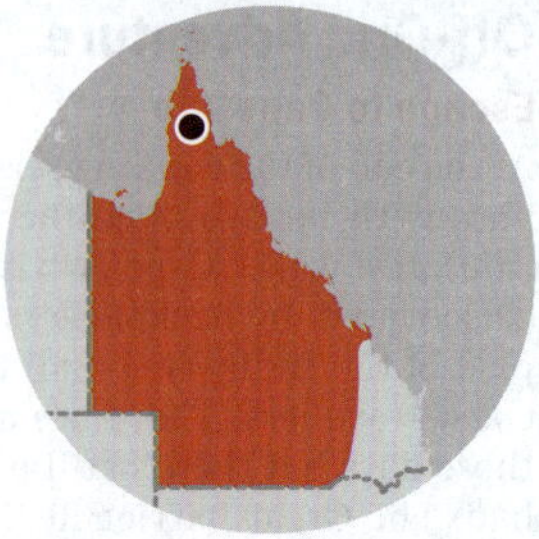

REMOTE ADVENTURE | HISTORICAL HOT SPOT | OUTBACK CHARACTERS

Places

Coastal Cooktown, considered the gateway to Cape York, is an easy-going place with good accommodation, dining, beaches and gardens. It's a small town with a big history: for thousands of years, Waymbuurr was the place the local Guugu Yimithirr and Kuku Yalanji people used as a meeting ground. It was here in 1770 that Lieutenant (later Captain) James Cook beached the *Endeavour*, which had earlier struck a reef offshore from Cape Tribulation. Cook's crew spent 48 days repairing the damage, making Cooktown Australia's first (albeit transient) non-Indigenous colony.

Rugged and remote, Cape York Peninsula has one of the wildest tropical environments on the planet. The overland pilgrimage north to 'the Tip', the northernmost point of mainland Australia, is an exhilarating 4WD trek into one of the country's last great frontiers, while the area around Laura is home to the Quinkan rock-art sites, recognised by UNESCO as some of the world's finest.

GETTING AROUND

You'll want your own wheels to go exploring up here. Sealed roads will get you to Cooktown and Laura, but to go any further north you'll need a 4WD, preferably a rugged one. Trans North runs buses between Cairns and Cooktown. Hinterland Aviation flies between Cairns and Cooktown, while Skytrans, REX Regional Express and QantasLink operate flights into the main communities on Cape York. Cooktown itself is small and relatively easy to navigate on foot. Getting around becomes a whole different ball game in the Wet.

Cooktown

TIME FROM CAIRNS: **4HR**

Cooktown weekends are quiet; visit during the week for more signs of life.

Australia's first reconciliation

Believed to be the site of the first recorded reconciliation between Indigenous Australians and Europeans, **Reconciliation Rocks** is just a two-minute walk from Charlotte St. Wander among the public art and reflect upon the generosity of locals when Cook and his crew stole some darts (spears).

Deep dive into Cooktown's past

A former convent built in 1899, the **Cooktown Museum** *(nationaltrustqld.org.au/visitor-sites/Cooktown-Museum; adult/child $25/15)* explores rich stories of the region, covering Indigenous culture, social history, Cook's visit (the *Endeavour's* cannon and anchor are displayed here, recovered in 1969) and the Chinese contribution during the Palmer River gold rush.

After the gold ran out, Cooktown's population declined. During WWII, those who were left were evacuated. For more

insight into the boom-and-bust years of Cooktown, visit the **Cooktown History Centre** *(cooktownhistory.org.au; $8).*

Drive (or climb the bush trail from the Botanical Gardens and Cherry Tree Bay) to **Grassy Hill Lookout**, the 162m hill that Cook and naturalist Joseph Banks summitted, hoping to spot a passage out through the reefs in 1770. The 360-degree views of Cooktown, the Endeavour River and Coral Sea are wonderful, especially at sunset. The lighthouse was built in 1886.

TOP TIPS FOR THE TIP

Duration: Plenty of travellers spend months up here but definitely allow at least 10 to 14 days for the return journey from Cairns.

When to go: It's best between June and October. The peak period is July to August. If you want to avoid crowds, September and October are good, but it will be getting warm.

Booking camp sites: For Cape York's national parks, book online well in advance through the Queensland National Parks Booking Service *(book.parks.qld.gov.au).*

Be croc smart: Crocs inhabit Cape York's waterways; heed warning signs and be vigilant when around water. Never leave food or discard scraps near water.

Alcohol restrictions: Applies to all visitors; in some communities, alcohol is banned completely and cannot be carried in. Fines can be huge.

EATING IN COOKTOWN: OUR PICKS

Balcony Restaurant: The balcony here overlooks the main street; enjoy pub-style meals, cold beer and sunset views. *11am-2pm & 5-10pm* **$$**

Jackey Jackey Thai: Authentic Thai food (don't be put off by appearances!); perfect if you're over pub meals. *4.30-9pm Tue-Sat* **$**

Cooktown Bowls Club: Generous meals with views of the sunset and bowling greens; roast on Sundays. *noon-2pm & 5.30-8.30pm* **$$**

Cooktown Memorial RSL: Some of the best meals in town at the RSL (Returned & Services League of Australia) bistro. *10am-10pm Mon-Sat, to 6pm Sun* **$$**

BIODIVERSITY IN COOKTOWN & CAPE YORK

Cooktown sits at the southern gateway to the Cape York Peninsula bioregion, a rare convergence of ecosystems that makes it one of Australia's most ecologically diverse areas. The region features wet tropics and dry savannah woodland (Kalkajaka, also known as Black Mountain, is the meeting of the two), heathlands, windswept sandy dunes and wetlands. This variety supports more than 3300 vascular plant species and over 500 terrestrial vertebrates, including many rare or endemic species that attract botanists and zoologists alike.

From lush rainforest alive with the majestic southern cassowary to open savannahs where the endemic and endangered golden-shouldered parrot flits between termite mounds – travelling through this rugged country reveals how dramatically the landscape shifts, sometimes in the space of a single day's journey.

Gold-rush gardens and botanical art

The tranquil 62-hectare **Cooktown Botanic Gardens**, established in 1878 at the height of the gold rush, is one of Queensland's oldest. Stop by the gallery and cafe, **Nature's Powerhouse**, which has a superb collection of the late Vera Scarth-Johnson's botanical illustrations, and the excellent gift shop. Marked walking trails lead to Finch and Cherry Tree Bay.

Gourmet sunsets and colonial relics along the river

Cooktown can be steamy, but wander north along the esplanade to catch the breeze and soak up views of the river and Coral Sea. Walk towards the **Cooktown Powder Magazine** (a restored explosives storehouse from 1875) and you'll find a small **public splash park** that should keep the kids happy!

To get on the water, **Riverbend Tours** *(riverbendtours.com.au; adult/child $60/35)* runs sunset cruises, where you can partake in gourmet cheese and BYO wine. Keep your eyes peeled for crocs in the mangroves.

Wujal Wujal Falls & Bloomfield

TIME FROM COOKTOWN: **1HR**

If you can't tackle the Bloomfield Track from Cape Tribulation, Bloomfield is 2WD accessible from Cooktown. Driving north to south, the road is sealed all the way to Wujal Wujal.

Journey south for cultural falls and iconic pub yarns

Head south of Cooktown, pass the mysterious looming boulders of Kalkajaka (Black Mountain) and turn left at Shiptons Flat Rd. Drive through Rossville (home of the three-day **Wallaby Creek Festival** held in September) and continue to the peaceful **Black Cockatoo Gallery** *(blackcockatoogallery.com.au)*, open every day April to December, to enjoy the art, coffee and gardens. To reach **Wujal Wujal Falls**, follow the signs from the car park. It's a short, uneven scramble in (not recommended for the less agile) but truly impressive when it's pounding. Sacred to the local community, many of the waterfalls are reserved for female members only. Excellent guided tours with Indigenous women from the Walker family are available (call Kathleen on 07-4083 9100; bookings essential). There are crocodiles here so don't be tempted to swim.

On the way back, stop by one of Queensland's most iconic pubs, the **Lion's Den Hotel** (30km from Cooktown). It was established in 1875 and is still going strong – there's nothing

EATING IN COOKTOWN: OUR PICKS

Bektopia: Top coffee and the best view in town; brekkie and poke bowls and gluten-free/vegan options. *6.30am-2pm Mon-Fri* $

122 on Charlotte: Coffee, cake and gelato in the historic Cooktown bank, with lots of original features. *8am-2pm Mon-Fri* $

Shipwreck Bar & Cafe: An excellent all-day cafe with a deep, breezy verandah; try the Fijian curry for dinner. *9.30am-8.30pm Mon-Sat, to 3pm Sun* $

Lion's Den Hotel: Just 25 minutes south of Cooktown, Lion's Den serves up steaks the size of your face and atmosphere in spades; pizzas all day. *9am-late* $

PAUL HARDING/LONELY PLANET

Lion's Den Hotel

pretentious here! Folks from far and wide turn out in droves for live music on Friday and Saturday nights; this place is a must.

Laura

TIME FROM CAIRNS: **4HR**

At the end of the sealed road, Laura is the gateway to Cape York. It's 4WDs-only past here. But tiny Laura is worth a visit – it's home to Quinkan Country rock art, recognised by UNESCO as one of the world's top 10 rock-art sites.

Quinkan rock art

The Laura region is the home of the Ang Gnarra people, who are the Custodians of the Quinkan sites. The area boasts hundreds of rock-art galleries depicting the giant Quinkan spirit figures on the sandstone escarpments, where Ang Gnarra people used to spend the Wet in the comfort of the dry caves.

The excellent **Quinkan & Regional Cultural Centre** *(anggnarra.org.au)* in Laura covers the history of the region and offers insightful tours of the Giant Horse and Mushroom rock-art sites. Bookings essential for guided tours; closed Sundays. **Split Rock Gallery** *($33)* has self-guided access (signposted 12km south of Laura, via a steepish track) but a guided tour will provide a much deeper understanding of these ancient paintings.

For a truly magical immersive adventure, stay on Country with **Jarramali Rock Art Tours** *(jarramalirockarttours.com.au; from $350)*. Johnny Murison, a Western Yalanji man and host, welcomes all with open arms; you won't regret a single moment. Bookings essential.

Laura Quinkan three-day cultural festival

The biennial **Laura Quinkan Dance Festival** *(lauraquinkanfestival.com.au)* is believed to be the longest running Aboriginal cultural festival in Australia, with communities

TOP TIP

This is a place to go in the Dry (May to October here). Mobile-phone reception is limited to large towns, if at all. Carry a satellite phone, UHF or HF radio and/or a personal locator beacon in case of emergencies.

BEST INDIGENOUS ART CENTRES

Spaces can close for Indigenous sorry business; call ahead to avoid disappointment.

Kuku Bulkaway Indigenous Art Gallery: Small gallery in Cooktown showcasing the paintings, jewellery and weavings of Cape York region artists.

Hope Vale Arts & Cultural Centre: Excellent showcase of local Indigenous art in Hope Vale, a small community 40 minutes' drive north of Cooktown on sealed roads.

Quinkan & Regional Cultural Centre: Very informative and insightful displays about the region.

Western Cape Cultural Centre: A gallery packed with history, culture and art on the water in Weipa. Includes Aurukun camp dog sculptures.

Northern Peninsula Area Art Centre: Wonderful gallery and art centre at New Mapoon, between Bamaga and Seisia.

CHAMELEONSEYE/SHUTTERSTOCK

from across Cape York and the Torres Strait coming together to celebrate with music, dance, singing and cultural performances. Camping and campervan facilities are available on-site. Book ahead.

Cape York

TIME FROM CAIRNS: **2 WEEKS**

This is 4WD country, preferably during the Dry. Tackle the Tip yourself or take a tour.

DIY to the top of Australia

Driving to **the Tip** of Cape York is one of Australia's great adventures. The untamed landscape undergoes a spectacular transformation each year when the torrential rains of the wet season set in – rough, dry earth turns to rich red mud and trickling creek beds swell to raging rivers. The Great Dividing Range forms the spine of the Cape: tropical rainforests and palm-fringed beaches flank its eastern side; sweeping savannah woodlands, eucalyptus forests and coastal mangroves are on its west.

If sticking to the main (easiest) track during the Dry, anyone with a high-clearance 4WD, a sense of adventure and adequate experience and preparation can drive up 'Cape Corrugations' to the Tip. If that's you, take it on. If not, don't go.

If you're heading off the main track, it's essential to prepare. Carry spare tyres, tools, winching equipment, food and plenty of drinking water. Check up-to-date road conditions at *cook.qld.gov.au/services/roads/road-conditions-closures*. Mobile-phone service is very limited so consider taking a satellite

Old Telegraph Track

phone. Don't head into remote areas alone; travel in a convoy of at least two 4WD vehicles.

It's possible to hire a vehicle from **4WD Hire Cairns** *(4wdhirecairns.com.au; per day from $500)*, but double-check which routes you are allowed to drive.

Guided tours to the Tip

If you're travelling solo, nervous about driving or short on time, a tour is the best option. Most depart from Cairns or Cooktown between April and October and range from seven to 14 days with no more than 20 passengers. An early or late wet season may affect dates. The Torres Strait Islands are usually an optional extra. Transport can be by land, air and/or sea, while accommodation is camping or basic motels.

The Cape York Day Tour with **Daintree Air Services** *(daintreeair.com.au; from Cooktown $1799)* runs from April to November and is the world's longest scenic flight – it certainly packs a punch! You'll fly low over the reef and Cape York before a 4WD takes you overland to the Tip. Departures are also available from Cairns (from $1999).

The guys at **Cape York Motorcycle Adventures** *(capeyorkmotorcycles.com.au; from $2040)* have been offering fully supported dirt-bike adventures from Cairns to the Tip for 35 years. Trips range from three to eight days, including the epic Bucket List Tour (from $7940).

Far North Escapes *(farnorthescapes.com.au; from $4950)* runs five- to 16-day trips to the Tip of Cape York in rugged 4WD vehicles.

OLD TELEGRAPH TRACK (OTT)

The OTT follows the original telegraph line through the Cape York Peninsula, which was used to connect Cairns with Thursday Island. It operated from 1885 until 1962 with two wires. The line was upgraded to radio during WWII and was still in use as a telephone cable until 1987.

These days, it's a legendary 350km 4WD track that was featured on the *World's Most Dangerous Roads* TV series. While hardcore 4WDers consider it fun rather than dangerous, it's definitely tough going for the inexperienced. Many take the useful southern and northern bypass roads to dodge as much of it as they can. The OTT is accessible only during the Dry (May to October).

Torres Strait Islands

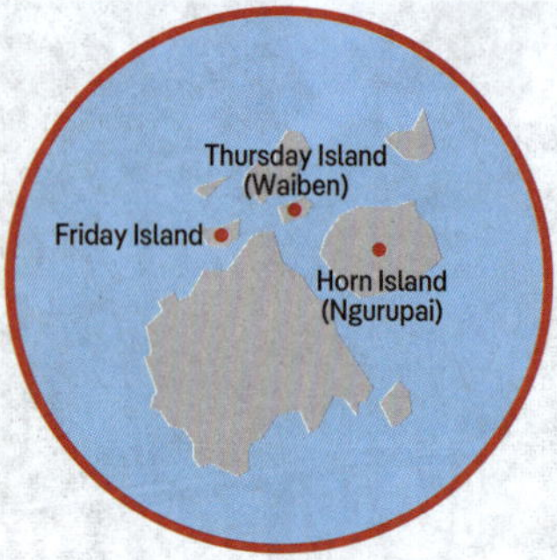

REMOTE ADVENTURE | INDIGENOUS CULTURE | INTRIGUING HISTORY

Scattered like stepping stones across 150km of turquoise sea between Cape York and Papua New Guinea, the 274 islands of the Torres Strait (Zenadth Kes) are rich in culture and history. Only 17 are inhabited and just a handful welcome visitors, but even a brief stay offers a window into one of Australia's most vibrant Indigenous cultures. Torres Strait Islanders, predominantly of Melanesian descent, have preserved their own languages and customs for thousands of years, living in close harmony with land and sea.

Fringed by coral reefs, mangroves and sandy beaches, the islands have a natural beauty matched by a dramatic past. Once a global source of pearl shell for buttons, the strait is also home to the RMS *Quetta* shipwreck. Military history draws visitors too, as the Torres Strait played a key role during WWII. Largely undeveloped for tourism, the region rewards those seeking culture, nature and history in equal measure.

Horn Island (Ngurupai)

TIME FROM HORN ISLAND AIRPORT: **10MIN**

If you're flying to the Torres Strait, you'll arrive at Horn Island Airport. The island's main drawcard is its WWII history – it was the second-most bombed site in Australia after Darwin.

GETTING AROUND

Thursday (Waiben or TI) and Horn (Ngurupai) are the most accessible and visited Torres Strait islands. Horn Island handles all flights (Qantas from Cairns and **Cape Air Transport** or **Hinterland Aviation** for inter-island services); Thursday Island is the administrative hub and main population centre. Travelling between the two is easy: **Time & Tide Transport** *(timeandtidetransport.com.au)* and **Rebel Marine** *(rebeltours.com.au)* run regular ferries; water taxis can be arranged after hours. Both also offer bus-ferry combo tickets from the airport. From the mainland, **Peddells Ferry Service** *(peddellsferry.com.au)* runs year-round from Seisia to Thursday Island; bookings essential.

Both townships are compact and walkable. Visitors with limited mobility may prefer wheels to reach Green Hill Fort or the cemetery. Hire a car or join a guided tour with Zenadth Kes Tours (p424). On Horn Island, **Torres Strait Heritage Museum** will get you to the WWII sites. For bespoke trips or excursions to outer islands, contact Strait Experience (p424) or Torres Strait Eco Adventures (p424).

JOHN CRUX/SHUTTERSTOCK

Thursday Island

Soak up WWII history

During WWII, Japanese aircraft attacked Horn Island several times. Civilians were evacuated, but around 5000 troops and airmen remained, including the Torres Strait Light Infantry Battalion – Australia's first and only all–First Nations army unit.

Military buffs shouldn't miss Torres Strait Heritage's engaging **In Their Steps Tour** *(torresstraittours.com.au; incl museum entry $95)*. It's a fascinating circuit of gun emplacements, the old airstrip, aircraft wrecks and other wartime sites. Bookings essential.

Run by Vanessa and Liberty Seekee, passionate custodians of the island's history, the **Torres Strait Heritage Museum** *(torresstraittours.com.au; $10)* is an excellent companion visit. Its photographs and artefacts illuminate this often-overlooked chapter of Australia's wartime story, alongside exhibits on Torres Strait culture, pearling and island life.

TOP TIP

Plan ahead, accommodation is limited and books out early. If need be, stay on Horn Island and catch the ferry to TI. Visit during the Dry (May to September here). There's no ocean swimming – crocs, sharks and stingers also call the Torres Strait home.

Thursday Island (Waiben or TI)

TIME FROM HORN ISLAND AIRPORT: **25MIN** +

The administrative capital of the Torres Strait, Thursday Island is just 3.5 sq km in size, with two relaxed main streets and a population of about 2800. It punches well above its weight when it comes to history and culture.

Culture on TI

The excellent **Gab Titui Cultural Centre** *(gabtitui.gov.au; free)*, near the wharf, has two gallery spaces dedicated to the display of both contemporary Torres Strait Islander and Aboriginal work and historical artefacts. Striking 'ghost nets' made from abandoned fishing nets and intricate pieces by contemporary artist Alick Tipoti are highlights. The gallery

GUIDED BY THE WINDS

It's almost always breezy in the Torres Strait, so it's little wonder that local life and language revolve around the winds. Kuki, the wet season (January–April), brings strong northwesterlies, heavy rain and steamy days. When dragonflies appear, Sager, the dry season (May–December) begins, marked by cooler southeast trade winds.

Two other winds, Zey and Nay Gay, can blow at different times of the year: Zey is a southerly that cools the ocean and the air, while Nay Gay, a northerly, signals the approach of turtle-mating season from October to December. It's the hottest, most humid time of year – and a reminder that in the Torres Strait, the winds don't just shape the weather, they shape life itself.

CYNTHIA A JACKSON/SHUTTERSTOCK

gift shop has a wonderful selection of books on Torres Strait history, original art, prints, clothing and jewellery.

Wander around the corner to **Island Stars** *(islandstars.com.au)* for a coffee and a crayfish toastie (TI's best!) and immerse yourself in the Migi Malu experience (from $100; three-course Ailan 'island' feast extra; bookings essential). It's an unforgettable traditional dance, storytelling and musical show and you'll personally meet the performers and feel part of the show. Don't miss the gallery of Torres Strait lino carvings and paintings; renowned artist Joey Laifoo is Island Stars' owner.

For more local art, visit **Rosie Ware Designs** *(rosiewaredesigns.com)* in Rosie's home studio perched high on Hargrave St; it has one of the best views of town. For other crafts and produce, **Port Kennedy Association Inc Mini Markets** are held fortnightly, on Saturdays from 8.30am to noon, in the Port Kennedy Hall on Douglas St.

Winds of Zenadth Indigenous dance festival

In September, every two years, TI bursts into colour for the **Winds of Zenadth Cultural Festival** *(torres.qld.gov.au)*, a

EATING & DRINKING IN THE TORRES STRAIT ISLANDS: OUR PICKS

Torres Hotel: 'Australia's Top Pub' – there are none further north! Plenty of seafood and cold beer; on Thursday Island. *11am-10.30pm Mon-Sat* **$$**

Grand Hotel: Tuck in to pub fare on the outdoor deck overlooking the ocean on Thursday Island; close to the wharf. *11am-9pm Sun-Thu, to 10pm Fri & Sat* **$$**

Wongai Beach Hotel: Horn Island's local joint, with typical pub-counter meals for lunch and dinner and a beer garden. *noon-9.30pm Sun-Wed, to 10pm Thu-Sat* **$$**

Gateway Torres Strait Resort: This Horn Island resort restaurant and bar serves dinner nightly; bookings essential. *dinner 6-9pm* **$$**

Green Hill Fort

four-day celebration of Torres Strait life and cultural identity. Communities from across the islands and mainland gather for dance, song, feasting and parades – it's one of Queensland's most vibrant Indigenous festivals and well worth visiting.

The 2025 event featured more than 60 performances by dancers and musicians, plus markets and street parades. Most of the action happens after the sun goes down (when it is substantially cooler) and the final day is the liveliest (and a public holiday). Book flights and accommodation early and note that extra night ferries run between Horn Island and TI during the event, making Horn Island an option for accommodation.

Forts, flags and local legends

Trek up the hill behind town to **Green Hill Fort**, built in 1891 to defend against a feared Russian invasion and one of Australia's most well-preserved forts. Here you can wander between gun emplacements and take in the superb sea views (it's the highest point on Thursday Island). There's also a small underground museum here that recounts the fort's history and strategic significance.

TORRES STRAIT 8: CLIMATE JUSTICE TRAILBLAZERS

In 2019, eight Torres Strait Islanders – the Torres Strait 8 – brought a landmark complaint to the UN Human Rights Committee, challenging Australia's failure to act on climate change. In 2015, the government had warned that some communities might need to relocate within decades, as rising seas threaten homes, cultural sites and graves. Although the High Court ruled against them, in September 2022 the UN Committee found that Australia was violating their human rights, marking the first time a UN body has held a government accountable for climate inaction affecting Indigenous peoples. Their fight highlights the impact of climate change on Torres Strait communities, from changing coastlines to the challenges of island life and the resilience of people their maintaining culture and traditions in a shifting environment.

EATING & DRINKING IN THE TORRES STRAIT ISLANDS: OUR PICKS

Ma:Kai: On Thursday Island, the best spot for a refreshing juice with locals on the waterfront. Don't miss the Beach Boy or Blind Melon. *6.30am-1.30pm* $

Island Stars: Snack on a crayfish toastie and immerse yourself in the art and dancing; a TI must-visit. *6am-1pm Mon-Sat* $

Thursday Island Bowls Club: Classic Sunday roasts, a top-notch beachside location, live music and loads of local character. *4.30-11.30pm Wed-Fri, 3-11.30pm Sun* $

Federal Hotel-Motel: Sip a cold one right on the water's edge on TI and don't miss the vintage wall murals. *hours vary* $

PUBLIC HOLIDAYS & CELEBRATIONS

These public holidays mark defining moments of island identity – and are a vibrant time to visit.

Torres Strait Flag Day: (29 May) Marks the official presentation of the late Bernard Namok Snr's flag in 1992.

Mabo Day: (3 June) Australia's first successful native title claim, led by Eddie 'Koiki' Mabo, when the High Court recognised traditional land rights on Mer (Murray Island).

Coming of the Light: (1 July) Commemorates Christianity's arrival at Erub in 1871 with enactments, church services, music and feasting.

Anniversary of the First Councillors Meeting: (23 August) Celebrates self-determination, marking the first formal meeting on Masig in 1937.

Winds of Zenadth Cultural Festival: (September) The final day of this biennial event begins with a lively street parade.

Take a leisurely walk (or call a taxi) to visit **Thursday Island Cemetery**, where the dead reflect Torres Strait's fascinating cultural mix. Some 600 Japanese pearl divers are buried here as is Bernard Namok Snr, who passed away at only 31 years of age, just 12 months after designing the Torres Strait Island flag.

It is easy to visit these sites independently but for a more in-depth perspective of the island's layered history, we recommend booking small, guided tours with local operators **Zenadth Kes Tours** *(torresstraitecoadventures.com.au; $40)* or **Torres Strait Heritage** *(torresstraittours.com.au; $45).*

Other Islands

TIME FROM HORN ISLAND AIRPORT: **35MIN**

With planning and permission, it's possible to explore beyond Horn and Thursday Islands.

Visit a pearl farm on Friday Island

A very accessible option, Friday Island (a 15-minute boat ride from TI) offers a window into the region's pearling past. Visit **Kazu Pearl Farm** *(bookings 07-4069 1268; incl TI pickup $70)*, where you'll learn about the delicate art of pearl cultivation, hear stories about when Torres Strait shell supplied over half the world's demand for mother-of-pearl buttons and share a Japanese morning tea on the picturesque deck. Bookings essential.

Go local with Strait Experience

Strait Experience *(straitexperience.com.au)*, a Torres Strait–owned company, takes travellers beyond the well-trodden path. Using deep local networks, Fraser and his team tailor trips to individual interests – arranging homestays and cultural visits to islands rarely open to outsiders. They also run one- and three-day round-trip packages from Cairns (from $2753).

Adventure in the Strait

Torres Strait Eco Adventures *(torresstraitecoadventures.com.au; from $250)* offers fishing charters in dazzling, remote waters and trips to seldom-visited islands like Goodes (with its 19th-century lighthouse) and Prince of Wales (Muralag) – take a dip in the majestic waterfalls during the Wet. Hammond Island (Kiriri; permission required) is an unsubmerged remnant of Australia's Great Dividing Range and the site of a former Catholic mission.

TRAVELSCAPE IMAGES/ALAMY

Kazu Pearl Farm

Mission Beach

GORGEOUS BEACH | WILDLIFE SPOTTING | OUTDOOR ACTIVITIES

TOP TIP

You may be surprised to find few people swimming at such a beautiful beach. Obey all posted warnings of stingers (jellyfish) and saltwater crocodiles. There are stinger nets at Mission Beach and at the northern end of South Mission Beach for those keen to get into the water.

This tropical enclave of enticing beach hamlets is a serene balance of yoga living, backpacker paradise and eco-escape, making Mission Beach a worthy detour. With Australia's highest density of cassowaries, you'll have the best chance to see this extraordinary bird here. Hidden among rainforest, Mission Beach is also one of the closest access points to the Great Barrier Reef and the gateway to Dunk Island. These are the traditional lands of the Djiru people.

The beach is a glorious 14km of sand, split into four distinct communities. The northernmost is Bingil Bay, with secluded beaches and a charming cafe. Mission Beach itself lies directly south, with a village of restaurants, bars, boutiques, accommodation and an excellent information centre. In the middle is Wongaling Beach, with a supermarket, school, pool and town facilities. South Mission Beach has holiday homes and a popular camping ground.

Looking for Cassowaries

The endangered flightless bird

Driving into Mission Beach from the Bruce Hwy, one of the first things you'll notice is the yellow road signs asking you to slow down due to the presence of cassowaries. You're on what is known as the **Cassowary Coast**, home to the country's

GETTING AROUND

The freedom of having your own wheels will be greatly appreciated in the Mission Beach area, especially when exploring, going to the supermarket and looking for cassowaries. Mission Beach Taxi and rideshare operators are other options. The Mission Beach village area is compact and easy to get around on foot; you'll want wheels to head south to Wongaling Beach and South Mission Beach. Outdoor companies often provide transfers, especially for activities such as rafting and skydiving. Heading offshore? There are boat transfers to Dunk Island and further afield if you're diving.

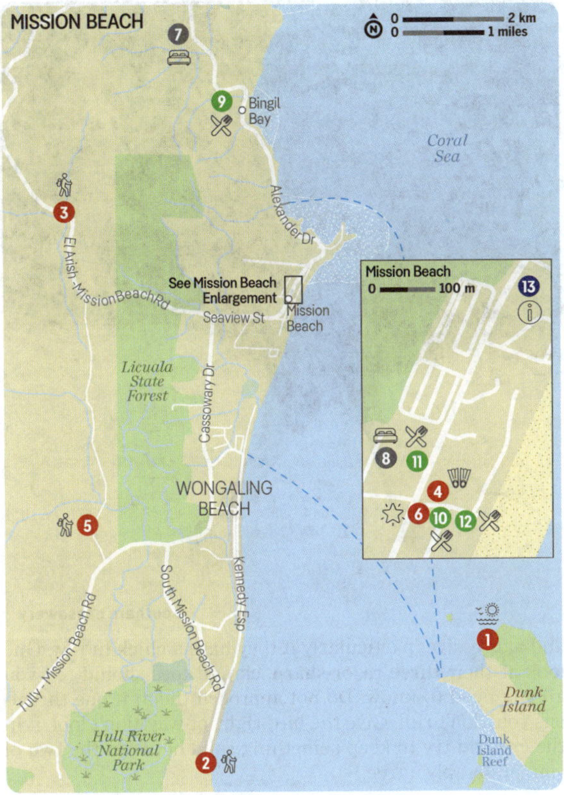

SIGHTS
1 Muggy Muggy Beach

ACTIVITIES
2 Kennedy Walking Track
3 Lacey Creek Track
4 Mission Beach Dive
5 Rainforest Circuit
6 Skydive Australia

SLEEPING
7 Jackaroo Treehouse Hostel
8 Rainforest Motel

EATING
9 Bingil Bay Cafe
10 Garage Bar & Brewhouse
11 Mission Beach Tavern
12 Plenty Restaurant & Bar

INFORMATION
13 Mission Beach Visitor Centre

highest concentration of these amazing endangered birds, and their biggest threat is...fast cars. So drive slow, keep your eyes open and if you're lucky, you may see one of these large, flightless birds walking roadside, through farm fields or gardens, or even swimming across a river. Early morning is the best time to spot them.

Of course, you can up your chances by taking a walk in an area around Mission Beach known to be frequented by cassowaries. Head to the **Mission Beach Visitor Centre** for the latest news and advice. The 1.5km **Lacey Creek Track**, about 6km west of Mission Beach on the El Arish Rd, is a good spot and a lovely family-friendly walk. The easy, graded 1.6km **Rainforest Circuit** in Licuala State Forest on the Tully Mission Beach Rd is also frequented by cassowaries. The **Kennedy Bay Walking Track** to Lugger Bay from the southern end of South Mission Beach is another possibility – check tide times before heading out on this easy track. As kids can be liberal with lunch handouts, you might also pay attention when passing the local school!

While seeing your first cassowary up close can be a captivating experience, keep in mind that they can be unpredictable

THE ENDANGERED CASSOWARY

This flightless prehistoric bird struts through the rainforest like something out of *Jurassic Park*. It can be as tall as a fully grown adult, has a bright-blue head, red wattles (the lobes hanging from its neck), a helmetlike horn, three clawed toes and shaggy black feathers similar to an emu.

The cassowary is an important link in the rainforest ecosystem. It's the only animal capable of dispersing the seeds of more than 70 species of trees whose fruit is too large for other rainforest animals to digest and pass. It is estimated that there are around 4000 cassowaries left in Australia.

Fun fact: the males incubate the eggs and raise the hatchlings.

Southern cassowary

and aggressive, particularly if they have a chick in tow. One look at their three razor-sharp, clawed toes should tell you all you need to know. Do not approach them; if one threatens you, don't run. Give the bird right-of-way, don't look it in the eye and try to keep something solid between the two of you, preferably a tree.

Adventures on Water

The quieter side of the Great Barrier Reef

Head to the outer Great Barrier Reef with **Mission Beach Dive** *(missionbeachdive.com.au; from $239)* for snorkelling and diving. With crystal-clear waters and fewer crowds than more popular destinations along the Great Barrier Reef, Mission Beach is a great place to explore. The closest reef is an hour away by boat and teeming with vibrant coral, tropical fish, turtles and even reef sharks gliding along the colourful underwater world. Mission Beach Dive also offers dive school courses for first-timers and those who need a refresher.

EATING & DRINKING IN MISSION BEACH: OUR PICKS

Plenty Restaurant & Bar: Views of the beach, an upmarket menu, cocktails and top service. *hours vary* $$

Mission Beach Tavern: Survey the village from the pub's terrace while enjoying a simple meal and a cold beer. Big TVs for sport. *10am-10pm* $$

Bingil Bay Cafe: This lavender-painted cafe has great breakfast and vegetarian options. Live music on Fridays. *7am-8pm Tue-Sat, 7am-4pm Sun* $$

Garage Bar & Brewhouse: Lively beer garden serving its house-brewed beers on tap, plus pizzas and tacos. Often live music on weekends. *3-9pm* $$

Island in the Sun

While the day away on Dunk Island

There are daily **boat transfers** *(dunkislandreefadventures.com; $75)* to Dunk Island, the island directly offshore from Mission Beach. The 30-minute transfer departs Clump Point at 8.45am and leaves Dunk Island at 4.30pm. Dunk features lush jungle, white-sand beaches and walking trails that criss-cross the island. offers secluded swimming and snorkelling spots just 45 minutes' walk from Clump Point. The challenging 7km Mt Kootaloo circuit meanders through rainforest and eucalypts before leading to the summit with a view over the Family Islands and the nearby mainland, taking two to three hours to complete. Food and accommodation are limited – Dunk Island Spit Restaurant is the sole restaurant and has limited hours, while camping is your only accommodation option. If you're interested in fishing, stop in the information centre – they'll gladly point you in the right direction.

Mission Beach from Above

Skydive to the beach

Consider a tandem jump with **Skydive Australia** *(skydive.com.au; from $379)*. Free fall from up to 15,000ft and take in views of the lush rainforest and Great Barrier Reef below. The golden sands of Mission Beach, right out front of the village, is the landing spot, making the experience a unique one for Australia. Skydive Australia has an office in the village. Not into jumping yourself? Head out to the beach to watch the exhilaration in people's faces as they land.

White-Water Adventures

Explore Tully's raging rapids

For rafting on the mighty Tully River in the Tully Gorge, companies generally provide transfers from Mission Beach for half- and full-day options. **Raging Thunder** *(ragingthunder.com.au; from $229)* is an excellent operator, running for over 30 years on the Tully River, with pickup and drop-off options from Cairns, Mission Beach and Tully. White-water rafting runs year-round, thanks to Tully's trademark downpours and the river's hydroelectric floodgates. Rafting trips are adrenaline-fuelled, coursing through grade 3 and 4 rapids, foaming against a backdrop of stunning rainforest scenery.

AUSTRALIA'S WETTEST TOWN

In Tully's town centre, you'll find their famous golden gumboot, opened in 2003. Standing an impressive 7.9m tall, it's the same height as the cumulative amount of rainfall recorded in Tully in 1950, an Australian record. The idea for a town gumboot came about as a rubber boot was awarded to the wettest town in Australia, according to which town had the most rainfall each year.

The towns of Tully, Innisfail and Babinda all vied for the title annually until Tully decided to erect its gumboot and grab it outright. Climb the spiral staircase, enjoy the historic photos of rainy years past across the district on the way up and take in the views of the town at the top.

Townsville

PARKS & GARDENS | NIGHTLIFE | DIVING

GETTING AROUND

Greyhound and Premier buses stop in Townsville, as does the *Spirit of Queensland* train. Once you're in Townsville, it's easily walkable, with popular attractions like the Strand and Castle Hill within the town's centre. Electric scooters are popular and can be found scattered around the city if you prefer faster transport. Translink (Kinetic) runs local bus services around Townsville as well.

Townsville is the largest city in north Queensland, an easy-going place dominated on one side by the towering Castle Hill and on the other by the waterfront promenade. Many visitors only have eyes for Magnetic Island, a 30-minute ferry ride away, but Townsville is a worthy destination on its own. Take the time to stroll the picturesque Strand, enjoying the ocean views, beaches and free lagoon, or partake in some of the best dining and nightlife north of Noosa. It's a lively town, with plenty to do inside and out. Townsville is a major gateway to the Great Barrier Reef and the country's only underwater art museum, with excellent reef and wreck diving nearby. A beautiful town, it's a great balance of city experiences and relaxed, oceanside enjoyment.

Climbing Castle Hill

Outstanding city views

It's just one of those things you have to do. This striking 286m-high pink granite **monolith** dominates Townsville's skyline and offers stunning 360-degree views of the city and across Cleveland Bay to Magnetic Island. Walk up via the rugged but paved 'goat track' (2km one way) from Hillside Crescent, or try the Cudtheringa Track (1.1km one way), accessed opposite the first car park at the bottom of Castle Hill Rd, for a more moderate incline. Otherwise, drive via Gregory St up the winding 2.6km Castle Hill Rd to the summit car park. A signboard up top details short trails leading to various other lookout points around the hill.

TOP TIP

Climb or drive to the top of Castle Hill to get an overview of town, then do the walk along the waterfront Strand from Memorial Gardens to Rock Pool. Townsville's **Visitor Information Centre** on Flinders St has maps and walking guides.

Back to Nature

Parks and wildlife

Townsville has some beautiful tropical botanic gardens. Heritage-listed **Queens Gardens** *(townsville.qld.gov.au; free)* has ornamental plantings at the base of Castle Hill, with shady lawns perfect for picnicking and a rose garden to

HIGHLIGHTS

1 Museum of Tropical Queensland

SIGHTS

2 ANZAC Memorial Park
3 Army Museum of North Queensland
4 Castle Hill
5 Foreigner
6 Jezzine Barracks
7 Maritime Museum of Townsville
8 Museum of Underwater Art
9 Ocean Siren Sculpture
10 Perc Tucker Regional Gallery
11 Queens Gardens
12 Strand Waterfall

ACTIVITIES

13 Adrenalin Dive
14 Strand Rock pool
15 Strand Water Park
16 Tobruk Memorial Baths

SLEEPING

17 Coral Lodge
18 Rambutan
19 Yongala Lodge

EATING

20 A Touch of Salt
21 Cowboys Leagues Club
22 Garden of Eating
23 Grandma's
24 Jam Corner
25 Longboard Bar & Grill
26 Spirited Goat

DRINKING & NIGHTLIFE

27 Hooch & Fellow
28 Molly Malones
see 18 Rambutan
29 Tiny Mountain Brewery
30 Townsville Brewing Co

SHOPPING

31 Strand Night Market

INFORMATION

32 Visitor Information Centre

Home of the North Queensland Cowboys rugby league team

EATING IN TOWNSVILLE: AFFORDABLE EATS

Grandma's: Cute, plant-filled spot serving a long list of shakshukas, pancakes and blintzes for breakfast and lunch. *7am-2pm Mon-Fri, 7am-3pm Sat & Sun* **$$**

Longboard Bar & Grill: The coolest place in Townsville for a light meal and a drink overlooking the water. *11.30am-9pm* **$$**

Rambutan: Lively rooftop bar restaurant overlooking the hotel's pool (guests only), with wood-fired pizzas, seafood, steaks and cocktails. *noon-10pm* **$$**

Cowboys Leagues Club: Two restaurants with a soundproof indoor/outdoor kids area, as well as a sports bar featuring a 12m TV. *9am-2am Sun-Thu, 9am-4am Fri & Sat* **$$**

explore. Originally set up as trial acclimatisation garden for European colonies, its collection now focuses on colourful flowers, foliage and fruit in the tropical colonial garden. Check out the on-site aviary, home to a variety of native Australian birds such as cockatoos, lorikeets and finches.

About 17km south of Townsville, **Billabong Sanctuary** *(billabongsanctuary.com.au; adult/child $52/35)* is an eco-certified wildlife park that offers up-close-and-personal encounters with Australian wildlife – including koalas, cassowaries, crocodiles and dingoes – in natural habitats. You could easily spend all day here, with feedings, shows and talks every half-hour. The sanctuary provides an intimate experience, centred on a lagoon, with shady walkways that invite lingering.

Townsville's Museum Trail

History, culture and fun

The **Museum of Tropical Queensland** *(museum.qld.gov.au; free)* provides a family-friendly snapshot of this diverse region, from the rainforest and reefs to the story of the shipwrecked *Pandora*, the ship sent to capture the *Bounty* mutineers.

The **Maritime Museum of Townsville** *(tmml.org.au; adult/child $12/6)* is a window into Townsville's seafaring past, including information about the area's involvement in both world wars. With a gallery dedicated to the wreck of the *Yongala,* exhibits on north Queensland's naval industries and tours of the decommissioned patrol boat *Townsville,* it's a great stop to learn about some of the town's history.

Contemporary **Perc Tucker Regional Gallery** *(townsville.qld.gov.au; free)* is housed in a stately 1885-built former bank, with special exhibits often in the vault. Exhibitions focus on north Queensland artists, but the gallery also showcases national and international exhibitions. Check to see if a floor talk, lecture or performance lines up with your visit for a more intimate look into the art space of Townsville.

The **Army Museum of North Queensland** *(amnq.org.au; free)* is a wonderfully informative museum located in the Jezzine Barracks. Run by volunteers, the multigallery museum is well organised into three distinct galleries, housing collections and historic artefacts dating from the late 1800s to the modern day. The museum's focus on the defence efforts of north Queensland provides a real sense of place.

Where the Ocean Meets the Imagination

Dive into the Museum of Underwater Art

Created in 2020, Australia's only underwater art installation is a sight to behold. The **Museum of Underwater Art** (MOUA; *moua.com.au)* consists of the Coral Greenhouse, a large structure with more than 20 individual sculptures 16m below the surface. The installation is slowly attracting coral and marine life, holding the Guinness World Record for the

TIPS FROM A TOWNSVILLES LOCAL

Paul Crocombe, director of **Adrenalin Dive** (p434), shares his tips on the reef and the region. *@adrenalindive*

Favourite dive sites: John Brewer Reef has some good corals and Yongala Reef is a top-10 wreck dive. Wheeler Reef is exceptionally good; the Palm Islands have some great diving but aren't as well known. The reef here is in good condition; there's been less impact from the big cyclones than further north.

Favourite spots on land: Magnetic Island is a must-see with its national park and koala colony. Mt Spec and Crystal Creek in Paluma are also really pretty areas.

Favourite place for a drink: Seaview Hotel has good water views and the Ville (resort casino) has a nice deck. C-Bar is also a good restaurant-bar on the water.

STROLLING THE STRAND

This easy, flat walk follows the Strand's waterfront esplanade, with fine views of Magnetic Island all the way.

START	END	LENGTH
Visitor Information Centre	Army Museum of North Queensland	3.3km; 1hr

Starting at Townsville's ❶ **Visitor Information Centre** (p430), walk down Flinders St, the main nightlife strip, past the ❷ **Museum of Tropical Queensland** and on to the southern end of the Strand at ❸ **ANZAC Memorial Park**, with its war memorials and outlook to the Breakwater Marina.

Just past Mariner's Dr is the ❹ **Tobruk Memorial Baths**, the town's main pool and training ground for numerous Olympians. Kids will also love the adjacent and free ❺ **Strand Water Park**, a great place to cool off. Continue on to Strand Park, where the jetty is popular with locals casting a fishing line and you can view the ❻ **Ocean Siren sculpture** (p434), part of MOUA. It's only another 500m to the ❼ **Strand Rockpool**, a wonderful free swimming lagoon with lawns, mini beaches, lifeguards and the excellent Rockpool Pavilion restaurant. Stop in at Tan Lines Distillery to sample their vodka and gin.

The final area is the beautifully redeveloped hilltop Kissing Point Fortifications, with views of Magnetic Island and the (somewhat rare) chance to see turtles and ❽ **Jezzine Barracks**, a 19th-century fort that was in use until 2006. The site is now a series of parks, boardwalks, monuments and public artworks, as well as the ❾ **Army Museum of North Queensland**.

TOWNSVILLE AT WAR

Due to Townsville's advantageous location in the Pacific, it became an important military base during WWII. With a major military base housing up to 90,000 Australian, American and other Allied service personnel, the town was a staging ground for operations in the Southwest Pacific. In July 1942, Townsville's city and harbour were subjected to three air raids by flying Japanese boats.

Although the damage was minimal, it highlighted the town's strategic location. One of the town's major fortifications, Kissing Point Fort, played a key part in the town's coastal defence. Built in 1891 on a rocky headland, it's speculated the fort got its name due to ships' keels 'kissing' the ocean floor at the shallow navigable points.

GABRIEL GUZMAN/SHUTTERSTOCK

largest underwater art structure. A short swim from here are the Ocean Sentinels, eight statues in 5m of water, that represent Australian individuals who've played key roles in advancing marine science and conservation. The museum's primary mission is to bring attention and awareness to the Great Barrier Reef and the challenges it faces. The catch is that it's two hours by boat from Townsville at John Brewer Reef so you'll need to book with a tour operator to get here. To truly appreciate MOUA you need to dive, though snorkellers are welcome. On days with good visibility, snorkellers can see the top of the greenhouse and other portions of the museum. **Adrenalin Dive** *(adrenalindive.com.au; from $384)* runs trips for divers and snorkellers, including introductory dives.

If you prefer to stay land-based, walk down the Strand promenade to check out the 4m-high **Ocean Siren sculpture**. Modelled after Takoda Johnson, a young Wulgurukaba girl, she acts as a siren for the warming seas and a symbol of youth shaping the future. Illuminated, the sculpture's colour changes based on the average daily water temperatures of the reef.

EATING IN TOWNSVILLE: TOP END

Garden of Eating: Wayne and Adele have been running this restaurant for decades; innovative menu with plenty for dietary-restricted diners. *hours vary* **$$$**

Spirited Goat: Located on the Strand, serving simple but elegant meals. Great wine list and cocktails. *6am-9pm Tue-Sat, 6.30am-6pm Sun, 6am-3pm Mon* **$$$**

Jam Corner: Celebratory breakfasts and desserts, plus a set menu and à la carte lunch and dinner. *hours vary* **$$$**

A Touch of Salt: Award-winning modern Australian cuisine in a sophisticated setting, with a menu that changes with the seasons. *5-10pm daily, plus noon-2pm Fri* **$$$**

***SS Yongala* shipwreck**

Dive to the Yongala

Tragic history meets world-class diving at the SS *Yongala*

The SS *Yongala* was an English-built steamship that made numerous voyages around Australia in the early 20th century. It tragically sank in a cyclone while passing through the Great Barrier Reef between Mackay and Townsville in 1911 (one year before the *Titanic* sank); 122 passengers and crew lost their lives. It wasn't until nearly 50 years later that the wreck was discovered and identified. Today, it's regarded as one of Australia's best wreck dives, sitting at a depth of 14m to 28m, covered in coral and home to turtles, fish, rays and more. As the largest and best-preserved wreck in Australian waters, it's a worthy spot for dive enthusiasts. **Adrenalin Dive** *(adrenalindive.com.au; from $489)* in Townsville runs day trips here for certified divers. **Yongala Dive** *(yongaladive.com.au; $320)* runs trips from its dive lodge on Alva Beach, located 100km southeast of Townsville but only a 30-minute boat ride to the dive site.

TOWNSVILLE'S BEST NIGHTLIFE

Townsville attracts a diverse crowd and has many opportunities for a big night. Nightlife is concentrated in two locations – Flinders St and the Strand. Flinders is the main stretch, full of cocktail bars, Irish pubs and nightclubs, attracting a younger crowd and those looking for a night of dancing and club vibes. It can get pretty wild here, so solo travellers may not be comfortable.

The Strand is more laid back, with a focus on bars with ocean views, small plates and a more discerning crowd. Like most places, nightlife kicks off on Fridays and Saturdays, with live music at many spots. The Strand Park is also host to many events throughout the year.

DRINKING IN TOWNSVILLE: OUR PICKS

Townsville Brewing Co: Craft brewery housed in an 1880s post office. Reserve ahead for a brewery tour. *noon-10pm Mon-Thu, noon-11pm Fri & Sat*

Tiny Mountain Brewery: The industrial, airy setting is the perfect place to enjoy crisp beers, with a popular happy hour. *4-11pm Mon-Wed, 11am-11pm Thu-Sun*

Hooch & Fellow: Award-winning cocktail bar serving up creative drinks in a cosy setting with knowledgeable and friendly staff. *6pm-midnight Tue-Sat*

Molly Malones: A classic Irish pub with live music every Friday and Saturday. *3-10pm Tue-Thu, noon-3am Fri, 3pm-3am Sat*

Beyond Townsville

Follow the road north of Townsville to detour to national parks, waterfalls, country towns and island hiking.

Places

GETTING AROUND

Greyhound and Premier buses between Townsville and Cairns stop at Ingham and Cardwell, as does the *Spirit of Queensland* train. To explore Paluma Range National Park and Wallaman Falls, you'll need your own transport. Hinchinbrook Island can be reached by pre-arranged boat from Cardwell or the small harbour town of Lucinda. Charters Towers is on the Flinders Hwy; it has Greyhound services three times a week and the twice-weekly *Inlander* train service.

Travelling between Townsville and Mission Beach? There's no need to rush, especially if you have your own wheels. Explorations off the Bruce Hwy include the freshwater swimming holes and waterfalls of Paluma Range National Park and Wallaman Falls. Access the uninhabited Hinchinbrook Island by boat from Cardwell or Lucinda and you'll see it's a remote wilderness in every sense. Well-prepared hikers can challenge themselves with the famous multiday Thorsborne Trail. Come to Ingham for the wildlife spotting at Tyto Wetlands and stay for the Italian heritage. For something different, you can head inland to the classic gold-rush town of Charters Towers or lesser-known Ravenswood, where ghost tours are part of the attraction.

Paluma Range National Park

TIME FROM TOWNSVILLE: 1HR

Hike, swim and spot platypuses in a mountain paradise

The **Paluma Range National Park**, located approximately 65km northwest of Townsville, serves as the southern gateway to the Wet Tropics World Heritage Area. It's a great spot for hiking, swimming, camping and platypus spotting.

From the northern access route off the Bruce Hwy, head to **Big Crystal Creek**. Rocks create a natural slip and slide in this freshwater swimming spot, accessible via a 500m walk to the water from the car park. Nearby Paradise Waterhole is another favourite swim spot. Further north off Jourama Rd is **Jourama Falls**, a spectacular cascade accessed by a 3km round-trip hike.

The southern access route (Mt Spec Rd) snakes up the mountains to tiny Paluma Village; stop off at **Little Crystal Creek**, a picturesque swimming hole with a cute stone bridge, picnic area and waterfalls. The area has experienced serious landslides and may be closed; check with the visitor centre before exploring.

Ingham & Around

TIME FROM TOWNSVILLE: 1½HR

Heritage meets natural wonders and majestic waterfalls

Ingham is a cane-cutting centre with a proud Italian heritage, though the main attractions here are natural. In town, the 120-hectare **Tyto Wetlands** has 4km of walking trails and attracts around 240 bird species and hundreds of agile wallabies. Access the wetlands boardwalk at the **Hinchinbrook Visitor Information Centre**.

Australia's longest single-drop waterfall, the majestic 268m **Wallaman Falls**, is 51km west in the Girringun National Park. Drive to the top; the lookout is next to the car park.

The Nywaigi are the Traditional Custodians of the land around Ingham. **Mungalla Aboriginal Tours** *(mungalla aboriginaltours.com.au; adult/child $99/80)*, based at Mungalla Station 15km east of Ingham, runs insightful tours about the Aboriginal culture and pioneering history of the station.

Hinchinbrook Island

TIME FROM TOWNSVILLE: 3HR

A challenging hike through pristine wilderness

Australia's largest island national park (399 sq km) is ideal for bushwalkers. Granite mountains rise from the sea and wildlife creeps through the foliage, while long sandy beaches and tangles of mangrove curve around the eastern shore. Hinchinbrook forms part of the traditional lands of the Bandjin and Girramay peoples.

To best enjoy the island, plan well in advance to hike the **Thorsborne Trail**, a challenging 32km coastal track from Ramsay Bay to George Point. It requires at least three nights to complete; return walks of individual sections are also possible. You need to be completely self-sufficient to camp at any of the trail's seven national park sites; there are limited or no facilities and no water. Book early for coveted spots during the winter hiking season – only 12 people are permitted to start the trail each day.

TRANSPORT TO HINCHINBROOK

Hinchinbrook Island can only be accessed by boat from Cardwell's Port Hinchinbrook Marina (trips to Ramsay Bay) or from Lucinda, which is close to the southern tip of the island (advanced bookings are recommended).

Hinchinbrook Island Cruises *(hinchin brookislandcruises.com.au; $240)* runs return hiking transfers from Cardwell, dropping off at Ramsay Bay and picking up at George Point.

Absolute North Charters *(absolute northcharters.com.au; $210)* has return hiking transfers from Lucinda, 27km northeast of Ingham, starting at either end of the trail. They also have return trips between Lucinda and George Point for short-term hikers.

Hinchinbrook Island Tours *(hitours.com.au)* runs half-day cruises (adult/child $165/125) and sunset excursions (adult/child $60/40).

Note: most boat operators provide transfers for multiday hikers only; day trips are uncommon.

EATING IN INGHAM: OUR PICKS

JK's Delicatessen: An Italian deli and cafe with a range of gourmet meats, cheeses and homemade lasagne. *7am-3pm Mon-Fri, 7.30am-1.30pm Sat* $

Wild Local: Award-winning fishmonger serving fresh seafood to enjoy in-house or takeaway, plus a cafe specialising in coffee and organic ice cream. *8.30am-7.30pm* $

Lees Hotel: This local institution inspired the Slim Dusty song 'A Pub with No Beer' after American soldiers drank the place dry. *10am-10pm* $$

Fiori With Love: A cafe set in a florist shop serving sandwiches, salads and homemade cakes. Gluten-free and vegetarian options. *8.30am-4pm Mon-Fri, 8.30am-noon Sat* $

JOANNA HUMPHRYS/SHUTTERSTOCK

Picnic Bay

TOP EXPERIENCE

Magnetic Island

Magnetic Island ('Maggie' to her friends) is justifiably popular. Over half of this mountainous island's 52 sq km is national park, with cycling, scenic walks and abundant wildlife, including koalas and rock wallabies. A 30-minute boat ride from Townsville, the island is known for its gorgeous beaches and bays, lively dining options and a laid-back attitude that you can't help but adopt when arriving.

DON'T MISS

- Picnic Bay
- Horseshoe Bay
- Forts Walk
- Butterfly Walk
- Florence Bay
- Alma Bay
- Rock wallabies
- Snorkelling

Island Walks

Magnetic Island has some excellent bushwalks, especially in the northeast, where trails from Horseshoe Bay connect isolated beaches and coves such as Balding Bay, Radical Bay and Florence Bay. One of the island's most popular trails is the **Forts Walk** (2.8km, 1½ hours return). The remains of the fortifications here were built during WWII to protect Townsville from naval attack. Keep your eyes peeled; sightings of wild koalas snoozing in the trees are almost guaranteed.

PRACTICALITIES

● *magneticislandguide.com.au*

Stroll through the **Butterfly Walk**, a 100m walk through a migratory resting place for blue tiger butterflies. You'll need to walk slowly and quietly to avoid disturbing the hibernating butterflies. It's best visited between April and July.

In Picnic Bay, the **Hawkings Point Track** (1.2km return, trailhead at the end of Picnic St) takes you up to a lookout with views of the east coast. Serious walkers can tackle the easy but long 16km return walk to **West Point** from Picnic Bay. Follow a rugged dirt road to access the isolated west-coast beaches and tidal wetlands.

Horseshoe Bay

Horseshoe Bay is the largest bay on the island, named for its 3km-long horseshoe-shaped beach. With a strip of restaurants overlooking the beach and a stinger net (from November to May), it's a popular spot to watch the sunset or swim. A short walk from the shore along the main road is **Bounce Magnetic Island** *(staybounce.com/locations/magnetic-island; tours from $50)*, which houses a koala and wildlife park. Daily park tours are from 10.30am, 12.30pm and 2.30pm, and free daily lorikeet feeding takes place at 4.15pm near the bar.

Picnic Bay

Picnic Bay is one of the most low-key spots on the island, dominated by a community of friendly locals. There's a stinger net (from November to May) and the swimming is superb. At low tide from the beach, scout the wreck of *George Rennie*. The little village is a great spot for a nice meal or to enjoy a few brews at the bay's pub or brewery. There's also a historic jetty, if you'd like to throw in a line or simply contemplate the sea.

Arcadia Village

Only five minutes' drive from the Nelly Bay ferry terminal lies **Arcadia**, home of a popular hotel pub and two of the island's prized bays. Geoffrey Bay is home to allied rock wallabies, best viewed on Bremner Point, a short walk from the village. Although wild, they come out like clockwork at around 5pm. This bay is also the starting point for the Geoffrey Bay Snorkel Trail, with four numbered surface floats to outline the trail. Coral, fish and clams are on display down below and the *Moltke* shipwreck can be seen on a clear day. For strong swimmers, venture slightly off the trail to see a WWII aeroplane propeller and engine block, the only remains from a 1943 crash. Hire snorkel gear from **Pleasure Divers** *(pleasuredivers.com.au; per day from $30)* in Arcadia.

Just over the headland of Geoffrey Bay lies Alma Bay, a popular place for swimmers due to its year-round lifeguard patrols and calm waters. The family-friendly spot is often regarded as one of Queensland's best beaches.

GETTING AROUND MAGGIE

Translink (Kinetic) runs local bus services around the island, but hiring open-top vehicles or scooters is a popular way to get around. With one main road linking Horseshoe Bay and Picnic Bay (end-to-end it's a 20-minute drive), it's easy to zip around. Most hire vehicles must stay on or near the main road – hire a 4WD if you want to head off-road to West Point.

TOP TIPS

- The best time to visit is during the dry season, from May to November.
- Though a day trip is easy to do, stay at least overnight to soak in the relaxed island experience.
- Don't skip the great dining and bar experiences. Picnic Bay houses a brewery, a fine-dining spot, a pub and more, while Horseshoe Bay has a variety of beach-front spots. Plenty more options are dotted around the more populated bays.
- If you're arriving after 8pm, pack a dinner or eat in Townsville – the island's kitchens close earlier than on the mainland.
- Bring cash if you plan to ride the bus.

Airlie Beach

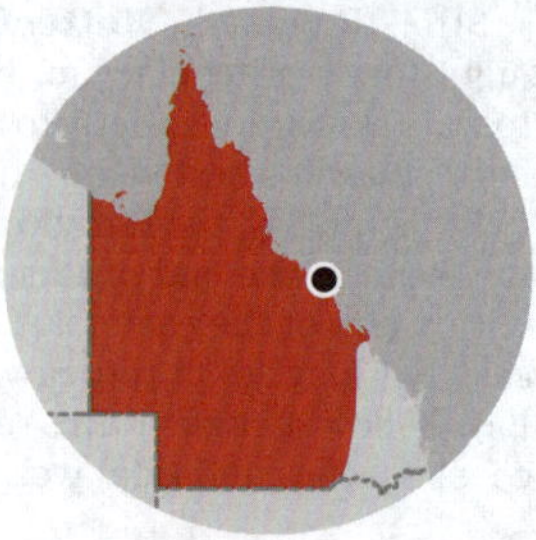

ISLAND VIEWS | HIKING | BACKPACKER BLISS

TOP TIP
The main visitor centre for the region is in Proserpine and bookings for activities can be made there. There are also many private information centres on the main strip in Airlie Beach where you can book tours and activities, but be aware that these agencies are commission-based.

Airlie Beach is the main gateway to the legendary Whitsunday Islands, with a backpacker vibe in the town centre and million-dollar yachts bobbing in the nearby marinas. Numerous hostels, beer gardens and tour operators are strung along the short stretch of Shute Harbour Rd, bookended by the marinas of Coral Sea and Port of Airlie.

There's a small beach just west of the sailing club, but the safe spot for swimming is next door at the patrolled stinger-free Airlie Lagoon. Numerous tours to the Whitsundays and the inner Great Barrier Reef depart from here – booking offices on Shute Harbour Rd have friendly staff and brochures.

The Ngaro and Gia peoples are the Traditional Custodians of this coastal area and also lived seasonally on the islands, as evidenced by discoveries of stone tools, fish traps and rock art. Cook named the islands when he sailed through in 1770, but didn't land here.

Take the Turtle Boardwalk

Stroll along the Bicentennial Walkway

The **Bicentennial Walkway** is an easy 4km return track that meanders through marinas with views of the Whitsundays. Pick up the trail at the lagoon and walk towards Coral Sea

GETTING AROUND

Greyhound and Premier buses both detour off the Bruce Hwy to Airlie Beach, also stopping at Proserpine. Whitsunday Transit connects Proserpine, Cannonvale, Abell Point Marina, Airlie Beach and Shute Harbour throughout the day, useful if you're staying outside Airlie Beach; there are several stops in the centre.

There are airports near Proserpine, Shute Harbour and on Hamilton Island.

Scamper is an island water-taxi service carrying passengers from Shute Harbour, 10km east of Airlie Beach, to camp sites on South Molle, Whitsunday and Hook Islands. Cruise Whitsunday has regular ferries to Hamilton Island (via Daydream).

VANESSA PFAJFER/SHUTTERSTOCK

Airlie Beach

Marina, carrying along until Cannonvale beach, your end point. The walk takes about an hour each way and hugs the coast through a mix of wooden boardwalks and concrete pavement, making the relatively flat path wheelchair accessible and great for prams.

Keep your eyes peeled along Pioneer Bay, the section affectionately known as 'turtle boardwalk', for sea turtles. These special creatures sometimes make guest appearances, especially around dawn and dusk and are easier to spot in calm waters. If not, console yourself with sights of cockatoos and kookaburras along the way.

Hiking in Conway National Park

Tropical rainforest near Airlie

This serene national park encompasses the Conway Peninsula, once the hunting grounds of the Giru Dala and still home to large swathes of lowland tropical rainforest, remote mangroves, rocky uplands, and pandanus and paperbark woodlands. The Whitsunday Transit bus from Airlie Beach to Shute Harbour (operating once or twice hourly) can drop you off at the Mt Rooper car park, the trailheads for these two hikes. The 4.2km **Swamp Bay Traverse** ends at the coral-strewn beach overlooking the Molle Island group, a moderate walk

EATING IN AIRLIE BEACH: OUR PICKS

BOHO Cafe: With dazzling views across Pioneer Bay, this health-conscious cafe packs in boat-tour customers for an early breakfast. *6.30am-1pm* $$

Ramen in May: Sweet Japanese restaurant specialising in *tonkotsu* ramen (noodles in broth), plus gyoza and tea. *11.30am-2.30pm & 4.30-8.30pm* $

Cafe One 3: This family-run cafe is all about wholesome vegetarian and vegan dishes. It opens early for breakfast. *6.30am-1pm Mon-Fri* $

Whitsunday Sailing Club: The sailing club has a waterfront location and a great menu spanning the globe. *11am-9pm Wed-Sun* $$

AIRLIE BEACH
Airlie Beach
Ocean View Ave
Shingley Dr
Mazlin St
Shute Harbour Rd
Airlie Cres
Begley St
Lamond St
Waterson Way
Airlie Bay
Airlie Creek
Coral Sea
0
200 m
Armit Island
Hayman Island
Dryander National Park
See Airlie Beach Enlargement
Airlie Beach
Cannonvale
Riordan Vale
Jubilee Pocket
Swamp Bay
Shute Harbour
North Molle Island
South Molle Island
Coral Sea
Cid Island
Sugarloaf
Thomas Island (55km)
Pelican Island
Long Island
Molle Islands National Park
Whitsunday Passage
Pine Island
The Narrows
Conway National Park
Bonavista
Proserpine River
Wilson Beach
Conway
Conway Beach
Repulse Bay

HIGHLIGHTS
1 Armit Island
2 Hamilton Island
3 Hook Island
4 Lindeman Island
5 Long Island
6 South Molle Island
7 Whitehaven Beach

SIGHTS
8 Catseye Beach
9 Cedar Creek Falls
10 Escape Beach

ACTIVITIES
11 Bicentennial Walkway
12 Big Fury
13 Charter Yachts Australia
see 13 Cumberland Charter Yachts
see 19 HeliReef
14 Lady Enid
15 Mt Rooper Circuit
16 Ocean Rafting
17 Red Cat Adventures
18 Salty Dog Sea Kayaking
19 Skydive Airlie Beach
20 Solway Lass
21 Spion Kop Lookout
see 15 Swamp Bay Traverse
see 16 Whitehaven Xpress
22 Whitsunday Dive Adventures
23 Whitsunday Sailing Adventures

SLEEPING
24 Coral Sea Resort
25 Heart Hotel & Gallery
26 Kipara
27 Magnums

EATING
28 BOHO Cafe
29 Cafe One 3
30 Little Vegas Burger & Bar
31 Ramen in May
32 Sorrento
33 Whitsunday Sailing Club

DRINKING & NIGHTLIFE
34 Northerlies Beach Bar & Grill
35 The Pub

TRANSPORT
36 Cruise Whitsundays
37 Island Transfers
see 37 Scamper

MATTHEW JAMES FERGUSON/SHUTTERSTOCK

TOP EXPERIENCE

Whitsunday Islands

There's a magic about the 74 islands that make up the Whitsundays. The moment you set eyes on Whitehaven Beach from the Hill Inlet Lookout or savour the sunset from a yacht deck, you'll understand why. This is island-hopping and sailing territory, but also perfect for hikers, campers and resort loungers. Whatever your tropical island fantasy, you should find it here.

DON'T MISS

- Whitehaven Beach
- Hamilton Island
- Hook Island
- Long Island
- South Molle Island
- Lindeman Island
- Island camping

Whitehaven Beach

On Whitsunday Island, **Whitehaven Beach** is a pristine 7km-long stretch of blinding sand (at 98% pure silica, some of the whitest in the world), framed by lush vegetation and a brilliant sea in multihued shades of blue. Head straight up to the lookout at Hill Inlet, an easy, 700m walk uphill, where the views across the swirling sands and turquoise waters paint a magical picture that changes with the light. Down on the beach, you can swim and snorkel in crystal waters and look out for lemon sharks. Almost every day tour from Airlie Beach stops here (it's about two hours by boat).

PRACTICALITIES

- *tourismwhitsundays.com.au*

Hamilton Island

The most developed of the Whitsundays, **Hamilton Island** has an airport, large marina, waterfront restaurants and a range of exclusive luxury accommodation. This is also one of the only islands that isn't a national park. Make a day trip of the island – **Cruise Whitsundays** *(cruisewhitsundays.com; return $135)* has nine daily ferries from Airlie Beach. Hike the bushwalking trails around the island, or head to **Catseye Beach** for **water sports** *(hamiltonisland.com.au; from $22)* like stand-up paddleboarding, kayaking or parasailing. **Escape Beach** is Hamilton's prettiest. Golf buggies can be hired to get around.

Hook Island

Hook is the second-largest island in the group and vies with neighbouring Whitsunday for day-trip popularity, mainly as an anchorage for snorkelling. Good beaches and coves are dotted around the island, and sites such as Manta Ray Bay and Butterfly Bay are popular snorkelling stops. There are basic camping grounds located at Maureen's Cove, Steen's Beach, Curlew Beach and Crayfish Beach.

Long Island

Mostly classified as a national park, thickly forested **Long Island** has secluded white-sand beaches, lots of adorable wild rock wallabies and 17km of walking tracks. There are two luxury resorts here (Palm Bay is open to day-trippers), plus the Sandy Bay camp site overlooking a sheltered beach. Get here via private transfer from Shute Harbour to Palm Bay with **Island Transfers** *(islandtransfers.com; day trip from $89)*, which offers daily departures and takes about 30 minutes.

South Molle Island

The largest of the Molle Islands group – the closest major islands to Airlie Beach – **South Molle** is criss-crossed by 15km of walking tracks with some superb lookout points. Check out the hike to **Spion Kop Lookout**, an easy-to-moderate 4km return with views of the islands and water below. There are two partially shaded camping grounds, as well as one basic camping ground, each on the tiny Planton and Denman satellite islets. Day-trippers and campers can get to South Molle with the **Scamper water taxi** *(whitsundaycamping.com.au; return from $90)*, starting the 30-minute journey from Shute Harbour.

Almost-Private Exploring

For those interested in lesser-known islands to explore on a bareboat charter, **Lindeman Island** is the best known of the 13 coral-fringed specks in the Lindeman Islands National Park. Nature photographers and hikers are the main visitors, as the island's resort remains closed. The sea-claimed volcano has splendid empty bays, reefs for snorkelling and over 16km of walking trails.

ISLAND CAMPING

There are basic national park camp sites on South Molle, Whitsunday, Hook, Henning, Long, Lindeman, Shaw, Repulse and Smith Islands. You must be self-sufficient and book camping permits in advance. **Scamper** *(whitsundaycamping.com.au; one way from $45)* runs a water-taxi service direct to camp sites on Hook, Whitsunday and South Molle Islands from Shute Harbour and also hires out camping gear and kayaks.

BAREBOAT OR GUIDED TOUR?

If you've come to the Whitsundays to sail, there are plenty of operators, but be warned: this is the most popular activity, so book ahead or try to get on last-minute stand-bys. Most tours are guided, meaning all you need to do is be a good passenger. For bareboat sailing charters, at least one member of your party must be able to demonstrate that they can operate and navigate a vessel. For non-sailors, crewing on a yacht is the best way to work for your cruise – look out for 'crew wanted' notices in Airlie Beach or ask at the sailing club.

HOW TO PICK A TOUR

Tours vary from half-day to full-day and multiday adventures. Multiple days are perfect for exploring more islands and having more time for activities like snorkelling or diving, depending on the type of trip you choose. If you prefer to sleep on land, get seasick easily, or are tight on time, a half- or full-day adventure might be best.

Little-visited **Armit Island** in the northern Whitsundays awaits yachties in the know, with a fringing reef, secluded anchorage, nesting birds from October to March and a peaceful, facility-free beach camp site accessible to those on boats.

Sailing Tours

Experience the Whitsundays in fashionable style by sailboat. There are many operators, all with various time lengths (half-day, full-day, multiday trips), sizes and types of boat. If you're unsure what you're after, **Whitsunday Sailing Adventures** *(sailing-whitsundays.com)* books directly with a range of owner-operated vessels and price points and can also set you up for sea kayaking, on-land exploring, diving and snorkelling. Keep in mind that many sleeping quarters are bunk-style and can increase feelings of seasickness. Pack some anti-seasick pills just in case!

For bareboat charters, **Charter Yachts Australia** *(charteryachtsaustralia.com.au; from $670)* is a respected operator offering classic bareboat charters from Airlie Beach at competitive rates (with a five-night minimum). **Cumberland Charter Yachts** *(cy.com.au; from $607)* is an established bareboat charter company offering sail- and engine-powered yachts and catamarans (with a three-night minimum).

For those longing for something more historic, **Solway Lass** *(solwaylass.com.au; from $740)* is an authentic square-rigged 28m tall ship with three-night trips.

CHAMELEONSEYE/SHUTTERSTOCK

Ocean Rafting

Day Trips

Adventures abound in the Whitsundays, but don't fret if you only have a day. There are plenty of different ways to enjoy the islands, with most day trips visiting Whitehaven Beach and Hill Inlet Lookout on Whitsunday Island. Tour operators depart from Airlie Beach and most have complimentary shuttle services from accommodation in town. Snorkel gear is included if that's part of your itinerary.

Ocean Rafting *(oceanrafting.com.au; adult/child from $209/138)* operates two day trips, with the distinctive yellow semi-rigid inflatables that can park right on Whitehaven Beach. These boats hold from 25 to 32 passengers, creating a more intimate experience. They're also the only tour operator with direct access to Hill Inlet beaches, meaning less walking and more beach time.

Red Cat Adventures *(redcatadventures.com.au; from $199)* is an established family-run operation with tours to Whitehaven and a sailing catamaran to Langford Island Sandbar.

Whitehaven Xpress *(whitehavenexpress.com.au; from $225)* is a popular boat, perfect for those who want maximum beach time. This tour gives you the longest time on the beach and includes a classic Aussie beach BBQ.

Big Fury *(magicwhitsundays.com; adult/child from $220/175)* runs speedboat tours to Whitsunday Island with snorkelling and a fresh buffet lunch.

Lady Enid *(iconicwhitsunday.com.au)* is a stately, adults-only cruising yacht that does day trips to Whitehaven Beach (from $285), including snorkelling and a guided walk, as well as sunset cruises (from $99).

Human-Powered Fun

If you'd like to remain on top of the water, **Salty Dog Sea Kayaking** *(saltydog.com.au; adult/child from $120/100)* has half-day, full-day and six-day guided tours, plus kayak hire, departing from Shute Harbour.

For an underwater adventure, **Whitsunday Dive Adventures** *(whitsundaydiveadventures.com; from $399)* runs dive trips around the islands. You can stick close to Airlie to explore the fringing reef around the islands, or head to the outer reef of the Great Barrier Reef, a three-hour boat journey.

Great Barrier from Above

Jump from 15,000ft on a tandem skydive with **Skydive Airlie Beach** *(skydive.com.au; from $369)* for up to 60 seconds of free fall. For those who want to enjoy the views without the adrenaline, **HeliReef** *(helireef.com.au; per person from $300)* runs scenic helicopter flights. Checking out the famous Heart Reef (a reef shaped like a heart) is an iconic Whitsundays experience.

TOP TIPS

- Ask at Airlie Beach booking offices about last-minute cancellations or stand-bys for sailing trips.
- Carry some anti-seasickness medication if you're prone.
- Sunscreen and insect repellent are musts for relaxing on deck and during island bush walks.
- Avoid holiday periods; it's easier to get on a boat in September and October or March and April.
- Day tours run to Whitehaven Beach, Hook Island and Langford Island; multiday sailing trips visit more islands.
- The dry season (May to October) is the best time to visit due to cooler days and lower rainfall.

AIRLIE BEACH & THE WHITSUNDAYS SAILING TIPS

Ross Chisholm is the sailing manager at the Whitsunday Sailing Club, which welcomes non-members to its bar and bistro. He shares his tips for the Whitsundays and Airlie Beach. *whitsundaysailingclub.com.au*

If you're interested in sailing, the best time to sail the Whitsundays is May to September, which has the most consistent breezes and flatter waters. Be aware of the tides year-round as they can vary by as much as 4m.

A favourite destination is Thomas Island, west of the Whitsundays near Bowen; it's less well known and has a lovely anchorage. In Airlie, I recommend the Sailing Club, which has a great restaurant and the Anchor Bar, a friendly place with good views.

MICHAEL XIAOS/SHUTTERSTOCK

Cedar Creek Falls

that takes about two hours to complete and can be linked to the **Mt Rooper Circuit**. The ascent of Mt Rooper is a moderate-to-hard 5.3km return trip with a 221m gain, and should take around three hours.

A half-hour drive south from Airlie towards Proserpine, you can take a freshwater dip to cool off in **Cedar Creek Falls**. The cascading rocky waterfall is a 200m well-signposted stroll from the car park and is surrounded by cedar forest. It's best to visit after a big rain so the falls are flowing. If you don't have your own car, tours leave from Airlie Beach.

EATING IN AIRLIE BEACH: OUR PICKS

Little Vegas Burger & Bar: For classic American-style burgers or fish tacos, this Pop-Art-style main-street spot is the place to be. *noon-3pm & 5-9pm* $

Northerlies Beach Bar & Grill: It's worth the 7km trip west of Airlie (take the courtesy bus) for lunch and drinks at this shorefront pub with great views. *11am-8pm* $$

Sorrento: With views of the Coral Sea Marina, plus Italian food and a relaxed vibe, it's hard to beat this spot at sundown. *11.30am-9pm Tue-Sun* $$

The Pub: Just off the backpacker strip, The Pub has sea views from its terrace, an eclectic crowd and live music four nights a week. *11am-late* $$

Beyond Airlie Beach

The Whitsunday Coast stretches from cane country around Mackay to mango country at Bowen. Head inland for adventures in Eungella.

While the Whitsunday Coast is the main attraction in this region, there are worthwhile detours to break the journey. Mackay is the main town in a large cane-growing region and with its Art Deco architecture, streetart and easy access to the coast, it's a welcome stopover. It is on the traditional lands of the Yuwibara people. North of Mackay is Cape Hillsborough National Park, where rainforest meets ocean. Half an hour south of Mackay, Sarina Beach is a coastal enclave popular with locals. Inland, the big attraction is Eungella National Park, roughly 80km west of Mackay, where platypuses pop up in rivers, and leisure activities include hiking to waterfalls and swimming holes at Finch Hatton Gorge.

Places

GETTING AROUND

Greyhound and Premier buses stop at Sarina, Mackay and Bowen daily. Mackay Transit Coaches has several services around the city, many leaving from Caneland shopping centre and connecting the city with the harbour, airport and northern beaches. There's no public transport to Eungella; if you don't have your own car, tour companies in Airlie Beach and Mackay run day trips.

Mackay

TIME FROM AIRLIE BEACH: **2HR**

Heritage walks, Art Deco gems and a historic lagoon

Sitting at the heart of vast sugar-cane plantations, Mackay is a prosperous regional hub. The town's main draw is its proximity to Eungella National Park, though its easy-going tropical vibe, free swimming lagoon and handsome building facades make it a worthy stopover.

Mackay's Art Deco architecture dotted around the town centre – check out the Ambassador Hotel, Palace Hotel and Australian Hotel – owes much to the devastating cyclone of 1918, which flattened many of the town's former buildings. Stop in the visitor centre next to the lagoon for a pamphlet on the town's heritage walk. The contemporary gallery **Artspace Mackay** *(artspacemackay.com.au; free)* showcases works from local and visiting artists, including pieces by the Indigenous Lockhart River Art Gang.

Cape Hillsborough National Park

TIME FROM AIRLIE BEACH: **1½HR**

Rainforest meets the sea

With 10.75 sq km of protected land making up **Cape Hillsborough National Park** and the surrounding waters a part of the Great Barrier Reef Marine Park, Cape Hillsborough

BOWEN'S CLAIMS TO FAME

This small coastal fishing town is famous around Australia for its bounty on land and sea. A 10m-tall statue of a ripe mango at the visitor centre along the Bruce Hwy greets motorists on the way in. It gets busy here during fruit-picking season from April to January, with the area producing a large amount of tomatoes and mangoes, along with fresh seafood coming in from the marina.

Baz Luhrmann shot his epic movie *Australia* here in 2007, turning Bowen's historic streets into 1940s Darwin and casting locals as extras. Sadly, there's nothing left of the film set. Check out the information plaques near Bowen's *Little Mango* statue at the jetty entrance in town for photos and stories of the town as a set.

is a great stop. The diverse landscape is home to colourful birds, the vibrant Ulysses butterfly and six species of kangaroo and wallaby. Look for wallabies on Casuarina Beach at dawn and dusk, coming to the shore to feast on the all-you-can-eat mangrove seed pod buffet. It's not unusual to see tourists trying to feed them, which may look cute but can harm them – human food can lead to malnutrition and disease. Sand bubbler crabs decorate the beaches with their patterns at low tide and there are plenty of sea creatures to observe in the rock pools.

Scenic tracks through a rainforest and hidden coves

To fully explore Cape Hillsborough, take a hike. The **Beachcomber Cove Track** starts at the day-use area before climbing over a ridge and dropping into a secluded bay. This 2.2km track is moderate, but if the tide is high you'll need to return the way you came. For an easy, kid-friendly walk, the 40-minute **Diversity Boardwalk** meanders through mangroves and vine thickets. The challenging **Andrews Point Track** (5.2km, 2½ hours return) climbs from rainforest to ridgeline for rewarding views of the coast and even turtles down below if you're lucky.

Bowen

TIME FROM AIRLIE BEACH: **1HR**

Snorkel granite bays and walk the low-tide sandbars

Drive or walk to the top of Flagstaff Hill Lookout, which offers a 360-degree view of the area including the northern Whitsundays islands. North Head Island and its historic lighthouse are easy to spot and it's also a great place to view humpback whales during their winter migration.

There are some secluded beaches and bays northeast of the town centre, including the stinger-free **Queens Beach** and **Horseshoe Bay**, a snorkellers' favourite. Framed by granite outcrops, it's the perfect place for beginner snorkellers to explore fringing reefs, due to the easy accessibility straight off the beach. High tide is best for finding large schools of parrotfish, while low tide is perfect for coral viewings. During winter's low tide, walk to the **North Head Lighthouse**, which is connected to the mainland by a sandbar. Sea turtles, sea stars and feather stars can be seen along the walk and you might spot a dugong in the distance. Be sure to wear reef shoes.

EATING & DRINKING BEYOND AIRLIE BEACH: OUR PICKS

9th Lane Grind: Popular brunch spot on Mackay's 'eat street'. Eclectic breakfast and lunch plates, plus great coffee and sweet treats. *6.30am-3pm Mon-Sat* $$

Eimeo Pacific Hotel: Overlooking the beach 15km north of Mackay centre, this is a historic place for a drink at sunset. *10am-8pm*

Dispensary: An intimate experience in Mackay, with modern Australian cuisine. *6am-2.30pm Sun & Mon, 6am-10.30pm Tue-Thu, 6am-midnight Fri & Sat* $$$

360 on the Hill: Sitting atop Flagstaff Hill in Bown, this authentic Italian restaurant serves pizza, pasta, tiramisu and more. *7am-4pm Sun-Wed, 7am-9pm Thu-Sat* $$

MARTIN VALIGURSKY/SHUTTERSTOCK

Horseshoe Bay

Eungella National Park

TIME FROM AIRLIE BEACH: 2HR

Platypuses and mountain views

You have an excellent chance of spotting platypuses in the rivers and creeks of the mountainous Eungella National Park, located on the traditional lands of the Widi and Yuwi peoples. The park covers nearly 500 sq km of the lofty Clarke Range, but visitor activity is largely limited to two separate areas: the waterfalls and swimming holes of Finch Hatton Gorge and the established hiking trails and camp sites around Broken River. There are stunning views from Eungella village high up in the mountains.

Don't miss the **Sky Window Circuit** (250m), a level, easy loop offering great views of the Pioneer Valley. At Broken River, two easy interlinked loops meander through the rainforest and along the river, where platypus viewing is best in the early morning or evening. Carry on to the **Rainforest Discovery Circuit** (780m) and further onto the Granite Bend Circuit, a moderate 1.6km walk through Livistona palms, with plenty of birdsong to keep you going.

At **Finch Hatton Gorge**, a gorgeous 2.8km return trail leads through the rainforest to Araluen Falls, with its tumbling waterfall and deep swimming hole. Carry on to the Wheels of Fire track, a moderate 4.2km return, which takes you to Wheels of Fire Falls, a series of cascades ending in another deep swimming hole.

Finch Hatton village has a shop, cafe and pub, but the most popular pit stop is the **Pinnacle Hotel**, 10km east, famous for its pies and pub meals.

THE ELUSIVE PLATYPUS

Platypuses are one of only two Australian monotreme mammals (echidnas are the other), meaning they're mammals that lays eggs. Endemic to Australia, they're remarkable swimmers, able to dive and find food underwater for several minutes. With duck-like bills, furry bodies, webbed feet and beaver-like tails, it's easy to see why! They're mostly nocturnal, so your best chance of seeing these shy creatures is at dawn or dusk; otherwise, they're usually found burrowed in riverbanks. Remain as still and quiet as possible and keep an eye out for air bubbles, which indicate the platypus is feeding on the river bottom. They store food in their little cheek pouches, surfacing to eat. Their diet is made up of insect larvae, swimming beetles, tadpoles and water bugs.

Outback Queensland

DINOSAUR TRAILS | STARGAZING | EPIC CAMPING

Places

West of the Great Divide beckons a vast land of myth and folklore, of treeless black-soil plains, dinosaur fossils and zillion-hectare cattle stations. Of boom and bust, where rain transforms the western Channel Country and red desert dunes, only to slink away again leaving cracked claypans, broken dreams and skeletons.

The bitumen, straight and narrow, vanishes into the hazy blue horizon while dusty, corrugated tracks promise unseen adventures. Towns are few and far between and mobile-phone coverage is negligible. The stars are deafening. This is the land of Australian stories, of heroes and villains and ghosts that haunt distant waterholes. Of a 60,000-year-old culture foundering on the jagged reef of colonialism.

Travellers, nomads, gypsies and wanderers are all welcome here. Come the adventurous or just the plain curious. Just make sure you have spare fuel and water. The distances are immense, the heat intense, the locals friendly and the beers never colder.

☑ TOP TIP

Don't rely on generic internet maps in the outback – they're notoriously inaccurate. Have a good GPS app (Avenza, Garmin etc) and back it up with a quality paper map of your intended route. HEMA's Great Desert Tracks are excellent. Carry a personal locator beacon or satellite phone and don't drive at night.

Cloncurry

TIME FROM TOWNSVILLE: **8½HR**

Flynn of the outback

Reverend John Flynn chose Cloncurry in the 1920s as the home for his newly conceived flying medical service, the world's first air ambulance, which later became the Royal Flying Doctor Service (RFDS), still an essential service today for regional Australians. Learn more about John Flynn and the birth of the RFDS at the **John Flynn Place Museum** *(experience cloncurry.com; adult/child $13/9)*. Consider a combined ticket

GETTING AROUND

While there are sporadic train and plane services to Mt Isa, Longreach and Charleville from the coast, you'll need a car to explore the outback properly, preferably a 4WD. The main highways are sealed, but most of the sights are not. There are recognised through-routes, particularly the **Matilda Way**, best for heading north from the southern states via Bourke (NSW), Longreach and Cloncurry, and the east–west routes of the **Overlander Way** (Townsville to Tennant Creek, NT, via Mt Isa) and the **Warrego Way** (Brisbane to Birdsville). More adventurous options include the Birdsville Track (from SA) and the Plenty Hwy (from NT), both requiring serious off-road skills and planning.

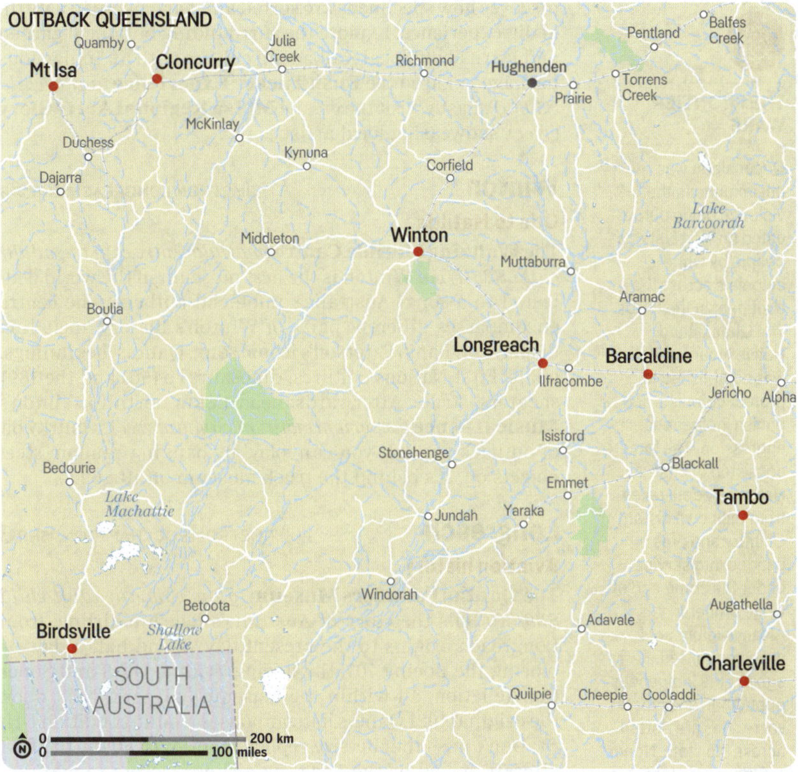

(adult/child $19.50/13.50) with **Cloncurry Unearthed** (aka the visitor centre), which showcases local minerals and history.

Mt Isa

TIME FROM CLONCURRY: 1½HR

Mining lifestyle

Outback at Isa *(outbackatisa.com.au)* in the visitor centre has several attractions that you can explore in a day. On the Underground Tour at **Hard Times Mine** *(adult/child $85/50)* you'll experience life as a miner. Don a protective helmet and cap lamp to explore 1.2km of tunnels complete with fuming, roaring, rattling machinery. At the **Riversleigh Fossil Discovery Centre** *(adult/child $19.50/11.50)* examine fossils,

EATING IN MT ISA: OUR PICKS

Bambino Espresso: Start the day with a prawn and spanner-crab omelette at this funky local specialising in innovative soul food. *6am-2pm* **$$**

Giuseppe's Cantina: Try the pear, walnut and Gorgonzola linguine at this excellent Italian fine-dining experience attached to Ibis Styles. *5.30-9pm Mon-Sat* **$$$**

Adobo Avenue: Unexpected, authentic, delicious Filipino food. Try the signature chicken adobo or *palabok. 11am-9pm Mon-Sat* **$$**

Xtra Mile: Great brunch choice with healthy drinks and dishes catering for all diets including gluten-free and vegan. *6am-2pm Mon-Fri, 7am-1pm Sat* **$$**

THE FRONTIER WARS

Queensland was not immune to the violence being perpetuated on First Nations people by white colonials across the continent in the 1800s. The Queensland Native Mounted Police was established to protect colonists and punish Indigenous aggression. The force consisted of First Nations people taken from their own distant Country and press-ganged into service under the command of white officers.

Many violent acts were committed against the Indigenous population and massacre sites are dotted across the state. None are more poignant than the 'last stand of the Kalkadoon' at **Battle Mountain** (Mt Remarkable, northwest of Cloncurry) in 1884, where a group of between 150 and 600 Kalkadoon warriors, armed with spears, charged the muskets of the Native Police and suffered horrendous casualties.

discover how specimens are sorted and participate in a virtual dig experience. Explore the surrounding botanical garden and learn about local Kalkadoon culture with an Indigenous heritage guide on the **Bush Tucker Experience** *(adult/child $50/30)*. Lastly, visit the on-site **Mt Isa Regional Art Gallery** *(free)*, showcasing local artists.

Winton

TIME FROM LONGREACH: **2HR**

Ode to Matilda

The **Waltzing Matilda Centre** *(matildacentre.com.au; adult/child $35/17)* in Winton is the first museum in the world dedicated to a song: Australia's unofficial anthem. The centre encompasses different parts of Winton's history, including displays on Banjo Paterson's iconic song, Qantas' beginnings, opals, First Nations cultures, dinosaurs (p456) and the 1891 shearers' strike. Afterwards, head 1.8km north to Winton's **Musical Fence** *(experiencewinton.com.au; free)*, a quirky bit of outback art that you can 'play' by banging random steel objects on. It's behind the truck museum off Rte 62.

Longreach

TIME FROM ROCKHAMPTON: **15HR**

Aviation history

The **Qantas Founders Museum** *(qfom.com.au; adult/child $39/30)* tells the story of Australia's flagship airline, from Longreach origins to the present day. Spend half a day exploring the Boeing 707, the Boeing 747, the DC-3 and Super Constellation, all within the museum's airpark. Next door, the original 1921 Qantas hangar houses a mint-condition DH-61. Don't miss the life-size replica of an Avro 504K, the first aircraft owned by the fledgling airline. Tickets range from museum-only entry up to $250 for exclusive small-group tours.

The life of a stockman

In a beautifully conceived, multi-arched building, the **Australian Stockman's Hall of Fame** *(outbackheritage.com.au; galleries only adult/child $40/25)* pays tribute to outback pioneers, early explorers, stockmen and First Nations peoples. Themed galleries cover Aboriginal Songlines (a sung or spoken memory map), outback folklore, the 'Long Paddock' (stock routes), Unsung Heroes and immersive displays of station life. The premium **Stockman's Experience** *(adult/child $99/50)*, at 9am, 9.30am, 11am and 11.30am from April

'Waltzing Matilda's' first public performance was here

EATING IN WINTON & LONGREACH: OUR PICKS

Little Star Indian Restaurant: Good vegetarian options at this local curry favourite in Longreach that also does pizzas, burgers... you name it... *4-9pm* **$$**

Lost Poet: The funkiest brekkie in Winton comes toasted with a side of books and the best coffee in town. *6.30am-2.30pm Tue-Fri, 8am-noon Sat* **$**

Kynda Cafe: With açaí bowls, spirulina oats and yummy Spanish eggs, hipster has come to Longreach! *7am-4pm Mon-Fri, to 2pm Sat, to 11am Sun* **$$**

North Gregory Hotel: Classic outback pub fare with interesting updates like Moroccan chicken salad and pork-belly noodles. *11.30am-2pm & 5.30-8pm* **$$**

ALEX CIMBAL/SHUTTERSTOCK

Qantas Founders Museum

to early October, includes a live show complete with horses, muster dogs, whip cracking and storytelling.

Barcaldine

TIME FROM LONGREACH: **70MIN**

Strike for your rights

Barcaldine, at the junction of the Landsborough and Capricorn Hwys, gained its place in Australian history in 1891 when it became the headquarters of a major shearers' strike. The **Australian Workers Heritage Centre** *(australianworkers heritagecentre.com.au; adult/child $25/13)* honours Australia's workers – past, present and future – who help preserve the country's heritage and culture. There's a variety of exhibits spread over 14 halls on 2 hectares of landscaped grounds.

Tambo

TIME FROM CHARLEVILLE: **2HR**

Birds, bears and chooks

The oldest outback town is perhaps the quirkiest. Tiny Tambo (population 318), founded in 1863 (as Carrangarra, but renamed five years later), makes a pleasant overnight stop on the A2 between Charleville and Barcaldine. There's a shady picnic area, walking tracks and a bird hide at **Tambo Dam** and a self-guided heritage trail along the main street.

QUEENSLAND EXPLORER PASS

Overseas visitors to Queensland (including those on working holiday and student visas) are eligible to purchase rail passes for unlimited travel on Queensland's long-distance trains up to a period of one ($299) or two months ($389). These passes are valid for all regional trains except the *Gulflander* and the Kuranda Tourist Train. You could visit Charleville (on the *Westlander*), Longreach and Winton (on the *Spirit of the Outback*) and Cloncurry and Mt Isa (on the *Inlander*).

However, given there are no direct rail routes between these disparate outback towns, travelling from Longreach to Mt Isa by train would take almost a week via Rockhampton and Townsville (and include the *Spirit of Queensland*). But what a most excellent trip! See *queensland railtravel.com.au.*

EATING IN BARCALDINE, TAMBO & CHARLEVILLE: OUR PICKS

On the Rocks: Quality Charleville outback fare. It's the Vietnamese-flavoured dishes like potato-wrapped prawns and *bò kho* that stand out. *6-8pm Mon-Sat* $$

Ridgee Didge Cafe: The best of Barcaldine – generous Turkish rolls and fair-dinkum coffee made with love. *7.30am-2pm Mon-Fri, from 8am Sat & Sun* $

Fanny Mae's: Good coffee, toasted sangas and light meals in pleasant surroundings on the A2 in Tambo. *7am-2pm* $

Heinemann's Bakery: Simple brekky and lunches, with plenty of takeaway pastry options, in Charleville. *5am-3pm Mon-Fri, 6am-noon Sat & Sun* $

THE AUSTRALIAN DINOSAUR TRAIL

Discover 110-million-year-old dinosaur bones, ancient fish fossils and thousands of giant dinosaur footprints on this easy drive through outback Queensland.

START	END	LENGTH
Flinders Discovery Centre	Lark Quarry Conservation Park	505km; 3 days

Before starting, purchase a three-day pass to all sites from **Australian Age of Dinosaurs** *(australianageofdinosaurs.com; adult/child $155/90).*

In Hughenden visit ❶ **Flinders Discovery Centre** and say 'G'day' to Hughie, a life-size replica of a Muttaburrasaurus (herbivore) skeleton and the pterodactyl-like Queensland pterosaur. You'll also find over 3000 fossil specimens from the Cretaceous period.

Roughly 115km west is Richmond, a small outback town home to ❷ **Kronosaurus Korner**, both a museum and research facility. This region was once an inland sea and here you'll see (and perhaps discover your own!) marine remains from over 100 million years ago. The museum runs guided fossil digs in the surrounding countryside and also supplies the information and permits to mount your own dig.

The third stop on the Dinosaur Trail is 255km south, near Winton. Here you'll find the ❸ **Australian Age of Dinosaurs**, a natural history museum that holds annual dinosaur fossil hunts and also has the largest fossil lab in the country.

Head a further 110km south to ❹ **Lark Quarry Conservation Park** and take the guided 45-minute tour showcasing 3300 fossilised footprints. These footprints are a snapshot of a dinosaur stampede – 95 million years ago, roughly 150 small dinos (chicken to emu sized) scattered along a lakeshore trying to get away from a larger predator. The findings here inspired the stampede scene in *Jurassic Park*.

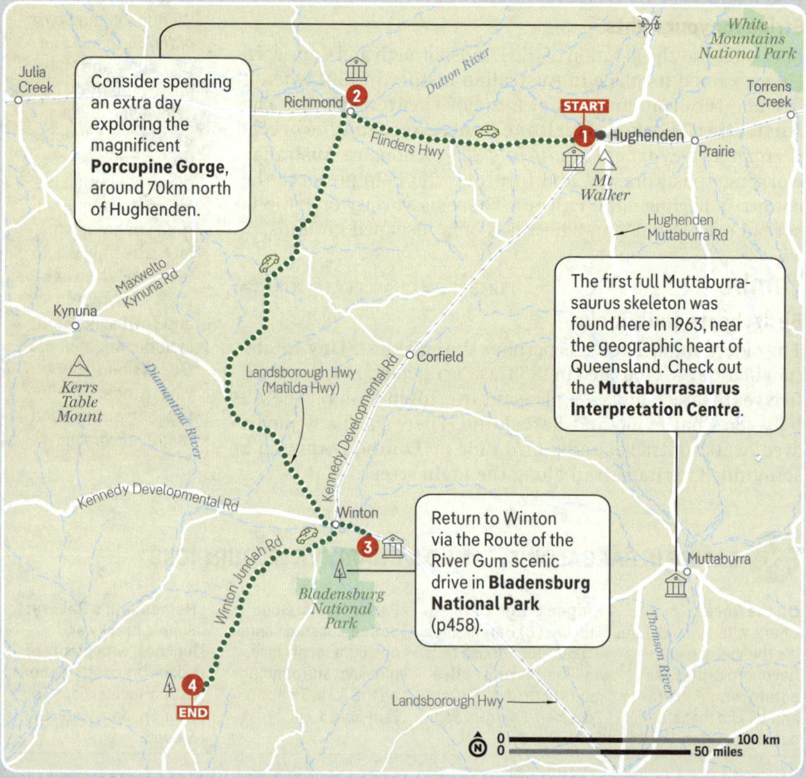

However, the town is most famous for its teddy bears and chicken races. Yep. **Tambo Teddies** *(tamboteddies.com.au),* three doors down from the pub, was conceived as a way to use up excess wool, and the beautifully hand-sewn bears have become a desirable souvenir for many travellers.

And only in the Aussie outback would coloured chickens race around a pub beer garden every night at 5pm (from April to October), raising money for charity. Check it out at the **Royal Carrangarra Hotel** *(royalcarrangarrahotel.com.au).*

Charleville

TIME FROM BRISBANE: **9HR**

Under the Milky Way

Contemplate the galaxies through high-powered telescopes at the **Cosmos Centre** *(cosmoscentre.com),* a unique observatory and planetarium where hour-long guided sessions reveal the wonders of our own sun (by day; adult/child $25/18) and the Milky Way (evening; adult/child $40/20). There's also daytime planetarium viewings (adult/child $12/8) and on cloudy nights you'll end up in there as well.

Birdsville

TIME FROM CHARLEVILLE: **9½HR**

Outback zeitgeist

A *very* long way from anywhere, Birdsville (population 110) is burnt into the Australian psyche as the epitome of remoteness. In Channel Country at the end of the legendary Birdsville Track across the Simpson Desert from South Australia, it's known for its historic pub (built in 1884), annual race meeting and desert rock festival.

A beer and a selfie at the photogenic and typically offbeat **Birdsville Hotel** *(birdsvillehotel.com.au)* is mandatory for most travellers. The place really gets loose during the **Birdsville Races** *(birdsvilleraces.com),* first held in 1882 and now run each September, when vast hordes of people arrive from all directions and planes park across from the pub like cars.

A newer though no less energetic festival is the **Big Red Bash** *(bigredbash.com.au),* a musical extravaganza held in early July on the edge of the Simpson Desert, 35km west of town.

Birdsville by road is at least eight hours from anywhere. **Rex** *(rex.com.au)* flies twice a week from Mt Isa and Brisbane, or consider a charter flight.

MIN MIN LIGHTS

Deserted outback roads are spooky places at night. Stories of strange lights appearing to follow people have haunted the Channel Country for over a century and featured in Indigenous stories for much longer, and from as far away as the Pilbara and South Australia, though ground zero for sightings is the lonely Winton–Boulia road, where the old **Min Min Hotel** once stood.

Possible explanations have included insect bioluminescence (unlikely), marsh gas (there's no marsh), aliens (?) and the refraction of truck headlights hundreds of kilometres away through a temperature inversion layer of cold air (plausible, though this doesn't explain the earlier Indigenous sightings). If you are followed, the lights are reportedly benign, though don't attempt to follow them. You may not come back.

HELP ME PICK:

Outback Queensland National Parks

Where the vast, flat, treeless brownness of the Queensland outback is broken up by a shift in terrain or vegetation, say a crumbling ancient ridge, or a gorge lined with Livistona, perhaps a few coolabah-ringed billabongs or the uniform march of infinite red sand dunes, chances are it's a national park. They come in all shapes, sizes and degrees of accessibility. But one thing they all have in common is a stunning natural environment waiting to be discovered.

Where to Visit if You Like...

Easy Access

Combo Waterhole Said to be the actual billabong of 'Waltzing Matilda' fame, Combo is easily accessed via 2WD on a sealed road 13km south of Kyuna off the Landsborough Hwy. From the car park it's a pleasant 1.3km stroll to the waterhole where there's abundant birdlife. No camping.

Bladensburg National Park Accessible by 2WD from nearby Winton, this park offers scenic drives, billabong camping and the sobering Skull Hole, site of a massacre of the local Koa/Guwa people in the late 1800s.

Walking & Wildlife

Carnarvon Gorge National Park A magnificent gorge below towering sandstone cliffs in the Central Highlands has a great selection of shady day walks as well as the showpiece Carnarvon Great Walk (six days, 87km, from March to September). However, most sights are in the gorge itself and can be visited in one long day, though an overnight camp at Big Bend would be a highlight of any trip.

Idalia National Park Look for yellow-footed rock wallabies and plum-headed finches on the graded walks traversing ancient gorges, rocky escarpments and mulga woodland, 115km southwest of Blackall.

Relaxing by a Billabong

Lochern National Park Discover myriad birdlife while camped by Broadwater Waterhole, 133km southwest of Longreach.

Diamantina National Park This large, remote park in Channel Country between Winton and Birdsville is the perfect place to camp and unwind for several days. The minimalist landscapes are best explored by 4WD and offer plentiful wildlife, good fishing and killer sunsets. Or you can rattle your car some more on the 90km **Warracoota Circuit Drive**.

A Bit of Everything

Welford National Park Red sand dunes, scenic drives, spinifex, rocky escarpments, wildlife, big sunsets and camping by the Barcoo near Windorah.

Epic Adventures

Munga-Thirri National Park Closed December to mid-March, this 10,120-sq-km swathe of red dunes by the NT border west of Birdsville is the biggest, wildest and remotest national park in Queensland. It encompasses the banana-side of the Simpson Desert; you will need a fully-tooled, high-clearance 4WD (preferably two), to be adept at sand driving and to be totally self-sufficient. Crossing the dunes to Poeppel Corner where three states intersect will take all day. Crossing the full Simpson into northern SA, usually five.

HOW TO

When to go April to September is the best time to travel. The heat can become life-threatening in summer. Not to mention the flies.

How to book Book all camp sites and the Carnarvon Great Walk online at *book.parks.qld.gov.au*.

What to avoid Rain! Most of these parks become inaccessible in wet weather. Keep an eye on the forecast and on what's happening in nearby catchment regions.

Top tip Be prepared for bush camping with minimal facilities. Take plenty of water, two spare tyres and good binoculars for the wildlife. Download the Central West Queensland guide from *parks.qld.gov.au*.

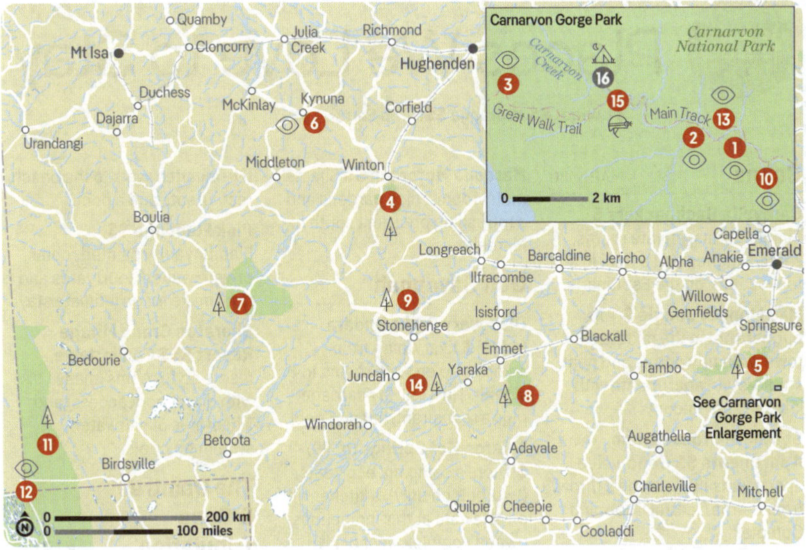

SIGHTS	see **15** Boowinda Gorge	**8** Idalia National Park	**13** Wards Canyon
1 Amphitheatre	**5** Carnarvon Gorge National Park	**9** Lochern National Park	**14** Welford National Park
2 Art Gallery	**6** Combo Waterhole	**10** Moss Garden	**ACTIVITIES**
3 Battleship Spur	**7** Diamantina National Park	**11** Munga-Thirri National Park	**15** Cathedral Cave
4 Bladensburg National Park		**12** Poeppel Corner	**SLEEPING**
			16 Big Bend Campground

Carnarvon Gorge: Day, Overnight or Great Walking?

The delights of the wonderfully lush Carnarvon Gorge are best sampled on foot, with most attractions easily visited in a day walk. From the visitor centre, the Main Gorge Track follows the canyon floor upstream to **Big Bend Camping Ground** (19.4km return). Along the way, short side-tracks lead to the soothing **Moss Garden** (7km return) and impressive **Amphitheatre** (8.6km return), the exquisite tree ferns of **Wards Canyon** (9.2km return) and the rock-art sites of the **Art Gallery** (10.8km return) and **Cathedral Cave** (18.2km return).

The mostly flat, sometimes sandy **Main Gorge Track** contains creek-crossing, rock-hopping and full-sun sections, so bring a hat, water, snacks and good walking shoes. Side-gorges can be steep, though expect decent rock or steel stairs, nice shade and benches for resting.

To allow more exploration time, consider camping overnight at Big Bend ($7.50 per person).

The excellent multiday Carnarvon Great Walk is suitable for anyone with time, medium fitness and hiking gear. From narrow **Boowinda Gorge** near Big Bend, a steep 550m climb ascends **Battleship Spur** to the plateau you'll spend the next five days traversing. The well-marked trail links camp sites that are four to six hours apart, the only places where water is usually available. Nights above 1000m on the plateau can be cold.

Guided day walks in the lower canyon are offered by **Australian Nature Guides** *(carnarvongorge.info; per person from $80)*.

Places We Love to Stay

$ Budget $$ Midrange $$$ Top End

Cairns

MAP p380

Caravella Backpackers $ Simple dorms, private rooms, shared kitchen and a pool in a top location on the Esplanade.

Mad Monkey Jungle $ Top budget spot in the middle of town, with tidy dorms and neat studio-style apartments with kitchen and balcony.

Southern Cross Atrium Apartments $$ Good-value apartments just a stone's throw from Cairns Central Shopping Complex.

Bay Village Tropical Retreat $$ Good-value, well-located, self-contained rooms for families who don't need more than a pool and somewhere to sleep.

Floriana Boutique Hotel $$ Restored Art Deco boutique hotel on the Esplanade, with a superb restaurant downstairs.

Cairns Plaza Hotel $$ One of Cairns' original high-rise hotels; recent renovations make it a good option in this price range.

Doubletree by Hilton $$$ Just what you'd expect: stylish, modern guest rooms with an enviable location on the Esplanade.

Atherton Tablelands

On the Wallaby $ Cosy, clean ecofriendly hostel in Yungaburra that feels like a home away from home; it also runs tours of the area.

Malanda Lodge $$ Just south of Malanda with extensive grounds, lovely rooms, a pool and the on-site Pickle & Smoke restaurant.

Mareeba Motor Inn $$ Simple motel rooms, nice gardens and a refreshing pool, just south of Mareeba.

Gulf Savannah

Discovery Parks Undara (p399) **$** Everything from camping to en suite rooms to sleeping in a railway carriage, plus a restaurant, bar and pool.

Talaroo Hot Springs (p399) **$** There's camping, eco-tents (two-person only), a kitchen and on-site cafe at this Indigenous-owned complex west of Mt Surprise.

Cobbold Gorge Village $ Choose from cabins, camping and caravanning if you're checking out the gorge; infinity pool and restaurant.

Chillagoe Cabins $$ Cabins with en suite bathrooms, separate bedrooms and air-con, plus a lovely pool and complimentary breakfast.

Croydon Club Hotel $$ Budget rooms in the old 1887 pub building and modern units beside the pool; also a restaurant and bar.

End of the Road Motel $$ Great location at Karumba Point; perfect when combined with the Sunset Tavern next door.

Burketown Pub $$ This outback pub has somewhat simple rooms with bathrooms, tasty pub grub and the coldest beer in town.

Port Douglas

Port Douglas Motel $$ A great family choice; two-bedroom options, fun retro furnishings, five minutes' walk to the beach, restaurants and a pool.

Pink Flamingo $$ Flamboyantly painted rooms, private walled courtyards and a pool make for an intimate stay.

Sheraton Grand Mirage Resort $$$ Comfortable, resort-style rooms (many with direct pool access) and 2 hectares of saltwater swimming pools.

The Daintree & Cape Tribulation

MAP p409

Daintree Beach Resort $ Camping and luxe glamping at Wonga Beach; an excellent on-site food truck has delicious tacos and drinks.

Cape Trib Beach House $ Clean dorms and rustic cabins in the rainforest by a pristine beach, plus a pool, restaurant and bar.

Rainforest Hideaway $$ This lovingly built solar-powered ecofriendly accommodation is a unique rainforest experience at Cape Trib.

Cooktown & Cape York

Orchid & Frangipani Suites $$ Two new suites with magnificent views at Lek's place, a short walk from the main street in Cooktown.

Mungumby Lodge $$ Located 25 minutes from Cooktown; cosy cabins with self-catering, nestled in the Greater Daintree where wildlife and waterfalls abound.

Sovereign Resort Hotel $$$ Breezy tropical-style rooms,

spacious two-bedroom apartments, gorgeous gardens and a pool, in Cooktown.

Torres Strait Islands

Wongai Beach Hotel $$ It's all here, with 21 self-contained units, a restaurant, bar and pool, on Horn Island.

Dugongs Rest $$ Brand-new cabins on Horn Island with complimentary breakfast and beautiful gardens.

Island Villas $$ Boutique self-catering accommodation on Thursday Island with a convenient location close to the main street.

Mission Beach MAP p427

Jackaroo Treehouse Hostel $ Tropical rainforest location with an on-site pool, bar and cafe.

Rainforest Motel $$ Tranquil motel rooms in the back of the village, only a short walk from the main Mission Beach.

Townsville MAP p431

Coral Lodge $ Quaint B&B, with a short walk into town. Friendly owners, spacious rooms and comfortable beds.

Rambutan $$ Cool hotel in the heart of the action on Flinders St, with comfy, large rooms surrounding the pool and rooftop bar.

Yongala Lodge $$ Housed in a lovely historic building with a private pool, Yongala is a short stroll from the Strand and city centre.

Magnetic Island

Bounce Magnetic Island (p439) **$$** Relaxed hostel in a rainforest setting with a pool and breezy bar, attached to a koala sanctuary near Horseshoe Bay Beach.

Peppers Blue on Blue Resort $$$ Overlooking the Nelly Bay marina, this is one of the island's premier addresses, with stylish rooms and an infinity pool.

Airlie Beach MAP p442

Kipara $ A budget alternative, with basic en suite cabins and larger villas, a pool, BBQs and camp kitchen. Set in the rainforest 3km east of Airlie.

Magnums $ In a lively central location surrounded by rainforest. Comfortable, quiet rooms and cabins with shared kitchens and BBQ areas.

Heart Hotel & Gallery $$ Boutique hotel in the heart of Airlie with quality fittings and luxurious bathrooms.

Coral Sea Resort $$$ Luxe resort overlooking the main marina west of Airlie, with sea views, garden views and suites with private verandah and spa.

Eungella National Park

Platypus Bushcamp $$ Rustic camp with sites for vans and tents, set in the Finch Hatton Gorge rainforest next to a platypus swimming hole.

Broken River Mountain Resort $$ Lovely retreat in natural gardens next to the Broken River's platypus-viewing platforms.

Cloncurry

Wagon Wheel Motel $$ A historic inn offering clean rooms, an attached restaurant and walking distance to most sights.

Mt Isa

Outback Motel $$ Clean, comfortable rooms a 10-minute walk from the city centre.

Barcaldine

Barcaldine Caravan Park $ Nice, grassy tent sites and clean amenities make for a pleasant overnighter.

Tambo

Tambo Mill Motel & Caravan Park $$ Airy rooms in a quiet park within walking distance of all attractions.

PAULINE MONGARNY/SHUTTERSTOCK

Sheraton Grand Mirage Resort, Port Douglas

For places to stay in Melbourne & Surrounds, see p534

SOUTHWESTIMAGESAUS/SHUTTERSTOCK

Above: Melbourne skyline; Right: Williamstown (p507)

THE MAIN AREAS

CITY CENTRE
Business meets pleasure on historic streets.
p468

SOUTHBANK & SOUTH MELBOURNE
High-rises, fine art, refined parks.
p481

ST KILDA & THE SOUTHERN SUBURBS
Beaches, bohemia and the bagel belt.
p487

RICHMOND & THE INNER EAST
Sport and art beside the river.
p494

CARLTON & THE INNER NORTH
Artsy and alternative.
p500

Researched by
Peter Dragicevich

Melbourne & Surrounds

AUSTRALIA'S CAPITAL OF COOL

Other Australian cities may be deemed to be glitzier, prettier and with far better weather, but none is as effortlessly cool as Victoria's capital.

Sophisticated, bohemian and cultured, Melbourne (Narrm) would be insufferable if it wasn't also down-to-earth, diverse and completely sports obsessed. The city's charms are subtle, not relying on the typical Australian clichés of sun and surf to sell itself. Instead, its appeal lies in the tight grid of graffiti-clad lanes and grand boulevards that form the city centre and the idiosyncratic ring of heritage neighbourhoods that encircle it – each of them endowed with hip cafes, restaurants and bars.

HYPERVISION CREATIVE/SHUTTERSTOCK

Before 1835, Narrm was a sleepy expanse of towering red gums, tea trees and ferns on the banks of the Birrarung (Yarra River) – part of the lands of the Wurundjeri people. That all changed with the arrival of a couple of British chancers from Tasmania, one of whom claimed to have purchased 2400 sq km of land around Port Phillip Bay from local chiefs while the other simply squatted and started building huts. Two years later, the colonial governor in Sydney sent a surveyor to sort out the mess and to draw up a town. In 1851, Victoria became a separate colony with Melbourne as its capital. Shortly after, gold was discovered in nearby Bendigo and Ballarat. The ensuing gold rush pumped money into the city, endowing Melbourne with many of the grand buildings that still grace the city centre today. Spare a thought for the Wurundjeri who, by 1863, were confined to a reserve in the Yarra Valley (in 1924, they lost even that).

Melbourne is now a city of 5.35 million people and is close to surpassing Sydney as Australia's biggest city. Migration has driven its grown and, as of the 2021 census, 36% of the population was born overseas (most notably in India, China, England and Vietnam). Visitors benefit from this diversity in myriad ways, the most obvious being Melbourne's extraordinary global food culture. The city has a Chinatown, Little Italy, Little Saigon, long-established Jewish neighbourhoods and one of the largest Greek communities outside of Greece. Add to that wine regions on three flanks and you've got a gastronomic destination that's up there with the best in the world.

WILLIAMSTOWN & THE WESTERN SUBURBS
Heritage and cultural diversity.
p507

GEELONG & THE BELLARINE PENINSULA
Wine, wool, wildlife and waves.
p511

MORNINGTON PENINSULA
Wineries, hot pools and beaches.
p517

YARRA VALLEY & THE RANGES
Vineyards and vistas.
p524

AROUND MELBOURNE

Find Your Way

Melbourne is a city that sprawls. Its concentric layers – city centre, inner suburbs, outer suburbs and satellite regions – cover a huge area, but it's relatively easy (albeit time-consuming) to navigate, thanks to good roads and public-transport networks. Options are more limited on the rural fringes.

TRAM

Trams are great for exploring the city centre and inner southern, eastern and northern suburbs, but there are no tram routes from the city centre to the western suburbs or to many parts of the outer suburbs. See *transport.vic.gov.au* for details.

FROM THE AIRPORT

Most flights arrive at **Melbourne Airport** *(melbourneairport.com.au)*, 21km north of the city centre, although some domestic services use **Avalon Airport** *(avalonairport.com.au)*, 52km southwest of the city centre. Both are served by taxis, rideshares and the efficient **SkyBus** *(skybus.com.au)* service.

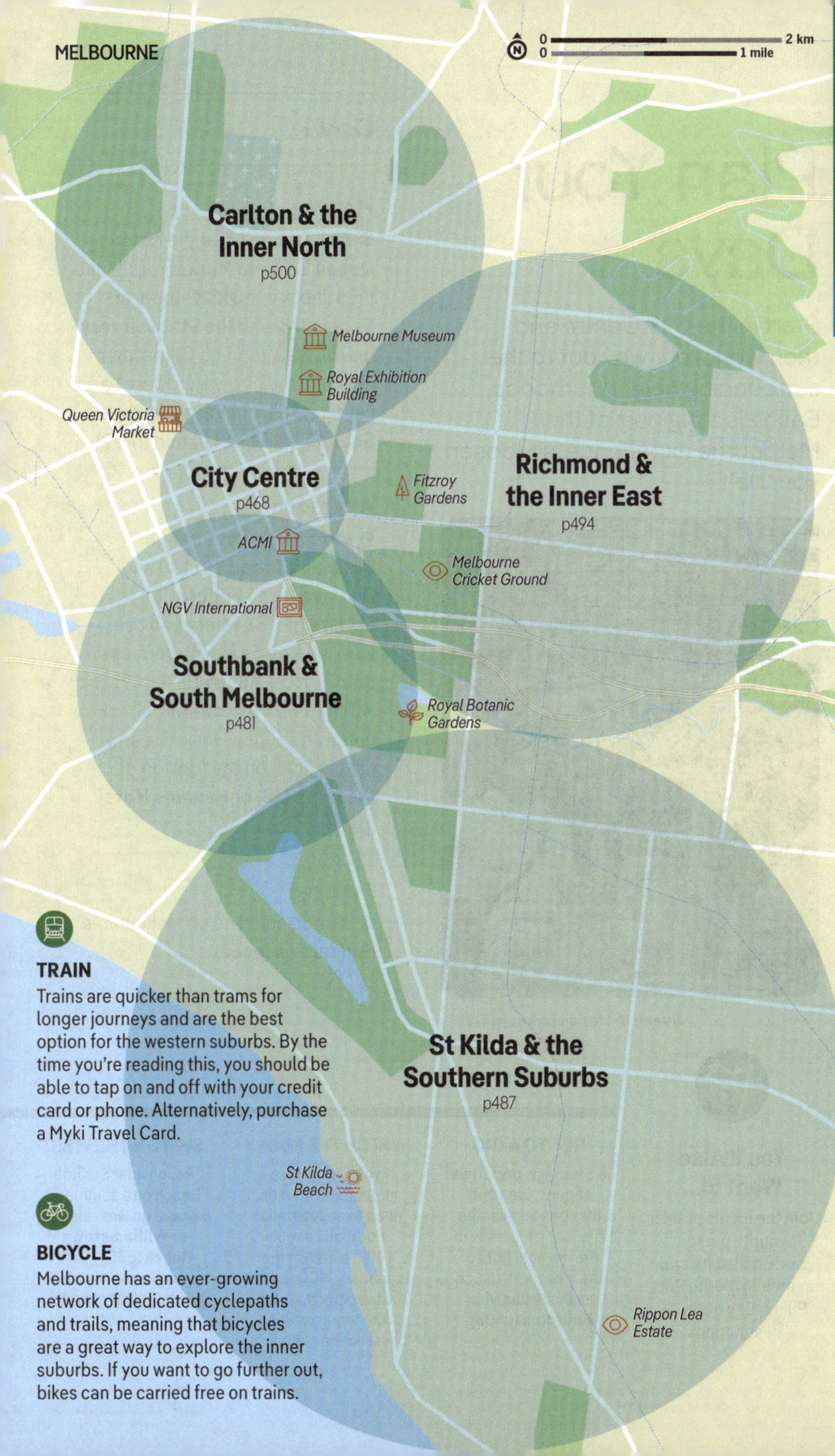

TRAIN

Trains are quicker than trams for longer journeys and are the best option for the western suburbs. By the time you're reading this, you should be able to tap on and off with your credit card or phone. Alternatively, purchase a Myki Travel Card.

BICYCLE

Melbourne has an ever-growing network of dedicated cyclepaths and trails, meaning that bicycles are a great way to explore the inner suburbs. If you want to go further out, bikes can be carried free on trains.

Plan Your Days

Start in the City Centre and then work your way out to the surrounding neighbourhoods. Eating is a big part of the Melbourne experience, so loosen your belt.

JAMES WK/SHUTTERSTOCK

Queen Victoria Market (p477)

Day 1

Morning

- Kick off the day at the historic **Queen Victoria Market** (p477) and then check out **Old Melbourne Gaol** (p478) and the **State Library** (p476). Walk through **Chinatown** (p475) to the buzzy Hardware La eating strip for lunch at **Hardware Société** (p469) or **Miznon** (p472).

Afternoon

- After lunch, cut through the **Block Arcade** (p474) and Degraves St to **Federation Square** (p473), where you can visit the **Koorie Heritage Trust** (p468), **NGV Australia** (p469) and **ACMI** (p472). Afterwards, check out graffiti-lined Hosier La and have a drink on the rooftop of the **QT** (p478) or **Hickens Hotel** (p478).

Evening

- Barhop and dine on fashionable **Flinders La** (p469).

You'll Also Want to...

Join the locals at their favourite pursuits, both in the city and in their favourite Port Phillip Bay getaway destinations.

GET TO A GIG

Live music is performed at pubs, bars and theatres all over the city, but especially in the hip hot spots of the inner north, such as the **Brunswick Ballroom** (p506).

WATCH THE FOOTY

If you want to see a Melbournian fired up, head to an Australian Football League (AFL) match at the legendary **MCG** (p496). Alternatively, watch the tennis at Rod Laver Arena (January).

SWIM IN THE WEST

Reconsider St Kilda Beach on a summer's day and go west instead to **Williamstown Beach** (p509) – it's usually less crowded and has cleaner water.

Day 2

Morning

- For breakfast, graze the food stalls in **South Melbourne Market** (p486) then wander down to the river. Call into **DFO South Wharf** (p485) for bargain shopping or head up to the **Skydeck** (p481). Stroll along Southbank and call into the **NGV International** (p484) before cutting through the Domain to the **Shrine of Remembrance** (p485) and **Royal Botanic Gardens** (p485).

Afternoon

- Catch a tram to **St Kilda** (p487) and have a late lunch by the beach. Afterwards, stroll along the sands to the pier and finish up at the **Hotel Esplanade** (p490).

Evening

- Stay south of the river for dinner and drinks around Chapel St.

Day 3

Morning

- Start your day with breakfast on Lygon St in Little Italy. Wander through **Carlton Gardens** (p505) to the **Melbourne Museum** (p505) and **Royal Exhibition Building** (p504) and then drop down to **Parliament House** (p476) and **St Patrick's Cathedral** (p475).

Afternoon

- Stroll through **Fitzroy Gardens** (p497) and grab some lunch at **Long St Coffee** (p495) in Richmond. Continue north into Abbotsford and walk along the Yarra River to **Abbotsford Convent** (p498) and on to **Yarra Bend Park** (p499).

Evening

- Spend your evening hopping between pubs and bars in Abbotsford, Collingwood and Fitzroy. Dinner could be at **Bowl Bowl** (p501) or **Zareh** (p501).

SEEK ART AT HEIDE

A wild garden, sculpture park and river frontage make the **Heide Museum of Modern Art** (p499) a worthwhile destination, even if you're not an art fan.

ENJOY A WINE TASTING

There are three wine regions to choose between that are within an hour's drive of the city, with the oldest and most famous being the **Yarra Valley** (p528).

DRIVE THROUGH THE DANDENONG RANGES

Take a day trip into the hills to visit mountain villages, botanic gardens and scenic viewpoints and to hike in **Dandenong Ranges National Park** (p532).

SOAK IN A HOT SPRING

Residents of the Mornington Peninsula have three favoured places to relax: the beach, a winery or the soporific waters of a **thermal spa** (p522).

City Centre

BUSINESS MEETS PLEASURE ON HISTORIC STREETS

TOP TIP

The **Melbourne Visitor Hub** *(whatson.melbourne.vic.gov.au)* at the Town Hall in Swanston St is open from 9am to 5pm daily and can supply tourism and transport advice, brochures and maps. There's also a volunteer-staffed **visitor booth** in Bourke St Mall and 'city ambassadors' stationed at Fed Square and Queen Victoria Market.

Apart from being a business precinct, the historic heart of Melbourne thrums with activity day and night. The grid of wide streets that comprises the city centre – and the innumerable lanes that link them – deserves to be a major focus of any Melbourne stay. Locals come here to shop, dine, party and catch a show, while travellers will find museums, galleries and heritage buildings by the dozen.

It was here in the 1830s, on the north bank of the Yarra River, that the city first started to take shape. The gold rush of the 1850s bequeathed it with its first grand buildings, while the 1880s boom times landed it the title 'Marvellous Melbourne'. Many buildings survive from this era, providing atmospheric settings for basement restaurants and rooftop bars. Flanking the river, Federation Square (Fed Square) is Melbourne's civic heart and the perfect place to start your explorations.

Meet Narrm's First People

Koorie Heritage galleries and walks

An essential stop for those interested in scratching the surface of the roughly 40,000 years of Indigenous culture in what is now Victoria, the headquarters of the **Koorie Heritage Trust** *(kooriehertiagetrust.com; free)* in Fed Square has free galleries displaying art and artefacts relating to the people of the 38 different language groups that live in the state. For a more intimate encounter, book ahead for the one-hour **Birrarung**

GETTING AROUND

This is the hub of Melbourne's public-transport system, serviced by trains, trams and buses. Though the city centre is flat and easily explored on foot, visitors can take advantage of the free tram zone that covers the area between the Yarra River (south), Spring St (east), La Trobe St and Queen Victoria Market (north) and Docklands (west). An announcement will warn you when you're about to leave the zone. Avoid driving here if you can, as there are Melbourne-specific transport rules (such as 'hook turns' to avoid blocking tramlines) that are confusing for out-of-towners.

BEN BRYANT/SHUTTERSTOCK

Ian Potter Centre: NGV Australia

Wilam Walk *(1pm on weekdays, adult/child $40/20)*, which explores the historical riverside gathering place that is now Birrarung Marr park.

The Nation's Best & Brightest

Homegrown art at NGV Australia

Encounter faces from the past, long-lost landscapes and the Aboriginal Dreaming in the heart of Fed Square. Traditional and contemporary, figurative and abstract, Indigenous and colonial – the **Ian Potter Centre: NGV Australia** *(ngv.vic.gov.au; free)* does a great job of representing the visual art of the island continent. Start downstairs in Wurrdha Marra and get lost in the mesmerising dots and swirls of Australian First Nations art. The name means 'Many Mobs' and speaks to the diversity of cultural traditions and forms represented, covering the gamut from bark painting to neon works.

Upstairs, there are galleries devoted to Australian art from the 19th century onwards, with Indigenous artists well represented here, too. Melbourne's own Heidelberg School features prominently, notably Tom Roberts' famous *Shearing the Rams* (1890) and Frederick McCubbin's monumental triptych *The Pioneer* (1904). Also fascinating are John Brack's scenes of 1950s Melbourne. Other big names to look out for include

Continued on p472

FLINDERS LANE

These days, Flinders La is one of the most vibrant parts of the city centre, home to a significant proportion of its best restaurants, bars, cafes, boutiques and commercial art galleries.

Originally called Little Flinders St, this historic strip had its name changed from 'Street' to 'Lane' in the 1940s, officially acknowledging the fact that the so-called rag traders (predominantly Jewish businesspeople involved in the textile and clothing trade) who had operated businesses here since the late 19th century had always called it 'the Lane'. Many of the multistorey warehouses and factories that once lined both sides of Flinders St have been demolished, but some survive in the stretch east of Swanston St.

Hardware La is one of the city's main eating strips

EATING IN THE CITY CENTRE: BEST CAFES

Brother Baba Budan: Serves just coffee and counter food, but both are excellent. There is only a handful of seats inside. *7am-5pm* $

Square One Rialto: Tucked beneath a tower block, this upmarket cafe delivers classic fare with a few Asian touches. *7.30am-4pm Mon-Fri* $

Higher Ground: Breakfast favourites and substantial, innovative lunches served within a cavernous red-brick power station. *7am-5pm* $$

Hardware Société: One of the city's best cafes, with excellent coffee and French-influenced menu. Sit on the lane or at the long communal table. *8am-2.30pm* $$

CITY CENTRE
0 200 m
0 0.1 miles
Franklin St
RMIT University
Mackenzie St
Russell St
Bowen St
Swanston St
American Doughnut Kitchen (400m); Queen Victoria Market (400m)
A'Beckett St
Literature Ln
Little La Trobe St
La Trobe St
State Library
State Library Victoria
Melbourne Central
Elizabeth St
Davisons Pl
Hayward La
Little Lonsdale St
Jane Bell La
Artemis La
Red Cape La
QV Square
Albert Coates La
ArtVo (2.3km)
Sutherland St
Drewery La
CHINATOWN
Guildford La
Hellenic Museum (250m)
Little Lonsdale St
Timothy La
Lonsdale St
Heffernan La
Celestial Ave
Caledonian La
Tattersalls La
Queen St
La Trobe Pl
Little Bourke St
Hardware La
Niagara La
Whitehart La
Rankins La
Russell Pl
Royal La
Higher Ground (550m)
Bourke St Mall
Kirks Ln
Union La
Royal Arc
Howey Pl
Carson Pl
Marvel Stadium (1km)
Bourke St
McKillop St
Block Pl
Dame Edna Pl
New Chancery Ln
Little Collins St
Block Arc
Block Ct
Town Hall
Regent Pl
Centre Pl
Manchester La
Swanston St
Savoy Hotel on Little Collins (500m)
Bank Pl
Collins St
Fulham Pl
Bligh Pl
Degraves St
Square One Rialto (250m)
Flinders La
Market St
William St
Queen St
Bond St
Flinders St
Sea Life (300m)
Prince Bridge

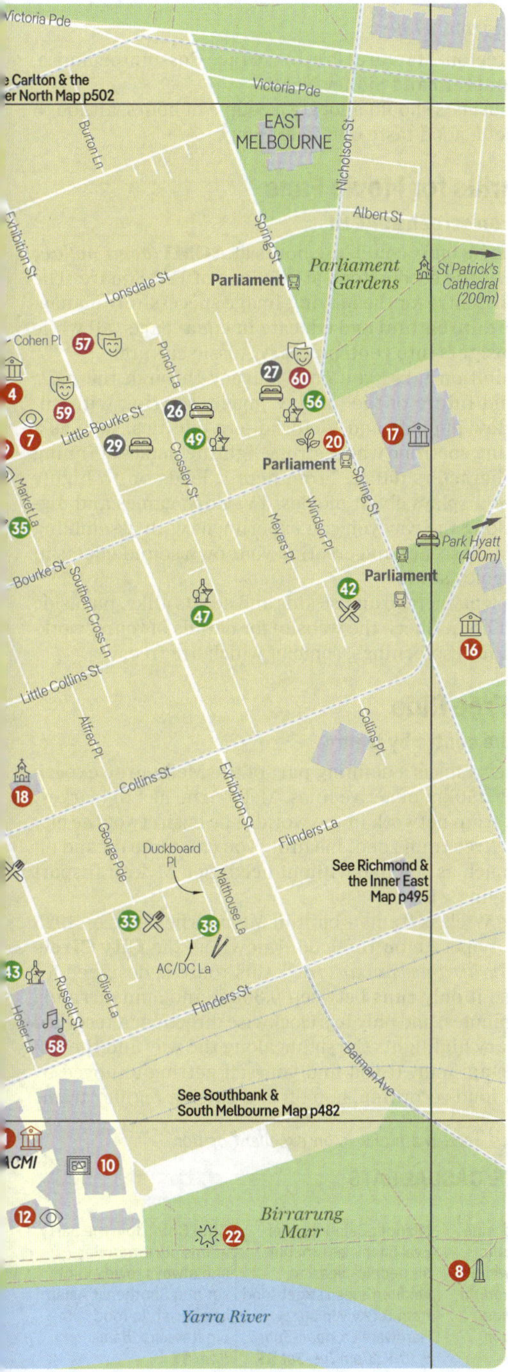

HIGHLIGHTS
1 ACMI
2 State Library Victoria

SIGHTS
3 333 Collins St
4 Chinese Museum
5 Curtin House
6 Eight Hour Day Monument
7 Facing Heaven Archway
8 Federation Bells
9 Flinders Lane
10 Ian Potter Centre: NGV Australia
11 Immigration Museum
12 Koorie Heritage Trust
13 Melbourne Town Hall
14 Nicholas Building
15 Old Melbourne Gaol
16 Old Treasury Building
17 Parliament House
18 St Michael's Uniting Church
19 Sum Kum Lee Trading Company Building
20 Tianjin Garden
21 Young & Jackson

ACTIVITIES
22 ArtPlay
23 City Circle Tram

SLEEPING
24 Bounce Melbourne
25 Hotel Indigo Melbourne Little Collins
26 Lancemore
27 Laneways by Ovolo
28 QT Melbourne
29 Rydges Melbourne
30 Space Hotel
31 Treasury on Collins

EATING
32 Brunetti Oro
33 Chin Chin
34 Embla
35 Flower Drum
36 Gimlet
37 Hardware Société
38 Lee Ho Fook
39 Miznon
40 Osteria Ilaria
41 Trattoria Emilia
42 Warkop

DRINKING & NIGHTLIFE
43 Apollo Inn
44 Bijou
45 Brother Baba Budan
46 Caretaker's Cottage
47 Cherry
48 Dessous
49 Double Happiness
50 Gin Palace
51 Heartbreaker
52 HER Rooftop
53 Hickens Hotel
54 Jayda
see 5 Rooftop
see 28 Rooftop at QT
55 Section 8
56 Siglo
see 5 Toff

ENTERTAINMENT
57 Comedy Theatre
58 Forum
59 Her Majesty's Theatre
60 Princess Theatre
61 Regent Theatre

SHOPPING
62 Craft
63 Emporium
64 Melbourne Central
65 Myer
66 Wunderkammer

INFORMATION
67 Melbourne Visitor Booth
68 Melbourne Visitor Hub

BEST CITY-CENTRE SHOPPING

Myer: The signature branch of Victoria's homegrown department-store chain is a heady nine-floor temple to consumerism.

Emporium: Seven-level shopping centre connected to Myer by a bridge, with a food court and basement gaming venue.

Melbourne Central: A lead shot tower (1890) rises incongruously beneath a glass cone at the centre of this sprawling 1990s shopping mall.

Craft: This boutique operated by a not-for-profit sells contemporary craft and design products made by local artisans.

Wunderkammer: Surprises abound in this 'Cabinet of Curiosities' selling taxidermy, fossils, feathers, insects in jars and antique lab equipment.

Continued from p469

Arthur Streeton, Margaret Preston, Grace Cossington Smith, Albert Namatjira and Sidney Nolan.

Art enthusiasts should allocate a couple of hours, although you can get a good taste of it in an hour.

Free Thrills for Movie Fans

Australia on screen at ACMI

Serious movie buffs could lose hours at **ACMI** *(acmi.net.au; free)*, one of the cornerstone attractions of Fed Square. The Australian Centre for the Moving Image successfully manages to entertain, enthral and educate in equal parts, all while offering insights into contemporary Aussie culture.

The exhibition takes you on a journey through the past, present and future of the moving image, starting with ancient shadow puppets and Victorian-era oddities, such as a mesmerising zoetrope where strobe lighting makes spinning cartoon characters dance. From here it leads on to highly interactive displays about movies, TV, video games and digital art. Along the way you can experiment with assembling your own film scenes and creating your own sound effects in a custom Foley studio.

There's plenty here to amuse kids and adults alike; put aside at least an hour. Check the website for details of tours, workshops and film screenings, some of which are free.

Take a Free Ride

Explore the centre by tram

Riding the trams is a defining part of the Melbourne experience. With 250km of active lines, Melbourne has the largest surviving tram network in the world. The entirety of the city centre is a 'free tram zone', meaning you can jump on and off them as much as you like without needing a Myki transport card or paying a cent.

Heritage W-class trams – built in Melbourne between 1923 and 1956 – operate on route 35. Known as the **City Circle Tram** *(yarratrams.com.au; free)*, this route is designed for tourists, so it only runs between 9.30am and 5pm (arriving every 12 minutes) and only in a clockwise direction. A recorded commentary highlights the sights along the way and the full loop takes an hour. If you find yourself getting annoyed by the overly loud recording, hop off and catch a regular tram.

'The Classics' feed-me menu is an excellent option

EATING IN THE CITY CENTRE: CASUAL EATS

Warkop: Toasted sandwiches are the speciality here, with Indonesian flavours making their way into many of them. Good coffee, too. *7am-3pm* **$**

Embla: Darkened wine bar serving fantastic food for grazing while drinking. *3pm-midnight Mon & Tue, from noon Wed-Sat, noon-5pm Sun* **$$$**

Miznon: Celebrity chef Eyal Shani has brought his people-pleasing Mediterranean street-food from Tel Aviv to buzzy Hardware La. *noon-3pm & 5.30-9.30pm Tue-Sat* **$$**

Chin Chin: Join the party at this ultra-popular and always rowdy joint serving Southeast Asian hawker-style food with big flavours. *11am-11pm* **$$**

A FLINDERS STREET STROLL

This short walk traverses Melbourne's civic heart, taking in some of the city's most famous buildings and public spaces.

START	END	LENGTH
Flinders St Station	Angel	1km; 1hr

Start at 1 **Flinders St Station**, Melbourne's most iconic building. You'd be hard-pressed to find a Melburnian who hasn't uttered the phrase, "Meet me under the clocks", referring to the row of timepieces above the steps leading up to the octagonal domed main entrance. On the diagonally opposite corner is 2 **St Paul's Cathedral**, a towering, sandstone, Gothic Revival, Anglican church (1891), designed from afar by British ecclesiastical architect William Butterfield. It's well worth calling in to see the ornate stained-glass windows, tiled floors, painted organ and mosaic high altar.

Cross over to 3 **Federation Square** (aka Fed Square), named in honour of the centenary of Australia's federation in 2001. The architecturally distinctive complex houses some of Melbourne's major cultural institutions within buildings clad in a fractal-patterned reptilian skin. Take the stairs at the far end to Birrarung Walk and then look for the old stairs to the right leading down to 4 **Flinders Walk**, which edges the Yarra River. Head up into multi-terraced 5 **Birrarung Marr**, one of Melbourne's most unique parks, which incorporates elements of Indigenous art and storytelling. End your walk at the 6 **Angel** – a 10m-high, three-legged, mosaic sculpture by Deborah Halpern – or continue to the MCG via the William Barak Bridge.

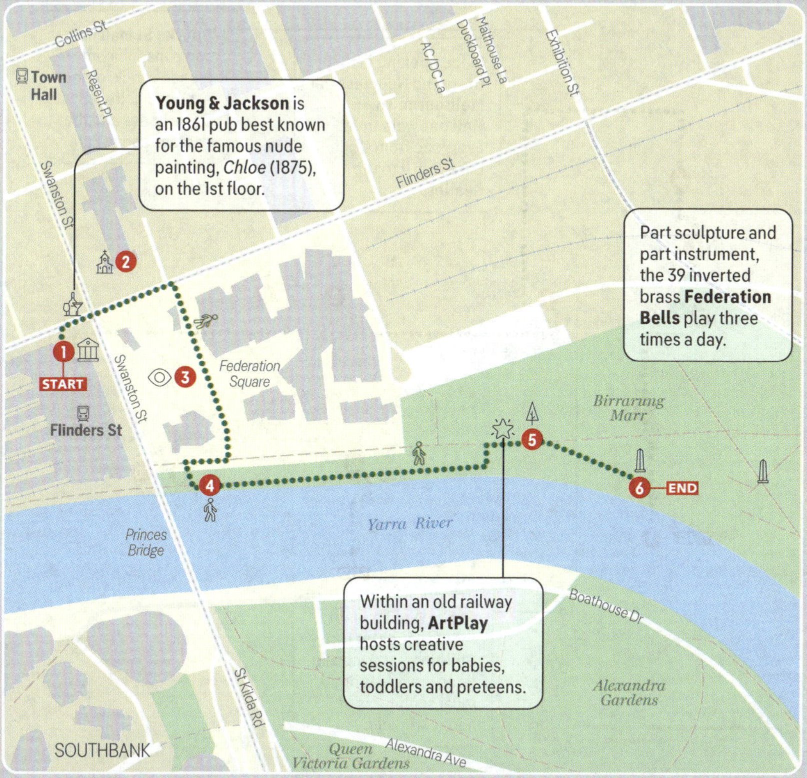

WALKING MELBOURNE'S ARCADES & LANES

Escape the city centre's orderly street grid on a stroll through its most interesting lanes and shopping arcades.

START	END	LENGTH
Degraves St	Hosier La	2km; 1hr

Start on ❶ **Degraves St**, an archetypal cafe-lined Melbourne la. Continue over Flinders La to enter narrow, food-lined ❷ **Centre Pl**. Cross Collins St and enter the ❸ **Block Arcade**, built in 1892 and featuring ornate plasterwork and mosaic floors. Ogle the window display at the famous ❹ **Tea Rooms** and then continue through the arcade to atmospheric ❺ **Block Pl**. Cross Little Collins St and enter the wonderfully ornate ❻ **Royal Arcade**. Look out for Gog and Magog, hammering away on either side of the clock under the dome. Turn right into Bourke St Mall and right again onto Swanston St. Detour through the ❼ **Manchester Unity Arcade** (1932), then turn left onto Collins St. Continue uphill to the 'Paris end', where you'll pass Gothic-style ❽ **Scots' Church** (1874) and the unusual Lombardic Romanesque-style ❾ **St Michael's Uniting Church** (1866). Turn right and right again into Flinders La and duck down ❿ **Duckboard Pl** to admire the streetart lining this and adjacent ⓫ **AC/DC La**. Continue along Flinders La and then turn left onto Melbourne's most photographed streetart hot spot, ⓬ **Hosier La**.

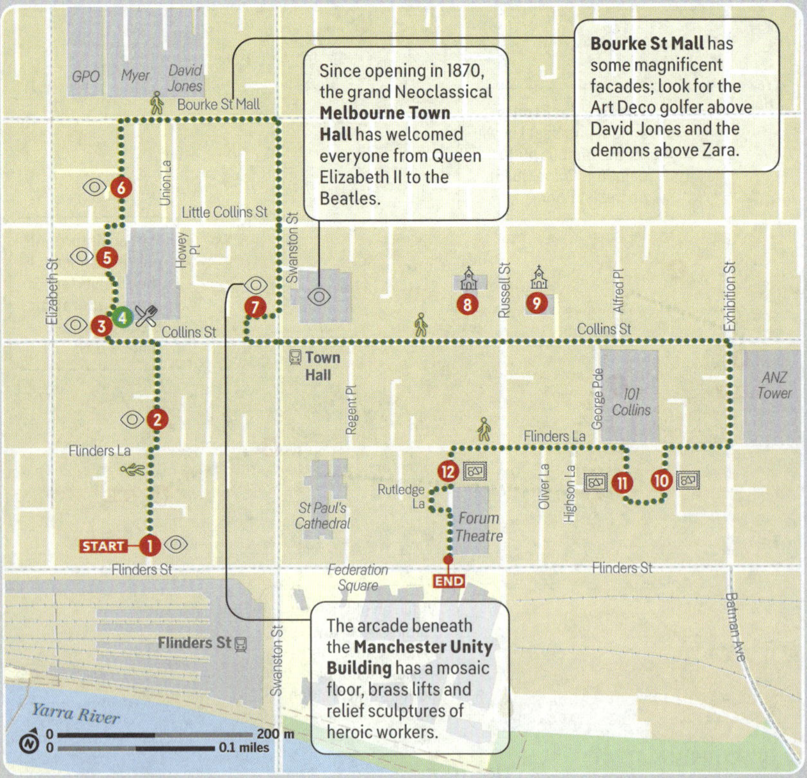

SUTHIKAIT TEERAWATTANAPHAN/SHUTTERSTOCK

St Patrick's Cathedral

Melbourne Goes Gothic

Divine architecture at St Patrick's Cathedral

Rated as one of the finest Gothic Revival cathedrals in the world, **St Patrick's Cathedral** *(stpatrickscathedral.org.au; free)* is an awe-inspiring sight – especially from the inside, where the side windows bathe the cavernous interior in a yellow light. The building of this bluestone Catholic cathedral took place between 1858 and 1897, but it wasn't officially completed until the sandstone spires were added in 1939. The interior stonework is extraordinary, especially in the elaborate side chapels.

Dumplings & Dragons

Wander the streets of Chinatown

Of all of Melbourne's ethnic enclaves, Chinatown is the most atmospheric. That's partly due to the four ornate archways that mark its entrances, positioned on Little Bourke St between Swanston St and dragon-filled **Tianjin Garden** on Spring St. There's a fifth, larger structure known as the **Facing Heaven Archway** which opens onto the small square at the centre of this stretch. It was built in China by traditional craftspeople and reassembled here.

BEST CITY-CENTRE HERITAGE THEATRES

Regent Theatre: Built as a picture palace in 1929, the opulent Regent hosts big-name musicals, opera, ballet, comedy and concerts.

Her Majesty's Theatre: The home of musical comedy since 1880 and still going strong, with a fantastic 1930s interior.

Princess Theatre: One of the city's most recognisable landmarks, this 1854 theatre mostly stages musicals and the occasional ballet.

Comedy Theatre: Built in 1928 with a Florentine facade and Spanish interior, this midsize venue is dedicated to comic theatre, stand-up and musicals.

Forum: One of the city's most atmospheric music and cinema venues, with a Moorish design featuring minarets, domes and dragons.

EATING IN THE CITY CENTRE: TOP END

If dining solo, opt for the kitchen counter

Gimlet: Contemporary European cuisine in a heritage space reminiscent of a Viennese cafe. Glamourous and pricy but not starchy. *noon-midnight* $$$

Lee Ho Fook: Housed in an old warehouse, this restaurant represents the best in modern Chinese-Australian culinary wizardry. *5.30-10.30pm Mon-Sat* $$$

Flower Drum: This Chinatown fine diner serves classic Cantonese cuisine in a charmingly old-fashioned ambience. *noon-3pm & 6-11pm Mon-Sat, 6-10.30pm Sun* $$$

Osteria Ilaria: Italian food with a Mod Oz sheen is on offer at this slick venue, along with an impressive wine list. *noon-10pm Mon-Sat* $$$

SIGNIFICANT CITY-CENTRE BUILDINGS

Parliament House: Opened in 1856, Victoria's grand Neoclassical state parliament building can be explored on free guided tours on non-sitting days.

Old Treasury Building: Designed by 19-year old JJ Clarke, this 1862 Renaissance-style structure shifted much of the gold-rush loot. It's free to visit.

333 Collins St: Built in the 1890s as a bank's headquarters, it's worth calling in to see the extraordinary Italian Baroque dome.

Curtin House: A cultural linchpin since 1922, it has housed the Community Party, Catholic Action and now bars, restaurants and a bookshop.

Nicholas Building: This landmark 1926 building is a bohemian base for vintage-clothing shops, artists' studios and artist-run galleries.

Chinese immigrants first arrived in substantial numbers during the 1850s, hoping to make a fortune in the colony they described as 'New Gold Mountain'. Melbourne's Chinatown was founded in the decades that followed and several grand buildings from this period still exist. The most impressive is the wedding-cake-like former **Sum Kum Lee Trading Company Building** at 112–114 Little Bourke St, now home to the Shanghai Village restaurant. This is one of many popular Chinese restaurants and bars operating in Chinatown today.

But Chinatown has more to offer than delicious dumplings. It's well worth setting aside an hour to explore the **Chinese Museum** *(chinesemuseum.com.au; adult/child $17/14)*, located in an old brick warehouse behind the archway on Cohen Pl. Start at level 3, which explores 200 years of Chinese Australian stories since the first known migrant arrived in 1818. The next floor down showcases 2000-year-old Han Dynasty antiquities on loan from a private collector. Make your way down to the basement and enter recreated gold-rush scenes, such as a rocking ship's cabin and cook shop, then follow the tail of the 65m-long processional dragon up to its 200kg head on the ground floor. In full flight during Lunar New Year, the dragon needs eight people just to hold up its head and more than 200 to operate it for the whole procession.

Beautiful Repository of Knowledge

Victoria's Neoclassical State Library

At the forefront of Melbourne's literary scene since 1856, the **State Library Victoria** *(slv.vic.gov.au; free)* is a hub of city life. There's free Wi-Fi and computer terminals and a series of inspiring rooms where anyone is welcome to quietly study, work or simply read for pleasure. The central **La Trobe Reading Room** is arguably the most beautiful room in Melbourne. When it was completed in 1913, its reinforced-concrete octagonal dome was the world's largest and its natural light continues to illuminate ornate plasterwork and studious Melburnians.

Visitors are welcome to quietly wander around and to visit the free galleries. Take the frescoed grand staircase up to the main reading room, then catch the painfully slow lift up to the 6th floor to gaze down on it from the balcony. You can then make your way down through the **Dome Galleries**, where you'll find fascinating free exhibitions – many on bookish themes. Be sure to visit the **Ian Potter Queen's Hall**, the

Sister establishment New Gold Mountain is upstairs; there's no sign

DRINKING IN THE CITY CENTRE: DARKENED DENS

Apollo Inn: The city's classiest cocktail joint is an homage to intimate, dimly lit New York–style bars. *5pm-1am Sat-Thu, 3pm-1am Fri*

Gin Palace: This moody cellar is the perfect place to grab a soft couch and hard liquor, with over 330 gins on offer. *4pm-3am*

Dessous: Claim a velvet chair in this atmospheric Victorian basement and relax over a cocktail and excellent bar snack or two. *5pm-late Tue-Sat*

Double Happiness: Tucked away in Chinatown, this little firecracker serves Asian-influenced cocktails. *5pm-midnight Mon-Wed, to 3am Thu-Sat*

WANDER THROUGH QUEEN VICTORIA MARKET

Spread over a 7-hectare site at the north of the city grid, 'Vic Market' has been a Melbourne institution since it first opened in 1878.

START	END	LENGTH
Meat and Fish Hall	Market Lane Coffee	1km; 1hr

Plan to visit when the market is in full flight (before 3pm on Tuesdays, Thursdays, Fridays, Saturdays or Sundays). Start in the 1 **Meat and Fish Hall** on the corner of Elizabeth and Victoria Sts and do a loop to view the extraordinary range of animal products sold here. Next, go through the door in the middle of the fish stalls to find yourself in the Art Deco 2 **Dairy Produce Hall**, built in 1929. Alongside bread and delicatessen items, here's where you'll find many of the market's most popular takeaway food stalls.

Exit onto Therry St and turn right towards the 3 **Fresh Flower Stall**. Cross Queen St to reach the open-sided Upper Sheds, dating from 1878. Turn left and enter through the final lane, 4 **String Bean Alley**, which houses some of the market's more upmarket stalls. At the end you'll find 5 **Palletus Radiata**, a stylised tree made from wooden pallets.

Cut through the centre of the market, where stalls sell everything from leather goods to Harley Davidson T-shirts. Turn right at B Shed, where you'll find yourself in the heart of the market's large 6 **Fruit and Vegetables** section. End your walk with a brew at 7 **Market Lane Coffee**.

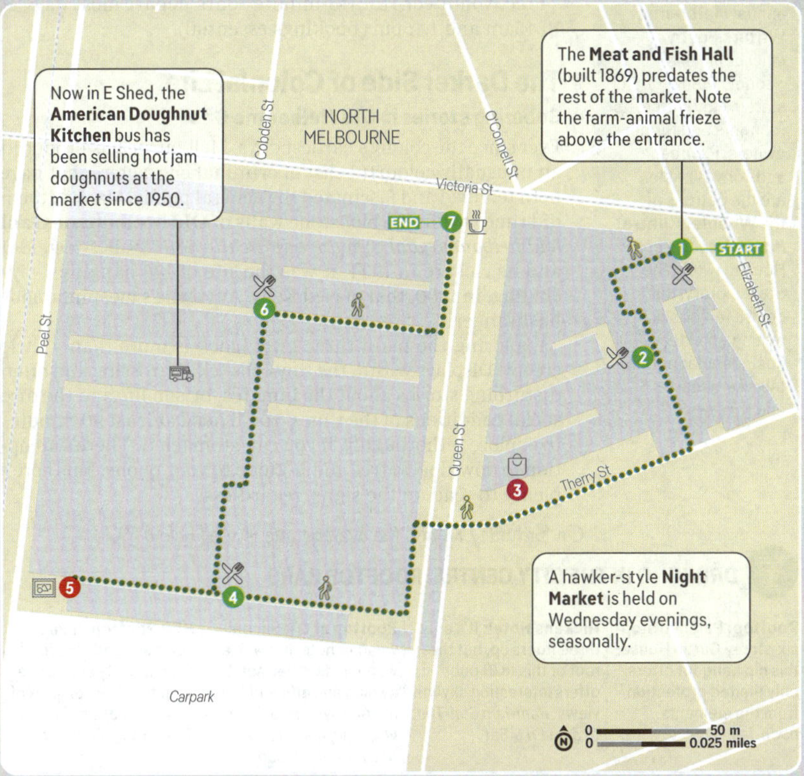

UNESCO CITY OF LITERATURE

In 2008, Melbourne was designated the first UNESCO City of Literature in Australia – and only the second in the world. It's a fitting accolade for a place whose residents consume more books, magazines and newspapers per capita than any other Australian city. The city's rich literary culture encompasses local publishers, independent bookshops, writers' organisations, journals and the annual **Melbourne Writers Festival** *(mwf.com.au)*.

Lonely Planet got its start in Melbourne. Its founders and former owners, Maureen and Tony Wheeler, are the patrons of the **Wheeler Centre** *(wheelercentre.com)*. Housed within the State Library, this centre for 'books, writing and ideas' hosts regular public talks by writers and thinkers.

MICHELLE BRITTAIN/SHUTTERSTOCK

library's original reading room, another light-filled space lined with soaring Ionian columns. Also notable is the **Redmond Barry Reading Room,** where the bullet-dented armour worn by outlaw Ned Kelly is on display.

Free, volunteer-run, 45-minute tours depart most days at 10.45am and 1.45pm (bookings essential).

The Darker Side of Colonial Life

Sobering stories in Old Melbourne Gaol

Ever since the colony's earliest days, Melbourne has produced an unusually colourful cast of criminal characters that have both terrified and fascinated the general public. Many of them did time within the bluestone walls of **Old Melbourne Gaol** *(oldmelbournegaol.com.au; adult/child $38/22)*. Between 1841 and its closure in 1924, it was the site of 133 hangings – including, in 1880, that of Ned Kelly, Australia's most infamous bushranger.

Exploring the main three-level block is more than a little creepy. Displays within the tiny cells tell engrossing and often disturbing stories about the inmates, prison life and the dire social conditions of the times. You'll need at least 90 minutes to explore it thoroughly, if you can stomach it. There's an option to download a free audio-guide to your phone, but there's plenty to read on the signs, regardless.

On Saturday nights, the average age is well below 30

DRINKING IN THE CITY CENTRE: ROOFTOP BARS

Rooftop: Perched atop six-storey Curtin House, this hip hangout offers only limited protection from the elements. *noon-1am*

Hickens Hotel: It's only three floors up, but the roof of this 1870 pub offers interesting skyline views. *11am-1am Sun-Thu, to 3am Fri & Sat*

Rooftop at QT: Slick all-weather hotel bar with a wooden deck, retractable awning and efficient heating system. *3-11pm Mon-Thu, noon-1am Fri & Sat, noon-11pm Sun*

HER Rooftop: Sample cocktails and Thai food amid the city skyscrapers atop the HER complex of venues. *11.30am-1am Sun-Thu, to 3am Fri & Sat*

Old Melbourne Gaol

Guided tours include the City Watch House Experience, where you'll be 'arrested' and thrown in the slammer (more fun than it sounds). If you're after an even scarier time, take the Hangman's Night Tour or an after-dark ghost tour. If you're on a budget, pick up the free *Outdoor Walking Tour* pamphlet from the ticket desk and explore just the old prison grounds, most of which are now part of RMIT University.

Melbourne's Multicultural Melting Pot

Family stories at the Immigration Museum

Melbourne is famously multicultural, with successive waves of immigration (British, Irish, German, Chinese, Italian, Greek, Jewish, Vietnamese, Indian and many more) shaping the city of today. While a whole museum dedicated to the subject might sound painfully worthy, the **Immigration Museum** *(museumsvictoria.com.au; adult/child $15/10)* lightens the tone through personal stories and memorabilia. Contentious subjects such as the White Australia Policy (1901–73) are covered, but the overall mood is more celebratory than po-faced. The upstairs galleries are given over to colourful artistic expressions of immigrant life, which included a recreated suburban video store when we last visited.

THE EIGHT-HOUR DAY

The unusual **Eight Hour Day Monument** near Old Melbourne Gaol celebrates an important victory for Victoria's workers.

During the the first half of the 19th century, many employees worked up to 14 hours a day, six days a week. In 1856, stonemasons working on the construction of Melbourne University walked off their jobs in protest over working conditions. This brought their employer, the Colony of Victoria, to the negotiating table and the result was an agreement that workers employed on public projects should only be required to work for eight hours a day. By 1860, most workers in Victoria had been granted an eight-hour day.

The monument sits diagonally opposite **Trades Hall**, the oldest union hall in the world.

Be prepared for cigar smoke on the terrace

DRINKING IN THE CITY CENTRE: WINE & COCKTAIL BARS

Bijou: Bottles completely line the walls of this corner bar and wine store. There's no list; the staff will let you know what's open. *noon-1am*

Jayda: Down the business end of town, little Jayda is the cocktail-serving sister of neighbouring Middle Eastern restaurant Maha. *4pm-midnight Thu-Sat*

Caretaker's Cottage: In the bluestone house where the caretaker of the neighbouring church once lived, this tiny bar serves a mean cocktail. *4pm-1am Mon-Sat*

Siglo: As well as having rooftop views over grand Victorian buildings, Siglo has a great wine and cocktail list. *5pm-3am Tue-Sat*

MELBOURNE'S BEST FESTIVALS & EVENTS

Formula 1 Australian Grand Prix: Four days of rev-head action in early March focussed on the circuit around normally tranquil Albert Park Lake.

Melbourne Food & Wine Festival: Hundreds of events in March, including the 'World's Longest Lunch', celebrate the city's exciting eating and drinking scene.

Melbourne International Comedy Festival: An enormous range of local and international comic talent hits town in late March for four weeks of laughs.

Rising: Cutting-edge theatre, music and dance events staged in the first half of June.

Melbourne Fringe Festival: Celebration of everything arty and experimental over 20 days from late September.

Plus, the Neoclassical building is worth a trip in itself. It was built in 1876 as the Customs House and its column-lined Long Room is a magnificent piece of Italian Renaissance–revival architecture. Allow an hour to explore.

Greece is the Word

Ancient treasures at the Hellenic Museum

Melbourne is said to have the biggest Greek population of any city outside of Greece, with around 174,000 people claiming Hellenic ancestry (near 4% of the population). Fittingly housed in a beautiful Neoclassical building that was once the Royal Mint, the **Hellenic Museum** *(hellenic.org.au; adult/child $16/free)* is a regular beneficiary of ancient treasures on loan from the homeland, making it one of Melbourne's best boutique museums.

Underwater but Dry

Eyeball sharks at Sea Life

A surefire hit with younger kids, **Sea Life** *(sealifemelbourne.com.au; adult/child from $38/28)* is a whizz-bang aquarium with walk-through tunnels offering a below-the-surface view of giant rays, gropers and sharks. Balancing out the cuteness factor somewhat is the colony of gentoo and king penguins, busily pottering about in their own icy enclosure.

Tickets are far cheaper online and if booked at least a day in advance. Add-ons include shark dives and behind-the-scenes experiences. You'll need at least 90 minutes to see everything.

DRINKING IN THE CITY CENTRE: LIVE-MUSIC BARS

Cherry: The city's most legendary rock bar has a downstairs dive bar and a dedicated band room upstairs. *7pm-3am Sun-Thu, 6pm-5am Fri & Sat*

Heartbreaker: A rockin' jukebox, pool table and raucous atmosphere are the hallmarks of this drinking den. *5pm-1am Sun-Tue, to 3am Wed, 3pm-3am Thu-Sat*

Toff: Within the boho confines of Curtin House, the Toff delivers DJs, intimate rock gigs and cabaret. *6pm-3am Mon, 5pm-5am Tue-Sat*

Section 8: A fenced off graffiti-covered corner in a back lane with a shipping-container bar, DJs and live musicians. *noon-11pm Sun-Wed, to 1am Thu-Sat*

Southbank & South Melbourne

HIGH-RISES, FINE ART, REFINED PARKS

South of the river, Melbourne's skyline is continually reaching new heights. In 2020, the Australia 108 building overtook the gold-tipped Eureka Tower to become the city's tallest (at 319m), but even that is due to be eclipsed by the 366m garden-shrouded STH BNK building that's currently under construction.

Once a gritty industrial zone servicing the nearby Docklands, Southbank has been rebuilt and rebranded as Melbourne's glitziest tourist precinct. The riverside promenade is peppered with big-name international restaurants, hotels, a convention centre and the distinct whiff of 'casino', but its Yarra River views and multiple top-draw arts institutions make it an essential part of any Melbourne itinerary.

Beyond here, South Melbourne has more of a heritage feel, with intricate wrought-iron awnings extending from Victorian-era shops that are now crammed with boutiques and cafes. Just across busy St Kilda Rd, the substantial green expanse known collectively as the Domain Parklands provides respite from the dense urban landscape.

TOP TIP

In summer, the **Royal Botanic Gardens** hosts the popular **Moonlight Cinema** *(melbourne.moonlight.com.au)* on its central lawn and the **Sidney Myer Music Bowl** is used for outdoor concerts. The city's main Anzac Day (25 April) and Remembrance Day (11 November) commemorations are held on the forecourt of the Shrine.

Head for the Heights

Ascend to the Melbourne Skydeck

Every great modern city worthy of the title has an observation deck atop a tower and Melbourne's inhabits the 88th floor of the 297m-high Eureka Tower. As you'd expect, the views from **Melbourne Skydeck** *(melbourneskydeck.com.au; adult/*

GETTING AROUND

Southbank and the Domain Parklands are only a short walk from the city centre. Trams are the main form of public transport here, although be aware that it's outside of the free tram zone. Lines 3, 5 and 6 head along St Kilda Rd, stopping right outside the NGV and edging the Domain. For South Melbourne Market, catch tram 12 or 96; for Melbourne Skydeck, exit the 58 at Crown Casino. Anzac Station opened near the Shrine in late 2025, with underground platforms for the Pakenham and Cranbourne rail lines.

HIGHLIGHTS
1 NGV International
2 Royal Botanic Gardens
3 Shrine of Remembrance

SIGHTS
4 ACCA
5 Alexandra Gardens
6 Arts Centre Melbourne
7 Buxton Contemporary
8 Domain Parklands
9 Government House
10 Ian Potter Centre: NGV Australia
see 8 Kings Domain
11 Melbourne Skydeck
12 Queen Victoria Gardens

SLEEPING
13 Coppersmith Hotel
14 Pan Pacific Melbourne

EATING
15 Chéri
16 Juniper
17 Lucia
18 Simply Spanish
19 St Ali

DRINKING & NIGHTLIFE
20 Boatbuilders Yard
21 Hophaus
22 Montague Hotel
23 Ponyfish Island

ENTERTAINMENT
24 Malthouse Theatre
25 Melbourne Recital Centre
26 Sidney Myer Music Bowl
27 Southbank Theatre

SHOPPING
see 16 Coventry Bookstore
28 DFO South Wharf
29 Lana Berg
see 15 Nest
30 NGV Design Store
31 South Melbourne Market

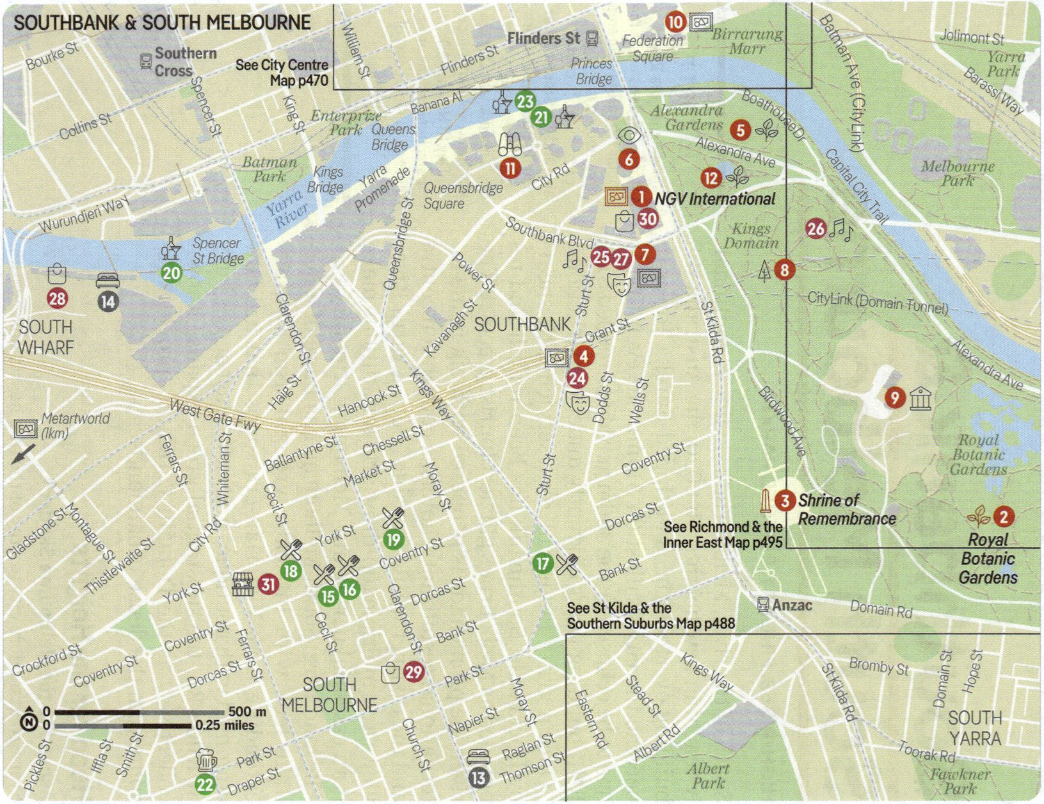

child from $33/21) are beyond incredible, offering a bird's-eye perspective of the languid Yarra River winding through the suburbs and city before emptying into Port Phillip. You'll need at least 30 minutes to take it all in.

The viewing floor is mainly enclosed, but a small corner of exposed deck gives you the opportunity to feel the force of the wind. Daredevils can pay $18 extra to enter the Edge, a glass cube that extends over the side of the building. You can also add on a virtual-reality experience, presenting a cinematic journey through Victoria's main sights.

Tickets are cheaper if bought online and in advance. The Skydeck doesn't open until midday but stays open until 9pm (10pm in summer).

Weird, Wonderful & Thought-Provoking

Southbank's contemporary art scene

NGV International isn't the only player in this part of town for art aficionados. Two major contemporary galleries are a short walk away and there's soon to be a third. Set to open in 2028 in a brand-new landmark building, **The Fox: NGV Contemporary** will be Australia's largest gallery dedicated to contemporary art and design.

Already in the neighbourhood are two of Australia's most exciting and challenging galleries, **Buxton Contemporary** *(buxtoncontemporary.com; free)* at Melbourne Uni's art school and **ACCA** *(acca.melbourne; free),* which occupies a fittingly sculptural building with a rusted exterior. Both galleries are closed on Mondays, with Buxton also closed on Sundays.

Melbourne's Green Zone

Wander through the Domain Parklands

If the sun is shining and you want to stretch out, all you need do is cross the Yarra River and disappear into the 123 hectares of lawns and formal gardens that form the **Domain Parklands** *(melbourne.vic.gov.au/domain-parklands; free).* Office workers slink here on their lunchbreaks, joining picnicking city dwellers, ball-kicking kids and a small army of pram-pushing parents on the expansive lawns and shady paths.

'The Domain' is actually a conglomeration of parks, starting with **Alexandra Gardens** (closest to Federation Square), which has lawns and a skatepark. Next up are the **Queen Victoria Gardens** (opposite the Arts Centre), where a regal statue gazes over a central pond.

BEST SOUTHBANK ARTS VENUES

Arts Centre Melbourne: Comprising Hamer Hall and the Theatres Building (with its distinctive spire), this is the city's premier performing-arts precinct.

Sidney Myer Music Bowl: A partly covered 1950s amphitheatre in the Domain, used for summertime events such as Carols by Candlelight.

Malthouse Theatre: This repurposed 1892 beer-making malthouse in Southbank has two theatre spaces used by its resident company.

Melbourne Recital Centre: Classical music and jazz venue that's home to the Melbourne Chamber Orchestra.

Southbank Theatre: Home of the Melbourne Theatre Company, with two stages and a geometric facade.

EATING IN SOUTH MELBOURNE: OUR PICKS

The mushroom congee is a hearty winter warmup

Lucia: Sophisticated contemporary Italian cuisine in a formal setting at the base of a modern office block. *noon-10pm Tue-Sat, to 5pm Sun* $$$

Chéri: The cake counter at this large patisserie cafe will have you reaching for your camera. Classic French breakfasts and Italian-influenced lunches. *8am-5pm* $

St Ali: Speciality coffees and creative food at this roastery cafe in a converted warehouse tucked down a side street. *7am-5pm* $$

Juniper: Near South Melbourne Market, this slender cafe has enticing counter food (filled baguettes, etc) and an eclectic menu. *8am-3pm* $

TOP EXPERIENCE

NGV International

The flagship branch of the National Gallery of Victoria, NGV International is more than just a gallery, it's a cultural and social institution. It's always filled with Melburnians milling about, meeting for lunch and shopping at the design store – and that's before you even hit the exhibitions. Those certainly don't disappoint, either.

ANNE CZICHOS/SHUTTERSTOCK

TOP TIPS

- For local art, head across the river to NGV Australia (p469).
- From June until September, the ticketed **NGV Friday Nights** give access to the annual Winter Masterpieces show. Food and drinks are available.
- Leave large bags in the free cloakroom.

Practicalities

- *ngv.vic.gov.au*
- 10am-5pm
- free

Monumental Modernism

Designed by local architect Sir Roy Grounds, the NGV building was controversial when it was completed in 1967 but has come to be respected as a modernist masterpiece. Entry is through a perfectly semicircular arch that opens onto a large water wall. Be sure to visit the Great Hall, on the other side of the foyer, with its vast stained-glass ceiling.

The Collections

You'll need at least a couple of hours to do the permanent collection justice. **Asian Art** takes up over half of the 1st floor, with Japanese and Chinese works assigned their own separate galleries. Spanning the 12th to 18th centuries, the **European Collection** (Titian, El Greco, Fontana, Rembrandt) starts on this floor and continues upstairs. The **International Collection** (Picasso, Rothko etc) picks up from the 19th century and is interspersed with a decorative-arts collection that includes whole suites of mid-century furniture.

Tours, Exhibitions & Events

Bookings aren't required for the free 50-minute highlight tours that kick off at 11am daily. Blockbuster exhibitions roll through with regularity and are ticketed separately. Check the website for talks, performances, specialist tours and other events.

Beyond here is the **Kings Domain**, a large expanse of lawn liberally peppered with mature trees and monuments. Here you'll find the Sidney Myer Music Bowl (p483), the Shrine of Remembrance and **Government House**. The latter was built between 1872 and 1876 as the official residence of Victoria's governors, modelled on Queen Victoria's Osborne House on the Isle of Wight. It remains one of the largest residences in Australia, with a whopping 240 rooms.

To the east is the horticultural highlight of the Domain precinct, the magnificent **Royal Botanic Gardens** *(rbg.vic.gov.au)*. Founded in 1846, these gardens are considered to be among the finest examples of Victorian-era landscaping in the world. Highlights include the fern gully, arid garden, Australian forest walk and the lawns, which slope down to a large ornamental lake. Check the website for details of free guided walks, Aboriginal heritage walks (adult/child $45/23), punting tours on the lake (for three adults $90) and 30-minute rides on the Explorer open-sided mini bus (adult/child $15/10).

Encounter the Anzac Legend

Stirring memories at the Shrine

The **Shrine of Remembrance** *(shrine.org.au; free)* is more than just a war memorial and museum. It is also an excellent introduction to one of the foundations of Australia's national identity. Australia only became a country in 1901 and WWI (1914–18) had an oversized role in shaping how the newly minted nation saw itself. The original Anzacs (Australian and New Zealand Army Corps) who fought in that conflict are celebrated for their resilience, mateship and good humour, all of which have come to epitomise the Aussie spirit.

This secular temple was built between 1928 and 1934 (much of it with Depression-relief labour) to honour the Victorians killed in WWI, but subsequently was extended to remember all who have served in war and peacekeeping roles since. The Classical design is partly based on the Mausoleum of Halicarnassus, one of the seven wonders of the ancient world. At its heart is the **sanctuary**, where a beam of sunlight illuminates a memorial stone at 11am on 11 November, the time and date when the fighting of WWI ended. Directly beneath the sanctuary is a sombre **crypt** lined with regimental flags. The brick vaults surrounding the crypt have been converted into an engrossing **museum** devoted to each of the conflicts in which Australian troops have been involved.

BEST SOUTHSIDE SHOPPING

DFO South Wharf: Bargain hunters will love this huge direct-factory-outlet complex full of big-brand clearance clothing and footwear.

NGV Design Store: The gallery's gift shop sells beautiful art books, cards, jewellery, ceramics, apparel and special-edition pieces themed to current exhibitions.

Lana Berg: One-off local boutique specialising in women's apparel, catering to a diverse range of body types.

Coventry Bookstore: Independent bookstore stocking local and international fiction; biographies; and travel, design, fashion and architecture titles.

Nest: In a light-filled space, Nest stocks a gorgeous range of homewares and gifts, from sheets to Aesop skincare.

'Aperitivo hour' stretches from 4pm to 6pm weekdays

DRINKING IN SOUTHBANK & SOUTH MELBOURNE: OUR PICKS

Montague Hotel: On a backstreet, this old corner pub offers craft beer, interesting wines and good food. *4-10pm Mon & Tue, noon-11pm Wed-Sun*

Hophaus: Enjoy a European brew with a view from the deck of this large bar above the Southbank promenade. *noon-11pm*

Boatbuilders Yard: On the revitalised South Wharf, the Yard attracts a mixed crowd of office workers and travellers for its waterside views and backyard vibe. *9am-10pm*

Ponyfish Island: Tucked below a bridge in the middle of the Yarra, this quirky place packs out on sunny days. *11am-1am*

BEST SONGS ABOUT MELBOURNE

'From St Kilda to Kings Cross' (Paul Kelly; 1985): Homesickness engulfs Melbourne's premier chronicler.

'Four Seasons in One Day' (Crowded House; 1991): Kiwi music legend Neil Finn has confirmed that the Domain he's singing about is Melbourne's. The weather certainly is.

'Accidently Kelly Street' (Frente!; 1992): Perky '90s indie pop celebrating the songwriter's new house in Richmond.

'Move On' (Jet; 2003): An introspective moment in Flinders St Station is captured on a down-tempo number by local rockers.

'Elevator Operator' (Courtney Barnett; 2015): Action takes place on the 96 tram and the rooftop of the Nicholas Building in this amusing indie-rock banger.

PHOEB/SHUTTERSTOCK

Oysters, South Melbourne Market

You'll need at least an hour to explore the complex, longer if you're a military buff. Be sure to check out the views from the upper balcony. Guided **tours** *(adult/child $20/10)* depart throughout the day.

Local Institution & Foodie Destination

Graze through South Melbourne Market

At the centre of neighbourhood life since 1867, **South Melbourne Market** *(southmelbournemarket.com.au)* has an outsized reputation for its food, especially its international selections (the Dim Sims stall has operated here since 1949!). It's possible to book a 90-minute specialist **Foodie Tour** *($79),* but there's plenty of enjoyment in simply wandering around and grazing as you go. Aside from Dim Sims' famous cricket-ball-sized dumplings, try the paella at **Simply Spanish** and freshly shucked oysters at one of the two oyster bars.

The market is open on Wednesdays, Fridays, Saturdays and Sundays, from 8am. Keep an eye out for night markets in summer.

St Kilda & the Southern Suburbs

BEACHES, BOHEMIA AND THE BAGEL BELT

St Kilda is Melbourne's tattered bohemian heart – a place that has featured in songs, novels, TV series and films, and where a young Nick Cave played gloriously chaotic gigs. The neighbourhood has taken on many roles over the years: 19th-century seaside resort, red-light district and punk-rocker hub among them. It's a complex jumble of boom-era Victorian mansions, raffish Spanish Moorish apartments, seedy side streets, a vintage roller-coaster and nostalgia-inducing theatres, flanked by wonderful dining options.

South from here are a string of beach suburbs stretching towards the Mornington Peninsula. Away from the water, St Kilda East, Balaclava and Elsternwick are home to a large proportion of Melbourne's Jewish population, many of whom fled Europe in the years immediately before and after WWII. Heading north are the cool eating and drinking hot spots of Windsor and Prahran, followed by well-heeled South Yarra and Toorak, spread along the banks of the river.

TOP TIP

The water quality at **Port Phillip Bay**'s beaches can be compromised for up to 48 hours after rain. If you're planning to swim, it's wise to check the regularly updated Beach Report page on the Environment Protection Authority website *(epa.vic.gov.au)*, which grades water quality as good, fair or poor.

Melbourne's Most Famous Beach

Soak up the St Kilda scene

It's crowded, there's usually no surf to speak of and the water quality can be dubious, but **St Kilda** is Melbourne's most

Continued on p490

GETTING AROUND

This is a large, spread-out area and you're best to use public transport to get around. St Kilda, Balaclava, Windsor, Prahran and South Yarra are well served by trams. Sandringham-line trains stop at South Yarra, Prahran, Windsor, Balaclava, Ripponlea, Elsternwick and Brighton Beach, while Frankston-line trains reach the southernmost beaches. Buses plug the gaps. Dedicated cycle lanes run along St Kilda Rd, and the 50km Bay Trail between Port Melbourne and Seaford is one of the most popular cycling and walking routes in the city.

HIGHLIGHTS
1 Melbourne Holocaust Museum
2 Rippon Lea Estate
3 St Kilda Beach

SIGHTS
4 Albert Park
5 Como House & Garden
6 Elwood Beach
7 Fawkner Park
8 St Kilda Botanical Gardens
9 St Kilda Pier
10 Victorian Pride Centre

ACTIVITIES
11 St Kilda Adventure Playground

SLEEPING
12 Cullen Melbourne – Art Series
13 Olsen Melbourne – Art Series
14 Ovolo South Yarra
15 Prince Hotel
16 Royce Hotel

EATING
17 All Things Equal
18 Cicciolina
19 Donovans

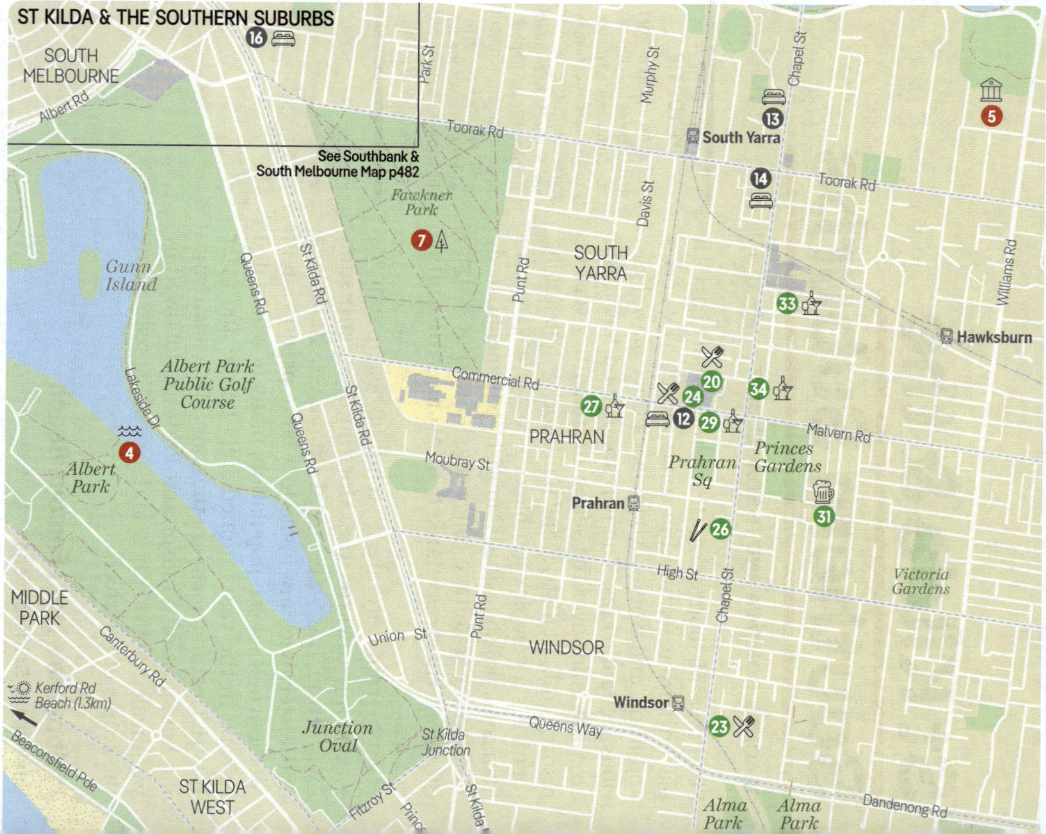

- **20** G McBean Family Butcher
- **21** I Carusi II
- **see 20** Maker & Monger
- **22** Monk Bodhi Dharma
- **23** Otakoï
- **24** Q Le Baker
- **25** Stokehouse
- **26** Suzie Q

DRINKING & NIGHTLIFE

- **27** Alps
- **28** Dogs Bar
- **29** Don's
- **30** Ellora
- **31** Flying Duck Hotel
- **32** Hotel Esplanade
- **33** Leonard's House of Love
- **34** Poof Doof
- **see 15** Prince Public Bar

ENTERTAINMENT

- **35** Luna Park
- **36** Palais Theatre

SHOPPING

- **see 10** Hares & Hyenas
- **see 24** Prahran Market
- **37** St Kilda Esplanade Market

Continued from p487

popular beach. On summer weekends, scantily clad young things preen on the golden sand while a constant progression of rollerbladers, joggers and cyclists zip along the promenade. Jutting out over the bay, **St Kilda Pier** offers a smashing view of the Melbourne skyline, best seen at sunset. The Edwardian-style kiosk at the end of the pier is a replica of the original, which burnt down in 2003.

Behind the beach, straggly palm trees sway and passengers on the Great Scenic Railway at **Luna Park** *(lunapark.com.au; single/unlimited rides $30/55)* scream their lungs out. Taking its inspiration from New York's Coney Island, this amusement park opened in 1912 and its wooden roller-coaster is the oldest of its kind still in service. The park only operates on Friday evenings, weekends, school holidays and public holidays. Entry is through the gaping mouth of 'Mr Moon', one of a trio of signature St Kilda structures.

Another is the large Art Deco **Palais Theatre** *(palaistheatre.com.au)* next door, which opened its doors in 1927 and still stages musicals, opera, comedy and concerts. Then there's the 1878 **Hotel Esplanade**, Melbourne's most famous pub and a much-loved live-music venue. Threatened with development in 1997, 'the Espy' was saved after a high-profile campaign by the community. On weekends and balmy summer nights, the joint heaves.

There are plenty of food and drink options on nearby Fitzroy and Acland Sts, but the best (and priciest) choices line the beachfront. On Sundays, the **St Kilda Esplanade Market** sets up along the road, with stalls selling high-quality arts and crafts from local makers.

St Kilda's Colourful Sister

Skyline views from Brighton Beach

For a different take on Melbourne beach culture, catch the train to **Brighton Beach Station**, 5km south of St Kilda. The train will deposit you mere metres from the sand, but the best beaches are north of here.

Turn right towards **Green Point**, a natural vantage point with fantastic views of the Melbourne skyline, then keep walking towards **Dendy St Beach**. Here you'll find the first of 82 brightly painted Victorian-era bathing boxes, beloved by social-media posters. These simple structures are privately owned and most families use them to store equipment,

ST KILDA'S LITTLE PENGUINS

Despite the great mass of humanity that converges here, St Kilda is home to a colony of around 1400 little penguins, which nest between the rocks in the breakwater that extends from historic St Kilda Pier.

As part of a pier redevelopment completed in 2025, a viewing boardwalk was built to separate the penguins from their many thousands of admirers. Access to the boardwalk is now restricted in the evening – which is when the penguins return to their nests – to those with tickets to one of the two viewing sessions (starting 30 minutes and 90 minutes after sunset, respectively). Tickets are free but book out months in advance; look for the St Kilda Penguins tab on *penguins.org.au*.

Scan this QR code to book tickets

EATING IN ST KILDA: BEST RESTAURANTS

I Carusi II: Family-friendly but still romantic, this Italian restaurant serves pasta and Neapolitan-style pizza to candlelit tables. *5pm-10pm Wed-Mon* $$

Donovans: St Kilda's top restaurant sits right on the boardwalk, serving modern Mediterranean fare. Prices match the views. *noon-3pm & 6-10pm Wed-Sun* $$$

Cicciolina: An ageing but still sexy St Kilda grande dame, Cicciolina serves Italian-accented dishes, including pasta, risotto, and meat and fish dishes. *noon-10pm* $$$

Stokehouse: Upstairs is an acclaimed fine-dining restaurant while downstairs is more relaxed. Floor-to-ceiling windows showcase bay views. *noon-midnight* $$$

F.MALIKI/SHUTTERSTOCK

Brighton Beach

such as beach furniture, kayaks, toys, towels and barbecues. Although there's no electricity or plumbing, sheds such as these can sell for more than houses (one in Portsea sold for a record $1.2 million in 2024).

The wood-clad **Dendy Beach Pavilion** won an architectural award when it opened in 2025. It houses a cafe, public toilets and the Brighton Life Saving Club. Beyond here are the broader sands of **Brighton Beach** proper, popular with families and stand-up paddleboarders for its (usually) calm waters.

Posh Nosh in Victorian Surroundings

Treat yourself at Prahran Market

While not as big or famous as Queen Vic or South Melbourne Market, **Prahran Market** *(prahranmarket.com.au)* more than holds its own on the snackable food front – although it does have a reputation for being pricier. It actually predates the other two, having been established in 1864 (albeit on another site). The grand facade dates from 1891, which is when it moved to this location.

Come with an empty stomach and not on Mondays or Wednesdays when it's closed. There's usually live music

SOUTHSIDE BEACHES: BEST OF THE REST

Most of these beaches are patrolled on summer weekends.

Kerford Rd Beach: Sandy beach with a pier that's close to the city centre and the Victoria Ave cafe strip.

Elwood Beach: Barbecue, picnic and play facilities close to the water; lots of sailing action to watch.

Half Moon Bay: Pretty beach in Black Rock with a pier that's popular for fishing.

Chelsea Beach: Clean sandy strip with a playground and shallow waters that's close to a train station; great for kids.

Frankston Beach: The last beach before the Mornington Peninsula, with very clear waters. It can get crowded in summer.

DRINKING IN ST KILDA: BEERS & GIGS

Hotel Esplanade: A St Kilda legend, with lots of areas to explore, including a famous live-music venue. *noon-11pm Sun-Thu, to 3am Fri & Sat*

Ellora: Rooftop bar with sea views, DJs on Saturdays and live music on Fridays and Sundays. *4-10pm Thu, to midnight Fri, 1pm-1am Sat, 1-11pm Sun*

Prince Public Bar: Queer-friendly, Art Deco pub with a central bar, live-music band room and wine bar next door. *7am-11pm*

Dogs Bar: Live-music pub with dog-friendly, outdoor tables that get soaked in afternoon sunshine. *5pm-midnight Thu & Fri, from 3pm Sat & Sun*

PRIDE IN THE SOUTH

While the northside has more gay bars, some of the most important LGBTIQ+ spaces and events are found south of the river. Opened in St Kilda in 2021, the **Victorian Pride Centre** *(pridecentre.org.au)* is mainly used to house community organisations, but visitors can access the social-enterprise cafe, coworking space and **Hares & Hyenas** bookshop.

The annual **Midsumma Festival** *(midsumma.org.au)* runs over three weeks from mid-January, kicking off with the Midsumma Carnival in Alexandra Gardens. The headline event is the Midsumma Pride March, which takes place along Fitzroy St in St Kilda a couple of weekends later.

Party-wise, **Poof Doof** is the city's most popular queer club night, operating out of Chasers Nightclub in Prahran on Saturdays.

JAGODAPATTERNS/SHUTTERSTOCK

Rippon Lea Estate

around lunchtime on weekends, which is when it's busiest. Recommended stalls include **Q Le Baker** for pastries, **G McBean Family Butcher** for its porchetta rolls and **Maker & Monger** for its cheese toasties.

Combine a visit with a stroll along Chapel St, the buzzy shopping strip linking South Yarra, Prahran and Windsor.

Beyond the Mansion Gates

House and garden at Rippon Lea

What do you do if you're a successful Victorian businessperson with wads of cash? How about buying 11 hectares on what was then the fringes of Melbourne and commissioning the city's best architect to build you a mansion surrounded by extensive pleasure gardens? Now operated by the National Trust, **Rippon Lea Estate** *(ripponleaestate.com.au; adult/child $15/9)* in Elsternwick is one of the finest historic houses and gardens in the country.

Built in the 1850s, the turreted mansion features the polychromatic brickwork and arches that architect Joseph Reed dubbed 'Lombardic Romanesque', inspired by his time spent

DRINKING IN SOUTH YARRA & PRAHRAN: OUR PICKS

Leonard's House of Love: Southern rock vibes and fairy lights in a bluestone cottage on a South Yarra side street. *5pm-1am Mon-Thu, noon-2am Fri-Sun*

Alps: Elegant little wineshop and bar with a rear garden in an unassuming patch of Commercial Rd. *3-10pm Mon-Fri, noon-10pm Sat & Sun*

Flying Duck Hotel: Upmarket brick-lined pub with a plant-filled conservatory and parklike beer garden in a Prahran back street. *noon-11pm*

Don's: Diminutive joint opposite Prahran Market serving simple but tasty bar food and pouring natural wines. *3-7pm Sun, 4-9pm Mon-Thu, 1-11pm Fri & Sat*

in northern Italy and reminiscent of his design for St Michael's (p474) in the city. It was subsequently refurbished in the 1930s by an heiress with a taste for Hollywood glamour, adding a swimming pool and painting over dark wood and marble columns with creamy-gold paint. It's worth paying extra for the **house tour** *(adult/child $10/5)* to see the over-the-top interiors and to get all the goss on the former owners.

The gardens were designed in the picturesque style, with paths winding around an ornamental lake, boathouse, lookout tower and large fernery. General admission also gives access to the servants' quarters below the house, which had been closed off and left in their original Victorian condition for decades before the Trust took over.

Set aside an hour to enjoy the gardens and a further 45 minutes for the house tour.

Tales of Horror & Hope

Elsternwick's sobering Holocaust Museum

Dedicated to the memory of the six million Jews murdered by the Nazis and their collaborators between 1933 and 1945, the **Melbourne Holocaust Museum** *(mhm.org.au; adult/child $18/14)* offers visitors a sobering but enriching experience. Founded by survivors in 1984, the museum won a major Australian architecture award when it was redesigned in 2023.

The main permanent exhibition, titled 'Everybody Had a Name', recounts the events of the Holocaust in historical panels and through personal stories illustrated by photographs, artefacts, newsreels and a disturbing scale model of Treblinka II built in the 1980s by a Melburnian survivor. Next to it, *In the Footsteps* is a multimedia installation allowing visitors to view video testimony by six local survivors. Contemplative spaces include the Memorial Room and the Garden of the Pillars of Witness, with its striking bronze sculptures and eternal flame.

As an alternative to the harrowing main exhibits, 'Hidden: Seven Children Saved' *(adult/child $12/10)* is specifically designed for children aged 10 years and over. It relates the incredible stories of seven Jewish children who attribute their survival to the kindness of others.

The museum is closed on Mondays, Saturdays and Jewish holidays. Set aside 90 minutes to do it justice.

BEST SOUTHSIDE PARKS

Albert Park: The large central lake is popular with rowers and boaters, while joggers and cyclists whiz around the 5km perimeter.

St Kilda Adventure Playground: Younger kids love the trampoline, mini Luna Park tunnel and 'fighter jet', while the older ones gravitate to the basketball court.

Como House & Garden: National Trust property in South Yarra (built 1847) with 2 hectares of urban pleasure garden remaining; garden admission is free.

St Kilda Botanical Gardens: Dating from 1859, this much-loved green space has treelined walkways, a rose garden and children's play areas.

Fawkner Park: A 19th-century park in South Yarra with playgrounds, formal paths and lawns.

EATING IN BALACLAVA, WINDSOR & PRAHRAN: OUR PICKS

All Things Equal: This veggie-friendly cafe in Balaclava provides jobs and training for people with disabilities. *8.30am-3.30pm Sun, Mon, Thu & Fri* **$**

Monk Bodhi Dharma: Hidden down a Balaclava alley, this vegetarian cafe serves tasty global dishes, all of which can be made vegan. *8am-3.30pm* **$**

Otakoï: Staff in folk costume serve authentic Ukrainian fare, such as dumplings, chicken Kyiv and honey cakes. *5-10pm Tue-Sat, plus noon-3pm Sat & Sun* **$$**

Suzie Q: Modern Chinese cuisine is the focus of this large, buzzy, neon-lit restaurant in Prahran. *5-11pm daily, plus noon-3pm Sat & Sun* **$$**

Richmond & the Inner East

SPORT AND ART BESIDE THE RIVER

TOP TIP

For an enjoyable walk alongside the Yarra River, follow the Main Yarra Trail from the Collingwood Children's Farm through Dights Falls Reserve, cross the river near the mouth of Merri Creek and then follow the Dights Falls Loop Trail to Studley Park Boathouse, accessed via Kane's Bridge.

East Melbourne is the most sporty part of the most sporty city in a sport-obsessed nation. The neighbourhood's southwestern skyline is completely dominated by the angular shapes of stadiums, none more imposing than the mighty Melbourne Cricket Ground. North from here are genteel streets of heritage residences centred on gorgeous Fitzroy Gardens. To the east, Richmond is a densely packed old suburb with some great cafes and 19th-century pubs.

The affluent neighbourhoods beyond here may be short on blockbuster sights, but there are less immediately obvious attractions on offer for those who choose to seek them out. Chief among these is the Yarra River itself, which winds its way through urban bushland, passing historic boathouses and grand old buildings. It's easy to walk or cycle alongside sections of river flats lined with red gum trees and catch glimpses of the landscape as it used to be.

Catch a Match

Witness Melbourne's sporting obsession

Melbourne is one of the world's great sporting cities. It has hosted both the Olympics and the Commonwealth Games, celebrates two annual public holidays linked to sporting events (the Melbourne Cup and AFL Grand Final) and has a disproportionate number of world-class sporting venues – most

GETTING AROUND

A footbridge connects the Jolimont sporting precinct to Birrarung Marr park in the city centre. Richmond Station is a major train junction, with five lines stopping there. Other useful stations include North and West Richmond, Jolimont, Glenferrie and Victoria Park. Tramlines cross through East Melbourne, Cremorne, Richmond and Hawthorn. Buses are useful for getting to Abbotsford Convent (or you can walk from Victoria Park Station in 15 minutes) and the Heide Museum (take the Hurstbridge train to Heidelberg and switch to bus 903 from there).

HIGHLIGHTS
1 Abbotsford Convent
2 Fitzroy Gardens
3 Melbourne Cricket Ground

SIGHTS
4 AAMI Park
5 Australian Sports Museum
6 Collingwood Children's Farm
7 Cooks' Cottage
8 Johnston Collection
9 Melbourne Park
10 Museum of Desire
11 St Patrick's Cathedral
12 Yarra Bend Park

ACTIVITIES
13 Studley Park Boathouse

SLEEPING
14 Park Hyatt

EATING
15 Black Gold
see 6 Farm Cafe
16 Flour Child
17 Long St Coffee
18 Minamishima
19 Tarts Anon

DRINKING & NIGHTLIFE
20 Bodriggy Brewing Co.
21 Corner Hotel
22 Dr Morse
23 London Tavern
24 Lulie Tavern
25 Retreat Hotel
26 Royston Hotel
27 Union House

A set omakase menu is offered for $325 per person

EATING IN RICHMOND: OUR PICKS

Long St Coffee: Hidden down a dead-end lane, this friendly place serves good coffee and reasonably priced food. *7.30am-2.30pm Mon-Fri, 8am-1pm Sat* **$**

Black Gold: The toasted sandwiches are legendary at this plant-filled cafe on a unassuming back street. The menu is unexpectedly creative. *7am-3pm* **$**

Flour Child: Pizza, pasta, *polpette* (meatballs) and a buzzy, youthful vibe await in this pink-neon-lit Italian restaurant above Church St. *noon-11pm* **$$**

Minamishima: Arguably Australia's best Japanese restaurant, but be prepared to empty your pockets and book two months in advance. *6-10.30pm Tue-Sat* **$$$**

BEST BOOKS SET IN MELBOURNE

My Brother Jack (George Johnston, 1964): Brilliantly captures working-class family life in Melbourne during the world wars.

The Children's Bach (Helen Garner; 1984): The life of a suburban family is disrupted when a friend introduces them to Melbourne's bohemian underground scene.

The Slap (Christos Tsiolkas; 2008): The fallout from a single incident at a backyard barbecue in a Melbourne suburb reverberates through a group of friends.

Black Rock White City (AS Patrić; 2015): A migrant janitor has to deal with a series of disturbing incidents at a Melbourne hospital.

The Butterfly Women (Madeleine Cleary; 2025): Rollicking 19th-century whodunnit set in brothels of a notorious inner-city slum.

of which are crammed into the corner of East Melbourne known as Jolimont.

Chief among them is the legendary **Melbourne Cricket Ground** *(mcg.org.au)*, affectionally referred to as 'the MCG' or just 'the G'. In summer this vast oval stadium hosts cricket, while in winter the focus shifts to AFL (Australian Football League, Aussie rules or 'footy').

Just across the railway tracks is **Melbourne Park** *(melbournepark.com.au)*, home to the **Australian Open** *(ausopen.com)*, the first of tennis' four Grand Slam tournaments. At other times, basketball and netball take over the four main arenas (Rod Laver, Margaret Court, John Cain and Kia).

Right next door is **AAMI Park** *(aamipark.com.au)*, a striking honeycomb-framed stadium with a capacity of 30,000 that's home to the Melbourne Storm rugby-league team, the Melbourne Rebels rugby-union team and the Melbourne Victory and Melbourne City football (soccer) teams. It is sometimes referred to as the Rectangular Stadium (as opposed to the oval configuration used for AFL and cricket).

As if that wasn't enough, there's another 53,000-seater with a retractable roof, **Marvel Stadium**, across town in Docklands.

Regardless of the sport or venue, try to catch a match. You'll find plenty of passion on display at any of them, but for a quintessentially Melbourne experience, nothing beats watching AFL at the MCG. A standard mid-season ticket costs around $30. Australian Open tickets start at $49 for a 'ground pass', stretching to nearly $1500 for the men's final.

More than Memorabilia

Kick off at the Sports Museum

There aren't many museums where you can show off your athletic ability (or lack of it), but the **Australian Sports Museum** *(australiansportsmuseum.org.au; adult/child $38/17)* is more than just a repository for dusty trophies and team photos. The 'Game On!' section offers the opportunity to kick goals, shoot hoops, test your reactions and pit yourself against Olympians. Sports nuts, big and small, will love it.

Hidden away within the MCG, the museum focuses on Australia's favourite sports and historic sporting moments, with a particular emphasis on local obsessions: AFL, cricket, horse racing and the Olympics. There are Olympic medal and torch displays, sporting clips on rotation and even a hologram of late cricketing great Shane Warne. The most traditional

DRINKING IN RICHMOND: OUR PICKS

Union House: Zhooshed-up 1871 pub with French doors opening on to Swan St and a rooftop bar. *4-10pm Mon-Wed, noon-midnight Thu-Sat, noon-10pm Sun*

Corner Hotel: Downstairs is one of Melbourne's most popular midsize live-music venues; upstairs is a far less grungy rooftop bar. *noon-late Tue-Sun*

London Tavern: This 1921 corner pub is a favourite with locals, especially when the AFL's screening. The covered beer garden gets raucous on game days. *noon-11pm*

Royston Hotel: Craft beer dominates the taps at this 1970s-looking stone-clad pub near the river. *4-11pm Tue & Wed, noon-11pm Thu-Sun*

PAUL HARDING 00/SHUTTERSTOCK

AAMI Park

part is the **Melbourne Cricket Club Museum**, which has its own separate wing filled with treasured mementos.

Allow about an hour if you're a fair-weather sports fan; more if you're a cricket nut. Tickets can be combined with a 75-minute **guided tour** of the MCG, taking you behind the scenes and onto the boundary line *(adult/child incl Sports Museum $50/21, tour only $38/17)*.

East Melbourne's Beautiful Backyard

Stroll through Fitzroy Gardens

Aside from being one of Melbourne's most beautiful parks, **Fitzroy Gardens** *(melbourne.vic.gov.au/fitzroy-gardens; free)* has interesting sights scattered within its stately elm-lined avenues. The park was laid out in 1859 and has all of the picturesque elements you'd expect of a formal Victorian garden, including ponds, fountains, sculptures and a bandstand. On sunny days it's full of local kids racing about, parents pushing prams and couples canoodling in quiet corners. There's also a great little **playground** with a dragon slide and a giraffe swing.

UNUSUAL ATTRACTIONS

Johnston Collection: This 1860s East Melbourne mansion can only be explored on 90-minute tours. Different curators rearrange the house quarterly.

ArtVo: Immersive 'trick art' gallery in Docklands that will provide plenty of content for social-media posts.

Metartworld: Scrap-metal art gallery in Port Melbourne with virtual-reality experiences, a fluorescent starry-sky exhibition and a '9D flying cinema'.

Museum of Desire: Adult's-only immersive exhibition of erotic art in Collingwood with a 'boobie ball pit' among other risqué attractions.

RAAF Museum: Tells the story of the Royal Australian Air Force within a working military base.

You'll also find them in Prahran Market and Collingwood

EATING IN CREMORNE, ABBOTSFORD & HAWTHORN: CHEAP EATS

Bawa Cafe: You can order a Bloody Mary with your chilli scrambled eggs at this pleasant, plant-filled cafe in Hawthorn. *7am-3pm* $

Farm Cafe: Attached to the Collingwood Children's Farm in Abbotsford, this rustic cafe makes good use of the farm's super-fresh produce. *9am-3pm* $

Old Quarter: Five types of *pho bò* (beef noodle soup) are on offer at this lantern-strewn Vietnamese cheapie in Hawthorn. *10.30am-9pm* $

Tarts Anon: Tucked beneath a modern building in Cremorne, this bakery-cafe serves delicious sweet pastries, some incorporating Asian flavours. *8am-2.30pm* $

KULIN COUNTRY

It's thought that the area around Melbourne has been inhabited for over 40,000 years. It falls within the lands of the Kulin nation, a confederation of five groups, each speaking its own related language. Woiwurrung (or Woi Wurrung) was mainly spoken on the north side of the river, while Boonwurrung (Boon Wurrung or Bunurong) was spoken to the south and east (the two languages share 93% of their vocabulary).

The central part of Melbourne was built on the territory of the Wurundjeri, one of the Woiwurrung-speaking groups. Narrm (Naarm) was their name for the area where central Melbourne now stands, while the Boonwurrung used this word to refer to Port Phillip Bay. Narrm has now been widely adopted as an alternative name for the entire city.

BEN BRYANT/SHUTTERSTOCK

Cooks' Cottage

Worth seeking out is the 1930s Spanish Mission–style **Conservatory**, filled with colourful floral displays. Nearby is **Cooks' Cottage** *(adult/child $7.90/4.30)*, built by the parents of explorer James Cook in 1755 and shifted here from England in 1934. Tickets to view the interior are available at the garden's visitor centre.

Near the centre of the park is a cutesy miniature **Tudor Village**, a thanksgiving gift from a grateful London pensioner for food parcels sent by Melburnians following WWII. Right next to it is writer Ola Cohn's kooky carved **Fairies' Tree**, a 300-year old stump embellished in the 1930s with fairies, kangaroos, emus and possums.

Predating the park itself is the stump of a **scarred tree**, one of only six identified across Melbourne. Its oval-shaped scar was caused by a portion of its bark being removed by precolonial Aboriginal people, possibly to make a canoe.

Rural Retreat by the River

Art and animals at Abbotsford Convent

While all around them was being swallowed by the expanding city, the Sisters of the Good Shepherd preserved their 6.8-hectare slice of countryside at **Abbotsford Convent** *(abbotsfordconvent.com.au; free)* right up until 1975. It's now an arts, cultural and educational precinct, while the farmland has become the **Collingwood Children's Farm** *(farm.org.au; adult/child $20/10)*, where city kids can get acquainted with pigs, sheep, cows, goats and geese.

Tucked in a bend in the Yarra River, this impressive collection of heritage buildings (mainly dating from the 1880s to 1910s) is considered the most significant Catholic complex to ever have been built in Victoria. It once housed up to 1000 underprivileged women and children, along with 120 nuns and novices. After the convent closed, it became a university campus. Horrified at a proposal in 1997 to sell the site to a property developer, residents waged a campaign to save it.

The buildings now house more than 120 studios and shops, along with a gallery, a bakery and restaurants. Everyone's welcome to explore the gardens and roam the corridors. Regular events are held in the grounds, including the **Regional Farmers Market** *(donation $2)* on the second Saturday of the month.

A Cradle of Modernism

Admire art at the Heide Museum

It's fitting that the house of art patrons John and Sunday Reed in suburban Bulleen now functions as the **Heide Museum of Modern Art** *(heide.com.au; adult/child $27/free; closed mon)*, as the couple played an important role in the development of Australian modernism. Between the late 1930s and early 1960s, they opened their home to artists, including Sidney Nolan, Albert Tucker and Joy Hester, who lived and worked here.

One of the buildings is a modest farmhouse, while another is an architecturally significant home designed by David McGlashan and built in the late 1960s. The exhibitions staged across the site are uniformly excellent. An additional reason to visit is the sculpture park on the banks of the Yarra River. The on-site cafe is top notch, too.

BIRRARUNG: THE YARRA RIVER

Winding its way for 242km from the Yarra Ranges to its mouth at Port Melbourne, the Yarra River enters the city from the east before turning south at Yarra Bend and west again below Hawthorn.

'Yarra' is a Woiwurrung word meaning 'flowing water' but it was never their name for the river, that being Birrarung (meaning 'river of mists'). The misnaming came about in 1835, due to the confusion of the Surveyor-General during his conversations with the local people.

One of the best places to get out on the river is in the vicinity of **Yarra Bend Park**, where it's possible to hire rowboats, canoes and kayaks from two historic boathouses: **Studley Park** (1863) and **Fairfield** (1908).

DRINKING IN ABBOTSFORD: OUR PICKS

Bodriggy Brewing Co.: Abbotsford brewery with excellent craft beer (try the Utropia Pale Ale), Latin American food and live music. *noon-11pm Mon-Thu, to 1am Fri-Sun*

Retreat Hotel: Corner boozer that retains its original 1915 interior and blue-tiled exterior trim. *4-10pm Mon & Tue, noon-11pm Wed-Sun*

Dr Morse: Party bar with indoor and outdoor seating, DJs and live acts. *11.30am-11pm Tue-Thu & Sun, to 1am Fri & Sat*

Lulie Tavern: Free pool table, live music and a rooftop. *4-11pm Mon & Tue, noon-11pm Wed & Sun, noon-1am Thu-Sat*

Carlton & the Inner North

ARTSY AND ALTERNATIVE

TOP TIP
Take time to savour the village-style charms of North Melbourne. The main drag is Errol St, where wrought-iron verandahs still extend from Victorian shopfronts, giving it a country-town ambience despite its proximity to Melbourne's high-rise heart. It shirks that languid feel after dark, when the pubs and restaurants spring to life.

A museum and zoo are the big-ticket attractions here, but Melbourne's inner-northern suburbs are far less mainstream than that implies. They're also a hotbed of radical politics, cutting-edge art and the largest concentration of exciting eating, drinking and entertainment venues in the city.

Fanning out from the city centre, this is where the first residential suburbs sprouted in the 1850s, but the landscape still retains traces of precolonial times, particularly in Parkville's Royal Park, where the Wurundjeri and visiting tribes once camped and gathered together.

Nearby, intact Victorian streetscapes and dishevelled shopping strips teeming with bars and vintage shops sit cheek-by-jowl. Backstreet corners are home to welcoming neighbourhood pubs, many of which host live-music gigs; and student life thrives, thanks to the nearby University of Melbourne and RMIT University. These suburbs encapsulate the best that the city offers – they're multicultural, egalitarian and fun.

A Sign of Changing Times

Explore Collingwood's main strip

Collingwood has come a long way since its establishment in 1842, trading its 19th-century reputation as a home to noxious industries and notorious criminals for its present-day status

GETTING AROUND

North Melbourne, Carlton, Fitzroy and Collingwood are easy walks from the city centre but can also be reached via any Melbourne University tram, or trams number 57 (North Melbourne), 1 (Carlton), 11 (Fitzroy) or 86 (Collingwood). Brunswick can be accessed via train (Upfield line) or trams 1 or 19. Reach Northcote via tram 86 or by train (Mernda line). One of Melbourne's best cycle routes, the Capital City Trail, circles the inner north.

ADAM CALAITZIS/SHUTTERSTOCK

Victoria's Pride Street Party

as one of Melbourne's most fashionable inner-city suburbs. **Smith St** has always been its centre of gravity. In the early 20th century, its department stores drew customers from across the city and these days, it's a vibrant eating, drinking and shopping strip.

Many of the grand old department store buildings still exist, although most have been repurposed as apartments and this architectural bounty makes a stroll down Smith St and the streets immediately east a delight.

Don't miss **Collingwood Yards** on Johnston St, a cultural precinct in a former technical school that's home to galleries, a bookshop, a record shop, a bakery and bars. There's also a **Keith Haring mural**, painted by the late New York street artist on his visit in 1984; you'll find it on the wall at the end of the Johnston St block facing the Tote pub.

NORTHSIDE PRIDE

Melbourne has never really had the 'gay ghetto' that some other big cities have. Currently the largest cluster of LGBTIQ+ venues can be found in Fitzroy around Smith and Gertrude Sts. It's here that the annual **Victoria's Pride Street Party** *(midsumma.org.au)* is held in early February.

The mainstays of the Smith St scene are the conjoined **Mollie's Bar & Diner** (upstairs, known for its drag shows) and **Sircuit** (downstairs dance club). **Yah Yah's**, next door, attracts a younger, queerer crowd, especially on Thursdays for Thursgay.

The longstanding **Laird** in Abbotsford is a bastion of the bear and leather scenes, while **DT's Hotel** in Richmond is an old-style gay pub with a beer garden, drag shows and karaoke.

EATING IN COLLINGWOOD, CARLTON & PARKVILLE: OUR PICKS

CIBI: This combination homewares shop and cafe is a celebration of all things Japan, including traditional Japanese breakfast platters. *8am-4pm* $	**Stefanino Panino e Vino:** Italian sandwich joint that opens for hearty Friday dinners. *9am-3pm Tue-Thu, Sat & Sun, to 10pm Fri* $	**Bowl Bowl:** Spicy Sichuan dumplings and hand-pulled noodles are the mainstays of this friendly neighbourhood restaurant. *11.30am-10pm* $$	**Zareh:** Armenian, Lebanese and North African dishes are cooked over charcoal and wood in this upmarket restaurant. *5.30-11pm Wed-Sat* $$
Florian: Be prepared to wait for a table at this popular Carlton North cafe. The filled baguettes, sandwiches and pastries are worth it. 7.30am-3pm $	**Pidapipó:** All of the creamy gelato is whipped up in-store daily at this flagship store of a mini Melbourne chain. noon-10.30pm $	**Brunetti Classico:** A one-stop-shop for Italian cuisine, with drool-inducing cakes and pastries, and counters serving coffee, pizza and gelato. 5am-10pm $	**Residence:** Equal parts upmarket cafe and relaxed-but-lauded restaurant at the Potter Museum. 8am-4pm Mon-Fri, 11am-4pm Sat, plus 6-11pm Wed-Sat $$

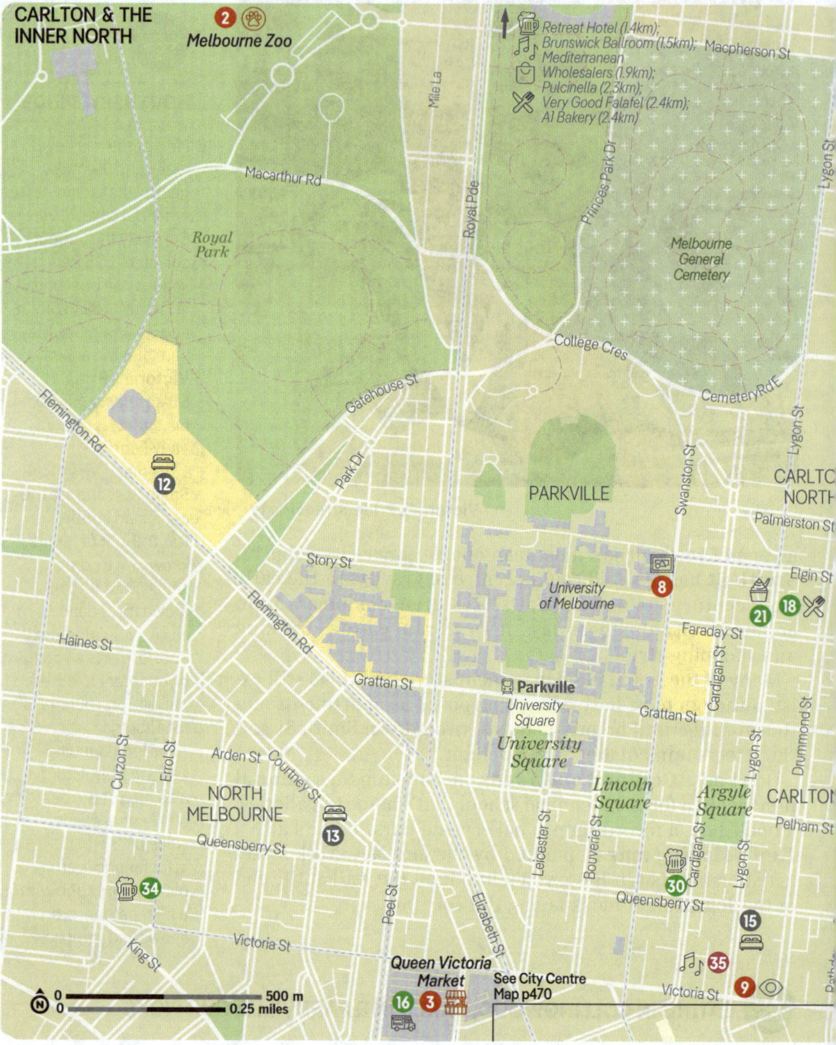

HIGHLIGHTS

1 Melbourne Museum
2 Melbourne Zoo
3 Queen Victoria Market
4 Royal Exhibition Building

SIGHTS

5 Carlton Gardens
6 Collingwood Yards
7 Keith Haring Mural
8 Potter Museum of Art
9 Trades Hall

ACTIVITIES

10 Fitzroy Swimming Pool
11 Fitzroy Victoria Bowling & Sports Club

SLEEPING

12 Larwill Studio
13 Little Drifter North Melbourne
14 Tyrian Serviced Apartments
see 6 Veriu Collingwood
15 Zagame's House

EATING

16 American Doughnut Kitchen
17 Bowl Bowl
18 Brunetti Classico
19 CIBI

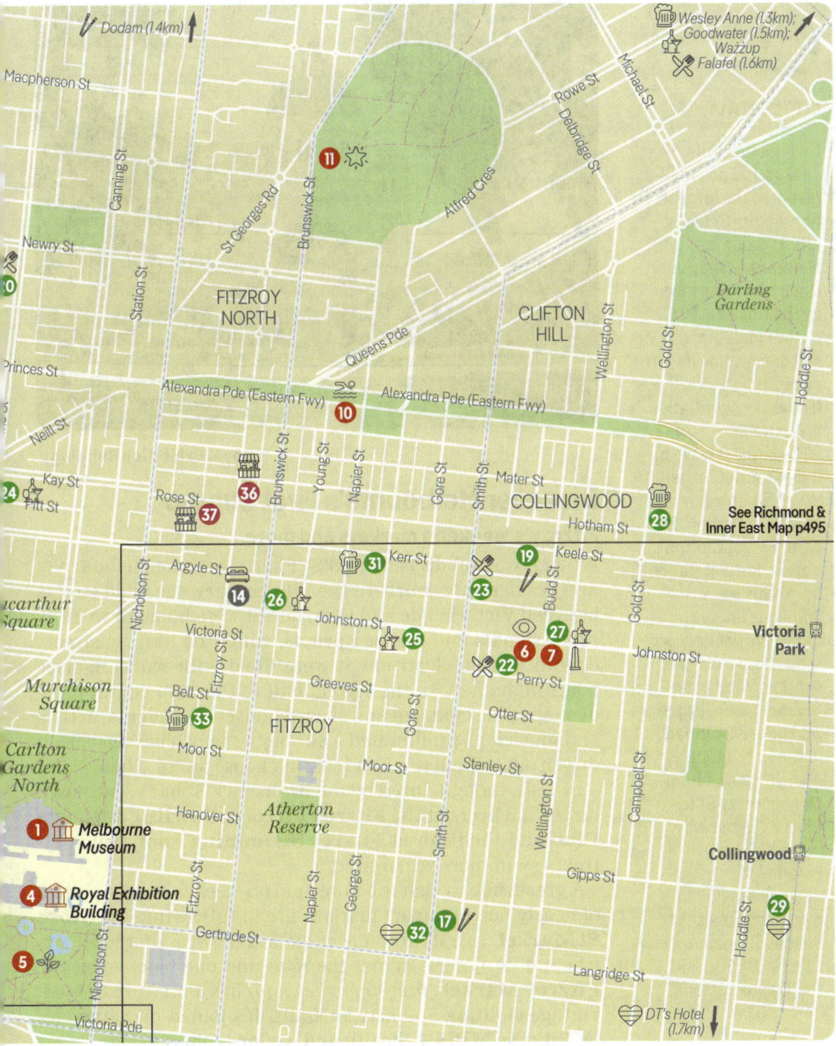

20 Florian
21 Pidapipó
see 8 Residence
22 Stefanino Panino e Vino
see 21 Tiamo
23 Zareh

DRINKING & NIGHTLIFE
24 Bar Bellamy
25 Bar Liberty
26 Black Pearl
27 Commis
28 Goldy's! Tavern
see 22 Hope St Radio
see 21 Johnny's Green Room
29 Laird
30 Lincoln
31 Marquis of Lorne
32 Mollie's Bar & Diner
see 7 Runner Up
see 32 Sircuit
33 Standard Hotel
34 Town Hall Hotel

ENTERTAINMENT
35 Curtin
see 32 Yah Yah's

SHOPPING
36 Fitzroy Market
see 36 Fitzroy Mills
37 Rose Street Market

LITTLE ITALY

Up until the 2011 census, Italians represented the largest non-Anglo-Celtic ethnic group in Melbourne. They've since been overtaken by the Chinese, but 6.7% of Melburnians still claim some Italian ancestry, which is the highest concentration in Australia.

The biggest wave of Italians arrived after WWII, when many settled in Carlton. By 1960, 25% of Carlton's population was Italian born. This Italian influence lingers today, particularly on the suburb's major shopping and entertainment strip, Lygon St. The area dubbed 'Little Italy' stretches along Lygon St from Queensberry St to Elgin St, especially in the block north of Faraday St.

Prominent Italian-owned businesses include Brunetti Classico (p501) and the **Tiamo** trattoria.

ALEX FONDA/SHUTTERSTOCK

Royal Exhibition Building

Discover Melbourne's First Suburb

Fitzroy's weekend markets and more

When it was subdivided in 1839, Fitzroy became Melbourne's first residential suburb. In the 19th century, the wide streets between Victoria Pde and Gertrude St were home to wealthy professionals and businesspeople, while the narrow streets downhill from Gertrude St were filled with working-class boardinghouses. In the second half of the 20th century, the demographic changed and shared houses of students, artists and musicians proliferated – although many have since been driven out by high rents and soaring house prices. These exiles still visit, though, lured by the Brunswick St bar scene, lawn bowls and beers at the **Fitzroy Victoria Bowling & Sports Club** and the beloved **Fitzroy Swimming Pool**, which attracts swimmers year-round.

A great time to visit is before 3pm on weekends, when a trio of nearly neighbouring markets are in full swing. The **Rose St Market** *(rosestmarket.com.au)* is a showcase for local artists and designers. Across the road and one block over, the **Fitzroy Market** *(fitzroymarket.com)* has a mixture of food, vintage clothing and artisan stalls. It's joined on Saturdays by **Fitzroy Mills**, a 'health and wellness' market.

To explore the suburb's rich Aboriginal history, download the **Fitzroy Aboriginal Walking Heritage Trail** map at *deadlystory.com*.

EATING IN BRUNSWICK & NORTHCOTE: CHEAP EATS

A1 Bakery: Frantically busy Lebanese bakery in Brunswick with ample seating, serving delicious savoury pies, platters, pizzas and wraps. *7am-5pm* $

Very Good Falafel: The Israeli-style falafel and salads live up to this Brunswick joint's name and then some. *11am-8.30pm Mon-Fri, to 5pm Sat* $

Dodam: Relaxed but classy Korean dining at this restaurant tucked beneath an apartment building in East Brunswick. *11am-3pm & 5-10pm* $

Ważżup Falafel: Friendly vegan place in Northcote serving wraps, pita pockets and other Palestinian specialties. *11am-9pm Tue-Thu & Sat, 4-9pm Fri, 11am-6pm Sun* $

Marvellous Melbourne on Display

World heritage at Carlton Gardens

Built for the 1880 International Exhibition, the UNESCO World Heritage–listed Royal Exhibition Building and surrounding **Carlton Gardens** retain their Victorian splendour but have been fully assimilated into the city's contemporary life.

Nowhere is this more apparent than in the angular modern building housing the **Melbourne Museum** *(museumsvictoria.com.au; adult/child $18/free)*. Most of the ground floor is given over to the **Bunjilaka Aboriginal Culture Centre**, where Indigenous stories are told through engaging interactive displays, artefacts and video testimonies. Upstairs, the **Melbourne Story** gallery spotlights the city's history from colonial times.

But what will really set young hearts aflutter is the extraordinary **Dinosaur Walk**, a lineup of 17 skeletons, ranging from quite large to enormous. It's just a teaser for **Triceratops: Fate of the Dinosaurs**, a very cool immersive experience using video projections to recreate a journey through a Cretaceous forest leading to a moodily lit 67-million-year-old skeleton dubbed Horridus.

Set aside at least a couple of hours to explore the museum. Guided tours of the **Royal Exhibition Building** *(adult/child $29/15)*, including its landmark dome, take place most days and can be booked at the museum's front desk or website.

In late March, the annual **Melbourne International Flower & Garden Show** *(melbflowershow.com.au)* takes over Carlton Gardens for five days, filling the Royal Exhibition Building with blooms. It's one of the city's major festivals, attracting more than 100,000 visitors.

Melbourne Uni's Edgy Gallery

Potter about the Potter Museum

After seven years of renovations and extensions, Melbourne University's **Potter Museum of Art** *(potter-museum.unimelb.edu.au; free)* reopened in 2025 and instantly reclaimed its esteemed place in the city's cultural life. The curators have at their disposal the largest university art collection in the country – over 18,000 works, running the gamut from Ancient Greek vases to videos. Many of the biggest names in Australian art are represented, including a broad range of Aboriginal artists. The gallery is closed on Sundays and Mondays.

ITALIAN MELBOURNE

Cristian Bonetto is the author of *Italo*, a guide to Italian Australia *@cristian_alessandro_bonetto*

Melbourne claims Oceania's largest, most vibrant Italian diaspora and its imprint on the city runs deep. The National Gallery of Victoria (p484) runs a dedicated NGV Italia program. It's most famous Italian masterpiece is Tiepolo's *The Banquet of Cleopatra*, best pondered before a happy-hour spritz at **Brunetti Oro** and dinner at acclaimed **Trattoria Emilia**, much loved by visiting Italian sports stars. For a local day out, catch the number 19 tram to Brunswick's **Mediterranean Wholesalers**, Australia's biggest Italian supermarket and a venerated Melbourne institution. A short walk away is **Pulcinella**, a bona fide Neapolitan bakery.

DRINKING IN THE INNER NORTH: BEST PUBS

Goldy's! Tavern: Collingwood pub with good food, a pool table, Monday trivia and a loyal local clientele. *3-11pm Mon-Thu, noon-1am Fri & Sat, noon-11pm Sun*

Marquis of Lorne: This Fitzroy stalwart is a northside favourite, known for its excellent food. *3-11pm Mon-Thu, noon-1am Fri & Sat, noon-11pm Sun*

Standard Hotel: Pulling pints in Fitzroy since 1865 and well known for its all-weather beer garden. *3-10pm Mon & Tue, noon-11pm Wed-Sun*

Lincoln: Carlton's favourite gastropub has been operating since 1854. Its lunchtime Sunday roast is one of Melbourne's best. *noon-11pm*

BEST INNER-NORTH GIG VENUES

Brunswick Ballroom: A converted hat factory with chandeliers and mirror balls, hosting live music, cabaret and comedy (capacity 468).

Town Hall Hotel: Grungy North Melbourne pub beloved for its live music, beer garden and unpretentious vibe. Great food, too.

Wesley Anne: Very cool Northcote pub in an old Methodist chapel, with a beer garden, live-music room and an arty vibe.

Retreat Hotel: This 1892 pub is a grungy outpost of old-school Brunswick, with nightly gigs and a popular quiz night.

Curtin: One of Australia's oldest pubs, with historic trade-union links, the Curtin in Carlton serves up fried chicken and live bands.

ARDANME/SHUTTERSTOCK

Melbourne Zoo

Where the Wild Things Are

Cuteness overload at Melbourne Zoo

As zoos go, this is one of the goodies. Not only is **Melbourne Zoo** *(zoo.org.au; adult/child from $55/29)* compact, well laid out, well connected to public transport and a smash hit with kids, its environmental credentials are first-rate (it was one of the first zoos in the world to be certified 'carbon neutral' and it's actively committed to fighting wildlife extinction). Accessibility is excellent, too.

Australian natives are well represented, but there are plenty of exotic family favourites as well, including gorillas, giraffes and tigers. The penguin and seal enclosures are particularly good, offering underwater views as the cute critters torpedo past.

You'll want to allocate at least half a day to justify the hefty admission charge (prices are slightly cheaper online). Children aged under four get in for free and under 16s are free on the weekends. Check the website for up-close animal experiences.

DRINKING IN THE INNER NORTH: BEST BARS

Commis: Cosy candlelit bar in Collingwood with free popcorn and interesting house cocktails. *5-11pm Tue-Sat*

Hope St Radio: Buzzy restaurant and bar combo in Collingwood. At night, fires are lit in the courtyard. *3-11pm Thu-Sun*

Runner Up: Inside Collingwood Yards, this bar has a roof terrace and DJs. *5-11pm Wed & Thu, 4pm-1am Fri, 1pm-1am Sat, 2-10pm Sun*

Bar Bellamy: A little Carlton wine bar serving cocktails and seasonal food. *3-9pm Sun, 5pm-1am Mon & Wed-Fri, 3pm-1am Sat*

Johnny's Green Room: Sunny Italian vibes permeate this rooftop bar above Lygon St in Carlton. The deck has great skyline views. *noon-11pm*

Bar Liberty: Fitzroy favourite serving innovative food and an expertly curated list of global wines. *5-11pm Tue-Sat, noon-5pm Sun*

Black Pearl: Cocktail bar that has been shaking and stirring in Fitzroy for more than two decades. *5pm-3am Wed-Mon*

Goodwater: Whisky, wine and cocktail bar in Northcote, with red-brick walls, rugs and a beer garden. *5pm-midnight Wed-Fri, 3pm-1am Sat, 2-11pm Sun*

Williamstown & the Western Suburbs

HERITAGE AND CULTURAL DIVERSITY

Melbourne's remaining working docklands divide the city from the historically working-class western suburbs. Venture here for multicultural feasts, one of Melbourne's better beaches and a distinctly off-the-tourist-path feel.

Just beyond the docks, the Maribyrnong River curls around the edge of shabby but loveable Footscray. Almost half of its population was born overseas, most notably in Vietnam, India and China. The suburb has long been known for it's good-value ethnic restaurants and increasingly for its craft breweries.

Heading south from Footscray are the gentrified residential nooks of Seddon and Yarraville, where you'll find some excellent neighbourhood bars and restaurants. Venture further south still and you'll hit historic Williamstown, a salty seafaring settlement with a popular beach and dozens of heritage buildings.

Melbourne's suburbia now sprawls far to the west. At its very extremity, Werribee Park evokes the era when this land was home to massive pastoral runs owned by the colony's establishment.

TOP TIP

The main access to Werribee Park is via the Princes Freeway (M1), which is also the direct route to Victoria's Surf Coast. If you are planning a drive down the Great Ocean Rd, visit Werribee on your way to the coast rather than on a dedicated day trip.

GETTING AROUND

Williamstown and Werribee line trains from the city centre travel via Footscray, Yarraville, Seddon and Spotswood. Tram services are limited, but buses fill the gaps.

Melbourne River Cruises *(melbcruises.com.au)* operates ferry trips between Southbank and Williamstown's Gem Pier on Saturdays and Sundays, with extra weekday services in summer and during school holidays. **St Kilda Ferries** *(stkildaferry.com.au)* services sail from St Kilda Pier to Williamstown and Port Melbourne three to six times daily.

A 'cyclist's highway' extends from Footscray to Docklands. The 26km Hobsons Bay Coastal Trail wends from West Gate Bridge via Williamstown to Skeleton Creek.

HIGHLIGHTS
1 Werribee Open Range Zoo
2 Werribee Park Mansion
3 Williamstown Beach

SIGHTS
4 RAAF Museum
5 Saigon Welcome Arch
6 Scienceworks
7 Shadowfax Winery
see 2 Victoria State Rose Garden
8 Vietnamese Museum Australia
9 Williamstown Botanic Gardens

EATING
10 Luxsmith
11 Ras Dashen
12 Slice Shop
13 T Cavallaro & Sons Pasticceria

DRINKING & NIGHTLIFE
14 Hop Nation
see 12 Mr West
15 Mrs Mutton's
16 Seddon Wine Store

ENTERTAINMENT
17 Flemington Racecourse

SHOPPING
18 Footscray Market

INFORMATION
19 Hobsons Bay Visitor Information Centre

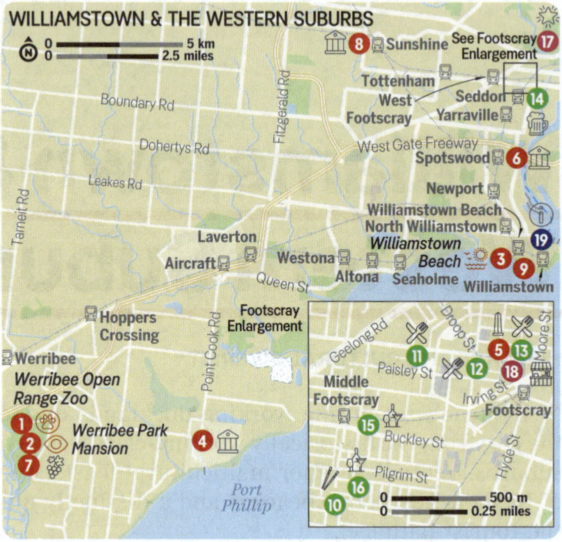

Mad Scientist Training Academy

Expand young minds at Scienceworks

Incorporating an old brick sewage-pumping station in Spotswood that resembles a French château, **Scienceworks** *(museumsvictoria.com.au; adult/child $15/free, incl planetarium $25/10)* keeps inquisitive kids engaged with interactive science displays. There are plenty of buttons to push, levers to pull, flaps to lift and weird facts to learn. The on-site planetarium splashes the universe onto a 16m-domed ceiling during 40-minute shows. You could easy spend a couple of hours here.

Melbourne's Best Beach

Historic charm and golden shores in Williamstown

It only takes 30 minutes to reach historic Williamstown, either by train from the city or ferry from St Kilda. Now a suburb of Melbourne, the town was once a contender for the site of Port Phillip's main settlement, due to its deep harbour (better water supplies eventually gave Melbourne the win).

EATING IN FOOTSCRAY & SEDDON: GLOBAL CUISINE

T Cavallaro & Sons Pasticceria: Italian bakery in Footscray that hasn't changed since 1956. Cannoli are filled to order. *8.30am-4pm Mon-Sat, to noon Sun* $

Ras Dashen: Budget Footscray restaurant beloved for its spicy Ethiopian stews and stir-fries served on spongy injera bread. *noon-9.30pm Wed-Sun* $

Slice Shop: Takeaway pizzeria serving exceptional Neapolitan-style pizza with chewy crusts. It delivers to Mr West bar. *4.30-9pm Tue-Sun* $$

Luxsmith: Head to this Seddon restaurant for tasty modern Asian food in upmarket surroundings. *5.30-10.30pm Tue-Sat, plus noon-3pm Fri & Sat* $$

Where Williamstown has the edge is in its **beach**, a broad stretch of coarse golden sand with a 1930s Moderne bathers' pavilion at one end.

Ferries dock alongside Gem Pier (1847) in the main town centre, where there are terrific views over the Melbourne skyline. Call into the **Hobsons Bay Visitor Information Centre** *(visithobsonsbay.com.au)* to pick up brochures outlining three themed walks exploring early-Colonial-era buildings in the handsome heritage streets. From here it's a 20-minute walk to the beach, cutting through the **Williamstown Botanic Gardens** (planted in 1860) along the way.

Join a Safari in Werribee

Drive through the Open Range Zoo

Meerkats greet you at the entrance to the 225-hectare **Werribee Open Range Zoo** *(zoo.org.au; adult/child from $55/29)* on the westernmost fringe of Melbourne. This is where Melbourne Zoo keeps the animals that really need space to spread out, such as the herd of nine Asian elephants that now have a 21-hectare enclosure to roam. Admission includes a guided tour in a wheelchair-accessible safari bus through the habitats of Asia, North America and Africa, spotting bison, rhinos, zebras and giraffes grazing on the savannah.

Tickets are cheaper online and children under 16 years enter for free on weekends and public holidays. Allocate half a day to make the most of it, but two hours as a minimum. It's easily to combine with a visit to the nearby Werribee Park Mansion and the RAAF Museum (p497).

A Pastoralist's Pride

Floral gardens and fine wine at Werribee Park Mansion

Located 35km west of the city centre, Werribee Park Estate was once completely surrounded by farmland, but these days suburbia is rapidly encroaching, with housing estates proliferating on this fringe of the city. The setting was very different in the 1840s when Scottish pastoralists Thomas and Andrew Chirnside acquired the land on which they would eventually build a grandiose 60-room Italianate mansion. These were some of the lands on which the Boonwurrung people hunted and fished, with few European colonists in the area.

Constructed in the 1870s, **Werribee Park Mansion** *(parks.vic.gov.au; adult/child $13/9)* is a vivid reminder of the opulent

LITTLE SAIGON

The Vietnamese are the fourth-largest migrant community in Melbourne, with 2% of the population born in Vietnam. One of the areas in Melbourne where this is most apparent is Footscray, especially in atmospheric **Footscray Market** and the streets surrounding it. In 2016, the City of Maribyrnong erected the **Saigon Welcome Arch** on Leeds St to celebrate the Vietnamese community's success in the suburb. This sculptural landmark features a stylised take on the traditional temple motif of a pair of cranes standing on the back of a turtle.

At the time of writing, the **Vietnamese Museum Australia** *(vietnamesemuseum.com.au)* was being completed in the nearby suburb of Sunshine. The striking new building was due to open its doors in 2026.

DRINKING IN FOOTSCRAY & SEDDON: OUR PICKS

Hop Nation: Popular craft brewery with a taproom in an old warehouse down an alley by the river in Footscray. *3-9.30pm Thu, noon-10pm Fri-Sun*

Mr West: Hip craft-beer and cocktail bar above a bottle shop on Footscray's sketchy pedestrian mall. *4-11pm Tue-Thu, to 1am Fri, 1pm-1am Sat, 1-11pm Sun*

Seddon Wine Store: A grown-up spot for wines by the glass, cocktails and sophisticated snacks, with bottles lining the walls. *11am-9pm*

Mrs Mutton's: Another bottle-shop bar, this one with a beer garden and good craft-beer selection. *3-6pm Mon, to 10pm Tue-Sat, 2-7pm Sun*

THE RACE THAT STOPS A NATION

The **Melbourne Cup** is one of the most famous horse races in the world. It's as much a social event as a sporting one, with people getting dressed up for champagne-fuelled festivities both at **Flemington Racecourse** and in bars around the city. That's facilitated by Cup Day (the first Tuesday in November) being a public holiday in Victoria.

However, not everyone's joining the party. In recent years the racing industry has come under criticism for horse deaths and contributing to the larger national issues of irresponsible alcohol consumption and gambling addiction. The 'Say Nup to the Cup' campaign encourages people to ignore the Cup but get together with friends anyway.

Werribee Park Mansion (p509)

lifestyles that the early pastoralists enjoyed. The entrance hall leads to a grand staircase and there's a library, dining room and billiard room to explore. It's all extremely grand, especially considering that the Chirnsides started out as squatters, as did many early-19th-century colonists who took possession of tracts of fertile land that they had no legal claim to.

After touring the house, explore the grounds, which were originally laid out by William Guilfoyle, director of the Melbourne Botanic Gardens. Here you'll find a heritage orchard and the **Victoria State Rose Garden**, where 5000 roses bloom in stages between October and May. Also within the estate is the **Shadowfax Winery** *(shadowfax.com.au)*, where from Wednesday to Sunday visitors can enjoy a tasting of its highly regarded wines before settling in for lunch.

Geelong & the Bellarine Peninsula

WINE, WOOL, WILDLIFE AND WAVES

For generations, Melburnians have been either making the drive or catching the ferry to the seaside villages of the Bellarine Peninsula for their summer escapes. It's an area that's known for it's beaches, historic towns and wonderful cool-climate wineries. A vintage train serves booze and the blues to rocking revellers, while other visitors prefer the company of seals and dolphins within the marine national park.

At the base of the peninsula sits Geelong, Victoria's second-largest city (population 283,000). Once known for its wool and paper mills, it has been quietly transforming itself into a tourist town over recent decades. Its waterfront promenade and beaches present a sunny face to the bay, backed by a heritage precinct full of Victorian-era warehouses and grand civic buildings. After dark, the car-free section of Little Malop St is every bit as buzzy as similar strips in big sister Melbourne.

TOP TIP

It's possible to circumnavigate Port Phillip Bay without any backtracking by catching the car ferry between Queenscliff (Bellarine Peninsula) and Sorrento (Mornington Peninsula). **Searoad Ferries** *(searoad.com.au; car & driver $86, passenger $20)* has hourly services during daylight hours; the crossing takes 40 minutes.

Indulge in Some Wooly Thinking

Visit the National Wool Museum

More interesting than it may sound, the **National Wool Museum** *(geelongaustralia.com.au/nwm; adult/child $13/8)* highlights the importance of the wool industry in shaping

GETTING AROUND

A car will give you the most flexibility, but it is possible to visit by public transport. It only takes an hour to get from Melbourne to Geelong on one of the regular train services. From Geelong there are buses to Portarlington, Queenscliff and Barwon Heads. Once you're on the Bellarine Peninsula there are various services that will shuttle you around the vineyards. **Port Phillip Ferries** connects Portarlington to Geelong and Melbourne. Cyclists can take advantage of the 35km Bellarine Rail Trail, which follows an old railway route from South Geelong to Queenscliff.

HIGHLIGHTS
1 Bellarine Railway
2 Fort Queenscliff
3 Portarlington Beach

SIGHTS
4 13th Beach
5 Bellarine Estate
6 Cunningham Pier
7 Curlewis Winery
8 Eastern Beach
see 8 Eastern Beach Fountain
9 Eastern Beach Mineral Spring
10 Farmdog Brewing @ McGlashan Estate
11 Geelong Botanic Gardens
12 Geelong City Hall
13 Geelong Gallery
14 Geelong Library
15 Geelong Waterfront Carousel
16 Hitchcock Memorial Rotunda
17 Indented Head
18 Leura Park Estate
19 National Wool Museum
20 Platform Arts
21 Point Lonsdale Rock Pools
22 Queenscliffe Historical Museum
23 Scotchmans Hill

ACTIVITIES
see 8 Children's Pool
24 Portarlington Mussel Tours
25 Q Train
26 Sea All Dolphin Swims

SLEEPING
27 Lon Retreat
28 Tasman Holiday Parks – Geelong

EATING
29 Basils Farm
30 Bistrot Plume
31 El Santo De Los Tacos
32 Staple Eatery & Deli
see 5 Texas BBQ @ Bellarine Estate
33 Tommy Gunns
34 Tulip
see 11 WYM (Where You Meet)

DRINKING & NIGHTLIFE
35 Beav's Bar
36 Geelong Cellar Door
see 34 Queen of the West

ENTERTAINMENT
see 1 Blues Train
37 Geelong Arts Centre
38 Piano Bar
39 Wool Exchange

TRANSPORT
see 24 Port Phillip Ferries
see 26 Searoad Ferries

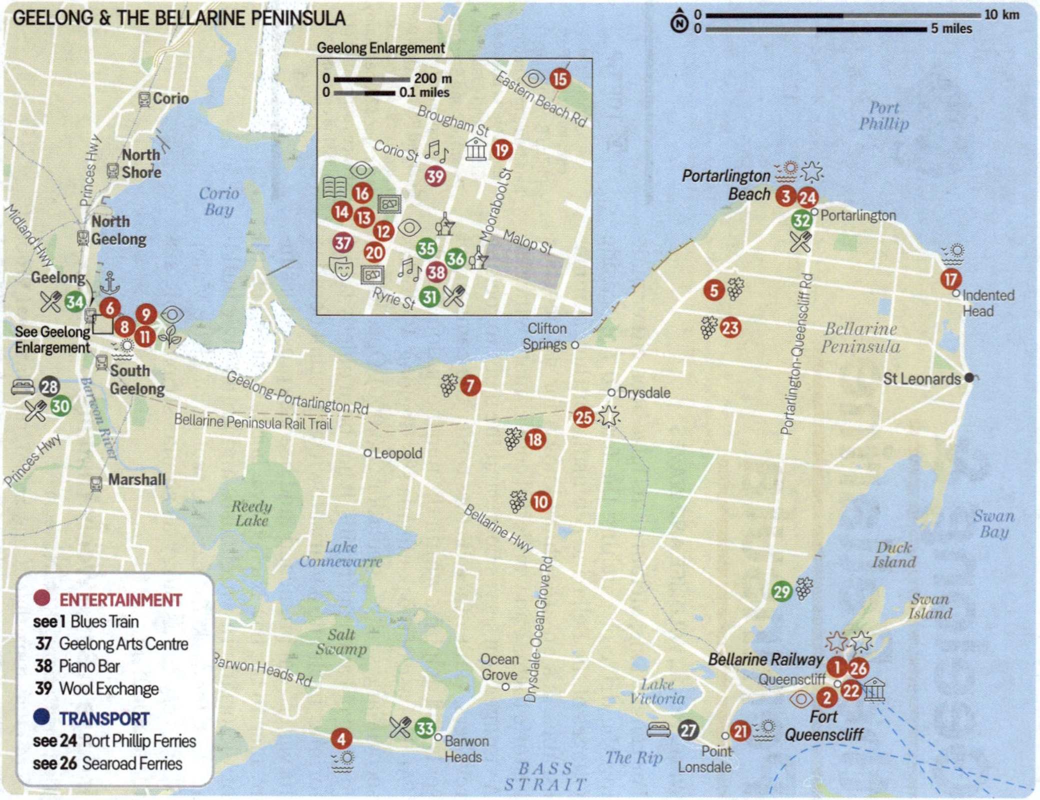

Geelong. Displays are split into themes such as 'On the Land, In the Factory' and 'Machinery in Action', the latter showcasing a massive 1910 Axminster carpet loom that gets chugging at regular intervals throughout the day. Technology, farming and fleece enthusiasts could spend an hour here.

Head up the Garden Path

Linger in Geelong Botanic Gardens

They're not overly large, but **Geelong Botanic Gardens** *(geelongaustralia.com.au/gbg; free)* sure are pretty. Entry is through the leaf-shaped 21st Century Garden, but the main part of the gardens was established in 1851, consisting of orderly paths winding around lawns, a rose garden and a conservatory. Tucked towards the back is Geelong's first Customs House, a one-room wooden cottage dating from 1838. It's one of the oldest buildings in the state.

An hour is plenty of time to see everything, including time for a coffee and pastry at WYM.

Mussels & Beach

Portarlington pit-stop or day trip

Facing Melbourne from the tip of the peninsula, Portarlington is a pretty little seaside town with a grand old pub and a shallow, sheltered **beach** that's great for kids. Its proximity to Bellarine's best wineries makes it a pleasant pit-stop on a driving tour, either for lunch or an overnight stay. But you don't need a car to visit, as **Port Phillip Ferries** *(portphillipferries.com.au; adult/child $22/13)* has twice-daily ferries that will whisk you here from Melbourne's Docklands in 70 minutes. On weekends, there's also a daily Geelong service. Once you arrive, there are plenty of options to shuttle you to nearby vineyards (see the ferry website for details).

Portarlington bills itself as the 'Mussel Capital of Victoria' and you'll see these sweet bivalves on lots of fancy menus in Melbourne. Departing from the same pier as the ferries, **Portarlington Mussel Tours** *(portarlingtonmusseltours.com.au; tours from $295)* has a range of foodie-focussed cruises heading out to the aquafarm to see the Australian blue mussels being brought up from the waters. Afterwards you'll be given a cooking demonstration so you know how to deal with them at home, followed by a feast of these and other local delicacies, all washed down with a selection of Bellarine wine.

WATHAURUNG COUNTRY

Geelong and the Bellarine Peninsula lie on the ancestral lands of the Wathaurung (Wadawurrung) people, one of the five constituent parts of the Kulin nation. Their territory stretches east to the Werribee River and north to beyond Ballarat. From 1835, their lands were progressively taken from them by British squatters who first settled around Geelong and started converting the bush to pasture.

A unique insight into precolonial Wathaurung life survives through the remarkable story of William Buckley, an escaped convict who lived among them from 1803 to 1835 and was accepted as one of their own. His account was given in an 1852 biography and was retold by Garry Linnell in *Buckley's Chance* (2019).

EATING IN GEELONG: OUR PICKS

WYM (Where You Meet): Kiosk cafe serving sandwiches, wraps and pastries within Geelong Botanic Gardens. *11am-3pm Sun-Tue, 9am-3pm Wed-Sat* $

Bistrot Plume: In suburban Belmont, this smart cafe-restaurant dishes up classic French dishes and tasty patisserie. *7am-2.30pm, plus 5.30-10pm Fri* $$

El Santo De Los Tacos: Hip cantina serving authentic Mexican street-food, beers and cocktails. *5-9pm Tue-Fri, noon-9pm Sat & Sun* $$

Tulip: Casual yet sophisticated Modern Australian dining, down an alley in Geelong West. *5.30-10pm Tue-Thu, noon-10pm Fri & Sat* $$$

GEELONG ON FOOT

Explore Geelong on this stroll through the historic city centre and along the sparkling waterfront.

START	END	LENGTH
Geelong City Hall	Children's Pool	2.5km; 1hr

Start outside the Neoclassical 1 **Geelong City Hall**, where two stately lions guard what is now the visitor information centre. On the adjacent corner, an elegant Spanish Mission–style courthouse now houses 2 **Platform Arts**. Beside it on Little Malop St is the quirky 3 **Geelong Arts Centre**, with its stylised theatre-curtain frontage. Directly opposite is an equally unusual building housing the 4 **Geelong Library**. Cut through Johnstone Park past the 5 **Hitchcock Memorial Rotunda** (1919) and the main entrance to the highly esteemed 6 **Geelong Gallery**.

Cross the busy roads and continue along Gheringhap St, then take the first right onto Corio St. On the right is the 1920s 7 **Wool Exchange**, where traders once auctioned wool. Many of the grand buildings in the area are former wool stores, including the 1872 bluestone around the corner housing the 8 **National Wool Museum** (p511).

Head down to the waterfront, where a glass pavilion protects an ornate 9 **Carousel** (1892). Outside you'll see the first of Jan Mitchell's 100-plus painted Baywalk Bollards, carved poles representing lifesavers, brass bands and bathing beauties. Turn right and walk past the marina to the golden sands of 10 **Eastern Beach**. At the far end, a wooden promenade loops around a netted section in front of a shallow 11 **Children's Pool**.

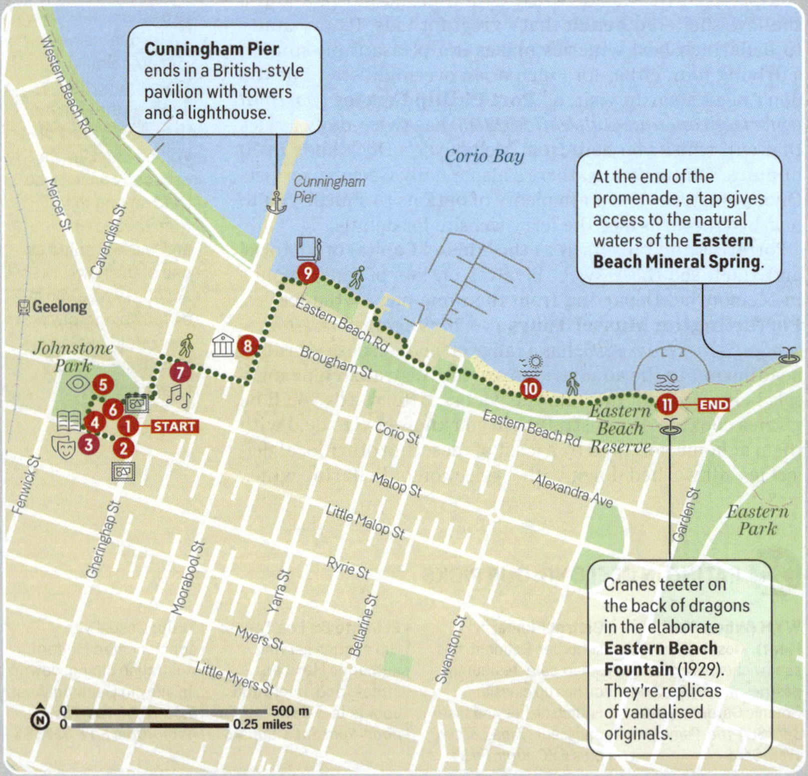

The Town that Never Changed

Wander Queenscliff's heritage streets

The literal end of the peninsula road (the ferries to the Mornington Peninsula depart from here), Queenscliff is a seaside town with a staggering 142 protected heritage buildings. Before you dash off on the ferry to the Mornington Peninsula, take some time to explore the lost-in-time streets lined with vintage shops, glorious pubs, pretty cottages and grand seaward-gazing mansions. It's worth poking your head into the interesting one-room **Queenscliffe Historical Museum** *(historyofqueenscliffe.com; free)* behind the information centre to learn the town's story.

Chief among the significant structures is **Fort Queenscliff** *(fortqueenscliff.com.au; adult/child $24/9)*, built in 1860 to defend the entrance to Port Phillip Bay and protect the shipping lanes to Geelong and Melbourne. Book head for a 90-minute guided tour (11am Friday to Monday plus 1.45pm on weekends; bring your passport).

Rocking the Rails

Ride the Bellarine Railway

If you've never danced and drunk on a heritage steam train before, here's your chance. Most Saturdays from October to May the **Blues Train** *(thebluestrain.com.au; $175)* rolls out of Queenscliff Station with a blues or roots band performing in each of its four carriages. The round trip takes four hours and includes nibbles and unlimited drinks (within legal sober-service rules). Check the website for performers and timings and book well ahead (it's popular). Day trips get the views, but night trips get more raucous.

If you'd rather get fed than blues-ed and boozed, the **Q Train** *(theqtrain.com.au; from $144)* has a three-hour culinary-focussed journey along the same rails, but starting in Drysdale.

Both of these services are operated by **Bellarine Railway** *(bellarinerailway.com.au; adult/child from $24/38)*, which also offers more family-friendly options.

Seeking Seals & Dolphins

Cruise the marine national park

Based in Queenscliff, **Sea All Dolphin Swims** *(dolphinswims.com.au; adult/child from $120/90)* presents the opportunity to get out on the waters of Port Phillip Heads Marine National

BEST BELLARINE WINERIES

Part of the Geelong wine region, the peninsula has over a dozen wineries that can be visited.

Bellarine Estate: Family winery that's also home to a gin distillery and a BBQ restaurant. Tastings $10, refundable upon purchase.

Scotchmans Hill: Tucked up a country lane but still extremely popular (book ahead). Tastings from $20.

Leura Park Estate: Busy, tourism-focussed cellar door offering do-it-yourself tastings ($15) in test-tubes.

Farmdog Brewing @ McGlashan Estate: In a rustic shed overlooking the vines, with tasting flights of wine ($24), gin ($32) and beer ($24).

Curlewis Winery: Book ahead for this intimate cellar door, which is only open on Sunday afternoons. Tastings are $15.

DRINKING IN GEELONG: OUR PICKS

Geelong Cellar Door: Lead-light windows and a copper counter add ambience to this cosy bar that showcases local wines. *noon-11pm Tue-Sun*

Beav's Bar: A former auction house, Beav's is decorated with religious prints and old couches. There's live music most nights. *4pm-1am Wed-Sun*

Queen of the West: Inviting old pub with a blue-tiled sports bar and a kids' playground in the beer garden. *4pm-late Tue-Thu, from 11.30am Fri-Sun*

Piano Bar: Who would've thought pop songs played on request on the piano would be so popular with young people? *6pm-midnight Fri & Sat*

Admission $10; book ahead for a table

BEST BELLARINE BEACHES

Kat Barber, Bellarine local, travel writer and creator of *@lovethebellarine*, shares some of her favourite spots around the peninsula.

Portarlington Beach: My favourite Bellarine beach for kids. It's shallow and has gentle bay waves and large shady trees. In summer, don't miss the famous jam-doughnut van.

13th Beach: My favourite walking beach is lovely, quiet, long and clean, and you can watch the surfers coming out of the water. It's dog-friendly.

Indented Head: It has a shipwreck, *The Ozone*, not far from the water, so you can snorkel around it. You can hire boats and beach boxes and it's a nice little cove.

Point Lonsdale Rock Pools: At low tide you can access the rock pools.

RUSS PHOTOGRAPHY/SHUTTERSTOCK

Pier, Queenscliff (p515)

Park searching for dolphins, seals and other marine life. Seal sightings are guaranteed, but dolphin sightings run at about an 80% success rate.

You can opt just for sightseeing (the cheaper option). Should you choose to swim, you'll be provided with a wetsuit and all the necessary snorkelling gear. Note, there are strict controls on swimming with dolphins in Australia, but some animal-welfare organisations still advise against it.

The trips take in Pope's Eye, the circular foundations of an unfinished military fort, which is home to an Australasian gannet–breeding colony. The water is shallow and it's a great place to spot colourful fish and marine life while snorkelling. The next stop is a visit to a permanent Australian fur-seal colony, which usually has about 30 to 40 young seals diving in the water, lounging around and being smelly.

EATING ON THE BELLARINE PENINSULA: OUR PICKS

Staple Eatery & Deli: Smart cafe in Portarlington serving wood-fired pizza on Friday and Saturday evenings. *8am-2pm, plus 6-9pm Fri & Sat* $

Tommy Gunns: Bistro fare with Sri Lankan flair in an old weatherboard house in Barwon Heads. *5-11pm Wed & Thu, noon-11pm Fri & Sat* $$

Texas BBQ @ Bellarine Estate: Enjoy live music and Texas barbecue at the oldest family-owned winery in the area. *noon-9pm Fri & Sat* $$

Basils Farm: Local seasonal produce is showcased at one of the peninsula's most scenic wineries, overlooking Swan Bay. *11.30am-4pm Thu-Mon* $$$

Mornington Peninsula

WINERIES, HOT POOLS AND BEACHES

Known to Melburnians as 'the Peninsula', this sun-dappled expanse has been a sybaritic summer playground for city dwellers since the 1870s, when paddle steamers carried holidaying passengers to Portsea and Sorrento.

Lying on the lands of the Boonwurrung people, the Peninsula was the site of a short-lived British penal colony in 1803. Later, after the establishment of Melbourne, the she-oak forests were converted into agriculture and the Boonwurrung people were dispossessed. It remains a significant agricultural region and the cultivation of cool-climate grapes, particularly chardonnay and pinot noir, is a major economic driver here.

The Peninsula has plenty to justify a multi-night stay, particularly during summer when the wild ocean beaches and the much calmer and safer bay beaches are powerful magnets for visitors. At other times of the year, the area's impressive local restaurants, cellar doors, spas, art galleries, gardens and walking tracks provide a wealth of experiences to enjoy.

TOP TIP

Powerful rips, reefs, big waves and unpredictable conditions characterise the Peninsula's ocean (back) beaches. Always swim and surf at patrolled beaches and stay between the flags. For patrol updates, refer to *beachsafe.org.au*, operated by **Surf Life Saving Australia**.

GETTING AROUND

You need your own transport to make the most of your time on the Peninsula, as public-transport options are limited.

Trains from central Melbourne terminate in Frankston, from where the 788 bus travels to Portsea via Mornington, Point Nepean Rd and Sorrento. The Stony Point train service travels from Frankston to Hastings, from where bus 782 travels to Flinders via Merricks and Point Leo. The Red Hill area is not serviced by public transport.

The terrain is hilly and road conditions can be dangerous, so cycling is challenging.

EATING ON THE PENINSULA: BEYOND THE VINEYARDS

Order curry in a hopper (rice-pancake bowl)

Flock Cafe: The wood-smoker works overtime at this humble little cafe attached to a vintage market in Rye. *9.30am-4pm Tue & Wed, 7am-4pm Thu-Mon* $

Red Gum BBQ: Pulled pork and meltingly tender brisket served with classic American sides in a massive Red Hill warehouse. *11am-8pm Tue-Sat, to 4pm Sun* $

Flat BLK: There's just coffee and counter food on offer at this little heritage cottage in Sorrento, including filled rolls, baguettes and croissants. *6.30am-3pm* $

Many Little: Exceptional Sri Lankan cuisine in Red Hill, either à la carte or showcased in a five-course set menu. *5-10pm Thu-Sun, plus noon-3pm* $$$

HIGHLIGHTS
1 Peninsula Hot Springs
2 Point Nepean National Park
3 Sorrento Back Beach

SIGHTS
4 Arthurs Seat State Park
5 Arthurs Seat Summit
6 Cape Schanck Lighthouse
7 Cranbourne Gardens
8 Eldridge Estate
see 5 Enchanted Adventure Garden
9 Fort Nepean
10 Funky Farm
11 Gunnamatta Beach
12 McClelland Sculpture Park & Gallery
13 Merricks Store
14 Mont Rouge Estate
15 Montalto
16 Moonlit Sanctuary Wildlife Conservation Park
17 Mornington Peninsula National Park
18 Mornington Peninsula Regional Gallery
19 Point Leo Surf Beach
20 Polperro
21 Port Phillip Estate
22 Portsea Back Beach
23 Pt Leo Estate
24 Quarantine Station
25 Rye Beach
26 Safety Beach
27 Shoreham Beach
28 Ten Minutes By Tractor

ACTIVITIES
29 Alba Thermal Springs & Spa
30 BayPlay

SLEEPING
31 Hamptons in Rye
32 Jackalope
33 Lancemore Lindenderry Red Hill
see 21 Port Phillip Estate
34 RACV Cape Schanck Resort
35 Treetops at Red Hill

EATING
36 Flat BLK
37 Flock Cafe
38 Many Little
39 Red Gum BBQ

DRINKING & NIGHTLIFE
40 Coffee Traders
41 Commonfolk Coffee
42 Jetty Road Brewery
see 42 JimmyRum Distillery
see 42 Little Rebel
43 Merchant & Maker
see 30 Portsea Hotel
see 42 TWØBAYS Brewing Co

INFORMATION
44 Baxter Service Station Pop Up Visitor Information Centre
45 Mornington Peninsula Visitor Information Centre

TRANSPORT
46 Arthurs Seat Eagle

A Point of Interest

Explore dramatic Point Nepean National Park

Encompassing all of the Peninsula's windswept western tip, **Point Nepean National Park** *(parks.vic.gov.au; free)* is a 560-hectare expanse of native bush crisscrossed with walking tracks and dotted with significant heritage buildings and gun embankments. Gnarled moonah trees, bent by the strong winds, dot most of the landscape; and local fauna, such as echidnas, black wallabies and snakes call the park home. Put aside half a day to do it justice.

There's a car park at the **Quarantine Station**, established in 1852, which also houses the visitor centre. Call in to collect maps of the various walking tracks and to explore the 50-odd heritage buildings. The complex was most recently used in the 1990s to shelter Kosovar refugees.

Near the tip of the point is **Fort Nepean**, which was built in stages from the 1870s and played an important role in defending Melbourne from military threats. It's claimed that the first British Empire artillery shots of WWI were fired from here, across the bow of a German freighter. Vehicles are only permitted to drive as far as the Gunner's Cottage car park, from where you can walk to the fort in about 40 minutes. Alternatively, a wheelchair-accessible bus (adult/child $12/8) shuttles between the Quarantine Station and Fort Nepean from 9am and 4pm daily.

Cycling is also a great option for getting around this vast park; hire bikes from Portsea-based **BayPlay** *(bayplay.com.au; from $40)* and collect from the Quarantine Station.

Continued on p522

BEST PENINSULA BEACHES

Sorrento Back Beach: Surf, swim and explore rock pools, or take the clifftop walk to Diamond Bay.

Rye Beach: Long, white-sand, bayside beach backed by scrub, across the road from shops and cafes.

Portsea Back Beach: Wild beach with surfing, swimming and ocean-fishing opportunities. Consistent breaks make it one of the Peninsula's top surfing spots.

Gunnamatta Beach: The Peninsula's most popular (and dangerous) surf beach, with consistently high swells and rocky reefs. Swim only when patrolled.

Point Leo Surf Beach: A relatively safe beach but suitable for swimming only when the tide is in. Good point and reef breaks in winter.

HELP ME PICK:

Peninsula Grape Grazing

Most of the peninsula's 200 small-scale vineyards and 50-plus cellar doors are located in the undulating hills between Red Hill and Merricks. The cool climate means that pinot noir, chardonnay and pinot gris are the predominant varietals (at 50%, 25% and 11% of plantings, respectively). Many of the estates have excellent cafes or restaurants attached, making this region as famous for its food as it is for its wine.

Where to Visit if You Love...

Exceptional Winery Dining

Ten Minutes by Tractor
Enjoy one of the tasting menus accompanied by the winery's excellent pinot noir and chardonnay in the stylish surrounds of this vineyard restaurant. The unusual name reflects the fact that the estate comprises three vineyards, each located 10 minutes apart by tractor. Wine tastings: $15 to $50.

Polperro An excellent restaurant serves a set four-course menu, mainly using produce from its own organic, biodynamic farm. Atmospheric tastings ($20 to $25) are in a small candlelit room at the back.

Spectacular Views

Port Phillip Estate Home of the acclaimed Kooyong Estate pinot noir and chardonnay (tastings $10), this remarkable architect-designed winery resembles the lair of a Bond villain. The views stretch over the vines to the ocean.

Eldridge Estate Enjoy a glass of its acclaimed chardonnay, gamay and pinot noir while admiring a vista of vine-clad slopes. It's only open on weekends and bookings are advised.

Sculpture on the Side

Pt Leo Estate This architecturally impressive winery and acclaimed restaurant overlooks a sculpture garden ($15) with 70-plus works by major artists and magnificent ocean views. Tastings start from $15, with a $10 refund on purchase; the whites are particularly good.

Montalto Wander the 1km sculpture-lined trail through the native bushland on this estate before enjoying a three- or four-course set menu in the restaurant, a pizza in the relaxed piazza overlooking the kitchen garden or a catered picnic in the grounds. Tastings: $15 to $20, refundable upon purchase.

Chocolate on the Side

Mont Rouge Estate
Attached to the Cocoa Rouge *chocolaterie*, here you can enjoy a wine tasting ($10, refundable upon purchase), as well as a reasonably priced lunch, followed by ice cream and pure-cocoa-butter chocolates.

One-Stop Shop

Merricks Store Housed in a 1924 general store, Merricks is split between a relaxed restaurant and a wine store. It's officially the cellar door for Elgee Park and Baillieu Wines, but it also showcases a slew of small producers that don't have their own cellar doors. Tastings are free.

DRINKING & NIGHTLIFE
1 Eldridge Estate
2 Merricks Store
3 Mont Rouge Estate
4 Montalto
5 Polperro
6 Port Phillip Estate
7 Pt Leo Estate
8 Ten Minutes By Tractor

HOW TO

When to go Some of the smaller wineries only open on the weekends, although many extend their hours in January when the Peninsula's buzzing.

Book ahead It's essential to book restaurants and advisable to book for tastings. Availability is better midweek and in winter but fewer places are open.

Taste wine Relax, this is Australia – nobody cares if you do it the 'right way'. Swirl your glass, take a good sniff... or not. It's up to you.

Budget Most cellars charge for tastings, but the fee is sometimes redeemable upon buying a bottle. Many winery restaurants only offer pricy set menus.

DIY or Guided Tour?

Exploring this region with your own transport allows freedom to pick and choose your wineries and decide how long to linger in each one. The downside is that someone in your group will need to be the designated sober driver.

If you opt to do this, pick up a printed copy of the extremely useful *Official Wine Touring Map* produced by the **Mornington Peninsula Vignerons Association** *(MPVA; morningtonpeninsulawine.com.au)*. Updated annually, the map is free and available from the helpful visitor information centres in Dromana, Sorrento and the Baxter Service Station. An interactive version with a 'create your own itinerary' function is available on the MPVA website.

Alternatively, there are plenty of guided tours and shuttle services available. For full details of what's on offer, check the **Visit Mornington Peninsula** *(visitmorningtonpeninsula.org)* or **Visit Victoria** *(visitvictoria.com)* websites.

Hop It *(hopit.com.au; Melbourne/Peninsula pickup $98/77)* has a weekend-only hop-on, hop-off shuttle service that departs from central Melbourne and visits many of the best cellar doors; you can choose four of these for stops. Alternatively, tour companies including **Elevate Wine Tours** *(elevatewinetours.com.au; incl Melbourne pickup from $220)* can tailor tours.

BEST FOR KIDS

Moonlit Sanctuary Wildlife Conservation Park: Endangered Australian critters on display near Pearcedale, at the base of the Peninsula. Night tours, too.

Enchanted Adventure Garden: Hedge mazes, tube slides, canopy walk, rope-scramble obstacle course and 'tree surfing' with zip lines.

Funky Farm: Private, family-run, wildlife sanctuary and petting zoo with kangaroos, wallabies, emus, wombats and farm animals (bookings required).

Safety Beach: As the name implies, this is a safe family-friendly beach with shallow waters and plenty of sand for castle construction.

Shoreham Beach: A protected family-friendly beach with safe and enjoyable swimming at mid- to high tide.

Continued from p519

Soak in Serene Surroundings

Relax in a hot spring

Aside from the wineries, the Mornington Peninsula's most popular drawcards are its mineral-rich geothermal springs. Set around ponds and climbing up a hill, **Peninsula Hot Springs** *(peninsulahotsprings.com; adult/child from $55/40)* is a wonderful place to while away a couple of hours or even a whole day, flitting between the mineral pools, spa centre, cafes and entertainment amphitheatre. While the spa centre is for adults only, the rest of the complex is very family-friendly. The most popular pool is set right on top of the hill, with views over the Peninsula. Prices are cheapest if you book ahead and arrive before 9am or after 6pm. Bring a towel, or hire one for $5; lockers are an additional $10.

A second centre, **Alba** *(albathermalsprings.com.au; adult/child from $95/80)*, opened nearby in 2022. If you've seen the HBO series *The White Lotus*, that's the vibe (wealthy people in white towelling robes in very stylish surrounds). Robes, towels and lockers are included in the price here.

To the Lighthouse

Walks in Mornington Peninsula National Park

Stretching from Portsea along a long sliver of wave-battered coastline to Cape Schanck and then inland to the Greens Bush area, **Mornington Peninsula National Park** *(parks.vic.gov.au)* has rewarding walks and spectacular surf beaches (Portsea Back Beach, Sorrento Back Beach and Gunnamatta Beach are the best).

For a taste, nothing beats the short walk around the still-operating **Cape Schanck Lighthouse** (built 1859) on the peninsula's remote southwest tip. Descend the steps of the boardwalk that leads to the craggy cape for outstanding views. Longer walks starting from here include the 5km-return **Bushrangers Bay Walk** and the epic 26km (two-day) **Coastal Walk** to London Bridge. The two-day **Two Bays Walking Trail** cuts across the Peninsula from Cape Schanck to Dromana, but you'll get the best of it if you just tackle the 9km middle section passing through Greens Bush.

DRINKING ON THE PENINSULA: BEST COFFEE

Little Rebel: The coffee at this roastery, located in a Dromana industrial estate, easily rivals the best in Melbourne. *6.30am-2pm Mon-Fri*

Coffee Traders: This outfit in Mornington is so serious about its coffee making that it also runs barista courses. *6am-3pm*

Commonfolk Coffee: Mornington roastery–cafe where the food is as good as the coffee. *6.30am-3.30pm Mon-Fri, 8am-3pm Sat & Sun*

Merchant & Maker: Across from the beach in McCrae, serving artisan coffee and a tasty menu combining cafe fare and Asian dishes. *7.30am-2.30pm*

Eagle-Eye Views

Fly to Arthurs Seat Summit

Accessed from a winding road between Dromana and Red Hill, the 314m-high lookout at **Arthurs Seat Summit** has sweeping views over Port Phillip Bay to the Melbourne skyline and beyond. For added thrills, you can glide here on the **Arthurs Seat Eagle** *(aseagle.com.au; adult/child return $31/21)*, a gondola-style cable car that will whisk you to the top in 15 minutes. It's wheelchair-accessible, pram-friendly and you can even transport your bike for an additional fee. Prices are cheapest online.

The summit is part of the 572-hectare **Arthurs Seat State Park** *(parks.vic.gov.au)*. Five walks of varying length and difficulty are outlined on its website, including the hour-long, 1.8km Summit Circuit Walk, starting at the lookout.

Red Dirt & Wildflowers

Australian flora at Cranbourne Gardens

Not strictly on the Peninsula but close enough and interesting enough to warrant a short detour, **Cranbourne Gardens** *(rbg.vic.gov.au; free)* is the outpost of Royal Botanic Gardens Victoria devoted exclusively to Australia's unique flora. It was created on the site of an old sand mine and includes a large patch of regenerating native bush surrounding the showcase Australian Garden.

Entering the garden, visitors are confronted with the truly breathtaking Red Sand Garden, an evocation of the arid landscape of the Red Centre. Other highlights include a 'Weird and Wonderful' garden with a bizarre bottle tree; and a rock-pool waterway where excited children love to hop from flagstone to flagstone in shallow waters that ebb and flow, referencing the life-giving passage of water through the Australian landscape.

More than 100,000 plants from 1900 varieties are on show here, including rare and threatened species. Set aside an hour to explore the Australian Garden and another hour if you're keen for a bushwalk.

THROUGH ARTISTS' EYES

The landscapes of the Mornington Peninsula have long inspired artists. Members of the famed 19th-century Heidelberg School painted *en plein air* here, most notably Arthur Streeton and Charles Conder.

In the 20th century, the beaches and cliffs of the dramatic coastline inspired artists including Violet Teague, Arthur Boyd, Albert Tucker and Dorothy Mary Braund. This rich heritage is reflected in several important art institutions and sites located on the Peninsula today, most notably the **Mornington Peninsula Regional Gallery** *(mprg.mornpen.vic.gov.au; free)* and the **McClelland Sculpture Park & Gallery** *(mcclelland.org.au; adult/child $15/6)*.

You'll find some interesting commercial galleries in Sorrento.

DRINKING ON THE PENINSULA: OUR PICKS

Jetty Road Brewery: Craft brewery in a very cool mural-covered warehouse in a light-industrial part of Dromana. *noon-10pm Mon-Sat, 11am-6pm Sun*

JimmyRum Distillery: A couple of warehouses down from Jetty Road, with cocktails, meals and rum tasting. *noon-9pm Thu-Sat, to 6pm Sun*

TWØBAYS Brewing Co: Gluten-free beer and pizza are served at its Dromana taproom, but only on weekends. *noon-5pm Sat & Sun*

Portsea Hotel: Faux-Tudor pub with a massive beer garden and lawn overlooking Port Phillip Bay. Live music and DJs, especially in summer. *11am-10pm*

Yarra Valley & the Ranges

VINEYARDS AND VISTAS

GETTING AROUND

Exploring these areas by car is the best option, as it will give you far more flexibility. Trains head as far as Lilydale in the Yarra Valley and Belgrave on the edge of the Dandenongs. Buses connect to towns including Coldstream, Yarra Glen and Healesville (bus 685 from Lilydale); Warburton (683 from Lilydale); and Sassafras and Olinda (688 from Upper Ferntree Gully).

East of the city, the Yarra River wends its way from its source in the Yarra Ranges through a gently undulating, vine-clad valley. This was the birthplace of Victorian viticulture and the Yarra Valley is now firmly established as one of the country's premier wine regions. Hemming in the valley to the south are the Dandenong Ranges, a forested tract of mountains reveals heritage villages and notable gardens.

Though close to Melbourne, the valley and ranges beat to a different drum. In the ranges, nature rules supreme and somnolent surrounds are a given, especially midweek. On weekends, the pace picks up, but the vibe stays low-key. The Yarra Valley has a bit more glitz to it, but remains resolutely rural – despite all the architectural showpieces housing cellar doors and pricy restaurants. There's plenty of stuff for the kids as well, including a popular steam railway and excellent wildlife park.

TOP TIP

These are popular weekend day-trip destinations. To avoid crowds and traffic jams, it's best to visit midweek – although some wineries may be closed. Yarra Valley restaurants are often booked solid on weekends and public holidays, so it's wise to book in advance. The same applies to accommodation.

Puffing Billy railway (p526)

F.MALIKI/SHUTTERSTOCK

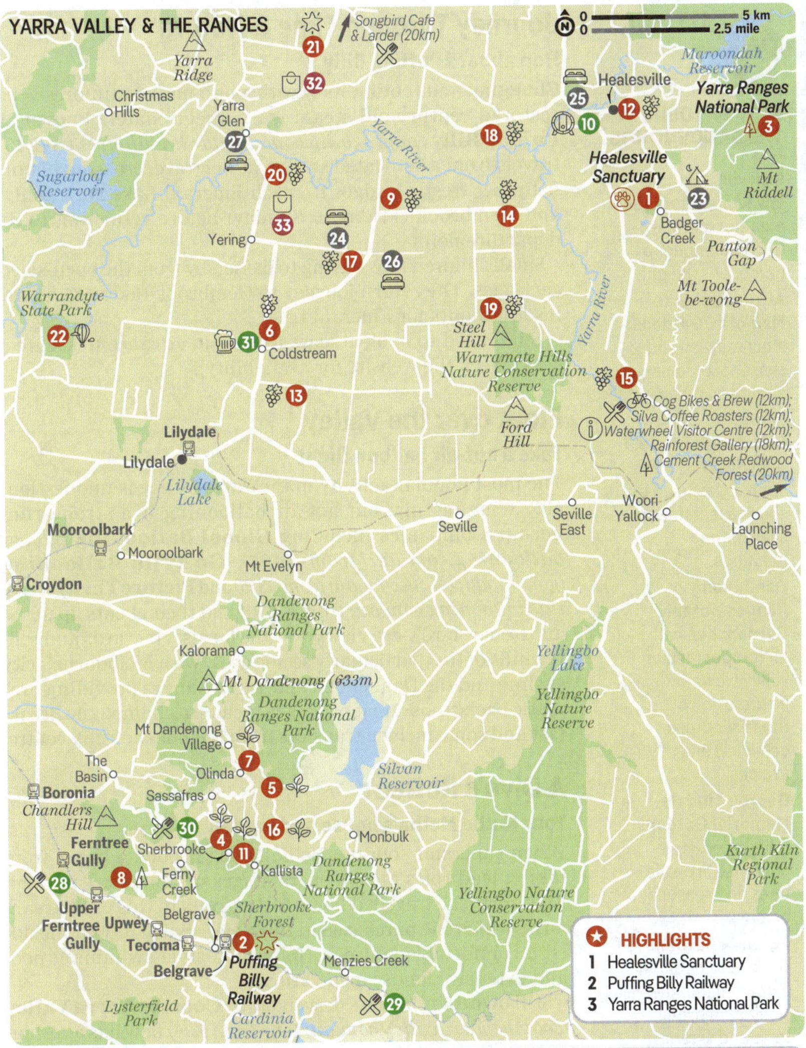

SIGHTS
4 Alfred Nicholas Memorial Gardens
5 Cloudehill
6 Coombe Yarra Valley
7 Dandenong Ranges Botanic Garden
8 Dandenong Ranges National Park
9 Domaine Chandon
10 Four Pillars
11 George Tindale Memorial Gardens
12 Giant Steps
13 Helen's Hill
14 Levantine Hill
15 Mac Forbes
16 Pirianda Garden
17 St Hubert's
18 TarraWarra Estate
see 18 TarraWarra Museum of Art
19 Yarra Yering
20 Yering Station

ACTIVITIES
21 Global Ballooning
see 20 Go Wild Ballooning
22 Picture This

SLEEPING
see 21 Balgownie Estate
23 BIG4 Yarra Valley Park Lane Holiday Park
see 20 Chateau Yering Hotel
24 Farmhouse at Meletos
25 RACV Healesville Country Club & Resort
26 Re'em Yarra Valley
27 Yarra Glen Grand Hotel

EATING
see 27 Harper & Ivy
see 14 Levantine Hill
28 Lorna
29 Paradise Valley Hotel
30 Proserpina Bakehouse
see 18 TarraWarra Estate Restaurant

DRINKING & NIGHTLIFE
31 Coldstream Brewery
see 24 Napoleone Cider Co

SHOPPING
see 12 Kitchen & Butcher
32 Yarra Valley Chocolaterie & Ice Creamery
33 Yarra Valley Dairy

BEST GARDENS IN THE DANDENONGS

Rich volcanic soil, low temperatures and plentiful rain make the Dandenongs a gardener's delight.

Alfred Nicholas Memorial Gardens: Mountain ash and seasonal blooms around an ornamental lake.

Cloudehill: Estate featuring 25 garden 'rooms' designed to showcase different seasons and plantings.

Dandenong Ranges Botanic Garden: Known for its spectacular valley views and its profusion of rhododendrons, camellias and azaleas.

George Tindale Memorial Gardens: Hill-station-style garden with exotic trees and seasonal blooms.

Pirianda Garden: Terraced woodland garden featuring significant exotic trees and shrubs.

Journey Through Time & Nature

Hop aboard Puffing Billy

Chugging and tooting its way through native rainforest, the restored century-old steam train affectionately known as **Puffing Billy** *(puffingbilly.com.au; adult/child from $42/21)* travels from a dedicated station at Belgrave, crossing historic timber trestle bridges to reach Emerald Lake Park (daily) and Gembrook (Friday to Sunday) before returning to its departure point.

Small children love waving to passersby from the open-sided carriages. The return journey to Gembrook takes 5½ hours; it's four hours for Emerald Lake.

You'll need to book at least 10 days in advance to secure a seat (check the website for availability).

Float over the Valley

Take a hot-air balloon flight

The most popular activity in the Yarra Valley is unquestionably wine tasting, but hot-air ballooning is a strong runner-up. Companies including **Global Ballooning** *(globalballooning.com.au; from $495)*, **Go Wild Ballooning** *(gowildballooning.com.au; from $375)* and **Picture This** *(picturethisballooning.com.au; from $379)* send their clients up in the air to enjoy bird's-eye views over the farms, vineyards and rolling hills of this particularly scenic area, with Melbourne's city skyline and the Dandenong and Yarra Ranges providing dramatic backdrops. Most packages include a champagne breakfast and some include transfers from Melbourne's city centre.

A Diva's Retreat

Tour Nellie Melba's house and garden

When superstar soprano Nellie Melba needed a break from taking lead roles on the opera stages of London, Paris and New York, she travelled home to Australia to this Coldstream farm, which she purchased in 1909. Her stylish retreat included a comfortable house, a Hollywood-style swimming pool and extensive landscaped gardens.

Still owned by Melba's descendants, **Coombe Yarra Valley** *(coombeyarravalley.com.au; tour from $35)* now has a restaurant and winery, but it's also possible to take a guided tour of Melba's house or its large, beautiful gardens. If visiting

Continued on p530

EATING IN THE RANGES: OUR PICKS

Proserpina Bakehouse: The best bakery–cafe in the Dandenongs. The loyal clientele dote on its cakes and pastries. *7am-4pm Wed-Mon* **$**

Lorna: Bright modern cafe with an eclectic menu in Ferntree Gully on the doorstep of the Dandenongs. *6am-4pm Mon-Fri, 8am-4pm Sat & Sun* **$**

Silva Coffee Roasters: Enjoy a speciality coffee flight and a delicious slice of cake in this roastery cafe in Warburton. *8am-4pm* **$**

Paradise Valley Hotel: On the Belgrave–Gembrook Rd, this pub is known for its excellent food and impressive wine list. *noon-9pm* **$$**

CYCLING THE WARBURTON RAIL TRAIL

This popular and well-maintained cycling trail follows the paths of two historic but now dismantled trainlines.

START	END	LENGTH
Yering Station	Warburton	47.5km; 4hr

The route stretches from Yering in the Yarra Valley to Warburton in the Yarra Ranges, though many people commence their ride in Lilydale, which is served by train from Melbourne. Featuring gentle gradients, the trails are sealed with fine gravel or asphalt.

Start your ride at 1 **Yering Station** (p528), the oldest winery in the Yarra Valley. Follow the path through bush and open pasture to Coldstream, the most picturesque pocket of the valley and on to the regional hub of 2 **Lilydale** (8.5km). Here you'll need to switch from the Yarra Valley Trail to the main Warburton Rail Trail. From here, continue southeast to 3 **Mt Evelyn** (7km) and then on through fern-lined gullies and remnant bushland past the small settlement of 4 **Seville** and on to 5 **Woori Yallock** (16km). You'll pass through the floodplains of the Yarra River (Birrarung), now rich grazing land, on this leg of the journey.

From Woori Yallock, the stage to 6 **Yarra Junction** (9km) follows the Yarra River closely. The final 8km stage continues to follow the river's course through native forest and wetlands to 7 **Warburton**, a pretty town nestled on the banks of the Upper Yarra in the shadow of stately Mt Donna Buang. The town has plenty of eating, drinking and sleeping options.

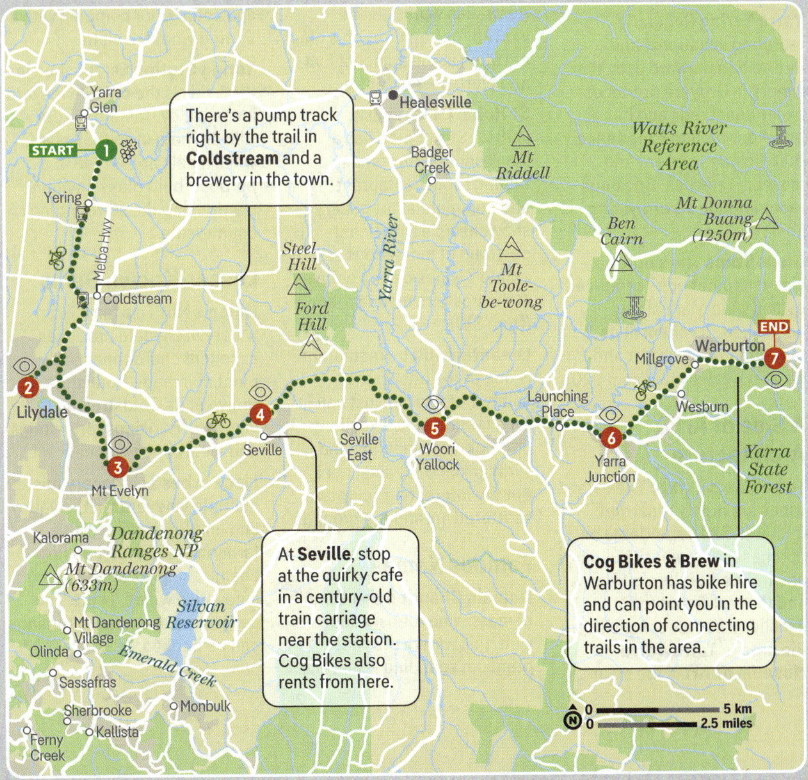

HELP ME PICK:

Yarra Valley Wineries

The Yarra Valley is home to more than 80 wineries, many of which have expert-led tasting experiences at their cellar doors *(wineyarravalley.com.au)*. A growing number also have top-notch restaurants, making a day spent touring here as satisfying for the stomach as it is for the palate. The area is recognised as Victoria's oldest wine region – the first vines were planted at Yering Station in 1838. Today, it is known worldwide for its cool-climate wines, especially chardonnay and pinot noir.

Where to Visit if You Love...

Outstanding Wine

Yarra Yering Regularly featuring in national and international award lists, this winery in Gruyere produces exceptional reds and has a one-hour tasting experience that includes current and museum releases. Bookings recommended *(yarrayering.com)*.

Giant Steps The single-vineyard pinot noirs produced by this winery are highly acclaimed. Try them at its tasting room, wine bar and shop in Healesville (from $20).

A Side of Art & Architecture

TarraWarra Estate The estate wines are highly regarded (tastings $20, refundable on purchase), the winery buildings are architecturally significant and the restaurant (p531) is excellent, but for some visitors, the on-site **TarraWarra Museum of Art** is the main drawcard ($18). Important Australian works can be viewed for free through a glass partition in the adjacent Eva and Marc Besen Centre.

St Hubert's Established in 1862, St Hubert's has a sleek semi-subterranean tasting room, restaurant and commercial art gallery showcasing a significant portfolio of Indigenous art. The estate's wines can be enjoyed in the upstairs tasting room (from $10).

Levantine Hill Its restaurant is one of the best in the valley, but you can just call in for a tasting of its excellent chardonnay, pinot noir and syrah (from $30) and check out the interesting sculpture scattered around the grounds.

Famous Names

Domain Chandon An example of mass wine tourism done well, this winery produces premium sparkling wines and has a restaurant, lounge bar and cellar door complex with a stirring vineyard vista.

Yering Station Established in 1838, this is the oldest vineyard in the valley. Tastings (from $15) are held in an 1859 shed, while meals are served in a purpose-built glass pavilion overlooking the surrounding countryside.

Lesser-Known Gems

Helen's Hill This family-run winery in Lilydale produces excellent chardonnay and pinot noir made from grapes grown at its Coldstream vineyard. Bookings for tastings and meals are essential.

Mac Forbes This winery has multiple vineyards in the valley and employs regenerative farming practices, reducing chemical inputs and creating innovative wines. There's no cellar door, but private tastings can be booked.

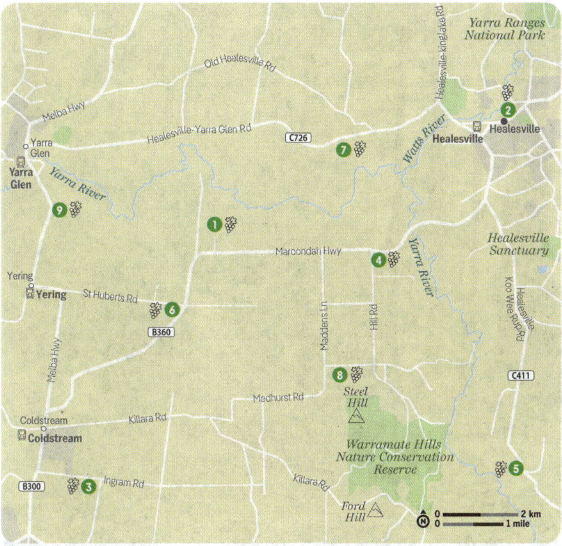

● DRINKING & NIGHTLIFE

1 Domain Chandon
2 Giant Steps
3 Helen's Hill
4 Levantine Hill
5 Mac Forbes Winery
6 St Hubert's
7 TarraWarra Estate
8 Yarra Yering
9 Yering Station

HOW TO

When to go The valley looks its best in spring or early summer when it's dry and warm but not too hot.

Book ahead It's essential to book restaurants and advisable to book tastings. Weekdays are quieter, but some cellar doors close on Mondays and Tuesdays.

Budget Most wineries charge for tastings and the best are expensive *(premium wines from $50)*. Some refund the charge if you purchase a bottle.

Pace yourself Most tastings are the equivalent of a glass of wine. If you're driving, be sensible – spread them out or spit it out.

Getting Around the Vineyards

As with the Mornington Peninsula (p520), you'll have more flexibility and control over your itinerary if you're touring the region with your own vehicle. If nobody is volunteering to be the sober driver, **Driven Indulgence** *(drivenindulgence.com.au; 8hr $400)* has a service where they'll provide one for you, but be sure to register their driver with your rental-car company.

Guided tours start at around $175 per day, but they usually only visit three or four of the less high-profile wineries. A better option is to sign up for the daily hop-on, hop-off bus tour offered by **Hop It** *(hopit.com.au; from Melbourne $98)*, which departs from central Melbourne, stops to take on additional passengers at Lilydale railway station and then heads into the valley to visit many of the best cellar doors (you can choose four to visit).

Some tour companies, including **Wine Compass** *(winecompass.com.au)* and the **Yarra Valley Touring Co** *(yarravalleytouring.com.au; day trip from Melbourne approx $650)*, can tailor car or minibus tours to your specifications but these are considerably more expensive than the public tours.

VineTours *(vinetours.com.au; incl bikes, lunch, tastings & pick up from Lilydale Station from $350)* has guided six-hour bicycle tours, starting in Woori Yallock.

BEST TRACKS IN THE DANDENONGS

Kokoda Track Memorial Walk: Also known as the 1000 Steps Walk, this steep 3km track starts at the main national park car park in Tremont.

Eastern Sherbrooke Forest Walk: There are some steep sections on this 6.6km forest walk where the melodious song of lyrebirds is regularly heard.

Sherbrooke Falls Loop: A 45-minute walk through mountain ash and tree ferns to a moss-covered cascade ('falls' is an overstatement).

Margaret Lester Walk: Wheelchair users can enjoy this 300m track through the forest, starting at Grants Picnic Ground in Kallista.

Birdsland Reserve: Another pram- and wheelchair-friendly track on gravel paths and boardwalks in a wetland reserve (2.8km).

ROBYN MACKENZIE/SHUTTERSTOCK

Yarra Ranges National Park

Continued from p526

in October or November, the garden tour is particularly rewarding, as this is when the roses, herbaceous borders and wisteria bloom.

Tours must be booked in advance and include food (either a Devonshire tea, high tea or lunch). Otherwise, just pop in for a tasting ($15, Wed-Sun) and to poke around the gallery of Melba memorabilia.

A Break from the Grapes

Gin tasting at Four Pillars

It's not all wine in the Yarra, as the hugely successful **Four Pillars** *(fourpillarsgin.com)* distillery in Healesville attests. As well as making award-winning gins, the distillery recycles the steamed oranges used in distillation to concoct delicious marmalades.

Call in for a tasting (six gins $15) or a 30-minute **tour** *(adult/child $30/10)*, or just grab a G&T in the on-site Beth's Bar or Jude's Gin Garden. Happy hour runs from 6pm to 8pm on Fridays, with half-price G&Ts, cocktails and G&T paddles. The booze-related gift shop is a good place to pick up a souvenir.

Australia's Cutest Furry & Feathery Things

Native encounters at Healesville Sanctuary

Healesville Sanctuary *(zoo.org.au; adult/child from $55/29)*, the rural sister of Melbourne Zoo, focusses exclusively on native species: koalas, kangaroos, wallabies, wombats, dingoes, platypuses, emus and all the ones you've never heard of.

Tucked within native bush, the park is large, leafy and very well laid out. The walk-through aviaries are particularly good, providing the rare opportunity to see superb lyrebirds. Keep an eye out for the critically endangered helmeted honeyeater – Victoria's state bird – the only bird endemic to Victoria alone.

Another point of difference of this park over other wildlife parks is the Australian Wildlife Health Centre, where you can watch lab work, checkups, surgery and postmortems taking place behind glass. It even has a kids' section labelled 'Future Vets', with dress-up materials and soft toys to practise on.

Put aside at least two hours for your visit. Tickets are slightly cheaper online and free for under 16s on weekends. Animal talks and free-flight demonstrations are free, or you can pay extra for a close-up animal experience with a Zoos Victoria keeper. Accessibility is excellent.

Nature's Gallery & Cathedral

Green attractions near Warburton

Set among tall trees on the banks of the Yarra River, the pretty town of Warburton is the gateway to some of the most popular parts of **Yarra Ranges National Park**. The park spreads over 76 sq km of the Great Dividing Range, including Mt Donna Buang (1250m), where locals go tobogganing in the snow in winter. Call into the **Visitor Centre** behind the giant waterwheel in Warburton for details of walks and cycling trails in the area.

A 10-minute drive up the mountain from Warburton will bring you to the **Rainforest Gallery**, a 40m-long wheelchair- and pram-accessible observation platform jutting out into the canopy of mountain ash and myrtle beech trees, 15m above the forest floor. Stairs lead down to a 20-minute walk circling a boardwalk at the base.

A completely different arboreal experience lies below the mountain, 10 minutes east of Warburton, at the **Cement Creek Redwood Forest**. Unlike the wild beauty of the rainforest above, here 1500 redwood trees were planted in orderly rows in the 1930s. Some are now 60m tall and there's an otherworldly cathedral-like quality in the hush beneath their towering canopy. In summer, it's deliciously cool.

OTHER YARRA VALLEY PRODUCTS

Kitchen & Butcher: Known locally as K&B, this deli in Healesville is a cornucopia of quality local produce, including cheese and artisan sausages.

Napoleone Cider Co: Apple and pear ciders made using estate-grown fruit. Available for tasting at the Punt Rd Wines cellar door in Coldstream.

Yarra Valley Chocolaterie & Ice Creamery: The name says it all. It also has branches on the Mornington Peninsula, the Great Ocean Rd and Bendigo.

Yarra Valley Dairy: This farm shop in Yering is known for its goat cheeses and Persian fetta.

Coldstream Brewery: Fronted by its naked 'shivering man' statue, this brew-pub in a converted wool store has beer- and cider-tasting paddles.

EATING IN THE YARRA VALLEY: OUR PICKS

In winter there's a roaring fire

Harper & Ivy: Friendly cafe in an historic bank building on Yarra Glen's main street. *7.30-11.30am Wed, 8am-3pm Thu, Sat & Sun, 8am-7pm Fri* **$**

TarraWarra Estate Restaurant: Multicourse modern-Australian dining at this acclaimed winery restaurant. *11am-5pm Wed-Sun* **$$$**

Levantine Hill: Middle Eastern spices marry with local seasonal produce in this modern Mediterranean restaurant overlooking the vines. *11am-5pm Wed-Mon* **$$$**

Songbird Cafe & Larder: This cheerful Kinglake cafe serves hearty country fare in substantial portions. *11am-7pm Wed-Fri, 9am-4pm Sat & Sun* **$**

DRIVING TOUR

Dandenong Ranges Drive

Generations of Melburnians have enjoyed regular Sunday drives east of the city to the forested Dandenongs (aka 'the Hills'). While the route we've suggested up Mt Dandenong is only 20km long, it can be turned into a 100km loop from central Melbourne (allow two hours total driving time). Pack your walking shoes, as you're going to want to stop for a stroll.

1 Dandenong Ranges National Park

It takes around 40 minutes to drive from the city to the **national park**, home to dense fern gullies, huge stands of mountain ash and vibrantly plumed native birds. Various walks start from the main car park, including the steep, slippery, 90-minute-return Kokoda Track Memorial Walk.

The Drive: Take the winding Mt Dandenong Tourist Rd up through the forest and turn right into Sherbrooke Rd (about 10 minutes).

2 Alfred Nicholas Memorial Gardens

Aspro painkiller tycoon Alfred Nicholas created this landscaped **garden** *(free)* in the grounds of his now-abandoned Art Deco house. The main path leads to an ornamental lake and waterfall. In spring the rhododendrons blaze red, while in autumn everything is golden.

The Drive: It's only a three-minute drive to the next stop. Backtrack to the Tourist Rd and turn right.

SUMMER360/SHUTTERSTOCK

Dandenong Ranges National Park

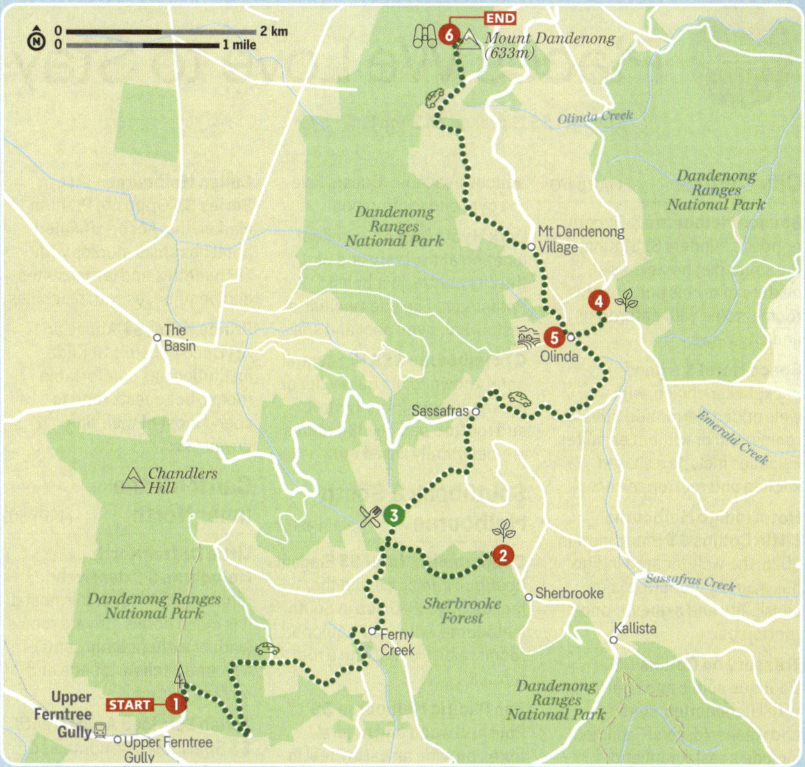

❸ Proserpina Bakehouse

Refuel at this excellent country-style **bakery**, where the counter is packed with old-fashioned sponge cakes, tarts and meat pies.

The Drive: Continue along the road for around 10 minutes, passing through the mountain village of Sassafras. Turn right when you reach Olinda.

❹ Dandenong Ranges Botanic Garden

You'll need to pay to enter this 50-hectare **garden** *(adult/child $12/6)* but it's worth it. It's home to the state's cool-climate collection, including over 15,000 rhododendrons, 12,000 azaleas, 3000 camellias and 250,000 daffodils.

The Drive: Backtrack to the village of Olinda (about three minutes).

❺ Olinda

Rustic Olinda was founded as a timber camp in 1855 before morphing into a proper settlement by 1870. The main street has a pie shop; pub; and stores selling hats, confectionary, soaps, crystals and speciality teas. Our favourite is Dr Quirky's Vintage Emporium.

The Drive: Continue up the Tourist Rd and follow the signs to SkyHigh, turning left onto Ridge Rd and left again onto Observatory Rd (about six minutes).

❻ SkyHigh Mt Dandenong

Enter **SkyHigh** *(weekdays $5, weekends $10)* for amazing views over Melbourne, Port Phillip Bay, the Yarra Valley and the Great Dividing Range from the highest point in the Dandenongs. The complex includes a bistro, cafe, English garden and **hedge maze** *(adult/child $8/6)*. From here you can backtrack to Ridge Rd and continue north, making your way down the mountain via a beautiful forested drive. It will take about an hour to return to the city.

Places We Love to Stay

$** Budget **$$** Midrange **$$$ Top End

City Centre

MAP p470

Bounce Melbourne $ Directly opposite Flinders St Station, this upmarket hostel has a mixture of dorms and private rooms, some with bathrooms and city views.

Space Hotel $ A good backpacker choice, with well-priced dorms and private rooms with or without en suites. Facilities include a shared kitchen and rooftop terrace.

Hotel Indigo Melbourne Little Collins $$ Brand-new in 2025, the well-located Indigo has a quirky modern design sensibility and a guests-only rooftop bar.

Treasury on Collins $$ Boutique suites and apartments with kitchenettes, seating areas and washer/dryers. Facilities include a restaurant and guest lounge. Prices drop on weekdays.

Laneways by Ovolo $$ Boutique hotel with a cool city vibe. The penthouse suite has a pinball machine and a private terrace with a Jacuzzi.

Lancemore $$ In a great location in Chinatown, near Parliament, this hotel has spacious rooms with work desks, a lobby lounge and a rooftop terrace.

Savoy Hotel on Little Collins $$ This 11-storey, 1866 hotel opposite Southern Cross Station is very comfortable, surprisingly well priced and very handy for the airport bus.

Rydges Melbourne $$ King rooms and suites on Exhibition St, with wheelchair-accessible options available. Guests love the gym and rooftop pool.

Park Hyatt $$$ An excellent location at the leafy end of the city centre, just behind Parliament. Facilities include a restaurant, gym, pool and spa.

QT Melbourne $$$ Hip central hotel known for its quirky decor, interesting art, friendly staff and rooftop bar. The 188 rooms are beautifully kitted out.

Southbank & South Melbourne

MAP p482

Coppersmith Hotel $$ Elegant boutique choice behind the facade of an 1870 pub in South Melbourne, with well-equipped rooms, a bistro-bar and a roof terrace.

Pan Pacific Melbourne $$ Polished wood and natural fibres provide an earthy feel in this luxurious hotel. Suites are huge and some have dazzling views.

St Kilda & the Southern Suburbs

MAP p488

Olsen Melbourne – Art Series $ Steps from South Yarra's boutiques and cafes, this art-filled choice has a cantilevered pool and studio suites with kitchenettes.

Royce Hotel $$ Longstanding boutique choice on St Kilda Rd near the Domain, with spacious rooms and a lovely bar and lounge.

Ovolo South Yarra $$ Rooms are on the small side but have pleasingly jaunty decor. There's a gym and self-service laundry.

Cullen Melbourne – Art Series $$ Opposite Prahran Market, this Accor-affiliated hotel has small studios with kitchenettes and larger suites and penthouses with balconies.

Prince Hotel $$ Above an Art Deco pub, this St Kilda institution has comfortable rooms, but guests tend to spend most of their time downstairs.

Carlton & the Inner North

MAP p502

Little Drifter North Melbourne $ Extensively refurbished in 2023, this hostel has clean dorms, private rooms (with or without bathrooms), a shared kitchen, lounge and rooftop terrace.

Tyrian Serviced Apartments $$ Spacious, self-contained one-, two- and three-bedroom serviced apartments in the heart of Fitzroy with balconies, Nespresso machines and washer/dryers.

Larwill Studio $$ The location is unusual (the hotel is attached to the Royal Children's Hospital) but rooms are well priced, especially considering the high standard.

Zagame's House $$$ A fully refurbished 1970s motel on Lygon St in Carlton, Zagame's offers comfortable rooms and suites and on-site parking.

Veriu Collingwood $$$ There's lots to like here, including a rooftop bar, heated swimming pool, gym, working spaces, and apartments with cooking and laundry facilities.

Geelong & the Bellarine Peninsula

MAP p512

Tasman Holiday Parks – Geelong $ Near the river in suburban Belmont, this large holiday park has a mixture of self-contained cabins and campervan sites.

Lon Retreat $$$ Spa hotel with seven luxurious suites on 100 hectares of rural and conservation land in Point Lonsdale on the Bellarine Peninsula.

Mornington Peninsula

MAP p518

RACV Cape Schanck Resort $$ Close to Gunnamatta Beach, this sleek multistorey resort has an indoor swimming pool, children's playground, bar and two excellent restaurants.

Hamptons in Rye $$$ Near the Peninsula Hot Springs, this quiet private guesthouse rents a studio apartment and two standalone cottages.

Treetops at Red Hill $$$ Two luxurious cottages on a vineyard with a micro-winery and landscaped garden.

Jackalope $$$ Rooms are as luxe as the hefty prices indicate. Facilities include an infinity pool overlooking the vineyard, a cocktail bar and two restaurants.

Lancemore Lindenderry Red Hill $$$ Set amid 14 hectares of vines and gardens, Lancemore is one of the most elegant accommodation options on the Peninsula.

Port Phillip Estate $$$ Six sleek suites with vineyard views, big beds and sitting areas are hidden underneath the public areas of this notable winery.

Yarra Valley & the Ranges

MAP p525

BIG4 Yarra Valley Park Lane Holiday Park $ Comfortable cabins, glamping pods and tents, en-suite caravan sites and camp sites. Swimming pool and jumping pillow, too.

Yarra Glen Grand Hotel $$ Comfortable en-suite rooms in a lovely old Italianate pub with tartan carpets and balconies trimmed with wrought iron. Continental breakfast included.

Farmhouse at Meletos $$ Channelling a Tuscan farmhouse vibe, the 23 rooms at this winery hotel are rustically luxurious. The best have vineyard views.

RACV Healesville Country Club & Resort $$ A golf course, spa, indoor pool, restaurant and bar are the major draws. Premium rooms have mountain views.

Balgownie Estate $$ On a vineyard outside Yarra Glen, this hotel has 70 rooms and suites, a restaurant, spa, indoor pool, steam room and gym.

Chateau Yering Hotel $$ The epitome of a country house hotel, this slightly faded but still tempting heritage-listed offering is set in gorgeous gardens.

Re'em Yarra Valley $$$ On the Helen and Joey Estate vineyard in Gruyere, this boutique hotel has rooms and suites with a patio or balcony.

PAUL HARDING 00/SHUTTERSTOCK

Rooftop bar at QT Melbourne, City Centre

Researched by
Jessica Korteman
and Paul Harding

Greater Victoria

COAST, MOUNTAINS AND COUNTRY ESCAPES

The view beyond Melbourne looks rather different. Experience Victoria's diversity with a trip to the countryside.

It's in regional Victoria that the state fully brings its varied terrain to the fore. Some of the most recognisable sections of coastline in the country can be found here, along with equally impressive landscapes most travellers are yet to discover. With beaches, bushland, mountains and agricultural plains all packed into a state that's small by Australian standards, Victoria has a lot to offer.

DIPEN KHADKA/SHUTTERSTOCK

Brushing up on gold-rush history will serve you well here. During the 1850s, more than a third of the world's gold production came from the Victorian goldfields. Under the gaze of global attention, momentous waves of migration and unprecedented wealth came together to weave a story of how Victorian communities were shaped by gold.

Today, quality dining is a big drawcard, with an emphasis on curated meals of local, seasonal ingredients. Opportunities to extend the palate through adventurous eating come in the form of numerous tapas-style plates and menus left to the creative flow of the chef. Boutique wineries and microbreweries are now an expectation on any beverage list.

It's all part of what the rural reaches of Victoria provide: a culinary culture that can hold its own and an expansive countryside to enjoy it all in. As you travel around, leave room in your bag for a picnic and plan to stay awhile.

THE MAIN AREAS

GREAT OCEAN ROAD
Iconic coastal views and walks.
p542

WARRNAMBOOL & THE SOUTHWEST COAST
Whale watching and ancient aquaculture.
p556

BENDIGO
Gastronomy and dancing dragons.
p563

BALLARAT
Gold-rush history and architecture.
p572

DAYLESFORD & HEPBURN SPRINGS
Mineral springs and cosy getaways.
p578

For places to stay in Greater Victoria, see p630

ALIZADA STUDIOS/SHUTTERSTOCK

Left: Cape Otway Lightstation (p552); Above: Boulders near Hanging Rock (p569)

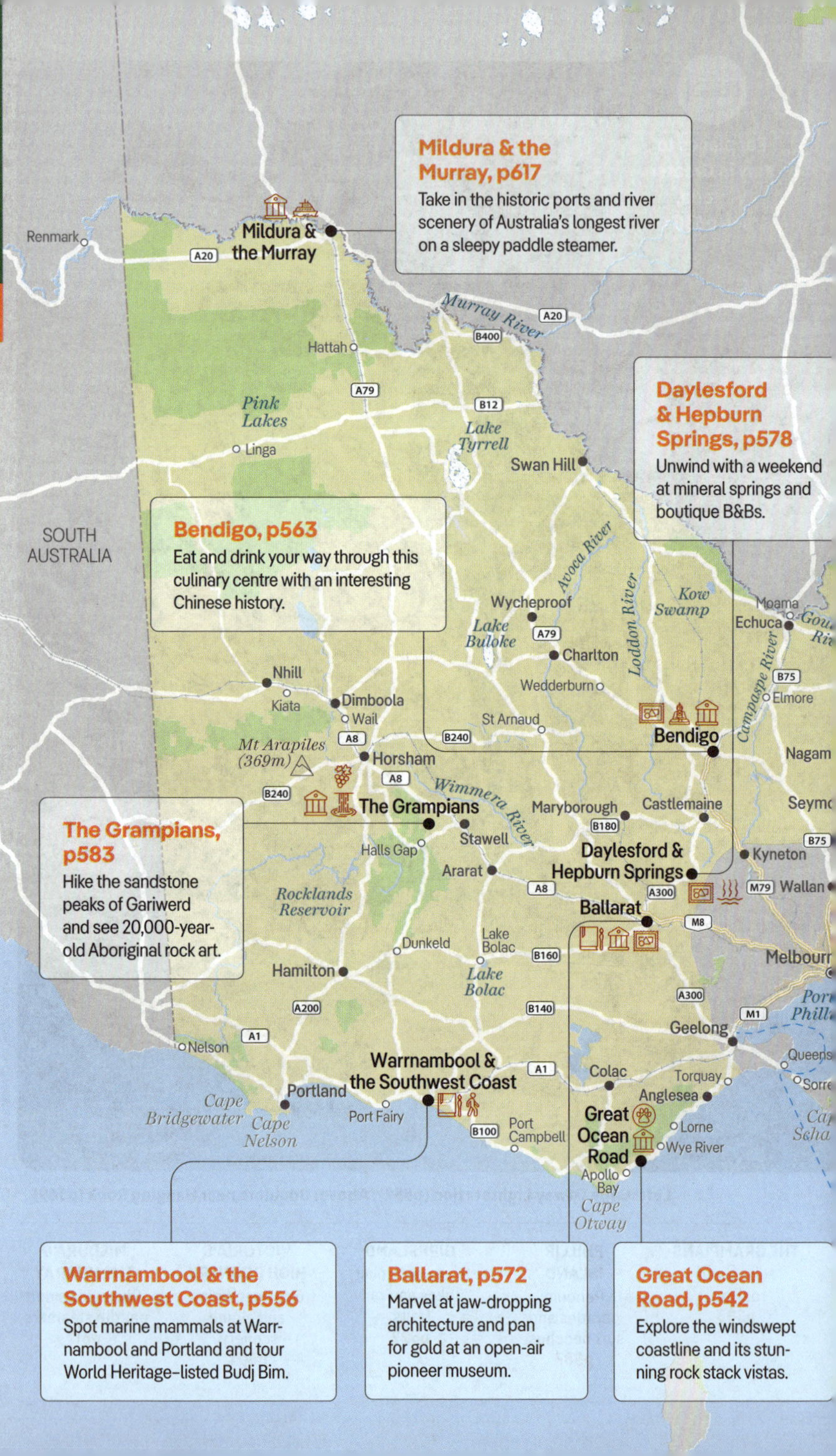
Mildura & the Murray, p617
Take in the historic ports and river scenery of Australia's longest river on a sleepy paddle steamer.
Daylesford & Hepburn Springs, p578
Unwind with a weekend at mineral springs and boutique B&Bs.
Bendigo, p563
Eat and drink your way through this culinary centre with an interesting Chinese history.
The Grampians, p583
Hike the sandstone peaks of Gariwerd and see 20,000-year-old Aboriginal rock art.
Warrnambool & the Southwest Coast, p556
Spot marine mammals at Warrnambool and Portland and tour World Heritage–listed Budj Bim.
Ballarat, p572
Marvel at jaw-dropping architecture and pan for gold at an open-air pioneer museum.
Great Ocean Road, p542
Explore the windswept coastline and its stunning rock stack vistas.
Renmark
A20
Mildura & the Murray
Murray River
A20
B400
Hattah
A79
B12
Pink Lakes
Linga
Lake Tyrrell
Swan Hill
SOUTH AUSTRALIA
Avoca River
Loddon River
Kow Swamp
Moama
Echuca
Campaspe River
B75
Elmore
Wycheproof
Lake Buloke
A79
Charlton
Wedderburn
Nhill
Kiata
Dimboola
Wail
St Arnaud
B240
Bendigo
Nagam
Mt Arapiles (369m)
A8
Horsham
A8
Wimmera River
B240
The Grampians
Stawell
Halls Gap
Maryborough
Castlemaine
B180
Seymo
B75
Kyneton
Daylesford & Hepburn Springs
A300
M79
Wallan
Ararat
A8
Ballarat
M8
Rocklands Reservoir
Dunkeld
Lake Bolac
B160
Melbourn
Hamilton
Lake Bolac
A300
A200
B140
Port Phill
M1
Geelong
Nelson
A1
Warrnambool & the Southwest Coast
A1
Colac
Torquay
Queens
Sorre
Anglesea
Portland
Great Ocean Road
Cape Bridgewater
Cape Nelson
Port Fairy
B100
Port Campbell
Lorne
Wye River
Apollo Bay
Cape Otway

Find Your Way

Victoria is one of Australia's smaller states, but it still has a lot of ground to cover. You'll find a mix of well-connected hubs and more locales that require a little more planning.

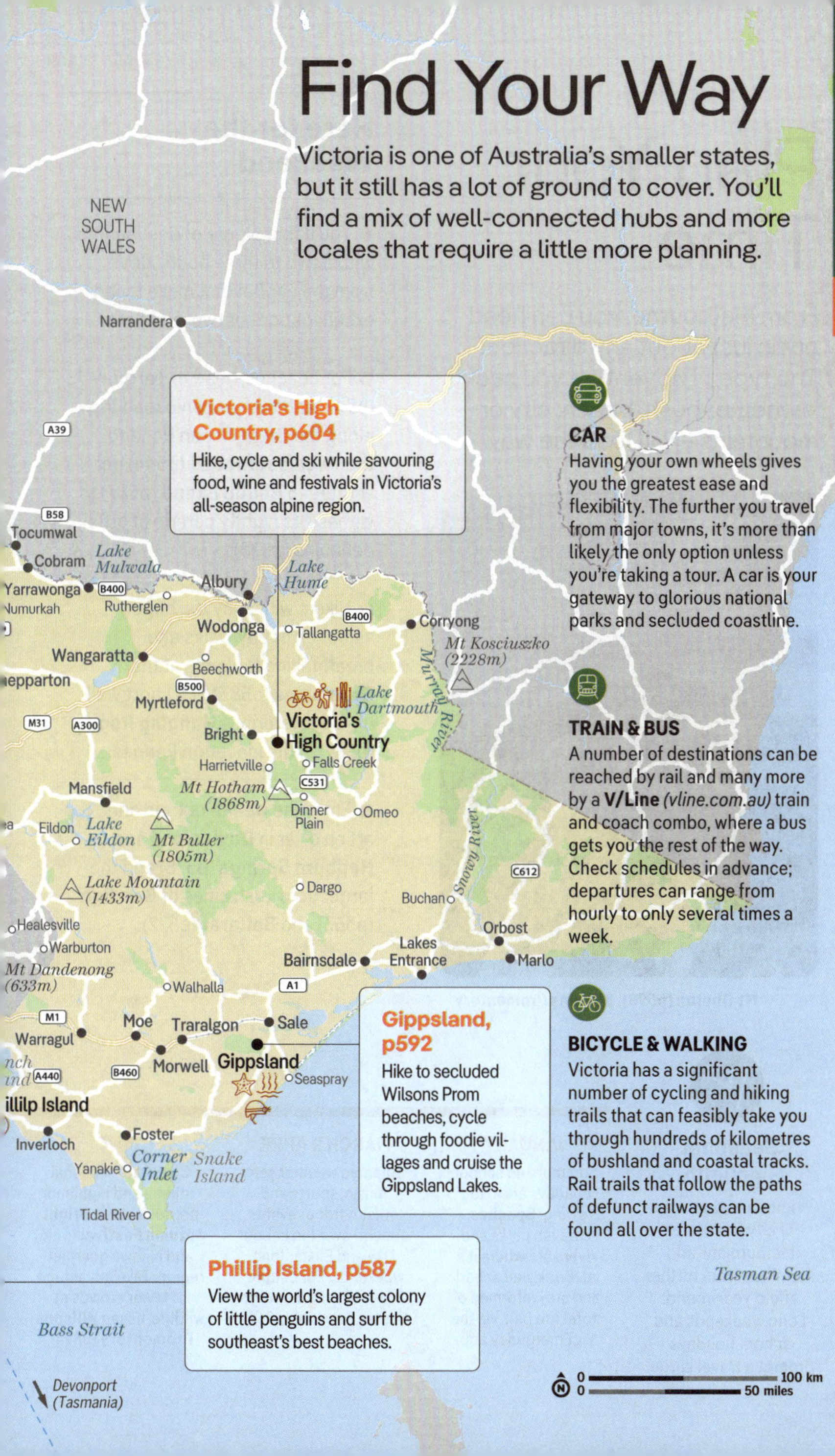

Victoria's High Country, p604

Hike, cycle and ski while savouring food, wine and festivals in Victoria's all-season alpine region.

Gippsland, p592

Hike to secluded Wilsons Prom beaches, cycle through foodie villages and cruise the Gippsland Lakes.

Phillip Island, p587

View the world's largest colony of little penguins and surf the southeast's best beaches.

CAR

Having your own wheels gives you the greatest ease and flexibility. The further you travel from major towns, it's more than likely the only option unless you're taking a tour. A car is your gateway to glorious national parks and secluded coastline.

TRAIN & BUS

A number of destinations can be reached by rail and many more by a **V/Line** *(vline.com.au)* train and coach combo, where a bus gets you the rest of the way. Check schedules in advance; departures can range from hourly to only several times a week.

BICYCLE & WALKING

Victoria has a significant number of cycling and hiking trails that can feasibly take you through hundreds of kilometres of bushland and coastal tracks. Rail trails that follow the paths of defunct railways can be found all over the state.

Plan Your Time

From Melbourne, you can head out in just about any direction. The type of adventure you seek – whether bush, beach, city or mountains – will lead the way.

NIC_JAMESS/SHUTTERSTOCK

Mt Oberon (p595), Wilsons Promontory

Here for the Weekend

- You'll find plenty of destinations within two to three hours' drive from the capital that make for an excellent one- or two-night stay.
- For beaches, head to **Torquay** (p542) and take a scenic road trip along the Great Ocean Road to the **Twelve Apostles** (p544) dor venture to **Phillip Island** (p587) to witness its nightly parade of little penguins (p590).
- Hikers will enjoy the huge selection of day walks and breathtaking lookouts at the **Grampians** (p583) or a short walk up the mysterious **Hanging Rock** (p569) in the Macedon Ranges.
- Enjoy the wealth of food and art on offer in **Daylesford and Hepburn Springs** (p578) and the larger gold-rush cities of **Bendigo** (p563) and **Ballarat** (p572).

Seasonal Highlights

Victoria has a range of city breaks for Melburnians and travellers from further afield year-round. Long weekends and school holidays prompt a travel surge.

JANUARY

Summer and school holidays are in full swing. **Beaches**, caravan parks and rivers are where it's at. Book well ahead and stay informed of 'total fire ban' via the VicEmergency app.

MARCH & APRIL

Splendid weather sees music, sports and other outdoor events abound over the Labour Day and Easter long weekends. For culture, don't miss the **Bendigo Easter Festival** (p563).

MAY

Celebrate seasonal foliage and highland produce at the **Bright Autumn Festival** (p616) and Milawa gourmet region. Take advantage of fewer crowds at wildlife-haven **Wilsons Promontory** (p594).

Five Days to Wander

- With a few more days at your disposal, extend your Great Ocean Road adventure with a trip to **Forrest** (p551), where you can mountain bike western Victoria's best trails and visit **Lake Elizabeth** (p551) to spot platypuses and glowworms. Or continue on to **Warrnambool** (p556) for whale watching and hot springs and tour **Budj Bim National Park** (p560) with Traditional Custodians of the land.

- In the **Grampians** (p583), add more time to hangout with the wildlife and view Aboriginal rock art. Explore the eastern side of the state with a trip to **Bright** (p614) for crisp mountain air and alpine cycling and the ski slopes of the **High Country** (p606) in winter.

One Week to Explore

- If you have a week to spare, you can take things slow in the extreme south of **Wilsons Promontory** (p594)with scenic coastal walks, pristine beaches and plentiful wildlife.

- Then head east for Gippsland's **Ninety Mile Beach** (p597) and wonderful coastal camping at **Cape Conran** (p601) or **Mallacoota** (p602).

- In the north, along the Victoria–NSW border, the **Murray** (p617) offers impressive river views and relaxed paddle-steamer rides in **Echuca** (p617), **Swan Hill** (p619) and **Mildura** (p621). From Mildura, venture into outback NSW with a night or two in **Mungo National Park** (p628) to visit an active archaeological site and observe wild emus roaming the plains.

JULY

Hit the slopes and enjoy alpine village life as **ski resorts** (p606) enter their peak season in the High Country or head to the dramatic coastline of **Warrnambool** (p556) to spot whales.

AUGUST

Pamper your way through the last of winter with a cosy escape by the fire and rejuvenating soak in Victorian spa country's mineral waters at **Daylesford and Hepburn Springs** (p578).

OCTOBER

The weather gets warmer as spring arrives. Dust off your hiking boots and admire the wildflowers in the **Grampians** (p584) or step aboard a paddle steamer for some **Murray River** (p617) fun.

DECEMBER

The end of year beckons and with it the beach. Hit the reset button on the **Great Ocean Road** (p542) or stay out late on **Phillip Island** (p587) for its nightly perambulation of little penguins.

Great Ocean Road

SCENIC DRIVES | COASTAL HIKES | NATIVE FOREST & WILDLIFE

Places

TOP TIP

This region can get very busy in the summer months. If driving, use slow-vehicle turnouts for photo ops and to let others pass; if hiking, book national parks' camp sites well in advance.

You've probably seen the wave-battered limestone rock stacks in tourist brochures, but that's only part of what makes the Great Ocean Road journey special. Around every spectacular turn, the wiggly road leads to surf beaches, coast-hugging hiking trails, wildlife-rich rainforest and dramatic cliffs.

Today it's tempting to think of the Great Ocean Road as a tourist attraction, but it was built in the early 20th century to connect remote fishing towns using much-needed labour by – and creating jobs for – returned WWI soldiers. It was a memorial to those workers long before it became Australia's coolest coastal drive.

Some of these once-remote fishing and farming communities are now lively tourist towns, but despite the summer crowds this is still wild territory, passing through the rugged Great Otway National Park. Venturing off the road, you can walk and camp on long-distance coastal trails where ocean views and deserted beaches are your daily canvas. Don't miss it!

Torquay

TIME FROM GEELONG: **30MIN**

The official starting point of the Great Ocean Road, Torquay has an infectious youthful surf, skate and street culture unlike anywhere else on this coast. In the 1960s, this small town began luring surfers to the legendary breaks at Bells Beach

Continued on p546

GETTING AROUND

The official Great Ocean Road is roughly 250km from Torquay to Allansford (near Warrnambool). Plenty of tour buses from Melbourne or Geelong can take you along the route and you can reach either end by V/Line train and bus to Torquay (via Geelong) or direct to Warrnambool. From there, nearly all the towns along the coast are served by public transport. **McHarry's Buslines** *(mcharrys.com.au)* runs daily services from Geelong Station to Apollo Bay via Torquay and the Great Ocean Road; change at Apollo Bay for another service to Warrnambool. As with any great road trip, though, the best way to experience the Great Ocean Road is in your own vehicle. Campervan hire is popular, or just pack a tent and some cooking gear as there are many camping grounds along the way. The route can be hiked or cycled via several linked walking paths, including the 100km **Great Ocean Walk** (p552) from Apollo Bay to the Twelve Apostles or the 44km **Surf Coast Walk** (p547) out of Torquay.

GREAT OCEAN ROAD
Geelong
Torquay
Bells Beach
Anglesea
Aireys Inlet
Fairhaven
Lorne
Anglesea Heath Reserve
Great Otway National Park
Angahook-Lorne State Park
Wye River
Kennett River
Wangara
Skenes Creek
Apollo Bay
Blanket Bay
Cape Otway
Great Otway National Park
Bass Strait
Bannockburn
Moriac
Barwon River
Inverleigh
Winchelsea
Lake Murdeduke
Deans Marsh
Barwon River
Birregurra
Forrest
Olangolah Flora & Fauna Reserve
Beeac
Colac
Lake Colac
Gellibrand
Beech Forest
Carlisle State Park
Lavers Hill
Glenaire
Johanna
Gellibrand River
Lake Gnarpurt
Lake Corangamite
Camperdown
Cobden
Princetown
Port Campbell National Park
Gibson Steps
The Twelve Apostles
Loch Ard Gorge
Port Campbell
The Arch
London Bridge
The Grotto
Peterborough
Timboon
Curdies River
Terang
Noorat
Mortlake
Hopkins River
Nullawarre
Bay of Islands Coastal Park
Allansford
Warrnambool
SOUTHERN OCEAN
A300
A1
B100
C146
C119
C155
C164
C165
B156
B120
0
20 km
10 miles

MAJONIT/SHUTTERSTOCK

TOP EXPERIENCE

Twelve Apostles

Port Campbell National Park is best known for the Twelve Apostles, towering limestone stacks that stand sentinel in the wild ocean less than 100m from the serrated coastline. They've changed over the years, shaped by weathering and erosion, and some disappeared completely. Visit at sunrise or sunset to enhance that feeling of awe and avoid the crowds.

DON'T MISS

- Gibson Steps
- Bay of Islands
- London Bridge
- Grotto
- Penguins

Why Twelve Apostles?

Despite the name, the Twelve Apostles are not 12 in number and, from all records, never have been. From the viewing platform, you can count seven, but some may obscure the others. Reach the boardwalk and viewing platform via the **visitor centre kiosk** in the large car park.

The Apostles are known as 'stacks' in geological parlance and they were originally called the 'Sow and Piglets'. In the 1960s, someone came up with a more catchy name and since

PRACTICALITIES

- *parks.vic.gov.au*
- visitor centre kiosk 10am-5pm, lookouts dawn-dusk

apostles come in a dozen, the number 12 was added sometime later. The two stacks on the eastern (Otway) side of the viewing platform are not technically among the Apostles – they're Gog and Magog.

Walk the Gibson Steps

Once you've stopped at the visitor centre, with its souvenirs and cafe and walked under the Great Ocean Road itself for the view of the Twelve Apostles, follow signs to the **Gibson Steps** (2.2km return). These 86 steps, hacked by hand into the cliffs by 19th-century landowner Hugh Gibson (and now replaced by concrete ones), lead down to wild **Gibson Beach**. The steps were closed to the public due to rock falls at the time of writing.

A Bird's-Eye View

Helicopters *(12apostleshelicopters.com.au; 15min flight from $195)* offer an unmatched aerial view of the Twelve Apostles, Loch Ard Gorge, the Sentinel, the Arch and London Bridge – a recommended splurge. They take off from behind the main car park. Do not attempt to fly a drone around here!

Great Ocean Road Detours

Look out for car parks leading to lesser-known geological sites and natural attractions, some just as photogenic while less crowded than the Apostles.

- **Loch Ard Gorge** Beach and blowhole with a backstory. Signboards tell the story of the two survivors of the *Loch Ard* shipwreck, who washed ashore here in 1878. From the car park, walk to lookout points over the gorge and the spectacular Island Arch. Steps down to the gorge and beach were closed in 2025 but should eventually reopen.
- **London Bridge** Once connected to the land, the 'bridge' eroded and collapsed in 1990, stranding two tourists who had to be rescued by police helicopter.
- **Grotto** One of the most photogenic stops; follow a 700m boardwalk and trail down steps to the surreal sight of the ocean and a blue pool, both seen through a huge natural porthole.
- **Bay of Islands** A beautiful sweep of bay with several limestone pillars, a beach to the left and caves to the right. It's a short walk with two viewpoints.

Visitor Booking & Fees

The Twelve Apostles have always been free to visit, but at the time of writing a $126-million redevelopment of the Visitor Centre Experience was underway. It's expected to be complete by the end of 2026. At that time, a new visitor fee will be introduced alongside a booking system to manage visitor numbers and parking at peak times. Check Parks Victoria for updates.

STAY FOR THE PENGUIN PARADE

Stay after sunset and bring binoculars to watch the parade of penguins on the sand below the viewing platform. Little penguins (*Eudyptula minor*, also known as fairy penguins) generally appear about 15 minutes after the sun goes down, waddling across the sand to their burrows.

About 800 penguins live at the Twelve Apostles. Fewer are at London Bridge, but you can get closer to the action.

TOP TIPS

- Visit in the morning or late afternoon to avoid the Melbourne tour-bus crowds (arriving between noon and 3pm). Evenings can get busy, with photographers vying for the best sunset shot.
- Nearby restaurants close at 8pm, so plan ahead or buy supplies and have a picnic or BBQ.
- Some nearby viewpoints offer even more spectacular views of the limestone stacks than the official lookout.
- Safety concerns by cautious authorities often lead to some limited access or closures, such as at Gibson Steps.

HIGHLIGHTS
1 Australian National Surfing Museum

SIGHTS
2 Fishermans Beach
3 Front Beach
4 Torquay Surf Beach

ACTIVITIES
5 Go Ride a Wave
6 Honu Honi Surf Camp
7 Point Danger Marine Sanctuary
8 SeaEarth Adventures
9 Southern Exposure Surf School
10 Torquay Surfing Academy

EATING
11 Fisho's
12 Ginger Monkey
13 Pholklore
14 Salty Dog Cafe

DRINKING & NIGHTLIFE
15 4 Pines
16 Bells Beach Brewing
17 Blackman's Brewery

SHOPPING
18 Garage Torquay
19 Ghanda Clothing
20 Quiksilver Factory Outlet
21 Reef Factory Outlet
see 20 Rip Curl Surf Factory Outlet
22 Surf City Plaza

Continued from p542
and brands like Rip Curl and Quiksilver gradually put it on the global map. Today, the Rip Curl Pro is the world's longest-running competitive surfing event, packing Bells Beach each Easter, and the sleepy town has grown apace. Torquay's entrepreneurial spirit is alive and well with boutique clothing shops, surf and skate outlets, coffee roasters, microbreweries and, naturally, surf schools.

Surf history

Start your Torquay exploration at **Surf City Plaza**, home to Rip Curl, Billabong, Quiksilver, Oakley, Roxy and more

EATING IN TORQUAY: OUR PICKS

Salty Dog Cafe: Open-air seafront cafe fires up early, with swimmers and beach walkers grabbing a coffee, waffle or smashed avo. *6am-3pm* $

Fisho's: Old Torquay on the Esplanade at its best, serving variations of fish and chips such as grilled squid and fish tacos. *noon-3pm & 5-8.30pm* $

Pholklore: Esplanade corner spot serving Vietnamese street-food including pho, around a shipping-container complex. *noon-3.30pm & 5-9pm* $$

Ginger Monkey: Rustic-chic cafe opposite Surf City Plaza; Torquay's best vegetarian food, big breakfasts and great coffee. *6am-3pm Mon-Fri, from 8am Sat* $$

surf and streetwear brands. Accessed through the visitor information centre is the excellent **Australian National Surfing Museum** *(australiannationalsurfingmuseum.com.au; adult/child $12/8)*, packed with history, photographs, the Surfing Hall of Fame and many surfboards. Exhibits include a collection of the famous Bells trophies, Simon Anderson's groundbreaking 1981 three-fin thruster, Mark Richard's retro airbrushed board art collection and the 'board room', showing the evolution of surfboard design.

Bells Beach and beyond

The powerful beach break at **Bells Beach** is part of international surfing folklore and the setting for Australia's premier surfing event, **Rip Curl Pro** *(ripcurl.com)*, since 1973.

The car park on the cliffs above the beach has a steady flow of cars and vans carrying not only surfers but curious observers wanting to check out the action below from the boardwalk lookouts. Surfers are usually skilled – Bells is not a place for beginners! – and there's always someone riding a wave. Other nearby surf spots you might hear about include Winki Pop, Southside and Jan Juc.

There are some great beaches closer to town, from **Fishermans Beach** with its early-morning swimmers and sailing club, to the family-friendly **Front Beach** and the town **Surf Beach** where you'll find the Surf Life Saving Club. If you want to learn to surf, there are numerous outfits offering lessons on these beginner waves. For nudists, nearby Point Impossible and Southside (near Bells Beach) are two of Victoria's three official clothing-optional beaches.

The Surf Coast on foot

The wonderful 44km **Surf Coast Walk** starts at **Point Impossible** 5km east of Torquay and follows the coast to **Fairhaven Surf Life Saving Club**, beyond Aireys Inlet. It's a scenic two-day coastal walk but there are no hiker-specific camping spots or bush camping, so plan a stop at Anglesea or tackle the trail in shorter sections. A great day hike is from Bells Beach to **Point Addis** (16km return). For a shorter walk from Jan Juc, park at **Bird Rock** and walk the 3.5km to Bells Beach. The 3.3km section from **Point Danger** in Torquay to Bird Rock is another excellent short introduction and can be cycled.

The **Koorie Cultural Walk**, off the Great Ocean Road near Point Addis, is a 2km bush trail (one hour return) with

SURF SCHOOLS

Torquay is a great place to learn to surf. Two-hour group lessons start at $70, with private lessons also available.

Go Ride a Wave: One of the longest-running surf schools with classes all along the coast. *(gorideawave.com.au)*

Honu Honi Surf Camp: Two- to seven-day surf camps including accommodation, yoga and meals. *(honuhoni.com)*

SeaEarth Adventures: Daily surfing lessons in Torquay and Anglesea. Also offers cycling, kayaking and climbing adventures. *(seaearthadventures.com.au)*

Southern Exposure Surf School: Daily two-hour surf lessons. *(southernexposure.com.au)*

Torquay Surfing Academy: Focuses on surfing at Torquay, Jan Juc and Point Addis. *(torquaysurf.com.au)*

DRINKING IN TORQUAY & AIREYS INLET: BEST BREWPUBS

Play a round of mini golf in between pints

Bells Beach Brewing: Giant vats provide a backdrop to the bar and a stage hosts live music most nights. *4-10pm Thu & Fri, noon-11pm Sat, to 8pm Sun*

Salt Brewing Co: Based at the excellent Airey's Pub, Salt brews half a dozen signature beers including Moby pale ale and Ink coffee stout. *11.30am-late*

4 Pines: A prime balcony surf-city spot and beer garden draw crowds for locally brewed beers; the food is also good. *11am-10pm Sun-Thu, to 11pm Fri & Sat*

Blackman's Brewery: A highlight of this Bell St brewery is the large family-friendly beer garden where you can sample 22 rotating tap beers. *noon-late*

TORQUAY RETAIL THERAPY

A smorgasbord of surf and ski shops is concentrated around Surf City Plaza. Head to **Baines Cres** for discount factory-outlet gear.

Ghanda Clothing: A local company that has expanded. Its huge warehouse sells discount surf and street clothing.

Quiksilver Factory Outlet: One of the original surf brands out of Torquay; also sells DC Shoes and Roxy.

Reef Factory Outlet: Sells slides and shoes.

Rip Curl Surf Factory Outlet: This Torquay original sells discount surf gear including wetsuits, bathing suits and towels.

Garage Torquay: Retro clothes, psychedelic old buses and campers, vintage skateboards and many more browse-worthy collectibles.

signboards showing how the Wathaurung people lived here for millennia. In 1836, a community of some 700 Wathaurung lived in the area. Tragically, by 1853, this number was reduced to a mere 35 as a direct result of European colonisation.

Anglesea

TIME FROM TORQUAY: **20MIN**

Anglesea is a lovely beach town made all the more appealing by the emerald Anglesea River, which meanders through town offering opportunities for canoeing, kayaking and bird watching. There's a great little backpacker hostel and some excellent dining.

Golf with the mob

Anglesea's undulating and well-manicured 18-hole **golf course** *(angleseagolfclub.com.au; 9/18 holes from $45/65)* would be unremarkable if not for the 300-odd mob of eastern grey kangaroos that have lived and grazed here since the course was established in the 1950s. You can play a round – the roos are accustomed to golfers – or take a **tour** *(adult/child $20/8)* in motorised golf carts. It's an only-in-Australia experience!

Aireys Inlet

TIME FROM TORQUAY: **30MIN**

This coastal hamlet is where the Great Ocean Road begins to open up and hug the coast at Fairhaven Beach. The lighthouse, a pub/brewery, gin distillery and an acclaimed restaurant are reasons to stop.

Climb the iconic lighthouse for panoramic vistas

Scale the 136 spiralling steps to the top of the beautiful 'White Queen' **Split Point Lighthouse** *(splitpointlighthouse.com.au; $12.50)* for sensational 360-degree coastal views. Built in 1891, the 34m-high lighthouse is still operational, though it's now fully automated. You can visit on self-guided tours (book online); a staff member awaits up top to field questions about the area's history.

Lorne

TIME FROM TORQUAY: **1HR**

Crowding around beautiful Loutit Bay and backed by steep hillsides of scented blue gum trees, Lorne has been the region's most fashionable resort town since the mid-19th century, when society types would make the arduous horse-drawn journey long before the Great Ocean Road was built. Today

EATING IN ANGLESEA & AIREYS INLET: OUR PICKS

Love House Anglesea: Enjoy amazing beach views and Asian-inspired share plates plus a full vegan menu. *5-9pm Wed & Thu, noon-10pm Fri & Sat* $$$

Poppies: Wholesome breakfasts, lunches, coffee and fresh local produce at a cafe/grocer in a lovely garden off Anglesea's main drag. *8.30am-3pm* $

Last One Inn: Food with a South American twist (BBQ on Sundays) and an awesome terrace in Anglesea. *4pm-late Thu & Fri, noon-6.30pm Sat & Sun* $$

a la grecque: An Aireys institution, this Greek taverna balances fine dining with home cooking and a coastal vibe. Meze plates and rack of lamb. *5-10.30pm* $$

RNDMS/SHUTTERSTOCK

Split Point Lighthouse

the town is still summer-holiday central – best visited outside the peak summer months.

Lorne's golden sands and historic coastal trails

Lorne's lovely main beach stretches south from the mouth of the Erskine River to the **Surf Life Saving Club**, where it's patrolled and is popular with stand-up paddleboarders, beginner surfers and boogie boarders. Wander the coastal **Shipwreck Trail** from the club to **Lorne Pier** where locals like to fish and stroll (though, sadly, the local fishing industry has ceased and trawlers no longer dock here). Back in town, wander cafe-lined Mountjoy St past the sea baths to the **Lorne Visitor Centre** with its free exhibition on the history and construction of the Great Ocean Road. It's a steep walk or easy drive up to **Teddy's Lookout** for a fine view of the Great Ocean Road carved into the forested hillside as it leaves Lorne.

Zip through the trees

Lorne's blue-gum-tree canopy is used to good effect at **Live Wire Park** *(livewirepark.com.au; zip line from $60)*, an adventure park with a state-of-the-art zip line and high-ropes tree courses. Book online.

THE WATHAURUNG & WILLIAM BUCKLEY

An insight into the lives of the Wathaurung people emerges through the story of William Buckley, an escaped convict who lived with the Wathaurung people from 1803 to 1835. They accepted this 'wild white man' as one of their own and he hunted and camped with them in present-day Point Lonsdale, Torquay, Anglesea and Aireys Inlet, becoming, as he described, 'as expert as any of them in spearing the kangaroo and taking fish'. His story is believed by some to lend its name to the Australian colloquialism 'you've got Buckley's chance' – meaning little or no chance. The less romantic version is that the saying comes from the name of a former Melbourne department store, Buckley & Nunn (that is, you have two chances – Buckley's and none).

EATING & DRINKING IN LORNE: OUR PICKS

Captain Hooked: Fish and chips on the beach is a Lorne summer tradition; this place uses fresh local seafood, from flake to chargrilled scallops. *11am-9pm* $$

Ipsos: Popular small taverna with a menu of mainly Greek-influenced sharing plates. Starters include grilled king prawns and octopus. *noon-10pm Thu-Mon* $$$

Totti's Lorne: The Lorne Hotel brings Italian trattoria to the coast with a range of antipasti plates, pasta dishes and local fish. *noon-10pm Thu-Mon* $$$

Brae: One of Australia's most lauded farm restaurants is a dining experience, with tasting plates and matching wines. *5-10pm Wed & Thu, noon-6pm Fri & Sat* $$$

In the village of Birregurra, 35km north of Lorne

WHEN TO HIT THE ROAD

The Great Ocean Road is a year-round destination, but it's still highly seasonal. Winter months (June to September) are low season, when you'll share the road mostly with locals, campervanners and the odd tour group, but the weather will likely be cold, at times raining and *very* windy on the coast – not ideal for hiking or camping. Prices and crowds are down but some attractions may close.

Summer school holidays (mid-December to early February) and Easter are peak, when caravan parks and tourist sights are impossibly crowded, prices are highest and traffic jams not uncommon. Visit in the shoulder months (October to November and February to April), preferably midweek. You'll still have to plan ahead, but you should get the best the Great Ocean Road has to offer.

F.MALIKI/SHUTTERSTOCK

Erskine Falls

Beautiful falls and riverside treks

About 10km northwest of Lorne, the cascading 30m **Erskine Falls** *(free)* can be seen from above via an easy five-minute walk from the car park to the viewing platform, but it's much better to take the slippery stone steps to its base (30 minutes return), where there's a photogenic pool (not suitable for swimming). A challenging 7.5km walking track follows the Erskine River (with multiple river crossings) all the way from Lorne to the falls.

Kennett River's koalas and glowworms

Half an hour south of Lorne, Kennett River is a coastal village with a caravan park, cafe and a large population of koalas – drive up Grey River Rd and look out for them in the trees. At dusk, continue for 6km up the same road for one of nature's great light shows. Once darkness descends, walk from the Grey River picnic area to caverns and walls lit up with glowworms, the remarkable bioluminescent larvae of a type of gnat.

EATING IN LORNE: BEST CAFES

Also hires out surf and boogie boards

Pit Stop Lorne: More takeaway than cafe, this American-diner-style place dispenses burgers, shakes and ribs from an Airstream food truck. *11am-9pm* $

Swing Bridge Cafe & Boathouse: Cafe with an appealing retro summer feel; it's at the historic 1934 swing bridge, a short walk to the beach. *7am-4pm* $

Lorne Central: Among Mountjoy Pde's cafes, this one has good coffee and pavement tables with Mod Oz cuisine. *7.30am-5pm Mon & Tue, to 10pm Wed-Sun* $$

HAH Cafe: Foreshore dining near the sea baths at a health-conscious cafe serving smoothies, bowls and jaffles. *8am-3pm Fri-Wed* $

Apollo Bay & Around

TIME FROM LORNE: **1HR**

Apollo Bay's broad, white-sand beaches and rolling hills frame a picturesque community of fisherfolk, artists, musicians and seachangers. This is one of the best bases for exploring the Otway Ranges and a good choice for budget travellers, with two excellent hostels and several camping grounds. Head up to **Marriners Lookout** for great views over the town and coast. The Gadubanud people are the Traditional Custodians of the region.

Walking with wildlife

Wildlife Wonders *(wildlifewonders.org.au; adult/child from $59/24)*, 5km from Apollo Bay, is a 12-hectare native-animal sanctuary accessed only on a guided walking tour, where you'll see free-roaming koalas, emus, swamp wallabies, sugar gliders, grey kangaroos and birdlife such as kookaburras. **Dusk and dawn tours** *(adult/child $95/75)* are more immersive, with a better chance of spotting shy wildlife, such as potoroos, bandicoots and pademelons, and include either dinner or breakfast.

Platypuses and mountain biking around Forrest

About 40 minutes' drive north of Apollo Bay (turn inland at Skenes Creek), the small town of Forrest is the base for an 80km network of mountain biking trails – some of the best in Victoria outside the High Country. Check out **Ride Forrest** *(rideforrest.com.au)* for maps and info. **Forrest MTB Hire** *(forrestbikehire.com.au; bikes from $88)* offers lessons; weekends only.

About 7km southeast of Forrest is scenic **Lake Elizabeth**, famous for its population of platypuses and surreal scenery of dead trees reaching out from the glassy water. A landslide in the 1950s blocked and flooded the Barwon River to form the lake. **Otway Eco Tours** *(platypustours.net.au; adult/child $95/60)* runs canoe trips at dusk and dawn to spot platypuses (and glowworms after dark). There's a camping ground here.

Cape Otway & the Ranges

TIME FROM APOLLO BAY: **30MIN**

Although the **Great Otway National Park** extends almost from Torquay to Lavers Hill, it's the section just past Apollo Bay where the Great Ocean Road really dives into the rainforest of

KEEPING WILDLIFE WILD

An abundance of wildlife lives along the Great Ocean Road, but human interaction affects it on a daily basis. Koalas and wombats have no street sense and often wander across the road, while kangaroos can come leaping from seemingly nowhere.

Avoid driving at dawn and dusk or slow down at these times. If you hit a wild animal, call **Wildlife Rescue** *(03-8400 7300)*; if it has a pouch, check it to see if any young have survived. Don't feed wild animals: human food can transmit disease, cause dietary deficiencies and may encourage aggressive behaviour. A good example is the scavenging sulphur-crested cockatoos flocking around Lorne – signs in multiple languages implore people not to feed them.

EATING & DRINKING IN APOLLO BAY: OUR PICKS

Apollo Bay Fishermen's Co-op: The best fish and chips in town is on the wharf; fresh seafood is sold in its Pascoe St shop. *11am-7pm Tue-Sun* $

Apollo Bay Distillery: Specialises in gin (masterclass $180) but is also a cosy pizza restaurant with large windows looking out to the beach. *11am-8pm* $$

Great Ocean Road Brewhouse: Taphouse pouring a range of craft beers. The front bar is a classic country-pub bistro. *11am-11pm Sun-Thu, to 1am Fri & Sat* $$

Graze: Specialises in local produce with a Modern Australian menu including duck fillet and charred octopus. Great wine and cocktail list. *5.30-9pm Tue-Sat* $$

BUILDING THE GREAT OCEAN ROAD

Construction began on the Great Ocean Road, an engineering marvel, in 1919 to open up the remote coastal communities between Anglesea and Apollo Bay, and was completed in 1932. Building the road was a monumental effort that involved more than 3000 workers, mostly returned WWI soldiers, initially using picks, shovels and crowbars.

At Eastern View (just after Fairhaven en route to Lorne), you'll find the *Diggers* sculpture depicting an ex-WWI-soldier labourer beneath the **Memorial Arch** (p554). Learn more from the history display at the Great Ocean Road Heritage Centre inside **Lorne Visitor Centre** (p549) and look out for the series of 15 commemorative plaques at points along the road between Torquay and Port Campbell.

the Otway Ranges. This area is rich in walking trails, wildlife (koalas are common) and waterfalls. The Gadubanud people are the Traditional Custodians of the region.

Rainforest walks

An easy stop off the GOR, the 800m **Maits Rest Rainforest Boardwalk** takes you through an ancient forest of giant mountain ash eucalypts, the tallest flowering plants in the world – for perspective, they would tower over the Sydney Opera House if they were side by side.

South of Beech Forest, off Binn's Rd, a small patch of towering California **redwoods** (giant sequoias) were planted in 1936, some more than 60m tall. Also in this area are a number of scenic waterfalls including **Hopetoun Falls** and **Beauchamp Falls**, which has a camping area.

Lighthouse on the Cape

Though no longer a working lighthouse, **Cape Otway Lightstation** *(lightstation.com; adult/child $22/9)* is the oldest surviving lighthouse in mainland Australia, built in 1848 without mortar by more than 40 stonemasons. There are sublime coastal views from its windy observation deck, while the **Telegraph Station** has fascinating displays on the 250km undersea telegraph-cable link with Tasmania, laid in 1859. It's a sprawling complex with plenty to see, from Aboriginal cultural sites to a WWII radar bunker built to detect potential Japanese threats, accommodation in original staff cottages and a cafe serving Devonshire teas (with giant scones).

Hike the coast

The incredible 104km **Great Ocean Walk** *(parks.vic.gov.au)* starts in Apollo Bay and heads west along the coast to the Twelve Apostles, passing spectacular clifftops, deserted beaches and the dense eucalypt forests of Great Otway National Park. Pre-book hiker-only camp sites online or choose from one of the 15 licensed tour operators that can do it all, from providing shuttles to delivering food or organising tours with yoga sessions and luxury accommodation.

Travellers with only a day to spare could walk the stunning 10km along cliffs and beaches from **Blanket Bay** to Cape Otway Lightstation, or the 7km from Princetown to the Twelve Apostles. There are several drive-in day-visitor or overnight camping areas, including **Aire River East** and **Johanna Beach**, which are linked by a 12.5km day walk.

Fly through the treetops

Deep in the forest about 10 minutes' drive west of the village of Beech Forest, the **Otway Fly** *(otwayfly.com.au; from $25)* is a remarkable 600m elevated steel walkway suspended high in the forest canopy. It includes a swaying lookout tower with a spiral staircase 50m above the forest floor. From the visitor centre, it's a 15-minute forest walk to the start of the walkway, so the whole circuit takes about an hour, but you can request a golf-cart shuttle service. Kids will enjoy the enchanted

DZUNG VU/SHUTTERSTOCK

Maits Rest Rainforest Boardwalk

forest along the way. For the more adventurous, the guided 2½-hour **zip-line tour** *(incl treetop walk from $135)* zooms you through the forest along a series of cables from elevated platforms; book online.

Port Campbell

TIME FROM APOLLO BAY: 1½HR

The closest town to the Twelve Apostles and other coastal rock formations, Port Campbell makes a decent accommodation base or pit stop for lunch or dinner. The Eastern Maar are the Traditional Custodians of the land.

Hit the beach and trails

Port Campbell is blessed with a lovely sandy beach bookended by cliffs and it's one of the few safe places for swimming along this tempestuous stretch of coast. On a sunny day, the water sparkles in iridescent shades of green and blue.

At the northern end of the beach, a **suspension bridge** leads to the start of the 4.4km **Port Campbell Discovery Walk**, a clifftop trail through heathland leading to scenic coastal lookouts. The almost 20km bike-friendly **Port Campbell–Timboon Trail** heads inland from the Great Ocean Road through forest and farmland. Turn off the Great Ocean Road about 1km west of town.

WHY I LOVE THE GREAT OCEAN ROAD

Paul Harding, Lonely Planet writer

As a Victorian, I've been visiting the Great Ocean Road since I was a kid. As an adult, with many summers or weekends spent at Lorne, Torquay and Wye River, I've never taken it for granted. Driving the road on a sunny day is always a thrill and camping, hiking and koala-spotting in the Otway Ranges are some of my fondest memories.

As a photographer, I love the changing light on the limestone cliffs, the solitary windswept lighthouses and those unexpected but frequent wildlife encounters. Fish and chips on the beach, watching graceful surfers in action, beers on the deck of a local brewpub and rainbows materialising out of the sea mist are all part of the road's story.

EATING & DRINKING IN PORT CAMPBELL: OUR PICKS

Barrels Bar: Fancy bar snacks such as whisky beef sliders, along with whisky-tasting paddles and stunning bay views. *2-8pm Mon-Fri, from noon Sat & Sun*

Port Campbell Hotel: The local pub beckons with an open fire, full bar, live music and pub meals (some vegetarian). *11am-1am Mon-Sat, noon-11pm Sun* $$

Grassroots Deli Cafe: A range of local beers, cider and wine by the glass or bottle. Grab some gourmet supplies for the road. *8am-3pm* $

Sow & Piglets: German beers are on the menu at this microbrewery and brewpub named after the Twelve Apostles' original nickname. *2-8pm*

Also a backpacker-friendly guesthouse

ROAD TRIP

Classic Great Ocean Road Drive

The Great Ocean Road (B100) is a 200km-plus coastal drive that can be done in as little as four or five hours but demands at least a couple of days. It's single-lane in each direction but there are many turnouts for slow vehicles – take it easy and enjoy the ride. This driving tour follows the most scenic 160km stretch between the Memorial Arch near Lorne and Peterborough.

1 Memorial Arch & Lorne

The **Memorial Arch** commemorating the building of the road is at Eastern View, about 12km before Lorne. From here, the road hugs the coast with fine beach views offering a taste of things to come. Enter Lorne (p548), packed with holidaymakers in summer but comparatively laid-back the rest of the year.

The Drive: The 45km drive from Lorne to Apollo Bay takes about an hour, but there are several turnouts with views and it's worth pausing in the tiny beach communities of Wye River, Kennett River and Skene's Creek.

2 Apollo Bay

Apollo Bay (p551) has a lovely white-sand beach and a pleasing strip of cafes, pubs and restaurants. If you prefer motels or hostels to camping, it's the best base for exploring Cape Otway and the northern Otway Ranges.

The Drive: It's a half-hour (30km) drive to spectacular Cape Otway – turn off the Great Ocean Road onto Lighthouse Rd 20km out of Apollo Bay. Stop at Maits Rest Rainforest Boardwalk (p552) about 4km before the turn off.

LKONYA/SHUTTERSTOCK

Lorne (p548)

3 Cape Otway

While the Great Ocean Road is a coastal drive, this leg may surprise you. Here the road heads inland through rainforest with towering native trees and fern gullies. Turn south for 10km to Cape Otway Lightstation (p552). The Great Ocean Walk passes through here and you can drive to several excellent beaches including Blanket Bay.

The Drive: It's about 70km (via Lavers Hill, allow 1½ hours) from Cape Otway to tiny Princetown. The road winds through undulating rainforest before opening up to farmland beyond Gellibrand. Your first glimpses of the coast come after the Princetown turn off, from where it's 7km to the Twelve Apostles.

4 Twelve Apostles

Stretching from Princetown to Peterborough, Port Campbell National Park features the road's finest scenery, including the Twelve Apostles (p544) and other dramatic limestone formations. There's designated parking at all attractions. At the Twelve Apostles, there's a large parking area and visitor centre with a tunnel under the road.

The Drive: The nearest town is Port Campbell (p553), 10 minutes from the Twelve Apostles. Stay on the coast road heading east for another 13km to Peterborough, from where you can explore some of the lesser-known coastal sights.

5 Peterborough

Little Peterborough is the last town before the road starts to head inland to Allansborough (the official end of the Great Ocean Road). There are some fine Shipwreck Coast viewpoints nearby including **Wild Dog Cove**, the **Bay of Martyrs** and the Bay of Islands (p545). From Peterborough it's 40 minutes to Warrnambool.

Warrnambool & the Southwest Coast

WHALE WATCHING | BEACH WALKS | INDIGENOUS CULTURE

Places

Victoria's southwest coast stretches beyond the Great Ocean Road and is far enough from Melbourne that most visitors are either travelling through to South Australia, looking out for migrating whales or heading to historic Port Fairy for one of its celebrated music festivals.

Warrnambool is the largest town on the Shipwreck Coast, a base for whale watching and other beach-based activities. Further west, Tower Hill is a wildlife-rich volcanic crater while Budj Bim Cultural Landscape is a culturally significant park and a fascinating place to connect with Traditional Custodians of the land. Portland, the last town of any size, is a wonderfully remote-feeling industrial port town and the start of the epic Great South West Walk to Nelson.

Warrnambool

TIME FROM GEELONG: **2½HR**

Warrnambool is a centre for whale watching and the main commercial centre for the agricultural southwest with some grand old buildings, historic sites, an acclaimed art gallery, numerous beaches and gardens – wander down Liebig St to find an eclectic dining, pub and cafe scene.

Logans Beach whale watching

Southern right whales come to mate and nurse their young in the waters near **Logans Beach** from June to October, breaching and fluking within view of the excellent 'Whale Nursery' platform. The males, yearlings and young adults remain further out to sea. Sightings are not guaranteed, but

GETTING AROUND

Warrnambool is an hour's drive west of Port Campbell on the Great Ocean Road and about 3½ hours' drive from Melbourne via the Princes Hwy (A1).

V/Line trains run daily to/from Melbourne via Geelong, and V/Line buses along the Great Ocean Road from Apollo Bay continue on to Warrnambool. There are also daily buses to Port Fairy and Portland. Still, having your own vehicle is the best way to explore this region, especially for Nelson and Budj Bim.

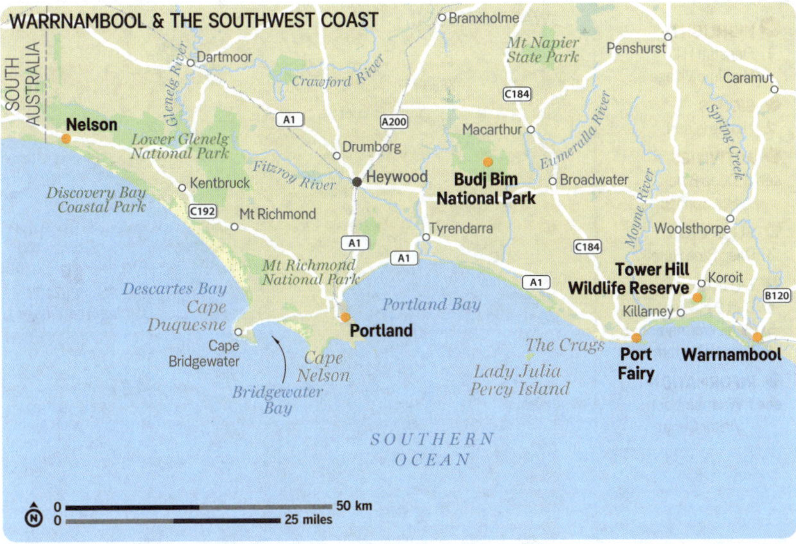

you can check **Warrnambool Whale Watch** *(facebook.com/warrnamboolwhalewatch)* for recent sightings.

Explore a historic maritime village

The world-class 'living museum' at **Flagstaff Hill** *(flagstaffhill.com; adult/child $20.50/9.50)* precinct is historic maritime Warrnambool at its best. The engaging shipwreck museum leads through to a compact and well-crafted reproduction of an 1870s port town, complete with an original lighthouse complex and a small lake. The village has ye olde shops such as blacksmiths, shipbuilders and a mini wharf, with costumed characters often going about their business. The nightly **Tales of the Shipwreck Coast** *(adult/child $33.50/18.50)* is a dazzling 70-minute sound-and-light show telling the tragic tale of the *Loch Ard* shipwreck.

Soak in hot springs

Deep Blue Hot Springs *(thedeepblue.com.au; weekday/weekend $55/66)* is a family-friendly year-round natural spa at the Deep Blue Hotel where a redevelopment has brought the naturally hot, mineral-rich water from the Dilwyn Aquifer outside

TOP TIP

For homemade ice cream, fudge, artisan cheese, malt whiskey and more, stop in at **Timboon**, 50km west of Warrnambool, a gourmet village on the 88km **Twelve Apostles Food Artisans Trail** *(12apostlesfoodartisans.com.au)*.

Handmade pasta and a solid cocktail and wine list

EATING & DRINKING IN WARRNAMBOOL: OUR PICKS

Simon's Waterfront: Trendy cafe facing Surfside Beach; seafront views along with seafood chowder, chicken parma, coffee and cocktails. *noon-8pm Wed-Sun* **$$**

Proudfoots Boathouse: Romantic spot on the Hopkins River in a heritage-listed boathouse. *11.30am-3.30pm Wed-Sat, from 11am Sun* **$$**

Hotel Warrnambool: Fine old country gastropub with bohemian character, wood-fired pizzas, Coorong steaks and a beer garden. *5.30-9pm Sat-Thu, from noon Fri* **$$**

Dart & Marlin: Popular bar and pizzeria make this Warrnambool's best Italian joint with stone-baked pizzas a highlight. *4.30-10pm Wed & Thu, noon-late Fri & Sat* **$$**

HIGHLIGHTS
1 Flagstaff Hill Maritime Village

SIGHTS
2 Middle Island

ACTIVITIES
see 3 Deep Blue Hot Springs

SLEEPING
3 Deep Blue Hotel

EATING
4 Dart & Marlin
5 Hotel Warrnambool
6 Simon's Waterfront

INFORMATION
see 1 Warrnambool Visitor Centre

into a series of pools and cascades up to 42°C. Book a two-hour session online for the outdoor Hot Springs Sanctuary, a series of rock pools, bubbling mineral baths, cave baths and the 'aroma pool'.

Ride the Rail Trail

The **Warrnambool to Port Fairy Rail Trail** *(portfairytowarrnamboolrailtrail.com.au)* is a reasonably flat 38km cycling path connecting these two seaside towns along a former rail line. The trail takes in the picturesque volcanic crater of Tower Hill and the blossoming town of Koroit, passing through swamplands and along the Merri River. A shorter option is the 1½-hour ride from Port Fairy to Koroit, which can still incorporate Tower Hill.

Tower Hill Wildlife Reserve

TIME FROM WARRNAMBOOL: **15MIN**

Hike the crater and spot wildlife

Turn off the main road about 12km west of Warrnambool and descend winding roads onto a bridge crossing the crater lake of a volcano into **Tower Hill** *(parks.vic.gov.au; free)*, the caldera of a long-erupted and dormant volcano and now a scenic wildlife reserve.

Signboards from the circular Robin Boyd–designed **visitor centre** (closed at the time of writing) detail a number of walks, the best of which is the 1.5km **Peak Walk** (30 minutes) to an elevated lookout revealing 360-degree views of the crater and lakes. An easier stroll is the flat 1.5km **Wagon Bay Loop**.

A highlight of Tower Hill is the native fauna that meander around the picnic area unperturbed by humans – you're likely to see koalas, kangaroos and emus up close in the wild and the wetlands are a haven for native birds.

Port Fairy

TIME FROM WARRNAMBOOL: **30MIN**

Port Fairy is a rare combination of coastal charm, well-preserved historic buildings and country-town cool, thanks to its impressive calendar of festivals, highlighted by the massively popular folk festival in March.

A historic port town

Historic buildings abound, including **Mills Cottage** *(nationaltrust.org.au; $5)* and **Mott's Cottage** *(nationaltrust.org.au; $5)*, both from the early 1840s. The **Stump** *(thestumpportfairy.com.au)*, aka the Caledonian Inn, holds the title of Victoria's oldest continuing licenced venue (c1844) and is still a great local pub. Across the bridge from Port Fairy's picturesque harbour, **Battery Hill** has cannons and fortifications positioned here in 1887 to protect the town from the unlikely but perceived threat of Russian warships.

In the 1850s, the town's **wharf** on the Moyne River was one of the busiest in Australia, serving as the main departure point for ships heading to England laden with wool, gold and wheat. Today, plenty of vessels still visit this photogenic marina, from luxury yachts to fishing boats, and you can buy seafood fresh from trawlers. Use the Moyne River footbridge to access **East Beach**.

Muttonbirds of Griffiths Island

Where the Moyne River meets the ocean and connected by a footbridge, **Griffiths Island** is home to a protected short-tailed shearwater (muttonbird) colony. From September to April, head

SHIPWRECK COAST

When sailing ships ruled the sea in the 18th and 19th centuries, this rugged coastline was treacherous, with 638 known shipwrecks between Cape Otway and Nelson. Only about a third have been discovered with the rest reported missing, never to be seen again.

Lighthouses were established along the coast from the early 19th century. The oldest remaining is Cape Otway Lightstation (1848; p552). You can also visit Cape Nelson Lighthouse (1884; p561) near Portland and **Griffiths Island Lighthouse** (1859) at Port Fairy. One of the most famous wrecks is the *Loch Ard*, which foundered in 1878 with two survivors. The site itself is at Loch Ard Gorge (p545) and the story of the wreck is told at the Flagstaff Hill (p557) in Warrnambool.

Historic Merrijig is said to be Victoria's oldest inn

EATING IN PORT FAIRY: OUR PICKS

Coffin Sally: Former coffin-maker's premises, now serving traditional thin-crust pizzas, craft beer and cocktails. *4.30-8.30pm Wed-Mon* $

Home Grown: Part super-brekkie cafe (coconut pancakes, chilli scrambled eggs), part Sri Lankan dining (dahl and curry bowls, mango lassi). *8am-3pm Thu-Mon* $

Yve Port Fairy: This restaurant in a charming historic building (Seacombe House) brings Italian deliciousness to breakfast and lunch. *8am-2.30pm Tue-Sat* $$

Merrijig Kitchen: Enjoy fine dining and history with a menu that owner-chef Tanya Connellan changes daily according to what's seasonal. *6-11pm Fri-Mon* $$

to the viewing platform to see them return to their nests at dusk: it's like something out of Alfred Hitchcock's *The Birds*.

Even out of season the island is worth a visit for its wheelchair-accessible 3km walking path, which passes the working **lighthouse** (1859; p559) and some lovely beaches.

Budj Bim National Park

TIME FROM WARRNAMBOOL: 1HR

Indigenous history and aquaculture

Budj Bim National Park *(parks.vic.gov.au)* – formerly Mt Eccles National Park – was inscribed on the UNESCO World Heritage List in 2019 as the only site in Australia designated 'cultural' because of its First Nations history. The Traditional Custodians, the Gunditjmara people, run an information centre, tour bookings and bush-tucker cafe at **Tae Rak Aquaculture Centre** *(budjbim.com.au; free; Wed-Sun)*, with displays on one of the world's oldest aquaculture systems on Lake Condah, some 50km inland from Portland.

The greater Budj Bim Cultural Landscape also takes in the Kurtonitj and Tyrendarra Indigenous protected areas, south of the national park and both accessible by guided tour. It's possible to see some of the sites at Budj Bim yourself and information boards are helpful, but having Gunditjmara guides explaining history from their perspective beats reading an information board. Oral history is vital to First Nations peoples and you can experience that firsthand with stories that have been passed down by ancestors on a guided **tour** *(budjbim tours.net; $89-199)*, ranging from a two-hour wetland tour to a full-day cultural walk.

Depending on the season, you might see eels, koalas, yellow-tailed black cockatoos, and copperhead and tiger snakes. There's a lovely camping ground at Lake Surprise on the east side of the park.

Portland & Around

TIME FROM WARRNAMBOOL: 1¼HR

Founded by Europeans as a whaling and sealing base in the early 1800s, Portland lies on the traditional lands of the Gunditjmara people. Colonial architecture and an industrial-sized port dominate the town, but there's plenty to do in this coastal region, from marine wildlife watching to beach and clifftop walks. Portland vies with Warrnambool as a whale-watching centre – check out **Whalemail** *(facebook.com/WhalemailPortland)* for viewing spots and recent sightings.

All aboard!

It's a little kitschy, but the **Portland Cable Tram** *(portland cabletrams.com.au; adult/child $24/12)* is a fun way to explore the town. The restored tram runs on a 7.4km return line four times a day from the depot on Bentick St.

MAREMMA GUARDIANS

Maremme, purebred white sheepdogs from Italy, were introduced to **Middle Island**, just offshore from Warrnambool's Merri River, in 2006 to protect the colony of little penguins from marauding foxes. In 1999, around 600 penguins lived on Middle Island, but as few as 10 had survived by 2005, as foxes had found a way to reach the island at low tide. The population was ravaged again in 2017 when some penguins arrived early for breeding before the maremme had been stationed on the island, but the population is now back to 150 or so. It's no longer possible to visit the island, but you may be able to see the guardian maremme when they're on leave at Flagstaff Hill (p557).

Scan this QR code for more on maremmas

DENNIS MACDONALD/SHUTTERSTOCK

Portland Cable Tram

Cape to cape

An easy circuit from Portland is to the twin capes of Nelson and Bridgewater. It's a 15-minute drive south to the spectacularly located **Cape Nelson Lighthouse** *(capenelsonlighthouse.com.au; tour adult/child $20/12)*, which has daily tours at 11.30am. Return to Portland, detouring to view the **gannet colony** *(pointdangergannets.com.au)*, Australia's only mainland colony, at Point Danger. Viewing is best between July and April and, during breeding season (September to March), volunteers run free guided tours from 5.25pm.

About 20km west of Portland, the tiny town of **Cape Bridgewater** has a lovely wheelchair-accessible **beach**. Continue along the road to the dramatic **Bridgewater Blowhole** (where the turbulent water shoots straight up when the weather's wild) and **Petrified Forest**. The 6.8km **Seal Colony Walk** along the clifftop offers distant views from the **viewing platform**. You might spot blue whales from here in season.

Embark on the Great South West Walk

The 262km signposted **Great South West Walk** *(greatsouthwestwalk.com)* begins and ends in Portland. The loop follows the coast west to Nelson and returns via an inland route; it takes between 10 and 14 days, but it can be tackled in smaller

TOP MUSIC FESTIVALS

Port Fairy Folk Festival: Australia's premier folk-music festival on the Labour Day long-weekend in March, showcasing international and national acts, with street buskers everywhere. *(portfairyfolkfestival.com)*

Aireys Inlet Music Festival: Aireys' music festival in March features local surf-coast bands and some well-known Aussie guest acts. *(aireysinlet.com.au)*

Port Fairy Jazz Festival: Three-day jazz fest in February since 2017, with musos at multiple indoor and outdoor venues around town. *(portfairyjazz.com.au)*

Port Fairy Spring Music Festival: An eclectic program of classical and contemporary performances on the second weekend of October. *(portfairyspringfest.com.au)*

EATING & DRINKING IN PORTLAND: OUR PICKS

Enjoy a coffee or wine on the terrace

Mac's Hotel: Portland's historic pub (1856), popular for cheap bar meals and more upmarket international flavours. *noon-2pm & 6-8.30pm* $$

Clock by the Bay: The former post office is known for its French-inspired cuisine and dishes made with fish bought straight off the boat. *9am-11pm* $$

Margaret & Agnes: Single-origin coffee and a contemporary brunch menu (homemade crumpets, sausage rolls, burgers). *7am-2pm Mon-Fri, from 8am Sat & Sun*

Bahloo Portland: In the original bluestone watchkeeper's house; hearty breakfasts, salad bowls, bagels and burgers. *7.30am-4pm Mon-Fri, from 8am Sat & Sun* $$

SURVIVAL STORY

The stone structures in Budj Bim were created long before many better-known world monuments such as the pyramids in Egypt and Angkor Wat in Cambodia. Despite serious obstacles – including a farmer removing the eel-smoking trees from the land, leaving only one (which was then struck by lightning) – this historic area stands firm.

A bushfire in 2025 tore through 20% of the park (leading to a highly controversial state-ordered koala cull). The story reaches back to the eruption of the Budj Bim volcano (formerly known as Mt Eccles), when an ancestral Creation being revealed itself in the landscape. With the area now protected as a national park, the story, from those who first told it, can continue.

WRIGHT OUT THERE/SHUTTERSTOCK

Glenelg River, Nelson

sections as day or overnight walks. One of the shortest sections is the **Enchanted Forest Walk**, a 3km out-and-back hike on the way to Cape Nelson. For long-haul hikers, there are 14 camp sites spaced roughly a day apart that can be booked through Parks Victoria.

All About Us Bus *(allaboutusbus.com.au; from $90)* offers pickup and drop-off shuttles to points along the walk. The excellent visitor centre at *(visitportland.com.au)* has maps and information.

Nelson

TIME FROM WARRNAMBOOL: **2HR**

Tiny Nelson is the end of the road in Victoria's southwest, only 4km from the South Australian border. The highlight here is the Glenelg River and the Discovery Bay estuary. There's no public transport, so you need your own wheels.

Paddling the Glenelg River

The Glenelg River flows through jagged limestone cliffs and gorges of the **Lower Glenelg National Park** *(parks.vic.gov.au)*, where a 75km stretch of scenic river is one of Victoria's best-kept secret adventures. A series of eight riverside camp sites is set aside for kayakers and canoeists and must be booked through Parks Victoria. **Nelson Canoe Hire** *(nelsoncanoehire.com.au; half/full-day single kayak $50/80, double kayak or canoe $55/90)* can sort you out for canoes, kayaks, transfers and camping. A two-day trip with camping starts at $140.

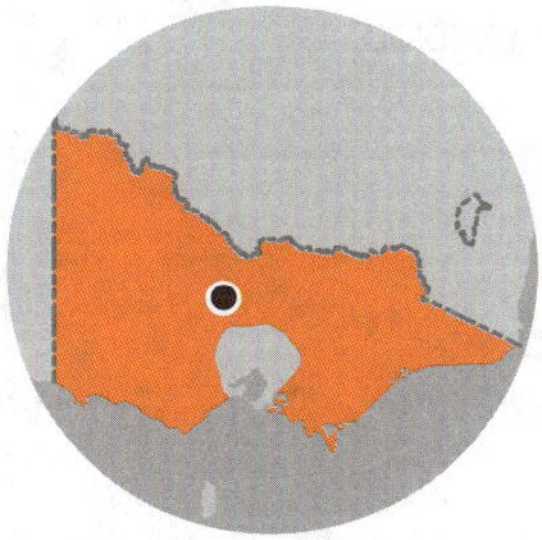

Bendigo

GASTRONOMY | ARCHITECTURE | PARADING DRAGONS

The central Victorian city of Bendigo has an unusually rich geology that saw its swift transformation from pastoral land to gold-rush boom town. More gold was found here from 1851 to 1900 than anywhere else in the world, leaving a legacy of grand architecture and gardens, epitomised by the stately Alexandra Fountain that still presides over the centre of town. The enduring Chinese culture, brought by Chinese diggers in the mid-19th century, is a point of difference from other places on the goldfields.

Today, Bendigo is Victoria's fourth-largest city and Australia's first UNESCO City of Gastronomy, a title in recognition of its exceedingly strong and diverse local food and wine culture. Meanwhile, the Traditional Custodians, the Dja Dja Wurrung people, with tried and true knowledge of Country, are breathing renewed life into lands and waterways adversely affected by gold-mining.

At Easter, Bendigo reaches the heights of exuberance when it hosts one of Australia's longest-running community events, its annual Easter Festival.

GETTING AROUND

Trains run from Melbourne to Bendigo in under two hours. Once in town, take local buses to get around (Myki card required) or hop on the **Vintage Talking Tram** (p566) to get between various points of tourist interest. If you have a car, you won't be bound to a timetable, but check parking signs. Spots may be time-restricted, metered or both.

An Easter Like No Other

Witness Bendigo's Gala Parade

The **Bendigo Easter Festival** *(bendigoeasterfestival.org.au)* has been a highlight of the city's calendar for over 150 years. Over the four-day Easter long weekend, an extensive lineup of events in Rosalind Park (p568) and the surrounding streets makes this Bendigo's busiest weekend of the year. Celebrations kick off on Good Friday with an 80,000-egg-strong Easter egg hunt, a carnival with kids' rides and games, live music and market stalls.

On Easter Saturday, the **Awakening of the Dragon** takes place at the Golden Dragon Museum (p565) to ritualistically 'wake' the main parade dragon, Dai Gum Loong (the world's longest imperial dragon), from slumber ahead of the following

TOP TIP

Book accommodation well in advance for the Easter long weekend. **Easter Festival** street processions (Saturday night and Sunday) are on a first-come, first-served basis. Bring something to sit on and arrive early to get your preferred spot.

HIGHLIGHTS
1 Bendigo Art Gallery
2 Golden Dragon Museum

SIGHTS
3 Bendigo Town Hall
4 Cascades Fountain
5 Central Deborah Gold Mine
6 Charing Cross
7 Guan Yin Temple
8 Lake Weeroona
9 Poppet Head Lookout
10 Rosalind Park
11 Tramways Depot
12 Tysons Reef
13 Vintage Talking Tram
14 Yi Yuan Gardens

SLEEPING
15 City Centre Motel
16 Julie-Anna Inn

EATING
17 Awaken Coffee
18 Brewhouse Cafe & Coffee Roasters
19 Crooked Kitchen
20 Woodhouse

DRINKING & NIGHTLIFE
21 Dispensary Bar & Diner
22 Ms Batterhams

ENTERTAINMENT
23 Ulumbarra Theatre

INFORMATION
24 Bendigo Visitor Centre

day's festivities. Expect spirited lion teams, drums and 100,000 firecrackers to rouse him. In the evening, a **Torchlight Procession** features illuminated floats, smaller lions and dragons, and concludes with a fireworks display.

On Easter Sunday, enjoy the main **Gala Parade**, when the winding and energetic approach of the city's resplendent dragon, covered in thousands of mirrored scales and beads, is announced along the parade circuit with ear-popping firecrackers. In our opinion, it's worth skipping the earlier floats to experience the pre-parade festivities in the Chinese precinct and Dai Gum Loong's exciting departure from the museum.

Bendigo's Showstoppers

View 100m dragons

When not parading Bendigo's streets during Easter, the dragons are 'sleeping' at the **Golden Dragon Museum** *(goldendragonmuseum.org; adult/child $16/10)* in the city's Chinese precinct. Visitors can view all three of Bendigo's historic main-parade dragons on permanent display throughout the year.

In the main hall, you are greeted by the imposing head of Dai Gum Loong extending out onto the blue carpeted floor representing the ocean. His 125m embellished body winds up and around the sloped gallery to the sky-blue of heaven, side by side with his retired predecessor Sun Loong. In the second hall is the heritage-listed Loong, Bendigo's inaugural parade dragon and the oldest intact processional dragon in the world.

Allow at least 30 minutes to explore the museum, including the displays on Bendigo's Chinese history and collection of rare Chinese antiquities. It's free to enter the adjacent **Yi Yuan Gardens** and **Guan Yin Temple**. The museum is closed on Mondays.

Explore Yaram Yaram

Take an Aboriginal cultural walk

See Bendigo, or Yaram Yaram in Dja Dja Wurrung (Djaara) language, from a First Nations' perspective on a cultural walk with a Djaara guide.

Next to **Bendigo Botanic Gardens** in White Hills, the 90-minute **Larni Garingilang** *(dumawul.com.au/tours; adult/child/under 10yr $85/55/free)* tour at the native garden of the same name, will introduce you to Indigenous uses of endemic plants, from sustenance and medicine to ceremony.

BENDIGO'S DRAGONS

The arrival of Chinese diggers at Dai Gum San (Big Gold Mountain) in the 1850s led to an unexpected cultural wealth celebrated in spectacular fashion at the city's annual Easter festivities. The first Bendigo Easter Fair (now festival) took place in 1871 as a charity event. Bendigo's Chinese community was key in the early development of a parade, fundraising for a permanent collection of costumes and regalia and then a processional dragon. The welcoming of Loong (Dragon) in 1901 established a tradition that has lasted more than 120 years. Loong appeared as the parade's star attraction until his retirement in 1970, when the mantle was handed to Sun Loong (New Dragon) and then to Dai Gum Loong (Great Golden Dragon) in 2019.

EATING IN BENDIGO: OUR PICKS

Crooked Kitchen: Gluten- and peanut-free kitchen with excellent cafe menu and delightfully unusual salads. Try the arancini. *8am-3pm Tue-Fri, from 9am Sat* $

Omari: Cafe with lunch and all-day breakfast menu overlooking the Larni Garingilang gardens. Choose the terrace when the weather's nice. *8am-3pm Wed-Sun* $$

Peppergreen Farm Cafe: Social enterprise supporting employment for people with disabilities; meals utilise fresh farm produce. *9am-3pm Mon-Fri, to 2pm Sat* $

Woodhouse: Book ahead for premium grass-fed and dry-aged steaks. Small, more inexpensive plates available at the walk-in bar. *hours vary Tue-Sat* $$$

CITY OF GASTRONOMY

Councillor Thomas Prince, City of Greater Bendigo Mayor 2025/2026, explains the region's gastronomy designation.

As Australia's first UNESCO Creative City and Region of Gastronomy, Bendigo and central Victoria share an indisputable reputation of diverse food cultures and communities committed to local, sustainable, delicious and creative produce.

The region's focus is shared across four key pillars: celebrate and elevate First Nations' cultures, creativity and knowledge; recognise our creativity, cultural diversity and innovation; improve health and wellbeing, particularly through healthy eating; and prioritise environmental sustainability, sustainable agriculture and food production to tackle climate change. Gastronomy is a fitting Creative City category for this region, with its strong focus on art, culture and celebrating local producers.

Learn about the garden's many symbolic cultural design elements and bear witness to how the reversion to traditional practices is revitalising habitats and healing Country.

The **Ulumbarra Central Business District Tour** *(adult/child/under 10yr $85/55/free)* starts at the iconic **Ulumbarra Theatre**, the first building in Victoria to be renamed an Aboriginal name. Venture through Rosalind Park (p568) for fascinating insights into its grey-headed flying fox population and its role as a significant gathering place. Learn about the impact of mining on Yaram Yaram's waterways and the Indigenous architectural design elements now integrated into some of the city's most prominent buildings.

Tours are held two to four times per month on Fridays and Saturdays (advanced booking essential). Both itineraries range from 2km to 2.5km and are suitable for wheelchair users and those with limited mobility.

Talking Transport

Ride a vintage tram

Bendigo's **Vintage Talking Tram** *(bendigotramways.com; adult/child $18/12.50)* is a hop-on, hop-off tourist tram, with audio commentary, that can ferry you between the Central Deborah Gold Mine (p568) in the city's southwest and **Joss House Temple** in the northeast. In between, it stops at **Charing Cross** (city centre), the **Tramways Depot** (location of the free Tram Museum and popular Tram Cafe), **Lake Weeroona** and **Tysons Reef**.

The commentary draws your attention to points of interest along the way and delves into Bendigo's mining history. Those who jump aboard Tram 918, known as the **Dja Dja Wurrung Tram**, will enjoy striking artwork by Djaara artist Natasha Carter and special commentary combining spoken word and song by Traditional Custodians. A full circuit back to your starting point takes one hour; however, all tickets are unlimited daily passes with the idea to get on and off to explore the city's attractions. Check the timetable (available online) in advance to plan your wanderings.

Tickets can be purchased from the **Bendigo Visitor Centre** *(bendigoregion.com.au)*, the Central Deborah Gold Mine, onboard with cash or card and online, and include access to the mine's 'Explore the Surface' above-ground self-tour. Note that Joss House Temple is only open on weekends. Wheelchair users should phone **Bendigo Tramways** *(03-5442 2821)* in advance so they can ensure an accessible tram is in operation on the day of your visit.

On Saturday nights, take the 90-minute **Groove Tram** *($25)*, a moving pop-up bar with live music (bookings essential). Other speciality trams operate throughout the year to coincide with special events.

MASTERSKY/SHUTTERSTOCK

Bendigo Tramways

Art from the Creek

Visit Australia's oldest working pottery

When Scottish gold-seeker George Duncan Guthrie arrived in Sandhurst (later known as Bendigo) in the late 1850s, he didn't know the creek beds would proffer a different kind of fortune. A trained potter, Guthrie instantly saw the value in the white clay along Bendigo Creek and established **Bendigo Pottery** *(bendigopottery.com.au; free)* in 1858, today Australia's largest and oldest working pottery producer.

Allow around 45 minutes to learn about the pottery's history at the on-site **interpretive museum** *(adult/child $8/4)*, which includes the oldest collection of wood-fired kilns in one location anywhere in the world. Paint your own cup, bowl or plate at your own pace in the **hands-on workshop space** *(per piece $25-35);* no bookings required. Your piece will later be glazed, fired and returned to you by post. Alternatively, grab a clay kit ($5) for some sculptural play. Guided wheel-throwing and decorating classes are available during Victorian school holidays (bookings essential).

The pottery precinct includes an **antiques centre** and an **artisanal village** of mini galleries and studios featuring the works and wares of local artists, along with food and wine producers. The pottery is closed on Tuesdays.

WHY I LOVE BENDIGO

Jessica Korteman, Lonely Planet writer

I distinctly remember when the Golden Dragon Museum opened in March 1991. I was a young primary schooler and seeing Sun Loong majestically positioned on the staircase is one of my earliest school-excursion memories.

While each year other kids made Easter bunnies, in Bendigo we crafted shimmering dragon scales and sang of 'waking' Sun Loong for the Easter Fair. It's amazing to look back and realise how special Bendigo's dragon culture truly is.

Many Bendigonians have an emotional attachment to the dragon they grew up seeing in the parade. For me, Sun Loong is representative of my childhood and now Dai Gum Loong is that dragon for the next generation.

DRINKING IN BENDIGO: COFFEEHOUSES & BARS

Try a tiger-nut-milk latte!

Brewhouse Cafe & Coffee Roasters: Speciality roasters serving quality coffee and a full breakfast and lunch menu. *6am-3pm Mon-Fri, from 7am Sat, from 8am Sun*

Dispensary Bar & Diner: In Chancery Lane, staff aim to find your new fave drink. Asian-Australian fusion plates designed for sharing. *noon-11pm Wed-Sat, to 3pm Sun*

Ms Batterhams: Classy lounge bar with decadent cocktails and a wine list for days. European-inspired seasonal menu. *5-10.30pm Mon, Wed & Thu, from noon Fri-Sun*

Awaken Coffee: Near the train station, top takeaway cafe for your morning brew. Make it breakfast with a toastie or pastry. *6.30am-2pm Mon-Fri, 8.30am-noon Sat*

MORE TO DO IN BENDIGO

Rosalind Park: Shady green space in Bendigo's city centre. See the Cascades Fountain and climb Poppet Head Lookout.

Central Deborah Gold Mine: Take a guided mine tour 61m underground. Tickets include an above-ground self-tour and gold panning.

Bendigo Art Gallery: A local institution since 1887, this free gallery houses both permanent and special exhibitions. Closed until early 2028.

Bendigo Town Hall: On Tuesdays and Sundays, tour the grand Town Hall with a volunteer guide. Book online *(bendigo region.com.au).*

Bendigo Water Sports: From November to April, rent a kayak or SUP at Crusoe Reservoir. Book online *(bendigo watersports.com.au).*

MIKE SEAMAN/SHUTTERSTOCK

Great Stupa of Universal Compassion

A Visionary Place of Worship

Marvel at the Great Stupa

Modelled on the Great Stupa of Gyantse, the 50m-wide and almost 50m-tall **Great Stupa of Universal Compassion** *(stupa.au; by donation)* is the largest stupa in the Western world. The stupa is the centrepiece of 85 hectares of bushland in the Whipstick Forest that is slowly being transformed into an off-grid village.

The long approach to the stupa provides an excellent sense of scale and the surrounding **Peace Park**, featuring memorials and symbols of many faiths, leaves plenty to explore on your way back. Inside, don't miss the collection of sacred Buddha relics and the **Jade Buddha of Universal Peace**, which was carved from an off-cut of 'Polar Pride', a huge 18-tonne boulder of jade unearthed in 2000 in northern Canada.

The stupa's interior is a work in progress and will eventually house six levels. Allow 1½ hours to explore the site at leisure.

Beyond Bendigo

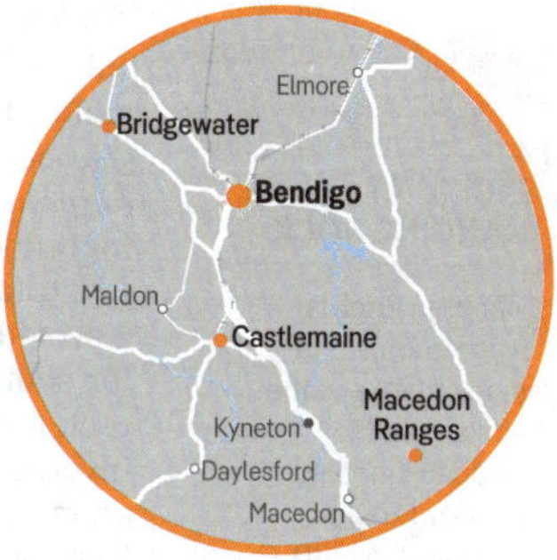

When a relaxed weekend calls, slow down with good food and wine, thought-provoking art and picturesque country views.

From Harcourt's delicious apples to Heathcote's strong wine scene, the greater region that makes up Bendigo's UNESCO City of Gastronomy presents a hyperlocal culinary trail for enthusiastic foodies and cyclists. Hop on a bike, pack a picnic or tour the wineries. Take a train to Castlemaine for community-centred dining and shopping or drive to Bridgewater on the Loddon River and ascend Mt Kooyoora with Traditional Custodians of the land.

Further afield, vineyards and elevated country vistas are the calling cards of the Macedon Ranges. About halfway between Bendigo and Melbourne, it's an easy day or weekend trip to bush and farming country. Drive to the lookout at the top of Mt Macedon or explore the fantastical lava formations at Hanging Rock.

Places

Macedon Ranges

TIME FROM BENDIGO: **1HR**

Climb a volcanic rock

Hanging Rock *(car $15, cyclist & walk-in $5)* is one of the world's rare examples of a mamelon, a rock formation caused by a volcanic eruption of thick, stiff lava through a narrow vent in bedrock. Its viscosity means it simply congeals in place, creating pinnacles, craggy overhangs, caverns and boulders that become even more dramatic through weathering.

Learn more about its formation six million years ago at Hanging Rock Reserve's free on-site **Discovery Centre**. From the trailhead behind the centre, it's only a 900m walk (about 25 minutes) to the upper reaches of the peak, but be prepared for steep stretches, rock scrambling and narrow passes. At the top, the haphazard result of the hardened lava offers numerous boulders and ledges from which to take in the view. Wear suitable footwear and watch your step.

Back down at the base, the reserve has plenty of barbecues and grassy areas for picnics. Before leaving, pay the park entry fee at the machines near the on-site cafe; you're issued a ticket needed to exit the car park. You must exit by 4.30pm (mid-April to August) or 5pm (September to mid-April), when the gate closes.

GETTING AROUND

Castlemaine and Woodend (for Hanging Rock) are most easily accessible from Bendigo by train. There are also established cycling trails to Castlemaine and Heathcote. The Bendigo–Heathcote PTV bus service has an external two-bike carry rack (first come, first served) for one way adventures.

To reach Hanging Rock from Woodend Station, it's a 10-minute drive or taxi ride. With limited public transport options, the Macedon Ranges are best explored by car.

PICNIC AT HANGING ROCK

Hanging Rock is a name known to many thanks to the acclaimed 1967 novel by Joan Lindsay, *Picnic at Hanging Rock*. Set in 1900, it's about a group of private-school girls who mysteriously go missing while on an outing to the rock on Valentine's Day. The story has captured the imagination of Australians for more than 50 years. Was there truth to the story? If so, what happened to the girls? The author never did much to clear up the matter and was often deliberately vague when asked. While many theories exist, the plot was entirely fictional. The book has been adapted into a film (1975) and a six-part mini-series (2018) of the same name.

Walk a llama

Take a three-hour stroll around Hanging Rock Reserve accompanied by your own llama with **Hanging Rock Llama Treks** *(facebook.com/hangingrockllamatreks; hangingrockllamas@bigpond.com; $75)*. The llamas are whip-smart and surprisingly docile, and you quickly settle into an easy-going rhythm.

In total, it's a relaxed llama-paced walk of about 5km, with a provided tea break in between and plenty of opportunities for selfies with your new friend, including with the iconic rock formation in the background. Best of all, you get to be involved in every aspect of handling your llama, from adding and removing the lead and tying them up at tea break to the issuing of 'llama lollies' for a job well done.

The entrance fee to the reserve is included in your tour. If you plan on also climbing Hanging Rock, Llama Treks can arrange for your second same-day visit to be free by informing the ranger. A shorter **Meet & Greet** *($30, child under 2yr free)* session and longer 12km trek on the **Domino Rail Trail** *($100)* are also available. Email them to make a booking.

Bridgewater

TIME FROM BENDIGO: **30MIN**

Ascend the 'Mountain of Light'

Take a two-hour **Kooyoora Cultural Tour** *(dumawul.com.au/tours; adult $195)* accompanied by a knowledgeable Dja Dja Wurrung (Djaara) guide on **Mt Kooyoora**, the 'Mountain of Light'.

Meet your guide at the lower picnic area for a cleansing smoking ceremony before ascending Mt Kooyoora in your private vehicle. Experience the privilege of having the mountain's landscape – the home of the mallee fowl, with its striking granite boulders, caves and culturally significant sites – interpreted by a Traditional Custodian. Learn how Djaara is putting Red Spirit back into Country and the significance and benefits of Djandak Wi (cultural burns). Participants must be able to walk comfortably for two hours and unassisted over uneven terrain for at least half an hour.

The tour is held twice a month on a Friday and Saturday. Once a month, there's the opportunity to visit Mt Kooyoora at night on the incredible **Sky Country Tour** *(per person $540)*, a two-hour cultural astronomy experience giving a Djaara perspective of the stars.

EATING & DRINKING BEYOND BENDIGO: OUR PICKS

Mill: Shopping, art and dining hub in Castlemaine. Find a brewery, winery, coffeehouse, bakery, ice creamery, sit-down dining and more. *hours vary*

Super Lekker: In Woodend, grass-fed and free-range beef burgers with gluten-free and vegan options. *noon-2pm Fri-Sun, 5-8pm Wed-Sat, to 7.30pm Sun* $

Axedale Tavern: Grab a drink or meal at this historic pub with a beer garden near the O'Keefe Rail Trail. *10am-11pm Wed-Fri, to 10pm Sat & Sun* $$

Bridgewater Hotel: Popular restored Art Deco pub on the banks of the Loddon River. *11.30am-9.30pm Wed & Thu, to 11pm Fri & Sat, to 4pm Sun* $$

JACKSONHU2207/SHUTTERSTOCK

Buda Historic Home & Garden

Castlemaine

TIME FROM BENDIGO: **25MIN**

Tour a historic home

Take a self-tour of **Buda Historic Home & Garden** *(budacastlemaine.org; adult/child $15/5; noon-4pm daily)*, the former home of the Leviny family. The family's patriarch, Ernest Leviny, a Hungarian-born silversmith, joined the throngs of hopeful diggers on the Victorian goldfields in the 1850s, only to realise his potential for wealth lay in creating jewellery from the finds of others rather than the toil of seeking it himself.

Ernest developed the 3-acre property with his second wife, Bertha, and their 10 children. They had six daughters, five of whom famously didn't marry and spent most of their lives at Buda, which was unusual for the times and evidence of the family's privileged position in society. Never pressured to wed nor in need of employment, the women focused on developing their artistic talents, including woodcarving, photography and metalwork, examples of which can be seen throughout the home and garden.

Ampl e interpretive signage, along with a 10-minute video, gives insight into the life and times of the Levinys, who occupied the property for 118 years across only two generations. Outdoors, view the impressive facade and wander the established garden. You'll need around one hour here.

MORE TO DO BEYOND BENDIGO

O'Keefe Rail Trail: Hire a bike from Bicycle Centre Bendigo and take this historic 50km cycling route to Heathcote *(railtrails.org.au)*.

Victorian Goldfields Railway: Heritage train linking the mining towns of Castlemaine and Maldon on Fridays, Sundays and select Saturdays. Book at *vgr.com.au*.

Pink Cliffs Geological Reserve: The moonlike formations of fine pink clay in Heathcote are a result of gold-mining in the 1880s.

Hanging Rock Winery: Pop in for a free wine tasting and to admire the sculptures from the 'Art in the Vines' exhibition. Open daily.

Goldfields Track: Walk (grade 4) or mountain bike (moderate) this epic 210km track from Bendigo to Ballarat.

Ballarat

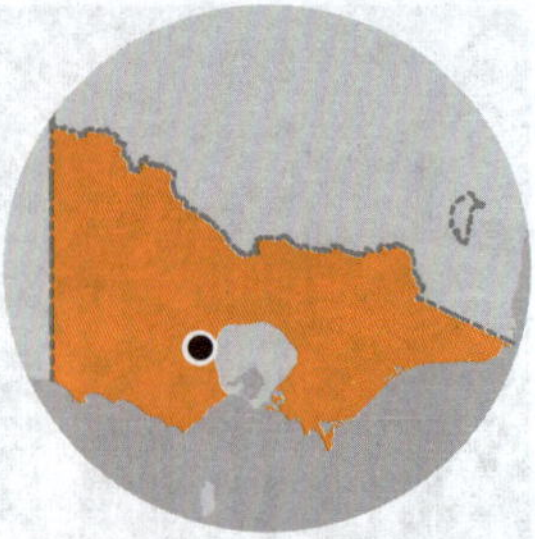

HISTORIC ARCHITECTURE | GOLD LEGACY | ART GALLERIES

TOP TIP

The city's street parking meters are connected, so you can use any machine to pay or top up. As long as you have time remaining, you can move your vehicle as many times as you like. Input your car registration number even if you're only using the free hour.

It didn't take long after the European discovery of gold at Clunes, just north of Ballarat, for the Victorian gold rush to recast this once sleepy bushland, a 'resting place' for the Wadawurrung people, into a mining superhighway. Ballarat was the world's richest alluvial goldfield during its peak in 1852 and 1853 and it shows through its towering Victorian-era architecture, made even more imposing atop the city's undulating streets.

Gold appears to have rolled down the steep slope of Lydiard St, from its illustrious art gallery to the historic Royal Hotel. You can imagine the candlelit Sugg lamps (two of which remain) allowing residents to dress up in their finery and promenade at night.

Aside from gold, modern-day Ballarat is gaining distinction for dining. Armstrong St North is considered the city's 'feast street', while Aboriginal art finds deserved prominence on the established art scene at Indigenous galleries such as Raintree Art and Perridak Arts.

Return to the Gold Rush

Experience Ballarat c1850s

One of Ballarat's longest-standing and most popular attractions, the 'living museum' of **Sovereign Hill** *(sovereignhill.com.au; adult/child $52.50/33)* is a recreated pioneer town

GETTING AROUND

Driving is the easiest way to explore. The town has a bus network, with routes starting and ending at Ballarat Station. The station has free all-day multi-storey car parking and metered parking spots offer one free hour per day.

E-scooters are a popular way to zip around town; use the **Neuron** *(rideneuron.com)* app to locate and hire one. During the warmer months, e-bikes are available from the train station via the same app. Sturt St has dedicated paths used by both bicycles and scooters; otherwise, use regular roads, not footpaths.

HIGHLIGHTS
1 Eureka Centre
2 Perridak Arts
3 Sovereign Hill

SIGHTS
4 Ballarat Botanical Gardens
5 Ballarat Tramway Museum
6 Lake Wendouree
7 St Patrick's Point

ACTIVITIES
8 Steve Moneghetti Track

SLEEPING
9 Craig's Royal Hotel
10 Victoriana Motor Inn

EATING
11 Fika Coffee Brewers
12 Kōsaten
13 Saigon Allée

DRINKING & NIGHTLIFE
14 Aunty Jacks

ENTERTAINMENT
see 3 AURA

TRANSPORT
15 Windmill Drive Car Park

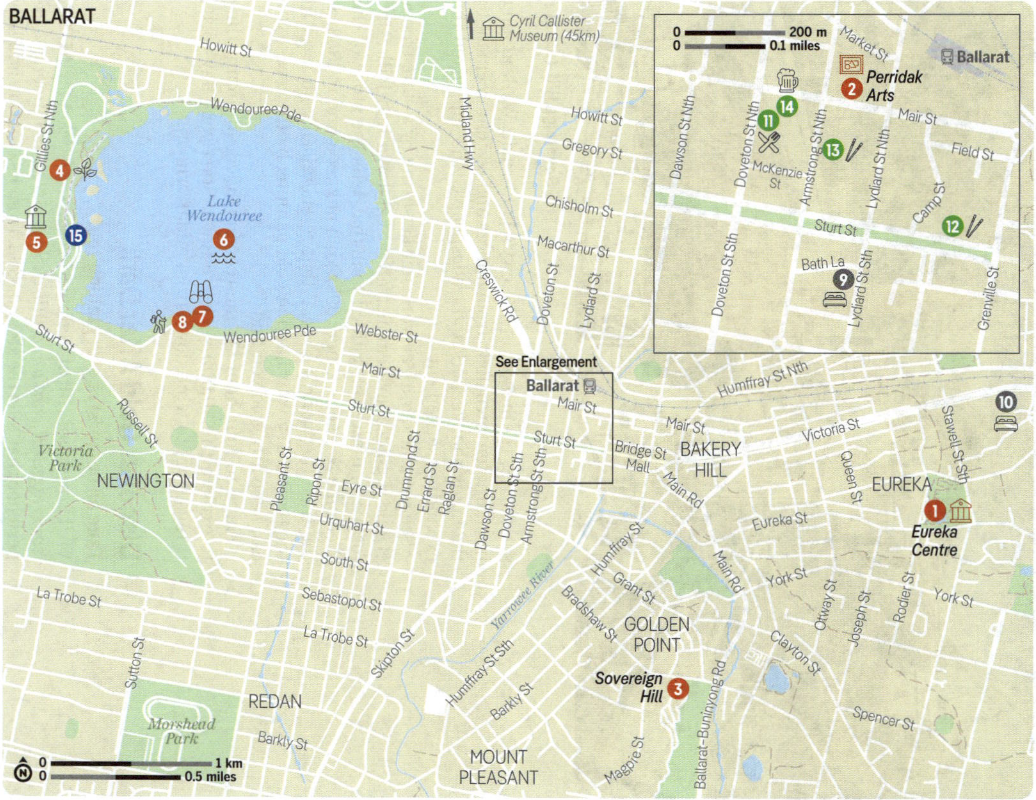

FILEDIMAGE/SHUTTERSTOCK

Sovereign Hill (p572)

set during the height of the city's gold rush. Walk among in-character townsfolk, from miners and law enforcement to the many shopkeepers and tradespeople who supported the expanding settlement.

See the blacksmith at work, musket-firing by a state trooper and a gold-pour demonstration. Go down Red Hill Mine for a 12-minute self-guided tour that tells the story of the Welcome Nugget – a huge 69kg gold nugget found in 1858, at the time the world's largest, that re-energised gold fever in the region. Try your hand at gold panning by the creek; you can keep any gold you find.

Three to four hours is the recommended minimum time to explore the 30,000-sq-metre town. Start your day early; things start to wind down from midafternoon.

Discover Gold After Dark

Take an immersive storytelling tour

Visit Sovereign Hill at night with a separate ticket for **AURA** *(sovereignhill.com.au; adult/child $45/24)*, an immersive experience that tells the story of gold, from its creation and how it shaped Ballarat, through a sound-and-light show.

Indoor diners have dishes delivered by 'train'

EATING & DRINKING IN BALLARAT: OUR PICKS

Aunty Jacks: Multilevel industrial brewpub serving house beer and a crowd-pleasing menu. *3-11pm Wed & Thu, noon-midnight Fri & Sat, to 9pm Sun*

Saigon Allée: Modern Vietnamese cuisine in the heart of the city's foodie precinct. Banh mi at lunch. *noon-2.30pm & 5-10pm Tue-Sat, 5-9pm Mon* **$$**

Fika Coffee Brewers: Top spot for breakfast and the morning caffeine hit. Try the 'Tradesman' egg, bacon, rocket and cheese bun. *6.30am-2pm Mon-Fri* **$**

Kōsaten: Japanese sushi, curry and noodle restaurant with indoor and outdoor seating. Order from a table-side screen. *11.30am-2.30pm & 5-9pm Mon-Sat* **$**

The outstanding 90-minute audiovisual presentation begins in an indoor 3D theatre before taking visitors through the site after dark in an open-air vehicle for further multisensory storytelling. Be sure to dress for evening weather. The experience is fully wheelchair-accessible (up to five wheelchairs per session).

An Uprising Remembered

Take a Eureka history lesson

The **Eureka Centre** *(eurekacentreballarat.com.au; adult/child $7/5)*, at what is believed to be the site of the Eureka Rebellion, takes visitors through the differing perspectives of the insurgency and, notably, houses the original Eureka flag. It is regarded as the 'birthplace of Australian democracy', as the incident resulted in an official inquiry into the administration of the goldfields and subsequently the abolition of the controversial monthly gold license and the start of other democratic reforms, such as voting rights for miners.

There's plenty of reading for inquiring minds via the central touchscreens; however, the signboards and a guidebook given upon entry provide a sufficient summary. Don't miss the fascinating short video about the flag's restoration. Around 1½ hours is ample to take in the centre and the surrounding **Eureka Stockade Memorial Park** with several monuments of remembrance. Same-day re-entry to the centre is permitted; the park is not ticketed.

Vintage Transport Reborn

Ride a historic tram

Ballarat Tramway Museum *(btm.org.au; adult/child $15/7)*, opened in 2022, is the culmination of decades of volunteer efforts to preserve Ballarat's tram history. When the city's trams were set to be decommissioned in 1971, a group of passionate locals formed the Ballarat Tramway Preservation Society, which ultimately brought a number of the city's abandoned tram cars back to working order.

Now operating next to the group's original 1974 depot in the Botanical Gardens (p576), it's the only entirely volunteer-run tram service on public roads in Australia. The museum displays several historical trams, including the only operational horse-drawn tram in Victoria. Tickets include a solar-powered heritage tram ride (20-minute return) along an original section of side track by Lake Wendouree (p576). An 'access' tram with a ramp runs on demand for wheelchair users and anyone with mobility needs.

Art for Change

Support First Nations artists

Owned and operated by the Ballarat and District Aboriginal Cooperative (BADAC), **Perridak Arts** *(perridakarts.com.au; free)* is a First Nations gallery and safe space for interested visitors to ask questions about the world of Aboriginal art. The

THE EUREKA REBELLION

The mass influx of diggers to the Central Victorian Goldfields brought the need for law and order. Yet the heavy-handedness of colonial government controls caused unrest to build over the gold-rush settlements. Of particular contention was the introduction of a prohibitively expensive license to pan or mine for gold.

When demands for change remained ignored, miners and their allies decided to resist authorities, in what is now known as the Eureka Rebellion, by building a hastily erected timber fort (stockade) at a strategic position in the east of Ballarat. On 3 December 1854, 276 soldiers and police caught rebels off-guard in a predawn ambush, resulting in the death of six soldiers and 22 rebels and several arrests for treason.

BALLARAT OR BALLAARAT?

You may notice that some of the city's older institutions spell Ballarat with a double 'a'. This is not a typo, but the official spelling of the city since its proclamation as a township in 1852.

From the Wadawurrung words *balla* ('reclining on the elbow') and *arat* ('place'), Ballaarat carries the meaning of 'resting place'. The spelling remained that way for 143 years, continuing through the transformation from township to municipality and then borough and later its declaration as a city in 1870.

It didn't become the City of Ballarat (single 'a') until 1994 when a local government amalgamation incorporated districts from outside the previous city bounds.

DOUBLELEE/SHUTTERSTOCK

gallery, opened in 2023, showcases the work of First Nations artists who are residents of Ballarat or have links to the area.

The city has a disproportionate connection to the Stolen Generations, as Aboriginal children from across Victoria were brought to Ballarat and its five orphanages under government assimilation policies. Now a growing number of those affected, along with their descendants and communities, are taking up creative endeavours as a form of grief exploration and healing, with the display and sale of their artwork supported through the gallery.

The artist receives 75% of the sales, while the remaining 25% goes back into BADAC programs that support the health and wellbeing of local Aboriginal communities. The gallery is a signatory to the Indigenous Art Code, ensuring the authenticity of each piece and adherence to a code of ethics for the fair and respectful treatment of First Nations artists.

Leisurely Ballarat

Take a lakeside walk

Adjoining **Ballarat Botanical Gardens**, stroll spectacular **Lake Wendouree** with its resident swans, lakeside cafes and dedicated walking track. Named after the Australian marathon runner, the 6km **Steve Moneghetti Track** around the perimeter of the 238-hectare lake is a favourite of walkers, runners, dog owners and stroller-wielding parents.

While technically the track starts and ends by **St Patrick's Point** on the southern shoreline, its circular nature means you can start anywhere. Our favourite section is the western side, easily accessible from Windmill Drive Car Park. Clear signage indicates your progression along the trail and

Steve Moneghetti Track, Lake Wendouree

distance to toilets and drinking fountains. Allow 1½ hours to fully circumnavigate the lake and take in the view at an average walking pace.

An Aussie Icon

Visit the home of Vegemite

Around 35 minutes by car from downtown Ballarat in the small town of Beaufort, the volunteer-run **Cyril Callister Museum** *(cyrilcallisterfoundation.org; adult/child $5/free)* celebrates all things Vegemite and the local man who invented this iconic Aussie spread. Situated in a retro 1950s petrol station, the museum displays donated Vegemite memorabilia, historical timelines and artworks made from Vegemite and toast. A range of licensed and museum-exclusive Vegemite products are available for purchase, including fudge, cookies and candles. On weekends, try the Vegemite meat pie baked in Sovereign Hill's brick ovens.

To get the most out of your visit, take the 1¼-hour **Vegemite History Tour** *($18)*, which includes a meet-and-greet history talk, a 25-minute video screening in Cyril's Cinema narrated by grandson Jamie Callister and a cuppa with a locally baked chocolate Vegemite treat. For some artistic fun, try your hand at Vegemite painting (or a play-dough creation) in a one-hour **Vegemite Thru Art** *($8)* experience. The 1½-hour **Cyril's Lab Science Tour** *($15)* for kids five years and older incorporates elements of the history and art tours, along with the chance to conduct a food science experiment and make (and taste) Vegemite 'caviar'. Proceeds go into funding university scholarships for budding rural scientists. The museum is open Thursday to Monday; online tour reservations essential.

HERITAGE TRAMS LIVE ON

Chris Phillips, Foundation Member of Ballarat Tramway Museum, shares the organisation's history.

I was at the first meeting of the Ballarat Tramway Preservation Society in May 1971. As a young man, I always enjoyed bouncing around on the city's trams and then one day, just like the steam trains, our electric trams were also disappearing.

Our thought was to try to preserve one tram, but we were able to convince government bodies to let us keep six. Now we have 11 original Ballarat trams and five former Melbourne trams, and continue to acquire and restore them.

In 1990, Tram 12 was rediscovered inside a house during construction of the Ballarat Hwy bypass, fitted with a washroom and storage and the saloon used as a bedroom.

Daylesford & Hepburn Springs

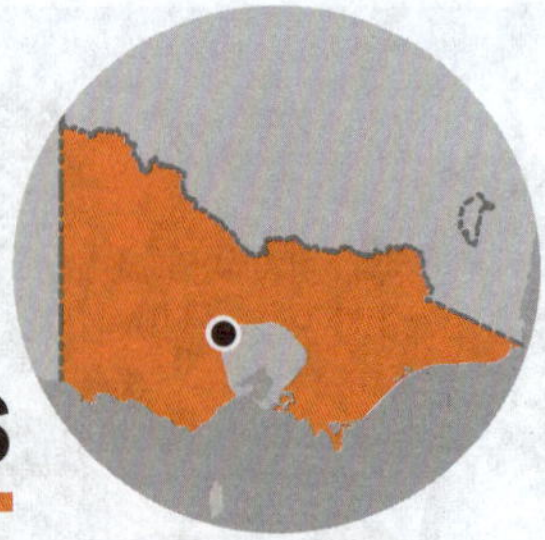

MINERAL SPRINGS | FOOD & WINE | ART & ANTIQUES

GETTING AROUND

Some points of interest are technically walkable, but you'll be getting your steps in. The area is hilly and you need a reasonably good level of fitness to get around on foot.

The towns are more easily explored by car or taxi. On weekdays, a town bus service connects Daylesford and Hepburn Springs with four departures daily. Some accommodation offers chauffeur or concierge services.

Reach Daylesford from Melbourne by taking the train to Woodend and then an onward coach service.

The twin towns of Daylesford and Hepburn Springs, just five minutes apart by car, developed differently from other central Victorian gold-rush settlements. The discovery of mineral springs here in the mid-1800s saw a culture around wellness evolve side by side with mining and when one threatened the other, it was the waters that won out.

Dubbed the 'spa capital of Australia', the region is the source of an incredible 80% of Victoria's mineral water. Whether you come to drink it or bathe in it, a visit to Daylesford and Hepburn Springs is all about rejuvenation.

Beyond the mineral springs, indulge in the elevated food and wine scene, soul-filling galleries and vintage retail therapy. It's largely a weekend tourist destination, with the high season in winter and cosy evenings by the fireplace the aim of the game. In March, it's the home of Australia's largest rural LGBTIQ+ pride event, the ChillOut Festival.

Wellness from the Source

Drink the mineral springs

Hepburn Mineral Springs Reserve was declared in 1865, the first of its kind in Victoria. The novel move was a preservation measure for the springs, which had quickly gained interest for their medicinal properties, against the artificial sluicing methods used to divert and control the flow of water during the region's gold rush.

The original 1908 brick building by the site of the old Pavilion Spring, the first uncovered by reserve namesake Captain John S Hepburn, is at the heart of the reserve. A popular meeting place at the turn of the 20th century, the building now functions as the **Pavilion Cafe**. About 150m from the cafe at the reserve's entrance, the historic **Hepburn Bathhouse & Spa** *(hepburnbathhouse.com; from $60)*, established in 1895 for mass public mineral bathing, remains open as a communal bathhouse offering a range of wellness and spa experiences.

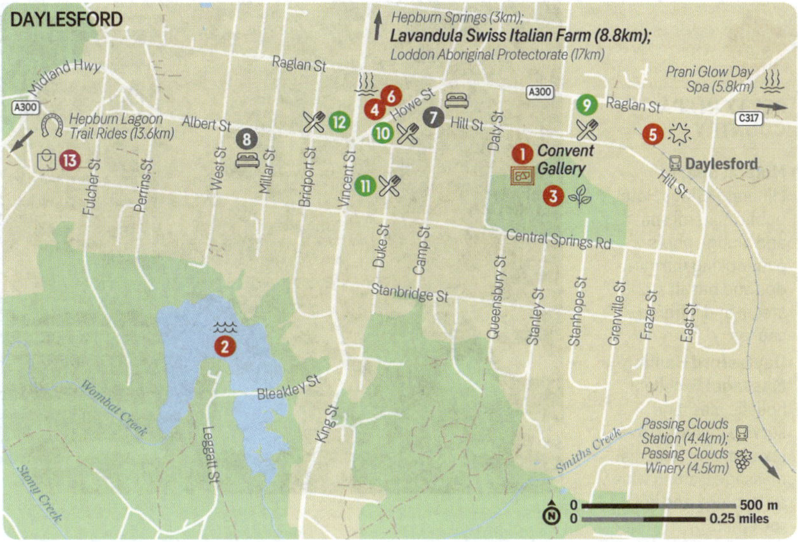

HIGHLIGHTS
1 Convent Gallery

SIGHTS
2 Lake Daylesford
3 Wombat Hill Botanic Gardens

ACTIVITIES
4 Daylesford Healing Massage
5 Daylesford Spa Country Railway
6 Daylesford Traditional Chinese Massage

SLEEPING
7 Central Springs Inn
8 Daylesford Central Motor Inn

EATING
see 1 Bad Habits Cafe
9 Cliffy's Emporium
10 Daylesford Hotel
11 Larder Daylesford
12 Vietnamese Kitchen

SHOPPING
13 Amazing Mill Markets
see 5 Daylesford Sunday Market

From the reserve's car park, visitors can fill up their drink bottles from **Locarno**, **Soda**, **Sulphur** and **Wyuna** springs along the creek bed or take a 30-minute hike through bushland to **Argyle Spring**. Each spring has its own tasting notes and it's interesting to compare them – expect some bold flavours. Most springs in the reserve tend towards the sodium bicarbonate type and hence are quite effervescent. They are accessed via a hand pump; once the water starts flowing, best practice is to pump it 10 times before drinking from it. The reserve's springs are part of **Victoria's Mineral Springs Trail** *(mineralspringsvictoria.com.au)* of 39 publicly accessible mineral springs.

TOP TIP

It's best to plan your restaurant meals ahead of time to avoid disappointment or a lengthy wait, especially on weekends, in these popular tourist towns. Most restaurants can be easily booked online. Some require credit card details to secure a reservation.

A Djaara Perspective

Take an Indigenous cultural walk

From Hepburn Mineral Springs Reserve car park, venture through bushland and old mining country to experience **Nyerna Djayi Wurreka**. Meaning 'Listening to Country Speak', this upgraded cultural walk, opened in August 2025 along the established Argyle Spring trail, is a collaboration between Dja Dja Wurrung Clans Aboriginal Corporation (DJAARA) and Parks Victoria. Over the 2.8km trail, eight 'pause points' – featuring interpretive signage, sculptural works by Djaara artists and resting spots – invite visitors to

RELAX IN SPA COUNTRY

Mineral Spa: At Mineral Springs Hotel, public mineral spa and plunge pools overlooking the garden and basalt stone, steam and infrared saunas.

Daylesford Healing Massage: Excellent, holistic massage service including relaxation and remedial massages, along with reflexology and hot-rock therapy.

Daylesford Traditional Chinese Massage: Combines remedial Tui Na techniques with other popular styles of massage. Cupping therapy is also available.

Sauk Head Spa: In Hepburn Springs, Japanese-inspired head spa service with rejuvenating scalp treatments.

Prani Glow Day Spa: Less than a 10-minute drive from downtown Daylesford, traditional Thai ritual meets modern healing techniques.

DREAMSCAPE STELL/SHUTTERSTOCK

engage with their surroundings through sight, sound and smell, and reflect on Djandak (Dja Dja Wurrung Country) through an Indigenous cultural lens.

Start at the **Manna Gum Welcome Sculpture** by the electric BBQs, then proceed down to Wyuna Spring (p579) to enter the trail. It takes around 30 minutes to reach Argyle Spring (p579), one of the pause points, where you can taste water from the mineral spring, listen to the flow of Wild Cat Creek and peer up at the bush canopy from wooden lounge chairs. On the return, continue straight at the trail fork (point 4) to take a slightly different route for the final interpretive display and artwork. This is a grade 3 hike with some slopes, stairs, and uneven and rocky terrain, so don sensible footwear. While the hike can be completed in an hour, allow an additional 30 minutes to participate in the signage prompts as intended. Toilets are available at the car park.

For a special experience, time your visit for an **Argyle Spring Walking Tour** *(dumawul.com.au/tours; $150)* to hike the trail with a Djaara guide, who can provide further cultural insights and interpretations to deepen your understanding of Djandak.

Back in the Habit

Admire art in a nunnery

The grand Victorian-era building on Wombat Hill at the edge of the Botanic Gardens, now known as the **Convent Gallery** *(conventgallery.com.au; adult/child $10/5)*, began its days as a private residence during the 1860s gold rush. It later had a short-lived life as a presbytery before becoming the home of the Presentation Sisters, an order of Irish nuns who reopened it as the Holy Cross Convent and Boarding School in 1892 and called the convent home for almost 90 years. Today,

Lavandula Swiss Italian Farm

the carefully restored building has been given new life as a prestigious art gallery and events space.

Visitors can self-tour the building's four floors, which include seven gallery spaces of changing exhibits and learn about the life and times of the Presentation Sisters, from the old music room in the basement to the chapel and the former infirmary and bell tower where a panoramic view of Daylesford and the Central Highlands awaits. **Bad Habits Cafe** is available on-site.

An Ode to Europe

Visit a lavender garden

A 10-minute drive from Hepburn Springs in Shepherds Flat, **Lavandula Swiss Italian Farm** *(lavandula.com.au; adult/child $5/1)* is situated on the former dairy farm and homestead of Swiss-Italian miner Aquilino Tinetti, who was initially leased the land in 1861 under a Victorian government scheme to persuade miners to stay and farm. He was later joined by his wife, Maria and their 13 children, and the 100-hectare property served four generations of the Tinettis before being revitalised as a publicly accessible European-style farm and garden, renowned for its signature lavender.

Pack a picnic to enjoy on the lawn when the weather's nice (or pre-order a picnic basket) and say hello to the farm's alpacas, emus and highland cows. Try huge lavender scones and European-style cuisine at **Maria's Trattoria**, wine by the glass and grazing plates at **Tinetti's Wine Bar** and fresh baked goods and take-home preserves from the **Post Office Deli & Larder**. Buy handcrafted bath and body products featuring lavender oil from the farm's harvest at the **Farm Shop**, with further shopping available in the **Homestead Store** housed in the original Tinetti home. The farm is open daily.

SWISS-ITALIAN INFLUENCE

The 1850s and 1860s brought gold seekers from all over Europe to the Central Victorian Goldfields, and the Daylesford and Hepburn Springs region in particular saw a wave of migration from both sides of the Swiss-Italian border. These migrants mostly came from the Italian-speaking Swiss cantons of Ticino and Grisons and the northern Italian provinces of Piedmont and Lombardy. With only a few finding fortune on the goldfields, the Swiss-Italian migrants turned to farming, trades and small business. The Italian names still seen today are a legacy of their significant contribution to early town development, from the Old Macaroni Factory and Hotel Bellinzona to street names such as Crippa and Vanina and the Locarno mineral spring.

MORE IN DAYLESFORD & HEPBURN SPRINGS

Lake Daylesford: Do a lap of this picturesque lake near town on the 2.8km (one-hour) 'Peace Mile' walk.

Daylesford Truth-Telling Tour: An eye-opening two-hour tour to the Loddon Aboriginal Protectorate Station with a Djaara guide. *(duma wul.com.au/tours)*

Alice's Journeys: Walking tours of Daylesford and Hepburn Springs on Fridays and Saturdays.

Hepburn Lagoon Trail Rides: A short drive from Daylesford, take a two-hour horse ride through the Wombat State Forest.

Daylesford Sunday Market: Small outdoor market offering local produce and wares. Stalls wind down by lunch.

Amazing Mill Markets: Secondhand and vintage items for sale at a huge indoor market complex.

RUSTY TODARO/SHUTTERSTOCK

Daylesford Sunday Market

Moving Heritage

Take a vintage train ride

On Sundays, take the one-hour return **Daylesford Spa Country Railway** *(dscr.com.au; adult/child $22/18)* from heritage-listed Daylesford Station within the grounds of the Daylesford Sunday Market to Bullarto, the highest operating railway station in Victoria.

The train starts through open farmland before chugging its way up through the tall timbers of the Wombat State Forest. **Bullarto Station** sits at 747m above sea level and is a replica of the 1930s station that once stood here. You'll be given around 15 minutes to get off and take photos. Book online in advance to secure your preferred train; remaining tickets are available at Daylesford Station.

The en route station of **Passing Clouds**, servicing **Passing Clouds Winery**, is on-demand only. Inform the conductor on embarkation if you'd like to stop here. Wine tastings are available at the cellar door and, by advanced reservation, a **Train Wine Dine** *(passingclouds.com.au; $200)* package for a boozy Sunday lunch.

EATING & DRINKING IN DAYLESFORD: OUR PICKS

Larder Daylesford: On the main street, this early opener is a good choice for a cafe breakfast and morning coffee. *7.30am-3.30pm* $$

Daylesford Hotel: Country-style pub with excellent wood-fired pizza for eat-in or takeaway from the pizza drive-thru. *noon-8.30pm Wed-Mon, from 4pm Tue* $$

Cliffy's Emporium: Cosy up for an ethically sourced brunch by candlelight near the Sunday Market. Try the signature eggs Benedict. *8am-3pm* $$

Vietnamese Kitchen: At the Daylesford RSL, Southeast Asian cuisine (including soups, rice, curry and noodle salads) in a pub setting. *11.30am-8pm Thu-Sun* $$

The Grampians

DRAMATIC SCENERY | HIKING | ROCK ART

Home of the Jardwadjali and Djab Wurrung peoples, Grampians National Park (also known by its Indigenous name of Gariwerd) has an Aboriginal cultural history dating back at least 22,000 years. Their ancient presence can be seen within the caverns and overhangs of these great sandstone ranges in the form of culturally significant rock art. Containing 80% of the Aboriginal rock art found in Victoria and the largest collection in southeastern Australia, Gariwerd is a place of reverence for Traditional Custodians extending to Creation stories of the Dreaming.

The dramatic peaks and craggy outcrops are the result of more than 400 million years of geological activity. Flowing rivers deposited sedimentary layers of rock, which eruptions on the southwestern volcanic plains shaped and tilted, resulting in Gariwerd's cauliflower-like escarpments. Whether you drive to a lookout or hike to one, the view is nothing short of astounding.

Places

TOP TIP

Camping, rock climbing and bouldering are permitted only in designated areas. Camping grounds with fees must be booked online before arrival and special rules apply to dispersed campers, including no campfires. When in doubt, contact Parks Victoria *(parks.vic.gov.au)*.

Halls Gap & Central Grampians

TIME FROM MELBOURNE: **3HR**

Visit the town baths

The small township of Halls Gap in the Central Grampians is the park's main tourist centre. From the back of Halls Gap car park, a trailhead from within the Botanical Gardens (p584) leads to shallow rock pools, the **Venus Baths** (grade 2). Bring a towel and wear a swimsuit underneath if you plan to sit and splash around in the pools on warm days. There are no toilets or changing rooms on the trail, so use the facilities at the car park. On the return, continue on the loop track by crossing the bridge over Stony Creek. The whole circuit is 2.3km and takes 30 minutes to one hour.

GETTING AROUND

Reach the town of Halls Gap from Melbourne via train to Ballarat or Ararat and then a connecting bus, or a bus from Warrnambool.

The Grampians are a hiking destination, with trails starting right from the centre of Halls Gap. Your wanderings will be limited, however, to how far your feet can take you. Access to a vehicle is by far the easiest way to explore and gets you up the windy mountain roads to the car parks for popular trailheads and lookouts.

OTHER THINGS TO DO IN HALLS GAP

Halls Gap E-Bike Hire: Rent an Ibosa e-bike to explore on shared bike paths. Walk-ins only; last rental 3pm daily. *(hallsgapebikehire.com)*

Grampians Adventure Golf: Family-friendly 18-hole mini-golf course in shady surrounds with on-site cafe and gallery.

Halls Gap Botanical Gardens: Informative signage about how First Nations peoples use native plants and thought-provoking 'treasure hunt' for kids.

Wildlife Art Museum of Australia (WAMA): Environmental art facility with a changing exhibition space and small native garden. Open Friday to Monday.

Halls Gap Recreation Reserve: In the late afternoon, this sports oval is a popular spot to view the Gap's resident kangaroos.

Hike the Grand Canyon

From the Venus Baths, continue onto **Splitters Falls** and link up with the popular Grand Canyon and the Pinnacle hike on the **Wonderland Loop** (grade 4). The 9.6km circuit can be completed in four to five hours and returns to Halls Gap via a rocky gully and stringybark forest, culminating with a series of steep steel steps. Toilets are available at Wonderland car park.

For an easier route, drive to Wonderland car park, less than 10 minutes from Halls Gap, where you can either do the **Grand Canyon Loop** (grade 3) in 20 to 40 minutes or continue from the top of the canyon to the **Pinnacle Lookout** (grade 3) for spectacular views over the Wonderland Range and Lake Bellfield. A highlight of the trail is **Silent Street**, a long and narrow pass with sheer rock walls. Grand Canyon included, the 4.2km return journey takes two to 2½ hours.

See the park's largest waterfall

MacKenzie Falls, the largest waterfall in Gariwerd, is accessed from MacKenzie Falls car park, a further 25-minute drive northwest of Wonderland car park. Either take the trail to **MacKenzie Falls Lookout** (grade 2), an easy 1.9km walk that takes around 40 minutes return, or the steep 1.2km, one-hour out-and-back track to the base of MacKenzie Falls (grade 3) to bask in the negative ions of the powerful 35m falls from water level. A toilet block is located by the trailheads.

Hollow Mountain & Northern Grampians

TIME FROM HALLS GAP: **45MIN**

Marvel at Indigenous rock art

In the Northern Grampians, find two Aboriginal rock-art sites on grade 2 walking tracks. **Gulgurn Manja Shelter** is a gradual uphill 1.5km out-and-back hike (30 minutes return) starting at Hollow Mountain car park. Once you emerge onto the open granite, continue straight to rejoin the bush path. Within a few metres, the caged shelter featuring handprints of young people reveals itself.

Ngamadjidj Shelter, a 15-minute drive away near **Stapylton Campground**, is a 900m loop walk (20 minutes) through flat bushland. Meaning 'white person', Ngamadjidj is the only art site in Gariwerd to depict solely white figures. To minimise time on bumpy, unsealed roads from Halls Gap, avoid Mt Zero Rd and instead link up with the Western Hwy.

Roaming robots will serve your dishes

EATING & DRINKING IN HALLS GAP: OUR PICKS

Flame Brothers: Lively smokehouse and bar serving smoked meats, burgers and a cafe breakfast. *7.30am-9pm Fri-Mon, from noon Tue-Thu* **$$**

Paper Scissors Rock Brew Co: Good selection of beers on tap (most gluten-reduced), tasty food options and live music events. *noon-8pm*

Livefast Cafe: Nice spot for a coffee and toastie, or something from the lunch and all-day breakfast menu. *7am-4pm Mon-Fri, to 5pm Sat & Sun* **$$**

Spirit of Punjab: Popular Indian restaurant with an extensive menu and easy online orders for takeaway. *5-9.30pm daily & noon-2.30pm Fri-Sun* **$$**

DZUNG VU/SHUTTERSTOCK

MacKenzie Falls

Embark on an epic hiking adventure

A three-minute drive from Hollow Mountain car park, the parking area serving **Mt Zero (Mura Mura)** is the trailhead for the **Grampians Peaks Trail (GPT)**. This incredible 12-night/13-day hike spans 164km through the entire length of the national park from Mt Zero Trailhead in the north to Dunkeld in the south. This is a grade 4 to grade 5 hike and requires preparation. The entire GPT was reopened to hikers following the 2024–25 bushfires, but some camp sites in the central and southern sections remained closed, so affected trails will be for day hikes only until their staged reopening. See *parks.vic.gov.au* for the latest.

Dunkeld & Southern Grampians

TIME FROM HALLS GAP: **45MIN**

Hike the southern peaks

The **Piccaninny (Bainggug)**, just north of Dunkeld, is one of the most popular hikes in the Southern Grampians. There are two approaches, both grade 3, through uphill open forest – one from Grampians Tourist Rd (east) and the other from Victoria Valley Rd (west). Both trails are around 2.5km and take one to 1½ hours return, merging for the final ascent to the summit, with excellent views of Mt Abrupt and Dunkeld.

For a bigger challenge, but doable with a reasonable level of fitness, try **Mt Abrupt (Mud-dadjug)** or **Mt Sturgeon (Wurgarri)**. Both are grade 4 hikes (7km; 2½ to three hours return) through woodland and rocky terrain, with stunning views. None of these trailheads have toilets, so stop at **Dunkeld & Grampians Visitor Information Centre** in town before you head out.

GPT PREPARATION

If you plan on hiking the **Grampians Peaks Trail**, you'll find excellent resources by searching at **Parks Victoria** *(parks.vic.gov.au)*. Dedicated books, such as *The Grampians Peaks Trail* by Julie Mundy and Debra Heyes and *Grampians Walks* by Monica and Phil Coleman, are also available for purchase online.

Those looking for logistical assistance should check out tour operator **Grampians Peaks Walking Company** *(grampianspeaks.com.au)*, an entity of **Absolute Outdoors** *(absoluteoutdoors.com.au)* offering guided walks along with support services for independent GPT hikers, including shuttle buses, food drops and gear rental. Hike-in **camping grounds** *(from $53.30)* must be booked and paid for in advance via Parks Victoria.

TRAIL & ACCESSIBILITY INFO

Halls Gap Visitor Information Centre and the **Parks Victoria** *(parks.vic.gov.au)* office, a five-minute drive from Halls Gap at the site of the closed Brambuk Cultural Centre, are open daily to assist with planning your stay. Visitors are encouraged to check the Parks Victoria website, for any changed conditions.

Wheelchair users and those with limited mobility can experience some otherwise inaccessible trails by booking at least one week in advance for one of the park's two motorised **TrailRiders** *(03-8427 3541; volunteer@parks.vic.gov.au)*. This all-terrain wheelchair service is free and operated by volunteers. See 'All Abilities' on the Parks Victoria website for information on trails with wheelchair, stroller and TrailRider access.

Scan this QR code for more on accessible trails

Learn the region's explosive past

A 20-minute drive south of Dunkeld at the foot of extinct volcano Mt Rouse, **Penshurst Volcanoes Discovery Centre** *(volcanoesdiscoverycentre.com.au; per person/family $10/20)* provides surprising insights into the region's Newer Volcanics Province. Learn about the volcanic plains – which stretch 19,000 sq km from Melbourne across western Victoria to the Mt Burr Range in southeastern South Australia and incorporate more than 430 individual volcanoes – through immersive and interpretive displays. The centre is open on Fridays, Saturdays and Sundays and every day of the Victorian school holidays. Allocate an hour here, though you could spend much longer.

Afterwards, do a self-drive tour of **Mt Rouse (Collorrer)**, first stopping to view the gigantic crater, just two minutes' walk from the car park, before driving up to the lookout, accessed via a 100-step steel staircase, for panoramic views. The lookout is less than 10 minutes from the Discovery Centre.

Stawell & Surrounds

TIME FROM HALLS GAP: **25MIN**

See a one-of-a-kind Aboriginal artwork

Bunjil's Shelter, near Stawell, is the only physical depiction ever found of the wedge-tailed eagle creator deity Bunjil and is considered one of the most significant Indigenous cultural sites in southeastern Australia. Creator of the land, water, plants and animals in Dreaming stories, Bunjil is depicted along with two dingoes in a small alcove at the base of a large granite boulder, just 150m from the car park.

Tour an undergound wine cellar

A 15-minute drive from Stawell, visit the **Seppelt Great Western Winery** for a fascinating 50-minute **Underground Cellar Tour** *(seppeltgreatwestern.com.au; adult/child $28/10)*. Known as 'the drives', this 3.5km network of tunnels was hand-dug and can store up to three million bottles of wine. Learn the incredible history of this subterranean wine maze, hear fantastical celebrity stories and visit an underground wine museum. Afterwards, an included wine tasting for those of age is offered at the cellar door. Tours depart at 11am, 1pm and 3pm daily (book online).

Phillip Island

PENGUINS | SURF BREAKS | MOTOR RACING

Once a remote and sparsely populated rural farming island surrounded by the Southern Ocean, today Phillip Island is one of Victoria's most popular tourist destinations thanks to its colony of little penguins, world-class motor-racing circuit and some exceptional surf beaches.

About 140km south of Melbourne by road, the island (called Millowl by its Traditional Custodians, the Yalluk Bulluk people) is still pretty sleepy most of the year but fills to capacity over summer months and during big race events.

Cowes is the main town on the north side of the island, connected to the Mornington Peninsula by a pedestrian ferry, but there are smaller waterfront communities scattered around: Newhaven, across the bridge from San Remo; Cape Woolamai, the surfing community with a small knot of shops and cafes and the island's favourite surf beach; Smiths Beach and Sunderland Bay, with more surf beaches; and Rhyll, a small town on the inlet east of Cowes.

TOP TIP

At the **Phillip Island Visitor Information Centre** *(visitbasscoast.com.au)* in Newhaven you can book tickets for most attractions (bundles for multiple sights are cheaper). Take care on hazardous surf beaches and only swim between the patrolled flags.

Ocean-View Boardwalks

Windswept wildlife spotting

Weather conditions at the tip of the Summerland Peninsula can vary wildly and it's usually blowing a gale, but the views from the 500m winding **Nobbies Boardwalks** are

GETTING AROUND

It's possible to access the island via V/Line coach from Melbourne or the passenger-only **Western Port Ferries** *(westernportferries.com.au; $16.50)* service from Stony Point on the Mornington Peninsula direct to Cowes, but the best way to explore is by car or on a day tour. The island is connected to the mainland by a single bridge linking San Remo with Newhaven. If you're arriving on public transport, you can hire an e-bike from **Super Cruzer** *(phillipislandebikehire.com.au)* or call the **Phillip Island Taxi Service** *(13 10 08)*.

HIGHLIGHTS
1 Penguin Parade

SIGHTS
2 Churchill Island Marine National Park
3 Berninneit
4 Churchill Island Heritage Farm
5 History of Motorsport Museum
6 Koala Conservation Reserve
7 Nobbies Boardwalks
8 Phillip Island Chocolate Factory
9 Purple Hen Winery

ACTIVITIES
10 Big Wave Complex
11 Cat's Bay
12 Island Surfboards
13 Philip Island Go Karts
14 Smiths Beach
15 Summerland Beach
16 Woolamai Beach
17 YCW Beach

EATING
18 Bani's
19 Grenache Wine Bar
20 Island Whole Foods
21 Isola di Capri

DRINKING & NIGHTLIFE
22 Ocean Reach Brewing
see 24 Rusty Water Brewery
23 Wooli Tavern

ENTERTAINMENT
24 A Maze'N Things

INFORMATION
25 Phillip Island Visitor Information Centre

TRANSPORT
26 Western Port Ferries

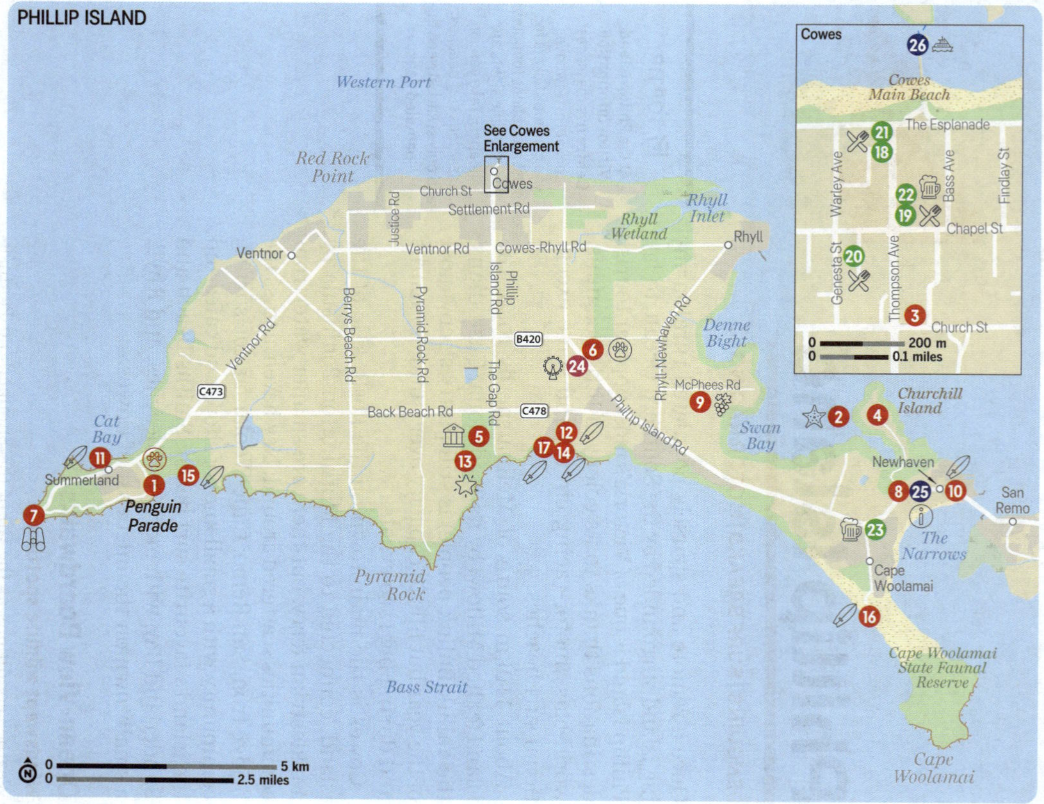

consistently spectacular. From this vantage point, you'll see the offshore rock formations known as **The Nobbies**, as well as **Seal Rocks**, home of Australia's largest colonies of fur seals.

Phillip Island for Families

Fun for the kids

With a maze, illusion rooms, mini golf, puzzle island, magic shows and rope course, whacky **A Maze'N Things** *(amazenthings.com.au; day pass adult/child/family $52/39/162)* is understandably popular with kids; there's also a lolly shop and a cafe for frazzled parents.

Like Willy Wonka's come to life, Panny's **Phillip Island Chocolate Factory** *(phillipislandchocolatefactory.com.au; adult/child/family $23/15/68)* is a chocolate shop, working factory and gallery of chocolate sculptures from the statue of David to an entire model village and interactive games.

Wildlife from the Treetops

Meet the local koalas

Treetop boardwalks at the **Koala Conservation Reserve** *(penguins.org.au; adult/child/family $17/8.50/42.50)* ensure that you get pretty close to the 15 resident koalas (all named!), some rescued from bushfire-affected areas. Interactive displays at the information centre and guided **tours** *(adult/child $60/30)* enrich the visitor experience, as do sightings of wild wallabies, echidnas and native birds; book in advance for tours. Children are well catered for, with a nature-play area and a digital quest followed via QR codes.

Experience Living History

Nature and nostalgia on Churchill Island

The historic 19th-century farm buildings and activities at **Churchill Island Heritage Farm** *(penguins.org.au; adult/child/family $17/8.50/42.50)* offer an insight into the early days of farming here with demonstrations of blacksmithing, cow-milking, sheep-shearing and whip-cracking; the website has a full list of timings. There's a **farmers market** on the first Saturday morning of the month.

The 670-hectare **Churchill Island Marine National Park** *(parks.vic.gov.au)* is an important habitat for many bird species and can be explored on boardwalks (free) of varying lengths that loop through the mangroves, salt marshes and

YALLUK BULLUK LAND

The Boonwurrung (aka Bunurong) people are the Traditional Custodians of this part of Victoria. Their Country stretches from the Werribee River west of Melbourne to Wilsons Promontory in Gippsland.

Phillip Island is the home of the Yalluk Bulluk group of the Bunurong, who call the island Millowl. Traditionally, they spent the summer months here feasting on shellfish, fish, small marsupials and muttonbirds. The multipurpose **Berninneit** *(basscoastculturalvenues.com)* cultural centre in Cowes (Berninneit means 'gather together') has rotating exhibits and shows.

Elsewhere on the island, the title of a parcel of land on the richly biodiverse Rhyll Inlet was transferred to the Bunurong Land Council Aboriginal Corporation in 2023 – the first land handback to the Bunurong since European colonisation.

EATING IN COWES: OUR PICKS

Isola di Capri: Great Italian place facing the Cowes foreshore; homemade pasta, innovative pizzas and gelati served next door. *11am-9pm, reduced hours winter* $$

Island Whole Foods: This cafe's 100% plant-based menu has a devoted local following for vegan breakfasts, smoothie bowls and coffee. *9am-3pm Wed-Mon* $

Bani's: Central, modern Greek restaurant serving some of the best food on the island, from slow-cooked lamb shoulder to takeaway souvlaki. *noon-9pm Thu-Tue* $$

Grenache Wine Bar: With a lengthy wine and gin list and a seasonal bistro menu, Grenache is a popular evening haunt. *5-9pm Tue-Thu, to 11pm Fri & Sat* $$

TOP EXPERIENCE

Penguin Parade

The sight of dozens, or even hundreds, of cute little penguins *(Eudyptula minor)*, also called fairy penguins or blue penguins, waddling up the beach almost on cue after sunset is one of Australia's great wildlife experiences. Summerland Beach has the world's largest colony of little penguins, so book a prime viewing spot for the nightly event and enjoy the show.

FERRY FERDINANDUS/SHUTTERSTOCK

Start at the Visitor Centre

A massive state-of-the-art **visitor complex** provides your entry to the beach with a giant car park, educational interactive displays, a cafe and amphitheatres that hold up to 3800 spectators. Arrive well before sunset to secure a good spot – staff will direct you out to the beach. There's a range of premium ticket options that get you closer to the penguin colony with an experienced guide.

The Penguins Are Coming

This is the largest colony of little penguins in the world – up to 32,000-strong after summer breeding. They live in burrows on Summerland Beach and make their way into the ocean each day for feeding. Strong and graceful swimmers, they return like clockwork after sunset – instinctively under cover of approaching darkness to avoid predation (the beach is dimly lit for viewing). Check times when booking and arrive an hour beforehand.

The **Ultimate Adventure Tour** *($125)* is the premium choice as you'll join one of the reserve's nature guides on the beach itself (minimum age 16). The **Penguins Plus** *(adult/child $90/45)* ticket gives access to a prime viewing grandstand. Another premium option is the **underground viewing** *(adult/child $100/50)*, where you can observe from penguin perspective (and it's slightly warmer in winter!)

TOP TIPS

- Book well in advance for premium viewing tickets.
- Weekdays outside holiday periods see fewer crowds.
- Dress warmly in the cooler months.
- While summer months are warmest, sunset can be as late as 9pm.
- Photography is not allowed during the parade.

Practicalities

- *penguins.org.au*
- adult/child/family from $33/16.50/82.50

mudflats; two wheelchair-accessible walking trails, the 4.5km **Churchill Island loop** and the 2km **North Point loop** cover the rest of the island.

Surfing Phillip Island

Hit the island waves

One of Victoria's top surfing destinations, Phillip Island is also one of Australia's 19 National Surfing Reserves (NSR). Southside beaches are suitable for beginners (Smiths Beach) and expert board riders (Woolamai Beach). A good first stop is the **Big Wave Complex** *(thebigwavecomplex.com.au)* in Newhaven, where you'll find Rip Curl, Islantis surf shop and backpacker accommodation. For surfboard hire and lessons, head to **Island Surfboards** *(islandsurfboards.com.au; group lessons $75, hire per day from $40)* at Smiths Beach. There's another branch in Cowes.

Motorcycle Dreams

Go-karting and race history

Petrolheads love Phillip Island's motor-racing circuit, home to a host of motor-racing events on two wheels and four. Sadly for the island economy, the Australian leg of the world Motorcycle Grand Prix, held here since 1997, was due to move away from Phillip Island after the 2026 season. At the visitor centre, you'll find the **History of Motorsport Museum** *(phillipislandcircuit.com.au; adult/child/family $20/13/67.20)* with displays of Grand Prix–winning motorbikes and memorabilia dating back to 1928.

For something more immersive, try **go-karting** *(phillipislandgokarts.com.au; per 10min from $40)* around a scale replica of the track on single or tandem go-karts (minimum age 12). Book online.

BEST PHILLIP ISLAND SURF SPOTS

Woolamai Beach: Known internationally for its constantly changing and challenging beach surf breaks, this is also the island's most scenic beach.

Smiths Beach: The island's premier barrelling reef break is sometimes mellow enough for novices; a surf school operates from here.

Summerland Beach: Renowned reef breaks that work in the largest of swells.

Cat's Bay: High-quality left- and right-hand reef breaks north from Summerland.

YCW Beach: Gentle, consistent waves and excellent breaks directly east of Smiths Beach.

DRINKING ON PHILLIP ISLAND: OUR PICKS

Rusty Water Brewery: A range of pale and golden ales are on offer (a tasting paddle of four costs $15); best known for its Shipwreck IPA. *11.30am-10pm Tue-Sun*

Wooli Tavern: Cape Woolamai is a fun little surfing community and the local pub is the place for a beer, bar meal and a live band on weekends. *noon-late*

Ocean Reach Brewing: Taphouse in Cowes pouring regular and seasonal beers brewed on the island. *4-9pm Wed-Fri, from noon Sat, noon-4pm Sun*

Purple Hen Winery: Head to this vineyard in Rhyll to enjoy its signature pinot noir, grazing platter and views over Western Port Bay. *11am-4.30pm Thu-Mon*

South Gippsland

WILD BEACHES | FOODIE VILLAGES | RAIL TRAILS

Places

GETTING AROUND

While public transport is useful for reaching main towns – V/Line trains travel between Melbourne and Bairnsdale and buses hit all the towns between Nyora and Yarram – you'll need your own wheels to explore independently and to visit the national parks. By car from Melbourne, the most common routes are via the Princes Hwy (A1) when heading east to Lakes Entrance or the South Gippsland Hwy towards Leongatha.

Gippsland occupies all of southeast Victoria between the mountains and the coast but is neatly split into two regions – South and East Gippsland. East of Phillip Island, South Gippsland is something of a surprise packet with its string of pretty coastal villages such as Kilcunda, Cape Paterson, Venus Bay and Walkerville. Venture inland to find rolling farmland and charming, artistic towns where markets, gourmet food stores, galleries, distilleries and live music scenes abound. Rail trails link many of these towns for cyclists and walkers.

The star attraction here, though, is Wilsons Promontory National Park, better known as 'the Prom', where bushwalking, eye-popping coastal scenery and secluded white-sand beaches conspire to form one of Australia's finest outdoor adventures.

Kilcunda to Inverloch

TIME FROM PHILLIP ISLAND: **30MIN**

Bunurong coastal drive

There are some wonderful ocean vistas on the drive between Phillip Island and the coastal holiday town of Inverloch. At Kilcunda, the dramatic Southern Ocean views really open up and there are walking trails down to the surf beach. The **Bass Coast Rail Trail** *(railtrails.org.au)* runs through here to Wonthaggi – check out the impressive **Bourne Creek trestle bridge** along the trail just past Kilcunda.

Turn south at Wonthaggi to hit the coast again at Cape Paterson and the **Bunurong Marine & Coastal Park** *(parks.vic.gov.au)*. Follow the winding 14km coastal drive stopping at car parks that lead to secluded beaches such as **Eagles Nest**, **Shack Bay** and the **Caves**, where dinosaur fossils and a footprint can be seen at low tide. There's good snorkelling at the Caves, while the **Oaks** is popular with local surfers. Most beaches are accessed via stairs, so they're not wheelchair-accessible.

Loch Brewery & Distillery

Great Southern Rail Trail

TIME FROM PHILLIP ISLAND: **1HR**

Cycle through foodie towns

The **Great Southern Rail Trail** *(gsrt.com.au)* is a 100km-plus cycling and walking trail that can be done in stages or paralleled by car, stopping in some of South Gippsland's quintessential foodie towns.

The official start point is tiny **Nyora** but more interesting is the first stop at **Loch**, a cute historic village with a range of gourmet eateries plus the excellent **Loch Brewery & Distillery** *(lochbrewery.com.au)* in an old bank building and the tasting room at nearby **Gippsland Wine Company** *(gippslandwinecompany.com)*. Larger towns en route include **Korumburra** and **Leongatha**. On Saturdays, **Meeniyan** *(meeniyan.org.au)* has a music gig at the town hall. **Fish Creek** is a popular stop on the way to Wilsons Prom with a brilliant Art Deco **pub** *(fishcreekhotel.com.au)*, quality winery and **cidery** *(gurneyscider.com.au)*. The original finish line was **Port Welshpool**, with the longest jetty in the region, but the trail now continues via Alberton to Yarram (p596; north) or **Port Albert** (south), another quaint fishing village.

Continued on p596

TOP TIP

South Gippsland has several rail trails (cycle or walking paths along former railway lines), which are a lovely way to get from A to B away from the busy roads and more are in development. Bikes can be hired at towns such as Leongatha and Meeniyan.

Stock up here if you're cycling the rail trail

EATING & DRINKING IN SOUTH GIPPSLAND: OUR PICKS

Kilcunda Ocean View Hotel: The Killy has sweeping ocean views from the terrace and pub classics like chicken parmas and steaks. *noon-late Thu-Sun* $$

KGS Kilcunda: The beloved general store has rebranded but still serves sublime all-day breakfasts, burgers and shakes. *6.30am-2.30pm* $

Port Albert Wharf Fish & Chips: Its seafront location in Port Albert is great but the fish and chips are legendary. *11am-2.30pm Mon-Thu, to 7.30pm Fri-Sun* $

Meeniyan Store: Quality country purveyor stocking local craft beers, Loch gin and Prom Coast ice cream; great coffee and local bakery pies. *8am-3pm* $

JULIA KULESHOVA/SHUTTERSTOCK

Squeaky Beach

TOP EXPERIENCE

Wilsons Promontory

The 'Prom' is one of Victoria's most rewarding national parks for walkers and the southernmost part of mainland Australia. This is a wonderland of unfenced wilderness, white-sand beaches, wildlife, and hiking trails long and short. The Brataualung people from the Gunaikurnai nation are the Traditional Custodians of this land.

DON'T MISS

- Tidal River
- Norman Beach
- Mt Oberon
- Waterloo Bay
- Squeaky Beach
- Wilsons Promontory Lighthouse
- Sealers Cove

Get Oriented at Tidal River

The official (now unstaffed) entry to the Prom is about 7km south of the village of **Yanakie**. From there it's about 30km to **Tidal River**, the hub and main accommodation base with the Parks Victoria office, a general store, cafe, cinema, camp sites and cabins. Accommodation bookings should be done online; in peak holiday periods, accommodation is usually booked out well in advance or available on a ballot system.

Prom Beaches

All of the Prom's beaches have dangerous rips (undercurrents), so swimming here beyond your waist is generally not

PRACTICALITIES

● *vic.gov.au/places-to-see/parks/wilsons-promontory-national-park* ● day visitors free ● Tidal River visitor centre 10am-noon & 2-4pm advised. Some of the best beaches are close to Tidal River, reached either via walking trails or a short drive to dedicated car parks. **Norman Beach**, hemmed in by Pillar Point and Norman Point, is the largest and most popular stretch of sand, patrolled in summer. North of here is the aptly named **Squeaky Beach**, then **Picnic Bay** and **Whisky Bay**. South of Tidal River, it's an easy coastal walk to **Little Oberon Bay** along the Oberon Bay Walking Track.

Day Walks

One of the great things about the Prom is the wealth of easy short walks, either from Tidal River or from numerous car parks.

- **Lilly Pilly Gully Nature Walk** Easy 5km (1½-hour) return walk through heathland and eucalypt forest.
- **Squeaky Beach Nature Walk** Moderate 5km (two-hour) return stroll from Tidal River through coastal tea trees and banksias to a sensational (and squeaky) white-sand beach.
- **Prom Wildlife Walk** Signposted 2.3km (45-minute) loop trail 14km south of the park entrance with good potential for kangaroo, swamp wallaby and emu sightings.
- **Big Drift Walk** A 2km walk from Stockyard Campground at the park entrance, these spectacular sand dunes are best viewed at sunrise or sunset.

You'll need a decent level of fitness and preparation to tackle these longer hikes:

- **Sealers Cove** Popular 19km hike (six hours) through pristine forest and boardwalks leading to a gorgeous sandy cove.
- **Vereker Outlook** From Five Mile Rd car park (6km, two hours' return) through varied bush landscapes and past granite boulders, with fantastic coastal views.
- **Mt Oberon Summit** From the Telegraph Saddle car park, this moderate-to-hard 7km-return walk is an ideal hiking introduction to the Prom, with panoramic views.

Overnight Walks

For all overnight walks, arrange a **camping permit** *(parks.vic.gov.au; per person per night $7.90)* in advance online, but you'll still need to check in at the Tidal River visitor centre before heading off.

The **Southern Prom Hike** is a two-day walk that starts at Telegraph Saddle and heads down Telegraph Track to overnight at beautiful Little Waterloo Bay (12km, 4½ hours). The next day, walk on to Sealers Cove and return to Telegraph Saddle (20km, 7½ hours).

Lighthouse Walk is a moderate 51km circuit across to Sealers Cove from Tidal River, down to Refuge Cove, Waterloo Bay and the lighthouse, then back to Tidal River via Oberon Bay. Allow three days and coordinate your walk with tide times, as creek crossings can be hazardous.

SANCTUARY PROJECT

The **Prom Sanctuary Project** is a long-term initiative by Parks Victoria, Traditional Custodians and conservations groups to protect the park's wildlife and habitat by eradicating introduced predators such as foxes, to successfully re-establish endangered native wildlife and create a 'climate-change refuge'. In essence, it will make this Victoria's largest conservation sanctuary for native creatures.

TOP TIPS

- Leave pets at home – they're prohibited in the park.
- Even outside peak season, plan to visit on a weekday when there are fewer visitors.
- Weather conditions can change rapidly, even in summer. If camping or hiking, be prepared with suitable clothing, footwear and food and water.
- Some trails and beaches are wheelchair-accessible; mobility aids such as beach wheelchairs are available free of charge from the Tidal River visitor centre.
- Parks Victoria provides social scripts for adults and children on the autism spectrum, downloadable from the website.

LATROBE VALLEY POWER STATIONS

The Latrobe Valley, bisected by the Princes Hwy between Moe and Sale, is known for its reserves of brown coal, industrial towns and coal-fired power plants that have historically provided most of Victoria's energy. The two main operational power stations, with their giant steam-belching stacks, are strangely impressive sights. **Yallourn**, between Moe and Traralgon, is due to close by 2028; **Tyers Lookout** has panoramic views of the massive power station and valley below. **Loy Yang**, 7km south of Traralgon, is Australia's largest open-cut coal mine. Drive up to **Jack Vines Lookout** for jaw-dropping views of the mine and power plants, or drive right through the mine site on the Hyland Hwy. It's expected to close by 2046 as Victoria transitions to wind and solar renewable energy.

ROBERT HARDING VIDEO/SHUTTERSTOCK

Continued from p593

The hilliest stretches for cyclists are Meeniyan to Fish Creek and Fish Creek to Foster, while the easiest are Nyora to Loch and Korumburra to Meeniyan.

Korumburra

TIME FROM PHILLIP ISLAND: **1HR**

Step back in time

On the site of a historic coal mine, **Coal Creek Village** *(coalcreekcommunityparkandmuseum.com; free)* is a revelatory re-creation of a 19th-century mining town, like a mini Sovereign Hill – but with barely any tourists! It's a real surprise to walk through the visitor centre and into a street full of beautifully preserved or restored buildings, including a blacksmith, Korumburra's old courthouse, a war museum and the fabulous ye olde general store. Volunteers (sometimes in costume) greet visitors, usually in the store, but you're welcome to roam around at your leisure. It's great fun for families and a testament to community conservation. Open Friday to Monday and daily during the school holidays.

Yarram

TIME FROM KORUMBURRA: **1HR 20MIN**

Streetart town

The small town of Yarram is worth a stop to explore the prolific street art of Mongolian-born Heesco Khosnaran who collaborated with residents and local businesses to paint 25 murals around town, including eye-catching portraits of locals, leading to the tag of **'Heesco Town'** *(heescotown.com)*. A highlight is the town's water tower, painted with whales, koalas and beautiful Indigenous and Japanese patterns.

Corrigan Suspension Bridge

The Great Southern Rail Trail goes as far as Yarram, so you can cycle here all the way from Nyora or the short section from Port Albert.

Tarra-Bulga National Park

TIME FROM YARRAM: **45MIN**

Walk through mountain ash forests

Tarra-Bulga National Park is a remote and hilly pocket of giant mountain ash trees, fern gullies and ancient myrtle beeches that is just far enough off any beaten track to be virtually unknown to most tourists, but still easily accessible via narrow winding roads from Traralgon or Yarram. You'll hear the calls of lyrebirds, pilot birds and yellow-tailed black cockatoos, but otherwise there's a sense of silence. The park forms part of the Gunaikurnai cultural landscape where legend has it that Borun the Pelican (the first Gunaikurnai man) travelled while carrying his bark canoe from the mountains to the sea.

Short but enthralling walks fan out from the car park at **Tarra-Bulga Visitor Centre** *(parks.vic.gov.au)*, including to the **Corrigan Suspension Bridge** (1.2km return, 40 minutes) or the 2.4km return **Lyrebird Ridge Track** through mountain ash forests. The longer and more difficult **Forest Track walk** (4.4km return) finishes the circuit and takes you back to the visitor centre. Although there's no camping here, self-contained campers sometimes overnight in the car park as there are toilets and BBQs. The visitor centre is open on weekends.

NINETY MILE BEACH

Ninety Mile Beach is a romantically named narrow strip of dune-backed sand punctuated by the lagoons of the **Gippsland Lakes Coastal Park** *(parks.vic.gov.au)* and stretching unbroken for more or less 90 miles (150km) from near McLoughlins Beach to the channel at Lakes Entrance.

The area is great for surf fishing, camping and long beach walks, though the crashing surf can be dangerous for swimming, except where patrolled at Seaspray, Woodside Beach and Lakes Entrance. The subtidal sandy expanses have one of the highest levels of species diversity anywhere in the country, with 860 species found in 10 sq metres.There's free beach camping (basic facilities) at **Flamingo Beach** and **Golden Beach** and Parks Victoria sites at **Paradise Beach**.

East Gippsland

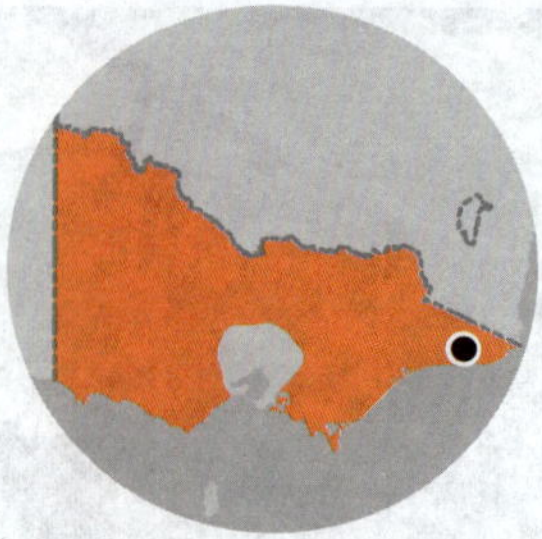

LAKE CRUISES | REMOTE CAMPING | RAIL TRAILS

Places

From the commercial hub of Bairnsdale, the Princes Hwy dips towards the coast at holiday towns like Paynesville, Metung and the family favourite, Lakes Entrance. This is the Gippsland Lakes region, where a network of saltwater lakes and lagoons inspire boating and fishing, and the dunes of Ninety Mile Beach conceal secluded spots for beach camping.

Past Lakes Entrance, the traffic thins and towns get smaller and further apart as you enter a wilderness area of spectacular coastal national parks and old-growth forest. In the far east, Mallacoota is a gorgeous little community with an end-of-the-world feel. Much of this region has never been cleared for agriculture and it contains some of the most remote and pristine national parks in the state. Native timber logging was officially banned on public land in Victoria in 2024.

Raymond Island

TIME FROM BAIRNSDALE: **15MIN**

Walk the Koala Trail

With a human population of fewer than 600 people and a koala population of more than 300, **Raymond Island** is one of the best places in Australia to see these furry marsupials in the wild.

To get to the island, catch the regular five-minute public ferry (free for cyclists and pedestrians) from the tiny town of Paynesville on Lake King. Walk to the park across from the ferry to start the signposted 1.2km **Koala Trail**, which takes you through residential streets to **Raymond Island Gippsland Lakes Reserve** *(parks.vic.gov.au)*, a wonderful revegetated tract of forest with its own walking trail. Look up to spot koalas snoozing or munching on eucalyptus leaves.

GETTING AROUND

V/Line trains run from Melbourne to Bairnsdale. From there, V/Line coaches will get you to Lakes Entrance, Orbost, Marlo and Genoa, from where a local bus operates to Mallacoota a few times a week. To get to any of the national parks and to explore with any degree of flexibility, you'll need a car. It's about 240km (three hours) from Bairnsdale to Mallacoota.

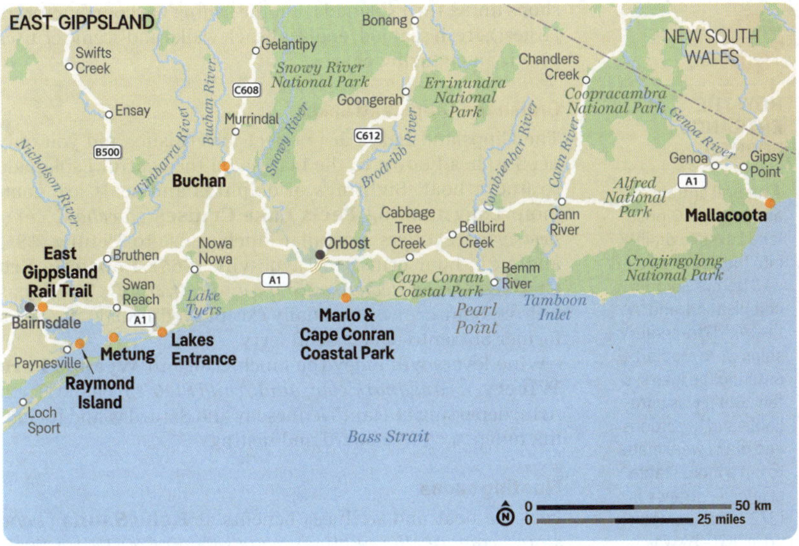

East Gippsland Rail Trail

TIME FROM PAYNESVILLE: **15MIN**

Cycle from Bairnsdale to Orbost

North of the coast, this scenic 96km walking and cycling **path** *(eastgippslandrailtrail.com.au)* runs along the former railway line between Bairnsdale and Orbost, passing through Bruthen and Nowa Nowa and close to several other small communities. By bike, the trail can comfortably be done in two days (even one day on an e-bike), but allow longer to explore the countryside with a detour on the 17km **Gippsland Lakes Discovery Trail** *(railtrails.org.au)* to Lakes Entrance.

Highlights include the 27km from Bruthen to Nowa Nowa through the Colquhoun State Forest and across the 276m Stony Creek trestle bridge, and the final 38km from Nowa Nowa to Orbost. Towards the end, you pass the partially restored **Snowy River Rail Bridge**, an almost 1km-long trestle bridge. When the community-led restoration is complete, you'll be able to walk or cycle the length of the bridge.

Orbost-based **Snowy River Cycling** *(snowyrivercycling.com.au; e-bikes per day from $110, bike & rider transfers $350)* runs a range of multiday cycling tours.

TOP TIP

Pull in at **Kalimna Lookout** or **Jemmy's Point Lookout** for super views over Lakes Entrance and Ninety Mile Beach. Other good Gippsland Lakes views are from the cliffs at **Nyerimilang Heritage Park** or a cruise boat.

Lakes Entrance

TIME FROM BAIRNSDALE: **35MIN**

Your first view of Lakes Entrance as you drive down from the elevated Kalimna area is spectacular, with the shallow Cunninghame Arm waterway separating the town, Ninety Mile Beach and the rugged ocean. This is Gippsland family-holiday central – in summer, a packed-out tourist town with a strip of motels, caravan parks, mini-golf courses and souvenir shops lining the Esplanade. But the fishing harbour (Victoria's largest), fresh seafood, endless beach walks and scenic cruises give it an enduring charm.

Cruise the Gippsland Lakes

The Gippsland Lakes are perfect for cruising and you only need to head down to the marina on the central Esplanade to find a boat. Sightings of dolphins and seals are common. Longstanding **Peels Lake Cruises** *(facebook.com/peelscruises)* offers a popular lunch cruise to Metung ($85) and a 2½-hour cruise to Paynesville ($65). **Lonsdale Eco Cruises** *(lonsdalecruises.com.au; adult/child $70/45)* has a three-hour cruise (1pm daily except Wednesday) aboard a former Sorrento–Queenscliff ferry.

Wine lovers will enjoy the lunch cruise to **Wyanga Park Winery** *(wyangapark.com; adult/child $120/45)* on the North Arm, departing at 11am Wednesday and Saturday and including lunch, a cheese board and tastings.

Floating sauna

Feel the heat and wellness benefits at **Koho Sauna** *(kohosauna.com.au; 1hr public/private session $40/150)*, a floating wood-fired sauna where you can raise a sweat then jump straight into the waters of the Cunninghame Arm to cool off (then repeat). Reinvented from the former Floating Dragon restaurant, it's a stunning modern design but an ancient process. Public sessions are shared but limited to four people. Open Thursday to Sunday by appointment.

HOW THE ENTRANCE FORMED

A natural entrance allowing the Gippsland Lakes to drain into the ocean existed well before European colonisation, and by the mid-19th-century ships were regularly entering the lake system. But it was unreliable and hazardous and plans were made to cut a more stable artificial entrance in 1872. It was completed in 1890, by which time a town called Cunninghame had been established, attracting steamboats and holidaymakers as well as serving the timber industry. The town was renamed Lakes Entrance in 1915. In addition to retaining its early reputation as a popular place for tourists and retirees, Lakes Entrance today has the largest fishing fleet in Victoria and is the hub of the Gippsland Lakes.

Metung

TIME FROM LAKES ENTRANCE: **20MIN**

Soak in the hot springs

The subterranean geothermal waters that feed **Metung Hot Springs** *(metunghotsprings.com; from $65)* have been around forever but have more recently been developed into a fabulous sprawling spa complex with numerous public and private pools, some with views over the lakes. Admission is valid for the full day from your booked time and includes access to hot pools in the Lagoon Precinct, Bathing Ridge and Hilltop Escarpment, as well as individual barrel baths and a lakeside sauna. There's even accommodation (p630) in glamping tents. The water is 45°C at its source 500m below the surface, but the pools are a few degrees lower.

EATING IN LAKES ENTRANCE: OUR PICKS

Try the 'Taste of Sodafish' set menu ($69) for the full experience

Off the Wharf: Fresh seafood dishes, straight from the boat; it's behind the Lakes Entrance Fishermen's Co-op on Bullock Island. *9am-4pm Tue-Sun* $$

Wyanga Park Winery: Arrive on a boat cruise or drive here to enjoy local food paired with the winery's own bottles. *10am-5pm Sun-Thu, to 9pm Fri & Sat* $$

Servo: Opposite Lakes Entrance's footbridge is this sprawling former petrol station serving drinks and pub food. *noon-6pm Sun-Thu, to 9pm Fri & Sat*

Sodafish: Waterfront dining doesn't get better than this floating harbour restaurant; fresh seafood is paired with Gippsland wines. *noon-3pm & 5-9pm* $$$

Metung Hot Springs

FILEDIMAGE/SHUTTERSTOCK

Buchan

TIME FROM LAKES ENTRANCE: **40MIN**

Subterranean wonders

Victoria's most amazing limestone caverns, **Buchan Caves** *(parks.vic.gov.au; tour adult/child $26.60/15.60)* have been dazzling visitors with their natural fantasy world of glistening calcite formations for over 100 years.

There are daily one-hour guided tours of Royal and Fairy Caves, or you can time your visit to see both. Royal has more colour, a higher chamber and dripping candle-like formations, while Fairy has more delicate decorations and potential fairy sightings. Both are spectacular. Buchan Caves Reserve is a pretty spot with shaded picnic areas, walking tracks, grazing kangaroos and a camping ground.

The Gunaikurnai people are the Traditional Custodians and the reserve is jointly managed with Parks Victoria, which runs the cave tours; check the schedule online and book at least a day in advance.

Marlo & Cape Conran Coastal Park

TIME FROM LAKES ENTRANCE: **1HR**

Beaches, brews and bushland

Detour off the highway to Marlo, a pretty coastal hamlet at the mouth of the Snowy River. There's a fabulous **pub**

METUNG'S LEGEND ROCK

Metung is one of the prettiest towns on the Gippsland Lakes, with the main road caressing Bancroft Bay where boats bob in the marina. In the water in front of Metung Yacht Club lies **Legend Rock**, a significant site for the Gunaikurnai people.

The story goes that fishermen from the Tatungalung group had hauled in many fish with their nets but ate more than their share while neglecting to feed the dogs. As a way of punishment, the women – guardians of social law – turned them to stone.Two similar rocks were blown up to make way for the coast-hugging Metung Rd. This formation was saved when community members and Gippsland and East Gippsland Aboriginal Cooperative issued an injunction.

DRINKING IN EAST GIPPSLAND: TOP PUBS

Marlo Hotel: Savour an afternoon beer on the wooden verandah of the Marlo Hotel (1886), with views of the Snowy River flowing to the ocean. *11am-midnight*

Metung Hotel: Iconic pub with big windows and a terrace deck, making the most of the water views over Bancroft Bay. *11am-late*

Lake Tyers Beach Tavern: Relaxed pub on Ninety Mile Beach. Craft beers on tap and local fish and chips on the waterfront terrace. *10am-late*

Buchan Caves Hotel: Call in for a beer and parma at the 1882 Buchan pub; it burned down in 2014 but was rebuilt after a community crowdfunding campaign. *11am-late*

TOP EAST GIPPSLAND NATIONAL PARKS

Snowy River National Park: Deep gorges carved through limestone and sandstone by the Snowy River on its route from the Snowy Mountains in NSW.

Errinundra National Park: Victoria's largest cool-temperate rainforest and one of East Gippsland's most outstanding natural areas with three granite outcrops.

Croajingolong National Park: Pristine beaches, inlets, estuaries and forests for camping, walking, swimming and surfing. Point Hicks was the first part of Australia to be spotted by Captain Cook and the *Endeavour* crew in 1770.

Cape Conran Coastal Park: Blissfully undeveloped part of the coast with long stretches of remote white-sand beaches. The 19km coastal route from Marlo to Cape Conran is bordered by banksia trees.

MAGGIE MCGUINNESS/SHUTTERSTOCK

(marlohotel.com.au) here, some lovely deserted beaches and, on the remote road to Cape Conran, **Sailors Grave Brewing** *(sailorsgravebrewing.com)* where you can taste the craft beers in a surreal bushland setting (open Wednesday to Sunday).

Continue along the coastal road bordered by banksia trees, grass plains, sand dunes and the ocean, to **Cape Conran Coastal Park** *(parks.vic.gov.au)*. If there's a more pristine, undeveloped yet accessible beach in Victoria, do let us know. The long stretches of remote white sand seem to go on forever and dolphins dance in the waves. This is a place for beach walks, bushwalks, spotting wildlife, swimming and snorkelling. It's an easy 15km drive back to the A1 highway.

The Aboriginal Gunaikurnai people are the Traditional Custodians of Cape Conran.

Mallacoota

TIME FROM LAKES ENTRANCE: 2½HR

Out on the water

The state's most easterly town, snuggled on the vast Mallacoota Inlet, is surrounded by the tumbling hills and beachside dunes of Croajingolong National Park. You'll be treated to long, empty surf beaches, tidal estuaries and swimming, fishing and boating on the inlet. Take a stand-up paddleboard on the estuary or head out on an eagle-spotting **boat cruise** *(mallacootacruises.com; $50)* aboard the MV *Loch-Ard*. There are plenty of ways to play in the water. Visit **Surf Shack** *(surfshack.com.au)* for ideas and equipment hire.

Mallacoota Inlet

Stay in an island lighthouse

The windswept 154-hectare **Gabo Island** is home to seabirds and Australia's second-largest colony of little penguins. It has an operating red-granite **lighthouse** (1862); you can stay in the old lighthouse caretaker's **cottage** *(parks.vic.gov.au)* but it requires a minimum of three nights (sleeps up to eight people). Getting to the island by chartered boat also requires some planning and minimum numbers. Contact **Wilderness Coast Charters** *(04-1739 8068; for up to 6 people $990)*.

Bushwalking in Croajingolong

The eastern end of remote **Croajingolong National Park** *(parks.vic.gov.au)* surrounds Mallacoota but the mighty park stretches west to Bemm River along 100km of coastline. Since 1977, these landscapes and ecosystems have been a UNESCO World Biosphere Reserve, with 70 types of native wildflowers, 52 kinds of mammals and 250 bird species. This area was badly affected by 2019–2020 bushfires and later floods, and while the forest is recovering, some areas remain closed. From Mallacoota, you can drive 15km south via Secret Beach to **Shipwreck Creek** camping ground, from where there are lots of short bushwalks.

SAVING OLD-GROWTH FOREST

East Gippsland is renowned for its remote national parks and the old-growth forest protected within them, but until recently it was also known for its logging and timber industry. Towns like Orbost and Cann River were built on timber milling, but logging of native forest on public land was officially banned by the Victorian state government in 2024 after years of environmental pressure. Discoveries of threatened species such as the endangered Leadbeater's possum (Victoria's faunal emblem), which is only found in mountain ash forests of Victoria's central highlands, led to buffer zones and eventually the statewide ban. Logging is still permitted on private land and on plantations, but these days you'll see far fewer logging trucks pounding the roads.

Victoria's High Country

ALPINE SPORTS | FOOD & WINE | HISTORIC TOWNS

Places

The Great Dividing Range provides a mountain playground for skiers and snowboarders in winter, and bushwalkers and mountain bikers in summer. The main resort peaks of Mt Buller, Mt Hotham and Falls Creek receive a blanket of fairly reliable snow in the brief winter season, but the scenery is unrelentingly spectacular across the Victorian Alps year-round.

For many travellers, though, it's the valleys, vineyards and farmland below the mountaintops where the real all-season essence of the High Country plays out. Historic gold-rush towns appear like pop-up movie sets, while easy long-distance rail-trail cycling routes, epic horseback adventures, gourmet food and wine regions, frequent festivals and spectacular bursts of autumn colour – hello Bright! – draw awestruck visitors throughout the year. You can be as active or as indulgent as you want here: the High Country rarely disappoints.

TOP TIP

Hiking or cycling in the Victorian Alps can be dangerous. If you get lost, use the **Emergency Plus** *(emergencyplus.com.au)* app to call for help. If heading to remote areas with no phone coverage, carry an EPIRB (distress beacon).

Mansfield & Around

TIME FROM MELBOURNE: **2½HR**

Mansfield is the gateway to the Southern Alps and Victoria's largest snowfields at Mt Buller, but is an exciting all-season destination in its own right, with horse riding and mountain biking popular in summer and a buzzing atmosphere in winter when the snow bunnies hit town.

Horse riding in the High Country

Mansfield is the base to live out your High Country horse-riding fantasies, with trail rides to suit all abilities. **Watson's Mountain Country Trail Rides** *(watsonstrailrides.com.au)* and **McCormacks Mountain Valley Trail Rides** *(mountainvalleytrailrides.com.au)* are two experienced

GETTING AROUND

The High Country lies east of the Hume Hwy (M31) between Melbourne and Albury Wodonga and this is the quickest route to most towns. A more interesting and scenic drive from Melbourne is through the Yarra Valley and Ranges via Healesville, Alexandra and Yea. V/Line offers train/bus connections to most of the towns via Melbourne; in winter, there are direct bus services to the ski resorts from either Melbourne or the gateways towns, but getting around parts of the region can be problematic without a car.

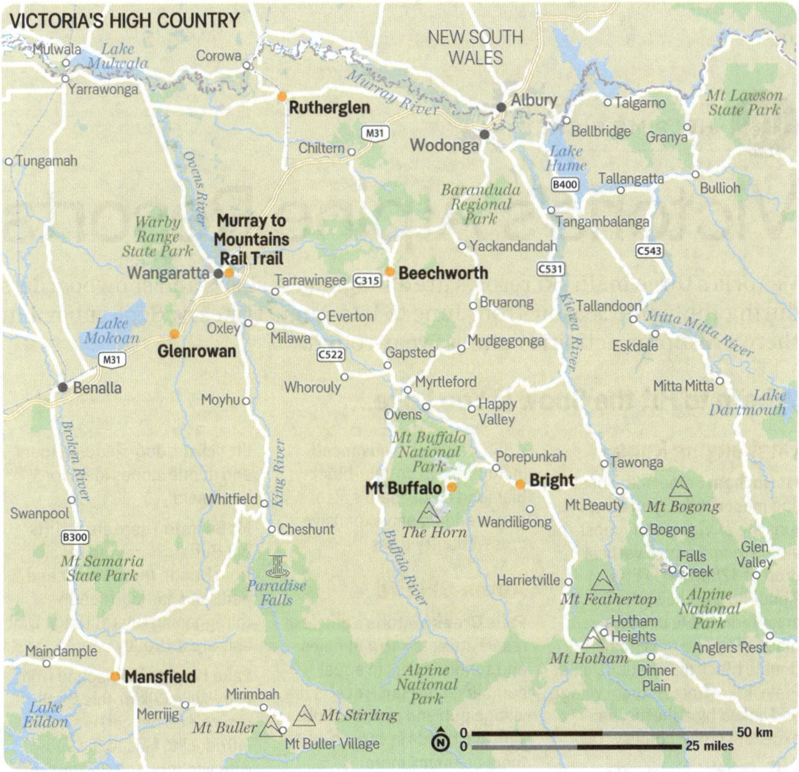

operators offering everything from one- or two-hour trail rides for beginners (from $75/120) to full-day rides and multiday 'Man from Snowy River' adventures that take you deep into the High Country to Mt Stirling and beyond.

Cycle the Great Victorian Rail Trail

If two wheels are more your thing, the 134km **Great Victorian Rail Trail** *(greatvictorianrailtrail.com.au)* from Mansfield to Tallarook is great for cyclists – as well as walkers and horse riders. As if the scenery wasn't enough, a series of 27 art installations appear like 3D apparitions at points along

Continued on p610

EATING & DRINKING IN MANSFIELD: OUR PICKS

Mansfield Regional Produce Store: Popular rustic store-cafe with a changing blackboard menu, locals wines and artisanal produce. *8.30am-5pm* **$$**

Mansfield Coffee Merchant: This cavernous modern space is the place for coffee lovers with beans roasted on-site, plus good breakfasts. *6am-3pm* **$$**

Mansfield Hotel: Mansfield has three fine country pubs but we like this big corner landmark (1862) with an outdoor courtyard terrace. *noon-8.30pm* **$$**

Anvil Brewing: Mansfield's newest brewery has three signature beers on tap, plus guest beers, a pub-style menu and pizzas. *noon-late Thu-Sun* **$$**

HELP ME PICK:

Victoria's Alpine Resorts

Victoria's three main ski resorts are a magnet for skiers and snowboarders during the 'white season' from June to late August or early September, but there are alpine activities almost year-round.

Where to Hit the Snow if You Love...

Challenging Runs

Mt Hotham Some of the best and most challenging downhill runs are at Victoria's highest alpine resort, with a vertical drop of 428m and 14 lifts. About 80% of the ski trails are intermediate or advanced black-diamond runs (four double black diamonds). Dinner Plain, 10km from Hotham village and linked by a shuttle, has excellent cross-country trails.

Falls Creek Combining a picturesque alpine setting with impressive slopes, Falls has excellent downhill skiing, 15 lifts and a vertical drop of 267m, plus 65km of groomed cross-country trails. You can even heli-hop across to Hotham.

FILEDIMAGE/SHUTTERSTOCK

Mt Buller

Mt Buller Victoria's largest resort, with 19 lifts and a vertical drop of 430m across 300 hectares of skiable terrain – 55% of runs are advanced including two double-black-diamond runs. There's also dog-sledding and expansive cross-country trails.

Apres-Ski Life

Falls Creek Victoria's glitziest resort attracts snow bunnies and serious skiers in equal numbers. The **Man Hotel** is the village pub and nightlife hub with live bands in season, but there are many more.

Mt Buller With over 7000 beds and plenty of day-trippers, nightlife here is robust and the village atmosphere is always vibrant in snow season: the **Kooroora Hotel** pub and the bar at the **Arlberg** are reliable options.

Mt Hotham Plenty of ski-in/ski-out apres-ski cafes and nightlife venues like the **General** pub and the **Dinner Plain Hotel**.

Family Fun

Mt Buller Generally considered the most family-friendly of the 'big mountains', Buller has gentle runs around the village, snow play areas, dog-sledding tours and a cinema.

Mt Baw Baw Victoria's smallest downhill skiing resort and the closest to Melbourne. There are seven lifts, relatively cheap lift tickets, dog-sledding tours and gentle slopes ideal for beginners.

Mt Buffalo There are no lifts but Buffalo is easy to reach from Bright, free to enter and park, and has kid-friendly tobogganing runs at Dingo Dell and Cresta Valley.

Lake Mountain Reached from Marysville (21km), this small resort ($68 per car) is all about introducing kids to the snow with a tobogganing area, cross-country skiing and a restaurant.

Off-Mountain Gateways

Bright/Harrietville Bright is the main access town for Hotham and Falls Creek, with plentiful accommodation, transport options and snow-gear hire. Harrietville is smaller but closer to Hotham.

Mt Beauty/Tawonga A base and gateway for Falls Creek, with a small number of accommodation places, camping and the Falls Creek Coach Service.

Mansfield/Merrijig Mansfield is the main town before Mt Buller, with a range of accommodation and services, including the winter bus service with Mansfield Mt Buller Buslines *(mmbl.com.au)*.

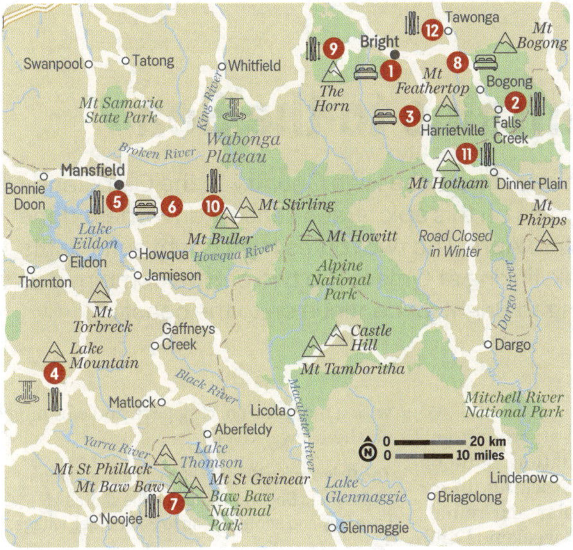

SIGHTS

1 Bright
2 Falls Creek
3 Harrietville
4 Lake Mountain
5 Mansfield
6 Merrijig
7 Mt Baw Baw
8 Mt Beauty
9 Mt Buffalo
10 Mt Buller
11 Mt Hotham
12 Tawonga

HOW TO

When to go Victoria's snow season officially starts in early June and runs into September, depending on snow cover. Peak is July/August and weekends are at a premium. Spring skiing on a sunny day in September is as good as it gets. Avoid school holidays in early July.

Book ahead If staying on-mountain at Falls, Hotham or Buller, you'll need to book accommodation and parking permits in advance (best through dedicated online booking sites). Hassle-free day trips run from gateway towns in winter.

Transport If driving in winter, you must carry and fit chains where required; parking (resort permit) is expensive and snow driving isn't easy! Winter bus services run from gateway towns and there are direct shuttles from Melbourne to the main resorts.

On a budget You can't avoid the main expenses such as gear hire and lift tickets. To keep costs down, stay in shared accommodation or off mountain, take the bus or car-pool, self-cater at the resort supermarket and visit midweek and early or late in the season.

Hiking & Biking Green Season

The mountains attract adventurous types after the snow melts – mostly hikers and mountain bikers. The websites for all resorts have detailed 'summer' pages.

Mt Buller is one of Victoria's great gravity mountain biking destinations, with the Northside Express chairlift carrying riders and bikes on weekends through summer. The 46km-long Australian Alpine Epic is for advanced mountain bike riders. Buller also has Victoria's only via ferrata, a high-altitude climbing course, at Rockwire *(rockwire.com.au)*.

Hotham is legendary for its day and multiday hikes, including the 37km Alpine Crossing, the challenging 22km-return Feathertop–Razorback trail and the full-day Huts Walk. Easier is the Mt Hotham Summit Walk (3.5km return), with views of Feathertop and Razorback.

Falls Creek has 50km of gravity-fed bike trails; a mountain bike shuttle service operates on weekends. It's also popular for trail running and hiking around Rocky Valley Lake.

ROAD TRIP

From Mountains to the Sea

Take the backroad shortcut from the High Country to the Gippsland coast over the mountains on this epic 'green season' drive, best done between November and April. The two routes from Bright summit Mt Hotham or Falls Creek, linking at Omeo. The two can be combined as a scenic loop returning to Bright, or continue on to the coast at Lakes Entrance.

1 Bright

Bright (p614) is the ideal starting point with plenty of accommodation, outdoor activities and shops for stocking up on supplies and fuel. It's popular year-round, so book ahead and avoid weekends and school holidays if possible.

The Drive: It's a steep and winding 32km drive to Mt Beauty in the Kiewa Valley, with alpine views from Tawonga Gap and Sullivans Lookout.

2 Mt Beauty

At the foot of Victoria's highest mountain, **Mt Bogong** (1986m), Mt Beauty is the gateway to Falls Creek. It's a small community with a mountain biking park and camping on the Kiewa River.

The Drive: It's a winding 15km on Bogong High Plains Rd to Bogong Village on the shores of Lake Guy and another 17km to Falls Creek village.

3 Falls Creek

Falls Creek (1842m) combines alpine views with a summer mountain biking scene and hiking across the Bogong High Plains. A bike shuttle service operates on weekends in summer and daily in January. Short walks off the main road lead to historic cattle-droving huts.

DARIA NIPOT/SHUTTERSTOCK

Mt Beauty

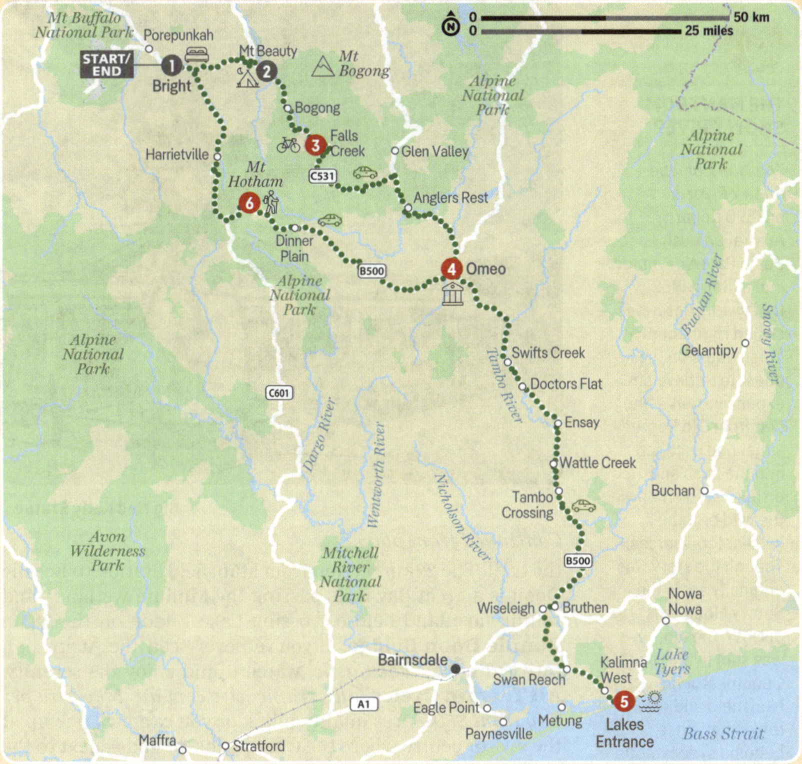

The Drive: The road beyond Rocky Valley Dam generally opens a month or two after snow season ends; check in advance. It's around 50km to Anglers Rest, home to camping areas and a pub, then another 28km to Omeo.

4 Omeo

Omeo was a booming gold-mining town in the late 19th century; today it's an important High Country service town with many of the grand buildings remaining, including the post office and courthouse. Grab a picnic and check out the mountain biking streetart near Livingstone Park.

The Drive: Loop back to Bright, or continue south on the Great Alpine Rd following the Tambo River via Swifts Creek, Ensay and Bruthen to the coast at Lakes Entrance, a 130km drive.

5 Lakes Entrance

You've made it – the mountains to the sea! Savour the view as you drive into Lakes Entrance – the namesake lakes and ocean beyond are stunning on a sunny day.

The Drive: To return to Bright, take the alternative route via Omeo and Mt Hotham. From Omeo, the road climbs gently eastward for 55km via Dinner Plain to Mt Hotham.

6 Mt Hotham

Mt Hotham (1862m) is a much more open summit than Falls Creek, with incredible alpine views on a clear day. The Hotham village pub is usually open in summer. Heading towards Bright, you'll enjoy some of Victoria's most expansive alpine vistas. Diamantina Hut is the starting point for the Razorback–Feathertop trail. From Hotham, the road winds down for 30km to Harrietville village, then another 20 minutes to Bright.

THE MAN FROM SNOWY RIVER

The Man from the Snowy River is an 1890 poem by Australian bush poet Banjo Paterson, made into a film in 1982, that vividly describes skilled High Country horse riders on their quest to retrieve an expensive colt – 'the colt from Old Regret' – that had escaped into the bush and disappeared among the wild brumbies (wild or feral horses). Though the story was originally set in the Snowy Mountains of NSW, the film was shot in the High Country around Mansfield and the region has since become synonymous with the theme. The northern Victorian town of Corryong also claims local stockman Jack Riley as an inspiration for the poem and celebrates with the annual **Man from Snowy River Bush Festival** *(bushfestival.com.au)*.

PAUL HARDING 00/SHUTTERSTOCK

Big Ned Kelly Statue

Continued from p605

the trail. The 22km section from Mansfield Station to Bonnie Doon is a great day ride, passing the Mullum wetlands and rolling farmland before crossing Lake Eildon on the 385m **Bonnie Doon Bridge**. If you've never seen the Australian satirical movie *The Castle,* watch it and enjoy the serenity. **All Terrain Cycles** *(allterraincycles.com.au; bike hire per day from $50)* hires quality bikes, or you can pick one up at the visitor centre where the trail begins (or ends), next to the old railway station.

Family fun with interactive animal encounters

On mostly cage-free grounds 10km south of town, **Mansfield Zoo** *(mansfieldzoo.com.au; adult/child $22/14)* is great for families with young kids. Collect a bucket of feed pellets on entry and you can hand-feed most of the free-roaming or fenced animals that include deer, wallabies, llamas, goats and slobbering camels. There are native animals like wombats and dingoes, while non-native species include African lions (feedings at 1.30pm on weekends), American bison and meerkats.

Thrilling trails and cross-country mountain biking

Victoria's largest winter-sports resort, **Mt Buller** *(mtbuller.com.au)* is also a great summer mountain biking destination. A network of 100km of cross-country trails around the summit and 60km of single-track and exhilarating downhill, gravity and flow trails are usually open from the first weekend of December to the end of April.

From 27 December to mid-February, the **Northside Express** *(all-day lift & trails access adult/child $88/66)* chairlift operates from Horse Hill on weekends, lifting you and your bike up to the plateau. All Terrain Cycles can arrange bookings and mountain bike hire.

In a bushranger's footsteps

The 62km 'shortcut' from Mansfield to King Valley on Whitfield Rd is a lovely subalpine drive with some super views at its crest. The road winds up into the hills via Tolmie to **Powers Lookout**. Signboards tell the fascinating story of the 19th-century 'gentleman' bushranger (outlaw) Harry Power, an associate and mentor of a young Ned Kelly, who used this remote clearing as a hideout and vantage point. Two viewpoint decks offer stupendous views over the King Valley and the mountain ranges. It's a further 20km downhill to the small town of Whitfield in the heart of the valley.

Glenrowan

TIME FROM BRIGHT: **1HR 10MIN**

Glenrowan would be an unremarkable little town, bypassed by the Hume Hwy, if not for its association with bushranger Ned Kelly. But it's also a mini wine region, with several cellar doors and a brewery north of town.

It's all about Ned

Ned Kelly is Australia's most famous bushranger (an Australian term for a 19th-century highway robber) and Glenrowan was the scene of his last stand. The main street is lined with Kelly attractions, starting with the 6m-tall rifle-wielding **Big Ned Kelly Statue**.

The excellent **Ned Kelly Discovery Hub** *(free)*, a circular viewpoint and visitor centre set in a leafy park, includes a **museum** *($5)* with panels and an immersive theatre experience explaining the siege in graphic detail.

Ned Kelly Memorial Museum & Homestead *(katescottageglenrowan.com.au; adult/child $12/2)*, behind Kate's Cottage gift shop, displays a dusty collection of Kelly memorabilia, replica suits of armour and a re-creation of the Kelly home.

Kellyland *(kellylandglenrowan.com; adult/child $34/25)* is an over-the-top but strangely captivating animated performance where Kelly's story is told in a series of rooms by a cast of surprisingly lifelike animatronic characters. It culminates in a smoky shoot-out and the hanging of Kelly, which may be too scary for young children. Check out the murals on the side of the building.

Rutherglen

TIME FROM BRIGHT: **1½HR**

Closer to the Murray than the mountains, Rutherglen is wine country. Combining marvellous gold-rush-era buildings (gold was discovered here in 1860) with northern Victoria's most celebrated winemaking tradition, the town's historic main street is a photogenic strip of antique dealers, leafy cafes and classic country pubs. Head up to the **Big Wine Bottle**, a former water tower, for good views and check out the **silo art** near the visitor centre where the Murray to Mountains Rail Trail runs past.

KELLY'S LAST STAND

A notorious bushranger and cop killer, Ned Kelly is probably Australia's best-known folk antihero, considered something of a Robin Hood figure. Born in Beveridge in 1854 of Irish descent, Ned was in trouble with the law from a young age, culminating in the shooting of two police officers at Stringybark Creek. With a reward on his head, Kelly and his gang held 60 locals hostage at the Glenrowan Hotel with a scheme to ambush a trainload of police and trackers. But the police were tipped off and a shoot-out ensued, with Ned walking out in his homemade suit of armour. Shot in the legs, Kelly was captured alive, tried in Melbourne and hanged in 1880. His death mask, armour and the gallows on which he died are on display in the Old Melbourne Gaol.

TOP RUTHERGLEN WINERIES

Rutherglen Estates: De Bortoli's large cellar door, restaurant and accommodation complex is in town. Also an Aboriginal art gallery.

All Saints Estate: The heritage-listed 19th-century castle facade greets you at this historic winery and gardens; tours ($35) at 10am and 11am.

Morris: The oldest winery in Rutherglen (1859), Morris still produces some of the best fortified wines in the region.

Stanton & Killeen Wines: Century-old winery known for its durif-shiraz blend, rosé and vintage ports. Picnic in lovely grounds.

Cofield Wines: Near the Murray River at Wahgunyah, Cofield adds sparkling wines into the mix.

Cycle between cellar doors in this wine hub

Thanks to the warm and dry climate, the Rutherglen region is famous for its fortified wines (port and muscat) and heavy reds (durif, bold shiraz and grenache) with a dozen or so wineries and cellar doors scattered around a compact area: you can easily visit a swag of wineries in half a day by bicycle.

Start at the **Rutherglen Wine Experience** *(explore rutherglen.com.au)*, where you can pick up maps, cellar-door info and hire **bikes** *(half/full day $30/40)*. The 34km **Wine Loop** takes you past some of the region's top wineries and includes a stretch of the Murray to Mountains Rail Trail to Wahgunyah on the Murray River.

Murray to Mountains Rail Trail

TIME FROM MELBOURNE: **2HR 40MIN**

Scenic off-road cycling

The **Murray to Mountains Rail Trail** *(railtrails.org.au)* is Victoria's second-longest bike path and one of the High Country's best walking/cycling trails for families or casual riders. It's sealed and relatively flat much of the way and passes through rural scenery of farms, forest and vineyards, with views of the alpine ranges.

The original 94km trail runs from Wangaratta to Bright via Myrtleford and Porepunkah. A section of the trail then heads northwest from Wangaratta to Wahgunyah via Rutherglen and another from Bright to Harrietville, completing the true Murray-to-mountains experience. An excellent branch trail runs from Everton to Yackandandah (48km) via Beechworth (17km) and there are shorter rides to Milawa and Oxley.

Beechworth-based **Bike Hire Company** *(thebikehire company.com.au)* rents bikes, including e-bikes, which can be delivered anywhere along the trail.

Beechworth

TIME FROM BRIGHT: **1HR**

Beechworth was built on gold and is listed by the National Trust as one of Victoria's two 'notable' towns (the other is Maldon) thanks to its well-preserved gold-rush past, historic honey-coloured granite buildings, spooky gaol and connections to the Kelly family and other bushranging folklore. The Beechworth area is the ancestral homeland of the Dhudhuroa people.

Pair your beer with Mexican Food - tacos, burritos or quesadillas

EATING & DRINKING IN RUTHERGLEN: OUR PICKS

Caffeine N Machine: Dozens of shiny old motorcycles decorate this welcoming industrial-style cafe, open early for a caffeine fix. *6.30am-5pm* $

Pickled Sisters Café: Light-filled main-street cafe that uses local produce in its regularly changing menu. *10am-9pm Thu-Sat, to 4pm Sun & Mon* $$

Parker Pies: Local bakery known for its gourmet pies (emu, venison, kangaroo, crocodile) along with your standard steak and mushroom. *8am-5pm* $

Convent Brewery: In the historic Rutherglen Convent, this excellent brewery has five craft beers and a cider on tap. *noon-late Fri-Sun*

MILAWA & KING VALLEY TOURING

By bike or car, spend a day touring the High Country's premier gourmet food region and a prosperous cool-climate wine region noted for Italian varietals.

START	END	LENGTH
Milawa	Whitfield	70km; 3hr to 1 day

In the village of Milawa, 1 **Brown Brothers** is the region's oldest (1889) and best-known winery, with a welcoming cellar door, tours and a fine restaurant with a grazing menu. Only 2km north, pick up some flavour-filled jars at 2 **Milawa Mustards**, then continue on to 3 **Milawa Cheese Company** where you can enjoy a cheese-tasting experience; also stop by the Milawa Bread cafe and bakery next door. If you like olives, detour 10km east to the lush groves at 4 **EV Olives** to taste its oils, olives and tapenades (call 0400 005 609 for appointment).

Head back along the Snow Rd through Milawa towards Oxley to reach 5 **Sam Miranda** winery, which has a cellar door and a fine-dining restaurant (bookings essential); the rows of vines produce a range of Italian wines. Turn south for 15km to the little village of Moyhu for quality meals served at its rustic country pub, the 6 **Moyhu Hotel**.

Continuing south, you're now in the King Valley as the road starts to parallel the King River. It's about 20km from Moyhu to 7 **King River Brewing**, a lovely German-style beer garden with a taphouse in an old tobacco kiln. Ask about the seasonal brews. It's another 5km to Whitfield where you'll find 8 **Dal Zotto Wines**, famous for its prosecco. Finish your tour with dinner at Whitfield's 10 **Mountain View Hotel**.

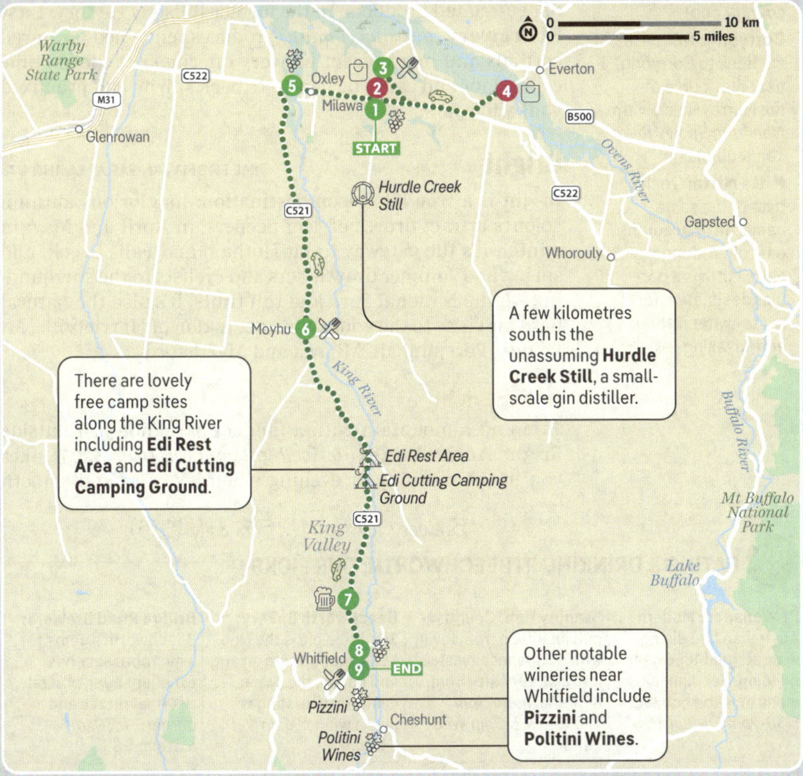

HISTORIC HIGH COUNTRY TOWNS

Chiltern: Like an old-time movie set, tiny Chiltern is one of Victoria's most historic townships, with 19th-century buildings and antique shops.

Yackandandah: 'Yack' is a gorgeous former gold-mining village with two pubs, great cafes and antique shops lining High St.

Stanley: Just a 10-minute drive from Beechworth, this village is worth the detour for its 1854 country pub.

Corryong: Trout fishers flock to Corryong, near the source of the Murray River, with *Man from Snowy River* connections.

Mitta Mitta: On the river of the same name, an hour southeast of Wodonga, Mitta Mitta is a popular destination for white-water rafting and kayaking.

Historic and spooky Beechworth

Beechworth's Historic Precinct on Ford St is a photogenic collection of 19th-century buildings including the old **Telegraph Office** and the **Courthouse** *(explorebeechworth.com.au; adult/child $15/12)*, where guided tours and the **Kelly Trials Exhibition** take place daily. Also worth a visit is the **Burke Museum** *(adult/child $8/6)* with gold-rush relics and an arcade of shopfronts preserved as they were around 150 years ago. Tickets for both can be purchased at the visitor centre, where you can also ask about guided walks.

Beechworth's old **gaol** *(theobg.com.au; tour adult/child $28/22)* can be visited on guided tours packed with fascinating tales of its most infamous inmates – namely Ned Kelly, his family and sympathisers. Tours start at 10am, 11am, noon and 1.30pm. For the spookiest tours in town, head to the **Beechworth Asylum**, a decommissioned psychiatric hospital on Mayday Hills south of the centre. **Asylum Ghost Tours** *(asylumghosttours.com; from $48)*, nightly from Thursday to Sunday, tell supernatural stories and historical tales.

Bees and brews

Don't leave Beechworth without checking out two of its epicurean experiences. The **Beechworth Honey Shop** *(beechworthhoney.com.au)* sells locally produced honey and all sorts of bee-related products. In the former Billsons Factory, **Last St Brewery** *(billsons.com.au)* produces renowned flavoured cordials and more recent brewery offerings; at the sublime cellar door and cafe, you can taste beer, spirits and premixed vodka flavours.

Bright

TIME FROM WANGARATTA: **1HR**

Bright is a true all-season destination: its glorious autumn colours attract droves of 'leaf peepers' in April and May; in winter, it's the gateway to Mt Hotham and Falls Creek; and spring and summer draw hikers and cyclists to the surrounding Alpine National Park and rail trails. It's also the natural base for visits to the wider gourmet region of Harrietville, Mt Beauty, Porepunkah, Milawa and Myrtleford.

Active Bright

Jump off a mountain with a tandem paraglide just outside Bright. **Active Flight** *(activeflight.com.au; from $225)* takes you in the morning or evening when it's calm and smooth

Brewery tours at 11.15am daily ($15)

EATING & DRINKING IN BEECHWORTH: OUR PICKS

Provenance: Modern Australian fine dining in an elegant 1856 bank building. Set dinner menu must be booked. *5.30-9pm Fri-Sun* **$$$**

Stanley Pub: Country pub just 10km from town, with a Japanese twist and a sweet cafe (from 8.30am). *noon-3pm Thu-Sun & 6-8pm Wed-Sat* **$$**

Beechworth Bakery: Signature pie is the Ned Kelly, topped with an egg and bacon; the sweet custardy bee-sting is also a winner. *6am-6.30pm* **$**

Bridge Road Brewers: Beechworth's gem of a microbrewery has excellent beer, pretzels, gourmet pizzas and burgers. *11.30am-8.30pm* **$$**

PAUL HARDING 00/SHUTTERSTOCK

Beechworth Honey Shop

and you get to experience flying for about eight to 10 minutes before touching down. **Bright Flight** *(brightflight.com.au; from $225)* can land you in a vineyard.

Bright's **Mystic Bike Park** *(elevationmystic.com; pass per day/week $20/50)* is a popular community mountain bike park, with some 500m of vertical drop and stunning views. It's accessible for beginners and experts but experienced riders should consider the **Gravity Uplift Pass** *($100)*.

Starting at Howitt Park, the **Canyon Walking Track** takes you 2.5km to a suspension bridge over the Ovens River and a small rocky canyon. For a longer walk, continue along to the second bridge. Alternatively, hire bikes in Bright and hit the **Wandiligong Bike Path** for an easy 12km return ride.

Mt Buffalo

TIME FROM BRIGHT: **45MIN**

Mt Buffalo is an easily accessible year-round destination. In winter it's a tiny, fee-free family-friendly resort, with enough snow for tobogganing runs and cross-country skiing around Dingo Dell and Cresta Valley. In summer, it's a hub for bushwalking, mountain biking, road cycling, rock climbing and camping at Lake Catani.

ALL-SEASON BRIGHT

Selena Blair-Holt from the legendary Bright Brewery (p616) says life in Bright rarely slows down.

I love that there's always something going on here and every season has its own appeal. People travel from all over Australia to see the autumn leaves change colour; in winter we have a thriving snow economy with visitors heading to the mountains. Summer is the busiest time in Bright. The Ovens River is great for swimming and kayaking and we're lucky to have Mystic Park for mountain bikers. Some of my favourites are **La Cigale** for soups and cheese platters, Tomahawks (p616) for burgers and lamb ribs, **Hometown** for pizza, **Basils** for a fancy meal and **Billy Button** winery.

EATING AROUND BRIGHT: COUNTRY PUBS

Wandi Pub: Great pub meals of steaks, parma and pizza, local craft beers and a country-pub vibe; in Wandilong, 7km south of Bright. *noon-late* $$

Alpine Hotel: The Alpine has a reliable bistro menu, bar meals and the fancier Tigre Vita with three-course degustation. *noon-2pm & 5.30-8.30pm* $$

Porepunkah Pub: Social hub where steaks sit alongside veggie options and craft beers flow. The rail trail runs past. *from 4pm Mon-Wed, from noon Thu-Sat* $$

Happy Valley Hotel: On the rail trail in Ovens, near Myrtleford, with a beer garden and an atmospheric dining room serving pub classics. *noon-2pm & 6-8pm* $$

TOP HIGH COUNTRY FESTIVALS

Tastes of Rutherglen: A weekend of indulgence in March; shuttle bus links the wineries.

Roam Rutherglen: Australia's original wine festival (formerly Winery Walkabout) in June; huge event of music, food vans and wine tasting.

Bright Autumn Festival: Markets, music, open gardens, scenic convoy tours and a popular gala day celebrate Bright's autumn colours in April or May.

Brighter Days: Charitable car, motorbike and music festival draws petrol-heads and big Aussie bands to Bright on Labor Day weekend (March).

Spring Ditch!: In March, this music and food festival in the village of Stanley, 10 minutes' drive from Beechworth, is classic country fun.

FILEDIMAGE/SHUTTERSTOCK

Mt Buffalo Chalet

Hit the trails

For much of the year, road cyclists use Buffalo as a training run. It's around 34km from Porepunkah to Cresta Valley on the sealed Mt Buffalo Rd – the remaining few kilometres to Horn Lookout are unsealed.

A wide range of marked hikes criss-cross Buffalo, many leading to waterfalls and lookouts. A good first stop is the historic **Mt Buffalo Chalet**, a former resort and gardens that closed in 2007 but has been preserved with government funding. A cafe is proposed to open here. From the car park, wheelchair-accessible steel walkways lead to superb lookouts. The **Gorge Walk** is an easy 2.5km stroll from here, or you can set out on the 4km **Lake Catani Track**. One of the park's best day hikes is the 12km **Big Walk** from the Eurobin Picnic Area at the base of the mountain to the Gorge car park. Allow eight hours up and back.

EATING & DRINKING IN BRIGHT: OUR PICKS

Live music sessions on Sundays

Tomahawks: Cosy cafe and well-stocked bar serving share plates and small dishes such as tacos or fried squid. *noon-11pm Wed-Sun* $$

Reed & Co: Two chefs-turned-distillers use local botanicals, with gin-tasting tours, a Japanese restaurant and the great Sixpence Cafe. *from 1pm Tue-Sat*

Ringer Reef Winery: Drink in the Mt Buffalo views in Porepunkah while enjoying live music and grazing platters with wine tastings. *noon-5pm Thu-Tue*

Bright Brewery: Established brewery-restaurant with an exciting range of beers, huge terrace, good food and riverside location. *11.30am-10pm*

Mildura & the Murray

RIVER VIEWS | PADDLE STEAMERS | FRUIT & WINE

Spanning more than 2500km and three states, the mighty Murray is Australia's longest river and one of the world's great waterways. It's continuously navigable for almost 2000km, making it the third-longest navigable river on the planet, after the Amazon and the Nile.

The river is a natural divide and the Victoria–NSW border mostly follows the course of the Murray, although technically the river itself is part of NSW, with the state border at the top of the southern bank. When visiting Victorian Murray towns, you can therefore expect to be flitting between the two states multiple times a day.

Echuca is Australia's paddle-steamer capital and a popular destination for cruises from its historic wharf. Swan Hill, 150km away, has an open-air riverbank pioneer museum, while 220km further you'll reach sunny Mildura with its fruit farms and vineyards made possible thanks to Murray irrigation.

Places

TOP TIP

Unlike in Echuca and Swan Hill, paddle steamers in Mildura don't operate daily. Confirm the current schedule online ahead of your visit *(paddlesteamers.com.au)*.

Echuca

TIME FROM MELBOURNE: **3HR 10MIN**

Wander Echuca's heritage-listed wharf

Venture into the **Port of Echuca Discovery Centre** *(portofechuca.com.au; free)*, on the site of the old Evans Sawmill, to learn more about Echuca's river history. Start inside for interpretive displays, then continue out to the refurbished heritage-listed wharf, now an open-air museum, to peruse more exhibits and view the paddle steamers. Look out for the docked 160-year-old PS *Adelaide,* the world's oldest working wooden-hulled paddle steamer. Plan for around one hour.

GETTING AROUND

The river towns along the Murray are most conveniently explored by car. Local bus services in Echuca, Swan Hill and Mildura are available but may have limited departures. If using public transport, check schedules in advance to avoid getting caught out *(transport.vic.gov.au).*

Echuca and Swan Hill can be reached by train from Melbourne. Mildura's train station is freight only and hasn't served passenger trains since 1993; take a bus to Mildura Station from Swan Hill or take the Sunraysia Hwy bus route via Ballarat.

PADDLE STEAMERS: WHY ECHUCA?

Echuca's port precinct was instrumental to the development of Australia's wool, timber and river trades in the latter half of the 19th century. Surrounded by red-gum forests, Echuca quickly gained a reputation for its high-quality timber and became a shipbuilding hub and the port of choice for many wool suppliers, knowing guaranteed return cargo from the fast-churning timber mills awaited their paddle steamers at Echuca Wharf. By 1895, around two-thirds of the paddle steamers and barges working on the Murray system had been built in Echuca-Moama. Today, vessels like the PS *Pevensey* and PS *Emmylou* – both featured in classic 1980s Australian TV miniseries *All the Rivers Run*, filmed on-site – continue Echuca's paddle-steamer legacy.

MASTERSKY/SHUTTERSTOCK

PS *Emmylou*, Echuca

While visitors can walk the historical street in front of the port anytime, access to the wharf is limited to the Discovery Centre's opening hours (9am to 5pm daily).

Ride a historic paddle steamer

There are several ways to chug along the Murray in Australia's paddle-steamer capital. Through the Port of Echuca (p617), PS *Pevensey*, which starred as the fictional PS *Philadephia* in acclaimed TV miniseries *All the Rivers Run*, is available for one-hour **cruises** *(adult/child $35/15)* at 10.15am, 11.30am and 1.30pm daily, along with a 2.45pm departure on weekends and select weekdays. From around October to April, weekly 90-minute **sunset cruises** *(adult/child $55/30)* are available on a seasonal schedule.

Murray River Paddlesteamers *(mrps.com.au; adult/child $35/15)* runs one-hour cruises on the 114-year-old PS *Canberra*, with three departures daily (10.15am, 11.30am, 1.15pm) and a fourth (2.30pm) on demand. Choose **Port to Plate** *(adult/child $120/15)* to add a two-course lunch or dinner at **Echuca Distillery** near the port precinct, or **Wharf to Winery** *(adult/child $110/30)* for a two-course lunch with a

EATING & DRINKING IN ECHUCA: OUR PICKS

Johnny & Lyle: Cafe breakfast and lunch menu with indoor/outdoor seating. Great option for gluten-free diners. *6am-3pm Mon-Fri, from 7am Sat & Sun* $$

Niko Niko: Casual Japanese-Korean restaurant, serving Korean fried chicken, bento boxes and sushi. *11am-2.30pm Tue-Sun, plus 5.30-8.30pm Wed-Sat* $$

Noodle Canteen: Filling, fast and affordable Asian-style noodles. Geared for takeaway, with a few dine-in seats. *11.30am-9pm Tue-Sat, 4-9pm Sun & Mon* $

Port 53: Creole and Cajun restaurant by the port. Check out the seasonally changing $15 'cheap eats' weekday lunch menu. *noon-2.30pm & 6-10pm Tue-Sat* $$

glass of wine and complimentary wine tastings at **Morrisons Winery Riverside Restaurant**.

The 113-year-old **PS *Melbourne*** *(psmelbourne.com.au)* returned to Echuca in late 2025. See the website for the latest.

Take a guided port tour

Gain a better understanding of Echuca's role in riverboat trade history in the 50 years leading up to Federation on a one-hour **Guided Walking Tour** *(adult/child $15/10)* of the port precinct, departing at 11.30am and 1.30pm daily. On Wednesdays and Saturdays at 8pm, learn the port's darker and otherworldly secrets on the **Port After Dark Tour** *($30)*, a one-hour guided walking tour by lantern light; minimum age is 16. Book both tours via *portofechuca.com.au*.

Explore the Murray's Mexican side

One hour by car from central Echuca in the town of Strathmerton, **Cactus Country** *(cactuscountry.com.au; adult/child $25/10)* is a private collection of more than 4500 species of cacti and succulents from around the world. Set on 8 hectares of arid landscape, this 'little piece of Mexico on the Murray' is Australia's largest cactus garden, taking visitors through cacti of the Andes, Arizona and Central America over eight trails, with several more in development.

To assist your self-tour, download the garden guidebook and watch the video tour by garden founder Jim Hall (QR codes on-site). At 11am, join an expert on a one-hour **guided tour** *($29)*. The guide is only on-site on days with bookings (minimum of two participants), so reserve in advance.

The restaurant menu includes nachos, tacos and cactus treats. Try the handcrafted cactus ice cream, featuring the fruit of the prickly pear, Peruvian apple and golden torch varieties from the garden on a rotational basis. Expect to spend 1½ to two hours. Closed Mondays and Tuesdays.

Swan Hill

TIME FROM MELBOURNE: **4¾HR**

Experience a historic township

The main tourist attraction of Swan Hill, the city's **Pioneer Settlement** *(pioneersettlement.com.au; adult/child $33.50/23.50)* was one of the first living history museums of its kind in Australia. In what started with the acquisition of the 1876 paddle steamer *Gem*, the recreated Mallee townscape on the banks of the Murray at Horseshoe Bend showcases relocated buildings and machinery from the turn of the 20th century.

Hop aboard the docked *Gem*, visit the town lolly shop, see the blacksmith at work and don a period costume in the drapery to take an old-timey photo in the parlour. Horse-drawn carriage and vintage-car rides are included with entry. A minimum of three hours is recommended to explore the 3-hectare site, open daily. Tickets are valid for two consecutive days and there's an on-site cafe.

THE EVOLUTION OF ECHUCA WHARF

The 1870s saw the wharf's busiest years, processing a total of 240 paddle steamers in 1872 and more than 1000 logs a week in nearby timber mills. It was dubbed the 'Chicago of the South', as arriving vessels often resorted to underhanded tactics to get their shipments of wool and wheat unloaded first. The three-level wharf underwent extensions to meet the intense demand through the 1880s, but improved rail transport, economic depression and the arrival of automobiles led the river industry into decline. During WWII, most of the wharf was dismantled to supply firewood to munitions factories in Melbourne. In 1974, the port precinct was revitalised as a tourist attraction, with the addition of the Port of Echuca Discovery Centre in 2013.

LAKE BOGA & WWII

Many visitors are surprised this tiny town by the Murray was a significant WWII base. However, it was precisely its remoteness and physical attributes that made Lake Boga the perfect location for the flying-boat repair depot. Importantly, it was far enough inland that Japanese aircraft couldn't reach the depot without needing to land and refuel, and had a sufficiently large body of water surrounded by flat, obstacle-free countryside for safe alighting. Coupled with an adjacent rail line and highway and electricity access from Swan Hill, simply put, Lake Boga ticked all the boxes. Only in the 21st century are we learning the depot's full scope of operations, including the covert 'black cat' missions, held to 60 years of secrecy.

CANDYAPPLERED IMAGES/ALAMY

Float on a 130-year-old steamer

From Horseshoe Bend Wharf at the Pioneer Settlement, take a one-hour cruise on the **PS *Pyap*** *(pioneersettlement.com.au; adult/child $29/20)*. Built in 1896, the paddle steamer once operated as a floating general store servicing over 60 settlements along the Murray. Cruises depart at 2.30pm daily, with an additional 10.30am departure on weekends and Victorian school holidays. General admission to the settlement is not required to take the cruise, but there are discounts for multi-tickets. Phone 1800 981 911 for bookings (required) or use the online contact form for enquiries.

Nightly laser shows and vintage treats

At night, the Pioneer Settlement reopens for immersive 30-minute **multimedia laser shows** *(adult/child $30/21)* incorporating water, laser lights, sound, special effects and the river setting as its backdrop. Two shows are available, alternating each night (at 8.30pm). '**Legends of the Mallee**' (Monday, Wednesday, Friday, Sunday) depicts stories from Traditional Custodians the Wamba Wamba and Wadi Wadi peoples, European exploration and nearby Lake Boga during WWII, while 'Heartbeat of the Murray' (Tuesday, Thursday, Saturday) is a journey through 30 million years of the Murray's history. After the show, patrons can purchase sweets from the settlement's vintage lolly shop.

If you're in Swan Hill for a couple of nights, there's a 25% discount for booking both shows. Reservations are required; phone 1800 981 911 or enquire online.

PS *Pyap*, Swan Hill

Visit a secret military base

A 10- to 15-minute drive from Swan Hill, **Lake Boga Flying Boat Museum** *(flyingboat.org.au; adult/child $18/10)* on the shores of Lake Boga is housed on the site of the former No 1 Flying Boat Repair Depot of the Royal Australian Air Force (RAAF). Operating from 1942 to 1947, this previously top-secret military base played a key role in Australia's defence against the Japanese in WWII, providing refuge and servicing facilities for flying boats (a type of seaplane with a waterproof hull for buoyancy) of Allied forces.

At this fascinating museum, see a restored Catalina A24-30 with an impressive 104ft wingspan, along with over 500 pieces of other WWII memorabilia. Time your visit for the 15-minute **Amazing Facts History Talk** (10am, 11am, 12.30pm, 2pm and 3pm), watch a 20-minute history movie and search war records of anyone who has served Australia in the past. Check out the original **underground communications bunker**, which has been returned to its wartime state and showcases the vital work of the Women's Auxiliary Australian Air Force (WAAAF) at the facility. Allow one to 1½ hours to fully explore the museum, open daily.

Mildura

TIME FROM SWAN HILL: **2HR 40MIN TO 3½HR**

Explore Mildura's irrigation legacy

Mildura's history as an irrigation colony began with the arrival of Canadian brothers George and William Benjamin (WB) Chaffey, who established the first irrigation scheme in Australia in present-day Mildura in 1888. It was no easy

ATTRACTIONS AROUND SWAN HILL

Riverside Park: By the river off Monash Dr, enjoy manicured lawns, picnic facilities and the Family Fun Park.

Giant Murray Cod: Next to the railway station, view a gigantic fish sculpture, one of Australia's famed 'big things'.

Art Gallery of Swan Hill: Open daily, this redeveloped gallery by the Pioneer Settlement stages changing exhibitions. Entry is by donation.

Lake Tyrrell Viewing Platform: Take in the incredible terrain of this pink salt lake from the dedicated boardwalk. Top spot for stargazing.

Silo Art Trail: Tour some of the impressive regional silo art murals, such as those at Lake Boga, Sea Lake and Nullawil.

HIGHLIGHTS
1 Rio Vista

SIGHTS
2 Feast Street
3 Langtree Mall
4 Lock 11
5 Lock Island
see 1 Mildura Art Gallery
6 Mildura Riverfront
7 Mildura Weir Lookout
8 Rio Vista Park
9 Trail of Lights

ACTIVITIES
10 Weir Track

SLEEPING
11 Mildura City Gate Motel

EATING
12 Baghdad Kitchen
13 Blk.mlk Specialty Coffee
14 Italian
15 Jessica Rabbit Cafe
see 12 Seoul Chicken & Beer

DRINKING & NIGHTLIFE
see 15 TOL Bar

ENTERTAINMENT
see 1 Mildura Arts Centre

SHOPPING
16 Sunraysia Farmers' Market

TRANSPORT
17 Mildura Station
18 Mildura Wharf

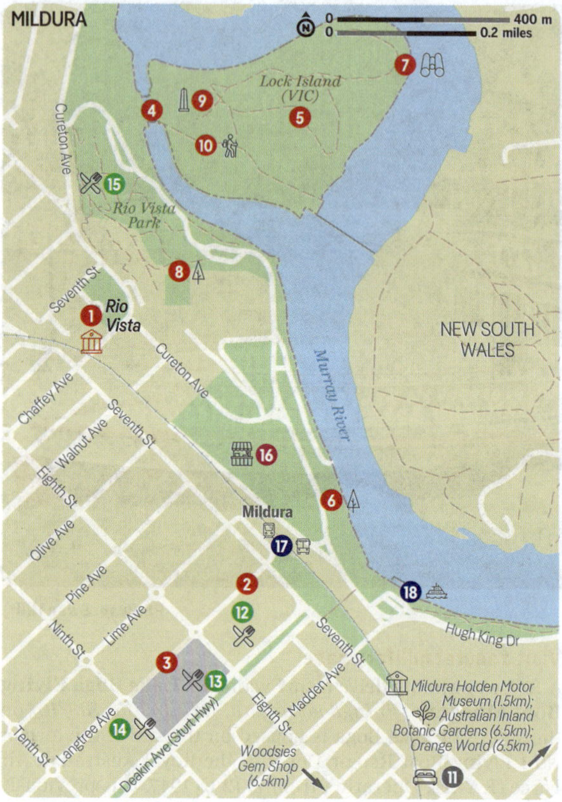

task harnessing the waters of the Murray for farming, but the Chaffeys' ambition landed them early success and the following year WB began constructing a grand Queen Anne–style residence with a distinct California feel, which he named **Rio Vista** (River View).

Despite the scheme's demise only a few years later, bankrupt WB, unable to find a buyer for the elaborate home, stayed on in Mildura and even became the borough's first mayor in 1920. Today, visitors can enter the historic home for free as part of the **Mildura Arts Centre** *(milduraartscentre.com.au)*. A section of the residence has been restored and styled to the

Complimentary lentil soup and tea

EATING & DRINKING IN MILDURA: OUR PICKS

Italian: Delectable made-to-order sandwiches filled with quality deli ingredients on house-made ciabatta. *9am-3pm Mon-Fri, 6.30-9.30pm Sat* $

Blk.mlk Specialty Coffee: Modern cafe brunch and burger menu; top choice for the morning caffeine fix. *7am-2pm Mon-Fri, from 8am Sat & Sun* $$

Seoul Chicken & Beer: Casual Korean fried chicken and BBQ restaurant with robot servers. *5-9.30pm Mon-Sat & noon-2.30pm Fri & Sat* $$

Baghdad Kitchen: Charcoal-grill Middle Eastern cuisine; try the falafel and kebab wraps. *noon-3pm & 5-10pm Wed-Fri, noon-10pm Sat & Sun* $$

times of the Chaffeys, while the rear is now the **Mildura Art Gallery**. Expect to spend 30 to 45 minutes here. Rio Vista is part of the **Chaffey Trail** *(thechaffeytrail.com.au)*, a collection of 12 sites across the Mildura region with a historical connection to the enterprising brothers.

See a lock in action

In **Rio Vista Park**, find **Lock 11**, one of 26 locks that now exist between the Murray's mouth in Goolwa (SA) and Echuca, allowing artificial regulation of river levels. The average difference in water level between upstream and downstream at Lock 11 is 3.6m. The best way to understand how a lock works is to see it in operation, a process that takes 15 to 20 minutes.

Paddle steamers move through Lock 11 at 11am, 12.30pm, 2pm and 3.30pm on cruising days, while it's possible to see private vessels go through every half-hour (pending bookings) between 8am and 4.30pm daily (except 11.30am and noon on weekends and public holidays). If you want to go through the lock on a private vessel, you need to call the duty officer on 03-5055 3402 the day before to make a free booking.

Walk to Lock Island

When Lock 11 is not in operation, you can cross it via metal bridgeways to **Lock Island**. Unique to this junction, it's the only site on the Murray where a lock and weir are separated by an island. From the lock, it's a five-minute walk through bushland to the **Mildura Weir Lookout**. For this most direct route, head to your right past the Lock 11 sign (written in rocks) and around the picnic table; up the path you'll see a sign for the **Weir Track**. There are various marked bush trails on the small island, which you can freely explore from 6am to 4.30pm. Outside these times, the bridgeways are locked except to paid ticket holders of the Trail of Lights exhibition.

Take an illuminated night walk

On Thursday, Friday and Saturday nights, Lock Island becomes the setting for the **Trail of Lights** *(mildura.com/lights; adult/child $45/25)* installation. By British artist Bruce Munro, also responsible for Uluru's Field of Light (p880), the exhibition features 12,500 firefly lights as well as illuminated 'gone fishing' sculptures over five self-toured bush trails.

Access to the island and all paths, which vary in length from 950m to 2.2km, are wheelchair- and pram-accessible with assistance. **Trail 4** (1.1km) and **Trail 5** (950m) have been especially designed with accessibility in mind. It's best to book ahead online, though tickets may be purchased (pending availability) at the on-site box office.

On exhibition evenings, an 'activation space' in Rio Vista Park offers food and drinks at **Jessica Rabbit Cafe** and **TOL Bar** and a place to wait for your specified entry time. Use the toilets here as there are none on the island. Most visitors spend about an hour exploring the light trails. The exhibition is expected to continue until at least April 2028, in conjunction with sister installation FOSO at the **Perry Sandhills** (p626).

THE CHAFFEYS: SUCCESS OR FAILURE?

Impressed by George and WB Chaffey's successful irrigation endeavours in the US state of California, 1880s Victorian Premier Alfred Deakin invited the duo to Mildura to irrigate the Murray River for farming. In 1893, however, despite the most abundant fruit season yet, severe drought lowered the river to unnavigable levels. In the absence of a railway, the harvest could not get to market and the year's profits were left to rot.

Farmers, unable to recover from the financial loss, left Mildura in large numbers and by the end of 1895, the irrigation scheme was over. Bankrupt, George returned to California to start over, while WB stayed to face a Royal Commission into the scheme's downfall.

MORE THINGS TO DO IN MILDURA

Mildura Riverfront: Walk or cycle the riverfront parks and playgrounds. Jaycee Park hosts Sunraysia Farmers' Market twice a month.

Orange World: An entertaining one-hour tractor tour of a working citrus farm at 10.30am, 11.30am and 2.30pm daily (closed February).

Australian Inland Botanic Gardens: Free gardens near Orange World, with Sturt desert peas in bloom almost year-round.

Woodsies Gem Shop: Explore the gem collection of Aladdin's Cave, then spend some time trying to escape the challenging hedge maze.

Mildura Holden Motor Museum: See the brand's evolution from the first model to its last in a showroom of up to 35 Holdens.

JESSICA KORTEMAN/LONELY PLANET

Rio Vista (p622)

Cruise through a working lock

From **Mildura Wharf** (not to be confused with Lock 11 and Mildura Weir), take a cruise with **Mildura Paddle Steamers** *(paddlesteamers.com.au; adult/child $45/20)* on the only paddle vessels to pass through a working lock in Australia. Two-hour cruises on the PV *Rothbury* (or PV *Mundoo*) operate on Tuesday, Thursday, Saturday and Sunday at 10.50am and 1.50pm, with the opportunity to pass through Lock 11 twice. Prior reservation is required; book online or call *(03-5023 2200, 03-5018 8380)*. Check the website for changes to the schedule and for lunch, dinner and special-event cruises.

Eat through a street

Langtree Ave is known as Mildura's **Feast Street** for its concentration of eateries. Find a range of cuisine, including Spanish, Italian, Indian, Korean and Irani, with many restaurants offering streetside terraced parklets for permanent outdoor dining – perfect for enjoying a glass of regional wine on a balmy summer's evening or by the warmth of a standing heater during winter. While 'Feast Street' is technically the top of Langtree Ave from **Mildura Station** to **Langtree Mall**, you'll find more restaurant, cafe and bar options further down and in the surrounding streets.

MORE RIVER ADVENTURES

Follow the course of the Murray from Mildura into South Australia. Venture into **the Riverlands & the Murraylands** (p764) to explore Australia's largest wine-producing region and experience some of the world's darkest star-filled skies.

Beyond Mildura & the Murray

The Murray River is the natural frontier between Victoria and NSW. Make a quick crossing and the rest of NSW awaits.

The Victorian farming community of Mildura is the gateway to the southwestern corner of Outback NSW. From here, it's a quick jaunt to Wentworth for more river play and sandhills, while the Silver City Hwy can take you to the historic mining town of Broken Hill.

A separate road northeast leads to the World Heritage–listed Mungo National Park, one of the most significant Aboriginal archaeological sites in the country. It was the discovery of the 42,000-year-old remains of Mungo Man and Mungo Lady here in the 1960s and '70s that completely rewrote the science on the longevity of Aboriginal presence across the continent. Rise with the sun and see kangaroos and emus starting their day in the morning light.

Places

Wentworth p625

Mungo National Park p628

Wentworth

TIME FROM MILDURA: **30MIN**

Explore an iconic river junction

In Wentworth, two of Australia's great rivers meet: the Murray and the Darling. The country's third-longest river, the 1472km-long Darling officially begins its journey between Brewarrina and Bourke in northern NSW, making its way down the entire state before meeting its confluence here, just north of the Victorian border.

Carrying more water than the Darling, the Murray's dominance forces the course of the Darling westward, which has resulted in the forming of a narrow spit of land known as **Junction Island**. This island sandbar was the site of a well-known interaction between Captain Charles Sturt and a group of Paakantji, the 'peoples of the Darling', during his expedition of the Murray River in 1830.

View the island from **Junction Viewing Tower** at Junction Park, via a spiral staircase, or explore it on foot by crossing the bridge at the end of Ski Reserve Rd. The serene 2km out-and-back **Murray–Darling Junction Island Walk** (45 minutes to one hour) features plentiful birdlife, interpretive signage and a viewing platform.

GETTING AROUND

You can get to Wentworth by public bus from Mildura, but a car gives you the most flexibility.

Mungo National Park has no public transport options. The tracks into and around the park are bumpy and unsealed. A 2WD will suffice in dry conditions, but consider a 4WD for greater confidence in more challenging terrain. For those who don't want to drive, several tour companies operate out of Mildura.

PHOTODIGITAAL.NL/SHUTTERSTOCK

Perry Sandhills

Learn Wentworth's pioneer history

Constructed between 1879 and 1881, what is now **Old Wentworth Gaol** *(adult/child $8/4)* served to control the many perceived misdemeanours of inhabitants of expanding colonial settlements, fuelled by the bustling riverboat trade and mining. The premises, made from an estimated one million handcrafted bricks, operated as a jail until 1927 and later became an annex of the local school. It's considered the most intact original jail of its kind in New South Wales. Self-tour the cells, the prisoner's yard and amenities blocks and take a souvenir photo in replica wooden shackles.

Over the road, **Wentworth Pioneer Museum** *(adult/child $8/4)* is a local history museum housing over 3000 artefacts with an interesting megafauna display and short documentary on the catastrophic 1956 Murray River floods. Combo tickets are available for both attractions (adult/child $14/6), open daily.

Ride sand and sound waves

Less than a 10-minute drive from downtown Wentworth, find 162 hectares of windswept sand dunes known as the **Perry Sandhills**. Once the home of giant megafauna, today's desert-like landscape of constantly evolving hills is a popular site for sandboarding. Boards can be hired from **Intersport Mildura** *(per day $25)*.

At night until April 2028 (planned), the sandhills will host an immersive sound-and-light experience by artist Bruce Munro, entitled **Fibre Optic Symphonic Orchestra (FOSO)**. Eighty illuminated Hills Hoist clotheslines resembling orchestra pits and representing different instruments will be synchronised with a symphonic score by acclaimed composer Nainita Desai. FOSO is a joint installation with Mildura's **Trail of Lights** (p623; *mildura.com/lights*).

DRIVE THE MUNGO LOOP TRACK

Venture beyond the main attractions on this self-drive tour to the outer reaches of the park.

START	END	LENGTH
Mungo Visitor Centre	Mungo Visitor Centre	70km; 2–4hr

Explore the interpretive displays and download the free 'Mungo Stories' app at the **1 Mungo Visitor Centre** (p628) to gain access to cultural videos by Traditional Custodians. Three story markers are behind the centre. When ready to depart, head east, following signs to the **2 Walls of China** (p629), around a 15-minute drive. From the car park, it's about five minutes on foot along a boardwalk to the lunette viewing platform. Two Mungo Stories can be found here.

Exit the car park and take a left, along the signposted 'self-drive' track. Ten minutes away, popular sunset spot **3 Red Top Lookout** (p629)offers an alternative perspective of the lunette from a viewing platform and another Mungo Story. Near the halfway point, you reach the **4 Mallee Stop**, a 500m loop walk through Mallee eucalyptuses on the park's east side and five minutes' drive on, **5 Belah Campground** (p631).

On the northern rim, take the out-and-back detour to **6 Vigars Well** to ascend the sand dunes. As you venture west, you'll reach the **7 Zanci Homestead**. Check out the woolshed for interpretive signage on the area's pastoral history. From here, it's less than 10 minutes back to the visitor centre. Toilets are located at the visitor centre, the Walls of China and Vigars Well.

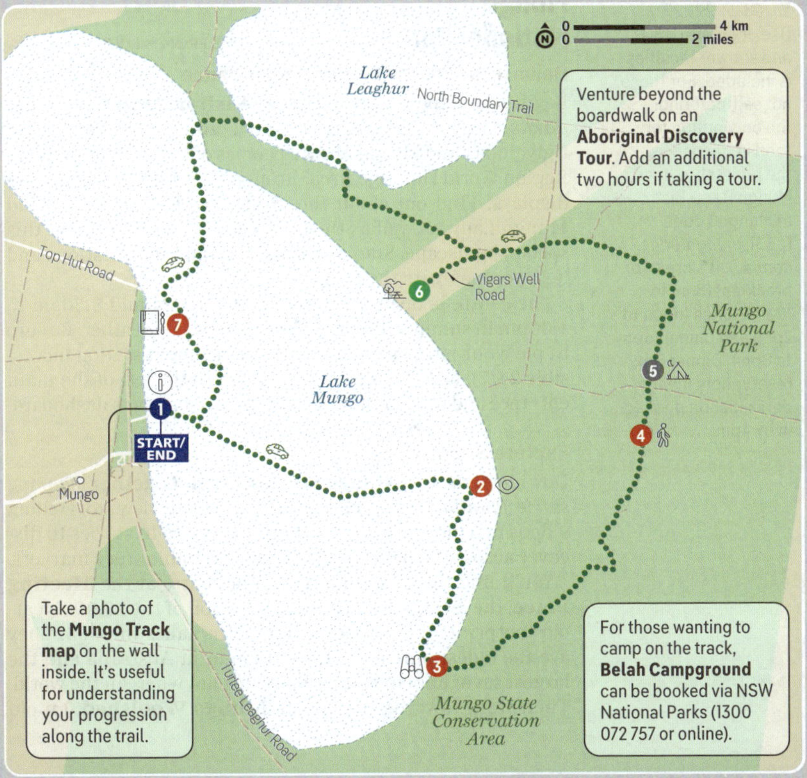

MUNGO: NEED TO KNOW

Mungo National Park is jointly managed by the NSW National Parks and Wildlife Service (NPWS) in collaboration with Elders from the three Aboriginal tribal groups of the area: the Paakantji, Ngiyampaa and Mutthi Mutthi peoples. An $8 park entry fee (per standard vehicle per day) applies, payable on arrival at Mungo Visitor Centre *(nationalparks.nsw.gov.au; 03-5029 7297)*. Use of on-site BBQ and shower facilities is included. For those not self-catering, the only option for food in the park is the privately owned Mungo Bar & Bistro at Mungo Lodge (p631; *mungolodge.com.au*). It's open for breakfast (8am to 10am), lunch (noon to 2pm) and dinner (6pm to 8pm). Dinner is by reservation; meal orders must be phoned in by 4pm.

NICK FOX/SHUTTERSTOCK

Mungo National Park

TIME FROM MILDURA: **1½HR**

Delve into Mungo's cultural significance

Begin your exploration at **Mungo Visitor Centre** *(nationalparks.nsw.gov.au; free)* to learn about the Paakantji, Ngiyampaa and Mutthi Mutthi peoples of the Willandra Lakes Region World Heritage Area through the centre's interpretive displays. Find out about the discovery of Mungo Man and Mungo Lady, as well as the flora and fauna that inhabit this special landscape. Staff are on hand to answer questions and help you navigate the park.

The centre is open daily from 8am to 4pm and 8.30am to 4.30pm in summer, but may close in extreme weather. Be sure to pay your park entrance fee at the payment station (accessible 24/7), found under the verandah to the left of the main entrance and display the 'vehicle copy' on your car's dashboard.

Explore Mungo by app

Download the free **Mungo Stories: Walk Together** *(sharingstoriesfoundation.org/mungo-stories)* app to view storytelling videos by Traditional Custodians. There are 10 stories to discover across the park, triggered by scannable story markers.

You'll find three behind the visitor centre at the **Meeting Place**, the location of a partial recreation of the 20,000-year-old footprints discovered at Willandra Lakes in 2003. They are the oldest human footprints found in Australia and the largest set of human ice age footprints anywhere in the world. Then walk towards the on-site **Mungo Woolshed**, an old

Walls of China

shearing shed originally built in 1869. Within metres you'll reach the trailhead of the **Foreshore Walk**, a 2.5km trail with interpretive signage through saltbush plains and sandy dunes (1½ hours return), where you'll find a further three stories.

Other stories are located at the Walls of China (boardwalk), **Red Top Lookout** and **Mungo Lookout**.

Visit an active archaeological site

At Lake Mungo, visit the **Walls of China**, a Mungo highlight, on a two-hour guided daytime or sunset experience with **Aboriginal Discovery Tours** *(visitmungo.com.au/discovery-tours; adult/child $50/35)*. Named after Chinese workers who built a woolshed in the region in the mid-1800s, this series of otherworldly clay formations on sandy dunes is the result of erosion caused by land clearing since European arrival.

Don't be deceived by the swathes of blue on your map: Lake Mungo hasn't seen water for 15,000 years and what remains is continually being moved and shaped by the elements, revealing calcified trees and fossilised lake life. The groundbreaking discovery of Mungo Man and Mungo Lady, two of the oldest ritual burials to be found outside Africa, happened at the now dry lakebed.

You'll meet your First Nations guide at the visitor centre, before proceeding in convoy in your own vehicle (around 15 minutes) to the 'lunette', a reference to the Walls' resemblance to a moonlike landscape. This is an active archaeological site and place of immense cultural significance, so access beyond the boardwalk viewing platform (a couple of hundred metres from the car park) is with an authorised guide only.

PREPARE FOR YOUR MUNGO ADVENTURE

Lance Jones, Ngiyampaa Elder and Discovery Guide at Mungo National Park, shares how to visit the park.

Access to Mungo is condition-dependent and rain can quickly cause road closures. Confirm what's open within the park online *(nationalparks.nsw.gov.au)*. For roads into Mungo, see the websites of the local shires of Wentworth *(wentworth.nsw.gov.au)*, Balranald *(balranald.nsw.gov.au)* and Central Darling *(centraldarling.nsw.gov.au)*.

Book your accommodation online before arrival, including camping grounds. Carry plenty of food and water and fill up on fuel as there are no supermarkets or petrol stations within Mungo.

For your safety and in respect to the Traditional Custodians, only enter areas open to the public and follow all park signage.

Places We Love to Stay

$ Budget $$ Midrange $$$ Top End

Aireys Inlet

Sunnymead Hotel $$ Award-winning modern reimagining of an old motel yells refined fun with its poolside bar, intimate restaurant and day spa.

Apollo Bay & Around

YHA Eco Beach $ Architect-designed hostel with eco credentials, great lounge areas, multiple kitchens, a pool table and rooftop terraces.

Warrnambool

MAP p558

Deep Blue Hotel $$ Combine you stay with the hot-springs sanctuary at this modern beachfront hotel. Amenities include a restaurant/bar and tennis court.

Port Fairy

Pelican Waters $ Stay in a converted 1980s suburban train carriage, camp or choose a cabin at this holiday park. It has all the mod cons and is on the rail trail.

Drift House $$$ An intriguing mix of 19th-century grandeur and 21st-century design, Drift House is a must for architecture lovers and a place to treat yourself.

Portland & Around

Cape Nelson Lighthouse $$ Indulge your fantasy of living in a remote, windswept lighthouse keeper's cottage. The cottages (which date to 1884) have been refitted with mod cons but retain their maritime charm.

Phillip Island

Island Accommodation $ At the Big Wave complex in Newhaven, this backpacker setup has dorms, private rooms, two large kitchens, a cafe and rooftop deck.

Wilsons Promontory

Tidal River Campground $ The main accommodation base at Wilson's Prom has camp sites, limited powered sites and cabins; book in advance online.

Lakes Entrance

Eastern Beach Tourist Park $ More spacious and family-friendly than most Lakes caravan parks, this is still walking distance from the beach and town centre.

Eight Acres $$ The perfect farmstay with a glamping village, pool and cracking luxury camp kitchen with a fireplace. Don't miss the morning feeding of the farm animals.

Metung

Metung Hot Springs Glamping $$$ Check into a waterfront safari-style tent next to natural hot springs and take full advantage of the thermal joy.

Cape Conran Coastal Park

Banksia Bluff Camping Area $ Shady camp sites under banksia trees. Look out for surfing dolphins and plenty more Aussie wildlife. Facilities include cold 'bush' showers.

Mallacoota

Mallacoota Foreshore Holiday Park $ Sprawling around the Mallacoota Inlet, this is one of the most sociable and scenic caravan parks around.

Mansfield & Around

Mansfield Travellers Lodge $ One of the few High Country backpacker hostels. The dorms are great value year-round and there's a kitchen, laundry, drying rooms and games room.

Alzburg Resort $$ With a heated pool, tennis courts, ski hire, tidy motel rooms and family-sized apartments, the Alzburg is a bargain.

Beechworth

Freeman on Ford $$$ In the 1876 Oriental Bank, enjoy five-star Victorian B&B luxury in six beautifully renovated rooms, right in the heart of town. Lovely gardens and outdoor pool.

Bright

Bright Velo $$ These central heritage rooms and motel-style rooms are well priced and set up for cyclists, with bike storage and guest common room.

Odd Frog $$ Architect-designed boutique treehouses in bushland on the outskirts of town, with eco features and designed with romantic getaways in mind.

Mt Buffalo

Lake Catani Campground $
A stunning summer camping ground with flush toilets, hot showers and spacious bush sites. Winter stays are possible without water.

Bendigo

MAP p564

Larni Yirrip Campground $
Djaara-led designed camping ground with 12 individual spaces on raised platforms for tents and swags. Book via Parks Victoria.

Julie-Anna Inn $$ Opposite Lake Weeroona on the tram line, this excellent motel features spacious rooms backing onto a central garden and pool.

City Centre Motel $$ Friendly and clean downtown motel with budget and accessible room options and EV charging facilities.

Ballarat

MAP p573

Victoriana Motor Inn $ On the Sovereign Hill side of town, this budget motel is a good choice for those with a car.

Craig's Royal Hotel $$
Ballarat's first licensed venue, ostentatious downtown hotel dating from 1853. The 'classic' rooms on weekdays are the most wallet-friendly.

Daylesford & Hepburn Springs

MAP p579

Central Springs Inn $$
Comfortable country-style motel within walking distance to Daylesford's main drag, Vincent St.

Daylesford Central Motor Inn $$ Reasonably priced motel with all the basic amenities in a quiet spot near the centre of town.

The Grampians

Halls Gap Lakeside Tourist Park $ Large caravan park by Lake Bellfield with year-round outdoor wood-fire heated pool. Powered and unpowered camp sites and budget cabins available.

Halls Gap Log Cabins $$ Fully equipped self-contained cabins perfect for a family or group stay. Wood-burning fireplaces from May to October. Two-night minimum stay may apply.

Mildura & the Murray

MAP p623

Mildura City Gate Motel $
Spotless motel conveniently located across from the paddle-steamer wharf. The fridge comes stocked with breakfast essentials.

Caledonian Hotel-Motel $$
Near Echuca train station, these spacious, well-appointed rooms are delightfully more hotel than motel for the price point.

BIG4 Swan Hill $$ Two caravan parks with camp sites and cabins. Choose Riverside to be near the Pioneer Settlement, while Swan Hill has a popular splash park for kids.

Mungo National Park

Mungo Shearers' Quarters $
Next to the visitor centre, excellent private bunk-style rooms with air-con and heating and shared kitchen and bathroom. BYO sleeping bag and pillow.

Main Campground & Belah Campground $ Main camp, a short drive from the visitor centre, caters for tents and caravans. Belah is more remote and for tents only. Book via Parks NSW.

Mungo Lodge $$ Choose from tents, cabins and family rooms at this privately run lodge a 10-minute drive from the visitor centre. Convenient on-site restaurant.

ERIC MIDDELKOOP/SHUTTERSTOCK

Cape Nelson Lighthouse, Portland

For places to stay in Tasmania, see p708

BENNY MARTY/SHUTTERSTOCK

Above: Cradle Mountain-Lake St Clair National Park (p691); Right: Farm Gate Market (p638)

THE MAIN AREAS

HOBART
Australia's best-looking capital city.
p638

THE SOUTH
Convicts, cheese, cider and wilderness.
p660

EAST COAST
Beaches, wildlife, whisky and wine.
p668

Researched by
Andrew Bain and
Charles Rawlings-Way

Tasmania

ANCIENT WILDERNESS, GASTRONOMY AND CONVICT HISTORY

This compact, zesty island is loaded with wild wonder, brutal history, exquisite wines, handcrafted beers, salt spray and lonesome beaches. Oh, and those whiskies...

Up until the end of the last ice age around 12,000 years ago, Lutruwita / Tasmania – now Australia's large, mountainous island state – was connected to the mainland via a land bridge. When the ice melted and sea levels rose, the Palawa, Tasmania's Aboriginal people, had Lutruwita to themselves.

In 1642, Abel Tasman became the first European to spy the island, which he named Van Diemen's Land after his boss back home. Whalers and sealers visited the outer islands of Van Diemen's Land regularly, but it wasn't until 1804 that the British set up shop at Sullivans Cove, the site of modern-day Hobart. The British built their new colony using convict labour, transporting around 80,000 hapless souls here, until transport ceased in 1853 and the colony was renamed Tasmania. By this stage, the Palawa had been dispossessed and demoralised, many forcibly repatriated to Flinders Island. Convict ruins remain...

DAVID STEELE/SHUTTERSTOCK

Over 40% of Tasmania is protected by either national park or World Heritage status and the island's entire southwest corner is a primeval old-growth wilderness unchanged since the time of Gondwanaland. From the squeaky white sand and lichen-splashed granite of the east coast to the snowy alpine plateaus of Cradle Mountain-Lake St Clair National Park, hiking, biking and kayaking opportunities abound.

These days, most visitors come to experience Tasmania's unique wilderness, wildlife and architectural treasures and to engage with its scintillating arts scene and show-stopping food and drink. Come on down!

LAUNCESTON
Wine, food and history.
p679

CRADLE COUNTRY & TAKAYNA / TARKINE
World-class wilderness, mountains and hiking.
p687

MIDLANDS, LAKES & WILD RIVERS
Colonial heritage, distilleries, fly-fishing and rafting.
p701

Find Your Way

Tasmania is compact by Australian standards, but getting from A to B usually takes longer than you think. Roads are rarely straight or dual carriageway, bus services are infrequent and passenger trains are extinct. But it sure is scenic!

Cradle Country & Takayna / Tarkine, p687

The famed Overland Track kicks off at Cradle Mountain. To the west are the sublime Takayna / Tarkine forests and the final frontier: the wild West Coast.

Launceston, p679

A UNESCO City of Gastronomy and Australia's third-oldest European settlement, 'Launnie' is a welcoming place with foodie delights and valley hillsides glistening with grapes.

Midlands, Lakes & Wild Rivers, p701

Georgian villages, whisky distilleries, the lonesome trout-filled lakes of the Central Plateau and the wildest ride of all, the majestic Franklin River.

East Coast, p668

Squeaky white-sand beaches, orange lichen-encrusted coves, curious wildlife and glorious vineyards make for a mesmerising road trip. Pack the mountain bike.

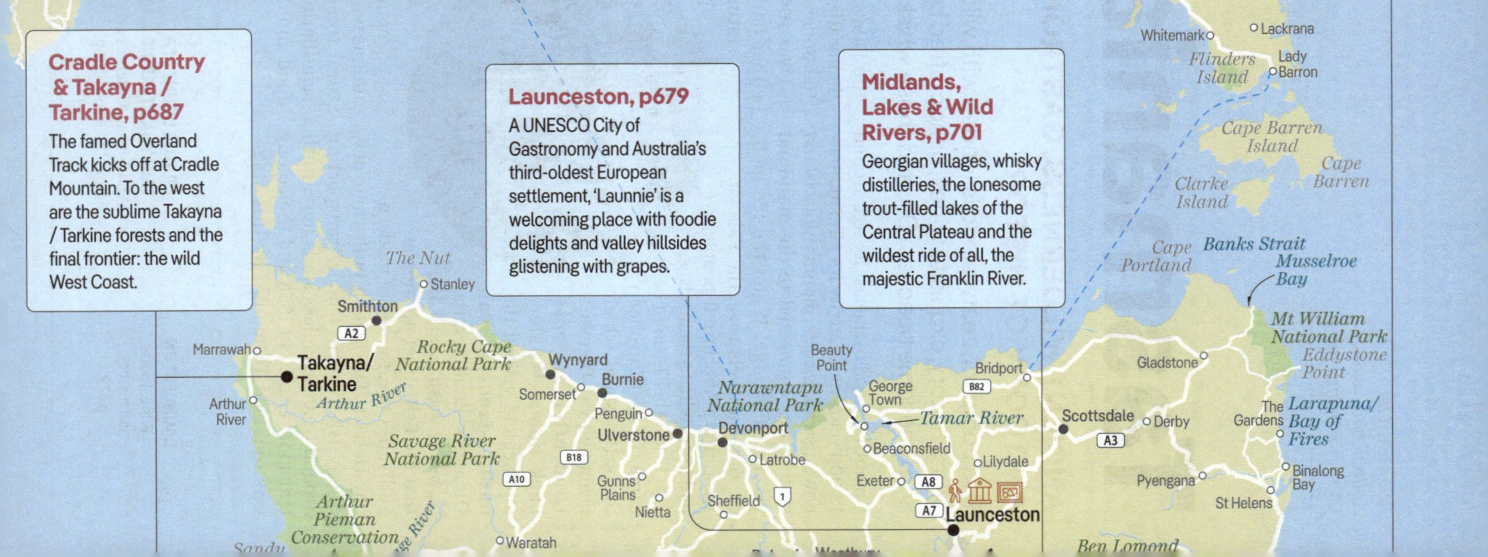

CAR

Having your own wheels is the best way to explore the island: you can either bring your own on the ferry from Victoria or hire one from rental agencies at all the major airports.

FERRY

Apart from the *Spirit of Tasmania* linking Devonport and Geelong on the mainland, there are ferries on Hobart's River Derwent, across to Bruny, Maria and Flinders islands and along Lake St Clair.

BUS

Regular coach services link Hobart, Launceston and Devonport. Outside these areas, services are more sporadic and some places might only see a weekly connection, if any. Private shuttles service most of the popular bushwalking destinations.

The South, p660

Draw a line under 43°S and you'll find convict ruins, gourmet food, caves, rivers, the wild Southern Ocean and remote Southwest wilderness.

Hobart, p638

The island's photogenic capital sits between the deep River Derwent estuary and omnipresent 1271m Kunanyi / Mt Wellington. Great art, food and bars.

Plan Your Time

Only here for a weekend? Make Hobart or Launceston your base. Most hire cars can be left at either airport, so there's no need for a full circuit (unless you want to, of course!).

HP HONEYWOOD/SHUTTERSTOCK

Kunanyi / Mt Wellington (p651)

Hobart in a Weekend

- Grab a croissant and coffee in **Battery Point** (p649), then walk to **Salamanca Market** (p645) and lose a few hours in the throng. Take the ferry to **MONA** (p642) for amazing art and tapas at **Moorilla Wine Bar** (p643). A drink on the lawn is *de rigueur* before the return ferry to the city. Hit the bars in **North Hobart** (p653), then devour **Flippers** (p649) fish and chips down at the waterfront.

- On Sunday, get your coffee with a bao from the **Farm Gate Market** (p638) before driving to the top of **Kunanyi / Mt Wellington** (p651) for incredible views over the city, the River Derwent and beyond. Check out historic **Richmond** (p655) and the **Coal River Valley wineries** (p655) on your way back to the airport.

Seasonal Highlights

Tasmanians love a festival. There's usually something happening somewhere, most months of the year - and if there isn't, somebody will invent a party, which is exactly how Dark Mofo materialised.

JANUARY

Hobart is one big party with the **Sydney to Hobart** (p647) yachts and the **Taste of Summer**. Let your hair down at the **Cygnet Folk Festival**.

FEBRUARY

Launceston rocks out to three days of quality booze, fab food and big-name music acts at **Festivale** in City Park, with decidedly family-friendly vibes.

MARCH

It's harvest time around the island, as grape vines turn golden. The **Taste of the Huon** food fest in Ranelagh is the perfect taster of the Huon Valley produce.

East Coast in a Week

● From Hobart, head for **Turrakana / Tasman Peninsula** (p660), dive into convict history at **Port Arthur Historic Site** (p662) and bag a coastal walk. **Maria Island** (p668) is calling: ferry out from Triabunna and spend a night with the wombats. Back on the main island, hit some **wineries** (p671) on the way to **Freycinet National Park** (p672). Burn off some carbs on the Wineglass Bay walk, before staying overnight in **Bicheno** (p670).

● Next stop is **St Helens** (p675), where mountain bikers can hit the forest trails. Detour to **Pyengana** (p676) for some cheese; stay overnight in **Binalong Bay** (p708). Check out the mountain biking trails in **Derby** (p677) or the **Tamar Valley wineries** (p684), before your final night in historic **Evandale** (p683).

West Coast in a Week

● From **Launceston** (p679), head to pretty **Deloraine** (p689) and walk along the gentle riverbank or the more up-tempo Liffey Falls. Check out the caves at **Mole Creek Karst National Park** (p690) en route to famous **Cradle Mountain** (p691), where the alpine peaks and tarns deserve at least two days. Truck north to **Stanley** (p694), with its impressive **Nut** (p694), little penguins and precious cache of historic buildings.

● Immerse yourself in rainforest on the **Tarkine Drive** (p696), then return to civilisation in **Strahan** (p697), where you can cruise across colossal Macquarie Harbour and into the Tasmanian Wilderness World Heritage Area (TWWHA). Take lonely Lyell Hwy back to **Hobart** (p638), passing the iconic **Franklin River** (p706) and **Leeawuleena / Lake St Clair** (p707), Australia's deepest lake, en route.

JUNE

Rip off your clothes and take the icy plunge: Hobart goes all elemental, unhinged and Gothic during **Dark Mofo** (p647).

JULY

Brightening up winter in the northwest, the four-day **Devonport Jazz Festival** fills venues and stages with all things bee-bop, trad, Dixieland, big-band and free-form.

OCTOBER

The edgy biennial **Unconformity** (p699) arts festival has a touch of the MONA, messing with your mind against Queenstown's lunar backdrop. Take the trip.

NOVEMBER

Sunshine in the sky and by the bottle at the **Bicheno Food & Wine Festival**, over a fun springtime day. Great seafood and live tunes.

Hobart

AVANT-GARDE ART | MOUNTAIN TRAILS | FOOD SCENE

☑ TOP TIP

Central Hobart is great for a cheap and delicious lunch: Elizabeth St Mall and Collins St are prime terrain for noodles, rice and curries. Less obvious are the arcades: try the Bank of Us Centre on Collins St or Bank Arcade off Liverpool for sushi, dumplings and more curries.

Hobart's buzzy city centre is the place for a cheap lunch and some outdoor gear for your next adventure. Just downhill, the waterfront delivers excellent restaurants and high-end hotels. Salamanca Place is here, too, a row of 1840s sandstone warehouses now home to galleries, cafes, restaurants and bars. Salamanca Market has been happening here every Saturday morning since 1972.

Behind Salamanca is photogenic Battery Point, Hobart's first suburb – host to historic houses, cafes, galleries and pubs. After dark, the restaurant strip in adjacent Sandy Bay has more of a pulse.

Epic Kunanyi / Mt Wellington offers hike/bike trails and lookouts (wow!). Below Kunanyi, South Hobart hosts the long-running Cascade Brewery and UNESCO-listed Cascades Female Factory Historic Site.

The bohemian North Hobart restaurant and bar strip is a recipe for a fun night out, while a short drive north is the fabulous, irreverent, enriching and unsettling MONA, the Museum of Old and New Art.

Farm Gate Foraging

MAP P640

Get it straight from the growers

A Sunday morning stroll down Bathurst St between Murray St and Elizabeth St is a weekly Hobart ritual. The excellent **Farm**

GETTING AROUND

Hobart Airport is 18km (about 25 minutes) from central Hobart. **Skybus** *(skybus.com.au; single/return $22.50/41)* coaches meet every flight and service six city locations. Budget $40 to $45 for a rideshare to Salamanca.

The easiest way to negotiate the city centre, waterfront and Salamanca area is on foot. Parking is a royal pain: save the car for out-of-town excursions or a trip up Kunanyi / Mt Wellington. There are plenty of e-scooters lying around, but most people use them for novelty value rather than actual transport. Metro bus services and the **Red Decker** *(reddecker.com.au)* hop-on/hop-off sightseeing bus connect the main inner suburbs.

TRABANTOS/SHUTTERSTOCK

Tasmanian Museum & Art Gallery

Gate Market *(farmgatemarket.com.au)*, running 8.30am to 1pm, offers sustainably produced mushrooms, bespoke pasta, artisan loaves, crumbly cheeses and expertly cured salamis. A jaunty selection of food vans serve interesting breakfasts of bao, *murtabaks* (pan-fried flatbreads), wallaby burritos and congee...although not everyone needs a gin tasting at 8.30am. A sunny seat with a coffee and a sourdough doughnut might be more your speed? Either way, stock up on picnic provisions for your Sunday drive.

Hobart History

MAP P640

TMAG is an essential Hobart museum

In a sprawling complex of colonial-era buildings between Davey St and Macquarie St, the **Tasmanian Museum & Art Gallery** *(TMAG; tmag.tas.gov.au; free)* is quintessentially Hobart, zeroing in on Tasmanian history, art, culture and natural science. Learn about the ill-fated thylacine (Tasmanian tiger) and the Black War between the colonists and Tasmania's Aboriginal people. Come to grips with Hobart's inexorable ties with Antarctica and learn some words of palawa kani, Tasmania's reconstructed Aboriginal language. Free 40-minute tours run Friday to Sunday and cover art gallery highlights (11am), TMAG's historic buildings (noon) and museum highlights (2pm). Lots of kid-focused exhibitions; cool courtyard cafe. Closed Mondays April to December.

Convict Heritage in the City Centre

MAP P640

Explore Hobart's original gaol

The courtrooms, cells and gallows at the **Hobart Penitentiary** *(nationaltrust.org.au/places/penitentiary; tours adult/child*

Continued on p645

TOP SHOPS

Fullers Bookshop: In this UNESCO City of Literature, Fullers leads the way. Australia's oldest independent bookshop (1920), with a lovely cafe and great staff.

Cool Wine: An excellent selection of cool-climate Tasmanian wine (plus a few global interlopers, if they're good enough).

Tommy Gun Records: For all your vinyl, secondhand CD, studded-leather wristband and heavy-metal T-shirt requirements.

Mountain Creek Outdoors: The best of the outdoors shops clustered around the corner of Elizabeth St and Bathurst St. Go wild.

Eumarrah: Follow Hobart's many hippies into this excellent whole-foods shop. Spices, nuts, teas and buckets of grains to go.

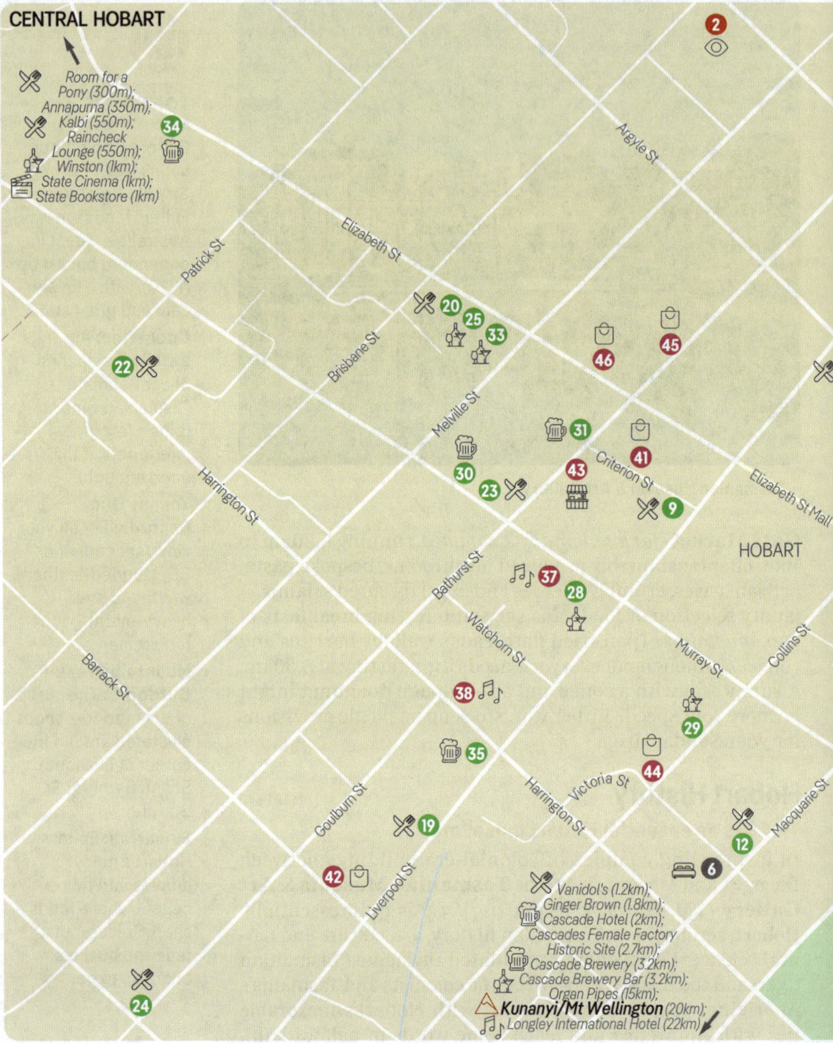

SIGHTS
1 Constitution Dock
2 Hobart Penitentiary
3 Lark Distillery
4 Mawson's Huts Replica Museum
5 Tasmanian Museum & Art Gallery

SLEEPING
6 Astor Private Hotel
7 Henry Jones Art Hotel
8 Tasman

EATING
9 Criterion Street Cafe
10 Customs House Hotel
11 Daci & Daci
12 Fico
13 Fish Frenzy
14 Flippers
15 Institut Polaire
16 Mures
17 Pigeon Whole Bakery
18 Pilgrim Coffee
19 Scholé
20 Stagg Midtown
21 Street Eats @ Franko
22 Templo
23 Urban Greek
24 Westside Laundry

DRINKING & NIGHTLIFE
25 Grinners Dive Bar
26 Hobart Brewing Co
27 Hope & Anchor
28 In the Hanging Garden
see 7 IXL Long Bar
29 Lucinda Wine Bar
30 Mountain Culture
31 New Sydney Hotel
32 Rosie in My Midnight Dreams
33 Rude Boy
34 Shambles Brewery
35 Shamrock Hotel
36 Telegraph Hotel

ENTERTAINMENT
37 Altar Bar
38 Pablo's Cocktails & Dreams
39 Sydney to Hobart Yacht Race
40 Theatre Royal

SHOPPING
41 Cool Wine
42 Eumarrah
43 Farm Gate Market
44 Fullers Bookshop
45 Mountain Creek Outdoors
46 Tommy Gun Records

TRABANTOS/SHUTTERSTOCK

TOP EXPERIENCE

Museum of Old & New Art

Think, eat, drink, feel. The provocative Museum of Old and New Art (MONA) at Berriedale is David Walsh's crazed ode to his hometown – simultaneously delivering a magnificent 'up yours' to the art-world establishment. Explore the challenging, the rare, the ancient, the horny and the downright disgusting as you wander through dim-lit stone galleries cut into a promontory above the River Derwent.

DON'T MISS

- *Snake*
- *MONA Confessional*
- *Chamber of Pausiris*
- *Amarna*
- *Cloaca Professional*
- Drinking in the dimness
- Live music on the lawn
- Burgers in the sun
- Ferry ride

The Backstory

MONA mastermind David Walsh grew up in nearby Glenorchy and turned his mathematical genius to professional gambling – and made a pile of money. An avid art collector, he originally bought the on-site **Moorilla Estate** winery, then launched MONA in 2011. MONA is now the largest private art gallery in the southern hemisphere and has boosted tourism and Tasmania's general self-esteem immeasurably – the so-called 'MONA effect'. The ever-expanding MONA world also includes **Moo Brew** brewery (off-site); **Manky Sally's** bar in Salamanca (Moo Brew's public face – try the pilsener); the fabulously unhinged **Dark Mofo** (p647) winter festival; luxury accommodation and even a recording studio. Visionary and rogue in equal measure, Walsh isn't short on ideas or ambition.

PRACTICALITIES

● *mona.net.au* ● non-Tasmanian adult/child $39/free, Tasmanian adult/child $5/free ● 10am-5pm Thu-Mon

Must-See MONA

It's hard to know where to start at MONA. Perhaps the best approach is to suspend preconceived ideas of a 'plan', wander through the subterranean, dim-lit galleries and see what kind of fun comes your way.

There are, of course, some must-sees in the vast collection here. Don't bypass **Snake** by Sidney Nolan, a 46m-long array of 1620 panels exploring the connections between myth and modernity; and the **Chamber of Pausiris**, containing the coffin and mummy of a 2000-year old Egyptian.

Other essentials include the very cathartic **MONA Confessional**, in which you can broadcast your sins anonymously to random listeners far above; James Turrell's aboveground archi-light installation **Amarna**, active at sunrise and sunset (stick around); and every kid's favourite, the aromatic **Cloaca Professional** poo machine. The machine gets fed in morning; the poo comes out around 2pm.

Then there are the regularly rotating, head-tripping guest exhibitions. Lost in time, space, art and darkness, three hours can pass at MONA and you still won't know how to get back to daylight.

EMBRACE THE O

To make any sense of MONA's label-less artworks, you'd be well advised to download the 'O' app to your phone – a marvel of geospatial programming that reveals all you ever needed to know about the artwork you're standing in front of. And probably a few things you didn't. It's also useful for finding the exit. BYO headphones (there's audio).

Fine Wine, Fine Food

There are some ace places to eat and drink at MONA – it's all part of the experience.

- **Heavy Metal Kitchen** Indulgent burgers, grilled-meat sandwiches, charred cauliflower and hot chips for lunch on the lawn. Rock on.
- **Moorilla Wine Bar** Moorilla winery was here for ages before MONA showed up. Outside the museum entrance, it's share plates, coffee and drinks in the sun. Plenty of vegan; open all day.
- **Void Bar** Gasping for a Manhattan and some crunchy jalapeño corn? Follow the live music into the half-light, 17m underground. Museum admission applies.
- **Faro Bar + Restuarant** Fine dining in a light-filled space, with massive glass windows overlooking the river. The menu changes constantly: high-end and superb. Lunch and dinner, too.
- **Source** Five-star lunch service in an immaculate restaurant, with river views and top Tasmania ingredients (ooh, oysters). Fixed-price menus or à la carte.

Architecture as Art

Once you've ogled the art and eaten and drunk your fill, kick back on the lawn and check out *mona.net.au/museum/architecture*. Along with David Walsh's take on the colourful Pharos wing, there's an entertaining interview with architect James Pearce from designers Fender Katsalidis, explaining the thinking behind the architecture and the museum's amazing site. Then head back to the bar.

TOP TIPS

- You can drive to MONA, but the ferry is much more fun. Book the Posh Pit for champagne and canapes.
- For most people, a decent half-day at MONA is plenty.
- For some exhibits (eg *MONA Confessional*), you need to queue up via the O. When it's your turn, the O will let you know.
- Tasmanians get into MONA for free, but still have to book and pay a $5 deposit. Bring ID.
- Bike it to MONA from Salamanca in 50 minutes, along the Intercity Cycleway.
- Some of MONA's exhibits are, well, pervy. If you blush easily, ask which rooms to avoid. Ditto if you're strobe-averse.

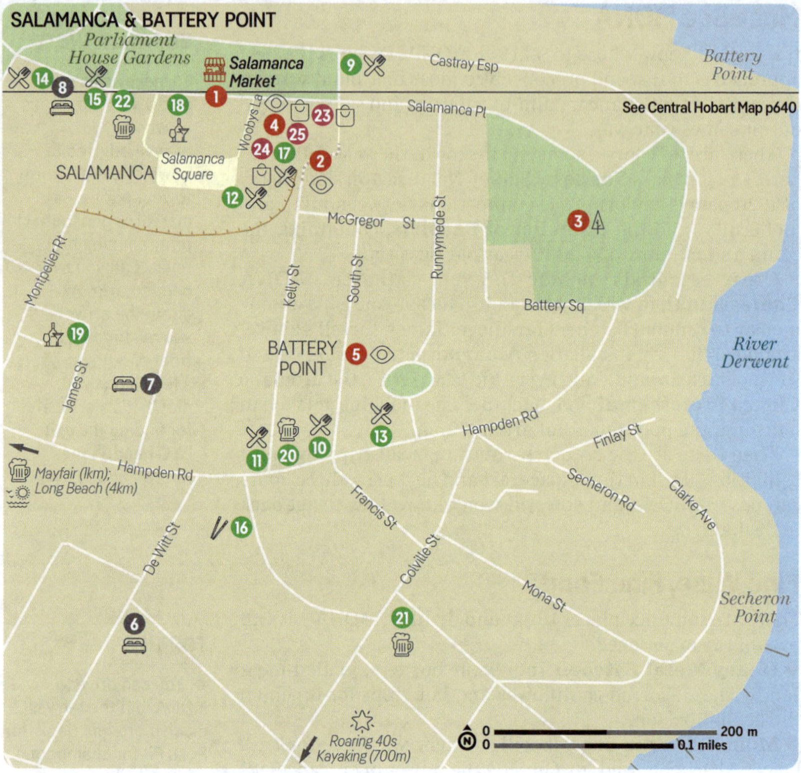

HIGHLIGHTS
1 Salamanca Market

SIGHTS
2 Kelly's Steps
3 Princes Park
4 Salamanca Arts Centre
5 South Street

SLEEPING
6 De Witt Apartment
7 Montacute
8 Waterman's Hotel

EATING
9 Blue Eye
10 Da Angelo
11 Jackman & McRoss
12 Machine Laundry Cafe
13 Magic Curries
14 Manky Sally's
15 Retro Cafe
16 Three Japanese
17 Tricycle Cafe & Bar

DRINKING & NIGHTLIFE
18 Jack Greene
19 Preachers
20 Prince of Wales Hotel
21 Shipwrights Arms Hotel
22 Whaler

SHOPPING
23 handmark
24 Kudelka Shop
25 Salamanca Wool Shop

EATING IN CENTRAL HOBART: CAFES & DECADENT DINNERS

MAP P640

Pilgrim Coffee: Exposed bricks, timber beams and distressed walls. Expert coffee. *6.30am-3pm Mon-Fri, to 1pm Sat & Sun* $

Criterion Street Cafe: Enduring downtown favourite: a short menu on a short street. Order the corn fritters. *7am-3pm* $

Pigeon Whole Bakery: Beaut baguettes, breads and biscuits. Sit in the window with your coffee and watch the city scenes. *7.30am-3pm Mon-Fri, to 1pm Sat & Sun* $

Westside Laundry: This reinvented laundromat does bagels and sandwiches by day, morphing into a NYC-inspired bar by night. *7.30am-3pm Wed-Mon, plus 5-9pm Thu-Sun* $

Continued from p639

from $35/20), aka 'the Tench', had a hellish reputation in the 1800s. Most of Tasmania's 75,000 convicts passed through here. The barracks and main yard are long gone, replaced by Hobart's rather stylish 1980s ambulance HQ – but the Penitentiary's beautiful red-brick 1834 chapel remains solidly intact. Visits are by 90-minute 'Unshackled' tours; book well ahead. Not spooky enough? Sign-up for a 90-minute Ghost Tour. Outside along Campbell St are remnants of the old sandstone prison wall, amazingly high where it connects to the chapel and continuing in fragments all the way to Bathurst St.

Royal Performances

MAP P640

Catch a show at Australia's oldest theatre

Hobart's endearing **Theatre Royal** *(theatreroyal.com.au; tours adult/child $20/10)* is Australia's oldest still-functioning theatre, where thespians have been treading the boards since 1837. Seating 700, it's still the centre of Hobart's performing-arts scene, hosting contemporary drama, comedy, dance and live music. Jump online and see who's playing, or take a 75-minute guided tour and hear stories of the theatre's chequered past, including the resident ghost 'Fred' and the 1984 fire that ravaged the building. Enter via the impressive new Hedberg UTAS performing arts centre next door; the box office is here, too.

Salamanca Market Mayhem

MAP P644

Great food, even better people-watching

What started out as a couple of hippies selling raspberries in 1972 has evolved into a kilometre-long frenzy of food and commerce that consumes all of Salamanca Place every Saturday morning (8.30am to 3pm), rain or shine – Tasmania's number-one tourist attraction. With thousands of people here every week, **Salamanca Market** *(salamancamarket.com.au; free)* is something to behold: give yourself at least a few hours to wander its length and back again, a slow-shuffling circuit down one side of the stalls then back down the other. The cafes overflow, the buskers are in fine voice and (even when it's cold and wet) the atmosphere is downright convivial. Don't miss it.

TIPS FROM THE LORD MAYOR

Rt Hon Cr Anna Reynolds, the Independent Lord Mayor of Hobart, was elected in 2018, only the third woman to ever hold the position. *@annareyno*

Hobart is such a vibrant, creative and down-to-earth small city, set in a stunning landscape ranging from alpine country to sandy beaches.

Street Eats @ Franko: On a Friday night in summer, it's a lively mix of everything Hobart.

Stagg Midtown: Serves my favourite coffee in a thriving part of the city centre.

Institut Polaire: A celebration of Hobart's connection to Antarctica and has amazing food and drinks.

Organ Pipes: On Kunanyi / Mt Wellington, get up close to the 'face' of Hobart, with views rivalling the Pinnacle. A Hobart favourite for over 100 years.

EATING IN CENTRAL HOBART: CAFES & DECADENT DINNERS

MAP P640

Templo: Unpretentious but classy, Templo is a Hobart treasure. Just 20 seats, so book in advance. *noon-2pm Fri-Sun & 5.30-9pm Wed-Sun* **$$**

Urban Greek: You'll smell the charcoal seafood before you see it. Succulent Mediterranean dishes and good Greek beer. *5-9pm Wed-Mon* **$$**

Scholé: Groundbreaking chef Luke Burgess has transformed this skinny, heritage shopfront into his latest restaurant-wine bar. *4-8pm Tue, 5.30pm-midnight Wed-Sat* **$$**

Fico: Amazing Italian. Paired wines take the flavours of the 'feed me' menu to another planet. *6-8pm Thu-Sat, noon-1.30pm Sun* **$$$**

SHIFTING SHORELINES

It's hard to imagine now, but Salamanca's warehouses were once a lot closer to the water than they are today. No, the warehouses haven't moved – but the shoreline has: the broad concrete apron encircling the whole of Sullivans Cove is largely built over reclaimed land.

Merchants were once able to sail their ships right up to a beach in front of the warehouses to offload/load their goods with ease. On the other side of the Cove, Hunter St is built on top of Hunter Island, once connected to the rest of Hobart via a narrow causeway. Look for the brass discs set into the concrete road tracing the line of the causeway below.

RICHARD SOWERSBY/ALAMY

Artfully Salamanca

MAP P644

A vibrant artistic hub of galleries, studios, and shops

Running since 1975, the **Salamanca Arts Centre** *(salarts.org.au; free)* is a vital hub of Hobart's artistic life, maintaining a hectic program of launches, events and performances – always as progressive and socially inclusive as they are creative. There are dozens of commercial artists' studios, retail spaces, cafes and galleries here, too. Don't miss **handmark** for exquisite ceramics, glass, jewellery, paintings and sculpture; the **Salamanca Wool Shop** for nice knits; the **Kudelka Shop**, home to works by mildly anarchic local cartoonist Jon Kudelka; and a coffee at **Tricycle Cafe & Bar**.

DRINKING IN CENTRAL HOBART: OLD PUBS & COOL BARS

MAP P640

New Sydney Hotel: Open fires, creative food, live-music jams, a dozen craft beers and ciders, and no screens. Winner. *noon-10.30pm Mon-Sat, 4-10pm Sun*

Shamrock Hotel: Old-school downtown boozer with hefty meals, all-comer vibes and zero posturing. Change is overrated. *11am-10pm*

Hope & Anchor: Australia's oldest continually licensed pub (1807) has suitably refused to gentrify. Nautical mood, cold beer. *noon-9pm*

Mountain Culture: Backed by investor Pat Cummins, the Australian Test cricket captain, this craft-beer hall is a post-work paradise. *hours vary*

Lucinda Wine Bar: Gorgeous, candlelit Lucinda is just begging you to come inside. French small plates, fine wine and conversation. *4pm-late Tue-Sat*

Grinners Dive Bar: Loud rock, craft beer, tacos and late-night street tables. Fun! *4pm-midnight Sun & Mon, noon-midnight Tue-Thu, noon-4am Fri & Sat*

In the Hanging Garden: Multi-level laneway complex with greenery, performance spaces and hole-in-the-wall eats. *11am-9pm Sun-Thu, to midnight Fri & Sat*

Rude Boy: Fried chicken and cocktails. Ramp up the rowdiness with rum BBQ sauce and cherry sour beer. Reggae rules. *4pm-midnight Tue-Sat*

Salamanca Arts Centre

In the Winter Dark

MAPS P640 & P644

Get loose at Hobart's decadent midwinter festival

The brainchild of the twisted minds out at **MONA** (p642), **Dark Mofo** *(darkmofo.net.au; prices vary)* is a winter arts-and-culture fest held in June each year. Focused on the waterfront, Dark Mofo revels in all things unhinged, Gothic and blood-red, and attracts visitors from around the world. Everything from the Tasman Bridge to Salamanca's warehouses is bathed in red light, with glowing red crosses studding the city. There's nonstop live music and performance art – shocking, sublime and downright weird. There's a new lineup every year, but three events are constant: the indulgent multi-night **Winter Feast** at Princes Wharf 1; the **Burning of the Ogoh-Ogoh**, a ritualistic bonfire of fears; and the festival-closing **Winter Solstice Nude Swim** at Long Beach in Sandy Bay. Book tickets in advance; leave your inhibitions elsewhere.

Recreating Antarctica

MAP P640

Life inside Sir Douglas Mawson's hut

On the waterfront next to Constitution Dock, **Mawson's Huts Replica Museum** *(mawsons-huts-replica.org.au; adult/child*

YACHT ROCK

Arguably the hardest open-ocean yacht race in the world, the Rolex **Sydney to Hobart Yacht Race** *(rolexsydneyhobart.com; free)* has been running since 1945, departing Sydney every Boxing Day and finishing at Hobart's Constitution Dock several days later.

The city is abuzz with anticipation from 27 December onwards, as sails materialise in the River Derwent and the waterfront bars start heaving with sunburned sailors.

For landlubbers, the classic Sydney to Hobart encounter is to promenade slowly (with ice cream) past the moored yachts, ooh-ing at expensive equipment and dreaming of the open-ocean glories. Or just head to the effervescent **Race Village** hub near Constitution Dock and have a beer instead.

EATING AT SALAMANCA & THE WATERFRONT: CAFE SCENES

MAPS P640 & P644

Retro Cafe: Masterful breakfasts, salads and burgers; laughing staff, jazz and the whirr of the coffee machine. *7.30am-4pm Mon-Fri, from 8am Sat & Sun* $

Daci & Daci: Slick bakery-cafe that's a hit with the local parliamentarians. Take your cake to the streetside deck. *7am-5pm* $

Tricycle Cafe & Bar: Artful nook inside the Salamanca Arts Centre serving cafe classics (ace muffins) and local wines. *8.30am-4pm Mon-Sat* $

Machine Laundry Cafe: Washing machine, killer coffee and plates of spicy potato hash. Live like a uni student in Salamanca Sq. *7.30am-3pm* $

WHO'S FOR A DRINK?

Hobart has always been a hard-drinking town – and nowhere more so than the waterfront. When in Rome...

START	END	LENGTH
Whaler	Hobart Brewing Co	1.5km; 2hr

Start with a pint at the rollicking, unpretentious **1 Whaler**, which has been pouring ales under various names since 1829 (mention 'Knopwood's Retreat' and older Hobartians tend to smile). The crew here is an egalitarian mix of tourists, tradies and suits – come as you are. Next up is the colonial-era **2 Customs House Hotel**, dating from around 1846, with an old-school public bar and a scattering of outdoor tables with water views.

Keeping your left hand on the shopfronts, shamble into the **3 Telegraph Hotel**, a swanky Art Deco drinking hole on the next street corner, reborn a few years ago with a rooftop bar, live music and good-looking drinkers. Craving a bite? Weave around to Brooke St Pier (via the mildly exciting Watermans Dock water-level walkway), where a corned-beef sandwich (OK and a pepperberry margarita) from **4 Rosie in My Midnight Dreams** will right your rudder.

Next, make a quick detour to **5 Lark Distillery** for a warming dram, before onwards to **6 IXL Long Bar** inside the luxe Henry Jones Art Hotel. Watch the sun sink slowly behind Kunanyi / Mt Wellington with jazz and further libations. Decamp around the back of the art school to **7 Hobart Brewing Co**. This big red shed serves excellent beers and the outside fire pits (mostly) repel Hobart's chilly night air.

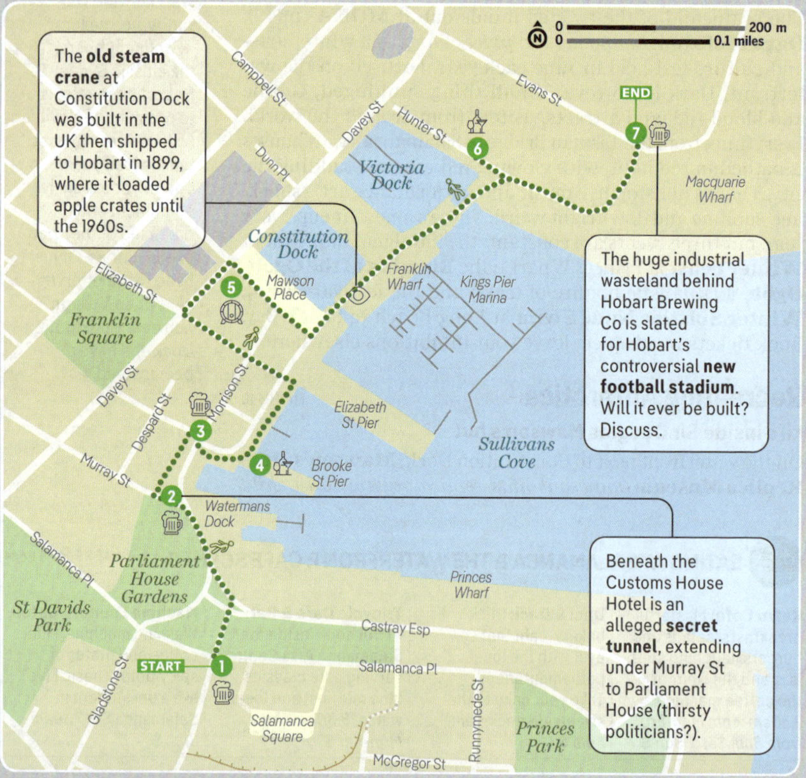

STEVE WATERS/GETTY IMAGES

Sullivans Cove

$15/5) is a model of one of the huts that Sir Douglas Mawson's Australasian Antarctic Expedition team, which set sail from Hobart, hunkered down in from 1911 to 1914. The replica is painstakingly exact (Mawson's tiny keyboard, a sledge and an ice axe are actually originals) and a knowledgeable guide is on hand to answer your Antarctic enquiries. Imagine 18 men living here, surviving on penguin stew. The original hut is still at Commonwealth Bay in Antarctica.

Hidden Battery Point

MAP P644

Historic cottages and quiet parks with a maritime soul

Beyond the Hampden Rd cafes, **Princes Park** is where Battery Point's gun battery once stood, built in 1818 to protect Hobart from the imagined threat of invading fleets of Americans, Russians, French, Dutch... The invasion never happened, the cannons are long gone and Princes Park is now a peaceful spot for a picnic or a snooze in the sun.

Skinny little **South Street**, off Hampden Rd, is crowded with historic timber and stone cottages that aren't particularly consistent or in particularly good condition. But South St just oozes maritime soul – the essence of Battery Point.

At the bottom of adjacent Kelly St, the foot-worn 1840 **Kelly's Steps** are named after one-time Hobart harbourmaster James

HOBART'S ARCHITECTURAL HERITAGE

Fred Ward, Director of 1+2 Architecture, shines a light on Hobart's historic buildings. *@1+2architecture*

Hobart has largely preserved its architectural heritage. Notable treasures include the cottages of **Battery Point**, one of Australia's most intact Georgian suburbs; and the early-19th-century stone **warehouses and factories** around **Sullivans Cove**. Many have been thoughtfully repurposed into modern hotels, restaurants and apartments. A great example is the former IXL Jam Factory, now the **UTAS School of Creative Arts**. Other highlights include the Tasmanian Museum & Art Gallery (p639), within one of Australia's finest collections of colonial buildings; and the exquisitely restored Theatre Royal (p645), a testament to meticulous heritage preservation.

EATING AT SALAMANCA & THE WATERFRONT: SEAFOOD

MAPS P640 & P644

Flippers: Fish-shaped Flippers is the pick of the floating fish punts in Constitution Dock, serving fresh, sea-salty fish and chips. *9.30am-9pm* $

Mures: A dockside regular. Upstairs is high-end; downstairs has oysters, ice-cream cones to go and the best seafood chowder in town. *8am-9pm* $$

Blue Eye: Seafood linguine, char-grilled octopus, sashimi, garlic-butter abalone – all sluiced down with Tasmanian wines and beers. *noon-10pm Tue-Sat* $$$

Fish Frenzy: Family-friendly fish and chips, inside and outside Elizabeth St Pier. Seagulls loiter with intent. *11.30am-8pm* $$

RACHAEL BOWES/SHUTTERSTOCK

Observation shelter, Kunanyi / Mt Wellington

Kelly and traverse the formerly impassable quarry face between Battery Point and Salamanca.

But sometimes it's transient occurrences that give Battery Point its character: a little pile of seashells on a doorstep, or a graffiti poem on a pub wall: 'Three flag-swept days/Ships monstrous and transitory/Heroes I could not captain'.

See Hobart from the Sea

MAP P644

Paddle through Sullivans Cove with a floating lunch

Clear, calm mornings on Sullivans Cove are perfect for sea kayaking – especially if you've got zero experience! **Roaring 40s Kayaking** *(roaring40skayaking.com.au; tours adult/child $140/85)* runs a 2½-hour paddling trip most mornings between October and April, suitable for all skill levels and kids over seven. The put-in is at Sandy Bay's Short Beach, then the trip heads north around Battery Point into Sullivans Cove. You'll paddle right into Constitution Dock for a floating fish-and-chip lunch. Day and multiday trips also available.

EATING IN BATTERY POINT: OUR PICKS

MAP P644

Jackman & McRoss: Famous Battery Point bakery-cafe: breakfast, brunch, breads and baked delights. Footpath tables when it's warm enough. *7am-5pm* $

Da Angelo: This classic *ristorante* packs out each night (book ahead). Pastas, pizzas and Carlton Football Club fandom. *5-9.30pm daily, plus noon-2.30pm Fri* $$

Three Japanese: Atmospheric Japanese: try the pork-belly charcoal skewers. Scary sake selection. *5.30-9pm Tue-Sun* $$

Magic Curries: Sip a cold Kingfisher beer in these magically coloured interiors and await your face-meltingly hot beef vindaloo. Excellent vegetarian, too. *5-9.30pm* $$

Hobart's Very Own Mountain

MAP P640

Towering mountain beacon with panoramic views and trails

Majestically sky-high or mysteriously shrouded in cloud, 1271m-high **Kunanyi / Mt Wellington** *(wellingtonpark.org.au; free)* is so large it generates its own weather patterns. Dappled with winter snow, Kunanyi is Hobart's beacon, its protector, its playground and its weather barometer...and the views from the top are awesome! At the summit car park, put on every layer of clothing you own and dash to the curvy-roofed **observation shelter**. Pinnacle Rd is often closed due to winter snow: check *hobartcity.com.au* for live road-closure updates.

The mountain is criss-crossed by a web of hiking paths, bike tracks, horse-riding trails and fire roads. Popular tracks include the Radfords Track, Pinnacle Track, Fern Glade Track, Pipeline Track, the steep Zig Zag Track and the excellent **Organ Pipes Circuit** (four hours, 9.2km), looping below Kunanyi's trademark dolerite cliffs. Check out *greaterhobarttrails.com.au* for info. Expect rapid weather shifts: this ain't no walk in the park (well, it is, but you know what we mean – be prepared, even for the shortest mountain walk).

Australia's Oldest Beers

MAP P640

Tour a brewery and sample the good stuff

Standing in startling, Gothic isolation next to the Hobart Rivulet, **Cascade Brewery** *(cascadebreweryco.com.au; brewery tour $38, historic tour adult/child $23/12)* is Australia's oldest brewery (1824) and is still pumping out superb beers. Daily one-hour tours dive into the beer-making process, with a tasting paddle at the end (try the pale ale). Under-18s aren't permitted on the main brewery tour (take the family-friendly historic tour instead) and brewery machinery might not be running if you're here on a weekend (brewers have weekends, too). Wear flat, closed-toe shoes. Want to skip straight to the liquid stuff? Cascade Brewery Bar (p652) is across the road.

Notorious Strumpets & Dangerous Girls

MAP P640

Haunting convict women's stories

The UNESCO World Heritage-listed **Cascades Female Factory Historic Site** *(femalefactory.org.au; adult/child $35/20, 1hr tour $40/22)* in South Hobart was where female

CAPTAIN BLOOD

Legendary swashbuckling actor Errol Flynn was born in Battery Point, first showing his handsome, future-moustachioed face at the Queen Alexandra Hospital on Hampden Rd on 20 June 1909. Flynn lived in Hobart, where his father was a professor of biology, until he was sent to school in London at the rather pivotal age of 14. Flynn went on to become a dashing Hollywood superstar, lighting up the screen in films like *Captain Blood* (1935), *The Charge of the Light Brigade* (1936) and *The Adventures of Robin Hood* (1938).

A notorious drinker and philanderer (his bedroom antics inspiring the phrase 'In like Flynn'), he expired prematurely while visiting Canada in 1959, aged just 50. Listen to Australian Crawl's 1981 song 'Errol' for further insights.

DRINKING IN BATTERY POINT & SANDY BAY: BEST FOR BEERS

MAP P644

Try the Killer Raspberry fruited sour ale

Prince of Wales Hotel: Battery Point's POW is an architectural poke-in-the-eye, but it does cracking pub food. *11am-10pm Sun-Thu, to midnight Fri & Sat*

Mayfair: Enduring Sandy Bay pub with live music, craft beers and vegan bar snacks. *3-10pm Mon-Thu, noon-11pm Fri & Sat, noon-10pm Sun*

Shipwrights Arms Hotel: Near the old Battery Point shipyards, 1846 'Shippies' has had a slick makeover, but the front bar is still sea-salty. *noon-11pm*

Preachers: Uphill from Salamanca, this backstreet beer garden (complete with old bus) has beaut brews and burgers. *noon-midnight*

WHALES IN THE DERWENT

In the 1830s, Hobart-ians joked about walking across the River Derwent on the backs of whales and complained about being kept awake at night by whales cavorting offshore. A glance across the river from Sandy Bay might reveal any number of spouting blowholes and splashing flukes. In typical Tasmanian style, the ensuing whaling boom was catastrophic, driving local populations of southern right and humpback whales to near extinction. Though still rare, the occasional forgiving whale returns to the Derwent during their June–July northbound and October–November southbound migration. If you spy one, call the Parks & Wildlife Service whale hotline on 0427 942 537.

MARCUS MOK/ALAMY

convicts were incarcerated and put to work in vile conditions. Around 12,500 women were transported to Tasmania and during its peak years of operation between 1828 and 1856, the Female Factory could hold up to 1200 women. Admission includes a 45-minute guided tour of the hauntingly spare yards with their interpretive installations; or book a one-hour themed **Notorious Strumpets and Dangerous Girls** tour, telling the tales of seven resilient convict women. See the website for tour times; kids' tours also available.

Arthouse at the State

MAP P640

A legendary 1913 cinema with 11 screens and rooftop films

The old **State Cinema** *(statecinema.com.au; adult/child $22/17)* dates back to 1913, when it opened as one of Tasmania's first purpose-built picture houses. These days there are 11 screens here (including a rooftop screen), showing films from the latest three-hour epics to shaky handheld documentaries. The adjacent **State Bookstore** is one of Hobart's best; there's a cafe out the back, too. You could exist in here indefinitely.

EATING & DRINKING IN SOUTH HOBART: OUR PICKS

MAP P640

Cascade Brewery Bar: At the foot of Kunanyi / Mt Wellington, with heritage gardens and brewery views. Tasting paddles and classic pub grub. *11am-9pm*

Vanidol's: Modern Asian, with a Thai twist. Try the *namtok* warm BBQ chilli-beef salad. *11am-2pm & 5-8.30pm Tue-Sat* $$

Ginger Brown: The pick of the Macquarie St cafes. Great baked eggs and coffee; kid- and cyclist-friendly. *7.30am-3pm Mon-Fri, from 8.30am Sat & Sun* $

Cascade Hotel: There were a dozen pubs in South Hobart once; Cascade Hotel (1846) is the last one. Super seafood, schnitzels and Cascade beer. *10am-9pm*

Cascade Brewery (p651)

Botanic Royalty

MAP P640

Historic cool-climate gardens with 200 years of heritage

Over the leafy Domain from North Hobart, the lush, sloping **Royal Tasmanian Botanical Gardens** *(rtbg.tas.gov.au; free)* are Australia's second-oldest (1818), featuring 14 hectares of local and cool-climate exotic plants, some more than 200 years old. Wander between the Subantarctic Plant House, the endemic Tasmanian Collection and collections of Chinese and Japanese plants – or just snooze on the lawns.

BEST LIVE MUSIC

Big-name bands hit MyState Bank Arena in Glenorchy or the city-centre Odeon. Sold out? Go here:

Republic Bar: North Hobart mainstay for singer-songwriters, open-mic nights, covers bands and touring rock interlopers.

Pablo's Cocktails & Dreams: Hidden, atmospheric, late-night jazz bunker off Harrington St in the city.

Altar Bar: Touring and local metal, alt-rock and dance acts in the city centre.

Jack Greene: A few Salamanca bars have live acoustic troubadours; Jack Greene is the pick of the bunch.

Longley International Hotel: Pub over the back of Kunanyi / Mt Wellington, attracting surprisingly big names (no neighbours to annoy).

EATING & DRINKING IN NORTH HOBART: OUR PICKS

MAP P640

Room for a Pony: Wood-fired pizzas and heated tables outside; beer and nachos inside. *7am-2.30pm Mon & Tue, to 9pm Wed, Thu & Sun, to midnight Fri & Sat* $$

Raincheck Lounge: Conversation and boho vibes flow freely at this pioneering North Hobart cafe-bistro-bar. Kid-friendly, too. *7am-3pm* $$

Annapurna: The best curry joint in North Hobart (there are a few). Try the balti prawns, tandoori lamb cutlets or veggie thali. *5-9.30pm* $$

Kalbi: Superbly spicy Korean soups, fired chicken and *pa jeon* (green onion pancakes). Gets busy – book ahead. *noon-2pm Thu-Sat & 5-9pm Tue-Sun* $$

Winston: Raffish corner pub with craft beer, a pool table and US-style eats (don't skimp on the Carolina Reaper chilli mayo). *4-10.30pm*

Shambles Brewery: Shamble into Shambles, down Elizabeth St, for a pint of the house pale. *4-10pm Wed & Thu, noon-midnight Fri & Sat, to 8pm Sun*

T-Bone Brewing Co: Down on the corner, T-Bone's quirky ales should impress. Love the barrel-aged stout. *4-9pm Wed, 2-9pm Thu, 2-11pm Fri & Sat, 2-8pm Sun*

Willing Bros: Cosy wine bar with a fantastic vino selection and sophisticated share plates. Classy, classy. *4.30-10pm Wed-Sat*

Beyond Hobart

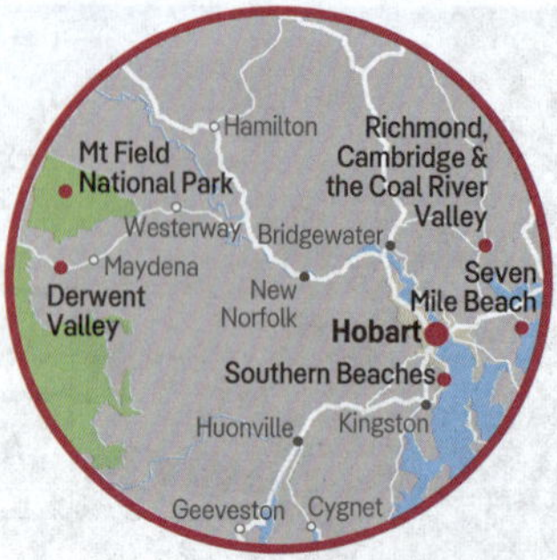

Places

GETTING AROUND

You'll need your own vehicle to fully explore this area. Public buses from Hobart run to Seven Mile Beach, Taroona, Kingston Beach and Blackmans Bay; to Richmond via Cambridge and the Coal River Valley; and to New Norfolk, several times daily. Day tours run to Richmond and Mt Field National Park (there's no public transport here), while minivan booze tours hit the wineries, distilleries and breweries in the Derwent and Coal River valleys.

Hobart isn't huge: head in any direction and you'll soon discover beaches, wilderness, vineyards and historic towns.

Right next to Hobart Airport is achingly deserted Seven Mile Beach – 7 miles of sandy, safe swimming. Nearby is Cambridge, home to the world's best whisky (seriously) and the lovely Coal River Valley wineries. Continue up the valley to historic Richmond, which looks for all the world like a teleported Kentish village.

Northwest from Hobart, the fertile fields around New Norfolk and the Derwent Valley are striped with hops and vines, while Mt Field National Park delivers some true wilderness: waterfalls, fagus and alpine tarns.

A string of beaches run south from Hobart to Taroona, where the sheer Alum Cliffs mark a divide before the seductive arc of Kingston Beach. Pack your snorkel to meet the underwater locals at Tinderbox.

Seven Mile Beach

TIME FROM HOBART: **25MIN**

Seven miles and a single hill

Out near the airport, a short drive through backstreet beach shacks then a short walk through the dunes delivers you to one of Tasmania's most underrated beaches, the aptly named **Seven Mile Beach** (yep – it's 7 miles long), with safe swimming and an occasionally surfable point break. A walk here is guaranteed to blow out the cobwebs; chances are it'll be just you and a few dog walkers.

On the western end of Seven Mile Beach is the formidable **Single Hill** *(greaterhobarttrails.com.au)*. At just 200m high it ain't alpine, but the ascent is a real workout! The 5.3km return track zig-zags up the slope, with increasingly eye-popping views. Catch your breath at the top and survey the scene from Kunanyi / Mt Wellington to the airport and across 7 miles of sand.

TOM JASTRAM/SHUTTERSTOCK

Seven Mile Beach

Richmond, Cambridge & the Coal River Valley

TIME FROM HOBART: **25MIN**

Bridging two centuries

Richmond's defining feature is the 1823 **Richmond Bridge** *(ccc.tas.gov.au)*, the oldest still-functioning bridge in Australia. Built by convicts, it's a massive structure that doesn't look like it's going anywhere anytime soon. The golden stone, manicured lawns and Coal River ducks are picture-perfect, although, in typical Tasmanian style, the bridge has a dark history too: it's purportedly haunted by the 'Flagellator of Richmond', George Grover, murdered here in 1832.

Wildlife, local and imported

Fifteen minutes from Richmond, **Bonorong Wildlife Sanctuary** *(bonorong.com.au; adult/child $35/20)* is a 24/7 wildlife rescue and rehabilitation centre. Bonorong is not a zoo, but it's a great place to see some wildlife: Tasmanian devils, quolls, bettongs, pademelons and kangaroos. Tours and animal encounters run regularly.

Closer to Richmond, **Hobart Zoo & Aquarium** *(hzaa.com.au; adult/child $37/21)* offers a more traditional zoo experience (on a Hobart scale), with a couple of imperious lions, snakes,

COAL RIVER VALLEY BOOZE TOURS

North of Seven Mile Beach, the Coal River Valley wine scene is booming. Wine time!

Coal River Wine Hopper: Hop-on/hop-off Coal River Valley winery tours, with hourly pickups at liquid hot spots.

Aging Barrel: Winery tours to the Coal River, Derwent and Huon valleys (and combos thereof), including lunch.

Drink Tasmania: Whisky, wine, cider and beer across the Huon, city and Coal River Valley.

Derwent Experience: 'Ultimate Tasmanian Tasting Tour' of the Derwent and Coal River valleys: gins, ales, wines and ciders, plus a cheesy lunch.

Boutique Wine Tours: Combine Coal River Valley wineries with a MONA visit, returning on the ferry.

DRINKING IN THE COAL RIVER VALLEY: BEST WINERIES

Frogmore Creek: Quality dining and cool-climate wines in a mod space that can get busy (better book). Try the iced riesling. *10am-5pm*

Puddleduck Vineyard: Relaxed escape revolving around a duck pond, with zesty vinos (try the 'Bubbleduck') and kid-friendly eats. *10am-5pm*

Pooley Wines: Sip top Coal River pinots inside the heritage cellar door or outside by the vines. Wood-fired pizzas, too. *10am-5pm*

Craigow Vineyard: Unpretentious and low-key with a farm-cottage cellar door, Craigow bottles up brilliant whites. *11am-4pm Sat & Sun, by appointment Mon-Fri*

RICHMOND RIVERSIDE RAMBLE

The main street in Richmond is heaving with shops and attractions (and people). See it, then unearth some historic backstreet gems.

START	END	LENGTH
Richmond Bridge	Richmond Bridge	2.5km; 1hr

From the Richmond Bridge car park, admire the six sandstone arches of handsome 1 **Richmond Bridge** (p655), Australia's oldest still-functioning bridge (1823). Cross the Coal River and veer left. The elegant, elliptical 2 **Old Courthouse** (1825) by the village green harks back to Richmond's penal past.

Thirsty? Duck into the sandstone 3 **Richmond Arms Hotel** (1888; formerly the 1827 Commercial Hotel), then cross the road to the former 4 **Congregational Church** (1875), now private accommodation.

Pass noble, symmetrical 5 **Oak Lodge** (1842), fronted by twin oaks and now a National Trust history room. Turn left down Blair St, then zigzag past heritage houses to Torrens St and the sombre 6 **Pioneer Cemetery** (1845), with its 40-plus graves.

Next up is Norman-style 7 **St Luke's Anglican Church** (1834), Australia's oldest Anglican church, where the convict carpenter's handiwork earned him his freedom. At the end of Bathurst St, the intact, unrestored 8 **Richmond Gaol Historic Site** is a sobering reminder of the inhumane treatment of convicts in Tasmania.

Wander down to the shallow, reedy 9 **Coal River** and follow the pathway back to Richmond Bridge. The timber platform over the water marks the optimal photo op. Back at the car park, if you still have gas in the tank, wander up the hill to 10 **St John the Evangelist Church**, the oldest Catholic church in Australia (1836).

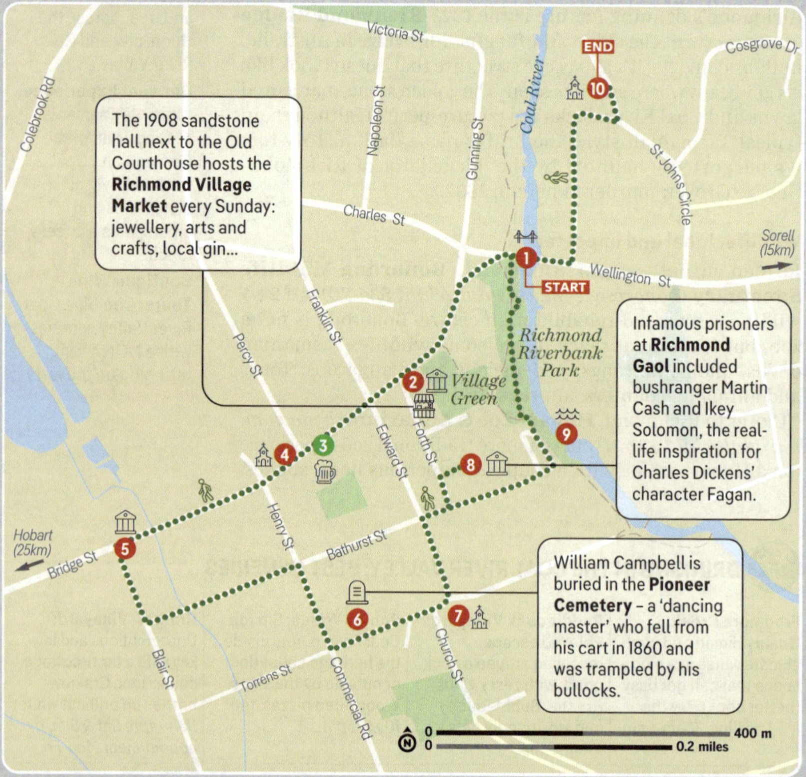

exotic birds, monkeys, meerkats and a room of aquarium tanks. Kids love the enthusiastic keeper talks.

Award-winning whisky in a sleek industrial setting

The industrial backblocks of Cambridge aren't necessarily where you'd expect to find the world's best whisky. But **Sullivans Cove** *(sullivanscove.com; tours/tastings $70/30)* is exactly that. Inside this black-box building, passionate distillers bottle up the world's best single-malt whisky (2014) and the best single-cask single malt (2018 and 2019), as adjudged at the World Whiskies Awards – the first distillery outside Scotland or Japan to wear the 'Best Single Malt' crown. Book a 90-minute tour (2pm daily) or a 30-minute tasting (10am daily) in the rather stylish bar.

Derwent Valley

TIME FROM HOBART: **35MIN**

How does your garden grow?

Inside the walled exercise yard of New Norfolk's old Willow Court asylum, the **Agrarian Kitchen** *(theagrariankitchen.com; tours adult/child $30/15)* cultivates an organic, sustainable garden to supply its restaurant. Informative one-hour tours run Fridays to Sundays, explaining the garden's workings (recycled and composted; no chemical fertilisers or pesticides). The result is nutrient-packed, super-fresh fruit and veg served straight to your plate. An indulgent range of **cooking classes** is also available, focusing on everything from charcuterie to cheesemaking. Book ahead.

Fresh berry picking and ice cream in Westerway

At tiny, evocatively named Westerway, en route to Mt Field National Park, is **Westerway Raspberry Farm** *(lanoma.com.au; from $18 per kg berries)*. Stop by for a berry ice cream, or wander into the fields with a bucket and pick your own strawberries, raspberries, blackberries, boysenberries and blackcurrants – straight from the bushes. Open December to February.

Mt Field National Park

TIME FROM HOBART: **1½HR**

Rainforests, waterfalls and alpine moorlands

The equal-oldest national park in Tasmania (along with Freycinet, founded in 1916), Mt Field is part of the vast

WHISKY HISTORY

With misty highlands, abundant barley, clean-running water... even peat, Tasmania has all the hallmarks of Scotland, the home of fine single-malt whisky. It's little wonder that whisky-making has taken off here, with spectacular results. But it wasn't until 1992 that Bill Lark, the godfather of Tasmanian whisky and founder of Lark Distillery (p648), successfully lobbied to have an archaic law banning backyard distilling overturned.

The ruling had been in place since 1839 when Governor Franklin's wife Lady Jane objected to Hobart's drunken ways. In the ensuing decades, only the odd moonshiner (some of them very odd) would dare distill anything remotely alcoholic. Now there are 70-plus distillers on the island, producing winning whisky, gin, rum – even sheep's whey vodka. Oh Lady Jane...

EATING IN RICHMOND & THE COAL RIVER VALLEY: OUR PICKS

Coal River Farm: Valley cheeses and chocolates; the Washed Rind will knock your socks off. Breakfasts, pies, share plates and coffee, too. *9am-5pm* $$

Wicked Cheese Co: Puts some bite into its cheeses; try the pepperberry cheddar. Platters, burgers, wines and beers. *10am-4.30pm* $$

Richmond Bakery: Country-town bakery: pies, pastries, sandwiches, muffins and cakes. Curried scallop pie, anyone? *6am-5pm Mon-Fri, from 7am Sat & Sun* $

Richmond Arms Hotel: Chunky sandstone pub (1888) serving old-school grub. Steak time. Live music in the beer garden. *8am-9pm* $$$

POETIC JUSTICE

Mt Field National Park is named after Barron Field (1786–1846), a dispute-prone English lawyer, scholar and poet. In 1817, Field arrived in Sydney to take up a posting as judge of the Supreme Court of NSW. In 1819 he presided over the first sitting of the Supreme Court of Van Diemen's Land, as Tasmania was then known, but he's better known for publishing Australia's first book of poetry that same year: the 12-page *First Fruits of Australian Poetry*.

Sundry disagreements led to Field's recall to England in 1824, followed by further postings (and squabbles) in Ceylon and Gibraltar – none of which extinguished his poetic fires. In 1841 he published another book of poems, *Spanish Sketches*.

ACROPOLYPSEPHOTOGRAPHY/SHUTTERSTOCK

Russell Falls

Tasmanian Wilderness World Heritage Area (TWWHA) – an accessible introduction to the wild southwest, just 90 minutes from Hobart.

Around the **Mt Field National Park Visitor Centre** *(parks.tas.gov.au; day pass per person/vehicle $24/48)* are damp groves of temperate rainforest: tree ferns, moss, myrtle beech and towering mountain ash. Hidden in the greenery are a series of exquisite waterfalls. A wheelchair-accessible 1.4km return track leads to the park's big-ticket attraction, the multitiered, photogenic **Russell Falls**. For a longer, more challenging circuit (two hours, 6km) continue up to **Horseshoe Falls**, a pair of twin falls deep in the forest; and **Lady Baron Falls**, a set of gentle cascades. Don't miss the short **Tall Trees Nature Trail** in a copse of mountain ash on the way.

For a closer encounter with the TWWHA, take the 30-minute twisting drive up unsealed Lake Dobson Rd from the visitor centre to **Lake Dobson**. Here on park's high exposed moorlands, the 12km, full-day **Tarn Shelf Track** takes you into the wilds. Australia's most southerly ski field is here, too: the very low-key **Mt Mawson** *(mtmawson.info; day pass adult/*

DRINKING IN THE DERWENT VALLEY: BEER, CIDER, WINE & WHISKY

Two Metre Tall: Farm brewery producing small-batch, hand-pumped ales and ciders. BYO picnic; on-site BBQs. Is brewer Ashley actually 2m tall? *noon-4.30pm Fri-Sun*

Plenty Cider: There's plenty of hazy, small-batch cider at this cidery in Plenty, using valley fruits. Love the apple and cherry combo. *11am-4pm Sat & Sun*

Derwent Estate: Sample a dozen wines in Derwent's 1820s cottage tasting room. The Shed restaurant is here, too. *11am-5pm*

Bush Inn: Who wouldn't want to drink a beer in Tasmania's oldest continually licensed pub? Nobody, that's who. In New Norfolk. *11am-10pm* *child $50/25)*. Rope tows run on weekends and school holidays when there's enough snow.

The turning of the fagus

There aren't many deciduous native trees in Australia – Tasmania's deciduous beech, *Nothofagus gunii*, is one of them. It's a straggly, gnarly shrub found only above 800m elevation in high-rainfall, alpine areas like Mt Field National Park. In autumn, its leaves turn a riot of yellow, orange and russet red and catching the 'turning of the fagus' creates a buzz on the socials. Head up twisty Lake Dobson Rd within the national park to the **Tarn Shelf** and **Lake Fenton** to witness the spectacle. The fagus does its thing any time from March to May, with the colours lasting several weeks.

Southern Beaches

TIME FROM HOBART: **20MIN**

Hike the Alum Cliffs Track

From **Taroona Beach**, with its BBQs, playground and boat ramp, follow the foreshore track south to hidden little **Hinsby Beach**, a perfect patch of sand at the base of the impressive Alum Cliffs. From the far end of the beach, pick up the 8km (return) **Alum Cliffs Track** *(greaterhobarttrails.com.au)*. Initially heading inland, the track climbs through coastal scrub and a few backstreets to the **Shot Tower** *(parks.tas.gov.au; adult/child $10/4)*. Built in 1870, this 58m circular tower (still one of the tallest buildings in Tasmania!) was designed to create ammunition: molten lead shot pellets were dropped from the top, forming perfect spheres as they fell to cool in a cold cauldron below. Take the creaky 259 steps to the top, scan the horizon, then hit the tearoom. From here, the track heads around the clifftops to handsome **Kingston Beach**. Swim out to the pontoon, then retreat for some fish and chips and a beer at the pub.

Snorkel the underwater trail at Tinderbox Marine Reserve

Follow the coast road 10km south from Blackmans Bay to sweet little **Tinderbox Beach**. Strap on your snorkel and explore the underwater trail along the reefs of **Tinderbox Marine Reserve** *(parks.tas.gov.au; free)*. There are usually plenty of fish here – wrasse, leatherjackets, seahorses and crayfish – although the trail's original submerged plaques are now somewhat hard to read.

QUEEN MARY OF TAROONA

Taroona's most famous ex-resident is Mary Elizabeth Donaldson, the present Queen of Denmark. The classic Cinderella story goes something along the lines of 'The Crown Prince of Denmark walked into a bar...' The rest is history. The bar was Sydney's Slip Inn during the 2000 Sydney Olympics: Mary was having a drink with a girlfriend when in popped Frederik André Henrik Christian, first in line to the Danish throne.

A secret courtship ensued, before the couple married in Copenhagen Cathedral in 2004. Mary learnt Danish and had four children, and when Frederik's mum abdicated in 2024, the royal couple ascended the throne. Back in the day she went to Taroona High School and lived on Morris Ave – a very long way from Copenhagen.

EATING & DRINKING IN KINGSTON BEACH: OUR PICKS

Salty Dog: This 1960s waterfront tavern has been reborn, Miami-style, serving refined dishes and old faves. Live beer-garden bands on Sundays. *8am-9pm* **$$**

Robbie Brown's: Beachfront wine bar serving tasty brunches, share plates and pub-style dinners. Order the rosti Benedict. *hours vary* **$$**

Boho: Bohemian style in the gift shop, extending through to a leafy courtyard cafe. Killer coffee, wine, open fire, happy days. Kid-friendly, too. *7.30am-3pm* **$**

Eb+Flo: Bright water-facing cafe serving simple soups and sandwiches. The takeaway coffee window does a roaring trade. *7am-4pm* **$**

The South

WILDERNESS | CONVICT HISTORY | FOODIE ENCOUNTERS

Places

TOP TIP

Time-poor visitors can tick off most of Bruny Island's must-sees in a long day. If you're planning on staying a while, book camping and accommodation well in advance – see *brunyisland.com.au* or *brunyisland.org.au* for options. Bring all your groceries with you, as supplies are limited (non-existent on North Bruny).

Just an hour from Hobart you'll find the staggering coastal landscapes, outdoor adventures and historic sites of Turrrakana / Tasman Peninsula. The World Heritage–listed Port Arthur Historic Site is here too, an infamous 19th-century convict colony.

A popular day tour or weekend getaway from Hobart, Bruny Island has some great foodie distractions, but it's largely low-key and agricultural: most tourists head to South Bruny, with its sparkling beaches and bays and towering sea cliffs.

Still harbours, heritage villages and misty valleys – the Huon Valley is the apple-producing heartland of the Apple Isle, also producing cherries, pears, apricots, wine, mushrooms and, of course, cider! Hartz Mountains National Park and Hastings Caves aren't far inland; further south, magnificent Recherche Bay sits on the doorstep of Southwest National Park. The only sealed road into Southwest National Park runs between Maydena, a small logging community reinventing itself as a mountain-biking hub and far-flung Strathgordon. Are you out there, thylacine?

Turrakana / Tasman Peninsula

TIME FROM HOBART: **1HR**

Coastal walk along spectacular sea cliffs

Designed for people who like a modicum of comfort with their wilderness, the 48km, four-day **Three Capes Track** *(parks.tas.gov.au; adult/child $625/495)* meanders along the spectacular sea cliffs within Tasman National Park. Nights are spent in comfortable, architect-designed cabins, achievable

GETTING AROUND

Turrakana / Tasman Peninsula is an hour from Hobart via Sorell; driving is ideal, though tours and daily Tassielink buses reach Port Arthur and Nubeena. There's no public transport on Bruny Island; take a tour or the car ferry from Kettering. Many island roads are unsealed.

Tassielink serves the Huon Valley, but a car will get you to national parks, caves and coastlines. The Southwest requires a vehicle or a pricey bushwakers' shuttle; Par Avion flies South Coast Track walkers to Melaleuca.

Three Capes Track

distances apart. The one-directional walk kicks off at Port Arthur Historic Site, with a cruise to **Cape Raoul** (the first cape) before the walking starts at Denman Creek. Views along the way are phenomenal, especially at **Cape Pillar** and **Cape Hauy** (pronounced 'hoy'). The track ends at photogenic **Fortescue Bay**; celebrate with a swim before the bus takes you back to Port Arthur. The track is walkable year-round – book well in advance. Several companies run fully guided tours, staying in luxury private lodges at equally luxurious prices.

Geological wonders and sea spray blooms along the coast

At the northern end of Pirates Bay, a short trail leads to a rocky coastal terrace, the **Tessellated Pavement** – curiously eroded into what looks like tiled paving. Just south of Teralina / Eaglehawk Neck, follow the signs through **Doo Town** village to the **Blowhole**, where sporadic bursts of sea spray bloom into the air. Nearby, within **Tasman National Park** *(parks.tas.gov.au; day pass per person/vehicle $24/48)*, short walks lead to **Tasman Arch** (a cavern-like natural bridge) and **Devil's Kitchen** (a rugged 60m-deep cleft).

Continued on p665

SOUTHERN KAYAKING

Ewan Blyth, wilderness adventure guide, shares his favourite paddling locales. *@ballaghblyth*

Turrakana / Tasman Peninsula: With sea caves, fur-seal colonies, white-bellied sea eagles, deserted beaches and tall sea cliffs, this is the paddle of a lifetime. Launch from Fortescue Bay; for experienced sea kayakers.

Franklin: For a more serene experience, slide your kayak onto the mirror-like Huon River at Franklin at dawn. Glide silently along glassy waterways and get up close to native birdlife at Egg Island Reserve.

Blackmans Bay: South of Hobart, paddle past aptly named Fossil Cove to the Tinderbox Marine Reserve and Tinderbox Beach (8km) where you can put out or return the same way. Great for newbies; pack a mask and snorkel.

EATING & DRINKING ON TURRAKANA / TASMAN PENINSULA: OUR PICKS

Doo-Lishus: Tasmania's best fish and chips? Unexpected caravan at the Doo Town Blowhole. *10am-5.30pm* $

Cubed: Enjoy views with your coffee at this restored, solar-powered 1957 caravan at Pirates Bay Lookout. Good biscuits. *9am-3pm Thu-Mon* $

Bangor Vineyard Shed: On a hilltop at Dunalley is this excellent vineyard, the cellar door doubling as an oyster-focussed restaurant. Fab riesling. *10am-5pm*

McHenry Distillery: Bush distillery near Port Arthur creating classic gins, whiskies and beers, with seasonal variations. Tours and lodgings, too. *noon-4pm*

MR IN CHARGE/SHUTTERSTOCK

TOP EXPERIENCE

Port Arthur Historic Site

Nowhere does Tasmania's grim convict past feel so tangible than at the World Heritage–listed Port Arthur Historic Site. Green lawns and neat cottages create an English-village vibe between the ruins – but even the impressive visitor centre can't gloss over historical, and more recent, horrors. This is a place to show human reverence and respect, from a time when these were in short supply.

DON'T MISS

- Penitentiary
- Commandant's House
- Separate Prison
- Church
- Boat tour to the Isle of the Dead
- Free talks
- Scorpion Rock lookout

Why Here?

The British established a small timber-milling settlement at Port Arthur in 1830 and began transporting their unwanted criminals here by the boatful. This process continued until transport ceased in 1853, the prison finally closing in 1877. Port Arthur had a harsh reputation: miscreants from other colonial prisons often ended up here. Port Arthur was considered escape-proof, as it was cut off from the rest of Tasmania by narrow Teralina / Eaglehawk Neck, where fierce guard dogs

PRACTICALITIES

- *portarthur.org.au* ● adult/child/family $53/26/117
- 9am-5pm

and tales of shark-infested waters deterred escape. The site was abandoned in the late 1890s. Despite its redemption as a major tourist site (the ruins are undeniably amazing), Port Arthur remains a sombre place. Compounding this mood are memories of April 1996, when a deranged young gunman murdered 35 people here and injured 19 more. UNESCO World Heritage status was assigned to Port Arthur in 2010, along with four other Tasmanian convict sites.

Explore the Main Buildings

Most visitors head first to the **Penitentiary**, the massive standalone sandstone facade that was once a flour mill, yet ended up housing 484 prisoners. The well-preserved **Commandant's House** is nearby, the refinement and comfort on display a poignant counterpoint to the squalor afforded to the convicts. The well-preserved **Separate Prison** and adjacent **Asylum** are mute reminders of punishment ideology; after being subjected to the psychological torture of the former, prisoners often ended up in the latter. On higher ground, away from the prison buildings, the **Church** indicates the role religion played in prisoner reformation.

Between the Ruins

The Historic Site covers 136 hectares, gently sloping down to tranquil Carnarvon Bay. Several formal gardens appear as you wander around, including the **Civil Officer's Gardens** below the Church and the hedged **Government Gardens**, complete with fountain. The **Officers Gardens** extend behind **Trentham Cottage**, itself with a fine example of an English cottage garden. The most poignant garden, though, is the small **Memorial Garden**, commemorating those who lost their lives in the 1996 massacre.

Isle of the Dead

The final destination for many Port Arthur inmates – the oddly tranquil **Isle of the Dead**, a small island in Carnarvon Bay – was the penal colony's cemetery. The majority of the 1100 graves here are unmarked. The boat trip included in your ticket goes out to the island, but you can't get off unless you've paid for the additional **tour** *(adult/child $30/15)*. The isle is just off Point Puer, site of the first boys' prison in the British Empire.

Tours & Talks

To get the most out of your visit, listen to the experts. Free talks are held at various times throughout the day outside the Penitentiary, Commandant's House, Church and Separate Prison; check times online. Other value-added guided tours are available for an additional cost, including the after-hours **Ghost Tour** *(adult/child $35/18)*. For 90 minutes a noir figure carrying a lantern leads you through the ruined buildings, relating tall tales and true.

PYDAIRRERME PEOPLE

Port Arthur lies on the lands of the Pydairrerme people of the larger Paredarerme language group, centred on Oyster Bay. Middens and artefacts have been found here and across the peninsula, even on formidable, cliff-wrapped Tasman Island. Following an all-too-familiar pattern, European contact proved deadly for the Pydairrerme and only one name was ever recorded – Poetigwerlayde, sent to Wybalenna on Flinders Island, fate unknown.

TOP TIPS

- Climb up to **Scorpion Rock** lookout on the path behind the Church for an excellent view over the entire site.
- Your entrance ticket is valid for two days – don't feel rushed to see it all at once.
- Take the Isle of the Dead tour for a 40-minute guided walk around the cemetery island.
- Is the classy 1830 restaurant open again? It was closed when we visited, but the cafe was doing a roaring trade.
- Don't miss **Remarkable Cave** nearby; or to really blow away the sombre vibes, take the four-hour return walk to timelessly beautiful **Crescent Bay**.

BRUNY ISLAND FOOD TOUR

Bruny Island is a gorgeous natural realm of beaches and sea cliffs...or forget all that and enjoy an indulgent foodie day trip.

START	END	LENGTH
Bruny Island Ferry	Bruny Island Ferry	100km; 1 day

Roll off the ferry from Kettering and follow the main road to 1 **Get Shucked Oysters**. Grab a shucked dozen from the drive-through or sit on the deck and slurp in the sun. Not far away, pull into 2 **Bruny Island Cheese Co** for some outstanding cheese, beer and sourdough. Settle in for a lazy lunch, or continue to 3 **Bruny Island Honey** for tastings, a scoop of honey ice cream and a jar to go.

Keep heading south to 4 **the Neck** and burn off some calories on the steep steps to the 5 **Truganini Memorial**, with dazzling isthmus views. Approaching Adventure Bay, take your pick from sumptuous chocs at 6 **Bruny Island Chocolate Co** or a punnet of juicy raspberries at 7 **Bruny Island Raspberry Farm**. Maybe both. Backtrack and head for Alonnah. Pull over to see if the 8 **Bruny Baker** has filled his retro roadside fridges with his daily sourdough loaves. Leave some coins and keep rolling. In Alonnah, prime yourself for a cold beer, a hot local cider and some fish and chips at 9 **Hotel Bruny**; or continue to Lunawanna for 10 **Bruny Island Premium Wines**, Australia's most southerly vineyard.

Weave your way back to North Bruny for a final snifter of Tasmanian whisky at the 11 **Bruny Island House of Whisky**, then roll back onto the ferry.

Continued from p661

Convict heritage, off the beaten track

The amazing Port Arthur Historic Site gets all the attention – and rightly so. But for a less visited, low-key convict encounter, detour to the **Coal Mines Historic Site** *(coalmines.org.au; free)*, 28km north of Port Arthur. Convicts worked in abominable conditions, before the mine closed in 1848 on 'moral and financial grounds'. Walking tracks loop through the ruins. The crumbled sandstone barracks, overlooking the water, are particularly evocative; the solitary confinement cells are tortuously small and dark. To get here, from the town of Premaydena, take the signposted turn off (the C341) 13km northwest to Saltwater River.

Crossing the Dog Line

Beyond Dunalley, **Teralina / Eaglehawk Neck** is the second isthmus you'll cross heading south to Port Arthur, this one connecting the Forestier Peninsula to Turrakana / Tasman Peninsula. In convict days, the 100m-wide Neck had a row of ornery dogs chained across it to prevent convicts from escaping – the infamous **Dog Line** *(eaglehawkneck.org; free)*. Rumours were told of shark-infested waters to discourage swimming. Remarkably, despite these measures, several convicts made successful bids for freedom. Today you can check out a ferocious-looking **dog sculpture**, without much bite.

Huon Valley

TIME FROM HOBART: **30MIN**

Celebrating all things apple

It's hard to miss **Willie Smith's Apple Shed** *(williesmiths.com.au)*, right on the Huon Hwy at Grove on the approach to Huonville from Hobart – a celebration of all things *Malus domestica* (the good ol' domestic apple). Packed into one large shed is an apple museum, a rollicking cider house, a restaurant serving pub favourites (go for the Reuben sandwich) and a distillery making – of course – apple liqueurs. On Friday nights, Willie's turns into a live-music venue and there's a local **craft market** on Saturday mornings. You'll find Willie Smith's cider on tap in pubs across Tasmania these days: is cider making a comeback?

FAST FOOD

All along the Huon Valley roadsides, particularly the B68 between Huonville and Cygnet, you can pull over and buy farm-fresh produce from makeshift (or sometimes sophisticated, illuminated and refrigerated) roadside apple stalls. These usually take the form of tin sheds out the front of farms, stocked with bags of whatever is in season: pears, apricots, peaches, blueberries, blackberries, raspberries, boysenberries, strawberries, potatoes, peas, beans, bottled juice and, of course, apples. It's an honesty system – grab your bag, drop some coins in the box (or often, scan a QR code to pay) and drive off brimming with vitamin C. As a rough guide, a bag of fresh apples sells for about $4. Bargain!

EATING & DRINKING IN THE HUON VALLEY: OUR PICKS

Summer Kitchen Bakery: On the Ranelagh crossroads, the pies and sourdough loaves here are legendary. *7.30am-4pm Mon-Fri, from 8am Sat & Sun* $

Red Velvet Lounge: Cygnet's fave coffee-and-cake hangout; also pizzas, pasta, salads and pies. Live music Fridays. *8am-4pm Mon-Thu, to 8pm Fri & Sat, 9am-3pm Sun* $$

Lost Captain: Huonville taphouse-restaurant in a beautiful riverside homestead. Order a pint of the Huon River Brown Ale and head for the brazier. *noon-9pm*

Frank's Cider House & Cafe: Family-run cider house in Franklin, with Huon heritage dating back to 1836. Live music on Sundays. *10am-5pm, to 4pm Jun-Aug*

JEAN-MICHEL HUON DE KERMADEC

Born into French naval royalty in 1746, de Kermadec served in the American War of Independence before joining Bruni d'Entrecasteaux on a 1785 voyage to the Far East on the *Resolution*. He again accompanied D'Entrecasteaux in 1791 as second-in-command, on a voyage to find the missing French explorer La Perouse and his ships *L'Astrolabe* and *Boussole*. Given command of the *Esperance*, together with D'Entrecasteaux (on the *Recherche*) they arrived in 1792 at what is now **Recherche Bay** near Cockle Creek, where they carried out surveys and scientific experiments and even planted a small garden.

Huonville, the Huon River, Huon Valley and Huon pine and the village Kermandie near Geeveston, are all part of Kermadec's legacy.

Woodworking magic in Franklin

Marvel at the carpentry skills on display at the **Wooden Boat Centre** *(woodenboatcentre.com; tours adult/child/family $15/5/35)* on the Huon riverbanks in Franklin. Inside, exquisite boats are produced using salvaged, recycled and sustainable Tasmanian timbers, each one a work of art. Take a 40-minute tour for an in-depth appreciation of the centre's place in the local community: a volunteer guide will walk you through the workshop, where you can watch boats being cobbled together and catch a glorious whiff of Huon pine.

Alpine walks in Hartz Mountains National Park

From Geeveston, take the Arve Rd then partly unsealed Hartz Rd into the 121-sq-km **Hartz Mountains National Park** *(parks.tas.gov.au; day pass per person/vehicle $24/48)*, an alpine wilderness that's part of the Tasmanian Wilderness World Heritage Area. **Waratah Lookout** is an easy five-minute shuffle from the road. Other well-surfaced short walks include **Arve Falls** (20 minutes return) and **Lake Osborne** (40 minutes return). The steeper **Lake Esperance** walk (1½ hours return) takes you into beautiful high country.

An amazing cave

Around 15km from Southport is **Hastings Caves & Thermal Springs** *(parks.tas.gov.au; adult/child $24/12, pool only $5/2.50)*, a state reserve where you can descend into the half-light below conical Adamsons Peak on a 45-minute guided tour through Newdegate Cave – the largest (publicly accessible) dolerite cave in the country. Tours run hourly from 11am to 3pm on a first-come, first-served basis. Take a dip in the thermal pool afterwards.

Drive to the bottom of Australia

Beyond Hastings, the C636 begins its lonely journey south to the bottom of Australia. Tiny communities crop up along the way – first **Lune River** then **Ida Bay**, where the asphalt runs out. **Catamaran** is a loose affiliation of fishing shacks alongside the soft-lulling waves of **Recherche Bay**, before you cross Cockle Creek into Southwest National Park...and there's no more road. You're as far south as you can get in Australia without a boat or a backpack.

EATING & DRINKING IN THE FAR SOUTH: OUR PICKS

Wild Bird: Progressive, pocket-sized Dover cafe serving breakfast burgers, pumpkin-and-pesto toasties and good coffee. *8am-2pm Thu-Sat, 10am-1pm Sun* $

rocket@TheEndOfTheRoad: Wacked-out water tank at the end of the Huon Hwy in Southport, selling excellent coffee and muffins. *9am-3.30pm seasonal* $

Masaaki's Sushi: In Geeveston, Japanese chef Masaaki boxes up Tasmania's best bentos. Takes a winter break. *from noon Sat* $$

Southport Hotel: Duck in for a beer, if only to say you've enjoyed one in Australia's most southerly pub. Pool tables and shoeless fishermen. *noon-9pm*

Maydena

TIME FROM HOBART: 1¼HR

Mountain bike trails and gravity runs through alpine forests

Carved into the forest on the side of a mountain, **Maydena Bike Park** *(maydenabikepark.com; full-access day pass adult/child $120/100)* offers over 85 mountain-bike trails catering for all skill levels, from rank amateur to hard-tailed pro (plus lessons if you're in the former category). Over 100km of trails include plenty of gravity runs – though there are some climbs for the masochistic and adventure runs with river crossings. Shuttle buses 'uplift' riders to several different drop-off points and there's a dizzying array of access-pass options. There's a cafe-bar here too, plus repair ships, bike-wash booths and a classy mountaintop restaurant for sunset dinners in summer. Takes a winter break.

Southwest National Park

TIME FROM HOBART: 2HR

Wild southern trails from Melaleuca to Cockle Creek

The best-known walk in the Southwest is the 85km **South Coast Track** *(parks.tas.gov.au; national park fees apply)*, running along the wild southern edge of Tasmania between Melaleuca and Cockle Creek at the southern end of the Huon Valley. Allow six to eight days to reach Cockle Creek. **Par Avion** *(paravion.com.au)* flies bushwalkers into/out of Melaleuca and there's vehicle access to Cockle Creek. If you don't have a spare week at your disposal, the last (or first) day of the South Coast Track makes a brilliant four-hour return walk from Cockle Creek to **South Cape Bay** and back.

DROWNING OF A LAKE

The unique pink quartzite beach of original **Lake Pedder**, immortalised in the photos of Olegas Truchanus, lies 15m below the current waterline, created by dams on the Huon and Serpentine rivers in 1972.

Opposition to the damming at the time was the first mainstream environmental battle in Tasmania and though ultimately unsuccessful, it was the birth of the Australian conservation movement and the Tasmanian Greens, the world's first Green political party.

The battle alerted the rest of Australia to the beauty of the Southwest wilderness and both the Greens and the conservation movement were better organised (and ultimately successful) for the next battle, a decade later, over the proposed damming of the Franklin River.

EATING & DRINKING IN THE SOUTHWEST: OUR PICKS

Best coffee in the Southwest

Summit Restaurant: MBP's 1100m-high Summit Restaurant is open sporadically over summer; book ahead. *hours vary* $$$

Maydena Eats: Take a seat at the Giants' Table & Cottages diner in Maydena for pub-style dinners and beers on tap. *5-9pm Wed-Sun* $$

Twelvetrees Bar & Restaurant: The bar-restaurant at Strathgordon's Pedder Wilderness Lodge is the only sign of life after 6pm. *hours vary* $$

Patio: Maydena Bike Park has an on-site bar-cafe: breakfasts, burgers and beers. *8.30am-7pm Thu & Sun, to 8pm Fri & Sat*

East Coast

BEACHES | WINE | MOUNTAIN BIKING

Places

Maria Island National Park is a car-free, carefree haven – a top spot for walking, wildlife watching, cycling, camping and delving into Darlington's UNESCO-listed convict ruins. You'll meet kangaroos, Cape Barren geese, an 'insurance' population of Tasmanian devils and ever-present wombats. The East Coast Wine Trail kicks off nearby, while Freycinet National Park holds famous Wineglass Bay, craggy granite peaks and uncrowded trails. Bicheno is a fishing port that's all but put its feet up and become a seaside holiday town – one of the most likeable in Tasmania.

Further north, St Helens feels alive and lived-in – no tourism fakery here – adding to its mountain biking enticements. Larapuna / Bay of Fires is a short hop away, with its white sand and orange lichen-clad boulders, best explored on guided walks. Inland, Derby thrives as Australia's top mountain biking town, while offshore, Flinders Island distils wild Bass Strait coastlines, mountains and fine food into an easy-going, adventurous escape.

Maria Island National Park

TIME FROM TRIABUNNA: **30MIN**

Convict history and heritage in Darlington

Step off the ferry at Darlington's pier and almost immediately you pass the island's oldest building, the 1825 **Commissariat Store**, now housing displays and information on the island.

Above the bay is **Darlington**, officially the World Heritage-listed Darlington Probation Station. Built in 1830, the **penitentiary** is one of the few buildings remaining from the

GETTING AROUND

From the wharf in Triabunna, ferries head to Maria Island. Tassielink buses run between Hobart, Bicheno and Coles Bay (for Freycinet National Park); Calow's Coaches ply the same route, extending to St Helens. To explore Larapuna / Bay of Fires, you'll need your own wheels. MTB Express runs transfers to Derby from Launceston airport, often combined with trail shuttle packages. From Launceston, it's a 1½-hour drive to Derby; from St Helens it's one hour. Sharp Airlines flies to Flinders Island from Launceston and Melbourne.

island's first convict period (1825–32), before it was abandoned in favour of Port Arthur. During the island's second convict era from 1842 to 1850, more than 66 prisoners were crammed into each room. Things are a little cosier these days with the penitentiary serving as rustic **accommodation** *(parks.tas.gov.au; up to 2 people $44)*, with six-bunk rooms (with wood heaters), shared bathrooms and coin-operated showers. There's also camping at the base of **Darlington's lawns** *(parks.tas.gov.au; camping for 2 people $13)* – regularly visited by Tasmanian devils – as well as further-flung **Frenchs Farm** *(free)* and **Encampment Cove** *(free)*.

TOP TIP

Prepare ahead – you can't buy food or drink on Maria Island. Self-catering overnight visitors can stock up at Triabunna's **Spring Bay IGA**.

EATING BEFORE & AFTER VISITING MARIA ISLAND: OUR PICKS

Fish Van: Fresh seafood so close to the Triabunna fishing fleet that the van is almost afloat. *11am–6.30pm* $

Elly's Tasting Table: Orford's best cafe serves all-day breakfasts; be sure to try Elly's own salted-caramel popcorn. *8am–2pm* $$

Darlington Vineyard: Cheese platters team with local wines in Orford at the east coast's southernmost vineyard. *11am–4pm Thu–Sun* $$

Aquila Art Lounge: Savoury pancakes and Thai dishes prepared with garden ingredients inside a Triabunna home. *hours vary* $$

DEVIL ISLAND

In the 1960s, Maria Island was chosen as a sanctuary in an attempt to save threatened species such as Forester kangaroos and the Bass Strait subspecies of wombat from extinction. There was an irony of sorts to the project – this island once used to imprison convicts now being employed to release animals – but it was an unbounded success. History repeated itself in 2012, when 28 Tasmanian devils – all free of the dreaded devil facial tumour disease (DFTD) – were released on the island to serve as a geographically isolated insurance policy in the hope of saving the fast-declining population. Numbers on the island have since increased to more than 100 animals. These days, you're unlikely to encounter any wild devils on Tasmania's mainland, but chances are excellent on Maria.

TRAN QUI THINH/SHUTTERSTOCK

Painted Cliffs

Wander among wildlife

Forget spending binocular-wielding hours stalking wildlife. Simply step out onto the lawns that run down to the shores from Darlington and you'll be all but stepping over wombats (we counted 132 one day), Forester kangaroos and Cape Barren geese. Tasmanian devils have made a habit of hanging out around the Darlington camping ground and the grasslands around the airstrip north of Darlington are good for roo and wallaby sightings. Bird watchers will be happy to know that 11 of Tasmania's 12 endemic bird species have been sighted on the island.

Island rambles

At the southern end of Hopground Beach, the naturally patterned, sandstone **Painted Cliffs** (one hour's walk from Darlington) are the island's signature scene. Other walks include a two-hour loop to the **Fossil Cliffs** and then up Skipping Ridge to climb the rugged peak of **Bishop and Clerk** (599m; around four hours return from Darlington) for bird's-eye views over Darlington and Tasmania's east coast. The island's most challenging hike is to its highest point, 711m **Mt Maria**. The seven-hour return hike delivers brilliant views over the island's narrow isthmus and far beyond.

To see the island from toe to tip – Haunted Bay to the Fossil Cliffs – join the luxury guided four-day **Maria Island Walk** *(mariaislandwalk.com; from $3050).*

Bicheno

TIME FROM HOBART: 2½HR

Penguin power

Bicheno's wildlife stars are the little penguins that waddle onto local beaches around dusk. They're often seen around the Blowhole (p674) and at Redbill Beach (p674) and Waubs Beach (p674), but the only sure sightings come on a guided experience

Continued on p674

DRIVE THE EAST COAST WINE TRAIL

The East Coast Wine Trail encompasses 14 vineyards, many around Swansea and many family-owned with distinctive cellar-door experiences.

START	END	LENGTH
Boomer Creek	Devil's Corner	45km; half-day

Near the wine trail's southern end, ❶ **Boomer Creek** is a small, family-owned vineyard with its own olive grove. Platters, craft beer, local tea and juices are also on offer, with views over Schouten Island and Freycinet Peninsula. Swap wine for salt at ❷ **Tasman Sea Salt**, where sea water is evaporated and crystallised in a remarkably simple yet unique process. The premium tour concludes with tastings at neighbouring Mayfield Estate vineyard.

From the ❸ **Mayfield Bay Conservation Area** picnic/camping area beside the highway, take the five-minute walk to see the Three Arch Bridge, one of Tasmania's lesser-known convict-built bridges. Next up, the 22-hectare ❹ **Milton Vineyard** offers tastings in an elegant weatherboard cottage, with views over a small lake. The cellar-door restaurant, A Tale Among the Vines, uses produce from the winery's own farm.

Continuing north, tastings at ❺ **Spring Vale Vineyard** take place in a convict-built 1842 stable. Apéro Bistro, a French-Australian restaurant, is here, too. The cellar door of farm-based ❻ **Gala Estate** is inside Cranbrook's old timber post office, with plenty of rustic touches.

Beyond Cherry Tree Hill, wind down the slopes to ❼ **Devil's Corner**. Wine tastings can be combined with wood-fired pizza and local seafood from on-site food vendors. Climb the lookout tower for views over Moulting Lagoon to the Hazards mountains in Freycinet National Park.

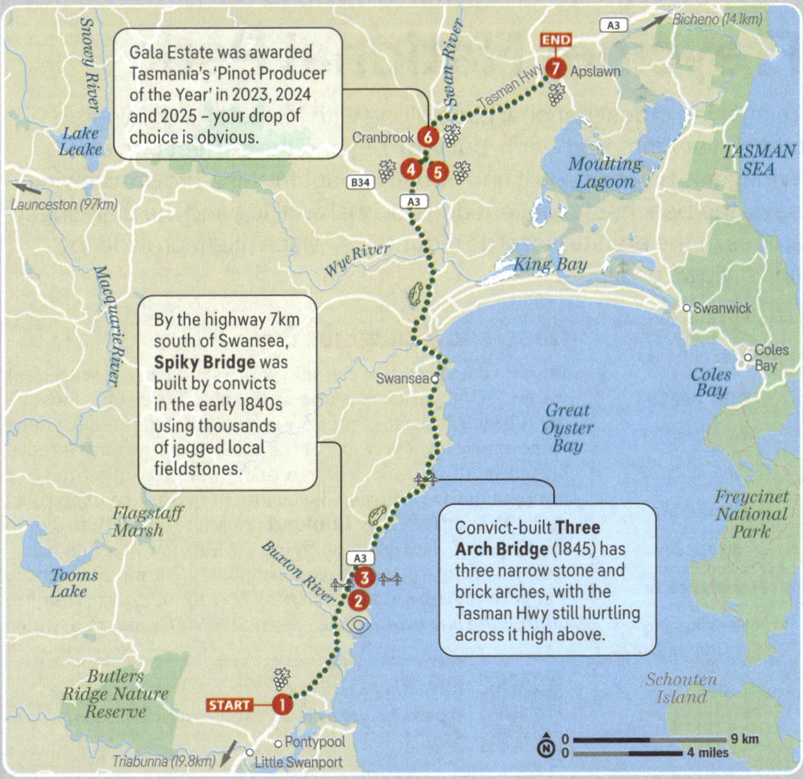

WATA51/SHUTTERSTOCK

Sleepy Bay

TOP EXPERIENCE

Freycinet National Park

Tasmania's oldest national park (along with Mt Field) is dominated by one very famous beach, but look beyond the perfect curve of Wineglass Bay and you'll find equally beautiful, less-crowd-drawing bays and beaches, excellent coastal bushwalking and the pink-tinged slopes of the granite Hazards mountains, which might provide the finest views of all.

DON'T MISS

- Wineglass Bay
- Cape Tourville
- Evening kayak tour
- Sleepy Bay
- Friendly Beaches
- Wineglass Bay Cruises

Cheers to Wineglass Bay

With its curvaceous arc of talc-white sand fringed with clear waters, Wineglass Bay is unquestionably Tasmania's most famous beach and one of the very symbols of the state. Just don't come expecting a lazy day at the beach. Getting onto its celebrated sands requires a 6km return walk, crossing through a low pass in the Hazards. The majority of visitors pull up short at the **Wineglass Bay Lookout** (2.6km return) clipped onto the slopes of the Hazards, giving a wide view over the bay.

If you want to reduce your step count, jump aboard the **Freycinet Aqua Express** *(freycinetaquaexpress.com.au; adult/child one way $75/60, return $120/100)* water taxi, which

PRACTICALITIES

● *parks.tas.gov.au* ● day pass per vehicle/person $48/24

heads to Hazards Beach five times daily. From here, you can walk across the isthmus to Wineglass Bay in less than 30 minutes. **Wineglass Bay Cruises** *(wineglassbaycruises.com.au; adult/child from $200/125)* runs daily five-hour boat trips from Coles Bay around the southern point of Freycinet Peninsula and into Wineglass Bay.

Locally based **Freycinet Air** *(freycinetair.com.au; per person $325)* operates 25-minute scenic helicopter flights, providing the upstairs look at the bay.

Other Walks Around Wineglass Bay

The **Wineglass Bay and Hazards Beach Circuit**, one of the state's 60 Great Short Walks, follows the main walking route to Wineglass Bay, but instead of retracing your steps back over the Hazards, take the trail that crosses the isthmus to parallel Hazards Beach. From here, the 11km circuit rounds the western base of the Hazards to return to the Wineglass Bay car park.

Freycinet's grandest adventure on foot is the **Freycinet Peninsula Circuit**, a two- to three-day, 27km loop of the park. Setting out from the Wineglass Bay car park, it can be walked in either direction, taking in Hazards and Cooks beaches on the Great Oyster Bay coastline, crossing Mt Graham and striding the length of Wineglass Bay. Camping and water supply need planning.

Beyond Wineglass Bay

The 20-minute wheelchair-accessible circuit around **Cape Tourville** is one of the national park's most popular short walks. There are glimpses into the mouth of Wineglass Bay and it's a good spot to see migrating whales.

Down the slopes from the Cape Tourville car park, a smaller car park marks the start of the 500m return walk to **Sleepy Bay**. A well-formed track leads through the forest – keep an eye out for the occasional echidna – before a stepped trail continues down to a compact and rocky bay with lichen-encrusted rocks and turquoise waters.

In the park's north, stretching in a long sandy line, the **Friendly Beaches** provide a long stretch of unbroken beach walking.

Adventures on the Water

Freycinet Adventures *(freycinetadventures.com.au; adult/child $145/115)* runs three-hour guided kayaking trips, crossing Coles Bay to the granite toes of the Hazards, passing a former granite quarry and stopping in at quixotic Honeymoon Bay.

For more water play, hire a SUP from **Freycinet Paddle Boards** *(freycinetpaddleboards.com.au; half/full day $50/70)* and go exploring on Coles Bay's (usually) sheltered waters. It also rents out sit-on-top kayaks as well as gear for snorkelling, fishing, camping and surfing.

A BLOOD-RED GLASS

See Wineglass Bay from above or on a map and it seems obvious that it was named for its curvaceous shape – but it was in fact named for the presence of a whaling station at the bay's southern end in the early 19th century. When whales were butchered here, the bay's waters were stained wine-red with blood.

TOP TIPS

- The national park visitor centre is one of the best informed in the state, so be sure to drop in when you arrive at the park.
- If you fancy camping at Richardsons Beach or Honeymoon Bay for the summer season (18 December to 10 February), plan ahead. Sites are so prized that they're allocated by a ballot, which is drawn in early August. Ballot applications can be made through the park website.
- Avoid parking issues at the Wineglass Bay car park by walking or cycling to the trailhead along a 4km shared-use path from the visitor centre.

BICHENO'S BEACHES & ISLANDS

Waubs Beach: Nearest to Bicheno town centre, this relatively safe ocean beach is good for swimming on calm days.

Redbill Beach: Bicheno's main surf beach is one hop north of Waubs Beach, with a 1km-long stripe of sand.

Diamond Island: Off Redbill Beach's northern end, this granite outcrop, connected to the mainland by a sandy isthmus, becomes accessible by foot at low tide.

Rice Pebble Beach: Tucked-away beach, accessed from the Blowhole car park. Compact and sheltered cove with coarse sand.

Denison Beach: Stretching for almost 10km north of Bicheno and more rugged and exposed than the beaches near town. Often impressively deserted.

SHAM_P/SHUTTERSTOCK

Continued from p670

with **Bicheno Penguin Tours** *(bichenopenguintours.com.au; $55)*. The one-hour tours visit a private area behind a beach with a rookery that's home to around 350 of the world's smallest penguins. Penguin numbers peak from November to January.

Blowholes and boulders

From **Redbill Beach** at Bicheno's northwestern edge, the **Foreshore Footway** is a 3km (one way) stroll along beaches and rock platforms. Highlights include **Waubs Beach** and the **Gulch**, a deep and clear ocean ravine separating Governor Island from the Bicheno shoreline. At the **Blowhole**, swells squeeze into cracks in the shore, surging skyward as geysers of white water.

Bicheno is punctuated by a couple of granite-studded hills, including **Whalers Hill**, an easy 10-minute climb from a signed pullout on Foster St to a pair of lookouts (any whales?).

From the **Douglas-Apsley National Park** car park, 12km west of town at the end of Rosedale Rd, it's a short stroll (15 minutes return) to a freshwater swim at **Apsley Waterhole**,

Bicheno Brewing Beers are made on site

EATING & DRINKING IN BICHENO: OUR PICKS

Le Coq: Bicheno's finest restaurant, Francophoning the town one pork rillette and cannellini bean stew at a time. Date-night material. *5-9pm Tue-Sat* **$$$**

Lobster Shack: Crack open half a cray and enjoy the elevated views of the Gulch, Governor Island and the fishing fleet. *11am-7pm* **$$**

Bicheno Beer Co: Buried behind Blue Edge bakery, with fire-warmed beer garden, brewing shed and regular boiler-maker BBQs. *2-9pm Fri & Sat, 1-5pm Sun*

Farm Shed: A full suite of east-coast wines combined with cheese and charcuterie platters. *10am-5pm*

Blowhole, Bicheno

while one of Tasmania's 60 Great Short Walks loops out from the waterhole through **Apsley Gorge** (four to five hours), with swim options aplenty.

St Helens

TIME FROM HOBART: **3¼HR**

Mountain biking around St Helens

Following in the well-rutted trails of nearby Derby, St Helens is quickly developing into one of Australia's best mountain biking towns. St Helens' hero trails are the 27km **Dreaming Pools** and, primarily, the isolated **Bay of Fires** trail. Around five hours is needed to complete this 42km trail, beginning at a trailhead atop the Blue Tier mountains, which is served by shuttles from both St Helens and Derby – the networks bleed into each other at this high point.

The trail network offers everything from family-friendly experiences to trails suitable for seasoned riders. Bike hire and shuttles, which typically cost $10 per run or $50 for unlimited uplifts in a day, can be arranged through **Gravity Isle** *(gravityisle.com)* or **Vertigo MTB** *(sthelens.vertigomtb.com.au)*.

EAST COAST WHALE TRAIL

With around 40 cetacean species – whales and dolphins – frequenting Tasmanian waters, the east coast is often a grandstand to whale activity. Humpback and southern right whales, in particular, are regularly sighted during their annual migrations. Between May and July they head north from Antarctica to give birth in warmer South Pacific waters, returning south from September to December. The East Coast Whale Trail is a series of 14 recommended viewing locations along the coast. Stops feature information boards about the whales. Around St Helens, there are stops at Beerbarrel Beach, Burns Bay and the Gardens, while Shelly Point, 15km south of town, has binoculars to assist with your whale viewing. Find more information at the Break O'Day Council website *(bodc.tas.gov.au)*.

EATING & DRINKING IN ST HELENS: OUR PICKS

Movies screen daily at Easy Tiger's cinema

Social: Choose between the retro lounge and the fire-warmed beer garden for craft beer and the likes of Balkan arancini. *3-8pm Wed & Thu, to 10pm Fri*

Lifebuoy Cafe: Nautically themed setting for breakfast and lunch in a space shared with a homewares store. *7am-2pm Mon-Fri, to 1pm Sat* $$

Skippers: The freshest of seafood, served from a floating restaurant moored beside the fishing fleet. *11.30am-2.30pm Wed, Thu & Sun, to 7pm Fri & Sat* $$

Easy Tiger: What do you get when you combine a craft brewery, cinema, burger joint and bar? Ever-eventful Easy Tiger. *8am-10pm*

DUAL PLACE NAMES

The Bay of Fires could easily have taken its name from the fiery orange lichen that lights up the granite headlands along this 29km-long sweep of white sand and crystal-clear seas. But it was, in fact, named for the fires of Aboriginal people sighted by Tobias Furneaux when the HMS *Adventure* sailed past in 1773. To the Tasmanian Aboriginal people, however, the Bay of Fires area was known as Larapuna.

In 2013, Larapuna / Bay of Fires was among a group of six spots in Tasmania to be officially recognised as places with Aboriginal or dual names (English and Aboriginal). They were the first of a growing list of places with dual names. At the time of writing, 44 places around Tasmania have officially adopted dual names, including Wukalina / Mt William.

AMELIE B/SHUTTERSTOCK

Larapuna/ Bay of Fires

Historic dairy and high waterfalls in emerald valleys

About 26km west of St Helens, tiny Pyengana (Pie-en-gah-na – an Aboriginal word describing the meeting of two rivers) slumbers in an impossibly emerald-green valley with some interesting diversions. They've been making cheese in the valley since 1895, a tradition now upheld by **Pyengana Dairy** *(pyenganadairy.com.au)*. The area has some beautiful waterfalls, including **St Columba Falls** (30 minutes return), one of Tasmania's highest.

Larapuna/ Bay of Fires

TIME FROM ST HELENS: **15MIN**

Isolated beaches, prolific wildlife and summit views

Reaching almost to Tasmania's northeast tip, isolated **Mt William National Park** *(parks.tas.gov.au; day pass per person/vehicle $24/48)* features long sandy beaches, prolific wildlife and the eponymous **Wukalina / Mt William**. Standing 216m above sea level, it's more a glorified hill, but it still affords views over the stunning coastline and the southern Furneaux Islands. A one-hour return trail to the summit departs from the Wukalina / Mt William car park.

EATING & DRINKING AROUND THE BAY OF FIRES: OUR PICKS

Lease 65: Grab your oysters from the waterside farm shed and head for your favourite Bay of Fires beach. Cash only. *11am-3pm Mon-Fri* $

Hub – Seaside: Great deck views as far as Eddystone Point and a large roster of wood-fired pizzas and local craft beers. *noon-8pm* $$

Gladstone Hotel: Classic pub grub – hello rissoles and mixed grill – by the edge of Mt William National Park. *5.30-8pm daily, plus noon-2pm Wed-Sun* $$

Priory Ridge Wines: Generous tastings of seven wines ($15) from the east coast's northernmost vineyard inside a rustic shearing shed turned cellar door. *hours vary*

Guided indigenous walks through coastal landscapes

Hike the coastline from Wukalina / Mt William to Eddystone Point on the four-day guided **Wukalina Walk** *(wukalinawalk.com.au; $3295)*, run by the Tasmanian Aboriginal community. The walk delves into bush tucker, middens, Aboriginal culture and the history and striking beauty of this fabled coastline. Expect cultural activities, including weaving and kelp-basket making and learning about the history and language of the Tasmanian Aboriginal community.

The vibrant Larapuna / Bay of Fires coastline springs to intimate, colourful life on the five-day, four-night **Bay of Fires Signature Walk** *(taswalkingco.com.au; from $2995)*. Setting out from Boulder Point in Mt William National Park and concluding at the walk's luxurious Bay of Fires Lodge near Ansons Bay, highlights include a night at a secluded beach camp, lunching in the dunes behind the Eddystone Point Lighthouse and kayaking on Ansons River. Fine food and wine included.

Derby

TIME FROM ST HELENS: **1HR**

Some of the world's best mountain biking

The hub of Derby's mountain biking scene is the **Blue Derby Trail Network** *(ridebluederby.com.au)*, named for the town's proximity to the Blue Tier mountain range and featuring more than 125km of trails.

A favourite short loop is a combination of the green (easy) **Axehead**, **Relics** and **Sawtooth** trails, climbing through a tight (but simple) set of switchbacks known as Twisties and passing **Tasty Trout Falls**. Shuttle runs close to town include Black Stump, from where you can access flowing downhill runs such as **Flickity Sticks Upper** (and the connecting Flickity Sticks) and **Return to Sender** (both blue, or intermediate). For the more skilled and airborne, the black (difficult) **Air-Ya-Garn** branches off Return to Sender for a faster, jump-filled return to Derby. Further afield, standout trails include **Blue Tier** and **Atlas** (both blue).

For shuttles and gear rentals contact **Vertigo MTB** *(vertigomtb.com.au)*, **Bark Off Biking** *(barkoffbiking.com.au)* and **MADMTB** *(madmtb.com.au)*.

Lake-top sauna

Balanced on a pontoon atop forest-framed Briseis Hole – aka Lake Derby – the **Floating Sauna Lake Derby** *(floatingsauna.*

DERBY'S MOUNTAIN BIKING HISTORY

Derby first shone as a tin-mining centre, but today it's the town that mountain biking reinvented. After the mines closed in the 1940s, Derby virtually slipped from the map – the highway passed through it, but few people found a reason to even stop. With the opening of the Blue Derby Trail Network in 2015, the air was pumped back into the town's tyres.

Derby quickly became one of the world's most revered mountain biking destinations and in 2017 and 2019 it hosted rounds of the Enduro World Series. In an island state that's quickly become Australia's standout mountain biking destination, the breadth and diversity of Derby's trail network has been often challenging but remains unparalleled. It's all about the flow.

EATING & DRINKING AROUND DERBY: OUR PICKS

Tin Timbers Cafe: Licensed cafe luring bike riders down the Valley Ponds trail to Branxholm for its home-baked gourmet pies. *hours vary* $

Hub: A mountain biker's two best friends – craft beer and wood-fired pizza – in a warm cottage setting. *noon-8pm* $$

LOT 40: Cafe out front, party (bar, brewery, distillery) out back at this cavernous venue at the town's heart. *hours vary*

Weldborough Hotel: Isolated 1876 country pub by the end of the Blue Tier mountain bike trail. A good selection of craft beers. *11am-late* $$

EXPLORING FLINDERS ISLAND

Flinders Island Adventures: Book a fishing charter with this local outfit, which also runs walking tours, including a seven-day all-inclusive guided walk. Also half- and full-day 4WD and luxury van tours.

Flinders Island Dive: There's great diving and snorkelling in the clear waters around the island, especially amid the sea caves, shoals and reefs. Fishing tours also offered.

Flinders Island Aviation: Scenic flights over the craggy peaks of Flinders and the surrounding isles, ranging from 30-minute highlight flights to longer customised air tours.

Tasmanian Expeditions: Guided multiday walking adventures on Flinders Island. Accommodation is in comfortable coastal eco-camps.

Roaring 40s Kayaking: Seven-day paddling trips along Flinders Island's shores and outlying islands.

com.au; $55) is a wood-fired surprise that can ease the fatigues of mountain biking or simply be enjoyed as an indulgent pleasure.

Flinders Island

TIME FROM LAUNCESTON: **35MIN**

Explore the islands' whaling and Indigenous history

Graced with an elevated location above Emita Beach on Flinders' west coast, the volunteer-run **Furneaux Museum** *(furneauxmuseum.org.au; $10)* records the history of the Furneaux Islands. Around the grounds are whalebones, blubber pots and rusty ship propellers, evidence of Flinders' whaling history. The interior focuses on local flora and fauna, muttonbirding and the stories of longstanding island families. The museum's Aboriginal section includes beautiful shell necklaces and a display about nearby **Wybalenna**, the misguided 'settlement' where 134 Tasmanian Aboriginal people were exiled from mainland Tasmania in 1834.

Walks along a colourful coastline

With three of the state's 60 Great Short Walks, Flinders Island punches above its weight as a bushwalking destination. Foremost among the trio is the 1½-hour circuit around **Trousers Point**, beginning near **Trousers Point Beach**, a mountain-backed cove lined with eroded and lichen-covered boulders.

Castle Rock is the destination for the second Great Short Walk. From Allports Beach, it takes around 1½ hours to reach the hulking boulder plugged in the sands of Marshall Beach, following a series of beaches along the way.

Flinders Island's third Great Short Walk is also its most challenging – the four- to five-hour return hike to its highest point, the 756m **Strzelecki Peaks**. It's a steep and strenuous walk, though there's nothing overly technical about the route, and the views over Trousers Point and well beyond are definitely worth the effort.

EATING & DRINKING ON FLINDERS ISLAND: OUR PICKS

Flinders Island Bakery: Try curried scallop pies and savoury sausage rolls at this friendly spot favoured by locals. *8am-4pm Mon-Fri* $

Missing Goose: A rotating roster of dishes, cocktails and its takeaway Pizza Qube next door. *9am-8pm Thu-Sun* $$

Furneaux Tavern: Focused on local produce and seafood. Dine in or grab takeaway fish and chips. *5.30-8pm daily, plus noon-1.30pm Thu-Sun* $$

Interstate Hotel: Whitemark's historic pub. Coffee and cake in the morning, pub standards at night. Book for dinner. *7.30am-1.30pm & 5-7.30pm Mon-Sat* $$

Launceston

HISTORY | FOOD | FESTIVALS

It's hard to imagine a city more likeable than Launceston. 'Launnie', as the locals call it, is large enough for a bit of urban buzz, but small enough for country congeniality to be the rule rather than the exception. Tasmania's second-largest city revels in its standing as a UNESCO City of Gastronomy – one of only two in Australia – while the cityscape is a mosaic of architectural styles, making every street a strip of discovery.

Few cities have Launceston's natural edge, with deep and powerful Cataract Gorge slicing through the hills improbably close to the city centre. Museums and galleries showcase everything from thylacine tales to Port Arthur prison doors and Salvador Dalí sketches, while the global gastronomic badge means the restaurant, cafe and bar life is top notch, with produce as fresh as the Tassie air. Launnie loves a good festival, so keep an eye out for food, beer or art celebrations as you journey.

Alexandra Suspension Bridge (p681)

GETTING AROUND

Central Launceston is compact and walkable. Its free Tiger Bus service was discontinued in 2025, but Metro buses operate through the city and suburbs. Options for transport to and from Launceston Airport include a shuttle-bus service operated by **Wild Island Adventures** *(wildislandadventure.com; $27)*. A taxi to or from the airport will cost around $40.

TOP TIP

In 2021, Launceston was awarded City of Gastronomy status by UNESCO. Discover the region's bountiful produce at **Harvest**, a Saturday morning market held in a city car park (71 Cimitiere St). Expect craft beer, cider, honey, salmon and more. Many of the producers and suppliers are organic and sustainable.

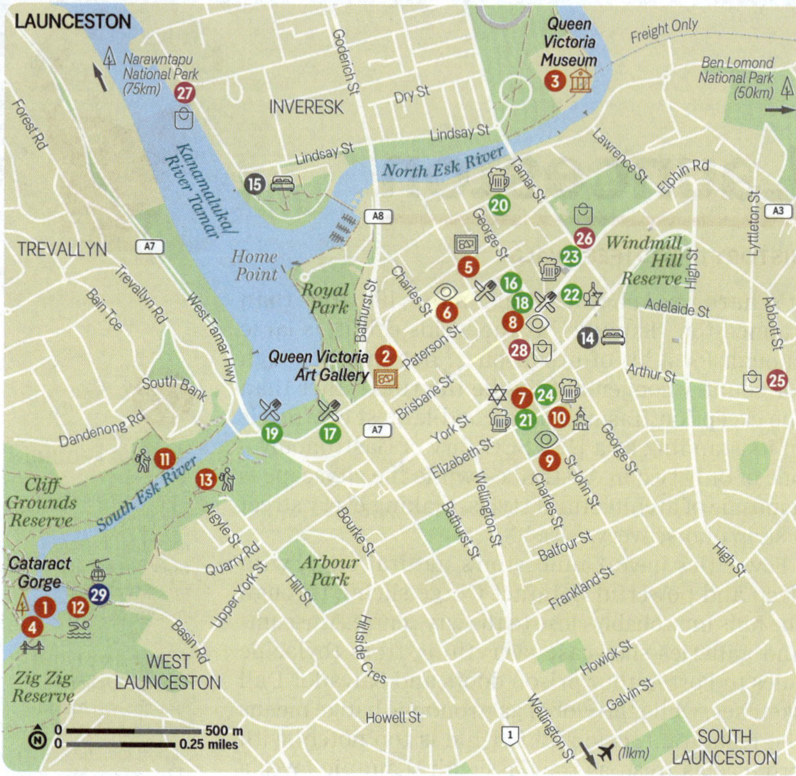

HIGHLIGHTS
1 Cataract Gorge
2 Queen Victoria Art Gallery
3 Queen Victoria Museum

SIGHTS
4 Alexandra Suspension Bridge
5 dAda mUse
6 Henty House
7 Launceston Synagogue
8 Majestic Theatre
9 Milton Hall
10 St Johns

ACTIVITIES
11 Cataract Walk
12 First Basin Pool
13 Zig Zag Track

SLEEPING
14 Change Overnight
15 Peppers Silo

EATING
16 Black Cow Bistro
17 Cataract on Paterson
18 Stelo @ Pierre's
19 Stillwater

DRINKING & NIGHTLIFE
20 Boag's Brewery
21 Du Cane Brewery & Dining Hall
22 Midnight Rambler
23 Royal Oak Hotel
24 Saint John Craft Beer

SHOPPING
25 Alps & Amici
26 Design Tasmania Shop
27 Glass Manifesto
28 Spotted Quoll
see 7 Stockton & Co

TRANSPORT
29 Gorge Scenic Chairlift

In 1956, Stelo fired up Australia's first commercial espresso machine

EATING IN LAUNCESTON: OUR PICKS

Stillwater: Fine dining harnessing local ingredients in a restored 1830s flour mill by the mouth of Cataract Gorge. *10am-10pm Mon-Sat* $$$

Black Cow Bistro: Classy steakhouse offering the best of Tasmania's beef and Wagyu in an Art Deco former butchery. *5.30-10pm Mon-Sat* $$$

Cataract on Paterson: Local favourite, with the chance to cook your own steak and seafood on a 400°C volcanic stone. *5pm-late* $$$

Stelo @ Pierre's: Smooth-as-velvet Italian dining to go with the velvet-covered ceiling. The house-made pasta is the hero. *11am-3pm Tue-Fri & 5.30-11pm Tue-Sat* $$$

Launceston's Outdoor Playground

Hike and swim in Cataract Gorge

Launceston's natural advantage, **Cataract Gorge**, is where the South Esk River, the dolerite cliffs and the bush feel a million miles from the city, even if it's only around 1km from the centre. You can hike the gorge's riverside trails, ride the world's longest single-span chairlift and take a dip in the outdoor swimming pool.

Cataract Gorge's green heart is First Basin, where the gorge widens and the city comes to play. It's straddled at one end by the **Alexandra Suspension Bridge**, built in 1904 and home to the world's longest single-span chairlift (457m), the **Gorge Scenic Chairlift** *(gorgechairlift.com.au; adult/child one way $15/10)*, which crosses the South Esk River – Tasmania's longest river – from the lawned southern banks to the Victorian-style garden on the northern banks.

Set within the grassed southern bank is **First Basin Pool**, a public swimming pool that's typically filled with water and open from November to March.

First Basin is connected to Kings Bridge and ultimately the city centre, by the **Cataract Walk** and Zig Zag Track. Both are around 1km in length, but are very different in nature. The Cataract Walk is the flatter, gentler option, running along the cliffs on the northern bank, providing good views of the river and the gorge's dolerite columns. The **Zig Zag Track** takes a more venturesome approach, with some steep pinches as it burrows into the gorge along the southern bank.

For a cultural (and natural) perspective on the gorge, join a guided walk with **Wallaby Walkabout Tours** *(launcestonwalkingtours.com.au; $45)*, with First Nations guide Geoff McLean.

Launceston's Cabinet of Curiosities

See thylacines, shipwrecks and art at QVMAG

Australia's largest regional museum, the **Queen Victoria Museum** *(QVMAG; qvmag.tas.gov.au; free)* is a real treasury of Tasmanian time. There are the requisite dinosaurs and megafauna, but pride of place goes to an exhibition on the cherished thylacine. Don't miss the original cell doors from Port Arthur and the gallery on the *Sydney Cove*, Australia's oldest-known shipwreck, which ran aground on Preservation Island in Bass Strait in 1797.

BEST TASMANIAN-MADE SHOPPING

Glass Manifesto: Venture out to riverside Kings Wharf for high-quality glass art from Anne Clifton and Peter Bowles, whose creations feature in galleries across the world.

Stockton & Co: A lovely collection of design, homewares and art from the likes of Tassie-favourite Tom Samek.

Spotted Quoll: A treasure trove of unique Tasmanian-made items, from clothing to gin kits to glassware cut with Tasmanian scenes.

Design Tasmania: Design Tasmania's store is effectively a gallery within a gallery, with works of wood, fine jewellery, ceramics and glass.

Alps & Amici: Launceston's top gourmet stop, from its house-made granola to ready-made meals by the chef owner.

DRINKING IN LAUNCESTON: OUR PICKS

Saint John Craft Beer: Eighteen taps of predominantly Tassie craft beers, with thirst-generating tacos and burgers. *noon-late*

Du Cane Brewery & Dining Hall: Wood-fired pizza and locally brewed beers. Try the Turning of the Fagus Hazy Pale. *noon-9pm*

Royal Oak Hotel: Launceston's best traditional pub. Live music from country and folk through to local noise merchants. *3pm-late Wed-Sat*

Midnight Rambler: Bourbon 'n' blues in a suitably well hidden, unsigned and grungy speakeasy-style bar. *5pm-2am Fri & Sat*

HISTORIC ARCHITECTURE

Geoff McLean, the history buff and walking guide behind Wallaby Walkabout Tours, shares some of his favourite Launceston buildings. *@wallaby_walkabout_tours*

St Johns: This 1824 Colonial Gothic-style Anglican Church was the first brick building in Launceston.

Milton Hall: An 1842 Greek Revival-style building that was once a church. Also the birthplace of the Australian flag.

Launceston Synagogue: One of Australia's longest-operating synagogues. Wonderful heritage and distinctive Egyptian-style architecture.

Majestic Theatre: Completed in 1917, Launceston's first purpose-built cinema features a wonderfully distinctive Grecian architectural style.

Henty House: A prime example of post-Modern Brutalism – a great future-classic building to view and experience.

TRABANTOS/SHUTTERSTOCK

Queen Victoria Art Gallery

The museum's artistic sibling, the **Queen Victoria Art Gallery** *(qvmag.tas.gov.au; free)*, occupies a separate site and is home to the First Tasmanians Gallery, showcasing shelters, tools and bush foods used by Tasmanian Aboriginal people, including kelp water carriers and beautiful rice-shell and maireener-shell necklaces. Colonial paintings, including works by John Glover, are the pride of the rest of the collection in a meticulously restored 19th-century building on the edge of Royal Park.

Raise a Glass to Boag's

Visit Launceston's historic brewery

James Boag's beer has been brewed on William St since 1881. Visit the heritage **Boag's Brewery** *(jamesboag.com.au; tours $37)* on a guided 1½-hour tour packed with history and anecdotes about northern Tasmania's most famous beer. The tour is a walk through the brewhouse and the brewing process, now largely automated other than the taste testers (dream job alert!), before finishing with – likely the reason you're here – a tasting session of three beers. Book online for daily departures at 11am, 1pm and 3pm.

A Surreal Collection of Art

Australia's largest Salvador Dalí collection

Launceston is probably not the place where you expect to find one of the world's largest collections of Salvador Dalí drawings, but that's the delight of **dAda mUse** *(dadamuse.com.au; ground floor/2nd level free/$10)*. Acquired over 35 years by a Launceston eye surgeon, the world-class collection now totals around 1500 artworks, a small portion of which is on display across the two levels of the 1842 Johnstone and Wilmot building. Book ahead for guided **tours** *($25)* through the collection on Saturday mornings.

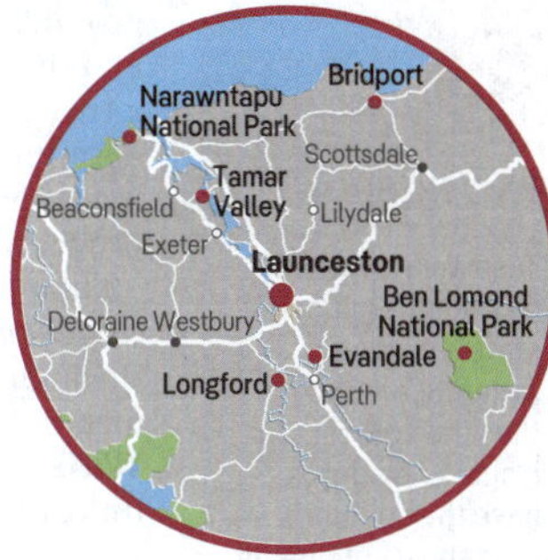

Beyond Launceston

Discover an intersection of convict history, wine culture, world-class golf and an often-overlooked alpine area.

Places

Launceston is ringed by reminders of a significant colonial heritage. Lifestyles of the 19th-century rich and famous feature at Clarendon Estate near Evandale, while Longford hosts the World Heritage–listed farms of Woolmers Estate and Brickendon. Look up and Tasmania's second-highest peak looms in ski-able Ben Lomond National Park.

A terrain of rolling vineyards, orchards and stands of native forest, the Tamar Valley is intersected by the wide Kanamaluka / Tamar River, running 64km north from Launceston. Along both sides of the river, more than 30 vineyards form the Tamar Valley Wine Route.

To the north on Bass Strait, Bridport is one of Australia's top golfing destinations, while Narawntapu National Park has wildlife and walks aplenty.

Evandale

TIME FROM LAUNCESTON: **20MIN**

Tasmania's grandest colonial home

Heading down the elm-lined driveway of **Clarendon Estate** *(nationaltrust.org.au/places/clarendon-estate; adult/child $25/10)* is like stepping onto the set of *Gone with the Wind*. With its imposing columns, the 1838 mansion built for wool grower and merchant James Cox is furnished in period style and open for self-guided visits.

The coach house out back is particularly beautiful, built with convict-made bricks and imported tiles. The estate is also home to the **Australian Fly Fishing Museum**.

Longford

TIME FROM LAUNCESTON: **20MIN**

World Heritage–listed estates

Two colonial farms on Longford's outskirts form part of UNESCO's Australian Convict Sites World Heritage listing.

Woolmers Estate *(woolmers.com.au; adult/child $25/4)*, a pastoral estate built by Thomas Archer in 1817, remained in the ownership of the Archer family until 1994. Its lovely

GETTING AROUND

Having your own transport is recommended for exploring outside Launceston. Tassielink's Launceston to Cressy bus, which runs up to nine times a day, stops in Evandale and Longford. A winter shuttle bus runs from Ben Lomond National Park's lower car park up the mountain. Visiting much of the Tamar Valley, especially vineyards, by public transport is impractical; take a winery tour or get someone sensible to drive.

grounds include a rose garden featuring thousands of roses and the oldest shearing shed – a rare if not unique example of a two-storey shearing shed – still in use in Australia. Guided 45-minute tours meander through the homestead, still furnished with the family's possessions, or you can explore the property's convict buildings.

Thomas' brother William established nearby **Brickendon** *(brickendon.com.au; adult/child $20/8)* in 1824. Wander through its convict-built farm village and heritage gardens, meeting the farm animals as you do. The 2.8km **Convict Trail Walk**, crossing the Macquarie River on a suspension bridge, links the two properties, if you fancy a walk.

WHY NO SNOW?

Tasmania is Australia's southernmost state – next stop, Antarctica – and thus the coldest. So it should by rights have the country's best snow conditions, right? Wrong. Snowfall on Ben Lomond (and even more so at the more southerly Mt Mawson) are flukey and snow is never guaranteed, even in the depths of winter.

There are two main reasons for this unreliability of snow. Wrapped in mild seas, Tasmania has a temperate maritime climate, keeping conditions on the island warmer than you might expect. It's also a relatively low-lying island – Ben Lomond's ski slopes top out below 1600m (and Mt Mawson's at little more than 1300m), while mainland ski resorts such as Falls Creek and Thredbo have higher ski runs at 1800m to 2000m.

Ben Lomond National Park

TIME FROM LAUNCESTON: 1HR

Tasmania's top ski field

Around 50km east of Launceston, **Ben Lomond National Park** *(parks.tas.gov.au; day pass per person/vehicle $24/48)* is Tasmania's only alpine resort, offering its most reliable (albeit not very reliable) skiing. **Ben Lomond Snow Sports** *(tasmania.ski)*, at the foot of the ski slopes, has lodge accommodation and offers lessons and equipment hire. Snow coverage can be patchy, but the ski season generally runs from early July to late September. Three 'snow guns' top up the natural snow. Downhill skiing, snowboarding, cross-country skiing and tobogganing are all available when the conditions are right. See *benlomond.org.au* for snow reports and webcams.

Bridport

TIME FROM LAUNCESTON: 1HR

Tee up at Barnbougle

Sitting 5km east of town, **Barnbougle** *(barnbougle.com.au)* is a trio of links-style golf courses that almost single-handedly put Tasmania on the world golf map. The Dunes is a challenging par-71 links course in rolling coastal sand dunes, while Lost Farm is a 20-hole links challenge 4km down the road. Bougle Run is a 14-hole short course. They're popular courses, so book well ahead.

Tamar Valley

TIME FROM LAUNCESTON: 30MIN

The Tamar's bubbly side

Sparkling wines thrive around Pipers Brook and Lebrina, along the Tamar Valley's eastern edge, with the bubbly stuff here

EATING & DRINKING AROUND EVANDALE & LONGFORD: OUR PICKS

Clarendon Arms: Classic 1847 Evandale pub with a lovely beer garden and warming British-pub-style food. *9am-4pm Wed, to 5pm Thu, Fri & Sun, to late Sat*

Ingleside Cafe: Spacious cafe inside Evandale's 1867 municipal offices, with a sunny side courtyard. *7am-5pm Mon-Fri, 8am-4pm Sat & Sun* $

Woolmers Restaurant: Take a light lunch in Woolmers' elegant dining room, wrapped around a 1927 Wolseley vintage car and rose garden. *10am-3.30pm Wed-Sun* $$

Ernest & Ernesto: Enjoy the Cuban-themed clutter (and excellent coffee) of this Longford espresso and dessert bar. *7.30am-2pm Tue-Fri, from 9am Sat*

FILEDIMAGE/SHUTTERSTOCK

Ben Lomond National Park

among the finest in the world. In 2024, **House of Arras** *(houseofarras.com.au)* winemaker Ed Carr was named Sparkling Winemaker of the Year at the International Wine Challenge, adding to a long list of global gongs won by this Pipers Brook winery. Book ahead at its cellar door, where options range from tastings ($35) to a Wine and Wildlife Tour ($195) that wanders through the vineyards in search of grapes and native critters. Also seek out sparkling-only **Jansz** *(jansz.com.au)*, where tastings take place in the large, light-filled Jansz Wine Room. Choose from introductory ($15) and estate ($20) tastings of four wines, or the ultimate tasting ($30) of all six Jansz sparklings.

Further south in Lebrina, **Clover Hill Wines** *(cloverhillwines.com.au; tastings $25)* has a beautiful rammed-earth and rusted-steel cellar door looking out over the winery's natural amphitheatre of vines. Tastings range across eight sparkling wines, including six exclusive to the cellar door. Little more than a flying champagne cork away is appointment-only **Apogee** *(apogeetasmania.com; tastings $20)*, a small vineyard from the doyen of Tasmanian winemaking, Dr Andrew Pirie, who planted one of the state's first vineyards nearby in 1974.

TASMANIAN WINE VARIETALS

Tasmania is a cool-climate wine region, where you're more likely to encounter the gentility of pinot noir than big, bolshy syrahs and cab savs. In 2025, 48% of the grapes planted around Tasmania were pinot noir, making this by far the most common grape grown around the state. Next in the queue was chardonnay, representing 29% of the Tasmanian plantings. In a sign of the changing times, pinot gris slipped past sauvignon blanc in 2023 to become the third most prolific grape, now accounting for 8% of the Tassie vines (to sauvignon blanc's 6%). In the wider scheme, the Tasmanian industry remains boutique, with the state's estimated crush in 2025 being less than 19,000 tonnes, or just 1.2% of Australia's total crush.

EATING AROUND THE EAST TAMAR: OUR PICKS

Lock Shop Cafe: Stop in at this unusual cafe, a retro-furnished former petrol station attached to a safe-making business. *7am-2pm Mon, Thu & Fri, from 9am Sat & Sun* $$

Clover Hill Wines: Pair a wine tasting with a multi-course, Japanese-style *omakase* (chef's choice) dining experience. *noon-2pm Sat & Sun* $$$

Delamere Vineyards: Pick your own lunch picnic items (and blanket) from the open pantry at this Pipers Brook cellar door. *10.30am-4.30pm Thu-Mon* $$$

Hillwood Farmgate: Grab breakfast, scones or muffins on a working berry farm, with pick-your-own berries in summer. *9am-5pm* $$

WHERE ARE THE WOMBATS?

Narawntapu National Park has long been dubbed 'Tasmania's Serengeti', in reference to the wealth of wildlife that roams the marsupial lawns of Springlawn. At dawn and dusk it can look almost like a sporting crowd of Forester kangaroos and wallabies, but not so many years ago it also teemed with wombats, cute nuggets of fur that blithely strolled the heavily nibbled lawns. Today it's rare to spot a wombat here, with a sarcoptic mange outbreak decimating the population in the 2010s.

The good news? Camera surveys in 2025 revealed that wombats might be returning – the cameras captured 35 wombat visits into the observed areas, compared with just three recorded visits in 2022. Perhaps there's hope on these Serengeti plains?

TKPANGJOSEPH/SHUTTERSTOCK

Kangaroo, Narawntapu National Park

Narawntapu National Park

TIME FROM LAUNCESTON: 1HR

Wildlife by the waves

Narawntapu National Park *(parks.tas.gov.au; day pass per person/vehicle $24/48)* – once moonlighting under the less appealing name of Asbestos Range National Park – presents a combination of open plains, wetlands and woodlands in which almost the full suite of Tasmanian native creatures thrives.

At dusk especially, marsupials including Forester kangaroos, Bennett's wallabies and pademelons emerge to graze on the neatly trimmed lawns at Springlawn, offering some of the easiest wildlife viewing in the state. Popular walking trails, all setting out from the park visitor centre at Springlawn, include a climb to 114m **Archers Knob** (two hours return) for a view over the park and beyond, a short stroll to a **bird hide** peeping across the lagoon at Springlawn, or a 21km coastal traverse that runs the shoreline length of the park (seven to nine hours).

Long **Bakers Beach** is good for sandy strolls, while **Badger Beach** has perhaps the best swimming, but careful attention should always be paid to tide times. Equine adventures with **Cradle Country Adventures** *(cradleadventures.com.au; from $399)* include a three-hour ride along Bakers Beach and a three-hour Grass Tree Bush Ride. It can also arrange overnight accommodation at historic Bakers Beach Homestead.

EATING AROUND THE WEST TAMAR: OUR PICKS

River Cafe: With the Tamar lapping near its doors, this licensed Beauty Point cafe has a seafood-strong lunch menu. *8.45am-4pm Fri-Mon, to 3pm Tue-Thu* $$

Ducks: Head to the deck for Tamar views and dishes such as prawn and cheese linguini or crumbed scallops. *noon-3pm Tue-Sun, plus 5.30-8.30pm Fri & Sat* $$$

Timbre Kitchen: Menus at this excellent vineyard restaurant change daily according to what local backyard growers deliver. *11am-4pm Thu & Sun, to 10pm Fri & Sat* $$$

Exeter Bakery: A Tamar staple, with pies that range from wallaby to curried scallop and even Jack Daniel's whisky. *7am-3pm Mon-Sat* $

Cradle Country & Takayna / Tarkine

REMOTE WILDERNESS | OUTDOOR ADVENTURES | RUGGED HISTORY

Devonport is many visitors' first taste of Tasmania as they roll off the *Spirit of Tasmania* ferry from the mainland. World Heritage–listed Cradle Mountain is a priority destination, but mix up your journey there with stops in arty Deloraine, cave-riddled Mole Creek, historic Stanley and pocket-sized Rocky Cape National Park, fuelled by local cheese, ice cream, truffles, whiskey and beer from the fertile northwest. King Island awaits offshore, with world-class golf and even more cheese.

Tasmania's wild west is a land of endless ocean beaches, tannin-tinted rivers and ancient rainforests. Framing the island's rugged northwest tip is stunning Takayna / Tarkine, one of the planet's greatest wilderness areas and a region of deep cultural significance to Tasmania's Aboriginal community. Further south, isolated mining towns reach critical mass around Zeehan and Queenstown (good mountain biking), while nearby Strahan sits on vast, undeveloped Macquarie Harbour, six times the size of Sydney Harbour.

Places

TOP TIP

It rains seven out of 10 days around Cradle Mountain (and snows more than 50 days a year), so carry warm clothing and wet-weather gear regardless of the sky's appearance.

Devonport

TIME FROM LAUNCESTON: 1¼HR

Light and culture on Mersey Bluff

Standing atop Mersey Bluff, Devonport's red-and-white-striped **lighthouse** illuminates the entrance to the Mersey River, where there are sometimes decent enough waves to draw surfers. From the base of the lighthouse, there are good coastal views, but the real treasure here is a scattering of petroglyphs scratched into the rock around the bluff. Start with a self-guided tour through the **Tiagarra Cultural Centre** *(tiagarra.com.au; adult/child $10/5),* one of the oldest

GETTING AROUND

From the *Spirit of Tasmania* ferry terminal, it's a 5km drive into Devonport. A car is a great asset here – the wilderness awaits. Kinetic buses will get you to Mole Creek, Deloraine and Stanley. Bushwalkers heading to Cradle Mountain will need to book a private shuttle. From the Cradle Mountain visitor centre, shuttle buses run to Dove Lake (limited cars only after hours – no campervans). Sharp Airlines and Rex Airlines fly to King Island. Kinetic's west-coast bus connects Queenstown with Strahan, Zeehan and Rosebery.

Aboriginal keeping places in Australia, telling the story of Tasmanian Aboriginal life and survival. Afterwards, set out on the 10-minute **Tiagarra Walking Track**, which begins from beside the centre and loops around the bluff. White marker posts along the track denote the locations of the petroglyphs.

Explore maritime history and pilot a ship simulator

Housed in the former harbour master's residence (c 1920), the **Bass Strait Maritime Museum** *(bassstrait.museum; adult/child $12/5)* is a small but worthwhile museum displaying the maritime history of Bass Strait and Devonport. Among its large collection of ship and ferry models is the 'Our First Mariners

EATING & DRINKING IN DEVONPORT: OUR PICKS

Laneway: This hip cafe offers stellar all-day breakfasts and the sense of being one of Devonport's cool kids. *6am-3pm* **$$**

Elegance Lounge Seafood Bar & Grill: Locally caught seafood accented with Sri Lankan spices. *noon-2pm & 5-9pm* **$$**

Mrs Jones: Long lounge space upstairs at the Surf Life Saving Club, with great views matched by the food. *5.30-9.30pm Wed-Mon, plus noon-3pm Fri-Sun* **$$$**

Empress Craft Beer: Friendly craft-beer bar with 14 taps and surprises from Australia and around the world. *2-9pm Tue-Thu, noon-midnight Fri & Sat, to 8pm Sun*

Sea Country People' display, looking at Tasmania's Aboriginal seafarers and canoe-building traditions. The knockout exhibit is an interactive simulator that allows museum-goers to sail the SS *Woniora* in or out of the Mersey River mouth – choose between a clear day and a stormy night.

A historic railway trip through time

Take a 30-minute railway ride into history aboard the **Don River Railway** *(donriverrailway.com.au; adult/child $20/15)*. The diesel locomotive runs along the historic Melrose Line beside the Don River (on the hour from 10am to 2pm, Thursday to Sunday), cruising past well-preserved signal boxes and other heritage railway buildings. From Monday to Wednesday you can still visit the interesting museum with its locomotives and brightly painted rolling stock – you don't have to be a trainspotter to enjoy what is the largest collection of rail history in Tasmania.

Family-friendly beach with white sand and calm waters

At the western foot of Table Cape, an hour west of Devonport, **Boat Harbour Beach** is a brilliant contrast of white sand pincered by black rock. With zhooshed-up shacks rising almost directly from its sands and the cliffs of Table Cape slipping away in the distance, it has worthy claims to being the most beautiful beach in Tasmania. The usually calm seas are patrolled in summer and perfect for kids and families. At the time of writing, a new community hub with Surf Lifesaving Club, cafe and BBQ and picnic areas was under construction, so watch this space.

Rugged coastal caves and ancient cultural landscapes

Stretching west of Boat Harbour for a rugged 12km along Bass Strait, **Rocky Cape National Park** protects a broad cape known to Tasmanian Aboriginal people – who made their homes in seaside caves here thousands of years before European colonisation – as Pinmatik. Drive out to the squat lighthouse on the cape's tip for excellent Bass Strait views and set out on nearby short walks to large **North Cave** (15 minutes return) and smaller **South Cave** (10 minutes return). Out of respect for the Tasmanian Aboriginal community, do not enter the caves.

Deloraine

TIME FROM DEVONPORT: **35MIN**

Artsy riverside sculptures along the Meander River

Framed around the languid curves of the Meander River, Deloraine has an artsy inclination – headlined by November's annual **Tasmanian Craft Fair** that attracts creative types from all around Australia – but you can follow the **Great Western Tiers Sculpture Trail** *(greatwesterntiers.net.au/sculpture-trail)* at any time. The trail spreads as far as Mole Creek, Meander and Liffey, but the greatest concentration is in Deloraine, with almost half of the 16 sculptures clustered along the banks of the river in town. A 1km loop walk between

DEVONPORT'S BEST BEACHES

Mersey Bluff Beach: Devonport's main beach is patrolled during summer. Public toilets, changing rooms, electric BBQs and an excellent children's playground are close by.

Back Beach: Accessed via Coles Beach Rd, this quiet unpatrolled beach is tucked into the western foot of Mersey Bluff.

Coles Beach: Popular, though unpatrolled, swimming beach framed with rock. There are public toilets, picnic shelters and an outdoor shower.

East Devonport Beach: A quieter option on the eastern side of the Mersey River.

Lillico Beach: Around 7km west of Devonport with no sand, but lots of penguins coming ashore over its stones every evening.

TASMANIA'S TOWN OF MURALS

In the 1980s, Sheffield, 38km northwest of Deloraine, was a typical small Tasmanian country town experiencing rural decline, but astute townsfolk decided to paint large murals on walls around town. A few decades later, Sheffield has become a veritable outdoor art gallery. More than 160 large-scale murals enliven the townscape, many depicting scenes from the district's pioneer days.

Courtesy of the town's annual **International Mural Fest**, held in early November, the number and diversity of colourful outdoor artworks increases every year. The very first mural and still one of the most striking, is on the wall of the Masonic Lodge on High St, depicting Gustav Weindorfer (p694) in ponderous mode in a hut filled filled with native animals.

the road bridge and the footbridge upstream by the caravan park reveals seven major sculptures.

Hunt out a truffle

In winter, Tasmanian thoughts inevitably turn to open fires, whisky...and truffles. Australia's first black truffles were harvested at the **Truffle Farm** *(thetrufflefarmtasmania.com.au; tours from $125)* in 1999 by Tim Terry and today the property is run by Tim's daughter, Anna. The farm has the traditional winter truffles but also summer truffles, meaning the hunt goes on almost year-round (December to September). Tours conclude with the likes of truffle pizzas and truffle toasted sandwiches. Nearby **Truffles of Tasmania** *(trufflesoftasmania.com.au; tour $120)* also has winter truffle-hunt tours (June to September) that include tastings of fresh truffles and other truffle products.

Mole Creek

TIME FROM DEVONPORT: **50MIN**

National parks, underground and above

Among the 500-plus caves in **Mole Creek Karst National Park** *(parks.tas.gov.au; cave tours adult/child $19/10)*, two can be visited on tours operated by rangers. **Marakoopa Cave** is the larger cave, with glowworms, while the subterranean formations in compact **King Solomons Cave** are more densely clustered.

The diminutive town of Mole Creek also makes a good base for hiking trips into **Walls of Jerusalem National Park**, an isolated Central Plateau park with glacial lakes and a ring of peaks ('the walls') with biblical names. The walls are hard to reach in a day-long return walk, but make for excellent overnight hikes.

Meet Tasmanian devils and wombats

At the western edge of town, the privately owned **Trowunna Wildlife Sanctuary** *(trowunna.com.au; adult/child $35/20)* has a strong focus on conservation. Wildlife includes Tasmanian devils, wombats, quolls and raptors and you can also wander among wallabies. Informative 45-minute tours (11am, 1pm and 3pm) get you up close to devils and wombats and you'll also see devils being fed in a no-holds-barred display of bared teeth and bones being crunched. You can even take part in day-long **workshops** *($500)* on devil or wombat care.

EATING & DRINKING AROUND DELORAINE: OUR PICKS

Frank & Lotti: Salads, top coffee and whatever has been freshly baked that day – quiches, cakes, or perhaps pork chipotle pistachio sausage rolls. *8am-2pm Mon-Sat* **$$**

T's: Paddock-to-plate Chinese dining, with heritage-breed lamb and pork from the owner's farm. Say hi to Bella the robot waiter. *11.30am-2pm & 5-8pm Thu-Sun* **$$**

Sailors Nook: Deloraine's newest cafe has grown from a food truck into a cool corner cafe, complete with 'Naughty Corner'. *8am-2pm Thu-Sat, from 9am Sun* **$$**

Bush Inn Brewhouse: Try a Turbo Red IPA with one of the house sourdough pizzas at this craft brewery inside an 1848 former pub. *noon-9pm Wed-Sat*

Dove Lake

Cradle Mountain-Lake St Clair National Park

TIME FROM DEVONPORT: 1½HR

Hike through mossy rainforests at the Cradle Mountain

Best walked in a clockwise direction, the well-formed 6km (two to three hours) **Dove Lake Circuit**, pooled at the foot of Cradle Mountain, is the classic half-day out in **Cradle Mountain-Lake St Clair National Park** *(parks.tas.gov.au; day pass per person/vehicle $24/48)*. The boat shed near the circuit's end frames Tasmania's most famous mountain scene.

From Cradle Mountain Lodge, the **Pencil Pine Falls** track (10 minutes return) descends through mossy rainforest to a lookout platform overhanging Pencil Pine Creek. The **Enchanted Walk** (20-minute circuit) heads along both banks of Pencil Pine Creek in a narrow, moss-covered gorge. Pencil Pine Falls can also be seen from the accessible **Rainforest Walk** (10-minute circuit), which departs from the ranger station.

For a taste of the Overland Track, follow the track's opening steps along Ronny Creek (keep an eye out for wombats) and ascend past Crater Lake to the chain-assisted final climb to lofty Marions Lookout (p693; two to three hours return), looking down onto Dove Lake and across to Cradle Mountain.

THE WORLD BENEATH OUR FEET

Deb Hunter, recently retired owner of Wild Cave Tours, has been caving around Mole Creek for 50 years.

Of all the densely cavernous karsts in Australia, Mole Creek has become probably the most desired destination because it's so convenient. You can stay somewhere in comfortable accommodation and there's not going to be a five-hour bushwalk to get to a cave. Mole Creek caves are famous for the beauty and abundance of their mineral formations and you won't see better than in the two show caves. The style of those caves and the passion of the guides is enough for 99% of people. If you want to explore further, there are four caving clubs in Tasmania and they welcome newcomers.

EATING & DRINKING AROUND MOLE CREEK: OUR PICKS

Wandering Trout: Off-grid craft brewer with convivial 'host's table' dinners and accommodation upstairs. *4-10pm Wed-Sun*

Mole Creek Hotel: Bar meals with a small list of German specials, weekend dinner pizzas and a fascination with the Tassie tiger. *noon-2pm & 6-8pm* $$

Mole Creek Takeaway: Burgers and other fried nibbles (and the only coffee in town) behind the glass wall of the visitor centre. *8.30am-5pm Sun-Thu, to 6pm Fri & Sat* $

Hearth of Chudleigh: Cafe-cum–antique emporium looking like a cross between a 1950s store and your grandpa's farmhouse. *11.30am-5pm Wed-Sat, noon-7pm Sun* $

FILEDIMAGE/SHUTTERSTOCK

TOP EXPERIENCE

The Overland Track

From Ronny Creek near Cradle Mountain south to the shores of Lake St Clair, Tasmania's alpine Overland Track is Australia's premier multiday walk. On a six-day, 65km journey past five of Tasmania's 10 highest peaks, look forward to diverse terrain – including rainforest, gorges and alpine moors – on trails that weave through the most spectacular mountain scenery Tasmania can deliver.

Starting at Ronny Creek

During the hiking season (October to May), the Overland Track can only be walked north-south, setting out from **Ronny Creek**, 7km from the Cradle Mountain visitor centre. Walking to Ronny Creek along the Cradle Valley boardwalk is an option, but few hikers want to add to the load ahead, so catch the shuttle bus to Ronny Creek.

DON'T MISS
- Marions Lookout
- Pelion Hut views
- Mt Ossa ascent
- Mersey River waterfalls

Best Time to Go

The best time to walk the track is during Tasmania's summer and early autumn (December to April), when the weather is warmer, days are longer and alpine plants are in flower. A permit system operates during the hiking season and the number of people setting out each day from Ronny Creek is

PRACTICALITIES
● *parks.tas.gov.au/explore-our-parks/cradle-mountain/overland-track* ● adult/child $300/260

capped. If your preferred day is already booked out, check with guided-walk operators for vacancies on departures. During the winter off-season (June to September), walker numbers are naturally reduced, but this period of snow and ice is only recommended for more experienced bushwalkers.

How Difficult Is the Walk?

The Overland Track is classified as grade 4 (bushwalking experience recommended). Tracks may be long, rough and steep. Directional signage may be limited, though it's not as challenging as other Tasmanian trails such as the South Coast Track and Frenchmans Cap. The Overland Track largely threads through the mountains, rather than grinding over them, reducing the amount of ascent and descent, though there's still plenty of walking at altitudes above 1000m on exposed plateaus. If you have experience with multiday hikes and a solid fitness base, it's an achievable independent adventure. Inexperienced hikers should join a guided walking group. The track is not recommended for children under eight.

What to Pack & Accommodation

Year-round the weather can be very changeable; be equipped with footwear and technical apparel covering all four seasons. If you're hiking independently, you'll need to carry all your food and you're required to carry a tent in case of emergency. There are six public huts for independent hikers along the track, each with camping nearby. Huts are typically rustic affairs with wooden bunks, composting toilets and space for cooking and eating, though a couple have had upgrades in recent years.

Recommended Detours

The track is stitched with detours to mountain summits, waterfalls and lakes. Cradle Mountain (p694) is an obvious goal for many and it's passed on the first day out from Ronny Creek, a short distance beyond **Marions Lookout**. From Kitchen Hut, the side track to Cradle's summit crosses scree fields and requires some scrambling. From Pelion Gap, just beyond Pelion Hut (night three, normally), side trails veer off to **Mt Pelion East** and **Mt Ossa**, Tasmania's highest peak (1617m). Be aware that Ossa is a four- to six-hour side trip from the gap. The easiest side trips are to a trio of Mersey River waterfalls – **Hartnett Falls** (one hour) and the twinned **D'Alton Falls** and **Fergusson Falls** (one hour) – on the section between Kia Ora Hut and Windy Ridge (typically the penultimate day).

Ending at Narcissus & Lake St Clair

The final stretch of the Overland Track is from Narcissus to Cynthia Bay, 17.5km along the shores of Lake St Clair, but most hikers jump on the ferry from Narcissus across the lake to end at the Lake St Clair visitor centre. Book the ferry online with *lakestclairlodge.com.au*.

GUIDED WALKS

Several excellent operators offer guided hikes along the Overland Track. The plushest option is the Cradle Mountain Signature Walk with **Tasmanian Walking Company** *(taswalkingco.com.au; from $4495)*, staying in its private huts. It also offers an eight-day winter crossing. **Tasmanian Expeditions** *(tasmanianexpeditions.com.au; from $3395)* runs camping-based hikes plus special family and winter trips, along with self-guided walks that include all transfers, food and logistics.

TOP TIPS

- A fee-based permit system is in place from 1 October to 31 May, with departures limited to a maximum of 34 independent hikers a day.
- Bookings for each season open in early July and places fill fast, so try to book early.
- A valid national parks pass is needed for walking year-round.
- Campfires are banned on the track. Carry a fuel stove for cooking.
- Cradle Mountain Coaches and eGuide run transfers from Devonport, Launceston, Deloraine, Sheffield and Hobart to Cradle Mountain, returning to the same places (or back to Cradle Mountain) from Lake St Clair.

THE WEINDORFERS' LEGACY

Gustav Weindorfer was an Austrian immigrant fundamental to the preservation of the Cradle Mountain area. In 1910, he built Waldheim, a wooden cabin, and with his wife, Kate, lobbied successive governments to preserve the area. Despite the challenging access to the region, the Weindorfers promoted Cradle Mountain to visitors, and Kate's botanical expertise and knowledge of the local flora and fauna deepened their appreciation of the landscape.

Following her death in 1916, Gustav moved permanently to Waldheim and dedicated his life to conservation. Cradle Mountain became a scenic reserve in 1922 an was declared a national park in 1971. The original Waldheim was replaced in 1976, but remains a poignant tribute to the Weindorfers' legacy.

JANELLE LUGGE/SHUTTERSTOCK

Climbing **Cradle Mountain** summit is a challenging full-day affair (eight hours return) and, beyond Kitchen Hut, transforms into a rock-hop and scramble. The reward? Sublime views all the way to Mt Ossa (Tasmania's highest mountain) and beyond.

Not up for a walk? **Cradle Mountain Canyons** *(cradlemountaincanyons.com.au)* takes you paddling across Dove Lake in a hand-built King Billy pine kayak, viewing Cradle Mountain from a water-top perspective.

Meet Tasmania's cutest carnivores

Located among the visitor facilities in Cradle Valley, **Devils@Cradle** *(devilsatcradle.com; adult/child $27.50/15)* is a conservation-focused centre for Tasmanian devils, spotted-tail quolls and eastern quolls. Housing up to 50 devils, the sanctuary is open all day for self-guided visits, keeper tours (10.30am and 3pm) and feeding tours (1pm), but try to schedule an evening visit when the animals are most active and the bush resounds with their banshee screams.

Stanley

TIME FROM DEVONPORT: 1½HR

Climb Stanley's iconic landmark

Known to the area's Aboriginal people as Moo-Nut-Re-Ker and labelled 'Circular Head' by explorer Matthew Flinders, the **Nut** is the 12-million-year-old plug of an extinct volcano and

Its more refined counterpart, Highland Restaurant, is in the same building

EATING AROUND CRADLE MOUNTAIN: OUR PICKS

Elements: Simple breakfasts and lunches (bacon-and-egg muffins, burgers, croissants) at the park visitor centre. *8.30am-4.30pm* $

Altitude: The house restaurant at Cradle Mountain Hotel has Tassie tastes such as Cape Grim beef and Huon Valley trout. Or perhaps a sweet-potato steak? *5-9pm* $$$

Hellyers Restaurant: Refined fireside dining using ingredients from Tassie producers at Cradle Mountain Wilderness Village. *noon-3pm & 5-7.30pm* $$$

Tavern Bar & Bistro: Popular three-tiered tavern with pub classics, a pool table and two open fires adding warmth and mood. *noon-late* $$$

The Nut

at 143m in height it can be seen for many kilometres around Stanley, which sprawls across its base.

To reach the summit of the Nut, either hike up the short, sharp and steep 20-minute **Zig Zag Track** or climb aboard the old-school **chairlift** *(thenutchairlift.com.au; adult/child one way $14/9, return $21/14)*. Once you're atop the Nut, with its windswept and wind-pruned plateau (with one conspicuous stand of trees), a 2km walking track circles the summit. It's particularly worth catching the chairlift down, when it provides the best views.

King Island

TIME FROM BURNIE: **35MIN**

Sample cheese, beer and whisky

If King Island is known for any one thing, it's food. **King Island Dairy** *(kingislanddairy.com.au)* is one of Australia's most revered names in cheese and, after almost closing in 2024, it was purchased by new owners and continues to produce its award-winning cheeses.

Occupying a tin shed in the paddocks midway between Currie and Grassy, the **King Island Brewhouse** taproom has six beers, from session ales to a stout and an alcoholic ginger beer. Friday night is wood-fired-pizza night.

The island is home to two distilleries. Contact Heidi Weitjens at the **King Island Distillery** *(kingislanddistillery.com)*

STANLEY'S MOST FAMOUS SON

South of the Nut, almost beside the Ship Inn (p709), **Lyons Cottage Historic Site** is a modest dwelling that was the birthplace of Australian Prime Minister Joseph Lyons (1879–1939). He's still the only Tasmanian to ascend to the highest political office in the country and was the first Australian prime minister to die while holding the post. Reputedly a very relaxed individual, Lyons was often depicted as a genial and laid-back koala in newspaper cartoons during his tenure and his sudden death shocked the nation during Easter in 1939. In 1943 his widow Enid Lyons was the first woman to be elected to Australia's House of Representatives and also the first woman appointed to the federal cabinet.

EATING & DRINKING IN STANLEY: OUR PICKS

Hursey Seafoods: Takeaway fish and chips downstairs, bistro dining upstairs, with seafood fresh off its own boats. Takeaway all day. *noon-2.30pm & 5.30-8pm* $$

Stanley Hotel: Steak and seafood both come with low food miles at this popular pub that dominates Stanley's streetscape. *noon-8pm* $$$

Marleys: Popular cafe with views out to Tatlows Beach as you tuck into spicy abalone or a salad of beef, haloumi, nuts and fruit. *7am-4pm Fri-Tue* $$

Stanley Wine Bar: Settle into an antique armchair and enjoy the cabinet-of-curiosities surrounds, from steampunk to uranium glass. *5-9pm Thu-Sat*

EXPLORING THE TARKINE DRIVE

This wonderfully remote drive explores a section of coast as wild as any in Tasmania and disappears deep into the Takayna / Tarkine rainforest's northern reaches.

START	END	LENGTH
Marrawah	Smithton	180km; 4hr

Fill up on petrol in Smithton or Stanley, as there's no petrol available along this fully sealed drive. From 1 **Marrawah**, it's 15km to 2 **Bluff Hill Point Lighthouse**, an excellent vantage point for a first taste of the coast's wild energy. Continue south for 10km to 3 **Gardiner Point**, a natural frontier so wild it's earned the title of Edge of the World. Further south, by the shack village of Nelson Bay, 4 **Sundown Point State Reserve** features a 2km walk to ancient petroglyphs. Approaching the fishing-shack community of 5 **Couta Rocks**, the drive turns inland to pass the northern entry to the 6 **Western Explorer Road**. The Tarkine Drive now meanders through temperate rainforest with recommended stops 17km ahead at 7 **Kanunnah Bridge**, ideal for a picnic beside the fast-flowing Arthur River and nearby 8 **Sumac Lookout**, with elevated Arthur River views. Two short rainforest walks (30 and 40 minutes) and overnight parking for caravans and campervans are highlights at 9 **Julius River**, 6km ahead, while platypuses are sometimes seen on the 30-minute walk at 10 **Lake Chisholm**.

The drive's standout feature, the collapsed sinkhole at 11 **Trowutta Arch**, is reached after a further 50km of forest-framed driving. From the arch, it's 31km north to 12 **Smithton**.

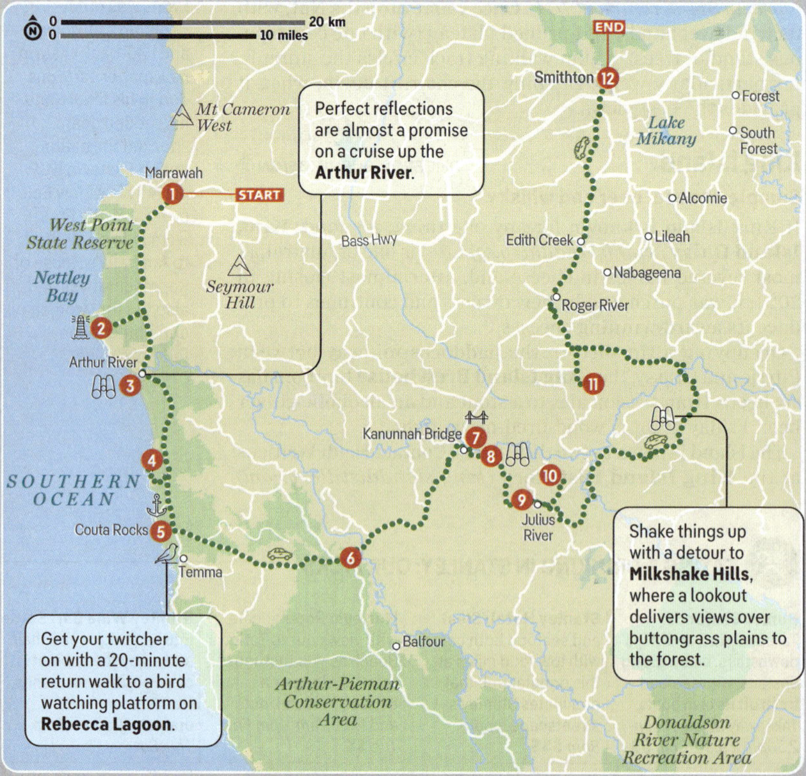

FILEDIMAGE/SHUTTERSTOCK

Strahan

to tour her original spirits shed by Currie's racecourse. The island's coolest bar, owned and operated by the similarly named **King Island Distillery Bass Strait** *(kingislanddistillery.com.au)*, is curiously inside the tiny airport.

Play Australia's best golf course

With a little imagination, it's not hard to picture King Island as a golf green in the middle of a very large water hazard. Fittingly, **Cape Wickham Golf Links** *(capewickham.com.au; 9/18 holes from $108/180)*, almost wrapped around the toes of its namesake lighthouse, was named Australia's best golf course by *Australian Golf Digest* in 2024. Close behind on the list of top golf courses, at No 13, was **Ocean Dunes** *(oceandunes.com.au; 9/18 holes from $100/160)*, just to Currie's north.

Strahan

TIME FROM DEVONPORT: **2¾HR**

Macquarie Harbour and Gordon River adventures

Early each morning, Strahan's harbourside is thronged with visitors boarding ships bound for Macquarie Harbour and the Gordon River. The dense rainforest lining the river and the perfection of its reflections make it an unforgettable experience. A stop at Heritage Landing includes a fully accessible boardwalk into a clearing created when a 2000-year-old Huon

THE RESTAURANT WITH NO FOOD

By the water in Currie Harbour, the **Boathouse** is a dining venue like no other. Known locally as 'the restaurant with no food', the brightly coloured boatshed with a sunny dining room and rustic outdoor tables is the best place to enjoy King Island's excellent local produce. It has a BBQ, compact kitchen, plates, cutlery and seriously eclectic decor – think chandeliers hanging among fishing nets.

FoodWorks in Currie puts together picnic and BBQ hampers perfect for the occasion (24-hour notice required) – pick one up, pop an LP on the Boathouse's 1970s turntable (complete with a rag-tag collection of old vinyl records) and enjoy perhaps the finest island picnic of your life. Just don't forget to do the dishes.

EATING ON KING ISLAND: OUR PICKS

Island Larder: KI's best coffee, great cakes and the likes of chilli scramble eggs and breakfast burritos. *7am-2pm Mon-Wed & Fri, 8am-1pm Sat & Sun* **$**

Oleada: Italian-accented dining in a tiny, map-covered Currie restaurant, with local island produce right down to the gins and beers. *6-10pm Wed-Sat* **$$$**

Wild Harvest: Five-course degustation dining in shearing-shed-chic surrounds at this restaurant poised high above Grassy Harbour. *6-10pm Sat* **$$$**

Chefanie's at View: Salt-and-pepper squid, karage chicken and roast specials overlooking Currie's golf course. *3-6.30pm Thu & Fri, 10am-4pm Sat* **$$**

TASMANIA'S FAMOUS TIMBER

No tree is more emblematic of Tasmania than the shaggy Huon pine. One of the planet's slowest-growing and longest-living trees, a Huon pine can take 2000 years to reach 30m in height and can live to 3000 years. Prized for its rich, golden hue and rot-resistant oils, it was plundered by loggers and shipbuilders in the 19th century.

Today, it's illegal to harvest Huon pine – those lovely Huon pine items you see for sale are made from ethically salvaged timber that washes down the rivers. One 2000-year-old beauty can be viewed during Gordon River cruises. Huon pine was central to the early colonisation of the west coast – Sarah Island was selected as the site for a convict station so that convicts could fell Huon pines for shipbuilding.

WILLOWTREEHOUSE/SHUTTERSTOCK

West Coast Wilderness Railway

pine fell. The final stop is **Sarah Island**, where entertaining guided tours tell the story of the first and most notorious penal colony in Van Diemen's Land.

Two companies – **Gordon River Cruises** *(gordonrivercruises.com.au; adult/child from $155/75)*, operating *Spirit of the Wild* (aka the Grey Boat) and **World Heritage Cruises** *(worldheritagecruises.com.au; adult/child from $155/70)*, operating the *Harbour Master II* (aka the Red Boat) – offer similar itineraries. There's plenty of scope for viewing from outdoor decks and both companies include lunch on the six-hour tours.

Watch Australia's longest-running play

Back in Strahan, continue the convict theme at **The Ship that Never Was** *(0476 651 089; roundearth.com.au; ship@roundearth.com.au; adult/child $30/5)*, an entertaining 1¼-hour, two-actor performance telling the picaresque tale of a group of convicts who escaped from Sarah Island in 1834 by hijacking a ship they were building. Premiering in 1994, it's the longest-running play in Australia. Nightly performances begin at 5.30pm from September to May. Book ahead .

EATING IN STRAHAN: OUR PICKS

Coffee Shack: Strahan's best coffee, home-style baking and toasties in a tin shack opposite the cruise-boat terminal. *6am-2pm* $

Risby Cove: Book ahead for calming harbour views and a short menu reliably featuring local fish, beef and house-made gnocchi. *5.30pm-late* $$$

Charlotte's at Franklin Manor: Fine French dining in a historic guesthouse; a five-course set menu, plus a wine tasting to extend the evening. *5.30-11pm Tue-Sat* $$$

View 42°: Harbour views and an evening buffet, including a Tasmanian salmon platter and an artisan meat board. *7-9am & 6-8.30pm* $$$

Queenstown

TIME FROM DEVONPORT: **2½HR**

Rails and rainforest

When the **West Coast Wilderness Railway** *(wcwr.com.au)* was built in 1896, the steam train and its tortuous route through remote country were a marvel of engineering. It clings to the steep-sided gorge of the King River, passing through dense rainforest across 40 bridges. At the time of writing, two trips were departing from the 1890s train station in Queenstown. The 1½-hour **Lynchford Express** *(adult/child from $50/30)* travels from Queenstown to Lynchford, a former gold-mining town. **Rinadeena, Rack & Rainforest** *(Heritage/Wilderness carriage from $95/130)* is a three-hour rail trip continuing past Lynchford to Rinadeena, making the steep 3km climb on a rack-and-pinion line to Rinadeena Saddle. Trips also run from Strahan.

Mountain biking on Mt Owen

Amid Queenstown's rugged landscapes, mountain biking is growing in popularity and the focus here – in contrast to forested trails elsewhere in Tasmania – are mountain tracks coursing along and down the exposed ridges and slopes of **Mt Owen** *(mtb.westcoasttas.com.au)*. More than 35km of trails include beginner-friendly loops and challenging, plunging descents. As a general rule, the easiest trails are on the lower half of the mountain, while the blacks and blues – the more difficult trails – are high up and require shuttles, which are operated by **RoamWild** *(roamwild.com.au; from $85)*. Bike hire can be arranged through **West Coast Ride** *(westcoastride.com)* in the main street.

Zeehan

TIME FROM DEVONPORT: **2¼HR**

Explore Tasmania's 'Silver City'

Once a self-proclaimed 'Silver City' of 27 pubs and 10,000 people, Zeehan (population now 720) is anchored by the **West Coast Heritage Centre** *(wchczeehan.com.au; adult/concession $25/20)*, housed in the 1894 School of Mines & Metallurgy and a showcase of the town's silver-flecked glory days. Highlights include a vast collection of minerals, the chance to burrow beneath the buildings in an underground mine simulation and stepping into the **Gaiety Theatre**. At the time of its construction in 1898, the theatre was the grandest building on the west coast and one of Australia's finest theatres. Sit in its old seats and watch the surviving remnants of one of two B&W silent movies: either *Jewelled Nights* (1926)

THE GRAVEL

They breed 'em tough out here. So tough, in fact, that Queenstown's historic **football oval** is known as 'the Gravel'. When laid out in 1880, the oval was covered in gravel to withstand the area's heavy rain. Pollution from the mine also made it difficult for grass to take hold. In 1969 the surface was changed to (slightly) less abrasive silica from the nearby Mt Lyell Copper Mine, but it remains a challenging place to play. Cuts, scrapes and lost skin are all but guaranteed for players.

It's the home ground of the Queenstown Crows, playing in West Coast Tasmania's Darwin Football Association. A good time to catch a match here is during the biennial **Unconformity** *(theunconformity.com.au)* festival in October (odd-numbered years).

EATING & DRINKING IN QUEENSTOWN: OUR PICKS

Moonscape: Wine bar and cafe with a sunny beer garden. Burrata and flatbread pizzas team with craft beers. *3-8.30pm Wed & Thu*

Tracks Cafe: Coffee and breakfast before a railway adventure, or one of its own Mt Lyell Mongrel lagers afterward. *7.30am-8pm Mon-Sat, 8am-3.30pm Sun* **$$**

Orange Pete's: Step into the very orange world (orange recliners, rusted walls) of the orange-suited Pete for a warm welcome, toastie and coffee. *5.30am-3.30pm* **$**

Empire Hotel: Hearty pub standards in the hotel dubbed the 'grand old lady of the west coast'. *noon-2pm & 6-8pm* **$$**

TASMANIA'S NEXT BIG WALK?

On the heels of the success of the **Three Capes Track** (p660) on the Tasman Peninsula, Tasmania's next 'iconic walk' project is squarely fixed on the Tyndall Range, a line of mountains reaching to almost 1200m between Queenstown and Rosebery. Proposed to be a three-day, 28km hut-based hike, the trail will run north–south from Lake Plimsoll to the old Lake Margaret Power Station. The two huts along the route are expected to replicate their plush cousins on the Three Capes Track (rather than the more basic Overland Track–style huts). Critics of the proposal note that the wetter, colder, more uncomfortable hiking conditions on the west coast might deter many hikers. The track is slated to open in 2029.

Montezuma Falls

or *The Story of the Kelly Gang* (1907), which was the world's first feature film.

Rosebery

TIME FROM DEVONPORT: **2HR**

Hike to Tasmania's highest waterfall

The base-metal mining town of Rosebery is more fondly known for its proximity to Tasmania's tallest waterfall, 104m-high **Montezuma Falls**. To see the waterfall, drive 2km southwest out of Rosebery and turn off to Williamsford, another abandoned mining town. The easy three-hour, 11km return walk follows the course of an old forest tramway to the falls. It can also be cycled on a mountain or gravel bike. Venture onto the swing bridge for views of the falls and a forested chasm.

EATING IN ZEEHAN: OUR PICKS

Pitstop Cafe: Diner-style cafe, appended by a vintage motorbike workshop – a favourite with touring motorcyclists. *9.30am-1.30pm Thu & Fri, to 12.30pm Sun* **$**

Big Z Cafe & Restaurant: Opened in late 2025 with simple offerings of toasties, burgers and spring rolls. *8am-2pm Tue-Fri & Sun, to 2.30pm Sat* **$$**

Carol's on Wheels: Food truck serving homemade pies and egg-and-bacon rolls from among the outdoor locomotives of the Heritage Centre. *7.30am-5pm Mon-Fri* **$**

Heemskirk Motor Hotel: Straight-up pub grub – parmi, steak burger, roast of the day – at this large pub on Zeehan's outer edge. *noon-10pm Mon-Sat, to 8pm Sun* **$$**

Midlands, Lakes & Wild Rivers

COLONIAL HERITAGE | FLY-FISHING | WHITE-WATER RAFTING

Straw-coloured plains, hawthorn hedgerows, rows of poplars, grand homesteads – Tasmania's Midlands have a distinctly English feel. This is old-school Tasmania, tracing the route between Hobart and Launceston hammered out by convict gangs in the early 1800s. These days, travellers can take a break at some sublime whisky distilleries.

Heading west, Tasmania's wild and windswept Highland Lakes sit above the clouds (and trees) at around 1050m – a stark, rocky expanse pockmarked by waterways brimming with trout.

West of the Highland Lakes, Australia's deepest lake lies waiting at the southern end of Cradle Mountain-Lake St Clair National Park. Leeawuleena / Lake St Clair is the finishing line for the legendary Overland Track (lots of hungry hikers). There are some great day walks here, too.

Further west again, the majestic Franklin-Gordon Wild Rivers National Park is as wild as the name suggests. Rafting the Franklin River is undoubtedly Tasmania's most exciting, once-in-a-lifetime adventure.

TOP TIP

For a quick glimpse of the fabled Franklin River, take the Nature Trail (1km) from a picnic area on the Lyell Hwy about 25km west of Derwent Bridge. The easy, accessible loop track passes through lush forest before following the fern-lined mossy riverbank back to the road.

Time for a Wee Dram?

Whisky tasting in the Midlands

Around 30km north of Hobart at Pontville, **Lark Distillery** *(larkdistillery.com)* occupies the historic 1830s Shene Estate,

GETTING AROUND

Daily buses running between Hobart and Launceston cruise the well-trafficked Midland Hwy (A1) and stop at the main Midlands towns. You'll need your own car to explore the Highland Lakes – and if you've got access to a 4WD, even better (lots of dirt roads). Derwent Bridge and Leeawuleena / Lake St Clair are 2½ hours from both Hobart and Launceston by car (the latter via the Central Plateau). The Hobart–Queenstown coach service trucks along the Lyell Hwy through Derwent Bridge twice weekly, while private bushwalker shuttles connect Leeawuleena / Lake St Clair with Hobart, Launceston and Cradle Mountain.

HIGHLIGHTS
1 Franklin-Gordon Wild Rivers National Park
2 Tasmanian Trail

SIGHTS
3 Australasian Golf Museum
4 Callington Mill Distillery
5 Collingwood Bridge
6 Convict Brick Trail
7 Cradle Mountain-Lake St Clair National Park
8 Four Corners of Ross
9 Lark Distillery
10 Leeawuleena/ Lake St Clair
11 Old Kempton Distillery
see 6 Red Bridge
see 8 Ross Bridge

ACTIVITIES
see 5 Franklin River Rafting
see 10 Larmairremener Tabelti
12 Miena Village Guiding
see 3 Ratho Farm
see 5 Tasmanian Expeditions
see 5 Water By Nature

SLEEPING
see 12 Great Lake Hotel
see 4 Oatlands Free Camping
13 Pumphouse Point
see 3 Ratho Farm
see 8 White Croft Cottage

EATING
see 4 Bunch
see 2 Central Highlands Lodge
14 Derwent Bridge Wilderness Hotel
see 12 Great Lake Hotel
see 14 Hungry Wombat Cafe
see 4 Kentish Hotel
see 10 Lake St Clair Lodge
15 Mood Food
see 13 Pumphouse Point
see 8 Ross Hotel
see 8 Ross Village Bakery
see 3 Sealy's Store
see 6 Sweet Brew

DRINKING & NIGHTLIFE
16 Lawrenny Estate

INFORMATION
see 10 Leeawuleena/ Lake St Clair Visitor Information Centre

TRANSPORT
see 10 Lake St Clair Ferry

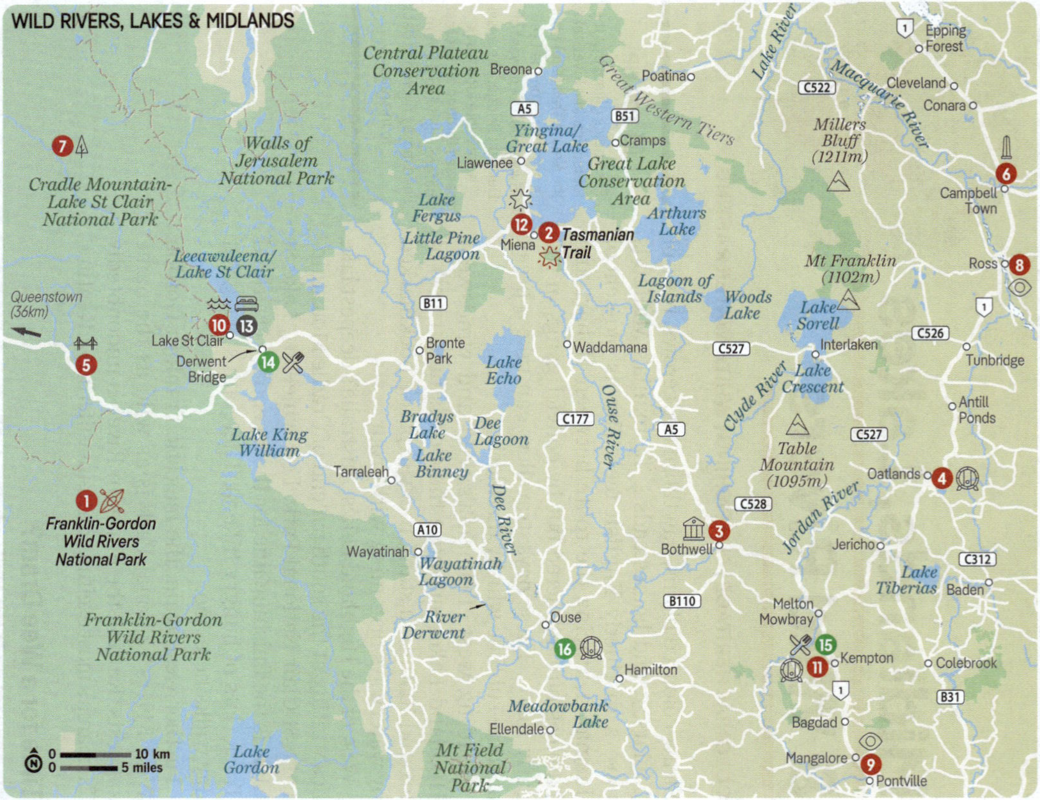

some 16 hectares of fields and heritage buildings the size of a small village. The distillery is open for tastings from 10am to 4pm, with tours at noon and 2pm daily.

Why settle for a bottle when you can own your own cask? **Old Kempton Distillery** *(oldkemptondistillery.com.au)* in the grand old 1842 Dysart Manor house is where you can sample whisky flights, take a tour (11am and 1.30pm daily), grab a cafe feed or purchase a 20L, 50L or whopping 100L tub of sunshine.

The windmill-fronted **Callington Mill Distillery** *(callingtonmill.com.au)* in Oatlands produces world-class single-malt whiskies using cutting-edge, innovative technology. Come for a guided tour (noon daily), a whisky flight, lunch in the excellent restaurant or a chance to blend your own signature whisky. Even if you don't like whisky, it's worth a wander: the owners have spent millions restoring the 1837 windmill, stables and old cottages on the estate. There's a great kids' playground adjacent and the glass-and-steel distillery building itself is a stunner.

Australia's Third-Oldest Bridge

Magnificent convict masonry at Ross

The oft-photographed **Ross Bridge** *(visitross.com.au)* over the Macquarie River is the third-oldest bridge in Australia (1836). Designed by colonial architect John Lee Archer, it was built by two convict stonemasons, James Colbeck and Daniel Herbert, who were granted pardons for their efforts. Herbert chiselled the 186 intricate carvings decorating the arches, including Celtic symbols, animals and notable people (such as Governor Arthur and Anglo-Danish convict Jorgen Jorgensen, the farcical ex-king of Iceland). At night the bridge is lit up – the carvings shimmer with spooky shadows.

Choose Your Destiny

Visit a Ross landmark

Feeling a bit aimless? Life lacking direction? Get some guidance down at the **Four Corners of Ross**. Here at the Church St and Bridge St crossroads, your soul can choose from four directions: 'Damnation' (the old jail, now a private residence), 'Recreation' (the Town Hall), 'Salvation' (the Catholic Church) and 'Temptation' (the pub). For most visitors, it's not a very challenging decision to make.

THE FATHER OF TASMANIA

Strung-out Kempton, 50km north of Hobart and bypassed by the main highway, was founded in 1838, making it one of the state's earliest European settlements.

Originally known as Green Ponds, it was later renamed after one-time resident and notorious rabble-rouser Anthony Fenn Kemp. Kemp was a charismatic dude: one-half egotistical bankrupt with scant moral fibre, one-half progressive patriot who was critical in Tasmania's evolution from convict dump to independent colony. Fleeing debts in England, he became a dedicated pastoralist, merchant and political sabre-rattler. Never far from controversy, he made as many friends as enemies and left behind more than a dozen children – a fact that has seen him dubbed the 'Father of Tasmania'.

Love the house Embezeller Gin

EATING & DRINKING IN THE MIDLANDS: OUR PICKS

Mood Food: The original and best Mood Food (Tasmanian roadhouse franchise) is on the highway north of Kempton. Burgers, truckers, country music. *24hr* $

Bunch: The pick of the Oatlands cafes, serving pizzas, soups and deli-style sandwiches. Beer and wine; sunny footpath tables. *8.30am-4pm* $

Kentish Hotel: Oatlands' last pub is hanging in there, with beer-garden burgers and adjunct coffee shop. *9am-10pm Wed-Sat, to 3pm Sun* $$

Old Kempton Distillery: Hearty Midlands fare to augment the single malt: soups, beef-and-whisky pie, sausages and sticky date pudding. *10am-4pm* $$

SUCCUMB TO TEMPTATION IN ROSS

Take a walk around the Ross streets and riverbanks and discover the town's key historic sites.

START	END	LENGTH
Four Corners of Ross	Ross Hotel	3km; 1hr

From the ❶ **Four Corners of Ross** (p703), head south past the 1891 ❷ **Town Hall** (aka 'Recreation') uphill to the 1885 ❸ **Uniting Church**, with heaven-sent country views. Truck back downhill past the ❹ **Tasmanian Wool Centre** (buy a beanie), then turn left to reach ❺ **Ross Bridge** (p703) and its 186 intricate carvings (how many animals can you spot?).

Follow the trail south along the Macquarie River, passing some interesting churchyard ruins, to arrive at the ❻ **Ross Female Factory**. Check out the Superintendent's Cottage and the bleak yards behind it.

Follow Portugal St, cross the railway line, then a path alongside a stone wall (all rather Yorkshire). On the hilltop beyond Park St is ❼ **Old Ross Burial Ground** (1835). Several British Redcoats are among the subterranean, plus Daniel Herbert the Ross Bridge convict stonemason (died 1868, aged 67).

Backtrack through the rambling ❽ **Anglican Pioneer Cemetery** and ❾ **Ross Catholic Cemetery**. Head north along Park St, turn left onto Bridge St, right onto Bond St, then left again onto Badajos St. The noble ❿ **St John's Anglican Church** dates from 1869.

Follow Church St to the 1847 ⓫ **schoolhouse** and admire the beautiful 1889 ⓬ **post office** across the street, with its elegant wrought-iron portico. Finally, succumb to 'Temptation' with a cold pint at the 1835 ⓭ **Ross Hotel**.

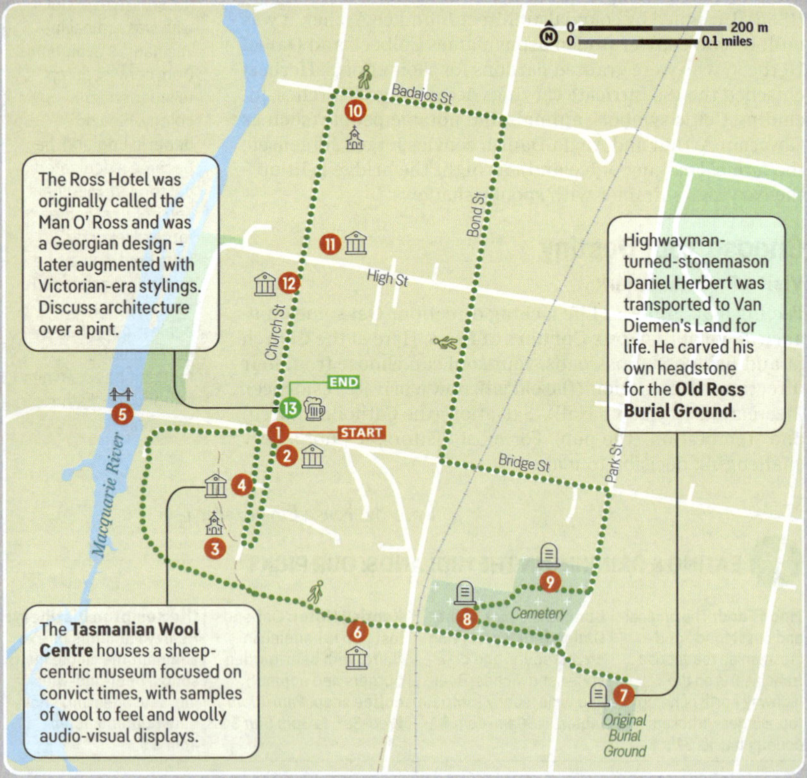

Red Bricks of Campbell Town

One convict-built bridge, hundreds of convict stories

The convict-built bridge across the slow-moving Elizabeth River at Campbell Town was completed in 1838, making it almost as venerable as the Ross Bridge. Locals call it the **Red Bridge** because it was built from more than 1.5 million red bricks, baked on site. The red-brick theme continues along the town's main street, where the **Convict Brick Trail** *(northernmidlands.tas.gov.au)* is set into the footpath. Each brick details the crimes, sentences and arrival dates of convicts such as Ephram Brain and English Corney, sent here for sins as various as stealing potatoes, bigamy, murder and being an 'indefatigable burglar'.

Fly-Fishing Nirvana

Wade into a misty lake and hook a trout

Catching brown and rainbow trout in the Highland Lakes should be as easy as getting your feet wet – but you still need timing and skill! There are also sustainability-informed restrictions on fish size, daily catch allocations and the types of tackle permitted in various areas in different seasons; the **Inland Fisheries Service** *(ifs.tas.gov.au)* sells licences and offers priceless advice.

Engaging a professional fly-fishing guide for lessons or a guided trip is a stellar idea; try **Rod & Fly Tasmania** *(rodandfly.com.au)*, **Miena Village Guiding** *(mienaguidingtasmania.com.au)* or **Trout Guides & Lodges Tasmania** *(troutguidestasmania.com.au)*. Prices range from $600 to $900 per person per day. And don't forget your licence!

Tee-Off in Bothwell

The oldest golf course outside Scotland

At Bothwell on the eastern edge of the Highlands, Scottish heritage runs deep: the town has adopted tartan street signs and is obsessed with golf. Next to the visitor centre, the **Australasian Golf Museum** *(ausgolfmuseum.com; $5)* has a putting green where you can test old-style clubs and a stupendous selection of golf-themed Jim Beam bourbon decanters (sadly, empty). The oldest golf course outside Scotland is in Bothwell too, rolled out of the dust at **Ratho Farm** *(rathofarm.com/golf; 9/18 holes $35/50)* in 1822 by Scottish settlers. It's an eccentric 18-hole prospect: watch out for sheep, hedges, hay bales and fences

SHADOWS OF THE PAST

The Midland Hwy between Hobart and Launceston is Tasmania's main north–south link road – and it comes with a rich history. The next time you're driving this way, keep an eye out (not you, driver) for the 16 large silhouette sculptures adorning the hills and roadside verges between Tunbridge and Kempton. The project, by artists Folko Kooper and Maureen Craig, illustrates snippets of the highway's history, including stagecoaches and bushrangers, convict chain gangs, a surveyor, even a pack of thylacines (Tasmanian tigers). However, the quirkiest two are the travelling hangman and a policeman wheeling a drunk in a wheelbarrow. For some background on the artists and detail on the sculptures, check out *southernmidlands.tas.gov.au/shadows-of-the-past*.

EATING & DRINKING IN THE MIDLANDS: OUR PICKS

Sweet Brew: Top Campbell Town coffee, plus fat blueberry muffins, toasties and spinach-and-fetta *börek* (Balkan pastry). *7.30am-2pm* $

Ross Village Bakery: Towering slabs of vanilla slice, pies and sourdough baked in an 1860 oven. Courtyard, inside or footpath tables. *8.30am-3pm Wed-Sun* $

Ross Hotel: In the process of culinary reinvention when we visited: pizza in the beer garden will suffice. *11.30am-10pm Wed, Thu & Sun, to 11pm Fri & Sat* $$

Callington Mill Distillery: Exquisite menu showcasing the best of Tasmania: super steaks, even better pulled-lamb ravioli. *10am-5pm* $$$

THE GENTLE ART OF FLY-FISHING

Brad Harris, ex-editor of *FlyLife* magazine, shares some insider tips.

Tasmania has three distinct seasons for trout fly-fishing.

In spring, when lakes are flooded and fish feed around the edges, dawn and dusk are optimal casting times. Summer brings hatching mayflies and beetles – match your fly colour to the insect. Try a dark brown Parachute Emerger or yellow/green Foam Beetle.

In autumn on the lakes, try Beetle or small Mayfly dry flies or Woolly Bugger and Stick Caddis wets. During drizzly weather, look for water with mayflies and on sunny days sight-fish in shallow clear lakes and rivers. Don't mix the two.

Pack a 9ft 5-weight rod with floating line and learn to cast in the wind. Polarising sunglasses are essential!

(local rules: if you hit a fence, you can replay the shot without penalty). There's convict-built accommodation here, too.

Cycle the Tasmanian Trail

Bike across Tasmania, coast to coast

Rambling between Devonport and Dover for 480km, the multi-use **Tasmanian Trail** *(tasmaniantrail.com.au; membership $70)* follows backroads, forestry tracks and private paths across farmland, river valleys, forests and the stark Central Plateau. Riders of all skill levels can tackle it, but there are a few tough sections and several (possibly dodgy) river crossings – not to mention some serious altitude gain. The trail sidesteps national parks and major towns, but it's never far from a cosy bed. Most riders take 10 to 14 days to complete the route, but if you don't have that kind of time, Miena in the middle of the Highland Lakes is a handy staging post. The trail is managed by volunteers who sell a guidebook via membership and supply keys to locked gates and amenities. You don't need to book and the trail is navigable in either direction. Hot tip: the southwesterly wind is better behind you than in your face (ride north).

Rafting the Franklin River

White-knuckled, white-water adventure

White-water rafting trips on the Franklin River within **Franklin-Gordon Wild Rivers National Park** *(parks.tas.gov.au; day pass per person/vehicle $24/48)* depart from **Collingwood Bridge** on the Lyell Hwy, 40km west of Derwent Bridge and take eight to 10 days end-to-end. Be prepared for wet, cold, adrenaline-packed days, riverside camps, sublime scenery and quite a few portages. It's an unforgettable journey (at $4K-plus, you won't be forgetting anything in a hurry), passing the narrow **Irenabyss**, the scary **Great Ravine** and famed **Rock Island Bend**, pinup for the 'No Dams' campaign. No experience is required, but this is one trip you should do with experienced professionals; try **Franklin River Rafting** *(franklinriverrafting.com)*, **Tasmanian Expeditions** *(tasmanianexpeditions.com.au)* or **Water by Nature** *(franklinriver.com)*.

EATING & DRINKING IN THE HIGHLANDS: OUR PICKS

Sealy's Store: A warming wood heater, proper coffee and interesting pies and soups in an 1850 corner store in Bothwell. *9am-3pm* $

Great Lake Hotel: Ace pub fare (pizzas, steaks, schnitzels, wallaby burgers) in Miena, with serves as big as the 4WDs in the car park. *11am-9pm Wed-Sat, to 3pm Sun* $$

Central Highlands Lodge: Cold beers, hearty food, friendly locals and a roaring fire welcome weary fisherfolk. *11am-9pm* $$

Lawrenny Estate: At Ouse, a Highlands' southern access town, this early-1800s estate bottles limited-release single malts and crystal-clear gins. *10am-4pm*

ANDREW BAIN/ALAMY

Franklin River

Australia's Deepest Lake

Walk the shores of Leeawuleena / Lake St Clair

More sightseer than mountaineer? Within Cradle Mountain-Lake St Clair National Park (p691), many walks around the 215m-deep, shimmering **Leeawuleena / Lake St Clair** *(parks.tas.gov.au; day pass per person/vehicle $24/48)* don't require an Overland Track Permit or a week in the mountains – just some decent shoes and a national parks pass. From the **Visitor Information Centre** at Cynthia Bay (5km from Derwent Bridge), the excellent cultural **Larmairremener Tabelti** trail runs through myrtle beech forest to the confluence of the Cuvier and Huegel rivers (aka 'Watersmeet'; 3.5km return). Or get out onto the lake onboard the **Lake St Clair Ferry** *(lakestclairlodge.com.au; one way $55)* to Narcissus Bay then walk back along the shore – an excellent 17.5km day walk. The ferry runs at 9am, 12.30pm and 3pm.

SAVING THE FRANKLIN

Franklin-Gordon Wild Rivers National Park was the site of Australia's biggest environmental battle – the Franklin River Blockade of the early 1980s. Despite national park and World Heritage status, Tasmania's Hydro Electric Commission (HEC) pushed plans to dam the Franklin, sparking mass protests. In 1981, 46% of Tasmanians scribbled 'No Dams' across their ballot papers in a referendum. In 1982, dam construction began, prompting hundreds of protesters to blockade the Franklin. Over 1400 people were arrested in protests that gained global attention. The issue became central to the 1983 federal election, won by the Labor Party on a 'No Dams' platform. The new government halted the dam, enshrining World Heritage protection for the Franklin and Gordon rivers.

EATING & DRINKING APRÈS WILDERNESS: OUR PICKS

Hungry Wombat Cafe: On the highway by the Derwent Bridge roadhouse: satisfying burgers, bacon rolls, toasties and hot chips. *8.30am-4.30pm* $

Derwent Bridge Wilderness Hotel: Favourite for a post-Overland Track feast, the steaks are all you've fantasised about over your dehydrated noodles. *11.30am-8pm* $$

Lake St Clair Lodge: Fresh off the boat from Narcissus, burgers, beers and hot chips have never looked so good. *8am-8pm* $$

Pumphouse Point: The best meals west of Hobart, in spectacular accommodation that you'll never forget...literally ON Leeawuleena / Lake St Clair! *hours vary* $$$

Places We Love to Stay

$ Budget $$ Midrange $$$ Top end

Hobart

MAPS p640 & p644

Astor Private Hotel $ Old-world charm in a classic 1922 red-brick guesthouse on Macquarie St. Clean rooms, shared bathrooms, on-site steakhouse.

Montacute $ Boutique backpackers with a choice of small dorms, mixed or same-sex, in a lovely Battery Point building. Shared bathrooms.

Waterman's Hotel $$ Stylish hotel above ground-zero Salamanca (read: not super-quiet). Rooms go heavy on the old timbers and exposed sandstone.

Henry Jones Art Hotel $$$ In the restored IXL Jam Factory overlooking Victoria Dock, you'll keep company with revolving art exhibitions. Rooms are suitably extravagant.

Tasman $$$ High-end Hobart at its height: fabulous rooms, from Art Deco to heritage to up-to-the-second contemporary. Bars and eats on-site.

De Witt Apartment $$$ Three-bedroom, artfully renovated shopfront in the heart of Battery Point; perfect for small groups or families.

MONA Pavilions $$$ Expect lots of glass, crazy angles, cavernous beds, spa views, offbeat art, Derwent solitude – and MONA right next door.

Turrakana / Tasman Peninsula

Stewarts Bay Lodge $$$ Self-contained log cabins at Port Arthur; different sizes (sleeping up to six), with bush or water views. On-site restaurant to boot.

Bruny Island

43 Degrees $$$ Unique 'aircraft-hanger' spa studios at the northern end of Adventure Bay beach, all with verandahs and impeccable eco credentials.

Bruny Boathouse $$$ Overlooking Satellite Island in Alonnah, this bright, stylish option sleeps four in two bedrooms. Pub and coastal trail nearby (choose your destiny).

Huon Valley

Huon Valley Caravan Park $ On Mountain River, walking distance to Ranelagh, with grassy powered/unpowered sites and kayaking on the nearby Huon.

Roundhouses $$ Eco-luxe circular straw-bale cottages near Cygnet, with a zero-carbon-footprint attitude. One for guests, one for the owners. Stylishly sustainable.

Maydena

Giants' Table & Cottages $$ A cluster of lovingly restored, self-contained workers' cottages near a pond frequented by platypuses. Maydena Eats diner is here, too.

Bicheno

Bicheno by the Bay $$ Self-contained motel units, flash new waterfront units and cosy A-frame chalets in a bushy oceanside setting.

Swansea & Freycinet National Park

Swansea Beach Chalets $$ Oceanfront self-contained chalets at the northern end of Jubilee Beach – the front line of chalets all but overhang the beach.

Freycinet Lodge $$$ Cradled within the park, with wooden cabins discreetly dotted along the coast and through the bush. Direct access to Richardsons Beach and Honeymoon Bay.

Larapuna / Bay of Fires

Bay of Fires Bush Retreat $$$ Boutique glamping enlivened by birdsong in a forested setting a few minutes' drive from Binalong Bay.

Derby

Tin Dragon Cottages $$ Five eco farmstay cottages at Branxholm's edge. Fon Hock cottage has a cute outdoor spa, while Settlers Hut, set in native bush, sleeps four and is geared towards mountain bikers.

Tin Mountain $$$ A trio of stylishly elevated units, sleeping up to eight and peering down onto the Ringarooma River. A trail rolls right by the doors.

Flinders Island

Crayshack $$$ Killiecrankie beach shack turned luxe hideaway, with views across the bay, three bedrooms, outdoor bath and a quaint old outhouse.

Launceston

MAP p680

Change Overnight $$ Dark and MONA-esque, this funky hotel in a converted warehouse has a big heart – a portion of your payment goes to your choice of one of nine causes.

Peppers Silo $$$ Check into a 1950s grain silo. To get the full rounded-silo effect, book a Gorge River room, facing the city and gorge.

Longford

Woolmers Estate $$ Sleep in World Heritage–listed lodgings in Woolmers' six self-contained farm cottages, giving you out-of-hours freedom to wander.

Tamar Valley

Rosevears Hotel $$ Two lines of glass-fronted apartments on the slope above the pub with long river views. A cut above the standard hotel accommodation.

Trig $$$ Perched on the lower slopes of Mt Arthur near Lilydale, these two well-spaced eco-cabins (one a converted shipping container) are a perfect romantic retreat.

Devonport

Cove $$ Two lines of adult-only clifftop chalets, 6km west of Devonport, that wrap around the cove of the name with wild Bass Strait views and penguin visitors in the evening.

Cradle Mountain-Lake St Clair National Park

Discovery Parks Cradle Mountain $ Campground etched into the bush, with options running from tent sites to dorm beds to newly installed premium mountain cabins.

Cradle Mountain Wilderness Village $$$ Timber chalets grouped among native bush, with a warming lounge bar, complete with board games, for mellow après-hike wind-downs.

Stanley

Ship Inn $$$ It's all style and sauveness in this wonderfully restored historic property, formerly the Bayview Hotel, with a seamlessly curated blend of heritage and modernity.

King Island

Kittawa Lodge $$$ Kittawa's two standalone one-bedroom lodges with rugged coastal views are King Island's most luxurious place to stay.

Strahan

Risby Cove $$$ Luxury suites and waterfront corrugated-iron cottages – any more Harbourside and they'd be afloat – inspired in design by beach sheds.

Wheelhouse Apartments $$$ Perched above Strahan, this brace of high-end townhouses has wrap-around windows framing superb views over Macquarie Harbour.

Queenstown

Mt Lyell Anchorage $$ This 1890s two-bedroom weatherboard home and the neighbouring two-bedroom cottage, have been transformed into stylish guesthouses steps from the major sights.

Midlands, Lakes & Wild Rivers

MAP p702

Oatlands Free Camping FREE Down by Lake Dulverton with the ducks; you're allowed a stay of 72 hours. There are toilets and a shower nearby (plus Callington Mill Distillery).

White Croft Cottage $$ Timber-lined, one-bed self-catering cabin with peaceful agrarian views, just a block from the Ross pub. The outdoor bath is a winner!

Ratho Farm $$$ Mixture of convict-built buildings/barns renovated into rooms and cabins of various capacities on a beautiful, historic farm/golf course just outside Bothwell.

Pumphouse Point $$$ Exclusive and exquisite; the place to contemplate the wilderness through floor-to-ceiling windows by a raging fire with a glass of Moët. Leeawuleena / Lake St Clair.

Great Lake Hotel $$$ On the Miena crossroads, the Great Lake has a selection of spacious self-contained rooms or cheaper 'fishing cabins' with shared facilities.

Researched by
Josh West

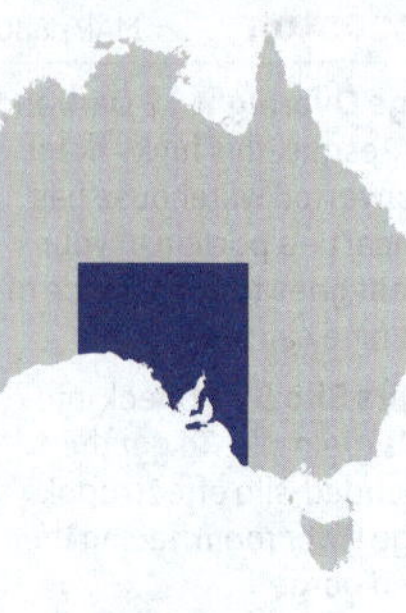

Adelaide & South Australia

WINE, WILDERNESS AND FESTIVAL FUN

THE MAIN AREAS

ADELAIDE
Year-round festival hub.
p716

THE RIVERLAND & MURRAYLANDS
Sun-soaked river country.
p764

ADELAIDE HILLS
Leafy walks and cool-climate wines.
p731

CLARE VALLEY & MID NORTH
Heritage towns and hiking trails.
p770

BAROSSA VALLEY
Internationally celebrated red wines.
p737

YORKE PENINSULA
BPioneer history meets coastal hideaway.
p776

MCLAREN VALE & FLEURIEU PENINSULA
Historic coastal towns and cellar doors.
p743

PORT LINCOLN & EYRE PENINSULA
Seafood and coastal wilderness.
p780

KANGAROO ISLAND
Wild, untouched beach scapes.
p749

FLINDERS RANGES
Ancient adventure-ready terrain. **p786**

MOUNT GAMBIER & LIMESTONE COAST
Underground discoveries await.
p757

COOBER PEDY
Desert opal-mining mecca.
p793

South Australia honours its sunny, fertile terrain with a flourishing food culture, age-worthy wines and an ambitious festival calendar.

Ease your way into South Australia, an ancient land of sun-soaked contrasts. Some see the landscape as extreme, others as balanced. Either way, from the arid outback to vine-lined valleys, you'll find escapes and adventures aplenty.

Far from the hustle of Australia's eastern states, the driest state on the planet's driest inhabited continent cools its heels by savouring life's pleasures: sophisticated cuisine, vibrant festivals and SA's most famous export: wine. Adelaide sits among the great wine capitals of the world, producing 80% of Australia's premium drops, with around 340 cellar doors sprinkled across 18 picturesque wine regions.

Beyond the vineyards, the state rolls out a gallery of postcard backdrops. Explore Kangaroo Island's wildlife-rich parks, vast frontier panoramas along the Yorke and Eyre peninsulas, ancient ochre peaks in the Flinders Ranges, citrus-streaked banks on the Murray River and the Limestone Coast's volcanic caverns. Amid these natural wonders, the state is known for its innovative festivals and forward-thinking ideals.

South Australia has long upheld its progressive values: sanctioning trade unions in 1876, allowing women to run for parliament in 1894, trailblazing women's suffrage, and becoming the first Australian state to ban racial and gender discrimination, legalise abortion and decriminalise same-sex relations. Today, its energy grid runs on a world-leading average of wind and solar and is on track for 100% net renewables by the end of 2027.

For places to stay in Adelaide & South Australia, see p798

DARYL LEACH/SHUTTERSTOCK

River Torrens (p716), Adelaide

Find Your Way

A large state in the heart of a colossal continent, South Australia's communities scatter across vast distances. Much of the action can be found in the southeast, within two hours of Adelaide.

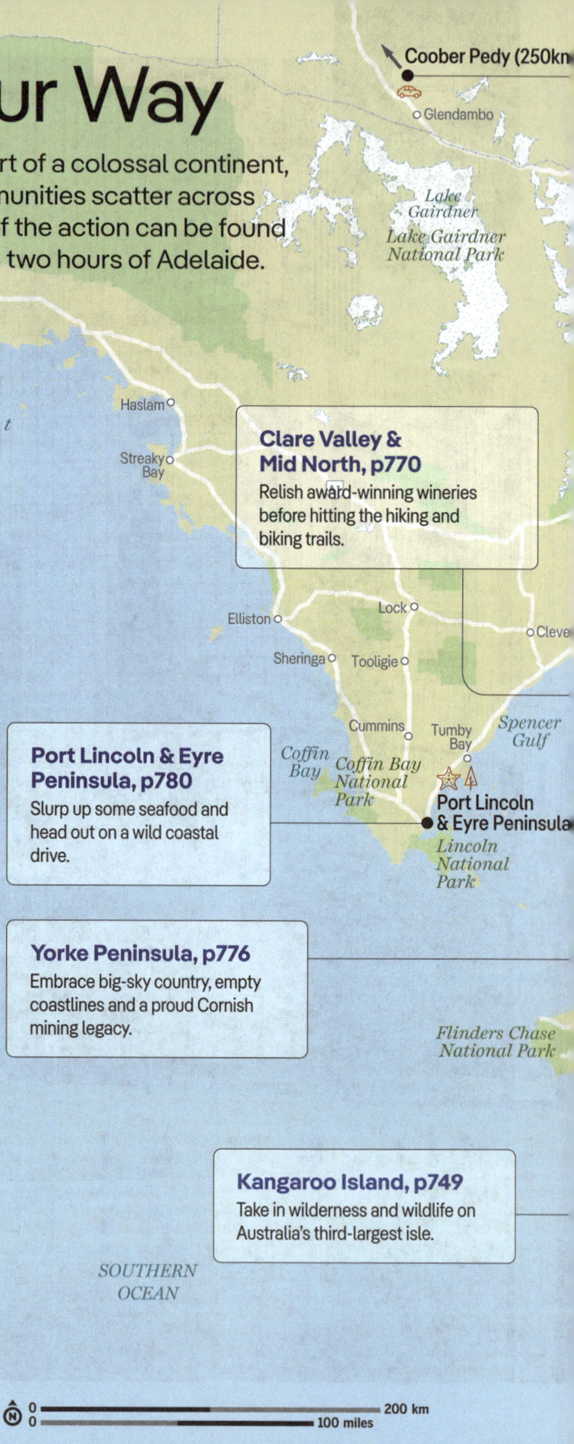

CAR

Private vehicles and guided tours unlock the best of SA's outlying regions. Public transport beyond Greater Adelaide is either limited or absent, making it difficult to seek out secluded beaches, less-trodden trails and off-the-beaten-path wineries without your own wheels.

METRO TRAIN, TRAM & BUS

Adelaide Metro trains service four lines and two spurs: Adelaide's north (Gawler), northwest (Outer Harbor and Grange), south (Seaford and Flinders) and southeast (Belair). The iconic Glenelg tram glides west from the city to the metro coast; buses fill the gaps.

COACH

LinkSA's buses connect all major towns on the Fleurieu Peninsula, with Stateliner chipping in for runs to Riverland, Mount Gambier and longer Eyre Peninsula trips. Yorke Peninsula Coaches services communities on 'Yorkes', plus the east coast of Kangaroo Island via the ferry.

Coober Pedy, p793
Uncover precious gems in this remote subterranean town.
Flinders Ranges, p786
Jagged peaks and fossil-filled boulders rise above semi-arid valleys.
Barossa Valley, p737
One of the most famous wine regions in the world. Shiraz, anyone?
The Riverland & Murraylands, p764
Sit back, unwind and watch the Murray River roll by.
Adelaide, p716
Clear your weekend for trendy bars, chic dining and festival treats.
Adelaide Hills, p731
Forested slopes and cellar doors on Adelaide's doorstep.
McLaren Vale & Fleurieu Peninsula, p743
Breathe the briny air across wineries and coastal escapes.
Mount Gambier & Limestone Coast, p757
Admire heritage streets, then explore underground caves.
Vulkathunha-Gammon Ranges National Park
Lake Frome
Flinders Ranges
Ikara-Flinders Ranges National Park
Lake Torrens
Flinders Ranges
Hawker
A87
Cradock
Quorn
Port Augusta
Iron Knob
Wilmington
Mt Remarkable National Park
Melrose
Whyalla
A32
Olary
Port Pirie
Jamestown
Gladstone
Spalding
A32
Port Broughton
Burra
Clare
Clare Valley & Mid North
Wallaroo
Mintaro
Auburn
Moonta
Morgan
Port Wakefield
Eudunda
Waikerie
Renmark
Maitland
Kapunda
Blanchetown
Barmera
Berri
Yorke Peninsula
Gulf St Vincent
Gawler
Swan Reach
The Riverland & Murraylands
Minlaton
Mt Pleasant
Barossa Valley
Adelaide
Warooka
Edithburgh
Adelaide Hills
Murray Bridge
Innes National Park
Tailem Bend
Pinnaroo
Mclaren Vale & Fleurieu Peninsula
Goolwa
Lameroo
Kangaroo Island
Kingscote
Cape Jervis
Victor Harbor
Big Desert Wilderness Area
Meningie
Coonalpyn
Cape Gantheaume Conservation Park
Tintinara
A8
Salt Creek
Keith
Coorong National Park
Bordertown
B1
Kingston SE
Naracoorte
Robe
Beachport
Millicent
Nangwarry
Mount Gambier & Limestone Coast

Plan Your Time

Adelaide's jam-packed festival calendar beckons throughout the year. In between celebrations, uncover the state's vibrant wine regions, coastal communities and wilderness reserves.

MYPHOTOBANK.COM.AU/SHUTTERSTOCK

Vineyard, Adelaide Hills (p731)

If You Only Have One Day

- Roll into Adelaide as the weather mellows in early autumn and festivities kick off. Grab breakfast at **Adelaide Central Market** (p724) before riding the free tram to **North Terrace** (p725) for a late-morning amble through whichever museum or gallery catches your eye.

- Venture to the **Adelaide Hills** (p731) for a winery tour, or get your blood pumping on a ridge-top walking trail, finishing at fauna-filled **Cleland Wildlife Park** (p734). Grab lunch at one of the Hills' much-loved heritage pubs.

- Back in Adelaide, fuel up at **Golden Boy** (p722), **Ông** (p725) or **Restaurant Botanic** (p725) in the East End. After dark, soak up the **Mad March**'s (p727) festival vibes – either quirky Fringe comedies, daring theatre performances or world music at WOMADelaide.

Seasonal Highlights

SA is known for its hot, dry summers – beach days and evening sea breezes provide relief. Mild weather graces autumn and spring, while winter's frosty grip impacts the state's vineyards.

JANUARY

Join locals lining suburban streets and vineyard-lined backroads to watch the world's best cyclists fly by during the **Tour Down Under** (p728), then follow the crowd to the afterparty in Victoria Sq.

MARCH

Milder nights bring a collision of **Mad March**'s (p728) arts festivals: **Adelaide Fringe**, **Adelaide Festival** and **WOMADelaide** energise city streets.

APRIL

Help celebrate the harvest's end: bold reds in the Barossa, crisp whites in the Adelaide Hills and Clare, and a bit of everything in McLaren Vale.

Three Days to Travel Around

- Pick up a picnic at **Adelaide Central Market** (p724) and take in a museum along **North Terrace** (p725), then devour your bounty in the nearby **Botanic Gardens** (p726). Spend the afternoon sweltering on a **city beach** (p720) or exploring the cooler **Adelaide Hills** (p731). City festivals and restaurants await in the evening.

- On the second day, travel north to the shiraz-loving **Barossa** (p737) or riesling-rich **Clare Valley** (p770), soaking in the vine-covered countryside by car, bike or private tour.

- Continuing north on day three, raise a sweat on bushwalking and mountain bike trails in **Mt Remarkable National Park** (p774) or push on to the red earth and saw-toothed peaks of **Ikara-Flinders Ranges National Park** (p790); you'll need another day to drive back.

If You Have More Time

- You can't rush **Kangaroo Island** (p749) in summer; spend a minimum of three days **beach-hopping** and gawking at its untamed beauty. Beforehand, stock up on supplies on the **Fleurieu Peninsula** (p743), grabbing a few bottles of McLaren Vale's finest and immersing yourself in the quirky **d'Arenberg Cube** (p743). Nearby, Southern Fleurieu's **coastal parks** (p745) are lush, sandy and often steep, requiring a full day of sweaty exploration. Alternatively, there's a spread of surf and swim beaches to get you into the water.

- In winter, make a beeline north for **Flinders Ranges'** (p790) warm days. Rattle through the outback on a **heritage train** (p788), hike the sunlit folds of **Ikara (Wilpena Pound**; p790) and trace the imprints of Earth's earliest animals at **Nilpena Ediacara National Park** (p789).

MAY

Indulge your taste buds at **Tasting Australia** (p728), with culinary exhibitions popping up in Victoria Sq and across SA's wine regions.

JUNE

Roll into Melrose for the gloriously mud-splattered **Fat Tyre Festival** (p775), where Mt Remarkable's single-track runs fast and loose. Whale sightings are common along the Eyre and Fleurieu Peninsulas.

SEPTEMBER

As temperatures warm and spring wildflowers blossom, late September brings ideal conditions for hiking in the Adelaide Hills and **Deep Creek National Park** (p745) on the Fleurieu Peninsula.

OCTOBER

Shucking blades at the ready for Ceduna's **Oysterfest** (p785), over a long weekend on the Eyre Peninsula's west coast.

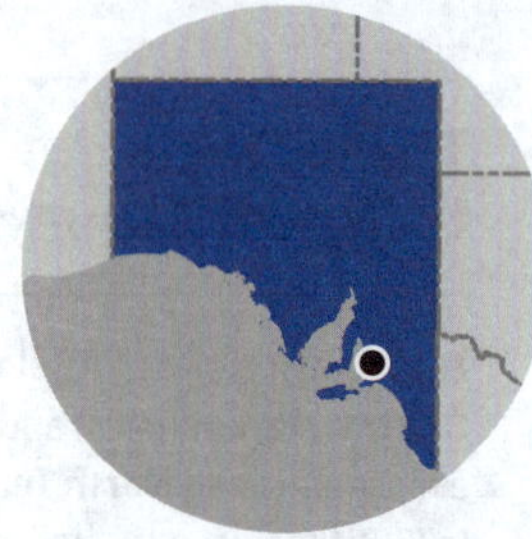

Adelaide

FESTIVAL HUB | FOODIE CULTURE | BEACH DAYS

TOP TIP

To enjoy free travel through the city centre, hop on the tram that runs gratis between South Tce, the Entertainment Centre, Festival Plaza and the Botanic Gardens. Four free loop buses circle the city – 99A and 99C on weekdays, while 98A and 98C extend the route up to North Adelaide including weekends.

While the eastern capitals jostle for size and spectacle, Adelaide moves to a steady, more grounded rhythm – one that has echoed across this plain long before Colonel Light mapped the city's grid in 1837. In Kaurna Country, this place is known as Tarntanya, a meeting ground where neighbouring groups gathered to trade, share stories and hold ceremony.

Dubbed Australia's 'big country town', Adelaide's cultured and casual self-image gestures towards the days of free colonisation. Adelaidians may highlight their convict-free past, but the conservative origins of the 'City of Churches' proved more inhibitive than progressive. Now, the vibe has shifted with festivals spilling across all seasons and forgotten laneways glowing with wine bars and global flavours.

Adelaide's renewal stretches beyond its leafy centre, with warehouse cafes, uncrowded beaches and traffic that rarely lingers. Compact and convenient, it's a rare capital – big enough to buzz, small enough to breathe.

Riverside Sojourn

MAP P718

Explore the River Torrens

Skirting north of Adelaide's central grid, the River Torrens (Karrawirra Parri) has long shaped the city's story. Flowing steadily from the Adelaide Hills west to the metro beaches,

Continued on p722

GETTING AROUND

Transport options from Adelaide Airport are easily navigable – rental cars, taxis, Ubers and Metro buses all line up just outside the terminal. Grab a metroCARD from the vending machine left of the plaza exit (coins, notes and Eftpos accepted) and hop straight onto the city's air-conditioned bus network reaching most of the suburban sprawl. Lines run from around 6am to midnight. Trains branch north and south, and the city's heritage tram glides west from the city centre to seaside Glenelg. Adelaide's grid layout, growing bikeway network and pancake-flat terrain makes it great for cycling.

SIGHTS

1 Adelaide Dolphin Sanctuary
2 National Railway Museum
see 3 Port Adelaide Lighthouse
see 2 South Australian Aviation Museum
3 South Australian Maritime Museum

ACTIVITIES

4 Adelaide Scuba
see 1 Adventure Kayaking SA
see 3 Port River Cruises
5 Stand Up Paddle SA
6 TreeClimb Adelaide

SLEEPING

7 Largs Pier Hotel
8 Watson
9 West Beach Parks

EATING

10 Bandit Pizza and Wine
see 8 Coffee Institute
see 3 La Popular Taqueria

DRINKING & NIGHTLIFE

see 7 Largs Pier Hotel
11 Palais Hotel
see 2 Pirate Life Brewing
12 Seacliff Beach Hotel
13 Shapeshifter Brewing Co
14 Threefold Distilling
15 West Beach Surf Club

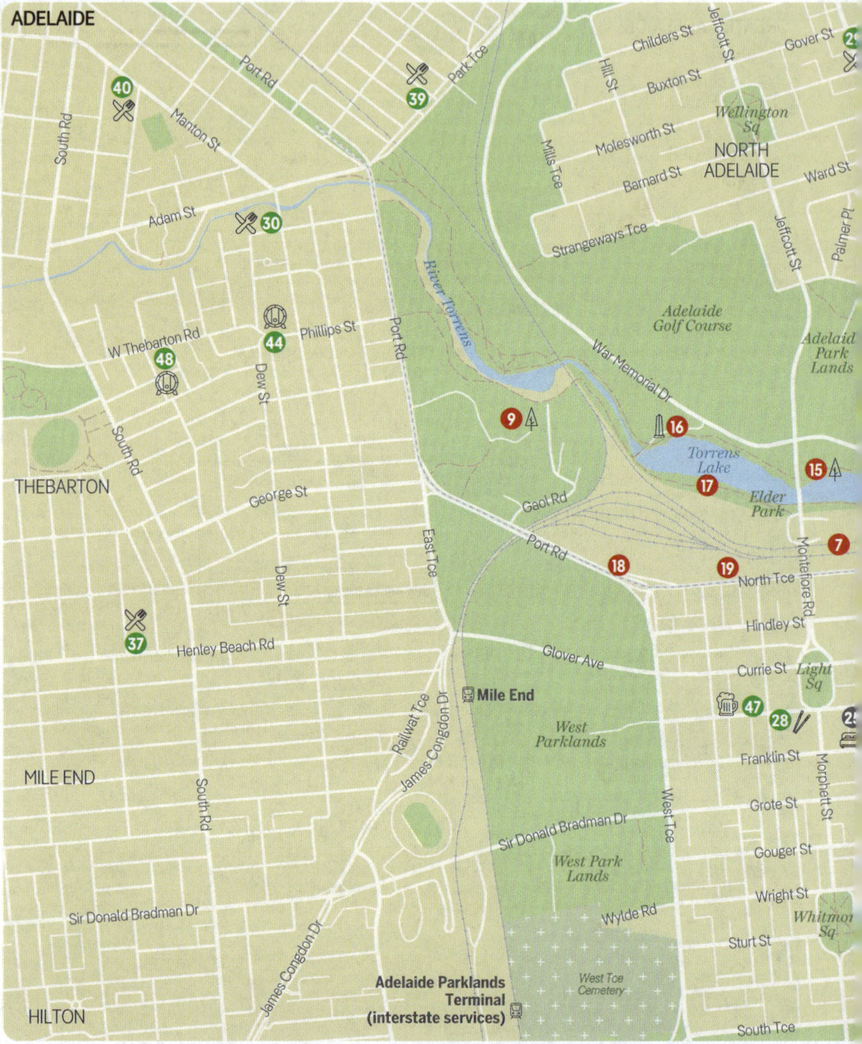

HIGHLIGHTS

1 Adelaide Central Market
2 Adelaide Oval
3 Art Gallery of South Australia
4 South Australian Museum

SIGHTS

5 Aboriginal and Torres Strait Islander War Memorial
6 Adelaide Botanic Gardens
7 Adelaide Convention Centre
8 Adelaide Zoo
9 Bonython Park
10 Botanic Park
11 Bradman Collection
12 Elder Park
13 Kaurna Reconciliation Sculptures
14 Memorial headstone
15 Pinky Flat
16 Pirltawardli statue
17 red gum trees
18 Royal Adelaide Hospital
19 SAMHRI
20 State Library of South Australia
21 Talking Our Way Home sculpture
22 Tiled mural
23 Victoria Park

ACTIVITIES

24 Captain Jolleys Paddle Boats
see 24 Popeye
see 2 RoofClimb Adelaide Oval

SLEEPING

25 Adelaide Central YHA
26 Mayfair Hotel
27 Oval Hotel

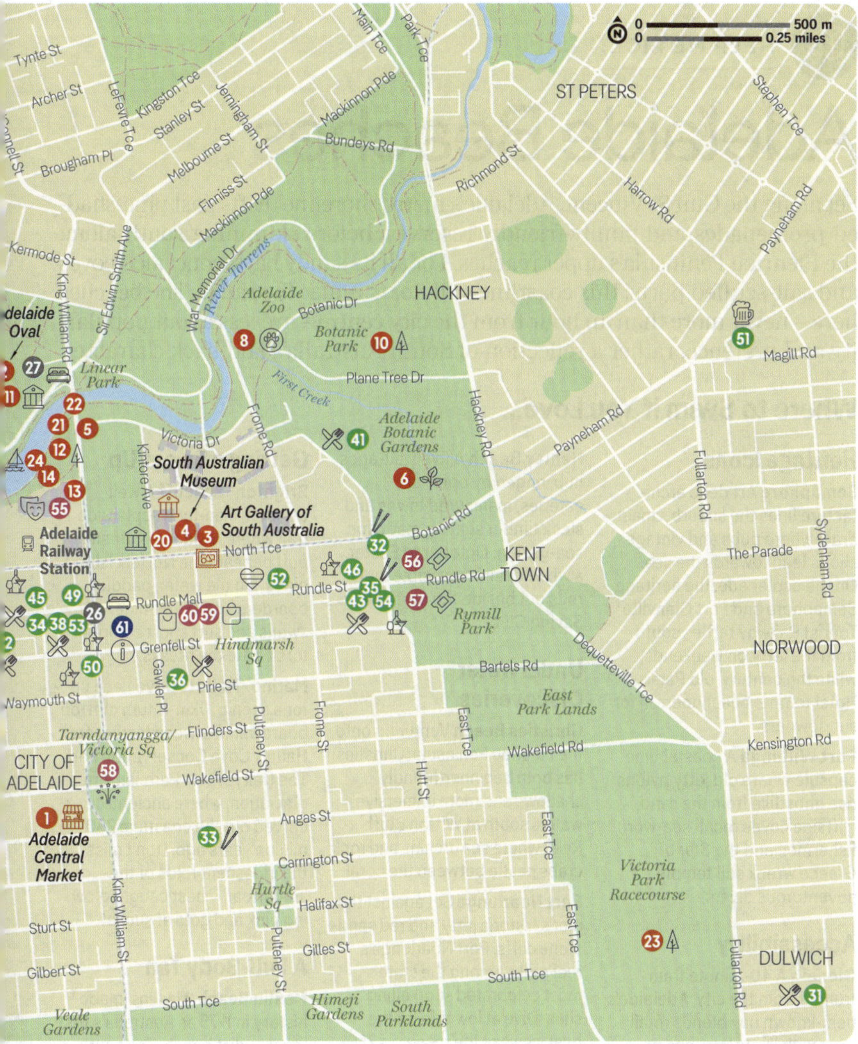

● **EATING**
- 28 Adelaide Pho
- 29 Bakery on O'Connell
- 30 Bloom
- see 1 Central Market Arcade
- 31 Corner Store Cafe
- 32 Golden Boy
- 33 Kiin
- 34 Leigh St
- 35 Ông
- 36 Osteria Oggi
- 37 Parwana Afghan Kitchen
- 38 Peel St
- 39 Plant 4
- 40 Pony and Cole
- 41 Restaurant Botanic
- 42 Sunny's Pizza
- 43 Vardon Ave

● **DRINKING & NIGHTLIFE**
- 44 Ambra Spirits
- 45 Bank Street Social
- see 39 Bowden Brewing Company
- 46 BRKLYN
- 47 Grace Emily Hotel
- 48 Imperial Measures
- 49 La Buvette Drinkery
- 50 La Louisiane
- 51 Little Bang Brewing Company
- 52 Mary's Poppin
- 53 Memphis Slim's House of Blues
- 54 NOLA Adelaide
- see 34 Udaberri

● **ENTERTAINMENT**
- 55 Adelaide Festival Centre
- see 55 DreamBIG Children's Festival
- 56 Garden of Unearthly Delights
- 57 Gluttony
- 58 Tasting Australia

● **SHOPPING**
- 59 Adelaide Arcade
- 60 Regent Arcade

● **INFORMATION**
- 61 Adelaide Visitor Information Centre

HELP ME PICK:

Adelaide Beaches

Set along the Gulf St Vincent, Adelaide's metro shoreline drifts past pine-shaded promenades and family-friendly reserves, before skimming south along the Fleurieu Peninsula's upper reaches. For all its sandy bays, concealed coves and salt-scuffed ports, this coastline still floats under the radar. The beaches here – never more than an hour from the city centre – are less about popularity and pretence, rather a reflection of South Australia's laid-back character.

Where to Swim if You Love...

Heritage Icons

Semaphore Art deco architecture lines the suburb's main drag, where pubs and vintage shops lean towards the sea. On the esplanade, the heritage Semaphore and Fort Glanville Tourist Railway rattles south from the jetty on weekends, while the century-old Palais Hotel tempts beachgoers in for sundowners.

Port Willunga A coastal time capsule where old jetty pylons rise ghostlike from the sand, cliffside caves recall sea-worn fishermen and the *Star of Greece* wreck still tempts adventurous divers.

Accessibility

Glenelg A 40-minute tram trundle from the city, Adelaide's best-known bay blends retail buzz with lively bars and a wide, walkable shore, plus a beach-access mat north of the jetty all summer long.

Henley Beach A lively all-ages hub, ringed by open-air eateries, manicured lawns and sleek timber seating made for sea-gazing. October to Easter, a wheelchair-accessible mat rolls out beside the Surf Life Saving Club.

Underwater Discoveries

Christies Beach Venturing onto the Fleurieu Peninsula, Christies has both beginner-friendly shallows and more immersive waters south at Witton Bluff Reef, where sea urchins and rock crabs nestle between the coral.

Port Noarlunga Set against the pier's historic jetty and red sandstone cliffs, Port Noarlunga's reef ranks among the state's most celebrated snorkelling sites. Dive at low tide for the best views of the reserve's 250+ species.

Getting a Sweat Up

Brighton–Seacliff A well-trodden, 4km-long esplanade trail where residents huff and puff beneath the Norfolk Island pines. On the water, paddle-boarders kiss the summer swells and surf sport competitors battle the breaks.

Marino–Hallett Cove Lace up for a scenic 10km-return clifftop boardwalk between Marino and Hallett Cove Conservation Park. The trail reveals Permian-era glaciation, where ancient ice carved out the coastline 280 million years ago. Don't miss the iridescent folds of the 'Sugarloaf' – best caught glowing pink and gold at sunset.

A Full-Body Tan

Maslin Beach 'Maslins' made history in 1975 as Australia's first legal nudist beach. The southern end has a discreet car park and sandy path leading below sandstone cliffs – a secluded spot to bare all.

HOW TO

When to go With mild shoulder seasons, Adelaide's coastline comes alive from November to April, once the sun has warmed the Southern Ocean waves.

Getting there Most of Adelaide's beaches link neatly by tram, bus and bike, though having a car makes slipping away to the quieter stretches much easier.

Before you go SA's metro coast experienced a rare algal bloom event in 2025. Before swimming, check algalbloom.sa.gov.au for beach updates.

Cheap eats With free BBQs and grassy reserves edging the sand, beach days come cheap and easy. Pack in, pack out and don't burn the snags!

SIGHTS
1 Brighton
2 Christies Beach
3 Glenelg
4 Hallett Cove
5 Henley Beach
6 Maslin Beach
7 Port Noarlunga
8 Port Willunga
9 Semaphore

Making the Most of the Coast

Adelaide Beaches *(adelaidebeaches.com.au)* is handy for planning. See *beachsafe.org.au/sa* for patrolled beach timetables.

Cycling the Coast Park Path – a 70km trail winding by coastal scrub and seaside suburbs – rewards with the most complete picture of Adelaide's beach scape. A flat, paved 32km section runs between Outer Harbor Station (20km northwest of central Adelaide via train) and Marino Rocks Station (18km southwest), from where rail services on the Seaford line run you back to the city. You can also bail out halfway through at Grange Station. Adelaide's trains welcome bicycles; buy your ride a concession fare during peak hours. **Spinway Adelaide** *(spinwayadelaide.com.au; from $15)* operates self-service bike stations at West Beach, Glenelg and Brighton.

Adelaide Metro links Fleurieu's metropolitan beaches (Christies Beach, Port Noarlunga, Aldinga) by bus but travel times can be long for day-trippers. Still, the quiet sands make a worthy escape. For SUP hire in Brighton, call **Stand Up Paddle SA** *(standuppaddlesa.com.au; per hour from $40)*. Seasoned divers can pre-book kit and tank hire *(per day from $80)* or a sea-bound boat dive *(6hrs from $129 excluding equipment)* with **Adelaide Scuba** *(adelaidescuba.com.au)* in Glenelg, or hire a snorkel and mask *(3hrs $15)* from **Go2Dive** *(go2dive.com.au)* in Port Noarlunga.

A CITY INSIDE A PARK

Adelaide claims to be the only city on Earth built entirely within a park. Conceived in 1837, the Adelaide Park Lands were a radical idea at the time – a planned public greenbelt, not a gated preserve for the elite. Spanning more than 760 hectares (twice the size of New York's Central Park), this ribbon of green encircles the whole city, blending heritage gardens, walking trails and open fields.

Within its borders, you'll find Adelaide Botanic Gardens (p726) and Adelaide Zoo; the River Torrens threads the northern parklands. In the east, **Victoria Park** (Pakapakanthi) hosts motor racing, festivals and Sunday joggers. Picnickers, playgrounds and concerts fill Bonython Park (Tulya Wardli) out west.

Continued from p716

its banks hold 45,000 years of Kaurna history. They also mark the place where colonial Adelaide first took root. Follow the Kaurna Walking Trail to trace this history.

Riverside lawns and wheelchair-friendly paths make for a peaceful 3km amble between Adelaide Zoo and the boating lakes of **Bonython Park**, passing heritage bridges, Adelaide Oval and whatever festival has taken over **Elder Park** en route.

From the landing in the park, you can get on the water too. Take a leisurely, 30-minute weekend pedal aboard one of **Captain Jolleys Paddle Boats** *(captainjolleys.com.au; $25 per boat)*, then enjoy a 45-minute return cruise aboard the iconic **Popeye** riverboat *(thepopeye.com.au; adult/child from $27/18)* riverboat with Devonshire tea in hand – or something stronger on a wine or gin cruise.

Sporting Soul of the City

MAP P718

Experience the historic Adelaide Oval

Framed by stately Moreton Bay figs, heritage pavilions and sweeping hill views, **Adelaide Oval** (Tarntanya Wama) or 'the Oval' is rightly lauded as one of the world's prettiest sporting grounds. From Australian Football League blockbusters and day-night Test match cricket, to international music acts lighting up the city skyline, its calendar runs year-round.

Go behind the scenes on a 90-minute guided **stadium tour** *(adelaideoval.com.au/tours; adult/child $29/18)*. Wander through players' changing rooms, commentary boxes and heritage-listed stands steeped in sporting folklore. Explore the **Bradman Collection** – a trove of personal artefacts, photographs and memorabilia tracing Don Bradman's rise from backyard prodigy to global cricketing icon. You'll even step inside the century-old scoreboard, best caught in full swing, with operators still madly assembling numbers by hand, during a domestic four-day Sheffield Shield cricket match (October to March). For a 360-degree bird's-eye view across the stadium and city, climb above the turf on a **RoofClimb Adelaide Oval** *(roof climb.com.au; adult/child $119/89)* – pricier on match days.

Panda-monium

MAP P718

Observe wildlife at Adelaide Zoo

Nestled within the city's northeast parklands, **Adelaide Zoo** *(adelaidezoo.com.au; adult/child $48/26)* is Australia's second-oldest zoo and one of its most charming. It houses

EATING IN ADELAIDE: CITY CENTRE

MAP P718

Bakery on O'Connell: Bakehouse upholding SA's proud pie floater tradition – a contender for the state's best. *24hr* $

Adelaide Pho: No-frills Vietnamese nook dishing out steaming bowls of soul-warming broth. *11am-3pm & 5-9pm Mon-Sat* $

Sunny's Pizza: Hand-stretched pies fired from a 1972 Bedford truck, with Solomon St's neon-lit energy spilling onto the pavement. *5pm-late* $$

Golden Boy: Vibrant Thai with communal tables, cosy booths and punchy plates loaded with herbs, chilli, citrus. *hours vary* $$$

KAURNA WALKING TRAIL

Find your Adelaide bearings along the River Torrens and reflect on Kaurna Country before and after European settlement.

START	END	LENGTH
Adelaide Festival Centre Plaza	Pirltawardli statue	2km; 30min

Begin by the 1 **Kaurna Reconciliation Sculptures**, anchoring Adelaide's landscape in five stone elements symbolising connection to Country. Cross King William Rd to the 2 **Aboriginal and Torres Strait Islander War Memorial**, a bronzed tribute to First Nations veterans. Head north to the River Torrens, then turn west through the underpass to find a 3 **tiled mural** declaring 'You are standing on Kaurna Land'.

Along the riverbank, pause at 4 **Talking Our Way Home sculpture**, a floating origami boat with a Kaurna-language inscription. 5 **Adelaide Oval** (Tarntanya Wama) dominates the skyline across the water, a once significant Kaurna ceremonial site, Dreaming track and trade route. In Elder Park find the 6 **memorial headstone** of Kaurna Elder Doris May Graham (1912–2004), a tireless advocate for reconciliation. Beyond the footbridge, look to the northern bullrushes for 7 **Pinky Flat**, a camping site for Kaurna families until the early 1900s. Past Morphett St Bridge, 8 **red gum trees** *(karra)* bear scars where bark was cut for traditional tools and carvings. Cross at Torrens Weir to the 9 **Pirltawardli statue** ('brush-tailed possum house'), marking the site of South Australia's first mission with the Kaurna people (1838), where language and phraseology were recorded and exchanged.

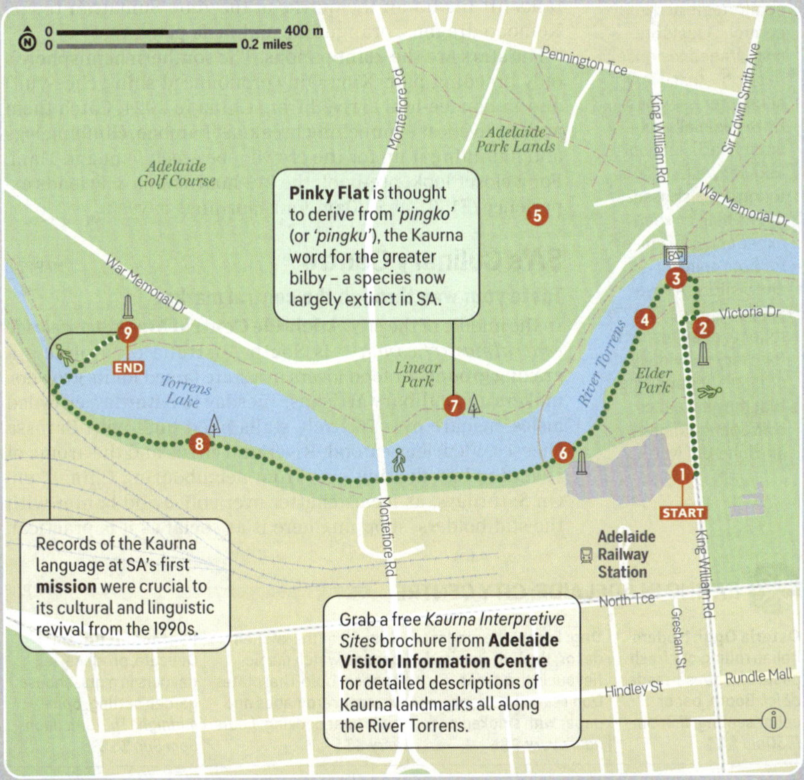

ANIMAL WELFARE

Justine Partoon, Animal Welfare and Research Manager at Zoos SA

At Zoos SA, we put animal welfare first in everything we do. Every encounter begins with choice – animals decide if and how they'd like to be involved. Our keepers pay close attention to body language and behaviour, adjusting experiences to make sure each animal feels comfortable and in control. Guests are encouraged to notice this, too – that every encounter is shaped by the animal's voluntary participation. Regular welfare monitoring and risk assessments help us keep experiences positive for both animals and visitors. Above all, this approach reflects deep respect for every individual creature, recognising that they have their own agency, dignity and inherent worth.

STEVE LOVEGROVE/SHUTTERSTOCK

Adelaide Central Market

hundreds of species across eight leafy hectares. Shady paths link up rainforest and wetland aviaries, reptile and nocturnal houses, and nature playgrounds. Free walking tours depart hourly from the main gate between 10am and 3pm. Keeper talks lift the lid on the quirks of the zoo's Sumatran tigers, Komodo dragons, orangutans and little penguins.

The stars are the giant pandas. The southern hemisphere's only breeding pair, Xing Qiu (pronounced shing chee-yull) and Yi Lan (ee-lun) arrived from China in 2024. Catch them at their liveliest – munching breakfast bamboo, climbing logs and hamming it up for the crowd – between 9am and 11am. For a closer look, pre-book the 2½-hour Panda & Friends experience ($150), at 8.30am four mornings a week.

SA's Culinary Centre

MAP P718

Taste your way through the central market

In the middle of the city, **Adelaide Central Market** *(adelaidecentralmarket.com.au)* is South Australia on a plate – a grazing ground for food lovers in a state famed for its growers, makers and culinary artisans. Tuesday to Saturday, crowded aisles ensnare over 70 lively stalls piled high with Barossa cheeses, Fleurieu seafood, Riverland citrus and the aroma of steaming bao floating over from neighbouring Chinatown. On Saturdays, as locals chatter over coffee and banter with the stallholders, shopping here is as social as it is practical.

EATING IN ADELAIDE: CITY CENTRE

MAP P718

Osteria Oggi: Modern Italian rolling out fresh pasta and house-made *dolci*. Booth, bar or cellar seating. *11.30am-11.30pm* $$$

Ông: Forget the modest decor; the Viet-inspired flavour is the event. Don't skip the crispy rice paper with smoked pork. *hours vary* $$$

Kiin: Sit at the kitchen bar and watch magic happen: bold Thai plates, charcoal aromatics and high-heat cooking. *hours vary* $$$

Restaurant Botanic: Delicate, produce-led flavours in a glasshouse garden setting. *6pm-midnight Thu-Sat, noon-5pm Sun* $$$

Need some contextual relish? Listen to the free 50-minute self-guided audio tour exploring 150 years of market history on Spotify or Audible.

Next door, the longstanding **Central Market Arcade** is being redeveloped as a mixed-use dining and retail precinct. Due for completion in late 2026, it promises to extend Adelaide's edible hub even further.

Adelaide's Cultural Heartbeat

MAP P718

Discover North Terrace

Of the four roads circling Adelaide's city grid, North Tce is by far the busiest. To the west, steel and glass dominate: the **Royal Adelaide Hospital**, the jagged **SAMHRI** nicknamed 'Cheesegrater' and the sweeping curves of the **Adelaide Convention Centre**. East of King William St, however, the street softens beneath ornamental trees and sandstone facades, where heritage-listed galleries, libraries and museums welcome visitors daily.

If politics and people are your thing, the **State Library of South Australia** *(slsa.sa.gov.au; free)* houses the **Centre of Democracy**. This free, compact exhibition explores women's suffrage, voting for equality, land rights and the challenges that have shaped Australian democracy – with South Australia leading the charge on many reforms. Nip into the Mortlock Wing before moving on; its soaring gallery, wrought-iron balconies and polished cedar staircases have made it one of Adelaide's most photographed interiors since opening in 1884.

A two-minute walk east, the **South Australian Museum** *(samuseum.sa.gov.au; free)* sprawls over five evolutionary floors, covering megafauna, prehistoric fossils and intrepid Antarctic journeys. Seek out the 11m-long giant squid and the mighty skeletal frame of a sperm whale. The museum's centrepiece **Australian Aboriginal Cultures Gallery** displays more than 3000 cultural items from the world's largest collection of First Nations artefacts, curated in close collaboration with the communities it represents.

Next door, carve out at least two hours for the **Art Gallery of South Australia** *(agsa.sa.gov.au; free)*. Since 1881, its halls have showcased works by European masters and bold contemporary artists, including the first Australian acquisitions by an Aboriginal artist in 1939: Albert Namatjira's *Illum-Baura (Haasts Bluff)*. Today, over 45,000 pieces span centuries and continents. Check the website for Auslan-interpreted events, dedicated quiet exhibitions and self-guided tours (including audio described and Auslan) of the Elder and Melrose wings.

WELCOME TO KAURNA COUNTRY

The expansive Adelaide Plains, stretching north and south between the foothills and sea, are the country of the Kaurna (pronounced 'gar-na') people. At the heart of this landscape lies Tarntanya (Red Kangaroo Place), once sweeping grassland and now home to Adelaide. Colonisation profoundly reshaped Kaurna life, displacing communities from their lands and silencing language for generations. In recent decades, a cultural revival has taken root in Adelaide. The Kaurna language, first recorded in the 1840s by missionaries, has been reawakened and now weaves through public art, song and ceremony. Across Adelaide dual place names, including for city squares and parks, reclaim this presence.

DRINKING IN ADELAIDE: CITY CENTRE

MAP P718

Bank Street Social: Exposed brick vault featuring SA wines and beers, Aussie gins and whiskies. Friday night DJs. *hours vary*

Memphis Slim's House of Blues: Blues and roots basement pouring American bourbon, pool and live blues. *hours vary*

Grace Emily Hotel: Character pub with cosy fire, warm service, live music and SA beers on tap. *4pm-late Mon-Fri, from 6pm Sat*

La Louisiane: Moody speakeasy serving up even moodier jazz, French canapés and swagger aplenty. *5pm-late Tue-Sat*

ARCADES & LANEWAYS

Adelaide Arcade: Rundle Mall's Victorian showpiece from 1885 features mosaic floors, cedar shopfronts and a fortnightly ghost tour ($49).

Regent Arcade: Heritage-listed arcade (1928) pairing a light-filled canopy with geometric tiling, stylish cafes and boutiques.

Peel Street: The Peel packs restaurants, bars and kerbside tables into one narrow, urban-cool strip in the West End.

Leigh Street: Parallel to Peel, Leigh brings a bluestone facade, wine bars and late-night kitchens that spill onto the laneway pavers.

Vardon Avenue: Brick facades, ironwork and a chic cafe culture in a pedestrian pocket in the East End.

TRABANTOS/SHUTTERSTOCK

Urban Eden

MAP P718

Relishing Adelaide's botanic gardens

At the far eastern end of North Tce, a pair of ornate wrought-iron gates open into **Adelaide Botanic Gardens** *(botanicgardens.sa.gov.au; free)*, a 50-hectare pocket of calm. Join a free daily walking tour at 10.30am to get your bearings, or wander at will between glasshouses and grand avenues of Moreton Bay figs. Step inside the 19th-century **Palm House**, a jewel of Victorian iron and glass; pause by the lily pond to see the colossal leaves of *Victoria amazonica;* and step through the canopy in the **Bicentennial Conservatory**, Australia's largest single-span glasshouse. In summer, lawns in the gardens make a shady refuge for picnickers and daydreamers. Next door, late November to mid-February, **Botanic Park** (Tainmuntilla) turns into a beanbag-strewn stage for after-dark film screenings at **Moonlight Cinema** *(adelaide.moonlight.com.au; from $25)*.

DRINKING IN ADELAIDE: CITY CENTRE

MAP P718

NOLA Adelaide: New Orleans–inspired haunt in back alley Vardon Ave, slinging whisky, craft beer and Creole-Cajun staples. *hours vary*

Udaberri: Laneway bar channelling Basque vibes with pintxos (tapas), charcuterie and gin cocktails. *4pm-late Mon-Fri, from 5pm Sat & Sun*

BRKLYN: Late-night Rundle St staple with clever cocktails and craft taps. Book a seat before the balcony fills. *5pm-late Mon-Fri, from 1pm Sat & Sun*

La Buvette Drinkery: Gresham St's French nook pours natural wines and artful canapés. Slip in before 5pm to beat the post-work crush. *hours vary*

Palm House, Adelaide Botanic Gardens

Canopy Climbs

MAP P717

Scale Adelaide's lofty gums

Within the leafy sweep of Adelaide's southern Park Lands, **TreeClimb Adelaide** *(treeclimb.com.au; adult/child $49/36.50)* threads a high-flying maze of log bridges, rope ladders and zip lines through the canopy. Five routes and 52 challenges, plus a kids-only course for climbers over 1m, offer 80 to 120 minutes of balance-testing and nerve-steadying fun, all in the safety of a harnessed treetop playground.

Mad March

MAP P718

Adelaide's creative festivals collide

Condensing Australia's premier performing-arts festivals into a single month might sound mad, but it's a strategy that's shaken Adelaide's sleepy stereotype. 'Mad March' heralds an energy shift – a season of laughter and late nights that turns the city into a stage.

WHY I LOVE ADELAIDE

Josh West, Lonely Planet writer

Raised in the languid rhythms of the South Australian countryside, I've come to appreciate a city that hums rather than shouts. Adelaide balances urban convenience with effortless access to leafy bushwalks, clean beaches and Australia's leading wine regions. It's no secret that the city took a while to find its momentum, but it's now rolling. Since relaxing its licensing laws in 2013, more than 150 new venues have sprung to life, giving Adelaide a new confidence without losing its sense of community, humility or calm. For someone who grew up under big country skies, cities can feel close and crowded. But Adelaide breathes differently – easy to leave, easier still to come home.

EATING IN ADELAIDE: SUBURBAN BRUNCH

MAPS P717 & P718

Corner Store Cafe: Classic corner cafe serving Asian-inspired dishes, just east of the city in Dulwich. *7.30am-2.30pm Mon-Fri, from 8am Sat & Sun* **$$**

Pony and Cole: West of the city, quirky brunch dishes are cooked up in a busy Hindmarsh storehouse. *7.30am-3.30pm Mon-Fri, 8.30am-2.30pm Sat & Sun* **$$**

Bloom: Thebarton's riverside cafe is known for its wood-fired plates and bougie brunches. *7.30am-3.30pm Mon, Thu & Fri, 8am-4pm Sat & Sun* **$$**

Coffee Institute: This Walkerville institution peddles the northeast's most famed breakfasts, burgers, bagels and coffee. *7am-3pm Mon-Sat* **$$**

From mid-February, **Adelaide Fringe** *(adelaidefringe.com.au; free to $120)* takes over the city. Often cited as one of the world's biggest arts festivals, comedians, cabaret acts, circus performers and musicians are stuffed into clubs, pubs and laneways during hundreds of shows over 30 nights. You'll find much of the action in the two eastern Park Land hubs: **Gluttony** and **Garden of Unearthly Delights**. If you're hopping between gigs, plan for proximity – everything gets busier after dark.

In early March, **Adelaide Festival** *(adelaidefestival.com.au; free to $200)* raises the curtain on international dance, drama, opera and literary events at venues all over town. It's right at the top of Australia's creative calendar, drawing world-class talent from across the globe. A big part of the lineup, **Writers' Week** is a local favourite, running ticketed events and free forums, bringing authors and readers together to exchange ideas and inspiration.

It all crescendos beneath the giant Moreton Bay figs of Botanic Park (p726) at **WOMADelaide** *(womadelaide.com.au; from $170)*, a four-day celebration of multilingual music, movement and global rhythm. Families and free-spirited souls sprawl across the lawns on the first weekend of March each year. Kids' craft zones, dance workshops and pop-up performers add to the festival's nightly headline acts.

ADELAIDE'S BEST NICHE FESTIVALS

DreamBIG Children's Festival: A biennial celebration for families, packing shows, workshops and installations across two lively weekends in May.

Illuminate Adelaide: Light and art collide as international artists transform North Tce into a glowing open-air gallery in July.

SALA: In August, the South Australian Living Artists Festival exhibits the work of local artists in galleries, cafes, libraries, community halls et al.

OzAsia: In October, Adelaide celebrates its Asian connection with parades, live music and a fragrant Lucky Dumpling Market in Elder Park.

Tarnathi: This three-month program (October to December) spotlights contemporary First Nations artists and a much-celebrated art fair.

Rest of the Fest

MAP P718

Embracing Adelaide's events calendar

Adelaide's festival calendar fills the city's social diary year-round, barely pausing for breath. In January the city zips into Lycra as the **Tour Down Under** *(tourdownunder.com.au)* launches the UCI WorldTour from its base in Victoria Sq (Tarntanyangga). Over several stages, men's and women's cyclists sweat it out through the Adelaide Hills, Barossa and Fleurieu Peninsula, with city sprints, roadside barbecues and vineyard vantage points drawing locals in droves.

Come May, **Tasting Australia** *(tastingaustralia.com.au)* takes on Victoria Sq, hosting the country's longest-running celebration of food and flavour. This 10-day feast delivers pop-up kitchens, long lunches and ticketed masterclasses. Satellite events spill into regions statewide, showcasing the best of Barossa reds, Limestone Coast seafood and Adelaide Hills produce.

EATING IN ADELAIDE: SUBURBAN DINING

MAPS P717 & P718

Parwana Afghan Kitchen: West of the city, Thebarton's Afghan favourite serves homely dumplings, dahls, chickpea curries and SA's best eggplant. *hours vary* $$

Plant 4: Northwest, Bowden's industrial-chic foodie warehouse hosts regular markets and global eateries. Kids' playground too. *hours vary* $

Bandit Pizza and Wine: Slinging smooth beats and cosy booths, stylish slices and Italian bites, south of the city in Hyde Park. *5-11pm* $$

La Popular Taqueria: This is the Port Adelaide go-to for authentic tacos, imported tequila and mezcal. *5.30-9pm Tue-Fri, noon-2.30pm & 5.30-9pm Sat* $$

Adelaide Fringe

When winter settles in, June brings warmth with the **Adelaide Cabaret Festival** *(cabaret.adelaidefestival centre.com.au),* a three-week spectacle of sass and song at the **Adelaide Festival Centre**. Locals rug up for late-night shows by the river, while international headliners share the stage with emerging acts and sharp-as-a-whip satirists.

Rounding out the year, November's **Feast Festival** *(feast.org.au)* paints the city in Pride during a two-week riot of LGBTIQ+ art, identity and unapologetic self-expression. Come for the open-air drag shows and street parties, but save some sparkle for **Picnic in the Park** – the feel-good finale with market stalls, bars and the much-loved Feast Dog Show, where dressed-up pups steal the spotlight. For glittery vibes on Friday and Saturday nights year-round, pop into **Mary's Poppin**.

Sea, Air & Rail

MAP P717

Visiting Port Adelaide's transit-rich museums

Conversations about Port Adelaide usually start with football – locals are quick to declare loyalty or loathing for the suburb's AFL team. But beyond the sporting divide, the currents here are far older. One of South Australia's first settlements (1840), 'the Port' blends maritime grit with slow-burn renewal centred around three heritage museums, all open daily.

PUTTIN' ON THE FRITZ

South Australia's colonial heritage, shaped by free German and British settlers, left behind more than architecture and vineyards. It gave rise to a language all its own. For example, the term 'fritz': a humble processed meat (think Devon), said to have been invented by a Lobethal butcher by the same name, is only found in SA lunchboxes. Linguistically, South Aussies also stand apart – that broad 'A' in 'dance', 'plant' or 'graph' nods to old Adelaide gentility, breaking from Australia's famed flat vowels. Even ordering a beer can trip up outsiders. Here, a 285ml pour is a *schooner* (a pot or middy in the eastern states), a 425ml glass is a *pint* (a schooner elsewhere) and a true English *imperial pint* hits 568ml.

DRINKING IN ADELAIDE: SUBURBAN BREWERIES

MAPS P717 & P718

Pirate Life Brewing: Microbrewery turned Port Adelaide powerhouse with pub bites and 24 brews on tap. *11am-10pm Sun-Thu, to midnight Fri & Sat*

Little Bang Brewing Company: Industrial-chic Stepney tapshed slinging wings, tacos, burgers and craft beer. *3-10pm Wed & Thu, 11am-11.30pm Fri & Sat, to 8.30pm Sun*

Shapeshifter Brewing Co: Findon favourite pouring IPAs and stouts, backed by rotating taps. Food trucks too. *4-9pm Wed, to 10pm Thu, noon-10pm Fri & Sat, to 6pm Sun*

Bowden Brewing Company: Classy Bowden tap house pushing flavour boundaries. Hoppy regulars, lemonade and sours. *noon-11pm Fri & Sat, to 9pm Sun, 4-10pm Tue-Thu*

BIRTHPLACE OF AUSTRALIAN GIN

Mar Farreras from Kangaroo Island Spirits provides insights into the gin industry. *@kangarooislandspirits*

South Australia is a foundational pillar of the country's gin industry. The Barossa Valley is its beating heart, yielding a delicate grape-based ethanol that pairs flawlessly with the state's native botanicals. From imaginative inclusions – oyster shells by **Never Never Distilling Co**, fruits by **Threefold Distilling** and seasonal blends by **Storytellers Distillery** – to modern extraction methods through vacuum distillation, SA leads. Whether visiting city distilleries like **Imperial Measures** or **Ambra Spirits**, or ferrying across Backstairs Passage to Kangaroo Island Spirits, options set taste buds ablaze.

Just down from the wharf on Lipson St, start with the **South Australian Maritime Museum** *(maritime.history.sa.gov.au; adult/child $22.50/9)*, home to the nation's oldest nautical collection dating to 1872. Across three creaky floors, you'll find salt-bleached instruments, figureheads and shipwreck artefacts, including the 'Best Bower' anchor from HMS *Investigator*, jettisoned in the harbour by explorer Matthew Flinders in 1803. Free weekend guided tours depart at 11am and 2pm.

A short stroll south, the **National Railway Museum** *(nrm.org.au; adult/child $19/7)* is a tribute to the heyday of Australian rail. Step inside the SAR 750 Class locomotive 752, the last of its kind; climb aboard a restored Redhen railcar, once a classic suburban commuter; and explore the museum's triple-gauge collection, reportedly the largest of its type in the world.

Continuing south, the **South Australian Aviation Museum** *(08-8240 1230; saam.org.au; adult/child $17/7.50)* shifts the view skyward. Inside two vast hangars sit 27 impressive aircraft, including the rare WWII light bomber *Fairey Battle I* (N2188), one of four such surviving planes in the world. Call ahead for guided cockpit tours led by volunteers who will talk you through dials, throttles and share flight lore pulled straight from South Australian skies.

Mangroves & Sea Mammals

MAP P717

Paddling Adelaide's dolphin sanctuary

North of Port Adelaide's industrial reaches, the **Adelaide Dolphin Sanctuary** is home to a 10,000-year-old mangrove forest, seagrass meadows, an eerie ship graveyard and around 40 bottlenose dolphins. Paddle out with **Adventure Kayaking SA** *(adventurekayak.com.au)* on a 90-minute guided kayak tour (adult/child $55/35) departing from Garden Island Boat Ramp. Kayaks and SUP boards are also available for hire here (two hours from $39). Always give passing dolphins a 50m buffer.

Prefer to let someone else do the work? **Port River Cruises** *(portrivercruises.com.au; adult/child $88/55)* launches 90-minute tours from alongside **Port Adelaide Lighthouse**, four times daily between 9am and 3pm year-round; twilight trips depart weekends October to January.

DRINKING IN ADELAIDE: OCEANFRONT ALES

MAP P717

Largs Pier Hotel: This Art Deco icon has spent 140 years watering, feeding and hosting beachgoers drifting in from Largs Bay. *7am-9pm*

Seacliff Beach Hotel: Heritage pub pouring cold pints and SA wines. Its balcony sunsets lure Seacliff's day-swimmers. *8am-midnight*

West Beach Surf Club: Breezy hangout serving cold beer on West Beach's blissfully bare foreshore. *8.30am-9pm Mon-Fri, from 8am Sat & Sun*

Palais Hotel: On Semaphore's sands, this century-old staple stays up late, a rarity along the Adelaide coast. *9am-2am Tue-Sat, to midnight Sun & Mon*

Adelaide Hills

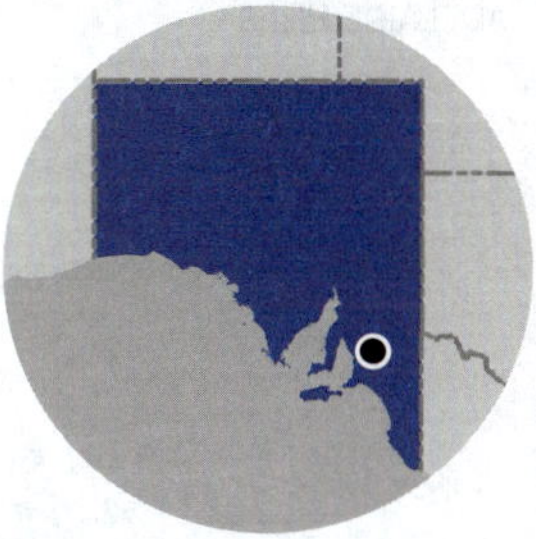

FOOD & WINE | NATURE TRAILS | HISTORIC VILLAGES

As Adelaide's eastern sprawl dissolves into pockets of stringybark and blue gum, the land swells upward into the Adelaide Hills. Tucked into the Mt Lofty Ranges – on the ancestral Country of the Peramangk and Kaurna peoples – the landscape here offers sweet reprieve from the summer heat of the plain below.

A leafy canopy throws shade over meandering dirt trails and quiet backroads, linking storybook villages with wind-brushed lookouts. The early English gentry built their cool-weather retreats around Stirling and Aldgate; many live on as lively pubs and boutique stays. German immigrants fleeing religious persecution settled Hahndorf and Lobethal, leaving behind stone cottages, Lutheran spires and stone-fruit orchards that still perfume the valleys each spring.

Just 30 minutes from Adelaide's city centre, the Hills feel worlds away – a green realm of mist, moss and morning birdsong. Come for a lazy day's wandering and don't expect to head home early.

Handpicked Goodies

Harvest your own fruit

Savour the seasons in the Adelaide Hills the old-fashioned way: by plucking sun-warmed fruit at the source. Wander beyond the farm gate for a behind-the-shed glimpse at your favourite produce, to meet growers and sample the day's pick.

November to April, the sweet perfume of strawberries fills the air at **Beerenberg Strawberry Farm** *(beerenberg.com.au; adult/child $5/free)*. Families have handpicked these crimson jewels in Hahndorf for generations. Basket brimming, wander back to the farm shop to weigh and purchase your haul (per kilo $13.50).

Cherry season follows, painting hillsides ruby red from mid-November to January. During **Summer Cherry Fest** *(cherriessa.com.au)*, a dozen or so orchards – mainly around Lenswood – swing open their gates for pick-your-own adventure. Prices vary between growers (and seasons), but expect to

GETTING AROUND

Like all of SA's regions, having a car is the best way to explore. The Hills has several public transport routes, but few accommodate remote wineries and orchards. Metro's buses connect Adelaide city to key towns Mt Barker, Stirling and Hahndorf, and pass popular sites like Mt Lofty Summit and Cleland Wildlife Park; timetables thin out fast beyond the main corridor. You can also cycle between Woodside and Birdwood on the 22km-long Amy Gillett Bikeway.

TOP TIP

Expect to see a lot of Lycra-clad bums. Weekend cyclists tackle the tight, narrow slopes up through Norton Summit and Mt Lofty Old Freeway. Allow extra driving time.

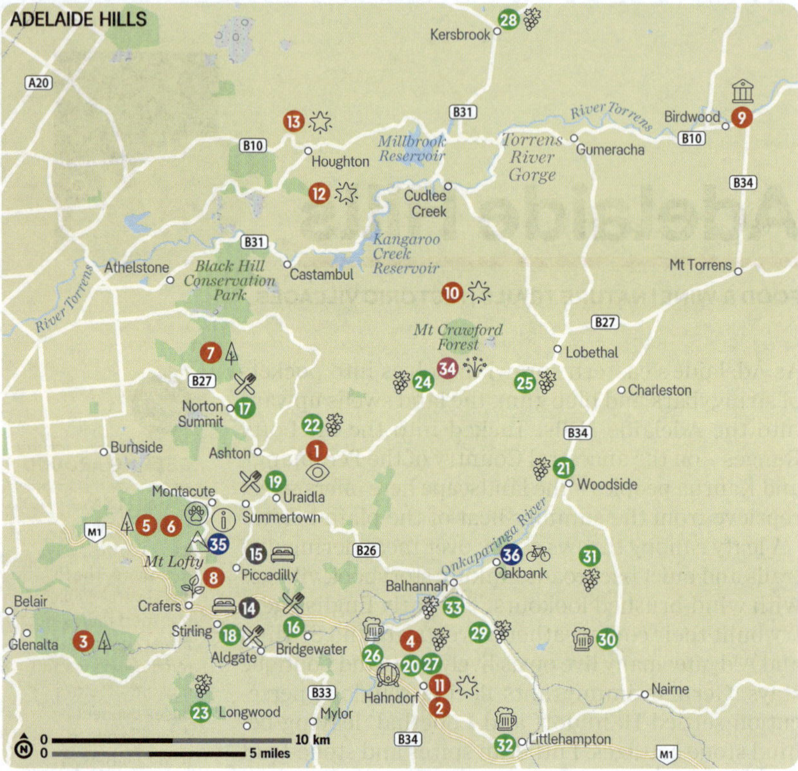

SIGHTS
1 Basket Range
2 Beerenberg Strawberry Farm
3 Belair National Park
4 Cedars
5 Cleland National Park
6 Cleland Wildlife Park
7 Morialta Conservation Park
8 Mt Lofty Botanic Garden
9 National Motor Museum

ACTIVITIES
10 Fox Creek Bike Park
11 Hahndorf Walking Tours
12 Paracombe Premium Perry
13 Willabrand Orchard

SLEEPING
see 8 Sequoia Lodge
14 Sticky Rice Villas
15 Woodhouse Adventure Park

EATING
16 Bridgewater Inn
17 Scenic Hotel
18 Stirling Hotel
19 Uraidla Hotel

DRINKING & NIGHTLIFE
20 Ambleside Distillers
21 Bike About
22 BK Wines
23 Deviation Road
24 Gentle Folk Wine
25 Golding Wines
26 Grünthal Brew
27 Hahndorf Hill Winery
28 Kersbrook Hill Wines
29 Lane Vineyard
30 Lot 100
31 Murdoch Hill
32 Prancing Pony
33 Shaw + Smith

ENTERTAINMENT
34 @Lenswood Pick Your Own
see 9 Bay to Birdwood

INFORMATION
see 11 Adelaide Hills Visitor Information Centre
35 Mt Lofty Summit Visitor Information Centre

TRANSPORT
36 Amy Gillett Bikeway

DRINKING IN THE HILLS: WINERIES

Shaw + Smith: Leaders in cool-climate craft, Balhannah's benchmark cellar delivers hallmark sauvignon blanc and chardonnay. *11am-5pm*

Lane: Hahndorf icon known for chef-led tastings, including a signature blend-your-own experience. *10am-5pm*

Golding Wines: Family-run Lobethal winery blending single-vineyard pours, garden dining and wood-fired fare in a barn. *11am-5pm*

BK Wines: One of Basket Range's only cellar doors; edgy skateboard art meets Hills' biodynamic rebellion. *noon-5pm Sat & Sun, from 3pm Fri* pay around $5 to $10 entry, plus $15 to $18 per kilo for picked fruit. February to April, fig foragers flock to **Willabrand Orchard** *(freshfigs.com.au; adult/child $20/free)* at Glen Ewin Estate in Houghton to savour sticky-sweet fruits straight from the tree.

As the air cools between late February and May, **@Lenswood Pick Your Own** *(atlenswood.com.au; adult/child $6/3)* is the pick for apple-laden fun – meet the growers, fill your basket (per kilo $4 to $5) and taste autumn fresh from the tree. Around the same time, pears peak in the northern Adelaide Hills at **Paracombe Premium Perry** *(paracombepremium perry.com.au)*, ripe for scooping up for a sweet $4 a kilo.

Cool-Climate Vintages

Drinking in the Hills wine region

Unlike the robust reds shaped by the hot and dry climates of the Barossa Valley and McLaren Vale, the Adelaide Hills craft their character in cooler air. Mid-altitude slopes and steady rainfall shape wines of finesse and restraint. Sauvignon blanc and chardonnay remain faithful stalwarts, though local shiraz and pinot are equally poised.

Stretched along a narrow 70km corridor, Adelaide's nearest wine country is a patchwork of over 50 cellar doors tucked among peaks and gullies. Much of the buzz centres on the Hills' small-batch vanguard – sustainable makers championing biodynamic wines. Since the early 2000s, **Basket Range** has become the noted hub of the natural wine movement, its cellar doors few but fiercely independent.

Seek out the likes of **Commune of Buttons**, **BK Wines**, **Gentle Folk**, **Lucy M Wines** and **The Other Right** at Hills' pubs and restaurants. For a deeper dive, grab the latest *Adelaide Hills Cellar Door Guide* from the **Adelaide Hills Visitor Information Centre** *(adelaidehills.org.au)* in Hahndorf. Better still, embrace July's chilly skies at the **Winter Reds** *(adelaidehillswine.com.au)* wine festival – a cosy weekend of tasting masterclasses, chef collabs and clinking glasses across the region.

Sun-Dappled Trails

Hiking in the Hills

Climb into the Hills and the temperature drops, the air freshens and the landscape flips to eucalypt green. Well-marked, mid-distance trails weave through Mt Lofty Ranges' cooler

BEST TOURS IN THE ADELAIDE HILLS

Trailhopper: Hop-on/hop-off winery tour bus looping around 10 wineries. Pickup and drop-off in central Adelaide. *trailhopper.com.au*

Ambler Touring: Locally guided outings through heritage villages, boutique wineries and farms. Transfers included. *amblertouring.com.au*

Small Batch Wine Tours: Curated, small-group visits to hand-picked cellar doors, with lunch, tastings and door-to-door service. *smallbatchwinetours.com.au*

Bike About: E-bike cruises between Beerenberg, Udder Delights, Shaw+Smith and The Lane Vineyard, with tastings and produce pickups along the way. *bikeabout.com.au*

Escapegoat: Beginner-friendly mountain biking tours dropping from Mt Lofty into bushland valleys, with a glide-by of Cleland Wildlife Park en route. *escapegoat.com.au*

DRINKING IN THE HILLS: WINERIES

Hahndorf Hill Winery: Hahndorf's Austrian-inspired boutique pouring Grüner Veltliner and Zweigelt. End with ChocoVino pairings. *10am-5pm*

Murdoch Hill: Oakbank's modern-country cellar door pours bright, textural wines amid rolling paddocks and grazing cattle. *11am-4pm Thu-Tue*

Kersbrook Hill Wines: Northern Hills winery championing offbeat white shiraz poured from its relaxed roadside cellar. *10am-5pm Sat-Thu, to 9pm Fri*

Deviation Road: Landscaped cellar door on Longwood's slopes; *méthode traditionnelle* sparkling and cool-climate reds. *10am-5pm*

heights, ideal for stretching your legs between cellar door visits. Perched at the top, around 20 minutes' drive from Adelaide's city centre, get your bearings at the **Mt Lofty Summit Visitor Information Centre**, where maps, hot coffee and local tips set the tone. From here, the **Waterfall Gully Track** plunges down the ranges' western flank, with Adelaide's most notorious climb waiting on the way back up from the bottom car park. This 8km-long return grind rewards sweaty persistence with sweeping city-to-sea views.

For slightly gentler slopes, drive for 10 minutes down the eastern flank from the info centre to **Mt Lofty Botanic Garden** *(botanicgardens.sa.gov.au; free)*, where the 7.5km-long **Heysen Trail Mt Lofty circuit** loops between switchbacks, ferny gullies and rhododendron groves. From the car park here, a series of shorter walking trails offers easier ambles beneath the gum canopy.

Fifteen minutes north along the range, **Morialta Conservation Park** hides a crumpled landscape of stringybark forests, ochre-streaked gorges and rangey lookouts peering over Adelaide. The standout track here is the 7.3km **Three Falls Grand Hike**, looping past a trio of seasonal waterfalls and clifftop paths before returning neatly to the car park.

BEST HILLS HIKES

Melanie Sjoberg, Friends of Heysen Trail volunteer, shares her favourite Adelaide Hills trails.

Wine Shanty Track: This 10km trek climbs through Cleland National Park, connecting meandering paths lined with swaying stringybarks and thicketed understory. Birds call as you pass startled roos and occasional koalas.

Warren Tower Hike: Northeast of Adelaide, Warren Conservation Park's explosion of spring wildflowers is a drawcard along 9km of rugged landscape. Your legs get a workout traversing a slice of the Heysen Trail; expansive vistas from the tower summit.

Section 4: Yurrebilla Trail: The 8km trail between Norton Summit and Morialta Conservation Park presents a 300m elevation gain, with lookouts and waterfalls.

Walk on the Wild Side

Get up close to Australian wildlife

In the centre of **Cleland National Park** *(parks.sa.gov.au; free)*, just 20 minutes uphill from Adelaide's city centre, **Cleland Wildlife Park** *(clelandwildlifepark.sa.gov.au; adult/child $34.50/19)* offers a quick escape in the wild. Spanning 35 leafy hectares, the sanctuary is managed by National Parks SA and shelters around 130 native species, from western grey kangaroos and yellow-footed rock wallabies to wombats, Tasmanian devils and a chorus of native birds. Daily keeper talks and feeding sessions are included in your entry ticket; hands-on encounters like the reptile experience ($20.50) or echidna feeding ($34) can be booked in advance. Several koala interactions are available too, but it's worth noting that koala handling remains a controversial practice and Cleland is among the few Australian parks still offering it.

EATING IN THE HILLS: PUB GRUB

Stirling Hotel: Long-loved pub icon-turned-upscale retreat, pairing refined local dining with five chic suites overlooking leafy Stirling. *8am-9pm* **$$**

Bridgewater Inn: Order a bridgey burger and a frosty pint and linger longer by the riverfront beer garden. *10am-10pm Mon-Fri, to 2am Sat & Sun* **$$**

Scenic Hotel: A Lofty Range-top beer garden with a wine list featuring the Hills' best biodynamic drops. *noon-11pm Tue-Sun, from 2pm Thu* **$$**

Ask to visit 'The Tank' underground cellar

Uraidla Hotel: Heritage Uraidla pub championing paddock-to-plate with its own bakery and brewery. *11.30am-10pm Mon-Fri, to 11pm Sat & Sun* **$$**

HYSERB/SHUTTERSTOCK

Kangaroo, Cleland Wildlife Park

Hahndorf Heritage

Australia's oldest German settlement

Embracing the title of Australia's oldest surviving German settlement, Hahndorf trades heavily on its settler heritage. Even as cafes and wine bars multiply along the main street, the town's half-timbered facades, chestnut-lined avenues and old-world fare keep its heritage alive and well. For context beyond the bratwurst, **Hahndorf Walking Tours** *(hahndorfwalkingtours.com.au; from $49)* leads gentle 1km-long guided rambles, revealing tales behind the steepled churches and sandstone shopfronts.

Just north of town, the **Cedars** *(heysen.org.au; adult/child $22/8)* is the historic homestead of artist Sir Hans Heysen (1877–1968). Open Tuesday to Sunday, one-hour guided tours of Heysen's wonderfully preserved family home, gardens and light-filled studio hung with some of his iconic works offer an intimate glimpse into the life and legacy of one of Australia's foremost landscape painters.

THE EARS OF A GIANT

Glancing southeast from Adelaide, two distinct peaks rise from the skyline about a kilometre apart: Mt Lofty and Mt Bonython. A Kaurna Dreaming story tells us that these twin summits form the ears of ancestor-creator Nganno. The story tells of Nganno's journey across Kaurna Country and how, after being fatally wounded in battle, he lay down to die, his body becoming the sweep of the Mt Lofty Ranges. Today, the Yurrebilla Trail traces this mythic ridgeline for 54km, linking five conservation parks through shaded fire tracks, winding footpaths and ridge-top roads. A favourite among long-distance runners and sure-footed hikers, it offers a moving connection between the region's ancient storylines and modern trails.

DRINKING IN THE HILLS: BREWHOUSES & DISTILLERIES

Ambleside Distillers: Hahndorf's modern-day moonshiner runs gin-blending masterclasses. *noon-6pm Mon & Wed-Fri, from 11am Sat & Sun*

Prancing Pony: Award-winning craft beers, brewhouse tours and build-your-own tasting paddles between Mt Barker and Hahndorf. *hours vary*

Grünthal Brew: Verdun microbrewery pouring ales alongside funky shared plates built around Hills produce. *10am-4pm Mon-Wed, to 5pm Thu & Sun, to 10pm Fri & Sat*

Lot 100: Looks like a beer hall, acts like a cosmopolitan brasserie. Collective of cider, beer and gin makers, north of Nairne. *11am-5pm Wed-Sun*

BEST BIKE TRAILS

Fox Creek Bike Park: SA's premier moutain biking hub in Cudlee Creek with 50km of downhill, cross-country and all-terrain single-track for riders of all ages. And it's free!

Cleland National Park: Gravel riders get their fix on winding fire trails linking ridge-top lookouts and fern-lined gullies.

Belair National Park: Pedal through native woodlands and picnic clearings, or tackle the 13km-long Adventure Trail just outside Belair.

Old Freeway to Mt Lofty: Adelaide's signature road-cycling workout: a 9km climb from Glen Osmond to the summit, averaging 4.7%.

Amy Gillett Bikeway: Named after an SA cycling legend, this leafy, 22km-long sealed trail between Woodside and Birdwood follows a former rail line.

MYPHOTOBANK.COM.AU/SHUTTERSTOCK

Hahndorf Old Mill Hotel

Drive Through Time

Visit the National Motor Museum

Australia's remarkable knack for keeping classics on the road has earned a reputation among vintage vehicle aficionados. Birdwood's **National Motor Museum** *(motor.history.sa.gov.au; adult/child $22.50/9)* keeps the engine running on this motoring heritage: collecting, restoring and showcasing the nation's penchant for Sunday drives. More than 400 vehicles chart the story, from steam carriages to high-octane racers. Exhibits highlight everything from Alice Anderson's trailblazing all-women garage to the arcade racing zone where you can spin the wheels on *Night Driver* (1976), *Daytona* (1977) and *Road Rash* (1991).

Each October, Birdwood's quiet streets spark to life for the **Bay to Birdwood** *(baytobirdwood.history.sa.gov.au)*. Watch on for free as 1500 vintage machines rumble from Barratt Reserve (West Beach in coastal Adelaide), climbing through the Hills to the museum – a honking great tribute to Australia's love affair with the open road.

Barossa Valley

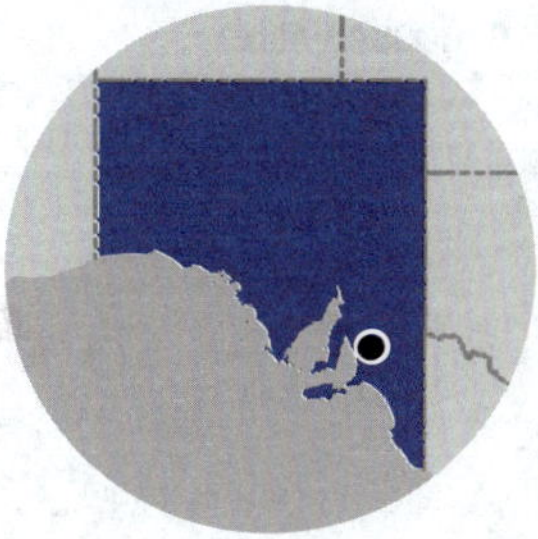

DISTINGUISHED WINES | VITICULTURAL HERITAGE | GERMAN TRADITION

Arguably Australia's most famous wine region, the Barossa Valley remains a vinous pilgrimage the world over. Its church spires and biergartens still lend a German lilt – the legacy of Lutheran settlers who fled persecution and arrived armed with faith, fortitude and a few well-travelled vine cuttings.

Shielded from phylloxera's devastation, the valley's original vineyards have aged into a knotted tangle of timber and history, none older than Freedom Block at Langmeil Winery in Tanunda, planted in 1843. Beneath these roots lies a much older story: that of the Peramangk, Ngadjuri and Kaurna peoples, whose connection to this land runs even deeper than the wine.

These days, Barossa's agricultural edges are softening with sheds reborn as gin bars, stone cottages as lux stays. But amid the *mettwurst* and *bienenstich*, the brass bands and 175-year-old Liedertafel choir, the valley still beats to a Teutonic rhythm: steady, proud and unmistakably Barossan.

TOP TIP

Visit March to May when crowds ease, it's cooler and vines blush gold. In April odd-numbered years, the Barossa Vintage Festival celebrates the harvest with a week of parades, boozy lunches and cellar door revelry.

Palms & Port

Stroll through Seppeltsfield's historic grounds

In Barossa's western reaches, **Seppeltsfield Road** *(seppeltsfieldroad.com)* unfurls like a stately procession – an aristocratic avenue flanked by 5km of Canary Island date palms. At

GETTING AROUND

An hour north of Adelaide via the expressway, the Barossa Valley is an easy day trip. The scenic detour is east through the Adelaide Hills, swapping freeway blur for sun-dappled gums. Can't find a designated driver? Catch an Adelaide Metro train to Gawler, then trundle by LinkSA bus through Lyndoch, Tanunda, Nuriootpa and Angaston. **Barossa Taxis** *(barossataxis.com.au)* can ferry you between cellar doors – or grab a bike to stitch together towns along the vine-striped 40km Barossa Trail between Gawler and Angaston.

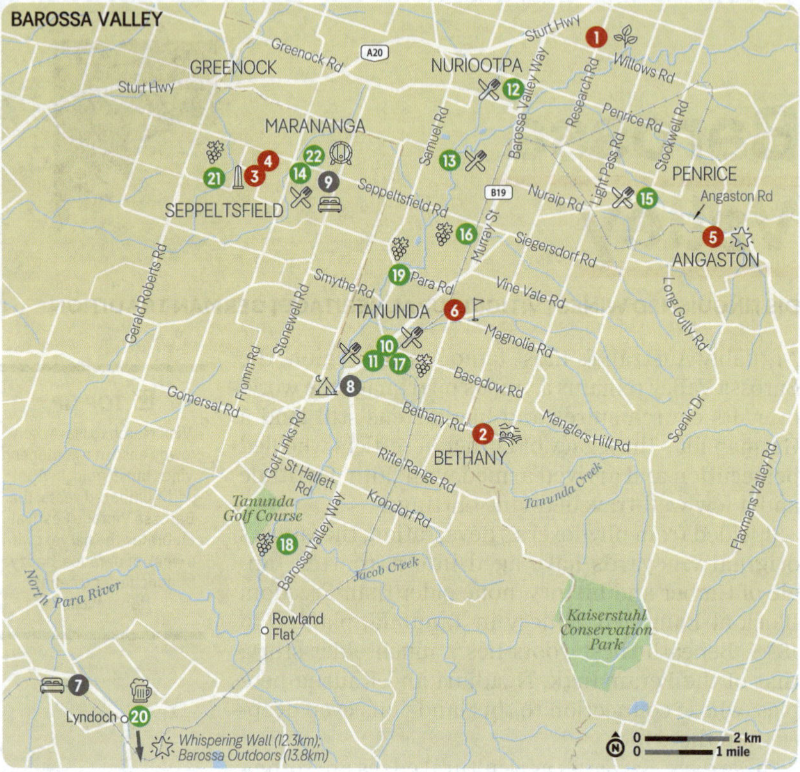

SIGHTS
1 Barossa Bushgardens
2 Bethany
3 Seppelt Family Mausoleum
4 Seppeltsfield Road

ACTIVITIES
5 Barossa Adventure Station
6 Barossa Bowland

SLEEPING
7 Barossa Shiraz Estate
8 Discovery Parks Barossa Valley
9 Louise

EATING
10 Apex Bakery
see 5 Barossa Valley Cheese Company
11 Browns Barossa Donuts
see 10 fermentAsian
12 Fleur Social
13 Maggie Beer's Farm Shop
14 Staġuni
see 11 Vino Lokal
15 Vintners Bar & Grill

DRINKING & NIGHTLIFE
see 10 Bar: Musque
16 Chateau Dorrien
17 Château Tanunda
18 Jacob's Creek
19 Langmeil Winery
20 Ministry of Beer
21 Seppeltsfield
22 Seppeltsfield Road Distillers

SHOPPING
see 15 Barossa Farmers Market

EATING IN THE BAROSSA VALLEY: OUR PICKS

Browns Barossa Donuts: Fluffy brioche buns bursting with cream, jam, custard and chocolate in Tanunda. *8.30am-2pm Wed-Fri, from 9am Sat* $

Barossa Valley Cheese Company: Angaston cheesemonger turning curds to gold. Try silky, medal-winning La Dame. *10am-4pm Wed-Mon* $

Vintners Bar & Grill: Barossa icon between Nuri and Angaston, delivering refined ambience and regional flavours. *noon-2.30pm & 6-9pm Mon-Sat* $$$

Staġuni: Maltese-inspired share plates, blue-cheese mussels and local drops in a 1922 Marananga schoolhouse. *noon-6pm Fri-Mon, 6-9pm Thu* $$$

its heart sits **Seppeltsfield** *(seppeltsfield.com.au)*, a winery established in 1851 and one of Australia's most atmospheric estates. A free self-guided history trail connects its storied past to its creative present, with 10 walkable audio stops (beginning at the main entrance) creating an hour-long wander through 170 years of winemaking lore. Along the way, the **Centennial Cellar** reveals century-old barrels of fortified port and **JamFactory Craft + Design** showcases artisans shaping glass, metal and clay. **Prohibition Distillery** brings a spirited edge with its gin tastings infused with local botanicals; **Vasse Virgin** tempts with olive-oil skincare and one-hour perfumery workshops ($100; bookings essential).

Visitors craving more speed can join a 90-minute Segway tour ($145) looping around the grounds and up to the **Great Terraced Vineyard**, with sweeping valley views. For another vantage point, climb on foot up the hill to the Grecian-style **Seppelt Family Mausoleum**, a serene lookout honouring one of Australia's great wine dynasties since 1927 – a fitting finale to this living Barossa landmark.

Cooking Royalty

Visit Maggie Beer's Farm Shop

Five minutes south of Nuriootpa, **Maggie Beer's Farm Shop** *(maggiebeersfarmshop.com.au)* has been the culinary home of Australia's first lady of food since 1979. Step into Maggie's TV studio kitchen for a live cooking demonstration ($60), complete with a non-alcoholic sparkling and tastings fresh from the pan. Beyond the demo, the Farm Eatery Cooking School runs hands-on classes and lively cocktail masterclasses keep things lively.

Outside, settle by the lake with pâtés, chutneys and gourmet ice cream from the on-site shop and watch resident turtles bake in the sun. True to Maggie's paddock-to-plate ethos, the shop sources most ingredients from local Barossa producers, many of whom trade at the Saturday-morning **Barossa Farmers Market** in nearby Angaston. It's a feast for the senses here: orchard-fresh apples, artisan breads, honey, olive oil and small-batch preserves. The region's cottage-industry flavours in their tastiest form.

BEFORE BAROSSA

Long before a clerical error labelled this region as Barossa Valley instead of Barrosa (after Spain's Battle of Barrosa), this land was, for millennia, the ancestral and cultural nexus for the Peramangk, Ngadjuri and Kaurna people. The traditional owners expertly cultivated the landscape, employing controlled burnings to regenerate vegetation and creating the foundation for today's fertile fields.

By the mid-19th century, however, First Nations' numbers had drastically declined as they were displaced by European settlers, ravaged by introduced diseases and impacted by ecological changes. Few cultural remnants remain; Barossa's only documented rock engravings are hidden within the Kaiserstuhl Conservation Park.

EATING IN THE BAROSSA VALLEY: OUR PICKS

Fleur Social: Nuriootpa cafe-florist serving speciality coffee and light bites in a bright, arty space. *6.30am-2pm Mon-Fri, 7.30am-noon Sat* $

Apex Bakery: Historic Tanunda bakehouse that nails in the basics: crusty loaves, meat pies and choc doughnuts. *7am-4.30pm Mon-Fri, 8am-2pm Sat* $

Vino Lokal: Tanunda's Murray St wine bar pairs Barossa craftsmanship with curated seasonal menus. *8am-4pm Thu, Sun & Mon, to late Fri & Sat* $$$

fermentAsian: Classy Viet-inspired fare among Tanunda's German-Australian bistros. *6-9.30pm Wed, noon-2.30pm & 6-9.30pm Thu-Sat, noon-2.30pm Sun* $$$

HELP ME PICK:

Barossa Valley Wineries

Blessed with hot, dry summers and cool, moderate winters, the Barossa is built for grapes that like a challenge. More than 150 wineries thrive in this compact, 25km-long valley – one of Australia's oldest – famed for its timeless trio of shiraz, grenache and cabernet sauvignon. Look beyond the big reds to find cellar doors offering far more than a tasting bench; they deliver experiences as memorable and intoxicating as the wines themselves.

Where to Sip if You Love...

Barossa Icons

Rockford Wines Famously bottled without bar codes, Rockford's boutique range has a limited presence in shops, relying instead on a devoted fanbase to buy directly from its winery on Tanunda's outskirts.

Henschke For 150-plus years, this Keyneton stalwart has guarded Barossa's winemaking soul. Breaking ground in the 1950s with single-vineyard bottlings, Henschke unveiled the now-legendary Mt Edelstone and Hill of Grace shiraz. These wines rewrote the script for Barossa reds.

Peter Lehmann Wines Founded in Tanunda in 1979 by its eponymous winemaker, this relaxed riverside cellar door hits a modern chord as a concert favourite. Past gigs include Chris Isaak, James Blunt and The Killers.

International Names

Jacob's Creek One of Australia's most recognisable wine brands, Jacob's Creek pairs global reach with Barossa roots. Its Rowland Flat estate showcases the heritage, hospitality and easy-drinking style that made it world-famous.

Yalumba Australia's oldest family-owned winery (1849), Yalumba has long flown the Barossa flag abroad – its elegant shiraz and pioneering viognier are well known internationally. At home in Angaston, its cellar door sits inside the original brandy bond store.

Long Lunches

Hentley Farm Building on its reputation for punchy single-block shiraz, Hentley delivers an adventurous avant-garde degustation in Seppeltsfield. The intimate Atrium restaurant sets the scene for a slow, indulgent affair – destination dining at its most decadent.

Seppeltsfield Tour the winery grounds, then settle in for a long lunch at light-filled FINO. Progressive Australian plates honour SA's small-scale producers.

Otherness Wines Breaking from Barossa's big-red tradition, this polished Angaston micro-producer was born from a collaboration of experimental winemakers. The relaxed wine bar–restaurant serves small-batch drops and seasonal dishes.

Rolling into Bed

Alkina Wine Estate Savour complimentary tastings and access to the kitchen garden at refined farmstay lodgings steeped in luxury.

Kaesler Wines Steps from the winery cellar door, Kaesler's courtyard cottages are within easy access to everything Nuriootpa has to pour. Three suites feature king beds and en-suite bathrooms; the Cottage Suite adds a spa bath.

HOW TO

When to go Visit in late spring or early autumn for soft light, mild days and fewer tour buses. Winter brings frosty air, but fireside reds have a warming charm.

Book ahead Many wineries welcome spur-of-the-moment visits, but boutique cellar doors often need notice. Plan ahead and save the sighs for the sunsets.

Budget Most cellar doors charge for tastings, though fees are often redeemable on purchase. Barossa hospitality runs a notch above Adelaide's – in polish and in price.

Don't cram your plan Between tastings, long lunches and lazy vineyard strolls, Barossa afternoons slip away fast. Start early and limit the cellar-door crawl to a five.

SIGHTS
1 Alkina Wine Estate
2 Henschke
3 Hentley Farm
4 Jacob's Creek
5 Kaesler Wines
6 Kellermeister
7 Kies Family Wines
8 Otherness Wines
9 Peter Lehmann Wines
10 Rockford Wines
11 Seppeltsfield
12 St Hallett
13 Yalumba

TRANSPORT
14 Barossa Bike Hire

Navigating Wine Country

A self-guided drive through the Barossa's 90-odd cellar doors is tempting, but someone has to drive; let someone else take the wheel. From Adelaide's CBD, **Trailhopper** *(trailhopper.com.au; from $89.95)* runs a hop-on, hop-off shuttle along a budget-friendly loop around 10 wineries. The seven-hour route includes stops for coffee, lunch and boutique browsing. Linger where you please and rejoin the next bus when the mood (or glass) calls.

For something slower and more personal, valley local Kym Farley at **Bespoke Barossa Tours** *(barossabespoketours.com.au; from $950 for two)* curates one-on-one day trips that include tasting fees, wine pairings, gourmet lunch and transfers. Expect small producers, vineyard stories and the kind of access that only a born-and-bred Barossan can unlock.

Cyclists can tackle sections of the scenic Barossa Trail, a 40km-long, sealed and mostly flat path from Gawler to Angaston, passing cellar doors en route including **Kies Family Wines**, **St Hallett**, **Kellermeister** and Jacob's Creek. Delivery service by **Barossa Bike Hire** *(barossabikehire.com; from $50)* makes bike hire a breeze; it has hybrid and e-bikes, helmets and maps. Cycling under the influence (blood alcohol concentration of 0.05% or higher) is illegal in SA.

FAMILY FUN

Barossa Bowland: Who'd have thought dinosaur-themed mini golf would become a Barossa icon? This prehistoric putt-putt (adult/child $16/14) and bowling alley keeps everyone entertained.

Barossa Outdoors: Explore Warren Reservoir's forest-lined shores by kayak. Guided two-hour paddles (from $79) include gear, instructions and photo stops.

Barossa Adventure Station: Angaston's free playground precinct blends rail heritage with monster slides, flying fox, bouldering wall and wheelchair-friendly trampolines.

Whispering Wall: At Williamstown's famous Whispering Wall, words carry 140m across the dam – a quirky, acoustic and free marvel delighting kids, baffling adults.

Château Tanunda: Enjoy a round of croquet (from $20) on Château Tanunda's manicured lawns – old-world fun for the modern family.

NICK RAINS/GETTY IMAGES

Vineyards (p740), Barossa Valley

Reflective Blooms

A quiet moment in Barossa Bushgardens

On Nuriootpa's outskirts, **Barossa Bushgardens** *(barossabushgardens.com.au; free)* celebrate the valley's native landscapes in miniature. Uncover 7 hectares of shady trails and picnic corners, with interpretive signs offering insights into 130+ local plant species.

Hard-packed paths keep the space accessible for wheelchairs and prams. Kids can roam the Nature Play zone and a dementia-friendly garden offers sensory calm. Run by volunteers, the community gardens are free to explore. Pick up a *Traditional Uses* trail map to trace how First Nations peoples drew food, tools and medicine from plants along the track.

Heritage Trails

Trace Barossan history

Explore the valley's past with **Barossa Heritage Trails**, a free app providing a digital guide through the region's quaint villages and vine-lined backroads. Featuring interactive driving maps, walking routes and short audio tales, it unpacks history across eight story-rich locations, including a 4km-long, 23-stop wander past slate cottages and old workers' huts in Barossa's first settlement from 1842, **Bethany**. Download a trail, tap play and let the valley lead you through time.

DRINKING IN THE BAROSSA VALLEY: WINE ALTERNATIVES

Ministry of Beer: Family-run Lyndoch brewery offering 16 taps, barrel-aged sours, cider and dog-friendly gardens. *11am-7pm Wed-Sun, noon-6pm Mon*

Seppeltsfield Road Distillers: Sip a Shiraz gin or myrtle martini on SRD's Marananga deck – very Barossan. *11am-5pm Sat-Thu, to 6pm Fri*

Chateau Dorrien: Outside Nuriootpa, this old-school cellar crafts sweet, quandong-infused honey mead. *11am-4pm Mon-Fri, 10.30am-4.30pm Sat & Sun*

Bar: Musque: A shimmering wall of 400+ bottles light up this Tanunda gin bar, a shrine to SA distillers. *4pm-late Mon, Tue & Fri, from 1pm Sat & Sun*

McLaren Vale & Fleurieu Peninsula

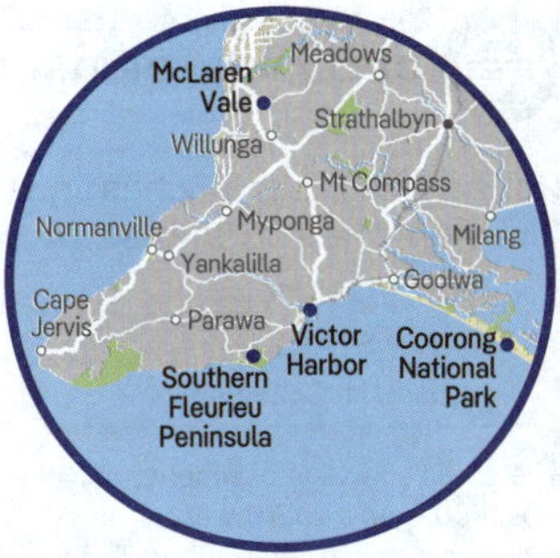

COASTAL WILDERNESS | HISTORIC PORTS | WINE COUNTRY

Striped with vineyards, almond groves and wheat fields tumbling towards Gulf St Vincent, Fleurieu is Adelaide's weekend playground. Just beyond the city's southern edge sprawls McLaren Vale – the historic cradle of SA wine, where the state's first vines went into the soil back in 1838. These days, the Vale still pours with confidence, balancing cellar-door sophistication with dirt-under-the-fingernails farm gates. Like the capital to its north, this is Kaurna Country.

Push south across the tail end of the Mt Lofty Ranges and you slip into Ngarrindjeri Country – a coastline of restless surf and wild beauty. Parks brim with kangaroos and wetlands with birdlife, while clifftop trails and wave-polished beaches line the Encounter Coast. Scattered among it all lie Victor Harbor, Port Elliot and Goolwa – historic harbour towns made for sea breezes and slow exhales.

Places

McLaren Vale

TIME FROM ADELAIDE: **40MIN**

Lose yourself in the d'Arenberg Cube

The product of winemaker Chester Osborne's wild imagination, The **d'Arenberg Cube** *(darenberg.com.au/darenberg-cube; from $20)* is an eccentric, surprising cellar door – a towering, half-turned black-and-white Rubik's Cube. Soaring five storeys above the vines, this quirky, outside-the-box building is McLaren Vale's most recognisable architectural landmark.

Inside its enigmatic exterior, the puzzles keep coming. Explore the ground-level **Alternate Reality Museum**, containing a psychedelic 360-degrees video multiverse, curious

TOP TIP

The peninsula might be blessed with more beaches than you can count, but don't assume they're all swimmable – hidden rips lurk beneath the calm. It's safest to swim at patrolled beaches such as Moana, Aldinga, Normanville, Chiton Rocks, Port Elliot and Goolwa. Check *surflifesavingsa.com.au* for times.

GETTING AROUND

Adelaide Metro trains run frequently to Seaford, where buses connect south to McLaren Vale and Willunga. LinkSA coaches run regularly from Adelaide to Victor Harbor via Encounter Bay, Port Elliot, Middleton and Goolwa; limited services continue to Cape Jervis (for the Kangaroo Island ferry) before turning back towards Adelaide, stopping at Myponga, Yankalilla and Normanville. Public transport is scarce, so plan ahead. A car (or organised tour) is the only practical way to explore the area's beaches, parks and trails.

CELLAR DOOR DRIVE

Rolling vines, lazy lunches and bold architecture define the cellar doors of McLaren Vale's northwest.

START	END	LENGTH
Chalk Hill Collective	Chapel Hill	9.5km; 4–5hr

There's no shortage of wineries in McLaren Vale – over 80 – yet its northwest corner distils the experience into five standout producers, all within 10km of each other. Just east of the McLaren Vale township, begin at 1 **Chalk Hill Wines**, a winery sharing spectacular hilltop views with **Never Never Gin Distillery** and **Cucina di Strada**'s Italian street eats. There's coffee, mocktails and desserts for designated drivers – everyone can drink in the landscape.

Down the hill, broad windows at 2 **Maxwell Wines** frame the winery floor below, allowing you to watch the action. Wander the hedge maze between tastings or sample the estate's traditional mead, sourced from the display beehive in the foyer. A few minutes north, the 3 **d'Arenberg Cube** (p743) is McLaren Vale's eccentric wine temple. By contrast, d'Arry's Verandah Restaurant next door cooks up classy food and far less chaos.

Further on, 4 **Coriole Vineyards** plays it humble in the tasting room but outside in the courtyard, a rambling English-style garden is made for lush long lunches with vine view. Up the road at 5 **Chapel Hill**, an 1865 ironstone chapel sets the scene for tastings that feel almost ceremonial – arched frames splashed with stained-glass colour, vaulted ceilings and a polished timber bar.

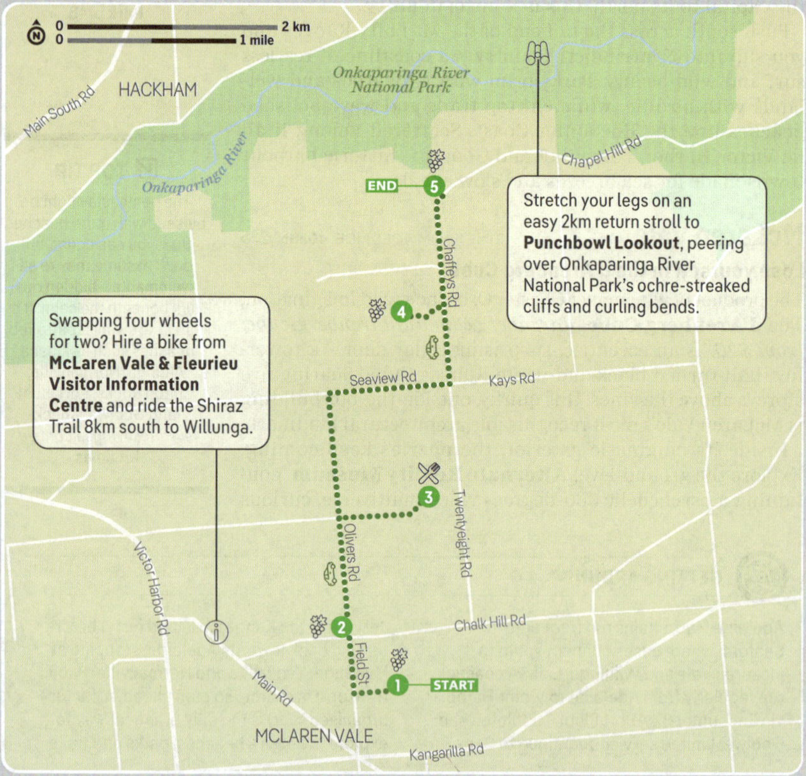

tactile installations, eclectic ephemera and a virtual fermenter. Ascending the cuboid to Level 2, Dalí diehards can access the **Dalí at d'Arenberg** exhibition ($10 on top of the entry price) displaying surrealist prints and sculptures on loan from Switzerland alongside works by Australian artist Charles Billich. Level 3's **Sensorial Circus Café** serves punchy, share-style plates with offbeat flair.

The sun-lit penthouse doubles as the tasting suite for d'Arenberg's 200-hectare vineyard; red and white pours are included in the general entry price. Pull up at the glass-topped bar or pre-book a mix-your-own session (from $120) at the blending bench. Either way, soak in vine-swept views across the valley. Don't miss the fabulously bizarre bathrooms on Level 1.

Southern Fleurieu Peninsula

TIME FROM ADELAIDE: 1½HR

Day walk in Deep Creek National Park

The largest pocket of wild country left on the Fleurieu, **Deep Creek National Park** *(parks.sa.gov.au; vehicle $13.90 per day)* is a sanctuary of cliffs, forest and sea that acts as a natural barrier against human intrusion. Within its boundaries biodiversity blooms, with over 400 native plant species, 110 bird species, 11 mammal types and countless reptiles, fish and insects – many threatened or rare.

It's also home to some of South Australia's best coastal bushwalks. Accessibility is front and centre at **Goondooloo Ridge**, a gentle, hard-packed trail with sweeping views over Backstairs Passage to Kangaroo Island (p749). Wheelchair-friendly restrooms and wide paths make this a rare stretch of wilderness open to almost everyone. On the drive down from Adelaide, **Fleurieu Coast Visitor Centre** in Yankalilla has free all-terrain wheelchairs to borrow; bookings essential (08-8558 0240).

Options abound for bushwalkers. **Forest Circuit Walk** (2.6km) loops inland from **Stringybark Campsite** (next to site 10) through remnant woodland alive with rosellas. The **Aaron Creek Hike** (6km return) traces rocky clifftops and ferny gullies out to the ocean. If you're carrying a tent, stay overnight at **Wuldi Krikin Ngawanthi/Eagle Waterhole** *($31.30)*, one of the park's best backcountry campgrounds. The **Deep Creek Circuit** (10.5km) steals the show. Starting near Tapanappa Lookout, it dips past seasonal waterfalls, traces sea cliffs and tunnels through stands of ancient *Xanthorrhoea* (native grass tree).

VINEYARDS FOR DAYS

Often overshadowed by SA's headline wine regions, the Fleurieu Peninsula sprawls for 100km south of Adelaide. Four subregions carry different characters, mesoclimates mellowed by the ocean's Mediterranean influence.

Closest to the city, **McLaren Vale** hugs the peninsula's northwest and is SA's star cradle of shiraz and innovation. To the east, cool southerlies sweeping off Lake Alexandrina temper family-run vineyards in **Langhorne Creek. Currency Creek**'s famed sauvignon blanc benefits from the same marine gusts off the Southern Ocean. Down south, the rising **Southern Fleurieu** region blends beaches, bushland and boutique vineyards stretching below the Mt Lofty Ranges to the peninsula's tip.

EATING IN MCLAREN VALE: WINERY DINING

Harry's Deli: Casual yet refined dining at Wirra Wirra's historic cellar door. Coffee, takeaway or lazy lunches. *10am-4pm Mon-Sat, from 11am Sun* $$

Vigna Bottin: Authentic Italian winery restaurant serving handmade pasta, rich sauces and delicate desserts. *noon-4pm Thu-Mon* $$

Maxwell Wines: SA's award-winning benchmark for winery restaurants and degustation theatre. *noon-5pm Fri & Sun, noon-5pm & 6.30pm-late Sat* $$$

Coriole Vineyards: Tasting menus and à la carte dining sourced from local producers; finest dining views in the Vale. *noon-2.30pm Thu-Mon* $$$

BEST FLEURIEU TOURS

Gone Awol: E-biking, stand-up paddle-boarding and wine tasting in McLaren Vale. *goneawol.com.au*

Trailhopper: Hop-on/hop-off winery bus circling 15 McLaren Vale spots across five boozy hours. Adelaide transfers. *trailhopper.com.au*

Big Heart Adventures: Guided five-day treks along the rugged, 74km-long Wild South Coast Way. Pack-free, ocean-view stays, gourmet grub and Adelaide transfers. *bigheartadventures.com.au*

Victor Harbor Walking Tours: Cheerful 90-minute strolls through Victor Harbor's heritage streets and across to Granite Island. *victorharborwalkingtours.com.au*

Waitpinga Farm Quad Bike Adventures: Guided 60- to 80-minute quad-bike tours across the grassy plains of a historic Southern Fleurieu farm. *waitpingafarm.com*

MAJONIT/SHUTTERSTOCK

For quick context, download the free **SA National Parks Tours** app, which weaves Ramindjeri (one of 12 Ngarrindjeri clans) stories through these ancient lands. Look for 'Wild South Coast Way' once downloaded.

South coast surf and sun

Motor south beyond Sellicks and things quickly get wilder. Down here, the coast needs a plan and a car, and rewards in spades. Tucked into the remote headlands of **Newland Head Conservation Park**, neighbouring **Waitpinga Beach** and **Parsons Beach** delivers serious surf for serious riders. Waitpinga's left- and right-hand swells break deliciously over both reef and beach, while Parsons has you covered for steep drops and powerful closeouts. At both spots, watch for powerful rips. Check the forecast, know your exits and don't paddle out alone.

Further east past Victor Harbor, the breaks mellow by patrolled beaches at **Goolwa**, **Chiton Rocks** and **Horseshoe Bay** (possibly SA's most picture-perfect cove), welcoming swimmers and less-seasoned surfers. **Surf & Sun** *(surfandsun.com.au)* runs beach lessons on the Middleton sand (from $65) and hires out SUPs and surfboards (from $25). Book well ahead in summer.

EATING IN MCLAREN VALE: OUR PICKS

Willa Coffee Shop: Willunga brunch cottage with dog-friendly courtyard garden, fuelling locals and passing cyclists. *hours vary* **$$**

Pizzateca: Destination pizzeria outside McLaren Vale, shaded by giant red gums and summery parasols. *noon-5pm Sun & Mon, to 7.30pm Fri & Sat* **$$**

Star of Greece: Clifftop institution perched above Port Willunga beach, pairing ocean views with two-course seafood plates. *noon-10pm* **$$$**

Pearl: A relaxed, sea-breezy diner with front-row views of Sellicks Hill's creamy red cliffs. Pure Fleurieu theatre. *hours vary* **$$$**

Granite Island

Victor Harbor

TIME FROM ADELAIDE: 1¼HR

Explore the granite isle

A day trip to lichen-crusted **Granite Island** is about as Fleurieu as it gets. From Victor Harbor's foreshore, a 630m-long concrete causeway has replaced the creaky timber original that connected the island since 1874. Take a stroll or hitch a ride on the Clydesdale horse-drawn **tram** *(horsedrawntram.com.au; adult/child $20/15)*, an 1894 vintage. It clops across roughly every 45 minutes.

Once ashore, **Kaiki Walk** loops 1.9km around wind-battered bluffs and sculpted granite tors. Grab a hot drink from the **Granite Island Recreation Park Café** and allow two leisurely hours to soak up the breezy seascape. Stay until dusk and you might spot the isle's little penguin colony shuffling up the northeast shore. Keep your distance and pack a red-light torch for nighttime viewing.

Watch whales

Late May to October, endangered southern right whales drift into Victor Harbor's sheltered bay for a seasonal congregation of courting, calving and socialising before the long swim south. The Southern Fleurieu's coastal lookouts make fine vantage

SA'S ALGAL BLOOM

First sighted off Fleurieu Peninsula in March 2025, South Australia's worst algal bloom on record began as a streak of discoloured water near Murray Mouth. Fuelled by warm seas, stagnant conditions and nutrient-rich run-off, the microscopic dinoflagellate *Karenia mikimotoi* (and later *Karenia cristata*) multiplied, spreading north into Gulf St Vincent and along Adelaide's metropolitan beaches.

The bloom stripped oxygen from the water, suffocating marine life and leaving a heavy toll on fishing, tourism and coastal communities. At the time of research, the bloom remained active with tentative signs that the waters were beginning to normalise. Stay across official updates at *algalbloom.sa.gov.au*. Check in with *beachsafe.org.au* for real-time safety alerts along patrolled beaches.

EATING ON FLEURIEU: FARMGATE PICNIC PRODUCE

Willunga Farmers Markets: The region's weekend stop for artisan breads, farm-fresh veg and ready-to-eat treats in Willunga. *8am-noon Sat* $

McCarthy's Orchard: Family-run vineyard and cider farm stocking pears, apples and other in-season goodies in their McLaren Flat cool room. *24hr* $

Peninsula Providore: Taste award-winning olive oil pressed in Tooperang. Pick your own April to June. *11am-4pm 1st Sat & Sun of month* $

Fleurieu Cherries: Seasonal pick-your-own orchard south of Willunga, tree-fresh cherries bursting under summer skies. *Dec-Jan* $

COORONG COUNTRY

Dana Shen, Ngarrindjeri practitioner, artist and bushwalker

When I see the pelicans wheeling over the Coorong, I know I'm home and I feel the spirit begin to heal. This is Ngarrindjeri Country – my Country – and being here feels like I've reconnected to my broader self. Never far from coastal communities, the Coorong draws its wildness from the restless sea – a moody spirit forever shaped by the surging tide. Its light, colours and weather can change hour by hour, framing how you feel and move through the landscape, so bring your all-weather gear. It's a place for slow walks, quiet reflection and listening – really listening – to the sounds of wind, waves and wildlife, far removed from the outside noise.

points, with regular sightings from the **Bluff** near Encounter Bay, **Freeman Lookout** in Port Elliot and **Basham Beach** just outside Middleton.

Running for 30km between Encounter Bay and Goolwa, the **Encounter Bikeway** strings these viewpoints together. Rent a bicycle on the foreshore at the **Spinway Victor Harbor** self-service station *(spinwayadelaide.com.au; per 1/2/24 hours $15/28/38)*. Chuffing alongside this, the steam-powered **Cockle Train** *(steamrangerheritagerailway.org; variable fares)* rattles along the coast between Victor and Goolwa on Australia's oldest public railway from 1854. Plan your heritage fix for a Wednesday, weekend or during SA's school holidays.

Or take to the water. Departing from the Granite Island causeway, **Big Duck** *(thebigduck.com.au; from $80)* runs 90-minute whale-watching trips; boats keep a safe distance under strict approach guidelines. Outside whale season, cruises encounter resident New Zealand fur seals, Australian sea lions and bottlenose dolphins.

Back on dry land, the family-friendly **South Australian Whale Centre** *(sawhalecentre.com.au; adult/child $5/4)*, beneath the Victor Harbor Visitor Centre, dives deep into the species' science and spectacle, with multimedia exhibits, fossil digs and the enormous skull of a southern right whale.

West Coast of Coorong National Park

TIME FROM ADELAIDE: 1¼HR

Cruising Coorong's wetlands

Stretching 145km southeast of Goolwa, **Coorong National Park** *(parks.sa.gov.au)* shelters a vast saltwater lagoon behind the slender Younghusband Peninsula. This is a sanctuary for waders and waterfowl, recognised as a 'Wetland of International Importance' under the Ramsar Convention.

From Goolwa Wharf, **Spirit of the Coorong** *(spiritofthecoorong.com.au)* runs half-day cruises (adult/child $120/90) exploring quiet inlets, sand islands and untouched shorelines. For the full picture, join a day-long voyage between October and May (adult/child $165/115) that includes a First Nations–led walk through ancient midden sites, a traditional smoke ceremony and cultural interpretations.

Launching from Hindmarsh Island, **Canoe the Coorong** *(canoethecoorong.com; from $115)* paddles these waters by kayak. Tours bundle all the essentials – gear, picnic lunch and bush-tucker walks. Kayak and camping kits are also available for overnight, self-guided trips.

EATING ON THE SOUTHERN FLEURIEU: WATERFRONT ICONS

Flying Fish Cafe: Horseshoe Bay's beachfront kiosk dishes up fish and chips. There's also a neat diner if you've packed more than swimwear. *9am-3pm* $

Anchorage Hotel: Heritage seaside pub serving hearty meals and cold beer steeped in Victor Harbor's maritime charm. *noon-2pm & 5.30-8pm Wed-Sun* $$

Kuti Shack: Fronting Goolwa Beach's dunes and serving brunch fare with pipis, Fleurieu wines and relaxed coastal vibes. *8am-3pm Thu-Sun* $$

Coorong Cafe: An improbably remote beach shack dishing out Coorong mullet, hot chips and strong coffee at Murray Mouth. *11am-3pm Thu-Mon* $

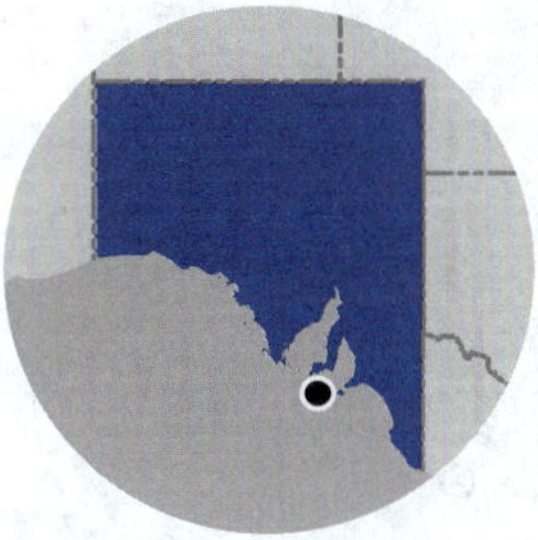

Kangaroo Island

PROLIFIC WILDLIFE | BEACH DAYS | ISLAND ESCAPE

It's rare to find a world-renowned holiday destination without a frenzied crowd. Yet, the million-dollar beach scapes and pristine wilderness on Australia's third-largest island feel refreshingly tranquil. Despite its global allure, Kangaroo Island (KI) remains humble, raw and delightfully underdeveloped. Unsealed roads, unreliable phone reception, early shop closures and a 45-minute ferry from the mainland help maintain the rural pace. When explorer Matthew Flinders first rounded the coast in 1802, he found the island uninhabited – except for its rampant wildlife (Aboriginal artefacts would later tell a different story). Today, over a third of the island is dedicated to conservation and national parks.

Offsetting the unrefined charms of its wild habitats is KI's indulgent side: sophisticated clifftop cabins, sumptuous degustations and creative artisanship all come with the territory. But these luxuries adapt to the insouciance of island time – a speed worth embracing.

TOP TIP

Kangaroo Island is surprisingly vast, with less infrastructure than you might expect. Outside its main towns, phone reception is patchy; Telstra offers the best coverage. Download GPS maps before hitting the road.

GETTING AROUND

It's 1¾ hours by car from Adelaide to Cape Jervis, where SeaLink ferries sail to Penneshaw on the island's east coast; a daily bus runs the same route, taking 2½ hours. Tight on time? QantasLink's 30-minute flights from Adelaide land near Kingscote, the island's sleepy hub. Public transport on the island is virtually non-existent. **Peninsula Coaches** *(peninsulacoaches.com.au)* run twice-daily shuttles between Kingscote and the ferry; otherwise, hire a car, join a tour or bring your own wheels. Most main roads are sealed, while gravel backroads and wildlife call for slow, steady driving.

Paws, Claws & Feathers

Encounter KI's iconic land-based animals

Alongside Flinders Chase National Park (p752), the 2023-hectare **Hanson Bay Wildlife Sanctuary** *(hansonbay.com.au)* is your best bet to see KI's animals in the wild. Fifty-minute guided **koala walks** *(adult/child $28/14)* thread through native blue gum habitat and 90-minute **nocturnal tours** *(adult/child $85/45)* draw out tammar wallabies, possums and echidnas among the crepuscular crowd.

Located centrally off South Coast rd, companion sites **Raptor Domain** *(kangarooislandbirdsofprey.com.au; adult/child*

HIGHLIGHTS
1 Flinders Chase National Park
2 Seal Bay Conservation Park

SIGHTS
3 Admirals Arch
see 3 Cape du Couedic Lighthouse
4 Cape Willoughby Lightstation
5 Clifford's Honey Farm
6 Emu Bay Lavender Farm
see 22 Emu Ridge Eucalyptus Oil Distillery
7 Hanson Bay Wildlife Sanctuary
8 Kangaroo Island Wildlife Park
9 Kelly Hill Caves Conservation Park
10 Little Sahara
11 Raptor Domain
12 Remarkable Rocks
13 Rocky River Precinct

ACTIVITIES
see 13 Heritage Walk
14 Ironstone Hill Hike
see 14 Kangaroo Island Ocean Safari
15 Kangaroo Island Outdoor Action
see 14 Kangaroo Island Sculpture Trail
16 Kangaroo Island Wilderness Trail
see 14 Penneshaw Penguin Centre
see 13 Platypus Waterholes
17 Snake Lagoon Hike

SLEEPING
18 Chapman River Campground
see 13 Postmans Cottage
19 Southern Ocean Lodge
20 Tea Tree Campsite

EATING
21 Amadio Wines
see 21 Cactus
22 Emu Ridge Cafe
see 14 Fat Beagle Coffee Shop
23 Fig Tree
see 14 Millie Mae's Pantry
see 14 Penneshaw Pub
24 Rockpool Café
see 16 Rocks Cafe
25 Samphire
see 21 So Sando
26 Sunset Food & Wine
see 21 Tirage
27 Vivonne Bay General Store

DRINKING & NIGHTLIFE
28 Bay of Shoals Wines
29 Dudley Wines
30 False Cape Wines
31 Islander Estate Vineyards
32 Kangaroo Island Spirits

SHOPPING
see 31 Kangaroo Island Wool

INFORMATION
see 16 Flinders Chase Visitor Information Centre

$30/20) and **Kangaroo Island Wildlife Park** *(kangarooislandwildlifepark.com; adult/child $35/20)* pair animal experiences with insights from the on-site wildlife rescue centre homing many of KI's injured and orphaned natives. Others, like the American alligator, are more curious additions.

Where Sea Lions Play

Meet the locals at Seal Bay Conservation Park

Around 45 minutes southwest of Kingscote, **Seal Bay Conservation Park** *(parks.sa.gov.au; adult/child $20/12)* is a safe haven for endangered Australian sea lions. Fewer than 12,000 remain worldwide, making this one of the few spots on Earth to watch them snuggle in the sand and ride the surf. Join a 45-minute **beach tour** *(adult/child $42/23.70)* led by rangers who discuss conservation efforts protecting the sea lions

Continued on p754

FIRST NATIONS CONNECTIONS

For thousands of years, Kangaroo Island was home to First Nations people. Before rising seas cut it off 3000 to 10,000 years ago, the island formed part of the Country of the Narungga, Kaurna (who call the island Karta Pintingga) and Ngarrindjeri (Nurrungaui) peoples. They still hold strong ties today. Archaeological sites reveal middens, hearths and stone tools – evidence of a rich cultural life that thrived here long before European arrival. Oral history passed down through mainland Aboriginal groups reflects an enduring connection to place. Now protected heritage sites, these locations are a reminder of deep time and care for Country. A free exhibit of artefacts and tools can be seen inside Emu Ridge Cafe (p756).

DRINKING ON KANGAROO ISLAND: WINERIES

False Cape Wines: Enveloped by gums in central Dudley Peninsula, this revamped cellar door has an award-winning wine list, with scenery to match. *11am-5pm*

Dudley Wines: Sip a Dudley Bubbly and take in the mainland vista from the deck of this pioneering Penneshaw winery. *10.30am-4.30pm Thu-Mon*

Bay of Shoals Wines: Waterfront vines and seafood platters highlight this producer's maritime heritage, overlooking the bay just north of Kingscote. *11am-5pm*

Islander Estate Vineyards: Cosy Cygnet River tasting room showcasing cool-climate wines and thoughtful food pairings. *noon-5pm Thu-Tue*

Remarkable Rocks

TOP EXPERIENCE

Flinders Chase National Park

At the western edge of the island, Flinders Chase National Park is among Australia's oldest recognised parks, established in 1919. Through fires, floods and human interference, this isolated environment and its native inhabitants have shown steadfast resolve. Whimsical geological formations and woodland bushwalks steal the show, but delve deeper and you'll uncover adaptability and resilience scarred into its skin.

DON'T MISS

- Kangaroo Island Wilderness Trail
- Remarkable Rocks
- Admirals Arch
- Cape du Couedic Lighthouse
- Rocky River Trails
- Snake Lagoon Hike
- Bushfire regeneration

Rocky River Bushwalking Trails

A slew of rewarding bushwalks branch out from the **Rocky River Precinct**, 4km west of the park entrance. Once a working farm, the area now teems with kangaroos, wallabies, echidnas and Cape Barren geese scuttling through the undergrowth. Trails vary from shady to exposed; bring sun protection and plenty of water. A central, 2km-long, wheelchair-friendly corridor links several tracks through fire-scarred sugar gums, leading north to a flat 2km loop around **Platypus Waterholes** (use the car park off Shackle Rd for faster access). To spot koalas, follow the 1.5km **Heritage Walk** loop; scan treetop branches and look below for the telltale sign of fresh green scat.

PRACTICALITIES

- *parks.sa.gov.au/parks/flinders-chase-national-park*
- adult/child $14.40/8.30
- dawn-dusk; Flinders Chase Visitor Centre 9am-5pm

Admirals Arch & Cape du Couedic Lighthouse

The scrub-lined road south of the Rocky River Precinct leads to Cape du Couedic Lighthouse. You can't access the century-old wayfinder, but interpretative boards in the upper car park chronicle its storm-battered history. From here, three walking trails disappear into the heath: a 2.8km-return clifftop walk to Weirs Cove, with faraway views to Remarkable Rocks; a 550m-long heritage wander through lighthouse lore; and a 1.9km loop via the lower car park, which links to a series of boardwalk switchbacks (wheelchair-friendly until the lookout). At its end, past a colony of long-nosed fur seals, a spiral staircase lands at the stalactite-strewn archway of Admirals Arch, carved by millennia of ocean muscle.

Remarkable Rocks

At Kirkpatrick Point, just east of Cape du Couedic, the much-admired, Dalí-esque Remarkable Rocks defy gravity's grasp atop a windswept plateau. Centuries of Southern Ocean storms have sculpted this exhibition of giant granite boulders into its current contours. Devote at least 30 minutes to searching its hidden corners and secret passages. A wide, wheelchair-friendly boardwalk leads to an accessible viewing platform, with excellent views of the rocks and distant Casuarina Islets.

Kangaroo Island Wilderness Trail

KI's big-ticket bushwalk is the five-day **Kangaroo Island Wilderness Trail** (*parks.sa.gov.au/experiences/kiwt; $205*), a 66km-long trek through raw terrain. Setting out from the **Flinders Chase Visitor Information Centre**, the remote Class 4 trail threads through wildflower-strewn scrub, white-sand bays, sheer coastal cliffs and habitat teeming with the park's iconic wildlife, finishing at **Kelly Hill Caves Conservation Park**. Four camp sites break up the journey, each with communal kitchens, fire pits or combustion fireplaces, woodpiles, rainwater tanks and toilets. Self-reliance is essential, but the rewards are unforgettable.

Sample a trek section on the 4km-return **Snake Lagoon Hike**, following a rock-pooled creek to the dramatic beach mouth. To experience the Wilderness Trail's final day's sloping mallee woodland, walk 14km out-and-back from Kelly Hill Caves to **Tea Tree Campsite** for free.

Bushfire Regeneration

Summer fires of 2019–20 burnt through 96% of the park. Imagine the black landscape, then marvel at the scrub's regrowth. Signs along Rocky River's trail corridor and displays at Flinders Chase Visitor Information Centre reveal vegetation resilience and returning wildlife.

NOT SO NATIVE NATIVES

Under threat on the mainland, koalas and platypuses were introduced to the island in the 1920s and flourished without natural predators – so much so that koalas were devouring the manna gum canopy. To protect the native vegetation and maintain a balance, a contentious sterilisation program began in 1997, regulating koala numbers to sustainable levels.

TOP TIPS

- The park is a long way from the eastern amenities. Plan meals and consider staying overnight near the west coast.
- Stop by the visitor centre to purchase tickets (if you haven't bought them online) and check which bushwalks are open.
- Arrive at sunset, after the crowds have thinned, to photograph Remarkable Rock's fiery lichen.
- Phone signal is weak to non-existent; free wi-fi is available at the visitor centre.
- Planning to visit Flinders Chase and catch tours at Seal Bay (p751), **Kelly Hill** and Cape Willoughby Lighthouse (p756)? Save money with a **Kangaroo Island Tour Pass** (*parks.sa.gov.au/book-and-pay/kangaroo-island-tour-pass*).

CARING FOR ISLAND LIFE

There's a reason Kangaroo Island is dubbed the Galápagos of Australia. Its remote setting, 15km from the mainland, provides refuge for vulnerable species like the glossy black cockatoo, duck-billed platypus, Rosenberg's goanna and Kangaroo Island dunnart. Much of the open landscape is unfenced – take care on roads to protect roaming creatures.

Home to the world's oldest bee sanctuary, KI safeguards the purest strain of Ligurian bee, introduced from Italy in 1881. To preserve this precious ecosystem, leave all honey and pollen products on the mainland. Other contraband include used beekeeping tools and equipment, unwashed or dirty potatoes and declared pests like foxes, rabbits and weeds.

Continued from p751

and their quirks. A wheelchair-accessible path (900m round trip) to the lookout provides an elevated perch over the colony.

Penneshaw's Wild Shores

Watch dolphins skim and penguins waddle home

Penneshaw's wildlife story plays out from surf to shoreline, day to night. Twice daily, **Kangaroo Island Ocean Safari** *(kangarooislandoceansafari.com.au; adult/child $88/55)* heads out on 75-minute coastal cruises along the Dudley Peninsula, skimming the chop in search of bottlenose dolphins and long-nosed fur seals. Two-hour swim experiences are also on offer, though research suggests close human interaction can influence marine mammal behaviour and breeding.

After dark, the focus shifts ashore as little penguins waddle home from a hard day's fishing. Guides from the **Penneshaw Penguin Centre** *(penneshawpenguincentre.com; adult/child $31/19)* lead nightly one-hour clifftop walks, scanning rocky burrows for the world's smallest penguins. Pack a jacket – it gets chilly on the rocks.

Wilderness Adventures

Dive into all-action experiences

The island's wild south coast is a playground for nature explorers. In Vivonne Bay, family-run **Kangaroo Island Outdoor Action** *(kioutdooraction.com.au)* runs guided and self-paced adventures ranging from wilderness quad biking (from $177 for 80 minutes) to river kayaking (from $47 for three hours). Just east, the same crew runs **Little Sahara** *(littlesahara.com.au)*, a base for sand-boarding and tobogganing ($37 for three hours) on a vast, naturally occurring inland dune field. Bundle experiences for a cheaper, full-on adventure fix.

Island Underworld

Limestone and light shows at Kelly Hill Caves

Just shy of Flinders Chase National Park (p752), an otherworldly network of underground caves is safeguarded by

EATING ON KANGAROO ISLAND: EAST-COAST DINING

So Sando: Playful, flavour-packed brunch dishes stand out at this Kingscote cafe. *7.30am-2.30pm Wed-Sun* **$$**

Cactus: A lively Kingscote cafe serving great coffee, mountainous pancakes, fresh juices and KI brews. *7.30am-2.30pm* **$$**

Sunset Food & Wine: Modern Australian, best timed with sunset's slow burn. *6-10pm Wed, from noon Thu & Fri, from 5.30pm Sat Dec-May* **$$$**

Samphire: Classy American River restaurant with market-fresh seafood and paired drinks. *6.30am-10.30pm Wed-Sat* **$$$**

Millie Mae's Pantry: Cosy brunch spot near the Penneshaw ferry port; a concise delicious menu and KI-made produce. *7.30am-4pm* **$$**

Penneshaw Pub: This 100-year-old institution serves hearty meals, local beers and front-row seats to Backstairs Passage's restless waves. *11am-11pm* **$$**

Tirage: New Kingscote wine bar blending simple sophistication with local and Australian drops. *3-10pm Wed-Fri, from 4pm Sat & Sun* **$$$**

Amadio's Vino e Cucina: Authentic trattoria serving pasta and pizzas baked in a wood-burning oven. *noon-2.45pm & 5-9pm Wed-Sun* **$$$**

BEACH DRIVING TOUR

Open roads on this beach-hopping journey link Kangaroo Island's turquoise coves and wild surf breaks with camping, wildlife and jaw-dropping scenery.

START	END	LENGTH
Antechamber Bay	Emu Bay	295km; 1–2 days

Begin at 1 **Antechamber Bay**, where the Chapman River flows onto 4.2km of snow-white sands fronting Australia's mainland. Drive 27km west to bushland-fringed 2 **Brown Beach**. Bush camps, hot showers and a short walk to dazzling white 3 **Island Beach** tempt. Just off Hog Bay Rd, 12km southwest, 4 **Pennington Bay** is prime surf territory.

Around 88km west, 5 **Vivonne Bay** shines with turquoise water, fishing boats and safe swimming near the jetty. West again by Kelly Hill Caves, the eastern headland of hourglass-shaped 6 **Hanson Bay** obscures a stunning cove, excellent for surf-fishing and strolls.

Turning up West End Hwy, North Coast Rd delivers a trio of standout beachfronts with free BBQs, toilets and picnic shelters. Gum-lined slopes drop to a cove at 7 **Western River Bay**, sea caves tucked in the western headlands. Motoring 22km east, 8 **Snelling Beach** rolls out 660m of classic surf from a roadside lookout before descending into Middle River. Another 16km on, 9 **Stokes Bay** hides KI's best secret – a twisting boulder tunnel opening onto ivory sands and a sheltered rock pool. The broad sweep of 10 **Emu Bay** invites a relaxed beach drive and leisurely end to the circuit.

For those new to ocean plunges, the **Kingscote Tidal Pool** gives the same salty vibes with protection from the shifting currents.

Staying near **Island Beach**? Choose a holiday home with kayaks included to make the most of Nepean Bay's sparkling waters.

A DAY ON DUDLEY

Julie Helyar, False Cape Wines, shares recommendations for KI's Dudley Peninsula. *@falsecapewines*

Start in Penneshaw with brekkie at Millie Mae's Pantry (p754) or **Fat Beagle Coffee Shop**, then walk it off on **KI's Sculpture Trail**. If you want to keep burning the calories, head east to the 4km **Ironstone Hill Hike**, where dolphins can be seen frolicking in the cove – for a closer look, join a KI Ocean Safari cruise (p752). Next, set your GPS for Antechamber Bay, where gorgeous beach and river strolls await. Thirsty? Dudley Wines (p751) offers stunning mainland vistas. Otherwise, join a historic **Cape Willoughby Lighthouse** tour. By now, you've earned your lunch. Set among charming vines, prepare for a gourmet platter and a tasting paddle at False Cape Wines (p751).

Kelly Hill Caves Conservation Park *(parks.sa.gov.au; adult/child $30/18).* Of almost 300 known caves across Kangaroo Island, Kelly Hill is the only cave complex open to the public. Join a one-hour ranger-led tour to a stalactite-strewn chamber, 15m underground. An ultra-impressive audio-visual light show traces the island's formation to the present day.

Farmgate Exports

Savour the island's unique produce

Kangaroo Island is blessed with fertile soils and abundant sunshine, cultivating its orchards, fields and a proud farmgate culture. Here, a rare, isolated strain of Ligurian honeybee thrives among the uninfected flora and GMO-free crops. The honey trade is buzzing here, with three local beekeepers providing tours, tastings and sweet-toothed treats. Jenny's honey ice cream at **Clifford's Honey Farm** *(cliffordshoney.com.au),* a 20-minute drive south of Kingscote, is the standout.

A five-minute drive away, **Emu Ridge Eucalyptus Oil Distillery** *(emuridge.com)* manufactures 100% pure Australian eucalyptus oil, picked, steamed and refined from the Kangaroo Island Narrow Lead Mallee. Used as a natural antiseptic, insect repellent and decongestant, this plucky little product was one of the country's first exports. Set aside 15 minutes for a self-led **distillery tour** *(adult/child $4/2),* then breathe in its gum-perfumed gallery cafe, **Emu Ridge Cafe**.

Heading back north to Kingscote, champions of island artisanry **Kangaroo Island Wool** *(kangarooislandwool.com)* and **Emu Bay Lavender Farm** *(emubaylavenderfarm.com.au)* deserve a stop.

Distilled Wisdom

Mixology masterclasses at KI Spirits

As Australia's first dedicated gin distillery, **Kangaroo Island Spirits** *(kangarooislandspirits.com.au; from $130),* 10km southwest of Kingscote, knows a thing or two about creating smooth blends. Curated masterclasses by the internationally recognised moonshiner delve into the country's gin history and the science and native aromatics that underpin it all. Book in advance to create your own signature blend across two botanical-infused hours.

EATING ON KANGAROO ISLAND: REMOTE FEEDS

Vivonne Bay General Store: Minutes from Vivonne Bay beach, pull up a chair on the deck for a whiting burger, crispy calamari or cold beer. *9am-3.30pm* $

Rock pool Cafe: Stokes Bay's seafood shack serves salt and pepper squid, pan-seared prawns and island wines. *11am-5pm Tue-Sun Sep-May* $$

Rocks Cafe: Swanky Eftpos-only cafe in Flinders Chase Visitor Centre serving baguettes, ice cream and lunch specials. *9.30am-3pm* $$

Fig Tree: Epicurean adventure beneath a 120-year-old fig, across from Snelling Beach. *noon-3pm Wed-Fri, 11am-5pm Sat & Sun Nov-Apr* $$$

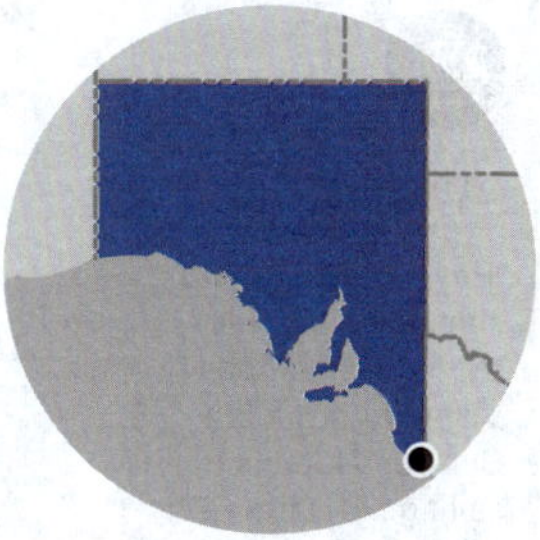

Mount Gambier & Limestone Coast

LAKES & SINKHOLES | WINE REGION | COASTAL CRUISES

Sprawled across the flatlands below an extinct volcano, Mount Gambier is the major service centre along South Australia's lengthy Limestone Coast. Rising from traditional Buandig Country, the town took shape in the mid-1800s as an agricultural and railway hub. But the town's true wonders lie underground, from the cobalt shimmer of Blue Lake to suburban sinkholes and limestone caves that tunnel below the town.

North from here, the Limestone Coast spans the traditional lands of the Bindjali, Pinechunga and Ngarrindjeri peoples – a broad sweep of olive-hued plains between the lower Murray and the Victorian border. Drift off the highway and you'll find surf-lashed beaches in Robe and Coorong National Park, cabernet-rich vineyards in Coonawarra and the fossil-laden underworld of Naracoorte Caves. Both natural and human history runs deep here. While the landscapes may seem quiet at first glance, look closer and the stories beneath the surface reveal themselves.

Places

TOP TIP

Everyone wants to see the luminous colours of Mount Gambier's Blue Lake, which turns big-time blue in the warmer months (late November to February/March). But if you visit between April and October, the lake will look much like any other – a steely grey. Timing is everything.

Mount Gambier

TIME FROM ADELAIDE: **4HR**

Caves, lakes and sinkholes

A couple of kilometres south of the city centre, Mount Gambier's volcanic complex holds the region's star attraction: **Blue Lake** (Warwar), a roughly 5000-year-old cone now filled with water.

GETTING AROUND

Driving between Adelaide and Mount Gambier, the Dukes Hwy (A8) is the most direct, but the coastal Princes Hwy (B1) through Coorong National Park is infinitely more scenic. Fuel up in Kingston SE or Meningie before you enter the Coorong: top-ups are unreliable in between. Stateliner buses ply these routes, stopping in Penola, Robe, Naracoorte and Meningie. You can save a few hours with a flight to the regional airport or take a V/Line bus over the border from Victoria. But if you want to explore, hike or linger in small towns, your own wheels are essential.

LADY NELSON

'Hey, what's that old ship doing outside the Mount Gambier Visitor Information Centre?' Not much sailing... But the original version of the **HMS *Lady Nelson*** (this one's a replica) sailed a long way indeed. She was built in London in 1799, specifically to survey the Australian coast. As Lieutenant James Grant sailed towards South Australia on 3 December 1800, he observed a modest mountain through his telescope: Mount Gambier ahoy! It was the first place in SA to be given a British name. The *Lady Nelson* was eventually scuppered by pirates in Indonesia, but Mount Gambier locals have a long memory: they commissioned this much-loved replica in 1986 to celebrate SA's 150th birthday.

This shimmering 70-odd-metre-deep phenomenon turns an insane hue of luminous blue in summer. Perplexed scientists think the colour change has to do with calcite crystals, suspended in the water, which form at a faster rate during the warmer months. You can loop around the lake on foot, following the crater's paved, wheelchair-friendly trail (3.6km).

The geologic awe continues at **Cave Garden** (Thugi), a 50m-deep sinkhole right in the middle of town, with the odd suicidal shopping trolley at the bottom. East of here, **Umpherston Sinkhole** (Balumbul) is a free, ivy-draped cavity tucked behind the lumberyards; you could row a boat

DRINKING IN MOUNT GAMBIER: BEST FOR BEERS

Mount Gambier Hotel: The main pub, on the main corner. For an easy-going beer and a reliable schnitzel, you really can't go wrong. *7.30am-late*

Woolstore Brewery: Occupies (you guessed it) an old wool store, pouring seasonal stout and hard lemonade. *3-9pm Thu, to 8pm Fri, noon-8pm Sat, to 6pm Sun*

Little Rippa Brewing Co: On the rural fringe, this breezy shed has plenty of quiet nooks for boisterous ales. *noon-10pm Fri & Sat, to 5pm Sun, 5-9pm Thu*

Jens Town Hall Hotel: Time-warping Jens dates back to 1884. The interior design is somewhat more recent and good for an unpretentious ale. *8am-late*

across it some years ago before an earthquake lowered the water table. Just west of town, **Engelbrecht Cave** *(visit mountgambier.com.au; adult/child $21/10.50)* is a meandering cave system extending beneath Jubilee Hwy and 19 local houses; guided 45-minute tours lead you down the stairs to this popular dive sight.

Beneath the waterline

Exploring beyond town, the freely accessible **Little Blue Lake** (actually greenish), 16km south, is a picture-perfect, 45m-deep sinkhole with a swimming pontoon. Want to dive deeper? Nearby **Kilsby Sinkhole** *(kilsbysinkhole.com; from $99)* is a prime snorkelling spot on a private sheep farm. Further south near the coast, **Piccaninnie Ponds** (undergoing restoration at the time of research) and **Ewens Ponds** *(parks.sa.gov.au; from $16.50)* are conservation parks, where you can scuba dive into glass-clear, bone-cold depths (minimum of two people). Ask about permits and gear hire at **Mount Gambier Visitor Information Centre**.

Heritage architecture and art

Mount Gambier's streets are lined with heritage shopfronts, halls and cavernous Victorian-era pubs, wrapped in wedding-cake ironwork balconies. An archi-essential here is the grand Romanesque **Riddoch Arts & Cultural Centre** *(theriddoch.com.au; free)*, the town's cultural pacemaker. Built as a theatre in 1906, it's now home to one of Australia's best free regional art galleries, with exhibitions, installations and community displays, open from 10am daily.

Penola & the Coonawarra Wine Region

TIME FROM MOUNT GAMBIER: **40MIN**

Wine tasting in Coonawarra

When it comes to spicy cabernet sauvignon, it's plain foolish to dispute the virtues of the Coonawarra wine region with its *terra rossa* (red earth) soils. Most of the region's 20-something cellar doors are strung along Riddoch Hwy, rolling north from Penola. If this lineup feels daunting, there's a cluster of six standout wineries – each with its own signature style – branching off Memorial Dr, 10km from Penola. Linked by the 5km-long **Coonawarra Wineries Walking Trail**, it's a fine half-day wander through vines.

CRATER RIM WALKS

Blue Lake (Warwar): Mount Gambier's most famous crater, this gentle, wheelchair-friendly circuit (3.6km) offers superb lookouts.

Valley Lake (Ketla Malpi): This 4.2km 'Mountain Trail' circuit rides ridges and crests to link lake views with the lofty Centenary Tower.

Leg of Mutton Lake (Yatton Loo): A 1.8km loop squeezed between Blue and Valley lakes, reborn with regenerating bushland and a tangle of leafy tracks.

Mt Schank: Rugged 2.4km climb (1038 steps) to the summit, with 360-degree views of crater, farmland and distant coast, 18km south of Mount Gambier.

Lake Edward: Secluded 2.5km forestry loop 32km northwest of Mount Gambier featuring the area's best-preserved volcanic maar.

DRINKING IN COONAWARRA: BEST CELLAR DOORS

Bellwether Wines: An irreverent cellar door in an 1868 stone shearing shed, with glamping tents out back to match the artsy vibe. *noon-4pm*

Brand's Laira: Refined yet welcoming winery, some parts dating to 1893. The rosé here is summer in a glass. *9am-4.30pm Mon-Fri, 11am-4pm Sat & Sun*

Majella Wines: Four generations deep in Coonawarra's soil, Majella's relaxed cellar door pours gutsy reds like The Musician, a shiraz-cabernet. *10am-4pm*

Rymill Coonawarra: Fronted by a statue of two rebellious steeds, Rymill rocks the boat by turning out super sauvignon blanc. *10am-5pm*

AUSTRALIA'S YOUNGEST VOLCANOES

Mount Gambier and Mt Schank rose in fire 4300 to 4600 years ago, making them among Australia's youngest volcanoes. Long before geologists arrived, the Buandig people told of Craitbul, their ancestor who lit his hearths across the land – first at Mt Muirhead, then Mt Schank and finally Mount Gambier. But rising waters drowned his fires to form the crater lakes that shimmer here today. The story carries the weight of memory, written in its pocked and folded earth.

At **Riddoch Arts & Cultural Centre** (p759; *11am & 2pm Mon-Fri, 11am Sat & Sun*), free daily screenings of *Craitbul and Volcano – The Movie* bring the landscape's fiery origins to life.

Penola's saints and sinners

Perky little Penola may be ground zero for Coonawarra wine tasting, but it's also famous for its ties to the Sisters of St Joseph of the Sacred Heart, a Catholic order cofounded in 1866 by Australia's first saint, Mary MacKillop. Dive into her story at the **Mary MacKillop Interpretive Centre** *(mackilloppenola.org.au; adult/child $8/free)*, a jaunty building with gregarious entrance pergola and oodles of info. The Woods MacKillop Schoolhouse, Australia's first school for children from lower socioeconomic backgrounds, is also here.

One street north, narrow **Petticoat Lane** has a chequered past. From the mid-1880s to early 1900s, this was the poor side of town, rife with nocturnal pursuits earning it nicknames like 'Fun Alley' and 'Lovers Lane'. A blind eye was turned until 1935 when bright street lights were installed to calm its lusty urges. Now just a handful of ramshackle timber-slab cottages remain; you can freely wander some (allow an hour), others are bookable for overnight stays. Pick up a free 'Walk with History' map at the **Penola Coonawarra Visitor Information Centre**.

Naracoorte

TIME FROM MOUNT GAMBIER: 1¼HR

Delve into fossil-filled caves

The World Heritage–listed Naracoorte Caves are SA's only UNESCO site – though the Flinders Ranges (p786) are hoping to join them soon. The discovery of an ancient fossilised marsupial here in 1969 raised palaeontological eyebrows around the world. David Attenborough even turned up here to film his 1979 BBC series *Life on Earth*.

Naracoorte Caves National Park *(naracoortecaves.sa.gov.au)* now protects 28 limestone caves, including **Alexandra Cave** *(adult/child $27.50/16.50)*, curiously named **Stick-Tomato Cave** *(adult/child $13/8)* and **Victoria Fossil Cave** *(adult/child $39/23)*. At the main entrance, **Wonambi Fossil Centre** *(free entry with cave ticket)* zooms in on life-sized reconstructions of extinct animals, including a giant echidna, *Diprotodon australis* (koala meets grizzly bear) and *Megalania prisca* – 500kg of aggressive goanna lizard.

Beachport

TIME FROM MOUNT GAMBIER: 1¼HR

Coastal drives and calm swims

Beachport is a holiday town on the up – part-fishing haven, part-seaside hideaway. From July to October, barefooted locals

EATING IN PENOLA & COONAWARRA: OUR PICKS

Pipers of Penola: A classy, intimate dining room inside a 1908 church. Superb seasonal fare and wine list. *6-9pm Wed-Sat, 8.30-11am Sun* $$$

Royal Oak Penola: A huge tartan-carpeted dining room serving upmarket pub grub: burgers, curries and schnitzels. *noon-2.30pm & 5.30-8.30pm* $$

Ottelia: Off the highway north of Penola, metal-and-glass Ottelia is one of SA's best secrets. Super sharing plates and pizzas. *11am-3pm Thu-Mon* $$

Upstairs at Hollick: Sit on this winery verandah on a warm afternoon for luscious dining, views and Hollick tastings. *11.30am-2.30pm Fri-Sun* $$$

GEORGECLERK/GETTY IMAGES

Naracoorte Caves National Park

cast from the jetty, beach or reef-rocks, chasing snapper and whiting. The real lure, however, is chasing Southern Ocean views west of town for 8km along the **Bowman Scenic Drive**. Lookouts perch above surf-worn cliffs as beaches unfurl below, including **Salmon Hole**, a brilliant turquoise bay and rare oceanfront swimming refuge, sheltered by beach rock.

The road rumbles north into the coastal fringes of **Beachport Conservation Park**, but you'll need a 4WD to tackle its jagged terrain. Inland, float free and easy in **Pool of Siloam**'s salty lagoon or wander the forested, 1.5km-long **Lake Wooley loop**, tucked just inside the conservation park entrance.

Robe

TIME FROM MOUNT GAMBIER: 1½HR

Heritage streets and dramatic seascapes

Robe is a cherubic little fishing port and holiday hot spot. The sign saying 'Drain L Outlet' as you roll into town doesn't promise much, but history buffs are in for a treat: Robe's heritage-listed limestone buildings date from the 1840s to 1870s. Caledonian Inn (p799) is a stately 19th-century stone pub on the main street, its upstairs rooms fitted with

Ask if the lobster's in. Delicious!

EATING ON THE LIMESTONE COAST: OCEANFRONT DINING

Bliss by the Sea: Just off Kingston SE's foreshore, this coastal nook peddles great coffee and house-baked treats in the old courthouse. *7am-2pm* $$

Waterfront Cafe at the Jetty: Casual diner pairs breezy waterfront tables with locally caught seafood and wraps in Beachport. *7am-3pm* $

Robe Hotel: Right on the shore, Robe Hotel is older than it looks (1847). Sport on the big screens, pub grub on your plate. *10am-11pm* $$

Salt Cafe & Bar: Grab a window seat in SA's southernmost eatery. Seafood with a smile in Port MacDonnell. *8am-4pm Mon-Thu, to 9pm Fri-Sun* $$

THE LONG WALK TO BALLARAT

Robe set up shop as a fishing port in 1846 and is one of SA's earliest settlements. During the 1850s gold rush in Victoria, Robe boomed when the Victorian government whacked a $10-per-head tax on Chinese gold miners arriving to work the goldfields. Thousands of Chinese miners dodged the tax by landing at Robe, then walking 400km to Bendigo and Ballarat in Victoria; 16,500 arrived between 1856 and 1858, with 10,000 in 1857 alone. But the arrivals stalled soon after, when the SA government instituted its own tax on the Chinese. The 'Chinamen's wells' along their route (including one in the Coorong) remain today, as does a memorial to past Chinese arrivals on the Robe foreshore.

RAPHAEL CHRISTINAT/SHUTTERSTOCK

shipwreck-salvaged doors. Smaller but no less appealing is the upstanding little **Customs House** *(adult/child $3/free)* from 1863, now a maritime history museum. Robe's self-guided **Town Heritage Trail** strings together 31 of these landmarks along 3km of walkable backstreets. Grab a free map from the **Robe Visitor Information Centre** *(robe.com.au)*.

The story continues for 6km west of town on the well-signed, wheelchair-friendly **Robe Scenic Trail**. The frayed limestone shoreline makes for a spectacular stroll, particularly when the Southern Ocean waves are surging into Guichen Bay. After seven shipwrecks were recorded here in 1853 alone, the town erected its guiding red-and-white **Obelisk** atop slowly eroding cliffs at Cape Dombey. Nearby, the ruins of Robe's **Old Gaol** similarly deteriorate under the sun and salt. The trail's planned loop back to town was unfinished at the time of research, leaving a breezy 20-minute amble through the backstreets to the start.

East Coast of Coorong National Park

TIME FROM MOUNT GAMBIER: 1¾HR

Detours into the wetlands

In Ngarrindjeri country, the fecund **Coorong National Park** is a lagoon landscape curving along the coast for 145km between Kingston SE (south), Meningie (north) and Goolwa

Obelisk, Cape Dombey

(west). A complex series of soaks and salt pans, it's separated from the sea by the chunky dunes of the Younghusband Peninsula. More than 200 waterbird species thrive here.

Princes Hwy scuttles through Coorong, but you can't see much from the road. For a deep dive, take the 13km unsealed **Coorong Scenic Drive**. Signed as Seven Mile Rd, it starts off Narrung Rd, 10km southwest of Meningie, and takes you right into the landscape with its stinky lagoons, sea mists, rusty fishing shanties and wild emus. The road rejoins Princes Hwy 10km south of Meningie.

With a 4WD, you can access **Ninety Mile Beach**, a well-known surf-fishing spot with the no-frills **Ocean Beach Campground** *(parks.sa.gov.au; from $19.10 per night)* pegged out behind the foredunes. The easiest ocean access point is 42 Mile Crossing, 3km off Princes Hwy and 19km south of Salt Creek.

STORM BOY

Based on the 1964 Colin Thiele novel of the same name, *Storm Boy* (1976) is a much-loved film about a young boy's difficult relationship with his reclusive father and his heartwarming friendship with a pelican called Mr Percival. Filmed around Coorong and in nearby Goolwa, the film propelled 11-year-old Greg Rowe and Aboriginal actor David Gulpilil to stardom and ushered-in a golden age of Australian cinema. *Storm Boy* was remade in 2019, but to lesser acclaim: if you want to get a feel for Coorong National Park before you get there, sit down in front of the 1976 version. Pleasingly, Mr Percival lived to the ripe old age of 33 and died at Adelaide Zoo in 2009.

COORONG CRUISES & CANOES

For a watery perspective on the northern side of the park, try **Spirit of the Coorong** (p748) or **Canoe the Coorong** (p748) boat tours, based in Goolwa on the Fleurieu Peninsula.

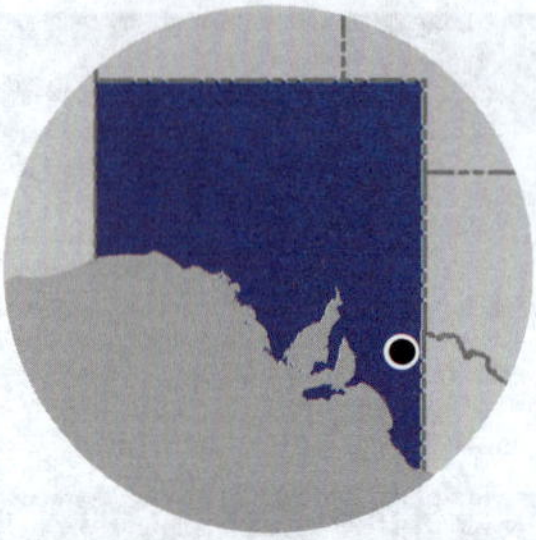

The Riverland & Murraylands

RIVER VIEWS | WINE & PRODUCE | NIGHT SKY

Flowing west from the Victorian border, the incredible Murray River begins its winding 600km descent through South Australia to the Murray Mouth near Goolwa, where the river meets the sea in Ngarrindjeri Country.

The northern section, known as the Riverland, stretching from Renmark and Paringa in the east to beyond Morgan in the west across Erawirung, Ngawait and Ngintait lands, is Australia's largest wine-producing region. With almost 1000 wine grape growers, dozens of wineries and cellar doors and countless licensed venues, relaxing with a glass in hand is a huge part of its appeal. This is also a centre for citrus, stone fruit, almonds and olives, so pack a farm-to-table picnic and enjoy it at one of the many riverfront parks.

South of Blanchetown in Ngangurakú and Peramangk territory, the Murraylands brings some of the world's darkest skies and incredible stargazing opportunities at the Dark Sky Reserve. Camp beneath the galaxies and enjoy the show.

TOP TIP

To prevent the spread of fruit fly and other pests, fresh unprocessed fruit and vegetables (among others) can't be taken into the Riverland. Rather than tossing your produce into the quarantine bins, buy locally instead. For more info on restricted items, see *fruitfly.sa.gov.au.*

GETTING AROUND

Having your own wheels is the easiest way to explore at your own pace. Free and on-demand, 24-hour ferries transport you and your vehicle across the river in 12 locations. To tour wineries without driving, book a bus or river tour – the latter allows you to go from boat to brew at some riverside establishments. The river itself has its own range of transport and leisure options, from historic paddle steamers and easy-going cruises to overnight kayak adventures.

THE RIVERLAND & MURRAYLANDS

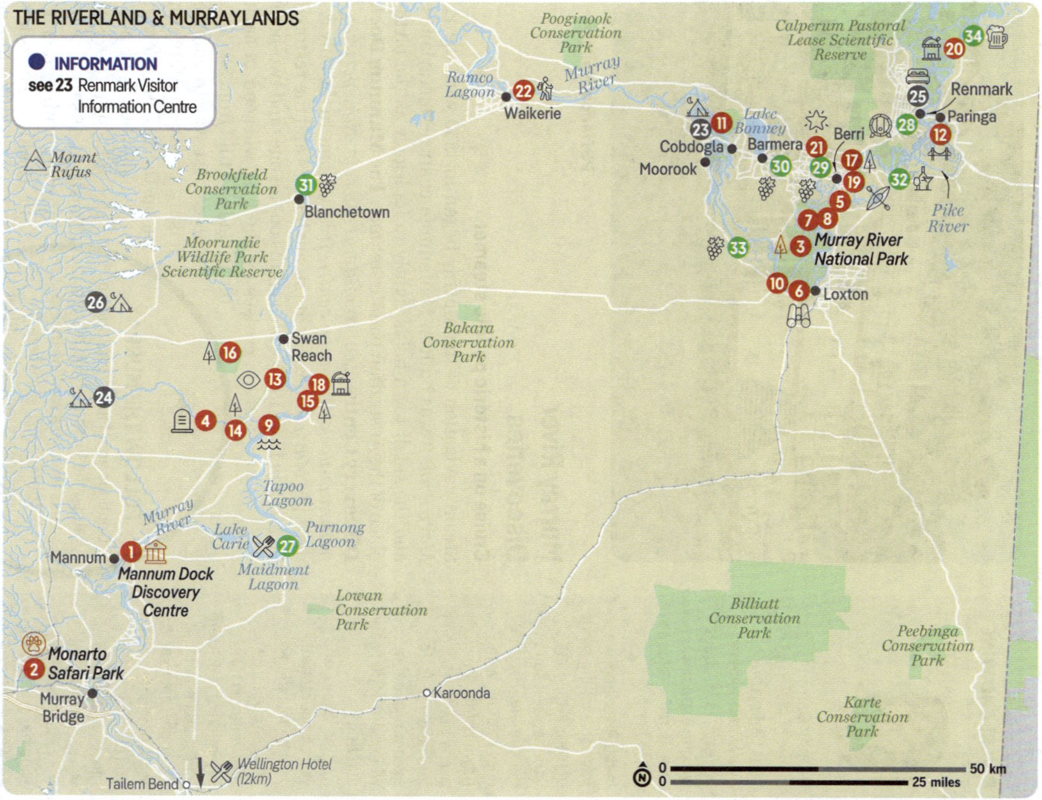

INFORMATION
see 23 Renmark Visitor Information Centre

HIGHLIGHTS
1 Mannum Dock Discovery Centre
2 Monarto Safari Park
3 Murray River National Park

SIGHTS
4 Black Hill Cemetery
5 Gurra Gurra Creek
6 'Heaven' Clifftop Viewpoint
7 Katarapko Creek
8 Lock 4
see 6 Loxton Historical Village
9 Marne River Mouth
10 Milich's Landing
11 Nockburra Creek
12 Paringa Bridge
13 River Murray International Dark Sky Reserve
14 Shell Hill Reserve
15 Sunnydale
16 Swan Reach Conservation Park
17 Wilabalangaloo Reserve

ACTIVITIES
18 Big Bend Lookout
19 Canoe Adventures Riverland
20 Heading Cliffs Lookout
see 1 Juggle House Experiences
see 6 Loxton Pioneer Playground
21 Monash Adventure Park
see 12 Riverland Boat Hire
22 Waikerie Cliff Top Walk

SLEEPING
see 12 Frames
23 Kingston-on-Murray Caravan Park
24 Meldanda Campsite
25 Murray River Queen
26 Towitta Campground
see 34 Wilkadene Cottage

EATING
27 Bowhill General Store
see 1 Pretoria Hotel

DRINKING & NIGHTLIFE
28 23rd Street Distillery
29 919 Wines
30 Bassham Wines
31 Burk Salter
32 Riverland Wine Centre
see 1 Roylancer Distillery Co
see 28 St Agnes Distillery
33 Whistling Kite Wines
34 Woolshed Brewery

RIVERLAND WINE

Bronny Caire, owner of Riverland Wine Centre (p769; *riverlandwinecentre.com.au*), talks about what to expect when sampling the region's wines.

In the Riverland, we have an exciting range of Mediterranean varieties as it suits our climate. They are easy to drink, with flavours that aren't overly bold. You won't find heavy reds, for example, and the whites are light, zesty and fruity.

At the Wine Centre, you can put together your own tasting and sample three to four vintages from a selection of red, white and sparkling wines. We represent over 25 local producers and you can buy by the glass or the bottle. We like to promote the region's smaller winemakers; in doing so, we strive to leave the most sustainable environmental footprint possible.

NORMAN ALLCHIN/SHUTTERSTOCK

PS *Marion*, Mannum

Murray River Discoveries

Cruise on a historic paddle steamer

Steam navigation of the Murray began in 1853 with the PS *Mary Ann*. It was built in Mannum in central Murraylands, and the small town holds tightly to its legacy as the birthplace of the Australian paddle steamer. The **Mannum Dock Discovery Centre** *(exploremidmurray.com.au/experience/mannum-dock-discovery-centre; free)* is home to the only remaining *Mary Ann* relic – its steam boiler – and the restored PS *Marion* from 1897, which chuffs out on one- and two-hour cruises on the first weekend of each month (adult/child from $35/20).

The easiest way to enjoy a leisure cruise in Mannum is on the PW *Mayflower*, the oldest working paddle wheeler in SA, built in 1884. Ninety-minute cruises depart on Tuesday, Thursday, Saturday and Sunday (adult/child $35/20).

A rekindled interest in the region's paddle-steamer

FOLLOW THE MURRAY

Continue your Murray exploration along the Victoria–NSW border. Pass through a working lock in **Mildura** (p619), see where the Murray meets the Darling River in Wentworth and explore Echuca's historic paddle-steamer wharf.

DRINKING IN THE RIVERLAND: FARMGATE WINE TASTINGS

Whistling Kite Wines: Premium organic and biodynamic wines and crispy weekend pizzas. No appointment tastings. *11am–4.30pm Thu–Mon*

Burk Salter: Boutique winery near Blanchetown offering tastings and tours aboard a restored 1927 Chevrolet truck. *11am–4.30pm Sat & Sun*

919 Wines: Family-owned winery and cellar door in Berri specialising in fortified wines and organically certified table wines. *10am–5pm Wed–Sun*

Bassham Wines: An impressive range of reds and whites, plus surprises like the fortified black currant liqueur. *10am–5pm* history has seen funding campaigns and thousands of volunteer hours put into returning previously defunct vessels to their former glory. Upstream in Renmark, the fully restored **PS *Industry*** *(psindustry.org.au; adult/child $35/12)* from 1911 cruises about 20 times per year. For a gold-coin donation you can also explore it dockside, behind the **Renmark Visitor Information Centre** *(renmarkparinga.sa.gov.au)*.

Go with the Flow

Paddling adventures in the Riverland

Contrary to SA's claim as the driest state in the world's driest inhabited continent, the Riverland's **Murray River National Park** *(parks.sa.gov.au)* offers a cool contradiction. Calm currents invite a slow journey through mirrored lagoons, creeks and wetlands – best in early autumn with warm days, cool swims and fewer houseboats than Easter's busy spell.

Gurra Gurra Creek's sheltered launch site, just off Bookpurnong Rd near Berri, makes an ideal starting point for a kayaking expedition. From here, the Murray ambles along at about 1km/h. Count 25km or two to three days to get to **Milich's Landing** near Loxton, navigating **Lock 4** and the **Katarapko Creek** anabranch where you'll find a string of riverside **campgrounds** *(parks.sa.gov.au; from $14.90 per site)* promising gum-shaded serenity and starry skies. Make the return trip upstream along the main river or organise a pickup. For kayak and camping hire, transfers and guided tours, pre-book with **Canoe Adventures Riverland** *(canoeadventure.com.au; from $106 per day min. two kayaks)*.

Alternatively, guests at **Kingston-on-Murray Caravan Park** *(komcaravanpark.com.au)* can hire two-seater canoes (per hour from $12.50) and slip straight into nearby **Nockburra Creek** – arguably, the Riverland's most immersive birdlife-rich wetland. Prefer a powered option? **Riverland Boat Hire** *(riverlandboathire.com.au)* rents roomy pontoons for groups up to 12 (half-day hire from $400) – just bring a driver's licence. Boats depart just south of the landmark **Paringa Bridge**.

Venture into the Dark

World-class star-gazing over dinner

Similar to a World Heritage listing for the night sky, the 3200 sq km **River Murray International Dark Sky Reserve** is Australia's first and one of only a small number worldwide.

FAMILY FUN

Monash Adventure Park: Impressive free park with a range of play equipment, maze, wave bridge and BBQs. A winner for all ages.

Loxton Historical Village: An immersive streetscape (adult/child $12/6), with relocated and recreated buildings preserving pioneer history. *thevillageloxton.com.au*

Loxton Pioneer Playground: A two-minute drive from Loxton Historical Village, this free playground sports a huge climbing frame for big kids.

Monarto Safari Park: Largest open-range safari park outside Africa, with lions, rhinos and giraffes.

Free Ferry Ride: The Murray's dozen ferry crossings, from Cadell (north) to Wellington (south), turn any drive into an adventure.

DRINKING IN THE RIVERLAND & MURRAYLANDS: BREWERIES & DISTILLERIES

Woolshed Brewery: Muthro's converted riverside shearing shed with creative beers, hard lemonade and a shady deck. *11am-5pm Wed-Sun*

23rd Street Distillery: Spacious indoor-outdoor setup in Renmark with a variety of spirits. Tastings, tours and masterclasses. *10am-4pm Sun-Wed, to 10pm Thu-Sat*

St Agnes Distillery: Whisky, gin and brandy tapped and tasted at Angove Family Winemakers in Renmark. *10am-5pm Mon-Fri, 11am-4pm Sat & Sun*

Roylancer Distillery Co: Mannum moonshiner, sampling smooth vodka and single malt whisky on the main drag. *10am-4pm Fri & Sat*

SILO ART TRAIL

Ditch the highway and follow a backroad gallery of silo murals celebrating the characters, animals and stories that have shaped the countryside.

START	END	LENGTH
Paringa	Coonalpyn	364km; 5hr

Start at 1 **Paringa** where artists Jack Fran and Sam Brooks have turned the silos into a river-front storybook. Four giant figures rise from the concrete, layering local heroes with snippets of Murray life: paddle steamers, pelicans and the river's steady rhythm. Cross Paringa Bridge, 82km west, to 2 **Waikerie**. Two clifftop towers salute the region's wildlife: a blue yabbie and regal regent parrot, drawn from the river and mallee below.

Turning south, wheat fields and mallee woodlands fill the skyline. Follow a graded backroad for 65km to near-ghost town 3 **Galga**, where local artist Sam Loxton has honoured the district's wartime medics and soldiers, among them nurse Vivian Bullwinkel, survivor of the 1942 Bangka Island massacre. His mural at 4 **Copeville** splashes with paddock inspiration: a rose-cheeked galah and a brace of Clydesdales ploughing through golden wheat.

Back on the bitumen at 5 **Karoonda**, this working silo lives up to its artwork, busy with merinos and kelpies. Another 70km southeast, 6 **Lameroo**'s twin silos form a stunning 2025 diptych contrasting rural progress and preservation. Finally, swing 91km southwest to 7 **Coonalpyn** where Guido van Helten's montage of local school kids remains one of the state's most recognised public artworks.

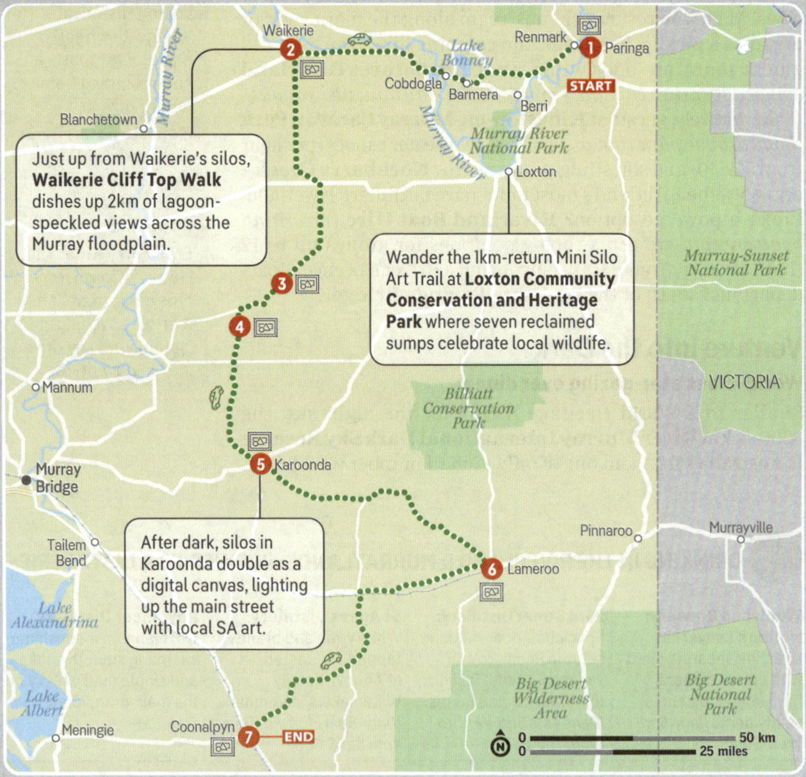

Measured on a scale of zero to 22, the night's darkness here is exceptional, reading around 21.8 to 21.99.

A simple pair of binoculars is enough to get started, but guided tours with telescopes and expert know-how really elevate the view. Setting off from Mannum, 90-minute sunset dinners with **Juggle House Experiences** *(jugglehouse.com.au; adult/child $299/255)* take in the constellations with astronomer commentary. Before booking, check the moon phase – too much light spoils the sparkle.

Top spots for peaceful, crystal-clear stargazing include **Big Bend Lookout**, **Meldanda Campsite** *(adult/child $5.50/2.20 per night)* near Cambrai, the reserve's core site in **Swan Reach Conservation Park** *(free off-grid camping, access by 4WD)*, **Towitta Campground** *($10 per night)* near Sedan, **Black Hill Cemetery**, the riverside reserves in and around Walker Flat (such as **Sunnydale** or the **Marne River mouth**), **Shell Hill Reserve** near Wongulla, or directly from the river on your own houseboat between Younghusband and Blanchetown.

Lions in the Landscape

Roaming Monarto Safari Park

Spread across 1500 hectares in Ngarrindjeri Country, **Monarto Safari Park** *(monartosafari.com.au; adult/child $54/30)* is one of the largest open-range zoos outside Africa – a vast slice of savannah in South Australia's mallee heartland. Home to more than 50 exotic and native species, the park's conservation work spans lions, cheetahs, rhinos and a vital breeding program for Tasmanian devils. Free hop-on hop-off buses with helpful volunteers on board shuttle between the park's seven hubs, arriving every 15 minutes (the last bus leaves the visitor centre at 3pm). Wheelchair-accessible stops make for easy exploring and 12km of walking tracks link enclosures for those who like to roam on foot.

For an extra fee, keeper-led encounters deliver rare insights into Monarto's animals – from meeting ring-tailed lemurs (adult/child $75/60) to hand-feeding Asian elephants ($500). Otherwise, time your lap with the seven free keeper presentations, starting at the chimpanzee platform at 10.30am (on weekends and public holidays). Allow at least five hours if you want to catch them all.

BEST RIVER LOOKOUTS

Waikerie Cliff Top Walk: This 1.7km-long clifftop track wanders along a late-1800 European settlement path, with views to Waikerie's lagoons.

Big Bend Lookout: View high cliffs around this magnificent bend in the river, 10km south of Swan Reach. Great stargazing perch with telescope pads.

Heading Cliffs Lookout: Climb stairs to the Riverland's most iconic watchtower, a 15-minute drive from Renmark.

Wilabalangaloo Reserve: A 1km sweep of sandstone cliffs rises 30m to a riverfront viewing platform, just north of Berri.

'Heaven' Clifftop Viewpoint: This roomy clifftop lookout above Loxton gazes towards Katarapko Island and houseboats at Habel's Landing.

EATING & DRINKING IN THE RIVERLAND & MURRAYLANDS: RIVERSIDE BITES

Bowhill General Store: The Murray's most surprising stop: coffee, burgers and river views in Bowhill. *8.30am-5pm Tue-Sat, 9am-4pm Sun* $

Riverland Wine Centre: Clifftop cafe over a floodplain lookout, pouring 35-plus local drops with regional platters. *11am-4pm Thu-Tue* $$

Pretoria Hotel: Historic Mannum pub with a shady beer garden to watch paddle steamers drift by. *10am-10pm Sun-Thu, to midnight Fri & Sat* $$

Wellington Hotel: One of SA's oldest pubs. Hearty fare, cold beer and ferry views before the Murray enters Lake Alexandrina. *11am-late* $$

Clare Valley & Mid North

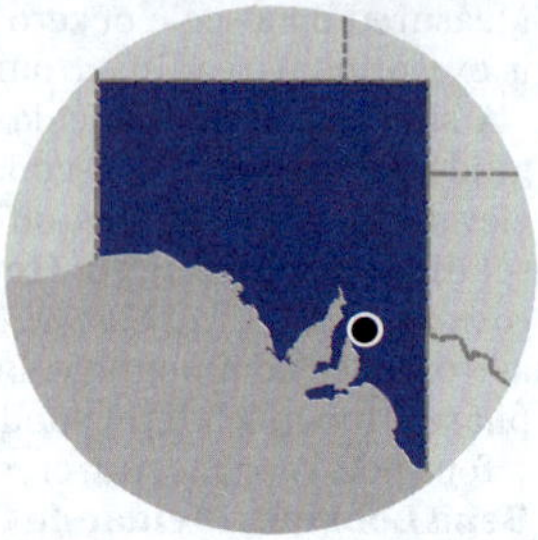

WINE COUNTRY | PIONEER HERITAGE | OUTDOOR ADVENTURES

GETTING AROUND

Having your own wheels – two or four – provides the most flexibility, especially beyond Clare's inner valley and further north. From Adelaide, it's a 90-minute drive along the Northern Expressway (M2), then 90 minutes to Melrose. Car-free travellers can leave Adelaide on Peninsula Coaches' Mid North service. Bike rentals are available in Clare, Auburn and Melrose.

Creased between fertile plains to the west and parched country rolling east, Clare Valley serves as the Mid North's epicurean heart and launchpad to the red-rock ranges and bluebush plains stretching north.

Set on Ngadjuri Country, this pocket of South Australia is threaded with stone cottages and heritage pubs across a string of historic villages, blending old-world charm with a thriving food and wine scene. Shaped by the copper boom of 19th-century Burra, the region's story took root earlier. Explorer John Horrocks planted the valley's first vines at Penwortham in 1840. Today 11 recognised soil types stretching 25km between Auburn and Clare yield wines of remarkable diversity, from renowned rieslings to full-bodied reds.

Beyond the vineyards, the Mid North fans out. Mountain biking trails carve through the ridge lines, hikers ascend Mt Remarkable's forested slopes, and stone-built towns trade in slow lunches and wide verandahs.

Divine Fermentation

Visit the sacred cellars of Sevenhill

In 1851 migrating Jesuit priests laid the foundations of **Sevenhill Cellars** *(sevenhill.com.au)* and, in doing so, helped shape Clare Valley's winemaking legacy. Their divine mission – crafting sacramental wine for the Eucharist – is still faithfully honoured today. Beyond this calling, their cellar door, 1.5km northeast of Sevenhill, pours an award-winning range of table wines. Pop in for a tasting ($10 redeemed on purchase).

Or book ahead for an 80-minute Weikert Cottage Riesling Experience ($80) – a guided tasting of pre-release, current and aged drops with an explanation of valley winemaking traits. Afterwards, pick up a free *Heritage Trail* map to wander an hour-long circuit through Sevenhill history – from underground cellars and a Jesuit crypt to the soaring Gothic silhouette of St Aloysius' Church.

TOP TIP

While the town of Clare (rather than the wider valley) covers day-to-day needs, more charming experiences lie beyond its main drag. Seek out the valley's country hospitality, but check availability and opening hours well in advance – call ahead to confirm a booking.

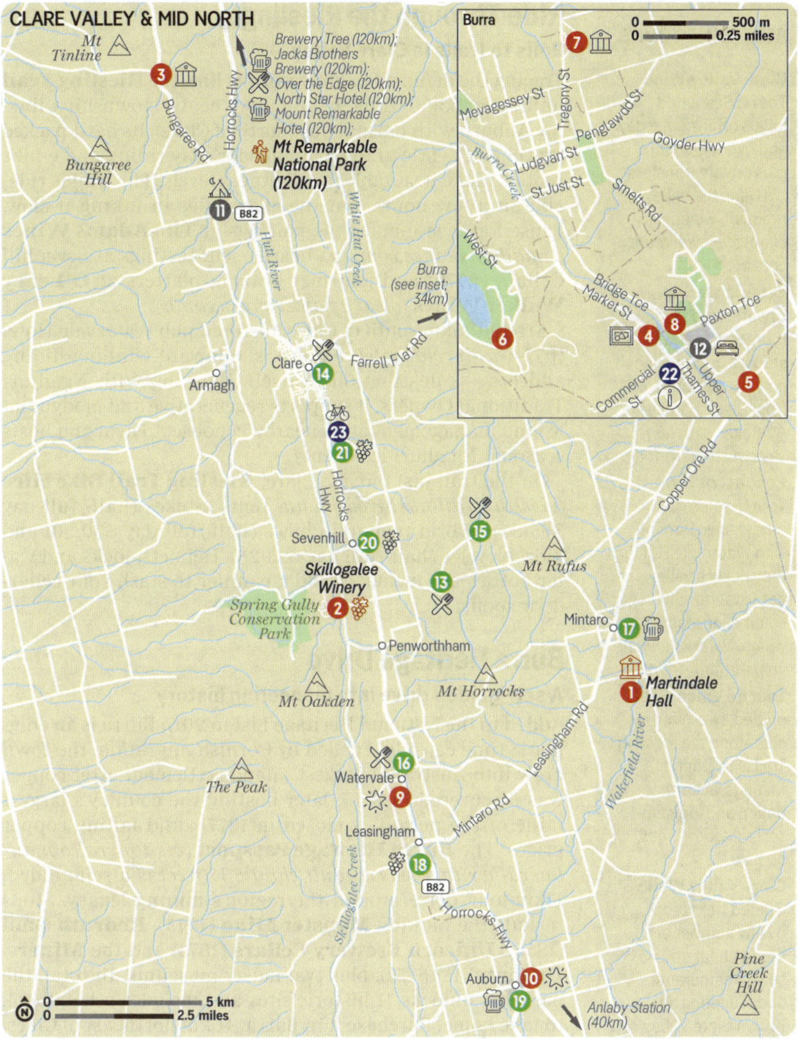

HIGHLIGHTS
1 Martindale Hall
2 Skillogalee Winery

SIGHTS
3 Bungaree Station
4 Burra Regional Art Gallery
5 Miners' Dugouts
6 Monster Mine
7 Redruth Gaol
8 Unicorn Brewery Cellars

ACTIVITIES
9 Penobscot Farm Tour
10 Tour de Vines

SLEEPING
11 Bukirk Glamping
12 Paxton Square Cottages

EATING
13 Bush DeVine Winery Restaurant
14 Mr Mick
15 Slate Restaurant
16 Watervale Hotel

DRINKING & NIGHTLIFE
17 Magpie & Stump Hotel
18 O'Leary Walker Wines
19 Rising Sun Hotel
20 Sevenhill Cellars
see 20 Sevenhill Hotel
21 Tim Adams Wines

INFORMATION
22 Burra Visitor Information Centre

TRANSPORT
23 Riesling Trail Bike Hire

BEST WINE TOURS

Clare Valley Wine Tours: Seasoned locals offer single-day and overnight tours, plus private transfers between the valley's premium wineries. *clarevalleywinetours.com.au*

ExperienceSA: Chauffeured tasting tours with four winery stops, a gourmet lunch and transfer options from Clare, Barossa or Adelaide. *experience-sa.com.au/clare-tours*

Penobscot Farm Tour: Explore biodynamic farming with Watervale Hotel, then enjoy a valley degustation with sommelier-matched wines. *watervalehotel.com.au/farm-tours*

Tour de Vines: Self-guided, two-night cycles along the Riesling Trail with lunches, tastings, accommodation and logistics sorted. *tourdevines.com.au*

Clare Valley Walk: Guided treks loop by any number of the 24 cellar doors, seven restaurants and four pubs on the 100km Clare Valley Wine and Wilderness Trail. *clarevalleywalk.com.au*

Ride Through the Riesling

Rails to trails in Clare Valley

Tracing the defunct Spalding railway line, the **Riesling Trail** unfurls for 33km through the valley's central townships, linking Auburn with Barinia (just north of Clare). Its hard-packed gravel and gentle gradients make for easy riding and e-bike rentals make it suitable for all fitness levels. The trail is rideable in a few hours, but the charm lies in taking it slow. Pause for cheese-and-wine pairings at **Tim Adams Wines** *(timadamswines.com.au)*, heaven-sent tastings at Sevenhill Cellars (p770) and gourmet grazing platters at **O'Leary Walker Wines** *(olearywalkerwines.com)*.

Around 15km south of Clare, restored pub Watervale Hotel (p774; *watervalehotel.com.au*) is an award-winning dining address – a destination in itself. Working with Ngadjuri Traditional Owners, it supports regenerative and biodynamic land management at its nearby Penobscot Farm and hosts seasonal Ngadjuri-led events.

On the trail just outside Clare, **Riesling Trail Bike Hire** *(rieslingtrailbikehire.com.au)* rents e-bikes (half-/full day $65/85), hybrid/mountain bikes (half-/full day $30/50) and kids' bicycles (half-/full day $25/25). Helmets, locks and water bottles are included; add a pannier to stash your cellar-door spoils.

Burra Heritage Drive

A self-guided drive into pioneering history

Added to the National Heritage List in 2017, Burra is an enigmatic time capsule. Fuelled by Cornish migration, the town grew into Australia's largest inland settlement after copper was discovered in 1845, later hosting the country's largest mine of the period. It closed in 1877, amid falling copper prices. The **Burra Heritage Passport** *(visitburra.com.au/burra-heritage-pass; adult/child $35/free)* is a self-guided, 11km-long drive around the region's mining legacy. Stops include the hulking **Monster Mine** (1845), **Redruth Gaol** (1856), **Unicorn Brewery Cellars** (1873) and the **Miners' Dugouts** (1846–51), plus two musty museums. In total, the passport unlocks 11 historic sites and includes a handbook to take home. Purchase it in Burra, 40km northeast of Clare, at the **Burra Visitor Information Centre** *(visitburra.com)*.

EATING IN CLARE VALLEY: WINERY DINING

Mr Mick: Contemporary tapas dining in a refurbished stone distillery, just off the Riesling Trail in Clare. *noon-3pm Sat-Thu, from 6pm Fri* $$$

Skillogalee Winery: Chic lunches at their nearby Barrel House; dining to return to the revamped cottage cellar door in 2027. *noon-3pm Thu-Sun* $$$

Bush DeVine Winery Restaurant: Smart seasonal plates and wine pairings at Paulett Wine's classy bistro, sublime views included. *11am-4pm* $$$

Slate Restaurant: Modern Australian menu celebrating regional flavours and award-winning riesling inside Pikes Winery. *hours vary* $$$

BACKROAD WINERY DRIVE

Slip off the main drag and follow the gum-studded backroads to Clare Valley's vineyard hideaways.

START	END	LENGTH
Hill River Wines	Sussex Squire	25km; 1 day

With most cellar doors welcoming visitors daily between 10am and 5pm, you've got seven hours to swirl and sip. Point your designated driver towards 1 **Hill River Wines**, a family-run estate in rolling farmland, a 10-minute drive southeast of Clare. Celebrated for crisp, fruit-driven rieslings and velvety shiraz, it pours complimentary tastings overlooking a lake.

Head 4km south to 2 **Pikes Wines**, a Clare icon pairing estate-grown wines with pilsners and pales from the next-door brewery. Sample its signature 'traditionale' riesling or dry Luccio sangiovese rosé. Around the corner, 3 **Paulett Wines** pairs a cool-climate riesling with standout dishes like kangaroo bresaola with watermelon in its Bush DeVine Winery Restaurant. If you have an extra hour, detour east to heritage village 4 **Mintaro**. Otherwise, cross Horrocks Hwy to the valley's western flank and 5 **Kilikanoon Wines**, famed for intense, age-worthy grenache. Up the road, 6 **Skillogalee Winery** charms with a stone cottage and rustic-chic restaurant. A short drive west leads to 7 **Jeanneret Wines** where small-batch drops and an on-site brewery back onto Spring Gully Conservation Park. End 8km north at 8 **Sussex Squire**, an intimate, husband-and-wife cellar door atop a vine-draped hill selling limited-release shiraz, grenache and malbec.

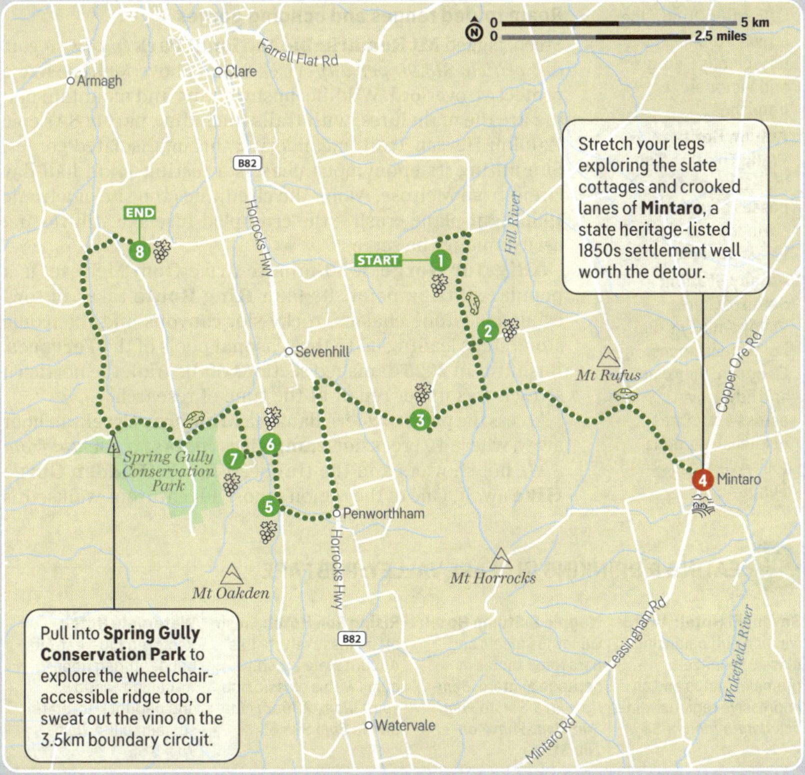

HERITAGE ARCHITECTURE

Martindale Hall: Ornate plasterwork, a grand staircase and slate floors grace this 1879 Mintaro manor. Downton Abbey meets Aussie bush. Closed Tuesday.

Bungaree Station: Bungaree's 1841 bluestone homestead and outbuildings anchor a historic pastoral complex, 12km north of Clare. Self-guided tours.

Burra Regional Art Gallery: The former Post and Telegraph Office (1860), now the region's top free gallery, blends Georgian and Victorian flourishes.

Auburn Heritage Walk: This free 2km loop through Auburn passes bluestone cottages and elegant 19th-century facades.

Anlaby Station: South of Clare Valley, Anlaby's 1860 homestead spans Georgian, Victorian and Edwardian styles across 4 hectares of English gardens; tours Wednesday and Sunday.

Historic Melrose

Wander a small-town sweetheart

Spend half a day wandering the streets and soaking up local heritage in picture-perfect Melrose, the oldest town in the Flinders Ranges. Founded snug in the elbow of Mt Remarkable in 1853, it offers a sublime mix of well-preserved architecture, two classic country pubs, quality accommodation, mountain bike trailheads and parks with actual grass (you won't see much of this further north).

Download the *Historical Melrose* brochure *(melrose-mtremarkable.org.au/history-of-melrose)* for a low-down on old buildings around town, including the towering-stone backstreet **Jacka Brothers Brewery** and impressive 300-year-old **Brewery Tree** (a river red gum).

Ten minutes' walk along the town's main drag Stuart St, the **Melrose Heritage Museum** *(melrosemuseum.com; adult/child $12/5)* occupies the old courthouse (1862) and Melrose's former police HQ. From here local cops once patrolled as far as the Northern Territory! A superb Nukunu exhibition in the former stables reveals perspectives long absent from the colonial narrative.

Hiking Mt Remarkable

Roam folded ranges and echoing gorges

Steep, jagged **Mt Remarkable National Park** *(parks.sa.gov.au; vehicle $13.90 per day)* rises 960m above Melrose like a protective overlord. Wildlife, bushwalking and mountain biking are the main lures, with trails (including part of SA's epic 1200km Heysen Trail) meandering through isolated gorges. Summiting its eponymous peak is a testing 14km half-day climb from Melrose. Along the circuit lies the site of a tragic 1980 light-plane crash – the crumpled fuselage still resting eerily among the scree.

Alligator Gorge, a 30-minute drive from Melrose, is a popular starting point. Its 9km **Ring Route** takes in towering sandstone chasms, rocky slot canyons and the iconic stone steps leading up to the seasonal pools of the **Terraces**. Bushfires in 2025 damaged sections of the trail; the northern stretch was under repair at the time of research.

Access the park's western flank via **Mambray Creek**, an hour away, where 49 creekside **camp sites** *(parks.sa.gov.au; from $33)*, hot showers and the trailhead for the **Hidden Gorge Hike** await. One of the region's most adventurous walks, this

EATING & DRINKING IN CLARE VALLEY: PUB FARE

Sevenhill Hotel: Award-winning pub balancing classic schnitzels, premium plates and an impressive regional wine list. *11am-midnight* $$

Magpie & Stump Hotel: Generous meals and parasoled tables in heritage Mintaro. *8am-11pm Fri & Sat, to 9pm Sun, 11am-9pm Mon-Thu* $$

Rising Sun Hotel: Fresh off a classy refurb, this Auburn stalwart still hums with a classic pub spirit. *11am-9.30pm Mon-Sat, to 5pm Sun* $$

Watervale Hotel: Restored 150-year-old pub featuring floor-to-ceiling windows and paddock-to-plate sustainability. *11am-9pm* $$$

DONNA LATOUR/SHUTTERSTOCK

Alligator Gorge

rugged 17km-long loop undulates between red cliffs, stringybark forest and range-top views across the Southern Flinders.

Biking Mt Remarkable

Grind up, fly down and revel in all things mountain biking

Mountain bikers are well catered for on Mt Remarkable. Widely considered one of South Australia's premier trail-riding networks, its hills are etched with around 80km of track. This slope also marks the start of the 38km **Mt Remarkable Epic Trail**, a fast-flowing ribbon of mountain biking singletrack that packs in more than 1500m of backcountry climbing. For mountain bike info, maps, hire, spares and repairs, head to **Over the Edge** *(otesports.com)* in Melrose. In June wheel yourself into the **Melrose Fat Tyre Festival** *(facebook.com/melrosefattyre)* for a weekend revelling in all things mountain biking.

GOYDER'S LINE

Just off Main North Rd, 3km north of Melrose, is a monument heralding the presence of Goyder's Line. George Woodroffe Goyder drew an imaginary line across the map of SA in 1865, delineating drought-prone land to the north and agriculturally viable land (with more than 10in of annual rain) south. The line arcs up from the Victorian border through Burra and Orroroo, darts down through Melrose, across the top of the Yorke Peninsula and slices off the Eyre Peninsula about halfway down. Over time, Goyder's estimations have proved reliable – farmers ignored his advice at their peril. But all this was before climate change. Where would he draw the line today?

EATING & DRINKING IN MELROSE: OUR PICKS

Jacka Brothers Brewery: This reborn 1878 brewery is an architectural wonder, as are its wood-fired pizzas. *11am-9pm Fri & Sat, to 5pm Sun, Wed & Thu* $$

Over the Edge: Bagels, rolls, sandwiches, baked beans, cake and coffee – morning fuel for every mountain biker. *9am-5pm* $

North Star Hotel: A noble 1854 pub renovated in city-meets-woolshed style, serving hefty steaks and schnitzels. *kitchen: noon-2pm & 6-8pm* $$

Mount Remarkable Hotel: Melrose's 'bottom pub' plates up solid burgers and seafood. *noon-2pm & 6-8pm* $$

Yorke Peninsula

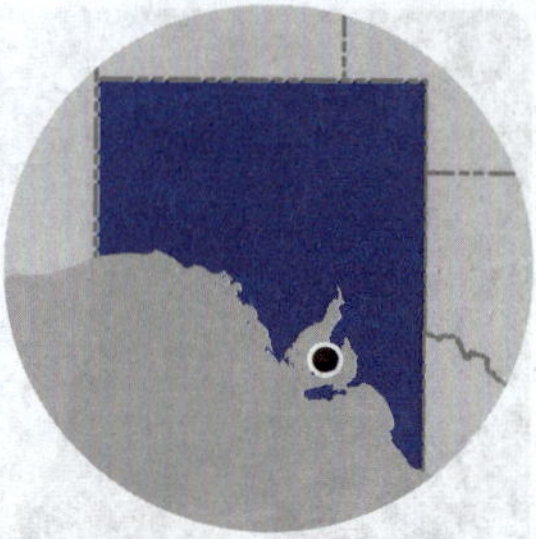

MINING HERITAGE | SEASIDE TOWNS | COASTAL WILDERNESS

TOP TIP

Few places in SA fish as well as Yorke Peninsula: yellowfin whiting in the shallows, tommies (Australian herring) and garfish off the jetties, and blue swimmer crabs scuttling into shore across the warmer months. Before you cast, download the **SA Fishing app** *(pir.sa.gov.au/recfishingapp)* to check bag and size limits.

Narungga Country since time immemorial, the boot-shaped Yorke Peninsula has more recently become prime holiday terrain for beach-bound Adelaideans: sandy towns with caravan parks abound. Come for a weekend, stay a while longer...

For history buffs, the northwestern end of 'Yorkes' has a trio of towns called the Copper Triangle: Moonta (the mine), Wallaroo (the smelter) and Kadina (the service town). Settled by Cornish miners, this area drove the regional economy after a copper boom in the 1860s and is still the peninsula's commercial heartland. Strewn with industrial relics and heritage stone buildings, it's an architectural and archaeological wonderland.

In big-sky country east and south, things are much more agricultural and laid-back, with rolling wheat fields, sleepy holiday hubs, remote surf breaks, wandering wildlife and an empty coastline, including isolated Dhilba Guuranda-Innes National Park on the pointy end of the peninsula's boot.

Into the Copper Triangle

Explore heritage-listed copper mines in Moonta

When copper was discovered near **Kadina** in 1859, mining fever swept across the northern Yorke Peninsula. **Moonta** followed Kadina's lead in 1861, when a local shepherd discovered

GETTING AROUND

An easy drive northwest of Adelaide, figure on two hours to reach Yorke Peninsula's northern areas. Driving is the best way to get around, but the peninsula is long and thin – don't expect to get too far down its length in a day. Roads are uncrowded and super scenic. Yorke Peninsula Coaches runs buses between Adelaide and the main towns. **Copper Trails Bike Hire** *(coppertrailsbikehire.com; adult/child $35/25 for two hours)* in Moonta rents electric and regular bikes to tour the town and copper-mine ruins.

HIGHLIGHTS
1 Dhilba Guuranda-Innes National Park
2 Moonta Mines National Heritage Area

SIGHTS
3 Berry Bay
4 Chinaman's Beach
5 Flaherty Beach
6 Hughes Enginehouse
7 Inneston
8 Miner's Cottage
9 Moonta Bay
10 Moonta Mines Museum
11 North Beach
12 Richmans Enginehouse
13 Shell Beach
14 Stansbury
see 14 Stansbury Museum
15 Wauraltee Beach
16 West Cape

SLEEPING
17 Bayside Glamping
18 Point Turton Caravan Park

EATING
19 Cafe Deluxe
see 17 Marion Bay Tavern
20 Smelter
21 Taste the Yorke

DRINKING & NIGHTLIFE
22 Barley Stacks Wines
see 14 Dalrymple Bar & Restaurant
23 Sunny Hill Distillery
24 Watsacowie Brewing Company

SHOPPING
25 Old Sweet Shop

INFORMATION
see 1 Dhilba Guuranda-Innes National Park Visitor Centre
26 Moonta Visitor Information Centre
see 14 Southern Yorke Peninsula Visitor Information Centre

TRANSPORT
27 Copper Trails Bike Hire

a copper-lined wombat burrow. Cornish miners arrived in the thousands: by 1870, Moonta was the second-biggest town in SA after Adelaide and the Moonta copper mine was one of Australia's richest. **Wallaroo** completed the 'Copper Triangle', with its huge copper smelter.

These days, Kadina (ka-dee-na) is a sprawling service town with some impressive copper-era civic buildings. Wallaroo is a major grain port and fishing town: the shiny Copper Cove Marina is full of expensive boats, there are plenty of pubs full of laid-back drinkers.

Moonta leans hardest into its past, calling itself 'Australia's Little Cornwall'. On the edge of town, **Moonta Mines National Heritage Area** *(moontaheritage.com.au; free)* makes for an interesting few hours of archaeological exploration. It's the cornerstone of the region's UNESCO World Heritage bid in 2024, partnering with Burra's own Cornish mining precinct (p772). Pick up a map at the **Moonta Visitor Information Centre** *(moontatourism.org.au)* and wander. Four main trails (each 2.5km), mostly flat and hard-packed for wheelchair access, weave among the relics; steeper side

YORKE'S SWIM-READY BEACHES

Moonta Bay: Safe, shallow and sparkling, this family favourite has calm turquoise water, long sand flats and an L-shaped jetty ready for summer plunges.

North Beach: Wallaroo's long, hard-packed beach is built for 4WD cruising – over 2km of drive-on sand beside calm, swimmable water. Take air out of your tyres first!

Flaherty Beach: West of Warooka, this tidal stunner serves up white sand and Yorke's warmest waters – ideal for waist-deep wading and envy-inducing photos.

Berry Bay: A twin-cove beauty south of Corny Point with a remote campground and dolphins cruising beyond the sheltered shallows.

Wauraltee Beach: A short hop south of Minlaton, this calm, secluded sweep feels miles from anywhere. Made for sunset lingering.

OZITRAVELER/SHUTTERSTOCK

Dhilba Guuranda-Innes National Park

tracks climb above the old pits. Highlights include **Moonta Mines Museum** *(adult/child $10/4)*, once a grand school with 1100 pupils; the sugary **Old Sweet Shop** across the road; and a fully restored **Miner's Cottage**. Above the scrub, standing guard over the old diggings, tower the Cornish remnants of **Richmans Enginehouse** and **Hughes Enginehouse**. If you're here during May in an odd-numbered year, **Kernewek Lowender** *(kernewek.org)*, aka the Copper Coast Cornish Festival, plates up plenty of hot pasties.

Beach-Town Perfection

Take a break in Stansbury

Towards the southern end of the peninsula's east coast, little **Stansbury** is the kind of place you come for a weekend and end up buying a beach house. The town has everything you might conceivably need for a holiday: a beach, jetty, corner-store deli, caravan park, pub, golf course, Norfolk Island pines swaying in the breeze...oh and a neat little **history museum** *(adult/child $5/1)* in the old schoolhouse. Take it all in along the **Stansbury Coastal Walk** – a breezy, waterbird-filled trail

EATING & DRINKING ON YORKE PENINSULA: OUR PICKS

Cafe Deluxe: A bohemian coffee bunker in central Kadina, with retro furniture and ace cakes. *7am-noon Mon, Tue & Sat, to 4pm Wed-Fri* $

Smelter: Rock 'n' roll cafe in Wallaroo plating up big breakfasts, vegan tofu scrambles, steak sandwiches and proper coffee. *7am-3pm Tue-Sun* $$

Dalrymple Bar & Restaurant: Stansbury's foreshore pub serves excellent pub-style curries, steaks and pizzas. *11.30am-2pm & 5.30-8pm* $$

Taste the Yorke: Moonta's brunch staple delivers excellent coffee, bruschetta, scones and classic Cornish pasties. *8am-4pm* $$

skirting tidal flats and pelican haunts, with wheelchair-accessible sections and clifftop views sweeping across Oyster Bay. Grab a map from the **Southern Yorke Peninsula Visitor Centre** *(stansbury.com)* on Towler St.

End-of-Land Wilderness

Explore Dhilba Guuranda-Innes National Park

The bottom of the boot is largely sheltered from the Southern Ocean's fury by Kangaroo Island, but the surf does reach the peninsula's south coast at far-flung **Dhilba Guuranda-Innes National Park** *(parks.sa.gov.au; vehicle $13.90 per day)*. Expect tumultuous shores, quirky industrial history and sheer cliffs plunging into indigo waters, plus ospreys, emus, kangaroos – and flies in summer (head nets advised).

Possible rips and hefty swells make swimming anywhere here dangerous, but the much-photographed rock pool at **Shell Beach** in the park's northeast corner hides a cool, calm dip. Find it tucked among granite ledges on the beach's eastern side; turn right at the foot of the stairs from the campground.

The standout surf is at **Chinaman's Beach** (3.5km west of the park's visitor centre) and **West Cape** (another 14km on), two of SA's more advanced breaks and regular hosts of the annual Yorkes Classic surf competition.

Between the two, the abandoned gypsum-mining town of **Inneston** is a real curio – home to 200 people in the early 1900s, but zero by 1970. Nosey for 2km around its ghostly remains on the flat **Inneston Historic Walk**, looping past the stables, post office, weedy cricket ground and silvery blue gypsum lake that once kept this place alive. Want to stay a while? The park has five self-contained heritage **cottages** *(from $135)* in Inneston and seven bushy camp sites (from $26.60) beyond.

THE PENINSULA FINGER

Something strange happens below a certain latitude on the Yorke Peninsula (and on adjacent Eyre Peninsula and Kangaroo Island too, interestingly): drivers in oncoming vehicles consistently raise their index fingers from their steering wheels in cheery acknowledgement of your passing. It's a country courtesy, as if to say 'G'day mate. Have a good one!' Stew in city-side cynicism and ignore them if you want. Or slip into a country state of mind and see who can deliver the 'peninsula finger' first, making new friends and spreading goodwill along highways and byways as you cruise happily across Yorkes.

MORE COPPER COUNTRY

For more mid-19th-century copper-mining ruins around SA, head to atmospheric **Burra** (p772) near Clare Valley wine country, or isolated **Blinman** in the Flinders Ranges.

EATING & DRINKING ON YORKE PENINSULA: OUR PICKS

Watsacowie Brewing Company: The bar food at this Minlaton craft-beer shed is almost as good as its red ale. *11am-6pm Wed, Thu, Sat & Sun, to 7pm Fri*

Barley Stacks Wines: South of Maitland, this breezy tin-shed cellar door pours cherry-ripe shiraz from its rustic bar. Weekend pizzas and tunes. *10am-5pm*

Sunny Hill Distillery: Pastoral views complement the spirits and liqueurs at this farmhouse distillery, on a hilltop near Arthurton. Call if they're open. *hours vary*

Marion Bay Tavern: Surveying the bay, this glass-fronted tavern is a top spot for sundowners and all-day wood-fired pizzas. *11am-late Sun-Thu, from 10am Fri & Sat*

Port Lincoln & Eyre Peninsula

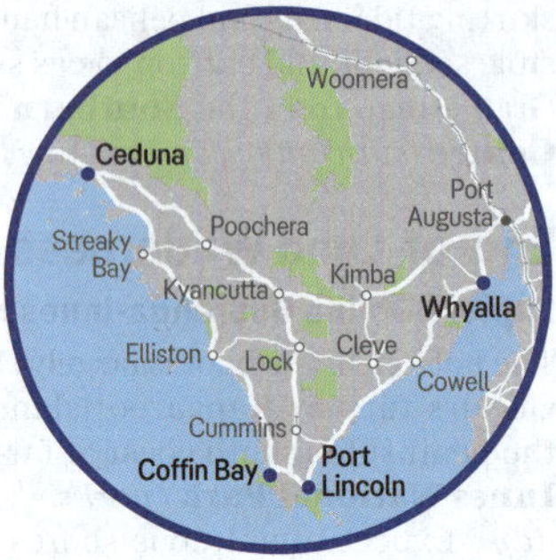

WILDLIFE | COASTAL WILDERNESS | LOCAL HISTORY

Places

GETTING AROUND

With the Spencer Gulf ferry crossing suspended indefinitely, the long-haul drive via Port Augusta is your sole driving option from Adelaide. Stateliner runs regular services along Eyre's east coast to Port Lincoln, plus an inland route to west-coast towns Streaky Bay, Smoky Bay and Ceduna. Regional Express and Qantas operate 50-minute flights from Adelaide to Port Lincoln Airport, 14km north of town. Big-name car-hire companies operate here.

Overlooking broad Boston Bay, Port Lincoln sits raffish and proud at the southern tip of the Eyre Peninsula. Dubbed 'Tuna Capital of the World', it is a prosperous fishing town, with one of Australia's largest commercial fleets bobbing in the marina and a per-capita millionaire count that locals claim beats anywhere else in the country. Tuna dollars power the place, but the vibe is far from conservative – rather, energetic and forward-looking, buoyed by seafood and salt air. Slurp oysters or tuck into freshly caught whiting, then drift between grassy foreshore and the town's lively old pubs and eateries.

Beyond Lincoln (as locals call it), a string of laid-back beach towns line the coast. Eyre Peninsula, home of the Nauo, Barngarla, Wirangu, Mirning and Kokatha peoples at the time of European settlement, is a vast straw-coloured wedge of wheat fields, oyster farms and weather-beaten horizons – as large as Uruguay or Florida.

Port Lincoln

TIME FROM ADELAIDE: **7HR**

Experience raw coastal landscapes

Like the Limestone Coast in the southeast of the state, the shorelines around Port Lincoln (and heading further west towards Ceduna) are craggy and strewn with caves, chasms and grinding surf. Around 13km south of Port Lincoln, sea-salty **Lincoln National Park** *(parks.sa.gov.au; vehicle $13.90 per day)* is no exception: here you'll find roaming emus, roos, brush-tailed bettongs and lazy goannas, set against safe swimming coves, vast dunes, bush campgrounds (from $23.20) and pounding surf beaches. May to October, migrating southern right whales cruise past.

That same dramatic coastline rolls into neighbouring **Whalers Way**, an improbably scenic coastal drive featuring blowholes, cliffs, islands, rock pools and crevasses for 14km along a remote spit of private land. Ever seen a 2.6-billion-year-old rock? Here's your chance (just off Cape Carnot, Eyre Peninsula's most southwesterly point). Before leaving

RUGLIG/SHUTTERSTOCK

Baleen Rock pool, Whalers Way

Port Lincoln, pick up a vehicle permit ($40 per day, camping included) from **Port Lincoln Visitor Information Centre** *(portlincoln.com.au)*.

Observe sharks and sea lions

Port Lincoln is synonymous with sharks – the scariest scenes in *Jaws* were filmed here. Boston Bay is a vast body of water, three times the size of Sydney Harbour, and with this much water to live in (and fish to eat), it's no surprise that the local sea lion and great white shark populations are significant. Local operator **Calypso Star Charters** *(sharkcagediving.com.au)* can take you out for a meet-and-greet. Full-day trips to the nearby **Neptune Islands** *($565 including breakfast, lunch, snacks and hot drinks)* get you kitted up in a steel cage as the big toothy fish glide past. Sightings vary with the seasons; check recent shark activity on its website. Five-hour trips with swimming with sea lions (adult/child $215/155) are also available. Note that research suggests that human interaction with sea mammals potentially alters their behavioural and breeding patterns.

ALMOST ADELAIDE

British explorer Matthew Flinders sailed the HMS *Investigator* into Boston Bay on 25 February 1802, planted the flag for King George III and named the place Port Lincoln after his home county of Lincolnshire. French rival Nicolas Baudin showed up a couple of months later and named it Port Champagny, but Flinders' name stuck.

In 1836 esteemed surveyor Colonel William Light was looking for a decent place to build the new South Australian capital. Kangaroo Island was looking good, as was Port Lincoln, with its vast harbour. But Light noted the absence of a free-flowing river on the craggy islands offshore and decided the surrounding hills were infertile. Adelaide got the gig.

EATING IN PORT LINCOLN: OUR PICKS

Rogue & Rascal: A convincing impersonation of a big-city cafe, with good coffee, beer and wine. *7am-3pm Mon-Fri, to 1pm Sat & Sun* $$

L'Anse: See the patisserie chefs in action, then tuck into the delicious array of flaky pastries. *7.30am-3pm Mon-Fri, from 8am Sat & Sun* $

Del Giorno's: Busy eatery with big breakfasts and top-notch pizzas, pastas and seafood. *7.30am-late Mon-Sat, from 8.30am Sun* $$

Pier Hotel: The best pub on the waterfront, the Art Deco Pier has bountiful beer, live music and reliable seafood. *8am-late* $$

ROAD TRIP

West-Coast Wilderness Drive

Stretching 362km between Coffin Bay and Streaky Bay, Eyre's west-coast drive captures the best of Australia's wild, salt-kissed fringes. Cliffs fall sharply into the Great Australian Bight, cerulean rock pools sparkle at low tide and limestone caves crash with thunderous swells. Wildlife sightings are common. Should the bitumen call further, the horizon rolls into the vast Nullarbor and onto Western Australia.

1 Coffin Bay National Park

West of Coffin Bay, wild **Coffin Bay National Park** (*parks.sa.gov.au; vehicle $13.90 per day*) teems with seabirds, roos, emus and fat goannas. Whales are common in winter and the bay has the world's highest density of resident dolphins. Enjoy ocean views at Point Avoid, walks and kayaking in Yangie Bay. To explore the rest of the park, you'll need a 4WD.

The Drive: Cruise north onto Flinders Hwy. The first 40-minute leg turns west just before Coulta, following signs to Greenly Beach.

2 Mt Greenly

Rising steeply and untamed from farmland flats, the rocky slopes of Mount Greenly are best suited to the sure-footed. The 4.5km, two-hour return hike to the summit delivers Southern Ocean and hinterland views. Soak afterwards in oceanfront rock pools on Greenly Beach.

The Drive: Drive two hours north, breaking in Elliston to refuel tank and stomach.

GASTON PICCINETTI/SHUTTERSTOCK

Murphy's Haystacks

3 Talia Caves

The Southern Ocean gouged two great amphitheatres at **Talia Caves** *(free)*. A 30m-long, timber stairway dips to **The Woolshed**, a vast sandy-floored chamber sloping to a surging inlet (cautious footing needed). About 1km south along the cliffs, **The Tub** is a window on a 30m-deep sinkhole, waves frothing below.

The Drive: Drive 40 minutes north through agricultural plains and coastal scrub. Veer west off the highway into Murphy's Haystack car park.

4 Murphy's Haystacks

The west coast's rock stars are the globular **Murphy's Haystacks** *($4)*, an improbable congregation of 'inselbergs' – colourful, weather-sculpted granite outcrops that have stood here for some 1.5 billion years. Allow 20 to 30 minutes to admire their whimsical forms up close.

The Drive: Allow 35 minutes to follow the gravel road west, then south, flanking Baird Bay's emerald waters.

5 Point Labatt Conservation Park

Perched above the rugged coastline, Point Labatt Conservation Park provides a rare (and free) glimpse of the country's largest mainland colony of endangered Australian sea lions. Bring binoculars.

The Drive: Returning past Baird Bay, follow Seale Bay Rd north, moving beyond Streaky Bay's wheat fields onto Cape Bauer.

6 Cape Bauer Loop Scenic Drive

This 38km, two-hour driving loop from Streaky Bay ventures into windswept dune country – islands, beaches, reefs, blowholes, limestone cliffs and endless ocean. Grab a map at **Streaky Bay Visitor Information Centre** *(streakybay.com.au)*.

BEST SWIM SPOTS

Greenly Beach: Natural oceanfront rock pool topped up by westerly swells, assuring calm, protected water for summer floats, a 30-minute drive north of Coffin Bay.

Venus Bay: Family-friendly cove 76km south of Streaky Bay, with gentle surf, sandy shallows and a jetty for jumping.

Donington Beach: Sandy strip in Lincoln National Park, with safe snorkelling and a 6.2km-long walking trail by Cape Donington Lighthouse.

September Beach: Also in Lincoln NP, popular for calm water, snorkelling and nearby camp sites.

Laura Bay Conservation Park: Paddle, beachcomb and spot seabirds on Laura Bay's twin beaches, shallow, sheltered and fringed with mangroves; 21km south of Ceduna.

Port Lincoln's working-class museums

If the clouds open up while you're in Port Lincoln, don't despair: there are distractions to keep your head dry. Chart Port Lincoln's history of boat-building, sailing and whaling at the tin-shed **Axel Stenross Maritime Museum** *(axelstenross.com.au; adult/family $10/20)*, just north of town on the shores of Boston Bay; look for the marooned 1946 tug *Nabilla* by the highway. Named after the super-capable Finnish seaman who lived here from 1927 to 1980, the museum overflows with refurbished boats and salty relics – set aside an hour to soak it all in.

If you're in town on a Wednesday, the **Port Lincoln Railway Museum** *(eprps.org.au; adult/child $8/3)* occupies the heritage-listed Port Lincoln railway station building from 1927 and the paraphernalia-filled freight shed. A trainspotter's paradise, it shines a light on how this vast peninsula was opened up by rail expansion in the early 1900s.

Whyalla

TIME FROM ADELAIDE: **4HR**

Swim with giant cuttlefish

Eyre Peninsula's east coast carries a sleepy reputation, marked by quiet fishing towns and straw-coloured fields rolling gently into Spencer Gulf. But off the coast, an underwater world shimmers with psychedelic colour. Each winter, between May and August, thousands of giant cuttlefish gather near **Point Lowly** (25 minutes from Whyalla), flashing hypnotic patterns across the rocky reef in a dazzling courtship display. Brave souls can enter the chilly waters from the shoreline at **Stony Point**, 5km west of Point Lowly Lighthouse, with guided dive and snorkel tours available through **Whyalla Dive Shop** *(whydive.com.au; adult/child from $216/160)*. For a dry option, **Cuttys Tours** *(cuttys.au; adult/child $64/42)* runs a 45-minute, wheelchair-accessible glass-bottom boat cruise, also launching from Stony Point.

Coffin Bay

TIME FROM PORT LINCOLN: **30MIN**

Join an oyster farm tour

If you don't like oysters, Coffin Bay mightn't be for you – these slippery bivalves are the town's culinary lifeblood. Take a 90-minute tour with **Oyster Farm Tours** *(oysterfarmtours.com.au; $60)* to see what all the fuss is about. Wade into the water, harvest your own native Angasi oysters and learn to

DRINKING IN PORT LINCOLN: LOCAL PRODUCERS

Port Lincoln Brewing Co: Cosy beer garden with wood-oven pizzas, weekend gigs, Oyster Stout and Cage Diver IPA. *hours vary*

West Coast Distilling Co: Excellent local gin inside a fabulous, red-brick Art Deco railway building. *noon-6pm Wed, Thu & Sun, to 10pm Fri & Sat*

Jump Ship Brewing: Jump ship to Port Lincoln's industrial backstreets for crafty taps, tacos and tapas. *noon-10pm Wed-Sat, to 8pm Sun*

Boston Bay Wines: Raise a riesling on Port Lincoln's northern outskirts. Watch whales glide through the bay in winter. *11am-5pm*

shuck 'em, sitting on a semi-submerged tour deck called Salt Water Pavilion. If this gets your juices flowing, head four hours up the highway to Ceduna in early October for **Oysterfest** *(cedunaoysterfest.com.au)*, the undisputed king of Australian oyster parties.

Ceduna & the Far West

TIME FROM PORT LINCOLN: **4HR**

Ceduna's First Nations arts centre

Aboriginal artists from South Australia's far west, including isolated communities Oak Valley, Yalata, Scotdesco and Koonibba, draw on traditions stretching back thousands of years. **Ceduna Arts & Culture Centre** *(artsceduna.com.au; free)*, open weekdays, carries that lineage today, supporting over 140 artists in transforming these ancient forms into contemporary canvases, prints and ceramics. Drop in and watch creativity in real time, then browse the gallery and take home a piece stitched with desert, sea and Country. At the time of research, the centre was relocating to new premises just behind the foreshore. Its Facebook page *(facebook.com/ceduna aboriginalartsandculturecentre)* has the latest on progress and local exhibitions. Until then, the free **Mint Bush Gallery** on McKenzie St is stocking a selection of artists' works.

Whale watching at Head of Bight

It's 480km from Ceduna to the Western Australian border. About 280km down the road (three hours' drive), you'll arrive at the turn off for the spectacular, 120m-high Bunda Cliffs at **Head of Bight** *(headofbight.com.au; in-season adult/child $20/9)* – literally at the head of the vast Great Australian Bight. Viewing platforms, ramps and boardwalks here (all wheelchair-accessible) overlook a major southern right whale breeding ground. Whales migrate here from Antarctica, and between June and October there's a very good chance of spying some cavorting offshore. Check with **Ceduna Visitor Information Centre** before you make the trek: it has up-to-date info on whale sightings.

GULLIVER'S TRAVELS IN CEDUNA

According to the map coordinates in Jonathan Swift's famous 1726 novel *Gulliver's Travels*, the islands of St Peter and St Francis, a few kilometres off the coast of Ceduna in the Nuyts Archipelago, are where the tiny folk of Lilliput reside. It's likely Swift drew inspiration from the adventures of 158 Dutch sailors aboard the *Het Gulden Seepaart*, a Dutch East India Co ship that navigated these waters in 1627. Drive or a walk out to **Pinky Point Lookout** in Thevenard, Ceduna's weather-beaten port suburb, and squint towards the southern horizon. St Peter Island might be visible, though the Lilliputians certainly aren't...but wouldn't life be dull without a little bit of imagination?

EATING ON THE WEST COAST: OCEANFRONT DINING

Oyster HQ: Devour oysters, tapas, chowder and cake at the best spot in town, right on Coffin Bay's esplanade. *10.30am-7pm* $$

Drift: Taking in Streaky Bay's cove from the deck, grab seafood, salads and tasty big breakfasts. *9am-2.30pm Tue, Wed & Sun, 9am-2.30pm & 6-8.30pm Thu-Sat* $$

Streaky Bay Hotel: Streaky's red-brick 1866 pub is great for a beer, a steak or a hefty schnitzel. *7-9am, noon-2pm & 6-8.30pm* $$

Ceduna Oyster Barn: Pick up a box of freshly shucked molluscs and head for Ceduna's foreshore. *11.30am-3.30pm Mon, 10am-7pm Tue-Fri* $$

Flinders Ranges

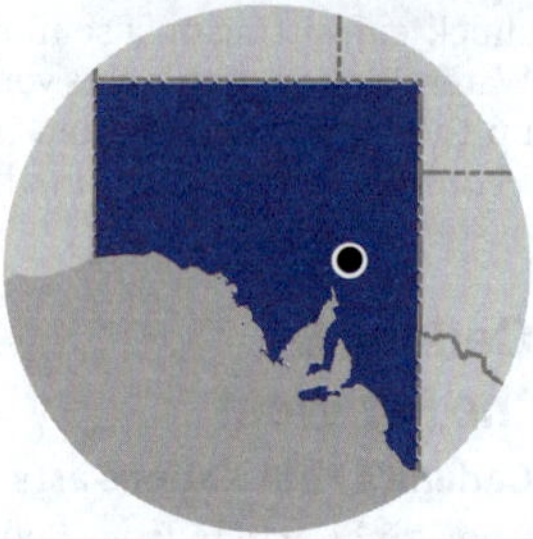

MOUNTAIN WILDERNESS | HISTORIC TOWNS | COUNTRY PUBS

TOP TIP
Don't underestimate the desert. Towns like Port Augusta and Quorn feel urbane at times, but you're right on the edge of Australia's vast central deserts. Driving times can be lengthy. Pack plenty of water and ensure your vehicle can handle highway heat before hitting the road.

Known simply as the Flinders, this ancient mountain range is an iconic South Australian environment. Jagged peaks and escarpments rise up north of Port Pirie and track 400km north to Mt Hopeless. The colours here are remarkable: as the day stretches out, the mountains shift from mauve mornings to ochre-red sunsets. Emus wander across roads and yellow-footed rock wallabies bound from fossil-filled boulder to boulder. Come for the wilderness, stay for the county hospitality: there are some cracking good country pubs down below the ridge lines here.

The northern Flinders Ranges are home terrain for the Adnyamathanha peoples who traditionally prized these peaks for their red ochre deposits, used in medicines and rituals. Further south, the lands of the Nukunu extend from Port Pirie to Quorn; and Barngarla Country, running west from Hawker towards Port Augusta and the Eyre Peninsula.

Gateway to Arid Lands

Desert life at Port Augusta's Arid Lands Botanic Garden

Framed by the Flinders' westernmost peaks, Port Augusta sits at the top of Spencer Gulf – a natural gateway to the Eyre Peninsula and desert where only resilient plant species survive.

GETTING AROUND

Exploring the Flinders under your own steam or on a guided tour is best. Cycling is possible in cooler months, but distances and exposure make it impractical for many. The major roads into Quorn, Hawker, Wilpena Pound and Parachilna are sealed, but others are mostly gravel (navigable in a regular car if you take it slow). Check unsealed road conditions with the **Department for Infrastructure and Transport** *(dit.sa.gov.au/outbackroads)* or call the Outback Road Report (1300 361 033) – after rain, there are often wash-outs and road closures.

HIGHLIGHTS
1 Ikara-Flinders Ranges National Park

SIGHTS
2 Australian Arid Lands Botanic Garden
3 Beltana
4 Hammond
5 Heritage Blinman Mine
6 Kanyaka Station
7 Nilpena Ediacara National Park
8 Razorback Lookout
9 Wilson
10 Woolshed Flat

ACTIVITIES
see 5 Wadna

SLEEPING
11 Discovery Resorts Wilpena Pound
12 Rawnsley Park Station
13 Teamsters Campground
14 Trezona Campground

EATING
see 11 Discovery Resorts Wilpena Pound
15 Flinders Food Co
see 5 Miners Crib Cafe Bakery
see 12 Woolshed Restaurant

DRINKING & NIGHTLIFE
16 Cradock Hotel
17 Flinders Gin Distillery
see 5 North Blinman Hotel
18 Prairie Hotel
see 3 Royal Victoria Hotel

INFORMATION
see 17 Flinders Ranges Visitor Information Centre
see 11 Wilpena Pound Visitor Information Centre

TRANSPORT
see 17 Pichi Richi Railway

QUORN'S CINEMATIC STREETS

Is Quorn (pronounced 'corn') a film set after the crew has gone home? With as many jeering crows and abandoned rail sleepers as people, this little outback town has a dusty, well-weathered vibe. But pub-lined Railway Tce and its broad backstreets are certainly photogenic – a virtue recognised by location scouts for iconic Australian films such as *Gallipoli*, *The Shiralee*, *The Tracker* and *Sunday Too Far Away*.

Wander the streets and scope out your next big-screen epic. There are a couple of decent eateries and **Flinders Gin Distillery** *(flindersgin.com.au; $20 tastings)*, so you'll have somewhere to sit while you compile your notes.

JOSH WEST/LONELY PLANET

Nilpena Ediacara National Park

Get the vegetative low-down a couple of kilometres north of town at the excellent **Australian Arid Lands Botanic Garden** *(aalbg.org; free)*. Expect 250 hectares of sand hills, clay flats and desert botany, with a bird list nudging 150 species. Explore on your own, observing wildlife from two purpose-built hides. Trails range from a wheelchair-friendly, 500m wander through the Eremophila Garden, to a 4.5km-long loop to Red Cliff Lookout. One-hour **guided tours** *(adult/child $10/6)* depart from the visitor centre at 10am weekdays. Its cafe is a sweet spot to refuel.

All Aboard the Outback Explorer

Riding the Heritage Pichi Richi Railway

When the first train rattled out of Port Augusta for Quorn in 1879, it marked South Australia's push into the outback and the birth of the original *Ghan* narrow-gauge railway line. The legendary route would eventually crawl its way north to Alice Springs (p850). It has since been rebuilt further west, but a lovingly restored stretch survives as the **Pichi Richi Railway** *(pichirichirailway.org.au)*.

Riding the trains that still roll out of Quorn railway station, also home to the **Flinders Ranges Visitor Centre** *(flindersranges.com)*, is a wholesome throwback: polished leather seats, carriage captains recounting history, plumes of steam rising through Flinders' jagged peaks. The

Take cash; the wi-fi doesn't always work out here

EATING IN NORTHERN FLINDERS: OUR PICKS

Discovery Resorts Wilpena Pound: The in-house restaurant puts a creative spin on beef, kangaroo and barramundi. *7-9.30am, noon-2pm & 5.30-8.30pm* $$$

Flinders Food Co: Hawker's cool cafe sasses up the town with saltbush lamb tacos and tiramisu French toast. *7.30am-3pm & 5.30-8pm Tue-Sun* $$

Woolshed Restaurant: Chic dining at Rawnsley Park Station, north of Hawker. Arrive for happy hour (4.30pm) and order the roo. *5.30-8.30pm* $$$

Miners Crib Cafe Bakery: Pies, pasties, coffee and quandong pie – fuel for a big day of Blinman copper mining. *9am-4pm Mon-Sat, to 3pm Sun* $

Pichi Richi Explorer *(adult/child $76/38; 2½ hours return)* turns back at **Woolshed Flat**, but not before tea and scones in the old schoolhouse. Just pack a layer; the trundle turns breezy when passengers drop the window for photos.

Blinman's Copper Credentials

Visit the historic copper mine

About an hour north of Wilpena along a sealed road, Blinman – one of SA's highest towns at 610m – is a charming relic of its mining heyday. The place owes its existence to the copper ore discovered here in 1859 and the smelter built in 1903 to process it. But the boom went bust and 1500 folks booted it out of town. The old copper diggings live on as **Heritage Blinman Mine** *(heritageblinmanmine.com.au; adult/child $40/20)*. Excellent 50-minute tours delve into its subterranean stopes and gaping cavities; book ahead as it can get busy. Above ground, a self-guided loop with interpretive boards guides you around 1km of kilns, shafts and the open-cut lookout.

The Origin of Life

Explore Nilpena Ediacara National Park

Formally ratified in 2004, the Ediacaran Period (635 to 541 million years ago) became the first new geological timescale added in 120 years, its recognition secured by fossils found in Flinders' long-vanished seabed. First unearthed by geologist Reg Sprigg near the eponymous Ediacara Hills in 1946, the ancient imprints are the oldest record of complex life on Earth. The site now lies within **Nilpena Ediacara National Park** *(parks.sa.gov.au)*, a saltbush-speckled expanse that was formerly a pastoral station. Access, mid-March to December, is by guided tour only. Meet your ranger guide at the park entrance, one hour north of Hawker.

A three-hour **Fossil Field Exploration Tour** *(adult/child $170/102)* takes you out to active dig sites where slabs of fossil-stamped seabed are revealed in situ. Back at the visitor precinct (the remodelled blacksmith's), the experience ends at *Alice's Restaurant Bed*: a 10m-long slab of fossilised seafloor brought to life with immersive light, sound and narration, tracing the rise of early multicellular life. Fully accessible, the interactive display allows visitors to encounter life's earliest etchings up close and can also be experienced on the two-hour **Ediacara Experience Tour** *(adult/child $85/51)*.

FLINDERS' FORGOTTEN TOWNS

Kanyaka Station: Stone chimneys and tumbledown cottages in a once-thriving station, 26km south of Hawker.

Wilson: Right above Kanyaka, boards interpret Wilson's rubble and preserved walls of the stationmaster's cottage.

Farina: This town, 220km north of Hawker, had two breweries, a church and brothel in the 1880s. Volunteers fight to keep its ruins upright; the bakery fires seasonally.

Beltana: Surveyed in 1873, Beltana's interpretive panels tell Adnyamathanha, Afghan and European stories, 134km north of Hawker. The pub reopened in 2025 after 68 years.

Hammond: All but abandoned, 40km southeast of Quorn: a church, store and pub with no beer.

DRINKING IN NORTHERN FLINDERS: OUTBACK PUBS

Prairie Hotel: Parachilna's iconic highway watering hole also has a brewery in the front bar. Unbeatable Fargher lager. *11am-9pm Tue-Sun*

Cradock Hotel: A brisk 27km drive south of Hawker, this roadside haunt is great for beer, pizza and tunes. *11am-late Tue-Sat, to 3pm Sun*

Royal Victoria Hotel: Beltana's pub is back pouring after 68 dry years. Simple country cooking and home brews, deep in the outback. *Mar-Nov*

North Blinman Hotel: Chunky slate floors, old-time photographs and cold beer collide at this 1869 'pub in the scrub'. *10.30am-late*

BMPHOTOGRAPHER/SHUTTERSTOCK

Bunyeroo Gorge Scenic Drive

TOP EXPERIENCE

Ikara-Flinders National Park

An SA icon, semi-arid Ikara-Flinders Ranges National Park is laced with craggy gorges, saw-toothed ranges and creek beds. Scenic drives and walks reveal abundant wildlife and wildflower-specked plains. Abandoned homesteads and Adnyamathanha rock art add a human layer to 800 million years of geological strata, now central to Flinders' bid to join UNESCO's World Heritage list.

DON'T MISS

- Adnyamathanha Tour
- Tanderra Saddle Hike
- Brachina Gorge
- Bunyeroo Gorge
- Razorback Lookout
- Scenic Pound flight

Ikara Hikes

The park's big-ticket item is 80-sq-km natural basin **Ikara** (Wilpena Pound), an astonishing, sunken elliptical valley ringed by gnarled ridges. Don't let anyone tell you it's a meteorite crater. The easiest way to get a look inside is via the 7km-return walk from Discovery Resorts Wilpena Pound (p788) to Wangarra Lookout; count around three hours via the forlorn Hills Homestead. The harder, near-full-day, 19km-long circuit up Tanderra Saddle along the ridge of St Mary Peak (Ngarri

PRACTICALITIES

- *parks.sa.gov.au/parks/ikara-flinders-ranges-national-park* • vehicle $13.90 per day • open year-round

Mudlanha) is brilliant, albeit a thigh-pounding scramble at times. Restrict your climbing to the ridge and, out of respect fot its traditional significance, don't venture to St Mary Peak itself. For a shorter challenge, the up-and-back track (5.6km) to Mt Ohlssen Bagge delivers one of Ikara's great panoramas. Before hiking, grab maps, snacks and trail updates at **Wilpena Pound Visitor Information Centre**.

Adnyamathanha Tours

For a deeper understanding of the park's living heritage, explore with a First Nations guide. At **Wadna** *(wadna.com.au)*, just outside Blinman, a 50-minute drive north of Ikara, tag-along tours are led by Adnyamathanha man Kristian Coulthard. Short to full-day tours are layered with modern history, geology and Dreaming stories (Yura Muda). Locations include **Sacred Canyon** *(adult/child $120/65)*, where petroglyphs and paintings still cling to sandstone walls; and **Dingly Dell** *(adult/child $110/55)*, featuring engravings of prehistoric creatures dating back 40,000 years. Tours are personal, powerful and get booked out – reserve in advance or call 0428 545 566 for last-minute availability. Hand-carved artefacts by Kristian and woven pieces, jewellery and artworks by other local makers are sold in the Wadna shop.

Back at **Wilpena Pound Resort**, visitors are welcome to join a free 'Welcome to Country' tour, departing daily at 4.30pm (March to November) or 6pm (December to February). Meet on the lawn in front of the reception; no bookings required, but call ahead (1800 805 802) to confirm it's running.

Scenic Drives

Spanning 950 sq km, this park is big-sky country writ large, with several geology-rich drives threading through the landscape. Beyond park entry, there is no additional fee to access these gravel trails, typically safe (with care) for high-clearance 2WDs. Check road conditions with Wilpena Pound Visitor Centre before driving off.

Bunyeroo Gorge Scenic Drive (31km) sets off 5km north of Wilpena Pound Visitor Centre; a sign on Flinders Ranges Way points you west. Take three leisurely hours to navigate the track's steep climbs, tight turns and creek crossings. Highlights include the Flinders' most photographed vista at **Razorback Lookout** (aim for sunrise to see the Heysen Range glowing fiery red) and the colour-banded cliffs of Bunyeroo Gorge.

The track eventually bumps into Brachina Gorge Rd, halfway along the **Brachina Gorge Geological Trail**, stretching 20km east-west between Flinders Ranges Way and Brachina Gorge. Slicing through the Heysen Range, Earth's history is laid bare in sedimentary layers spanning 650 to 520 million years. Look for a golden spike (actually a bronze plaque) set into the rock at Enorama Creek, 500m east of **Trezona Campground**. This Global Boundary Stratotype Section and Point (GSSP) marks the start of the Ediacaran Period (635–541 million years ago) – the only one of its kind in the southern hemisphere.

ADNYAMATHANHA DREAMING

Land and nature are inseparable for the Adnyamathanha Traditional Owners – collectively, the 'Hill People' made up of Wailpi, Kuyani, Jadliaura, Piladappa and Pangkala – who've traded and enriched stories to explain the Flinders' spectacular landscapes. The rugged walls of Ikara (Wilpena Pound), for example, are the bodies of two *akurra* (giant snakes) who swallowed those taking part in an initiation ceremony. Too full to move, they willed themselves to die, their bodies forming the landmark.

TOP TIPS

- Late winter into spring is prime time: while the coast chills, the Flinders sits in the mid-20s with wildflowers spilling across the plains. Summer is scorching; many trails and tours close.
- Aim for Razorback Lookout or Stokes Hill at dawn when the first light ignites mountain ranges red.
- Camp away from the lights of Wilpena Pound Resort to witness some of Australia's darkest, starriest skies.
- Brachina Gorge is prime yellow-footed rock wallaby territory – late afternoon is best.
- Pack a red-light torch for after-dark walks – it won't disturb nocturnal wildlife.

Both drives complete a six-hour circuit back to the highway. Better still, roll out a swag overnight at Brachina Gorge, one of the Flinders' best spots for spotting yellow-footed rock wallabies. **Teamsters Campground** *(from $26.60)* is a popular choice.

Scenic Flights

Take in a bird's-eye read of deep-time geology from the air. **Chinta Air** *(chintaair.com.au; from $210)* runs fixed-wing flights – 20-minute joy rides to hour-long loops – over the park from **Rawnsley Park Station** *(rawnsleypark.com.au)*. Pilots double as guides, pointing out ridge tops and ancient seabeds you'd struggle to recognise from the ground. Flights run on demand with a two-person minimum. Bookings are essential. If you've got time (and budget), longer flights stretch north into the outback or east to **Kati Thanda-Lake Eyre**.

Multiday Trek

Australia's longest-marked hiking trail, the free, two-month **Heysen Trail** (1200km), starts on the Fleurieu Peninsula and saves its most dramatic terrain for the park's northern reaches. The journey strings together valleys, rocky creek beds and three steepling hauls to ABC Range, Razorback Lookout and Bridle Gap on the Pound's southern rim. Camp sites break the hike into days of 10km to 20km; food drops, logistics and scorching summer temps require extra planning this far north.

Big Heart Adventures *(bigheartadventures.com.au; $3780 including transfers, meals and off-trail beds)*, offers guided daypack-only treks taking in the trail's final 85km across seven epic days.

UNESCO NOMINATION

Together with Vulkathunha-Gammon Ranges and Nilpena Ediacara (p789) national parks and historic pastoral lands, Ikara-Flinders Ranges National Park anchors the region's World Heritage bid. Recognised globally for its geological and palaeontological importance, the Flinders is seeking to become Australia's 22nd UNESCO site – and SA's second (after Naracoorte Caves; p760). A decision is expected by 2027.

HEATHER RUTH ROSE/SHUTTERSTOCK

Kati Thanda-Lake Eyre

Coober Pedy

LIFE UNDERGROUND | OPAL MINING | DESERT DETOURS

Arriving in cosmopolitan Coober Pedy (there are dozens of nationalities here, including the local Kokatha and Arabana peoples), parched desert becomes riddled with holes and piles of dirt. The reason for all this rabid digging is opals – the 'fire in the stone'. Discovered nearby in 1915, these gemstones turned the small town into a mining mecca. With swarms of flies, no trees, 50°C summer days, cave-dwelling locals and rusty car wrecks, you might feel you're in a post-apocalyptic wasteland, but it sure is interesting! The desert around town is jaw-droppingly desolate, a fact not overlooked by international filmmakers who've come here to shoot end-of-the-world epics like *Mad Max Beyond Thunderdome, Red Planet, Ground Zero, Pitch Black* and the slightly more believable *Priscilla, Queen of the Desert.*

GETTING AROUND

Coober Pedy is a nine-hour, 845km dash into the desert from Adelaide. If you can't face the endless highway (a really well-maintained road), Regional Express flies here several times weekly. Hire a car at the airport or bum a ride into town and explore on foot. Most of the main sights are walkable; just bring a big hat and water.

Fire in Stone

Uncover opal mines, old and new

Opal mining is Coober Pedy's economic lifeblood: a good percentage of the population spends its time tunnelling underground or 'noodling' through piles of rubble above, looking for leftover gems. For a terrific introduction to these artful practices – plus local history, fossils, desert habitats, Aboriginal culture and ecology – duck underground into the **Umoona Opal Mine & Museum** *(umoonaopalmine.com.au; free)*, one of the town's only wheelchair-friendly dugouts. Daily **tours** *(adult/child $15.50/8.50)* dig deeper still.

A two-minute drive away is **Old Timers Mine** *(oldtimersmine.com.au; adult/child $15/5)*, a honeycomb of underground passages, first mined in 1916. Take a self-guided tour in the museum and discover a recreated 1920s underground home. There's a free noodling pit too, for post-tour discoveries. To see a functioning operation, visit **Tom's Working Opal Mine** *(tomsopalmine.com; from $15)*, 2km southwest of town. Guided and self-guided tours involve donning a yellow hard hat to explore square- and round-cut mine shafts. You can also see a

TOP TIP

Even when it's face-meltingly hot in summer, subterranean temperatures never exceed 23°C – no air-con is required in underground hotels. Some places to stay have above-ground and underground rooms.

HIGHLIGHTS
1 Old Timers Mine

SIGHTS
2 Big Miner
3 Big Winch
4 Big Winch 360
5 Catacomb Anglican Church
6 Catholic Church of St Peter & St Paul
7 Faye's Underground Home
8 Spaceship
9 Umoona Opal Mine & Museum

ACTIVITIES
10 Coober Pedy Wellness Labyrinth

SLEEPING
11 Desert Cave Hotel
12 Lookout Cave Underground Motel

EATING
see 4 Big Winch 360 Cafe & Bar
13 CK Confectionaire
14 John's Pizza Bar & Restaurant
15 Outback Bar & Grill

ENTERTAINMENT
16 Coober Pedy Drive-In

INFORMATION
17 Coober Pedy Visitor Information Centre

'blower', a 'bosun chair' and 'black lighting' in action – Coober Pedy mining must-haves. Check summer hours: even miners take a break when it gets too hot out here.

A Matter of Faith

Visit Coober Pedy's underground churches

With so many nationalities in town, it's no surprise that a mix of religions is practised. Statue-filled nooks and hushed classical music lend sweet appeal to Coober Pedy's first underground church, the diminutive **Catholic Church of St Peter & St Paul** on Hutchison St. Over the hill to the north, **Catacomb Anglican Church** is a simple, cross-shaped bunker with pews aplenty. About 3km east of town, the **Serbian Orthodox Church** is Coober Pedy's most impressive subterranean church, with intricate carvings, stained glass and a gorgeous vaulted ceiling. Flip the lights off on your way out.

Big Winch 360

Tuck into a movie and meal with views

Wondering what the big bucket is up on the hill? It's the **Big Winch**, an oversized reproduction of a mining tool with knockout views extending all the way over Coober Pedy to Kanku-Breakaways Conservation Park. Inside, **Big Winch 360** *(bigwinch360.com.au; adult/child $25/15)* is a slick wrap-around cinema experience unpacking the history of the town and its sundry mining characters. Alongside the 40-minute 'circlevision' film, you'll find a decent cafe (p797): order a cheeseburger, a glass of vino and enjoy the sun setting over the town's rooftops.

Cave-Dwelling Characters

Explore eccentric underground homes

Glimpse how some locals live on a tour of an underground home. Featured in *Mad Max Beyond Thunderdome*, **Crocodile Harry's** *($10)* wildly eccentric underground abode was once home to Arvid Blumenthal, a Latvian-born runaway (quite possibly a Nazi) who poached crocs in Queensland for many years before moving to Coober Pedy. The interior is spangled with graffiti, sculptures, artworks, posters, hats, carvings and relics of his love life. Find it about 6km northwest of town, beyond the golf club (not the Thunderdome).

Back in town, **Faye's Underground Home** *($20)* is more modest. It was hand dug by three women in the 1960s and is now a time-warp museum. A window on Coober Pedy life in the last century, it's a little flowery decor-wise, but the living room swimming pool is a winner.

Break Away from It All

Drive a desert loop

Got a hankering to get out of town? An interesting 70km loop on sometimes-rough, unsealed roads takes you to **Kanku-Breakaways Conservation Park** *(parks.sa.gov.au; vehicle $13 per day)*, 32km north of Coober Pedy. A stark but colourful

QUIRKY COOBER PEDY

Opal Fields Golf Club: West of town, look for glimmering opal as you tee off – the fairways are covered in mining spoils.

Coober Pedy Drive-In: SA's last remaining drive-in cinema flickers to life on Friday or Saturday night (sometimes both).

Spaceship: This intricate, unexpected leftover prop from the film *Pitch Black* crash-landed on Hutchison St.

Big Miner: Coober Pedy's *Big Miner* is a lanky lad – 6m of earnest metallurgy in front of a Simos St opal shop.

Coober Pedy Wellness Labyrinth: Near Coober Pedy Oval, this circular stone labyrinth makes for a mindful moment.

ODNADATTA TRACK

Once an Aboriginal trading route linking artesian springs, later hijacked by the steam-era *Ghan* railway, this track now serves 4WD adventurers.

START	END	LENGTH
Marla	Marree	615km; 3–5 days

Two hours north of Coober Pedy, head west from 1 **Marla**, a service town on the Stuart Highway with 24-hour fuel, pub grub and motel beds. Stock up – the first stop isn't for at least four sun-baked hours. Only attempt this drive in the cooler months and check dit.sa.gov.au/outbackroads first.

In 2 **Oodnadatta** the cult-status Pink Roadhouse offers fuel, food and quirky characters. Grab a key here for the town's free Railway Museum. An hour or so later, stretch your legs at 3 **Algebuckina Bridge**, a relic from the *Ghan*'s glory days. Don't wander far: the 130-year-old sleepers aren't trustworthy.Two to three hours on, 4 **William Creek** appears as a dusty speck with a legendary pub, campground and outback flyer **Wrightsair** *(wrightsair.com.au; from $390)*. Scenic flights sweep over Kati Thanda-Lake Eyre's oft-dry expanse and the marbled red folds of the Anna Creek Painted Hills. Around three to four hours of salt pans and historic sidings take in 5 **Coward Springs** artesian spa, a lookout over 6 **Kati Thanda-Lake Eyre South** and a dusty 1.1km walk around the surreal recycled artworks of 7 **Mutonia Sculpture Park**.

Final stop 8 **Marree** clings to its rail heritage, with rusting relics and a storied hotel. **Arid Air** *(aridair.com.au; from $495)* lifts off here too, arcing over the mysterious 4.2km tall desert-etched Marree Man.

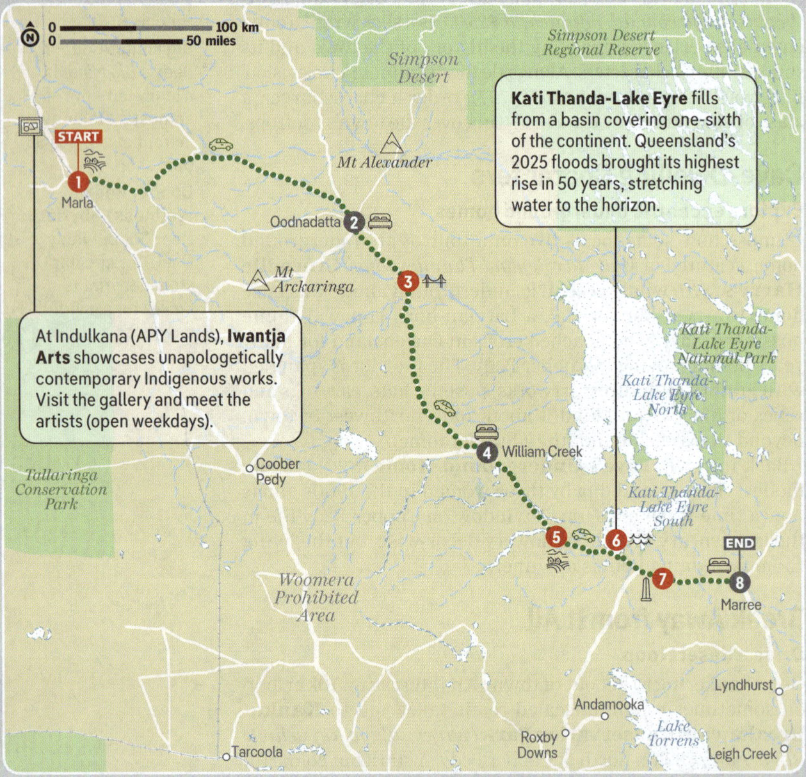

Kanku-Breakaways Conservation Park (p795)

sweep of arid hills, mesas and scarps rises from the desert plain, glowing red-gold at sunset from the Antakirinja lookout.

Entry permits are available via a QR code from **Coober Pedy Visitor Information Centre**; ask for good driving directions while you are here. From the national park, continue south past the dog fence built to keep dingoes out of southeastern Australia, and the surreal, table-like **Moon Plain** on the Coober Pedy–Oodnadatta Rd. The earth here has an oddly crusty, fractured surface: if it's been raining, give this stretch a miss.

LOOKING FOR OPAL IN COOBER PEDY

Brilyanz Mance from Umoona Opal Mine and Museum *(umoonaopalmine.com.au)* takes us underground.

Coober Pedy's opal fields are actually extremely dangerous, with over one million unmarked shafts, some 30m deep. The safest way to visit is on a guided or self-guided tour through any of the town's original mines. Or try 'noodling' (aka fossicking) when you sift through surface rubble looking for opal that may have been missed. The public noodling area in town is safe, free and open 24/7: people have found stones worth $4000 here. You can't detect opal underground, so opal mining is truly a game of luck. I like to think that there could be billions of dollars' worth of opal out there, just waiting to be unearthed.

EATING IN COOBER PEDY: BEST BITES

CK Confectionaire: Cafe-bakery by day; Filo-Asian fusion by night. This is Coober Pedy's only dugout diner. *hours vary* $$

Outback Bar & Grill: An upbeat petrol-station diner serving roasts, pastas, burgers and beer! *8am-9pm Mon-Sat, to 8pm Sun* $$

John's Pizza Bar & Restaurant: Table-sized pizzas, hearty pastas and heat-beating gelato. We have a winner! *10am-late* $$

Big Winch 360 Cafe & Bar: Check out a movie next door, then sip a glass of wine with your wrap or salad. *9am-3pm & 5.30-9pm* $$

Places We Love to Stay

$ Budget $$ Midrange $$$ Top End

Adelaide

MAPS p717 & p718

West Beach Parks $ Expansive shorefront complex featuring camp sites, cabins and spacious beach shacks; brimming with kid-approved activities.

Adelaide Central YHA $ An upgrade from your run-of-the-mill hostel with relaxed lounges, squeaky-clean dorms and an industrial-sized kitchen.

Largs Pier Hotel $$ An Art Deco stalwart with front-row sunsets over Adelaide's west coast. Plush beds, pub fare and a deep wine list.

Mayfair Hotel $$$ Old-world sophistication on King William St with polished rooms, a downstairs breakfast buffet and rooftop cocktails.

Oval Hotel $$$ Inside Adelaide Oval's eastern wing, guests enjoy ultra-modern suites and views over one of Australia's most storied sporting arenas.

Watson $$$ Artsy complex in Walkerville with lap pool, 24-hour concierge and complimentary bikes for River Torrens cruising.

Adelaide Hills

Woodhouse Adventure Park $ Grassy campgrounds, tents and cabins backed by a kid-friendly obstacle course in Picadilly.

Sticky Rice Villas $$$ Architect-designed villas in Stirling, best bundled with Sticky Rice's Asian-inspired cooking classes for couples.

Sequoia Lodge $$$ Crafers' luxe retreat offers 14 adults-only suites, each with a hilltop balcony and access to a serene, spring-fed hot pool.

Barossa Valley

MAP p738

Discovery Parks Barossa Valley $ Tanunda's gum-shaded caravan park spans camp sites, glamping and cabins, plus a water park.

Barossa Shiraz Estate $$$ Six charming cottages on a vineyard-wrapped estate in Lyndoch. Tours, transfers and artisanal treats included.

Louise $$$ A proposal-ready retreat in Marananga pairs fine dining with a private outdoor rain shower, sauna and infinity pool.

McLaren Vale

Redhens $$$ Two tastefully restored Redhen railcar carriages perch above Blewitt Springs' undulating vineyards.

Old Chaff Mill Retreat $$$ Sellicks Hill grain mill reborn as an elegant B&B, trimmed with burnt timbers and wide, panoramic windows.

Southern Fleurieu Peninsula

Port Elliot Beach House YHA $ Breezy beachside hostel, a short walk from the famous Port Elliot bakery, set within the historic Arcadia Hotel.

Beach Huts Middleton $$ A dozen stylish beach-hut cabins fan around a shared lawn, shaping a cosy, boutique-village feel.

Kangaroo Island

MAP p750

Chapman River Campground $ Twelve delightfully untouched camp sites sit beneath the shade as the Chapman River gently drifts out to Antechamber Bay.

KI Dragonfly Guesthouse $ Channelling your trendy aunt's spare room, this Kingscote guesthouse comes with communal rooms, fruit trees and a herb garden.

Postmans Cottage $$ Heritage cottage rebuilt after the 2020 fires; Flinders Chase National Park's wildlife is just outside your door. Two-night minimum stay.

Southern Ocean Lodge $$$ KI's once-in-a-lifetime retreat has 25 cliff-hugging suites, a lavish spa and exceptional on-site restaurant.

Mount Gambier

Old Mount Gambier Gaol $ Refurbished prison buildings make for an atmospheric hostel-style stay.

Colhurst House $$ An 1878 mansion B&B built by Welsh migrants; old-fashioned without being twee.

Penola & the Coonawarra Wine Region

Alexander Cameron Suites $$ Stylish motel rooms in Penola with well-tended gardens and rural Australian styling.

Bellwether Glamping $$ A rustic-luxe glamping nook beneath towering gums, conveniently close to a cellar door.

Robe

Lakeside Tourist Park $ Right on Lake Fellmongery with plenty of grass, basic cabins and flashy villas.

Caledonian Inn $$ This historic inn (1859) has bright, upstairs pub rooms with doors pulled from an old shipwreck.

Coorong National Park

Dalton on the Lake $$ Generous in spirit, this two-bedroom lakeside B&B is the pick of Meningie's offerings.

Coorong Cabins $$$ Two self-contained rental houses, right on the waterfront within the national park.

The Riverland & Murraylands MAP p765

Wilkadene Cottage $$ Cosy riverside cottage with fully equipped kitchen by the Woolshed Brewery near Renmark; sleeps up to six.

Murray River Queen $$ Now moored in Loxton, this refurbished paddle steamer is a unique floating stay delivering river-view rooms.

Frames $$$ Five-star property in Paringa specialising in luxury stays. Its 'wetland and wildlife' safari is a highlight.

Houseboat Hirers Association $$$ Choose from over 60 houseboat listings, moored from Murray Bridge to Paringa *(houseboatbookings.com)*.

Clare Valley & Mid North p771

Mambray Creek Campground (p772) **$** Enjoy the simple joy of a post-hike hot shower deep in the bush at this Melrose creekside site in Mt Remarkable National Park.

Under the Mount $ Part share-house, part hostel in Melrose, with a common love of mountain biking uniting guests.

Paxton Square Cottages $$ Rubble-walled miner's cottages, modernised and brightened, sit a short stroll from Burra's cafes and pubs.

Bukirk Glamping $$$ Adult-only bohemian bell tents with a shared fire pit, camp kitchen, pool and barnyard company, just outside Clare.

Yorke Peninsula p777

Point Turton Caravan Park $ On the lower west coast, a super-friendly caravan park overlooking the sea.

Bayside Glamping $$$ A lantern-lit hideaway in Marion Bay, right on the doorstep of Dhilba Guuranda-Innes National Park. Four-walled options here, too.

Port Lincoln & Eyre Peninsula

Discovery Parks Streaky Bay Foreshore $ Just west of Streaky Bay, this shallow waterfront caravan park is ready to keep kids entertained.

Streaky Bay Motel & Villas $$ A tidy row of older-style motel units, plus a complex of family-size villas that are much more 'now', in Streaky Bay.

Limani Port Lincoln $$ Self-contained, self-check-in stays right on the waterfront overlooking Boston Bay in Port Lincoln.

Cobble + Stone $$ Four ocean-view units sit on Boston House's lush wedding venue grounds in Port Lincoln; best for midweek stays.

Ikara-Flinders Ranges National Park MAP p787

Rawnsley Park Station $$$ This rangy homestead just south of the national park has everything from tents to luxe eco-villas, plus a restaurant.

Discovery Resorts Wilpena Pound (p790) **$$$** Motel-style rooms, a campground with plush safari tents and a tempting pool and bar – all within the national park.

Coober Pedy MAP p794

Lookout Cave Underground Motel $$ A cave with a view? This dugout hotel gazes over the desert with 18 cool, cave-carved rooms above town.

Desert Cave Hotel $$$ The Desert Cave delivers some much-needed luxury, plus a pool. Above- and below-ground rooms.

ALEXANDRE.ROSA/SHUTTERSTOCK

Lookout Cave Underground Motel, Coober Pedy

For places to stay in Darwin & the Top End, see p843

FRERD78/SHUTTERSTOCK

Above: Karlu Karlu / Devils Marbles (p839); Left: Nourlangie (p816), Kakadu National Park

Researched by
Anthony Ham

Darwin & the Top End

OUTBACK WONDERS AND WILD ADVENTURES

Everything seems to happen on a grand scale in this part of the world, a frontier where Indigenous stories and epic landscapes are at the centre of nearly every experience.

Most journeys up in the Top End of the Northern Territory begin in Darwin (Garramilla). Lapped by the cyan Timor Sea, Darwin is an intriguing city with an end-of-Australia feel, at once outback Australia unvarnished and a fascinating, culture-rich place to spend a few days. Expect brilliant weekend markets, top-notch museums, beautiful green spaces and an enticing culinary scene that is equal parts Asian and Aussie.

An easy boat ride offshore from the city, the Tiwi Islands are an intriguing escape from city life into a world of art and traditional culture. Elsewhere, within a day's drive of the Territory's capital are three of Australia's most celebrated, most beautiful national parks – Kakadu, Litchfield and Nitmiluk (Katherine Gorge). Each is its own magical realm, awash in towering red-rock escarpments and waterfalls, floodplains and billabongs, rock art and iconic Australian wildlife. Travel beyond and you enter frontier country – Arnhem Land, with its big horizons, natural beauty and powerful Indigenous story; or Victoria River with its wildly beautiful scenery, vast cattle stations and barely known national parks. Down into the deep south, the Karlu Karlu / Devils Marbles are one of those natural wonders you only find in the outback.

Underlying it all, infusing these astonishing landscapes with meaning, is a soulful Indigenous presence, which you can learn about on Aboriginal-led tours, draw near to at art centres and immerse yourself in at fabulous festivals.

THE MAIN AREAS

DARWIN
The Top End's tropical capital.
p804

LITCHFIELD NATIONAL PARK
Waterfalls, waterholes and walks.
p821

ARNHEM LAND
Rock art, culture and Aboriginal culture.
p828

KATHERINE & NITMILUK NATIONAL PARK
Gorgeous gorges and Aboriginal art.
p832

Find Your Way

Darwin, p804
The vibrant, tropical capital is a great place to ease into Territory life before setting out to explore the Top End.

Arnhem Land, p828
One of the world's most raw and remote wilderness areas, this storied Indigenous landscape is best visited on a tour.

CAR
Hitting the road is the best way to experience the Northern Territory – ideally take a 4WD if you're planning to venture off sealed roads. Read up on outback-touring safety before you start the engine.

BUS
Greyhound runs at least one service per day between Darwin and Alice Springs, with stops at just about every Stuart Highway town in between. Katherine Coaches runs services to out-of-the-way places.

Crocodiles can inhabit all waterways in tropical areas. Swimming is not recommended.

Litchfield National Park, p821
This incredibly popular national park south of Darwin can be visited on a day trip, or camp and take your time.

Katherine & Nitmiluk National Park, p832
The outback town of Katherine, home to some great art centres, is the gateway to Nitmiluk (Katherine Gorge).

ANDY333/SHUTTERSTOCK

Nitmiluk National Park (p832)

Plan Your Time

Many attractions can be visited in a day from Darwin, though factor in long drives to get where you want to go.

If You Only Do One Thing

- Fly into **Darwin** (p804) to explore the city's rich cultural offerings and markets. After a couple of days, travel to **Litchfield National Park** (p821); day tours are possible from Darwin, but we prefer renting a car, staying overnight in Batchelor and getting an early start to beat the crowds. And two nights in **Kakadu National Park** (p812) is a minimum.

A Week to Play With

- After visiting **Darwin** (p804) and **Litchfield** (p821), spend more time in **Kakadu** (p814), enjoying **Marrawuddi Arts & Culture** (p819), **Ubirr** (p814), **Nourlangie** (p816) and the **East Alligator River** (p816); on your way out take a **Yellow Water Cruise** (p818) and swim at **Maguk** (p817) and **Gunlom** (p817). Head south to **Katherine** (p832) and then explore the sublime gorges and hiking trails of **Nitmiluk National Park** (p834).

Seasonal Highlights

THE DRY (MAY–SEP)

Sunny days, mild temperatures and bearable humidity make this the ideal time to travel. Festivals at every turn across the Top End.

THE BUILDUP (OCT)

Rising temperatures and stifling humidity prompt locals to pray for rain. Vote for your favourite noodle soup during the **Darwin International Laksa Festival** (p810).

THE WET (NOV–APR)

Heat and mosquitoes can dampen your enjoyment. Some roads become impassable after flash floods and land routes into Arnhem Land are usually closed until April.

CYCLONE SEASON (NOV–APR)

Top End cyclones can wreak havoc with travel plans – they're worse along the coast, but rains can reach far inland.

Darwin

HISTORY AND CULTURE | NATURE | FABULOUS FOOD

TOP TIP

At Doctor's Gully, off the northern end of the Esplanade, **Aquascene** *(aquascene.com.au)* is best known for its high-tide fish feeding. If you don't have an appetite for the show, come here instead to enjoy coffee and fresh-baked bagels at Darwin Bagels Co (open since 2023), along with the sea views.

Australia's only tropical capital city and gateway to the Top End, Darwin (Garramilla) occupies the traditional lands of the Larrakia Aboriginal people and gazes out across the Timor Sea. It's closer to Bali than Bondi and feels removed from the rest of the country, which is just how the locals like it.

There are many Darwins, not all of them appealing. In places, Darwin is the Top End unvarnished and Mitchell St is a loud and somewhat tired backpacker hangover from decades past. But look a little further and you'll encounter a city languid and vibrant in equal measure. Darwin is brimful of markets, green spaces, fabulous cuisine, touchstones of Indigenous culture and outstanding museums. And we love the NT capital's cosmopolitan mix, with more than 50 nationalities represented here.

Best of all, Darwin is the starting point of grand adventures into what lies beyond.

Eat, Shop & Eat Some More

Darwin's magical markets

It's worth planning your visit around Darwin's markets – they're one of the best things about being here.

The biggest and most popular is the **Mindil Beach Sunset Market** *(mindil.com.au)*, open 4pm to 9pm, Thursday to

GETTING AROUND

Compact and relatively flat, Darwin is Australia's easiest capital to navigate on foot – or with e-scooters and e-bikes, which make it easier to whizz around town, especially in the heat of the day. Free local buses (main terminus on Harry Chan Ave) service the surrounding suburbs of Fannie Bay, Parap and beyond.

Greyhound buses run south to Alice Springs and interstate; and the *Ghan* luxury sleeper train runs between Darwin and Adelaide. Book ahead for car hire, especially for campervans and 4WDs; try Britz or Adventure Rentals. Ensure you have the correct permits before venturing out to national parks or Aboriginal lands (p811).

MICHAEL BEGANI/SHUTTERSTOCK

Mindil Beach

Sunday from late April to October. Food – starring native ingredients and Southeast Asian flavours – is the main attraction. Arts and crafts stalls bulge with handmade jewellery, rainbow tie-dyed clothes, Aboriginal art and wares from Southeast Asia. As the sun nears the horizon, half of Darwin descends on the market, with BYO chairs and picnic rugs.

Darwin's other top markets are year-round. On Saturday from 8am to 2pm, the compact, food-focused **Parap Village Market** *(parapvillage.com.au)* at Parap Shopping Village, 4km north of the city centre, is the place for a stellar Southeast Asian feed (Mary's Laksa is a cult local favourite).

Held on Saturday and Sunday (7am to 2pm), the **Rapid Creek Market** *(rapidcreekmarkets.com.au)* is Darwin's oldest market. Located at the Rapid Creek Business Village, 7km north of Parap, this Asian marketplace is where tropical fruit and vegetables mingle with swirls of spices and satay smoke.

Also on Sunday is **Nightcliff Market**, in the Nightcliff Shopping Centre from 8am to 2pm. Browse clothes, arts and crafts, grab a feed or indulge in a Thai massage.

Continued on p808

IS IT SAFE TO SWIM IN DARWIN?

There hasn't been a fatal crocodile attack at a Darwin beach in over 120 years, but there's still a chance of meeting a 'saltie'. A bigger problem is deadly jellyfish, which makes swimming very risky between October and May. Unlike in tropical Queensland, there are no stinger nets here.

If you do decide to swim, head to **Mindil Beach**, Nightcliff or Casuarina (part of the latter is clothing-optional); all patrolled by local surf-life-saving clubs in the Dry. You can swim year-round without fear of stingers in Lake Alexander, an easy cycle from the centre at **East Point Reserve**, and at the Beach and Wave Lagoon (p809) in the Darwin Waterfront Precinct.

EATING IN DARWIN: BEST CAFES

Aboriginal Bush Traders Cafe: Tasty contemporary dishes with a bush-tucker twist, either in taster plates or breakfasts. *7am-2pm Mon-Fri* **$$**

Speaker's Corner Cafe: Spilling out of Parliament House onto a waterfront terrace, cafe with sandwiches, salads, hot specials. *7.30am-3pm Mon-Fri* **$$**

Laneway Speciality Coffee: Great coffee and all-day breakfast in leafy industrial space at this Parap favourite. *7am-3pm Mon-Fri, 7.30am-3pm Sat, 7.30am-2.30pm Sun* **$$**

Sweet Brew & Co: A banging brunch menu makes this cafe worth the short trek up the Stuart Highway from the city centre. *6.30am-2pm Mon-Sat, 7am-2pm Sun* **$$**

★ **HIGHLIGHTS**
1 Deckchair Cinema
2 Mindil Beach Sunset Market
3 Royal Flying Doctor Service

SIGHTS
4 Crocosaurus Cove
5 Darwin Convention Centre
6 Darwin Military Museum
7 Darwin Waterfront Precinct
8 East Point Reserve
9 Mindil Beach
10 Museum & Art Gallery of the Northern Territory
11 Sky Bridge

ACTIVITIES
12 Aquascene
13 Darwin Gourmet Tours
14 Darwin Harbour Cruises
15 Northern Territory Indigenous Tours
16 Sea Darwin
17 Wave Lagoon

SLEEPING
18 Adina Apartment Hotel
19 Palms City Resort
20 Vibe Hotel

EATING
21 Aboriginal Bush Traders Cafe
22 Chok's Place
23 CHOW!
24 Ella by Minoli
25 Frying Nemo
26 Hanuman

27 Laneway Specialty Coffee
28 Pee Wee's at the Point
29 Speaker's Corner Cafe
30 Sweet Brew & Co

DRINKING & NIGHTLIFE
31 Charlie's of Darwin
32 Darwin Ski Club
33 Discovery Darwin
34 Stone House Wine Bar & Kitchen
35 Trader Bar

ENTERTAINMENT
see 9 Beer Can Regatta
see 5 Darwin Aboriginal Art Fair
36 Darwin Festival
37 Darwin Railway Club
see 13 Happy Yess
38 National Indigenous Music Awards

SHOPPING
see 15 Aboriginal Bush Traders
39 Mason Gallery
see 10 Museum & Art Gallery of the Northern Territory
40 Nightcliff Market
see 27 Outstation Gallery
41 Parap Village Market
42 Rapid Creek Market
see 31 Sister7

INFORMATION
43 Tourism Top End

TRANSPORT
44 Britz Australia

DARWIN'S BEST FESTIVALS/ EVENTS

Darwin Festival: Mainly outdoor arts-and-culture festival celebrates music, theatre, visual art, dance, cabaret in August. *darwinfestival.org.au*

Darwin Aboriginal Art Fair: At **Darwin Convention Centre**, three-day August fair showcases Indigenous art from communities throughout NT. *daaf.com.au*

Darwin Fringe Festival: Eclectic, local performing and visual arts at various venues for 10 days in July. *darwinfringe.org.au*

Beer Can Regatta: Festival featuring races for boats made out of beer cans, at Mindil Beach (p805) June–July. *beercanregatta.org.au*

National Indigenous Music Awards: August celebration of First Nations artists and music at Gardens Amphitheatre. *nima.musicnt.com.au*

JANELLE LUGGE/SHUTTERSTOCK

Continued from p805

Movies by Moonlight

Relax at Darwin's Deckchair Cinema

Watch a film under the stars while reclining in a deckchair, surrounded by tropical gardens. During the Dry, the Darwin Film Society runs the fabulous daily **Deckchair Cinema** *(deckchaircinema.com; adult/concession/child/family $19/15/10/44)* just a short stroll from the Waterfront Precinct, below the southern end of the Esplanade on Jervois Rd. There's a licensed bar, a snack kiosk and a different local caterer serving food every night from 5.45pm, or you can bring a picnic (no BYO alcohol) to enjoy at the seating area overlooking the harbour. If you arrive early, reserve a deckchair with one of the cushions piled up near the bar. The daily film begins at 7pm; there are usually double features on Friday and Saturday nights.

The Outback's Air Ambulance

Learn about the Royal Flying Doctor Service

The **Royal Flying Doctor Service** (RFDS; *rfdsdarwin.com.au; adult/child/family $30/17/85)* museum on Stokes Hill Wharf is a particular highlight. There's a hologram cinema experience, virtual-reality glasses that enable you to relive in

After dinner at Pee Wee's take a stroll along the foreshore

EATING IN DARWIN: OUR PICKS

Frying Nemo: Consistently ranked among Australia's best fish and chips; waterside in Stuart Park. *5-8pm Mon-Thu, noon-2pm & 5-9pm Fri-Sun* $

Ella by Minoli: The *MasterChef* alumni's Sri Lankan–inspired dishes are perfectly suited to sultry Darwin's weather. *5-11pm Tue-Sat* $$

Hanuman: High-class city-centre performer, reliable for smart-casual nights out. Great Indian and Thai cooking. *6-10pm Sat-Tue, noon-2.30pm & 6-10pm Wed-Fri* $$$

Pee Wee's at the Point: Classic Darwin dining, with dishes like wild-caught barramundi with macadamia, herb and lemon myrtle by the water. *4-11pm Tue-Sat* $$$

Darwin Waterfront Precinct

frightening detail the 1942 Japanese bombing raid on Darwin Harbour, a decommissioned Pilatus PC-12 aircraft from the Royal Flying Doctor Service, a live map showing the current location of RFDS planes and a series of touchscreens that take you through the story of the RFDS and Darwin during WWII.

Waterfront Waves

Cool off in giant wave pools and lagoons

The turn-of-the-21st-century redevelopment of the old **Darwin Waterfront Precinct** transformed the city. At its heart is the **Wave Lagoon** *(waterfront.nt.gov.au; adult/child/family $8/6/25)*, a giant wave pool and artificially made **Beach** (fed by filtered seawater). It's all surrounded by lush green lawns, hotels and a decent collection of restaurants.

The **Sky Bridge**, an elevated walkway at the south end of Smith St, connects the waterfront to the rest of the city centre for pedestrians.

Indigenous Art & Cyclone Tracy

World-class Indigenous art and a powerful cyclone

The superb **Museum & Art Gallery of the Northern Territory** *(MAGNT; magnt.net.au; admission free)* in Fannie Bay is home to beautifully presented galleries of Top

DARWIN'S BEST INDIGENOUS ART SHOPPING

Aboriginal Bush Traders: Not-for-profit with beautifully curated selection of products, from earrings to bush foods.

Outstation Gallery: In Parap, Outstation works directly with remote Aboriginal art centres in the presentation and promotion of works by their artisans.

Mason Gallery: Browse bold dot paintings from the Western and Central Desert regions, as well as works from Arnhem Land and Utopia.

Sister7: Small gallery on Smith St representing 17 female Aboriginal artists and weavers.

Museum & Art Gallery of the Northern Territory: There's a small shop on-site at this excellent gallery; check that it and the museum haven't moved to new premises.

DRINKING IN DARWIN: OUR PICKS

Trader Bar: Serving Darwin's best cocktails since 2016. Cool cafe by day, cocktail bar on Friday and Saturday. *7.30am-11am Sun-Thu, 8am-midnight Fri & Sat*

Stone House Wine Bar & Kitchen: Part of Darwin's new trickle of sophistication, with a European-wine-bar feel. *3-10pm Mon-Thu & Sat, noon-11pm Fri*

One Mile Brewing Company: Enjoy this microbrewery's tasting bar, showcasing some of the Top End's tastiest beers. *4-8pm Thu & Fri, noon-8pm Sat*

Charlie's of Darwin: Sip locally distilled gin right next to the copper still in a terrific central location. *3-11pm Wed & Thu, to 1am Fri & Sat, to 10pm Sun*

LAKSA OBSESSION

Closer to Malaysia's Kuala Lumpur than Sydney, Darwin often looks north for cultural and culinary inspiration. And if there's one dish that defines Darwin, it's laksa. In 2019 the city launched its inaugural **Darwin International Laksa Festival** *(darwinlaksafestival.com.au)*, a month-long event in October to celebrate the spicy Malay noodle soup. As part of the festival, the Laksa Festival Food Tour encourages people to vote for their favourite laksa venues. On the last Sunday of October, the Laksa Festival Finale is a celebration of all things laksa, culminating in the Laksa Festival Awards. **Chok's Place** (Smith St) and **CHOW!** (Darwin Waterfront) have both won the coveted Golden Bowl several times.

End-centric exhibits. A large section is devoted to Cyclone Tracy, which hit Darwin in the early hours of Christmas Day 1974. By Christmas morning, 71 people had been killed and just 400 of Darwin's 11,200 homes were still standing. You can enter a dark room and listen to the whirring sound of Tracy at full throttle – a sound you won't forget in a hurry.

MAGNT's changing Indigenous art exhibitions are a highlight. After a change of government in 2024, the future of a city-centre custom-built gallery (Northern Territory Art Gallery) to showcase Indigenous art has been cast into doubt. The collection is world-class. Ask at **Tourism Top End** for the latest.

Relive the Bombing of Darwin

Wartime history through immersive military displays

An air-raid siren sounds every 20 minutes at the innovative **Darwin Military Museum** *(darwinmilitarymuseum.au; adult/child/family $20/10/45)* at the tip of East Point, signalling the beginning of a short film bringing one of Darwin's darkest days to life: 19 February 1942, when the area was attacked by 188 Japanese aircraft during two separate raids.

The main museum building covers the bombing of Darwin (the only Australian city ever bombed), with other military relics strewn around the grounds. Download the free Darwin Military Museum ('Defence of Darwin Experience') app for a self-guided tour.

The museum of the Royal Flying Doctor Service (p808) also has a VR experience of the bombing.

Take a Tour of Darwin

Embark on guided walks, gourmet tours sunset cruises

Uncover Darwin's secrets on a walking tour with **Walk Darwin** *(walkdarwin.com.au; per person $35-79)*, with a range of themed tours, from Darwin's hidden secrets to its WWII history.

Food is central to understanding the city, so join **Darwin Gourmet Tours** *(darwingourmettours.com; three-/four-hour per person incl meals $189/249)* for a delicious introduction to local cuisine on a Gourmet Food & Art Tour.

Take in an epic Darwin sunset from the water with **Darwin Harbour Cruises** *(darwinharbourcruises.com.au; lunch/dinner cruises from $88/125)* or **Sea Darwin** *(seadarwin.com; per person $65-369)*. The latter also runs the eight-hour **Turtle Tracks** tour (May to September), taking groups out beyond Darwin Harbour to beautiful Ngulbitjik (Bare Sand Island) at sunset to see turtles laying their eggs; come late in the season and you may see hatchlings emerge.

CLAUDINE VAN MASSENHOVE/SHUTTERSTOCK

Darwin Military Museum

For tours beyond Darwin (eg to Kakadu and/or Litchfield), **Ethical Adventures** *(ethicaladventures.com.au*; tour prices vary*)* and Aboriginal-owned **Northern Territory Indigenous Tours** *(ntitours.com.au)* are both highly recommended; the latter offers exclusive access to traditional Aboriginal lands and it runs the half-day women-and-girls-only **Muku Women's Morning Tour** *(adult/child $296/148)* to Berry Springs.

Get Close to Crocs

Dip into Crocosaurus Cove

Some of the largest saltwater crocodiles in captivity inhabit the aquariums and pools at **Crocosaurus Cove** *(crocosauruscove.com; adult/child/family $40/25/122)*. You can even opt to be lowered right into a pool with the crocs in the transparent **Cage of Death** *(one/two person $195/295)*. If you share concerns held by animal-welfare experts about the use of wildlife for human entertainment, this urban zoo on Mitchell St might not be for you.

DRINKING IN DARWIN: BEST FOR LIVE MUSIC

Darwin Ski Club: Darwin's best location for a sunset beer, in Fannie Bay, with live music from 5pm most nights. *noon-10pm Mon-Fri, from 11am Sat & Sun*

Happy Yess: This not-for-profit venue hosts great live acts on weekend nights in the Browns Mart theatre precinct. *9am-1am Fri-Sat*

Darwin Railway Club: Big supporters of Darwin's live music scene, this Parap social club pulls class acts. *4-11pm Mon-Fri, 3pm-midnight Sat, 3-10pm Sun*

Discovery Darwin: Darwin's biggest nightclub hosts a big night out with decent DJs. *9pm-4am Fri & Sat, from 10pm Sun-Wed*

Beyond Darwin

Darwin may be a destination in its own right but the city's hinterland is special, from the Tiwi Islands to the Arnhem Highway en route to Kakadu.

Places

GETTING AROUND

SeaLink *(sealink.com.au/tiwi-islands; adult one way/return $62/124, child $34/67)* runs a daily return ferry from Darwin's Cullen Bay Marina to the Tiwi Islands during the Dry, with three departures weekly most weeks in the Wet – check the online timetable for details. The trip to Wurrumiyanga on Bathurst Island takes 2½ hours; there's a kiosk on board. **Fly Tiwi** *(flytiwi.com.au)* also has daily flights to Bathurst Island (30 minutes). The Arnhem Highway branches off towards Kakadu 34km southeast of Darwin.

You needn't venture far from Darwin to uncover some real gems and this part of Darwin's hinterland has some of the best tour possibilities in the Top End.

The Tiwi Islands – Bathurst Island and Melville Island – are an 80km boat trip north of Darwin and home to the Tiwi Aboriginal people. A visit here is one of the cultural highlights of the Top End.

Southeast of Darwin, the Arnhem Highway (Rte 36) connects the city to Kakadu National Park. While many travellers stop for little more than petrol along the way, there are a number of worthwhile sights and activities in the Adelaide River and Mary River regions en route if you have time, from serene wetland cruises to hands-on Aboriginal cultural experiences. The highway traverses the traditional lands of numerous Aboriginal groups.

Tiwi Islands

TIME FROM DARWIN: 2½HR

Discover vibrant Tiwi culture through art and workshops

The Tiwis ('We People') have a distinct culture and today are known for producing vibrant art (particularly screen-printed textiles, paintings and carvings) and the odd champion Aussie Rules football player.

The main settlement is Wurrumiyanga in the southeast of Bathurst Island, founded in 1911 as a Catholic mission. On Melville Island the settlements are Pirlangimpi and Milikapiti. Tourism is restricted on the islands, home to around 2350 people (more than 86% Indigenous). Most travellers visit on one of the daily organised tours from Darwin.

SeaLink offers several options, although interaction with the local community tends to be limited. Tours run only in the Dry (usually sometime in April or May until September). The **Tiwi by Design** *(adult/child from $469/399)* tour is the pick – it includes permit, welcome ceremony, lunch, visits to a local museum and church, and an art workshop, where you get to screen-print your own tea towel or T-shirt.

Arnhem Highway

Watch the local footy

One of the Territory's top sporting events, the **Tiwi AFL Grand Final** is held in July; check online for the latest schedule (it used to be in March). Held on Bathurst Island, this sporting spectacular displays the Tiwis' passion for Aussie Rules football. Thousands come from Darwin for the day, which coincides with the **Tiwi Annual Art Sale**. Book your ferry trip well in advance.

Arnhem Highway

TIME FROM DARWIN: **30MIN TO 1½HR**

Spot prolific waterbirds and reptiles in lush wetlands

As the Arnhem Highway peels away west of the Stuart Highway and heads for Kakadu, wetlands in elemental greens and blues unfurl to the far horizon on either side of the road. **Fogg Dam Conservation Reserve** *(nt.gov.au/parks/find-a-park/fogg-dam-conservation-area)* fills with water and prolific numbers of waterbirds after rains and numbers are highest between December and July.

A couple of flat, easy nature walks (2.2km and 4.4km) fan out from the main car park through monsoon forest and woodlands to viewing decks over the water lilies. As you go, watch for one of the 250,000 water pythons thought to live here – that's an estimated 800kg of snake for every square kilometre. The dam walls are closed to walkers (due to crocodiles).

The turn off for the reserve is about 15km southeast along the Arnhem Highway from the **Humpty Doo Hotel**. NT Parks Pass required.

Continued on p820

MILLION-DOLLAR FISH

Introduced to boost Top End tourism during the Wet, the **Million Dollar Fish competition** *(milliondollarfish.com.au)* sees barramundi tagged and released in five main fishing regions: Arnhem Land, Darwin, Kakadu, Katherine and the Tiwi Islands. With tags on approximately a dozen fish worth $1 million and a further 99 tagged fish worth $10,000, it's Australia's richest fishing competition. A few prize-winning fish are reeled in each season, but a $1 million 'barra' has yet to be bagged, with most of the tagged fish likely ending up in the bellies of local crocs. You must be registered for the season (1 September to 31 March; free) to be eligible to claim a prize.

SLJONES/SHUTTERSTOCK

Ubirr

TOP EXPERIENCE

Kakadu National Park

One of Australia's signature landscapes is a marriage of Top End magnificence and soulful human presence. Across its escarpments and floodplains, billabongs and waterfalls, rock-art sites and croc-filled rivers, Kakadu is an ancient story on the lands of the Bininj/Mungguy people. This is a world with timeless gravitas, a magical place of wildlife and big horizons. And its Indigenous story is always centre stage.

DON'T MISS

- Ubirr rock art
- Nardab Lookout
- Cahill's Crossing
- Guluyambi Cultural Cruise
- Maguk
- Gunlom
- Yellow Water Cruises
- Jim Jim Falls
- Scenic Flight

Ubirr's Rock Art & Sunset Lookout

Magnificent, spiritual **Ubirr**, 42km north of the Arnhem Highway via a sealed road, is home to one of Kakadu's most famous rock-art sites. Coming here feels like wandering into a poignant history book of Kakadu's extraordinary human and natural history.

Spread over five main galleries, layers of rock-art paintings, in various styles and from various millennia, command mesmerising stillness. Dominating the walls and rock shelters

PRACTICALITIES

● *kakadu.gov.au* ● 7-day Kakadu Park Pass adult/child/family $25/12.50/65

are images of kangaroos, tortoises, fish, even a thylacine, all painted in X-ray and dating back at least 8000 years. Predating these are the paintings of mimi spirits: cheeky, dynamic figures who, it's believed, were the first of the Creation Ancestors to paint on rock. And look for the yam-head figures, where the head is depicted as a yam on the body of a human or animal; these date back around 15,000 years.

The magnificent **Nardab Lookout** is a 250m scramble accessed from the main gallery. Surveying the lush floodplain, watching the sun set in the west and the moon rise in the east is humbling to say the least. The site closes right after sunset.

There's another stunning rock-art site at Nourlangie.

Magical Nourlangie

The sight of Nourlangie, this looming outlier of the Arnhem Land escarpment, makes it easy to understand its ancient importance to Aboriginal people. Its long, red-sandstone bulk, striped in places with orange, white and black, rises from the surrounding woodland in stepped cliffs, with sublime rock art down below.

A 2km looped walking track (open 8am to sunset) takes you first to the **Anbangbang Shelter**, used for 20,000 years as a refuge and canvas. Next is the **Anbangbang Gallery**, featuring vivid Dreaming characters repainted in the 1960s. Look for the dangerous **Nabulwinjbulwinj**, a dangerous spirit who likes to eat females after banging them on the head with a yam. From here it's a short, steep walk to **Gunwarddehwarde Lookout**, with views of the Arnhem Land escarpment.

An easier short walk (600m return, 30 minutes) climbs a gradual slope to **Nawurlandja Lookout**, which gives excellent sunset views of the Nourlangie rock area. Another pleasurable short stroll is the picturesque **Anbangbang Billabong Walk** (2.5km loop, 45 minutes), around a lily-filled billabong and through paperbark swamp.

For something more challenging, there's always the challenging **Barrk Walk** (12km loop, five to six hours) or the walk to **Nanguluwur Gallery** (3.5km return, 1½ hours); the latter showcases very early dynamic style work, X-ray work and a good example of 'contact art' – a painting of a two-masted sailing ship towing a dinghy.

CAMPING IN KAKADU

There are more than 20 campgrounds in Kakadu National Park; some are free, while those with more facilities require fees paid in cash (per adult from $6–15), so don't forget to bring change. With sites available on a first-come, first-served basis, arrive early in the Dry to snag a good spot. There's a supermarket in Jabiru and a small store in Cooinda, but they're expensive; bring everything you'll need from Darwin, especially drinking water. Alcohol is permitted only in the Mardukal campground, near Cooinda. You can also camp at several privately run holiday parks in Jabiru and at Cooinda.

Kakadu & Its Crocs

It may be small, but there can be few more dramatic frontiers in Australia. **Cahill's Crossing**, a shallow causeway near Ubirr, which is impassable when the tide's in, crosses the **East Alligator River** from Kakadu National Park on the west bank to Arnhem Land to the east. And watching you as you cross is the river's healthy and rather prolific population of saltwater crocs. Check tides in advance to time your visit.

Catch the action from another angle on a **Guluyambi Cultural Cruise** *(kakaduculturaltours.com.au; adult/child $89/56)* run by Kakadu Cultural Tours. Departing May to October from the upstream boat ramp on the East Alligator River just east of Cahill's Crossing, these Aboriginal-led cruises (three departures daily in the Dry) are a wonderful way to see

TOP TIPS

- Buy your Kakadu Pass online or from Bowali Visitor Information Centre or Cooinda Lodge.
- Day (and longer) tours to Kakadu are possible from Darwin, but driving is easy, roads are sealed and having your own wheels means more freedom.
- The park is open throughout the Wet, but some sites and access roads are seasonal. Some car-rental companies won't let you drive the unsealed access road to Gunlom – check the fine print of your contract.
- Check the **Kakadu Access Report** *(kakadu.gov.au/access)* for the latest road, campground and visitor site closures.
- Fuel is available at Cooinda and Jabiru.

crocodiles and a little of Arnhem Land from the riverbank, listening to Dreaming stories and learning about traditional uses for plants and animals as you go. There's even a bit of rock art to admire on your way upriver.

Hikes near Cahill's Crossing

Mainly sticking to a boardwalk, the **Manngarre Monsoon Forest Walk** (1.5km return) starts by the downstream boat ramp just south of Cahill's Crossing and winds through heavily shaded vegetation, palms and vines.

A short stroll south of the upstream car park, the **Bardedjilidji Sandstone Walk** (2.5km) takes in wetland areas of the East Alligator River and misshapen eroded sandstone outliers of the Arnhem Land escarpment. Look for rock wallabies and the chestnut-quilled rock pigeon.

Swimming in Waterholes

When it comes to Top End waterholes, dreamy **Maguk** (Barramundi Gorge) is simply glorious. The 2km-return walk in from the car park follows a crystal-clear, pandanus-lined creek, but you'll need to resist the urge to dive in (crocs) until you reach the top pool. Count on about an hour's walking, plus swimming time. The 10km unsealed road in here (off the Kakadu Highway, 50km south of Cooinda Lodge) is lined with golden termite mounds; there's a bush camp site just before the car park.

Another 40km along the Kakadu Highway is the turn off to **Gunlom** (Waterfall Creek Falls), reached by a 37km unsealed road. The site includes the pool at the base of the falls,

WATCHING WILDLIFE IN KAKADU

Saltwater crocodiles: Cahill's Crossing over the East Alligator River.

Dingoes: Ubirr, Jabiru and along the Kakadu Highway.

Black wallaroo: Nourlangie Rock.

Short-eared rock wallabies: Early morning around Ubirr.

Northern quolls: Possible at night near Border Store.

Northern brown bandicoots: Watch for them if driving at night.

PAUL HARDING 00/SHUTTERSTOCK

View from the top of Gunlom Falls

THE SIX SEASONS OF KAKADU

Local Aboriginal people recognise six seasons in the annual cycle.

Gudjewg: (January to March) The Wet proper, with violent thunderstorms and hot, moist conditions.

Banggerreng: (April) Storms (known as 'knock 'em down' storms) flatten the spear grass, which – during the course of the Wet – has shot up to 2m high.

Yegge: (May to June) The season of mists, when the air starts to dry out. The wetlands and waterfalls still have water and most tracks are open. The first firing (burning off) of the countryside begins.

Wurrgeng: (June to mid-August) The late Dry, beginning in July, is when animals, especially birds, gather in large numbers around shrinking billabongs.

Gurrung: (mid-August to September) The end of the Dry and the beginning of another cycle.

Gunumeleng: (October to December) The buildup to the Wet. Humidity increases, the temperature rises to 35°C or more and mosquitoes reach near-plague proportions. By November the thunderstorms have started.

CHRISTINA FINK/SHUTTERSTOCK

Jim Jim Falls

a campground and a track to the natural infinity pool at the top of the falls.

Yellow Water Cruise

Just off the Kakadu Highway, 58km south of Jabiru, Cooinda is a popular base for exploring the southern part of the national park. The highlight here is one of the guided year-round **Yellow Water Cruises** *(kakadutourism.com; adult/child $130/90)* that drift along the South Alligator River and through Yellow Water Billabong in search of wildlife. The scenery's superb and there are crocs, prolific birdlife and much more.

Purchase tickets from Cooinda Lodge Kakadu (p845); a shuttle bus will take you from here to the tour's departure point. Two-hour cruises depart at 6.45am, 9am and 4.30pm; 1½-hour cruises leave at 11.30am, 1.15pm and 2.45pm. The best ones are at sunrise and sunset, when the wildlife's at its most active. Departures are less frequent during the Wet.

Get Cultured in Cooinda

An easy 1km walk from the tourism hub at Cooinda Lodge Kakadu is the excellent **Warradjan Aboriginal Cultural Centre** *(kakadutourism.com; free)*. Open daily, its excellent displays include artefacts and other cultural displays that illustrate the stories Traditional Custodians wish to share with visitors. You'll also be introduced to the 'six seasons' of Kakadu, all with a background soundtrack of chants and didgeridoos. The attached gift shop is a rich resource of Aboriginal art, homeware and more.

Chasing Waterfalls

Remote and spectacular, two Kakadu falls epitomise the rugged Top End. **Jim Jim Falls**, a sheer 215m drop, is awesome after rain (when it can only be seen from the air), but its waters shrink to a trickle by about June, though you can still swim in the pool at the base of the falls. Similarly impressive **Twin Falls** flows year-round, but there's no swimming.

These two impressive waterfalls are reached via a good unsealed road that turns south off the Kakadu Highway between Nourlangie and Cooinda – you'll need a 4WD and the road is usually closed in the Wet. Once you arrive at either site, expect some clambering around boulders or a climb to the viewpoints.

Fly Over Kakadu

Kakadu Air *(kakaduair.com.au; 30min flight adult/child $159/129, 60min $259/209, helicopter per person $245-495)* has both fixed-wing and helicopter scenic flights, and both are a wonderful way to get a sense of the sheer scale and beauty of Kakadu and Arnhem Land.

Departures are possible from both Jabiru and Cooinda.

The Jabiru Rebrand

Founded as a mining town back in 1982, Jabiru's growth in population and services was always tied to the Ranger uranium mine just up the road. The mine closed in January 2021, although the subsequent massive cleanup and rehabilitation of the landscape will last for more than a decade.

Six months after the mine closed, the federal government officially handed back the town to its Traditional Owners. The NT Government, in conjunction with Mirarr Traditional Owners, launched an ambitious plan to transform Jabiru into Kakadu's tourism hub.

Change happens slowly here and Jabiru remains a languid, if fascinating place, where Aboriginal people make up one-quarter of the town's population. The brilliant **Marrawuddi Arts & Culture** is the town's showpiece and one of the best galleries of Top End Indigenous art you'll find anywhere.

KAKADU ROCK ART

Kakadu has more than 5000 rock-art sites, which date from 20,000 years to 10 years old. Rock paintings have been classified into three periods: Pre-estuarine, which is from the earliest paintings up to around 6000 years ago; Estuarine, which covers the period from 6000 to around 2000 years ago, when rising sea levels brought the coast to its present level; and Freshwater, from 2000 years ago until the present day.

The backdrop to it all – the canvas, if you like – is the circuitous Arnhem Land escarpment. This dramatic 30m- to 200m-high sandstone cliff line forms the natural boundary between Kakadu and Arnhem Land and winds 500km through eastern and southeastern Kakadu. Creeks cut across the rocky plateau and, in the wet season, tumble off it as thundering waterfalls. These water sources would have been sites of seasonal settlements, where many of the artists would have lived.

CROC JUMPING?

One of the most popular activities in the Arnhem Highway region involves taking travellers out on a boat on the Adelaide River and enticing otherwise wild saltwater crocodiles to leap from the water to snatch hunks of meat held above them. There are some concerns with these tours, typically advertised as day trips from Darwin, on animal-welfare grounds. While operators claim to closely monitor their activities to avoid creating an unnatural dependence upon humans for food, the ethics of baiting wild animals to perform for entertainment and profit are murky. Concerns remain that staged interactions between human beings and crocs can have dangerous consequences for other kinds of pleasure craft (including fishing boats) in the area.

Continued from p813

Take a cultural or ecological tour

Family- (and 100% First Nations–owned) **Pudakul Aboriginal Cultural Tours** *(facebook.com/PudakulNT; per person from $150)* runs an excellent two-hour cultural tour through Limilngan-Wulna Land from its base just off the Arnhem Highway, 45 minutes from Darwin. The expert local Aboriginal guides take you through everything from spear-throwing and didgeridoo lessons to bush-tucker and bush-medicine guided walks. Add an art lesson to paint your own souvenir, or book the 30-minute experience separately. It also has a full-day, Aboriginal-guided, rock-art tour from Darwin, with tours possible to Litchfield and Kakadu as well.

While most wildlife tours focus on croc-jumping, **Adelaide River Tours** *(adelaiderivertours.com.au; day tour per person $190-240)* gets our vote for the best wildlife tour on the Adelaide River. Yes, you'll see crocs, but also kangaroos, buffaloes and charismatic bird species. It's a family-run operation and they'll pick you up from your Darwin hotel.

For tours with either company, don't just turn up and hope to join an existing tour; advance bookings are essential.

One of the Territory's best wetland boat tours

Wonderful boat excursions with **Wetland Cruises – Corroboree Billabong** *(wetlandcruises.com.au; tour adult $75-225, child $45-115)* show the Mary River Wetlands in all their glory. You're almost guaranteed to see crocs, as well as plenty of birdlife, and learn loads of fun facts along the way. There are 90-minute morning cruises and lunch or sunset cruises, along with full-day excursions from Darwin, including transfers.

The departure point is a 90-minute drive from Darwin; a shuttle bus is available from **Corroboree Park Tavern** (85km from Darwin), which is useful if you have a hire car that you're not permitted to drive on the unsealed side road (20km) to the billabong.

Discover a remote national park

Blink and you'll miss the skinny section of **Mary River National Park** *(nt.gov.au/parks/find-a-park/mary-river-national-park)* that crosses the Arnhem Highway. This wetland region is famous for its crocs, birdlife and barra (barramundi) fishing (best with your own boat). There is also a handful of short walks and two rollicking 4WD tracks: the 32km **Wildman Track** linking Rockhole and Wildman Rds, and the **Hardies Track**, aka the long way from the Arnhem Highway to Corroboree Billabong (25km each way).

Accessible by dirt road, riverside **Couzens Lookout** is the park's most atmospheric camping area; anglers usually opt for **Shady Camp**, next to a boat ramp further north.

Litchfield National Park

SPECTACULAR WATERFALLS | WILD WALKS | SUPERB SCENERY

If it weren't for Kakadu, spectacular Litchfield would be a world-famous icon of the Top End. The park is a spiritual and significant site for Maranunggu, Koongurrukun, Werat and Warray Aboriginal peoples, and the rock formations and natural swimming pools are simply stunning. Litchfield is also smaller and more manageable than Kakadu.

The 1500-sq-km national park encloses the spectacular Tabletop Range, a wide, sandstone plateau edged by rugged cliffs. The waterfalls that pour year-round off the plateau's edge are a highlight of the park, feeding crystal-clear cascades and plunge pools cleared of crocodiles at the beginning of the Dry. The only downside is that, given its proximity to and ease of access from Darwin, it's often busy and the only road through the park can be full of tour buses. Even so, it remains a beautiful place and certainly one of the best spots in the Top End for bushwalking, camping and especially swimming.

Termite mounds (p822)

MONA K-R/SHUTTERSTOCK

GETTING AROUND

Just a 90-minute drive south from central Darwin, the park's main attractions are all 2WD-accessible, but you'll be able to see more – including the surreal Lost City (p824) – with a 4WD. Litchfield Park Rd, the main sealed road through the park, peels off Cox Peninsula Rd near Berry Springs and ends at Batchelor to the south. There are petrol stations in both of these gateway hubs, with more sleeping and dining options in Batchelor. Several Darwin-based operators run day-tours to Litchfield, including a stop at Berry Springs Nature Park (p825); Ethical Adventures also has a '4WD Adventure' option.

HIGHLIGHTS
1 Florence Falls
2 Tabletop Track
3 Wangi Falls

SIGHTS
4 Litchfield National Park
5 Lost City
6 Magnetic Termite Mounds
7 Surprise Creek Falls
8 Tjaynera Falls
9 Tolmer Falls

ACTIVITIES
10 Bamboo Creek Tin Mine
11 Buley Rockhole
12 Cascade Pools Walks
13 Greenant Creek Walk
14 Walker Creek
see 14 Walker Creek Walk

SLEEPING
15 Hideaway Litchfield
16 Litchfield Tourist Park

EATING
17 Litchfield Cafe
see 16 Litchfield Tourist Park
18 Rum Jungle Tavern
see 3 Wangi Falls Kiosk

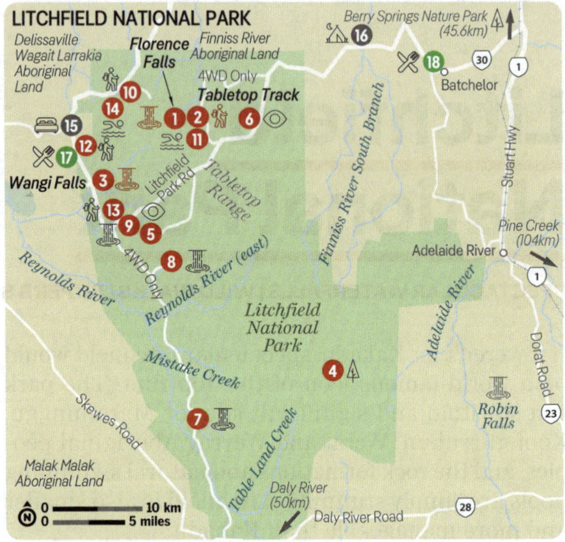

Nature's Tombstones

Litchfield's magnetic termite mounds

Termite mounds line roadsides, dot the plains and, with quirky Territorian humour, they're often dressed with brightly coloured clothing and hats. But perhaps the most photogenic of them all are in Litchfield.

About 17km after entering the park from Batchelor and the first main site you come to on the main route through the park, you arrive at what looks like a field of golden tombstones rising up from a wide, flat plain. These giant wedge-shaped **mounds** made by magnetic (or compass) termites are perfectly aligned to regulate temperature, catching the morning sun, then allowing the residents to dodge the midday heat. There's a short boardwalk with interpretative signage; don't miss the giant mounds made by the aptly named cathedral termites between the car park and the main road.

TOP TIP

If you can, stay overnight close to Litchfield (eg in Batchelor) and enter the park at sunrise. For the whole day, you'll be an hour ahead of the tour buses coming in from Darwin and all of Litchfield's sights are so much better without the crowds.

Immerse in Nature

Camping in Litchfield National Park

Litchfield National Park's camping areas are among the NT's best, making a good case for exploring the park slowly over several days. There are six camping areas inside the park, with top billing going to **Florence Falls** and **Wangi Falls** for 2WD accessibility and hot showers; the former's east-facing sites come with stellar views. Near the park's northern entrance, **Walker Creek** has walk-in tent sites only. The trio of creekside campgrounds at Central Valley have dirt-road

LITCHFIELD'S WATERFALLS BY CAR

Water cascading over red cliffs is something of a Litchfield motif – this driving tour takes you through the park's best.

START	END	LENGTH
Batchelor	Wangi Falls	68km; 1hr

Slip into your swimwear and enter the national park from the south (near Batchelor), bound for ❶ **Buley Rockhole**, 8km from the magnetic termite mounds. Find your own personal rock pool in this gentle cascade.

Beyond Buley, it's another 3.4km to ❷ **Florence Falls**. From the car park, it's a 15-minute, 135-step descent to the beautiful pool surrounded by monsoon forest, where the twin falls flow year-round. Alternatively, you can see the falls from a lookout, 120m from the car park.

From Florence Falls car park, double back to the main road and drive 18.5km to the spectacular ❸ **Tolmer Falls**, which are for looking at only. A 1.6km return track (45 minutes) offers beautiful views of the 42m-high falls pouring into the valley below.

It's a further 7km along the main road to the turn off for ❹ **Wangi Falls** (pronounced 'wong-guy'), which lies a further 1.6km up a side road. The falls flow year-round, spilling either side of a huge rocky outcrop and filling a large swimming hole fringed by monsoon forest. The lovely 1.6km-return Wangi Falls Walk takes you to a viewing platform at the base of the falls, through a monsoon forest, then via stairs up to the escarpment.

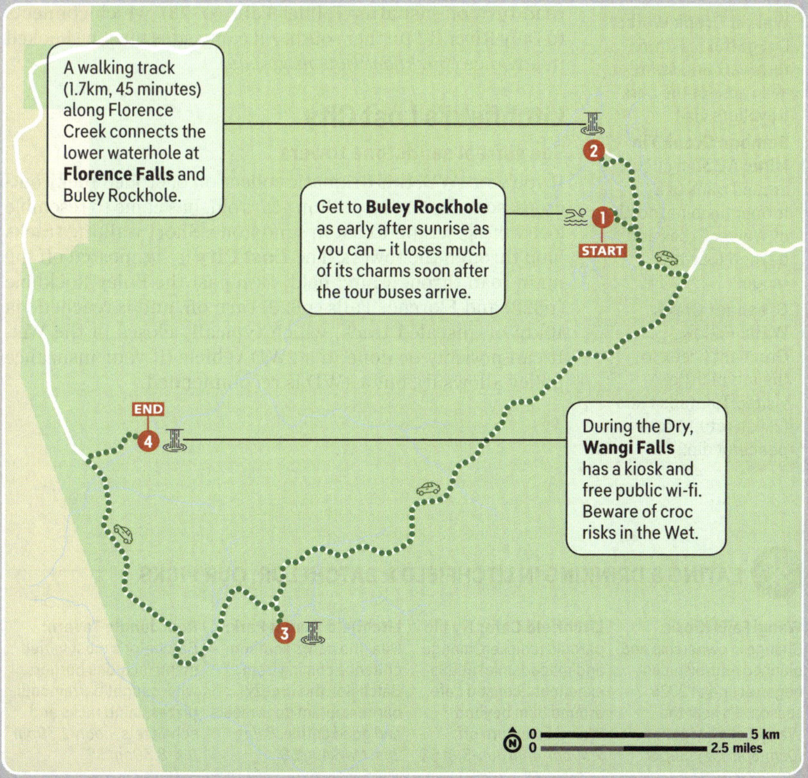

BEST WALKS IN LITCHFIELD NATIONAL PARK

Tabletop Track: A topographic map and emergency communication method are essential on this dramatic 39km circuit (two to five days) for experienced bushwalkers.

Cascade Pools Walks: Easy 2.6km-return Lower Cascades Walk to Curtin Falls, or loop back via Upper Cascades (3.3km total). You can swim at both.

Walker Creek Walk: Delightful 3.5km-return walk and swim in an area of the park travellers visit.

Bamboo Creek Tin Mine: A 330m circuit around ruins of a former tin mine, north of Walker Creek and beyond tour-bus range.

Greenant Creek Walk: Follow Greenant Creek to the top of little-visited Tjaetaba Falls (2.7km return) for a peaceful dip.

BMPHOTOGRAPHER/SHUTTERSTOCK

Wangi Falls (p822)

access (off the road to the Lost City), with a 4WD required to access the more remote **Tjaynera Falls** (Sandy Creek) and **Surprise Creek Falls** campgrounds, both along the dirt-road turn off just after Tolmer Falls (p823), which connects to Daly River Rd further south. All camp sites must be booked in advance *(parkbookings.nt.gov.au).*

Litchfield's Lost City

See surreal sandstone towers

If you've a 4WD, this dramatic collection of eroded rocky outcrops, some up to 500 million years old, has come to resemble a city of skyscrapers cast in sandstone. Short walking tracks loop through the towers. The **Lost City** is signposted off the main road through Litchfield, 4km past the Buley Rockhole (p823) and Florence Falls (p823) turn off, and is reached via 10km of unsealed track, which typically closes in the Wet. It can possibly be done in a 2WD vehicle (if your insurance policy allows it), but a 4WD is recommended.

EATING & DRINKING IN LITCHFIELD & BATCHELOR: OUR PICKS

Wangi Falls Kiosk: Change in ownership and planned refurbishment began at end of 2025 season. It's near the Wangi Falls car park. *10am-3pm May-Sep* $

Litchfield Cafe: Try filo parcels (chicken, mango and macadamia) at this excellent licensed cafe, around 8km beyond Wangi Falls turn off. *9.30am-4pm Jun-Sep* $$

Litchfield Tourist Park: Near the park's southern entrance coming from Batchelor, this breezy bar-restaurant does meals and good coffee. *8am-2pm May-Aug* $$

Rum Jungle Tavern: Batchelor's most varied menu includes burgers, wild-caught barramundi, pizzas, lamb racks and schnitzels. *noon-2.30pm & 6-8.30pm* $$

Beyond Litchfield National Park

Places

Watch the tour buses rush past, oblivious to the charms of Litchfield's hinterland, with echoes of the gold rush and stunning natural oasis.

If you're in the Litchfield area for more than a day trip from Darwin, then Batchelor, Berry Springs and Pine Creek are worth a day or two of your time. They offer fascinating windows on local life.

Bucolic Batchelor, on the lands of the Kungarakan and Warrai, is now the gateway town for Litchfield National Park, with plentiful accommodation. Just up the road, Berry Springs, on Kungarakan Country, has a spectacular spring and a popular zoo.

A little further afield, 145km south of Batchelor, Pine Creek is a former gold-mining outpost and a quietly pretty town where the traditional lands of the Wagiman and Jawoyn Bolmo, Matjba and Wurrkbarbar people meet.

GETTING AROUND

Greyhound buses from Darwin to Alice Springs stop in Adelaide River (32km south of Batchelor) and Pine Creek, but you won't get much further without a car; most people visit the area on a road trip or tour from Darwin. Near the Kakadu Highway and Umbrawarra Gorge turn offs, Pine Creek makes for a pleasant place to spend the night while exploring the area. There are petrol stations in all of these towns.

Berry Springs

TIME FROM LITCHFIELD NATIONAL PARK: **40MIN**

Waterholes and native bushland

If you want to see where Territorians in the Top End go to relax, head for the wonderful waterholes of **Berry Springs Nature Park** *(nt.gov.au/parks/find-a-park/berry-springs-nature-park)*. It's only 50km south of Darwin and very popular with locals; it's much quieter on weekdays.

The park consists of a beautiful series of spring-fed swimming holes shaded by paperbarks and pandanus and serenaded by abundant birds; native flowers bloom here in March and April. The **Water for Life Walk** (1km, 30 minutes) loops through monsoon vine forest and bushland.

Facilities include a kiosk, a picnic area with BBQs, toilets, changing sheds and showers. And there are large grassed areas to lounge around on between swims, as well as a small kiosk open from 11am to 2pm from April to the end of October.

To get here, turn off the Stuart Highway 48km south of Darwin; it's then about 10km to the park.

THE HOODED PARROT

Australia has, at last count, 53 parrot species, one-sixth of the world's total. Around 20 of these are either found (or possible) in the Territory and most roam over vast reaches of the land. But one, the hooded parrot, a beautiful bird with a turquoise front, golden shoulders and a black hoodie, has an extremely small range. Found only from Pine Creek to Mataranka and from Pine Creek to the Arnhem Land escarpment, this uncommon bird is quite the prize for birders. They are sometimes spotted in the small park that runs through the heart of Pine Creek, or on any of the town's lawns when the sprinklers are turned on.

EA GIVEN/SHUTTERSTOCK

Berry Springs (p825)

Meet the Top End's signature wildlife

If zoos are your thing, the vast **Territory Wildlife Park** *(territorywildlifepark.com.au; adult/child $39.50/20)* delivers. Its relaxed bush setting promises lots of opportunities to see Top End wildlife; everything from reptiles or birds to dingoes and northern brown bandicoots. The aquarium has a clear tunnel that takes you through aqua-scaped exhibits that include a 4m saltwater crocodile.

The park is a five-minute drive from Berry Springs Nature Park. Wear comfortable walking shoes and bring a bicycle or scooter for kids, or use the free shuttle train that runs continuously on the park's 4km loop road. Wheelchairs are also available.

Batchelor

TIME FROM LITCHFIELD NATIONAL PARK: **15MIN**

Learn Batchelor's backstory

Many travellers breeze through Batchelor, but if you're not in a rush, pick up a copy of the *Batchelor Heritage Walk* at the **Batchelor Visitor Centre** *(visitlitchfieldnt.com.au)* on Takarri Rd to guide your steps on a history-focused amble. The **Batchelor Museum** *(batchelormuseum.org.au; adult/child $5/free)*, also on Takarri Rd, covers the WWII years, when Batchelor became an important base for Allied air operations and the region's Aboriginal heritage.

If you're lucky enough to be in town on the second Sunday of the month from April to December and the weather's fine, the little **Batchelor Market** *(facebook.com/batchelormarkets)* showcases local foods and produce, as well as a few arts and crafts sprinkled throughout.

Pine Creek

TIME FROM LITCHFIELD NATIONAL PARK: 1¾HR

Relics of the gold rush

Established in 1889 after gold was discovered in the 1870s by construction workers on the Overland Telegraph Line, now-sleepy Pine Creek retains a clutch of historic buildings from the era. Among them is the rustic **Pine Creek Museum** *(nationaltrust.org.au; adult/child $5/free)*, housed in Australia's oldest prefabricated corrugated-iron building; it only opens weekday mornings. Shipped from England and erected in 1889 as the home of the mining warden in nearby (and long-ago-abandoned) Burrundie, it was moved to Pine Creek in 1913.

The old train station is now the **Railway Museum** *(adult/child $5/free)*, but you'll be lucky to find it open; mornings are most likely. Otherwise, drive or walk up the short-but-steep hill off Moule St to the **Enterprise Pit Mine Lookout** over the old open-cut mine, now full of water (135m deep!). There are good views over the surrounding countryside.

More gold rush–era relics can be found along the 79km **Northern Goldfield Loop** trail that takes you along dirt roads from Pine Creek to Adelaide River.

Explore an isolated gorge

About 3km south of Pine Creek on the Stuart Highway is the well-signposted turn off to the dramatic red cliffs of **Umbrawarra Gorge Nature Park**. It has a safe swimming hole (which can stagnate by September), a little beach and a basic campground. The Wagiman people speak for this land; look carefully and you'll see Aboriginal art on the gorge walls. The 1km walk along the water's edge is easy, but will have you clambering over boulders every now and then.

The gorge is 22km down a corrugated dirt road (just OK for 2WDs in the Dry; 4WD only in the Wet). Bring plenty of water and mosquito repellent.

A MINING MASSACRE

The harsh living conditions in the Territory goldfields are of little significance when compared to those of the era's Aboriginal peoples. In 1884, following the killing of several non-Indigenous miners by Wulwulam/Woolwonga men, the entire Wulwulam/Woolwonga people were thought exterminated in one of the most devastating massacres of Indigenous peoples carried out across the country from 1788 until the 1930s. Nearly 130 years later, an 1889 census document was found, showing that at least one member of the Wulwulam/Woolwonga clan, a child named Jennie, had survived. In 2014 a memorial plaque was installed in Burrundie, on the traditional lands of the Wulwulam/Woolwonga people, in the company of her descendants.

EATING & DRINKING IN PINE CREEK & BERRY SPRINGS: OUR PICKS

Mayse's Cafe: Diner-style spot in Pine Creek with sandwiches, homemade sausage rolls, burgers, mango smoothies. Decent coffee. *8am-2pm Mon-Sat* $

Crazy Acres Kiosk: Inside Berry Springs Nature Park. Sandwiches, local pies and homemade ice cream. *11am-3pm Mon-Fri, 10am-4pm Sat & Sun Apr-Oct* $

Lazy Lizard Tavern: Select a tune on the jukebox and settle in for a pub meal at this Pine Creek caravan-park restaurant. *noon-3pm & 6-8pm* $$

Berry Springs Tavern: The burgers and parmigiana (chicken or eggplant) are reliable from extensive menu. Happy hour at 5pm weekdays. *10am-9.30pm* $$

Arnhem Land

ROCK ART | 4WD ADVENTURE | INDIGENOUS EXPERIENCES

Places

One of Australia's last wilderness areas and an Aboriginal homeland of great spiritual power – the two very often go hand in hand – Arnhem Land is a destination for dry-season adventurers. This is a land of raw, undeveloped coastlines and abundant wildlife. It's a hauntingly beautiful, even mysterious, place; its red earth, azure seas and bottle-green woodlands are the backdrop to a fascinating, soulful human story.

Arnhem Land's population of fewer than 16,000 people comes mostly from the Yolŋu Nation of East Arnhem Land and other Traditional Custodians. This is their land and you're here only with their permission (permits are required). Most people live on outstations, but there are also Indigenous art centres, including some of Australia's best, and a fine festival to anchor your visit. Travelling out here requires careful planning, but the rewards can be transformative.

Gunbalanya (Oenpelli)

TIME FROM DARWIN: **3½HR**

Arnhem Land art centre

Best arranged in advance, tours of Injalak Hill are run out of **Injalak Arts** *(injalak.com; free)* in Gunbalanya (Oenpelli); check the website or call 08-8979 0190 to confirm opening hours. One of Australia's best Indigenous art centres, it's a wonderful place to pick up paintings on bark, canvas and paper, woodcarvings, textiles and handwoven pandanus basketry. If you're lucky, you can watch some of the artists at work.

GETTING AROUND

If you're travelling far enough to warrant an overnight stay (ie beyond Gunbalanya/Oenpelli), you'll need to organise accommodation (which is in short supply) in advance. Most travellers visit on a tour, which will include the necessary permit(s) to enter Aboriginal lands. If you're self-driving, a 4WD, plenty of fuel (petrol stations are scarce), enough food and water in case of an emergency and a satellite phone are essential. Most visitors to East Arnhem Land arrive from Darwin at Gove Airport in Nhulunbuy, serviced by **Airnorth** *(airnorth.com.au)*. The road across Cahill Crossing from Kakadu and on to the Cobourg Peninsula is only open in the Dry; other roads within Arnhem Land can also flood in the Wet.

XERO9/SHUTTERSTOCK

View from Injalak Hill

Rock-art treasures

West Arnhem Land's blockbuster rock-art site, **Injalak Hill** *(Tom Long Dreaming; tour adult/child$95/65)* is an hour's drive from Jabiru and 5km from the town of Gunbalanya (Oenpelli). Covering just about every inch of a sandstone monolith, this magnificent collection of rock art, with most works in X-ray style, tells a rich story of Aboriginal life spanning tens of thousands of years. Doubling as an ancient burial ground, it's a deeply sacred and spellbinding place.

Cobourg Peninsula

TIME FROM DARWIN: 12–15HR (car) OR 1HR (plane)

Accessible only by 4WD (or boat or charter flight) and only possible to visit with a permit (apply six weeks in advance), the Cobourg Peninsula on the traditional lands of the Arrarrkbi people sees very few visitors, which adds considerably to its sense of raw beauty and isolation. It's only open and accessible from May to October.

Wildlife of sea and land

The waters of **Garig Gunak Barlu National Park** *(nt.gov.au/parks/find-a-park/garig-gunak-barlu-national-park; one-week camping permit for five people & one vehicle $232.10)*, which covers most of the peninsula, are home to six of the world's seven species of marine turtle. Watch for the northern snake-necked turtle in the park's inland billabongs. Whales, dolphins, various shark species and saltwater crocodiles are all found in the waters off the coast – swimming here would be extremely dangerous.

ARNHEM LAND INSPIRATION

Another Country (2015): Renowned actor David Gulpilil (1953–2021) introduces his hometown, Ramingining, in this quietly powerful documentary.

An Intruder's Guide to East Arnhem Land (Andrew McMillan; 2001): One of the best books written about the region.

Balanda: My Year in Arnhem Land (Mary Ellen Jordan; 2005): Honest chronicle of 14 months living and working in Maningrida.

Healing Stone: The Best of Yothu Yindi (2012): Fine album introducing Arnhem Land's groundbreaking Yolŋu band; includes enduring hit 'Treaty'.

Naku Dharuk: The Bark Petitions (Clare Wright, 2024): Tells how Yolŋu petitions written on bark against bauxite mining in the 1960s changed Australia's history.

Mammal species, though elusive, include the likes of dingoes, echidnas, northern brown bandicoots and adorable sugar gliders. The park is also home to more than 200 bird species.

Staying overnight

You can't come here without staying overnight and the silence that descends after darkness falls is truly special.

There is a designated camping area at **Smith Point** with showers, toilets, BBQs and limited bore water; generators are allowed in one section. But the best place to stay is **Cobourg Coastal Camp** *(cobourgcoastalcamp.com.au)* around 30km south, used exclusively by **Venture North Safaris** *(venturenorth.com.au)* on its brilliant land-based and fishing tours. Outside the park, Wiligi Outstation (p845; *wiligi arnhemland.com.au; camping/room $33/275*) is an excellent alternative, with permanent tents, cabins and camping.

The history of Port Essington

On a remote inlet across the water from the park headquarters, the surprisingly well-preserved ruins of **Victoria Settlement**, also known as Port Essington, are the third and final failed attempt by the British Navy to establish a colony in Australia's Top End in the early 19th century. Conical ironstone chimneys rise above the otherwise low-slung ruins. Upon the order to disband in 1849, 11 years after the settlement was founded in this remote, isolated, unforgiving environment, 61 souls had perished. Unless you have your own boat, the only way to visit is with Venture North Safaris.

Nhulunbuy

TIME FROM DARWIN: **14HR** (car) **OR 1½HR** (plane)

The wildly beautiful coast and country of East Arnhem Land is well off the beaten track: key to its appeal for intrepid travellers. About 3350 people live in the region's main settlement, Nhulunbuy, built to service the bauxite mine here. Some of the country's most respected art comes out of this region, too, including bark paintings, carved mimi-spirit figures, yidaki (didgeridoos), woven baskets and mats, and jewellery. Admire/purchase local art from the **Buku-Larrŋgay Mulka Art Centre & Museum** *(yirrkala.com)*, 20km southeast of Nhulunbuy in Yirrkala.

If you're headed to Groote Eylandt, don't miss **Anindilyakwa Arts** *(anindilyakwaarts.com.au)*.

Attend the Garma Festival

Held in northern East Arnhem Land in August, the four-day **Garma Festival** *(yyf.com.au/garma-festival)* is Australia's largest Indigenous cultural gathering; a celebration of Yolŋu life and culture that includes ceremonial performances, storytelling, film screenings, yidaki healing, bushcraft lessons and much more. Its Key Forum hosts important discussions between government and local leaders.

CRAIG R_AU/SHUTTERSTOCK

Rainbow Cliffs, Nhulunbuy

Serious planning is required to attend, so start early. The festival site is a 30-minute drive from Nhulunbuy. Or you can tackle the 675km drive from Katherine; 4WD essential. Festival accommodation is in tents; BYO linen.

Bremer Island / Dhämbaliya

TIME FROM DARWIN: 1½HR + 15HR

Take a day trip to Banubanu

If beachfront glamping at **Banubanu Beach Retreat** *(banubanu.com)* on beautiful Bremer Island / Dhämbaliya, a 45-minute boat ride from the Gove Peninsula, is not in your budget, why not visit for the day? The retreat has a day-trip option with return **transfers** *(weekdays/weekends $149/179)*, or you can pay a small fee (per person $30) to head over in your own boat to stroll the island's empty beaches, kayak through crystalline waters, or simply kick back and savour a meal at Banubanu's Seabreeze Restaurant.

ARNHEM LAND PERMITS

Arnhem Land's strict visitor-permit system is designed to protect the environment and sacred sites. The process has been streamlined and can be completed online. If you're visiting as part of a tour, the operator will make the necessary arrangements.

If you're travelling independently, apply (in advance) through the **Northern Land Council** *(nlc.org.au/permits)* for the Central Arnhem Highway, Gunbalanya (Oenpelli) and West Arnhem Land; the **Dhimurru Aboriginal Corporation** *(dhimurru.com.au/permits-information.html)* for East Arnhem Land; and **Parks & Wildlife** *(nt.gov.au/parks/find-a-park/garig-gunak-barlu-national-park)* for the Garig Gunak Barlu National Park. Permits usually take two to three days and most are free.

Katherine & Nitmiluk National Park

GORGE TOURS | WILD SWIMS | INDIGENOUS ART

TOP TIP
Spend some time talking (and planning) with the people at Nitmiluk Tours at the Nitmiluk Visitor Centre to see the full range of tour possibilities, including adventure swimming, self-guided canoe trips and multiday wilderness expeditions.

Katherine is best known for Nitmiluk National Park, northeast of the town. Apart from being an obvious base for exploring the national park – one of the Territory's biggest attractions that's famous for its string of spectacular gorges – the sunbaked outback town also has a handful of interesting features worth a day or half-day of your time.

Katherine has long been an important meeting place, standing as it does where the traditional lands of the Jawoyn, Dagoman and Wardaman come together. Roads also converge here from Darwin, Western Australia and Alice Springs; you'll certainly feel like you've arrived somewhere if you've just made the long trip up the highway from Alice Springs – Katherine's namesake river is the first permanent running water on the road north of Alice Springs.

The Nitmiluk Visitor Centre at the entrance to Nitmiluk Gorge is a great place to begin your visit to the park; there's another visitor centre in Katherine.

GETTING AROUND

Katherine is 317km south of Darwin along the Stuart Highway; the turn off to **Leliyn** (Edith Falls) in the northern section of Nitmiluk National Park (p834) is 44km before Katherine. **Greyhound** *(greyhound.com.au)* buses from Darwin to Alice Springs stop in Katherine; **Katherine Coaches** *(katherine coaches.com.au)* also runs services to/from Darwin and remote communities. **Airnorth** *(airnorth.com.au)* flies to Darwin, Alice Springs and Tennant Creek from Katherine's small airport. You'll want a car to get around the spread-out town and out to the national park (Nitmiluk Gorge is 30km east of town), but local taxis and hire cars are also available. Nitmiluk Tours runs **Jatbula Trail** *(nitmiluktours.com.au/gorge-experiences/gorge-tours/jatbula-trail-transfer)* transfers.

KATHERINE & NITMILUK NATIONAL PARK

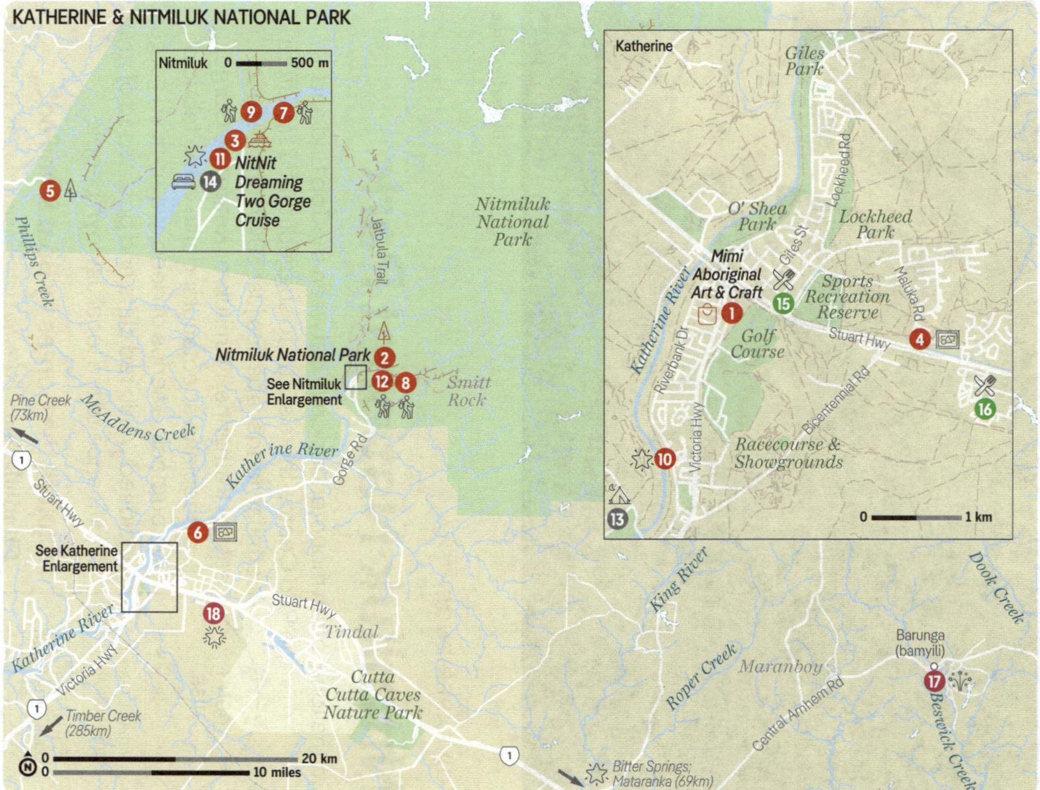

HIGHLIGHTS
1 Mimi Aboriginal Art & Craft
2 Nitmiluk National Park
3 NitNit Dreaming Two Gorge Cruise

SIGHTS
4 Godinymayin Yijard Rivers Arts & Culture Centre
5 Leliyn (Edith Falls)
6 Top Didj Cultural Experience & Art Gallery

ACTIVITIES
7 Baruwei Lookout & Loop
8 Butterfly Gorge
9 Jatbula Trail
10 Katherine Hot Springs
11 Nitmiluk Tours
12 Windolf Walk

SLEEPING
13 Big4 Breeze Holiday Parks Katherine
14 Cicada Lodge

EATING
15 Black Russian Caravan Bar
see 14 Cicada Lodge
16 Maiden's Lane
see 11 Nitmiluk Cafe

ENTERTAINMENT
17 Barunga Festival
18 Katherine Outback Experience

INFORMATION
see 15 Katherine Visitor Information Centre
see 11 Nitmiluk Visitor Centre

KAREL STIPEK/SHUTTERSTOCK

Butterfly Gorge

TOP EXPERIENCE

Nitmiluk National Park

On the long, often monotonous drive between the Top End and the Red Centre, there's little to suggest that a signature Australian landscape lies just 30km off the road, east of Katherine. Nitmiluk, or Katherine Gorge, is a deep and spectacular defile in the fabric of the outback, a series of deep, water-filled gorges enclosed within red cliffs and possessed of great significance to the local Jawoyn people.

DON'T MISS

- Two Gorge Cruise
- Nabilil Dreaming Sunset Dinner Tour
- Ancient Garlarr One Gorge Safari
- Baruwei Lookout & Loop walk
- Jatbula Trail
- Footsteps of Our Ancestors Tour
- Take a scenic flight
- Butterfly Gorge walk
- Swim at Leliyn (Edith Falls)

Explore the Gorges by Boat & on Foot

Nitmiluk Tours *(nitmiluktours.com.au)* runs gorge tours from the boat jetty. Advance bookings are essential. The two-hour **NitNit Dreaming Two Gorge Cruise** goes to the second gorge and visits a rock-art gallery (including an 800m walk), usually with a swim along the way.

The four-hour, dry-season-only **Three Gorge Cruise** does the same as the two-gorge cruise but continues on to the third gorge.

PRACTICALITIES

● *nt.gov.au/parks/find-a-park/nitmiluk-national-park* ● entry free ● open year-round

Also popular from May to October is the **Nabilil Dreaming Sunset Dinner Tour**, which comes highly recommended, taking in two gorges and a rock-art gallery and topped off with a sumptuous bush-tucker-inspired feast as the gorges glow scarlet at sunset.

Indigenous guides lead all tours. For an even deeper cultural experience, the excellent 2½-hour **Ancient Garlarr One Gorge Safari** takes you through men's and women's traditional stories, rock art, crafts and local plants, with time for a swim as well. Or the five-hour **Footsteps of Our Ancestors Tour** focuses on Jawoyn traditional activities like basket weaving, spear throwing, making fires, painting and didgeridoo playing.

Check the website for prices and departure times. There's wheelchair access to the top of the first gorge only.

Hike the Trails of Nitmiluk

Nitmiluk is one of northern Australia's best hiking destinations. There are dozens of trails extending over 120km. These are our favourites.

The **Baruwei Lookout & Loop** begins near the visitor centre and climbs steadily to the lookout (1.8km, one hour) for stunning views. The trail then loops more gently back to the visitor centre (4.8km, two hours). In the same area, **Windolf Walk** (8.4km, 3½-hours) is a moderately challenging hike to the first gorge, with swimming at the waterfall at Southern Rockhole when water levels allow.

For something a touch more challenging, **Butterfly Gorge** (12km return, 4½ hours) weaves through monsoon rainforest to a deep-water swimming spot along the second gorge.

But the real prize in these parts is the epic, celebrated **Jatbula Trail** (66km one way, five days) to Leliyn (Edith Falls). A ferry service takes you across the gorge, whereafter you climb the Arnhem Land escarpment, passing swamp-fed Biddlecombe Cascades, Crystal Falls, the Amphitheatre and Sweetwater Pool.

Take a Scenic Flight

If you're craving the aerial view, Nitmiluk Tours runs the **Nitmiluk Heli-Art Adventure** *(per person $753)* for one hour, 40 minutes. It takes you in a helicopter as far as the 13th Gorge (with soul-stirring scenery en route) and a rarely seen rock-art site. Building on this, the **Nitmiluk Ultimate Adventure** *(per person $1289)* lasts an extra hour and includes a touchdown in a remote wilderness waterhole for a swim. Ask also about its eight-minute buzz over the first gorge.

Swim at Leliyn (Edith Falls)

Reached off the Stuart Highway 40km north of Katherine and a further 20km along a sealed road, **Leliyn (Edith Falls)** is a picturesque, safe haven for swimming and hiking. The huge pool at the base of the falls is only 100m from the car park. It's one of the Territory's least-known gems.

LANDSCAPE & CULTURE

Nitmiluk consists of 13 deep sandstone gorges that were first formed 23 million years ago by the Katherine River on its journey from Arnhem Land to the Timor Sea. The gorge lies on the lands of the Jawoyn people, who jointly manage Nitmiluk with Parks & Wildlife. 'Nitmiluk' means 'Place of Cicadas' in the Jawoyn language.

TOP TIPS

- Most hiking trails are open April–September.
- In the Dry the tranquil river consists of sedate pools separated by rock bridges. In the Wet, an awesome torrent churns through the gorge.
- **Jatbula Trail** can only be done one way (ie you can't walk from Leliyn/Edith Falls to Katherine Gorge), is closed October– April and requires at least two walkers.
- At **Leilyn (Edith Falls)**, behind the pool is a leafy picnic area adjacent to a pleasantly landscaped and popular campground. A kiosk on the edge of the car park has basic supplies.
- Overnight hikers must register at **Nitmiluk Visitor Centre**.

THE BARUNGA STATEMENT

At the Barunga Festival (p841) in 1988, on the bicentennial of white settlement in Australia, two senior Aboriginal elders, Galarrwuy Yunupingu and Wenten Rubuntja, presented then-prime minister Bob Hawke with a statement of principles for Indigenous rights and aspirations. Painted upon a more-than-1m-long piece of wood, it became known as the Barunga Statement. In response, the prime minister stated that he hoped to conclude a treaty with Aboriginal people by 1990. The encounter became the inspiration for the hit song 'Treaty' by Yothu Yindi. Prime Minister Hawke's final act as prime minister was to hang the Barunga Statement in Parliament House in Canberra, where it remains. Aboriginal people are still waiting for their treaty.

An Urban Spa for the Ages

Bathe in Katherine Hot Springs

Bitter Springs (p844) may be bigger on social media, but **Katherine Hot Springs** is also excellent and much more accessible; there's a wheelchair ramp (call 08-8972 5500 for the ramp access code).

Within the township in Katherine South, this natural thermal spring fringed by greenery meanders alongside the Katherine River, its shallow gin-clear pools (with an average temperature of 25°C) inviting a relaxing soak. Arrive early enough (it's open 7am to 7pm) and you might score a private float.

Aboriginal Art Fest

Visit Katherine's excellent art centres

In Katherine South, but just south of the Stuart Highway, the Aboriginal-community-owned and not-for-profit **Mimi Aboriginal Art & Craft** *(mimiarts.com)* has a large gallery space and two studios where you might spot regional artists at work.

In Katherine East, the expanded-in-2024 **Godinymayin Yijard Rivers Arts & Culture Centre** *(gyracc.org.au)* is dedicated to showcasing works by Indigenous and non-Indigenous artists from the Big Rivers region.

Just off Gorge Rd on the way to Nitmiluk Gorge, **Top Didj Cultural Experience & Art Gallery** *(topdidj.com)* showcases Katherine's largest collection of Indigenous art for sale. It's open April to September and by appointment the rest of the year.

An Outback Experience

Horse around to country tunes

Operating during the Dry off the Stuart Highway southeast of town, the **Katherine Outback Experience** *(katherineoutbackexperience.com.au; adult/child $84/45)* is a two-hour show about horse training and working dogs, but expect your host, country music star Tom Curtain, to burst into song without warning at some stage.

EATING & DRINKING IN KATHERINE: OUR PICKS

Black Russian Caravan Bar: This cutesy caravan serves NT's best street-food with great coffee, thick-cut toasties and pastries. *6.30am-2pm* $

Nitmiluk Cafe: Katherine River views from the deck at the Nitmiluk Visitor Centre, while tucking into a light meal with outback ingredients. *7am-2pm* $

Maiden's Lane: In Katherine East, this cafe (same owners as Caravan Bar) serves great burgers, brunch, coffee. *6am-2pm Mon-Fri, 7am-2pm Sat & Sun* $$

Cicada Lodge: The best place to stay in this part of the NT also has its best kitchen, with designer, three-course meals for nonguests for $125 per person. *7-9pm* $$

Beyond Katherine & Nitmiluk National Park

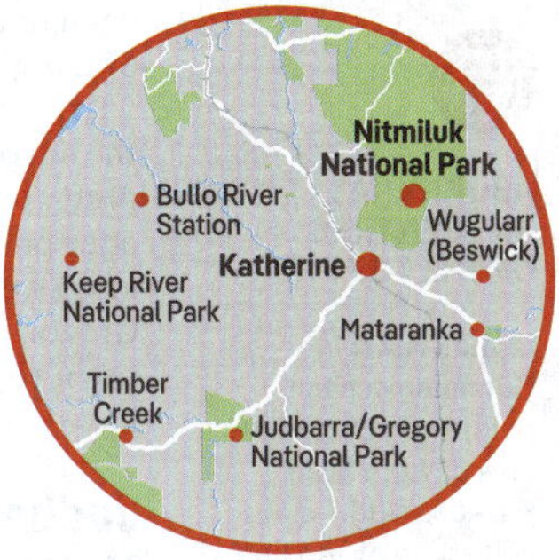

Pretty special country awaits you beyond Katherine and Nitmiluk, from the Victoria River and remote national parks to deep down into the heart of the continent.

Places

Connect with Aboriginal culture, float in hot springs or bump along isolated 4WD trails – you can do it all here, where the tropical north melts into the arid outback.

Detour off the Stuart Highway before Katherine to find one of the NT's least touristy Aboriginal art centres and experiences. Just 70 minutes south of Katherine on sealed roads, Mataranka and Bitter Springs provide an idyllic taste of Elsey National Park, the setting of the renowned colonial-era autobiographical novel, *We of the Never Never*. Southwest of Katherine, the sealed Victoria Hwy connects to Kununurra in WA and is one of Australia's most underrated outback roads, passing by two lesser-known national parks, a storied cattle station and superb escarpments.

Timber Creek

TIME FROM KATHERINE: **3¼HR**

Visit a remote Victoria River town

With a population of barely 300 and the only 'town' in the 514km between Katherine and Kununurra, Timber Creek feels like a glimpse of an old frontier. Most travellers stop only long

GETTING AROUND

Like most of the NT, this region is most easily explored with your own vehicle, ideally a 4WD if you're planning to explore national parks beyond Elsey or the Victoria River. Greyhound has a daily service from Darwin to Kununurra via Katherine, but the bus passes through the region at night, so to enjoy the views, book Katherine Coaches' daytime service. Katherine Coaches also services Wugularr (Beswick). Greyhound buses to/from Darwin and Alice Springs stop in Mataranka.

ABORIGINAL ART CENTRES OF THE TOP END

Injalak Arts: In Gunbalanya (Oenpelli) and accessible on a day trip from Kakadu. World-class collection of Top End styles/genres.

Mimi Aboriginal Art & Craft: Small, well-curated and Aboriginal-run; its collection befits its Katherine location – between desert and tropics.

Marrawuddi Arts & Culture: Centrepiece of Jabiru's rebirth, Marrawuddi has an especially fine selection of Arnhem Land bark paintings and pandanus basketry.

Buku Larrŋgay Mulka Art Centre: In far east of Arnhem Land, this remote centre showcases mostly Yolŋu art.

Ghunmarn Culture Centre: In Wugularr (Beswick), both first-class gallery and shop for local art.

enough to refuel body and vehicle, but we reckon it's worth an overnight stop to revel in the small-town isolation.

Drive up to **Escarpment Lookout** for sweeping views of the surrounding country, or detour to **Policeman's Point**, a pretty overlook alongside the Victoria River where local police once posted lookouts for fugitives drifting downriver; birders also swear by this place to look for the prized Gouldian finch. Gregory's Tree is another worthwhile stop and ask around town to see if the sunrise and/or sunset cruises on the river have resumed.

Judbarra / Gregory National Park

TIME FROM KATHERINE: **4HR**

Discover an unknown masterpiece

Ripe for 4WD exploration during the Dry, **Judbarra / Gregory National Park** *(nt.gov.au/parks/find-a-park/judbarra-gregory-national-park)* is vast, covering 12,860 sq km, and utterly magnificent.

It's a little like travelling to a barely visited echo of the Kimberley, with tabletop escarpments in deep red hues separated by ancient river valleys snaking south. Also like the Kimberley, Judbarra has a stirr Indigenous story and it encompasses the traditional lands of numerous Aboriginal groups, among them the Ngarinyman, Karrangpurru, Nungali, Malngin, Wardaman, Ngaliwurru and Bilinara.

The park is accessible from the Katherine-to-Kununurra highway, and one of the park's many campgrounds, **Big Horse Creek**, just off the highway next to the mighty Victoria River near Timber Creek, will give you a taste of what the park has to offer. For example, worthwhile walks include the 500m-returnable to **Gregory's Tree**, 9km from the campground or 15km from Timber Creek. The tree occupies a sacred Aboriginal site, where the dates of English explorer AC Gregory's 1855–56 North Australia Expedition were carved into a boab tree by expedition artist Baines.

But the real drama of this special place is found south off the highway and down beyond where the paved roads end. A fabulous detour is the 54km gravel track off the Victoria Hwy to **Jasper Gorge**, one of the park's (and the NT's) most spectacular corners. The **Parks & Wildlife office** *(08-8975 0888)* in Timber Creek can provide park and 4WD notes, and a map to the various walks, camping spots, tracks and the historic homestead and ruggedly romantic original stockyards.

And one final thing: this is croc country; swimming isn't safe in these parts.

Bullo River Station

TIME FROM KATHERINE: **5½HR**

Conservation meets cattle

Drive north off the highway down a 75km-long driveway to **Bullo River Station** *(bulloriver.com.au)*. Open April to September, it's a beautiful drive through the Pinkerton Range and down across the floodplains to the station headquarters shaded by boab trees. Made famous by then-owner

TOP EXPERIENCE

Karlu Karlu / Devils Marbles

Of the many weird-and-wonderful landscapes found across the Australian outback, none seem quite so otherworldly as the Devils Marbles (Karlu Karlu in Warumungu). They're a long way from anywhere and the presence of these great piles of gigantic rocky boulders (some with a diameter of 6m) amid what is otherwise a largely featureless desert only adds to their almost preternatural beauty.

PUYALROYO/SHUTTERSTOCK

Sacred Stories

The Karlu Karlu / Devils Marbles were returned to the Alyawarre Traditional Owners in 2008. They believe that the great granite boulders, a sacred site, are the eggs of the Rainbow Serpent, the Creator spirit in most stories of the Dreaming.

The Marbles carry great spiritual significance for other Aboriginal groups of these desert regions, including the Kaytetye, Warumungu and Warlpiri. Signposts make it very clear where you can explore and photograph; some areas are off-limits, due to their importance in traditional beliefs.

Exploring on Foot

There are five signposted walks around the Karlu Karlu / Devils Marbles, including the 20-minute, 400m **Karlu Karlu Walk** and the 1½-hour, 4km **Nurrku Walk**, which is excellent for escaping the crowds. If you've only time for one walk, make it the 30-minute, 800m **Mayijangu Walk** that unfurls from the day-use area to the campground, with a 20-minute, 350m add-on up to **Nyanjiki Lookout**; the views from up here are superb.

As you go, watch for boulders sliced in half: such are the extremes of temperature out here that the boulders undergo an ongoing 24-hour cycle of expansion and contraction.

TOP TIPS

- The Karlu Karlu / Devils Marbles are 105km south of Tennant Creek/ 412km north of Alice Springs.
- Plan to visit in your own wheels and, if staying overnight, you'll need camping equipment and supplies.
- The nearest motel is in Warumungu, 9km south along the Stuart Highway.

Practicalities

- *nt.gov.au/parks/find-a-park/karlu-karlu-devils-marbles-conservation-reserve*

Sara Henderson in her 1993 memoir of life on Bullo, *From Strength to Strength*, the property is now a groundbreaking partnership between its private owners and the not-for-profit Australian Wildlife Conservancy *(AWC; australianwildlife.org)*. Put simply, it combines a commercial pastoral operation with a tourism project and intensive conservation measures.

Only those with a confirmed reservation can enter the property, but staying here and exploring the station could just be a highlight of your trip.

THE SAVANNAH WAY

The sealed Victoria Hwy – part of the Savannah Way, which stretches 3700km between Broome (WA) and Cairns (Queensland) – runs 513km from Katherine to Kununurra in Western Australia. With its sandstone outcrops and boab trees rising out of the semiarid plains, this part of the world is sometimes called the East Kimberley and it is a stirring precursor to the glorious red-rock landscapes of the Kimberley further west.The only town en route is tiny Timber Creek (290km from Katherine). Fuel, meals and camping are also available at the Victoria River Roadhouse, 200km from Katherine. Note that fruits, vegetables, nuts and honey cannot be taken across the state border into WA.

Keep River National Park

TIME FROM KATHERINE: **5HR**

Discover the natural drama of Keep River

One of the Northern Territory's best-kept secrets, remote **Keep River National Park** *(nt.gov.au/parks/find-a-park/keep-river-national-park)* lies alongside the WA border, making Kununurra the closest town, 46km to the west. Used by the Miriwoong and Gajirrabeng peoples for thousands of years, this relatively small park packs some seriously epic scenery into its 574.37 sq km, with Aboriginal rock art and surreal sandstone formations – reminiscent of the Bungle Bungle Range in WA's Purnululu (Bungle Bungle) National Park – among its highlights.

Apart from the sheer beauty of this magical place, Keep River's appeal lies in its accessibility. There are two basic, shady, 2WD-accessible (in the Dry) camping areas in the park – one at **Goorrandalng**, 18km from the park entrance; the other at **Jarnem**, 32km from the entrance. From Goorrandalng, a 2km loop trail weaves through a soul-stirring sandstone habitat. From Jarnem, a 7km loop track takes you to an Aboriginal rock-art site, as well as a spectacular lookout. Other short walks leading off the main access road reveal traces of historic Aboriginal occupation.

Keep an eye out for local critters, including the short-eared rock wallaby, white-quilled rock pigeon and sandstone shrike-thrush with its peachy buff.

Wugularr (Beswick)

TIME FROM KATHERINE: **1¼HR**

Admire Top End art

To see genuine Aboriginal art produced by local communities, take the 59km, all-weather detour off the Stuart Highway to the small community of Wugularr (Beswick) on Jawoyn Country.

The main attraction in the town itself is the **Ghunmarn Culture Centre** *(djilpinarts.org.au; free)*, which displays local paintings and didgeridoos painted in the West Arnhem Land style, as well as fibre crafts and other creations. Usually open on weekdays during the Dry (call ahead to check), the centre also features the **Blanasi Collection**, a permanent exhibition of absolutely stunning artworks by the late artist David Blanasi and other Elders from the region. Attached is **Djilpin Arts**, a small shop where you can purchase paintings,

PIERDEST/SHUTTERSTOCK

Rock art, Jarnem loop trail

handmade jewellery, woven baskets and other handicrafts, with profits supporting the community.

Explore authentic culture and splendid falls in Wugularr

From early May to mid-September, it's worth lingering overnight in Wugularr (Beswick) and really getting a sense of what this otherwise-closed community is all about. Attached to the cultural centre are the stilted, architecturally arresting **Djakanimba Pavilions** *(djilpinarts.org.au/stay)*, swathed in corrugated iron on the outside, spacious and supremely comfortable within. There's no restaurant, but there's a small supermarket a short walk away and each room has a microwave and fridge.

At the centre, join a weaving workshop and expert local guides also run day tours to magical **Melkulumbu (Beswick Falls)** and/or **Bullocky Head**. Both are stunning and the latter is also a scenic (and sacred) ceremony site. Each takes an entire day, which costs $295 per person per tour. Groups are invariably small and they're worth every dollar.

All experiences must be booked in advance through the centre *(djilpinarts.org.au/experience)*.

Indigenous arts and culture at the Barunga Festival

Second in significance only to the Garma Festival (p830) and much more accessible, the **Barunga Festival** *(barunga festival.com.au)* happens in three days over a wonderful long weekend in mid-June. Barunga, 30km east of Wugularr (Beswick), showcases traditional arts and crafts, dancing, music, workshops, film screenings, sporting competitions and more. Bring your own camping equipment; alternatively, visit for the day from Katherine.

WE OF THE NEVER NEVER

Few outback stories captured the national imagination like *We of the Never Never*, Jeannie Gunn's account of life on Mataranka's Elsey Station; made into a film (1981).

Gunn arrived in the NT from Melbourne in 1902 with her husband, Aeneas, who was to take up the manager's position at Elsey Station. Only a year after their arrival, Aeneas died of malarial dysentery.

Jeannie returned to Melbourne and recorded her Top End experiences in the memoir-novel, published in 1908. Today, her depiction of Aboriginal peoples may seem antiquated, although she did voice the (then-unpopular) opinion that white settlers had stolen their land.

Jeannie was awarded an OBE (Order of the British Empire) in 1939 for her contribution to Australian literature.

MATARANKA TO ALICE SPRINGS DRIVE

The Stuart Highway is still referred to as 'the Track'. It's dead straight and gets progressively drier and flatter the further south you go.

START	END	LENGTH
Mataranka	Alice Springs	1075km; 11–14hr

Begin in ❶ **Mataranka** (p844), followed by tiny ❷ **Larrimah** (p844), then continue another 93km to the ❸ **Daly Waters Pub**, where the pub's interior is decorated with business cards, bras, banknotes and memorabilia from passing travellers.

Pass the Carpentaria Highway to Borroloola, then drive past ❹ **Newcastle Waters** and ❺ **Elliott**, each with a roadhouse with fuel and hot chips, as needed.

At ❻ **Threeways Roadhouse**, the road to Queensland branches away to the east; most travellers pull over here, desperate for human company. ❼ **Tennant Creek** may only be home to a couple of thousand souls, but it feels like a metropolis after driving 567km from Mataranka.

Spend as long as you can at ❽ **Karlu Karlu / Devils Marbles**, 96km south of town.

It's all about the UFOs at the ❾ **Wycliffe Well Roadhouse** – they apparently fly over here with astonishing regularity. Signs depict alien figures. At the time of research, the roadhouse had been closed for a number of years.

Further south is ❿ **Barrow Creek Hotel**, one of the highway's oddball outback pubs, where travellers have left notes, photos, bumper stickers and knickknacks.

There's fuel at ⓫ **Aileron Roadhouse**, where the owner's collection of Albert Namatjira watercolours adorn the bar and dining area.

From Aileron, it's a short 135km hop down the asphalt to ⓬ **Alice Springs**.

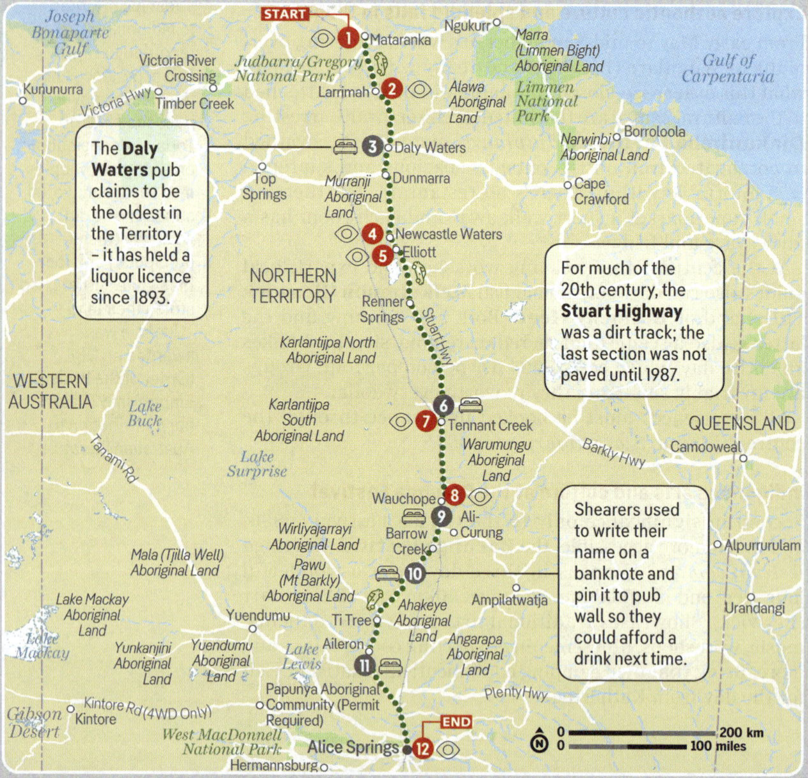

INNE WAGEMANS/SHUTTERSTOCK

Hot springs, Mataranka (p844)

LAST STOP LARRIMAH

Once upon a time, the railway line from Darwin came as far as Birdum, 8km south of tiny Larrimah. That's about as good as it ever got for Larrimah, on the traditional lands of the Wubalawun people, until the mysterious 2017 disappearance of local larrikin (hooligan) Paddy Moriarty. What followed was a 2017 podcast *Lost in Larrimah* and the 2021 book *Larrimah* (both about the disappearance and its aftermath). A 2023 two-part Netflix documentary *Last Stop Larrimah* then followed the ensuing investigation and the unravelling of a tiny outback town (population 11 or 12). Stop for a pint at the Larrimah **Pink Panther Hotel** (which sold to new owners in September 2025) just off the Stuart Highway, 75km south of Mataranka.

Mataranka

TIME FROM KATHERINE: **1¼HR**

Follow the Never Never trail

In the small highway town of Mataranka, 108km south of Katherine on the lands of the Najig and Guyanggan Nganawirdbird peoples, the **Never Never Museum** *(adult/child $5/2.50)* has displays on the northern railway, WWII and local history. Across the road from the museum, life-size figures representing the *We of the Never Never* book's main characters populate the park along the Stuart Highway in the town centre.

Lonely **Elsey Cemetery**, around 20km south of Mataranka and signposted off the Stuart Highway, is a poignant footnote to the story. Many of the larger-than-life characters from the book are buried here, among them Aeneas Gunn (alongside a memorial to his wife), Henry Peckham, John MacLennan and Tom Pearce. The last (barely visible) remains of the original **Elsey Station Homestead** (destroyed during roadworks in the 1940s) lie around 1km to the south, near the end of the gravel track.

Outside the entrance to the **Mataranka Homestead Resort** (9km east of Mataranka) is a rickety **replica homestead**, constructed for the filming of *We of the Never Never*, which is screened daily in the resort bar.

Spring into Elsey National Park

It's not difficult to understand how the pair of crystal-clear, aquamarine springs fringed by subtropical greenery in **Elsey National Park** *(nt.gov.au/parks/find-a-park/elsey-national-park)* became famous on social media. Named for the taste of its mineral-rich waters, which hover around 32°C, **Bitter Springs** is the most scenic of the two, with its sensitively designed tourism infrastructure (several sets of stairs leading into the springs, connected by a footpath) allowing its natural beauty to shine. Better yet, it's only 3km from Mataranka along the sealed Martin Rd, with an easy 500m loop encircling the main Livistona palm–lined thermal pool.

Beside the **Mataranka Homestead Resort** (9km from Mataranka on the sealed Homestead Rd), **Mataranka Thermal Pool** is also accessed via an easy 500m loop trail. There's a bit more infrastructure here (read: more concrete), upgraded in 2023, tending to make it more popular among travellers with kids. It can also be more crowded. Both springs flood in the Wet, making them off-limits for swimming until cleared of crocs.

Places We Love to Stay

$ Budget $$ Midrange $$$ Top End

Darwin

MAP p806

Discovery Parks Darwin $ Pitch a tent, park your van (all sites are powered) or check into a cabin amid landscaped gardens, 10km east of Darwin.

Vibe Hotel & Adina Apartment Hotel $$ Choose from smart hotel rooms or studio, one- or two-bed apartments in this popular two-in-one waterfront property.

Palms City Resort $$ Central but quiet and occupying a palm-filled garden, this place has outstanding rooms and especially good villas with echoes of Asia.

Kakadu National Park & Jabiru

Cooinda Lodge Kakadu $$ This sprawling lodge is the tourism hub for this corner of Kakadu, with a restaurant, pool, rooms, campground and glamping safari tents.

Anbinik Kakadu Resort $$ Aboriginal-owned caravan park in Jabiru offering a range of tropical-design bungalows, cabins and suites in lush gardens. It only opens April to October.

Mercure Kakadu $$$ Known locally as 'the Croc', this hotel is designed in the shape of a crocodile. Rooms are clean and comfortable if a little pedestrian for the price.

Mary River

Breeze Holiday Parks Mary River $ This relaxing riverside bush retreat just off the Arnhem Highway has camping and simple safari tents.

Bamurru Plains $$$ This remote slice of ecofriendly luxury on the Mary River floodplains has canvas-topped lodgings with hardwood floors, wraparound views and high levels of comfort. Guests fly in from Darwin.

Litchfield National Park & Batchelor

MAP p822

Litchfield Tourist Park $$ Just 4km from Litchfield National Park, this friendly, leafy caravan park has a great range of accommodation options.

Hideaway Litchfield $$$ In Rakula on the park's western fringe, with luxury two-tier villas that blend perfectly into the bushy surrounds.

Pine Creek

Pine Creek Railway Resort $$ This charming boutique hotel has modern rooms and a dining room harking back to romantic rail journeys of yore.

Arnhem Land

Davidson's Arnhemland Safari Lodge $$$ Tasteful, high comfort in West Arnhem Land, Davidson's has safari tents on stilts, good food and a gorgeous setting.

Walkabout Lodge $$$ The motel-style rooms would be overpriced elsewhere, but they're not bad value for Nhulunbuy. There are also 12 powered camp sites.

Wiligi Outstation $$$ On a remote outstation near Garig Gunak Barlu NP, Wiligi has lovely eco tents with views and shady waterfront camp sites.

Katherine & Nitmiluk National Park

MAP p833

BIG4 Breeze Holiday Parks Katherine $ A well-manicured caravan park in South Katherine with plenty of shady sites, a bistro and a great swimming pool.

Cicada Lodge $$$ This 18-room luxury riverside lodge near the gorge entrance melds modern sophistication, Jawoyn themes and high-class cooking.

Timber Creek

Timber Creek Travellers Rest $$ The only place to stay in town has shady camp sites and simple but clean rooms and cabins.

Wugularr (Beswick)

Djakanimba Pavilions (p841) **$$** Four attractive guest rooms attached to Djilpin Arts sit on stilts, with louvred windows to catch the prevailing breezes.

Mataranka

Little Roper Stockcamp $ Just 2km from Mataranka Thermal Pool, this welcoming caravan park provides a taste of outback station life, with campfire dinners.

Territory Manor Motel & Caravan Park $ A class act just off the Stuart Highway, with comfortable rammed-earth rooms, shady campground and bistro.

Researched by
Ivy Carruth

Uluru & the Red Centre

AUSTRALIA'S BEATING HEART

Venture deep into central Australia's outback, where dramatic landscapes and living culture define the desert's soul. The country's spirited heart is here.

Perhaps the nation's most iconic Indigenous homeland, the Red Centre is a place of ancient Songlines, ochre quarries and sacred monoliths where stories live in the rock itself. At its heart is Uluru, rising from the desert floor with an unshakable presence, even more so paired with the Kata Tjuta's underrated splendour.

Anchoring the region is Alice Springs, a frontier town with a creative pulse. Its galleries and nearby art centres carry traditions that stretch across deserts and generations, while just beyond town lie the spectacular gorges and clefts of the MacDonnell Ranges. Walk to Simpsons Gap at dusk, see the midday light blaze through Standley Chasm or cool off at Ellery Creek Big Hole. Ormiston Gorge shelters ghost gums and hidden pools, while the Ochre Pits reveal sacred colour still quarried for ceremony.

BENNY MARTY/SHUTTERSTOCK

The Larapinta Trail threads along these ranges, leading to the summit of Mt Sonder for panoramic desert views. To the south, Rainbow Valley's sandstone bluffs blow carmine and marigold, while Palm Valley shelters prehistoric plants found nowhere else. Kings Canyon in Watarrka National Park impresses with its sheer rock walls and rim-talk walks, and a brief stop at Hermannsburg hints at a mission past and an enduring tradition of Albert Namatjira's watercolour painting.

From vast desert plains to ancient escarpments and deep cultural connections, central Australia is a landscape that stirs the soul and rewards curious travellers – the remote, raw and radiant outback. Welcome to the Red Centre.

THE MAIN AREAS

ALICE SPRINGS
Desert city with great galleries.
p850

WEST MACDONNELL RANGES
Dramatic ridgelines ideal for hiking.
p862

KINGS CANYON
Culture and wild walks.
p871

ULURU-KATA TJUTA NATIONAL PARK
Home of Australia's most famous rock.
p876

For places to stay in Uluṟu & the Red Centre, see p883

KELLY SOUTH AUSTRALIA/SHUTTERSTOCK

Left: Palm Valley (p868), Finke Gorge National Park;
Above: Simpsons Gap (p864), Tjoritja / West MacDonnell National Park

Find Your Way

The main regional centres of Alice Springs and Yulara (Uluṟu) are easy enough to get around on foot, by bicycle or bus, but you'll want a car (preferably a 4WD) to explore further afield.

BUS

At Uluṟu, a hop-on/hop-off bus shuttles between sites. Alice Springs has a small town-bus network. For travel between Alice and Uluṟu, options include AAT Kings or Emu Run (p854) transfers, though most visitors drive or join multiday tours.

CAR

Central Australia opens up behind the wheel. A 2WD handles Alice Springs, the West MacDonnell Ranges, Kings Canyon and Uluṟu on sealed roads. Take a 4WD for unsealed tracks. Plan fuel stops carefully as services can be sparse.

Kings Canyon, p871

Kings Canyon stands out for its cliffs and gorges; explore on foot, take a scenic flight or dive into local Aboriginal culture.

Uluṟu-Kata Tjuṯa National Park, p876

Experience Aboriginal culture and hike through the dramatic scenery of Australia's most soulful landforms.

West MacDonnell Ranges, p862

The red ridgelines, cliffs and gorges rank among Australia's most spectacular massifs, with great hiking and camping.

Alice Springs, p850

Australia's only true desert city, with great art galleries and museums and the start of many Red Centre adventures.

BENNY MARTY/SHUTTERSTOCK

Watarrka National Park (p871)

Plan Your Time

Avoid visiting between November and February, as extreme heat can make outdoor activity unsafe. Many operators close for the season. We recommend April to October for a better experience.

If You Only Do One Thing

- Fly into Yulara, or drive from **Alice Springs** (p850) to **Uluṟu-Kata Tjuṯa National Park** (p876). With myriad ways to experience **Uluṟu** (p878) and **Kata Tjuṯa** (p878), from art installations to gourmet dining, plan on spending at least two full days here. Choose from guided walks, scenic flights and experiences that reveal why these monoliths hold spiritual and geological significance.

A Week to Play With

- Spend a couple of days in **Alice Springs** (p850), called the cultural crossroads of the desert. Hire a campervan and head out to **Uluṟu-Kata Tjuṯa National Park** (p876). En route, stop where your heart calls you – **Rainbow Valley** (p858), **Kings Canyon** (p871) or **Ormiston Gorge** (p867) – as you make your way through the gobsmacking landscapes of **West MacDonnell Ranges** (p862).

Seasonal Highlights

SPRING

Wildflowers erupt after winter rains. Daytime temperatures are ideal for multiday hikes. Uluṟu's waterholes fill; Kings Canyon opens up without the summer's punishing heat.

SUMMER

Dawn walks become essential – by 10am, heat reigns. The desert glows vermillion against bruised purple skies. Fewer tourists mean solitude at sacred sites.

AUTUMN

The season locals choose – it's the most forgiving. Temperate days invite gorge swims and crisp nights demand layers while granting clear stargazing skies.

WINTER

This is peak season; book well ahead and expect crowds. Campfires are essential – the mornings crack with frost. Venture to Ormiston Gorge or Trephina for space.

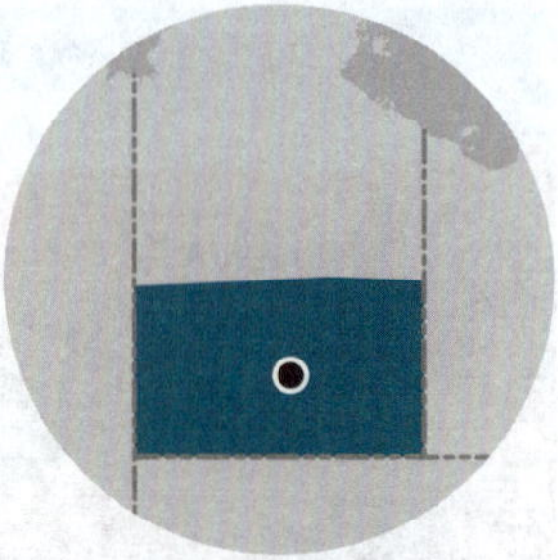

Alice Springs

ABORIGINAL CULTURE | DESERT WILDLIFE | MOUNTAIN PANORAMAS

TOP TIP

If you're heading out after dark, particularly on weekends, it's wise to take a taxi back to your hotel. While crime in Alice Springs isn't quite as alarming as headlines suggest, it pays to be cautious once night falls, especially around the town centre.

Alice Springs – known as Mparntwe to the Arrernte Traditional Owners – is no ordinary outback town. Roughly a quarter of its people are Indigenous, giving the city a cultural heartbeat you won't find elsewhere. The desert sun seems to shine on cue most days and under that golden light you'll find a heady mix of experiences: a remarkable cluster of First Nations art galleries, a hands-on desert wildlife park and a surprisingly eclectic food scene. It's easily worth a couple of days to soak it all in.

But Alice is also the launchpad for the outback's big-ticket adventures. The East and West MacDonnell Ranges rise right from its edge, hiding red-walled gorges, shady waterholes and trails that wind through primordial stone. A half-day's drive gets you to Uluṟu or Kings Canyon, two of the country's most iconic landscapes, making Alice both a destination in itself and the gateway to central Australia.

Desert Art in Depth

Browse First Nations art galleries

Mbantua Gallery *(mbantua.com.au; free)* offers one of Alice Springs' most grounded introductions to Arrernte art and culture. Indigenous-owned and run by local families, the gallery champions central Australian artists, with a strong focus on

GETTING AROUND

If you're venturing outside the city centre, having a car makes things simpler. The heart of town is compact enough, but many sights sit further afield and, with the desert heat often cranking up during the day, a quick drive or taxi trip (no rideshares here) is usually the smarter choice.

A car or campervan also unlocks the wider region, putting the East and West MacDonnell Ranges comfortably within reach and letting you shape your own itinerary. Otherwise, several operators run day trips to both ranges, with the West Macs particularly well served.

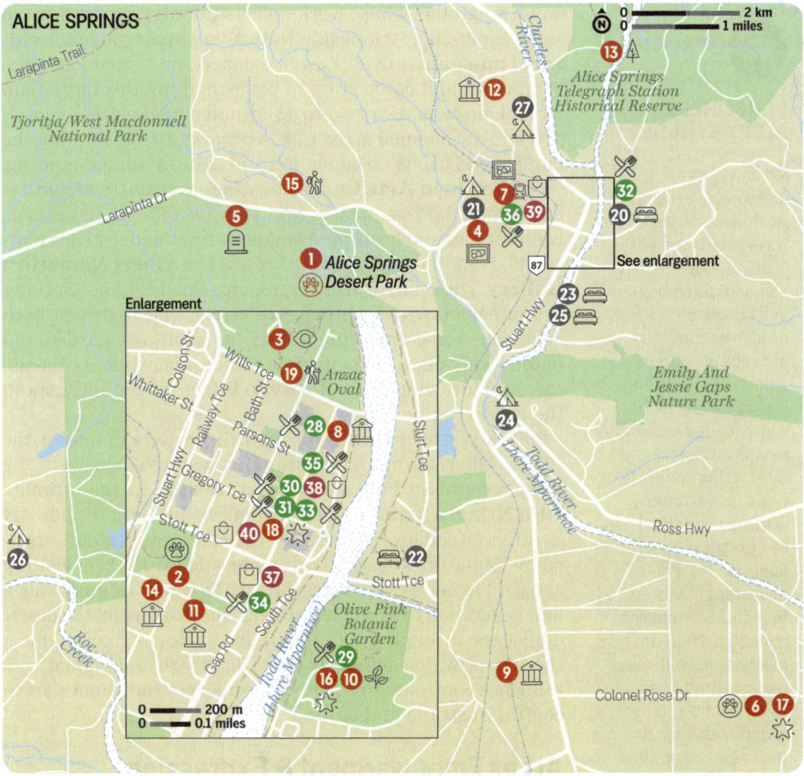

HIGHLIGHTS

1 Alice Springs Desert Park

SIGHTS

2 Alice Springs Reptile Centre
3 Anzac Hill
4 Araluen Arts Centre
see 4 Central Australian Aviation Museum
5 Grave of John Flynn
6 Kangaroo Sanctuary
7 Mbantua Gallery
8 Megafauna Central
9 National Road Transport Hall of Fame
see 9 Old Ghan Heritage Railway Museum
10 Olive Pink Botanic Garden
11 Royal Flying Doctor Service Base
12 School of the Air
13 Telegraph Station
14 Women's Museum of Australia

ACTIVITIES

15 Art Tours of Australia
16 Ayeye Atyenhe Art
17 Earth Sanctuary
18 Emu Run Experience
19 Lions Walk Trail

SLEEPING

20 Alice Lodge Backpackers
21 Alice Springs Tourist Park
22 Alice's Secret Traveller's Inn
23 Desert Palms Resort
24 Discovery Parks Alice Springs
25 Doubletree by Hilton
see 24 G'Day Mate Tourist Park
see 24 MacDonnell Range Holiday Park
26 Squeakywindmill Boutique Tent B&B
27 Wintersun Cabin & Caravan Park

EATING

28 Bakery
29 Bean Tree Cafe
30 Bella Alice
31 Epilogue Lounge
32 Flavours of India
see 8 Goods Coffee Shop
see 25 Hanuman Restaurant
33 Page 27 Cafe
34 Tea Shrine
35 That Little Cafe
36 Water Tank Cafe

DRINKING & NIGHTLIFE

see 24 Alice Springs Brewing Company

SHOPPING

37 Central Australian Aboriginal Media Association
see 36 Desert Dwellers
see 36 Iltja Ntjarra
see 31 Lone Dingo Adventure
38 Papunya Tula Artists
see 33 Red Kangaroo Books
39 Tangentyere Artists
see 36 Tjanpi Desert Weavers
see 30 Todd Mall Market
40 Yubu Napa Art Gallery

SONGLINES & STORY SYMBOLS

Art and story are inseparable in central Australia and they always have been. First Nations peoples used painting, ceremony and Songlines to pass on knowledge in the absence of written language. A Songline is an ancestral pathway encoded in song, mapping Country through the law of story and travel routes, with meanings held by Elders and specific families. Some of the elements are shared, though much remains restricted. Many dot paintings echo these narrative traditions, using symbols for waterholes, animal tracks and camp sites that carry layered meaning within each community. Around the mid-20th century, artworks from desert communities began circulating nationally, sparking broader interest in central Australia's cultural traditions. Today, you'll find them in galleries and museums worldwide.

women painters whose work reflects Country, storylines and lived experience. Alongside the gallery space, a small **cultural museum** provides useful context for Arrernte history, symbolism and connection to place, making this more than a quick browse. Allow 30 to 45 minutes to explore, longer if you join a scheduled artist talk. Artworks are for sale, but the emphasis is firmly on education and cultural understanding.

The **Araluen Arts Centre** *(araluenartscentre.nt.gov.au; adult/child $8/6)* showcases works across different Indigenous communities and hosts performances, films and festivals year-round. Plan some time here to browse the **Albert Namatjira Gallery**. The centre is the creative crossroads of Alice Springs' arts precinct, with rotating exhibitions that highlight both established and emerging artists. Its sculpture garden and outdoor installations invite slow wandering, while the on-site cafe and gift shop make it easy to linger longer and soak in the creative atmosphere.

Before Western Desert dot painting rose to fame in the 1970s, Albert Namatjira's luminous watercolours were the most recognised First Nations art. Nearby, at the intimate **Iltja Ntjarra** *(manyhandsart.com.au)*, or Many Hands Art Centre, you can browse fresh-off-the-easel watercolours created by Namatjira's descendants alongside works from visiting artists. The centre continues the artist's legacy by nurturing a new generation of Arrernte painters who reinterpret the desert landscape through colour and light. Visitors can often meet the artists, watch demonstrations and learn how Namatjira's influence continues to shape contemporary Indigenous art in central Australia and beyond.

Art as Empowerment & Expression

Visit women's and community art collectives

Run by the Ngaanyatjarra Pitjantjatjara Yankunytjatjara (NPY) Women's Council, **Tjanpi Desert Weavers** *(tjanpi.com.au)* features more than 400 Central Desert female weavers from 26 communities. Their skilled hands transform wild desert grasses into intricate fibre art and whimsical sculptures; *tjanpi* means 'wild harvested grass'. Each piece tells a story of connection to Country and community, blending traditional skills with contemporary creativity. Visitors can often watch artists at work or purchase directly from the gallery, supporting sustainable livelihoods and the continuation of a powerful, living art form unique to the Central Desert.

Awesome plant-based options under cooling shade trees

EATING & DRINKING IN ALICE SPRINGS: BEST CAFES

Goods Coffee Shop: Fresh fruit smoothies, toast with toppers and (everyone says it) the best coffee. Buy some beans. *7am-2pm Mon-Fri, 8am-noon Sat* $$

Bakery: Compact spot with artisan bread, gourmet sandwiches and house-made cordials. Pastries sells out; arrive early. *7am-2pm Wed-Fri, to noon Sat & Sun* $$

Tea Shrine: Asian-leaning cuisine and extensive (for Alice) vegan and vegetarian choices. The menu changes daily. *9am-4pm Mon-Sat* $$

That Little Cafe: Specialising in all things matcha and serving quick bites and small plates. Dine in or takeaway. *7am-2pm Mon-Fri, 8am-noon Sat & Sun* $$

MIKE GREENSLADE/AUSTRALIA/ALAMY

Araluen Arts Centre

The groundbreaking **Tangentyere Artists** *(tangentyere.org.au)* champions emerging and itinerant artists whose works capture the rhythm of life in Alice Springs' Town Camp communities. Their pieces balance grit and grace, translating everyday moments into vivid creative expression. Expect wearable textiles, handcrafted jewellery, painted skate decks and artist-made books that blur the line between art and storytelling. Each work carries a sense of place, resilience and individuality that's as contemporary as it is connected to Country.

Connect Through Creation

Sign up for art workshops

One of the most authentic ways to experience cross-cultural exchange on First Nations land is to sit with an artist as they create. **Ayeye Atyenhe Art** *(ayeyeatyenheart.com.au; classes adult/child $100/30)* takes that idea further. Led by acclaimed artists Marie Ryder (from the community of Santa Teresa) and Kevin Bird (Mulga Bore), the program offers 90-minute sessions four days a week at Olive Pink Botanic Garden. Each class is a rare opportunity to gain insight into technique and cultural traditions.

At Simpsons Gap, the desert's drama becomes your muse in a watercolour workshop led by **Art Tours of Australia**

A PRIMER ON ALICE'S PAST

Old Ghan Heritage Railway Museum: Rail buffs shouldn't miss the frontier-era refashioned locomotives.

Central Australian Aviation Museum: A trove of cultural remnants in the original Connellan Airways hanger.

National Road Transport Hall of Fame: Vintage cars, military memorabilia and, of course, space dedicated to the Australian-designed and built Kenworth trucks.

Megafauna Central: Check out the fossils and Indigenous artefacts housed here at Todd Mall. It's compact but rich in the geological past of this storied region.

Women's Museum of Australia: Located in the old gaol, this museum celebrates outback trailblazers and highlights the courage and grit of women in Australian history.

EATING & DRINKING IN ALICE SPRINGS: BEST CAFES

Page 27 Cafe: This Alice favourite has warm service and pours top coffee, juices and creative plates. *7am-2pm Mon-Fri, from 7.30am Sat & Sun* $$

Water Tank Cafe: Rustic water tank collides with vintage charm at this offbeat cafe serving hearty breakfasts and light midday meals. *8am-2pm Thu-Mon* $$

Epilogue Lounge: This urban, retro space has a decent wine list, live music sessions and local late-night vibes. *7am-2pm Tue-Sun* $$

Bean Tree Cafe: Head to the Olive Pink Botanic Garden for polished but bush-inspired outback brekkie and lunch. *8am-3pm Wed-Sat* $$

BEST TOURS FROM ALICE

Emu Run Experience: Tours to Uluṟu, Kings Canyon and through the West MacDonnell Ranges with smaller groups than most. Multi-awarded.

Sandrifter Safaris: Locally owned outback 4WD specialist with informative, amusing guides and ideal vehicles for Palm Valley's wild terrain. Includes tea and lunch.

Adventure Tours Australia: Hike, camp and eat fireside as guides decode Country's stories at Uluṟu, Kata Tjuṯa and Kings Canyon. Co-created with First Nations partners.

Trek Larapinta: Boutique trekking company running multiday hikes along the Larapinta Trail. Be ready to tackle moderate to challenging terrain for five to eight hours daily.

Art Tours of Australia: Explore Aboriginal-owned art centres and galleries on a half-day tour through Alice with an expert who connects the art to Country and culture.

BENNY MARTY/SHUTTERSTOCK

Thorny devil, Alice Springs Desert Park

(arttoursofaustralia.com; $175). Situated against towering red cliffs and ghost gums, you'll learn to capture the play of light and shadow that has inspired generations of central Australian painters. Guided by local artists, you'll mix colours that shift with each passing minute as the rocks glow and the sky softens. No experience is needed, just a willingness to slow down and look closely. By the end, you'll take home more than a painting – a vivid memory of this extraordinary landscape.

Up Close with Creatures

Resilient desert wildlife at conservation sanctuaries

Though central Australia is well and truly alive with creatures adapted to its fierce desert, many species are threatened. Encounter survivors at the **Alice Springs Desert Park** *(alicespringsdesertpark.com.au; adult/child $39/20)*, which recreates a series of habitats. Highlights include the immersive **Nocturnal House**, with an array of rare small mammals. Grab the free audio-guide and join a free ranger-led walk and talk, daily at 8.45am (times may change seasonally, so check before visiting). Don't miss the birds-of-prey show in the **Nature Theatre**; these run daily at 10.30am year-round, plus at 3pm between 1 March and 31 October.

The hands-on and educational **Alice Springs Reptile Centre** *(reptilecentre.com.au; adult/child $24.50/13.50)* is a must-see for all ages. The most dangerous animals, in the comfort of their habitats, include the taipans, death adders and the resident 3.3m resident saltwater croc, Terry. The centre runs daily meet-and-greet sessions where visitors can get to know friendly reptiles like rainbow pythons and blue-tongued lizards. Keepers share fascinating insights into desert adaptation, such as how snakes sense heat and the camouflage tricks of geckos. It's a lively, accessible way to understand the outback's often misunderstood creatures and appreciate the role they play in this fragile ecosystem.

The **Kangaroo Sanctuary** *(kangaroosanctuary.com; adult/child $105/95)* was the home paddock of *Kangaroo Dundee* (a BBC/National Geographic show about a kangaroo family). Guided sunset tours let visitors walk among rescued kangaroos while hearing stories about rehabilitation and release. The experience offers a rare, close-up look at Australia's iconic marsupial in a natural setting, inviting reflection on wildlife conservation and the challenges of balancing tourism with animal welfare in the desert environment. Open Wednesday to Friday; book ahead (no children under the age of seven).

Alice in the Sky with Diamonds

Stargazing in the desert

After dark (exact times vary with seasons), **Earth Sanctuary** *(earth-sanctuary.com.au; adult/child $60.10/41.10)* weaves Indigenous Dreaming stories with modern star science. Opt for the **Dinner & Star Tour** *(adult/child $141.30/70.65)* to enjoy dinner and drinks under festoon lights at sunset before cosying up to high-power telescopes under clear night skies. Set on a family-run property just outside town, the experience blends culture, sustainability and cosmic wonder. Perfectly positioned in the middle of nowhere yet only minutes from Alice Springs, the sanctuary provides crystal-clear views of the southern sky and its constellations. Guides point out celestial landmarks and explain how seasonal changes shift what's visible overhead, while sharing traditional sky lore and astronomy tips as the Milky Way blazes overhead. The best viewing is during the winter months.

Get Out & Beat Feet

Bushwalking around Alice Springs

Start with a leisurely wander through the **Olive Pink Botanic Garden** *(opbg.com.au; free)*, where more than 500 central Australian plant species are on display. These include bush foods and medicinal plants traditionally used by Arrernte people, such as native lemongrass, sour quandong and emu bush. The birdlife here is outstanding.

For something a little more strenuous, make your way to the **Telegraph Station** *(alicespringstelegraphstation.com.au; adult/child $16/6.75)*. This historic site was the vital

LOCAL FAVOURITES

Adam Utschink is an Alice local and tour guide. He shares his favourite places and can't-miss spots.

My number-one pick is the Desert Park, just 10 minutes from the town centre. It's easy to spend all day exploring and discovering. Every time I come I see something new. Don't miss the Nocturnal House.

Alice Springs' School of the Air (p856) is something different; it's the world's largest classroom and well worth a visit.

Olive Pink Botanic Garden is fantastic in the early morning. You'll spot heaps of black-footed rock wallabies and common wallaroo atop the hill at the back of the gardens warming up in the sun.

Walk to the Telegraph Station, where Alice began; it's 2km from town and a nice, easy trail.

EATING & DRINKING IN ALICE SPRINGS: OUR PICKS

Flavours of India: This humble family restaurant in Alice puts all its effort into cooking excellent pan-Indian dishes. *4pm-10pm* $$

Hanuman Restaurant: Easily Alice Springs' best restaurant, in the Hilton, serves Thai- and Indian-influenced dishes. *noon-2.30pm & 6-10pm Wed-Fri, 6-10pm Sat-Tue* $$$

Alice Springs Brewing Company: The outback's very own craft brewery, with ales, brewery tours and rowdy weekend nights. *hours vary* $$

Bella Alice: Authentic wood-fired pizzas and Italian fare in a casual setting at Todd Mall. Dietarians catered for. *6.30am-8.30pm Thu-Tue* $$

RED-DIRT SCIENCE & SPIRIT

Australia's outback earns its name from being 'out the back' of the settled coast – a vast, remote interior that feels like another world. Its famous red soil gets its colour from iron oxide, the same compound that gives rust its hue. Technically, much of it is sand rather than true soil and while it looks barren, it contains surprising nutrients that support hardy desert plants. Temperatures often soar above 40°C, yet the land teems with life adapted to its extremes. The red dust does stain clothes and skin, but travellers love it for that very reason – it's tangible proof of being somewhere wild, ancient and unmistakably Australian. There's simply nowhere else like it on Earth.

communications link between Darwin and Adelaide until 1932 and sits within 450 hectares of scenic parkland. Take the 30-minute circuit for panoramic views, then loop back past the original cemetery.

Foundations of the Frontier

Discover how remote outback children learn via radi

Few places capture the ingenuity of outback life like the **School of the Air** *(schooloftheair.net.au; adult/child $22/15)*, founded in 1951. This high-tech classroom network still delivers lessons to children on remote stations spread over the vast desert.

Long before video calls were the done thing, kids in remote areas across central Australia were logging in through crackling radios to learn their lessons from teachers in Alice Springs. For families living on cattle stations or in isolated communities, daily lessons meant education and socialisation without leaving home for months at a time. They also meant connection, routine and a chance to feel a part of the wider world.

A visit gives a clear picture of how it worked. Sit at old pedal-powered radios, listen to recorded lessons and see the evolution of distance education from analogue equipment to today's online classrooms. Exhibits share stories from students who grew up hundreds of kilometres from their nearest neighbour and from teachers juggling lessons and pastoral care. The museum highlights the resilience of both, along with the creativity required to deliver schooling across an area larger than many countries.

It's a fascinating stop for travellers curious about how people thrive in the remotest regions of Australia. You'll walk away with a deeper appreciation of resourcefulness and the ongoing importance of equal access to education.

The Outback Lifeline

Delve into the lifesaving history of the Flying Doctor

The **Royal Flying Doctor Service Base** (RFDS; *rfdsalicesprings.com.au; adult/child $22/15*) is an engaging museum that traces a century of lifesaving work across almost 1.25 million sq km. The RFDS is one of Australia's most important institutions, but the Alice Springs Tourist Facility makes it easy to understand, even if you've never heard of it.

Set in the original 1939 base, the museum explains how the Flying Doctor became a lifeline for anyone living in the outback – people whose closest medical practitioner might be a full day's drive away. Instead of signboard and text, the experience breaks it down in holograms, short films and personal stories that show how the service began in 1928 under Reverend John Flynn and how it still operates across the Red Centre today.

The museum's standout exhibits include a replica RFDS aircraft you can sit inside, the famous medical chests still stocked with supplies, and a VR experience that puts you in the back of the helicopter as a patient is airlifted. A small theatre screens

FRITZ16/SHUTTERSTOCK

Royal Flying Doctor Service Base

a short documentary that ties the whole story together. It's not a dry heritage display, but rather a practical look at how people survive in isolated areas and why the RFDS remains essential. Entry fees and the well-stocked shop support the service, so your visit helps keep it going. Guided tours leave every half-hour, with the last at 4pm.

About 7km west of town along Larapinta Dr, a small reserve marks the **resting place of Reverend John Flynn**, founder of the Royal Flying Doctor Service. His ashes lie beneath a granite boulder, though not the original, which was returned to the sacred Warumungu site it came from and replaced with one gifted by the Arrernte people. You'll need a car or tour to visit; it's not walkable from town.

Sunsets over Alice

Take in the views from Anzac Hill

As evening settles on Alice Springs, red cliffs of the West MacDonnell Ranges glow in a fiery wash of colour. The prime spot to take it in is from atop **Anzac Hill**, or Untyeyetweleye in Arrernte. From the summit, survey the gridded streets of town and out to Heavitree Gap. You can go via the **Lions Walk Trail** from Wills Tce or drive by taking Schwarz Cres off the Stuart Hwy, then Anzac Rd. Along with its sweeping 360-degree outlook, the hill is crowned by a stirring war memorial that gives this lookout its name.

BEST ALICE SPRINGS SHOPS

Central Australian Aboriginal Media Association: Look for CDs by central Australia's First Nations musicians.

Desert Dwellers: Maps, swags, tents, portable fridges, stoves and more.

Lone Dingo Adventure: Hiking and camping gear, satellite-phone rental, GPS equipment and more.

Papunya Tula Artists: Best of the First Nations art in Alice.

Red Kangaroo Books: One of the best bookshops in Australia for central Australian and First Nations titles.

Todd Mall Market: Buskers, craft stalls, Aboriginal art, jewellery and more dominate this occasional Sunday market.

Yubu Napa Art Gallery: High-quality paintings, textiles and Indigenous crafts.

Beyond Alice Springs

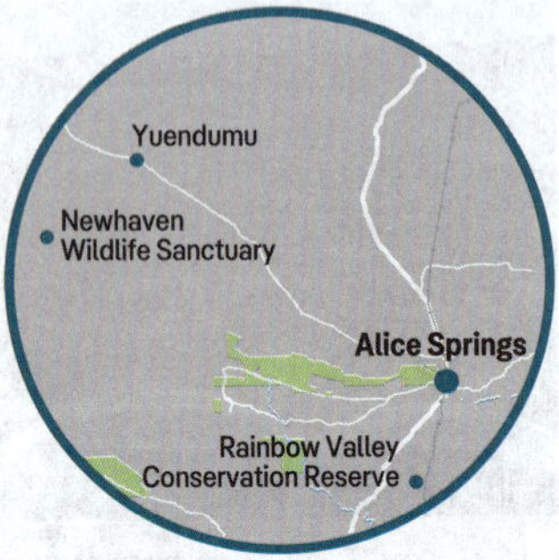

Alice is only the beginning; wonders await at Rainbow Valley, the Newhaven Wildlife Sanctuary and across the rugged East MacDonnell Ranges.

Places

Most visitors in the vast Red Centre make a frenzied beeline from Alice Springs to the West MacDonnell Ranges' showier (and busier) landscape. For true outback quiet and in the spirit of adventure, you should head east instead. Ghostly ruins and rough-hewn gorges branch from empty trails off the Ross Hwy, with the abandoned gold-mining town Arltunga and the petroglyph-rich N'Dhala Gorge waiting for you right where the road runs out.

To try another angle, take the Tanami Track northwest into the Great Sandy Desert. Here lies the Newhaven Wildlife Sanctuary, a remarkable home to 23 ecosystems, 363km from Alice. A 4WD is recommended for clearance and uneven, vastly wild terrain.

GETTING AROUND

There is no public transport of any kind to or inside the East MacDonnell Ranges.

Exploring the area is best done in a 4WD. While the Ross Hwy and a few key sites are fine for a 2WD, many tracks are unsealed and can become impassable after rain. Access to places like N'Dhala Gorge requires riverbed crossings and most rental companies won't cover a 2WD vehicle on unsealed roads.

Rainbow Valley Conservation Reserve

TIME FROM ALICE SPRINGS: 1HR

Witness sandstone bluffs that transform with the light

Positioned about 75km south of Alice Springs, **Rainbow Valley** (*nt.gov.au/parks; day pass adult/child $10/5*) is a conservation reserve on the traditional lands of the Arrernte people, who know it as Wurre. While Uluṟu, Kings Canyon and the West MacDonnell Ranges draw the crowds, Rainbow Valley offers a more contemplative, less-travelled experience. On approach, freestanding sandstone bluffs and cliffs rise from the sands, rather like ramparts of a lost city. At midday, the colours flatten and form can seem washed out, but linger into the golden hours and rocks take on an almost kaleidoscopic beauty – a geological marvel of earth colours running the full spectrum from cream to deep red.

There is no public transport to Rainbow Valley. From Alice Springs, all but the last 22km is along the sealed Stuart Hwy; the final stretch is unsealed and 4WD is a must. Day-trip and half-day tours operate from Alice; **Sandrifter Safaris** (*sandrifter.com.au; private tour $270*) stops here.

NEALE COUSLAND/SHUTTERSTOCK

Rainbow Valley

Wind-eroded sandstone and mirrored desert flats

Marked trails fan out from the car park and camping area, linking parched basins and multicoloured outcrops. The standout **Mushroom Rock Walk** is a wind-eroded sandstone feature with natural tunnels. It's an easy loop trek, mostly along a 1.4km boardwalk and should take 30 minutes to an hour. The **Claypan Walk**, also a cruisy loop and slightly longer at 1.8km, skirts the edges of the depression and offers views of the main bluff. After rains, these cracked-earth flats hold water and reflect the cliffs, creating mirror-like scenes and knockout photos.

Savour celestial views and desert stillness after dark

Rainbow Valley is far enough from Alice Springs for a proper dark-sky hit. Staying after dusk rewards you with a Milky Way arcing cleanly over the escarpment. Bring a tripod or rest your phone on a rock.

Arrive an hour before sunset to catch the pre-dusk blush on the **Hermannsburg Sandstone** and stay for the blue period when the rock turns a deep mauve. It's one of the easiest places in central Australia to get pro-looking shots without trekking.

If you're keen, picnic on Country in the designated area. Don't rush in and out just because the light has gone; the stillness and the quiet is part of the experience. The natural amphitheatre effect of the bluffs makes even small sounds feel heightened; listen for the rising chatter of desert birds, barking geckos and, of course, the yips of dingoes just out of sight. Breathe.

Ancient petroglyphs and sacred stories at Mushroom Rock

Rainbow Valley reveals its stories slowly, but visitors can tune in if they know where to look. On the short walk to Mushroom

AUSTRALIAN WILDLIFE CONSERVANCY

The Australian Wildlife Conservancy (AWC) manages more than 30 conservation properties nationwide, protecting over 120,000 sq km of threatened habitat across Australia's most diverse ecosystems. Set on the northern edge of the Great Sandy Desert, Newhaven Wildlife Sanctuary (p859) is a refuge for threatened wildlife and a major hub for desert conservation science.

At its heart, a 100-sq-km feral-free area protects species once extinct locally, including greater bilbies, golden bandicoots, brush-tailed and burrowing bettongs, central rock rats and mala (rufous hare-wallabies). Intensive monitoring, fire management and habitat restoration underpin the program's success, creating one of Australia's largest and most important rewilding projects.

Beyond the sanctuary, AWC ecologists continue to expand the range of endangered species and restore balance to this unique ecosystem.

EAST MACDONNELL RANGES BY CAR

Trace ancient Dreaming trails and frontier history on this rewarding eastbound drive through the rugged landscapes beyond Alice Springs.

START	END	LENGTH
Alice Springs	N'Dhala Gorge	136/125km with/ without 4WD; 3½hr

Drive south out of 1 **Alice Springs** through Heavitree Gap, before following the signs east to Ross Hwy. The first stop is 2 **Emily Gap (Anthwerrke)**, 16km out of Alice, a narrow gap that features in the Eastern Arrernte Caterpillar Dreaming trail. There are some well-preserved paintings on the eastern wall. You could walk the 8.2km (one way) Yeperenye Trail to 3 **Jessie Gap (Atherrke)**. Otherwise, it's an 8km drive. A further 27km brings you to 4 **Corroboree Rock Conservation Reserve**, an oddly shaped rock that plays a role in the Perentie Dreaming trail.

Some 77km after leaving Alice, 5 **Trephina Gorge** is arguably the most spectacular site along this stretch of Country. Take one of the three walking trails, but carry plenty of water. On the road in, you'll pass what's believed to be Australia's largest ghost gum tree, which may be 300 years old.

Just after the Trephina Gorge turn off, follow the signs to 6 **Arltunga Historical Reserve**. After 33km on an unsealed road, walk the hill to the old gold-mining ghost town of Arltunga, with lonely ruins and an end-of-the-road feel. Head back to the main road and if there's a festival on, take a detour to 7 **Ross River Resort**. From there, a 4WD-only track leads 11km southwest to 8 **N'Dhala Gorge**, a spot with nearly 6000 Aboriginal rock carvings, some dating back 10,000 years.

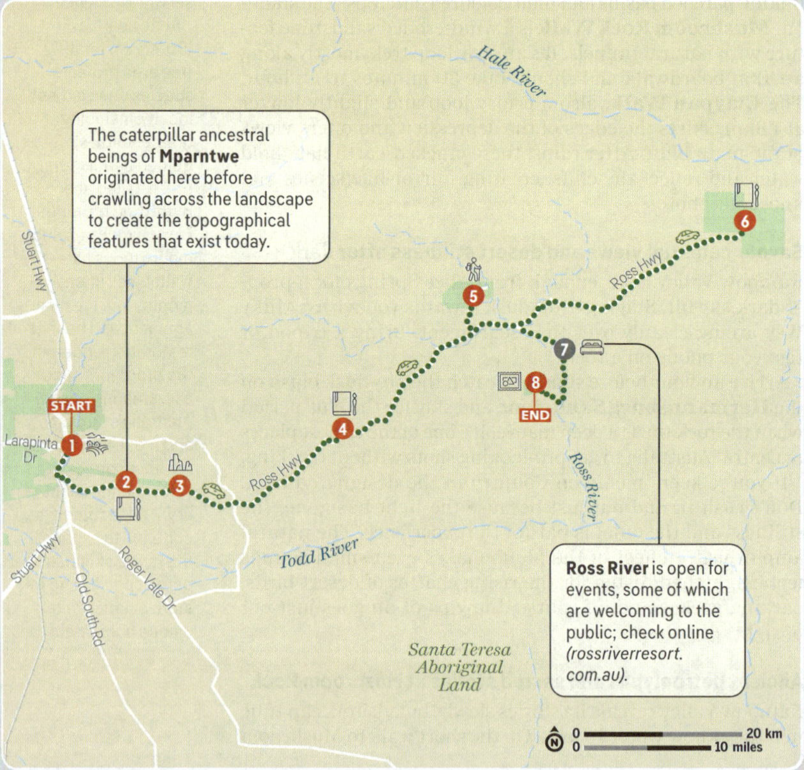

Rock, scan the sandstone for faint petroglyphs and small pickets of ochre hinting at earlier rock art. Keep an eye on the ground for spherical grinding stones, often easiest to spot where the track meets open rock.

The massif to the south, **Ewerre**, and its 50m buffer zone is a registered sacred site. You can't access it, but understanding that presence gives the landscape extra weight. Rangers and Southern Arrernte Traditional Owners jointly manage the reserve and interpretation signs at the day-use area help visitors grasp why this Country matters and how to explore it with respect.

Newhaven Wildlife Sanctuary

TIME FROM ALICE SPRINGS: **4HR**

A living conservation success story

Newhaven Wildlife Sanctuary *(australianwildlife.org; free)*, 136km west off the Tanami Track, sprawls over 2620 sq km and ranks among Australia's most important conservation projects. An inspiration for large-scale ecological restoration, it's turning the tide against feral cats, estimated at 15 million nationwide and each killing up to five native animals a night. At Newhaven, fences and science-backed programs give threatened species a fighting chance and the 83 reptiles and 170 bird species here are thriving. Milestones include reintroducing brushtail possums (2024) and golden bandicoots (2023), and the first red goshawk sighting in 30 years.

Sign in at the headquarters, then head for the simple **camping ground** *(adult/child per night $10/5)* or 'homestead', open April to September. Unpowered sites have showers, toilets and drinking water. At dusk, follow the marked path to the hilltop for unbroken outback vistas; take a jacket.

From the main info post, grab the latest map for 4WD self-drives, nearly 300km of routes looping through weathered salt flats and scrub. The **Lakes** (50km) and **Dunes** (40km) return tours are standouts. The Lakes route finishes with a short walk across a pristine creek to a dune-top lookout over Lake Bennett. Be prepared for water crossings.

Yuendumu

TIME FROM ALICE SPRINGS: **3-4HR**

Support Indigenous artists

The gritty, predominantly Warlpiri town of Yuendumu (population around 800), off the Tanami Track, is mainly utilised by travellers as a place to fill up on fuel and supplies. But its **Warlukurlangu Art Centre** *(warlu.com; free)* is one of the longest-established Indigenous arts cooperatives in the Territory and absolutely worth planning a visit around. Watch cultural custodians at work on the shady terrace and choose something to take home, or look into the volunteer program for deeper immersion and stay for a few days to pitch into the everyday needs of the centre. It's open Tuesday to Thursday and by appointment; call ahead.

TRUE CENTRE?

There are lots of different ways to measure the geographical centre of Australia, from the furthest point from the sea to the point where lines from the furthest compass points inevitably intersect. Each will, of course, give you a different answer.

The **Lambert Gravitational Centre** is where an Australian government commission determined the centre to be in 1988, during the 200-year anniversary of white settlement in Australia. It lies around 170km west of the Stuart Hwy in the Northern Territory's Deep South, 260km south of Alice and just 21km west of Finke (Aputula), along a signposted, sandy track. Remote and starkly beautiful, the site embodies Australia's vast, empty heartland. The spot is marked with a 5m-high version of the flagpole found on top of Parliament House in Canberra.

West MacDonnell Ranges

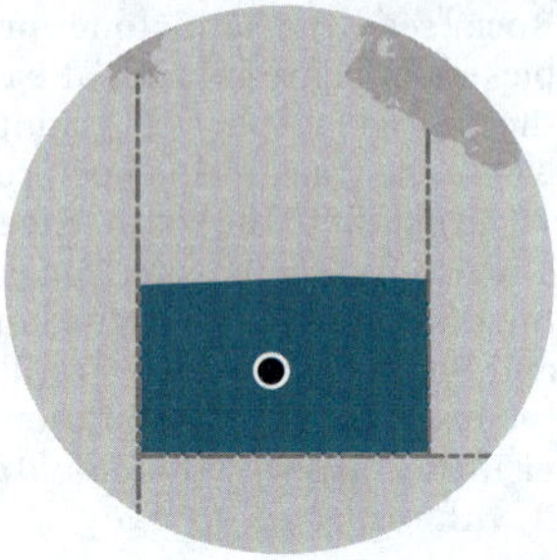

MAJESTIC SCENERY | COOLING WATERHOLES | DESERT CREATURES

TOP TIP

Most travellers spend just a day in the West MacDonnell Ranges, but if you have the time, try and spend two (or three) days exploring. Camp, or return to Alice Springs each night. You'll need a **Northern Territory Parks Pass** *(nt.gov.au/parks/parks-pass)* for most major sites across central Australia.

Few visitors expect such dramatic scenery in central Australia, yet the West MacDonnell Ranges rank among the country's most remarkable landscapes. Their rugged ridgelines resemble a giant reptile resting in the desert, split into two parallel ranges that shelter more than a dozen standout stops inside Tjoritja / West MacDonnell National Park. The best known – Simpsons Gap (Rungutjirpa), Standley Chasm (Angkerle Atwatye) and Ormiston Gorge (Kwartatuma) – blend striking geology with the stories of the Arrernte people. Simpsons Gap has a permanent waterhole and cliffs that glow at sunrise, while Standley Chasm is narrow and vertical, its walls igniting at midday. Near the heart of the range, Ormiston Gorge lures hikers with its challenging Pound Walk and deep, cool pool. Meanwhile, the Larapinta Trail links sacred sites and lookout points. Even a short section delivers sweeping views and a sense of vastness, especially when black-footed rock wallabies appear at dusk.

GETTING AROUND

Public transport doesn't run through the West MacDonnell Ranges, yet numerous Alice Springs operators offer half-, full- and multiday tours, either returning to town or linking on to Kings Canyon and Uluṟu.

Many car rentals in Alice limit mileage allowance (100km per day), with an extra fee charged per additional kilometre. Rugged and 4WD rentals will come at a premium due to demand. Contact the Alice Springs Visitor Information Centre for a list of companies and possibilities.

You can traverse almost the entire range on foot if you're game, on the 12- to 14-day Larapinta Trail.

HIGHLIGHTS
1 Ormiston Gorge
2 Simpsons Gap
3 Standley Chasm

SIGHTS
4 Ellery Creek Big Hole
5 Finke Gorge National Park
see 1 Ghost Gum Lookout
6 Glen Helen Gorge
7 Hermannsburg Mission
8 Mt Sonder Lookout
9 Ochre Pits
10 Palm Valley
11 Serpentine Gorge
12 Telegraph Station
13 Tnorala
14 Tylers Pass Lookout

ACTIVITIES
15 Bond Gap
16 Cassia Hill Walk
see 4 Dolomite Walk
see 1 Ghost Gum Walk
17 Larapinta Trail
18 Mt Sonder Southern Summit Walk
see 1 Ormiston Gorge Pound Walk
19 Woodland Trail

SLEEPING
see 1 Ormiston Gorge Campground
20 Redbank Gorge Campground
see 3 Standley Chasm Campground

SHOPPING
see 7 Hermannsburg Potters

INFORMATION
see 10 Alice Springs Visitor Information Centre

BUSH FOODS & FLORA

The West MacDonnell Ranges are home to hardy desert plants that have supported Arrernte people for thousands of years. Seasonal bush foods include *kampurarrpa* (desert raisins), *ilpengk* (native figs), *arlep* (wild tomatoes) and *akatyerr* (bush plums), which ripen after good rains.

Wattles provide edible seeds that can be roasted and ground, while the corkwood tree produces sweet nectar. Iconic species like ghost gums and spinifex dominate the landscape, each adapted to the heat, fire and low rainfall.

Many plants hold cultural and medicinal value and several are tied to specific Dreaming stories, with knowledge passed down through families. Collecting bush foods isn't appropriate for visitors, yet understanding their role in culture adds depth to how you see the landscape.

Watch Wallabies at Natural Pools

Find refuge in the cliffs at Simpsons Gap

Barely 20 minutes west of Alice Springs lies one of the outback's most accessible natural showpieces, **Simpsons Gap**. It sits within **Tjoritja / West MacDonnell National Park** *(nt.gov.au/parks; day pass adult/child $10/5)*. A short drive from the highway leads to the car park, where a level trail traces a dry riverbed lined with river gums and desert grasses. Boulders scatter the slopes and the cliffs glow ochre as the light shifts. This is prime territory for spotting black-footed rock wallabies, best seen as they emerge to sun themselves in early morning or at dusk.

A 15-minute stroll ends at a tranquil pool sacred to the Traditional Owners; swimming isn't permitted. Venture beyond the crowds on the 15.5km return **Woodland Trail** winding through mulga and porcupine grass to **Bond Gap**, another secluded waterhole where swimming is allowed. The **Cassia Hill Walk** climbs to a lookout where you can take in a grand sweep of the ranges. For a more gentle loop, the **Ghost Gum Walk** starts at the unstaffed visitor centre near the entrance. Interpretive signs along the path explain the area's geology and the significance to the Arrernte people. Bird watchers should keep an eye out for zebra finches, galahs and the occasional wedge-tailed eagle circling high above.

The site is open from sunrise to sunset, with shaded picnic tables, toilets and free gas BBQs near the car park. It's accessible to standard vehicles, though cyclists can reach it via the **Bike Path**, a 17km sealed route from Alice Springs that passes desert oaks and spinifex plains. Rangers advise bringing water, a hat and sturdy shoes, as shade is limited and summer temperatures can exceed 40°C.

Connect with First Nations Traditions

Journey into Standley Chasm's narrow gap

Standley Chasm *(standleychasm.com.au; adult/child $12/5)* is owned and managed by the local Iwupataka (Western Arrernte) community and is a sacred women's site; some areas are closed to visitors. It's only 50km west of Alice Springs and unlike any of the other gorges in the West MacDonnell Ranges.

Narrowest of the West MacDonnell canyons, Standley has sheer walls that rocket 80m skyward. The track to reach it (1.2km, 20 minutes) traces a creek bed flanked by ancient cycads, wattle and bush tomato. You can explore on your own, but we recommend one of the **cultural workshops** *(adult/child from $118/59)* with an Aboriginal guide, where you can make a day of it for cultural context and deeper connection to place. Workshops often include dot painting, traditional bush-tucker tastings and guided storytelling sessions led by Arrernte custodians. There's also a shaded cafe, gift shop and gallery selling locally made jewellery, paintings and carvings, with proceeds supporting the community. Entry fees help maintain the walking track and protect sacred areas. Dogs are not permitted within the reserve.

LADA LACINA/SHUTTERSTOCK

Black footed rock wallaby (p867)

Visiting earlier or later in the day offers gentler light and fewer crowds, or time your visit for midday when the sun perfectly illuminates the crevice as if it's lit from within; photographers deem it 'magic'. Before you depart, pop into the kiosk for a bite or a cool drink under the gum trees. Toilets, shaded picnic facilities and a small **camping ground** with powered and unpowered sites are available, as well as basic cabins for overnight stays. Wi-fi and phone reception are limited; plan ahead and bring cash for purchases.

Crossing the Land

Trek the rugged spine of the West MacDonnell Ranges

Australia has no shortage of iconic walks, but few rival the 223km **Larapinta Trail** *(larapintatrail.com.au)*. The trek is broken into 12 sections, each with challenge and reward; hike the whole thing in 12 to 14 days or devote a day to a single section. Beginning east in Alice Springs and ending west at Mt Sonder, it follows the spine of the West MacDonnell Ranges through sun-baked plateaus and tucked-away billabongs. The land links spiritually with Arrernte Dreaming: three caterpillars crossing the desert to create the West Macs, the East Macs and, between them, Mparntwe – Alice Springs. **Trek Larapinta** *(treklarapinta.com.au)* specialises in a variety of all-inclusive small groups, from three days to two weeks, with a 'leave no trace' policy. Trailheads are signposted, with camp sites, water tanks and drop toilets at most junctions. Hikers should carry paper maps and register intentions at the Telegraph Station (p855) in Alice Springs.

Walk from April to September for mild days and cool nights; summer temperatures can exceed 40°C. An NT Parks Pass is required; day walkers only need the Parks Pass, but if you're hiking overnight you must pay the multiday walking-trail fee (from $25 per person) and book a designated **camp site** *(parkbookings.nt.gov.au)*.

WATERHOLE WARNING

If you've swum in the Top End, you might rightly hesitate before diving into the West MacDonnell Ranges' waterholes, but rest easy: there are no crocodiles to be found here. The water's amber tint comes from natural tannins released by surrounding vegetation, not from murkiness, and it's clean and cool year-round. You might even spot small fish or freshwater shrimp darting in the shallows. Still, take care when entering, as the rocks can be slippery and the water deceptively deep in places. Always walk into the water first to test its depth and never dive. Some waterholes drop off suddenly. Prolonged exposure, especially in cooler months, can cause hypothermia, so limit time in cold water.

DREAMING STORIES

Dreaming stories (or Tjukurpa in the Central and Western Desert languages) are the foundation of Aboriginal culture, describing how the land, people, plants and animals were created by ancestral beings. In central Australia, these stories map every ridge, waterhole and rock formation, connecting Country to identity and law.

One well-known local story tells of the Kuniya and Liru, a python woman and venomous snake man whose battle at Uluṟu shaped the rock's contours. Dreaming stories are told by Traditional Owners, often through song, dance, art and ceremony. Some parts are shared publicly; others are sacred, known only to initiated custodians. Passed orally for tens of thousands of years, these stories preserve the world's oldest continuous culture and living relationship with the land.

KWEST/SHUTTERSTOCK

Ormiston Gorge

Swim in Red-Rock Shade

Immerse into Ellery Creek Big Hole

Ellery Creek Big Hole, 91km west of Alice Springs, may not have the soaring walls of other West MacDonnell waterholes, but it's easily one of the most inviting swims in central Australia. A large permanent pool shaded by towering scarlet escarpments, it's a popular and accessible spot for cooling off on a blazing summer day. The water here is cold year-round, fed by groundwater seepage through the ranges, and swimming is safe with no crocs present. Shaded picnic tables, gas BBQs, toilets and changing rooms are provided. The best time to visit is early morning or late afternoon when the light warms the cliffs and the crowds thin.

You'll enjoy being here most if you stay overnight at one of the camping spots. By mid-afternoon, most of the tour buses and day-trippers have moved on. As temperatures cool, take a hike along the **Dolomite Walk** (3km, 1½ hours return) through gently undulating bush country nearby. Bring insect repellent and a torch for after dark, and keep food secured as dingoes occasionally wander through camp. Fires are permitted only in designated areas and bookings for camp sites are made online. When silence and darkness descend, you might just see a dingo coming down to drink.

Parking is 2km off Namatjira Dr, down a dirt track that's usually accessible in a 2WD vehicle. Mobile coverage is patchy, so download maps in advance or pick up a printed one from the Alice Springs Visitor Information Centre (p862) before heading out.

West MacDonnell's Most Beautiful Gorge

Explore Ormiston Gorge

Ormiston Gorge is a hot spot for bird watchers, with the elusive spinifex pigeon and painted finch thriving in the area – perhaps because its deep pool holds water year-round. On hot afternoons, the rock face shifts through hues of orange and purple, and the waterhole, fringed with sand and ghost gums, offers a cool respite. The gorge twists and narrows as it leads into Ormiston Pound, a vast natural amphitheatre surrounded by red cliffs. The further you venture, the fewer people you'll share it with. It's also a key stop along the Larapinta Trail.

Of the many walks beginning at the car park, the standout is the **Ghost Gum Walk** (2.5km, 1½ hours), which climbs to the lookout, follows the ridge, then loops back via the waterholes. You may need to swim when water levels are high. The shorter option to the lookout and back is 1.2km or about 45 minutes. For something longer, try the **Pound Walk** (8.5 km, three to four hours), one of central Australia's most rewarding circuits. Walking tracks are well marked and graded, but sturdy shoes, water and sun protection are essential.

A simple seasonal kiosk operates daily from April to October, serving drinks, snacks and ice creams, and rangers are usually on site during peak months. The camping ground (p883) has shaded, unpowered sites, gas BBQs, hot showers and toilets. Bookings are required and swimming is permitted within the main pool. Pets, drones and fires are not allowed. Mobile coverage is limited and generators are prohibited to preserve the quiet. Access is 8km off Namatjira Dr on a good gravel road; no 4WD needed.

Soaring Cliffs & Rugged Ranges

Dramatic red cliffs mirrored in permanent waterholes

Glen Helen Gorge, where the ancient Finke River carves through the West MacDonnell Ranges, is among the region's most photogenic stops. Its resort and camping ground have been closed intermittently since 2023 due to water supply issues, so check online *(discoveryholidayparks.com.au)* before planning an overnight stay. Once here, stroll past boggy reed beds and tall eucalypts to the cool, permanent waterhole framed by towering red cliffs that blaze in the afternoon light. Swimming is permitted but the water is often icy, even in summer. Facilities include toilets, shaded picnic areas and gas BBQs near the car park. The site is accessible by 2WD year-round, though care is needed after rain.

A kilometre beyond the Glen Helen turn off, a signed access road climbs to the **Mt Sonder Lookout**, where sweeping ridgelines and the snaking Davenport Creek sprawl below. The view is superb at sunset and photographers often linger as the ranges turn gold to crimson. There's space for parking larger vehicles and interpretive panels explaining the area's geology and Indigenous significance.

WEST MACDONNELL WILDLIFE

Black-footed rock wallaby: Watch for them blending into the boulders, especially at Simpsons Gap.

Common brushtail possum: Spot them in river woodlands throughout the range. They're nocturnal, so most active at night.

Dingo: They're found throughout, but tend to stay out of sight until people leave; best spotted at dawn or dusk (in a quiet environment) around Ormiston Gorge or Ellery Creek Big Hole.

Euro or common wallaroo: Watch for them around Simpsons Gap or Ormiston Gorge, but as with the others, they're most likely spotted around dawn or dusk.

Red kangaroo: Keep an eye out, especially around sunset, near Simpsons Gap, along Larapinta Dr and Ormiston Gorge.

About 25km beyond Glen Helen, the Redbank Gorge car park marks the start of a 2km walk into a cool, cathedral-like chasm. From the same trailhead, keen hikers can tackle the **Mt Sonder Southern Summit Walk** (15.8km, six hours return). It's a steady 2km climb to the saddle, then a longer 5.5km ascent to the summit with panoramic desert views. Allow around 2½ hours for the descent. **Redbank Gorge** has basic camping facilities (p883) with toilets and fire pits (no water available). Bring a float or inflatable ring for the narrow water channels and a wetsuit if visiting outside summer. The final access road is unsealed and a 4WD is recommended.

Head Out in the Wild West

Venture out to Tylers Pass and Tnorala

Most travellers visit Redbank Gorge and Mt Sonder, then retrace the 175km back to Alice Springs. But if you continue via Hermannsburg or take the backroad to Kings Canyon, you'll find yourself at one of the outback's most dramatic vistas: **Tylers Pass Lookout**. From here, the land falls away into the seemingly never-ending desert interior, with the enigmatic ring of **Tnorala (Gosse Bluff)** easily dominating the horizon. A rough 5km 4WD track winds into the crater itself; you might think of it like driving into a sunken amphitheatre. Geologists say this ring is the eroded remnant of a meteorite impact 22km across and 2km deep that struck some 142 million years ago, when dinosaurs still reigned.

For the Indigenous Western Arrernte people, the land tells a much different story. Women once danced across the Milky Way and when one grew weary, she placed her beloved baby into a wooden basket. The basket (the curved constellation known as Corona Australis) then tumbled to Earth, forcing the rocks skyward, and the baby's parents – the morning and evening stars – continue to search for their lost child to this day.

Walking tracks meander across the sunken bowl, past desert oaks and wildflowers in season. The site feels hushed and not of this world. Few linger long, yet it's truly unforgettable. This is a landscape of shared strength, where science explains the cosmos in one way and culture in another.

Uncover a Palm-Filled Oasis

Wander through a Jurassic oasis of rare cabbage palms

Set within **Finke Gorge National Park** *(nt.gov.au/parks; day pass adult/child $10/5)*, about 120km southwest of Alice Springs, **Palm Valley** feels like a Jurassic mirage in the desert. Its claim to fame is 12,000 red cabbage palms, a species found nowhere else in the world. Believed to be living fossils, these survivors from a wetter era cling to life along the sandy valley floor and in spring-fed pockets that shift with the seasons. Their fan-shaped fronds and towering trunks contrast with the surrounding red rock, creating a scene that feels tropical amid the desert. The valley is also home to rare plant species like the MacDonnell Ranges cycad, desert quandong, plus zebra finches and the occasional perentie lizard.

WHY I LOVE THE WEST MACS

Ivy Carruth, Lonely Planet writer

I love the desolation of the West Macs because they feel like the outback at its most honest. The ridgelines glow copper fire in the morning, the gorges offer cool, surprising pockets of water and the walking tracks cut through Country that feels ancient in a way you don't need to name to understand. Every stop has its own character. Ormiston is a cathedral of stone. Ellery feels made for long, lazy swims and Standley carries stories older than anything on a map. Wildlife is everywhere if you slow down; rock wallabies flick across the scree and wedge-tailed eagles circle overhead. The West Macs remind me that the best parts of central Australia ask for nothing except that you look just a little closer.

BENNY MARTY/SHUTTERSTOCK

Finke Gorge National Park

A 4WD is essential to reach Palm Valley. The final 16km track from Hermannsburg follows the ancient Finke River bed and involves creek crossings, soft sand and rocky ledges. Allow two hours for the return trip and check road conditions, as flooding can make access impossible. The drive itself is part of the adventure, with ghost gums, wildflowers in season and soaring sandstone walls. Travelling in convoy or with a satellite phone is recommended, as mobile reception is nil. If you'd rather not drive, **Sandrifter Safaris** *(sandrifter.com.au; $259)* offers guided 4WD tours from Alice Springs.

Once here, the easiest hike is the **Arankaia Walk** (2km loop, one hour), which winds through the palm-studded valley before looping back over a sandstone plateau with sweeping views. For more distance, combine it with the **Mpulungkinya Track** (5km loop, two hours). There's also the **Mpaara Track** (5km loop, two hours), which traces Dreaming stories through the landscape and takes in the Finke River, Palm Bend and a cliff-ringed hollow. Facilities include a camping ground (p883) with toilets, picnic shelters and BBQs but no drinking water, so bring plenty. The park is accessible year-round, though winter offers cooler hiking conditions and clearer skies. Book camping online.

Explore Albert Namatjira's Town

Delve into art in historical Hermannsburg

The important First Nations community of Hermannsburg (Ntaria) lies 125km southwest of Alice Springs. Close to 90% of the town's population is Indigenous, predominantly Arrernte. The well-done **Hermannsburg Historic Precinct** *(hermannsburg.com.au)* pays tribute to artist Albert Namatjira (who lived here) and includes the site of the NT's early Lutheran **Hermannsburg Mission**. It was closed until further notice at the time of writing due to restoration.

ALBERT NAMATJIRA

Albert Namatjira (1902–59) was a Western Arrernte artist from Hermannsburg, west of Alice Springs, and one of Australia's most celebrated painters. Renowned for his luminous watercolours of the central Australian desert, he was the first Aboriginal artist to gain national acclaim. His distinctive style captured the rugged beauty of his homeland – native flora, red cliffs and incandescent light – with both precision and deep spiritual connection.

Namatjira's success challenged perceptions of Aboriginal art and identity during a period of harsh discrimination; in 1957 he became the first Aboriginal person granted Australian citizenship. His legacy endures through the Hermannsburg School of painters and the generations of Arrernte artists he inspired to share their Country through art.

HERMANNSBURG MISSION

Established on Western Arrernte Country in 1877 by Lutheran missionaries from South Australia, Hermannsburg Mission (p869) brought Christianity to the region and became one of central Australia's earliest permanent settlements. Despite the hardships and cultural clashes of the time, Hermannsburg fostered a rare, if complex, degree of cooperation between missionaries and the Arrernte people. Key figures included Pastor FW Albrecht and artist Albert Namatjira, whose watercolours later brought the landscape international recognition. The mission introduced education, pastoral work and art training, shaping cross-cultural exchange still felt today. It operated until 1982; today, the restored Hermannsburg Historic Precinct preserves its buildings, stories and evolving legacy of resilience, faith and creativity in the desert.

NIAL FULTON/SHUTTERSTOCK

Ochre Pits

The internationally acclaimed **Hermannsburg Potters** (*hermannsburgpotters.com.au*) is open to visitors by appointment only; book online. Otherwise, you can pause at the township for photos and look at the church and mission buildings from the roadside. The community asks travellers to remain mindful that this is an active settlement, not a museum, and to treat it as such. It's an essential stop for understanding central Australia's art and history.

Where First Nations Artists Found Pigment

Admire vibrant ancient ochre cliffs at this sacred site

Tjoritja / West MacDonnell National Park is home to one of central Australia's most vivid natural sights – the **Ochre Pits**. It's impossible for photos to capture their raw, layered beauty. Around 113km west of Alice Springs and 11km beyond **Serpentine Gorge**, these striped cliffs reveal ancient seams of white, yellow, green, red and violet-brown, each shade shaped by iron oxide and the slow passing of time. The site holds deep cultural significance for the Western Arrernte people, who have quarried here for millennia, using ochre in ceremony, body painting and artwork. It was once a major trade hub, with ochre from this quarry travelling hundreds of kilometres across desert Songlines and exchange routes.

Today, the pits remain open to visitors, though collecting is strictly prohibited. Interpretive signs near the viewing area explain their cultural and geological importance, and visitors are asked to stay on designated tracks. Just off Namatjira Dr, the walk from the car park takes only a few minutes along a flat, well-maintained path. There are shaded picnic tables, toilets and parking for small buses, and the site is accessible to standard vehicles. For the best colour and contrast, visit mid-morning or late afternoon when the low sun enhances the mineral bands. If you'd like a closer look, a short flight of stairs leads to the viewing platform at the base of the cliffs.

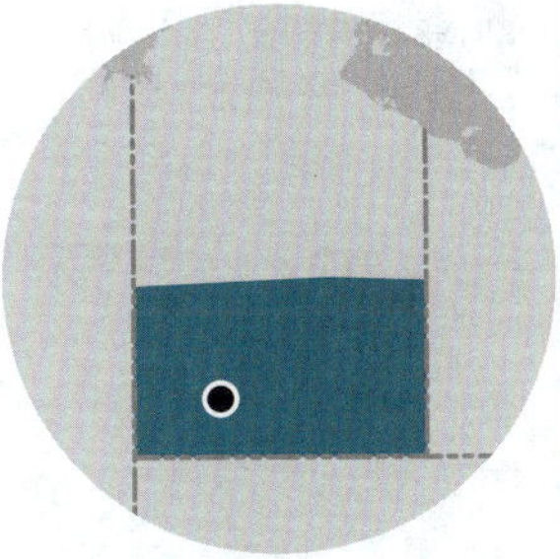

Kings Canyon

EPIC TREKS | STUNNING PANORAMAS | SCENIC FLIGHTS

Nothing prepares you for the first sight of Kings Canyon. One minute the road stretches deep across flat desert plain, the next you're standing before cliffs that create a glowing sandstone amphitheatre on a scale that staggers. This is Watarrka National Park, a place where living culture and geology meet in steadfast authority.

Kings Canyon reminds you how much the desert keeps its best stories tucked away from view. Its power lies in the surprise that such expanse and colour could be veiled until you're right at the edge. Climb the rim, of course, but don't stop there – it's custom-made for exploration. Meander through craggy rock landscapes and rest in shady outcroppings. Towering red walls soar up to 300m, revealing the Lost City domes and the cool, fern-fringed Garden of Eden below. Walks range from gentle creek trails to challenging rim climbs, each with interpretive signage.

GETTING AROUND

Most visitors to Kings Canyon come as part of a tour, with transport covered. If you're not on a tour, there's no public transport so you'll need your own wheels. Kings Canyon is 325km from Uluṟu and 328km from Alice Springs via the paved Luritja and Lasseter Hwys or 332km via the Mereenie Loop Rd, which requires a 4WD and permit; the latter is not available online, only in person via specific outlets including the Kings Canyon Resort (p883) reception or the Alice Springs Visitor Information Centre.

An Iconic Australian Walk

Ancient sandstone domes on the spectacular rim walk

You probably came to **Watarrka National Park** *(nt.gov.au/parks; day pass adult/child $10/5)* for the **Kings Canyon Rim Walk**. At 6km, the loop is not especially long, yet it usually takes three to four hours because the views will tempt you to pause again and again. Start early; sunrise is perfect. The walk closes at 9am if the temperature is forecast to exceed 36°C, so begin before that time. A shorter version of the Rim Walk, called the Kings Creek Walk (p872), stays open on hot days until 11am, but you'll miss most of the best views. Rangers recommend carrying at least 3L of water per person and wearing a hat, sunscreen and sturdy hiking boots. Free filtered water, toilets and a shaded rest area are available at the car park.

After a short walk to the base of the climb, a steep ascent along a rocky path takes you into the extraordinary landscape atop the canyon's lofty walls. The climb is strenuous but manageable for anyone of reasonable fitness. Once that first climb

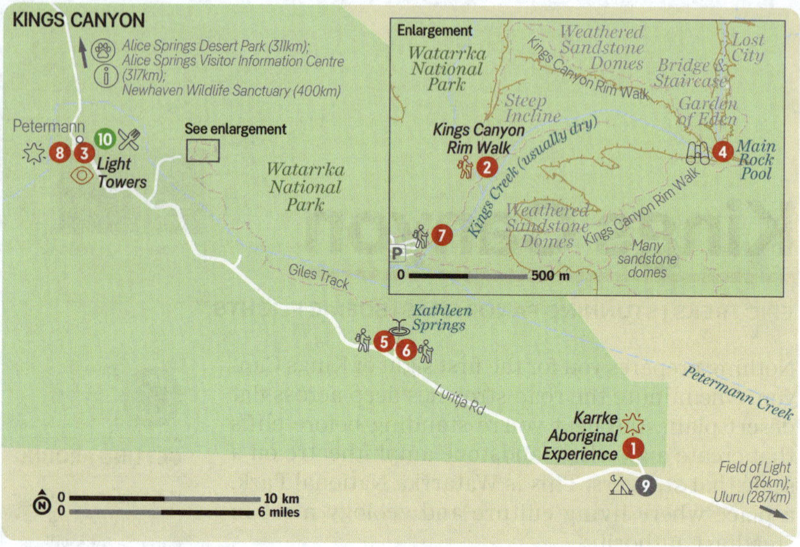

HIGHLIGHTS
1 Karrke Aboriginal Experience
2 Kings Canyon Rim Walk
3 Light Towers

SIGHTS
4 Garden of Eden

ACTIVITIES
5 Giles Track
6 Kathleen Springs Walk
7 Kings Creek Walk
8 Professional Helicopter Services

SLEEPING
see 8 Kings Canyon Resort
9 Kings Creek Station

EATING
see 3 Kings Canyon Bar & Grill
see 9 Kings Creek Station Cafe
see 3 Luritja Lookout Kiosk
10 Under a Desert Moon

TOP TIP

The sweet spot for visiting Kings Canyon is two full days. Dedicate one to the Canyon Rim Walk and another to exploring the other walks and adventures. Remember, there will be times, especially in blazing summer, when you'll want to simply relax and take it all in.

is behind you, the most demanding part of the walk is done. The trail then weaves across a clifftop, sometimes thrillingly close to the precipice, other times bending inland past sculpted sandstone. Several signposted lookouts along the rim offer sweeping views over the gorge and surrounding ranges.

A side track drops to the aptly named **Garden of Eden**, where ferns and ancient cycads grow beside a permanent waterhole – a cool pause amid the desert inferno. Returning to the rim, the path threads through beehive-shaped domes, weathered formations linked in Luritja tradition to the men of the Kuniya Dreaming. The circuit finishes with stirring views before a steady descent returns you to the car park. If walking in summer, plan to finish by 11am to avoid peak heat and note there's no shade or water available along the trail itself.

Roam the Country

Other Kings Canyon walks

If you've made time after the Kings Canyon Rim Walk, or want a gentler introduction, the **Kings Creek Walk** (2km return, one hour) traces the canyon floor beneath towering red walls. The path follows a stony creek bed to a viewing platform deep in the gorge. It's best walked in the early morning or late afternoon when the light softens the rock and the temperature drops. Carry water and wear sturdy shoes, as loose stones make footing uneven. Facilities include toilets, shaded picnic tables and a seasonal kiosk at the car park.

A little further afield, **Kathleen Springs Walk** (2.6km return, 1½ hours) is a quieter, wheelchair-accessible trail through a scenic valley with a waterhole at its head. The trail entrance is 10km east of the Kings Canyon car park. Interpretive signs tell stories of stockmen and Luritja Dreaming, making it ideal for families or those seeking a slower pace.

For die-hard trailblazers, the **Giles Track** (22km one way, overnight) links Kathleen Springs with Kings Canyon, skirting the George Gill Range. Before beginning the trek (you'll need to carry your own gear and supplies), register in the logbook at Kings Canyon Resort (p883). Camp sites are unserviced and hikers should carry at least 4L of water per person per day. The route is best tackled from April to September to avoid extreme heat.

A Sound-&-Light Spectacle

Experience the mesmerizing desert Light Towers

Building on the success of his celebrated Field of Light (p877) at Uluṟu, artist Bruce Munro unveiled a large-scale installation at Kings Canyon in April 2023. Known as the **Light Towers**, this immersive sound-and-light experience weaves the surrounding landscape into its spectacle, set to a soundtrack by Orlando Gough that shifts with the rhythm of the desert.

The installation features 69 towers made from 220 glass bottles filled with fibre-optic cables, creating a 360-degree field of shifting colour and sound. Each session lasts about 1½ hours and warm clothing is recommended in winter, as temperatures drop quickly after sunset. Light Towers operates year-round, with sunrise sessions offering a front-row seat to the canyon's cliffs glowing gold in first light, while evening showings coincide with the Milky Way arching above. It's a striking contrast between the celestial and the terrestrial and photographers should bring a tripod to capture the shifting hues.

Visits are only possible with a guide via Kings Canyon Resort (p883; *discoveryholidayparks.com.au; adult/child from $30/25*) and can be booked at sunrise, sunset or after dark. Sunrise and sunset options include food and drink packages. Bookings can be made online and numbers are limited to preserve tranquillity. Free parking is available for visitors staying at the resort or camping ground. The site is wheelchair-accessible and guided transfers can be arranged from the resort's reception.

Immerse Yourself in Desert Culture

Discover Karrke culture on an immersive guided walk

Let the **Karrke Aboriginal Experience** *(karrke.com.au; $99)* carry you into a living culture. Run by local Arrernte and Luritja people from the small community of Wanmarra,

THE MALA

The mala, a small marsupial once widespread across the Australian interior, is a name you'll hear often, especially in the First Nations stories attached to Uluṟu. Also known as the rufous hare-wallaby, the mala disappeared from the wild on the Australian mainland (a small island population survives in Shark Bay, off Western Australia) in the 1980s when the last survivors in the Tanami Desert were taken into captivity to form a breeding program at Uluṟu, Kings Canyon and Alice Springs Desert Park.

In recent years, some of these captive mala were released into a 100-sq-km exclosure at Newhaven Wildlife Sanctuary (p861). This first wild population of mala in half a century is now thriving.

FIRST NATIONS PEOPLE OF CENTRAL AUSTRALIA

Warlpiri: Encompassing much of the Tanami Desert north and northwest of Alice Springs; Yuendumu is a predominantly Warlpiri town.

Pintupi: Spanning the NT and WA, Pintupi Country lies west of the West MacDonnell Ranges, close to Kintore and Kiwirrkurra.

Luritja: Luritja Country spans part of the West MacDonnell Ranges and the area around Haasts Bluff and Mt Liebig.

Arrernte/Aranda: Traditional Owners of Mparntwe (Alice Springs) and large swathes of the West MacDonnell Ranges and to the south.

Pitjantjatjara/Aṉangu: Custodians of Uluṟu; their territory extends south into the Great Victorian Desert and the APY (Aṉangu Pitjantjatjara Yankunytjatjara) Lands.

BENNY MARTY/SHUTTERSTOCK

the Karrke journey is a one-hour walk-and-talk plunge into desert culture. Trace paths through scrub while your guide points out bush tucker and native medicines, shares the secrets (some of them) behind boomerang technique and invites you into the world of dot painting and ancestral stories. This is more than a demonstration or a passive observation; it's a chance to feel the legacy directly.

Reserve your spot directly on the website or book through Kings Canyon Resort (p883) or **Kings Creek Station** (p883; *kingscreekstation.com.au*) camping ground. Tours run Thursday to Sunday, typically at 10.30am and 1.30pm, and group sizes are kept small for a personal experience. The meeting point is 34km east of Kings Canyon on the Luritja Rd and parking is available for 2WD vehicles. Visitors are encouraged to bring a hat, water and cash for purchasing handmade jewellery or artworks created by community members. Photography is welcome, but some cultural content may be restricted.

EATING & DRINKING IN KINGS CANYON: OUR PICKS

Kings Canyon Bar & Grill: Wood-fired pizza, burgers and BBQ dishes are on offer at this Aussie-style bistro at Kings Canyon Resort. *11am-8.30pm* $$

Kings Creek Station Cafe: Cafe staples such as burgers, chicken parmigiana, fish and chips and more; next to the station's reception. *7am-6.30pm* $$

Luritja Lookout Kiosk: Light drinks and basic snacks available during the Light Towers sessions. Also open to outside guests. *sunrise & sunset* $

Under a Desert Moon: Open-air desert dining featuring a five-course dinner by campfire with locally inspired dishes. *from 6pm Wed-Sun Apr-Oct* $$$

Peter Abbott, a Southern Aranda man and tour guide, Karkke Aboriginal Experience (p873)

Look Down from Above

Soar above dramatic desert canyons on a helicopter flight

If you've ever toyed with the idea of a helicopter flight, Kings Canyon is the place to give it a whirl. From quick eight-minute dashes over the canyon's sandstone escarpments to half-hour arcs that take in the northernmost part of the George Gill Range, you're in for a treat no matter how long you soar. From above, the canyon reveals its truest form – a dramatic cleft in the outback that feels even bigger once you see how abruptly it slices through the plains. At sunrise and in late afternoon the desert glows in coppery crimson; book at Kings Canyon Resort (p883) or Kings Creek Station (p883).

Flights are operated by **Professional Helicopter Services** *(phs.com.au)* and range from about $150 for short scenic hops to $600 for extended journeys over Watarrka National Park. All tours include headsets for live commentary and sunrise flights are popular with photographers. Bookings can be made at the resort or online; availability depends on weather, so check ahead. Passengers under three fly free on a parent's lap and weight limits apply. The helipad sits five minutes from Kings Canyon Resort, with transfers available for guests. Flights run year-round from early morning until dusk and each pilot provides insight into the canyon's geology and Indigenous significance. In cooler months, the air is especially clear, giving breathtaking views of the West MacDonnell Ranges on the horizon.

MODERN ART INSTALLATIONS

There is a tendency among art critics, as among tourists, to see First Nations art as never-shifting or locked in the past. But the paintings and other artworks you see today are as diverse as the artists who create them. Sometimes this manifests in the emerging use of modern forms, such as the use of light to deepen our understanding of landscapes.

In 2016 the Indigenous-led **Parrtjima** light festival debuted on the Alice Springs calendar and non-Indigenous artist Bruce Munro inaugurated his celebrated Field of Light (p877) at Uluṟu. Seven years later, Bruce Munro brought Light Towers (p873) to Kings Canyon, cementing the Red Centre's role at the heart of innovative contemporary First Nations art in Australia.

Uluru-Kata Tjuta National Park

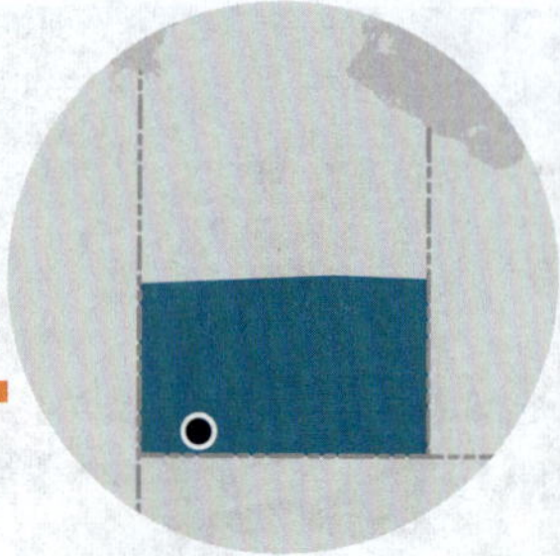

FIRST NATIONS GUIDES | ICONIC TERRAIN | HIKING

GETTING AROUND

The town of Yulara is the gateway to the national park and where Ayers Rock Resort is located. At the resort itself, a hop-on/hop-off bus makes getting around easy and is the only form of public transport.

Many travellers arrive in Yulara on a tour bus or at the dedicated regional airport; for others, it's a road-trip destination from Alice Springs (5½ hours if you don't take long stops). To venture out, you'll need your own wheels or to join a tour, which we recommend you book in advance.

Rising improbably from the desert, Uluru is a glorious monolith with an undeniable gravitas. Up close, its textures are strangely compelling, and from afar, it radiates a soulful countenance. For the Anangu people, the Pitjantjatjara and Yankunytjatjara Traditional Owners, Uluru is a realm of spiritual meaning with ties to enduring culture and story. In respect of its spiritual significance, climbing Uluru officially became illegal in 2019. Visitors can still explore it in countless ways: walk, cycle or Segway its base, take one of several guided tours with an Aboriginal ranger, watch as it glows at sunset or see its scale from the air.

Nearby, Kata Tjuta rises like a desert citadel, its domes sheltering superb walks into valleys and gorges that are highlights of any Red Centre journey. You could easily spend a relaxing week here, or see the best of it in three to four days if you prioritise.

The Living Story of Uluru

The spiritual heart of Anangu storytelling and art

Far more than a visitor stop, the **Uluru–Kata Tjuta Cultural Centre** *(uluru.gov.au; free)* holds the spirit of the park's storytelling and understanding. About 13km from the Car Sunset-Viewing Area (p879), it's the first place to visit before stepping onto Country. Built in 1995 under Anangu direction, the structure itself is part of the story; its curved, mud-brick walls represent Kuniya and Liru, two ancestral snakes whose epic battle shaped Uluru. Inside, bilingual exhibits, audio stations and videos explain Tjukurpa, the Anangu concept encompassing Creation stories, cultural law and spirituality. You'll also learn how Traditional Owners and Parks Australia jointly manage the park, blending ancient knowledge with modern conservation. Rangers hold free talks most mornings; photography inside the centre is restricted out of respect for cultural protocols.

In one wing, the free **Tjukurpa Theatre** screens a short film that brings the landscape's spiritual and geological history to

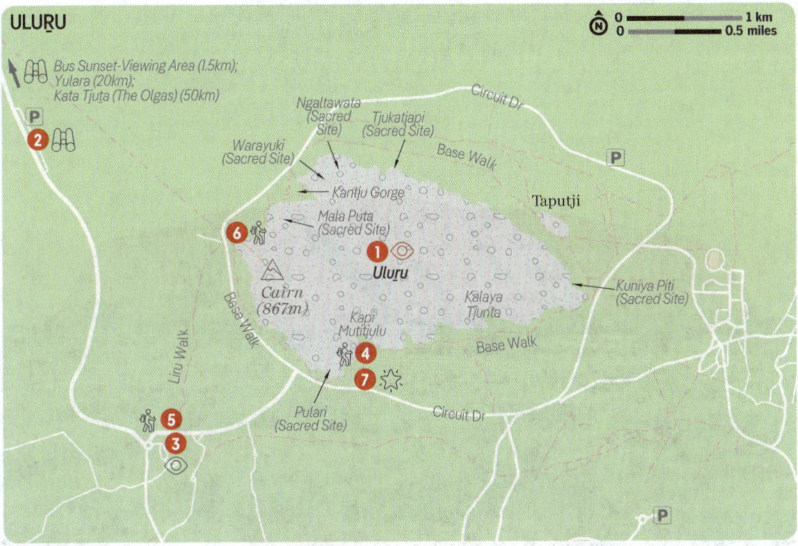

HIGHLIGHTS
1 Uluru

SIGHTS
2 Car Sunset-Viewing Area
3 Uluru-Kata Tjuta Cultural Centre
see 3 Walkatjara Art Centre

ACTIVITIES
4 Kuniya Walk
5 Liru Walk
6 Mala Walk
see 6 Ranger-Guided Mala Walk
see 6 Uluru Base Walk
7 Uluru Segway Tours

SHOPPING
see 3 Maruku Arts

TRANSPORT
see 3 Outback Cycling

life. Narrated by Anangu voices, it weaves archival footage, music and Dreaming stories into a moving interpretation of how this Country came to be. It's air-conditioned, a welcome respite from the desert heat, and a perfect primer before walking the base track (p879) or joining a ranger tour.

Within the centre you'll also find two Indigenous-owned galleries. **Walkatjara Art Centre** *(walkatjara.com; free)* showcases acrylic paintings by artists from the nearby Mutitjulu community, often inspired by local Dreamings such as Mala, Kuniya and Lungkata. Next door, **Maruku Arts** *(maruku.com.au; free)* presents carvings, *punu* (woodwork) and dot paintings created by artists from across central Australia. Maruku is a nonprofit art and craft collective of approximately 900 artists from many remote Anangu communities across the Western and Central Desert regions. Purchases support local artists directly, ensuring that culture, not commerce, remains the focus. Together, these spaces form the cultural and creative soul of the Red Centre.

TOP TIP

Travelling southwest by road to Uluru? Don't be fooled by Mt Connor, nicknamed 'Fool-uru', which appears at a roadside lookout with a rare phone signal 107km before Yulara. Uluru isn't visible until 20km or so before town.

After-Dark Wonders

The desert dark, three different ways

A visit to the **Field of Light** *(ayersrockresort.com.au; adult/child from $49.50/38)* begins at sunset, as darkness falls across

WIRESTOCK CREATORS/SHUTTERSTOCK

TOP EXPERIENCE

Uluṟu & Kata Tjuṯa

Standing sentinel over the endless horizons of Australia's Red Centre, soulful Uluṟu and Kata Tjuṯa seem filled with mysterious drama. Together, they have become icons of the outback: ancient and timeless, Uluṟu and Kata Tjuṯa are even more special in reality than what you've heard and they really do have to be seen to be believed.

DON'T MISS

- Uluṟu Base Walk
- Circle Uluṟu by bicycle
- Valley of the Winds Walk
- Ranger-Guided Mala Walk
- Sunset-Viewing Area
- Kata Tjuṯa Sand Dune Lookout
- Liru Walk

First Nations Culture

A guided tour with **SEIT Outback Australia** *(seittours.com; adult/child from $389/220)* – especially the immersive seven-hour Patji tour – offers a deeper understanding of Aboriginal culture through a local A<u>n</u>angu lens, with access to areas closed to other tours. It's an Indigenous perspective on bush tucker, life on the land and the history of the national park. Departure times and rates vary by season.

PRACTICALITIES

- *uluru.gov.au*
- 3-day/annual pass $38/50

The national park has two galleries showcasing Anangu artworks and sculpture at the cultural centre – Walkatjara Art Centre (p877; *walkatjara.com; free*) and Maruku Arts (p877; *maruku.com.au; free*). Watch the artists as they create, browse and learn from the creations including *punu* (using wood as the medium), dot paintings and more from over 500 artists in 20-plus remote communities.

Hike Uluru

The **Liru Walk** (4km return, 1½ hours) links the Uluru-Kata Tjuta Cultural Centre (p876) with the main Uluru car park. The fascinating, free, 1½-hour **Ranger-Guided Mala Walk** begins every morning from 8am October to April and 10am May to September, and requires no booking. The other walks – the **Mala Walk** (2km return, one hour) and **Kuniya Walk** (1km return, 45 minutes) – are part of an overarching circumnavigation of the rock: the **Uluru Base Walk** (10.6km, three to four hours).

Aside from a shadeless stretch on the Base Walk's north side (start early), you'll love the chance to examine the rich textures of the rock faces – Uluru's caves, waterholes (including **Mutitjulu**, home of the ancestral water snake), fissures and enigmatic rock formations laden with spiritual meaning.

Valley of the Winds Walk

Over at Kata Tjuta, the 7.4km, two- to four-hour Valley of the Winds loop is one of the great outback hikes. Following the inner gorges and dwarfed at every step by the surreal domes surging above you, this trail climbs to a saddle where you can return the way you came or – much better – continue on into the broader valleys of the range before looping back to where you began. Start at first light; if the weather is forecast to reach 36°C, trail access is closed, usually by 11am.

If you can't make the full walk, try the **Walpa Gorge (Tatintjawiya) Walk** (2.6km return, 45 minutes); look for rock wallabies.

Sunrise & Sunset Freebies

Few places in Australia flaunt a more spectacular sunset. Choose from the **Bus Sunset-Viewing Area** and Car Sunset-Viewing Area (p876), both wonderfully chosen (and free); bring refreshment and watch Uluru turn shades of red you never knew existed.

For Kata Tjuta, the **Kata Tjuta Sand Dune Lookout** is magnificent, with an unrivalled panorama of the anything-but-desolate range, although it's shadowed for the final half-hour. For another fine angle, drive 2km out on the Kaltukatjara (Docker River) road and simply park by the roadside as you watch while nature does its thing.

For sunrise, it simply must be **Talinguru Nyakunytjaku Lookout** with Uluru in the foreground and Kata Tjuta in the same frame. It's one of the best ways to start a day out here.

BIKE THE BASE TRACK

Follow the Uluru Base Walk on a bike from **Outback Cycling** *(outbackcycling.com: adult/child $80/65)*, which operates alongside the Uluru–Kata Tjuta Cultural Centre. Although the trails are not paved, they're flat, well maintained and usually in excellent condition except after heavy rains. Including the trip to/from the rental point, a full circumnavigation should be an easy 11km to 12km. Allow three hours.

TOP TIPS

- You can book most tours through the **Tour & Information Centre** on Town Sq in Yulara or online before you go.
- Plan your trip as early as you can: online flash sales *(ayersrockresort.com.au)* can cut accommodation rates by 75%.
- The Uluru–Kata Tjuta National Park entry fees are separate from the NT Parks Pass; children visit for free. If your visit spills into a fourth day, a free extension is granted.
- Plan to begin all activities that involve being outdoors soon after sunrise; park gates open just before then.
- Temperatures fluctuate wildly. Layers are best.

ULUṞU'S ALLURE

Once called Ayers Rock, Uluṟu reclaimed its original name in 1993 to honour and respect the Aṉangu Traditional Owners. Rising 348m from the desert floor, it's made of arkosic sandstone rich in feldspar, which glows deep red at sunrise and sunset. Its colour changes dramatically throughout the day, reflecting shifting light and weather. Scientists estimate two-thirds of the monolith lies underground and out of sight. Uluṟu is more than 600 million years old and about 9.4km around its base. For the Aṉangu, it's a sacred site woven with Tjukurpa (Creation stories) and living law.

Today, Uluṟu is one of Australia's most visited landmarks, celebrated for both its geological wonder and profound cultural significance.

the desert and Uluṟu fades into silhouette. In the foreground, over 50,000 poppy-like stems topped with glowing glass orbs create an awe-inspiring display of light and colour. Crowds fall silent, people gasp and the world melts away. Appropriately, it's known locally as *Tili Wiru Tjuta Nyakutjaku*, meaning 'looking at lots of beautiful lights'. Advance bookings are essential. The experience runs nightly, with transfers available from Yulara hotels. Wear sturdy shoes and warm layers, as evenings can be chilly even in warmer months. Tripods aren't permitted, but hand-held photography is encouraged and accessibility options are available on request.

Newly launched at Uluṟu is the **Wintjiri Wiṟu** *(ayersrockresort.com.au; adult/child $205/102.50)* light show, commanding a force of 1000 drones choreographed across the night sky to bring to life a chapter of the ancestral Mala story; Wintjiri Wiṟu means 'beautiful view out to the horizon' in the Pitjantjatjara language. Prepare for a moving, transcendent evening and a deep connection to this place of Country. The experience includes return transfers, refreshments and a three-tier viewing platform overlooking Uluṟu. Shows run most evenings, but are weather-dependent and often sell out days in advance.

Also not to be missed is an early-morning **Sunrise Journey** *(ayersrockresort.com.au; adult/child $125/75)*, becoming one with the day as light and laser projections ripple across the desert floor. The tale traces cycles of renewal, narrated by three Aṉangu artists in a modern retelling of Tjukurpa – Creation and cultural law stories. Guests are collected from the resort before dawn, with coffee, tea and breakfast provided. Bring a jacket and arrive camera-ready: sunrise over the red dunes is nothing short of extraordinary.

Eat Under the Stars

Savour gourmet desert dining under a starlit sky

A massive upgrade on a simple desert meal around a campfire, two desert dining experiences have become a special part of a visit to Uluṟu. Each offers a slightly different setup, but the unifying themes are desert views, locally inspired flavours, red sands underfoot and a sky dense with stars. Cultural storytelling remains at their heart. Both are hosted by **Voyages Indigenous Tourism Australia** *(voyages.com.au)* and can be booked online through the Ayers Rock Resort or at the resort's tour desk. Return transfers from Yulara hotels are included,

EATING & DRINKING IN YULARA: OUR PICKS

Kulata Academy Cafe: Staffed by trainees of Uluṟu's Indigenous training academy, Kulata does breakfast, coffee and light lunches. *7am-2pm* **$**

Ayers Wok Noodle Bar: This small takeaway place on the Town Sq does a fine pad thai, laksa, dumplings and stir-fries. *5-8pm* **$$**

Geckos Cafe: This popular cafe serves wood-fired pizza, kangaroo burgers and pasta as well as international meals. *7-10am & 11am-9pm* **$$**

Outback Hotel & Lodge: Two restaurants in one: buffet breakfast at Bough House and grilled meats at Outback BBQ & Bar. *6-10am & 5-9pm* **$$**

Sunset picnic, Uluṟu-Kata Tjuṯa National Park

but temperatures drop sharply after dark, so bring a jacket. Seating is communal for Sounds of Silence and intimate for Tali Wiru. Dietary requirements can be accommodated with advance notice.

The first option, **Sounds of Silence** *(ayersrockresort.com.au; adult/child $290/145)*, is a relaxed dinner beginning with canapés, followed by a three-course meal infused with native bush spices and local ingredients. Apart from the food, guests enjoy a didgeridoo performance at sunset before an astronomer guides you through the southern night sky, where the Milky Way glitters with almost supernatural clarity. The evening typically lasts four hours, with drinks included throughout, and the experience is available year-round except in heavy rain.

The second option, **Tali Wiru** *(ayersrockresort.com.au; $450)*, is a more refined fine-dining experience; the minimum age is 16. Running from April to October, it unfolds atop a dune with distant views of Uluṟu and Kata Tjuṯa. The four-course menu blends Japanese influences with surprising native ingredients such as desert limes and fermented quandong salsa. Premium wines and champagne accompany the meal, service is impeccable and, in place of an astronomer, a First Nations storyteller shares local Creation stories by firelight. Only 20 guests are seated per evening, ensuring an

ULUṞU & KATA TJUṮA TOURS

AAT Kings: Large-group bus tours, with lots of options to choose from.

Desert Awakenings Tour: Sunrise tour with First Nations storytelling and a traditional bush-dweller's breakfast.

Outback Sky Journeys: Look through a telescope at the outback sky with an astronomer.

SEIT Outback Australia: Small-group tours, including bush foods, sunset and sunrise tours.

Uluṟu Camel Tours: View distant Uluṟu and Kata Tjuṯa from atop a camel, with free farm visits.

Uluru Motorcycle Tours: Drawing near to Uluṟu on a Harley does have a certain cachet.

Uluṟu Segway Tours: Four- to five-hour tours along the Uluṟu Base Walk.

EATING & DRINKING IN YULARA: OUR PICKS

Mangata Bistro & Bar: This lobby cafe-bar in the Desert Gardens Hotel does small and big plates to share and barista coffee. *6-10am & 11am-9pm* **$$**

Arngulli Grill & Restaurant: Arguably Yulara's best restaurant, Arngulli is the place for fabulous, locally sourced dishes; dress nicely. *6-8.30pm* **$$$**

Ilkari Restaurant: Buffet breakfasts/dinners at Sails in the Desert: seafood, pan-Asian cuisine and a chocolate-fountain finale. *6.30-10.30am & 5.30-9.30pm* **$$$**

Walpa Lobby Bar: Good service and excellent food including seafood platters and Aussie bush ingredients. *dining 10.30am-5.30pm, drinks 5.30-9pm* **$$$**

WHAT ABOUT KATA TJUṮA?

About 56km west of Uluṟu, Kata Tjuṯa (meaning 'many heads' in Pitjantjatjara) comprises 36 immense domes of conglomerate rock rising up to 546m, taller than Uluṟu. Estimated to be more than 500 million years old, it is geologically distinct: Uluṟu is a single sandstone monolith, while Kata Tjuṯa formed from a mix of granite and basalt cemented by sand. Though less photographed, Kata Tjuṯa is equally sacred to the Aṉangu Traditional Owners, with many sites restricted to visitors. Walking trails such as the Valley of the Winds (p879) and Walpa Gorge (p879) reveal its vast scale and silence. The name 'the Olgas' came from 19th-century European explorers, but it was officially restored to Kata Tjuṯa in 1993; few locals still use the colonial term.

BENNY MARTY/SHUTTERSTOCK

Helipcopter tour, Uluṟu-Kata Tjuṯa National Park

intimate and atmospheric experience that ends beneath one of the clearest night skies on Earth.

Uluṟu from Above

Take it all in on a scenic flight

Operating out of Yulara, **Fly Uluru** *(flyuluru.com.au)* and **Professional Helicopter Services** *(phs.com.au)* each offer a choice of flight times and distances. Flights skim Uluṟu's flanks before widening to Kata Tjuṯa, 56km away. With extra time in the sky and a stretch of the budget, you might even set down on **Mt Connor** or reach Kings Canyon.

If helicopters aren't your style, or you want something a bit off-piste, Fly Uluru also operates small fixed-wing planes. These provide a steadier ride and usually come in cheaper (though with more folks aboard) than a chopper seat. Fixed-wing itineraries open up the possibility of covering greater distances, making an extended trip to the crater of, say, Tnorala more feasible. Morning flights offer calmer conditions and the best light for photography, while afternoon departures highlight the desert's deepening colours. Bring sunglasses, sunscreen and a camera with polarising filter for best results.

Most flights depart from the main Yulara airstrip, with transfers available from resort hotels. Advance booking is strongly recommended, especially during peak season from May to September. Uluṟu flights start at $155 for 15 minutes and longer jaunts that include Kata Tjuṯa (30 to 40 minutes) are from $345.

Places We Love to Stay

$$$ Top End $$ Midrange $ Budget

Alice Springs

MAP p851

Alice's Secret Traveller's Inn $ Easily among the best Alice hostels, with lots of info, quirky decor, a pool and plenty of fun.

Alice Lodge Backpackers $ Friendly, close to town, with decent dorms and rooms, and a pool – ideal budget digs.

Discovery Parks Alice Springs $ Powered and unpowered sites, several pools and a brand-new water park. Food trucks on site, plus snack bar and kids' club.

MacDonnell Range Holiday Park $ Probably Alice's biggest and best kept, this caravan park has grassy sites, cabins, villas and family-friendly facilities.

Alice Springs Tourist Park $ All sites are close to amenities, with well-equipped camp kitchens. Secure and well maintained with a small convenience shop in reception area for basics. This one is closest to town and pet-friendly.

Wintersun Cabin & Caravan Park $ Quietest of the sites; no pets. Pool, laundry, BBQ, dump point and free luggage storage. Staff are helpful with recommendations and local knowledge.

G'day Mate Tourist Park $ Lots of grass and shade trees make this a lovely and comfortable spot to spend the night. Super en-suite options and fast wi-fi. Walk to brewery and mini-mart.

Desert Palms Resort $$ Excellent value reigns at this quiet collection of attractive modern villas, with a good pool and lots of palms.

Squeakywindmill Boutique Tent B&B $$ Stay out bush in glamping-style en-suite tents; you're out of the way but only a 15-minute drive to town. Possible change in ownership; check online.

Doubletree by Hilton $$ This is widely considered one of Alice's top hotels; go for the pricier mountain-view rooms. Great facilities and restaurant.

East MacDonnell Ranges

MAP p863

Arltunga Bush Hotel $ Renovated in 2023, this camping ground is deliciously remote and well run. Make the most of your seclusion here; simply breathtaking.

N'Dhala Gorge Camping Ground $ Location is everything at this simple and largely shadeless camping area. Perfect for a good night's sleep close to the action.

Hale River Homestead at Old Ambalindum $$ Wonderful Hale River has a homestead, cottage, converted shed, bunkhouses and lovely camp sites. Good showers, too.

West MacDonnell Ranges

Ormiston Gorge Campground $ Great once the day-trippers leave; watch for dingoes after dark.

Redbank Gorge Campground $ One of the better West Macs camps; book ahead for one of the sites on the bluff overlooking the gorge.

Finke Gorge National Park Camping Ground $ Camp among the palm trees in this gorgeous spot; facilities are basic.

Kings Canyon

MAP p872

Kings Creek Station $$ Located 36km from the canyon, this family-run station offers top-notch glamping, cabins, camping, tours and meals.

Kings Canyon Resort $$$ You're 10km from the canyon at this sprawling resort, with excellent accommodation and restaurants.

Uluṟu-Kata Tjuṯa National Park

Ayers Rock Resort Campground $ The only budget accommodation at Yulara has crowded camp sites and cabins.

Outback Pioneer Hotel & Lodge $$ A quasi-budget hotel, Outback Pioneer has motel-style rooms, a pool and restaurants.

Desert Gardens Hotel $$$ The 4½-star Desert Gardens has supremely comfortable rooms with a lovely Scandinavian minimalist look.

Emu Walk Apartments $$$ This tidy self-contained accommodation in the heart of Yulara is close to everything.

Longitude 131 $$$ One of the best places to stay in the Red Centre, Longitude has uber-luxurious glamping tents within sight of Uluṟu.

For places to stay in Perth & Western Australia, see p1006

DRONE CHICKS/SHUTTERSTOCK

Natures Window, Kalbarri National Park (p965)

Researched by
Rosamund Brennan,
Emmylou Dzubiel
and Steve Waters

Perth & Western Australia

ETERNAL LANDSCAPES, ENDLESS COASTLINE AND RAW BEAUTY

A sun-kissed capital leading to vast outback gorges, ancient forests and some of the most biodiverse and pristine reefs on Earth.

It's difficult not to envy those who call Perth home. The city seems to glow with natural abundance – a coastline of pale sand and Indian Ocean blues, a river curling through sculpted parklands and sunlight that feels almost perennial. Yet Perth's appeal runs deeper, encompassing a sophisticated food and wine culture, a lively arts calendar, and neighbourhoods threaded with small bars and galleries. It's a coastal capital still closely tied to nature and it's the gateway to some of Australia's most extraordinary journeys.

South of the city, the Southwest region unfolds in a sweep of dramatic headlands and cool, sea-washed air. Here, cellar doors and kitchens celebrate world-class produce, surfers skim along perfect breaks and walkers trace clifftop trails above turquoise bays. Further on, ancient forests rise like cathedrals, where Noongar guides share stories shaped by millennia. Along the coast lie whale-watching lookouts, cool-climate vineyards, the treetop walkway of the Valley of the Giants and national parks protecting some of the planet's most exquisite beaches.

To the north, Western Australia widens into a monumental landscape. The Pinnacles, Kalbarri's ochre gorges, Shark Bay, Ningaloo, Karijini, the Kimberley and the beehive domes of Purnululu form a procession of outback icons. Here you can swim with whale sharks, trek to hidden pools beneath red cliffs or steer a 4WD across riverbeds and ancient ranges. Few places offer such breadth, beauty and sheer possibility.

THE MAIN AREAS

Find Your Way

Western Australia spans a vast corner of the continent, with Perth on its southwestern coast and remote regions stretching thousands of kilometres north and east. Distances are immense, so plan carefully around time, fuel and seasonal weather.

Carnarvon & the Gascoyne, p972
River-fed oasis of tropical fruit, outback stations and skies.

Exmouth & Ningaloo Coast, p974
Accessible reef experiences with whale sharks, snorkelling and quiet beaches.

The Pilbara, p979
Vast red landscapes shaped by ancient geology and enduring culture.

Broome & the Kimberley, p986
Broome's tropical beach life abuts the Kimberley's deep cultural landscapes.

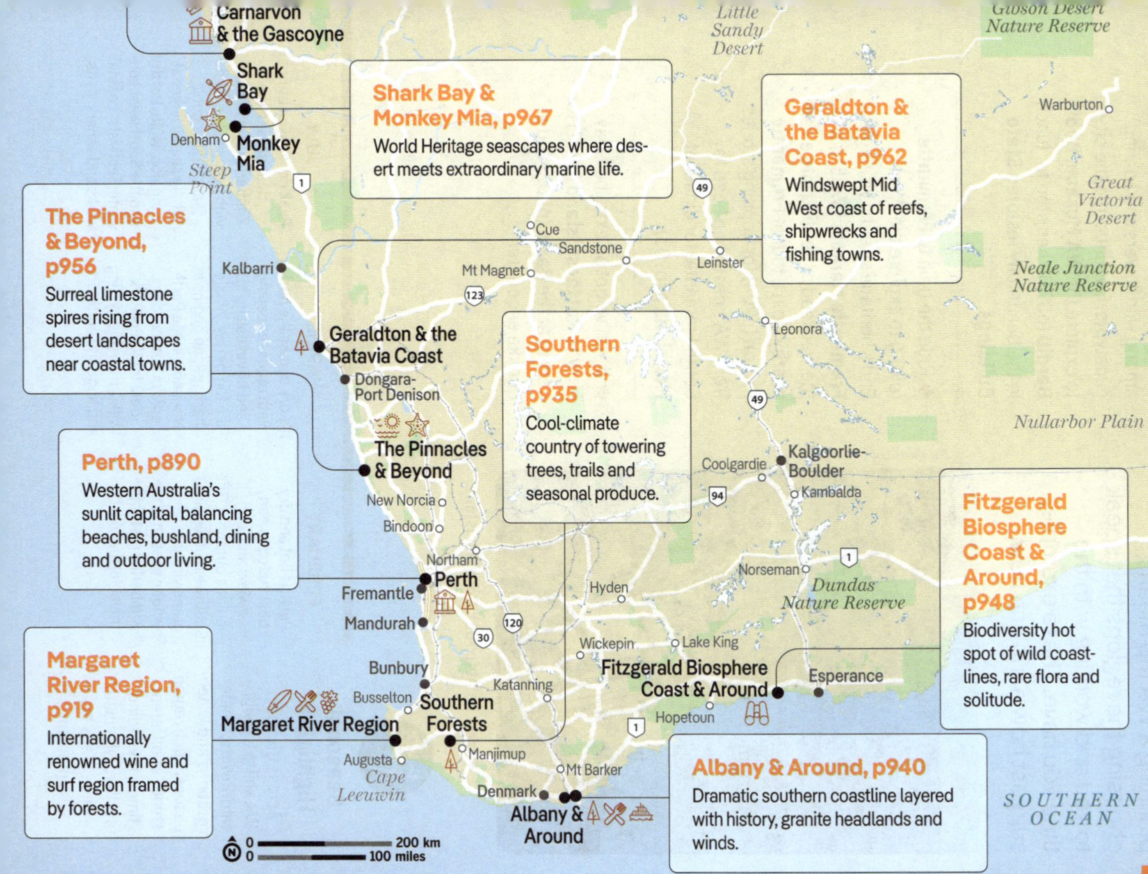

PLANE

Unless you have weeks to drive WA's coastline, flying is the most practical way to cover long distances. From Perth, regular flights reach Broome, Kununurra, Exmouth, Albany and Esperance, with charter services accessing more remote outback and coastal regions.

CAR & 4WD

Self-driving is one of the most rewarding ways to explore WA, with open roads leading to beaches, forests and dramatic outback scenery. A 4WD unlocks remote tracks and national parks, but even on sealed routes plan for long distances and check road conditions.

BUS

Transwa coaches connect Perth with many key regional centres, including Albany, Margaret River, Geraldton and Kalbarri. Services are comfortable and reliable, though timetables are limited, so trips need a little planning. Perth and Fremantle are also well covered by local buses for short-hop travel.

Plan Your Time

With so much variety (and distance) across the state, planning a WA trip means choosing the regions that speak to you and working with the time you have. These examples suggest how a trip can flow.

ANNALUCIA/SHUTTERSTOCK

Parker Point (p908), Rottnest Island

Pressed for Time

- If you only have a day or two, focus on Perth and Fremantle. Begin in **Perth** (p890) with a wander through **Kings Park & Botanic Garden** (p895), walking among wildflowers and soaring eucalypts. Continue into the city to explore the **WA Museum Boola Bardip** (p897), then stop for lunch in the beautifully restored **State Buildings**.

- Ride the train to **Fremantle** (p902) to explore the West End's heritage streets, visiting **Fremantle Markets** (p905) if it's the weekend or settling into a cafe nearby. Join a tour at **Fremantle Prison** (p904) for gripping stories from WA's past, then head to South Fremantle for dinner at **Madalena's** (p903).

- If you've got an extra half-day, ferry to **Rottnest Island** (p907) for a swim at the **Basin** (p908) and a quokka encounter.

Seasonal Highlights

Across the year, WA shifts through wildflowers, whale migrations and winery seasons. Each region shines at different times, rewarding travellers who match their plans to the moment.

FEBRUARY

Perth is hot and dry, best suited to early swims and long evenings outdoors. The Southwest moves into grape vintage, while cyclone season in the Kimberley restricts travel further north.

APRIL

It's dry across the north, with roads reopening and travel easing in the Kimberley. Whale shark season begins at Ningaloo, while Perth enjoys autumn days ideal for Kings Park walks, riverside cycling and lingering outdoors.

JULY

Peak dry season brings clear days to the Kimberley and Pilbara, with gorges accessible and nights cool. Whale sharks linger at Ningaloo, while Perth and the Southwest suit winter festivals, coastal walks and winery visits.

Five Western Days

- Five days is the ideal window to explore WA's Southwest and Great Southern regions, where forests, surf and vineyards sit within easy reach. Start in the **Margaret River Region** (p919), spending two days between winery lunches at **Vasse Felix** or **Cullen Wines** (p922), coastal walks to **Surfers Point** (p924)and visits to **Ngilgi** (p924) or **Mammoth Cave** (p927).

- Continue east into the **Great Southern** and settle in **Albany** (p940), exploring the granite cliffs of **Torndirrup National Park** (p944), **Misery Beach** and **The Gap** and **Natural Bridge** (p944).

- Head inland to wander among towering tingle trees in the **Valley of the Giants** (p944) before returning to Perth through rolling farmland and small country towns.

A Week to Spare

- A week gives you time to pair Perth with a taste of the Kimberley's spellbinding north. Fly into **Broome** (p986) and spend your first day easing into its tropical rhythm: wander **Chinatown** (p988), float in the calm water at **Town Beach** (p988) and watch sunset ignite the horizon at **Cable Beach** (p986).

- Hire a car and follow the red-dirt road up the **Dampier Peninsula** (p990), where white sands and flame-coloured cliffs meet the clearest water you've ever seen. For a deeper Kimberley moment, join a day trip into gorge country – **Windjana Gorge** (p1003) or **Tunnel Creek** (p1004) – where towering walls glow gold and ancient caverns breathe cool air. End with a dinosaur footprint walk at **Gantheaume Point** (p988) before flying south.

AUGUST

Wildflowers peak across the Mid West and Wheatbelt. Kings Park's displays begin, while the Kimberley enjoys dry-season conditions, with waterfalls flowing and gorges accessible before peak crowds arrive later.

OCTOBER

Spring warmth settles in, with wildflowers lingering along the Coral Coast and in Perth. Broome enjoys late dry-season conditions, while the Southwest suits hiking, wine tasting and early swims along sheltered bays and beaches.

NOVEMBER

Heat builds rapidly in the north, storms increase and remote roads begin closing as the Wet approaches. Down south, visitor numbers rise, while Perth enjoys warm, clear days ahead of statewide summer holidays.

DECEMBER

Summer begins with long days and festive energy across Perth and the Southwest. Beaches and Rottnest are busy, while inland forests offer cooler air and shade ahead of peak heat during the holiday travel season.

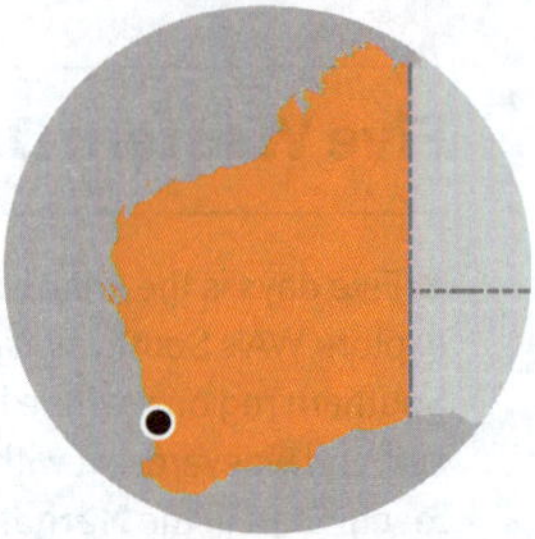

Perth

HERITAGE ARCHITECTURE | ART | EPICUREAN SCENE

GETTING AROUND

Central Perth is easily explored on foot. The CBD (central business district) merges with Elizabeth Quay and the Perth Cultural Centre, a distance of just over 1km from one end to the other. East Perth extends from here. Free CAT (Central Area Transit) buses run to Matagarup Bridge, where you can stroll over the Swan River to Optus Stadium. Other options include the hop-on, hop-off Perth Explorer or ride-share services. Central Perth is a transport hub for services to elsewhere in the city.

TOP TIP

Walk or catch the free Red CAT bus to **Heirisson Island**, a tranquil patch of parkland on the Swan River. Cross the **Boorloo Bridge** and follow the riverside paths, keeping an eye out for western grey kangaroos.

Perth – Boorloo in Noongar – is Western Australia's capital, home to big-ticket cultural institutions, shimmering Swan River views and an impressive gastronomic scene. Skyscrapers house the city's corporate muscle, but at street level the pace is gentler, with heritage facades, leafy walkways and streetart threaded through the grid.

To the north is the Perth Cultural Centre, a hub for contemporary art and theatre. Just south, Elizabeth Quay connects the skyline to the Swan River with waterfront bars and a steady buzz of locals and visitors. East Perth fans out towards Optus Stadium – the heart of Perth's sporting obsession – linked by the sculptural Matagarup Bridge and anchored by the Camfield, Australia's largest pub.

By day it's all about visiting Perth's premier museums and cruising the Swan River, but evenings beckon with cocktail bars and contemporary fine dining, which add a whole new level of sophistication.

Where the River Meets the City

MAP P892

Experience Perth's modern centre at Elizabeth Quay

Perth's multibillion-dollar plan to revitalise its city centre produced this gleaming waterfront precinct, unveiled in 2016. Overlooking the Derbarl Yerrigan (Swan River), **Elizabeth Quay** draws visitors for dining, riverside promenades and ferry departures. A well-signed interpretive trail offers background on the area, including its First Nations history. It also leads past major public sculptures: *First Contact*, by Laurel Nannup, reimagines the moment Noongar people first saw European ships as a giant bird-like figure rising from the water; and *Spanda*, by Christian de Vietri, forms a looping white gateway symbolising the connection between land, water and sky.

Families gravitate to the island playground and the **Elizabeth Quay Carousel** *(elizabethquaycarousel.com.au; from $8)*, an authentic Venetian-built piece that spins

Continued on p894

HIGHLIGHTS
1 Kings Park & Botanic Garden

SIGHTS
2 Boorloo Bridge
3 Cottesloe Beach
4 Heirisson Island
5 Hyde Park
6 Matagarup Bridge
7 Optus Stadium
8 Perth Zoo
9 Scarborough Beach

ACTIVITIES
see 7 Ozone
10 Warrang-Bridil – Swan River Cultural Tours

EATING
11 Chu Bakery
12 Daph's
13 Di Chiera Brothers Continental Store
14 Hobart Deli
15 Lulu La Delizia
16 Mummucc'
17 Neho
18 Peasants Paradice
19 Prophet
see 18 Sayers Sister
20 Sonny's Bar
21 Tsukaya

DRINKING & NIGHTLIFE
see 18 Bar Love

ENTERTAINMENT
22 Rosemount Hotel

EATING IN PERTH: BEST DINING

MAP P892

Ah Um: Hidden behind a record-listening bar, this chef-led spot serves inventive share plates with a creative seasonal focus. *from 5pm Wed-Sat* **$$**

Light Years Asian Bar & Diner: Bold flavours, crowd-pleasing share plates and lively cocktails in a heritage building. *noon-late* **$$**

Balthazar: Refined dining room showcasing WA produce and one of Perth's strongest wine lists. *noon-late Mon-Sat* **$$$**

Fleur: Romantic Royal Hotel dining room serving elegant, French-leaning seasonal dishes in a softly lit space. *from 5.30pm Wed-Sat* **$$$**

HIGHLIGHTS
1 Elizabeth Quay
2 WA Museum Boola Bardip

SIGHTS
3 Art Gallery of Western Australia
4 Bell Tower
5 Perth Institute of Contemporary Arts

ACTIVITIES
6 Foodloose Tours
7 Go Cultural Aboriginal Tours
8 Gondolas on the Swan
9 Hidden de Tours
10 Oh Hey WA
11 Swans on the Swan
12 Two Feet & a Heartbeat
13 Wild West Charters

SLEEPING
14 Adnate Perth
15 Akara Hotel
16 Alex Hotel
17 Como the Treasury

EATING
18 Ah Um
19 Balthazar
20 Fleur
21 Hifumiya
22 Island at Elizabeth Quay
23 Le Vietnam
24 Light Years Asian Bar & Diner
25 Long Chim
26 Miss Mi
see 25 Petition
27 Post

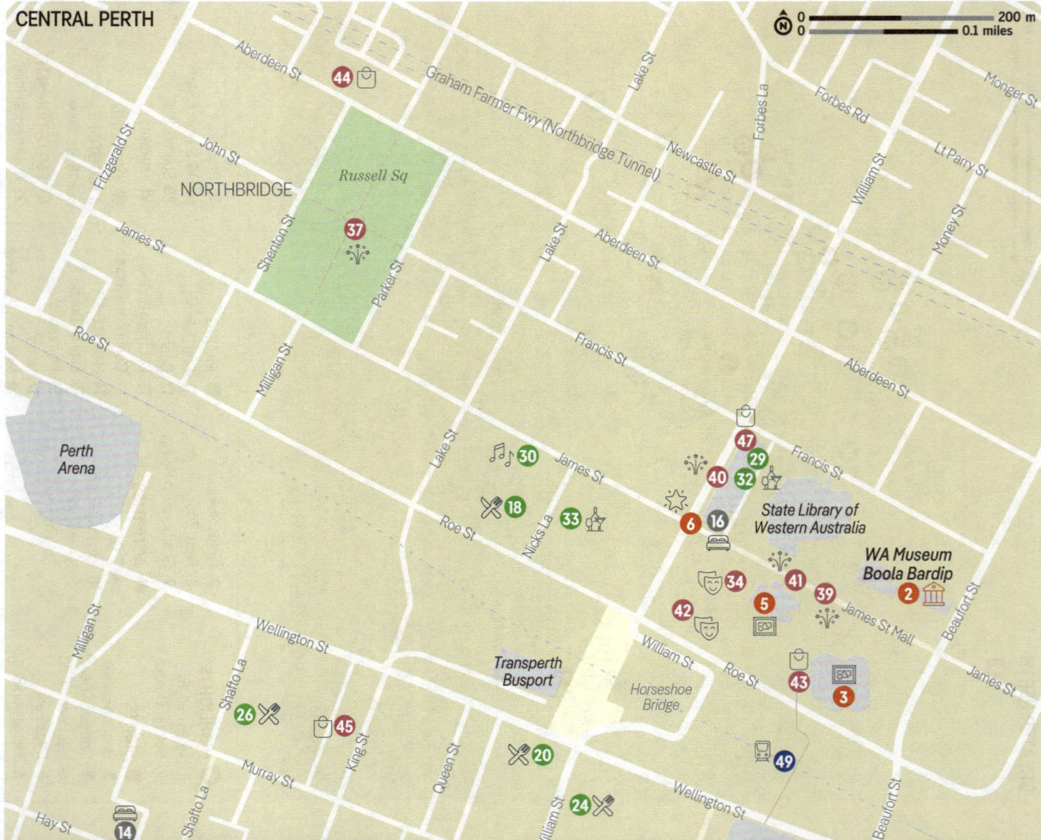

28 Twilight Hawkers Market
see 27 Wildflower

DRINKING & NIGHTLIFE
29 Alabama Song
see 18 Astral Weeks
30 Geisha
31 Howard's Groove
see 29 Joe's Juice Joint
32 Mechanics Institute
33 Sneaky Tony's
see 27 Telegram Coffee

ENTERTAINMENT
34 Blue Room Theatre
35 Boorloo Heritage Festival
36 Elizabeth Quay Carousel
37 Fringe World
38 His Majesty's Theatre
39 Perth Festival
40 PrideFEST
41 Revelation Perth International Film Festival
42 State Theatre Centre

SHOPPING
43 AGWA Design Store
44 Arrival Hall
45 Highs & Lows
46 Pigface Bookstore
47 Ruck Rover General Store

INFORMATION
48 Perth City Visitor Kiosk

TRANSPORT
49 Perth Station
50 Transperth Ferry

BEST PERTH WALKING TOURS

Perth City Visitor Kiosk: Volunteer-run 90-minute walking tours depart from the Perth City Visitor Kiosk; book ahead online at *visitperth.com/getting-around/walking-tours.*

Oh Hey WA: Two well-connected sisters run these urban-themed tours taking in underground secrets, architectural marvels and Perth's coolest new bars.

Two Feet & a Heartbeat: Arcades, laneways, coffee, art, cheese, whisky, crime and scavenger hunts: these guys have all angles covered.

Hidden de Tours: Booze-themed walking tours taking in Perth's hidden city drinking dens and gin bars.

Foodloose Tours: Guided food walks through Northbridge, sampling Asian eats, Italian baked goods, coffee and natural wines.

ADAM CALAITZIS/SHUTTERSTOCK

Continued from p890

on Fridays and weekends. Nearby, the **Island at Elizabeth Quay** *(theislandeq.com.au)* occupies the heritage-listed 1928 Florence Hummerston Kiosk, rebuilt brick by brick to house a modern bistro. Nearby, the **Bell Tower** *(thebelltower.com.au; from $15)* is home to historic London bells and an open-air lookout; you can also buy a ticket that includes the chance to chime the bells yourself.

Bold Collections Across Two Major Galleries

MAP P892

See world-class contemporary art

Just north of the city, the Perth Cultural Centre brings several major arts institutions together in one compact precinct. The **Art Gallery of Western Australia** *(artgallery.wa.gov.au; free)* is the standout, offering four levels of works by renowned local and international artists from the 1800s to today. The Indigenous galleries show multimedia and concept-driven pieces that blend cultural knowledge with new media. You'll also find strong displays of 20th-century Australian Modernists, including Nolan, Boyd and Drysdale. Free guided tours run most days; check times online or at the information desk. Nearby, the **Perth Institute of Contemporary Arts** *(pica.org.au; free)* offers a more experimental take, with bold installations and performance projects.

Try the Lobster tagliolini - it's to die for!

EATING AT THE STATE BUILDINGS: OUR PICKS

MAP P892

Wildflower: Perth's best fine-diner presents local ingredients attuned to the Noongar calendar's six seasons. *hours vary* $$$

Long Chim: Acclaimed Australian chef David Thompson's authentic Thai street-food flavours in a vibrant setting. *noon-late Tue-Sat* $$

Petition: Refined modern restaurant offering seasonal creative cuisine to go with its Wine Merchant and Beer Corner bars. *7am-late Mon-Fri, from 8am Sat & Sun* $$

Post: Fitting nicely into an elegant space, this *osteria* is open all day for contemporary breakfasts and its modern Italian degustation menu. *6.30am-10pm* $$$

Elizabeth Quay (p890)

Eucalypts, Wildflowers & City Views

MAP P891

Wander through Kings Park

Perched above the city on Mt Eliza (Kaarta Gar-up), **Kings Park & Botanic Garden** *(bgpa.wa.gov.au/kings-park; free)* is one of the world's largest urban parks, known for its wildflowers and expansive views over the Swan River. Wander the Lotterywest Federation Walkway, a treetop bridge that carries you through eucalypts and over a glass span above the forest. In spring the WA Botanic Garden bursts with rare plants from every corner of the state. For a quintessential Perth experience, enjoy a picnic on the grassy banks of Fraser Ave – sunset there is a must.

Out on the Swan

MAPS P891 & P892

Enjoy Perth's shimmering river

Whatever floats your boat, there are countless ways to enjoy the sparkling Swan River. From Elizabeth Quay, the **Transperth Ferry** *(transperth.wa.gov.au; from $3.50)* runs frequently to the Mends Street Jetty in South Perth, a short walk from **Perth Zoo** *(perthzoo.wa.gov.au; from $19.50)*. For a deeper immersion, **Wild West Charters** *(wildwestcharters.com.au; from $35)* runs 90-minute cruises past leafy riverside suburbs and stretches of Perth's 'millionaires' row'; you may well spot dolphins along the way.

BEST PERTH FESTIVALS

Fringe World: January–February festival bursting with comedy, cabaret, circus, music and boundary-pushing pop-up performances across the city.

Perth Festival: For more than 70 years this February/March arts festival has blended international acts with Noongar culture, theatre, music and large-scale contemporary works.

Boorloo Heritage Festival: Held each April, this city-wide program explores Perth's stories through tours, talks, exhibitions and community events.

Revelation Perth International Film Festival: Early to mid-July festival showcasing bold independent cinema, from WA productions to standout international films.

PrideFEST: Running each November, this LGBTQIA+ festival celebrates Pride, visibility and community through parades, parties, arts events, talks and cultural programming across Perth.

EATING IN CENTRAL PERTH: BEST ASIAN FOOD

MAP P892

Hifumiya: Authentic udon made from scratch. Try spicy miso pork or the Hifumiya original with bean curd. *11am-3pm Mon-Fri, to 4pm Sat, to 5pm Sun* $

Le Vietnam: Tasty pork-filled banh mi slathered with pâté, chilli and lemongrass to take away or enjoy in nearby Stirling Gardens. *10am-3pm Mon-Fri* $

Twilight Hawkers Market: Head to Forrest Place to taste multicultural Perth at a variety of Asian street-food stalls. *4.30-9.30pm Fri Oct-Apr* $

Miss Mi: Inventive takes on wok-fired Southeast Asian classics by Philippines-born chef Alex De Leon. *5.30-10pm Tue, Wed & Sat, noon-3pm & 5.30-10pm Thu & Fri* $$

INSIDER TIPS FROM AN ARTS LEADER

Anna Reece, artistic director of the Perth Festival *@perthfestival*

For me, Perth is best taken slow: carbs, parks and people-watching by day, sunsets and tunes by night. Start by joining the queue at **Chu Bakery** for pastries, then wander to **Hyde Park** to sprawl under the trees or loop the lakes. Head a few blocks to **Di Chiera Brothers** for a top-notch continental roll. Later, settle into the courtyard at the **Rosemount Hotel** for relaxed afternoon vibes and regular live music, or catch a big WA sunset with a beer on the verandah at North Perth Bowls Club. If you're still going, **Astral Weeks** is a tiny vinyl listening bar with cocktails and a hidden dining room.

YMGERMAN/SHUTTERSTOCK

Optus Stadium

Quirkier options include evening kayaking with **Go Go Active Tours** *(gogoactivetours.com.au; from $79)*, romantic rides with **Gondolas on the Swan** *(gondolasontheswan.com.au; from $340)* or a spin on the Swan Train with **Swans on the Swan** *(swansontheswan.com.au; from $55)*, a swan-shaped pedal boat that offers fun 20-minute whips around the river.

Outdoor Adventure & Sporting Glory

MAP P891

Take in Perth's sporting precinct

Taking centre stage in Perth's mining-boom renaissance is **Optus Stadium** *(optusstadium.com.au)*, an award-winning 60,000-capacity sporting arena. There's plenty to see even on non-game days: sports exhibits, behind-the-scenes tours and rooftop walks with city and Swan River views. The stadium's **Ozone VERTIGO experience** *(theozone.com.au; from $129)* places harnessed visitors on a platform 42m above the turf. Lift access and staff-assisted setup make this one of the more accessible high-adrenaline experiences in WA.

Shaped like intertwined rainbow serpents, **Matagarup Bridge** *(zipclimb.com.au; from $59)* offers a different taste of adventure, with a zip line across the Swan River and a climb to an open-air viewing deck with wide city views.

Perth's Indigenous Cultures

MAPS P891 & P892

Learn about Noongar culture and traditions

The Indigenous Whadjuk Noongar people have lived in Perth (Boorloo) for at least 45,000 years, so standing in Elizabeth Quay and reading how the *Aborigines Act 1905* (WA) barred Noongar people from entering central Perth until 1954 is as upsetting as it is vital to reflect upon. To learn more about Noongar culture and the impact of colonisation, seek out one of Perth's many Indigenous tours. Led by Noongar guide Walter

TOP EXPERIENCE

WA Museum Boola Bardip

Spanning natural, cultural and social histories, WA Museum Boola Bardip ('many stories') is one of Perth's most engaging attractions. Across multiple levels, you'll uncover everything from megafauna fossils to migrant diaries, meteorites and deep-sea creatures. Exhibits are hands-on, story-driven and rich in local detail, making this an ideal half-day stop for travellers seeking a deeper understanding of Western Australia.

Skeleton of a blue whale

Start with Country

Begin on the ground floor at the Welcome to Country hub, introducing Whadjuk Noongar boodjar (land). Interactive displays share the six Noongar seasons and links between climate, plants and animals. Close by, Ngalang Koort, Boodja Wirn gallery expands the story with contemporary Aboriginal voices, artworks and stories from across the state, offering vital cultural context.

Stories of Perth

Continue into the Reflections gallery, where early Perth and social-history displays trace WA's evolving identity, from landmark sporting moments to changing patterns of work, culture and community life across generations. Just beyond, enter Hackett Hall to see the 24m blue whale skeleton, a WA icon, suspended in mid-air.

Nature & People

Upstairs, Wild Life showcases WA deserts, forests and coasts through live reptiles, habitat displays and interactives. Nearby, Connections traces key migration stories across the Indian Ocean world, while Innovations highlights local breakthroughs in medicine, mining and maritime engineering. On level 2, finish in Changes and Origins, where geology, deep time, fossils and shifting land use reveal how WA's dramatic landscapes came to be.

TOP TIPS

- Time your visit for Nyumbi, a free 11am Saturday performance of Noongar song and dance and a smoking ceremony in the museum's forecourt.
- The museum offers free guided tours included with admission; sessions book out, so reserve a spot via the website.

Practicalities

- *visit.museum.wa.gov.au* • adult/child $15/free • 9.30am-5pm

PERTH'S ARCHITECTURE & URBAN ART

Historic streets, grand facades and bold streetart in one easy loop.

START	END	LENGTH
Perth Station	Perth Town Hall	2km; 1½hr

Begin at 1 **Perth Station**, dating to 1881, then walk into pedestrianised 2 **Forrest Place**. Framed by the GPO and Forrest Chase, this was once Perth's main civic meeting point. Look for the playful 'Big Cactus' sculpture and the heritage facades lining the square. Backtrack via the station to 3 **Yagan Square**, a meeting place honouring Noongar culture, where the 45m Digital Tower, the Yirin sculpture and other artworks reflect stories of Country.

Cross Wellington St to the 4 **Royal Perth Hotel**, a two-storey verandah pub from 1882, before slipping into 5 **Prince Lane** to see murals by leading Perth artists including Stormie Mills. Re-emerge onto 6 **King Street**, one of Perth's best-preserved gold-rush-era streets, lined with ornate balconies, narrow lots and handsome facades now filled with fashion boutiques and cafes.

Head south to 7 **Wolf Lane**, a pocket of large-scale murals backed by small bars and coffee spots. From here it's a short walk to 8 **London Court**, a quirky Tudor-style arcade from 1937 filled with boutiques and photogenic detailing. Continue to 9 **St Georges Terrace**, where polished glass towers sit beside early-20th-century facades. Finish at 10 **Perth Town Hall**, built by ticket-of-leave convicts in the 1870s and today neatly contrasted with the modern Justice Centre behind it.

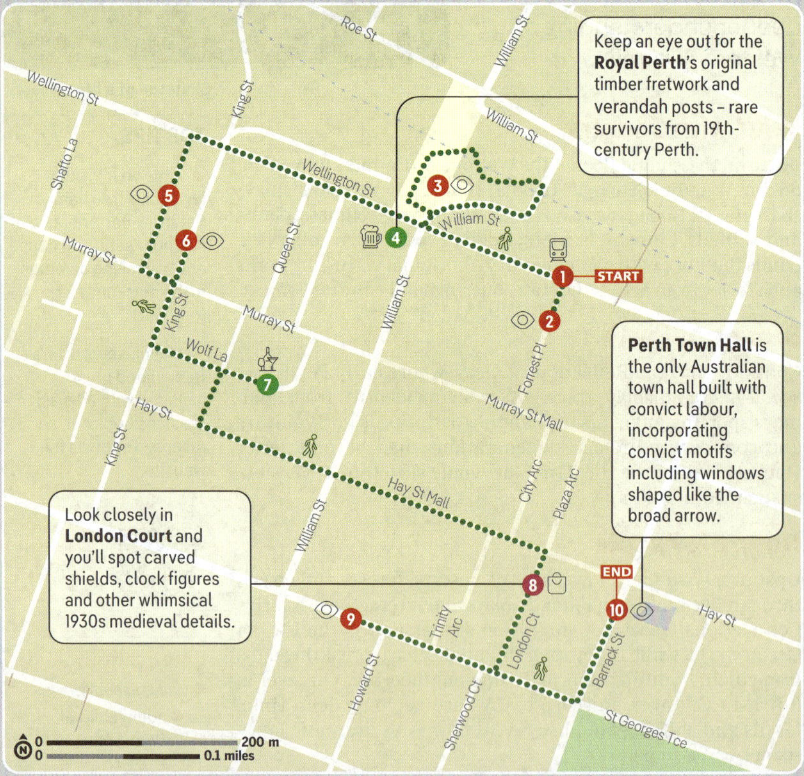

ARDANME/SHUTTERSTOCK

His Majesty's Theatre (p900)

McGuire, the 90-minute Goomup (Elizabeth Quay) Cultural Walking Tour with **Go Cultural Aboriginal Tours** *(goculturalcom.au; from $13.75)* delves into Dreaming stories and traditional songs and explains the deep cultural significance of the Derbal Yerrigan (Swan River) for Noongar people.

For deeper truth-telling, join **Warrang-Bridil** *(warrang-bridil.com.au; from $80)* with cultural leader Nick Abraham. His 60-minute 'Ancient Gateway to a Modern City' tour traces the river near Optus Stadium and Matagarup Bridge, outlining Noongar language, kinship and daily life before European settlement.

To explore independently, download the Karla Yarning walking trails from visitperth.com. 'This City Is Whadjuk Country' examines Noongar life before 1829, while 'Fighting for Families, Country, Rights and Recognition' focuses on post-1829 history – from the resistance of leaders Midgegooroo and Yagan to the Aboriginal protest movements of the 1930s and '40s and the creation of key Aboriginal organisations.

A Night Out in Northbridge

MAPS P891 & P892

Hit speakeasies, wine bars and dance floors

Northbridge's nightlife may get a bad rap for being backpacker central, but among the chaos you'll find some of Perth's best bars. Start with a Peaches & Cream Negroni at **Bar Love** *(barlove.com.au)*, a retro-leaning cocktail den. Continue to **Mechanics Institute** *(mechanicsinstitutebar.com.au)*, reached by a graffiti-spattered lane, with a terrace perfect for sinking back a few WA craft beers. Nearby, sibling dive bars **Alabama Song** *(lavishhabits.com.au/venues/alabama-song)* and **Joe's Juice Joint** *(lavishhabits.com.au/venues/joes-juice-joint)* deliver honky-tonk charm and late-night rock'n'roll. **Sneaky Tony's** *(facebook.com/sneakytonys)* is a speakeasy

PERTH'S BEST SHOPPING

Highs & Lows: A cult Perth streetwear store and sneaker institution, known for limited-edition drops, global collabs and a tightly curated edit of apparel and accessories.

Arrival Hall: A beautifully styled Northbridge showroom offering Scandinavian-inspired homewares, furniture, lighting and thoughtful lifestyle objects.

AGWA Design Store: Inside the Art Gallery of WA is a sharp edit of jewellery, ceramics, textiles and design pieces by leading Australian makers.

Pigface Bookstore: One of Perth's coolest new indie bookstores, with smart curation across fiction and non-fiction and a good selection of books by local authors.

Ruck Rover General Store: Northbridge favourite selling colourful apparel, accessories, cards and giftware by independent designers.

LKONYA/SHUTTERSTOCK

requiring a nightly password – check its social media for intel. For dancing, **Geisha** *(geishabar.com.au)* is the long-running favourite for house and techno.

Heritage Elegance & Fearless New Work

MAP P892

Explore Perth's theatre scene

Perth has a serious stage pedigree: Heath Ledger was born here and Hugh Jackman trained here. The ornate Victorian **His Majesty's Theatre** *(hmt.com.au; from $50)* presents ballet, opera and major touring productions, plus cabaret, jazz, comedy and burlesque in its smaller downstairs space.

Nearby, the **State Theatre Centre** *(artsculturetrust.wa.gov.au/venues/state-theatre-centre-of-wa; from $79)* is home to the Black Swan State Theatre Company and its sharp Australian drama and powerful First Nations storytelling. Just behind it, the **Blue Room Theatre** *(blueroom.org.au; from $27)* presents intimate, adventurous work from emerging artists, with a lively bar that draws a creative local crowd.

EATING & DRINKING IN PERTH: BEST CAFES & BRUNCH SPOTS

MAPS P891 & P892

Telegram Coffee: Brilliant espresso in the State Buildings' postal hall; minimal, sleek and serious about beans. *6am-4pm Mon-Fri*

Howard's Groove: City workers and speciality coffee lovers mingle for the CBD's best single-origin brew as well as Cuban sandwiches. *6.30am-2pm Mon-Fri*

Sayers Sister: Bustling Northbridge brunch spot with inventive plates, excellent filter options and well-textured milk coffees. *6.30am-2.30pm* $$

Hobart Deli: North Perth gem for strong brews, wholesome breakfasts, great toasties and genuine neighbourhood charm. *6.30am-2pm* $

Cottesloe Beach

Beach-Hopping in Cottesloe & Scarborough

MAP P891

Laze on two of the city's most loved beaches

Perth's classic city shoreline, **Cottesloe Beach** is a 1.5km stretch of soft sand backed by grassy terraces and heritage Norfolk pines. Swim between the flags (October to March) near the surf club; there's a shark net for extra peace of mind. Arrive early (before 10am on weekends or during summer) for parking or come by train to Cottesloe Station for an easy downhill walk.

With turquoise water and white sand, **Scarborough Beach** offers a buzzier, more youthful scene. Its skate park, surf schools and volleyball courts give it a So-Cal feel and the beachfront pool is perfect for cooling off. There's plenty of parking, but you can also take bus 990 from Perth Station.

REMEMBERING YAGAN

One of WA's great Noongar warriors, Yagan (born around 1795) and his father Midgegooroo, an Elder from south of the Swan River, together led a resistance campaign against the British invasion. In 1833 Midgegooroo was caught and executed by firing squad, while Yagan was shot a few months later by teenage settlers whom he had befriended. Brutally, Yagan's head was removed, smoked and sent to London, where it was publicly displayed as an anthropological curiosity. Yagan's head was buried in an unmarked grave in Liverpool in 1964; it was exhumed in 1993 and eventually repatriated to Australia and finally laid to rest in the Swan Valley in 2010, 177 years after his murder.

EATING IN PERTH: BEST SUBURBAN RESTAURANTS

MAP P891

Prophet: Lebanese favourite known for generous meze, charcoal-grilled meats and warm BYO hospitality that draws loyal locals. *5-9pm Mon, noon-3pm & 5-9pm Tue-Sun* $$

Sonny's Bar: Blends produce-driven cooking with a serious drinks program in a buzzing neighbourhood dining room. *4-10pm Wed & Thu, noon-late Fri-Sun* $$

Mummucc': Lively Wembley bar-restaurant serving generous Italian-leaning plates designed for sharing, with a strong wine list and an energetic crowd. *4pm-late Tue-Fri, noon-late Sat & Sun* $$

Lulu La Delizia: With a warm, bustling dining room, this Subiaco restaurant is devoted to regional Italian pasta traditions. *noon-3pm & 5-10pm Thu & Fri, 5-10pm Tue, Wed & Sat* $$$

Neho: Casual Vic Park favourite serving punchy Asian share plates, bold flavours and fast-paced energy; ideal for groups and relaxed weeknights. *5.30-9.30pm Sun-Thu, to 10pm Fri & Sat* $$

Tsukaya: Refined Japanese restaurant blending traditional technique with subtle Peruvian influences in an intimate Mt Hawthorn setting. *5.30-9pm Wed & Thu, to 9.45pm Fri & Sat* $$

Daph's: Leederville open-fire restaurant delivering seasonal tasting menus with punchy flavours in an intimate, low-key setting. *5.45-10pm Tue-Sat* $$$

Peasants Paradice: Cult city-fringe restaurant showcasing modern African flavours, generous hospitality and bold, soulful cooking. *5-8pm Tue & Sun, to 9pm Wed-Sat* $$

Beyond Perth

From Fremantle to Rottnest Island, Swan Valley, Avon Valley and Mandurah, Rockingham, explore beaches, wine country, towns and escapes.

Places

GETTING AROUND

Getting around beyond Perth is straightforward, with trains, ferries and cycling covering the basics, but a car will give you the most flexibility. Fremantle and Mandurah are walkable and bike friendly, and have regular rail connections from Perth. Ferries link the capital and Fremantle with Rottnest Island, which is car free. Swan Valley and Avon Valley are best explored by road, though scenic river cruises and limited train services offer slower alternatives.

Step beyond the city and Perth quickly gives way to a patchwork of coast, countryside and small-town life. Historic Fremantle blends port history with beaches, markets and a strong creative pulse, while Rottnest Island offers car-free cycling, sheltered bays and coral-fringed swims just offshore. Close inland, the Swan Valley pairs wineries and fresh produce with Indigenous culture and river walks, before the Avon Valley slows the pace further with heritage towns, wildflowers and long horizons. To the south, Mandurah and Rockingham combine estuaries, dolphins and surf beaches with an easy-going seaside rhythm. Each destination sits close to Perth yet feels distinct, rewarding travellers who slow down and explore a little deeper.

Fremantle

TIME FROM PERTH: **30MIN**

Once a gateway for migrants arriving by sea, Fremantle (Freo) – known as Walyalup in Noongar – has evolved into Perth's most spirited coastal enclave. Its 19th-century architecture, narrow streets and vibrant cafe culture tell the story of a city built on maritime grit, artistic ambition and multicultural roots. Today that heritage mingles with a creative, free-spirited energy, visible in the art, the markets and the easy rhythm of daily life that defines this seaside hub.

Wander the West End & Cappuccino Strip

Fremantle's West End is one of Australia's most atmospheric historic precincts, a compact grid of more than 250 heritage-listed buildings from the 1890s and early 1900s. Begin on **High Street**, where indie boutiques, small galleries and specialist bookstores sit behind ornate shopfronts. Pause at **New Edition Bookshop** *(newedition.com.au)* for local fiction, design titles and Fremantle histories, then continue to the restored **Moores Building Art Space** *(wfac.org.au; free)*, a former merchant warehouse hosting contemporary exhibitions, artist studios and a leafy courtyard cafe, **Moore & Moore** *(mooreandmoorecafe.com.au)*. Nearby, **Japingka** *(japingkaaboriginalart.com; free)* shows exceptional Indigenous works from across Australia.

RUBEN M RAMOS/SHUTTERSTOCK

New Edition Bookshop, Fremantle

Wander along High, Henry and Mouat Sts, admiring grand facades, iron-lace balconies and maritime flourishes that speak to the port's prosperous harbour days, then head to the Cappuccino Strip, a lively run of cafes, pubs and heritage shopfronts on South Tce. This stretch helped cement Fremantle's bohemian reputation in the 1980s and remains a vibrant spot for coffee and people-watching and soaking up the city's European-leaning street life.

Explore WA's oldest building and jail cells

The **Round House** *(fremantleroundhouse.com.au; entry by donation)* crowns Arthur Head, a limestone headland that once formed Fremantle's early defensive and maritime precinct. Completed in 1830–31, the compact eight-cell jail held Noongar prisoners, sailors and runaway crewmen before trial. Step inside the thick limestone chambers, then wander the courtyard to see remnants of early lock-up spaces and the original well. Climb to the lookout for sweeping views over Bathers Beach (p905) and the harbour. Time your visit for the daily 1pm cannon firing, a vivid echo of Fremantle's seafaring past.

TIPS FROM A LOCAL SPORTS STAR

Alex Pearce, captain of the Fremantle Dockers in the AFL *@freodockers*

I love how Freo feels like a big beach town. Little traffic, amazing beaches, food, coffee and access to a variety of art and culture hidden throughout the streets that I'm still discovering after 10 years of living here. Check out the Freo markets (p905) and once you've finished, explore the city on foot through the Cappuccino Strip and High Street towards Bathers Beach (p905). For breakfast, Good Things (p907) does an amazing chilli scramble and later on swing by Emily Taylor for spicy Asian-fusion share plates. In the evening, head to Mrs Brown (p906) to loosen up into a gig at iconic Mojos (p906).

The Wadjemup (Rottnest) yellowfin tuna is a must try

EATING IN FREMANTLE: BEST DINING

Vin Populi: Italian bistro dishing up handmade pasta and spritzes in a charming West End setting. *4pm-late Mon-Thu, from noon Fri-Sun* $$

Bread in Common: Converted warehouse that takes 'homemade' to new levels with its seasonal menu. *noon-10pm Sun-Thu, to 11pm Fri & Sat* $$

Emily Taylor: Asian-fusion restaurant serving dumplings and modern share plates with flair. *11.30am-10pm Mon-Fri, 9am-late Sat & Sun* $$

Madalena's Bar: Seafood-focused small plates and natural wine in a stylish seaside diner. *5-10pm Wed & Thu, noon-late Fri & Sat, noon-10pm Sun* $$$

FREMANTLE'S BEST TOURS

Two Feet & a Heartbeat: Award-winning walking tour revealing Fremantle's convict past, creative laneways and vibrant streetart scene.

Fremantle History Walking Tour: Step back in time with local historians uncovering Fremantle's maritime heritage and grand 19th-century architecture.

In Culture Tours: A powerful guided walk led by Whadjuk Noongar hosts sharing ancient stories, language and cultural knowledge of Walyalup (Fremantle).

Hidden deTours: Sip cocktails in tucked-away bars while exploring Freo's lane-ways and its thriving small-bar scene.

Fremantle Food Tours: A progressive five-course feast through Freo's best eateries, blending local flavours, drinks and stories of the port city.

JORDAN TAN/SHUTTERSTOCK

Fremantle Prison

Tour Fremantle Prison

Granted UNESCO World Heritage status in 2010, **Fremantle Prison** *(fremantleprison.com.au; adult/child $24/13)* is the largest convict-built structure in the country. Completed in 1855, it operated as WA's main high-security facility until 1991. Visits are only possible via in-depth guided tours, which explore harsh conditions, notorious inmates, riots and executions. You'll learn about the prison's convict beginnings through to the late 20th century, with the main cell block preserved almost exactly as it was on closing, while stepping inside solitary cells and seeing the gallows where the last execution occurred (in 1964). Other tours feature true-crime stories, torchlit night visits and boat trips through underground tunnels. You can even stay overnight at Fremantle Prison YHA Hostel (p1006; *yha.com.au*), set in the former women's cell block.

Take in Fremantle's salty seafaring atmosphere

At Fremantle Port, join the free **Port Walk** *(fremantleports.com.au; 10am Tue & Fri)* for an insider's view of this working gateway to the Indian Ocean. The port's maritime museums tell stories of trade, exploration and shipwreck.

DRINKING IN FREO: BEST PUBS

Gage Roads: Waterfront brewery pouring crisp ales and hazy IPAs overlooking Fremantle port. *11am-11pm* $$

Clancy's Fish Pub (p906)**:** Beloved institution for fish and chips, craft beers and live music. *noon-late Mon-Fri, 11.30am-late Sat, 11.30am-10pm Sun* $$

Local Hotel: South Fremantle favourite serving modern pub fare and WA brews in a heritage bar. *11am-late* $$

Running with Thieves: Cavernous brewery pairing house-made beers, gin and hearty plates. *11am-10pm Sun-Thu, to 11pm Fri & Sat* $$

The **WA Maritime Museum** *(museum.wa.gov.au/maritime; adult/child $15/free)* has exhibits including the *Australia II* yacht, which won the 1987 America's Cup, and a rare megamouth shark. Outside, tours of the Cold War–era **HMAS Ovens submarine** *(adult/child $15/7.50)* reveal life below deck on Fremantle's WWII submarine base.

Nearby, the **WA Shipwrecks Museum** *(museum.wa.gov.au/shipwrecks; free)* showcases artefacts from Dutch and British wrecks. The haunting story of the *Batavia*'s 1629 mutiny (p963) brings early European history vividly to life.

Browse Fremantle Markets

Dating to 1897, the **Fremantle Markets** *(fremantlemarkets.com.au; free)* remain the city's beating heart – a sensory feast of colour, sound and spice housed in a grand Victorian hall. More than 150 stalls brim with handmade wares, fresh produce and global street eats, from Balinese satay and bratwurst to açaí bowls and artisan gins, while lively buskers play outside. It fills up early, so arrive before 10.30am to browse in peace or grab picnic supplies for the beach. It's closed Monday to Thursday.

Convict-built galleries and leafy art courtyards

Built by convict labour, the neo-Gothic **Walyalup Fremantle Arts Centre** *(wfac.org.au; free)* is set among leafy grounds. Wander through the galleries; browse FOUND, where you'll find some of WA's best handcrafted gifts; or grab lunch in the courtyard and soak up the atmosphere.

The building began as the Fremantle Lunatic Asylum, but today it's one of the city's most open and communal spaces. Time your visit for Sunday Music, the free weekly concert series (October to March) from 2pm to 4pm in the front garden.

Relax at calm beaches and shaded picnic spots

Freo's coastline packs a lot into a small stretch. **South Beach** is an easy five-minute drive or relaxed cycle south of town, with calm water, shady Norfolk pines, grassy picnic areas and plenty of parking. **Bathers Beach**, tucked beside the port, offers soft sand, gentle waves and the novelty of booking a sunlounger on Australia's first licensed beach. For a little more room, head north to **Leighton Beach** – ride the Fremantle line to North Fremantle Station and stroll about 10 minutes to its big, open sweep of sand – or continue to **Port Beach**, a quieter local favourite with clear shallows and long views across to Rottnest Island.

WHY I LOVE FREMANTLE

Rosamund Brennan, Lonely Planet writer

Fremantle gets under your skin in the best way. It's a small port city, but it hums with creative energy and a perennial holiday vibe.

Having lived here for almost six years, some of my favourite spots are the ones you discover slowly – like the **Freo Farmers Market**, where you can taste delicious WA produce and watch the city wake up, or **Monument Hill Park** at sunset, when the harbour turns molten and the coastline drops away beneath you.

Freo's packed festival calendar – music, art, food, film – gives the city a year-round creative heartbeat. My top tip is to visit in spring, when warm days, quieter beaches and alfresco dining make exploring a joy.

EATING IN FREO: BEST CHEAP EATS

Sealanes: Classic fish-and-chip shop across from South Beach serving fresh local seafood to go. *noon-8pm Tue-Sun* $

Peggy's: Central Freo institution serving stacked schnitty subs, roast-pork rolls and a cult sausage-and-cheese muffin. *7am-3pm Mon-Fri, 9am-3pm Sat & Sun* $

Run Amuk: Freo favourite serving loaded gourmet hot dogs with quirky names and WA ingredients. *10am-9pm Tue-Sun* $

La Cabaña: South Freo taqueria famed for Baja-style tacos, ceviche and mezcal; there's a leafy courtyard. *hours vary* $$

FREMANTLE'S BEST FESTIVALS

Fremantle Biennale: Large-scale installations, performances and site-specific works in November.

Fremantle Street Arts Festival: Busking festival drawing acrobats, comedians and performers from around the world over Easter.

Hidden Treasures: Emerging and alternative bands play in rarely opened heritage spaces across the city in June.

Totally Lit: Authors, storytelling, workshops and public readings; September–October.

10 Nights in Port: Experimental theatre, music, storytelling and after-dark experiences in August.

Fremantle BeerFest: Local brewers, food stalls and live music pack the Esplanade for this lively November fixture.

Head out after dark

Fremantle's nightlife is soaked in music history. AC/DC frontman Bon Scott grew up here and the city's punk-to-psych lineage runs deep: Tame Impala, The Triffids and John Butler Trio were spawned here.

Start at **Mojos** *(mojosbar.com.au)* in North Fremantle, the hallowed indie band room where Tame Impala and John Butler cut their teeth. Then head to **Freo.Social** *(freo.social)*, the former home of the historic Fly by Night Club (founded 1986), now a major venue hosting touring acts and local favourites.

For something rawer, the **Buffalo Club** *(freobuffclub.org)* is a haven for experimental bands, while **Clancy's Fish Pub** *(clancysfishpub.com.au)* keeps things classic with weekly gigs and a crowd that spans generations.

Join a Noongar-led walking tour

Walyalup has long been a meeting place for Whadjuk Noongar people – a shoreline for ceremony, trade and stories long before Fremantle took shape. You can certainly feel that history with Whadjuk guide Steven Jacobs on his 90-minute **walking tours** *(inculturetours.com.au; adult/child $99/40)*. Steven opens with a Welcome to Country – a protocol delivered by Traditional Custodians of the land – then leads you through Bathers Beach (p905) all the way to Fremantle Port, bringing to life the stories and relationships tied to this stretch of coast. Bring your camera – the sunset at the end is worth capturing.

Browse Fremantle's freshest galleries

Fremantle's contemporary art scene is compact enough to explore in an afternoon but varied enough to keep you lingering. Start at **Vessel Contemporary** *(vesselcontemporary.org; free)*, an independent space in the old Naval Store showcasing ambitious, site-responsive contemporary art. Next, wander down to the limestone **Kidogo Arthouse** *(kidogo.com.au; free)*, a 19th-century kerosene store turned gallery on Bathers Beach with shows and events by local artists. Then head up High St to **David Giles Art Gallery** *(davidgilesartgallery.com; free)* for bold, expressive abstracts and work by dozens of WA painters. Finish at **PS Arts Space** *(psas.com.au; free)*, a vast heritage warehouse turned experimental project space in the West End.

Enjoy high-octane family fun at FOMO Freo

At the city's entertainment complex **FOMO Freo** *(fomofreo.com.au; games from around $14)*, **Strike Bowling** *(strikebowling.com.au)* and **Holey Moley** *(holeymoley.com.au)*

DRINKING IN FREO: BEST BARS

Darling Darling: Candlelit nautical bar pouring rum-forward classics and playful cocktails. *4pm-midnight Mon-Thu, noon-midnight Fri & Sat, noon-10pm Sun*

Ode to Sirens: A 1970s-infused lounge bar with natural wines, inventive cocktails and a warm vinyl soundtrack. *4pm-late Mon-Thu, noon-late Fri-Sun*

Strange Company: Buzzing small bar serving share plates, WA wines and craft beer in a sleek, modern space. *noon-midnight*

Mrs Brown: North Freo favourite with cosy couches, a leafy courtyard and a strong wine and whisky list. *4.30pm-late Mon-Thu, noon-late Fri-Sun*

LEANNE IRWIN/SHUTTERSTOCK

Kidogo Arthouse

deliver glowing lanes, themed holes and high-octane fun for kids. Just a 10-minute stroll away, **Esplanade Reserve** has a huge playground and the **Tourist Wheel Fremantle** *(touristwheelfremantle.com.au; adult/child $15/12)*, offering sweeping views over the port and coast. Mere steps away, the **Fishing Boat Harbour** is an ideal place to refuel with a gelato or classic fish and chips. If you're running out of ideas, stop by the **Fremantle Visitor Centre** *(visitfremantle.com.au; free)* for kids' maps and easy family-friendly ideas to keep your little ones occupied all day long.

Rottnest Island

TIME FROM PERTH: 1½HR

Though it's only 19km offshore from Fremantle, arriving at Rottnest Island (Wadjemup) feels like landing in a far-flung paradise of white-sand beaches and turquoise bays. Named 'Rottnest' after a 1696 Dutch explorer confused quokkas for giant rats, the island today owes its global fame to those photogenic marsupials. Long a favourite escape for Perth locals, 'Rotto' has recently become an international drawcard, with visitors flocking for the wildlife, beaches and laid-back island pace.

FREMANTLE'S BEST SHOPPING

Remedy Store: Beloved Freo institution packed with quirky gifts, natural skincare, design books and beautifully chosen homewares with a playful edge.

Kartique: Treasure trove of ethically sourced jewellery, textiles and vintage pieces from India and beyond, set inside a dreamy, world-traveller-style boutique.

Mills Records: A Fremantle classic since 1945, stocking new and secondhand vinyl, local releases, merch and turntable gear.

Vintage on High: One of the West End's best haunts for curated vintage clothing, retro accessories and one-off finds from local collectors.

Ginger Morris: Boutique mixing colourful fashion, fun accessories and small-batch WA labels – perfect for easy coastal style.

EATING & DRINKING IN FREO: BEST CAFES

Good Things: Bright, loft-style cafe known for well-crafted brews, friendly vibes and standout brunches. *6.30am-3pm Mon-Fri, 7am-3pm Sat & Sun* **$$**

Bib & Tucker: Beachfront spot for breakfast and smooth morning coffees, served alongside ocean views. *8am-10pm Wed-Sun* **$$$**

Little Lefroy's: Cosy South Freo cafe with eclectic art, all-day breakfast, great vego options and reliably good coffee. *6.30am-3pm* **$$**

Kerfuffle: Tiny corner cafe pouring quality coffee and matcha with pastries and pavement seating. *5.30am-12.30pm Mon-Fri, 6.30am-12.30pm Sat & Sun* **$**

THE SHIPWRECKS OF ROTTNEST

Rottnest's shallow reefs and shifting swells have claimed more than 13 vessels over the past two centuries. The *Uribes* (1942) rests in just a few metres of water at Thomson Bay and is often visible from the surface on calm days. At **Parker Point**, the *Shark* (1939) ran aground on a reef and is now one of the island's most popular snorkel sites. Near the Basin, the *Lady Elizabeth* (1878) sits in a sandy pocket after striking submerged rocks.

Some wrecks can be reached by a short swim or snorkel in light conditions, while others are for divers only. Pick up the free Shipwrecks Trail map from the **Rottnest Island Visitor Centre** for entry points, GPS marks and safety advice.

Meet adorable quokkas on a guided island walk

It's the cherub-faced quokka that draws most first-time visitors to Rotto. Their popularity exploded in the selfie era, especially after celebrity snaps with Chris Hemsworth and Margot Robbie. You'll often spot these adorable marsupials around **Thomson Bay**. For a deeper introduction, join a **Meet the Quokkas walking tour** *(rottnestisland.com; free)* run by Rottnest Volunteer Guides. Tours depart daily at 9.30am and 2.30pm from the **Salt Store** in the centre of the Thomson Bay settlement. Tours explore quokka behaviour, their bush-to-beach habitat and why they seem so comfortable around humans.

Quokkas appear unusually relaxed because they face almost no natural predators on Rotto and decades of tourist interaction have made them habituated to people. Still, they're wild animals: never touch or feed them – human food risks their health and natural behaviour. With around 12,000 quokkas on the island, you'd be very unlucky to leave without a sighting, but your best chances are early morning or late afternoon, when they're most active.

Discover marine life at these pristine island beaches

With more than 60 beaches, Rottnest is one of WA's best islands for swimming and snorkelling. The **Basin**, a natural ocean pool protected by a limestone shelf, is ideal for beginner snorkellers. **Pinky Beach** sits below **Bathurst Lighthouse** and is best in the morning before the wind picks up; snorkel around the rocky southern corner for the clearest water. For quieter swims, **Geordie Bay** has shallow turquoise water, while nearby **Parakeet Bay** offers easy off-the-beach snorkelling and **Little Salmon Bay** features the island's underwater snorkel trail.

Learn Wadjemup's tragic history

Noongar people have a deep ancestral connection to Wadjemup (Rottnest Island), with archaeological evidence showing Aboriginal presence more than 12,000 years ago – long before rising seas separated the island from the mainland. Yet from 1838 to 1931, Wadjemup became a prison for Aboriginal men and boys from across Western Australia. Many were incarcerated for minor offences or for resisting frontier expansion. More than 3700 men were imprisoned here and at least 370 died.

EATING ON ROTTO: BEST RESTAURANTS

Isola Bar e Cibo: On Thomson Bay, breezy Italian waterfront dining with handmade pasta, *crudo* and spritzes. *11.30am-8.30pm Wed-Mon* **$$**

Pinky's Rottnest Island (p911): Laid-back beach bar serving modern Aussie plates, cocktails, local wine and sunset views. *7am-8pm* **$$**

Sunsets Bar & Dining: All-day spot serving fish tacos, burgers and chilled drinks, with a rare elevated view over Rotto's shimmering salt lakes. *7am-10pm* **$$**

Lontara: Resort restaurant marrying Southeast Asian flavours with WA seafood and share plates made for long, lazy lunches. *noon-8.30pm Wed-Sun* **$$$**

A CYCLING TOUR OF ROTTO

A breezy island loop linking Rotto's best beaches, viewpoints and wildlife encounters on an easy half-day cycle.

START	END	LENGTH
Thomson Bay Settlement	Thomson Bay Settlement	22km; 3–4hr

Begin at ❶ **Thomson Bay Settlement** and follow the road north towards the historic ❷ **Bathurst Lighthouse**, offering views over the island's northeastern coastline. Zoom past the crystalline waters of ❸ **Pinky Beach** and continue to the ❹ **Basin**, one of Rotto's most popular swimming spots thanks to its natural limestone shelf and calm water.

Pedal on to ❺ **Longreach Bay** and ❻ **Geordie Bay**, both known for glassy shallows and family-friendly beaches that are perfect for a quick dip. Continue south to ❼ **Little Parakeet Bay**, then cut inland past the island's shimmering ❽ **Pink Lake**, where migratory birds often gather and wildflowers carpet the verges in spring, before looping back to the coast at ❾ **Little Salmon Bay**, home to Rottnest's underwater snorkel trail and some of the clearest water on the island.

Continue to ❿ **Parker Point**, a popular snorkelling stop with limestone ledges, reef fish and a shallow shipwreck just offshore, then ⓫ **Henrietta Rocks**, where a purpose-sunk wreck creates calm, protected waters ideal for beginner snorkellers. Return to Thomson Bay for a refreshing dip before stopping for a late lunch or heading back on the ferry.

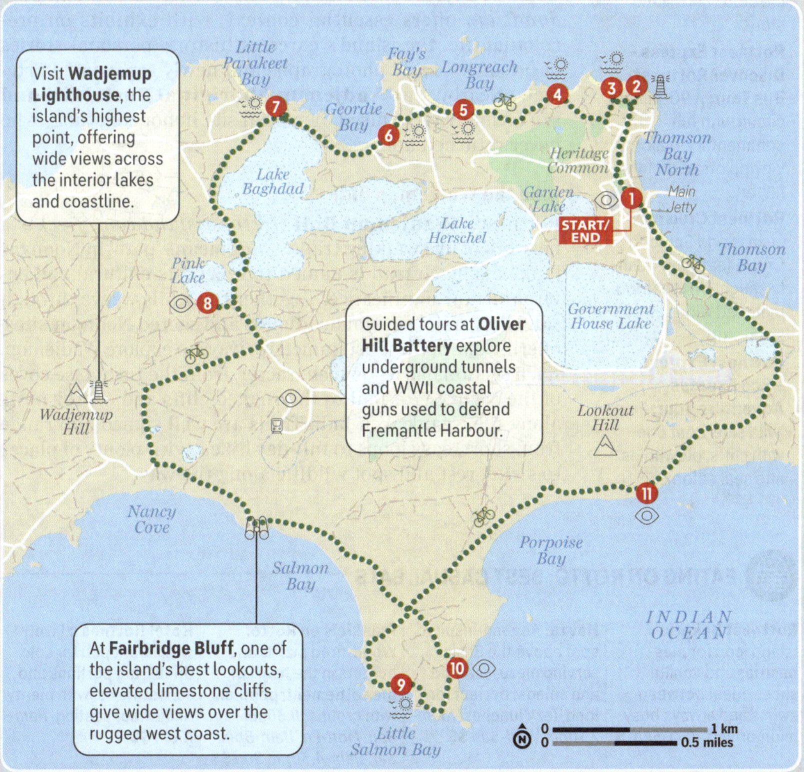

BEST ROTTNEST TOURS

Rottnest Voluntary Guides: Free daily walks covering quokkas, shipwrecks, early settlement and coastal ecology, plus ticketed Wadjemup Lighthouse and Oliver Hill tours.

Rottnest Snorkel: Guided tours to sheltered bays, reefs and coral gardens; equipment included.

Laura the Explorer Tours: Small-group e-bike adventures mixing beaches, wildlife stops and island stories.

Rottnest Express – Discover Rottnest Bus Tour: A 90-minute circuit with full commentary, major viewpoints and island history.

Rottnest Cruises: Luxe Island Seafood Cruise featuring freshly caught WA seafood, matched wines and a swim stop.

Rottnest Express – Eco Express Adventure Tour: Fast 'wild side' boat ride with cliffs, blowholes and seal colonies.

STARGRASS/SHUTTERSTOCK

Pinky Beach (p908)

The **Wadjemup Museum** *(rottnestisland.com; entry by donation)* offers essential context, with exhibits on precolonial life, the island's carceral history, personal stories of prisoners, early photographs and newly repatriated artefacts. Nearby, the **Wadjemup Aboriginal Burial Ground** is a formally recognised memorial site honouring those who never returned home.

Hike the Wadjemup Bidi

Rottnest's **Wadjemup Bidi** *(rottnestisland.com; free)* is a network of five walking trails – *bidi* means 'path' in Noongar language. Each trail is named to reflect its cultural and environmental significance. Together the trails weave through salt lakes, quiet coastal headlands and sacred Noongar sites, offering one of the most immersive ways to explore Wadjemup. Each section has its own character, from the turquoise coves of the Ngank Yira Bidi to the rugged cliffs and osprey nests along the Ngank Wen Bidi. Trails are well signed and range from short, easy loops to full-day hikes, with plenty of places to swim, rest and spot wildlife along the way.

EATING ON ROTTO: BEST CASUAL EATS

Rottnest Bakery: Island icon for pies, pastries and vanilla slices; ideal between swims and always busy midmorning. *7am-5pm* $

Havza: Aegean-inspired spot above the Basin serving meze, seafood and salads; perfect for long, lazy lunches. *10am-7.30pm Wed-Sun* $$

Frankie's on Rotto: Wood-fired pizzas and burgers in the heart of the settlement; popular with groups. *11.30am-8pm Mon-Fri, 11am-8pm Sat, 11am-4.30pm Sun* $$

Hotel Rottnest: Lively waterfront pub for cold drinks, big portions and sunset views, with plenty of outdoor seating. *11am-10pm* $$

Watch the sunset at Pinky's

Pinky Beach (p908) has long been the island's favourite place to watch the sun sink into the Indian Ocean. Just over the dunes sits **Pinky's Rottnest Island** *(pinkysrottnestisland.com.au; mains from $32)*, an open-air restaurant and bar where you can relax on the deck with fresh WA seafood as the sky turns pink and gold. Keep an eye on the horizon from June to October, when migrating whales are often seen breaching offshore. From late spring, Pinky's hosts live-music sessions on weekend afternoons.

Swan Valley

TIME FROM PERTH: **20MIN**

Delight in the 19th-century charm of this river settlement

Established in 1829, Guildford is the oldest of the Swan River settlements, predating both Perth and Fremantle. Its historic heart beats along **James Street**, where antique shops, bookstores and cafes spill from beautifully preserved 19th-century buildings. Packed with antiques and curios, **Jones of Guildford** is a favourite stop for treasure hunters, while the quirky **Museum of Natural History** *(academyoftaxidermy.com; adult/child $8/4)*, housed in the old Regent Theatre, showcases more than 2000 taxidermy specimens and fossils.

Built on an island-like patch of land encircled by the Swan and Helena Rivers, Guildford is made for walking. The **Swan Valley Visitor Centre** *(swanvalley.com.au)*, set within the 1866 courthouse, includes a small museum where artefacts and photographs trace the town's early years. It's also the starting point for tours of the convict-built **Guildford Gaol** *(swanguildfordhistoricalsociety.org.au; adult/child $5/3)*, available weekly on Wednesday, Friday and Saturday from 10am to 2pm, and four self-guided heritage trails that lead past 50 historic sites – from Taylor's Cottage and **St Matthew's Church** to grand 19th-century homes.

Discover Noongar food culture

Wardandi and Bibbulmun woman Dale Tilbrook offers her signature **Bush Tucker Talks & Tastings** *(daletilbrookexperiences.com.au; adult/child $90/45)* – the session to book for a practical introduction to Noongar food culture. Over two hours you'll handle native ingredients, learn simple ways to cook with them at home and taste wattleseed damper with finger-lime butter. Sessions run at **Maalinup Aboriginal Gallery** at **Mandoon Estate** *(mandoonestate.com.au)*, where Dale has welcomed visitors since 1998.

FROM COLONY TO CELLAR: A SHORT HISTORY

When British settlers arrived on Whadjuk Noongar land in 1829, they planted vines along the fertile banks of the Swan River, establishing Western Australia's first wine region. Vineyards soon spread around Guildford and Caversham, thriving in the valley's alluvial soils and Mediterranean climate. By the late 19th century, southern European families – many from Croatia and Italy – introduced robust grape varieties and traditional methods that give Swan Valley wines their distinctive depth and warmth.

Historic estates such as Houghton, Olive Farm and Nikola Estate remain at the heart of production, joined today by boutique winemakers crafting premium shiraz, verdelho and fortifieds from old vines.

DRINKING IN THE SWAN VALLEY: BEST WINERIES

Sandalford Wines: One of WA's oldest and best-known wineries offers tastings and premium blends at its historic estate. *10am-5pm*

Pinelli Estate Wines: Family-run Mediterranean-style winery producing award-winning reds and whites. *10am-5pm*

RiverBank Estate: This peaceful Caversham estate offers elegant small-batch wines and sweeping vineyard views. *10am-4pm Wed-Sun*

Olive Farm Wines: WA's oldest family-owned winery (established 1829) offers intimate tastings in a modern cellar door. *11am-5pm*

A DAY OUT IN THE SWAN VALLEY

Cruise through vineyards, heritage towns and art stops on this easy loop through WA's oldest wine region.

START	END	LENGTH
Guildford town centre	Motor Museum of Western Australia	5–6hr

Begin with a stroll along Guildford's historic ❶ **James Street** (p911), then head to ❷ **Mandoon Estate** *(mandoonestate.com.au; tastings from $10)*, a riverside winery combining fine dining, a craft brewery and the ❸ **Maalinup Aboriginal Gallery** *(maalinup.com.au; free)*. Next, sample bold, small-batch spirits at ❹ **Old Young's Distillery** *(oldyoungs.com.au; tastings $10)* or grab a paddock-to-pint ale at ❺ **Mash Brewing** *(mashbrewing.com.au; prices vary)*.

Pause for lunch at ❻ **Upper Reach Winery** *(upperreach.com.au; mains from $36)*, a tranquil riverside estate with a restaurant overlooking the Swan River. Enjoy seasonal dishes made from local produce alongside estate wines, then linger on the deck.

Continue to ❼ **Nikola Estate** *(nikolaestate.com.au; tastings from $10)*, one of the valley's oldest wineries, lined with jacarandas and steeped in local history, including the capture of notorious outlaw Moondyne Joe (p917). Finish at the ❽ **Motor Museum of Western Australia** *(motormuseumwa.com.au; adult/child $17.50/8)* in Whiteman Park, home to more than 200 vintage vehicles, including Daniel Ricciardo's first Red Bull racer.

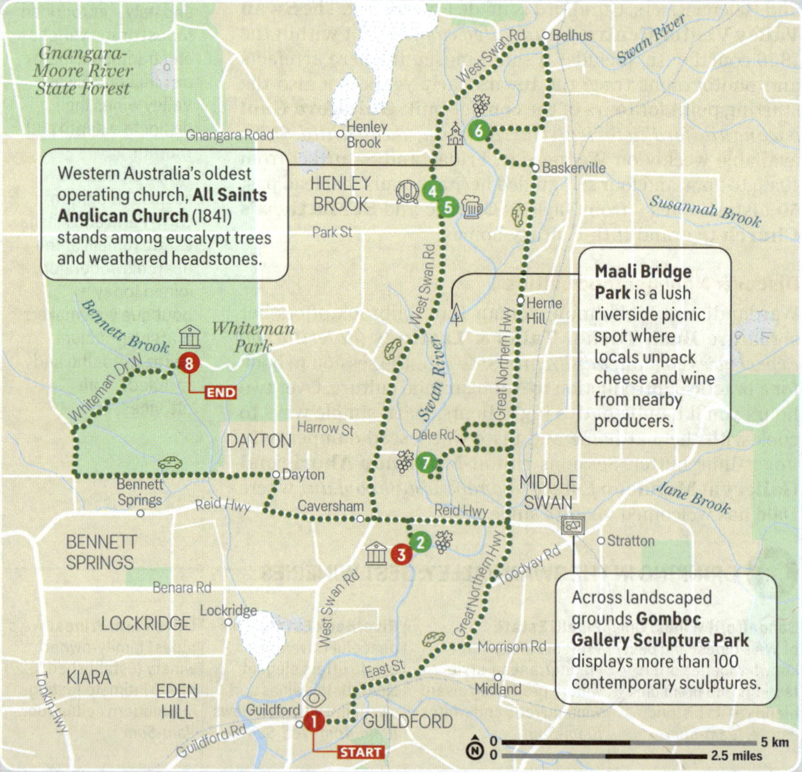

A descendant of the Wardandi-Bibbulmun peoples, Dale draws on teachings passed down by Elders alongside decades of her own research, depth that earned her the nickname 'the bush-tucker queen'. You'll walk through her bush-food garden, learn how ingredients like saltbush, sandalwood nuts and wattleseed are harvested and prepared, and discover easy ways to incorporate them into everyday cooking. The session naturally slows into a shared-table conversation, where travellers can ask questions and hear stories about the six Noongar seasons and how they shape life on Country.

Dale also works with chefs, schools and community groups to help bring native foods into mainstream Australian kitchens. Her gallery showcases authentic Aboriginal art and bush-food products.

Explore bushland trails, heritage trams and native wildlife

A short drive from Guildford, **Whiteman Park** *(whitemanpark.com.au; free)* is one of Perth's favourite outdoor escapes, spanning 40 sq km of bushland, with heritage attractions, picnic lawns and seasonal volunteer-run trams.

Ride a heritage **electric tram** *(petswa.org.au; free)* on a 30- to 40-minute loop, spotting restored timber trams and engines along the way. Explore walking and cycling trails where kangaroos and birdlife roam, then meet more than 200 native species at **Caversham Wildlife Park** *(cavershamwildlife.com.au; adult/child $36/17)*. Don't miss the **Farm Show** *(10am, 1pm & 3pm)*, where stockmen shear sheep, crack whips and milk cows, with visitors able to help feed lambs.

Taste the seasonal harvests

The Swan Valley's Mediterranean-style climate and rich soils make it one of Western Australia's most abundant regions for fresh produce and hands-on food experiences.

Start at the **House of Honey** *(thehouseofhoney.com.au; free entry)*, where you can watch bees at work before sampling single-origin jarrah honey and handcrafted mead. Just down the road, **Mondo Nougat** *(mondonougat.com.au; free entry)* offers a glimpse of traditional Italian nougat making in a glass-walled kitchen, plus complimentary tastings. Finish at **Grapes on Swan** *(facebook.com/grapesonswan; Dec-Apr)*, a family-run vineyard where visitors can pick their own sun-ripened table grapes straight from the source.

BEST SWAN VALLEY TOURS

d'Vine Wine Tours: Bookable by the seat; an entertaining option for solo travellers looking to enjoy the Swan Valley's highlights.

Out & About Wine Tours: Public and private tours with knowledgeable guides taking in small-scale and big-operation wineries. Also offers cruise options from Perth.

Swan Valley Tours: Choice of public and private tours, along with cruises for a day of indulgence.

Captain Cook Cruises: Arrive in style via a scenic Swan River tour; the variety of options includes an all-you-can-drink booze cruise.

Black Swan Tours: Sign up for a day all about beer, wine, coffee, chocolate and cheese.

EATING IN THE SWAN VALLEY: OUR PICKS

Rose & Crown: This Guildford pub, WA's oldest operating hotel (1841), has heritage character, a rambling beer garden and hearty gastropub fare. *11am-10pm* $$

Oscar's in the Valley: Upscale yet relaxed restaurant offering modern Australian cuisine showcasing fresh produce. *11am-5pm Wed, Thu & Sun, to 10pm Fri & Sat* $$

Henley Brook: Family-friendly tavern on a wide green paddock with wood-fired pizzas, craft beers and a weekend buzz. *11am-late* $$

Alfred's Kitchen: Guildford's late-night burger shack has been an institution since 1946. *5pm-midnight Sun-Wed, to 3am Fri & Sat* $

BEST MANDURAH TOURS

From Indigenous-led cultural experiences to dolphin cruises, e-bike adventures and beginner-friendly surf lessons, Mandurah's tour operators offer easy ways to explore the region.

Mandjoogoordap Dreaming: Local Bindjareb guide George leads tours offering interpretations of Mandurah's sea and land from an Indigenous perspective.

Mandurah Cruises: Most popular for its one-hour Dolphin & Scenic Marine Cruise but offers relaxed estuary, high tea and sunset cocktail cruises.

Bike Kiosk: E-bike tours to Mandurah's Giants ranging from three to four hours.

Star Surf+Skate: Runs surf lessons at Pyramids Beach in Mandurah for beginners and beyond.

Mandurah & Rockingham

DISTANCE FROM PERTH:
50MIN (MANDURAH),
40MIN (ROCKINGHAM)

Whimsical timber giants across Mandurah's landscape

Thomas Dambo's **Giants of Mandurah** *(giantsofmandurah.com.au; free)* have become a major draw, luring visitors from across Australia to seek out the renowned artist's whimsical recycled-timber sculptures. Dambo worked closely with Bindjareb Noongar Elders to ensure the trail respected local stories and the significance of the landscape.

Five giants are scattered across the region (plus a secret sixth unlocked via clues), creating a true treasure hunt. Each has its own personality: Little Lui watches over the estuary reeds, Seba's Song shelters beneath peppermint trees and Yaburgurt Winjan Cirkelstone sits among sculpted boulders. Allow at least half a day, wear sturdy shoes and be prepared for short walks on bush tracks.

The official guidebook from **Mandurah Visitor Centre** *(visitmandurah.com)* outlines routes, access points and clues. Sites are spread across Mandurah, so you'll need a car, or you can book into an e-bike, bus or boat tour.

Explore an abundant water world

Mandurah shines from both the water and shore. Its expansive estuary is best explored by boat, kayak or SUP, with dolphins and birdlife frequent companions. **Mandurah Cruises** *(mandurahcruises.com.au; from $42)* offers relaxed wildlife tours and sunset seafood cruises past wide inlets and quiet canals. On land, **Town Beach** is ideal for calm swims, while **Falcon**, **Avalon** and **Pyramids** offer wilder stretches, plus the 10km Halls Head Coastal Trail for easy walks or rides.

Trails and trains at Dwellingup

Just 40 minutes from Mandurah, **Dwellingup** delivers deep forest, river pools and adventure in one compact hub. Start at the **Forest Discovery Centre** *(forestdiscoverycentre.com.au; gold coin donation)*, where an 11m canopy walk lifts you into the treetops. For more action, **Treetops Adventure** *(treetopsadventure.com.au; adult/child $67/57)* runs zip lines and high-ropes courses, while **Dwellingup Adventures** *(dwellingupadventures.com.au)* hires mountain bikes, SUPs and kayaks for exploring Lane Poole Reserve. On weekends the **Hotham Valley Railway** *(hothamvalleyrailway.com.au; adult/child $31/16.50)* rumbles through the forest.

EATING IN MANDURAH: OUR PICKS

Flics Kitchen: Share wood-roasted lamb, pork belly and lobster brioche at Mandurah's most inventive dining room. *hours vary* $$

Boundary Island Brewing: Waterfront brewpub serving house-made beers with smoked meats and family-friendly energy. *hours vary* $$

Little Stiller: Gin and vodka microdistillery with water views, playful cocktails and bao. *11am-late* $$

Redmanna: Estuary-side favourite for seafood platters, crab and scallops. *11.30am-2.30pm & 5.30-9pm Wed-Sat, 11.30am-2.30pm Sun* $$$

ALEISHA ORR/SHUTTERSTOCK

Giants of Mandurah

Limestone cliffs and WA's largest penguin colony

Just 5km south of Rockingham, **Penguin Island** *(exploreparks.dbca.wa.gov.au; free)* sits 600m offshore in Shoalwater Islands Marine Park. The small conservation island is home to WA's largest little penguin colony, along with sheltered beaches, limestone cliffs and short coastal walks. Penguin numbers have declined and sightings are now mostly possible from January to February.

Perth Wildlife Encounters operates the **Penguin Island Ferry** *(penguinisland.com.au; return from $30)* and manages all visitor access. Due to sand build-up at the Penguin Island jetty, ferry services may be suspended at times – check the operator's website for current conditions. Confident paddlers can kayak across when the weather's calm.

Steady winds for kiteboarding

Kiteboarders head for Safety Bay, a coastal pocket just south of Rockingham, where steady winds blow from November to April. Try lessons with **West Oz Kiteboarding** *(westozkiteboarding.com.au)*, **Seabreeze Kitesurf School** *(seabreezekitesurfschool.com)* or **WA Surf** *(wasurf.com.au)*.

Avon Valley

TIME FROM PERTH: **70MIN**

Discover historic streetscapes and Avon Valley views

York mixes wide streets with a strong sense of heritage, making it an easy first stop on any Avon Valley trip. Start on Avon Tce, where balconied shopfronts, iron lacework and weathered brick facades form one of WA's best-preserved historic streetscapes. A highlight is the **York Motor Museum** *(yorkmotormuseum.com; from $14)*, a long-running favourite filled with classic cars, racing memorabilia and beautifully restored oddities.

A short walk away, the **York Courthouse Complex** *(nationaltrust.org.au; from $7)* adds deeper context with

ROCKINGHAM'S BEST TOURS

In Culture Tours: Walks through Rockingham and Cape Peron with Whadjuk guide Steven Jacobs, sharing Noongar stories, coastal culture and saltwater sites.

Capricorn Seakayaking: Kayak tours to Penguin and Seal Islands, exploring limestone reefs, marine wildlife and the sheltered Shoalwater coastline.

Sea Breeze Kitesurf School: Kitesurfing specialists also offering SUP tours, wing-foil lessons and yoga sessions around Safety Bay and Shoalwater.

Scubanautics Dive Academy: Scuba courses, Discover Dives, gear hire and free weekly guided shore dives; ask about diving the nearby *Saxon Ranger* wreck.

Skydive Australia: Tandem skydives over Shoalwater Islands Marine Park with ocean, island and coastline views.

A SHORT HISTORY OF THE AVON VALLEY

The Avon Valley's story stretches back thousands of years: the Ballardong Noongar people moved seasonally along the river for ceremony, food and trade. European settlement began in the 1830s, with York emerging as WA's first inland town and a base for farming families pushing east towards the Wheatbelt. Toodyay became a crucial convict outpost, housing ticket-of-leave men, police, chain gangs and notorious outlaws. The arrival of the railway transformed Northam into a key junction linking the goldfields and Perth, while flour mills, river crossings and homesteads multiplied across the district. Today heritage buildings, bridges and museums across all three towns reveal these layered stories of frontier hardship, expansion and adaptation.

RIC JACYNO/SHUTTERSTOCK

Northam Suspension Bridge

old cells, magistrates' rooms and stories of bushrangers and early policing. Pause in **Avon Park** for its shady lawns, picnic tables and riverside paths, then cross the Avon River on the **York Suspension Bridge**, a narrow pedestrian bridge built in 1906.

Take in York's sweeping landscape from above at **Mt Brown Lookout**, where the valley unfurls in wide layers of paddocks, ridgelines and distant hills. Sunrise and sunset are especially rewarding.

Ballooning above Northam

Just 30 minutes' drive from York, **Northam** is the ideal place to greet the day from above, with sunrise hot-air balloon flights drifting over patchwork farmland and the looping Avon River. Operators such as **Windward Ballooning** *(windwardballooning.com; from $369)* lift off before dawn, when the air is cool and the sky blushes pink. As the burner fires and the basket rises, the landscape opens out in soft layers – paddocks, creek lines, sheep trails and historic buildings glowing in the early light. After the flight, settle in with a relaxed French-style breakfast and a glass of sparkling – a longstanding ballooning tradition.

Northam's bridges and big art

Northam pairs its natural river setting with compelling cultural experiences. Start near the **Northam Suspension Bridge**,

EATING IN THE AVON VALLEY: OUR PICKS

Imperial Homestead: Generous modern Australian dishes in a restored 1880s hotel in York. *10am-9pm Tue-Sun* $$

Bellissimo York: Lively spot serving breakfast and lunch favourites plus Italian-leaning cafe fare. *7am-2.30pm Wed-Mon* $$

Lume Bar & Bistro: Popular Northam bistro with refined seasonal dishes a step up from classic pub fare. *11am-2.30pm & 5-9pm Mon-Sat, 11am-2.30pm Sun* $$

Riverside Hotel: Solid modern-pub meals in Northam with spacious indoor-outdoor seating. *5.30-8pm Mon & Tue, 11am-2pm & 5.30-8pm Wed-Sun* $$

one of the longest pedestrian suspension bridges in Australia, spanning 117m over the Avon River. Then, visit **Bilya Koort Boodja** *(bilyakoortboodja.com; adult/child $10/5)*, a riverside centre detailing Ballardong Noongar culture and the Avon's significance through interactive displays. From here it's a short drive to **Northam Silo Art** *(australiansiloarttrail.com/northam; free)*. Located on Northam–Toodyay Rd, these large-scale murals painted in 2015 on working grain silos helped launch Australia's silo art movement. Morning or late afternoon offers the best light.

Step back in time in Toodyay

Toodyay's history is best explored through two sites a short stroll apart. The **Newcastle Gaol Museum** *(toodyay.wa.gov.au; from $5)* reveals frontier policing through preserved cells, artefacts and stories of outlaws including Moondyne Joe, whose repeated escapes helped cement his local legend.

A short walk leads to **Connor's Mill** *(toodyay.wa.gov.au; from $5)*, a restored 1870s flour mill where original machinery still runs during demonstrations, showing how grain was processed for early settlers.

Together, the sites highlight Toodyay's early foundations: compact cells, workrooms, milling equipment and solid stone buildings shaped by convict labour.

Explore Avon Valley National Park

Just under half an hour southwest of Toodyay, **Avon Valley National Park** *(exploreparks.dbca.wa.gov.au; per vehicle $17)* protects dramatic bushland where wandoo, jarrah and marri woodlands meet high granite outcrops with sweeping views over the Avon Valley. The scenic **Bald Hill** area offers one of the best lookouts in the park. A handful of short walking trails lead through native forest and open country, with wildflowers in spring and plentiful birdlife year-round. Picnic spots and basic facilities sit near camping areas such as Bald Hill Campground. Roads within the park are unsealed and can be rough after rain, so check conditions before you set out.

Discover monastic New Norcia

Founded in 1847, the Benedictine monastic town of **New Norcia** rises unexpectedly from the bush. It remains home to a small community of monks whose routines still set the rhythm of the day. Visitors can explore on a self-guided wander or join a **Town Tour** *(newnorcia.com.au; from $15)* for

THE OUTLAW WHO OUTSMARTED THE VALLEY

Moondyne Joe – born Joseph Bolitho Johns – is the Avon Valley's most famous outlaw and a defining figure in Toodyay's frontier past. Transported from Britain as a convict in the 1850s, he became notorious for bush escapes, horse stealing and outsmarting the authorities across the rugged valley landscape. His most daring breakout in 1861, near modern-day Toodyay, cemented his legend as a local folk hero who used cunning rather than violence. Today his story helps illuminate the region's early policing, settler hardship and the vast, difficult country that shaped colonial life. Sites like the Newcastle Gaol Museum preserve his tale, while Toodyay's annual **Moondyne Festival** keeps his rebellious spirit alive in the Avon Valley.

EATING IN TOODYAY: OUR PICKS

Toodyay Bakery: Award-winning country bakery famed for its pies, sourdough and pastries, ideal for breakfast or a grab-and-go lunch. *6am-4pm* **$**

Cola Café & Museum: Retro 1950s-themed cafe for burgers, shakes and relaxed lunches, with a fun memorabilia collection. *9am-3pm Thu-Mon* **$**

Victoria Hotel: Historic 1890s pub-restaurant serving hearty modern Australian classics and sizeable plates in a restored heritage hotel. *11am-late* **$$**

Alicia Estate Winery & Restaurant: Scenic winery-restaurant offering German-Austrian dishes and long lunches in a rural setting. *10am-4pm Fri-Sun* **$$$**

A PLACE OF TRAUMA

New Norcia's peaceful exterior harbours a grim past. Founded in 1847 as a Benedictine mission, it became a place where Yued Noongar families were deeply disrupted, with children removed from Country and placed in missions.

Throughout the 20th century, inquiries and a Royal Commission documented serious failings in the care provided to Aboriginal children, along with historic allegations of child sexual abuse involving members of the Benedictine community. The order has since issued public apologies and participated in redress processes.

Today, parts of New Norcia acknowledge this difficult history through exhibitions and interpretation. Visitors encounter not only striking architecture and monastic heritage but also the deeper story of a town shaped by both devotion and harm – a legacy still felt by many.

CHAMELEONSEYE/SHUTTERSTOCK

Abbey Church

access to historic interiors including the **Abbey Church**, old colleges, the flour mill, cultural displays and architecture from Baroque to Byzantine.

With its carved altar and muted frescoes, the Abbey Church anchors the town centre, while the Spanish Quarter and old college buildings line broad, echoing avenues inviting slow exploration.

One of New Norcia's greatest surprises is its art – a little-known collection of religious works spanning centuries, displayed across the **New Norcia Museum & Art Gallery** *(newnorcia.com.au; from $12.50)*. The surrounding landscape adds to the atmosphere: golden paddocks, stands of eucalypts and the distant hum of bees in the monastery's olive trees. You can also try the monks' famous baked goods – including rustic loaves, nut cakes and *Pan Chocolatti* – sold at the **New Norcia Visitor Centre**.

WA MUSEUM BOOLA BARDIP

For truth-telling about the hardships and trauma endured by the Indigenous Noongar people since colonisation, visit Perth's **Boola Bardip** (p897) with its comprehensive coverage of communities across WA.

EATING IN NEW NORCIA: OUR PICKS

Salvado Roadhouse Cafe: Simple roadhouse cafe serving coffee, rolls, burgers and hot snacks. *7.30am-5pm* $

Monastery Guesthouse: A three-course 'Monastery Lunch' of hearty, home-style dishes is served in the guesthouse dining room; pre-booking required. *noon* $

New Norcia Visitor Centre: Pick up the monks' famed fresh bread, olive oil, biscotti and light grab-and-go snacks for an easy picnic in the grounds. *9.30am-4.30pm* $

New Norcia Hostel: Historic hostel dining hall – serves hearty meals – also hosts occasional ticketed long-table dinners; pre-booking required. *hours vary* $$

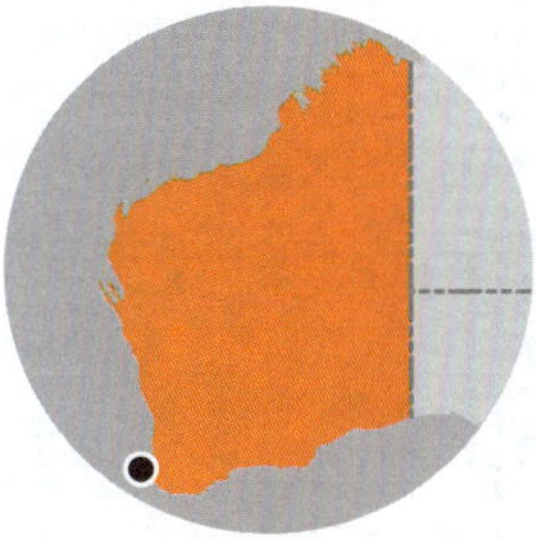

Margaret River Region

WINE | WILD BEACHES | HISTORIC CAVES

Though Margaret River is also a town – a great little community that's well worth checking out – it's better known as a region, famous not only for world-class waves and wineries but also as a gastronomic destination set among superb natural attractions. Stretching from Cape Naturaliste in the north to Cape Leeuwin in the south, it's a coastline of golden beaches, sublime surf and national park native forest, bookended by two iconic lighthouses.

The region is home to some of Australia's finest wineries, craft breweries and distilleries, all paired temptingly with acclaimed restaurants showcasing the best of Margaret River's gourmet produce. It's the first certified eco destination in WA and you'll find some of Australia's finest caves, beaches and bike trails here. Come springtime, there are wildflowers too and whales are regularly spotted off the coast.

Visit for family fun, a romantic getaway or that long-awaited group trip with friends.

TOP TIP

It pays to plan ahead: there are no petrol stations in Yalliungup or Cape Naturaliste, so be sure to fill up in Dunsborough if you intend to stay a few days there. Year-round, book all accommodation in the region well in advance.

Connecting with the Saltwater People

Engage with Indigenous Noongar culture

Translating as the 'saltwater people', the Indigenous Wadandi – one of the 14 language groups of the Noongar nation – are the Traditional Custodians of the Margaret River (Wooditchup)

Continued on p924

GETTING AROUND

Buses can get you here, but unless you're happy to base yourself in one spot you'll need your own car to explore the region in depth. There are direct flights from Perth, Melbourne and Sydney, so picking up a rental car at Busselton airport is now a viable option; book well ahead.

With an increasing network of cycling paths, biking is another good option; the **Hairy Marron Cafe** is ground zero for all your bike-hire needs. At the town of Margaret River there's an off-road bike path to Prevelly Beach, while the Wandandi Track leads you to Cowaramup and Witchcliffe.

SIGHTS
1 Aquarium
2 Aravina Estate
3 Beerfarm
4 Bob's Hollow
5 Bunker Bay Beach
6 Busselton Jetty
7 Canal Rocks
8 Cape Mentelle
9 Cape Naturaliste Lighthouse
10 Castle Bay Beach
11 Grove Distillery & Brewery
12 Happs Winery & Commonage Pottery
13 Injidup Natural Spa
14 Kathleen's Seat
15 LS Merchants
16 Margaret River Distilling Company
17 Meelup Beach
18 Point Picquet
19 Redgate Beach
20 Stella Bella
21 Sugarloaf Rock
22 Surfers Point
23 Voyager Estate
see 61 West Winds Distillers

ACTIVITIES
24 Cape to Cape Track
25 Hairy Marron Cafe
26 Koomal Dreaming
27 Lake Cave
28 Mammoth Cave
see 19 Margaret River Surf School
29 Naturaliste Charters
30 Ngilgi Cave
31 Yallingup Surf School

SLEEPING
32 8 Paddocks
33 Karriview
34 Southcamp Stays

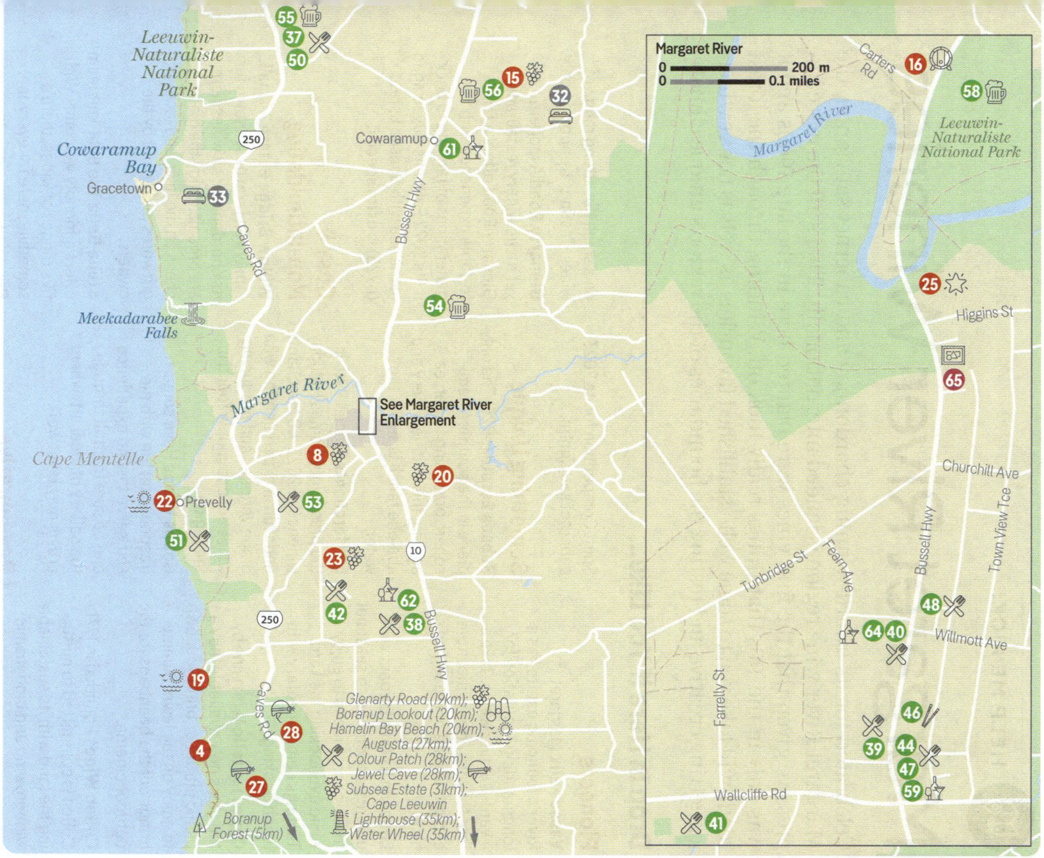

EATING

35 Burger Bones
36 Chow's Table
37 Cullen Wines
38 Dear Darnell's
39 de'sendent
40 Egberts
see 5 ilma Beach House
see 31 Lagoon Yallingup
41 Lasa
42 Leeuwin Estate
43 Mano Wraps
44 Margaret River Tuck Shop
45 Masseria Restaurant & Bar
46 Miki's Open Kitchen
47 Morries
48 Normal Van
49 Origins Market
50 Vasse Felix
51 White Elephant Cafe
52 Wills Domain
53 Xanadu

DRINKING & NIGHTLIFE

54 CBCo
55 Cheeky Monkey
56 Cowaramup Brewing Company
57 Eagle Bay Brewing Co
58 Margaret River Brewhouse
59 Pearl's Bar
60 Rocky Ridge Brewing
61 Strange Brew
62 Vintners
63 Wild Hop Brewing Company
64 Yonder

ENTERTAINMENT

65 REDSEA Gallery
66 Yallingup Aboriginal Art
67 Yallingup Galleries

HELP ME PICK:

Margaret River Wineries

Celebrated for its award-winning chardonnay and cabernet sauvignon, the Margaret River wine region is lauded internationally. That's all the more impressive given that the first vines were planted here in the late 1960s and it was only in the '90s that things really took off. Winding through the forest roads will take you to some well-established favourites as well as newer wineries getting creative and testing the boundaries of the region's unique climate.

Drop in Here if You Like...

Pioneers

Vasse Felix Margaret River's founding estate has a longstanding reputation for award-winning wines. Take a tour to learn about viticulture and get a taste of the region's history.

Leeuwin Estate Elegant wine pairings accompany a seasonal three-course menu to enjoy while overlooking the karri. Tastings complimentary with lunch bookings.

Cape Mentelle With wine by the glass now available, buy a picnic platter or bring your own to enjoy on the lawn. Summer brings out the beanbags for the outdoor cinema.

Cullen Wines Founded in 1971, Cullen is committed to nurturing the land with its sustainable winegrowing and biodynamic practices.

Xanadu Claiming the No 1 red wine in the world, Xanadu received a coveted trophy from the International Wine & Spirit Competition for its 2023 cabernet sauvignon.

Something Unique

Subsea Estate (p925) The only place in the southern hemisphere practising undersea ageing, this unique winery and abalone ranch is set by the water.

LS Merchants Placed 99th in the prestigious James Halliday wineries of 2025, LS Merchants finds fun in experimenting with grape varieties and producing wines not commonly found in the region.

Happs Wines Have some (responsible) fun with the self-serve tasting experience and be sure to stroll through the gallery of local art, where artists may be at work.

Regenerative & Organic Farming

Voyager Estate Using minimal input methods, single-estate Voyager has moved to focus on a small but strong range of wines. Tastings by booking only.

Glenarty Road A modern yet rustic winery restaurant, Glenarty Road offers a farm-to-table experience with five generations of farming to back it. Its 2022 Fathoms Cuvée aged in the sea with Subsea Estate (p925) is extra special.

Cosy & Non-Intimidating

Willow Bridge Estate A small, family-run farm best known for its chardonnay; all wines here are organic. Enjoy the giant chess on the lawn and local giftwares picked out by the owners.

Stella Bella The tight-knit team offers a friendly welcome. With five ranges of wines, there's something here for everyone. Bring your own picnic to enjoy with a glass.

HOW TO

Before you go Check the hours and locations of places you're interested in for a seamless journey with minimal backtracking.

Pace yourself There are 100-plus cellar doors in the region and moving between several can be tiring. Pick four to six per day to truly enjoy the experience.

Budget Many wineries charge a tasting fee, but it's usually refundable with a purchase. Budget $20 per winery to avoid unexpected expenses.

Don't be shy Wine tasting can be intimidating for newcomers, but cellar-door staff are happy to offer guidance and share their love of wine.

DRINKING & NIGHTLIFE

1 Cape Mentelle
2 Cullen Winery
3 Glenarty Road
4 Happs Winery & Commonage Pottery
5 Leeuwin Estate
6 LS Merchants
7 Stella Bella
8 Subsea Estate
9 Vasse Felix
10 Voyager Estate
11 Willow Bridge Estate
12 Xanadu

Be Your Own Guide or Choose a Tour

Making your own way around this stunning region allows for flexibility and the option to discover places as you go. If no one in your group is willing to volunteer as designated driver, though, there are plenty of tour companies to choose from. Most tours run from $170 and offer a mix of activities if you're interested in more than just wine.

Well-established tour group **Bush Tucker Tours** *(bushtuckertours.com)* stops at six iconic locations, including wineries, distilleries and breweries, and is sure to provide a fun day out. Another option that includes breweries is **Wine for Dudes** *(winefordudes.com)*. Don't let the name put you off: this bunch welcomes all and makes for a great introduction to wines and more by taking a more casual approach. If a truly gourmet experience is what you're after, **Waves of Wine** *(wavesofwinetours.com)* is your best bet. This boutique tour visits three wineries, with blind tastings and a gourmet lunch included.

For something a little outside the box, **Margaret River Discovery Co** *(margaretriverdiscovery.com.au)* weaves canoe rides, 4WD adventures and treks of the Cape to Cape track (p927) into a wine experience. The team at **All About Margaret River** *(allaboutmargaretriver.com.au)* also offers something beyond the wineries, with coffee tastings and forest walks in the mix.

MARGARET RIVER PROS

Surfers Point at Prevelly Beach lies at the epicentre of the coastal surf scene here and is home to the Margaret River Pro, the seventh leg of the World Surf League circuit. Reaching its 50th year in 2026, the event is held in May and attracts the world's very best to shoot it out at the iconic Southside, Main Break and Box. Waves here can reach up to 7.5m. It's thus one of the few places you'll see surfers wearing helmets; local shapers design specialised, stronger boards with more rocker for the conditions. Local favourite Jack Robinson took out top place in 2022 and 2024, and Willow Hardy and Jacob Willcox have also found success in the competition.

Continued from p919

region. Alongside Madjedbebe in Arnhem Land and Lake Mungo in New South Wales, this is one of the earliest sites of human occupation in Australia, with unearthed evidence of human settlement dating back over 40,000 years.

Koomal Dreaming *(koomaldreaming.com.au; adult $68-175, child $35-135)* is one of the best Indigenous culture tour operators. Tours (1½ to three hours) are led by Josh Whiteland, a local Wardandi man and natural storyteller whose ancestors were the last to live in the bush here in the 1960s. Tours take in a range of cultural experiences, including coastal walks to learn about the six Noongar seasons and journeying into **Ngilgi Cave** to hear traditional stories, learning to make a fire and didgeridoo performances.

Otherwise, the self-guided **Ancient Lands Experience** *(capesfoundation.org.au; adult/child $32/16)* at Ngilgi Cave (named after an ocean spirit who now resides in and protects the cave) provides in-depth information with interactive installations.

Surf's Up

Ride the perfect wave

Some 75 breaks dot this coastline of the Indian Ocean – including secret spots only accessible by 4WD – and it's where the likes of Taj Burrow and Jack Robinson grew up carving monster waves at Margaret River, Yallingup and Gracetown. This surf culture dates back to the late 1950s; those interested in its history can drop by **Aravina Estate** winery for the **WA Surf Gallery**.

The **Margaret River Surf School** *(margaretriversurfschool.com)* team keeps you feeling safe on the beginner-friendly shores of **Redgate Beach** and will have you popping up and riding the waves within hours with their hands-on guidance and expert advice. Just $65 gets you into a group lesson; private and individual options are also available. **Yallingup Surf School** *(yallingupsurfschool.com; $60-170)* is another great option a bit further north.

Bites with the perfect balance of sweet and savoury

EATING IN MARGARET RIVER: OUR PICKS

Egberts: Sweet little bakery-cafe slinging out the best croissants in town. *6am-1pm Tue-Sat* $

Normal Van: Some of the juiciest burgers with beer on tap and margaritas. Weekend brunches. *noon-8pm Thu, Fri & Mon, 8-11.30am & noon-8pm Sat & Sun* $$

Dear Darnell's: Quirky bar-restaurant in Witchcliffe with artistic interiors and seasonal cocktails. *noon-9pm Fri & Sat, to 8pm Thu & Sun* $$$

Lasa: Filipino-inspired takeaway joint serving treats like *bibingka* (steamed rice cakes). *8am-3pm Mon & Tue, to 8pm Wed-Sat, to noon Sun* $

Margaret River Tuck Shop: Go-to spot for wood-fired pizza and beautiful seafood dishes. Try the octopus. *5-10pm Thu-Mon* $$$

Morries: Modern Australian menu showcasing native and seasonal ingredients paired with stellar cocktails. *5-10pm Tue-Sat* $$$

Miki's Open Kitchen: Carefully crafted degustation of Japanese-style dishes and fine Japanese sake and whisky. *6-11pm Tue-Sat* $$$

de'sendent: A unique tasting menu brings the ultimate form of edgy fine dining to town. *4pm-late Wed-Sat* $$$

MARC WITTE/SHUTTERSTOCK

Redgate Beach

Get Crafty

Award-winning microbreweries and distilleries

Margaret River's craft beer and artisan booze scene is a beautiful complement to its wineries. Other than the **Brewhouse** *(margaretriverbeer.co)* in Margaret River town, all venues are set among wine country and are wonderfully rustic affairs with pastoral outlooks and family-friendly setups. **Beerfarm** *(beerfarm.com.au)* is one of the region's standouts for its seasonal ales to go with big IPAs, all poured within an old dairy shed overlooking paddocks. Brewing since 2004, **CBCo** *(cbco.beer)* is also one of southwestern Australia's originals and has 22 beers on tap; try its signature pale ale.

Wild Hop Brewing Company *(wildhopbeer.com.au)* sports reliable core brews and seasonals to be enjoyed with smoked meats in its bush setting. Other places to kick back with a cold one and a view are **Cowaramup Brewing Company** *(cowaramupbrewing.com.au)*, with pilsners and British-style ales; **Eagle Bay Brewing Co** *(eaglebaybrewing.com.au)* near Cape Naturaliste for a winning pale ale; and **Cheeky Monkey** *(cheekymonkey.com.au)* for hoppy beers on the lawn by the water.

UNDERWATER WINES

Inspired by pristine bottles of wine discovered in shipwrecks on the ocean floor, winemakers around Europe have been dabbling with the art of ageing wine below the sea and the process has made its way to Western Australia. With near-perfect conditions, such as low light and a consistent temperature and atmospheric pressure, the depths of the ocean make for a unique ageing location.

Together with a team of experienced winemakers in France, the crew at **Subsea Estate** experiment with a second fermentation process, utilising the natural movement of ocean currents at a depth of 20m with the activity of live yeasts, yielding a rare collection of wines with a flavour that cannot be created on land. Their collection includes land and sea ageing mixes and sea-aged-only wines.

DRINKING IN MARGARET RIVER & COWARAMUP: OUR PICKS

Pearl's Bar: Does superb local twists on classic cocktails in an intimate space. Enjoy small plates and charcuterie while you sip. *4pm-late*

Yonder: This cosy dive bar will attract you with its retro lighting, eclectic decor and top-notch cocktails. *5pm-late*

Vintners: This wine bar and restaurant attached to the cellar door for McHenry Hohnen in Witchcliffe has something for everyone. *hours vary*

For local wines with no cellar door

Strange Brew: Born of the team at Skigh Wine; visit for locally celebrated wines in a relaxed atmosphere. *2pm-late Thu-Mon*

SIX SEASONS OF THE WADANDI PEOPLE

The Wadandi people use a six-season calendar to understand the land and work in harmony with it. These seasons are indicated not by specific dates but by what is happening in the environment.

Birak, the 'season of the young', is when burning takes place for seed germination. *Bunuru,* the 'season of adolescence', is a time for fishing and white flowers. *Djeran,* the 'season of adulthood', is when native flowers are abundant and courtship ceremonies traditionally took place. *Makuru,* the 'season of fertility', is a time to move inland and shelter from the rains. *Djilba,* the 'season of conception', brings lush new growth from previous burning and abundant native foods. *Kambarang,* the 'season of birth', is when the orchids bloom and turtles and *gilgi* (crayfish) were traditionally hunted.

GAGLIARDIPHOTOGRAPHY/SHUTTERSTOCK

Cape Naturaliste Lighthouse (p928)

Grove Distillery & Brewery *(thegrovedistillery.com.au)* was the first in Margaret River to get the ball rolling for gins and vodka and today it's also known for its single-malt scotch and rums – enjoy overlooking its vines. For artisanal gins using native botanicals from wattleseed, bottlebrush and lemon myrtle to sea parsley, don't miss **Margaret River Distilling Company** *(distillery.com.au),* or **West Winds** *(westwinds distillers.com)* for its cocktail flight tastings.

Lighthouses & Rugged Landscapes

Be captivated by Cape Leeuwin

At Australia's most southwesterly point you'll find a different vibe to the rest of the Margaret River region, with the windswept romance of lighthouses, forlorn beaches and moody seascapes.

Augusta is the main town down this way and sits overlooking the inlet where the Blackwood River empties into the ocean. It offers an old-school seaside-holiday feel, with fish and chips, a ripper main pub and the very worthwhile historical museum.

The closest fine dining you can get to the beach

EATING BY THE COAST: OUR PICKS

White Elephant Cafe: Blissful beachside cafe overlooking Gnarabup Beach. *7am-3pm* $$

Lagoon Yallingup: Upmarket beachfront kiosk dishing up wild-truffle eggs on toast and delicious seafood lunches. *8am-3pm Wed-Sun* $$

Colour Patch: Enjoy a seafood lunch at this cafe with a restored early-1960s yacht serving as the bar. *8.30am-3pm Sun, Mon, Wed & Thu, to 8pm Fri & Sat* $$$

ilma Beach House: At Margaret River's northern tip, this stylish beach bistro on Bunker Bay has a menu of seasonal modern Australian dishes. *9am-4pm Thu-Mon* $$$

The highlight here is **Cape Leeuwin**, 9km south of Augusta, where you'll find mainland Australia's tallest **lighthouse** (39m; 1886) looking out to where the Indian Ocean meets the Southern Ocean. Guided **tours** *(capesfoundation.org.au; adult/child $22/10)* take you to the top of this still-operational beacon, where you'll be battered by gale-force winds while watching the waves crash below. Get safely out onto the water with **Naturaliste Charters** *(naturalistecharters.com.au; adult/child $105/65)* for whale-watching cruises from mid-May to August in Flinders Bay.

Caves Rd leads up from the southern tip of Cape Leeuwin, taking you through the remnant karri forest of **Boranup**, part of Leeuwin-Naturaliste National Park. Sadly, fires raged through here in 2021, but its southern sections remain intact. You can drive among its giant trees up to **Boranup Lookout** for superb coastal views. En route you'll pass **Hamelin Bay Beach**, a contender for the region's best patch of white sand and famous for its stingrays in the shallows.

Journey Below the Surface

Historic underground caves

The Margaret River landscape is a stunning sight, but there's still more to enjoy below the surface. Visitors can explore a select few of the region's 100-plus subterranean limestone caves, each with its own charm.

Near Augusta, **Jewel Cave** is the southernmost and largest of the caves open to visitors. To see ancient fossils of megafauna that once roamed Australia, head to **Mammoth Cave**, where the first 30m stretch is wheelchair accessible, or wander down into a sinkhole to stand mesmerised by dripping stalagmites reflected against the underground lake at **Lake Cave**.

Entry costs $25/12.50 per adult/child per cave and access is a mix of tour-guided and self-guided. Allow an hour to see each of the caves.

Rock Pools & Cape to Cape

Wander along the coast in Yallingup

With its surf, chilled-out locals and nearby wineries, the laid-back northern township of Yallingup offers a quintessential Southwest experience. It's where you'll find some of the best sections of the **Cape to Cape Track**, a 130km walking trail stretching from Cape Leeuwin to Cape Naturaliste. Taking

BEST COASTAL VIEWS FROM CAPE TO CAPE

Sugarloaf Rock: From here to the lighthouse is the start or finish of the Cape to Cape journey and offers spectacular views of the coast including 1km of timber boardwalk.

Redgate Beach: Peep down at the beautiful shoreline bookshelved by rocks and watch as surfers await their perfect wave.

Bob's Hollow: New boardwalks and steps lead down to a beachside cave and further down to turquoise waters.

Hamelin Bay Beach: A favourite beach destination in the south that's famous for stingrays. Expect expansive views along the shore and out to sea.

Water Wheel: Down by the Cape Leeuwin Lighthouse, wade into the rock pools here and enjoy an unbeatable sunset.

There's a snack bar with service for lawn picnics too!

EATING IN WINE COUNTRY: OUR PICKS

Glenarty Road (p920): At this set-menu restaurant, most of the produce is grown on-site, including its famous lamb. Bookings essential. *hours vary* **$$$**

Masseria: On Cherubino winery's stunning property, this elegant restaurant serves local ingredients in Italian-inflected dishes. *noon-4pm Wed-Sat* **$$$**

Wills Domain: Award-winning fine-diner overlooking the vineyard hills. *noon-3pm Thu-Mon* **$$$**

Chow's Table: Contemporary Malay Chinese cuisine in a relaxed, open restaurant beside House of Cards Wine. *11.30am-3pm Wed-Sun* **$$$**

WHALE HIGHWAY

For nature lovers, there's no better time to visit Margaret River than from August to November, when its wildflower blooms coincide with the whale migration season. At this time, its waters become a thoroughfare for humpbacks, southern rights, minke and blue whales, all on their journey from Antarctica up WA's coast to the Kimberley, where they turn around for the long voyage home.

For the northern winter migration (May to August) you're guaranteed to spot humpbacks from Cape Leeuwin in the south, while in the southern migration (late August to November), you'll see them in the north off Cape Naturaliste. Be sure to pack binoculars to really see the magnificent ocean giants in action.

most people five to eight days to complete, it offers scenic walks and natural coastal wonders.

A short 15-minute walk from **Kathleen's Seat** through flourishing bush will get you to the **Aquarium**, a stunning, protected rock pool popular with snorkellers for admiring the colourful sea life. Just east of here is **Canal Rocks**, another worthwhile stop where you can walk out along a footbridge to immerse yourself in spectacular rocky seascapes. A 10-minute drive back down Caves Rd takes you to **Injidup Natural Spa**, a lagoon-style rock pool that requires some easy clambering down to reach its refreshing waters. Sit and watch the spray of waves crashing against the rocks around you.

Lighthouse History & Whale Watching

Cruise up to Cape Naturaliste

Hidden away at Margaret River's far northern tip is the spectacular **Cape Naturaliste**, characterised by secluded white sandy beaches and its namesake **lighthouse**. Built in 1903, the lighthouse can only be entered on a **guided tour** *(capes foundation.org.au; adult/child $17/8)*, starting at the car park and departing every half-hour. With only 59 steps, the beacon's on the shorter side, but the views from up here overlooking Geographe Bay are astounding.

A 3.5km walk from the lighthouse brings you to the Sugarloaf Rock (p927) viewpoint, where you'll find Australia's most southerly breeding colony of red-tailed tropicbirds; bring along binoculars to see them diving offshore.

The beaches here are a big lure: **Meelup**, **Bunker Bay** (patrolled by a surf life-saving club on weekends from November to January) and **Castle Bay** all have talcum-white sands overlooking the calm turquoise waters of Geographe Bay.

This is a prime whale-watching area from winter to spring, with **Point Picquet** and the lighthouse platform making for great viewpoints. Alternatively, hop on a boat from nearby Dunsborough with **Naturaliste Charters** *(naturaliste charters.com.au; adult/child $95/55)* and cruise along the western side of the cape to spot humpbacks, southern rights and the occasional rare blue whale.

Family Fun in Busselton

Underwater and forest adventures

Extending 1.841km over the translucent waters of Geographe Bay, the 1860s-built **Busselton Jetty** *(busseltonjetty.com.au; adult/child $5/free)* is heritage listed as the longest timber jetty in the southern hemisphere. Enjoy a 25-minute stroll along the jetty's length, or jump on the **tourist train** *(adult/child $18/12)*, running on laid-out tracks along the timber piles (past people fishing for squid) all the way to the end.

At the jetty's endpoint lies a stunning **underwater observatory** *(adult/child $42/27)*, one of only six in the world. It allows visitors to plunge to the depths and witness a world

TRABANTOS/SHUTTERSTOCK

Tourist train, Busselton Jetty

teeming with marine life, all without getting wet. Tickets for the observatory include a return ticket on the train, a day pass to the jetty and a 45-minute guided tour leading you 8m underwater to 11 viewing windows, through which you can observe some of the 300 marine species that live down here. Note that the observatory may shut when weather conditions are rough, but walking along the jetty is still possible at those times.

For a bit of fun for the older kids, journey 15km out of town to **Forest Adventures** *(capesfoundation.org.au; adult/child $59/49)* for some adrenaline-filled exploits in the trees. There are six rope courses of varied difficulty, jam-packed with obstacle courses and zip lines through the towering trees; the highest point is 19m above the ground. A booking gives you 2½ hours, which is enough time to experience three courses of your choice.

BEST ART GALLERIES IN THE SOUTHWEST

REDSEA Gallery: Featuring a mix of local, interstate and international art, this gallery in Margaret River has something different in every corner.

Commonage Pottery: A vibrant hub for creatives at Happs Wines, with pottery, jewellery, glass art and paintings.

Yallingup Aboriginal Art: In front of the Yallingup Maze lies a beautiful collection of contemporary Aboriginal art by local Noongar artists with stories to tell.

Yallingup Galleries: In the heart of Yallingup, this gallery has stunning displays of work from a range of recognised Australian artists.

Bunbury Regional Art Gallery: Housed within a former convent, this gallery is well worth visiting for the annual Iluka Visions youth art exhibition.

EATING & DRINKING IN BUSSELTON: OUR PICKS

Rocky Ridge Brewing: Sustainable, net-zero microbrewery popular for its core range and new releases. *11am-7pm Sun-Thu, to 8pm Fri & Sat* $$

Origins Market: Indoor farmers market with a food hall showcasing local produce. *8.30am-9pm Thu-Sat, to 6pm Sun* $

Burger Bones: Some of WA's finest grass-fed beef cheeseburgers; vegan and vego options too. *11am-2pm & 4.30-8pm Fri & Sat, 11am-2pm & 4.30-7.30pm Wed & Thu* $$

Mano Wraps: Market stall turned bricks-and-mortar venue serving handcrafted buckwheat wraps with savoury or sweet fillings. *8.30am-3pm Mon-Sun* $$

Bunbury & Around

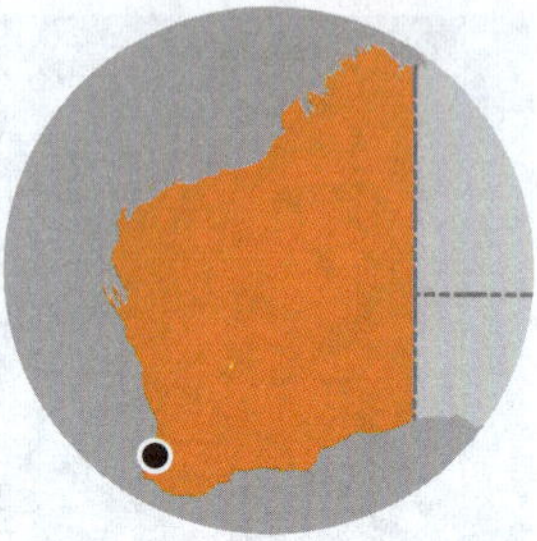

DOLPHINS | SWIMMING HOLES | MURALS

GETTING AROUND

A good network of buses will get you to and from Perth, and train services are expected to resume in 2026. There are also bus links to Collie, Margaret River, Pemberton and the south-coast towns of Denmark and Albany. In Bunbury, **Melo Velo** hires out bikes, or you can jump on a Beam e-scooter. There are also Uber, taxis and a network of local buses. In Collie there are taxis, or e-bikes for hire from Adventure Connections (p934). In all other places you'll need a set of wheels to get around.

TOP TIP

Bookings are essential for camping in **Wellington National Park**, so be sure to reserve your spot in advance online at *exploreparks.dbca.wa.gov.au.*

Bunbury, known as Goomburrup to the local Traditional Owners, may be WA's second-largest city, but with its turquoise waters and white sandy beaches it feels as relaxed as any of the state's coastal towns. It marks the starting point of the Southwest and forms an important juncture where the road splits between Perth, Margaret River and the Southern Forests and coast.

Home to a resident population of wild dolphins, Bunbury is best known for its Dolphin Discovery Centre. It's also home to regional WA's best art gallery and sandy walking trails that make the best of the coastal views.

Beyond Bunbury lies a treasure trove of backroad destinations, from the scenic hills and wineries of the Ferguson Valley to peaceful swimming spots in Wellington National Park and Collie.

There's fun for the kids too, with a village of gnomes, apple picking and a play park for all ages.

Dolphin Encounters & Marine Centre

Meet the dolphins at Koombana Bay

At the not-for-profit **Dolphin Discovery Centre** *(dolphin discovery.com.au; adult/child $23/13)*, a brilliant aquarium and interactive displays showcase geological, Indigenous and marine history.

In the bay you can experience an inquisitive community of bottlenose dolphins that swim right up to shore. A pod of some 60 females live free from captivity here; if the water's calm (no wind or rain) you have a good chance of seeing them in the morning between late October and late March.

From November to April you can **swim with the dolphins** *($220)* and a team of well-trained volunteers or jump on a **boat** *(adult/child $65/45)* departing multiple times daily to witness the dolphins frolicking in their home waters. Tickets can be

SIGHTS

1 Black Diamond Lake
2 Dolphin Discovery Centre
3 Donnybrook Apple Fun Park
4 Gnomesville
5 Green Door
6 Hackersley Estate
7 Lake Kepwari
8 Little Rock
9 Maidens Reserve Lookout
10 Minningup Pool
11 Potter's Gorge
12 Rapids
13 St Aidan Wines
14 Stockton Lake
15 Wellington Dam
16 Willow Bridge Estate

ACTIVITIES

17 Adventure Connections
18 Collie River Trail
19 Honeymoon Pool
20 Jabitj Trail

EATING

21 Bahlu Coffee & Acai Bar
22 Little Spencer Coffee Co
23 Market Eating House
24 White Elephant Thai

TRANSPORT

25 Melo Velo

EATING IN BUNBURY: OUR PICKS

Don't skip the dessert here!

Bahlu Coffee & Acai Bar: Take your pick of creative açai bowls or indulge in the pulled-pork sourdough toastie. *6am-2pm* $$

Little Spencer Coffee Co: Classic Aussie brunch fare with loaded cookies and freshly baked pastries. *6am-3pm Mon-Sat, 7am-2pm Sun* $$

White Elephant Thai: Enjoy generous serves that pack some heat amid walls of traditional Thai decor. *11.30am-2pm Wed-Sat, 5.30-8.30pm Tue-Sun* $$

Market Eating House: Divine shared and large plates comprising wood-fired dishes and seafood. *5.30-10pm Wed, noon-10pm Thu-Sat* $$$

BEST SPOTS TO TAKE A DIP

Former open-cut mines and free-flowing rivers make for great swimming spots.

Minningup Pool: Find locals pulled up along this section of the river and neighbouring 'Sandy' all through summer.

Lake Kepwari: 'Kepwari' means 'playing in water' in the local Willman language. You can jet ski, swim or canoe here.

Black Diamond: People travel from across WA for these turquoise waters. Remember to take your rubbish out with you.

Stockton Lake: This former open-cut mine, 7km east of Collie, is popular for jet skiing.

Honeymoon Pool: Known for its year-round icy waters; a swim here will get your blood flowing.

ALYBABA/SHUTTERSTOCK

Wellington Dam

purchased at the Dolphin Discovery Centre or on its website. Note there is considerable debate about whether these wild encounters are harmful to the dolphins.

Camping, Swimming & Bushwalks

Explore Wellington National Park

Sitting pretty beside the vineyards of the Ferguson Valley, **Wellington National Park** is home to the world's largest dam mural, *Reflections*. On **Wellington Dam**, the 34m-high, 367m-wide work was inspired by stories of local people and can be seen from the **Wellington Dam Lookout**.

You can easily spend a day here wandering through the bush on trails like the **Jabitj Trail**, (12km, two hours). Be sure to cool off at some of the best sections of the Collie River, like **Honeymoon Pool,** the **Rapids** or **Little Rock**. You could make a weekend of it and set up camp at the popular **Honeymoon Pool Campgrounds** *(exploreparks.dbca.wa.gov.au/site/honeymoon-pool-campground; adult/child $20/5)* or serene **Potter's Gorge** *(exploreparks.dbca.wa.gov.au/site/potters-gorge-campground; adult/child $20/5)* to bask in the flora and fauna of the park. Australian ringneck parrots are likely to greet you come morning.

Hit the Trails

Walk or cycle fantastic nature trails

In Bunbury, the **Maidens Reserve Lookout** provides sweeping views over the city on one side and pristine beaches on the other. There's a wheelchair-accessible ramp to the lower lookout and steps leading further up to the top; both locations take 20 minutes or so to reach from the car park. Five short trails have signage on Noongar culture and the surrounding environment.

DISCOVER HARVEY'S HERITAGE BY CAR

Take a scenic inland drive from Pinjarra along the Southwestern Hwy and explore Harvey on your way down south.

START	END	LENGTH
Harvey River Estate	Harvey Cheese	21.7km; 30min

Now an excellent winery, the ❶ **Harvey River Estate** has its roots in cattle and oranges. Harvey Fresh dairy milk and orange juice are stocked at almost every local supermarket and it began here with the Sorgiovanni family. They've sold the company now, but there's still the ❷ **Big Orange Tower**. Climb 62 steps to see historic photographs and take in the view over the orange trees.

Head east to the ❸ **Wildflower Ridge Walk**, a 1.4km loop trail with stunning views over the Harvey Dam Reservoir, before making your way to ❹ **Boola Bidi** for Aboriginal-made giftwares and accessories, or book an educational walking tour or cultural workshop in advance. Wander to the back of the building and grab a bite to eat or simply explore the beautiful gardens at ❺ **Stirling Cottage**, a replica of famed 'Snugglepot and Cuddlepie' (p934) author May Gibbs' home.

For more scenic views, stop at the ❻ **Harvey Dam viewing platform**. Just below, at the ❼ **Gibbs Pool Amphitheatre**, there are plenty of park benches, barbecues and a playground.

On your way out of town, end the Harvey experience at ❽ **Harvey Cheese**. Taste some locally made cheese or try a scoop from the popular Junction Icecreamery.

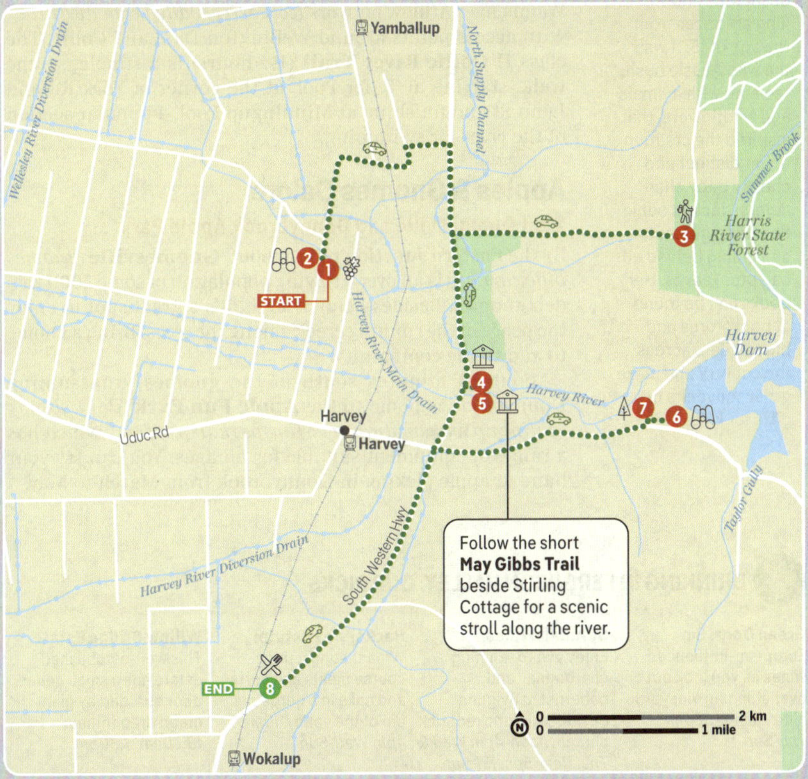

SNUGGLEPOT & CUDDLEPIE

May Gibbs' stories about the gumnut babies, the most iconic being Snugglepot and Cuddlepie, are beloved nationwide. Her works imagine the native flora of Australia as inhabitants of a fantasy bushland and have captivated Australian children for decades.

Gibbs spent her childhood years in Perth and the small township of Harvey, exploring the WA bushlands and winning art prizes from the age of 15. It was the wild Aussie bush, teeming with animals and wildflowers, that inspired the creation of her distinct and cheeky baby characters, decked out in flowering gumnuts and hiding behind eucalyptus leaves. Her books can be found at bookstores and big retailers across the country and make great souvenirs or gifts for kids.

BECAUZ GAO/SHUTTERSTOCK

Gnomesville

Hire an e-bike from **Adventure Connections** *(adventureconnections.com.au; half-/full-day from $95/135)* and hit the dirt on some of WA's best mountain bike trails on the Wambenger Arklow network *(collierivervalley.com.au/trails)*, with access points around Wellington Dam and Collie. The class II **Collie River Trail** (1½ hours) is a simple, serene walk, starting at Telfer Pool, at the corner of York Rd and Lynn St and finishing at Minningup Pool, a popular section of the river for swimming.

Apples & Gnomes Galore

Visit Gnomesville and Donnybrook Apple Park

By the Eastern Junction roundabout, **Gnomesville** *(gnomesville.com.au)* is an ever-growing population of some 5000 garden gnomes. Besides being a sight, it's a great spot to enjoy the peace of the running creek among the trees. Bring a gnome to add to the community.

About 20 minutes south of the gnomes, unassuming Donnybrook is home to the **Apple Fun Park** *(donnybrook-balingup.wa.gov.au/apple-fun-park.aspx; free)*, which has a range of equipment suitable for all ages. You can try your hand at apple picking in Donnybrook from March to May.

DRINKING IN FERGUSON VALLEY: OUR PICKS

Green Door: Sip European-influenced wines as you look out over stunning vineyard hills. *11am-4.30pm Thu-Sun*

St Aidan Wines: Enjoy award-winning chardonnay and cabernet sauvignon beside a historic redbrick church. *noon-4pm Wed & Thu, 11am-5pm Fri-Sun*

Hackersley Estate: Wine tastings, three-course meals and coffee and cake in a gorgeous dip of the valley. *10am-4pm Wed-Sun*

Willow Bridge Estate: This well-established estate has a small cellar door guarded by giant metal dragonflies. *10.30am-4.30pm*

Southern Forests

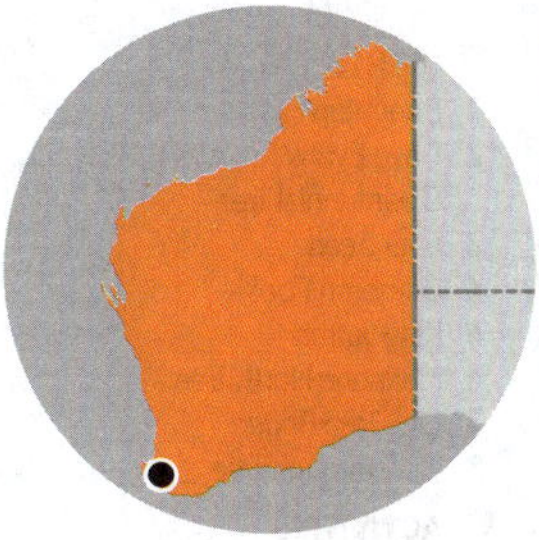

GIANT TREES | TRUFFLES | OUTDOOR ADVENTURE

Lesser known than the beaches and wineries, the ancient forests of WA's south and Southwest offer a stunning change of scenery as you detour inland for a whole new adventure. This region is defined as much by towering karri, jarrah and marri as it is by a succession of picturesque rural towns, each offering unique charm.

The journey starts with Balingup and tiny Greenbushes, a mining town turned sleepy hollow turned mining town again as it rides the wave of the lithium boom. From here you'll pass through sprightly Bridgetown, famous for its music festival; the working town of Manjimup, surrounded by dense forests and farm-gate produce; and, best of all, Pemberton – the perfect base for exploring the region's giant trees.

The mighty forests and flowing rivers have inspired many an artist in these parts. After bathing in the serenity of the region's unique natural charm, you just might be inspired too.

TOP TIP

Some useful online resources for visitors include **Southern Forests and Valley** *(southernforestsandvalleys.com)* and **Southern Forests Food** *(southernforestsfood.com)* for wine trails and gourmet stops.

Bushwalks & Golden Valleys

Admire spectacular foliage in Balingup and Greenbushes

At the entrance to the Southern Forests, **Balingup** makes a spectacular front door in autumn. The best place to experience the season's foliage is the **Golden Valley Tree Park**,

GETTING AROUND

Buses transit through Manjimup and Pemberton via Balingup, but if you plan to explore this region in depth you'll need your own wheels. That way you can detour down enticing side roads or stop anywhere that grabs your attention, whether for a photo stop or for a longer stay.

With that said, this area is made for walkers and cyclists, with the Bibbulmun and Munda Biddi trails immersing you among its karri forests. Mountain bikers will also be in for a treat, with plenty of trails leading through bushland around Pemberton.

SIGHTS
1 Beedelup Falls
2 Dave Evans Bicentennial Tree
3 Four Aces
4 Glenoran Pool
5 King Jarrah
6 Marianne North Tree
7 One Tree Bridge
8 Walkthrough Tree

ACTIVITIES
9 Pemberton Mountain Bike Park
10 Pemberton Pool
11 Pemberton Tramway
12 Understory Art & Nature Trail

EATING
13 Hound & Hunter
14 Treehouse Tapas & Wine
15 Wild at Heart

DRINKING & NIGHTLIFE
16 Jaspers

ENTERTAINMENT
17 State Timber Museum

INFORMATION
18 Northcliffe Visitor Centre
see 17 Manjimup Visitor Centre

TRANSPORT
19 Pemberton Pedals & Paddles

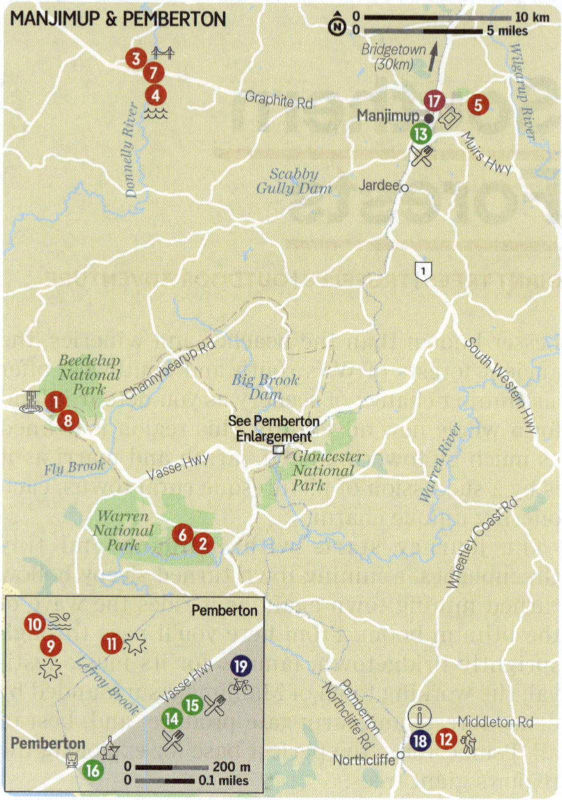

the largest arboretum in WA; it's been around for a century. Stroll among the deciduous trees while their stunning red, orange and yellow leaves fall around you.

Just 10km south of Balingup lies the quiet town of **Greenbushes**. Walk the one-hour looped bush track, punctuated by wildflowers and the calls of black cockatoos, from **Greenbushes Pool** to **Schwenkes Dam**, a historical mining pit turned wetland for birdlife. Alternatively, tackle the full 15km **Greenbushes Loop Walk** (five hours) that includes a small section of the Bibbulmun Track (p944).

The chestnut liqueur is a must-try

EATING & DRINKING IN BRIDGETOWN: OUR PICKS

Bridgetown Hotel: Superb 1920s pub open for lunch and dinner and with a cabinet of homestyle cakes made in-house. *11.30am-2.30pm & 5.30-8pm* **$$**

FATS: Standing for Food, Art, Toys, Santa, FATS does a roaring trade in bagels and coffee, sharing space with a toy store and Christmas shop. *9am-4pm* **$**

Barking Cow: Along Bridgetown's scenic streetscape is this popular cafe doing well-made coffees, brekkie rolls and Angus beef burgers. *8am-2pm* **$**

Cidery & Blackwood Valley Brewing Company: One of the main reasons to visit Bridgetown are the natural ciders and craft beers. *hours vary*

Golden Valley Tree Park (p935)

Fridgetown Festivals & Museums

Take in history and culture in Bridgetown

The grandest town in the region is historical **Bridgetown**, characterised by its pretty streetscape of 19th-century heritage buildings that sprang up during the gold rush. Wander down the main street to come across some of the funkiest cafes, museums and art galleries in the Southwest.

During the **Fridgetown Festival** *(fridgetownfest.com.au)*, the streets come alive for a fun-filled, winter-long calendar of events, while November brings the **Blues at Bridgetown Festival** *(bluesatbridgetown.com.au)*, luring in music lovers from far and wide. Book accommodation well ahead if you plan on joining the festivities.

At the unique and recently upgraded **Jigsaw Puzzle Museum** *(puzzletown6255.com.au)*, printing personalised jigsaws was a coming attraction at research time. Used as a police station until 1973, the **Bridgetown Police Station Museum** *(bridgetownhistoricalsociety.org.au)* touches on the treatment of Indigenous people during colonisation. It's open Wednesday, Friday and Saturday.

WHY I LOVE THE SOUTHERN FORESTS

Emmylou Dzubiel, Lonely Planet writer

The Southern Forests are the perfect escape when it feels as though life is getting on top of you. There's nothing like camping in the national parks, retreating to a chalet among the towering trees or waking up to the sweet song of magpies and falling asleep to the cackling laugh of a kookaburra.

In winter the misty forests take on a magical quality, while the warmer months are perfect for floating in rivers and picnicking among the wildlife. The towns are quiet and filled with quirky cafes, homemade jams and condiments, and unique artworks just waiting to be discovered. I always leave with a new treasure in hand, feeling calmer and more grounded than when I arrived.

EATING IN MANJIMUP & PEMBERTON: OUR PICKS

Jaspers: Intimate whisky bar with a menu of regional produce from garlic-and-butter marron to truffle-infused dishes. *noon-2pm & 5-9.30pm Tue-Sat* $$$

Wild at Heart: Go-to cafe for creative, house-made breakfasts and lunches from falafel plates to delicious cakes. *8am-2.30pm* $$

Treehouse Tapas & Wine: Popular, cosy bar offering Pemberton wines matched superbly with enticing tapas. *5-10pm Fri, 4-10pm Sat, 4-9pm Sun* $$$

The best pastries in Manjimup

Hound & Hunter: Makes the most of Manjimup's prized truffles, with gourmet pies, sausage rolls and pâté. *8.30am-2.30pm Mon-Sat, 9am-2.30pm Sun* $$

TOP FIVE SOUTHERN FORESTS FESTIVALS

Nannup Music Festival: Held over the Labour Day long weekend in March, with local and international talent, food, artisan markets and more.

Blues at Bridgetown: Come November, this sleepy town does blues and roots music. The iconic street party is a day not to be missed.

Truffle Kerfuffle: Bucket-list festival for foodies, in celebration of the world-famous black Périgord truffle.

CinéfestOZ: Held across the Southwest to promote local and Indigenous filmmakers.

Balingup Medieval Carnivale: Guests and performers don their finest medieval gear for archery, combat and pints of mead.

CHAMELEONSEYE/SHUTTERSTOCK

Pemberton Mountain Bike Park

The **Bridgetown-Greenbushes Visitor Centre** *(bridgetown.wa.gov.au)*, recently moved to the Heritage Railway station, is also worth a visit for its art gallery.

Art Meets Nature

Engage with unique artwork in Bridgetown and Northcliffe

Near Bridgetown's entrance is the **Perrier Sculpture Park** *(perrier.com.au)*, a wondrous display of works by acclaimed artist Kim Perrier in his front garden. Particularly eye-catching are the charcoal bodies and faces delicately carved into the trunks of trees. For entry, pop a $2 coin into the frog's mouth in the garden's centre.

In Bridgetown, wander down the stairs to the **Rabbit Hole** *(facebook.com/rabbitholebridgetown)*, where more of Perrier's charcoal faces hide in its backyard.

Journey 90km south of Bridgetown to Northcliffe, where Perrier's tree people make an appearance along the **Understory Art & Nature Trail** *(understory.com.au; adult/child $15/10)*, a 45-minute bushwalk featuring art installations nestled among native plants. Buy tickets at the **Northcliffe Visitor Centre**, which is also the entrance to the trail.

Forests Around Manjimup

Get to know karri and jarrah country

Before heading out to the magnificent trees around Manjimup, learn about their history at the **State Timber Museum** *(manjimupheritagepark.com.au; adult/child $5/2)*. Buy tickets at the next-door **visitor centre**.

Just northeast of town is a 600m-return bushwalk to the 500-year-old **King Jarrah**, standing 47m tall. En route you'll pass **Queejup's Birth Tree**, a section of the tree beneath which the legendary Noongar stockman was born; it was cut down for roadworks along Balbaraup Rd and transported here. Queejup was refused treatment at Busselton hospital for pneumonia, the ultimate cause of his death. Here you'll also read about Noongar culture during the colonial period.

Heading west, 22km from Manjimup is a remnant of **One Tree Bridge**, a karri log that timber workers felled to cross the 25m Donnelly River. Beside the main bridge that replaced it sits a suspension bridge used by riders and walkers on the Munda Biddi Trail and Bibbulmun Track. From here it's a 20-minute walk along a secluded bush path to the **Four Aces**, a row of four giant karri trees that rise 75m and are up to 400 years old. If the sun's out, bring your bathers for a dip in **Glenoran Pool**, one of the Southern Forests' many popular water holes for wild swimming.

By Tram, Bike or Water

Explore Pemberton

Hire a bike from **Pemberton Pedals & Paddles** at the general store and hit one of the 43 world-class trails zipping through karri forest at **Pemberton Mountain Bike Park**. A more leisurely way to explore the forests is aboard the **Pemberton Tramway**, which follows tracks built for the timber industry in the 1920s.

Or float peacefully in the **Pemberton Pool**, a natural lap pool and wider swimming area established in the 1920s, and appreciate the forest all around.

Historic Trees

Prepare to be stopped in your tracks

From Pemberton, a drive along the 12km **Heartbreak Trail** will take you to the **Marianne North Tree**, made famous by a painting, and the 65m-tall **Dave Evans Bicentennial Tree**, the last of three famous fire-viewing platform trees that's still safe enough to climb, at least to the first platform, 20m above the ground.

Venture 20km west of town to **Beedelup Falls** and walk 20 minutes to the **Walkthrough Tree**, where the artificial hole from 1971 is slowly closing over but can still be stepped through. In spring, spider orchids line the 15-minute scenic walk to the lookout and swinging bridge here.

SEASONAL BITES

Often referred to as the food bowl of WA, the Southwest boasts a diverse range of high-quality gourmet produce. Manjimup's home to the biggest producers of black Périgord truffles in the southern hemisphere, with 92% of Australia's truffles coming from the Southwest. Responsible for 85% of the state's production, Manjimup is also known for its bright, juicy cherries, available from late October to February.

Over in Pemberton, the climate, the soil quality and high water levels make the ideal environment for growing avocados – the town held its first festival in honour of the delicious breakfast favourite in November 2025. Carry cash and keep an eye out for roadside stalls selling fresh farm produce throughout the Southern Forests.

Albany & Around

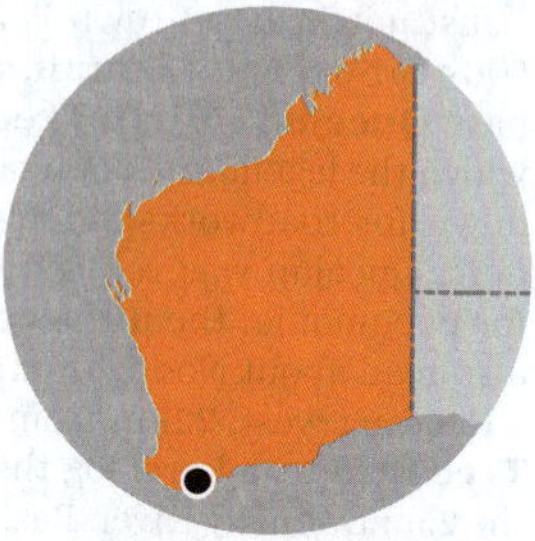

TREETOP WALK | BEACHES | WINERIES

☑ TOP TIP
To avoid the spread of dieback (p945) in these protected areas, use shoe-cleaning stations where available and stick to designated paths.

Welcome to Albany, WA's oldest town, a port city settled by the British in 1826 as a military outpost to thwart the perceived threat of French claims to the region. Formerly known as Kinjarling, a name still in use by the Indigenous Menang Noongar people and officially reclaimed by the City of Albany, the town is a perfect combination of modern convenience and country hospitality in one of the most picturesque locations along WA's coastline.

It remains a proud, working-class port, with whaling heritage, historical sights and nature-loving locals. Here you'll find some of the state's best museums covering its storied past, mixed with the urban culture of streetart trails, renowned restaurants, city beaches and superb coastal attractions.

Surrounding Albany is an enticing region of natural drawcards taking in sublime forest and stunning shores, with wineries and outdoor adventure adding to the appeal. Stirling Range and Porongurup national parks are also nearby.

Journey into Albany's Past

Indigenous and Anzac history

In 1914 Australia's first deployment of soldiers embarked from Albany on their perilous journey to the WWI battlefields. Part of the 250-hectare **Albany Heritage Park**, the **National**

GETTING AROUND

Daily flights from Perth and car-hire options make this the gateway town to the Great Southern region. **Albany Bicycle Hire** *(albanybicyclehire.com.au)* can arrange e-bikes for those tackling the Munda Biddi Trail.

Many sights within the city can be reached on foot, but without a car you'll need a taxi or local bus to get beyond that; see *pta.wa.gov.au/our-services/transregional* for schedules. Buses run to Walpole and Denmark, but without your own wheels, getting to the beaches, wineries and Valley of the Giants is tricky.

Local operators offering transport include **Naturally Walpole** and **Blue Wren**.

EMMA JONES/SHUTTERSTOCK

National Anzac Centre

Anzac Centre *(nationalanzaccentre.com.au; adult/child $25/11)* commemorates this history. You can take an interactive journey following the experiences of individual soldiers.

Albany's **Museum of the Great Southern** *(visit.museum.wa.gov.au/greatsouthern; free)* offers excellent coverage of Indigenous Menang culture, marine life, wartime history and Albany's evolution as a port city. Hop aboard the brig *Amity* for free or explore below deck for $5 ($2 for kids) and get a taste of what life was like on a convict ship.

Outside the visitor centre is a **statue of Mokare**. Read all about the Menang man's role as a guide and peace bringer with early settlers in the 1800s.

Join Noongar-run cultural tours with **Kurrah Mia** *(kurrahmia.com.au; adult/child $110/50),* where knowledgeable Larry Blight describes the lives of Indigenous communities some 40,000 years ago while pointing out their movements on Albany's spectacular backdrop.

Wander 15km northeast of town to the remains of innovative Indigenous fish traps at **Kaatboonup**; they're best viewed at low tide from the boardwalk.

Continued on p944

NATIONAL PARK FEES & PASSES

Purchasing a **national parks pass** *(shop.dbca.wa.gov.au)* is a good way to save some dollars while travelling in WA. The annual **All Parks Pass** *(per vehicle $130)* is the perfect all-rounder, allowing unlimited entry to all of WA's national parks for one full year. For shorter stays, the **Holiday Pass** *(per vehicle 5 days/14 days/4 weeks $30/50/70)* offers unlimited entry for a given period, while the **Annual Local Park Pass** *(per vehicle $30)* gives unlimited entry to a single national park; the latter is usually of most use to locals. Single entry into any of the national parks is generally $17 per vehicle.

EATING IN ALBANY: OUR PICKS

Bred co Sourdough Bakery: Flour is milled on-site from grains grown just 70km away to make gorgeous breads, pastries and sausage rolls. *6.30am-2pm* $

Ocean & Paddock: It ain't a proper seaside holiday without fish and chips and these guys do some of WA's best. *11am-8pm Tue-Sun* $$

Liberté: In a heritage hotel, this wonderful option pairs French-Vietnamese shared dishes with local wines. *11.30am-10.30pm Tue-Thu, to 11.30pm Fri, to midnight Sat* $$

Majuba: Exquisite modern European dishes draw on regional produce and seafood. Affordable lunchtime menu. *5-10pm Tue, noon-2pm & 5-10pm Wed-Sat* $$$

ALBANY & AROUND

- **SIGHTS**
- 1 Albany Heritage Park
- 2 Castle Rock Estate
- 3 Conspicuous Cliffs
- 4 Ducketts Mill Wines & Denmark Farmhouse Cheese
- 5 Duke's Vineyard
- 6 Gap
- 7 Greens Pool
- 8 Kaatboonup
- 9 Little Beach
- 10 Madfish Bay
- 11 Mazzoletti Beach
- 12 Misery Beach
- 13 Mt Barker
- 14 Museum of the Great Southern
- 15 National Anzac Centre
- see 6 Natural Bridge
- 16 Porongurup National Park
- 17 Statue of Mokare
- 18 Torndirrup National Park
- 19 Two Peoples Bay
- 20 Valley of the Giants
- 21 Waterfall Beach
- 22 William Bay National Park

- **ACTIVITIES**
- 23 Bibbulmun Track
- see 16 Granite Skywalk
- 24 Kurrah Mia
- 25 Naturally Walpole Tours
- 26 WOW Wilderness Ecocruises

SLEEPING
27 1849 Backpackers
28 Blue Wren Travellers' Rest YHA
29 Karribank
30 Six Degrees

EATING
31 Bred co Sourdough Bakery
32 Denmark Chocolate Company
33 Denmark Good Food Factory
34 Flame Trees
35 Ironwood Estate Wines
36 Kindfolk Coffee
37 Majuba
38 Mt Barker Country Bakery
39 Ocean & Paddock

DRINKING & NIGHTLIFE
40 Bar Tarifa
41 Denmark Tavern
42 Liberté

SHOPPING
43 Bartholomews Meadery

TRANSPORT
44 Albany Bicycle Hire

THE BIBBULMUN

If you're a hiker, chances are you've heard of the **Bibbulmun Track**, a 1000km walking trail inspired by a long-distance hike through the Victorian Alps and stretching from the hills of Kalamunda near Perth all the way down to Albany. It takes most people six to eight weeks to complete, with the fastest time (unsupported) recorded at just over 16 days by local hiker Cam Bostock.

Opened in 1979, this recreational bush track is named after the Bibbulmun, one of the 14 Noongar groups belonging to WA, who are known to have walked long distances across the Southwest for changing seasons and cultural activities. The name was chosen with the hope that trail walkers would move along it with the same connection and respect for *boodja* (land or country) as the Bibbulmun.

DARKYDOORS/SHUTTERSTOCK

Continued from p941

Albany's Wild Natural Playground

Visit Torndirrup National Park

Not far from Albany, **Torndirrup National Park** *(per vehicle $17)* includes stunning coastal attractions the **Gap**, a walkway leading over a clifftop with views down to the hypnotic froth of the Southern Ocean and **Natural Bridge**. Further along is **Bald Head**, a coastal trail (12.5km, eight hours) delivering extraordinary vistas.

Misery Beach is much nicer than it sounds (or these days, anyway) and was named Australia's best beach in 2022 by Tourism Australia. It's come a long way from the whaling days when washed-up offal stunk it out while staining its white sands red.

On the other side of Albany, the important **Two Peoples Bay** reserve housing the critically endangered noisy scrub bird has an unmanned interactive visitor centre to explore. Nearby **Little Beach** is another treasure.

Climb into the Treetops

Valley of the Giants canopy walk

The red tingle, a eucalyptus species endemic to the Walpole region, can grow 75m tall and live for over 400 years. Known as particularly fire resistant, they're unique for their buttressed bases that can span 25m. Get up close to them at the **Valley of the Giants**.

The main attraction is the **Treetop Walk** *(treetopwalk.com.au; adult/child $21/10.50)*, a superb 600m suspension walk leading 40m up through the canopy of old-growth forest so you can admire the towering trees from special viewpoints. A second section hosts the **Ancient Empire Walk** *(free)*, a ground-level nature trail on an elevated boardwalk. Free

The Gap, Torndirrup National Park

tours run at 11am and 2pm for those interested in learning more. Tingle root systems are shallow and incredibly sensitive, making both ground and treetop paths a protective way for visitors to walk among the trees.

Taste Your Way Through Denmark

Cheese, chocolate, honey and condiments

Denmark has a wealth of culinary delights. At **Ducketts Mill Wines** & **Denmark Farmhouse Cheese** *(duckettsmillwines.com.au; tastings $5)* you can taste eight very different cheeses; the blue and camembert are particularly impressive. Or enjoy a platter on the verandah with a glass of one of its award-winning wines.

Sample several types of European chocolate pistole at **Denmark Chocolate Company** *(denmarkchocolate.com.au)* and leave with some of its handmade bonbons or a bottle of chocolate liqueur.

See the bees at work at **Bartholomews Meadery** *(honeywine.com.au)* and try sweet mead, local honeys and flavoured honey products like black sesame honey.

At **Denmark Good Food Factory** *(denmarkgoodfoodfactory.com.au)*, taste heavenly fudge and a wide range of condiments, including spiced asparagus chutney.

DEADLY DIEBACK

Phytophthora dieback is a destructive plant disease that causes root rot, killing or causing the dieback of plants, hence the name. Caused by a group of introduced soil-borne water moulds (*Phytophthora*, meaning 'plant killer' in Greek), it can spread to different areas by direct contact from contaminated shoes and tyres and stock movement. Its rapid destruction of native vegetation directly affects wildlife and disrupts entire ecosystems.

Over 40% of WA's native plant species are susceptible to dieback and over 10,000 sq km are, sadly, already infected. To avoid the spread of dieback, be sure to stick to designated paths in bushland and keep shoes and tyres clean when moving between areas. The **Dieback Working Group Inc** *(dwg.org.au)* is a great resource.

EATING & DRINKING IN DENMARK: OUR PICKS

Kindfolk Coffee: A beautiful selection of wholesome homemade cakes and slices to enjoy with your morning cuppa. *7.30am-1pm Mon, Tue & Fri, 8am-1pm Sat & Sun* $

Flame Trees: At this stylish, moody venue, indulge in an intimate Mediterranean-influenced meal using local ingredients. *4-9pm Thu-Sat, 4-8pm Sun & Mon* $$$

Bar Tarifa: Boisterous Spanish-owned wine bar with atmospheric front bar and rooftop deck for tapas and vino. *5-10pm Tue-Sat* $$

Denmark Tavern: Local favourite and unpretentious pub with a great beer garden, craft beers and classic pub food. *11am-midnight Mon-Sat, to 10pm Sun* $$

WILDLIFE OF THE SOUTHWEST

The Southwest's stunning flora make up a big part of the region's status as a world biodiversity hot spot, but don't forget its other wildlife. Western grey kangaroos and brush-tailed and ringtail possums are common, while the black-gloved wallaby, quenda (southern brown bandicoot), chuditch (Western quoll), quokka and honey possum are also residents to keep an eye out for.

Emus always make for popular sightings, but there are 16 endemic bird species in the region, including the red-tailed black cockatoo, Carnaby's black cockatoo, western rosella and red-winged fairy wren. Reptiles include legless lizards, shinglebacks, southwestern snake-necked turtles and southern heath monitors. Stay well away from tiger snakes.

Coastal Wonders

Find your favourite beach from Denmark to Walpole

Around 20km west of Denmark you'll find a string of sublime beaches within **William Bay National Park**. Journey to **Greens Pool**, popular for its exquisite green-tinged turquoise waters and fine white sands enclosed by granite rocks.

A short drive further are **Waterfall Beach** and **Madfish Bay**. Head west for more long, isolated stretches of surf beach, including the 7km **Mazzoletti Beach** and **Conspicuous Cliffs**, with breathtaking lookouts onto passing whales from June to September.

Exercise great caution in the strong rips if you swim at these surf beaches.

Walpole on Water

Cruise the Nornalup Inlet

Step into Gary (Gazza) Muir's classroom on water with **WOW Wilderness Ecocruises** *(wowwilderness.com.au; adult/child $63.27/21.50)* in Walpole, which has even locals coming on board to enjoy the renowned lemon tingle cake and Gazza's Oscar-worthy storytelling. Absorb the history of this dynamic region, from tales of Tolstoy to Walpole's super quokkas, on this 90-minute cruise along the scenic waters of the Nornalup Inlet, with the option to trek through native bushland to a secluded beach.

WOW also runs day and multiday mountain biking, packrafting and hiking adventures.

A Ruggedly Beautiful Park

Hike the Stirling Range

Located 80km north of Albany, the 1156-sq-km **Stirling Range National Park** *(per vehicle $17)* is one of WA's premier hiking destinations. From late August to November you'll be treated to its stunning array of native blooms – over 1500 species of flora live here.

Its signature trail is **Bluff Knoll** (1095m; 6km return, three to four hours), the park's highest mountain, which rewards with astounding summit views. Before starting the trek, drive out to the Bluff Knoll Car Park and read about the significance of the mountain to Indigenous communities.

Other peaks include **Toolbrunup** (1052m; 4km return), **Mt Hassell** (848m; 3km return) and **Mt Trio** (856m; 3.5km return). The ridgeline trek from **Bluff Knoll to Ellen Peak** (28.8km, two to three days) will entice more serious, well-prepared hikers.

Vineyards & Wilderness in Porongurup

Feast your eyes on panoramic views

Only 40km north of Albany, **Porongurup National Park** *(per vehicle $17)* is a 24-sq-km tract of wilderness within easy reach of the city.

LEANNE IRWIN/SHUTTERSTOCK

Bluff Knoll

Most hikers are here for the memorable **Granite Skywalk** (4km return, two hours) that leads up to Castle Rock. Starting through karri, jarrah and marri forest, it's a fairly steep climb to reach the impressive Balancing Rock, from where there's a scramble over granite using handrails for the 7m-high enclosed-ladder climb to the top. Awaiting is a glass-panelled walkway that takes in far-reaching views over the coast and Stirling Range.

Surrounding the national park are Porongurup's wineries, with small, intimate cellar doors and unbeatable views.

THE SACRED BEAUTY OF BORONGUR

Many venture to the Porongurups to clamber their way up to the spectacular Granite Skywalk, but for Noongar people there's only one time to climb the mountains here. The Porongurup Ranges, known as Borongur to the region's original inhabitants, are a culturally and spiritually sacred site for Indigenous people.

In Aboriginal culture, people have multiple totems (spiritual emblems from nature connecting them to country, their nation and their people). Some are passed down from parents, while others are discovered. For thousands of years, young people reaching maturity have come to Borongur to discover their totem. Hiking by visitors is welcome, but always be respectful of the land's cultural significance.

Go Under the Wine Radar

Mt Barker's wine region

Around 50km north of Albany, lovely **Mt Barker** lies en route to Porongurup and Stirling Range National Parks. Its grape production contributes significantly to the 37% of WA's grapes that come from the Great Southern. Sample cool-climate varietals at a dozen or so cellar doors; the riesling, chardonnay and pinot noir are standouts.

EATING & DRINKING IN PORONGURUP: OUR PICKS

Castle Rock Estate: Small, family-run estate with uninterrupted views of the Stirling Ranges. *10am-4.30pm*

Duke's Vineyard: James Halliday awarded Australian Wine of the Year to a Duke's riesling and it's not to be missed. *11am-4.30pm Fri-Mon*

Ironwood Estate Wines: Boutique winery with a cafe attached to its cellar door. The orange-and-almond cake is a sure-fire hit. *11am-5pm Thu-Sun* $

Mt Barker Country Bakery: Next door to Porongurup, this popular bakery has award-winning pies and a range of sweet pastries worth travelling for. *5am-4pm* $

Fitzgerald Biosphere Coast & Around

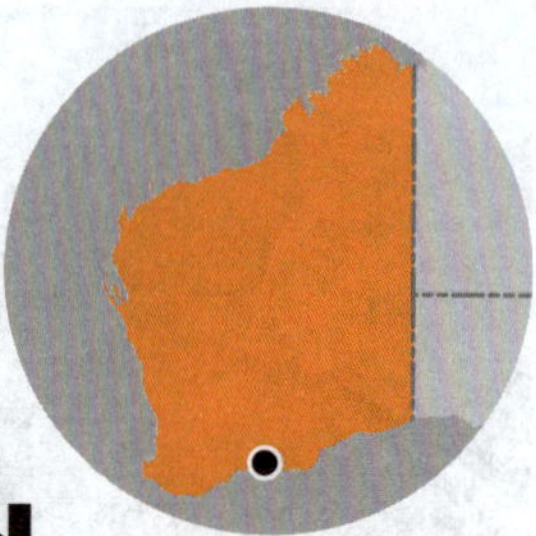

WHALES | BEACHES | WALKS

TOP TIP
There are no bins in the park; you'll need to carry out everything you take in. Stop by the **Bremer Bay Community Resource Centre** *(bremerbaywa.com.au)* or check the **park website** *(exploreparks.dbca.wa.gov.au)* for road conditions and closures.

Home to some of the nation's best beaches, this section of WA has a jaw-dropping effect, complemented by its laid-back coastal atmosphere.

It's a long drive between the south coast's major towns of Albany and Esperance, so it's fortunately that the area of Fitzgerald River National Park is perfectly positioned halfway. As WA's only biosphere reserve, it's much more than a convenient stopover; it's a destination in itself.

Joining onto the western section of the park is Bremer Bay, the best place in Australia to see orcas (killer whales), regularly spotted offshore during the summer months and bringing the crowds with them. On the eastern end is the coastal holiday town of Hopetoun, offering great camping and easy access to some of the park's highlights.

Further east, Esperance has one of the best coastal drives in the state, as well as some of the iciest waters.

Whale Watching in Bremer Bay

Orcas in summer, southern rights in winter

When it comes to cetaceans, Bremer Bay has double the luck: in winter southern right whales pass through and in summer it sees one of the largest congregations of orcas in the

GETTING AROUND

You'll need a car. All access points – Bremer Bay, Jerramungup and Hopetoun – are off the main highway, from where it's around a half- to one-hour drive south. Buses do run past the turn offs but only get you halfway to where you're going. Fitzgerald River National Park has a network of dirt roads leading to its walking trails, but a lot of the park is inaccessible during the winter months following heavy rainfall. To see orcas you'll need to organise a tour with a whale-watching operator.

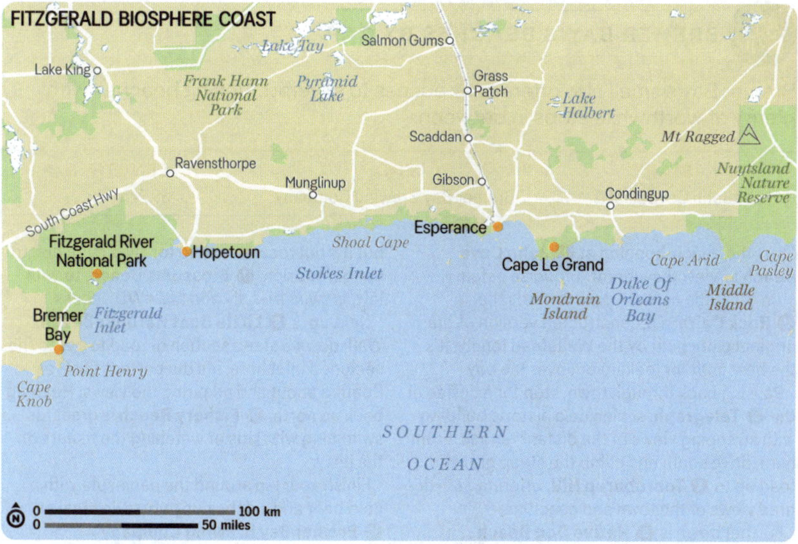

southern hemisphere. From December to April **Naturaliste Charters** *(naturalistecharters.com.au; adult/child $399/329)* runs eight-hour round-trip tours on which it says there's a 96% chance of seeing the orcas. An on-board pro photographer will take pictures on the day, so you can enjoy the sights with your own eyes. Book accommodation in Bremer Bay well ahead if you visit when the orcas do.

Wildflowers & Coastal Wilderness

Witness untamed beauty in Fitzgerald River National Park

Set over 3300 sq km of pristine wilderness, the UNESCO Biosphere Reserve of **Fitzgerald River National Park** *(parks.dpaw.wa.gov.au/park/fitzgerald-river; per vehicle $17)* is one of the world's most significant floral areas, with more than 1800 unique species of flora and half of WA's orchid species. The park is also home to 22 mammal and 184 bird species. A vast network of bushwalking trails, beautiful white-powder beaches, coastal drives and lookouts round out its appeal to nature lovers.

On the eastern side, the fully sealed southern section of Hamersley Dr runs through the park from Hopetoun to some of its nicest beaches (**Four Mile**, **Barrens**, **Mylies** and **West**) and **Cave Point** lookout. For downloadable maps, brochures and road-closure information, visit WA's **Parks and Wildlife website** *(exploreparks.dbca.wa.gov.au)*.

Hanging out in Hopetoun

Relax by the seaside

Even if there wasn't the national park on its doorstep, the township of Hopetoun is worth a visit. Not only can you easily

BREMER BAY'S BEACHES BY CAR

Bremer Bay's small size offers easy access to several stunning beaches with plenty of worthwhile stops in between.

START	END	LENGTH
John Cove Beach	Bremer Bay Brewing Company	39.2km; 1hr

Start the beach-hopping at 1 **John Cove Beach** to view the vibrant turquoise estuary. Turn off at the caravan park towards the 2 **Rock Cairn**, a reconstructed version of the original cairn built by the Wellstead family. It's the best spot for looking out over the bay.

Passing back through town, stop for a coffee at the 3 **Telegraph**, set inside a historic building with sweeping views of the distant ranges. From here, drive south and climb the steep gravel road up to 4 **Tooroburup Hill**, offering 360-degree views of the town and coastline.

Further down is 5 **Native Dog Beach Lookout**. 6 **Native Dog Beach** is to your right, but it's not recommended for swimming due to dangerous rips; 7 **Blossoms Beach**, to your left, is swim friendly and has 4WD access.

Next up is 8 **Little Boat Harbour Beach**. Walk down a steep section of road to get to the secluded inlet here; it's the perfect spot for floating about and admiring the views. Heading back up north, 9 **Fishery Beach** is great for swimming with kids or watching the fishers on the jetty.

Finish your lap around the peninsula with a cold beer and a delicious pub-style meal at 10 **Bremer Bay Brewing Company**.

KAREL STIPEK/SHUTTERSTOCK

Blue Haven

make day trips into its wilderness area, but the town's beaches feature soft white sands and aquamarine waters. Enjoy a meal at the local pubs and soak up the great outdoors.

Head 47km further east on an unsealed but 2WD-accessible road to **Starvation Bay**. Despite its name, the bay's a welcoming spot with family-friendly camping just metres from the water's edge and swimming lessons held every January.

Esperance's Great Ocean Drive

Gaze at miles of beautiful beaches

You're spoilt for choice when it comes to finding a good beach in Esperance. The best can be reached along a scenic 18km stretch of coastal road.

Start at the **Rotary Lookout (Taananeditj)**, a significant site for the Wudjari Traditional Owners. Follow the 20-minute Rotary Walk to the best seat in town, overlooking the coast.

Continue down Twilight Beach Rd to a string of blue-water beaches with dramatic white sand. Best for swimming are **West Beach**, **Blue Haven**, **Twilight Beach**, **Nine Mile Beach** and **Ten Mile Lagoon**, while **Fourth Beach** is popular for surfing. They don't call Esperance 'nature's ice bath'

THE PIRATE OF ESPERANCE

Esperance's Wudjari name, Kepa Kurl (Water Boomerang), refers to the shape of the bay. Archaeological finds on Middle Island suggest that it was occupied before the last ice age, when it was still part of the mainland. The town received its current name in 1792 when the *Recherche* and *Espérance* sailed into the bay to shelter from a storm. In the 1820s and 1830s the Recherche Archipelago was home to Australia's only pirate, **Black Jack Anderson**, an American whaler who supposedly jumped ship, living on Kangaroo Island before heading to Middle Island. From here, he raided ships, killed Aboriginal men and abducted their wives. He was eventually murdered in his sleep by one of his own men.

You can't pass up the vanilla slice here

EATING & DRINKING IN ESPERANCE: OUR PICKS

Lucky Bay Brewery: At the only brewery in WA sourcing barley direct from local farmers, enjoy a pint in the outdoor area. *11.30am-8pm Thu & Sat-Mon, to 9pm Fri*

Bistro Louis: A local favourite for French-inspired brunch and a good cup of coffee. *10am-2pm & 5.30-8pm Thu & Fri, 8.30am-2pm & 5.30-8pm Sat, 8.30am-2pm Sun* **$$**

Quarters: Contemporary Australian cuisine in a historic building moved all the way from Perth to Esperance. *10am-late Wed-Fri, 8am-late Sat & Sun* **$$$**

Bread Local: This place makes some of the best cakes and pastries in the Southwest. *8am-2pm Thu & Sat, to 4pm Fri* **$**

DISCOVERING WILDFLOWERS IN THE SOUTHWEST

Sue Leighton, Ravensthorpe Wildflower Show Coordinator *(wildflowersravensthorpe.org.au)*

When out looking for wildflowers, it's best to get away from main roads and head towards gravel pits, where more unusual plants are found. Remember to take only photos; it's against the law to pick them.

Ticks are prevalent here, so use insect repellent and wear gaiters over your footwear to help protect yourself. Snake bandages are also handy to have and can be found at most chemists. They could save your life.

Wildflowers bloom year-round, but they're most abundant from August to October. For two weeks in September the **Ravensthorpe Wildflower Show and Herbarium** showcases over 700 species of wildflower found in the Southwest.

TRAVELLINGDEDE/SHUTTERSTOCK

Lucky Bay

for nothing: the water temperatures remain fairly chilly but refreshing year-round.

Be sure to stop at **Chapman's Point** and **Observatory Point** along the way for phenomenal views above the beaches. Finish at **Eleven Mile Lagoon**, a local favourite for its rock pools. It's particularly beautiful at sunset.

Natural Wonders of Cape Le Grand

Hike between sublime beaches

With its luminous sapphire waters, it's no wonder **Lucky Bay** took out top spot in The World's 50 Best Beaches 2023. If it lives up to its name, you'll see kangaroos on its sands. (Don't feed them or get too close.)

Lucky Bay makes up part of **Cape Le Grand National Park**, where you'll find similarly stunning beaches at **Hellfire Bay** and **Thistle Cove**, along with **Le Grand Beach** and **Rossiter Bay** (4WD access only). All are interconnected along **Le Grand Coastal Hiking Trail** (15km one way), which meanders through wildflower-filled heathland and beaches. The hike up to **Frenchman Peak** (262m; 3km, three hours) is another popular walk.

Push on 75km further to the stunning **Wharton Beach**, a favourite with Esperance locals.

Kalgoorlie-Boulder & Around

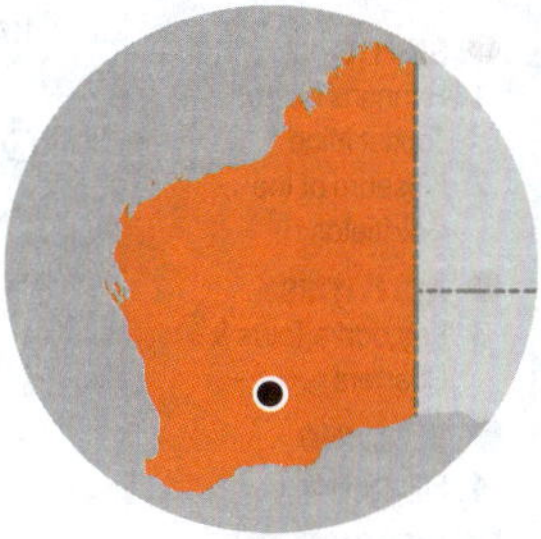

HERITAGE STREETS | GOLDFIELD HISTORY | OUTBACK ATMOSPHERE

When it comes to Aussie outback towns, names don't come much more iconic than Kalgoorlie. Emerging from vast, dusty ochre landscapes is this thriving goldfields settlement, WA's fifth-largest town, and it remains as vital today as when they first struck gold here back in the 1890s.

This region isn't just rich in gold; it's also rich with history. From the land's significance to Aboriginal communities to the diverse cultures that made their way into town for the gold rush, there's a lot to learn in this isolated town. Admire the unique flora in Kalgoorlie's arid landscapes and learn about the 12 languages that have been spoken on the plains of this region for centuries.

Inland, Hyden is another significant township whose surrounds are dotted with historical Indigenous and landscape sites, including the renowned Wave Rock. It's worth spending a night camping out under the stars here.

GETTING AROUND

Kalgoorlie is a major mining town where many workers are of the fly-in, fly-out (FIFO) variety, so it's better connected by flights from Perth than most other regional WA towns. Otherwise, it's a 597km drive (seven hours) across from the capital. The *Prospector* train runs daily from East Perth (seven hours).

Car is by far the best way of getting around, with rental options at the airport or downtown. You can hire bikes at the **visitor centre** *(kalgoorlietourism.com)*. Local buses and taxis are also an option.

Katter Kich can be reached by bus, but to explore other sites you'll need a car.

Prospecting Museums & Panning for Gold

Journey through decades of mining in Kalgoorlie

With its grand 19th-century streetscape lined with heritage buildings, little has changed in Kalgoorlie over the past 100 years.

The **Museum of the Goldfields** *(visit.museum.wa.gov.au/goldfields; free)* takes you back to where the rush began, when gold was discovered here in 1893. Fronted by the Ivanhoe-mine head frame, it's a treasure-filled stop with giant nuggets and gold bars displayed in its underground vault. Further north, **Hannans North Tourist Mine** *(hannans north.com.au; adult/child $18/10)* is one of Kalgoorlie's first registered mines. As well as learning about all the hardships of life on the mines, kids of all ages will want to clamber up to colossal 793C

SIGHTS
1 Hannans North Tourist Mine
2 Museum of the Goldfields

ACTIVITIES
3 Kalgoorlie Tours & Charters

SLEEPING
4 Palace Hotel

INFORMATION
5 Visitor Centre

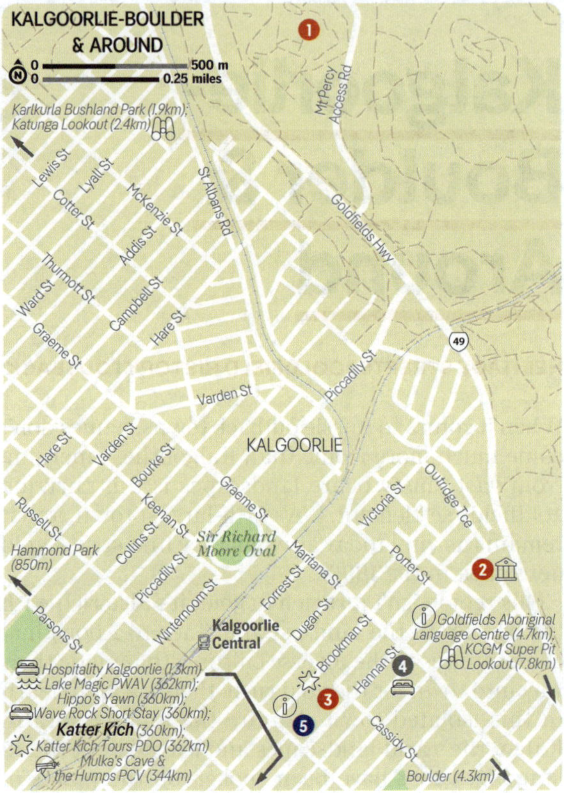

haul trucks and try their luck at panning for Kalgoorlie gold.

Further south, the **KCGM Super Pit Lookout** gives a birds-eye view of one of Earth's largest open-cut mines, a viewpoint that has changed over the years to accommodate the changing shape of the pit. Take a closer look into the Super Pit operations with **Kalgoorlie Tours & Charters** *(kalgoorlietours.com.au; adult/child $70/41)*

TOP TIP

Mobile phone service can be hard to come by when travelling through these inland towns. Come prepared with physical and offline maps, as well as plenty of snacks and water, and plan your stops in advance.

Bushwalks & Animal Sanctuaries

Explore the desert greenery

One of six regenerative zones forming a green belt around Kalgoorlie-Boulder, **Karlkurla Bushland Park** is part of the largest remaining area of intact Mediterranean climate woodland on Earth. An easy 30-minute walk along the paved trail here takes you to Kalgoorlie's highest point, **Katunga Lookout**, with panoramic views that stretch all around. There's well-placed signage along the 7km of sealed trails with information about the unique plants of the woodlands and their significance for Indigenous peoples. Nearby, **Hammond Park** is another popular place for respite in nature, with all

Katunga Lookout

manner of native wildlife roaming through and around the park; it's the perfect spot to picnic among the peacocks.

WA's Famous Katter Kich

See colossal Wave Rock

One of WA's most spectacular natural wonders, the wave-shaped rock 360km southwest of Kalgoorlie is known as **Katter Kich** *(Wave Rock; per vehicle $15)*. Streaked with colours created by runoff from local mineral springs, this crested granite wave stands at an impressive 15m high and 110m long. The acoustic effects are impressive, with sounds travelling its length.

The entrance fee, which can be paid at the kiosk or by using the car park ticket machine, includes a visit to the fantastic **Hippo's Yawn**, 1km east of Katter Kich. This granite cave, eroded from the base of a big orange boulder, does indeed resemble the gaping jaws of a yawning hippo. Noongar guide Michael Ward runs highly recommended morning and evening **Katter Kich Tours** *(katterkichtours.com.au; $110)*, connecting people to Country and teaching the ancient history of the land.

For an additional entrance fee (adult/child $10/5), you can visit chameleon-like **Lake Magic**, which, depending on the time, is a striking green, yellow or orange; it's very popular with Instagrammers.

Another site not to be missed is **Mulka's Cave** *(free)*. A further 18km north of Katter Kich, this is an immensely important cultural site for Nyaki-Nyaki people and one of WA's most significant rock art sites. Step into the chill of the cave before walking the hour-long Kalari Trail for expansive views.

SLEEPING LANGUAGES OF THE GOLDFIELDS

A staggering 12 Aboriginal languages are spoken across the Goldfields region, but colonisation and mining have, sadly, led to language loss in the area.

At the **Goldfields Aboriginal Language Centre** in Kalgoorlie, lost languages are not referred to as endangered or extinct; it's said they're sleeping and waiting to be remembered. Pitjanjatjara and Ngaanyatjarra are the strongest languages in this region because they're spoken way out in the desert, where there's been less interference. In Kalgoorlie many of the languages are in a recovery phase. The team here researches and documents regional languages and produces learning resources that can be purchased at the centre, along with Aboriginal-made items.

The Pinnacles & Beyond

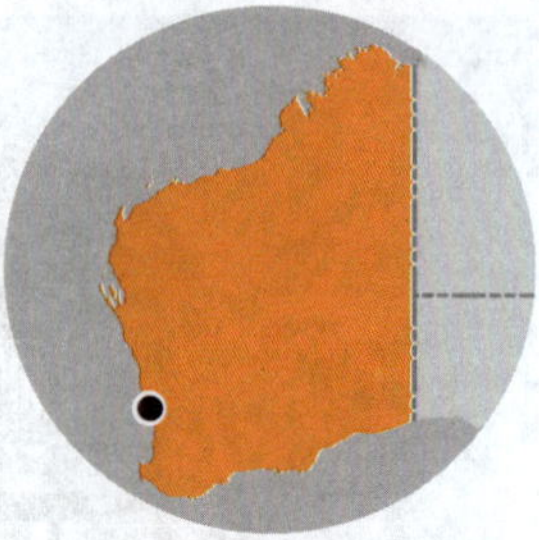

SURREAL LANDSCAPES | COASTAL SURROUNDS | NATIONAL PARKS

GETTING AROUND

The Pinnacles and Turquoise Coast region is an easy two- to three-hour drive north of Perth via the well-signed Indian Ocean Dr. Once you're in the region, expect short hops between sights, with sealed roads suitable for all vehicles.

Tour coaches run day trips from Perth, though services are limited and don't allow much time in surrounding towns.

TOP TIP

Most visitors make a quick dash to the Pinnacles, but the best way to experience the region is to slow down and follow the coast north, stopping at Lancelin's dunes, Jurien Bay's beaches and Green Head's wildflower lookouts before looping inland.

The majestic limestone pillars of the Pinnacles are one of WA's most captivating and surreal landscapes. Part of Nambung National Park – the Yued name means 'winding river' – the otherworldly spires jutting out dramatically from golden desert sands make for a spellbinding scene and will have you feeling like you've just landed on another planet.

If you were weighing up whether the Pinnacles were too far to travel to on their own merits, the fact that there are so many highlights on either side of them should put your decision beyond doubt.

Yanchep National Park is a popular stop to see koalas, while the Sunset Coast has the holiday towns of Guilderton and Lancelin, the latter with towering sand dunes. North of the Pinnacles, the Turquoise Coast takes you to the beach towns of Jurien Bay and Green Head before you head inland for wildflowers.

A Forest of Limestone Pillars

Visit the magical and mythical Pinnacles

A photographer's dream, the ancient, enigmatic lunarscape of the Pinnacles is as eerie as it is breathtaking, with sentinel-like spires rising as tall as 3.5m from the soft yellow sands like some long-lost ancient petroglyph forest. Scientists still can't be certain of its exact origin, though a leading theory suggests the pillars formed from shell-rich limestone that once covered the plain and, over millennia, was exposed and eroded. You can drive the one way 4km Pinnacles Desert Drive loop that runs by the formations, but for a fully immersive experience, head out on the walking trail (around 1km return).

At the park's entrance is the **Pinnacles Desert Discovery Centre** *(exploreparks.dbca.wa.gov.au; park entrance per vehicle $17)*, incorporating the visitor centre and fascinating displays on the park's natural history.

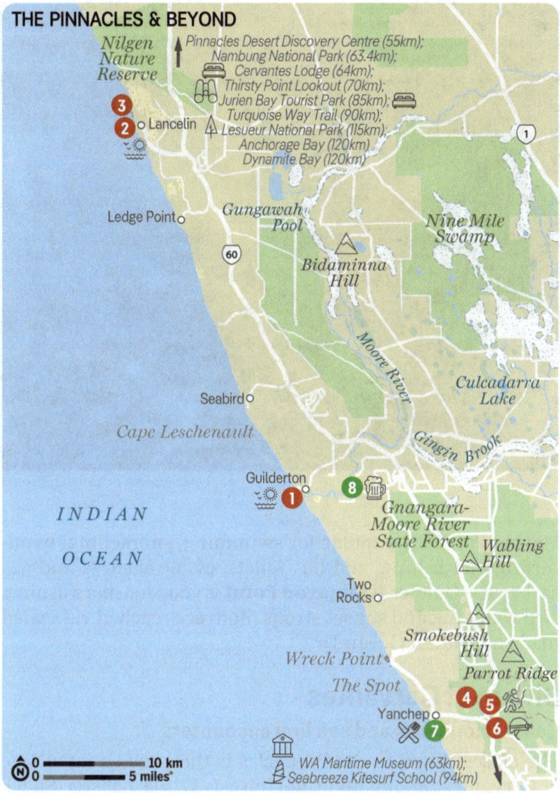

SIGHTS
1 Guilderton Beach
2 Lancelin Beach
3 Lancelin Island
4 Yanchep National Park

ACTIVITIES
see 1 Moore River Dinghy Hire
see 2 Perth Quad
5 Trees Adventure
6 Yanchep Crystal Cave

EATING
see 2 3 Emus
see 2 Café 6044
see 2 Endeavour Tavern
see 1 Moore River Cafe
see 2 Offshore Cafe
7 Orion Cafe
see 7 Yanchep Beach Lagoon Cafe

DRINKING & NIGHTLIFE
8 Moore River Brewing Co

INFORMATION
see 1 Guilderton Visitor Centre

Nambung's Unmissable Highlights

Lakes of ancient microbes and beaches

Other highlights of **Nambung National Park** *(exploreparks.dbca.wa.gov.au; per vehicle $17)* include **Lake Thetis**, one of the few places with living thrombolites (rock-like structures created by ancient microbes). Dating back more than 3000 years, these formations fringe the lake's edge and can be viewed on a 1.5km loop trail with interpretive signs along the way.

The park's coastal spots include **Hangover Bay**, a broad sweep of white sand and turquoise water within Jurien Bay

EATING IN THE PINNACLES: OUR PICKS

Lobster Shack: Famous for fresh crayfish, seafood plates and casual coastal dining right by the ocean in Cervantes. *11am-3pm* **$$$**

Cervantes Bar & Bistro: Friendly motel bistro serving hearty pub classics, local seafood and generous portions. *11am-10pm* **$$**

Club Cervantes: Welcoming community club offering affordable pub favourites, steaks and seafood in a laid-back dining room. *11am-8pm* **$$**

Seashells Cafe: In a relaxed beachfront setting, this cafe serves breakfast, lunch, coffee and sweet treats. *8am-2pm* **$**

BEST PINNACLE'S TOURS

Explore Tours Perth: Full-throttle day out combining the Pinnacles with sand-boarding in Lancelin, a Swan Valley winery lunch and close-up encounters with Aussie wildlife at Caversham. *exploretoursperth.com.au*

Lumineer Adventure Tours: Small-group sunset and stargazing adventures in the Pinnacles, complete with serious telescopes and knowledgeable guides. *lumineertours.com.au*

Australian Pinnacle Tours: Classic Perth day trips taking in the Pinnacles' otherworldly spires, with stops for koalas, sand dunes and golden-hour desert photography. *australianpinnacletours.com.au*

Sea Lion Tours: Book through Cervantes' Lobster Shack for unforgettable encounters with rare Australian sea lions – from the boat or while snorkelling. *lobstershack.com.au*

BRETT MONROE GARNER/GETTY IMAGES

Marine Park. It's popular for swimming, snorkelling, windsurfing and fishing, and has toilets, picnic shelters and gas barbecues. Quieter **Kangaroo Point** is good for shore fishing, bird watching and sunset strolls. Both are reached via sealed roads off Indian Ocean Dr.

Dive in at Cervantes

Coastal lookouts and sea lion encounters

The closest town to the Pinnacles is the crayfishing village of Cervantes, about 19km northwest. While Lobster Shack (p957) is its big drawcard, there's more to do here than eat seafood. Head to **Thirsty Point Lookout** for views over white dunes, turquoise shallows and offshore islands. Cervantes is also a practical base for sea lion snorkelling trips from nearby Jurien Bay.

A Town of Snorkelling, Sea Life & Cycling

Embrace Jurien Bay's outdoor attractions

Jurien Bay may look like a working town at first, but its picturesque foreshore quickly reveals a softer coastal side. Powdery sand and turquoise shallows invite relaxed swims and snorkelling around the jetty. There's plenty to do on

EATING IN JURIEN BAY: OUR PICKS

Sandpiper Tavern & Pizzeria: Seafood platters, wood-fired pizzas and sunset drinks amid a friendly atmosphere. *11am-2.30pm & 5-8pm* $$

Meraki: Cheerful brunch cafe known for excellent coffee, big burgers and its famous pancakes. *7am-2pm* $$

Oneh Jurien: Coastal-casual spot serving Asian-influenced share plates, bao and crisp cocktails. *11am-2.30pm & 5-8.30pm Tue-Sun* $$

Kakka Alley Brewing: Microbrewery with WA craft beers, seafood-topped pizzas and a lively beer-garden vibe. *noon-5pm Thu, to 7pm Fri & Sat, to 2.30pm Sun* $$$

Sea lion, Jurien Bay

land too, including the 14km **Turquoise Way Trail** along the foreshore. **Jurien Bay Adventure Tours** *(jurienbay adventuretours.com.au)* can kit you out with gear and bikes.

Jurien Bay Marine Park is the only major Australian sea lion breeding area on WA's west coast. **Sea Lion Charters** *(sealioncharters.com.au)* runs responsible tours where you can watch these agile puppies of the sea. The coastal path is ideal for cycling or strolling and the offshore reef creates calm pockets perfect for snorkellers and families.

Bloomin' Lovely Trails & Views

See wildflowers in Lesueur National Park

A 20-minute drive inland, **Lesueur National Park** *(explore parks.dbca.wa.gov.au; per vehicle $17)* has 900-plus plant species. From August to November, kwongan heath bursts with kangaroo paw, banksia, grass trees and orchids. The 6km **Yued Ponar Trail** is the standout walk, climbing through heath and woodland to views over the coast and plains. Easier options include the 2.5km **Gairdner Trail** and the 4km return to **Mt Lesueur's summit**. For a circuit, the 18.5km **Lesueur Scenic Drive** links lookouts, picnic spots and nature stops.

BEST JURIEN BAY TOURS

Jurien Bay Adventure Tours: Can sort you out for trips to the Pinnacles as well as nearby dunes and seasonal wildflowers.

Jurien Bay Oceanic Experiences: Offers dive courses and sea lion trips, or you can head out to catch lobster for dinner.

Skydive Jurien Bay: Take things up a notch with tandem skydives that include a beach landing.

Sea Lion Charters: Get a snorkel and mask for a view of Australian sea lions like no other.

Turquoise Safaris: Specialising in snorkel trips to visit a breeding colony of Australian fur seals.

EATING IN LANCELIN: OUR PICKS

Endeavour Tavern: Character-filled oceanfront tavern with a proudly local bar and a grassy beer garden for long, lazy afternoons. *11am-late* $$

Offshore Cafe: Old-school milk bar meets contemporary cafe and licensed bistro, complete with eclectic interiors and its famed stuffed grizzly. *7am-3pm* $

Café 6044: Stylish, polished venue serving juices, açaí bowls, bagels and good coffee to a steady beach crowd. *7am-3pm* $

3 Emus: Waterfront restaurant offering seafood plates and modern Australian dishes; big lawns and indoor-outdoor dining. *hours vary* $$

LANCELIN'S FISHING HERITAGE

Lancelin lies on Yued Noongar Country, along a coastline connected to Yued people for thousands of years. In the 1940s Lancelin was little more than a casual camping and shack-building spot for Perth families drawn to its rich crayfishing grounds. Commercial fishing grew in the 1950s and '60s, with boats like the *Trixen* – now preserved at the WA Maritime Museum in Fremantle (p905) – helping cement the town's reputation. Lancelin was gazetted as a township in 1950 and originally named Wangaree, a Noongar word meaning 'fish', reflecting the abundance found along this coast. It was renamed Lancelin in 1953 after nearby Lancelin Island. Today its fishing origins still shape the town's relaxed appeal, from its jetty to its working harbour.

BENNY MARTY/SHUTTERSTOCK

Koala, Yanchep National Park

Beach Walks & Swims

Dive into coastal bliss at Green Bay

Making up part of the Jurien Bay Marine Park, the beaches at dreamy **Green Bay** are dynamite – there's even one called **Dynamite Bay**, a regular nominee in Australia's top 20. It's one of three beaches that make up the **Three Bays Walkway**, a 2.5km one way coastal trail offering stunning views as it takes you from South Bay via Dynamite Bay to **Anchorage Bay** in the north.

Sandboarding & Kiteboarding

Jump on a board in Lancelin

Laid-back **Lancelin** feels like an outback town dropped beside the sea. Behind the township, a vast dune field rises into sharp white peaks. At the base of the dunes, sandboards can be rented from **Perth Quad** *(perthquad.com.au; from $10)*. Beginners should stick to gentler runs. Perth Quad also runs quad-bike and 4WD tours (from $139) across the dunes.

Steady summer breezes and a protective reef create ideal conditions for kitesurfers and windsurfers. Beginners are best suited to the sheltered waters near **Lancelin Island**, while experienced riders head to the exposed waves off **Lancelin Beach** and the offshore reef. There's no longer a dedicated kitesurf shop in Lancelin, so hire in Perth before you drive up. Try Seabreeze Kitesurf School *(915; from $90)*.

Where the River Meets the Ocean

Kick back in Guilderton

At **Guilderton** the Moore River meets the Indian Ocean, creating two distinct swimming options: **Guilderton Beach** and the often sandbar-sheltered river lagoon. Canoes, kayaks and paddle craft are available most days in summer at the Moore River foreshore car park, next to the boat ramp. **Moore River Dinghy Hire** *(0424 256 181; from $90)* rents small motorised dinghies from November to April.

Guilderton Beach is beautiful but exposed, so check conditions and avoid rips. Families base themselves beside the shallow river mouth, which stays gentle when the ocean is rough. At high tide the sandbar may shift – something to consider before wading out. The **Guilderton Visitor Centre**, open weekends only, provides maps, tide times and advice.

Koalas & Show Caves

Enjoy Yanchep National Park

Only 42km north of Perth, **Yanchep National Park** *(exploreparks.dbca.wa.gov.au/park/yanchep-national-park; per vehicle $17)* offers one of WA's few koala encounters. Native to Australia's east coast, koalas were introduced to the park in 1938 and now live in a small, naturalistic enclosure viewable from a short boardwalk.

Tours of **Crystal Cave** *(from $16)* reveal stalactites, stalagmites and underground chambers, while the **Trees Adventure** *(treesadventure.com.au; adult/child $69/59)* ropes course threads through the canopy on flying foxes. The **Aboriginal Cultural Experience** *(from $16)* introduces Whadjuk culture through storytelling and demonstrations.

THE GILT DRAGON

Of the 1600 shipwrecks strewn along WA's coastline, few evoke more intrigue than the *Vergulde Draeck* (Gilt Dragon). In 1656 this Dutch VOC ship, loaded with silver guilders bound for Batavia in the Dutch East Indies, met its fate off Guilderton. Of the 193 crew, 75 survivors reached the shore, believed to be the first Europeans to set foot on mainland Australia. Using the ship's boat, seven sailors journeyed 3000km to raise the alarm in Batavia. No trace of the other survivors has ever been found.

In 1931 two boys discovered guilders north of Moore River, leading to the town's naming. Then, in 1963, spear fishermen found the well-preserved wreck, finally unravelling the mystery of its whereabouts.

EATING IN MOORE RIVER & YANCHEP: OUR PICKS

Moore River Cafe: Relaxed spot serving burgers and fish and chips with river views. *8am-2.30pm Mon-Thu, to 6.30pm Fri, 7.30am-7pm Sat & Sun* $$

Moore River Brewing Co: Laid-back riverfront brewery in Caraban (near Guilderton) offering craft beers and pub-style meals. *hours vary* $$

Orion Cafe: Scenic cafe overlooking Yanchep Lagoon offering brunch classics, seafood plates and sunset dinners. *6am-8pm* $$

Yanchep Beach Lagoon Cafe: Easy-going beachside spot for coffee, burgers, fish and chips and cold drinks. *7am-6pm Mon-Wed, to 9pm Thu-Sun* $

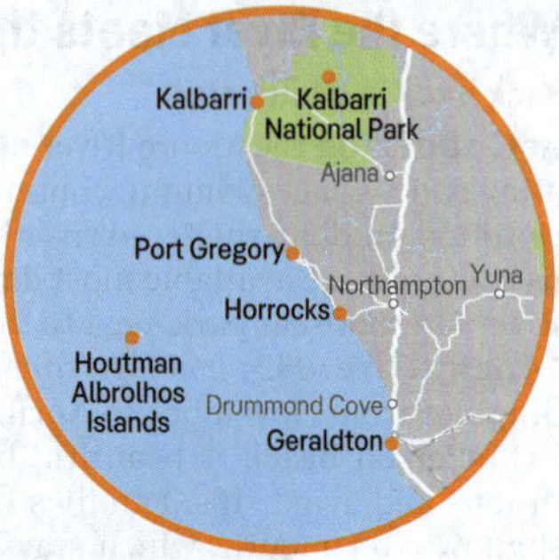

Geraldton & the Batavia Coast

SHIPWRECKS | BEACHES | HIKING

Places

TOP TIP

It's quicker to fly to Geraldton from Perth, but car hire is cheaper and easier to arrange in the capital and a 428km road trip along the incredibly scenic Indian Ocean Dr via Cervantes (p958) and the Pinnacles (Nambung National Park; p957) shouldn't be missed.

With its Mediterranean climate and beaches, bars, bike paths and restaurants, the laid-back port city of Geraldton, on Yamatji/Wajarri Country, is the perfect place to hole up for a few days, catch some sun and (over)indulge in some terrific dining. The city's museums and monuments celebrate a rich maritime history, and galleries showcase local arts and Indigenous culture.

The Batavia Coast stretches north, dotted with fishing villages and deserted white-sand beaches, and eventually ceding to crumbling Tumblagooda sandstone cliffs over 100m high, from where migrating whales can be spied in winter. This coast was notorious for wrecking the ships of the VOC (Dutch East India Company) if they strayed off-course on their way to Java.

Kalbarri, at the mouth of the Murchison River on Nanda Country, is a family-friendly resort town known for relaxed water sports, soaring sea cliffs and the magnificent gorges and wildflowers of Kalbarri National Park.

Geraldton

TIME FROM PERTH: **4½HR**

Shipping disasters

Delve into history at the **Museum of Geraldton** *(visit.museum.wa.gov.au; free)*, where multimedia displays showcase First Nations and early settler history and the area's unique

GETTING AROUND

Qantas and Nexus fly between Geraldton and Perth. TransWA runs three coaches a week between Geraldton and Kalbarri; Integrity drops off/picks up from Ajana on the highway, requiring a local **shuttle** *(dguyjourneys.com; $65)* into Kalbarri town.

To get around, you'll need your own vehicle unless you're on a tour. It's 156km from Geraldton to Kalbarri via the scenic coast road, while the Kalbarri Skywalk and gorges are another 37km, all on sealed, 2WD-friendly roads. Cycles and e-bikes can be hired in Geraldton but not Kalbarri.

DENNIS MACDONALD/SHUTTERSTOCK

Museum of Geraldton

endemic wildlife. The stunning Shipwreck Gallery brings to life the horrifying tale of the *Batavia* (1629). Download the museum's free **e-book** *(visit.museum.wa.gov.au/batavia-ebook)* for the full story. Over 1000 ships have been lost off the WA coast; many of those dating back to the 1600s belonged to the VOC and sank on their way to the Dutch East Indies. The WA Museums website has well-compiled databases of the known wrecks.

Be sure to visit the candy-striped **Point Moore Lighthouse**, erected in 1878.

On the hill overlooking town, the **HMAS *Sydney II* Memorial** tells the tale of the 1941 sinking of the cruiser in combat with the German raider *Kormoran*, killing all 645 crew. It is Australia's worst maritime disaster.

Heritage trails

Explore Gero's picturesque **foreshore** and historic backstreets on these downloadable self-guided **heritage trails** *(trailswa.com.au)* studded with interpretive panels relating the area's history. With themes including maritime history, the West End, public art and the waterfront, most trails take one to three

THE BATAVIA & AUSTRALIA'S FIRST EUROPEANS

The story of the Dutch ship *Batavia* is one of the more infamous in maritime history. After the ship sank off the Houtman Abrolhos Islands (p964) in 1629, the captain, Francisco Pelsaert, sailed off to find a rescue vessel in the Dutch East Indies. While he was away, mutinous crewmen raped and murdered the men, women and children who had been on the ship. When Pelsaert returned, he executed the murderers. Only two youths survived, Wouter Loos and Jan Pelgrom De Bye; exiled to a local beach, they lived out their lives with local Indigenous people. A plaque marks the spot where they came ashore at Wittecarra Creek by **Red Bluff Beach** south of Kalbarri.

EATING & DRINKING IN GERALDTON: OUR PICKS

Banh Mi Up: Tiny, hole-in-the-wall Vietnamese takeaway serving the best banh mi between Perth and Broome. *10am-3pm Mon-Fri, to 2pm Sat* $

Salt Dish: Innovative dishes and a killer wine list make for a perfect lunch. Red emperor and a sharp *fiano* – yum! *7am-3pm Mon-Thu, 7am-3pm & 5.45-10pm Fri & Sat* $$

Jaffle Shack: Gourmet jaffles (toasted sandwiches) in the foreshore park; kickstart your day with a brekkie or salmon one. *7am-3pm* $

Old Man & the Sea: Gero's rooftop bar is perfect for sunset viewing and not only because the cocktails come by the jug! *4-10pm Mon-Thu, from noon Fri-Sun* $$

hours; you'll never be far from refreshments or a sparkling beach. Several longer trails venture into the nearby countryside; you'll need a vehicle for the **Yamatji Drive** (195km), exploring Indigenous cultural sights, and the **Monsignor Hawes Trail** (named for the architect of the town's striking **cathedral** and many other regional churches). Hire bikes Monday to Saturday from **Revolutions** *(revolutionsgeraldton.com.au; half-/full-day $25/35)* and contact the **visitor centre** *(visitgeraldton.com.au)* for more information.

Art and architecture

Geraldton's wonderful **regional art gallery** *(artgallery.cgg.wa.gov.au)* hosts an engaging permanent WA collection and travelling exhibitions, while the attached visitor centre has a very useful printed public art trail map. Wander along Marine Tce from the distinctive colonial **courthouse** (1897) past the **Freemasons Hotel** (1895) down to **Yamaji Art** *(yamajiart.com)*, which showcases (and sells) local Indigenous works.

Horrocks & Port Gregory

TIME FROM GERALDTON: **1HR**

Pretty in pink

Heading north along the Batavia Coast towards Kalbarri, detour via **Horrocks**, a picturesque village on a lovely white sand **beach**. Continue north along the coast until you reach the extraordinary **Pink Lake** (Hutt Lagoon) just outside Port Gregory. The water is pink due to the presence of *Dunaliella salina*, an algae rich in beta-carotene, which is harvested here and used in food colouring and make-up. The lake is best viewed when the sun is directly overhead. Spring brings the most consistent colour.

Houtman Albrolhos Islands

TIME FROM GERALDTON: **½HR**

Snorkel the Leeuwin Current

Sixty kilometres from the mainland, 'the Abrolhos' are an archipelago of 210 islands, rocks and coral reefs; 189 are protected as a national park, and the remaining islands are used for commercial fishing purposes. The islands are an important refuge for wildlife including sea lions, green turtles, carpet pythons, migrating sea birds and the Tammar wallaby, while the surrounding waters, warmed by the Leeuwin Current,

KALBARRI'S BEST TOURS

Kalbarri Abseil: Abseil into spectacular Z-Bend Gorge, swim in the Murchison River and visit Nature's Window on this full-day tour.

D'Guy Journeys: Hunt wildflowers or walk Kalbarri's gorges, admiring the sea cliffs or the startling Pink Lake. *dguyjourneys.com*

Kalbarri Adventure Tours: Canoe, hike and swim in a remote section of the Murchison on a half-day adventure.

Kalbarri Wilderness Cruises: Join a 2½-hour wildlife cruise along the Murchison at sunset (November to May) or in the morning (April to October). *kalbarricruises.com*

Reefwalker Adventure Tours: Watch the sunset on a 90-minute cruise, or look for humpbacks from June to September.

EATING & DRINKING IN KALBARRI: OUR PICKS

Gorges Cafe: A good breakfast choice when the rest of the town is asleep. The smashed-avo rösti hits the spot. *7am-2pm Wed-Sun* $

Wild Ocean: Authentic and delicious Jakarta street-food served from a van opposite Kalbarri's main wharf. *5-7pm Sat & Sun* $

Little Leaf: Locally sourced produce mixed with love and turned into beautiful tapas and shared dishes. *7.30-11.30am & 5-8pm Tue-Sat* $

Finlay's: Tasty craft beers and premium seafood are on offer in this large, open space a few blocks south of the beach. *noon-10pm* $$

TOP EXPERIENCE

Kalbarri National Park

From the savagely eroded striped Tumblagooda sandstone cliffs falling into the Indian Ocean to the deep, rugged gorges of the winding Murchison River, the 1860 sq km Kalbarri National Park is a scenic wonderland offering walking trails for all capabilities. It's also a sanctuary for rare endemic plants and animals, with spectacular wildflower displays in August and September.

Sea Cliffs

South of Kalbarri, viewpoints such as **Natural Bridge**, **Island Rock**, **Shellhouse** and **Eagle Gorge** look out over the Indian Ocean from 100m-high Tumblagooda sandstone cliffs. The lookouts are connected by the wild, clifftop **Bigurda Trail** (8km one way), parts of which are wheelchair accessible, though it's mostly rough and unshaded. There's no drinking water, public transport or access fee here. In winter, migrating humpback whales can be seen offshore.

Skywalk

The park's biggest drawcard is the Skywalk, a pair of large, cantilevered, high-accessibility metal-mesh lookouts suspended over Murchison Gorge, providing uninterrupted views of the Murchison River 100m directly below. The Skywalk is in the main section of the park, 37km from Kalbarri.

River Gorges

From Loop car park, a steep walk leads to **Nature's Window** (800m return), a photogenic natural hole in the cliffs. The **Loop Trail** (9km, three hours) continues along the ridge before dropping to the riverbank and climbing back up to Nature's Window.

From Z-Bend car park, trails lead to the **lookout** (1.2km return), down to Z-Bend on the **river** (2.6km return) and to the impressive **Four Ways** (6km return).

WIRESTOCK CREATORS/SHUTTERSTOCK

TOP TIPS

- Start walking early to beat the heat; avoid November to March, which is very hot and fly-laden.
- Rare black-flanked wallabies are sometimes spotted at **Hawks Head lookout**.
- The easiest river access (700m return) is via **Ross Graham lookout** in the southeastern section.

Practicalities

- *exploreparks.dbca.wa.gov.au/park/kalbarri-national-park*
- per vehicle per day $17
- open sunrise to sunset

TRABANTOS/SHUTTERSTOCK

Chinamans Beach

contain many tropical species of sea creature and the most southernmost coral reefs in the Indian Ocean. No camping is allowed here. The easiest way to experience the Abrolhos is on a 'fly and flipper' day trip from **Geraldton** *(shineaviation.com.au; adult/child $545/460)* or **Kalbarri** *(kalbarriscenicflights.com.au; from $410),* which usually includes landing on **East Wallabi** island and snorkelling at **Turtle Bay**. Some tours include *Batavia* historical sites (p963).

Kalbarri

TIME FROM GERALDTON: **2HR**

Swim, surf, snorkel, repeat

Kalbarri has some idyllic sheltered swimming spots and none's better than the town favourite, **Chinamans Beach**, at the mouth of the Murchison RIver with gentle swell, shade, grass and barbecues. There are more sandy areas and facilities upstream along the Murchison, such as nearby **Main Beach** and the stretch opposite the IGA. Just south of town, **Blue Holes** offers good snorkelling, while surfers will want to try nearby **Siphon**, Red Bluff (p963) or the challenging but superb **Jakes Point**. The 8km dual-use **Melaleuca Trail** connects them all.

Shark Bay & Monkey Mia

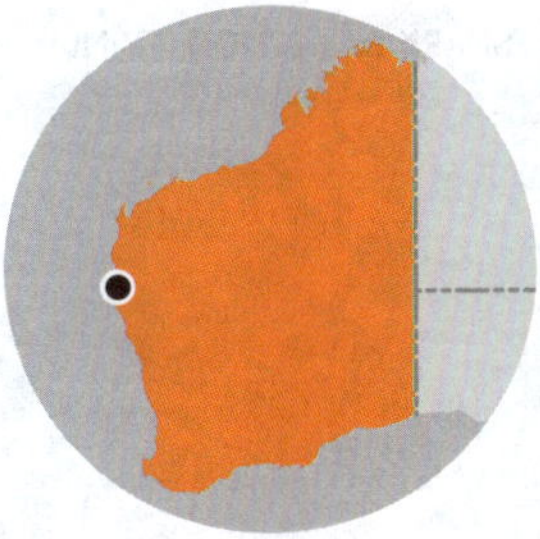

PRISTINE SEAS | WILDLIFE | INDIGENOUS CULTURE

With only minimal development, sheltered turquoise waters, lingering sunsets and kilometres of pristine desert coastline, Shark Bay World Heritage Area stretches from the Zutydorp Cliffs near Kalbarri to the Peron Peninsula and north to Carnarvon. These lands of the Nhanda and Mulgana people compose the westernmost edge of the continent and are steeped in Indigenous and European history.

On land and on water, efforts to protect endangered endemic wildlife are centre stage. Here you can swim with the famous dolphins of Monkey Mia, visit the remote wilds of Edel Land and Francois Peron and Dirk Hartog Island national parks, and engage with conservation efforts like Project Eden (whose predator-proof fence you'll pass through on your way here) and the Return to 1616 initiative.

Most people base themselves in Denham, with accommodation, fuel, groceries and the Shark Bay World Heritage Discovery Centre, where you can learn all about Shark Bay's unique ecosystems, wildlife and history.

Paddle to Your Own Tune

Paddle through calm lagoons and spot marine wildlife

Kayaking is the perfect way to explore the remote beaches, lagoons and stunning coastal scenery of Shark Bay. You'll see rays, turtles, dolphins and small sharks as you paddle along. **Little Lagoon** is a safe, family-friendly location close to Denham, while **Big Lagoon** in Francois Peron National Park is also excellent. From Monkey Mia (p971) you can explore the cape's eastern beaches and bays.

Hire kayaks from **Tasman Holiday Parks** *(tasmanholidayparks.com/au/denham-seaside; per hour from $30)* in Denham or from **Paddling Monkey Mia** *(paddlingmonkeymia.com; per day $50)*. Wula Gura Nyinda Eco Adventures (p969; *adult/child $225/190*) offers fully guided day tours.

GETTING AROUND

Rex flies daily from Perth to Shark Bay Airport. Integrity runs three coach services weekly between Perth and Exmouth (and further north), stopping at the Overlander Roadhouse (p970) on the North West Coastal Hwy, with a connecting shuttle (book ahead via Integrity) to Shark Bay.

Standard rental cars are available in Denham from **Shark Bay Car Hire** *(carhire.net.au)*, but you'll need your own high-clearance 4WD to explore Francois Peron National Park and Steep Point.

TOP TIP

The website *sharkbay.org* is a trove of information about the peninsula: natural attractions, parks, flora and fauna, conservation efforts, history, safe travelling and World Heritage qualifications. Download free visitor guides, maps and fact sheets.

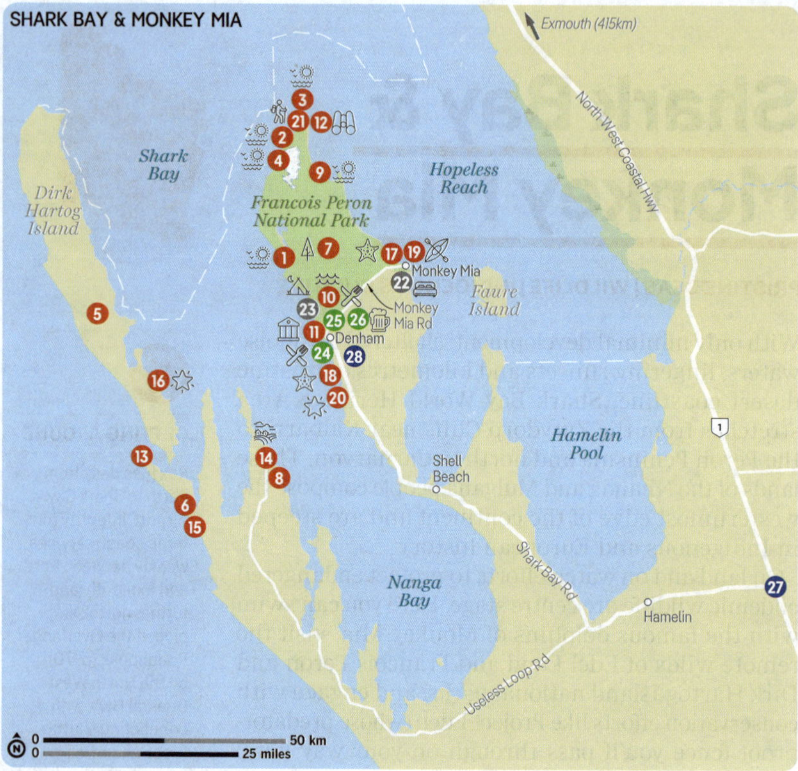

SIGHTS
1 Big Lagoon
2 Bottle Bay
3 Cape Peron
4 Cattle Well
5 Dirk Hartog Island
6 Edel Land National Park (Proposed)
7 Francois Peron National Park
8 Heirisson Prong
9 Herald Bight
10 Little Lagoon
11 Shark Bay World Heritage Discovery Centre
12 Skipjack Point Lookout
13 Steep Point
14 Useless Loop
15 Zutydorp Cliffs

ACTIVITIES
16 Dirk Hartog Lodge
17 Monkey Mia Conservation Park
see 11 Naturetime Tours
18 Ocean Park
19 Paddling Monkey Mia
20 Shark Bay Eco Tours
21 Wanamalu Trail
see 11 Wula Gura Nyinda Eco Adventures

SLEEPING
22 RAC Monkey Mia Dolphin Resort
23 Tasman Holiday Parks – Denham Seaside

EATING
see 18 Oceans Restaurant
24 Old Pearler Restaurant
25 Shark Bay Cafe

DRINKING & NIGHTLIFE
26 Shark Bay Hotel

TRANSPORT
27 Overlander Roadhouse
28 Shark Bay Car Hire

EATING & DRINKING AROUND SHARK BAY: OUR PICKS

Shark Bay Cafe: Unpretentious, with lots of outdoor space; the croissants and bagels are a great brekkie choice. *5.30am-8pm Sun-Fri, 7am-3pm Sat* $

Shark Bay Hotel: Known locally as 'The Old Pub', Australia's most westerly boozer has pub favourites and the perfect sunset beer garden. *meals noon-2pm & 5.30-8.30pm* $$

Oceans Restaurant: It's worth the drive out to the Ocean Park just for the delicious seafood chowder here. The view's not bad either. *9am-3pm* $$

Old Pearler Restaurant: Bookings are essential for this house built from shell bricks. Try the signature seafood platter. *5-9pm* $$$

Learning about Country

Experience local culture through guided adventures

Local legend and Nhanda man Darren 'Capes' Capewell, head of **Wula Gura Nyinda Eco Adventures** *(wulagura.com.au; 4WD or kayaking day tour adult/child $225/190)*, runs adventure and cultural tours around Shark Bay, including walking and 4WD tours of Francois Peron National Park, kayak and SUP tours along remote coastlines, and longer all-inclusive camping tours to **Steep Point** *(tour $1225 per person, three-day guided walk $1775)* or Dirk Hartog Island. The experience with Capes is a mix of history, storytelling and pure fun.

Touring Francois Peron National Park

Discover red cliffs, turquoise waters and abundant wildlife

Some of WA's loveliest and most deserted beaches wrap around **Wulyibidi** (Peron Peninsula; *park entry per car per day $17*), including **Bottle Bay** and **Cattle Well**, both great for swimming and kayaking, likewise the more sheltered **Herald Bight** on the eastern coast. However, the crowning glory is **Cape Peron**, where bay and ocean currents meet below towering red cliffs and bottlenose dolphins drive their prey into the shallows.

From Cape Peron, the scenic **Wanamalu Trail** (3.6km return) follows the clifftop south along the peninsula to **Skipjack Point Lookout**,, where you might spot dugongs, turtles, rays, sharks and dolphins.

The Heritage Precinct around the old homestead, complete with artesian hot tub, is 2WD accessible, but you'll need a 4WD to go any further. **Camp sites** *(adult/child $15/10)* are non-bookable. Indigenous-run Wula Gura Nyinda Eco Adventures and **Naturetime Tours** *(naturetimetours.com)* run full-day tours.

Heading West to Edel Land

Dramatic cliffs and Australia's westernmost mainland point

Edel Land National Park *(sharkbay.org)* encompasses **Steep Point**, the westernmost tip of the Australian mainland and the stunning, 200m-high **Zutydorp Cliffs**. Access is by a sandy, 140km 4WD track from Shark Bay Rd. Dirk Hartog Island is only an arm's length away. Drive from Denham in 3½ hours or tour with Wula Gura Nyinda Eco Adventures.

Beyond Be Dragons!

Watch the last sunset

Europeans named **Dirk Hartog Island** (Wirruwana; *exploreparks.dbca.wa.gov.au/park/dirk-hartog-island-national-park; free*) for the Dutch mariner who left a pewter plate nailed to a post in 1616. Once a sandy pastoral lease, the largest and westernmost of WA's islands is now a national

USELESS LOOP

On your drive along Shark Bay Rd you would have passed the turn off to Useless Loop, a closed salt-mining town of about 134 people (employees and their families) way out west on **Heirisson Prong**, one of Shark Bay's long tines. The track to Steep Point in Edel Land passes this way (and deteriorates somewhat rapidly thereafter). Apparently Louis de Freycinet's older brother Henri, aboard the Baudin expedition in 1801, christened the inlet Havre Inutile (Useless Haven) as he thought the entrance was blocked by a sandbar; it later proved to be only a temporary occurrence. The salt mined here is exceptionally pure: the surrounding seawater is 1.5 times as salty as the open ocean.

A WORLD HERITAGE DRIVE

Discover ancient lifeforms, beaches made of shells and sparkling turquoise waters on this drive from nowhere to definitely somewhere.

START	END	LENGTH
Overlander Roadhouse	Monkey Mia	183km; 2½hr

Leave the North West Coastal Hwy at the 1 **Overlander Roadhouse**, following Shark Bay Rd west for 29 lonely kilometres, then detour to 2 **Hamelin Pool**. Here you'll find stromatolites almost identical to organisms that existed 3.5 billion years ago. Until the boardwalks destroyed in a 2021 cyclone are repaired, you'll have to look with binoculars from the beach. Visit the nearby 3 **Hamelin Pool Caravan Park**, with its Telegraph Station (1884) museum and old shell quarry.

Return to the main road and enjoy increasing glimpses of Shark Bay over the next 55km. Pull into stunning 4 **Shell Beach**, where tiny cockleshells, densely compacted over time, were once quarried as building material for houses in Denham. Don't miss 5 **Eagle Bluff**, where you might spy loggerhead turtles, manta rays, sharks and even dugongs in the turquoise waters below the clifftop boardwalk.

Pull into 6 **Ocean Park**, an aquarium showcasing sharks, turtles and stingrays. Next stop is the 7 **Shark Bay World Heritage Discovery Centre** on Denham's scenic waterfront promenade. Head through the town to 8 **Little Lagoon** (p967), a circular lake behind the ocean dunes. Past the turn off to Francois Peron National Park, the road ends at 9 **Monkey Mia**.

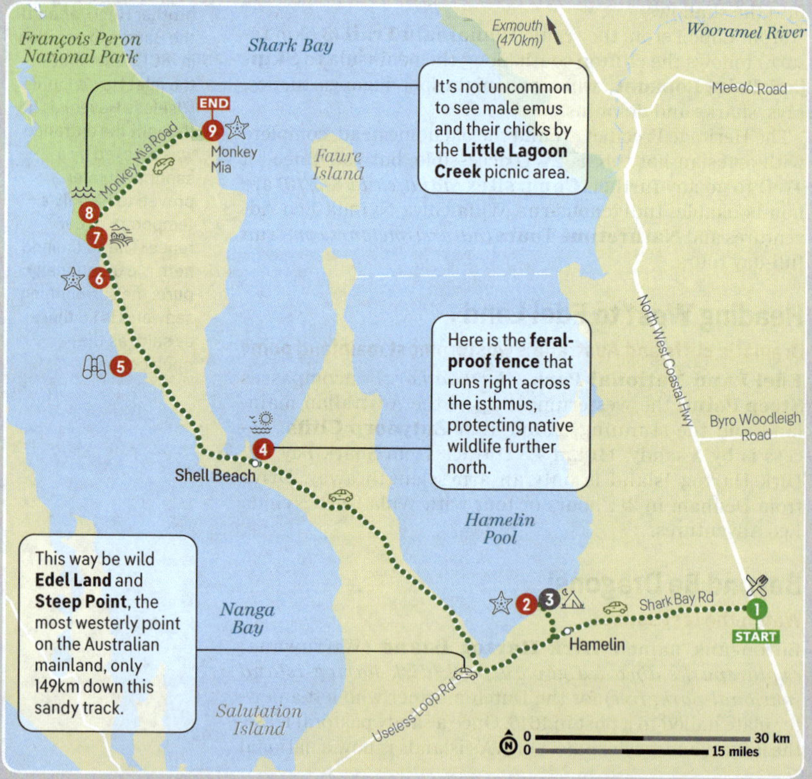

MAURICIOALEXIS22/SHUTTERSTOCK

Dolphin, Monkey Mia

park. Through the **Return to 1616** *(sharkbay.org)* initiative, it's being restored to its original state.

While high cliffs line the western coast, the sheltered beaches of the east are perfect for water activities. You can bring your own 4WD over on a barge from Steep Point, but it's cheaper and easier to take a day cruise from Denham.

If you want to witness the last sunset in Australia, you'll need to stay overnight – either **camping** *(adult/child $20/3)* or in the **lodge** *(three-night packages from $1755)*. **Shark Bay Eco Tours** *(sharkbayecotours.com; adult/child $299/239)* and the **Dirk Hartog Eco Lodge** *(dirkhartogisland.com.au; adult/child $300/235)* both run day trips. Book the barge through the latter.

Getting Close to Wild Dolphins

Witness Monkey Mia's famous visitors

Wild Indo-Pacific bottlenose dolphins have been turning up at the **Monkey Mia Conservation Park** *(exploreparks.dbca.wa.gov.au/park/monkey-mia-conservation-park; adult/child $15/10)* looking for a handout feed for over 50 years, and rightly or wrongly, this spectacle is hugely popular with visitors. The dolphins usually arrive around 7.45am. Don't expect to feed or touch them – feeds are handled by rangers and a small number of selected individuals.

MONKEY MIA DOLPHINS

Dolphin-feeding is illegal in Australia, but Monkey Mia is one of only four places with a special permit to continue the practice. How much this depends on the welfare of tourism as opposed to the welfare of the dolphins is open to debate.

Opponents, including those running long-term research projects at Monkey Mia, would like to see the feeding phased out, warning that dolphins can become dependent on humans and fail to pass the necessary hunting and survival skills on to their calves, who suffer an increased mortality rate compared to those with hunting mothers.

Supporters counter that hand-feeding at Monkey Mia accounts for only 5% to 10% of the dolphins' daily food needs and is important for research.

Carnarvon & the Gascoyne

SPACE | WILD SURF | BIG, BIG ROCK

Places

TOP TIP

The 26km Gascoyne Food Trail (also known as the Fruit Loop Trail) has nine stops covering both sides of the river that include produce stalls, farms, ice cream and even a cactus garden. Ask at the visitor centre for a brochure.

Heading north from the Overlander Roadhouse on the asphalt, it's 200km of semi-desert and not much else until you reach Carnarvon on Yinggarda Country, at the mouth of the Gascoyne River, where you'll find fertile fruit farms, strong First Nations culture, terrific windsurfing from October to April and the amazing Carnarvon Space & Technology Museum.

The Gascoyne, WA's longest river, only flows above ground for a third of the year, disappearing underground for the remainder, in effect creating a massive aquifer that's wonderful for farming. Less wonderful is its propensity for flooding.

North of town, the windswept Quobba Coast is the domain of rock fishers and hardcore surfers, drawn to its blowholes, great snorkelling, epic winter swells and breaks to die for.

In the Gascoyne's far inland corner is astonishing Burringurrah (Mt Augustus). Twice as large as Uluru and feeling a thousand times more remote, this ancient outcrop is adorned with rock art and walking trails.

Carnarvon

TIME FROM DENHAM: 3½HR

Relive historic space missions through immersive exhibits

In 1966 NASA helped build the giant Carnarvon OTC dish to relay communications from Gemini and Apollo space missions to mission control in Houston. In its present-day shadow is a **museum** *(carnarvonmuseum.org.au; adult/child $20/10)* dedicated to all things spacey. Learn about each Apollo mission and those of many deep-space probes; wander past racks of old electronics; engage in interactive displays; and ogle a full-size mockup of the lunar lander. But don't miss the Apollo 11 launch, lying on your back enclosed in a capsule.

GETTING AROUND

Rex flies daily to Carnarvon from Perth via Shark Bay and Integrity coaches pass through the town three times weekly between Exmouth and Geraldton. Your own wheels are essential out here. In good weather a 2WD will get you up to Gnaraloo and out to Mt Augustus, but check your rental car's policy about gravel roads and expect some corrugations. You'll probably have to carry extra fuel. As always in WA, a 4WD is usually the better option.

Explore Indigenous stories and bush tucker traditions

On Robinson St, the wonderful **Gwoonwardu Mia** *(gahcc.com.au)* cultural centre showcases the story of the five local First Nations language groups: the Yinggarda, Bayungu, Malgana, Thadgari and Thalanyji. There are permanent and travelling **exhibitions** *(adult/child $10/5)*, a bush tucker garden, a small training cafe, gift shop and an artist studio.

Wooramulla Eco Cultural Journeys *(wooramulla.com.au)* offers **two-hour walking tours** *(adult/child $80/55)* with Indigenous Yinggarda guides, exploring bush foods and First Nations interaction with the landscapes around Carnarvon. Longer 4WD tagalong tours into the Kennedy Ranges are also available.

Quobba Coast

TIME FROM CARNARVON: **1HR**

Powerful blowholes and world-class surfing breaks

North of Carnarvon, the wild, desolate coast road leads to several attractions. Left of the poignant **'King Waves Kill'** intersection, the **Blowholes** are a series of natural rock chimneys where surging seas funnel water through caves to shoot, geyser-like, high into the air. Nearby, the **Aquarium**, a sheltered lagoon, is a lovely snorkel at high tide.

Following the coast north, you'll come to **Red Bluff** on Quobba Station, the southernmost tip of Ningaloo Reef. The surf here is gnarly, but next door at **Gnaraloo** it's insane, with the epic **Tombstones**, a heavy, scary, left-hander reef break and one of the longest, roundest tubes in the world. For gentler action, Gnaraloo's **3-Mile Lagoon** offers some brilliant snorkelling.

Upper Gascoyne

TIME FROM CARNARVON: **6HR**

Climb this ancient island mountain for breathtaking views

In Wajarri country, 484km east of Carnarvon, **Burringurrah** (**Mt Augustus**; 1105m) is a giant inselberg (literally, 'island mountain') rising 715m above the surrounding plain. A 49km loop road (closed November to February) circles Burringurrah's base, giving access to walking trails and rock-art sites. Know your limitations: the challenging, shadeless **Summit Trail** (12.5km return, five to six hours) has claimed several lives. May to August is the best time to visit. The drive from Carnarvon via Gascoyne Junction takes six hours, from Meekatharra on the Great Northern Hwy only five hours.

DAWSON'S BURROWING BEE

Only found around the Gascoyne region, *Amegilla dawsoni* (or Moogadgurrah to the local Yinggarda) is one of Australia's largest and most curious bees. The solitary females dig several nests, some up to 30cm deep, in clay soil, depositing their eggs floating on a bed of nectar. The larvae hatch, eat the nectar and then remain dormant until early spring before emerging, mating and starting the cycle over again. Unfortunately, the females have a penchant for making their nests in the region's dirt roads and tourists can unknowingly negatively impact them. Moogadgurrah are culturally significant to Carnarvon's Indigenous population and the larvae were a prized food source. If you'd like more information about the bees, head over to Gwoonwardu Mia.

EATING IN CARNARVON: OUR PICKS

Kestrel Cafe: At One Mile Jetty are breakfast favourites with a view, but it's the Vietnamese-style lunches that are worth hanging around for. *8.30am-3pm Tue-Sun* **$$**

Old Post Office Cafe: Inhabiting the heritage post office; the evening pizzas bring in the punters. *8am-noon & 5-7pm Tue-Sun* **$**

Mar e Sol Cafe: Out by the port, tuck into a jalapeño omelette or a local seafood basket; indoor-outdoor seating and free wi-fi. *8am-2pm & 5-8.30pm Wed-Sat* **$$**

Bumbak's: Fabulous ice creams and smoothies made straight from farm fruit, as well as various preserves. *9am-4pm Tue-Sun* **$**

Exmouth & Ningaloo Coast

KAYAKING & SNORKELLING | WHALE SHARKS | COASTAL SCENERY

TOP TIP

Ningaloo can get heinously crowded in winter, especially the July school holidays. Pre-book everything including accommodation and whale shark tours well in advance. May to June is a better time to visit, as the coral's just spawned, whale sharks and humpbacks overlap and manta ray numbers are increasing.

The shark-fin-shaped North West Cape protrudes into the Indian Ocean at the bottom of WA's 'cyclone alley', the flat Pilbara coastline stretching all the way to Broome.

Here you'll find the magnificent, UNESCO-listed Ningaloo Reef, where you can swim with whale sharks from March to August. Inland, Cape Range National Park features dry limestone gorges and some appealing day walks. Further south, sand tracks follow the Ningaloo Coast (Nyinggulu) to family-friendly Coral Bay, Warroora and beyond.

The cape's only town, Exmouth is a wonderful hangout, with the best food scene between Perth and Broome. It's also the place to book last-minute tours, get your vehicle fixed, rent kayaks and snorkelling gear or just laze around drinking craft beers.

Wind, Water & Reptiles

Experience cyclone simulations and marine life exhibits

Exmouth's superb **Ningaloo Aquarium & Discovery Centre** *(ningaloocentre.com.au; adult/child $24/17)* can show you what it feels like to be in the middle of a cyclone. Cyclone Vance hit in 1999 and the 267km/h winds damaged 70% of the town. The showstopper aquarium has a 55,000L tank containing over 100 species of marine creature. Other notable exhibits detail the reptile denizens of Cape Range and explain Exmouth's historical connection to the US Navy.

GETTING AROUND

Qantas flies into Exmouth's Learmonth Airport daily; Integrity coaches stop in town three times weekly in both directions. Car hire is also available. Most roads are sealed, but even the unsealed ones are normally navigable by 2WD in fine weather. If you've booked a tour you'll most likely be met at the airport; otherwise there's a shuttle bus into town.

NORTH BY NORTH WEST

From high lookouts and deep gorges to stunning turquoise waters: explore North West Cape on this breathtaking scenic drive.

START	END	LENGTH
Exmouth	Exmouth	294km; 4–6hr

Pack the bathers and suncream and leave early from 1 **Exmouth**, heading south for 22km, then turn right onto Charles Knife Rd. Climb switchbacks with vertiginous views of Charles Knife Gorge until you reach 2 **Charles Knife Canyon Lookout** on the plateau. Return to the main road, then head back towards Exmouth, turning left to dramatic 3 **Shothole Canyon**, where the road ends at a picnic table surrounded by crumbling cliffs.

Pass back through Exmouth (grab a snack!), continuing north to 4 **Bundegi Beach** (p978) for a quick dip in the shadow of the VLF antenna array. Backtrack 3km to Yardie Creek Rd, then head northwest, turning right for the almost obscured 5 **SS *Mildura* Wreck**. Now on the west coast, check out the sets at 6 **Dunes**, the cape's best surf beach, before a short drive up to 7 **Vlamingh Head Lighthouse** offers exceptional views, sometimes of migrating whales.

Pull into 8 **Jurabi Turtle Centre** (p978) to learn about the Testurdines nesting on the nearby beach. Continuing south, pay your park fees at the entry station, then head for 9 **Mangrove Bay** bird hide. Don't miss swimming at 10 **Turquoise Bay** (p978), one of the loveliest beaches in WA. The asphalt ends at 11 **Yardie Creek**, where a boat trip explores the beautiful gorge. Exmouth is 88km back the way you came.

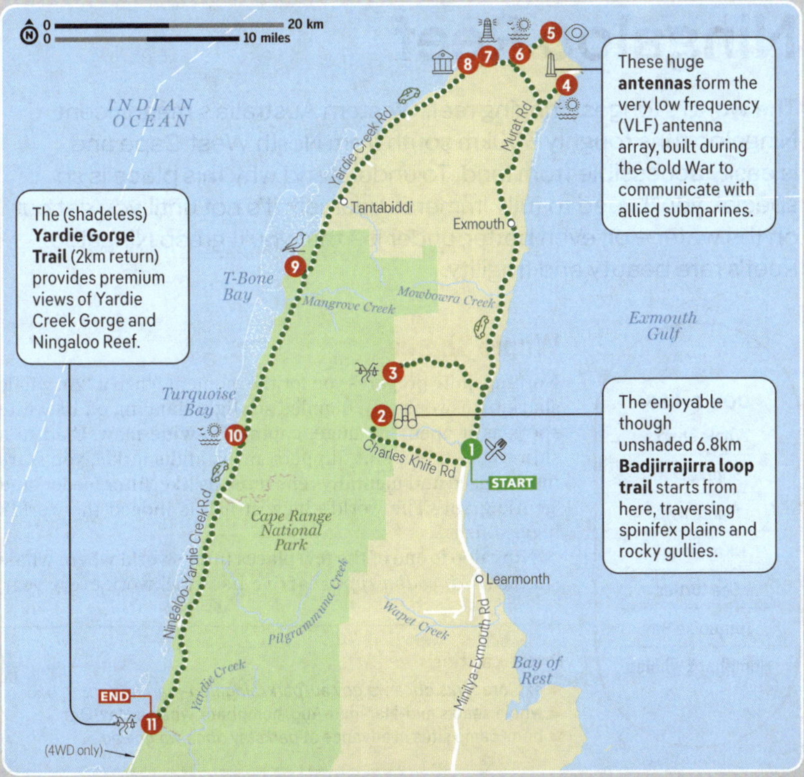

Whale shark, Ningaloo Reef

TOP EXPERIENCE

Ningaloo Reef

The world's longest fringing reef, Western Australia's magnificent Ningaloo runs roughly 300km south from North West Cape and is easily accessible from land. To understand why this place is so special, you'll need to fully immerse yourself: it's not until you get out on the water – or, even better, under it – that you'll grasp Ningaloo Reef's rare beauty and fragility.

DON'T MISS

- Whale sharks
- Snorkelling
- Manta rays
- Kayaking
- Sea turtles
- Turquoise Bay
- Humpback whales

Whale Sharks

Nothing quite prepares you for the moment when a 12m whale shark turns your way, dappled sunlight dancing off its white spots as it opens its huge, gaping 1m-wide maw. Clad in a skin-tight stinger suit, flippers, mask and snorkel, you stare mesmerised and mentally repeat terms like 'filter feeder' and 'gentle giant'. The world's biggest fish is indeed the world's biggest fish.

Ningaloo is one of the few places in the world where whale sharks *(Rhincodon typus)* arrive like clockwork every year,

Practicalities

- *exploreparks.dbca.wa.gov.au/park/ningaloo-marine-park*
- whale sharks mid-Mar–mid-Aug, humpback whales May–Oct
- book camp sites in advance at *parkstay.dbca.wa.gov.au*

just after the autumnal coral spawn, to feed on plankton and small fish. They're usually in the Ningaloo area from mid-March to mid-August, though later-season sightings (up to October) are becoming increasingly common.

There are numerous tour operators in Exmouth. Most will share the same spotter plane, meaning each company will take turns viewing a located fish. Strict protocols govern the interaction; most companies should have an onboard marine biologist. You'll also see manta rays, dolphins and sea turtles.

Tours are usually full day (eight hours) and include all necessary gear (including flotation devices if needed); lunch, snacks and refreshments are provided. Expect a warm-up snorkel on the inner reef before heading out to deeper water where the whale sharks are normally found. Once your operator has located a fish, you'll spend five to 10 minutes in the water, with a limit of 10 swimmers at any time. There should be several repeat opportunities throughout the day and another snorkel on the inner reef towards the end. Manta rays, dolphins and sea turtles are also commonly sighted. While tours won't operate in rough weather, bring appropriate medication if you're prone to seasickness. Prices (adult/child from $620/560) are similar across operators. **Kings** *(kingsningalooreeftours.com.au)*, **Ningaloo Whaleshark'n'Dive** *(ningaloowhalesharkndive.com.au)* and **Three Islands** *(whalesharkdive.com)* are all experienced outfits.

Humpback Whales

And you thought whale sharks were big!

From May to October, about 35,000 humpback whales *(Megaptera novaeangliae)* migrate along the WA coastline, heading north to their warm Kimberley calving grounds before returning south to feed on krill in the Antarctic summer. Exmouth Gulf is an important rest stop for mothers with calves.

Most Exmouth whale shark tour operators also offer full-day humpback tours in season that follow a similar patten: depart Tantabiddi for a warm-up snorkel on the inner reef before heading out into open seas to where a spotter plane has, with luck, identified a pod. If you want to get into the water (albeit from 250m away) with these mammoth creatures then you must be a competent swimmer aged over 13 years. Prices start at $550; just watching costs at least $300.

A shorter option is a two- or three-hour sunset wildlife cruise in Exmouth Gulf. which *may* spot humpbacks, dolphins, rays and other marine life. Usually snacks and sundowners (alcoholic drinks) are provided. These tours depart the Exmouth Marina. **Ocean Eco Adventures** *(oceanecoadventures.com.au; 2½-hour adult/child $139/109)* and **Ningaloo Discovery** *(ningaloodiscovery.com.au; two-hour sail adult/child $119/98)* are popular outfitters.

Failing that, you could drive up to Vlamingh Head Lighthouse (p975) with a pair of binoculars.

CITIZEN SCIENCE

There are several long-running ocean science projects that want to see your marine wildlife photos. **ECOCEAN** *(whaleshark.org.au)* has upload links to a 50,000-plus world-wide whale shark image library that hopes to track and identify individual creatures. Likewise, *happywhale.com* stores over a million whale images, while even sea turtles get a gig at the **Sea Turtle Observatory (STO)** Facebook group.

TOP TIPS

- Most tours leave from the Tantabiddi boat ramp 37km (30 minutes) from Exmouth on the western coast; check if your tour includes transfers.
- When booking a whale shark or humpback whale tour, check the fine print regarding weather cancellations or a no-show by your creature of choice. Usually you'll get another tour, but you might have to wait several days.
- If you badly want to see coral but baulk at snorkelling, a glass-bottomed-boat tour is the way to go. There are several operators. Tours range from an hour or two to half a day. Book at the **Ningaloo Visitor Centre** *(visitningaloo.com.au)*.

UNDERWATER HEATWAVE

Global ocean temperatures for 2024 were the hottest ever recorded, triggering Ningaloo's worst-ever coral bleaching event. Spilling into 2025, the full effects of this 'underwater heatwave', where water temperatures rose up to 4°C above normal, are still being investigated; shallower corals in particular are vulnerable to severe heat stress. An October 2025 survey of sites between Osprey and Tantabiddi revealed a 61% mortality rate, with staghorn *(Acropora)* and birds nest *(Seriatopora)* corals decimated.

Ningaloo Kayak Trails

Kayaking is one of the nicest ways to experience Ningaloo. Paddling at your own pace, you might see turtles, dolphins and manta rays up close. Parks & Wildlife has installed kayak-only moorings in four Ningaloo Sanctuary areas that offer superb snorkelling: **Osprey**, **Tantabiddi**, **Bundegi** and **Maud** (Coral Bay). Each zone has several moorings so you can safely snorkel and not lose your ride. Hire kayaks in Exmouth or off the beach in Coral Bay, or join a tour with **Exmouth Adventure Co** (*exmouthadventureco.com.au; full day $250*).

Nesting Turtles

During the December-to-March nesting season, join a two-hour guided tour run by the **Jurabi Turtle Centre** *(exploreparks .dbca.wa.gov.au/site/jurabi-turtle-centre; adult/child $25/10)* to see nesting green and loggerhead turtles on one of the beaches near the northern end of the peninsula. Tours depart at 6.25pm a few evenings each week; advance bookings are essential. If you have the time and a passion for conservation, consider volunteering with the **Ningaloo Turtle Program** *(ningalooturtles.org.au).*

Diving, Drifting & Bay Snorkelling

While there are epic scuba tours to **Lighthouse Bay** and the **Muiron Islands**, snorkelling is a much easier and cheaper and more fun way to experience Ningaloo. You'll be utterly transfixed by the bommie stacks, bulbous brains and delicate staghorn corals, crazily colourful fish and other exotic reef denizens such as rays and sea turtles. **Bundegi Beach**, **Lakeside** and **Turquoise Bay** are all primo sites; the latter has both bay snorkelling (good for all skill levels) or exciting drift snorkelling (for stronger swimmers; you 'ride' the current over the reef, exiting before you're sucked out to the open sea). Hire snorkel gear from **Exmouth Surf Centre** *(one/two or more days per day $15/10),* any of the dive shops around Exmouth shopping centre or from the **Milyering Discovery Centre** *(day/overnight $12/15).*

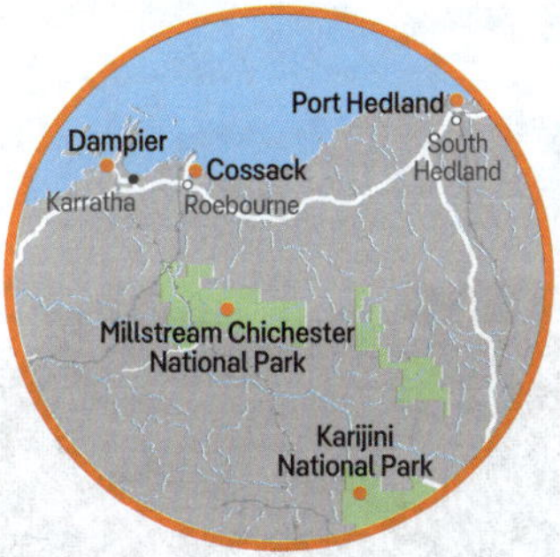

The Pilbara

DESERT LANDSCAPES | GORGES | INDIGENOUS CULTURE

At some point, every traveller needs to cross the vast, hot, mineral-rich expanse known as the Pilbara. Inland, the beautifully desolate 'roof of WA' is littered with ragged hills, spinifex and mines disgorging their bounty into kilometres-long freight trains that snake through mesas and bluffs of the Hamersley Range to the bustling ports and service towns along the coast.

It's inland that you'll find the gorges of Karijini, one of WA's most exquisite national parks, and the deep pools and rugged tors of less-visited though culturally rich Millstream Chichester. The mining towns of Paraburdoo, Tom Price and Newman bookend this region.

Infrastructure heavy, the coast east from Dampier also contains the petroglyphs of Murujuga, swimmable beaches at Hearson Cove and Point Samson, the commercial hub of Karratha, and historic towns such as Cossack and Roebourne. Even post-apocalyptic Hedland with its salt mountains, blast furnaces and railway yards hides an arty centre.

Places

TOP TIP

If you just want to get to or from the north quickly, the inland Great Northern Hwy between Perth and Port Hedland via the mining towns of Newman, Meekatharra, Mt Magnet and historic, cute-as-a picture Cue is much quicker than the coastal route.

Dampier

TIME FROM EXMOUTH: **6HR**

Millions of petroglyphs

Hidden among the curious piles of red rubble and massive gas-processing plants on Dampier's Burrup Peninsula is the planet's largest collection of petroglyphs (rock-art engravings). An estimated one to two million engravings, dating back 50,000 years, are found in the UNESCO-listed **Murujuga National Park**.

GETTING AROUND

Repeat the mantra: I must have my own wheels (preferably 4WD). It's 650 sealed kilometres from Exmouth to Karijini and driving it will take all day. Roads between Karijini/Tom Price and Millstream or Roebourne are unsealed and can be corrugated.

Integrity buses connect the coastal towns with Exmouth, Perth and Broome, and even Tom Price and Newman. Contact Flying Sandgroper (p985) for travel between Exmouth and Karijini.

Karratha, Port Hedland, Paraburdoo and Newman all have flights to/from Perth, while Nexus also flies between Karratha, Port Hedland and Broome.

JANELLE LUGGE/SHUTTERSTOCK

The easiest to visit are at Ngajarli (Deep Gorge), a turn off just before Hearson Cove. A 700m high-accessibility loop trail wanders past a menagerie of fish, goannas, turtles, ospreys, kangaroos and even a Tasmanian tiger. To gain an in-depth understanding of Ngajarli's cultural significance, join the 90-minute **Experience Murujuga tour** *(experience murujuga.com; adult/child $75/55; 8am Tue & Thu).*

Millstream Chichester National Park

TIME FROM DAMPIER: **2HR**

Cultural deep dive

Between Dampier and Karijini, the tranquil waterholes of the Fortescue River form lush oases at **Millstream**, while jagged peaks and flat-topped mesas hide hidden springs in the **Chichester Range**. This is Yindjibarndi Country, one of WA's most culturally significant areas, with 50,000 years of living, connected history. **Millstream Chichester National Park** *(exploreparks.dbca.wa.gov.au/park/millstream-chichester-national-park; per car $17)* is ground zero for Yindjibarndi culture, belief systems and Creation stories.

Millstream has the (unstaffed) visitor centre and museum in the old pastoral **homestead**, a short stroll from the laid-back

EATING IN THE PILBARA: OUR PICKS

Mean Bean: In Tom Price, fall upon a tasty burger whose bun doesn't self-destruct. *6.30am-1pm Mon-Fri, 8am-noon Sat* $

Silver Star Cafe: The brekkies and brunches in this old railcar in the centre of Port Hedland hit the spot. *6am-2pm Tue-Sun* $$

Soak: Dampier's best, with all-day tapas, excellent local seafood, meat and vego options and harbour views. *6am-3pm Mon-Thu, to 10pm Fri & Sat, to 9pm Sun* $$

Karijini Eco Retreat: Runs hot and cold depending on transient staff, but when they're good the modern-Australian dinners here are very good. *5.30-8pm* $$$

Millstream Chichester National Park

Miliyanha campground. There are several walking trails; don't miss the high-accessibility Wetlands walk to the sacred **Jirndarwurrunha Pool** (850m, 15 minutes – no swimming). Other trails lead to **Warrungunha lookout** and the swimming hole **Nhanggangunha** (Deep Reach Pool); you can also drive to both.

Towards Roebourne, **Mt Herbert** (600m, 20 minutes return) in the **Chichester Range** offers a superb 360-degree view over the tors, mesas and plains below, while the nearby **Python Pool** under a sheer cliff provides a welcome swim (if it's not algae tainted). The hot, rocky **Camel Trail** (8km one way) connects the two via **McKenzie Spring** and the **Cameleers Lookout**.

Port Hedland

TIME FROM KARIJINI: **3½HR**

Beauty and the beast

With giant mining apparatus silhouetted against the fierce Pilbara sun, Port Hedland certainly won't win a beauty contest. Nonetheless, the town's creative side shines. The **Courthouse Gallery** *(courthousegallery.com.au)* is an epicentre of tranquillity, championing local, Indigenous and WA art. Local Indigenous artists have also carved out a space at **Spinifex Hill Studio** *(spinifexhillstudio.com.au)*, where you can watch the process and purchase artworks. Afterwards, wander to **Marapikurrinya Park** and watch gigantic cargo ships move around the world's largest bulk-export port. The helpful **visitor centre** *(visitporthedland.com.au)* displays the shipping schedule.

BEST OF THE WARLU REST

Marble Bar: Burnt into the Australian psyche when 160 consecutive days topped 37.8°C (100°F); its annual **race day** is legendary.

Tom Price: WA's highest town (747m) called their local hill 'Mt Nameless'. Pity they didn't ask the Eastern Guruma, who have always called it **Jarndunmunha**.

Onslow: You have to love historic Onslow – a long way up a dead-end road – with beaches called **Sunrise** and **Sunset**.

Roebourne: The Pilbara's oldest town has some fascinating architecture, an interesting **art gallery** *(yinjaa-barni.com.au)* and a mosly Indigenous population.

Point Samson: There's a gorgeous beach, snorkelling at nearby **Honeymoon Cove**, a couple of campgrounds and some premium local seafood.

THE LOST ROCK ART OF JUUKAN GORGE

In 2020 the mining company Rio Tinto made international headlines for all the wrong reasons by legally dynamiting two 47,000-year-old rock art shelters in the Pilbara's Juukan Gorge to make room for the expansion of a nearby iron ore mine. The fact that Rio had the legal right to do it highlighted severe problems with state and federal environmental protection laws, and the company, universally pilloried, was keen to make amends. The Puutu Kunti Kurrama Pinikura (PKKP) Traditional Owners looked to France, where the famous Lascaux and Chauvet art caves have been painstakingly recreated, hoping that the same technology can be used to recreate Juukan in its entirety. Rio Tinto will be footing the bill.

Driving the Great Sandy

Heading 'up the track' (driving the Great Northern Hwy) to Broome from Port Hedland, there's 600km of almost nothing as you skirt the edge of the Great Sandy Desert. **Pardoo** *(pardooroadhouse.com.au)* and **Sandfire** *(facebook.com/sandfire.rh)* roadhouses break the monotony. Coastal stopovers include **Cape Keraudren** *(eastpilbara.wa.gov.au/our-region/tourism/cape-keraudren.aspx),* beloved by fishermen; the dazzling white **Eighty Mile Beach** (it's actually longer), with migrating shore birds and nesting turtles; utilitarian **Port Smith** *(portsmithcaravanpark.com.au)* and **Barn Hill station** *(barnhill.com.au)*; and the luxurious, book-ahead **Eco Beach** *(ecobeach.com.au).* Always check conditions before heading out and bring extra food, fuel and water, as bushfires or flooding can close the highway quickly.

Cossack

TIME FROM ROEBOURNE: **15MIN**

Walking with ghosts

Some 15km north of Roebourne, at the mouth of the Harding River on Ngarluma land, Cossack was once an important pearling centre (pre-dating Broome) and the region's main port. Unfortunately, the town was built in Cyclone Alley and was trashed by a storm in the 1880s; the port moved to Point Samson and the pearling north to Broome.

The heritage stone buildings were lovingly restored in the 1980s. Download the **Cossack Heritage Trail brochure** *(karratha.wa.gov.au/recreation-and-sports/cossack-heritage-trail)* and wander from the **old wharf** to **Galbraith Store** (500m return, 15 minutes) past the courthouse museum and schoolhouse. The separate **Drive Trail** includes **Tien Tsin lookout**; the **Pioneer Cemetery** with its poignant Japanese section commemorating Cossack's pearling past; and **Reader Head Lookout**, with views over the river mouth and alluring **Settlers Beach**.

The local Aboriginal corporation was running accommodation and a cafe in town, but all buildings were closed at research time due to a dispute with the state government.

INC/SHUTTERSTOCK

TOP EXPERIENCE

Karijini National Park

On Banjima, Yinhawangka and Guruma Country, among the dusty mines, spinifex plains and spiking temperatures of the Pilbara's iron-rich Hamersley Range, the glistening jewel of Karijini National Park lies waiting to be discovered. Nature here is on an epic scale, with orange gorges, narrow chasms, tranquil swimming holes, cascading waterfalls and shy rock wallabies hiding among the state's highest peaks.

DON'T MISS

- Hancock Gorge
- Dales Gorge
- Weano Gorge
- Hamersley Gorge
- Punurrunha (Mt Bruce)
- Knox Gorge
- Oxer Lookout

Weano & Hancock Gorges

Prepare to get wet! Weano Gorge and Hancock Gorge constrict to slot canyons where slippery chasms empty into plunge pools. Both gorges are easily combined into a fun afternoon's exploration (4.3km, two hours) and are accessed from the **Weano Picnic Area**, 10km from Karijini Eco Retreat (p1007).

Fire-damaged Upper Weano can be dry, but Lower Weano quickly shrinks into a tight, watery passage before spilling into the **Handrail Pool,** a circular pothole carved into the towering orange walls by swirling water. Back at the top of the Weano stairs, follow the clifftop path to **Oxer Lookout** over **Red Gorge** and the **Junction Pool** 130m below – the confluence of Joffre, Knox, Weano and Hancock Gorges. Next to the closed Junction Pool, a memorial honours SES volunteer

Practicalities

● *exploreparks.dbca.wa.gov.au/park/karijini-national-park* ● per vehicle per day $17 ● open year-round, but gorges may close due to adverse conditions

MEET THE NGADJI

The *ngadji* (western pebble-mound mouse; *Pseudomys chapmani*) is one of Karijini's more reclusive denizens – you might have passed its nest without realising. The mouse piles up literally thousands of pebbles around the hole to its underground den, which can contain as many as 25 mice. Punurrunha is a good place to spot mounds.

Jimmy Regan, who lost his life rescuing a tourist from the restricted zone of lower Hancock Gorge during a flash flood.

Steel ladders descend into Hancock Gorge, then some scrambling (or an easier swim) brings you to the relatively open Amphitheatre. Next, the narrow, slippery Spider Walk leads to the iridescent, emerald-hued Kermits Pool, where it feels as though you're swimming in the bowels of the planet.

Fortescue Falls & Fern Pool

Fortescue Falls and Fern Pool (Jubura) are everybody's favourite swimming holes in Karijini because of their closeness to Dales Gorge Campground (p1007) and permanent, spring-fed water. Most people descend the stairs from the car park directly, but a more interesting option is the full-circuit walk of **Dales Gorge** (4.5km, two hours). From the car park, after viewing the falls from the lookout, follow the clifftop Rim Walk path for impressive views until **Three Ways Lookout**, where you descend steeply into the gorge. At the bottom, turn right and follow the gorge on rock platforms along the stream. A large paperbark marks a nice swimming spot, or you can wait until you reach the falls, where a short, rocky ascent followed by 250m of shaded rainforest track brings you to the sublime Fern Pool, culturally significant to the local Banjima. Take the stairs, of which there are many, back to the car park.

Knox & Joffre Gorges

Out at Knox Gorge, a 1km track leads downstream past some delightful swimming holes to the restricted zone, but it's upstream that's worth exploring, with long, swim-through pools perfect for a hot afternoon.

RYAN HOI/SHUTTERSTOCK

Dales Gorge

Joffre Gorge and its falls are accessible via access road or directly from Karijini Eco Retreat. A lookout provides a view of the rarely flowing falls and the stagnant plunge pool at its bottom, the latter accessible by a series of very steep ladders. The water quality is usually poor.

Hamersley Gorge

Tucked into the park's far western corner, Hamersley Gorge is one of the most spectacular in Karijini: nowhere else are the massive geological forces that forged this landscape more evident. Sheer iron-red cliffs of banded, folded rock tower above cascades and swimming holes, none prettier than the exquisite Spa Pool. Descend from the car park (200m) to the sunny pool below the falls, where there's plenty of scope for further exploration by swimming downstream or boulder-scrambling upstream.

Allow a half-day return from Karijini retreat along mostly unsealed roads (2WD is OK). Combine a visit with a trip to **Tom Price** or to/from Millstream Chichester National Park (p980).

Kalamina Gorge

The park's least visited (public) gorge (due to its unsealed access road) is the wider, vegetated and picnic-friendly Kalamina; it's a great place to escape high-season crowds. You might not want to move from the waterfall and plunge pool at the bottom of the car park stairs, but the hike to **Rock Arch Pool** (3km return, 1½ hours) is one of Karijini's more rewarding wanders.

Restricted-Zone Tours

Hancock, Weano, Knox and Joffre Gorges have restricted zones that you can enter only with ranger permission, which usually means taking a commercial tour. Restricted-zone tours usually contain elements of rock climbing, abseiling, swimming and jumping off small cliffs. You'll spend a lot of time in the water, so wetsuits are mandatory. The payoff is an adrenaline-soaked day of extraordinary beauty in a place few travellers experience. **Space Chameleon** *(spacechameleon adventureco.com; from $295)* runs tours during the April, July and September school holidays; book well ahead.

Punurrunha

The hugely impressive Punurrunha (Mt Bruce; 1235m), WA's second-highest peak, is a much more interesting climb than the slightly higher Mt Meharry (1249m). From a car park past the western end of Banjima Dr, a well-marked trail (10km return, four to five hours) leads up Punurrunha's western flank and along rocky ridges and steep gullies to the flat-topped summit, which has exceptional 360-degree views of both Karijini and the adjoining Marandoo mine. Start early and take plenty of water, as there's almost no shade.

THE FLYING SANDGROPER

Part tour, part long-distance transfer, the hop-on, hop-off **Hoppa Bus** run by the **Flying Sandgroper** *(flying sandgroper.com. au; five days $895)* departs Exmouth every Monday, returning every Friday via Learmouth and Paraburdoo airports, Tom Price, Karijini and the Great Northern Hwy for Broome/Perth coach connections. Gorge tours are included. One- to five-day options offer total flexibility.

TOP TIPS

- Book Dales Gorge camp sites (p1007; adult/child $15/10) at *parkstay. dbca.wa.gov.au*
- Book stays at Karijini Eco Retreat (p1007; camping 2 people from $50) at *karijiniecoretreat. com.au.*
- December to February is unbearably hot during the day, with an increased bushfire risk and maddening flies.
- Swim in pools only if there's water flowing into them; stagnant water (common in Weano and Joffre Gorges) is a health risk.
- Wear closed shoes in the gorges; a cheap pair of reef shoes or sandshoes (find them in Exmouth or Carnarvon) is perfect.
- Don't underestimate how cold the water can be, even on a hot day.

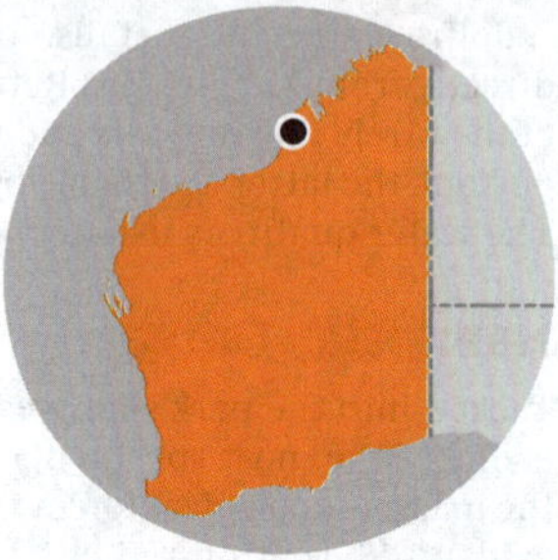

Broome

TURQUOISE WATER | SUNSET CAMELS | RED PINDAN

TOP TIP

Escape the high-season sunset crowds on Cable Beach and head to Entrance Point (p988) near the port. Or take unsealed Kavite Rd towards Gantheaume Point (p988) and search for sandy tracks leading to crumbling pindan clifftops. Park, pick a pozzie (position), sip your beverage and watch the cliffs turn molten red. You might even see whales.

Whether you've just flown in, jumped off a cruise ship or driven 600km across the Great Sandy, your first sight of Broome (Rubibi to the local Yawuru) will stay with you forever: brilliant turquoise waters, red pindan cliffs, deep blue skies and the long crescent of Cable Beach.

Broome is one of Australia's remotest towns; it's closer to Indonesia than to Perth or Darwin and that's reflected in its rich Indigenous, multicultural and pearling history.

Tourists flock to Cable Beach for the view of camels, sand and sunsets, but Broome is so much more than the place a telegraph cable from Java came ashore in 1899. It's mudflats and mangroves, dinosaur footprints and WWII relics. It's tiny Town Beach and pindan-smeared Reddell; it's the old tin shacks of Chinatown and the generations of ospreys nesting in the lighthouse; it's Saturday's Courthouse Markets, hunting for spices in Yuen Wing and that well-deserved, late-afternoon beer on Matso's verandah.

Ride into the Sunset

WA's most famous sands

Lots of travellers come to Broome with the romantic notion of riding a camel on **Cable Beach** at sunset, seduced by an

GETTING AROUND

Chinatown, Broome's principal shopping and cafe strip, is on Roebuck Bay, while Cable Beach and its resorts are on the Indian Ocean, 5km away; the airport runway's between the two. It's usually too hot to walk far, but you can hire almost anything on two or four wheels. Try **Broome Cycles** or **Broome Broome** car hire. A 4WD gives you more options out of town.

Integrity and **Greyhound** run long-distance coaches to Perth and Darwin respectively. A 'shoppers special' runs between Broome and Derby several times weekly. Qantas and Virgin fly daily to/from Perth. Qantas also flies direct to/from Sydney and Melbourne in high season. **Airnorth** flies to Darwin and Kununurra, Nexus to the Pilbara.

SIGHTS
1 Broome Museum
2 Cable Beach
3 Entrance Point
4 Gantheaume Point
5 Old Jetty
6 Reddell Beach
7 Roebuck Bay Lookout
8 Streeter's Jetty
9 Sun Pictures
10 Town Beach
11 WWII Flying Boat Wrecks

ACTIVITIES
12 Broome Camel Safaris
13 Jetty to Jetty Heritage Trail
14 Lurujarri Dreaming Trail
15 Red Sun Camels

SLEEPING
16 Bali Hai Resort & Spa
17 Beaches of Broome
18 Mangrove Hotel

EATING
19 Chi Mayi Kitchen
20 Good Cartel
21 Papá Fuego
22 Wharf Restaurant

DRINKING & NIGHTLIFE
23 Bay Club
24 Broome Closet
25 Matso's Broome Brewery
26 Moontide Distillery

ENTERTAINMENT
27 Town Beach Night Markets

SHOPPING
28 Magabala Books

INFORMATION
29 Broome Visitor Centre

TRANSPORT
30 Airnorth
31 Broome Broome
32 Broome Cycles
see 29 Greyhound
see 29 Integrity

image of camels crossing a reflected sky single file, backlit by a setting sun. Well, folks – that's exactly what you'll get.

Broome Camel Safaris *(Team Blue; broomecamelsafaris.com.au)* and **Red Sun Camels** *(Team Red; redsuncamels.com.au)* offer 30-minute **pre-sunset** *(adult/child $65/45)* – good for small kids – and one-hour **sunset** *(adult/child $130/80)* tours. Team Red also offers a quieter **morning ride** *(adult/child $100/70)*.

BEST KIMBERLEY FESTIVALS

Shinju Matsuri Festival of the Pearl: Broome's biggest festival pays homage to the pearl with parades, food, art, concerts, fireworks and dragon-boat races in August–September.

Mardi Gras: Broome's drag queens mount camels around February–March, while Kununurra gets its glitter on in late June.

Broome Fringe Festival: Grassroots spoken word, music, art and dance in the last week of May.

Ord Valley Muster: Kununurra goes off every May with a week of concerts, food, workshops, Indigenous culture and a rodeo.

Boab Festival: Derby's July celebration of the boab includes mud footy, crab races, street parades, art exhibitions and dinner on the mudflats.

Hunting Dinosaurs

Follow the tracks!

Broome's most publicised dinosaur footprints are found on the rocks below the cliffs at **Gantheaume Point** at low (less than 2.16m) tide. Difficult to recognise, these are just a fraction of the Dinosaur Coast Trackways that spread north for 80km. There are also footprints at nearby **Reddell Beach** and **Entrance Point**.

Download the *Dinosaur Coast* brochure from the **Broome Visitor Centre** *(visitbroome.com.au/see-and-do/dinosaurfootprints)* or, even better, install the **Dinosaur Coast Track Guide** app from *dinosaurcoast.org.au*, which suggests areas to search and aids in identification, then set off to explore the coast along Manari Rd.

Discovering Old Broome

Hear the stories and walk the walk

Broome's heart is the area known as **Chinatown**, with distinctive old tin 'shacks' turned into pearl shops, cafes and galleries. Wander back alleys such as Johnny Chi Lane (opposite Sun Pictures), then find your way to **Streeter's Jetty**.

It's here that the Yawuru self-guided **Jetty to Jetty Heritage Trail** *(yawuru.org.au/culture/the-jetty-to-jetty)* commences. Download the free app from the website, then start your audio tour, which includes 13 points of interest spread over 4km and ends at the **Old Jetty** at **Town Beach**. Each point is brought alive through vibrant stories and recollections by senior members of Broome's various cultural groups. The walk should take around 90 minutes, including an unscheduled but recommended detour to **Roebuck Bay Lookout** at the end of Frederick St.

EATING IN BROOME: OUR PICKS

Good Cartel: Drive through early for coffee and brekkie rice bowls and return later for serious ramen action at this local favourite. *6am-9pm* **$$**

Wharf Restaurant: No longer at the wharf but in Cable Beach; the seafood's still outstanding and the service still fluctuating. *noon-10pm* **$$$**

Papá Fuego: With a fabulous interior, this *parrilla* does delectable flame-grilled meats, tip-top seafood and potent cocktails. *5-9pm Tue-Sat dry season* **$$$**

Chi Mayi Kitchen: Hidden in a shady courtyard off Johnny Chi Lane just where you need a break. Try the barra tacos and delicious juices. *9am-3pm Mon-Sat* **$**

IACOMINO FRIMAGES/SHUTTERSTOCK

Camel riding, Cable Beach (p986)

Watching the Night Sky

See the Staircase to the Moon

Between April and October, the full moon's reflection shimmers across the mudflats of Roebuck Bay at low tide, creating a rippled illusion known as the Staircase to the Moon. At Town Beach it's accompanied by much frivolity: **night markets** *(broomemarkets.com.au)*, food, music and people lounging in fold-up chairs (or at the **Mangrove Hotel**). The phenomenon also happens at other Kimberley and Pilbara sites with east-facing mudflats, including along Crab Creek Rd near the Broome Bird Observatory (p992), **Cooke Point** in Port Hedland, Sunrise Beach at Onslow, **Hearson Cove** near Dampier and Reader Head Lookout (p982) at Cossack. Check visitor centre websites for dates.

Wrecks, Relics, Memorials & Movies

Journey through history

Continue diving into Broome's history at **Broome Museum** *(broomemuseum.org.au; adult/child $12/free)*, with quirky

Continued on p993

DRINKING IN BROOME: OUR PICKS

Bay Club: The Mangrove Hotel's casual outdoor bar is ideal for a beer overlooking Roebuck Bay and Staircase to the Moon viewing. *11am-10pm*

Broome Closet: Love the name, love the cocktails: hipster Melbourne done Broome style. *5-9.30pm Tue-Thu, 4pm-late Fri, 11am-late Sat*

Matso's Broome Brewery: Order a Chango (50/50 chilli/mango beer) and a smoked-croc souvlaki here and you're halfway to becoming a local. *11am-9pm*

Moontide Distillery: In Billingurr, Moontide uses Kimberley monsoonal rainwater and native botanicals in its gins. Tastings and tours available. *noon-5pm Fri-Mon*

HELP ME PICK:

Dampier Peninsula Hideaways

The sandy, scrubby Dampier Peninsula north of Broome is a favourite getaway for locals intent on spending a few days by a beach doing little other than catching seafood. These are the lands of the Bardi Jawi, Jabirr Jabirr, Nyul Nyul, Ngumbal and Goolarabooloo, of neat communities and family- or clan-run outstations, offering experiences from no-frills bush camping to luxury stays, bush tucker foraging and mud-crabbing, all in sight of sparkling waters visited by whales.

Where to Visit if You Love...

Exploring Indigenous Communities

Lombadina This postcard-pretty ex-mission on Thomas Bay offers cultural tours, kayaking, whale watching and accommodation. There's an arts and craft centre, a bakery, a white sand beach and a paper-bark church. The **Ardi Festival** is held here every winter.

Beagle Bay Sacred Heart Church The mother-of-pearl altar was built by Pallottine monks in 1918.

Ardyaloon (One Arm Point) Your access fee includes a tour of the aquaculture centre, which contains a *trochus* shell hatchery. The community has several gorgeous beaches, a store and fuel.

Stunning Coastal Scenery

Pender Bay Escape The clifftop camp sites overlooking this humpback calving site are stunning, as are the Indian Ocean sunsets. Andrew has a wealth of whale knowledge.

Goombaragin Eco Retreat High on red pindan cliffs overlooking Pender Bay, Goombaragin offers comfortable safari tents and a chalet. Don't miss the evening pizzas around the fire.

Family-Friendly Beachside Camping

Middle Lagoon At the end of a sandy track, Middle Lagoon has plenty of space, a swimming beach and basic cabins. You'll need a 4WD to reach it.

Gnylmarung Retreat On a shallow turquoise bay, this is the perfect laid-back spot to spend a few hours or a few days.

Smithy's Seaside Adventures Camp right on the Pender Bay beach at this no-frills place with million-dollar views.

A Hint of Luxury

Mercedes Cove At the tip of Pender Bay, this romantic place has its own private beach. No caravans, campers or day visitors are allowed. You'll need a 4WD to get here.

Resort Life

Cygnet Bay Pearl Farm Settle in to enjoy resort-style accommodation, a bar-restaurant and tours on the water or by chopper.

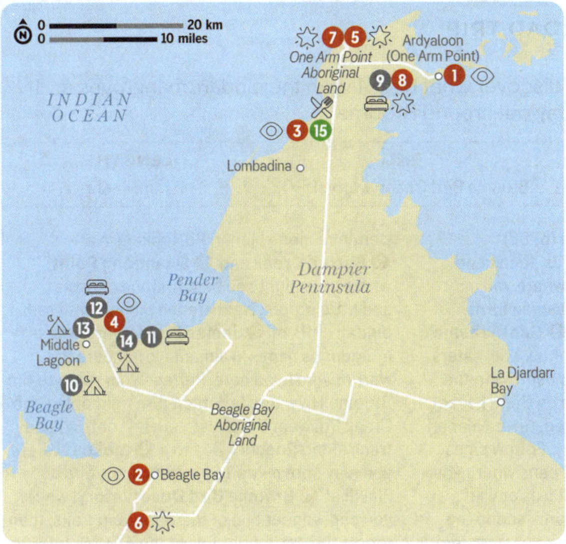

SIGHTS
1 Ardyaloon (One Arm Point)
2 Beagle Bay
3 Lombadina
4 Pender Bay

ACTIVITIES
5 Brian Lee Tagalong
6 Bunda Bunda NJ
7 Bundy's
8 Oolin Sunday Island

SLEEPING
9 Cygnet Bay Pearl Farm
10 Gnylmarung Retreat
11 Goombaragin Eco Retreat
12 Mercedes Cove
13 Middle Lagoon
14 Smithy's Seaside Adventures

EATING
15 Djarindjin Roadhouse

HOW TO

Book ahead Communities can close down quickly for any number of reasons, so booking ahead is a necessity. The *ardibeyondbroome.com.au* website has everything you need to know.

Access fee Most communities charge a small access fee for day visitors, usually payable at the community store or office.

When to go May to September is the normal tourist season; most places close November to March (the wet season).

Getting there There's a sealed road along the whole cape. Lombadina, Beagle Bay and One Arm Point are accessible via 2WD; you'll need a high-clearance 4WD for the rest.

Day Trip or Overnighter?

The full length of the Cape Leveque road is now sealed, drastically decreasing travel times to the Dampier Peninsula and providing for the possibility of a day trip – albeit a long one. You could easily visit Beagle Bay, Lombadina, Ardyaloon and Cygnet Bay by 2WD if you started early, with time for a quick dip.

An overnight stay allows for some essential parts of the Dampier experience: camping out on the pindan, watching a blazing Indian Ocean sunset or whales breaching in Pender Bay, or driving at 30km/h down a sandy track for an hour. More time allows you to get beneath the surface of this incredible place by engaging with locals and hearing their stories, or catching your own mud crab to cook over ashes and eat on the beach. Tours like **Brian Lee Tagalong**, **Bundy's** or **Bunda Bunda NJ** will broaden your understanding. Delve into mission history on the immersive **Oolin Sunday Island** tour.

Kooljaman Resort at Cape Leveque is permanently closed and the road blocked off, so the only dining options are at Cygnet Bay or the **Djarindjin Roadhouse**. Cultural tours leave from both these locations but must be booked in advance. If you don't have transport, Kimberley Cultural Adventures (p993) and Australian Pinnacle run day trips from Broome.

FEATHERED ROAD TRIP

Pack the binoculars and discover what birds live in the pindan, mangroves and mudflats on this scenic day out around Broome.

START	END	LENGTH
Town Beach	Broome Bird Observatory (BBO)	177km; 4–6hr

Start at lovely ❶ **Town Beach** (p988), frequented by pied butcherbirds, then head to ❷ **Entrance Point** (p988), where you may see white-faced herons and Caspian terns. Follow unsealed Kavite Rd to ❸ **Gantheaume Point** (p988), watching for rainbow bee-eaters on overhead wires and nesting ospreys in the point's lighthouse. Leave town on Cape Leveque Rd for 15km, turning left onto red, rutted Manari Rd into Goolarabooloo Country. Follow signs to ❹ **Willie Creek** across salt pans where you might spot emus, brolgas, bustards or wild horses. Just before the pearl farm, scope the mangroves (don't enter them!) for eastern reef egrets and honeyeaters. Double-barred and zebra finches are found in nearby thickets.

Continue along Manari Rd, looking in at ❺ **Barred Creek** and ❻ **Quandong Point**, where you might see beach-stone curlews and little egrets. Next are the magnificent red pindan cliffs of ❼ **James Price Point**, whose Indigenous name, Walmadany, honours the warrior who lived here. Retrace your route to the Broome Hwy, turn left, then turn right onto Crab Creek Rd. Near the coast, turn left onto a sandy track along Roebuck Bay to a ❽ **lookout** where you may spot myriad migratory shorebirds. Finish at ❾ **Broome Bird Observatory**, where you can wander one of the woodland trails, then report the day's sightings at the 6.30pm bird count.

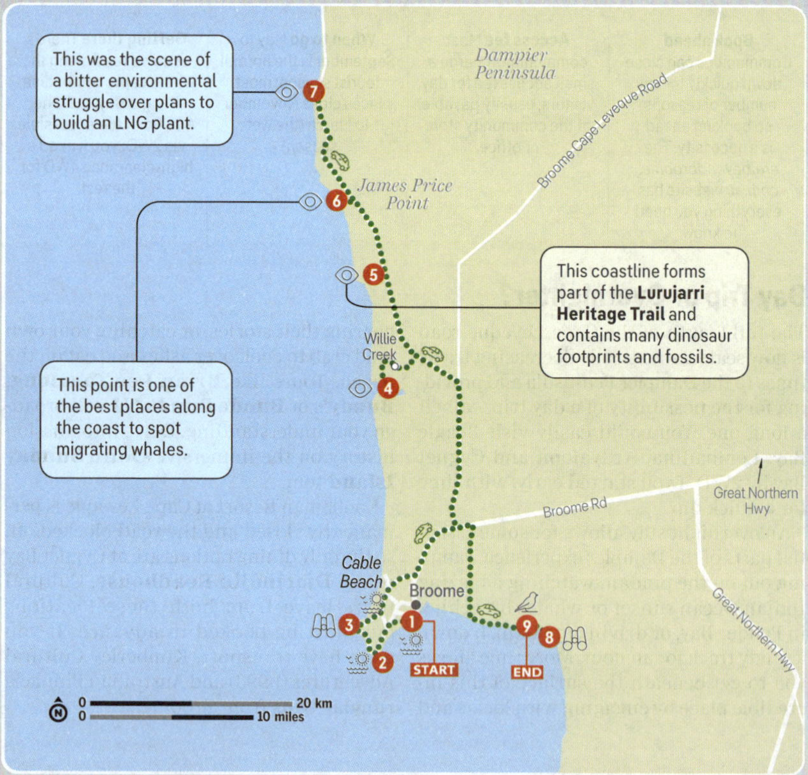

ALEX CIMBAL/SHUTTERSTOCK

Roebuck Bay Lookout (p988)

Continued from p989

pearling, photographic and WWII collections. Sunk in Roebuck Bay by Japanese Zeroes, the wrecked **WWII Flying Boats** can be visited at very low tide by walking out from Town Beach across the mudflats an hour before the tide goes out. Ask the museum for details and download the 'special dates' tide chart from the visitor centre (p988; *visitbroome.com.au/info/tides*).

The history of the **Sun Pictures** *(sunpictures.com.au)* building is the history of Broome itself; it's witnessed war, floods, low-flying aircraft (it's still on the airport flight path) and racial segregation. Take the 11am self-guided **audio tour** *(15 minutes; $5)*, then come back in the evening, sink into a canvas deck chair under the stars and watch a movie in the world's oldest picture garden, rejoicing that the high tide from Roebuck Bay no longer flows through the cinema.

BEST BROOME CULTURAL TOURS

Mabu Buru Tours: Broome local Johani Mamid runs Yawuru and Karajarri cultural tours that include song, dance and bush tucker foraging. *broomeaboriginaltours.com.au*

Jarndu Ngaank: Pat Torres, a Djugun and Jabirr Jabirr Elder, leads walking tours at Town Beach and a women-only tour at Reddell Beach. *jarndutoursbroome.com.au*

Kimberley Cultural Adventures: Learn about Nyul Nyul culture and Broome's history on tours with Robbie Dann. *kimberleyculturaladventures.com.au*

Lurujarri Dreaming Trail: Nine-day guided walk with the Goolarabooloo along the Songline from Cable Beach north to Coloumb Point. *goolarabooloo.org.au*

Magabala Books: Australia's leading Indigenous bookshop and publisher offers a cultural tour of the imagination, with stories for all ages. *magabala.com*

The Kimberley

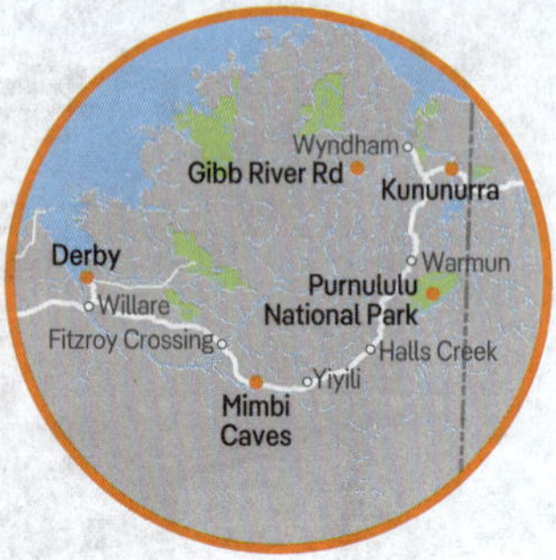

FIRST NATIONS CULTURE | HIDDEN GORGES | 4WD ADVENTURE

Places

TOP TIP
Roads close quickly: keep an eye on the weather, especially at either end of the Dry. Check conditions at *mainroads.wa.gov.au* (for the Great Northern Hwy and Gibb River Road), *sdwk.wa.gov.au* (for West Kimberley) and *swek.wa.gov.au* (for East and North Kimberley).

The vast Kimberley is nature at its wildest and most unforgiving. Over 1000km separates Broome from Kununurra, across plains of boab-studded savannah, ancient ranges, million-acre cattle stations, hidden springs and deep gorges. Hot and dry or hot and wet: take your pick. There are only two roads across the region and only one of them is open all year.

Almost as ancient as the landscape, Indigenous culture remains proud and strong throughout the Kimberley, with seasons intricately woven to the land. It's a culture of journeys and Songlines (sung or spoken memory maps) crisscross the land from coasts to deserts, recording waterholes and Creation stories, hunting spots and places to avoid. Travelling in the Kimberley is knowing the seasons and moving in harmony with them.

Most people visit during the Dry (May to September). Many places close during the Wet, but that's also a time of renewal, lush beauty and mighty storms.

Derby

TIME FROM BROOME: **2½HR**

Visit the Horizontal Falls

On a stretch of Talbot Bay in the Buccaneer Archipelago north of Derby, 11m tides rush through a pair of 10m- and 20m-wide coastal gaps, sometimes creating a 4m 'waterfall'. Accessible only by air or sea, the **Horizontal Falls** are a Kimberley highlight for many.

Seaplane tours depart Derby and Cygnet Bay regularly during the Dry, landing on Talbot Bay, where you'll transfer to a high-powered speedboat. There's an element of risk and

GETTING AROUND

Rent a 4WD unless you're content never to leave the Great Northern Hwy. The Gibb River Road is sealed for around 100km at both ends, but all the side and station access roads are still unsealed, many with often gnarly creek crossings. Most hire car companies don't allow you to take their 4WDs on the notoriously rough Kalumburu and Port Warrender (for Mitchell Falls) roads.

MARION CARNIEL/SHUTTERSTOCK

Horizontal Falls

people do get injured. Tour operators once 'rode' the tide change though the gorges, but the Dambimangari Traditional Owners consider the falls a sacred site, home to the Wongudd creator serpent; they ask that visitors respect Country and only pass through the falls on a neap (slack) tide. The magnificent views from the air are alone worth the trip. Short scenic chopper flights are also available from a pontoon in the bay.

Companies offering tours include **Horizontal Falls Seaplane Adventures** *(horizontalfallsadventures.com.au; from $1150)*. **Fly Broome** (*flybroome.com.au; from $860*) and **Broome Aviation** (*broomeaviation.com.au; from $885*) tours from Broome typically fly over the falls without landing.

Sculptures on the marsh

Rising up out of the flat salt marshes on either side of Derby are almost two-dimensional iron **sculptures**, designed to be viewed against the setting sun. They depict ringers (cowboys), football players, close-up faces and local totems like mud crabs, brolgas and stingrays. Their creator is local artist Mark Norval, whose **gallery** *(facebook.com/norvalgalleryderby)* is another reason to visit this often bypassed town.

Watch a catfish frenzy from the PumpHouse's deck

EATING IN KUNUNURRA: OUR PICKS

Hoochery Distillery: Open year-round, this rum distillery does great lunches during the Dry: the thick, smoky steak sanga is a standout. *hours vary May-Sep* $$

Wild Mango: Kununurrra's favourite brekkie spot has nourishing smoothies, great coffee and a wicked salmon eggs benny. *6.30am-2pm* $

Blak Tapas: This Indigenous-run cafe serves poke bowls, barra burgers and toasted sangers in a shady courtyard. *11.30am-2pm Mon-Fri, to noon Sat* $

PumpHouse: Outside, over the water, enjoy beautiful food, awesome cocktails and a sunset that keeps on giving. *4-9pm Wed-Sun, from 8am Sat & Sun* $$$

HELP ME PICK:

Kimberley Art Centres

Even the smallest First Nations community in the Kimberley has its own arts centre. Often the focal point of the community, these are important meeting places helping keep culture alive. Each part of the Kimberley has its own style, from the Wandjina (spirit beings) of the western Gibb to the X-ray paintings and Gwion Gwion figures of the far north, the bright acrylic dot style of the desert mobs and the traditional ochres of the East Kimberley.

Where to Go if You Love...

Traditional Ochres

Warmun Arts Discover the different ochres and the methods used to find and extract them. All work produced here uses pigments found locally. The nearby Bungle Bungles (Purnululu) are a common motif. *warmunart.com.au*

Dot Paintings

Yarliyil Gallery This Halls Creek gallery showcases the work of local artists using bright acrylics to paint in traditional and contemporary styles. You'll also find work by the Tanami desert mob from Kundat Jaru (Ringer Soak). *facebook.com/yarliyil.artcentre*

Warlayirti Artists Centre Down the Tanami Rd in Balgo, artists here bring the desert alive with vibrant colours and substrates including paper, glass and cloth. *balgoart.org.au*

Spirit Beings

Mowanjum This community near Derby are the Traditional Custodians of the Wandjina. Their art centre is shaped like one and there's an informative museum showing artefacts and a video about the spirit beings. Don't miss the May festival. *mowanjumarts.com*

Kira Kiro In far-flung Kalumbaru, this community paints the mysterious Gwion Gwion figures that are prolific in the far-flung north. It also depicts X-ray-style creatures including turtles and goannas. *facebook.com/kirakiroartists*

Imintji On the Gibb River Road, this tiny place has an art centre behind the local store featuring local Dreaming figures and other crafts. *imintji.com.au/art-centre*

Printmaking & Cultural Tours

Waringarri Arts At this centre in Kununurra, artists from the East Kimberley work with ochres and acrylics in traditional and contemporary styles; there are also etchings and lino prints. It stocks some Kira Kiro works from Kalumbaru. *waringarriarts.com.au*

Mangkaja Arts River and desert artists come together at this Fitzroy Crossing centre known for bright acrylics, dot style and forays into printmaking, textiles and basket weaving. *mangkaja.com*

Textiles & Homewares

Nagula Jarndu This saltwater women's cooperative of the Yawuru in Broome makes and sells exquisite screen- and block-printed textiles and other crafts. *nagulajarndu.com.au*

Marnin Studio Women from across the Martuwarra (Fitzroy River) region come to this safe place of sharing at Fitzroy Crossing. Look for the painted boab nuts. *marninstudio.com.au*

Lombadina Arts & Crafts Visit for beautiful hand-printed T-shirts and limited-edition prints. *lombadina.com/arts-crafts-centre*

Everything in One Place

Bungalow Near Town Beach in Broome, this centre represents artists from across the Kimberley and Central Desert. It holds regular exhibitions in its restored tin shack in Chinatown. *shortstgallery.com.au*

CHAMELEONSEYE/SHUTTERSTOCK

Mowanjum Aboriginal Art and Cultural Centre

HOW TO

Ring first Before heading down the Tanami or out on the Gibb, it pays to check that that remote gallery will actually be open.

Spend some time Many of the centres have artists in residence who will be happy for you to watch them work.

Do your homework Understand the lineal lines, as many of the current artists are second- or third-generation painters coming from a long line of established and well-respected artists.

Show respect Ask about the story the painting depicts. A particular mass of dots could represent the birthplace of the artist's mother.

Ethical Art Dealings

Buying from an Indigenous community owned and run art centre is the best way of ensuring that the original artist receives a fair price and is not being exploited. The centre should supply you with a certificate of authenticity listing the title of the work; the artist's name, skin name, clan or language group; their Country or community; possibly their date of birth; perhaps a brief family history or bio; an artist photo; and the story behind the artwork – what it is actually depicting. There should also be a unique catalogue number and this is important not only to prove provenance but also to ensure the artwork comes from where it's said to have come from. Last, there should be a description of the physical attributes of the piece, eg 'ochre on bark 115cm x 115cm', and a picture of the work.

The further removed you are from where the artwork was created, the greater the chance of artist exploitation. While there are reputable dealers and galleries out there, there are also total sharks. If buying from a dealer or gallery, ask for the certificate of authenticity from the original art centre the work was made at, *not* the dealer or gallery's own certificate. You can check if the reported art centre is legit at *oric.gov.au*. Be wary if the artist is on a wage producing works directly for the dealer or galley.

Piccaninny Creek

TOP EXPERIENCE

Purnululu National Park

The otherworldly sandstone 'beehive' domes of the Kimberley's fabled (and UNESCO listed) Bungle Bungle Range will take your breath away. Remote and inaccessible, the orange cliffs, palm-fringed gorges, spinifex plains, searing sunsets and abundant wildlife of Purnululu National Park, on the traditional lands of the Gija and Jaru people, make for an unforgettable experience.

DON'T MISS

- Cathedral Gorge
- Echidna Chasm
- Kungkalanayi Lookout Sunset
- Mini Palms Gorge
- Piccaninny Gorge
- Whip Snake Gorge
- The Domes

Northern Gorges

Start at the **Bloodwoods** picnic area and keep an eye out for northern rosellas and pied butcherbirds as you follow the Escarpment Trail to **Mini Palms Gorge** (4.4km return), one of the park's best day walks, where a boulder scramble leads to a Livistona palm sanctuary and viewing platform below towering cliffs. Decide whether to push on to Echidna Chasm on foot (7.2km return from the track junction) or go back to the Bloodwoods and drive; the latter is the sensible

PRACTICALITIES

● *exploreparks.dbca.wa.gov.au/park/purnululu-national-park* ● vehicle access $17, camping per night adult/child $15/7 ● Apr-Oct hot weather option. A dry creek bed leads to **Echidna Chasm** (2km return), a knife-thin cleft in the cliffs open to the sky. Widening to a chamber, the route constricts again to a tight scramble, eventually blocked by rockfall. Look up and marvel at the colours of the chasm walls overhead.

Southern Gorges

Day walks from the **southern car park** follow the dry bed of Piccaninny Creek. The **Domes** (700m), an easy loop track, brings you close to the 'beehives', but if there's an iconic view of Purnululu it's the massive orange cavern of **Cathedral Gorge** (2km return), a route mostly shaded until midmorning. Most people of average fitness can accomplish both walks.

Continuing along the main creek line will expose you to the full strength of the sun. The **Window** (6km return from the car park) is a photogenic natural hole in the surrounding cliffs. To sample the route to **Piccaninny Gorge**, follow the meandering, sandy creek bed, now broken up by smooth, eroded rock bands in fantastic and intricate shapes, to **Whip Snake Gorge** (10km return, three hours) with its small terminal pool, rock fig and possible visits from white-quilled rock pigeons.

Lookouts

Sunsets are sublime from **Kungkalanayi Lookout**, close to both the **visitor centre** and **Kurrajong Campground**. Visit during the day, then return with camp chairs and picnic snacks an hour before sunset. The sandstone cliffs turn molten red, while the spinifex plains shimmer soft and golden. For fewer people, **Stonehenge** near Bloodwoods is usually deserted. Sunrise by **Elephant Rock** on the way to the southern car park is rightly popular, though the view from **Piccaninny Creek Lookout**, past the Cathedral Gorge track junction, is simply spectacular as sheer walls and domes take on a deep orange glow.

Piccaninny Gorge Trek

The most challenging walk in the park, this magnificent hike (26km return, minimum two to three days) departs the southern car park and follows the hot, meandering dry bed of Piccaninny Creek into a pristine gorge system beginning at the **Elbow**. This is a true wilderness area without signage, amenities or track and should only be attempted by well-equipped, experienced hikers familiar with rough terrain; you'll need a permit ($20 per day) from the visitor centre. It's 13km (around four hours without stops) to the **camp site** at **1st Finger**. Exploring the five individual fingers (side gorges) will take extra time. Expect some scrambling, shady Livistona groves, sheer cliffs, swim-throughs, boulders and narrow slots. Don't underestimate the heat: leave at sunrise and bring a personal locator beacon and plenty of water (the latter *may* also be found in **Black Rock Pool** and at 1st Finger).

ACCESS BY ROAD OR PLANE

It's a rough, unsealed 53km from the Great Northern Hwy 130km north of Halls Creek to the visitor centre; due to permanent creek crossings, a high-clearance 4WD is mandatory. Scenic flights into or just over the park depart from Halls Creek, Warmun and Kununurra. Most tours include a visit to Echidna Chasm and/or Cathedral Gorge. An overnight stay increases the tour price dramatically.

TOP TIPS

- It takes over an hour to drive from Echidna Chasm to the southern car park, so pick the campground – northern **Kurrajong** or southern **Walardi** – nearest to your planned walk.
- Book camp sites before arriving at *parkstay.dbca.wa.gov.au*
- Start walking as early as possible, heading to your furthest point first to beat the heat (and groups!).
- Bring all water, food, fuel, sunscreen and camping gear; campfires are not allowed.
- Spend at least two nights, as it takes a full day to see most of the sights.
- Free camping is available outside the park at Spring Creek Rest Area on the Great Northern Hwy near the entrance road.

TACKLING YOUTH CRIME

Youth crime has blighted several Kimberley towns in recent years, with car theft, burglaries and vandalism by kids as young as 10. Most of it's opportunistic: the kids are bored with nowhere to go. Police have said that more arrests won't make a difference and that any solution should be community based. In response, Fitzroy Crossing's Marra Worra Worra Aboriginal Corporation has instigated a 'Night Place' program, which gives kids a safe place to go at night, get a feed, feel connected and play games like basketball. So far there's been an 85% drop in crime rates and other towns like Halls Creek are looking to do the same. Meanwhile, don't flash your valuables, don't wander around at night and always lock your vehicle, even when refuelling.

PHILIP SCHUBERT/SHUTTERSTOCK

Mimbi Caves

Spot diverse birdlife across unique natural habitats

Derby should be on every bird watcher's list, with its varied habitats of mangroves out by the pier (good for ospreys, herons, sea eagles); the unique **Derby Wetlands** (OK, they're sewerage ponds), where you might see hordes of whistling ducks; the **Joonjoo Botanical Trail**, hosting woodland birds such as honeyeaters, blue-winged kookaburras and little friarbirds; and the expansive **Munkajarra Wetlands** *(australiasnorthwest.com/explore/kimberley/derby/birdwatching)*, attracting migratory waders.

Mimbi Caves

TIME FROM FITZROY CROSSING: 1HR

Ancient limestone labyrinths and prehistoric fish fossils

Southeast of Fitzroy Crossing, just off the Great Northern Hwy on Gooniyandi land within Mt Pierre Station, is the vast subterranean labyrinth of Mimbi Caves. The caves, part of the limestone Devonian Reef, are rich in rock art and fish fossils. A tour typically lasts two hours. Book through Aboriginal-owned **Girloorloo Tours** *(mimbicaves.com.au; adult/child $90/45)*.

EATING IN DERBY: OUR PICKS

Neaps Bistro: Choose among açaí bowls, salmon eggs benny, smashed avo or a big Kimberley fry-up at this bistro attached to Derby Lodge. *hours vary* $$

Jila Gallery Cafe: Atmospheric courtyard dining and nightly gourmet pizzas (prawn, chilli, mango) that rock the place. *7-11am & 5-8pm Mon-Fri, 5-8pm Sat & Sun* $$

Boab Inn: Stop in for all the pub favourites: burgers, parmas, steaks and barra. *noon-2.30pm & 5-9pm Mon-Sat* $$

Sampey Meats: Be it a cryovac'd T-bone or some chilli biltong, they've got what you need to survive the Gibb. *8am-5pm Mon-Fri* $

THE OLD WAY TO WYNDHAM

Visit gorges, swimming holes, nature reserves and rock art on this historic 4WD route to a stunning lookout.

START	END	LENGTH
Kununurra	Kununurra	296km; 5hr

After admiring Kununurra's 1 **Diversion Dam**, head up the Great Northern Hwy and turn onto unsealed Valentine Springs Rd in the Ngamoowlaem Conservation Reserve. Swim at 2 **Middle Springs (Mayiba)**, beneath a small waterfall. Nearby 3 **Black Rock Falls** has a cliff stained black from cyanobacteria.

Follow Parry Creek Rd, once the route to Wyndham, into Parry Lagoons Nature Reserve and 4 **Telegraph Hill** with its outstanding view over the Ord floodplain. Descend the rough road to the bird hide at 5 **Marlgu Billabong**, where migrating birds arrive in the Dry, as well as local brolgas, jabiru and pelicans. Head across the flats for Wyndham, but on the outskirts turn onto King River Rd. Cross a large salt pan before climbing into the Cockburn Range, then take the Moochalabra Dam turn. After crossing a dry creek, park at a small turning circle and climb to an astonishing 6 **rock-art** gallery.

Return to the highway and continue towards Wyndham, turning right for the Bastion. The road winds 360m above Wyndham to the impressive 7 **Five Rivers Lookout** over Cambridge Gulf, a favourite sunset perch. Back in town, pass the 8 **Big Croc** and head to the port precinct and 9 **museum**. Return along on the asphalt, diverting to the tranquil 10 **Grotto** for a swim and, if time permits, the beautiful 11 **Wuggubun community** on the way back to Kununurra.

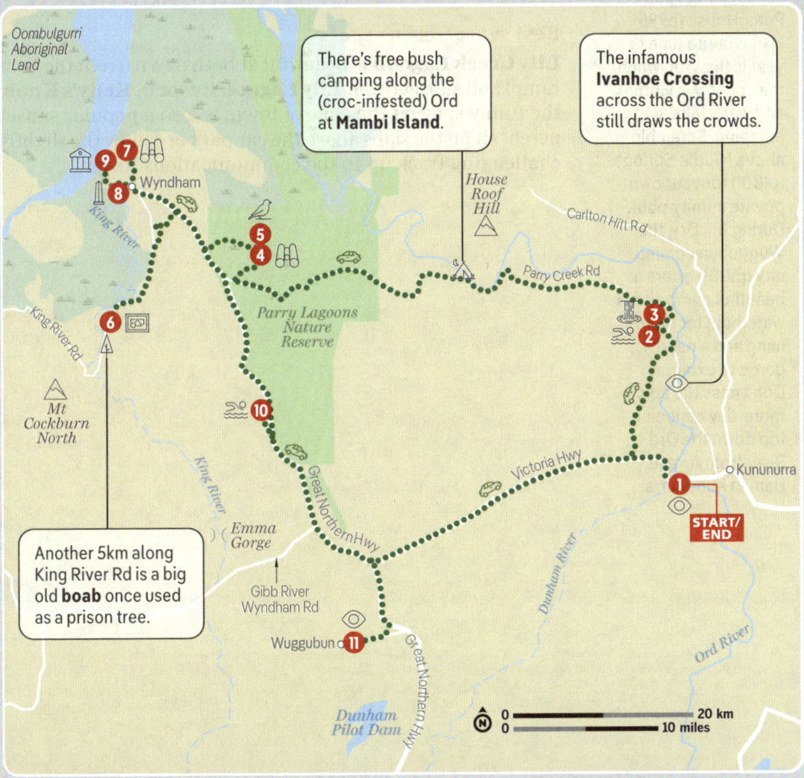

Kununurra

TIME FROM KATHERINE: **5½HR**

Canoeing the Ord on DIY adventure

Superb self-guided canoeing trips with **Go Wild** *(gowild.com.au; self-guided/guided $400/1950)* travel downstream on the **Ord River** from just below Argyle Dam to Kununurra, overnighting in designated camp sites complete with tent platforms and cooking equipment. Go Wild supplies all gear, including canoe, tent and cooler; you bring food, sleeping bag and bathers. You'll also get a map of the river detailing side hikes to gorges and swimming holes. Allow three days for the full descent. Go Wild also offers a five-day fully guided trip.

Explore sandstone formations on Indigenous-led tours

The sandstone cliffs and rock formations of **Mirima National Park** *(per vehicle $17)* – drive in, or walk in from Hidden Valley – on Kununurra's outskirts have been described as a miniature Bungle Bungles (p996). It's certainly easier to access than Purnululu. On Miriwoong and Gajerrong Country, the park has walks with interpretive signage; the closest to the car park is wheelchair accessible. The full circuit (5km) takes about 90 minutes. If you'd like to hear the stories firsthand, join a 2½-hour Indigenous-led tour from **Warringarri Arts Centre** *(waringarriarts.com.au/tours; adult/child $85/45).*

Best sunset gazing spots

Lily Creek Lagoon is beautiful at both dawn (from the boat ramp) and sunset (from **Lily Lagoon Resort**). **Kelly's Knob**, the funny spike at the edge of town, is also a popular sunset perch; sit on the slabs above the car park or follow the slightly challenging track up to the communications tower.

KUNUNURRA ADVENTURING

Dr Niki Teunissen, Kimberley ecologist based in Kununurra

Kununurra offers plenty for outdoor enthusiasts, from hikes among impressive rock formations to mountain biking, camping, canoeing and refreshing swims under stunning waterfalls. If you don't feel like leaving town, it's hard to beat a sunset dinner at the PumpHouse (p995). My favourite time of year is the Wet, when the country is vibrant and waterfalls are pumping. Scramble above Middle Springs (p1001) for your own private infinity pool. During the Dry, the Wuggubun community (p1001) offers a beautiful camp site, a waterhole for swimming and a nearby gorge to explore. Don't miss the epic three-day canoeing trip down the Ord River from Argyle Dam to Kununurra.

ANJAHENNERN/SHUTTERSTOCK

TOP EXPERIENCE

Gibb River Road

Epic, exhilarating, exhausting, a trip through the heart of the Kimberley on the legendary Gibb River Road ('The Gibb') is on every traveller's tick list. The 660km, mostly unsealed 4WD stock route linking Derby with the East Kimberley crosses huge cattle stations and dramatic gorge country. But it's the nights camping under the Milky Way that make this trip so memorable.

DON'T MISS

- Emma Gorge
- Punamii-unpuu (Mitchell Falls)
- Amalia Gorge
- Dimalurru (Tunnel Creek)
- Bandilngan (Windjana Gorge)

Western Gibb Diversions

An ancient Devonian limestone reef cuts across the western Gibb, containing several interesting national parks. Take unsealed Fairfield Leopold Downs Rd from its northern junction with the Gibb just before the Lennard River crossing to stunning **Bandilngan (Windjana Gorge) National Park** *(per vehicle $17)*, where several interpretive trails explore the base of 100m cliffs. Inside the gorge, spot numerous freshwater crocodiles basking by the pools of the Lennard River. It's sacred to the Bunuba, so swimming isn't permitted. There's a pleasant campground with showers nearby.

PRACTICALITIES

● *mainroads.wa.gov.au/travel-information/driving-in-wa/gibb-river- road/* ● usually open Apr-Oct, but check road reports.

GIBB TOUR COMPANIES

Kimberley Wild Expeditions *(kimberleywild.com.au; from $4615)* runs 11- and 14-day camping trips along the Gibb River Road and also includes the Bungle Bungles.

Kimberley Adventure Tours *(kimberleyadventures.com.au; from $3295)* passes through the Gibb on its 10-day Broome to Darwin camping trip.

Outback Spirit *(outbackspirittours.com.au; 16 days from $14,535)* has several luxury options visiting all the Gibb highlights.

Kimberley Outback Tours *(kimberleyoutbacktours.com.au; nine days from $7595)* runs tours aimed at a more mature crowd.

Further south, Fairfield Leopold Downs Rd weaves through the Napier Range past boab *(Adansonia gregorii)* groves and rocky ridges. Soon it'll be time to cool off at **Dimalurru (Tunnel Creek)**, an underground limestone cavern carved over millions of years by water flowing under the Napier Range. Extending for 750m, Tunnel Creek can only be explored during the Dry. Bring a decent torch and non-slip footwear as there's some scrambling and (possibly deep) wading. Look for rock art on the cliffs at the end.

Closer to Fitzroy Crossing than to the Gibb, **Danggu (Geikie Gorge)** was once the busiest of the Devonian Reef gorges, but it copped a beating from Cyclone Ellie in late 2022 and has only just reopened to sightseers.

North to Ngauwudu

Kalumburu Rd heads north from the Gibb to **Drysdale River Station**, your last fuel and supplies if you're heading on to Mitchell Falls. Check ongoing road conditions here. You'll need an **Uunguu Visitor Pass** *(adult/family five-day pass Apr-Oct $55/130)* from the **Wunambal Gaambera** *(wunambalgaambera.org.au)* covering the **Ngauwudu Road Zone**, which begins immediately after fording the **King Edward River**, 107km from Drysdale, on the Port Warrender Rd. There are two excellent rock art sites and a basic campground nearby, collectively called **Munurru**. Leave trailers here; the road across Ngauwudu (Mitchell Plateau) can be horrifically rocky and rutted.

Pass beautiful Livistona palm forests en route to the **Mitchell Falls campground**. Begin the walk to Mitchell Falls (10km return, three hours) early before the day heats up. Don't miss taking a refreshing dip in the beautiful pool below **Little Mertens Falls**, then search for rock art under nearby overhanging cliffs. **Punamii-unpuu (Mitchell Falls)** is a wonderfully photogenic set of cascading horseshoe falls and pools, though the water flow reduces to a trickle mid-Dry.

Eastern Gibb Gorges

El Questro Wilderness Park *(elquestro.com.au)*, a vast, 4000 sq km cattle station turned resort, is the Gibb's most touristed area. Hike into **El Questro Gorge** (with permanent, spring-fed pools), exciting **Amalia Gorge** with a lovely plunge pool or just soak in hot **Zebedee Springs** (morning only), under soothing Livistona palms. Day passes ($15) are available if you're not staying. Massive **Chamberlain Gorge** is best explored by **boat** *(adult/child $65/33)*.

Further down the Gibb, El Questro's **Emma Gorge** is a striking box canyon surrounded by the soaring orange walls of the Cockburn Range. Wear proper shoes and bring your bathers; a slippery, scrambling 40-minute hike leads to the terminal plunge pool, the prettiest in the Kimberley, with hanging moss gardens and crystal-clear water.

DRIVING THE GIBB

Fire up your 4WD and test your skills on this classic cross-country multiday drive through the heart of the Kimberley.

START	END	LENGTH
Derby	Kununurra	842km; 3–7 days

From ❶ **Derby** (p994), the first 119km of the Gibb to the Lennard River crossing are sealed. Over the river, pass Queen Victoria's Head, a regal-looking rock formation in the Napier Range. The road then straddles the Wunaamin Miliwundi Ranges, with good views from ❷ **Inglis Gap**. Take the rough dirt track to beautiful ❸ **Bell Gorge (Dalmanyi)**, where a spectacular horseshoe-shaped plunge pool will wash away the dust.

Grab diesel, toasties and some local art at tiny ❹ **Imintji Store**, then head for ❺ **Galvans Gorge**, where a lush plunge pool is protected by a Wandjina. Fuel up and grab a burger at ❻ **Mt Barnett**, then spend a night at ❼ **Mt Elizabeth** (p1007), a historic working cattle station with several interesting gorges and hearty communal dinners.

Drop into ❽ **Ellenbrae** for its legendary scones, then catch the majestic views from Cockburn Ranges lookout. Nearby, ❾ **Home Valley** (p1007) is a hospitality training venue for young Indigenous people; with restaurant, bar, pool and grass, it's a great place to overnight.

Cross the iconic ❿ **Pentecost River**, regain the asphalt, then follow the Cockburn Ranges past turn offs to El Questro and Emma Gorge, until the epic road ends with a whimper at a T-intersection. Turn left for Wyndham (p1001) or right to ⓫ **Kununurra** (p1002).

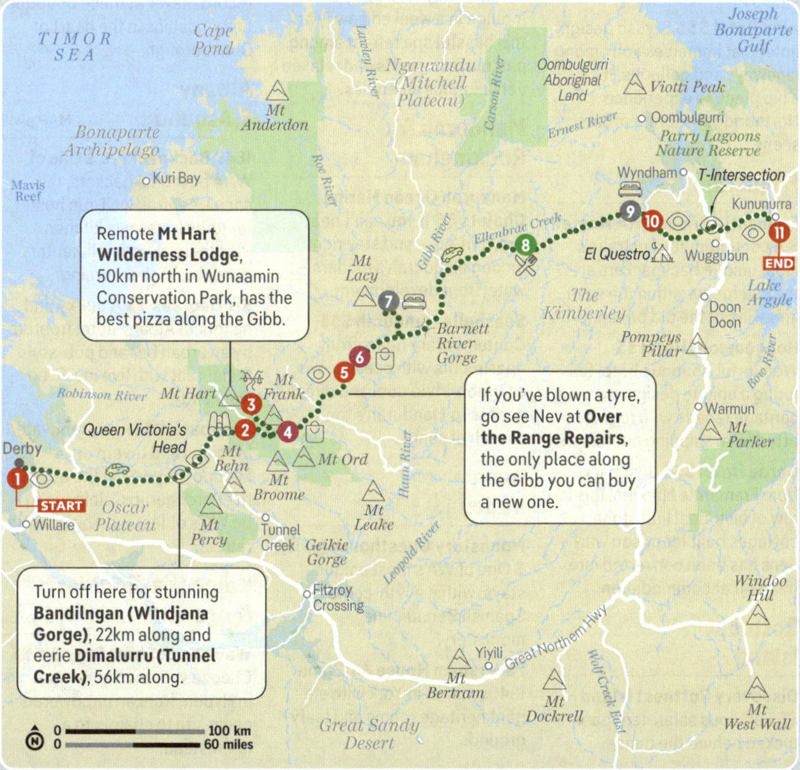

Places We Love to Stay

$ Budget $$ Midrange $$$ Top End

Perth

MAP p892

Akara Hotel $ Private rooms for under $100 is a good deal for central Perth. They're well located for main sights as well as Northbridge's nightlife.

Adnate Perth $$ Right in the heart of it, this hotel is decorated with a giant mural by renowned streetartist Adnate, alongside modern rooms with city views.

Como the Treasury $$$ Luxury hotel within the historic State Buildings' Baroque splendour with sleek, modern rooms and access to this wonderful dining precinct.

Alex Hotel $$$ Stylish design hotel that immerses you among laneways and galleries. It's a hip place to experience Northbridge's vibrant urban scene.

Fremantle

Fremantle Prison YHA Hostel $ A contender for Australia's most unique backpackers are the cell rooms within the woman's wing of the old prison.

Hougoumont Hotel $$ Wonderful boutique hotel featuring a unique design merging heritage facade with rooms fitted from shipping containers.

Garde Hotel $$$ Just back from Fremantle Markets, this row of historical limestone cottages built for prison wardens has been converted into five-star accommodation.

Rottnest Island

Discovery Rottnest Island $$ Fabulous safari-tent park tucked behind the dunes backing Pinky Beach with swimming pool and resort-style oceanfront bar-restaurant.

Lodge Wadjemup $$ A stylishly restored heritage lodge with contemporary, minimalist rooms and a lively cafe-bar, set in a quiet precinct overlooking the island's salt lakes.

Swan Valley

Discovery Parks Swan Valley $ Affordable, family-friendly holiday park with the usual setup of camp sites, cabins, swimming pool and playground.

Swan Valley Retreat $$$ Indulge in a weekend away at this blissful spa retreat among pastoral surrounds and relaxed yet luxurious amenities.

Mandurah & Rockingham

Mandurah Ocean Marina Chalets $$ If you can't beat 'em, join 'em – and stay right among Mandurah's modern waterfront development.

Seashells Mandurah $$$ Contemporary beachfront apartments with ocean views, a lagoon-style pool and direct access to Mandurah's top stretch of sand.

Avon Valley

Monastery Guesthouse (p916) $ One of WA's most unique stays: within a 19th-century Spanish Benedictine monastery.

Faversham House $$ Grand 1840s manor in York with elegant heritage rooms and leafy grounds.

Margaret River Region

MAP p920

Karriview $$ A multilevel lodge and tranquil chalets on a private Margaret River property surrounded by 16 hectares of bush and karri trees.

8 Paddocks $$$ Luxury chalets on a secluded Cowaramup property. Enjoy complimentary local beer and fresh farm eggs, plus there's a snack box so you can feed the adorable highland cows in the adjoining paddock.

Southcamp Stays $$$ Experience an intimate stay with minimalist design and a record player at these boutique timber cabins in the heart of Dunsborough.

Albany & Around

MAP p942

1849 Backpackers $ One of WA's best backpackers, this social, central, well-run hostel features a massive kitchen. Plus there are complimentary pancakes in the morning.

Six Degrees $$ A quirky and historical Albany hotel fronted by an urban bar and pub-style restaurant with live music on weekends.

Karribank $$ Newly renovated lodgings and tavern on a historic property in the quiet of the Porongurups, claiming to be WA's oldest running country retreat.

Kalgoorie-Boulder & Around

MAP p954

Wave Rock Short Stay $-$$$ Choose your own adventure in Hyden, from an unpowered camp site to chalets to a homestead.

Hospitality Kalgoorlie $$ Cosy rooms in a classic country-town motel with modern amenities and a restaurant serving generous pub-style and Filipino dishes.

Palace Hotel $$ Staying in a historic pub is the quintessential Kalgoorlie experience and this grand 1897 hotel delivers with plenty of local character.

The Pinnacles & Beyond

Jurien Bay Tourist Park $ Holiday park catering to solo travellers and families, with units and camp sites right on Jurien Bay's foreshore.

Cervantes Lodge $$ Run by the same folk who own the Lobster Shack are these well-priced rooms with a mix of private and family options.

Kalbarri

Gecko Lodge $$ The pick of Kalbarri's accommodation, this luxury B&B has morning muffins and spa-bath suites with balconies.

Shark Bay & Monkey Mia

MAP p968

RAC Monkey Mia Dolphin Resort $ Superb beachside place with campgrounds to high-end rooms, plus restaurant, bar, two pools, shop and tour-booking office.

Exmouth & Ningaloo Coast

DBCA Camp sites $ The 12 coastal campgrounds in Cape Range National Park, just behind the Ningaloo dunes, each have basic bush sites.

Ningaloo Lodge $$ An excellent deal, with small, cheerful rooms and well-equipped communal kitchen and laundry, plus barbecue, pool and palm-fringed courtyard.

The Pilbara

Dales Gorge Campground $ The best camp in Karijini, with large, shaded sites and a great location.

Karijini Eco Retreat $$$ Completely Aboriginal-owned, this retreat is a model for sustainable tourism with cheaper tents up to comfortable glamping, plus a restaurant.

AGENT WOLF/SHUTTERSTOCK

Karijini Eco Retreat, The Pilbara

Broome

MAP p987

Beaches of Broome $ An upmarket hostel, this popular place has dorms, air-con rooms, pool, bar and bike/scooter hire.

Broome Bird Observatory $ Tranquil bush camp sites, good amenities and plenty of birds are found 20km out of town, down unsealed Crab Creek Rd, by Roebuck Bay.

Bali Hai Resort & Spa $$$ Lush and with a touch of Zen, this small resort has gorgeously decorated studios and villas, plus spa and cafe.

The Kimberley

Mt Elizabeth Station $ Bush camping on a historic station, with plenty to see. Don't miss the evening communal meal.

Home Valley Station $ This hospitality training resort for local Balanggarra people has a range of accommodation and wholesome meals.

Larrawa Station $ Sunsets linger at this oasis between Fitzroy Crossing and Halls Creek; bush sites and basic amenities April to October.

Derby

Derby Lodge $$ Choice of clean, safe motel rooms or self-contained apartments; on-site bistro.

Kununurra

Hidden Valley Tourist Park $ Wonderful place with shady sites, cabins, mango trees and a pool, all within cooee of Mirima National Park.

Kimberley Grande Resort $$ Across the road from the lagoon, this stylish place has large rooms, a pool and a bistro.

Helinox

TOOLKIT

The chapters in this section cover the most important topics you'll need to know about in Australia. They're full of nuts-and-bolts information and valuable insights to help you understand and navigate Australia and get the most out of your trip.

Carnarvon Gorge National Park (p458)

STEVE WATERS/LONELY PLANET

Arriving

Most visitors reach Australia by air, typically via the major international airports of Sydney (Warrane), Brisbane (Meanjin) or Melbourne (Narrm). All state and territory capitals have an international airport, as do Cairns (Gimuy) and the Gold Coast. Hobart's only direct international route is to Auckland, New Zealand.

Visas

New Zealand passport holders are the only visitors exempt from applying for a visa or visa waiver (ETA) in advance of travelling to Australia. More than 30 nationalities are eligible for an ETA.

Customs

Australia takes biosecurity very seriously – don't forget to declare any food products, plants or seeds, and even muddy shoes (which will be cleaned for you, not confiscated, if needed).

Duty Free

You're allowed to bring 2.25L of duty-free alcohol into Australia. If you're travelling on a budget, it's wise to grab a few bottles at the airport upon your arrival, before you reach customs.

Wi-Fi & SIM Cards

All of Australia's international airports have free wi-fi, with SIM cards available for purchase, though SIM provider options can be limited.

Transport from the Airport to the City Centre

	SYDNEY	BRISBANE	MELBOURNE
TRAIN	from 11min; from $21	from 20min; $22.30	N/A
BUS	N/A	N/A	from 30min; $24.60
TAXI	from 20min; from $45	from 20min; from $67	from 25min; from $55

TOURIST REFUND SCHEME (TRS)

Did you spend $300 or more (including tax) at a single business in Australia within 60 days before your departing flight? That makes you eligible to claim a refund on the tax paid on the goods as you leave through the airport. You'll need to present the items – carried on board or, for checked items, shown to the Australian Border Force before you check in – along with a valid tax invoice. Arrive at the airport early, as you'll need time after security to lodge your claim; TRS queues can be lengthy.

FROM LEFT: FUSE/GETTY IMAGES, GOGLIK83/ISTOCK/GETTY IMAGES

Getting Around

Transport costs can quickly add up, but it's still much cheaper to use bus, train and light-rail networks in major cities rather than taxis or rideshares. A car is ideal (sometimes necessary) outside urban centres.

TRAVEL COSTS

Car rental
$55/day

Petrol
$1.75–1.80/L

Bicycle hire
from $20/hour

City train fare
$3–6 for a short trip

Local Networks

States and territories have independent transport networks; visit their websites or check their apps for timetables and fares. All capital cities have bus networks, and all but Darwin (Gulumerrdgen) and Canberra have trains. Sydney, Melbourne (as part of its tram network), Canberra and the Gold Coast have a light rail, and Sydney, Brisbane, Melbourne and Perth (Boorloo) have city ferries.

Transport Cards

States and territories also have their own transport cards. The Sydney metro area (including Newcastle) uses the Opal card, southeast Queensland has the Go Card, Melbourne the myki card, Perth the SmartRider card, Adelaide (Tarntanya) the metroCARD, Canberra the MyWay card, and Darwin the Tap and Ride card.

TIP

Carsharing is widespread across Australian cities. **GoGet** and **Pop Car** offer rates from around $10 per hour (plus joining fee), making it cheaper than hiring a car for short distances.

Driving Conditions

Australia is well connected by road, with sealed roads from north to south and east to west. Most are in good condition, but it's a good idea not to drive in rural areas after dark, to avoid hitting wildlife. A 2WD can handle some unsealed roads, but you'll need a 4WD to travel north of Cooktown or Broome, or into Arnhem Land.

DRIVING ESSENTIALS

Drive on the left

50

Speed limit is 50km/h in built-up areas, and up to 110km/h on other roads

.05

The blood alcohol limit is 0.05%

Electric Vehicles

Electric vehicles (EVs) still cost more to rent than petrol models in Australia, but you won't face range anxiety on an east coast road trip. Chargefox, Evie Networks and Tesla operate extensive fast-charging plugs across the Sydney–Brisbane–Melbourne corridor, with most high-speed chargers priced 50¢/kWh to 75¢/kWh. Download the PlugShare app for network maps.

Long-Distance Trains & Buses

Australia's extensive bus network is reliable and reasonably priced. Most buses have air-con, comfortable seats and decent toilets; all are smoke-free and some have wi-fi and USB chargers. Trains are slower and less frequent, with the more affordable category including services from Brisbane to Cairns, and Sydney to Brisbane, Melbourne and Canberra. The luxurious *Ghan* rail journey between Adelaide and Darwin is a once-in-a-lifetime trip.

Buying a Car

If you plan to stay several months and drive a lot, buying a car will probably be cheaper than renting one. Sydney and Cairns remain common hubs for backpackers finishing their travels and selling vehicles; hostel noticeboards and online marketplaces (such as *travellers-autobarn.com.au*) are the best places to look. Used-car prices remain high post-COVID and resale isn't guaranteed. Factor in registration, insurance and maintenance into your budget.

Money

CURRENCY: AUSTRALIAN DOLLAR ($)

Cards & Electronic Payments

TThere are ATMs just about everywhere and major credit cards are widely accepted, though there's often a surcharge for AMEX Cryptocurrency (particularly Bitcoin) is accepted at some major tourist destinations. Contactless payment, where you touch your credit or debit card against the reader rather than typing in your PIN, is now common.

Cash

Paying in cash is still widely accepted across Australia, but the option is decreasing. It's best to keep some cash on you, though, especially if you're travelling to small towns and remote areas. Australia also has a strong busking culture you might choose to support.

Taxes & Tipping

A 10% goods and services tax (GST) is automatically added to most purchases across Australia. Tipping isn't traditionally part of Australian etiquette and remains optional, but in bigger cities it's increasingly the norm to tip around 10% to 15% for good service at upmarket restaurants.

HOW MUCH FOR A...

major museum entry
usually free

concert or theatre show
$100

metered parking
up to $10/hour

major Gold Coast theme park entry
$109–124

HOW TO... Save Some Money

Booking flights and accommodation well in advance (with cancellation protection for peace of mind) and outside school holidays (which vary between states) is a great way to keep costs down. Major museums and galleries are typically free, and most cinemas offer discounts on Monday or Tuesday. Using public transport at off-peak times will also save you money. Flexible on when and where you explore? **Transfercar** *(transfercar.com.au)* relocations are worth a look.

TOLL ROADS

If you use a toll road in Sydney, Melbourne or Queensland, check **Linkt** *(linkt.com.au)* straight after your trip to pay any fees incurred – or risk copping a fine.

START SAVING

It's no secret that Australia is one of the most expensive places in the world to live, largely due to relatively high wages, strong consumer demand and the sheer cost of getting things across vast distances. That can make travelling here feel expensive, too, though visitors from the UK, Europe and the US often find their money goes further than expected when exchange rates are factored in. At the time of writing, the Australian dollar was buying £0.52/€0.59/US$0.71.

Accommodation

Camping & Glamping

Queensland national park camping grounds have Australia's cheapest rates at $7.50 per person, per night. Fees vary at national parks in other states and territories; at commercial camp sites they're around $35 for an unpowered site and from $45 for a powered site. Holiday parks offer caravan-friendly and tent sites plus standalone cabins for non-campers. Glamping outfits offer more luxuries, with prices to match.

Stay in a Lighthouse Keeper's Cottage

Australia's east coast hides some wonderfully moody lighthouse stays, where old keeper's cottages stare down the weather. Some of the most atmospheric include Byron Bay, Seal Rocks and Barunguba Montague Island in New South Wales, and Wilsons Promontory (hike-in, dorm only) and Cape Otway in Victoria.

Sleep on the Great Barrier Reef

Stay at one of the island resorts and glamping sites along the reef, camp in an island national park (only $7.50) or spend the night on a pontoon moored beside the reef. **Lady Musgrave Experience** *(ladymusgraveexperience.com.au)* offers glamping on the Southern Great Barrier Reef; **Cruise Whitsundays** *(cruisewhitsundays.com)* offers 'Reefsuites' (underwater rooms) and 'Reefsleep' (upper-deck swags) on the Central Great Barrier Reef.

Hostels

Backpacker hostels provide an affordable and sociable way of exploring Australia. There are clusters of them in cities and popular regional destinations – including Airlie Beach, Cairns, Byron Bay and Broome (Rubibi) – and they range from modest, family-run places to huge, custom-built party resorts. Dorm-bed prices start at around $30 and increase to $100 in flash city hostels, with private rooms also often available.

HOW MUCH FOR A NIGHT IN A...

camping ground
$7.50–50

hostel dorm bed
from $30

B&B
$150–220

Tiny Stays

Tiny-house accommodation has taken off around Australia. These camp-without-the-canvas stays – snug, self-contained twin-share eco-cabins – come with a price and comfort level that leans more boutique retreat than bush swag. **Unyoked** *(unyoked.co)* has a huge collection of sites along the east coast and around Perth, while **CABN** *(cabn.life)* has South Australia covered.

DO I AIRBNB?

Peer-to-peer accommodation rental companies such as Airbnb are ubiquitous across Australia. Travellers have benefited from the boost in accommodation choices, yet for many locals it has distorted property valuations, pricing them out of the area. Among the regional communities that have been upended by the trend is Byron Bay, where a hard-won 60-day cap on short-term accommodation rentals began in 2024. If you must use Airbnb, opting for a room in an owner-occupied property rather than a private property puts somewhat less stress on local housing demands.

CLOCKWISE FROM TOP LEFT: SHANA ESPINOZA/SHUTTERSTOCK, HOLLI/SHUTTERSTOCK, SHANA ESPINOZA/SHUTTERSTOCK, FAT JACKEY/SHUTTERSTOCK, FAT JACKEY/SHUTTERSTOCK

Family Travel

Travelling in Australia as a family can create highlights of a lifetime. Yes, distances are long, but there's much to see and do, from family-friendly beaches and other aquatic activities, theme parks and national parks to museums and wildlife parks where you can get a stellar view of the native creatures.

Wildlife Experiences

Zoo-going families will love **Taronga Zoo Sydney**, **Healesville Sanctuary** and **Australia Zoo**. Also offering close-up (but hands-off) views are koala sanctuaries including **Port Stephens Koala Sanctuary**.

For wild encounters, watch **penguins** arrive at sunset on Phillip Island, search out the sea lions on **Kangaroo Island** and spot whales along the east and west coasts between May and November.

Prams & Child Safety Seats

Cities and larger coastal hubs are pram-friendly; some smaller and outback towns may lack footpaths.

Safety restraints are compulsory for all children under seven. If you don't bring your own, major car-hire companies will supply and fit child safety seats from $6 per day, though availability and pricing vary widely.

BEST ATTRACTIONS FOR FAMILIES

Gold Coast Theme Parks (p312)
The 'big three' include **Wet'n'Wild**, **Warner Bros Movie World** and **Dreamworld**.

Rottnest Island (p907)
'Rotto' serves nostalgic barefoot holidays: quokkas, bike paths and no cars.

Questacon (p234)
Canberra's science hub is packed with interactive displays and experiments.

Sydney Harbour BridgeClimb (p79)
Kids over eight years and 120cm tall can join the urban family adventure.

Patrolled beaches
Keep the whole family safe and choose beaches with on-duty lifeguards.

Sun Safety

Australia's high UV levels can be especially harsh on babies and young kids. Cancer Council NSW recommends reducing your children's exposure to the sun, especially between 10am and 2pm (11am and 3pm daylight saving time).

Breastfeeding

Breastfeeding in public is legally protected across Australia, and it's widely accepted in everyday life. All cities and major towns also have public rooms where parents can breastfeed or change nappies (diapers).

KEEPING FAMILY TRAVEL COSTS DOWN

- Child concessions (and family rates) often apply to accommodation, tours, admission fees and transport, with some discounts as high as 50% off the adult rate. However, the definition of 'child' varies from under five, 12 or 18 years, so always check. Museums and galleries are often free.
- Another great way to keep costs down is staying at the country's coastal holiday parks, which typically offer easy beach access along with playgrounds and swimming pools to keep kids entertained without spending extra.
- Most cafes, pubs and restaurants have children's menus, or will provide a child-sized portion for a smaller price on request.

Health & Safe Travel

HEALTH CARE

Health-care standards are high in Australia, with the Medicare system covering Australian residents for some health-care cos Visitors from countries with which Australia has a reciprocal health-care agreement are eligible for benefits specified under the Medicare system; see *servicesaustralia.gov.au/reciprocal-health-care-agreements*. If you're not covered by Medicare, a short consultation with a local GP will usually set you back around $100.

Bushwalking & Bushfire Safety

Dehydration and hypothermia are real risks on a bushwalk, especially if you lose the track. Never walk alone and always tell someone your plans. Wear the right gear, carry plenty of water and snacks, and check the forecast conditions before you go. Bushfires are an increasing concern in warmer months, while localised floods are becoming common on the east coast – stay alert and come prepared.

Snakes & Spiders

Australia's snakes and spiders can loom large in travellers' imaginations, but statistically, they're nothing to fear. Encounters are rare, especially if you stick to marked tracks, avoid long grass and never poke around logs or rocks. Still, remote explorers should be sensible: carry a basic snake-bite kit, learn to use it and seek help immediately if bitten. Respect the bush and you'll be fine.

BE CROCWISE

Heading to Australia's tropical north? Be crocwise (*becrocwise.nt.gov.au*) at all times, and heed official advice during the stinger season from November to May.

BEACH SAFETY

RED-AND-YELLOW FLAGS

Swim between the flags; lifeguard on duty.

YELLOW FLAG

Caution required; potential hazards.

RED FLAG

Danger! No swimming.

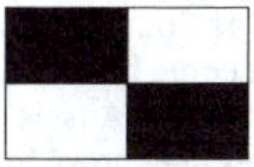

BLACK-AND-WHITE FLAG

Surfcraft riding area boundary.

FLOAT TO SURVIVE

From July 2024 to June 2025, Australia recorded its highest drowning toll on record, including 154 deaths at coastal locations. Rips remain the leading beach hazard. If you're caught in one, keep calm, lie back in the water, rotate your arms and legs in a circular motion and signal for help with an upraised hand. Always swim between the flags.

Drugs & Alcohol

As of 2026, cannabis remains illegal for recreational use across Australia. Possession of cannabis or other illicit drugs can still land you in serious legal trouble, including criminal charges or deportation if you're visiting from overseas. Police regularly conduct random breath and drug tests; driving (or cycling) under the influence of alcohol or drugs incurs heavy penalties.

FROM LEFT: BENNY MARTY/SHUTTERSTOCK, PIXEL-SHOT/SHUTTERSTOCK

Food, Drink & Nightlife

When to Eat

Breakfast (7am–9am) Typically toast, fruit with yoghurt or cereal, maybe eggs, and often latte.

Brunch (9am–noon) A popular weekend outing, usually a cooked, cafe-style late breakfast.

Lunch (noon–2pm) Anything from a salad, sandwich or sushi on the go to a pub meal or fancy lunch with wine.

Dinner (6–9pm) Anything from a light dish to a three-course meal.

MENU DECODER

Pie Always savoury, and purchased from a bakery. Sweet pies are identified by name (eg 'apple pie').

Parmi/parma/parmy Pub staple of crumbed chicken topped with tomato pasta sauce and cheese, served with chips (fries) and salad.

Damper Basic bread made from wheat flour, water and a pinch of salt, then baked in the coals of a campfire. Traditionally served with honey.

Burger with the lot Beef patty, bacon, cheese, lettuce, tomato, beetroot, egg and pineapple.

Barbie Barbecue – anything from sausages to steak, burgers, chops, seafood and/or veggies.

Snags Sausages – usually beef, sometimes chicken but rarely pork. Synonymous with budget BBQs.

Jaffle Closed toasted sandwich, made in a jaffle iron/machine (different to a sandwich press).

Chicken salt Savoury seasoning sprinkled on hot chips nationwide. Despite the name, most are vegan.

Where to Eat

Bakeries A popular breakfast or lunch stop with pies, pasties, sausage rolls, quiches and coffee, and usually also sandwiches.

Cafes Some people just come for coffee, but Aussie cafes are known for their sumptuous breakfast menus with wholesome options.

Pubs Many pubs have food specials on certain nights, making dining out more affordable.

RSLs Services clubs across the country (and RSL-run bowling clubs) are great for a budget pub-style meal.

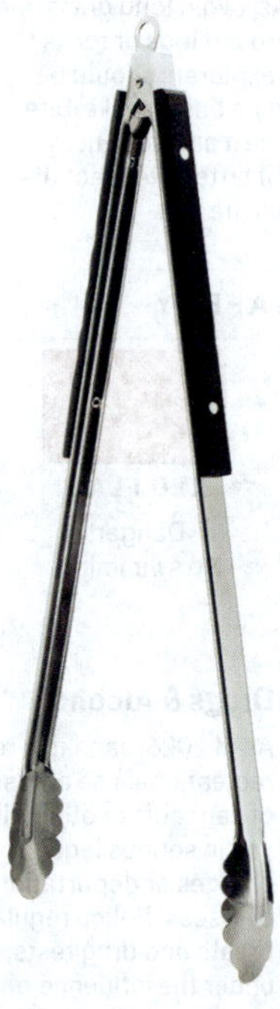

HOW TO... Nail Aussie BBQ Etiquette

Aussies love a BBQ; a tradition thought to date from the 1960s, when the 'chop picnic' – the act of resting a mesh grill over a fire with a few bricks to cook some chops – became part of the vernacular.

If you're invited to a 'barbie', your host might ask you to 'bring a plate'. This means a plate of food; if they don't specify, a salad or cheeseboard is a good bet. If you're instructed to simply 'bring yourself', bring your own drinks anyway, or at least a bottle for the host.

The host typically provides condiments and salads, and usually also bread for sausage sandwiches (BYO burger buns). When food is being provided, don't hog the prime cuts, and check that everyone has been served before going back for seconds. The dress code is always casual.

FROM LEFT: PAVEL KRUGLOV/SHUTTERSTOCK

HOW MUCH FOR A...

regular coffee
$5–7

pie at a bakery
$6–9

cafe breakfast or lunch dish
$18–32

glass of beer (425mL)
$8–14

wine at a bar
from $12

deli sandwich
$10–18

pub meal
$22–40

three-course meal at a good restaurant
$100–180

HOW TO... Choose an Australian Wine

Most Australian restaurants champion local produce, which increasingly extends to the wine list. If you're not familiar with local wine, what do you select?

Start with asking your server, who, if it's a nice restaurant, should always be able to recommend the perfect drop for your dish. And don't be shy about asking for a taste – most venues will oblige. If you prefer whites, Hunter Valley semillon and sauvignon blanc pair well with fresh seafood and salads; a buttery Margaret River chardonnay is a better match for fattier fare, like pastas with cream sauces; and Clare Valley riesling is a good choice for Asian-style dishes. Full-bodied Australian reds like shiraz and cabernet sauvignon, meanwhile, were made for enjoying with full-flavoured dishes and grilled meats, while lighter, more versatile pinot noir can be a good match for everything from grilled salmon to pork loin. Most Australian rosés are on the dry side.

Natural (aka minimal-intervention) wine is increasingly appearing on Australian wine lists. Among the most popular varieties are orange wines, the name given to white wines made with grapes left in contact with their skins anywhere from a few days to several months, creating a more textured and richly flavoured white. They pair well with a wide range of dishes; however, the theory that natural wine doesn't cause hangovers is sadly a myth.

Did You Know?

Australia has more than 2400 wineries in 65 wine regions around the country. The Northern Territory is the only state or territory without at least one working winery.

DRINKING LIKE AN AUSSIE

Australian attitudes to alcohol are changing. The younger generation is increasingly abstaining, and that's now more likely to be respected than mocked. That said, many Aussies still love a drink, with around 41% of the population enjoying a boozy beverage at least once per week.

Due to the high cost of alcohol in Australia, much of the drinking is done at home, often at BBQs. When Australians go out to drink, many start early. The climate lends well to weekend day drinking, so locals might 'call it a night' by dinnertime. Aussies are also partial to happy hours (typically 4pm to 5pm or 6pm). Queensland venues are not permitted to advertise happy hours outside the premises – call to check.

While pubs tend to get busy from around 6pm, some city bars don't get going until around 8pm. Most venues close by midnight or even earlier, especially in smaller towns, but in big cities some are open until as late as 3am – very few have a 24-hour licence. House wine is typically drinkable, but not memorable. Most pubs and bars have craft beers on tap along with big-brand lagers, and increasingly, low- and no-alcohol options. On the east coast, a 'beer' (425mL) usually means a schooner. The smaller 285mL glass is a 'pot' in Victoria and Queensland, a 'middy' in NSW, a 'handle' in Darwin, and in SA it's a 'schooner' ('pint' is their regular one).

Ordering is done at the bar, with rare exceptions; tipping isn't expected. However, if you pay in cash, dropping a few coins in the tip jar when the bartender is watching can go a long way.

Responsible Travel

Climate Change & Travel

It's impossible to ignore the impact we have when travelling; Lonely Planet urges all travellers to engage with their travel carbon footprint, which will mainly come from air travel. While there often isn't an alternative, travellers can look to minimise the number of flights they take, opt for newer aircrafts and use cleaner ground transport, such as trains. One proposed solution–purchasing carbon offsets–unfortunately does not cancel out the impact of individual flights. While most destinations will depend on air travel for the foreseeable future, for now, pursuing ground-based travel where possible is the best course of action.

The **UN Carbon Offset Calculator** shows how flying impacts a household's emissions

The **ICAO's carbon emissions calculator** allows visitors to analyse the CO2 generated by point-to-point journeys

Brunch for Equality

In Melbourne's Balaclava, **All Things Equal** is a social-enterprise cafe staffed by an all-abilities crew. Proceeds from its tasty vegetarian and pescatarian dishes – from smashed avo to barramundi fish cakes – go towards inclusive employment.

Support Wildlife Conservation

Visiting sanctuaries and nature parks helps protect some of Australia's most vulnerable species. Entry fees at the **Port Stephens Koala Sanctuary** (p168) go directly towards koala care. Not-for-profit **Phillip Island Nature Parks** *(penguins.org.au)* reinvests in research, rehabilitation and wildlife protection.

Care for the Coast

Heading for a shoreline stroll? **Take 3 for the Sea** *(take3.org)* encourages beachgoers to pick up three pieces of rubbish each visit – a small ritual that reduces the impact of pollution in the ocean.

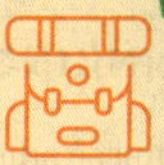

Australia is laced with low-impact rail trails to explore. Ride the **Northern Rivers Rail Trail** in NSW or the **Bass Coast Rail Trail** (p592) in Victoria.

Support artistic traditions with the purchase of works from Indigenous art centres such as **Iwantja Arts** (p796) in outback South Australia.

SUPPORT INDIGENOUS-OWNED TOURISM

Keeping experiences in Indigenous hands strengthens cultural authority and ensures communities benefit directly. Check who owns and leads the businesses you book, and look for operators who care for Country – like Mabu Buru Tours in the Kimberley.

CHOOSE SUSTAINABLE WINE PRACTICES

Knowing what's in your glass starts with the label. Certified organic and biodynamic wines follow strict, transparent environmental standards, while uncertified 'natural wines' can mislead. Without regulation, best practice relies on the ethos of the winemaker.

Avoid Feeding or Touching Wildlife

Human interaction can disrupt natural behaviours, make animals dependent on handouts and increase the risk of illness, injury, aggression and even abandoning their young. Observe from a distance and let them stay wild.

Re-Use & Re-Fill

Australia is gradually banning single-use plastics, including lightweight shopping bags, straws, cutlery and plates. Carry a reusable bag for errands and take a keep cup to cafes – it's widely accepted and often rewarded with a discount.

Explore with a Sustainable-Tourism-Certified Operator

Ecotourism Australia *(ecotourism.org.au)* certifies tourism operators, and also destinations (including Margaret River, p919), for having a well-managed commitment to sustainable practices. Look for its ECO Certified (for nature-based operators) and Sustainable Tourism Certified labels.

Visit a Carbon-Neutral Museum

The **Australian Museum** in Sydney is the first natural history museum in Australia to receive the Federal Government's Climate Active certification and is a certified carbon-neutral organisation.

Over half of Australia's plastic bottles end up in landfill. Tap water is safe almost everywhere here – refill rather than buy.

Upload wildlife photos to the iNaturalist app to help scientists better understand and protect Australia's natural world.

Green State

Tasmania isn't only physically green, with national parks covering more than 40% of the island state. It's also 100% self-sufficient in renewable energy, with a goal to generate 200% by 2040.

RESOURCES

lifeunhurried.com
Book sustainable stays across Australia.

farmersmarkets.org.au
Locate farmers markets around the country.

goodfish.org.au
Australia's first online consumer directory for sustainable seafood.

FROM LEFT: NATROT/SHUTTERSTOCK, SHAHIDPHOTOGHARAPHER/SHUTTERSTOCK

LGBTIQ+ Travellers

Australia is a popular destination for LGBTIQ+ travellers, with Sydney a big 'pink dollar' draw thanks largely to its epic Mardi Gras festival. Same-sex acts are legal nationwide and marriage equality has been recognised since 2017. Australians are generally open-minded about same-sex relationships, and acceptance of gender-diverse people is growing, though some hostility can occur in conservative neighbourhoods and rural areas.

Pride Events

The legendary annual **Sydney Gay & Lesbian Mardi Gras** (p110) draws huge numbers of visitors in February and March, as does Melbourne's **Midsumma Festival** (p492) in January and February. Australia's other major Pride events include Brisbane's **Melt Festival** (October), Alice Springs' **fabALICE** (March), Adelaide's **Feast Festival** (November; p729) and Tasmania's **TasPride** (February). Even Broome has a Pride festival, in March, with drag queens on camels. Visit the **Australian Pride Network** *(australianpridenetwork.com.au/lgbtiq-festivals)* website for a comprehensive directory of events nationwide.

RAINBOW NEIGHBOURHOODS

There are plenty of LGBTIQ+ neighbourhoods across Australia's cities. Connect with your community in the likes of Darlinghurst and Newtown in Sydney, Fitzroy in Melbourne, Fortitude Valley and New Farm in Brisbane, Northbridge in Perth, and North Adelaide. Beyond the capitals, Lismore (NSW) is affectionately known as Lesmore, and Daylesford is home of Australia's largest rural LGBTIQ+ Pride event, the **ChillOut Festival**.

Qtopia Sydney

Opened in 2024 within the old Darlinghurst Police Station, **Qtopia** maps the highs and lows of Australia's queer history, from Sydney's Mardi Gras and iconic drag performers to the HIV/AIDS crisis and 1978 Mardi Gras tragedy.

AUSTRALIA'S LESBIAN CAPITAL

There aren't any local gay bars, yet the outback city of Alice Springs is known as Australia's lesbian capital. Statistically speaking, the proportion of lesbian couples in the Australian Capital Territory (relative to all couples) is 65% higher than the nationwide average.

RESOURCES

visitgayaustralia.com.au
General information on gay-friendly businesses, places to stay and nightlife.

starobserver.com.au
Australia's longest-running publication for LGBTIQ+ communities.

planetdwellers.com.au
LGBTIQ+-focused travel agency and tour operator.

Accessible Travel

While accessible travel remains a work in progress in Australia, awareness of and services for travellers with limited mobility, blind or vision-impaired, deaf or hearing-impaired travellers and those with sensory sensitivities is increasing.

Sydney Opera House

Accessibility is well supported at the **Sydney Opera House**, including audio-described, Auslan-interpreted and captioned shows. A daily Mobility Tour provides step-free access and a deeper look at Australia's most iconic building.

Airport

Airports can provide assistance for those with accessibility needs, sensory or learning disabilities, or travellers with assistance animals; it's best to request assistance from your airline in advance. Visit the **Civil Aviation Safety Authority** *(casa.gov.au/operations-safety-and-travel)* for more info.

Accommodation

Legislation requires that new accommodation must meet accessibility standards and tourist operators must not discriminate. Facilities for wheelchairs are improving, and many operators now publish their accessibility credentials – **Big4 Holiday Parks** *(big4.com.au)*, for example, lists wheelchair-friendly cabins nationwide.

Toilets & Changing Places

Locate wheelchair-accessible toilets across Australia with the **National Public Toilet Map** *(toiletmap.gov.au)*. Travellers with high support needs can also access **Changing Places** *(changingplaces.org.au)* toilets in major cities.

Accessible Beaches & Surfing

Use the **Accessible Beaches** *(accessiblebeaches.com/beach-directory)* directory to locate beaches with matting, beach wheelchair hire, accessible parking and more, or ride a wave with the **Disabled Surfers Association of Australia** *(disabledsurfers.org)*.

RESOURCES

Tourism Australia *(tourism.australia.com)* The corporate arm of the tourism board has a handy directory of resources and contacts.

Travellers Aid *(travellersaid.org.au)* Help for Melbourne visitors with special needs.

Travel Without Limits *(travelwithoutlimits.com.au)* Australia's first and only disability-specific travel magazine.

SENSORY-FRIENDLY MUSEUMS

Sensory-friendly attractions are increasing in Australia, particulary at museums and galleries in capital cities including the **Melbourne Museum** and the **Museum of Contemporary Art** in Sydney. **Taronga Zoo Sydney** (p129) has special-access days.

ACCESSIBLE TRAVEL AGENCIES

Make trip planning easier with holiday providers like **Amplify Accessible Travel Specialists** *(amplifyats.com.au)* and Melbourne-based **TravAbility** *(travability.travel)*, or explore Sydney on a wheelchair-based tour arranged by **Australia in Style** *(australiainstyle.com.au)*.

Visiting the Outback

Exactly where Australia's outback starts and ends is hard to pin down on a map. But you'll know you're there when the sky yawns enormously wide, the horizon is unnervingly empty, and the sparse inhabitants you encounter are incomparably resilient and distinctively Australian. Out here, enduring Indigenous cultures, unique wildlife and intriguing landscapes await the modern-day adventurer.

WHEN TO GO

June through August is when the outback comes into its own. Clear skies, moderate daytime temperatures, cold nights and good driving conditions are the norm. It's also the best time to visit the tropical Top End and northern Western Australia, with low humidity and mild temperatures. September and October is prime time to head into the outback if you're into wildflowers. The MacDonnell Ranges near Alice Springs and the Flinders Ranges in northern SA erupt with colourful blooms. Summer temperatures can be debilitating, and the rains can make remote roads impassable.

ORGANISED TOURS

If you don't feel like doing all the planning and driving, a guided tour is a great way to experience the Aussie outback. These range from beery backpacker jaunts between outback pubs, to Indigenous cultural tours and multiday bushwalking treks into remote wilderness.

OUTBACK TRACKS

Another way to get from A to B in the outback is by detouring along historic cattle and rail routes. Some of these tracks are passable in a regulation 2WD, but a 4WD will make for a much more comfortable drive. Be prepared for minimal facilities, and don't attempt tougher routes during summer or if there's been recent flooding.

OUTBACK ROADHOUSES

Outback roadhouses emerge from the heat haze with some regularity. Most roadhouses sell 24-hour fuel; some have fry-up restaurants and accommodation out the back, including camp sites, air-conditioned motel-style rooms and/or basic cabins.

Outback Safety & Driving

Due to the lack of water, long distances between fuel stops and isolation, you need to be organised and vigilant in the outback, especially on sandy tracks.

- An emergency communication device, and enough water (5L per person per day, plus extra for the radiator), food, fuel and two spare tyres are essential.
- Avoid relying solely on generic online maps (Google, Apple) and carry a good paper-map backup (Hema).
- Check road condition reports before you go, and if you break down, stay with your vehicle.

Permits for Aboriginal Lands

In the outback, if you plan on driving through pastoral stations and Aboriginal communities, you may need to get permission first. This is for your safety; many travellers have tackled this rugged landscape on their own and required complicated rescues after getting lost or breaking down. Permits are issued by various Aboriginal land-management authorities. Processing applications can take anywhere from a few minutes to a few days.

Nuts & Bolts

OPENING HOURS

Banks 9.30am–4pm Monday to Thursday, to 5pm Friday

Bars 4pm–late

Cafes 7am–3pm

Nightclubs 10pm–4am Thursday to Saturday

Post offices 9am–5pm Monday to Friday; some also 9am–noon Saturday

Pubs 11am–midnight

Restaurants noon–2.30pm and 6–9pm

Shops 9am–5pm

Supermarkets 7am–10pm

Toilets

Larger petrol stations tend to have the best road-trip toilet facilities. National parks typically have non-flush, composting toilets; remember to close the lid.

Electricity

Type I 230V/50Hz

GOOD TO KNOW

Time zone
Three mainland zones: GMT +8, +9½ or +10 hours

Calling code
+61

Emergency number
000

Population
27.9 million

Smoking

Smoking is forbidden in all enclosed public places, and also some outdoor spaces, including outdoor areas in NSW where food is being eaten.

Internet Access

Good in urban areas, unreliable to nonexistent in regional areas. Free wi-fi at cafes is not as common as you might expect.

PUBLIC HOLIDAYS

New Year's Day
1 January

Australia Day
26 January

Labour Day
- First Monday in March (WA)
- Second Monday in March (Vic, Tas)
- First Monday in May (Qld, NT)
- First Monday in October (NSW)
- Second Monday in October (SA, ACT)

Easter
(Good Friday to Easter Monday inclusive) Late March or early April

Anzac Day 25 April

King's Birthday
Second Monday in June (last Monday in September in WA, first Monday in October in Queensland)

Christmas Day
25 December

Boxing Day
26 December

In addition, each state has its own public holidays, from Canberra Day to the Hobart Show Day.

THE AUSTRALIA

STORYBOOK

Our writers delve deep into different aspects of Australian life.

Parliament House, Melbourne (p476)

BEN BRYANT/SHUTTERSTOCK

A HISTORY OF AUSTRALIA IN 15 PLACES

The story of modern Australia began two and a half centuries ago with the arrival of British naval officer Lieutenant (later Captain) Cook. But the human history of Australia stretches much further back, with ancestral stories from the world's oldest living cultures describing the very creation of the land Down Under.
By Josh West

AUSTRALIA BECAME ITS own continent about 35 million years ago. Science also tells us that Australia's First Nations have inhabited it for at least 65,000 years, though from an Indigenous perspective of Creation, they have always been here. Drawing on early settler accounts, the book *Dark Emu* (2014), by Indigenous author and advocate Bruce Pascoe, effectively 'cancels' the theory that Indigenous Australians led a simple hunter-gatherer lifestyle. Instead, they are now recognised as sophisticated land managers and among the world's earliest known bakers.

Colonisation ushered in a darker chapter of Australia's history. From 1788, tens of thousands of convicted prisoners were transported from Britain and Ireland to serve their sentences in far-flung penal colonies. Frontier conflict and dispossession brought massacres and profound disruption to First Nations communities. More than a century after gaining formal independence from Great Britain, Australia is still reckoning with this legacy even as it moves forward as a country with much to be proud of.

From the outback to the coast, Australia's blockbuster landscapes are layered with deep time. Echoes of penal settlements, seafaring heritage, wartime activities and gold rushes linger in cities and country towns, while Indigenous cultures continue to pulse through this storied land.

1. Kakadu National Park

DEEP-TIME STORYTELLING

Few places on Earth reveal the past as vividly as the rock shelters at Ubirr and Nourlangie, vast open-air galleries in Kakadu National Park layered with artworks up to 20,000 years old, forming one of the longest continuous visual histories of any peoples. Some scenes record hunting, ancestors and powerful Creation beings; others depict changing coastlines and species, offering rare insight into deep environmental time as well as spiritual law. These Top End galleries sit within a continent-wide constellation of Aboriginal rock art, making Australia one of the world's richest repositories of site-based art and living cultural practice.

For more on Kakadu National Park, see p814.

2. Great Barrier Reef

GENESIS OF AN ICON

The world's largest coral reef system is a relatively young addition to the Australian landscape, formed over 7000 years ago when a coastal plain flooded during rapid sea-level rise, creating shallow regions for corals to grow. Aboriginal and Torres Strait Islander peoples have an enduring connection with the reef. Its 70 Traditional Custodian groups once lived on what is now the sea floor and cultural knowledge of this time's practices and sites still remains. Ancestral knowledge continues to play a role in safeguarding the reef today.

For more on the Great Barrier Reef, see p382.

3. Torres Strait Islands

FIRST TRADERS

Long before borders, Australia and New Guinea were joined in the supercontinent of Sahul. When the last glacial period ended some 8000 years ago, sea levels climbed, drowning the land bridge and dividing the two countries. Yet the remaining Torres Strait became a marine highway, not a barrier. Research on Papua New Guinea's Great Papuan Plateau has uncovered 3200-year-old marine shells carried from the Torres Strait – prestige items worn, traded and used to forge alliances. Distinctive pottery styles also moved between southern Papua, Torres Strait and northeastern Australia, while a shared cultural hero known as Sido or Souw appears in oral traditions across the seaway.

For more on the Torres Strait Islands, see p420.

Houtman Albrolhos Islands (p964)

PILOTEYES/SHUTTERSTOCK

4. Abrolhos Islands

HORROR ON THE HIGH SEAS

One of the worst horror stories in global maritime history unfolded on 4 June 1629, when the Dutch ship *Batavia* was wrecked on the Abrolhos Islands, off the coast of Western Australia. As the ship broke apart, around 300 of its 341 passengers made it ashore. When its commander, Francisco Pelsaert, sailed to Batavia (Jakarta) for help, senior official Jeronimus Cornelisz orchestrated a mutiny that resulted in the murders of 125 survivors. Pelsaert returned to find the mutineers in battle with the remaining survivors and subsequently tried and convicted Cornelisz and six of his men, who became the first Europeans to be legally executed in Australia.

For more on the Abrolhos Islands, see p964.

5. Botany Bay

A NEW CHAPTER

On 29 April 1770, life on the Australian continent changed forever when Lieutenant James Cook made the first landing of the *Endeavour* on mainland Australia at Botany Bay. In 1788 the First Fleet, a convoy of 11 ships, carried British officials, soldiers and convict prisoners to the lands of the people of the Eora Nation, with Governor Arthur Phillip establishing a penal settlement at Warrane on Gadigal Country and renaming it Sydney. Fast-forward 240-odd years and the New South Wales capital is a thriving city of some 5.5 million; its city centre is now one of the most culturally and linguistically diverse areas of the country.

For more on Botany Bay, see p88.

6. The Rocks

CONVICT SETTLEMENT

In Botany Bay, the Rocks marks the birthplace of European Australia. Here, the First Fleet built their first encampment, marking the start of Britain's penal colony and rapid dispossession of local Aboriginal people. Through the 19th century, the Rocks evolved into a crowded, working-class waterfront of sailors, wharf labourers, pubs and boarding houses, surviving outbreaks of disease, waves of immigration and calls for demolition. Today, its sandstone terraces, cobbled lanes and harbourside warehouses form one of Australia's most intact colonial precincts, a tangible, walkable gateway into the nation's modern story.

For more on the Rocks, see p78.

7. Cooktown

BIRTHPLACE OF RECONCILIATION

The Tropical North Queensland town of Cooktown is a small place with a big history: it was here on 17 June 1770 that Lieutenant Cook beached the *Endeavour,* which had earlier struck a reef offshore from Cape Tribulation. Cook's crew spent 48 days here repairing the damage and generally had amicable dealings with the local Guugu Yimithirr people. But a fight broke out when the British took a dozen green turtles from the river in violation of custom. An Elder prevented major bloodshed by making a peace offering – a gesture thought to be Australia's first act of reconciliation between Indigenous and non-Indigenous people.

For more on Cooktown, see p414.

8. Eden

WHALE TALE

The special relationship between the Thaua people of the NSW South Coast and killer whales preceded European settlement over many generations, with an ancestor known as Budgenbro, or Chief of Twofold Bay, said to have sung songs to a pod and called them towards the beach. Later, an orca known as Old Tom and his pod would help to herd baleen whales into the path of harpoons used by European settlers at Eden's Twofold Bay from 1895 to 1930. It's said that whalers felt so bad when Old Tom died that they funded the construction of the Eden Killer Whale Museum.

For more on Eden, see p214.

9. Adelaide

LAND OF THE FREE

The only Australian state capital city that wasn't settled by convicts, Adelaide (Tarntanya) was established in 1836 as a planned capital for free European settlers. There was so much optimism for the nation's first free settled colony of South Australia that no jail was included in the original plans. It quickly became apparent, however, that not everyone in the colony intended to be a law-abiding citizen and tenders were swiftly sought for a prison. South Australia was the first state to give women the vote in the 1890s and its capital has often been at the vanguard of political and social change.

For more on Adelaide, see p716.

10. Melbourne

GOLDEN GRID

Unlike Sydney, Victoria's capital was formally planned, its grid design conceived in 1837, paving the way for the ease of navigating Melbourne today. An important meeting place for the Kulin Nation, the site of modern-day Melbourne (Narrm) was established in 1835, three decades after an initial settlement at Sorrento on the Mornington Peninsula had been abandoned after just one year. The Victorian gold rush (1851 to late 1860s) prompted rapid growth, including a period of grand civic construction that blessed the city once briefly known as Batmania with some of its finest buildings, including Parliament House and the Treasury Building.

For more on Melbourne, see p463.

11. Rottnest Island

BEYOND QUOKKAS

Western Australia's favourite holiday island has a sobering backstory. Used by the Whadjuk Noongar people for important ceremonies and meetings when the island was connected to the mainland some 6500 years ago, Rottnest Island (Wadjemup) was later used for nearly a century as a prison and then a forced labour camp for Aboriginal males following colonisation, with almost 4000 Aboriginal men and boys from all over the state exiled here from 1838 to 1931. A key reason why 'Rotto' is significant to many Aboriginal communities today is its burial ground, where at least 373 Aboriginal prisoners lie in unmarked graves.

For more on Rottnest Island, see p907.

12. Beechworth

BUSHRANGER COUNTRY

No bushranger (outlaw) was more infamous than Ned Kelly. Born in Beveridge, a small town north of Melbourne, in 1854 or 1855, Kelly turned to bushranging at the age of 14. His (short) life of (often violent) crime in country Victoria would morph him into a cultural icon following

Beechworth Courthouse (p614)

his death by hanging at Melbourne Gaol in 1880, inspiring poems, books, movies and art, including Sidney Nolan's famed *Ned Kelly* series. In the old gold-rush town of Beechworth, you can visit the historic courthouse that saw over 40 trials for the Kelly family and see Kelly's morbid death mask.

For more on Beechworth, see p612.

13. Canberra

COOL CAPITAL

It took politicians more than a decade to agree on the site for Australia's capital. Canberra's location was determined, in part, by section 125 of the Constitution, which states that the seat of government should be within 100 miles (161km) of Sydney. But it wasn't the only factor: the fear of disease in Sydney, enemies from the sea, the availability of drinking water and even the cool climate played a role in the selection of Canberra, 285km from Sydney, over the country NSW town of Dalgety on 8 October 1908.

For more on Canberra, see p228.

14. Port Arthur

TRIUMPH OVER TRAGEDY

The sandstone ruins of the Port Arthur Historic Site cut a lonely figure on the Tasman Peninsula. Forming part of the UNESCO-listed Australian Convict Sites, this brutal convict prison turned tourist attraction set the tragic scene of modern Australia's worst mass murder. Just 12 days after a gunman killed 35 people in 1996, then–Prime Minister John Howard announced sweeping gun reforms that would change Australia.

For more on Port Arthur, see p662.

15. Uluṟu

SYMBOL OF HOPE

Formed around 500 million years ago, Uluṟu has more recently become a powerful symbol of the struggle for Indigenous rights. The local Aṉangu, to whom Uluṟu is deeply sacred, lobbied for decades for the rights to their traditional lands, which were officially handed back in 1985 by the Hawke Government. Climbing Uluṟu was subsequently banned in 2019. Uluṟu is also at the centre of the Uluṟu Statement from the Heart shared in 2017, which calls for the establishment of an Indigenous Voice to Parliament (an advisory body). A 2023 Indigenous Voice Referendum was ultimately unsuccessful, but the struggle for reform continues.

For more on Uluṟu, see p878.

MEET THE AUSSIES

We're a people of entertaining lingo and the best range of international cuisine you can find. EMMYLOU DZUBIEL introduces the modern Australian.

IF YOU'VE COME across an Aussie before, chances are you didn't understand 100% of what they said. You see, Australian English is a colourful language. Our expressive phrases, rolling off the tongue with an ease that sometimes sounds like lazy pronunciation, can glaze over a pair of untrained ears. With 31.5% of our nation born overseas, there's a multitude of languages across the land, not to mention the 120-plus Aboriginal languages. Given a myriad of facial features and skin tones, you could easily mistake a local for a tourist, but the moment you hear our outrageous slang and the drawn-out vowels of 'yeah-nah', there's no doubt: you've found yourself an Aussie.

We're coming into an age of second- and third-generation immigrants, Indigenous grandchildren of the Stolen Generation and mixed-ethnicity citizens with roots from a foreign land but a definitively Australian upbringing. While we certainly have our differences, there's one thing we can all agree on: the incomparable beauty of this island continent.

It's difficult to pinpoint what it means to be Australian and as you journey throughout this great land, you'll discover a population made up of an eclectic mix of cultures. First and foremost are the Indigenous communities, continuing connection with Country, healing scars from a colonised past and teaching newcomers how to survive this treacherous but generous land, the way they have since Europeans first arrived.

Out by the coast, you'll find the most relaxed of us. Mellowed out by the refreshing pull of the ocean waves and soft glow of sun-kissed skin, coastal dwellers enjoy an unhurried life on the famously picturesque shores. In the forests and hills are the peace-seekers – thriving communities of creatives who relish the quiet serenity of flowing rivers and towering eucalypts. Further inland are the rough 'n' tough – farmers working tirelessly to supply our nation with quality produce and miners decked out in hi-vis coated by an inescapable layer of red dust.

The capital cities house some of our most innovative minds and an immeasurable mix of international communities, bringing with them all manner of delicious cuisines and inspiring fusion food across the board. It's in these places that we are blessed with a world of flavours that have shaped the modern Australian food scene.

The truth is, being Australian means something slightly different to all of us. For some, it's the nostalgia of sweltering summers and a Peter's ice cream melting down your hands following an afternoon of jumping in rivers, lakes or oceans. For others, it's the welcoming heart of a country that brought safety and a new start. And for the Traditional Custodians of this land, it's a continuation of generations, carrying stories, traditions and a deep harmony with nature.

A Culturally Diverse Nation

Overseas migration has contributed to almost two-thirds of Australia's population growth. In 2024, 31.5% of Australia's population was born overseas, with people from almost every country in the world now calling Australia home.

CLOCKWISE FROM TOP LEFT: STUART WALMSLEY/GETTY IMAGES, AVIRUT S/SHUTTERSTOCK, GOOD KIND STUDIO/SHUTTERSTOCK, JAMES BRAUND/GETTY IMAGES

I'M A COUNTRY-TOWN GAL WITH AN INTERNATIONAL SOUL

Times are different now from when I was growing up in the small regional town of Collie in Western Australia: a mixed Aussie-Filipino kid binge-watching the cool surfer kids of *Blue Water High* and being mesmerised by the world of KPop. My snacks of choice were classic meat pies and mum's homemade *lumpia* (spring rolls). I wasn't exactly your typical country-town Aussie kid back then. In today's increasingly online world, the likes of BTS and KPop Demon Hunters have made their way onto almost every Australian screen and when I talk about *lumpia*, I rarely have to explain what it is. What was once an isolated continent has grown more diverse and education and media more inclusive, but the sentiment of being Australian remains the same. I'm grateful for this lucky country and I'm proud to call Australia home.

Laura Quinkan Dance Festival (p417)
CHAMELEONSEYE/SHUTTERSTOCK

MULTICULTURAL AUSTRALIA:

WHAT DOES THE COUNTRY LOOK LIKE TODAY?

Stained by a dark history of colonial oppression and racism, modern Australia is – slowly but surely – evolving into a colourful melting pot of cultures. By Sudeshna Ghosh

RIGHT BY SYDNEY'S busy Circular Quay waterfront thoroughfare is a small park. Fringed by jacarandas and overlooking the icons that have come to be synonymous with the city – the Opera House and Harbour Bridge – it isn't dissimilar to the many other city parks, except for one thing: a plaque at its steps commemorating the 11 ships that arrived from Great Britain in 1788.

Known as the First Fleet, this convoy transported more than 750 convicts, marking the official beginning of the colonisation of Australia. But this wasn't the first time that Europeans arrived at the shores of Terra Australis. Numerous European expeditions had banged up against the coast since the 1600s, many of them led by Dutch explorers. It was the British, however, who persisted. Recognising the commercial implications of extending the empire into the southern seas, the admiralty backed several voyages, including three critical ones led by Lieutenant (later Captain) James Cook between 1768 and 1779. These set the foundations for European settlement in Australia.

But long before this – at least 65,000 years by current accounts – Indigenous Australians had been calling this land their home. There are more than 250 language groups (commonly described as 'Nations') living here, with hundreds of different dialects and subcultures.

Australia's First Nations

The general consensus is that Indigenous Australians arrived on the continent via seafaring routes from Asia. Some recent genetics-based research also suggests a migration pattern from the Indian subcontinent. They were essentially hunter-gatherer tribes, but the culture featured complex social systems and sophisticated aquaculture and agriculture practices.

First Nations people in Australia are divided into two main groups: Aboriginal peoples of the mainland and Torres Strait Islanders. Hailing from a group of islands in the Torres Strait, the latter are of Melanesian descent and culturally distinct from Aboriginal Australians.

The conflict between Indigenous Australians and the conquest-hungry explorers is well documented. Colonisation in Australia led to the decimation of the Indigenous population – a result of ongoing frontier warfare, as conflict over land and resources escalated, as well as the spread of alien infectious diseases such as smallpox.

Today, the ramifications of the destruction of the First Nations' way of life are still being felt. Unresolved intergenerational trauma has resulted in First Nations

people being statistically more likely to struggle with unemployment, substance abuse and domestic violence.

'Some of today's well-meaning welfare systems have had a similar effect [as some of the crueller policies of before] and it has led to some terrible life patterns,' says Angela Woollacott, professor of history at the Australian National University.

'There's a direct correlation between the trauma of what our people have gone through and the high levels of substance and alcohol abuse. It was a form of escape for some people of the Stolen Generation like my own mother,' says Garry Farrar, a proud Wiradjuri man and a First Nations consultant for corporations. 'In some instances, trauma has affected our cultural storytelling. There's a wall holding us back from sharing important stories. So we've lost some of those stories forever.'

For a people that relied mainly on oral history (rock art notwithstanding), this is a great loss indeed. 'Our farming methods could have been better; our connections to water, land and vegetation were lost,' says Garry. 'We would be better at sustainability.'

Indeed, there's a lot to learn from 65,000 years' worth of wisdom gleaned from living and working with the land and water. The symbiotic link between humankind and the physical ecosystem takes on a spiritual character in Indigenous culture and is broadly described as 'connection to Country', an indelible part of the First Nations identity.

Unfortunately, this connection was lost in thousands of Indigenous Australians when they were forcibly taken from their homes as children by government authorities, in a bid to assimilate them into white society. These policies lasted from the 1910s until the 1970s, creating what's known as the 'Stolen Generation'.

Reconciliation is a Work in Progress

It was only in 1965 that First Nations people were granted suffrage. Since then, it's been a long, slow road towards reconciliation.

In 2008 Prime Minister Kevin Rudd issued a formal apology to Indigenous peoples, especially the Stolen Generations for the gross injustices meted out to them. In 2023 the country held a referendum proposing a change to the constitution that would recognise the First Peoples of Australia by establishing an Aboriginal and Torres Strait Islander Voice (a parliamentary advisory committee). The alteration was unsuccessful, with 60% of people voting 'no'.

However, there are green shoots. 'We haven't closed every gap, but it's on the agenda now – which is a positive,' says Garry. 'Corporate Australia is doing well with Reconciliation Action Plans, for example. Some communities are trying to resurrect lost languages. But there's a lot more work to be done.'

The Empire

While the general perception is that the majority of convicts who arrived from Europe were impoverished Irish and British people arrested for petty crimes, the convicts' cohort was more ethnically diverse – including people of African descent (some of the convicts who arrived through 80-odd years were former slaves).

Throughout the 18th and 19th centuries, people from other communities – including Pacific Islanders and Indians – also kept arriving through trade and maritime vessels, as Sydney was emerging as a major port. A little-known but significant group were the camel drivers from Afghanistan and northwestern British India, who accompanied the thousands of camels brought in to traverse the unforgiving Australian outback. The early cameleers, colloquially known as 'Ghans', played a vital role in the region's economic development and can be credited with planting the roots of Islam in Australia, including establishing the first mosques.

Meanwhile, the vastly reduced Indigenous populations came to live on the fringes of European society – literally and figuratively. Governance policies since the early 19th century focused on assimilation, with attempts to 'civilise' Indigenous people through education and evangelical missions often undertaken by force.

A Seismic Shift

One of the defining periods of Australia's multicultural history came in the 1850s, when the gold-rush era began. When gold was first discovered in New South Wales and Victoria, with it came a new wave of migrants. Over the next two decades, the country's population would double in size.

Immigrant 'diggers' arrived as free settlers from Britain and elsewhere in Europe, China and the US. Subsequent discoveries of gold in Tasmania, Queensland, the Northern Territory and Western Australia led to the proliferation of the migrant population across the country, while exponentially growing national wealth. Infrastructure development, from transport to cultural institutions, cemented Australia's appeal.

The gold-rush era led to economic changes and social, cultural and political development. The foundations for the Australian egalitarian ethos and culture of 'mateship' can be traced back to this period, when people from different social classes came together in search of a common goal, bound by a camaraderie created by shared hardships, and wealth was – theoretically – accessible to anyone.

'WHEN GOLD WAS FIRST DISCOVERED IN NEW SOUTH WALES AND VICTORIA, WITH IT CAME A NEW WAVE OF MIGRANTS.'

Panning for gold, Laura (p417)

HENK VRIESELAAR/SHUTTERSTOCK

The camaraderie went beyond the social, however. Progressive political thinking from the growing population laid the foundations for democracy in Australia.

This is also when the 'White Australia' policy took on clear contours, before becoming a formal immigration policy in 1901 (although it was never officially called as such). Chinese gold-rush immigrants were heavily discriminated against, with legislations in place through the 1800s restricting the number of Chinese immigrants who could sail into Victoria and NSW. (However, it didn't stop many from arriving on the shores of South Australia and making the difficult journey to Victoria overland.) Those who made it to the goldfields faced segregation, living in separate camps, with anti-Chinese sentiment running high.

In 1901 Australia became a federation, bringing the six disparate colonies into the fold of the Commonwealth. One of the first national policies was applying migration restrictions on non-Europeans. While there were no explicit laws, restrictions were implemented by giving immigration officials carte blanche to decide who got to enter the country. (The racially biased process usually involved unwelcome arrivals being given a dictation test in a language they didn't know.)

Subsequent federal government policies continued to reinforce the preference for Anglo-Celtic immigrants. Various government-assisted migration programs were put in place to encourage people from the British Isles to undertake the long, arduous and expensive journey Down Under. For example, under the so-called '10-pound Poms' scheme, people from the British Isles (and some of its colonies such as Malta) could migrate to Australia for as little as 10 pounds sterling, with the commitment to remain in the country for at least two years. The program, which fluctuated in popularity since its inception in 1945, only ended in 1982 (although the cost grew proportionately with the times).

However, the percentage of non-British arrivals continued to rise steadily, with small numbers from Greece, Italy and Yugoslavia – many of them fleeing post-war Europe in the 1920s and 1930s.

Rise of Multiculturalism

The birth of one of Australia's cultural icons, the milk bar, is an example of how the culture started to be shaped by immigrant populations. First opened in Sydney by a Greek migrant and inspired by American soda bars, the Australian milk bar served ice creams, milkshakes and chocolates. Greek-owned milk bars popped up all over the country and over time evolved into a corner-store-deli hybrid.

LEGRINIS BAR ESPRESS

After WWII, everything changed. The postwar era saw Australian immigration take on an entirely different complexion – albeit one still relatively pale.

The country needed to grow its population and arrivals from Old Blighty just weren't enough. So the government started a recruitment policy to attract the plentitude of displaced persons in postwar Europe, many of them from Central and Eastern Europe and the Baltic states. However, the goal was still to create a homogenous society and the going wasn't easy for all the new arrivals – even the ones from Europe.

'Anything "Australian" was put on a pedestal, even as everyone was trying to work out what it means to be Australian,' explains historian, anthropologist and social researcher Nonja Peters, herself the child of a Dutch immigrant family. 'In many cases, names were changed; you weren't allowed to learn your own language. People were starting to feel ashamed of their own backgrounds.'

'PERHAPS THE BEST EXPRESSION OF THIS MULTICULTURALISM IS IN AUSTRALIA'S FOOD. MODERN AUSTRALIAN CUISINE IS ONE OF THE MOST INTERESTING IN THE WORLD, ABSORBING INFLUENCES FROM THE MIDDLE EAST, CHINA, VIETNAM, JAPAN, GREECE AND ITALY, AMONG MANY OTHER INFLUENCES.'

Australia also started accepting refugees and asylum seekers from different countries from 1945 onwards (including Vietnamese and Lebanese asylum seekers who have become an integral part of Australia's social fabric, as well as Afghan refugees), although the approach towards their resettlement and offshore detention programs has been contentious. From the 1960s onwards, the White Australia policy began to be dismantled, with immigration gradually being opened up to non-whites, although it wasn't legally abolished until 1973.

Modern Australia

The official immigration policy from the 1970s onwards has been economically driven, with skilled migration programs aiming to fill gaps in the workforce; versions of this form of migration have endured to date, evolving according to the needs of the hour. This has led to an influx of people from different parts of Asia (including India) and Europe (including the mothership, Britain); it also grew a different kind of migrant community of educated white-collar workers.

While this brought about economic growth, discrimination didn't exactly disappear overnight and certain migrant communities were often isolated in their own pockets of suburban Australia.

However, the tide was definitely starting to turn and the focus had shifted from assimilation to a more integrative approach, helping to shape a truly cohesive multicultural society. This is amply evidenced by the diversity of colours, accents and cultural and religious institutions one can encounter in everyday Australia today, even in rural regions, and their largely peaceful coexistence.

Perhaps the best expression of this multiculturalism is in Australia's food. Modern Australian cuisine is one of the most interesting in the world, absorbing influences from the Middle East, China, Vietnam, Japan, Greece and Italy, among many other cultures. We have the various immigrant communities who have made this island their home to thank for this.

Even in the realm of food, though, Indigenous culture is still not adequately represented. While there are some high-end restaurants that are getting creative with native ingredients, we are a long way from mainstreaming Indigenous bush foods.

But, as with most other things, modern Australia is getting there.

Pellegrinis Espresso Bar, Melbourne (p463)

CHRIS PUTNAM/ALAMY

Melbourne Cricket Ground (p496)

OZITRAVELER/SHUTTERSTOCK

FOOTY: MORE THAN A GAME

In addition to the kangaroos, koalas and wombats, there's a uniquely Australian thing that you may never have heard of. Aussie Rules, known simply as 'footy', is Australia's preeminent sport. By Kat Barber

TO MANY AUSTRALIANS, footy is so much more than a game. It brings families together, provides hope, escape, excitement, joy and mateship. 'Who's your team?' is a common icebreaker at parties and friendships are often forged on sporting allegiances.

It's a national addiction. But footy can mean different things, depending on where you are.

In New South Wales and Queensland, 'footy' usually refers to the game of rugby league. The annual State of Origin clash between the best players from either state is a highly anticipated event on the calendar. Some people also use 'footy' to refer to the game of rugby union, just to add extra confusion into the mix. Meanwhile, football (the sport played by Messi and Ronaldo) is known as 'soccer' Down Under. But in the majority of states, 'footy' means the game of Aussie Rules, or AFL (Australian Football League).

History of the AFL

Aussie Rules was invented in Melbourne in 1858, as a way to keep cricketers fit in the off-season. Two teams of 18 players apiece kick, mark, handball and bounce the oval-shaped ball around the field before kicking a goal (six points) between two upright goalposts. A miss to either side is a 'behind' (one point). The game is fast-paced and full-contact, highlighted by the 'speccy' (a tactic that sees players launch off their opponent's back to catch a ball flying metres in the air), brutal bumps and tackles, and cries of 'BALLLL' if one player holds the ball too long.

The sport quickly spread throughout the country, with each colony creating their own league. However, its stronghold has always been the state of Victoria, where footy fever is inescapable. From footy-tipping competitions at workplaces to personalised team-colour number plates on cars and two massive stadiums in Melbourne, footy is to Melbourne what pizza is to Naples.

Today, the AFL is the most attended sport in Australia according to the Australian Bureau of Statistics, garnering huge crowds throughout the season. The league has 18 clubs, with 10 from Melbourne and surrounds, and all clubs have strong, loyal membership bases. Melbourne Football Club and Football Club are two of the oldest continuous sporting clubs in the world.

The Stadiums

When your team reaches the finals, footy fever peaks. The MCG (Melbourne Cricket Ground, known as the 'G) is an enormous stadium, just minutes from Melbourne's city centre, and it plays host to the Grand Final match. Over 100,000 passionate supporters fill the 'G on a Saturday in September. It's so captivating that a public holiday has been granted on the eve of Grand Final Day in Victoria. But throughout the year, certain rivalry matches such as the Anzac Day clash between Collingwood and Essendon always sell out. In fact, the 'G has one of the highest annual attendances of any stadium in the world.

'AUSTRALIANS ARE PROUD OF THEIR HOMEGROWN SPORTSPEOPLE AND FOOTY IS A UNIQUELY AUSTRALIAN THING THAT IS BEST EXPERIENCED FROM THE STANDS.'

Lauren Young, Alberton Oval, Adelaide (p716)

SPP SPORT PRESS PHOTO. /ALAMY LIVE NEWS/ALAMY

If you want to catch a match, head along to the MCG on a day when a Melbourne team is playing an interstate team and you'll be able to grab a ticket at the gate. Or you can watch a game at Marvel Stadium in Docklands, a newer Melbourne stadium, with a capacity of 53,000 and a retractable roof. Sydney, Brisbane, Adelaide and Perth also have AFL teams and thousands of passionate supporters.

A Spectator Sport

So why does footy have such a devoted and substantial following?

Well, as a spectator sport, it's pretty exciting. It's fast and free-flowing, with very little downtime. The players are incredibly athletic, combining speed, endurance, strength and ball skills. Plus, it's high-scoring, so there's always something to cheer about. But it's also a great show of mateship, both on the field and off. Friends who support rival teams will often watch a game together, families enjoy taking their kids to the footy and there is mutual respect.

It's also a pride thing. Footy is a truly local sport, invented and grown here. Australians are proud of their homegrown sportspeople and footy is a uniquely Australian thing that is best experienced from the stands.

The Women's Game

I grew up in a footy family – AFL, that is. From a young age, family gatherings were at footy matches, the footy fixture dictated weekend commitments and birthday cards from my Nan were always signed off with 'Go Roos' (our family are diehard supporters of the North Melbourne Kangaroos).

And when the AFL Women's (AFLW) league began in 2017, it spurred me on to have a kick myself. I quickly learned just how hard it is to kick, bounce and mark an oval ball. It's a brutal, exhausting and tough game to play. I decided not to quit my day job, but many other women have taken up the sport at a professional level and receive a salary that is just enough to live off.

Today, the AFLW competition has 18 teams and the skill level, professionalism and crowds grow with each season. Girls are taking up the sport at a rapid rate at junior levels. While AFLW games don't attract the same amount of fans as the men's league yet, this is sure to change over the coming years as sponsorship and investment grow. In soccer, however, the Australian Matildas' semi-final match at the 2023 Women's World Cup was the most-watched TV show in Australia ever, drawing 11.15 million viewers at its peak – a great boon for women's sport.

Women's or men's, the AFL is much more than a sporting competition; it's a piece of intangible cultural heritage that weaves itself into the fabric of Australian identity. The shared experience, passion and sense of belonging that the AFL cultivates extends long after the booming final siren signals the end of the match.

DEADLY & MISUNDERSTOOD:

AUSTRALIA'S WILDLIFE ISN'T OUT TO KILL YOU

Spiders under every seat, sharks off every beach, snakes behind every rock. What's really behind the legend? By Olivia Pozzan

ON A HOT summer day, swimmers drift between the flags while surfers sit beyond the break. The shark alarm pierces the air. A ripple of movement passes through the swimmers, but no one panics. They simply turn towards shore, wading out calmly as surfers paddle in. For many overseas visitors, this low-key reaction to danger is baffling. For Australians, it's just another day at the beach.

A Wild Country

Australia is stereotyped as a land filled with dangerous and venomous creatures, all ready to strike. It's a reputation fuelled by outback folklore, news headlines, films and documentaries. But the reality is far more nuanced. Although many of Australia's iconic species are considered dangerous, they are far more inclined to avoid humans than engage with them. The myth survives because it's an irresistible mix of fear and fascination.

Take snakes, the backbone of the country's deadly-animal folklore. The inland taipan is often described as the most venomous snake in the world, yet it's so reclusive that sightings are rare and bites almost unheard of. More visible are the eastern brown and tiger snakes, highly venomous species found in bushland, farms and suburban gardens. Yet most people will never come close to stepping on one. Snakes feel the vibration of a footstep long before they're seen, slipping away quietly into long grass or leaf litter. Most serious encounters involve pets, usually when they confront a snake in the backyard before it can retreat.

Spiders inspire their own brand of dread. The huntsman, with its dinner-plate legs, is a fixture in many Australian homes. Despite its appearance, it's harmless and most Aussies tolerate their uninvited roommate as a natural pest controller. Bites from venomous spiders like redbacks and funnel-webs are uncommon and most visitors are unlikely to see them.

Along the coast, where many people live, the cast of 'dangerous' creatures is well known. Sharks are part of life by the sea. Their presence doesn't clear the beaches, it simply adds a layer of awareness to the daily swim. In the tropical north, saltwater crocodiles and box jellyfish make many beaches unsuitable for swimming for much of the year. Locals adapt, turning to stinger nets, stinger suits or swimming pools.

In a land where nature sets the rules, Australians grow up with a healthy respect for its wildlife. Even the gentlest-looking animals are given a wide berth. Kangaroos aren't aggressive, but they can pack a powerful kick if they feel threatened. Koalas may look placid yet their claws make it clear they're wild animals, not cuddly toys, while the shy platypus has a venomous spur on each hind leg. Most wildlife would rather avoid humans. Trouble usually comes when people get too close.

Reality Check

In Australia, no one has died from a confirmed spider bite since 1979. Each year, on average, one to two snakebite deaths and one to three fatal shark attacks are reported. Given the millions of people who hike and swim here annually, the chance of a dangerous wildlife encounter is extremely low.

Pride in the Myth

So why does the 'deadly Australia' myth endure? Part of it traces back to the early British settlers, who arrived with no frame of reference for the continent's strange flora and fauna. They confronted a landscape unlike anything they had known – unfamiliar plants, large animals bounding through the scrub and venomous creatures hidden in the undergrowth. Fear filled the gaps in knowledge. Over time, though, the fearsome became familiar and settled into the background of everyday life.

For outsiders, however, shark attacks, snakebites and dramatic headlines continue to reinforce the idea of constant threat. Australians, with their wry sense of humour, play up the hype, even inventing imaginary drop bears to tease visitors.

'THE REAL STORY ISN'T ABOUT DANGER AT ALL. IT'S ABOUT VULNERABILITY.'

Threat or Threatened

But the real story isn't about danger at all. It's about vulnerability. Australia's wildlife faces pressures far more severe than any threat it poses. Habitat loss is among the most significant. Much of the nation's population is concentrated along a narrow coastal fringe – the very places where wildlife is most abundant. As cities grow, new housing estates replace bushland, fragmenting habitats and squeezing native animals into smaller spaces.

Climate extremes intensify the strain. Every year, floods, bushfires and drought push species to the brink, while conservation efforts struggle to keep pace. The 2020 Black Summer bushfires were an emotional turning point, burning through vast tracts of bush and forest, leaving billions of animals dead or displaced. It was a stark reminder of how fragile Australia's ecosystems really are. For all the talk of deadly creatures, much of Australia's wildlife survives on a knife-edge.

Ask any Australian and they'll tell you the country's wildlife is a source of national pride. Not because the animals are dangerous, but because they're extraordinary. They evolved over millions of years in isolation, giving rise to species unlike anything found elsewhere on Earth. Living alongside them has fostered a deeper respect for their behaviour and needs, and a clearer understanding of how human activity impacts their lives and habitats.

Visitors often arrive expecting danger around every corner. What they discover is something different: a country where nature is powerful but rarely hostile, where wildlife is ever-present but seldom intrusive, and where the relationship between people and animals rests on coexistence rather than fear.

This is Australia

From deserts to rainforests to rugged bushland, life has a unique rhythm here. Every day, somewhere, a snake slips across a backyard lawn and a huntsman claims its spot on a kitchen wall. Wildlife carries on as usual and people do as well. Down on the beach, swimmers return to the water as surfers paddle back out. It might look like casual indifference, but it's simply everyday life in a land of extremes.

Dr Olivia Pozzan is an Australian veterinarian with a focus on wildlife conservation and animal welfare. She has spent decades working with animals in diverse environments around the world.

Saltwater Crocodile

IAN SCOTT/SHUTTERSTOCK

STORYBOOK

AN ODE TO VEGEMITE

For travellers headed Down Under, tasting Vegemite is an unforgettable part of the Australian cultural experience.

By Lisa Martin

ON A COPENHAGEN winter morning, I stare out my window at the grey day ahead. But all it takes is one bite into my breakfast to be instantly transported to Australia. Each salty, umami bite brings me a bit of comfort and joy. It tastes like home.

For an Australian living in Denmark, Vegemite has become the secret weapon for surviving the dark gloom of Danish winter. A dark-brown spread that is a rich source of vitamins B1, B2, B3 and folate, the breakfast staple can be found in eight out of 10 Australian homes; 22 million jars are manufactured every year.

Initially, Australians weren't wild about the product, admits Jamie Callister, author of *Vegemite: The True Story of the Man Who Invented an Australian Icon* (2023) and the grandson of Vegemite's inventor, food scientist Cyril Callister. That changed in the 1940s amid wartime food rationing. Vegemite was sent to Aussie troops on the frontlines in WWII as a nutrition boost and buying it was marketed back home as a patriotic act.

Vegemite

Global conflict wasn't the only reason for its growth in popularity; at the time, Australia was trying to step out of the shadow of Great Britain and forge its own identity. The spread's reputation was cemented in 1954 with the release of the now-iconic jingle, 'We're Happy Little Vegemites', a true earworm. Vegemite has been celebrated in pop culture ever since – from the lyrics of Men at Work's song 'Down Under' to the children's book *Possum Magic* by Mem Fox.

You'll find Vegemite in the supermarket next to the peanut butter. But don't copy Mariah Carey and stick a spoonful in your mouth – it's not Nutella. First-time users are advised to add a small amount to a heavily buttered piece of bread or toast. Vegemite isn't only a breakfast food, though. You might find it baked into cheese scrolls at bakeries or as an ice-cream flavour, like the award-winning version at Dooley's in the Victorian coastal town of Apollo Bay. At the Cyril Callister Museum in Beaufort, northwest of Melbourne, you can tuck into Vegemite meat pies.

'THE SO-CALLED "BLACK GOLD" IS INTRINSICALLY LINKED TO THE AUSTRALIAN LARRIKIN SPIRIT – A MENTALITY OF BEING MISCHIEVOUS AND HAVING A DISREGARD FOR SOCIAL CONVENTIONS.'

FROM LEFT: JABIRU/SHUTTERSTOCK, J AL/SHUTTERSTOCK

High-end restaurants have jumped on the bandwagon – Sydney's King Clarence incorporates the spread into its popular drunken chicken-liver skewers. The Australian pop-up of lauded Danish restaurant Noma even once created its own homemade version.

Vegemite is also part of Australia's proud multicultural story. It's an easy entry point for new migrants to embrace Australian culture, with chefs adding it to cuisines including Malaysian, Mexican, Chinese and Vietnamese fare.

Despite its deep cultural significance, Vegemite has some high-profile sceptics – former US President Barack Obama described it as 'horrible', while Pope Leo XIV reportedly prefers another Aussie icon, Tim Tam biscuits. The polarising spread is also featured at Disgusting Food Museum's exhibitions in Sweden and Germany.

In 2025 there was even a Vegemite-related diplomatic crisis, when an Aussie-owned cafe in Toronto risked losing A$9000 worth of the delicacy because the product fell foul of Canadian food regulations. The trade dispute reached the agendas of both countries' prime ministers. Ultimately, the cafe owner was allowed to keep importing Vegemite, to the delight of his expat customers.

Jamie Callister, who never got to meet his grandfather, is sure he would be amused by Vegemite's colourful legacy. From its beginnings as an alternative to British Marmite, to its role in popular culture and current events, the so-called 'Black Gold' is intrinsically linked to the Australian larrikin spirit – a mentality of being mischievous and having a disregard for social conventions. In the book *The Changi Brownlow,* author Roland Perry recounts how Australian Peter Chitty smuggled Vegemite into the notorious Japanese prisoner-of-war camp in Singapore during WWII. When questioned by the guard, Chitty claimed that the dark-brown spread was actually boot polish.

Snow gum, Kosciuszko National Park (p248)

MICHAEL LESLIE/SHUTTERSTOCK

EUCALYPTS RULE

Deemed unattractive and of poor quality by early settlers, eucalypts define the Australian landscape and form an integral part of the country's identity. By Briar Jensen

ARRIVING IN AUSTRALIA 40 years ago from New Zealand, I initially struggled to see 'beauty' in the Aussie bush.

Unlike New Zealand's lush, moist, fern-filled forests or Europe's dark-green coniferous forests, the eucalypt woodlands of my new home were dry, untidy and sun-bleached. They gave off, as Murray Bail wrote in his 1998 award-winning taxonomic novel *Eucalyptus*, 'an inhospitable, unsympathetic air'.

And what did the term 'Aussie bush' mean exactly? Like 'the outback', it's vague vernacular that often has visitors stumped. Colloquially, it means anywhere beyond major metropolitan areas, but generally it refers to Australia's native forests. What sets Aussie bush apart from other forests of the world, however, is its monopolisation by eucalypts.

Eucalypts Reign

'No other landscape in the world is so dominated by one genus', writes Ashley Hay, author of *Gum: The Story of Eucalypts and Their Champions* (2021).

Commonly known as gum trees (due to sap-like resin oozing from some smooth-barked species), eucalypts have been here for at least 45 million years and make up 77% of our country's native forest trees.

'Most Australians can instinctively identify a eucalypt...by their overall "look, feel and smell"', says self-confessed eucalypt nerd Dean Nicolle, in the introduction to his reference books, *Taller Eucalypts for Planting in Australia* and *Smaller Eucalypts for Planting in Australia* (2016). Yet most Aussies don't realise there are over 900 species, almost all native to Australia.

They range from scrubby shrubs to towering sentinels (the mountain ash *Eucalyptus regnans* being the world's tallest hardwood). Some species define locales, like sculptural Sydney red gums found in Ku-ring-gai Chase National Park (p137), colourful-trunked snow gums in sub-alpine regions like Kosciuszko National Park (p248) and statuesque river red gums, the most prolific species, tracing water courses across the continent.

All belong to three genera: *Eucalyptus, Corymbia* and *Angophora*. Apart from a handful of easily identifiable varieties, trying to differentiate species is like decoding your DNA, involving minute differences in flowers and fruits (called gumnuts).

Single-trunked or multi-trunked (called mallee), their bark can be smooth, rough, mottled, shedding or a combination. There are some helpful descriptive group names, like ghost gums (bone-white trunks), ironbarks (hard, deeply furrowed bark), ribbon gums (bark strips dangling from branches) and scribbly gums (trunks traced with calligraphic etchings by moth larvae).

Internationally, eucalypts are perhaps most famous for the scent of their leaves. They contain oils that release aromas when crushed, from the distinctive eucalyptus scent to peppermint and lemon. Although classed as evergreens, gums lose a third of their leaves annually. The tannins from these leaves are also responsible for the tea-like hue of some of Australia's rivers, lakes and

waterholes, like North Stradbroke Island's aptly named Brown Lake (Bummiera, p301).

The bush isn't entirely muted-toned, though. Eucalypts are the world's tallest flowering plants, with blooms of massed, tightly packed stamens, resembling mini mopheads, mostly in creamy white. ('The colour of beer froth', writes Bail.) Yellow, orange, pink and red flowers are less common but more spectacular.

Tenacious and opportunistic, gums can sprout from rocks, their roots wedged in cracks, trunks oozing over the surface like candle wax for balance. Riverbank dwellers may have root systems exposed by gouging floods, yet they cling on.

Wildfire & Wildlife

It's believed eucalypts evolved in a regime of fire as our continent warmed. Some species need fire to trigger seed release or germinate underground seed. Consequently, eucalypts actively fuel fire with oil-rich leaves, dropped litter and flailing bark.

Post-burning, trees rebound quickly with new shoots sprouting from underground lignotubers (growths of food reserves) and epicormic buds beneath bark. Within weeks, blackened trunks are covered in verdant downy growth resembling fluffy dusters – evidence of this can be seen at spots such as Kangaroo Island (p749), South Australia, and the Blue Mountains (p138), New South Wales, both of which have been affected by bushfires in the last 10 years.

Fire is needed for Australia's landscape to regenerate, but uncontrolled bushfires can have devastating consequences, including on wildlife. One study found more than 320 species of invertebrates on a single river red gum (more than 4000 insects). That's not counting 300-plus vertebrates like possums, gliders, birds, bats and reptiles that shelter in their hollows and feed on their nectar and seeds, or aquatic species that hide and spawn amongst riverbank roots.

Koalas are the cutest eucalypt inhabitants, sleeping up to 18 hours a day wedged in tree forks. Their digestive system has adapted to extract maximum benefit from fibrous, low-nutrient gum leaves, though they must consume 200g to 500g a day.

The loudest forest-dwellers, though, are Australia's birds, renowned for their volume. Whipbirds pierce the air with namesake whip-cracking whistles and lyrebirds perform mimicry arias with operatic projection. Kookaburras cackling in unison resemble a laughter therapy session, while squawking parrots, caterwauling corellas and screeching cockatoos are as raucous as tanked-up footy fans at a Grand Final game.

But the iconic summer Aussie bush sound is millions of cicadas clacking a sonic Mexican wave so loud it reverberates inside your eardrums.

Indigenous Culture vs Settler Economy

If you take a tour during your time in Australia, you may hear Indigenous guides explaining how eucalypt forests were their supermarket, hardware store and pharmacy, providing food and material for shelters, tools, weapons, instruments and transport. It's no surprise to learn that eucalypts appear in Creation stories and are integral to spiritual practices, such as smoking ceremonies to cleanse, ward off bad spirits and provide protection.

They had myriad medicinal uses, too, from antiseptics and pain relief to treatments for infections and fevers. Australia's First Nations people understood that river red gums indicate underground water and knew which species' roots could be squeezed for drinking water.

Respecting nature's provisions, they harvested sustainably, taking only what was needed. Living 'scar trees' seen along the banks of the Murray River (p617), SA, show how carefully removed sections of bark for canoes or coolamons (bowls) didn't sacrifice the trees.

In contrast, within 24 hours of the First Fleet arriving in 1788, tradesmen and convicts were set to work felling trees for buildings, roads, bridges and jetties. Swathes of forest were cleared for farmland and fencing, and later for mine shafts, railway sleepers and steam engines.

Yet, as leisure-seekers explored the bush and pride in the fledgling colony grew, so too did their love for eucalypts. Gum leaves, flowers and nuts appeared as decorative motifs on furniture, pottery, jewellery, souvenirs, stamps and the $5 note.

Twentieth-century artists Hans Heysen and Albert Namatjira (p869), whose paintings hang in galleries around Australia, popularised landscapes highlighting eucalypts.

Meanwhile, photographer Harold Cazneaux immortalised their tenacity in a 1937 black-and-white image of a river red gum titled *The Spirit of Endurance* taken in the Ikara-Flinders Ranges (p786), SA, where the tree still stands today.

Aussie bush formed the backdrop for colonial-era writers Banjo Paterson ('Waltzing Matilda' bush ballad) and Henry Lawson, and more recently Tim Winton, Mark Tredinnick and Inga Simpson. May Gibbs' children's book about gumnut babies, *Tales of Snugglepot and Cuddlepie*, published in 1918 and never out of print, has become a gift-shop staple and her Sydney home, Nutcote, is now a museum.

Eucalypts make cameos in numerous lyrics, but the catchy folk song 'Home Among the Gum Trees' popularised by John Williamson is the most recognisable patriotic earworm. However, some international travellers may be more familiar with the opening words of a popular children's song, 'Kookaburra Sits in the Old Gum Tree'.

'NO OTHER LANDSCAPE IN THE WORLD IS SO DOMINATED BY ONE GENUS', WRITES ASHLEY HAY, AUTHOR OF "GUM: THE STORY OF EUCALYPTS AND THEIR CHAMPIONS" (2021).'

Koala, Kangaroo Island (p749)

THOMAS MORBEE/SHUTTERSTOCK

Conservation Is a Work in Progress

This love, however, came with negative side effects. Forestry flourished unregulated for many years as Australia became the world's leading producer of eucalyptus oil until the 1950s.

Today, Australia has one of the highest land clearance rates in the developed world, primarily for agriculture, mining and logging. It's demolished nearly 44% of forests and woodlands in the 200-odd years since settlement, which has increased soil salinity, affected biodiversity and fast-tracked extinctions.

Yet, thanks to passionate nature lovers, we have one of the world's oldest national parks, Royal National Park in NSW, established in 1879. Willing protestors from all walks of life have chained themselves to bulldozers and camped in treetops to protect forests from logging, dams and development, perhaps most famously in Tasmania (p633).

Recognition of the importance of gum trees is gradually increasing with National Eucalypt Day, public voting for Eucalypt of the Year and not-for-profit Eucalypt Australia offering fellowships for researchers, writers and artists.

Climate change may be their biggest threat, though. Increased bushfire frequency threatens some species by reducing the window for them to grow from seed to maturity and therefore reproduce.

Author Stephen J Pyne offers hope in his 1991 book *Burning Bush: A Fire History of Australia*. 'Eucalyptus is not only the universal Australian,' he writes, 'it is the ideal Australian – versatile, tough, sardonic, contrary, self-mocking, with a deceptive complexity amid the appearance of massive homogeneity; an occupier of disturbed environment; a fire creature.'

You need to walk among eucalypts to understand them: feel their magnitude, admire their painterly bark, caress their cool trunks, inhale their hot scent, hear their shivering leaves.

I've met matriarchal Sydney red gums, fulsome, dimpled and shedding bark like menopausal women in a hot flush, sticky red resin dribbling sweat-like down ochre-orange bark. I've been dwarfed, physically and historically, by ancient river red gums growing since before European settlement. And I've pressed my ear to a sapling gum and heard life-giving water gurgling through its vascular system.

It's been a slow smoulder getting to know the Aussie bush, but now my love of eucalypt forests burns as strong as the summer wildfires needed for their survival.

IF THESE WALLS COULD TALK: AUSSIE PUBS

Much more than a place for a beer, Australian pubs have unique identities, hallmarks and traditions that signal you're definitely drinking Down Under. By Jo Stewart

IT'S NO SECRET that Aussies are fond of drinking. Yes, you can wet your whistle at bars, restaurants and bottle shops across the country, but pubs are a goldmine if you want to delve into the culture, community and characters of wherever you land in Australia.

From rubbing shoulders with outback opal miners in Coober Pedy to enjoying a roast dinner by the fireplace at a quaint country pub in Tasmania, to having a 'Sunday Session' at a breezy beer garden in inner-city Brisbane or a late night at a grungy watering hole in the backstreets of Melbourne, there's a pub to suit every mood, taste and budget.

Pubs as Pop-Culture Landmarks

Firmly woven into the nation's identity, Australian pubs have spawned much more than hangovers. From 1971 thriller *Wake in Fright* to the cultural cringe of *Crocodile Dundee* (1986) and big-hearted 1994 classic *The Adventures of Priscilla, Queen of the Desert,* pubs have played a starring role in some of the nation's most influential films. They've even inspired a music genre: pub rock. During the 1970s and '80s, playing the pub circuit was a low-cost way to get your music out there, with bands like Cold Chisel, the Angels and INXS all cutting their teeth

Pictured clockwise from top left: Pub in Pemberton (p937); Chicken parmy, Glenmore Hotel (p87); 'Croc bar', The Grand Hotel, Cairns (p378); Larrimah Wayside Inn, Larrimah (p844)

playing mammoth sets at suburban pubs across the nation. Today, pub-rock songs are still played in old-school and country pubs, even if the live music scene isn't what it once was.

One cultural touchstone that baffles newcomers is the concept of popping into your local for a sneaky pint and coming home with a tray of fresh meat. Dating back to the 1940s, the meat raffle is a wartime phenomenon that's stuck around for good. Simply buy a ticket, wait for the winning numbers to be called and – bingo – you're now the proud owner of a tray of sausages (or 'snags' in Australia), steaks, lamb chops and more from the local butcher. A ubiquitous feature of Aussie pub culture, meat-tray raffles are held everywhere from flyblown wooden pubs patronised by farmers to beachside pubs in Sydney frequented by investment bankers.

A Peculiar Place in History

Whether acting as a makeshift court, improvised bushfire shelter or meeting place for the nation's leaders, pubs have played a vital role in Australia's social history. From gruesome to heroic, many significant events have gone down in pubs around the country.

In 1900 the body of a bushranger (outlaw) was laid out on a pub table during an inquest at the Caledonian Hotel in Singleton, New South Wales, while in 1983 Victoria's Macedon Hotel famously sheltered hundreds of locals during the devastating Ash Wednesday fires that claimed the lives of 75 people.

Then there's the pubs with unique identities tied up with cultural, political and social movements. In inner Melbourne, the John Curtin Hotel (named after Australia's 14th prime pinister) is where many political powerbrokers from the Labor Party have strategised, celebrated and commiserated over the years, including notorious beer-swiller Prime Minister Bob Hawke.

As its name suggests, Sydney's harbour-adjacent Fortune of War has its own place in the nation's military-cultural history. Built by a former convict, this pub – allegedly Sydney's oldest – has long been the first and last stop for sailors heading to and from war. Today, it's still a meeting place for veterans to share a lager on Anzac Day, followed by a wager on a game of two-up (a coin-toss game played on this special day). It doesn't get much more Australian than honouring your fallen mates with a beer and a gambling session at a pub poignantly called the Fortune of War, does it?

A Boozy Battleground

While many of us experience a warm welcome upon stepping into a pub, not everyone is greeted with a smile and frosty lager from a laid-back publican. Far from being an egalitarian paradise, pubs have been hostile environments for some.

Segregation was once commonplace, with women, foreigners, LGBTIQ+ and First Nations people having been excluded from entering pubs (or generally made to feel unwelcome) over the decades. Even by the 1960s, women still weren't allowed to drink in the public bar area in most states of Australia (instead, they were relegated to the 'Ladies Lounge' out the back).

The laws that excluded women were finally repealed in the 1970s after two plucky women chained themselves to the bar at Brisbane's Regatta Hotel. Today, that same pub is home to Merle's Bar, named in honour of one of the women who staged the protest. Oh, how times have changed.

Don't doubt it, accessing pubs is a serious business in Australia – so serious that in 1979 the closure of a beloved Newcastle pub caused one of the biggest riots in Australian history. When locals were told of the Star Hotel's imminent closure, thousands turned out to defend the none-too salubrious watering hole. The night ended in what is now known as 'the Star Hotel riot' – a violent clash between an estimated 4000 boozed-up customers and 40-or-so police officers. The subject of a documentary, song and many a tall tale told over an ale, the battle for the Star Hotel is now etched in Australian folklore.

More recently, creeping gentrification has got Aussie pubgoers talking, with rough-around-the-edges boozers being sold for a song to cashed-up developers who do a paint-by-numbers renovation that strips the space of all its character and charm. With one Australian billionaire pub baron now owning more than 80 pubs, this trend is unlikely to be reversed any time soon.

So get in the spirit of things and raise a glass at one of Australia's many character-filled pubs while you can. Who knows? You might even score a meat tray, too.

CLOCKWISE FROM TOP LEFT: RONAN O'CONNELL/LONELY PLANET, VANITA BARRETT-SMITH/SHUTTERSTOCK, PAUL HARDING/LONELY PLANET, PETAR B PHOTOGRAPHY/SHUTTERSTOCK

Boobialla

PFMPHOTOSTOCK/SHUTTERSTOCK

THE FIRST FOODS

A food trend 65,000 years in the making, the rise of native ingredients gives visitors and locals alike the chance to taste – and connect with – Indigenous Australia anew. By Max Veenhuyzen

THE CURRENT INTEREST in native ingredients isn't the first time Australia has looked to its own backyard for inspiration. Although macadamia nuts – native to Queensland – were first grown commercially in the 1880s, it wasn't until almost a century later that horticulturalists began to explore the viability of cultivating other native foods. The 1990s saw restaurants begin to serve ingredients such as kangaroo and bush tomatoes, only to be met with indifference, both then and during subsequent bush-food revivals. Then, around 15 years ago, the industry took another look at what was growing in its backyard and suddenly realised what a precious resource it had on its hands.

A new wave of interest in bush foods gripped Australia – only this time, it stuck. Perhaps it was due to the rise of hyper-local fine-dining restaurants such as Copenhagen's Noma, Pujol in Mexico and DOM in São Paulo. Perhaps it was eaters and cooks finally accepting that Australian food culture is just as worthy of recognition as other 'great cuisines' like French, Italian or Japanese. Perhaps it was a symptom of Australia's desire to (re)connect with its Indigenous culture. Or maybe it was all of the above.

Whatever the reason, it's safe to say these native flavours are on the way to becoming a permanent part of Australia's food culture. Each region of the country has its own unique foods and cultural practices, and the members of more than 250 Indigenous language groups protect and maintain a connection to the land spanning some 65,000 years and counting. For curious travellers keen to understand this place better, these homegrown foods make a fine starting point.

Modernising Ancient Ingredients

Once upon a time, native ingredients were regarded as medicine first and food second. Today, they are a chance for producers and consumers alike to connect with Indigenous Australian culture. Take, for instance, bloodroot. A relative of the kangaroo paw (the red-coloured floral emblem of Western Australia), bloodroot was traditionally used by the Noongar people to treat toothaches and mouth sores. Today, it's one of the botanicals used by the Margaret River–based Great Southern Distilling Company to produce its expressive gins. Distillers and brewers across Australia remain fervent advocates for using native flavours to create products that speak proudly to the joys of home-court advantage.

Boobialla – a native juniper – and citrussy green ants are some of the ingredients used by Larrakia man (and former professional footballer) Daniel Motlop to create the signature green-ant gin that helped put his spirit brand Seven Seasons

on the Darwin region map. Gamilaroi man and psychologist Dr Clinton Schultz and his wife Lozen Schultz are the founders of Sobah, a nonalcoholic craft-beer brewery and cafe on the Gold Coast that uses native ingredients such as lemon aspen and spicy pepperberry to add new dimensions to pilsners, IPAs and other popular beer styles.

Chefs have been equally taken by the no-holds-barred flavours of native ingredients. Once regarded as a weed by farmers, saltbush has found favour in cooking circles for its salty savour, especially when fried to accentuate its crunch. (Scientists believe that growing salt-tolerant edible native plants such as saltbush and Warrigal greens may be one option for farmers to commercially use land impacted by rising salt levels in the soil.) While some might baulk at the idea of eating the animals on a country's coat of arms, carnivores are appreciating the lean, gamey flavours of kangaroo and emu. Get your fix via kangaroo tartares, emu liver parfaits and other reworked French classics.

As you'd expect from an island nation, seafood such as crab, fish and shellfish featured prominently in coastal Indigenous diets. Yabbies – a native freshwater crayfish commonly found in farmers' dams around Australia – are served around the country in a range of styles and price points. Located in New South Wales' Southern Highlands, regional bakery Samuel Gee Pies and Pastries serves yabby pies, while dainty poached yabby tails served with garlic-scented custard are among the dishes one might have enjoyed at Quay, Sydney's late-lamented harbourside fine-dining restaurant.

'TODAY, NATIVE INGREDIENTS ARE A CHANCE FOR PRODUCERS AND CONSUMERS ALIKE TO CONNECT WITH INDIGENOUS AUSTRALIAN CULTURE.'

Connecting with Country

As thrilling as it is to be able to taste these unique ingredients in bars and restaurants, tasting them in the environment they came from completes the circle. Even more so if you've been welcomed to Country by an Elder who can share the cultural significance of these precious ingredients and place them in an Indigenous context. After all, what better teacher could a student ask for than somebody who has been entrusted with tens of thousands of years of knowledge?

Mark Koolmatrie, a Ngarrindjeri Elder, is the founder of Kool Tours and an excellent person to introduce you to the First Nations history and flavours of South Australia's Fleurieu Peninsula. Against the backdrop of Basham Beach, Koolmatrie will point out edibles such as zesty muntrie berries and coastal rosemary before culminating in a native-ingredient tasting including barramundi fish and local Goolwa pipis. In Queensland's Sunshine Coast, Simon Thornalley – a descendent of the Kaurareg people in the Torres Strait – and Jenna Griffiths operate Saltwater Eco Tours, a boutique tour company that runs intimate river cruises on the Mooloolaba canals in a historic sailing vessel. In addition to learning about the area's Kabi Kabi (Gubbi Gubbi) history, the tour is punctuated by terrific canapés and cocktails showcasing native flavours: oysters mornay made with mango macadamia cheddar, crackers freighting smoked barramundi, plus the signature lemon myrtle, gin and soda cocktail.

Less than half an hour from Perth's city centre is Maalinup Aboriginal Gallery. Found inside Swan Valley winery Mandoon Estate, Maalinup is the home of Dale Tilbrook, a Wardandi Bibbulmun woman with strong ties to the Indigenous food industry around Australia. She hosts regular tastings featuring teas, jams, chutneys and preserves, all accompanied by Tilbrook's pointed observations on Indigenous food and culture. Once the tasting is finished, browse the gallery's art and gifts and reflect on the many ways that Indigenous Australians connect to Country. More importantly, reflect on how the rest of us can help celebrate this astonishing, living culture.

Yabbies

LYNDA MACK/SHUTTERSTOCK

A GREAT AUSTRALIAN BITE: COUNTRY BAKERIES

A long history of colonisation and immigration has shaped the Australian food scene, giving rise to country-bakery classics that we all know and love. By Emmylou Dzubiel

IF YOU ASK a local 'What is Australian food?', the answer might be a lamington or a meat pie – two iconic treats found in any classic Australian bakery. Somewhere in the timeline, baked goods took over as the quintessential Australian fare and any local knows that a true Aussie road trip just isn't complete without your local bakery pit stop. Unsurprisingly, the runners of the show here are immigrant entrepreneurs and they've been pumping out perfectly baked pastry for decades.

The humble meat pie has risen in popularity since its introduction to the land by British settlers in the 18th century. Back then, the pie was a simple affair of meat, gravy and a pastry boat. Now, as bakers battle for the title of 'Australia's Best Pie', you can find all manner of fillings like satay chicken or fish amok – the winning masterpiece of 2023's national pie award, hailing from brothers Chan and Ryan Khun of Country Cob Bakery in Victoria. Since migrating to Australia, the Khun

 Pictured clockwise from top left: Pavlova; Banh mi sandwich; Doughnuts; Meat pie

CLOCKWISE FROM TOP LEFT: ARAZU/SHUTTERSTOCK, KIM DAVID/SHUTTERSTOCK, T RIZZA/SHUTTERSTOCK, BECAUZ GAO/SHUTTERSTOCK

family have been bringing the flavours of their Cambodian roots to country-town Australia, earning their fame status by taking out the 'Best Pie' title an impressive three years in a row, with 2023 as their fourth win. This winning streak may be a feat achieved only by them, but their story of immigrating to Australia to then running a local bakery isn't unique.

No matter how far you venture into this land, you'll find a myriad of immigrant-run shops, restaurants and services. According to the Australian Small Business and Family Enterprise Ombudsman, about a third of small-business owners today were born outside Australia and over half are considered second-generation immigrants. The research of Professor Jock Collins attributes the strong presence of self-employed immigrants to the difficulties that newcomers from overseas face with settling into a foreign land – from learning a new language to adapting their skills to meet new requirements. Many immigrants looking to make income turn to what they can offer to the public, often something from their homeland, and this is especially observed in the food sector.

'THEN THERE'S THE DESSERTS – VANILLA SLICE, LAMINGTONS AND JAM DOUGHNUTS. EVERYONE HAS THEIR FAVOURITE AND CLAIMS TO KNOW WHERE TO FIND THE BEST ONE'.

Lamingtons

NELEA33/SHUTTERSTOCK

Local bakeries are no exception. If you make your way around the continent, you'll discover local treasures run by the likes of Italian, German, Vietnamese and Jewish bakers, to name a few. In the case of the famous Pinjarra Bakery in Western Australia, the Pantaleo family proudly credits their Italian heritage to their passion for food, making use of strong family ties to provide a range of baked goods that many West Australians are willing to make a detour for.

The Vietnamese bakery boom is a well-known phenomenon that emerged in the 1970s and '80s following the Vietnam War. Many Vietnamese refugees fled to Australia seeking safety and ways to generate income for their families. For some, this came in the form of a countryside bakery, offering familiar goods to locals with the added touch of Vietnamese cuisine. With their history of colonisation by the French, the Vietnamese developed their version of the popular baguette, a softer and more economical bread that we now know as banh mi. These days, Australians might battle over where to get their hands on the best version of the generously filled rolls that have become a staple affordable lunchtime meal.

Then there's the desserts – vanilla slice, lamingtons and jam doughnuts. Everyone has their favourite and claims to know where to find the best one. Even as the pastry world develops into ultimate finesse, there will always remain something about a small-town Aussie bakery product that just hits the spot. One simply can't drive the country-town roads without sinking your teeth into at least one steaming-hot pie, lovingly doused in tommy sauce (ketchup), and burning your fingertips through the paper bag. The classic country-town bakeries of Australia have been built on the livelihoods of newcomers and the communities are all the richer for it.

INDEX

Map Pages **000**

Map Pages **000**

Map Pages **000**

Map Pages **000**

Map Pages **000**

Map Pages **000**

Map Pages **000**

'The first time I went to the Sapphire Coast (p210), I thought, seriously, why isn't everyone here? Empty beaches, great oysters, and unreal scenery.'
Natasha Bazika

'I love meeting friends for a sunset picnic at Kings Park among the eucalypts, or catching a gig in the botanical gardens (p895) in Perth.'
Rosamund Brennan

FROM LEFT: ANDREW BUESNEL/SHUTTERSTOCK RIC JACYNO/SHUTTERSTOCK

Mapping data sources:
© Lonely Planet
© OpenStreetMap http://openstreetmap.org/copyright

THIS BOOK

The 23rd edition of Lonely Planet's Australia guidebook was written and researched by Josh West, Brett Atkinson, Andrew Bain, Kat Barber, Natasha Bazika, Rosamund Brennan, Ivy Carruth, Peter Dragicevich, Emmylou Dzubiel, Anthony Ham, Paul Harding, Jessica Korteman, Ashlyn Oswalt, Charles Rawlings-Way, Chantae Reden, Rachel Tolosa Paz, Tiare Tuuhia and Steve Waters. Previous edition writers include Sarah Reid, Jayne D'Arcy, Trent Holden, Jessica Lockhart, Virginia Maxwell, Craig McLachlan and Mwende Mutuli Musau. This guidebook was produced by the following:

Destination Editor Jessica Lockhart

Coordinating Editor Brana Vladisavljevic

Production Editor Jennifer McCann

Image Editor Clara Monitto

Cartographer David Connolly

Assisting Editors Janet Austin, Sarah Bailey, Nigel Chin, Helen Koehne, Karyn Noble, Nicola Williams

Cover Researcher Sam Ubinas

Thanks Vojtech Bartos, Fergal Condon, Gwen Cotter, Corey Hutchison, Jenn Johnson, Alison Killilea, Kellie Langdon, Alison Lyall, Darren O'Connell, Graham O'Neill, Charlotte Orr, Gary Quinn, Kathryn Rowan, Saralinda Turner

MIX
Paper | Supporting responsible forestry
FSC™ C021741
FSC www.fsc.org

Paper in this book is certified against the Forest Stewardship Council™ standards. FSC™ promotes environmentally responsible, socially beneficial and economically viable management of the world's forests.

Published by Lonely Planet Global Limited
CRN 554153
23rd edition – Oct 2026
ISBN 978 1 83869 670 2

10 9 8 7 6 5 4 3 2 1
Printed in China